Inside

Microsoft®

SQL Server™
2000

Kalen Delaney,
based on the first
edition by Ron Soukup

PUBLISHED BY
Microsoft Press
A Division of Microsoft Corporation
One Microsoft Way
Redmond, Washington 98052-6399

Library of Congress Cataloging-in-Publication Data
Delaney, Kalen.
    Inside Microsoft SQL Server 2000 / Kalen Delaney.
      p. cm.
    Includes bibliographical references and index.
    ISBN 0-7356-0998-5
    1. Client/server computing. 2. SQL server. 3. Relational databases. I. Title.

    QA76.9.C55 D43 2000
    005.75'85--dc21   00-059280

Printed and bound in the United States of America.

5 6 7 8 9   QWT   6 5 4

Distributed in Canada by H.B. Fenn and Company Limited.

A CIP catalogue record for this book is available from the British Library.

Microsoft Press books are available through booksellers and distributors worldwide. For further information about international editions, contact your local Microsoft Corporation office or contact Microsoft
Press International directly at fax (425) 936-7329. Visit our Web site at mspress.microsoft.com. Send
comments to *mspinput@microsoft.com*.

Acquisitions Editor: David Clark
Project Editor: Rebecca McKay
Manuscript Editor: Ina Chang
Technical Editors: Marc Young and Jean Ross

For Dan,
forever.

Table of Contents

Table of Contents

Part II Architectural Overview

Table of Contents

Part III   Using Microsoft SQL Server

Table of Contents

Part IV Performance and Tuning

Table of Contents

FOREWORD

This is the definitive companion to Microsoft SQL Server 2000. The authors have combined the perspectives of the developer and the user into a readable and comprehensive guide. Ron Soukup led the SQL Server development team for a decade, and he continues to be one of its key architects. Kalen Delaney has been working with the application designers and developers for almost that long. This is their guide to why SQL Server is the way it is, and how it should be used. The guide complements the reference material in *SQL Server Books Online*.

The book begins with the inside story of how the PC database giant Ashton-Tate partnered with Microsoft and a startup (Sybase) to bring SQL to the OS/2 marketplace. The book then traces the amazing history of the product and the partners. This first-hand account makes this a must-read. I cannot think of a more amazing and entertaining story in our industry.

The book then takes the reader on a whirlwind tour of SQL Server, describing the key features and pointing out some highlights. It also goes "beneath the covers" and describes how SQL Server works inside. First-time readers might find this quite detailed, but it lays the groundwork for much that follows. Subsequent chapters explain how to design for SQL Server—giving sage advice on application design, database design, physical data layout, and performance tuning. This advice is based on watching customers use (and misuse) the product over many years. SQL Server and the Microsoft Windows environment are unique in many ways. These chapters cover the standard design issues but focus primarily on the things that are unique to SQL Server. Incidental to this, Ron and Kalen show many of the pitfalls and common errors that designers and programmers make. They also convey their sense of good and bad design. Anyone planning to do an implementation using SQL Server would do well to first read this book.

The book covers virtually all the extensions that SQL Server has made to the standard SQL language. Ron and Kalen take pride in describing these features. They often explain why features were introduced, how they compare to the competition, and how they work. This book is not an SQL tutorial, but it does an excellent job of covering the intermediate and advanced features of SQL and SQL Server. The descriptions are accompanied by detailed examples that are all on the companion CD.

The book also explains how to install, administer, and tune SQL Server. These chapters contain essential information that I have never seen explained elsewhere. It is very easy to get started with SQL Server—perhaps too easy. Some customers just install it and start using it without thinking much. Ron and Kalen walk the designer through (1) capacity planning, (2) hardware acquisition, (3) Windows, network, and RAID configuration, (4) SQL installation and licensing, (5) security policies,

(6) operations procedures, (7) performance measurement, and (8) performance tuning. The book provides a valuable checklist for anyone planning to set up or operate a SQL Server system.

The book devotes several chapters to understanding performance, concurrency, and recovery issues. Throughout the book, there is an emphasis on designing for client-server and Internet environments. In these environments, the server must process business-rules (stored procedures) or set-oriented requests, rather than record-at-a-time requests. The book explains traditional Transact-SQL stored procedures as well as user-defined external procedures and OLE Automation procedures.

The book gives a clear picture of how SQL Server transactions work. It first presents tutorial material on the ACID properties, isolation levels, and locking. It then explains how SQL Server does locking, logging, checkpointing, and recovery. It has a full chapter on how backup/restore works and how to protect your database from failures. The book also explains how SQL Server uses the Windows Cluster feature for high availability. This presentation is exceptionally clear. Understanding these issues is key to designing high-traffic and high-availability SQL Server servers.

SQL Server database replication is described in depth—especially the features that are new in SQL Server 2000. It also describes the many new features in SQL Server 2000 such as table-valued functions, variants, full-text indexing, data mining, data analysis, and multi-instance support.

In summary, this is the essential companion to SQL Server. It is an invaluable reference for the administrator and the designer—I look something up in it nearly every week. It is a first-hand account of how SQL Server works, why it works the way it does, and how to use it. We are all glad Ron and Kalen took the time to write this invaluable book. I certainly learned a lot from it. I hope you will too.

Jim Gray
Senior Researcher
Microsoft San Francisco Research Lab

Preface

The most wonderful thing about writing a book and having it published is getting feedback from you, the readers. Of course, it's also the worst thing. I wanted the previous edition, *Inside SQL Server 7.0*, to satisfy everybody, as impossible as that might sound. When I got e-mail from readers thanking me for the book, I would feel that all the time I put into it was well spent. When I got e-mail telling me that the book was not satisfactory, I would worry and fret and try to figure out how to make it better the next time. In fact, most of the negative comments were from people who complained about what wasn't included in the book, as if they were seeing the cup half empty instead of half full. As I said in my preface to the last edition, this book doesn't cover the entire product. The focus, as the name *Inside* implies, is on the core engine, in particular the query processor and the storage engine. The book doesn't talk about client programming interfaces, heterogeneous queries, or replication. In addition, some internal operations aren't discussed, such as security. However, unlike in the previous edition, I do include a discussion of the backup and restore operations. But I had to draw the line somewhere so the book wouldn't be twice as long and so I wouldn't still be writing it and avoiding calls from my editors asking when the next chapter would arrive.

For *Inside SQL Server 7.0*, I basically followed Ron Soukup's original outline. I made changes as required for the new version of the product, some of them quite substantial, but the organization was basically as it had been in the very first edition. In *Inside SQL Server 2000,* I've consolidated most of the information about indexes into a separate chapter. The previous editions discussed transactions, stored procedures, and triggers all in one chapter; with the addition of user-defined functions and new trigger capabilities in SQL Server 2000, I've split the discussion into two chapters. In the previous editions, query processing and tuning were combined into one huge chapter. I separated these topics into two chapters, one dealing with the internals of query processing and how the SQL Server optimizer works and the other providing suggestions for using what you've learned to write better performing queries. Finally, I combined two chapters dealing with Transact-SQL programming into one. When Ron's first edition came out in 1997, there were no good books on the market about complex programming using the Microsoft dialect of the SQL language. That is no longer true, and the suggested reading list at the end of this book mentions three excellent books about writing very advanced queries using Transact-SQL. I am grateful to the authors of those books for allowing me to minimize my discussion of programming and concentrate more on the workings of the SQL Server engine.

I hope you find value here even if I haven't covered every single SQL Server topic that you're interested in. You can let me know what you'd like to learn more about, and I can perhaps refer you to other books or whitepapers. Or maybe I'll write an article for TechNet or *SQL Server Magazine*. You can contact me via my Web site at www.InsideSQLServer.com.

As with the previous edition, this edition is not a new features guide or an upgrade book. However, I felt it necessary to compare areas of behavior where drastic changes occurred, in order to minimize confusion for people who have used the product for years. New users can simply ignore any references to what SQL Server used to do and appreciate the product for what it is today.

To help you appreciate SQL Server 2000 even more, the companion CD includes a complete reference to the Transact-SQL language, including all the system stored procedures. Although this reference is a Microsoft Word document, it is actually intended for use on line; many of the elements of a syntactic construct contain links to the further description of that element. When using the document on line, you can simply click on the colored element and you'll be repositioned to the place in the document with more details about that element. I am grateful to Frank Pellow for sharing this document. He has included his e-mail address in the document and invites comments and suggestions from readers.

Now comes the part I've looked forward to the most—thanking all the wonderful people whose enthusiasm and generosity have made writing this book not only possible but even a pleasure.

First on my list is you, the readers. Thank you, thank you, thank you for reading what I have written. Thank you to those who have taken the time to write to me about what you thought of the book and what else you want to learn about. I wish I could answer every question in detail. I appreciate all your input, even when I'm unable to send you a complete reply.

Thanks to Ron Soukup for writing the first edition and for giving me his "seal of approval" for taking on the subsequent editions. Thanks to my former editor at *SQL Server Professional Journal,* Karen Watterson, for opening so many doors for me, including passing on my name to the wonderful people at Microsoft Press.

The SQL Server development team at Microsoft has been awesome. David Campbell's assistance was invaluable, once again; in fact, I wouldn't sign the contract to write this new edition until he promised me that he'd still be available to answer my questions. In this edition, I went into more detail about the query processor and optimizer, and I am indebted to Lubor Kollar for his enthusiastic support. He actually seemed glad to see me when I stopped by his office, and he made me feel as if he valued my questions. Thank you, Lubor. Hal Berenson made valuable contributions to the sections on query processing. Most of the flowcharts in Chapter 15 are from his Tech·Ed presentation on query processor internals. As with the previous edition, Hal was also my primary resource for the update of the history section in Chapter 1. Thank you, Hal. Greg Smith, Gert Drapers, Euan Garden, Sameet Agarwal, Paul Randal, Eric Christensen, Cesar Galindo-Legaria, Wei Xiao, Michael Kung, and Giorgia Paolini opened their doors to me and responded to my (sometimes seemingly endless) e-mails. Goetz Graefe, Alan Brewer, Michael Zwilling, Darren Gehring, and Dan Meacham also offered valuable technical insights and information. I owe very special thanks to Fadi Fakhouri for the time he spent helping me understand the intricacies of SQL Server's full-text processing capabilities. Other members of the development team, including Damien Lindauer, Ganapathy Krishnamoorthy, Siva Raghupathy, Srikumar Rangarajan, Balaji Rathakrishnan, Sam Smith, Peter Carlin, Beysim Sezgin, Steve Lindell, Alazel Acheson, Susan Su, and Dana Burnell provided answers to my e-mails; I hope they all know how much I appreciated every piece of information I received.

I am also indebted to Steve Dybing and Bob Ward, who aren't really on the development team per se but whose patience and quick responses I appreciated more than I can say. And many thanks to Arvind Krishnan, who stepped to the plate in the bottom of the ninth and knocked the ball out of the park with all his help on the last chapter. If not for him, we might still be in extra innings. (I apologize to international readers and to the translators for the very American metaphor here.)

I owe more than just simple thanks to Richard Waymire for being a friend as well as a technical resource on the development team. Even though I don't cover most of his special areas in the book, he was unfailingly generous with his time and answers and quicker than anybody else in his response to my e-mailed questions. While writing this edition, I almost felt like a part of the development team myself. This was due not only to the generosity of the developers but also, in no small part, to Leona Lowry for finding me office space in the same building as most of the team and allowing interoffice mail to be sent to me through her. Thank you, Leona. The welcome you gave me was much appreciated.

I received tremendous support from Ryan Trout and Jeff Ressler of the SQL Server marketing team, who provided advance copies of whitepapers and sample exercises for exploring new features, as well as T-shirts and toys bearing the SQL Server logo. Ryan also arranged for the loan of a Toshiba laptop, loaded with Windows 2000 Server, so I could run my tests on a state-of-the-art machine. I am very grateful to Toshiba for their generous assistance. Thanks, Ryan, and thank you, Toshiba.

I found that other SQL Server trainers were the best help in digging into certain new behaviors and trying to figure out what was really happening. Thanks to Glenn Christiansen for posing so many puzzling questions and volunteering lots of technical insights. Writing this book wouldn't have been nearly so much fun without his help. Thanks also to Kimberly Tripp-Simonnet, Don Vilen, and Arthur Siu for many valuable suggestions on how to explain new behaviors. My editors at Microsoft Press deserve thanks also. David Clark, my acquisitions editor, got the ball rolling. Rebecca McKay, the project editor, made sure the chapters kept coming, and my terrific technical editors—Marc Young and Jean Ross—made sure those chapters turned out well. But, of course, Marc and Jean couldn't do it alone, so I'd like to thank the rest of the editorial team, including manuscript editor Ina Chang. I know you worked endless hours to help make this book a reality.

Some people might think that working as an independent trainer and writer can get lonely because I don't have coworkers to chat with every day in the office. But I've actually got something even better. As a SQL Server MVP, I work with over a dozen other SQL Server professionals to provide online support on the public newsgroups in the SQL Server forums. We share a private newsgroup with several Microsoft Support Engineers who serve as our interface with Microsoft, and through this newsgroup as well as various conferences, I have gotten to know this group personally. Boundless gratitude is due Itzik Ben-Gan for his amazing generosity, both professional and personal. In fact, his detailed scrutiny of the previous edition of the book earned him his role as a technical advisor of this edition. Thank you from the bottom of my heart, Itzik. I really couldn't have done this without you. Roy Harvey, Brian Moran, and Wayne Snyder offered much-needed moral support whenever I asked for it, and more importantly, when I didn't. B. P. Margolin was extremely generous with his comments on the previous edition and also provided the stored procedures for estimating table and index sizes, which are on the companion CD. To you guys and to the rest of the MVP crew—Neil Pike, Tibor Karaszi, Ron Talmadge, Tony Rogerson, Bob Pfeiff, Fernando Guerrero, Umachandar Jayachandran, Gianluca Hotz, Steve Robertson, Trevor Dwyer, Darren Green, Russell Fields, and our Microsoft support buddies Shawn Aebi, Steve Dybing, and Paul Wehland—I'd like to say that being a part of your team has been the greatest honor and privilege of my professional life. I could not imagine working with a more dedicated, generous, and talented group of people.

Most important of all, my family continues to provide the rock-solid foundation I need to do the work that I do. My husband, Dan, continues to be the guiding light of life and my inspiration for doing a job well. My daughter, Melissa, who has just returned from a year of world travel as a Watson Foundation post-graduate fellowship recipient, continues to be a role model for me as she expands her horizons and decides what she wants to learn about next. My three sons, Brendan, Rickey, and Connor, who are growing up to be generous, loving, and compassionate young men, have also recently decided to follow in my footsteps. Brendan is becoming a writer, although unlike me he is writing fiction. I eagerly await each new chapter of the novel he has in progress. Rickey learned to program in half a day this past summer, and after less than a month is writing more complex games than I ever wrote. And Connor is writing stories and acting in plays, which is not too different from what I do when teaching classes. My boys have been a source of countless hugs and kisses and I feel truly blessed to have them in my life.

Kalen Delaney, 2000

Preface to the Second Edition

I'll confess right here. I'm a SQL Server junkie. I want to know everything I can about how SQL Server works, exactly what the internal data structures look like, and what every bit in every status field means in the system tables. A full list of all the undocumented trace flags and DBCC commands would be my idea of the perfect birthday present.

I also feel like I was born to be a teacher. No matter how late I've been working or how hard it is to get myself out of bed in the morning, when I stand in front of a classroom, I'm in my element. I love sharing what I know about SQL Server, and I get even more excited when I have students who want to know about things that I've never even thought about.

When I was asked to write the update for Ron Soukup's masterpiece, my first thought was that no one besides Ron could do the topic justice. But then I decided to look at the challenge of the book as the ultimate training assignment, with thousands of students in the classroom. If I was going to write any book on SQL Server 7, this would be the one. The topics it covers are all the ones that I love learning about and sharing. The topics it doesn't talk about are the ones that I haven't spent too much time with and don't really consider myself an expert on.

In Ron's preface to the first edition, he likens his love for SQL Server to his love for a child. I'll go one step further. Writing this book was like carrying and delivering a child. Not too stressful at first (I never did have much morning sickness) and lots of eager anticipation. But during the last few months, I felt like it would go on forever. It would never end! But now it has, and you have this book in your hands and are reading it.

Ron's preface mentions that this book is *not* an introductory treatise on SQL Server, and I want to emphasize the same point. This book delves deep into the internal workings of SQL Server and expects that you, the reader, have some experience with the SQL language and SQL Server already, as well as a fair amount of general technical sophistication.

This book, as the name implies, deals with the way SQL Server works on the *inside*. SQL Server 7 includes a wealth of new peripheral tools, but you'll have to get the details about them in other books. This book doesn't talk about client programming interfaces, heterogeneous queries, or replication. There are also some internal operations that aren't discussed, such as security and database backup and restore.

I had to draw the line somewhere, or the book would have been twice as long and I would still be writing it and avoiding calls from my editors asking when the next chapter would be arriving. I hope you find value here, even if I haven't covered every single topic that you would like to know about. You can let me know what you'd like to learn more about, and maybe there'll be a second volume to this book one day. Or maybe I can refer you to other books or whitepapers. You can contact me through my Web site, at http://www.InsideSQLServer.com.

My editors insisted that this second edition wasn't supposed to be a new features guide or an upgrade book. However, I knew that lots of people who have used SQL Server for years would be reading this, and I felt it necessary to compare areas of behavior where drastic changes occurred. New users can just ignore any references to what SQL Server used to do and appreciate all the wonderful things it does now.

To help you appreciate some of the wonderful features even more, the companion CD includes a whitepaper section, which serves as a complete reference to the Transact-SQL language, including all the system stored procedures. Although this is a Microsoft Word document, it is actually intended for use on line, as many of the elements of a syntactic construct contain links to the further description of that element. When using the document on line, you can simply click on the colored element and be repositioned at the document with more details describing that element. I am grateful to Frank Pellow for sharing this document. He has included his e-mail address within the document and invites comments and suggestions from readers.

Now comes the part I have looked forward to the most (besides holding a published book in my hands). I get to thank all the wonderful people whose enthusiasm and generosity have made writing this book not only possible but almost a pleasure.

Thanks to Ron Soukup, for writing the first edition, and giving me his "seal of approval" for undertaking the second edition. Thanks to my editor at *SQL Server Professional Journal,* Karen Watterson, for opening so many doors for me, including passing my name on to the wonderful people at Microsoft Press.

The SQL Server development team at Microsoft has been awesome. David Campbell can never, ever be thanked enough, as far as I'm concerned. His enthusiasm for the book seemed to exceed my own at times, and his technical knowledge and clear explanations were priceless, as well as seemingly limitless. Goetz Graefe, Sameet Agarwal, Mike Habben, Wei Xiao, Nigel Ellis, Eric Christensen, Ross Bunker, Alazel Acheson, Lubor Kollar, and Shaun Cooper opened their doors to me and responded to (sometimes seemingly endless) e-mails. Cesar Galindo-Legaria, Peter Byrne, Greg Smith, Michael Zwilling, Jeff Alger, and Alan Brewer also offered valuable technical insights and information. Other members of the development team provided answers to e-mails, and I hope they all know how much I appreciated every piece of information I received. I am also indebted to Joe Marler and Bob Ward, who aren't really on the development team per se, but the technical information they were willing to share was just as valuable and their pride in SQL Server and dedication to the user community was evident in every e-mail I received from them.

A special thanks to several Microsoft program managers: Richard Waymire, for being a friend as well as a technical resource; David Marshall, for helping pull so many pieces together for the general architecture section in Chapter 3; Bob Vogt, who never seemed to tire of sharing all he could about his special projects, the Index Tuning Wizard, and SQL Server Profiler; and Hal Berenson, who was a tremendous help on the update of the history section in Chapter 1.

I received tremendous support from Ryan Trout and Tom Kreyche of the SQL Server marketing team, who provided advance copies of whitepapers, sample exercises for exploring new features, as well as T-shirts and toys bearing the SQL Server logo. Thank you so much for everything, especially your big smiles every time I stopped by.

Ryan Labrie made it possible for me to start down the long road of learning about SQL Server 7 shortly after the Beta 1 release by inviting me to help develop training materials for SQL Server 7. Rick Byham traveled down that long road with me as we worked together to produce the course, and we were able to spend every day for months doing nothing but learning about and playing with this powerful new version. I am grateful for that opportunity.

I found that other SQL Server trainers were the best help in digging into certain new behaviors and trying to figure out experientially what was really happening. Thanks to Glenn Christiansen for posing so many puzzling questions and Kimberly Tripp-Simonnet for wonderful ideas about how to explain things. Don Vilen deserves special thanks for trying to talk me out of writing this book; he said it would be much too much work. You were right, Don, but I did it anyway.

My editors at Microsoft Press deserve thanks also. Ben Ryan, my acquisitions editor, got the ball rolling. Michelle Goodman, the project editor, made sure the chapters kept coming, and my terrific technical editor, Dail Magee Jr., made sure they turned out well. But of course, Dail couldn't do it alone so I'd like to thank the rest of the editorial team, including many of you whom I never met. I know you worked endless hours to help make this book a reality.

Some people might think that working as an independent consultant and trainer would get lonely, as I don't have coworkers to chat with every day in the office. But I've got something even better. As a SQL Server MVP, I work with a dozen other SQL Server professionals to provide online support on the public newsgroups in the SQL Server forums. We share a private newsgroup with two Microsoft Support Engineers who serve as our interface with Microsoft, and through this newsgroup and yearly conferences and summits, I have gotten to know this group personally. Endless gratitude is due Neil Pike for his amazing generosity, both professional and personal. Neil, you are truly an inspiration. Roy Harvey and Brian Moran offered much-needed moral support whenever I asked for it, and more importantly, when I didn't.

To you three, and to the rest of the MVP crew: Tibor Karaszi, Ron Talmadge, Gianluca Hotz, Tony Rogerson, Bob Pfeiff, Steve Robertson, Trevor Dwyer, Russell Fields, and our Microsoft support buddies, Shawn Aebi and Paul Wehland, I'd like to let you know that being a part of your team has been the greatest honor and privilege of my professional life. I could not imagine working with a more dedicated, generous, and talented group of people.

There's another group of people without whose support and encouragement this book would have never seen the light of day. My husband, Dan, never faltered once in his absolute confidence in me and his endless encouragement. My multitalented daughter, Melissa, who will be graduating from Tulane University this spring, has always been an awesome role model for me. She's someone who can make up her mind to do something or learn something and then just do it. My three sons, Brendan, Rickey, and Connor, who are growing up to be generous, loving, and compassionate young men, have been the source of countless hugs and kisses and undreamed of patience and acceptance. I am truly blessed. It's done, guys, and now we're off to Disney World!

Kalen Delaney, 1999

Preface to the First Edition

For me, Microsoft SQL Server has been a labor of love. I lived and breathed this product for years, and I look at it not unlike how I look at my children—with immense love and pride. I've helped nurture the product from its infancy, through some very tough years, to its current success. I've lost many nights' sleep, upset that some customer was disappointed with it. Fortunately, I've also had many more thrills and moments of rejoicing—like when a customer speaks glowingly of SQL Server or when we win another award. Yes, the analogy to a child is the closest thing I can think of to describe my feelings about SQL Server. Like people who have always thought that one day they'd write the Great American Novel, I felt a need to finally put down in words some hopefully unique knowledge and *opinions* I have regarding SQL Server.

This book is *not* an introductory treatise on SQL Server, although it does include one introductory chapter (Chapter 2). In Chapter 1, I discuss the history of the product (which I lived), from SQL Server's inception and partnership with Sybase to its current success. But beyond these early chapters, the book is very detailed and written for those who want to dig deeply into SQL Server. This book is a suitable read for those who have worked with SQL Server for years already. It will also be of interest to experienced database professionals new to SQL Server who are developing or considering new development projects.

In this book, I focus on the "back-end" capabilities of the database engine. Topics include choosing appropriate hardware for SQL Server, effective use of the SQL language, writing correct queries, common mistakes, consistency and concurrency tradeoffs, data storage and structures, locking, and scrollable cursors. Performance considerations are covered throughout the book. The final chapters (Chapters 14 and 15) discuss specific performance issues, but because they assume that you've gained much knowledge from reading earlier chapters in the book, I strongly discourage you from jumping directly to those chapters.

When I planned the book, I felt it was necessary to describe how SQL Server works before going into the product's functional capabilities. But that presents a "chicken-or-the-egg" problem: what should I introduce first? I decided to include architectural information near the beginning of the book—Chapter 3 provides an in-depth discussion of how SQL Server works. If you are already familiar with the functional aspects of SQL Server, I think you'll benefit most from this chapter. If you are new to SQL Server, I encourage you to go back and read Chapter 3 again in a couple months after you've gained more familiarity with the product. I think you'll get a lot more out of it. Initially, simply try to absorb just the basics.

I've included little discussion of client programming issues, such as which development tools to use or details about ODBC programming. If you need information about these topics, see the Suggested Reading section near the end of the book. And I'm sorry to say that there is little discussion of the replication capabilities of SQL Server. (This is also a little embarrassing because I recently took charge of managing the Replication Unit within the SQL Server development team.) But, like software, this thing had to eventually ship, and replication ended up on the "cut" list. I promise that we're doing so many exciting new things in replication for the next version that I knew I would have to almost completely rewrite any replication section before long anyway. (And a very good whitepaper about SQL Server replication capabilities is included on the companion CD.)

This book has a healthy smattering of my personal opinions about many issues in software and database development. Software development is still at least as much an art as a science, and there are different schools of thought and different approaches. Healthy, even if heated, debate is one of the things that make software development so much fun. I elected to be pretty candid and direct with my opinions in many places, rather than keep the book bland and neutral. Some people will no doubt disagree strongly with some of my opinions. That's fine. I respect your right to disagree. But I do hope you can read and accept the book for its overall merits, even if you disagree with a few topics. And, of course, the opinions I present here are mine alone and not necessarily those of Microsoft.

Now I have many people to thank. Without the product, there would be no book. So my thanks must first be to my fellow SQL Server "old-timers," who bootstrapped the product. Working with you was an amazing, unforgettable experience. We worked 80 hours a week far more often than not, but we loved it. No one deserves more credit for SQL Server's success than Rick Vicik. I'm sure Rick is a genius, but he has the rare trait among those with genius IQs of being perfectly pragmatic. He's a doer, and no one works harder or more passionately. He led the development team by sheer example. And what a team. Without the other old-timers like Mike Habben, Lale Divringi, Peter Hussey, Chris Cassella, Chris Moffatt, Kaushik Chodhury, Dave Fyffe, Don Reichart, Craig Henry, Jack Love, Karl Johnson, Ted Hart, Gavin Jancke, Dan Tyack, Trish Millines, Mike Ervin, Mike Byther, Glen Barker, Bryan Minugh, and Heidy Krauer, there simply would be no Microsoft SQL Server today. And the early documentation team of Lesley Link and Helen Meyers, and the original marketing team of Dwayne Walker, Gary Voth, and Dan Basica, made SQL Server a product, not just software. It took this unique and special blend of people to make this product and to make it viable. There are, of course, many others of great talent who have joined the SQL Server team during the last few years. But if not for the extraordinary efforts of the original, very small team, there would be no SQL Server now. Be proud and always remember what we did together.

We needed and were backed up by a great customer support team, anchored by Andrea Stoppani, Gary Schroeder, Rande Blackman, Joe Marler, Vaqar Pirzada, Damien Lindauer, and James McDaniel (several of whom are now on the SQL Server development team). You often went above and beyond the call of duty. Thank you.

Turning toward the book, I want to extend special thanks to Lesley Link. Lesley did the huge job of editing this book entirely in her "spare time" (which meant many late nights and early Sunday mornings). She really committed to editing this book because of the pride and ownership she, too, feels in the product. But while I wrote the bulk of the book more or less on a sabbatical leave, Lesley edited while she continued in her more than full-time job as the manager of the SQL Server documentation team. There is no better editor in the business. And thanks to her production team, especially Steven Fulgham, Christine Woodward, Pat Hunter, and Rasa Raisys, for helping prepare the book.

Thank you to those who provided invaluable technical reviews of various sections, especially to Jim Gray, Rick Vicik, Mike Habben, Peter Hussey, Don Vilen, Dave Campbell, and Lale Divringi. The mistakes that no doubt remain are mine alone.

Special thanks go to Gary Schroeder, who authored the Microsoft internal documentation for the on-disk data structures that I made use of when describing disk and table formats. And thanks to Betty O'Neil, who revamped and reorganized much of the internal design documentation that I used as a resource when writing.

Finally, thanks to the staff at Microsoft Press: David, Lisa, John, and those of you I never met but knew were there, who guided me through the publication process.

This is the first book I've written. I've shipped a lot more software than books. I've learned there are a lot of similarities. Like the last 10 percent takes 90 percent of the time. And that when it's done, you always have this nagging feeling that you'd like to do some part over and could do it much better the second time around. After all the demands and grief I gave them over the years, I know that the documentation team that formerly reported to me has taken great delight in watching me write and seeing me struggle to complete this work. And just as software is never perfect, neither is this book. I've always found that fact painful in shipping software—I always want it to be perfect. And I find it painful now. I wish this book were perfect, and I know it's not.

But, as I always remind my development team, "Shipping is a feature." So, after a long labor, I have shipped.

Ron Soukup, 1997

System Requirements
for the Companion CD-ROMs

System

- PC with an Intel or compatible Pentium 166-MHz or higher processor
- Microsoft Windows NT Server 4.0 with Service Pack 5 or later, Windows NT Server 4.0 Enterprise Edition with Service Pack 5 or later, Windows 2000 Server, Windows 2000 Advanced Server, or Windows 2000 DataCenter Server operating system
- Minimum of 64 MB of RAM (128 MB or more recommended)

Hard drive space

- 95–270 MB for database server; approximately 250 MB for typical installation
- 50 MB minimum for Analysis Services; 130 MB for typical installation
- 80 MB for Microsoft English Query (supported on Windows 2000 operating system but not logo certified)

Other

- Microsoft Internet Explorer 5.0 or later
- Microsoft Word 97 or later
- Microsoft Excel 97 or later
- CD-ROM drive
- VGA or higher resolution monitor
- Microsoft Mouse or compatible pointing device

Part I

Overview

Chapter 1

The Evolution of Microsoft SQL Server: 1989 to 2000

In 1985, Microsoft and IBM announced "a long-term joint development agreement for development of operating systems and other systems software products." This announcement was the beginning of OS/2, a successor to the Microsoft MS-DOS operating system. OS/2 would be a more complete and robust operating system. It would exploit the powerful new personal computers based on the Intel 80286 processor. And it would allow multitasking applications, each with its own address space and each running in the safe ring 3 of the Intel four-ring protection scheme of the 80286. Machines sold in 1986 would be vastly more powerful than the original IBM PC (an Intel 8088–based machine) of just a couple years earlier, and OS/2 would signal a new age in harnessing this power. That was the plan.

OS/2 was formally announced in April 1987, with shipment promised by the end of the year. (OS/2 version 1.0 was released to manufacturing on December 16, 1987.) But shortly after the joint declaration, IBM announced a special higher-end version of OS/2 called OS/2 Extended Edition. This more powerful version would include the base OS/2 operating system plus an SQL RDBMS called OS/2 Database Manager. OS/2 Database Manager would be useful for small applications and would be partially compatible (although not initially interoperable) with DB/2, IBM's flagship MVS mainframe database, and with the lesser-used SQL/DS, which ran on slightly smaller mainframe computers using the VM or VSE operating systems. OS/2 Database Manager would also include Systems Network Architecture (SNA) communications services, called OS/2 Communications Manager. As part of its sweeping Systems Application Architecture (SAA), IBM promised to make the products work well together in the future. (OS/2 Database Manager later evolved into today's DB2/2.)

But if IBM could offer a more complete OS/2 solution, who would buy Microsoft OS/2? Clearly, Microsoft needed to come up with an answer to this question.

SQL Server: The Early Years

In 1986, Microsoft was a mere $197-million-per-year business with 1153 employees. (Ten years later, Microsoft had revenues of nearly $6 billion and almost 18,000 employees.) Microsoft's products were entirely desktop focused, and the main bread-and-butter product was MS-DOS. Client/server computing was not yet in the vernacular of Microsoft or the computer industry. Data management on PCs was in its infancy. Most people who kept data on their PCs used the wildly popular Lotus 1-2-3 spreadsheet application to keep lists (although many were discovering the limitations of doing so). Ashton-Tate's dBASE products (dBASE II and the recently released dBASE III) had also become popular. Although a few other products existed, such as MicroRim's Rbase and a relatively new product from Ansa Software called Paradox, Ashton-Tate was clearly king of the PC data products. In 1986, Microsoft had no database management products. (Beginning in 1992, Microsoft would go on to achieve tremendous success in the desktop database market with Microsoft Access and Microsoft FoxPro.)

IBM's Database Manager wasn't in the same category as products such as dBASE, Paradox, and Rbase. Database Manager was built to be a full-featured database (with atomic transactions and a full SQL query processor), more similar to traditional minicomputer-oriented or mainframe-oriented systems such as IBM's DB/2, or Oracle, or Informix. Microsoft needed a database management system (DBMS) product of the same caliber, and it needed one soon.

Microsoft turned to Sybase, Inc., an upstart in the DBMS market. Sybase hadn't yet shipped the first commercial version of its DataServer product (which it would do in May 1987 for Sun workstations running UNIX). Although certainly not a mainstream product, the prerelease version of DataServer had earned a good reputation for delivering innovative new capabilities, such as stored procedures and triggers, and because it had been designed for a new paradigm in computing: client/server.

As is true in all good business exchanges, the deal between the two companies was a win-win situation. Microsoft would get exclusive rights to the DataServer product for OS/2 and all other Microsoft-developed operating systems. Besides getting royalties from Microsoft, Sybase would get credibility from Microsoft's endorsement of its technology. Even more important, Sybase would gain a beachhead among the anticipated huge number of personal computers that would be running the new OS/2 operating system.

Because the transaction-processing throughput of these OS/2 systems wasn't expected to be high, Sybase could use the systems to seed the market for future sales on the more powerful UNIX system. Microsoft would market the product in higher volumes than Sybase could; it simply wasn't economically feasible for Sybase's direct sales force to deliver what would essentially be the first shrink-wrapped release of a full-fledged, blood-and-guts database to PC customers. Higher volumes would help Sybase win more business on UNIX and VMS platforms. On March 27, 1987, Microsoft president Jon Shirley and Sybase cofounder and president Mark Hoffman signed the deal.

In the PC database world, Ashton-Tate's dBASE still had the reputation and the lion's share of the market, even if dBASE and Sybase DataServer offered extremely different capabilities. To gain acceptance, this new, higher-capability DBMS from Microsoft (licensed from Sybase) would need to appeal to the large dBASE community. The most direct way to do that, of course, was to get Ashton-Tate to endorse the product—so Microsoft worked out a deal with Ashton-Tate to do just that.

In 1988, a new product was announced with the somewhat clumsy name *Ashton-Tate/Microsoft SQL Server*. Although not part of the product's title, Sybase was prominent in the product's accompanying information. This new product would be a port of Sybase DataServer to OS/2, marketed by both Ashton-Tate and Microsoft. Ashton-Tate had pledged that its much-anticipated dBASE IV would also be available in a server edition that would use the dBASE IV development tools and language as a client to develop applications (for example, order-entry forms) that would store the data in the new SQL Server product. This new client/server capability promised to give dBASE new levels of power to support more than the handful of concurrent users that could be supported by its existing file-sharing architecture.

Ashton-Tate, Microsoft, and Sybase worked together to debut SQL Server on OS/2. (This was the first use of the name *SQL Server*. Sybase later renamed its DataServer product for UNIX and VMS *Sybase SQL Server*. Today, Sybase's database server is known as *Sybase Adaptive Server*.)

The first beta version of Ashton-Tate/Microsoft SQL Server shipped in the fall of 1988. Microsoft made this prerelease version available at nominal cost to developers who wanted to get a head start on learning, developing for, or evaluating this new product. It shipped in a bundle known as the NDK (network development kit) that included all the necessary software components (provided that you were developing in C) for getting a head start on building networked client/server applications. It included prerelease versions of SQL Server, Microsoft LAN Manager, and OS/2 1.0.

RON'S STORY

In 1988, Ron Soukup was working for Covia, the United Airlines subsidiary that provided the Apollo Reservation System and related systems for airport and travel agency use. He had spent the previous five years working with the new breed of relational database products that had appeared on the minicomputer and mainframe computer scene. He had worked with IBM's DB/2 running on MVS; IBM's SQL/DS running on VM; and Oracle, Informix, and Unify running on UNIX. Ron viewed PC databases of the day essentially as toys that were good for storing recipes and addresses but not much else. He used a PC for word processing, but that was about it. At work, they were beginning to use more and more LAN-based and PC-based systems, and Ron had begun doing some OS/2 programming. When he heard of the NDK, with this new SQL Server product that had been mentioned in the trade press, he ordered it immediately.

The NDK was very much a beta-level product. It didn't have a lot of fit and finish, and it crashed a couple of times a day. But from practically the first day, Ron knew that this product was something special. He was amazed that he was using a true DBMS—on a PC!—with such advanced features as transaction logging and automatic recovery. Even the performance seemed remarkably good. Having used mostly minicomputer and mainframe computer systems, he was most struck by the difference in PC response time. With the bigger systems, even a simple command resulted in an inevitable delay of at least a couple of seconds between pressing the Enter key and receiving a reply. PCs seemed almost instantaneous. Ron knew PCs were fast for local tasks such as word processing, but this was different. In this case, at one PC he entered an SQL command that was sent over the network to a server machine running this new SQL Server product. The response time was a subsecond. He had never seen such responsiveness.

Ron's initial kick-the-tires trial was encouraging, and he received approval to test the product more thoroughly. He wanted to get a feel for the types of applications and workloads for which this interesting new product might be used. For this, Ron wanted more substantial hardware than the desktop machine he originally tested on (a 10-MHz 286 computer with 6 MB of memory and a 50-MB hard drive). Although SQL Server ran reasonably well on his desktop machine, he wanted to try it on one of the powerful new machines that used the Intel 80386 processor. Ron was able to procure a monster machine for the day—a 20-MHz 386 system with 10 MB of memory and two 100-MB disk drives—and was the envy of his division!

In 1987, Ron and a colleague at Covia had developed some multiuser database benchmark tests in C to help them choose a UNIX minicomputer system for a new application. So Ron dusted off these tests and converted the embedded C to the call-level interface provided in SQL Server (DB-Library) and ported these benchmarks to the PC. Ron hoped that SQL Server would handle several simultaneous users, although he didn't even consider that it could come close to handling the 15 to 20 simulated users they had tried in the earlier minicomputer tests. After many false starts and the typical problems that occur while running an early beta of a version 1.0 product, he persevered and got the test suite—2000 lines of custom C code—running on a PC against the beta version of SQL Server.

The results were amazing. This beta version of SQL Server, running on a PC that cost less than $10,000, performed as well and in many cases better than the minicomputer systems that they had tested a few months earlier. Those systems cost probably 10 times as much as the PC that Ron was using, and they needed to be managed by a professional UNIX system administrator. Ron knew the industry was in for a big change.

In May 1989, Ashton-Tate/Microsoft SQL Server version 1.0 shipped. Press reviews were good, but sales lagged. OS/2 sales were far below what had been expected. Most users hadn't moved from MS-DOS to OS/2, as had been anticipated. And about the only tool available to create SQL Server applications was C. The promised dBASE IV Server Edition from Ashton-Tate was delayed, and although several independent software vendors (ISVs) had promised front-end development tools for SQL Server, these hadn't materialized yet.

During the preceding six months, Ron had come to really know, respect, and admire SQL Server, and he felt the same about the people at Microsoft with whom he had worked during this period. So in late 1989, Ron accepted a position at Microsoft in the SQL Server group in Redmond, Washington. A few months later, he was running the small but talented and dedicated SQL Server development team.

KALEN'S STORY

Kalen Delaney saw the first version of Microsoft SQL Server at about the same time that Ron did. She started working for Sybase Corporation's technical support team in 1987. And in 1988, she started working with a team that was testing the new PC-based version of Sybase SQL Server, which a company in the Seattle area was developing for OS/2. Sybase would be providing phone support for customers purchasing this version of the product, and Kalen, along with the rest of the technical support team, wanted to be ready.

Up to that point, she had never actually worked with PC-based systems and had pegged them as being mere toys. Sybase SQL Server was an extremely powerful product, capable of handling hundreds of simultaneous users and hundreds of megabytes of data. Kalen supported customers using Sybase SQL Server databases to manage worldwide financial, inventory, and human resource systems. A serious product was required to handle these kinds of applications, and Kalen thought PCs just didn't fit the bill. However, when she saw a PC sitting on a coworker's desk actually running SQL Server, Kalen's attitude changed in a hurry. Over the next few years, she worked with hundreds of customers in her product support position and later in her position as Senior Instructor, using Microsoft SQL Server to manage real businesses with more than toy amounts of data, from a PC.

In 1991, Kalen and her family left the San Francisco Bay Area to live in the Pacific Northwest, but she continued to work for Sybase as a trainer and courseware developer. A year later, Sybase dissolved her remote position, and she decided to start her own business. A big decision loomed: should she focus primarily on the Sybase version or the Microsoft version of SQL Server? Because Microsoft SQL Server would run on a PC that she could purchase at her local Sears store with low monthly payments, and because she could buy SQL Server software and the required operating system in one package, the decision was simple. Microsoft had made it quite easy for the sole proprietor to acquire and develop software and hone his or her skills on a powerful, real-world, relational database system.

MICROSOFT SQL SERVER SHIPS

By 1990, the co-marketing and distribution arrangement with Ashton-Tate, which was intended to tie SQL Server to the large dBASE community, simply wasn't working. Even the desktop version of dBASE IV was quite late, and it had a reputation for being buggy when it shipped in 1989. The Server Edition, which would ostensibly make it simple to develop higher-performance SQL Server applications using dBASE, was nowhere to be seen.

As many others have painfully realized, developing a single-user, record-oriented application is quite different from developing applications for multiple users for which issues of concurrency, consistency, and network latency must be considered. Initial attempts at marrying the dBASE tools with SQL Server had dBASE treating SQL Server as though it were an indexed sequential access method (ISAM). A command to request a specific row was issued for each row needed. Although this procedural model was what dBASE users were accustomed to, it wasn't an efficient way to use SQL Server, with which users could gain more power with less overhead by issuing SQL statements to work with sets of information. But at the time, SQL Server lacked the capabilities to make it easy to develop applications that would work in ways dBASE users were accustomed to (such as browsing through data forward and backward, jumping from record to record, and updating records at any time). Scrollable cursors didn't exist yet.

NOTE The effort to get dBASE IV Server Edition working well provided many ideas for how scrollable cursors in a networked client/server environment should behave. In many ways, it was the prime motivation for including this feature in SQL Server version 6.0 in 1995, six years later.

Only two years earlier, Ashton-Tate had been king of the PC database market. Now it was beginning to fight for its survival and needed to refocus on its core dBASE desktop product. Microsoft would launch OS/2 LAN Manager under the Microsoft name (as opposed to the initial attempts to create only OEM versions), and it needed SQL Server to help provide a foundation for the development of client/server tools that would run on Microsoft LAN Manager and Microsoft OS/2. So Microsoft and Ashton-Tate terminated their co-marketing and distribution arrangements. The product would be repackaged and reintroduced as Microsoft SQL Server.

Microsoft SQL Server version 1.1 shipped in the summer of 1990 as an upgrade to the Ashton-Tate/Microsoft SQL Server version 1.0 that had shipped in 1989. For the first time, SQL Server was a Microsoft-supported, shrink-wrapped product, and it was sold through the newly formed Microsoft Network Specialist channel, whose main charter was to push Microsoft LAN Manager.

NOTE When version 1.1 shipped, Microsoft didn't see SQL Server as a lucrative product in its own right. SQL Server would be one of the reasons to buy LAN Manager—that's all.

SQL Server 1.1 had the same features as version 1.0, although it included many bug fixes—the type of maintenance that is understandably necessary for a version 1.0 product of this complexity. But SQL Server 1.1 also supported a significant new client platform, Microsoft Windows 3.0. Windows 3.0 had shipped in May 1990, a watershed event in the computer industry. SQL Server 1.1 provided an interface that enabled Windows 3.0–based applications to be efficiently developed for it. This early and full support for Windows 3.0–based applications proved to be vital to the success of Microsoft SQL Server. The success of the Windows platform would also mean fundamental changes for Microsoft and SQL Server, although these changes weren't yet clear in the summer of 1990.

With the advent of Windows 3.0 and SQL Server 1.1, many new Windows-based applications showed up and many were, as promised, beginning to support Microsoft SQL Server. By early 1991, dozens of third-party software products used SQL Server. SQL Server was one of the few database products that provided a Windows 3.0 dynamic link library (DLL) interface practically as soon as Windows 3.0 shipped, which was now paying dividends in the marketplace. Quietly but unmistakably, Microsoft SQL Server was the leading database system used by Windows applications. Overall sales were still modest, but until tools beyond C existed to build solutions, sales couldn't be expected to be impressive. It was the classic chicken-and-egg situation.

DEVELOPMENT ROLES EVOLVE

Microsoft's development role for SQL Server 1.0 was quite limited. As a small porting team at Sybase moved its DataServer engine to OS/2 and moved the DB-Library client interfaces to MS-DOS and OS/2, Microsoft provided testing and project management. Microsoft also developed some add-on tools to help make SQL Server 1.0 easy to install and administer.

Although a number of sites were running OS/2 as an application server with SQL Server or as a file server with LAN Manager, few were using OS/2 for their desktop platforms. Before Windows 3.0, most desktops remained MS-DOS based, with a well-known limit of 640 KB of addressable real memory. After loading MS-DOS, a network redirector, network card device drivers, and the DB-Library static link libraries that shipped with SQL Server version 1.0, developers trying to write a SQL Server application were lucky to get 50 KB for their own use.

For SQL Server 1.1, rather than shipping the DB-Library interface that Sybase had ported from UNIX to MS-DOS, Microsoft wrote its own, from scratch. Instead of 50 KB, developers could get up to 250 KB to write their applications. Although small by today's standards, 250 KB was a huge improvement.

> **NOTE** The same source code used for DB-Library for MS-DOS also produced the Windows and OS/2 DB-Library interfaces. But the MS-DOS RAM cram is what motivated Microsoft to write a new implementation from scratch. The widespread adoption of Windows 3.0 quickly eliminated the MS-DOS memory issue—but this issue was a real problem in 1989 and 1990.

With SQL Server 1.1, Microsoft provided client software and utilities, programming libraries, and administration tools. But the core SQL Server engine was still produced entirely by Sybase; Microsoft didn't even have access to the source code. Any requests for changes, even for bug fixes, had to be made to Sybase.

Microsoft was building a solid support team for SQL Server. It hired some talented and dedicated engineers with database backgrounds. But with no access to source code, the team found it impossible to provide the kind of mission-critical responsiveness that was necessary for customer support. And, again, fixing bugs was problematic because Microsoft depended entirely on Sybase, which had become successful in its own right and was grappling with its explosive growth. Inevitably, some significant differences arose in prioritizing which issues to address, especially when some issues were specific to the Microsoft-labeled product and not to Sybase's product line. Bugs that Microsoft deemed of highest priority sometimes languished because Sybase's priorities were understandably directed elsewhere. The situation was unacceptable.

It was a great day in the SQL Server group at Microsoft when, in early 1991, Microsoft's agreement with Sybase was amended to give Microsoft read-only access to the source code for the purpose of customer support. Although Microsoft's SQL Server group still couldn't fix bugs, they at least could read the source code to better understand what might be happening when something went wrong. And they could also read the code to understand how something was expected to work. As anyone with software development experience knows, even the best specification is ambiguous at times. There's simply no substitute for the source code as the definitive explanation for how something works.

As a small group of developers at Microsoft became adept with the SQL Server source code and internal workings, Microsoft began to do virtual bug fixes. Although they still weren't permitted to alter the source code, they could identify line-by-line the specific modules that needed to be changed to fix a bug. Obviously, when they handed the fix directly to Sybase, high-priority bugs identified by Microsoft were resolved much more quickly.

After a few months of working in this way, the extra step was eliminated. By mid-1991, Microsoft could finally fix bugs directly. Because Sybase still controlled the baseline for the source code, all fixes were provided to Sybase for review and inclusion in the code. The developers at Microsoft had to make special efforts to keep the source code highly secured, and the logistics of keeping the source code in sync with Sybase was sometimes a hassle, but all in all, this was *heaven* compared to a year earlier. Microsoft's team of developers was becoming expert in the SQL Server code, and they could now be much more responsive to their customers and responsible for the quality of the product.

OS/2 AND FRIENDLY FIRE

In 1991, Microsoft released SQL Server 1.11, a maintenance release. SQL Server was slowly but steadily gaining acceptance and momentum—and a long list of ISV supporters. Client/server computing wasn't widely deployed yet, but new converts appeared every day. Customer satisfaction and loyalty were high, and press reviews of the product were all favorable. Sales were generally disappointing, but this was hardly a surprise because OS/2 had continued to be a major disappointment. Windows 3.0, however, was a runaway hit. Rather than move their desktop platforms from MS-DOS to OS/2, huge numbers of PC users moved to Windows 3.0 instead. OS/2 hadn't become a widespread operating system as anticipated, and it was now abundantly clear that it never would be.

SQL SERVER'S LIMITATIONS AND THE MARKETPLACE

Microsoft SQL Server 1.11 clearly had a scalability limit. It was a 16-bit product because OS/2 could provide only a 16-bit address space for applications, and its throughput was hampered by OS/2's lack of some high-performance capabilities, such as asynchronous I/O. Even though an astonishing amount of work could be performed successfully with SQL Server on OS/2, there would come a point at which it would simply run out of gas. No hard limit was established, but in general, SQL Server for OS/2 was used for workgroups of 50 or fewer users. For larger groups, customers could buy a version of Sybase SQL Server for higher-performance UNIX-based or VMS-based systems.

This was an important selling point for both Microsoft and Sybase. Customers considering the Microsoft product wanted to be sure they wouldn't outgrow it. The large number of ISV tools developed for Microsoft SQL Server worked largely unchanged with Sybase SQL Server, and applications that outgrew OS/2 could be moved quite easily to a bigger, more powerful, more expensive UNIX system. This relationship still made sense for both Microsoft and Sybase.

The need for compatibility and interoperability made it especially important for Microsoft SQL Server to be based on the version 4.2 source code as soon as possible. Furthermore, a major features version hadn't been released since version 1.0 in 1989. In the rapidly moving PC marketplace, the product was in danger of becoming stale. Customers had begun to do serious work with Microsoft SQL Server, and new features were in great demand. Microsoft's version 4.2 would add a long list of significant new features, including server-to-server stored procedures, UNION, online tape backup, and greatly improved international support that would make SQL Server more viable outside the United States.

At the same time, Microsoft was working on a new SQL Server version that would sync up with the newest Sybase product on UNIX, version 4.2. When Microsoft SQL Server 1.0 shipped, Sybase's product was designated version 3.0. They had added some new features deemed necessary for the PC marketplace, such as *text* and *image* datatypes and browse mode. Sybase subsequently shipped version 4.0 for most platforms and version 4.2 on a more limited basis.

Meanwhile, in May 1991, Microsoft and IBM announced an end to their joint development of OS/2. Clearly, most customers were voting with their dollars for Windows, not OS/2. Microsoft decided to concentrate on future versions of Windows and applications for Windows. The announcement, although not a surprise, rocked the industry nonetheless. Microsoft was well underway in the development of a new microkernel-based operating system that was internally code-named *NT* (for "new technology"). This new system was originally envisioned as a future release of OS/2 and was sometimes referred to as *OS/2 3.0.* After the termination of joint OS/2 development, the NT project was altered to include the Windows user interface and the Win32 application programming interface (API), and it became known henceforth as Microsoft Windows NT.

The first version of Windows NT wasn't expected for two years. Microsoft SQL Server would eventually be moved to Windows NT—that was a no-brainer. But in the meantime, Microsoft had to continue developing SQL Server on OS/2, even though OS/2 was now a competitive product for Microsoft; there was no alternative. For the next couple of years, the SQL Server group got used to getting hit by friendly fire as Microsoft competed vigorously against OS/2.

SQL SERVER 4.2

Microsoft had been developing SQL Server 4.2 for the forthcoming OS/2 2.0, the first 32-bit version of OS/2. Since SQL Server 4.2 was also planned to be 32-bit, porting the product from its UNIX lineage would be easier because memory segmentation issues wouldn't be a concern. In theory, the 32-bit SQL Server would also perform faster. Many articles comparing 32-bit and 16-bit performance issues appeared in the press, and everyone assumed that the 32-bit environment would bring awesome performance gains (although few articles explained correctly why this might or might not be true).

The principal performance gain expected would be due to memory addressing. To address memory in the 16-bit segmented address space of OS/2 1.*x*, basically two instructions were required: one to load the correct segment and one to load the memory address within that segment. With 32-bit addressing, the instruction to load the segment was unnecessary and memory could be addressed with one instruction, not two. Because addressing memory is so common, some quick calculations showed that the 32-bit version might yield an overall performance increase of perhaps 20 percent or more, if all other operations were of equal speed.

THE 32-BIT PLATFORM: BIGGER ISN'T ALWAYS BETTER

Many people mistakenly believed that SQL Server needed to be running on a fully 32-bit platform to address more than 16 MB of memory. Under OS/2 1.*x*, an application could access a maximum of 16 MB of real memory; it could access more than 16 MB of *virtual* memory, but paging would result. In OS/2 2.0, an application could access more than 16 MB of real memory and avoid paging. This would allow SQL Server to have a larger cache, and getting data from memory rather than from disk always results in a huge performance gain. However, to the application, all memory in OS/2 was virtual memory—in both versions. So even the 16-bit version of SQL Server would be able to take advantage of the ability of OS/2 2.0 to access larger real-memory spaces. A 32-bit version was unnecessary for this enhancement.

Unfortunately, the early beta versions of OS/2 2.0 were significantly slower than OS/2 1.*x*, more than offsetting the efficiency in addressing memory. So rather than a performance gain, users saw a significant loss of performance in running Microsoft SQL Server 1.1 and preliminary builds of the 32-bit SQL Server 4.2 on OS/2 2.0.

OS/2 2.0 Release on Hold

Suddenly, the plans for the release of OS/2 2.0 by the end of 1991 were suspect. In fact, it was unclear whether IBM could deliver version 2.0 at all. At any rate, it appeared doubtful that OS/2 would ship any sooner than the end of 1992. The decision became clear—Microsoft would move SQL Server back to a 16-bit implementation and target it for OS/2 1.3.

Reworking back to 16-bit would cost the Microsoft developers about three months, but they had little choice. In the meantime, another problem appeared. IBM shipped OS/2 1.3, but this version worked only for its brand of PCs. Theoretically, other computer manufacturers could license OS/2 from Microsoft and ship it as part of an OEM agreement. However, the demand for OS/2 had become so small that most OEMs didn't ship it; as a result, buying OS/2 for other PCs was difficult for customers. For the first time, despite the seeming incongruity, Microsoft produced a shrink-wrapped version of OS/2 version 1.3, code-named *Tiger*. Tiger shipped in the box with Microsoft SQL Server and Microsoft LAN Manager, lessening the problem that the product was essentially targeted to a dead operating system.

Version 4.2 Released

Microsoft SQL Server version 4.2 entered beta testing in the fall of 1991, and in January 1992, Microsoft CEO Bill Gates (with Sybase's Bob Epstein sharing the stage) formally announced the product at a Microsoft SQL Server developers' conference in San Francisco. Version 4.2 truly had been a joint development between Microsoft and Sybase. The database engine was ported from the UNIX version 4.2 source code, with both Microsoft and Sybase engineers working on the port and fixing bugs. In addition, Microsoft produced the client interface libraries for MS-DOS, Windows, and OS/2, and for the first time it included a Windows GUI tool to simplify administration. Source code for the database engine was merged back at Sybase headquarters, with files exchanged via modem and magnetic tape.

Microsoft SQL Server version 4.2 shipped in March 1992. The reviews were good and customer feedback was positive. As it turned out, the source code for the database engine in this version was the last code that Microsoft received from Sybase (except for a few bug fixes exchanged from time to time).

After the product shipped, the Big Question for 1992 was, "When will a 32-bit version of Microsoft SQL Server be available?" The issue of 32-bitness became an emotional one. Many people who were the most strident in their demands for it were unclear or confused about what the benefits would be. They assumed that it would automatically have a smaller footprint, run faster, address more memory, and generally be a much higher-performing platform. But the internal work with a 32-bit version for OS/2 2.0 had shown that this wouldn't necessarily be the case.

SQL SERVER FOR WINDOWS NT

Contrary to what many people might assume, Microsoft senior management never pressured the SQL Server development team to *not* develop a full 32-bit version for OS/2. One of the joys of working for Microsoft is that senior management empowers the people in charge of projects to make the decisions, and this decision was left with Ron Soukup.

In early 1992, however, the development team faced some uncertainty and *external* pressures. On one hand, the entire customer base was, by definition, using OS/2. Those customers made it quite clear that they wanted—indeed, expected—a 32-bit version of SQL Server for OS/2 2.0 as soon as IBM shipped OS/2 2.0, and they intended to remain on OS/2 in the foreseeable future. But when OS/2 2.0 would be available was unclear. IBM claimed that it would ship by the fall of 1992. Steve Ballmer, Microsoft senior vice president, made a well-known pledge that he'd eat a floppy disk if IBM shipped the product in 1992.

The SQL Server team was now under pressure to have a version of SQL Server running on Windows NT as soon as possible, with prerelease beta versions available when Windows NT was prereleased. The SQL Server team members knew that Windows NT was the future. It would be the high-end operating system solution from Microsoft, and from a developer's perspective, Windows NT would offer a number of technical advantages over OS/2, including asynchronous I/O, symmetric

multiprocessing, and portability to reduced instruction set computing (RISC) architectures. They were champing at the bit to get started.

Although Microsoft had decided in 1991 to fall back to a 16-bit version of SQL
Server, Microsoft's developers had continued to work on the 32-bit version. By March
1992, just after shipping version 4.2, they saw that both the 16-bit and 32-bit versions
ran slower on the beta versions of OS/2 2.0 than the 16-bit version ran on Tiger (OS/2
1.3). Perhaps by the time OS/2 2.0 actually shipped, it might run faster. But then again,
it might not—the beta updates of OS/2 2.0 didn't give any indication that it was getting
faster. In fact, it seemed to be getting slower and more unstable.

For a product with the scope of SQL Server, there's no such thing as a small
release. There are big releases and bigger releases. Because resources are finite, the
developers knew that working on a product geared toward OS/2 2.0 would slow down
the progress of Windows NT development and could push back its release. Adding
more developers wasn't a good solution. (As many in the industry have come to learn,
adding more people is often the cause of, and seldom the solution to, software
development problems.) Furthermore, if Microsoft chose to develop simultaneously
for both OS/2 2.0 and Windows NT, the developers would encounter another set of
problems. They would have to add an abstraction layer to hide the differences in the
operating systems, or they'd need substantial reengineering for both, or they'd simply take a lowest-common-denominator approach and not fully use the services or
features of either system.

So Microsoft developers decided to stop work on the 32-bit version of SQL Ser-
ver for OS/2 2.0. Instead, they moved full-speed ahead in developing SQL Server for
Windows NT, an operating system with an installed base of zero. They didn't constrain
the architecture to achieve portability back to OS/2 or to any other operating system.
They vigorously consumed whatever interfaces and services Windows NT exposed.
Windows NT was the only horse, and the development team rode as hard as they could.
Except for bug fixing and maintenance, development ceased for SQL Server for OS/2.

Microsoft began to inform customers that future versions, or a 32-bit version,
of SQL Server for OS/2 2.0 would depend on the volume of customer demand and
that the primary focus was now on Windows NT. Most customers seemed to understand and accept this position, but for customers who had committed their businesses
to OS/2, this was understandably not the message that they wanted to hear.

At this time, Sybase was working on a new version of its product, to be named
System 10. As was the case when they were working on version 4.2, the developers
needed Microsoft SQL Server to be compatible with and have the same version number as the Sybase release on UNIX. OS/2 vs. Windows NT was foremost at Microsoft,
but at Sybase, the success of System 10 was foremost.

Although System 10 wasn't even in beta yet, a schedule mismatch existed between the goal of getting a version of Microsoft SQL Server onto Windows NT as soon
as possible and getting a version of System 10 onto Windows NT, OS/2 2.0, or both

as soon as possible. The development team decided to compromise and specialize. Microsoft would port SQL Server version 4.2 for OS/2 to Windows NT, beginning immediately. Sybase would bring Windows NT under its umbrella of core operating systems for System 10. Windows NT would be among the first operating system platforms on which System 10 would be available. In addition, Microsoft would turn the OS/2 product back over to Sybase so those customers who wanted to stay with OS/2 could do so. Although Microsoft hoped to migrate most of the installed customer base to Windows NT, they knew that this could never be 100 percent. They were honestly pleased to offer those customers a way to continue with their OS/2 plans, via Sybase. The SQL Server development team truly didn't want them to feel abandoned.

This compromise and specialization of development made a lot of sense for both companies. The development team at Microsoft would be working from the stable and mature version 4.2 source code that they had become experts in. Porting the product to a brand new operating system was difficult enough, even *without* having to worry about the infant System 10 code base. And Sybase could concentrate on the new System 10 code base without worrying about the inevitable problems of a prebeta operating system. Ultimately, System 10 and SQL Server for Windows NT would both ship, and the two companies would again move back to joint development. That was the plan, and in 1992 both sides expected this to be the case.

The SQL Server team at Microsoft started racing at breakneck speed to build the first version of SQL Server for Windows NT. Time to market was, of course, a prime consideration. Within Microsoft, the team had committed to shipping within 90 days of the release of Windows NT; within the development group, they aimed for 30 days. But time to market wasn't the only, or even chief, goal. They wanted to build the best database server for Windows NT that they could. Because Windows NT was now SQL Server's only platform, the developers didn't need to be concerned about portability issues, and they didn't need to create an abstraction layer that would make all operating systems look alike. All they had to worry about was doing the best job possible with Windows NT. Windows NT was designed to be a portable operating system, and it would be available for many different machine architectures. SQL Server's portability layer would be Windows NT itself.

The development team tied SQL Server into management facilities provided by Windows NT, such as raising events to a common location, installing SQL Server as a Windows NT service, and exporting performance statistics to the Windows NT Performance Monitor. Because Windows NT allows applications to dynamically load code (using DLLs), an open interface was provided to allow SQL Server to be extended by developers who wanted to write their own DLLs.

This first version of Microsoft SQL Server for Windows NT was far more than a port of the 4.2 product for OS/2. Microsoft essentially rewrote the *kernel* of SQL Server—the portion of the product that interacts with the operating system—directly to the Win32 API.

Another goal of SQL Server for Windows NT was to make it easy to migrate current installations on OS/2 to the new version and operating system. The developers wanted all applications that were written to SQL Server version 4.2 for OS/2 to work unmodified against SQL Server for Windows NT. Because Windows NT could be dual-booted with MS-DOS or OS/2, the team decided that SQL Server for Windows NT would directly read from and write to a database created for the OS/2 version. During an evaluation phase, for instance, a customer could work with the OS/2 version, reboot the same machine, work with the Windows NT version, and then go back to OS/2. Although it would be difficult to achieve, the developers wanted 100 percent compatibility.

The developers reworked SQL Server's internals and added many new management, networking, and extensibility features; however, they didn't add new external core database engine features that would compromise compatibility.

THE WINDOWS NT–ONLY STRATEGY

Many have questioned the Windows NT–only strategy. But in 1992, the UNIX DBMS market was already overcrowded, so Microsoft developers felt they wouldn't bring anything unique to that market. They recognized that SQL Server couldn't even be in the running when UNIX was a customer's only solution. Microsoft's strategy was based on doing the best possible job for Windows NT, being the best product on Windows NT, and helping to make Windows NT compelling to customers.

The decision to concentrate on only Windows NT has had far-reaching effects. To be portable to many operating systems, the Sybase code base had to take on or duplicate many operating system services. For example, because threads either didn't exist on many UNIX operating systems or the thread packages differed substantially, Sybase had essentially written its own thread package into SQL Server code. The Windows NT scheduling services, however, were all based on a thread as the schedulable unit. If multiprocessors were available to the system and an application had multiple runnable threads, the application automatically became a multiprocessor application. So the Microsoft SQL Server developers decided to use native Windows NT threads and not the Sybase threading engine.

The development team made similar choices for the use of asynchronous I/O, memory management, network protocol support, user authentication, and exception handling. (In Chapter 3, we'll look at the SQL Server architecture in depth and delve into more of these specifics. The point here is that the goals intrinsic to portability are in conflict with the goal to create the best possible implementation for a single operating system.)

For example, the developers ensured that there were no differences in the SQL dialect or capabilities of the Windows NT and OS/2 versions. The plan was for the future System 10 version to implement many new features. This release would be fundamentally a platform release. To emphasize compatibility with the OS/2-based 4.2 product and with the Sybase product line, Microsoft decided to call the first version of SQL Server for Windows NT *version 4.2*. The product was referred to as simply *Microsoft SQL Server for Windows NT* and often internally as *SQL NT*, a designation that the press and many customers also were beginning to use.

In July 1992, Microsoft hosted a Windows NT developers' conference and distributed a prebeta version of Windows NT to attendees. Even though SQL Server didn't exist yet at a beta level, Microsoft immediately made available via CompuServe the 32-bit programming libraries that developers needed for porting their applications from OS/2 or 16-bit Windows to Windows NT. Just as it had enjoyed success back in 1990 by providing the NDK to prospective Windows 3.0 developers, Microsoft sought the same success by providing all the necessary tools to would-be Windows NT developers.

COMMITMENT TO CUSTOMERS

Incidentally, at approximately the same time they were delivering the NDK to developers, Microsoft also shipped a maintenance release of SQL Server for OS/2 (and they shipped another the following year). In porting to Windows NT, the development team found and fixed many bugs that were generic to all platforms. Even though they wouldn't create new SQL Server versions for OS/2, they really meant it when they said that they didn't want to abandon the OS/2 customers.

By March 1993, Microsoft went a step further and made a public beta release; anyone (even competitors) could obtain this prerelease product, SQL Server Client/Server Development Kit (CSDK), for a nominal charge that essentially covered expenses. Microsoft set up a public support forum on CompuServe and didn't demand that participants sign a nondisclosure agreement. It shipped more than 3000 CSDKs. By May 1993, the volume on the support forum for the prerelease product exceeded that for the shipping OS/2 product. The feedback was highly positive: Microsoft had a winner. The dream of an eventual "client/server for the masses" was being realized.

In July 1993, Microsoft shipped Windows NT 3.1. Within 30 days, achieving their internal goal, the SQL Server development team released the first version of Microsoft SQL Server for Windows NT to manufacturing. Customer and press reaction was terrific. SQL Server for Windows NT was listed in many publications as among the top and most important new products of 1993.

In October 1992, Microsoft shipped the first beta version of SQL Server for Windows NT. The product was essentially feature-complete and provided a full Win32 version of all components. It shipped to more than 100 beta sites. For a database server, having 100 beta sites was unprecedented; the typical number of beta sites for such a product was approximately 10.

SUCCESS BRINGS FUNDAMENTAL CHANGE

SQL Server for Windows NT was a success by nearly all measures. The strategy of integrating the product tightly with Windows NT resulted in a product that was substantially easier to use than high-end database products had ever been. Sales were above the internal projections and increased as Windows NT began to win acceptance.

By early December 1993, much of the SQL Server customer base for the OS/2 operating system had already migrated to SQL Server for Windows NT. Surveys showed that most of those who hadn't yet upgraded to Windows NT planned to do so, despite the fact that Sybase had publicly announced its intention to develop System 10 for OS/2.

The upgrade from SQL Server for OS/2 to SQL Server for Windows NT was virtually painless. When applications were moved from one platform to the other, not only did they still work, but they worked better. SQL Server for Windows NT was much faster than SQL Server for OS/2, and most significant, it was scalable far beyond the limits imposed by OS/2. Within another nine months, Microsoft's SQL Server business had more than doubled, with nearly all sales coming on the Windows NT platform. Although they continued to offer the OS/2 product, it accounted for well below 10 percent of sales.

A FASTER SQL SERVER

Focusing the product on Windows NT had made the product fast. Studies conducted internally at Microsoft, as well as those based on private customer benchmarks, all showed similar results: SQL Server for Windows NT (running on low-cost commodity hardware) was competitive in performance with database systems running on UNIX (much more costly hardware).

In September 1993, Compaq Computer Corporation published the first official, audited Transaction Processing Council (TPC) benchmarks. At that time, on the TPC-B benchmark, well over $1000/TPS (transactions per second) was common, and it was an impressive number that broke the $1000/TPS barrier. Running on a dual-Pentium, 66-MHz machine, SQL Server achieved 226 TPS at a cost of $440 per transaction, less than half the cost of the lowest benchmark

---

ever published by any other company. The raw performance number of 226 TPS was equally astonishing. At that time, most of the TPC-B numbers on file for UNIX minicomputer systems were still below 100 TPS. Certainly a handful of numbers were higher, but all occurred at a price point of much more than $440/TPS. Just 18 months prior, the raw performance of 226 TPS was about as high as any mainframe or minicomputer system had ever achieved.

The implications were clear. SQL Server for Windows NT wasn't simply a low-end or workgroup system. Its performance was competitive with more costly UNIX systems, and the trend toward faster systems running Windows NT was unmistakable. The 66-MHz Pentium processors were the first generation of Pentiums from Intel. Much higher clock speeds were expected to emerge within a few months; hardware with additional processors was anticipated. Furthermore, Microsoft SQL Server for Windows NT would soon be available on RISC processors such as the DEC Alpha-AXP at 250 MHz and the MIPS R4400. The so-called *Moore's Law* (named after Gordon Moore, cofounder of Intel Corporation), which postulates that computing power doubles every 18 months, was clearly being proven true for the type of commodity hardware for which Windows NT and Microsoft SQL Server were designed. Microsoft took a serious look at what would be required to achieve 1000 TPS, definitely putting raw performance in the same league as even the largest systems of the day.

THE END OF JOINT DEVELOPMENT

Microsoft's success strained its relationship with Sybase. The competitive landscape of late 1993 was quite different from that of 1987, when Microsoft and Sybase had inked their deal. By 1993, Sybase was a successful software company, by most accounts second only to Oracle in the DBMS market. The credibility and visibility Microsoft brought to Sybase was far less important in 1993 than it had been to the upstart company of 1987. Similarly, Microsoft had grown a great deal since 1987. The growth wasn't just in revenues (although that was one of the great success stories of the industry) but also in the development of products for use with enterprise applications, such as Microsoft SQL Server, that Fortune 1000 companies could use as a platform on which to run their businesses.

The SQL Server development team had grown as well, from a handful of people in 1990 to more than 50 professionals (not including those in marketing, support, or field operations), with significant additional growth planned. The first-rate team of engineers knew database and transaction processing and the inner workings of SQL Server, and they were experts in developing for Windows NT. Microsoft now had the talent, size, motivation, and mandate, but it was still constrained in what it could do with the product: the 1987 agreement with Sybase had merely licensed to Microsoft the rights to the Sybase product. Because of this restricted agreement, Microsoft couldn't implement new features or changes without Sybase's approval. Contrary to what many people thought, Microsoft had no ownership stake in Sybase and could by no means simply call the shots.

Obviously, Sybase had different business needs and therefore different priorities than Microsoft. The development team at Microsoft might, for example, want to integrate SQL Server with messaging by using MAPI (Messaging API), but because this feature was specific to the Microsoft operating system, Sybase wouldn't be excited about it. As is always the case in development, many features *could* be implemented for every feature that is actually implemented: features specific to Windows NT didn't tend to interest Sybase as much as those that would benefit its UNIX products.

Sybase engineers had to confront the issue of portability to multiple operating systems. In fact, Microsoft's implementation of version 4.2 for Windows NT was already causing friction because Sybase was progressing with System 10 for Windows NT. Sybase was understandably implementing System 10 in a more portable manner than Microsoft had done. This was entirely rational for Sybase's objectives, but from Microsoft's perspective, it meant a looser bond with Windows NT. System 10 would not, and *could not,* perform as well on Windows NT as the product that had been designed and written exclusively for Windows NT.

Because of the economics involved, as well as the changing competitive landscape, the Microsoft/Sybase agreement of 1987 was no longer working. Microsoft SQL Server was now a viable competitive alternative to Sybase SQL Server running on UNIX, Novell NetWare, and VMS. Far from seeding the market for Sybase, Microsoft SQL Server was now taking sales away from Sybase. Instead of choosing a UNIX solution, customers could buy Microsoft SQL Server at a fraction of the cost of a UNIX solution, run it on less expensive PC hardware, and install and administer it more easily. Although Sybase earned royalties on sales of Microsoft SQL Server, this amounted to a small fraction of the revenue Sybase would have received if customers had bought Sybase products for UNIX in the first place. Microsoft and Sybase were now often vigorously competing for the same customers. Both companies recognized that a fundamental change in the relationship was needed.

On April 12, 1994, Microsoft and Sybase announced an end to joint development. Each company decided to separately develop its own SQL Server products. Microsoft was free to evolve and change Microsoft SQL Server. Sybase decided to bring its System 10 products (and subsequent versions) to Windows NT—the first time that the Sybase-labeled SQL Server would be available for a Microsoft operating system. (The original agreement gave Microsoft exclusive rights on Microsoft operating systems.) Both companies' products would be backward-compatible with existing SQL Server applications—however, the products would diverge in the future and would have different feature sets and design points. Sybase's product would be fully compatible with its UNIX versions. Microsoft's product would continue to be integrated with Windows NT as much possible. In short, the products would directly compete.

SQL SERVER PERFORMANCE: NO SECRET FORMULAS

Although Microsoft SQL Server is designed for and optimized for Windows NT, it uses only publicly documented interfaces. From time to time, articles or speakers suggest that Microsoft SQL Server uses private, undocumented APIs in Windows NT to achieve its performance. But this assumption is false, without exception. SQL Server's performance results from using the available and published Windows NT services without any compromise. This is something that other products could also do if developers were willing to dedicate themselves to doing the best possible job for Windows NT without making compromises for portability to other operating systems.

> **NOTE**   Although the Sybase product competed with Microsoft SQL Server, Microsoft encouraged and provided support for getting Sybase System 10 shipping on Windows NT as soon as possible because it was important to the acceptance and success of Windows NT. Such collaboration is typical; many such relationships are competitive on one level and cooperative on another.

THE CHARGE TO SQL95

As late as the beginning of 1994, the SQL Server development team had planned for the next version of the product to pick up the Sybase System 10 source code and new features. But the termination of joint development changed that plan. Sybase contributed no more code, and Microsoft released no System 10 product. Except for a couple of bug fixes, the last code drop received from Sybase was in early 1992 just as version 4.2 for OS/2 was shipping.

Time was at a premium. Besides promoting sales to new customers, Microsoft had to fight for its significant installed base. Sybase was to deliver System 10 for Windows NT later that year. That would be a potentially easy upgrade for Microsoft's installed customer base; so if Microsoft lost customers to System 10, they'd likely lose them forever.

Microsoft quickly planned for an ambitious release that was loaded with new features and performance improvements. It was tagged *SQL95,* borrowing the working moniker from the well-known upcoming Windows 95 release. Because the Big Question of 1994 was "What are your plans for replication?", replication became a keystone of the release. So did scrollable cursors, a feature that the developers had learned was necessary (from the ill-fated dBASE IV interface) to bridge the impedance mismatch between many record-oriented applications and a relational database. No mainstream DBMS product had yet provided a fully functional implementation of scrollable cursors in a client/server environment, and the SQL Server team believed that it was imperative to add this feature to the database engine. They had also been working on a dramatic new set of management tools, code-named *Starfighter* (today's SQL Server Enterprise Manager), which would also be included in the next release. The new feature list went on and on.

Microsoft's customers were clamoring to hear about the plans for SQL Server post-Sybase. So on June 14, 1994, Microsoft put together a briefing event in San Francisco for key customers, analysts, and the press. Jim Allchin, Microsoft senior vice president, walked the attendees through the plans for the future and for the SQL95 release. Attendees were impressed with the plans and direction, but many were openly skeptical of Microsoft's ability to deliver such an impressive product by the end of 1995.

> **NOTE**   Some industry press began to sarcastically refer to the planned release as SQL97 and even SQL2000. Internally, the development team was still targeting the first half of 1995. To outsiders, they were more cautious—after all, this is software development, which is still more art than science. Stuff happens, so the SQL Server team said nothing more ambitious than 1995. (Everyone assumed that the planned date was December 31, 1995, and that they'd miss that date, too.) The rampant skepticism only served to motivate the SQL Server team even more to show that they could deliver. After all, the team rightly felt that it had *already* delivered an impressive release independent of Sybase. But no one gave them credit for that, so they'd just have to show everyone.

The team worked incredibly hard, even by Microsoft standards, to make this deadline and still deliver a full-featured, high-quality product. The first beta was released at the end of October 1994. Although Starfighter was not feature-complete yet, the database server was complete, and because the server takes the longest lead time for beta sites to really stress it, they went ahead with the beta release. This release was followed by a series of beta updates during the next several months, along with gradual beta-site expansion, eventually surpassing 2000 sites.

For nine months, dinner was delivered each night for those on the development team who were working late—usually a majority. On June 14, 1995, the product was released to manufacturing. Microsoft SQL Server 6.0 (SQL95) had shipped within the original internal target date, much sooner than nearly everyone outside the team had expected. It was an immediate hit. Positive reviews appeared in nearly all the trade publications; even more significant, none were negative or even neutral. Even more important than the press reviews was customer reaction, which was terrific.

InfoWorld, in its second annual survey of the 100 companies with the most innovative client/server applications in the previous year, showed Microsoft SQL Server as the number-two database. SQL Server jumped from 15 percent to 18 percent of those surveyed as the database server of choice—for a virtual tie with Oracle, which dropped from 24 percent to 19 percent. Sybase rose from 12 to 14 percent. Three of the top 10 applications highlighted by *InfoWorld* were built using Microsoft SQL Server.

Of course, the SQL Server development team was happy to see this data, but they took it with a grain of salt. Other data could be interpreted to suggest that Microsoft SQL Server's presence was substantially less than the surveys indicated. And the team recognized that they were still relative newcomers. From a sales perspective, Oracle was clearly king of the hill, and Sybase, Informix, and IBM were also formidable competitors in the DBMS market. Microsoft had not previously been a significant competitive threat. But now it was, and all companies armed their sales forces with bundles of information on tactics for selling against Microsoft SQL Server. Sybase, Informix, and Oracle all promised hot new releases. Although the SQL Server team had been sprinting for nearly four years, now was certainly not the time to get complacent.

TEAM-BUILDING WITH TOP TALENT

Besides working hard on the development of version 6.0, Microsoft was also working to increase the size and strength of the team. It had built a small, crackerjack team that had delivered SQL Server for Windows NT, and this team was the core that delivered SQL95. But the team needed more people, more expertise, and exposure to broader ideas. So they went after top talent in the industry.

Microsoft attracted some industry luminaries—Jim Gray, Dave Lomet, and Phil Bernstein. They also attracted a lot of lesser-known but top development talent from throughout the industry. For example, DEC shopped its Rdb product around, looking to generate cash, and Oracle eventually spent a few hundred million dollars for it. But Microsoft didn't want to buy Rdb. Instead, it hired many of the Rdb project's best developers, augmenting this move by hiring several of the best recent masters' graduates who had specialized in databases.

THE NEXT VERSION

After shipping version 6.0, many team members took well-deserved vacations after months of working in crunch mode. But within a month, they were actively beginning work on SQL Server version 6.5. With any huge release like version 6.0, some features get deferred due to schedule constraints. And during the ambitious 18-month project, new demands had come up that weren't even conceived of as requirements when the project began. For example, the Internet and data warehousing both exploded in importance and demand in 1995. Version 6.5 added capabilities for both. It also included further ease-of-use improvements, gained certification for conforming to the ANSI SQL standard, and provided much richer distributed transactions.

Although version 6.0 was released to manufacturing in June 1995, on December 15, 1995, Microsoft shipped a feature-complete beta version of 6.5 to 150 beta sites. The production version of 6.5 was released to manufacturing in April 1996, a scant 10 months after 6.0 was released. The SQL Server team was not about to slow down.

THE SECRET OF THE SPHINX

Slowing down was never really an option. Even before SQL Server 6.5 was released, an entirely separate team of developers was hard at work on a brand new vision for Microsoft SQL Server. In 1993, Microsoft had decided that databases would be a core technology in the product line, and in late 1994, it began hiring expertise from DEC and other major vendors to work with Microsoft's Jet and SQL Server teams to plan components for a whole new generation of database technology. During 1995, the period when SQL Server 6.0 and SQL Server 6.5 were being released, this team was building a new query processor that was planned as a component for what was to become the Microsoft Data Engine (MSDE).

Development of the MSDE was enhanced by the simultaneous development of OLE DB, which allowed elements of the SQL Server core product to be developed as independent components. Components could then communicate with each other using an OLE DB layer. At the end of 1995, the new query-processing component was integrated into the SQL Server code base, and development of a brand new SQL Server, with the code name *Sphinx,* began in earnest. The team working on the query processor joined the rest of the SQL Server development team.

The development of this new generation of SQL Server had one overriding theme: to re-architect the entire database engine so that the SQL Server product could scale as much as its users wanted it to. This would mean upward growth to take full advantage of more and faster processors and as much memory as the operating system could handle. This growth would also have to allow for new functionality to be added to any of the components so that, for example, the query processor code could add an entirely new join algorithm to its repertoire as easily as a new hard drive could be added. In addition to the upward growth, SQL Server would also be expanded outward to support whole new classes of database applications. It would also need to scale downward to run on smaller systems such as desktops and laptops.

There were two immediate goals for the first version of this new re-architected system:

■   Full row-level locking with an extremely smart lock manager.

■   A brand-new query processor that would allow such techniques as distributed heterogeneous queries and efficient processing of ad hoc queries. (Ad hoc queries are a fact of life when you deal with data warehousing, Internet-based applications, or both.)

This brand-new SQL Server version 7.0 debuted in a limited beta 1 release in the fall of 1997. Beta 2 was made available to several hundred sites in December 1997. Because of the new architecture, all databases and the data structures they contained needed to be completely rebuilt during the upgrade process. Microsoft and the SQL Server development team were absolutely committed to making sure all customers would be successful in moving from SQL Server 6.5 to SQL Server 7.0. A program called the 1K Challenge was instituted, in which 1000 customers were invited to send copies of their databases to the SQL Server development team to be upgraded to version 7.0. A porting lab was set up in the building on the Redmond campus where the entire development team worked. Each week from February to August of 1998, four or five ISVs sent a team of their own developers to Microsoft to spend an entire week in the lab, making sure their products would work out of the box with the new SQL Server 7.0. The core SQL Server development engineers made themselves available to immediately isolate and fix any bugs encountered and to spend time talking to the ISVs about the best ways to take advantage of all the new features of SQL Server 7.0 to make their own products even better.

In June 1998, Microsoft publicly released SQL Server 7.0 Beta 3 from its SQL Server Web site, along with a set of exercises demonstrating many of the new features and capabilities of the product. An Internet news server was set up so that any Beta 3 user could report bugs and ask questions of the SQL Server development team. More than 120,000 sites received the Beta 3 version of SQL Server 7.0. This included companies directly requesting the product through the Microsoft Web site, MSDN subscriptions, and Microsoft Beta Program participants (who receive beta versions of all Microsoft products when they become available). And then at last, after almost four years for some of the earliest team members, SQL Server 7.0 was publicly announced at COMDEX in Las Vegas on November 16, 1998. By the time of the launch, more than a dozen sites were in full production with SQL Server 7.0, including Microsoft's internal SAP implementation and barnesandnoble.com, HarperCollins, CBS Sportsline, Comcast Cellular, and Southwest Securities. The SQL Server 7.0 development team released the product to manufacturing on December 2, 1998, using build 7.00.623.07, with a code freeze date of November 27, 1998. The product became available to the public in January 1999.

SOFTWARE FOR THE NEW CENTURY

As expected, the development team didn't stop working on SQL Server. Several planned features that had not made it into the SQL Server 7.0 release needed to be incorporated into the product. Other new features were already in the later stages of development in preparation for a version after 7.0. Two new code names were already in use: *Shiloh* was to be the version after 7.0, commonly assumed to be just a "dot" release like 7.5, and *Yukon* was the name given to the next major revision of SQL Server.

Initially, the SQL Server product managers were reluctant to predict widespread, immediate acceptance of SQL Server 7.0. Because it was basically a complete rewrite of the core engine code, many people might consider it a 1.0-level release. It was also anticipated that many potential adopters and upgraders would not be anxious to go to any release that ended in dot-zero and would want to wait for at least the first service pack. So initially, the Shiloh release was planned as just a "Super Service Pack." It would include perhaps a few new features that didn't get into 7.0 because of the shipping schedule, plus any bug fixes that were deemed too big for a normal, unnumbered service pack. The plan was to have a quick turnaround and release Shiloh no more than a year after the initial release of SQL Server 7.0.

Several factors came into play to change this initial vision of Shiloh. First, there seemed to be very little hesitation among the already installed user base to upgrade to the new SQL Server 7.0. Also, sales figures for new customers far exceeded even the most optimistic predictions. People were using SQL Server 7.0, and they liked it. Even after the public release of the product, Microsoft continued running the ISV lab in the building where the SQL Server developers worked, so feedback was ongoing and readily available to the development team. In general, the issues that came up as problems were easily fixable and a service pack for SQL Server 7.0 was released in May 1999. A second service pack was released in March 2000. There seemed to be no need for the "Super Service Pack" that Shiloh was intended to be.

A second factor that influenced a change in vision for the Shiloh release was customer requests. After referential integrity with cascading updates and deletes failed to make it into SQL Server 7.0, the product team heard loud and clear from the customer base that any further delay in adding this feature would not be tolerable. Customers also wanted better support for partitioned views and optimizer support for the star schema design used in data warehousing applications.

Finally, there was competitive pressure to make the next release bigger and better than originally planned. The Million Dollar Challenge issued by Larry Ellison of the Oracle Corporation pointed out a major piece of functionality that "they" had and "we" didn't. Adding materialized views to the product, which would allow SQL Server to meet this challenge, would be more than just a simple fix.

So the decision was made to have Shiloh be a full-blown release with at least an 18-month development cycle, but the version number would still be 7.5. The magnitude of the changes that would eventually find their way into this release was not immediately clear because the only absolute "must-have" at the outset was the cascading updates and deletes. It soon became clear that the release would grow beyond initial expectations. The team itself had grown substantially, spilling out of their original building on the main Microsoft campus into parts of two adjacent buildings. With a larger group of developers, a greater number of small to medium-size new features could be added to the product without seriously jeopardizing the planned release date. This book describes many of these new features.

In addition to having to add a substantial amount of new functionality, the development team also imposed upon themselves something they called "stretch goals." They declared an objective of a 20 percent increase in performance across the board, on all types of applications, but to give themselves something concrete to aim for, they extended this for specific applications. The main example of this was their goal to improve performance on the SAP R/3 Sales and Distribution benchmark by at least 40 percent. To do this, they had to make very specific changes in the optimizer that would directly affect the SAP queries but also benefit many other applications. At the Windows 2000 launch event in San Francisco on February 17, 2000, benchmark results were announced that demonstrated 6700 users for the Sales and Distribution benchmark, compared to 4500 users in SQL Server 7.0 for the same benchmark on the same hardware (an eight-way Pentium III-550). This represented a 48 percent improvement, and the goal had been well met.

After the development period was extended to a full 18 months, the decision was made to add another new feature. This decision was held in the strictest secrecy and wasn't even discussed with many high-level executives at Microsoft. The feature wasn't even addressed until after the release of Beta 1 in November 1999, and it was not announced publicly until the February launch of Windows 2000. Referred to internally by the code name *Coyote,* this secret project allowed SQL Server 2000 to support *distributed partitioned views* to allow unprecedented scalability in data management operations. It was this new feature that allowed the world-record-breaking benchmark results to be achieved and announced in San Francisco in February 2000.

Originally, these scalability features were scheduled for the version after Shiloh, but a close investigation revealed that many of the necessary components were already in place. These features included extensions to the optimizations of union views and the ability to update union views. Details of distributed partitioned views will be discussed later in the book.

The initial Beta 1 of Shiloh was released to a very small group of Early Adopters and serious beta testers in September 1999. Shortly after that, Microsoft announced that the official name of the product would be SQL Server 2000. There were two main reasons for this change. First, because of everything that was changing about the product, it was unrealistic to make it just a dot release (7.5); it really needed a whole new number. Second, if the product had gone with the name 8.0, it would be the only Microsoft BackOffice product that didn't use the name 2000. To conform to this companywide naming standard, the name SQL Server 2000 was announced. However, if you look at the internal version number using the *@@VERSION* function, you'll see that it returns the number 8.00.194.

It turns out that from the user's perspective, SQL Server 2000 introduces even more new functionality than did its immediate predecessor. SQL Server 7 had a completely rewritten engine, including brand-new storage structures, data access methods, locking technology, recovery algorithms, transaction log architecture, memory architecture, and optimizer. These, of course, are the things that this book describes in detail. But for the end user, developer, or part-time database administrator (DBA), the external changes and language enhancements in SQL Server 7 were minimal. SQL Server 2000 adds dozens of new language features as well as drastic changes to existing objects such as table constraints, views, and triggers that all developers and most DBAs will need to know about.

Because the internal engine changes are minimal, only two betas were planned. Beta 2, released in April 2000, was the widespread public beta and was sent to thousands of interested users, conference attendees, ISVs, and consultants. The SQL Server 2000 development team froze the code at build 8.00.194.01, on August 6, 2000, and released the product to manufacturing on August 9, 2000.

Internal SQL Server development is a never-ending story. Just as after the release of SQL Server 7, new capabilities were already well past the design stage, ready to be implemented. Features that didn't make it into SQL Server 2000, as well as continued improvements in scalability, availability, interoperability, and overall performance, continue to be addressed. The development team is using feedback from the beta forums and from early users of the released version of SQL Server 2000 to shape the future of Microsoft SQL Server.

Chapter 2

A Tour of SQL Server

Microsoft SQL Server 2000 is a high-performance client/server relational database management system (RDBMS). It was designed to support high-volume transaction processing (such as that for online order entry, inventory, accounting, or manufacturing) as well as data warehousing and decision-support applications (such as sales analysis applications). SQL Server 2000 runs on Microsoft Windows NT 4 or Microsoft Windows 2000 Server–based networks using Intel processors and can be installed as a personal desktop database system on machines running Windows NT Workstation 4, Windows 2000 Professional, Windows 98, and Windows Millennium Edition (Me). You can use the same CD to install one of the Server versions or the Personal version of SQL Server 2000. In addition, you can install multiple instances of SQL Server 2000 on the same computer, each with its own set of users and its own data. (I'll cover the details of multiple instances in Chapter 4.)

SQL Server 2000 actually has seven different editions available on different CDs: Standard Edition, Enterprise Edition, Personal Edition, Developer Edition, Windows CE Edition, Evaluation Edition, and Microsoft Desktop Engine (MSDE). (I'll discuss the differences between the editions in Chapter 4.)

> **NOTE** To simplify operating system designations, I'll use the following conventions. Windows NT/2000 means any of the following operating systems that support SQL Server 2000: Windows NT Server 4, Windows NT Server 4, Enterprise Edition, Windows NT Workstation 4, Windows 2000 Server, Windows 2000 Advanced Server, Windows 2000 Professional, or Windows 2000 Datacenter Server. If I need to refer specifically to just the server platforms, I'll use the designation Windows NT/2000 Server, which means any of the operating systems listed above except Windows NT Workstation 4 and Windows 2000 Professional. To refer to just the non-server operating systems, I'll use Windows NT/2000 Workstation. The designation Windows 98 includes both Windows 98 and Windows Me.

SQL Server 2000 also provides many client tools and networking interfaces for other Microsoft operating systems, such as Windows 3.1 and MS-DOS. And because of SQL Server's open architecture, other systems (such as UNIX-based systems) can also interoperate with it. SQL Server is part of the core of a family of integrated products that includes development tools, systems management tools, distributed system components, and open development interfaces, as shown in Figure 2-1. It's also a key part of Microsoft BackOffice.

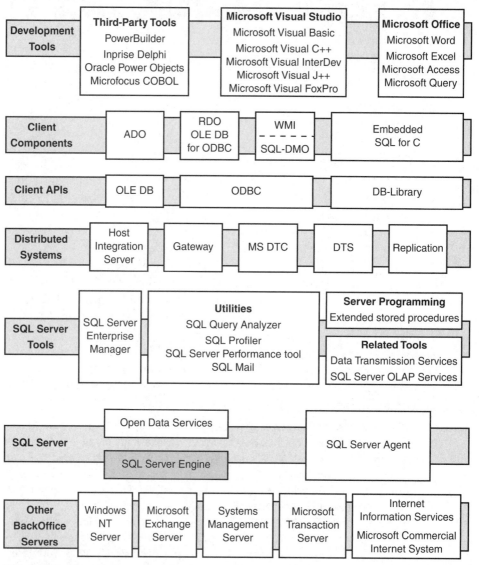

Figure 2-1. *The SQL Server family of integrated components.*

Most of this book focuses on the capabilities and uses of the SQL Server engine; this chapter provides an overview of the SQL Server family of components and describes the features and benefits of each component. Understanding these features and benefits will be helpful to you as you develop applications.

THE SQL SERVER ENGINE

The SQL Server engine supports a variety of demanding applications, such as online transaction processing (OLTP) and decision-support applications. At the core of its decision-support capabilities is Transact-SQL, Microsoft's version of Structured Query Language (SQL). Beneath this query language are the components that support transaction processing and recoverability.

Transact-SQL

SQL is a well-known, widely used data access language. Every mainstream database management system (DBMS) product implements SQL in some way. Transact-SQL (often referred to as *T-SQL*) is a powerful and unique superset of the SQL standard.

The SQL SELECT statement provides tremendous power and flexibility for retrieving information. Using SELECT, data from multiple tables can be easily chosen and combined and the results returned in tabular format.

Take a look at the following two tables from the *pubs* sample database. (This database, which I use in many examples in this book, is installed when SQL Server is installed. For brevity, I'll sometimes use an abbreviated amount of the data, as in this example.)

```
publishers Table
pub_id      pub_name                    city            state
0736        New Moon Books              Boston          MA
0877        Binnet & Hardley            Washington      DC
1389        Algodata Infosystems        Berkeley        CA


titles Table
title_id    title                                       pub_id
BU1032      The Busy Executive's Database Guide          1389
BU1111      Cooking with Computers: Surreptitious        1389
            Balance Sheets
BU2075      You Can Combat Computer Stress!              0736
BU7832      Straight Talk About Computers                1389
MC2222      Silicon Valley Gastronomic Treats            0877
MC3021      The Gourmet Microwave                        0877
MC3026      The Psychology of Computer Cooking           0877
```

The following simple SELECT statement logically joins the *titles* and *publishers* tables to retrieve the book titles with their corresponding publishers:

```
SELECT title, pub_name, city, state
FROM titles JOIN publishers
  ON titles.pub_id = publishers.pub_id
```

Here's the result:

```
title                        pub_name              city        state
-----                        --------              ----        -----
The Busy Executive's Database Algodata Infosystems  Berkeley    CA
Guide
Cooking with Computers:      Algodata Infosystems  Berkeley    CA
Surreptitious Balance Sheets
You Can Combat Computer Stress! New Moon Books      Boston      MA
Straight Talk About Computers Algodata Infosystems  Berkeley    CA
Silicon Valley Gastronomic   Binnet & Hardley      Washington  DC
Treats
The Gourmet Microwave        Binnet & Hardley      Washington  DC
The Psychology of Computer   Binnet & Hardley      Washington  DC
Cooking
```

The preceding query, a simple SQL statement, shows that standard SQL provides a powerful way to query and manipulate data. (In Chapters 7 and 10, I'll discuss SQL queries in much greater depth.)

The Transact-SQL language is compliant with the American National Standards Institute (ANSI) SQL-92 standard at the entry level. It offers considerably more power because of its unique extensions to the standard.

Transact-SQL Extensions

Transact-SQL provides a number of capabilities that extend beyond typical implementations of SQL. These capabilities allow you to easily and efficiently write queries that are difficult to write in standard SQL. You can, for example, embed additional SELECT statements in the SELECT list, and you can drill into a result set by further selecting data directly from a SELECT statement, a feature known as a *derived table*. Transact-SQL provides many system functions for dealing with strings (for finding substrings and so on), for converting datatypes, and for manipulating and formatting date information.

Transact-SQL also provides mathematical operations such as returning the square root of a number. In addition, you can use special operators such as CUBE and ROLLUP to efficiently perform multidimensional analysis at the database server, where the analysis can be optimized as part of the execution plan of a query. You can use the CASE expression to easily make complex conditional substitutions in the SELECT statement. Multidimensional (sometimes referred to as OLAP, or online analytical processing) operators, such as CUBE, and conditional expressions, such as CASE, are especially useful in implementing data warehousing solutions with SQL Server.

The Query Optimizer

In Transact-SQL, a cost-based query optimizer determines the likely best way to access data. This automatic optimization allows you to concentrate on defining your query criteria rather than defining how the query should be executed. For example, this nonprocedural approach eliminates the need for you to know which indexes exist and which, if any, should be used. Would it be more efficient to incur additional I/Os to read index pages in addition to data pages, or would it be better just to scan the data and then sort it? The optimizer automatically, invisibly, and efficiently resolves these types of important questions for you.

The query optimizer maintains statistics about the volume and dispersion of data, which it then uses to determine the execution plan that will most likely work best for the operation requested. Because a cost-based optimizer is by definition probability-based, an application might want to override the query optimizer in some special cases. In your application, you can specify *optimizer hints* that direct the choice of execution plan. In addition, you can use one of SQL Server's SHOWPLAN options to explain the chosen execution plan and provide insight into why it was chosen—this is information that allows you to fine-tune the application and database design.

The Programmable Server

Transact-SQL provides programming constructs—such as variables, conditional operations (IF-THEN-ELSE), and looping—that can dramatically simplify application development by allowing you to use a simple SQL script rather than a third-generation programming language (3GL). These branching and looping constructs can dramatically improve performance in a client/server environment by eliminating the need for network conversations. Minimizing network latency is an important aspect of maximizing client/server application performance. For example, instead of having the server return a value that the client needs to evaluate in order to issue a subsequent request, you can build conditional logic directly into the SQL batch file so that the routine is evaluated and executed entirely at the server.

You can use Transact-SQL to write complex batches of SQL statements. (A batch of SQL statements in a complex application can potentially be hundreds, or even thousands, of lines long.) An important capability of SQL Server 2000 is the T-SQL Debugger, which allows you to use SQL Query Analyzer to fully debug Transact-SQL routines, including stepping through the statements, setting breakpoints, and setting watchpoints on Transact-SQL variables.

Stored Procedures and Functions

Simply put, stored procedures and functions are collections of SQL statements stored in a SQL Server database. You can write complex queries and transactions as stored procedures and then invoke them directly from the front-end application. Whenever an ad hoc SQL command is sent to a database server for processing, the server must parse the command, check its syntax for sense, determine whether the requester has the permissions necessary to execute the command, and formulate an optimal execution plan to process the request. Stored procedures and functions execute faster than batches of dynamic SQL statements, sometimes dramatically faster, because they eliminate the need to reparse and reoptimize the requests each time they're executed. SQL Server supports stored procedures that let you store *groups* of compiled SQL statements on the server for later recall, to limit the overhead when the procedures are subsequently executed.

Stored procedures and functions differ from ad hoc SQL statements and from batches of SQL statements in that they're checked for syntax and compiled only the *first time* they're executed. SQL Server stores this compiled version in its memory cache and then uses the cached, compiled version to process subsequent calls, which results in faster execution times. Stored procedures and functions can also accept parameters, so they can be used by multiple applications using different input data.

Stored procedures and functions differ from each other in how they're used in your code. Stored procedures perform actions and usually contain all the error checking associated with that action. Many developers prefer to have each procedure perform a single, well-defined action. For example, a stored procedure might be written to insert a new order into the *orders* table, and the data must be checked for validity before the actual insert occurs. A function, on the other hand, returns a value, and that value can be used anywhere that any SQL statement can use a single value. For example, you can use a function in the list of items to return in the SELECT clause, you can compare it to other values in a WHERE clause, you can use it to generate a value for insertion in the VALUES clause of an INSERT statement, or you can use it to supply a parameter to a stored procedure or to another function. In addition, functions in SQL Server 2000 can return a table-valued result that you can use in a FROM clause. I'll discuss stored procedures and functions in detail in Chapter 11.

You can think of stored procedures as basic building blocks in database application development. Even if stored procedures provided no performance advantage (which, of course, they do), you'd still have a compelling reason to use them: they provide an important layer of insulation from changes in business practices. Suppose, for example, that a retailer maintains a mailing list for catalog distribution, which is used by multiple applications. After the applications are deployed, a change in criteria and logic (that is, the business rules) occurs, which affects which customers should automatically receive new catalogs. If the business rules were programmed directly into the company's applications, every application would need to be modified—probably an expensive and time-consuming operation. Furthermore, if multiple developers worked on the applications, the rules might not have been programmed with exactly the same semantics by every programmer.

A stored procedure, on the other hand, can be modified *once,* in seconds, at the server. An application need not be changed or even recompiled. The next time the application executes the stored procedure, the new rules are in place automatically.

In addition to providing a performance advantage, stored procedures can provide an important security function. By granting users access to a stored procedure but not to the underlying tables, you can allow them to access or manipulate data only in the way prescribed by the stored procedure.

Extended Stored Procedures

Extended stored procedures, which are unique to SQL Server, allow you to extend the programming capabilities provided by Transact-SQL and to access resources outside of SQL Server. Messaging integration, security integration, the ability to write Hypertext Markup Language (HTML) files (files formatted for use on the Internet), and much of the power of SQL Enterprise Manager (discussed later in this chapter) are all implemented using extended stored procedures. You can create extended stored procedures as external dynamic link libraries (DLLs). For example, you can write a DLL to establish a modem connection, dial the ACME Credit Service, and return a status value indicating credit approval or rejection. Also, you can build extended stored procedures using the Microsoft Open Data Services (ODS) API, which lets your stored procedures return self-describing result sets to the calling client applications, just as a normal stored procedure would.

Extended stored procedures allow even Microsoft to extend SQL Server. Good engineering practices dictate that if code doesn't benefit from being shared, it should be segregated and isolated. With this principle in mind, Microsoft added integration with messaging via the Messaging API (MAPI) as a set of extended stored procedures (*xp_sendmail*, *xp_readmail*, and so on) instead of directly modifying the SQL Server engine. Extended stored procedures allow you to add powerful features without risk of disrupting the core server engine. You can thus add more features quickly, with less risk of destabilizing the server. And because an extended procedure's DLL is loaded only if the procedure is executed, the memory footprint of SQL Server doesn't grow for services that aren't being used.

DBMS-ENFORCED DATA INTEGRITY

A database is only as useful as the user's confidence in it. That's why the server must enforce data integrity rules and business policies. SQL Server enforces data integrity within the database itself, guaranteeing that complex business policies are followed and that mandatory relationships between data elements are complied with.

Because SQL Server's client/server architecture allows you to use a variety of front-end applications to manipulate and present the same data from the server, it would be cumbersome to encode all the necessary integrity constraints, security permissions, and business rules into each application. If business policies were all coded in the front-end applications, *every* application would need to be modified *every time* a business policy changed. Even if you attempted to encode business rules into every client application, the danger of an application misbehaving would still exist. Most applications can't be fully trusted. Only the server can act as the final arbiter, and the server must not provide a back door for a poorly written or malicious application to subvert its integrity.

SQL Server uses advanced data integrity features such as stored procedures, declarative referential integrity (DRI), datatypes, constraints, rules, defaults, and triggers to enforce data integrity. Each of these features has its own use within a database; by combining these integrity features, you can make your database flexible and easy to manage yet secure.

Declarative Data Integrity

The ability to enforce data integrity based on the constraints you define when you create the database tables is known as declarative data integrity. The different kinds of declarative data integrity constraints correspond to the three fundamental aspects of data integrity: entity integrity, referential integrity, and domain integrity.

A central tenet of relational database theory is that every *tuple* of every *relation* (more colloquially, every *row* of every *table*) can be uniquely identified—a condition known as entity integrity. The attribute or combination of attributes (the column or combination of columns) that ensures uniqueness is known as the *primary key*. A table can have only one primary key. SQL Server allows you to designate the columns that make up the primary key when you define a table. This is known as a *PRIMARY KEY constraint*. SQL Server uses this PRIMARY KEY constraint to guarantee that the uniqueness of the values in the designated columns is never violated. It enforces entity integrity for a table by making sure that it has a primary key.

Sometimes more than one column (or combination of columns) of a table can uniquely identify a row—for example, an employee table might have an employee ID (*emp_id*) column and a Social Security number (*soc_sec_num*) column, both of whose values are considered unique. Such columns are often referred to as *alternate keys* or *candidate keys*. These keys must also be unique. Although a table can have only one primary key, it can have multiple alternate keys. SQL Server supports the multiple alternate key concept via *UNIQUE constraints*. When a column or combination of columns is declared unique, SQL Server prevents any row from being added or updated that would violate this uniqueness.

Assigning an arbitrary unique number as the primary key when no natural or convenient key exists is often most efficient. For example, businesses commonly use customer numbers or account numbers as unique identifiers or primary keys. SQL Server makes it easy to efficiently generate unique numbers by allowing one column in a table to have the *IDENTITY property*. You use the IDENTITY property to make sure that each value in the column is unique and that the values will increment (or decrement) by the amount you specify from a starting point that you specify. (A column with the IDENTITY property typically also has a PRIMARY KEY or UNIQUE constraint, but this isn't required.)

The second type of data integrity is referential integrity. SQL Server enforces logical relationships between tables with *FOREIGN KEY constraints*. A *foreign key* in a table is a column or combination of columns that match the primary key (or possibly an alternate key) of another table. The logical relationship between those two tables is the basis of the relational model; referential integrity means that this relationship is never violated.

For instance, the simple SELECT example shown earlier in the chapter includes a *titles* table and a *publishers* table. In the *titles* table, the column *title_id* (title ID) is the primary key. In the *publishers* table, the column *pub_id* (publisher ID) is the primary key. The *titles* table also includes a *pub_id* column, which isn't the primary key because a publisher can publish multiple titles. Instead, *pub_id* is a foreign key, and it references the primary key of the *publishers* table. If you declare this relationship when you define the table, SQL Server enforces it from both sides. First, it ensures that a title can't be entered in the *titles* table, or an existing *pub_id* in the *titles* table can't be modified, unless a valid publisher ID for the new *pub_id* is in the *publishers* table. Second, it ensures that no changes are made to a *pub_id* value in the *publishers* table without consideration of the referencing values in the *titles* table. It can do this in two ways. It can restrict changes to the *publishers* table so that a publisher can't be deleted or a *pub_id* value can't be changed if any titles in the *titles* table reference that publisher. Alternatively, it can cascade the changes through the *titles* table. So, if you were to delete a publisher, all rows in *titles* that reference that publisher would also be deleted. If you were to update a *pub_id*, all matching *pub_id* values in *titles* would be updated to the same value.

The third type of data integrity is domain integrity, in which individual data values must meet certain criteria. SQL Server makes sure that any data entered matches the type and range of the specified datatype. For example, it prohibits NULL values from being entered in a column unless the column explicitly allows NULLs. SQL Server supports a wide range of datatypes, resulting in great flexibility and efficient storage. It also supports the definition of CHECK constraints to define conditions that the data in a column must meet.

Datatypes

SQL Server datatypes provide the simplest form of data integrity by restricting the types of information (for example, characters, numbers, or dates) that can be stored in the columns of the database tables. You can also design your own datatypes (*user-defined* datatypes) to supplement those supplied by the system. For example, you can define a *state_code* datatype as two characters (CHAR(2)); SQL Server will then accept only two-character state codes. You can use a user-defined datatype to define columns in any table. An advantage of user-defined datatypes is that you can bind rules and defaults (which I'll discuss in the next two sections) to them for use in multiple tables, eliminating the need to include these types of checks in the front-end application.

CHECK Constraints and Rules

CHECK constraints and rules are integrity constraints that go beyond those implied by a column's datatype. When a user enters a value, SQL Server checks that value against any CHECK constraint or rule created for the specified column to ensure that only values that adhere to the definition of the constraint or rule are accepted.

Although CHECK constraints and rules are essentially equivalent in functionality, CHECK constraints are easier to use and provide more flexibility. CHECK constraints are the preferred mechanism for restricting values in a column; SQL Server provides rules primarily as backward compatibility feature. A CHECK constraint can be conveniently defined when a column is defined, it can be defined on multiple columns, and it has access to all of SQL Server's built-in functions. A rule, however, must be defined and then bound separately to a single column or user-defined datatype, and it has access only to built-in functions that don't reference database objects.

Both CHECK constraints and rules can require that a value fall within a particular range, match a particular pattern, or match one of the entries in a specified list. An advantage of CHECK constraints is that they can depend on either the value of another column or columns in the row or on the value returned by one of the built-in functions. A rule can't reference other fields. As an example of applying a CHECK constraint or rule, a database containing information on senior citizens could have the CHECK constraint or the rule "age column must contain a value between 65 and 120 years." A birth certificate database could require that the date in the *birth_date* column be some date prior to the current date.

Defaults

Defaults allow you to specify a value that SQL Server inserts if no value is explicitly entered in a particular field. For example, you can set the current date as the default value for an *order_date* field in a customer order record. Then, if a user or front-end application doesn't make an entry in the *order_date* field, SQL Server automatically inserts the current date. You can also use the keyword DEFAULT as a placeholder in an INSERT or UPDATE statement, which instructs SQL Server to set the value to the declared default value.

Triggers

Triggers are a special type of stored procedure. Stored procedures can be executed only when explicitly called; triggers are automatically invoked, or *triggered,* by SQL Server, and this is their main advantage. Triggers are associated with particular pieces of data and are called automatically whenever an attempt to modify that data is made, no matter what causes the modification (user entry or an application action).

Conceptually, a trigger is similar to a CHECK constraint or rule. SQL Server automatically activates triggers, constraints, and rules when an attempt is made to modify the data they protect. CHECK constraints and rules then perform fairly simple types of checks on the data—for example, "make sure the age field has a value between 0 and 120." Triggers, on the other hand, can enforce extremely elaborate restrictions on the data, which helps to ensure that the rules by which your business operates can't be subverted. Because triggers are a form of stored procedure, they have the full power of the Transact-SQL language at their disposal and they can invoke other stored and extended stored procedures. You can write a trigger that enforces complex business rules, such as the following:

Don't accept an order:

If the customer has any past due accounts with us

OR

If the customer has a bad credit rating by ACME Credit Service (with the trigger calling an extended procedure that automatically dials up ACME to get the credit rating)

OR

If the order is for more than $50,000 and the customer has had an account with us for less than six months

This integrity check is quite powerful. Yet the trigger to enforce it is simple to write. Triggers can also enforce *referential integrity,* ensuring that relationships between tables are maintained. For example, a trigger can prohibit a customer record from being deleted if open orders exist for the customer, or it can prohibit any new order for a customer for which no record exists. While you can do all this by declaring primary and foreign key constraints, triggers give you some added flexibility and functionality. Triggers allow you to supply your own error messages, which might be more useful than the default messages provided by SQL Server. Triggers also allow you to implement other forms of referential actions beside those available with the foreign key definition. I'll talk more about referential actions in Chapter 6, where I'll talk about constraints, and in Chapter 12, where I'll go into greater detail about triggers.

Triggers automatically execute whenever a specified change to a data object is attempted. A trigger executes once per statement, even if multiple rows would be affected. It has access to the before and after images of the data. SQL Server 2000 provides two kinds of triggers: "after" triggers and "instead-of" triggers. Instead-of triggers are what some people might call "before" triggers, but that name is not really accurate for SQL Server. An instead-of trigger defines actions to be carried out instead of the requested data modification. A before trigger would define actions to perform prior to the data modification. By default, if a table or view has an instead-of trigger defined for a particular modification operation (INSERT, UPDATE, or DELETE), that data modification does *not* take place. Instead, the trigger action is executed.

An after trigger executes after the data has been modified. The trigger takes further action such as rolling back the current transaction or carrying out special referential actions.

TRANSACTION PROCESSING

Transaction processing guarantees the consistency and recoverability of SQL Server databases. A *transaction* is the basic unit of work in SQL Server. Typically, it consists of several SQL commands that read and update the database, but the update is not considered "final" until a COMMIT command is issued.

Transaction processing in SQL Server ensures that all transactions are performed as a single unit of work—even in the presence of a hardware or general system failure. Such transactions are referred to as having the *ACID properties*: atomicity, consistency, isolation, and durability. In addition to guaranteeing that explicit multistatement transactions (such as those provided in the following DEBIT_CREDIT example) maintain the ACID properties, SQL Server guarantees that a single command that affects multiple rows also maintains the ACID properties.

Here's an example in pseudocode of an ACID transaction. (Note that error handling would be required to achieve the behavior described earlier.)

```
BEGIN TRANSACTION DEBIT_CREDIT
Debit savings account $1000
Credit checking account $1000
COMMIT TRANSACTION DEBIT_CREDIT
```

Now let's take a closer look at each of the ACID properties.

Atomicity

SQL Server guarantees the atomicity of its transactions. Atomicity means that each transaction is treated as all-or-nothing—it either commits or aborts. If a transaction commits, all of its effects remain. If it aborts, all of its effects are undone. In the previous DEBIT_CREDIT example, if the savings account debit is reflected in the database but the checking account credit isn't, funds will essentially disappear from the database; that is, funds will be subtracted from the savings account but never added to the checking account. If the reverse occurs (if the checking account is credited and the savings account is *not* debited), the customer's checking account will mysteriously increase in value without a corresponding customer cash deposit or account transfer. Because of SQL Server's atomicity feature, both the debit and credit must be completed or else neither event is completed.

Consistency

The consistency property ensures that a transaction won't allow the system to arrive at an incorrect logical state—the data must always be logically correct. Constraints and rules are honored even in the event of a system failure. In the DEBIT_CREDIT example, the logical rule is that money can't be created or destroyed—a corresponding, counter-balancing entry must be made for each entry. (Consistency is implied by, and in most situations is redundant with, atomicity, isolation, and durability.)

Isolation

Isolation separates concurrent transactions from the updates of other incomplete transactions. In the DEBIT_CREDIT example, another transaction can't see the work-in-progress while the transaction is being carried out. For example, if another transaction reads the balance of the savings account after the debit occurs, and then the DEBIT_CREDIT transaction is aborted, the other transaction will be working from a balance that never logically existed.

Isolation among transactions is accomplished automatically by SQL Server. It locks data to allow multiple concurrent users to work with data, but it prevents side effects that can distort the results and make them different than would be expected if users serialized their requests (that is, if requests were queued and serviced one at a time). This serializability feature is one of the isolation levels that SQL Server supports. SQL Server supports multiple degrees of isolation levels that allow you to make the appropriate tradeoff between how much data to lock and how long to hold locks. This tradeoff is known as *concurrency* vs. *consistency*. Locking reduces concurrency (because locked data is unavailable to other users), but it provides the benefit of higher consistency. (Chapter 14 provides much more detail about locking.)

Durability

After a transaction commits, SQL Server's durability property ensures that the effects of the transaction persist even if a system failure occurs. Conversely, if a system failure occurs while a transaction is in progress, the transaction is completely undone, leaving no partial effects on the data. For example, if a power outage occurs in the midst of a transaction before the transaction is committed, the entire transaction is automatically rolled back when the system is restarted. If the power fails immediately after the acknowledgment of the commit is sent to the calling application, the transaction is guaranteed to exist in the database. Write-ahead logging and automatic rollback and rollforward of transactions during the recovery phase of SQL Server startup ensure durability.

SYMMETRIC SERVER ARCHITECTURE

SQL Server uses a single-process, multithreaded architecture known as Symmetric Server Architecture that provides scalable high performance with efficient use of system resources. With Symmetric Server Architecture, only one memory address space is provided for the DBMS, eliminating the overhead of having to manage shared memory.

Traditional Process/Thread Model

To understand the architecture of SQL Server, it's useful to first understand the traditional architectures used by UNIX-based DBMS products. UNIX-based DBMS products are usually structured in one of two ways. One architecture uses multiple processes (or *shadow processes*), with one process per user, which makes the system quite resource-intensive. The second type of architecture employs a single process that tries to simulate an operating system threading facility by moving in a round-robin way among multiple requests, maintaining a stack for each request and switching to the specific stack for whatever unit is being executed.

> **NOTE** A *stack* is a last-in, first-out (LIFO) data structure that's kept in memory. It essentially serves as the control block for the executable unit on an operating system. (In Windows NT/2000, the basic executable unit is known as a *thread*, often called a *lightweight process* in other operating systems.) A thread stack stores status data such as function call return addresses, passed parameters, and some local variables.

In the first approach, because each process has its own address space, processes must resort to shared memory to communicate with one another. Unfortunately, shared memory is less efficient to use than the private memory of a process's own address space because of the weight of synchronization mechanisms (semaphores, mutexes, and so on) that are needed to avoid collisions while accessing shared memory. In addition, the implementation of stack switching and synchronized access to shared memory adds overhead and complexity. Adding complexity to a system is never good. The best way to avoid bugs in software and maximize performance is to keep code simple and, better yet, to write no new code when an existing tried-and-true service exists.

In the second approach, called simulated multithreading, the DBMS performs duties usually handled by the operating system. Typically, using such an architecture requires that the executing task be trusted to yield back to the system so another task can be run. If the task doesn't yield (because of software or hardware failure), *all* other tasks are severely—and perhaps fatally—affected.

SQL Server Process/Thread Model

SQL Server 2000 uses a scheduling architecture that's somewhere in between the two traditional approaches. Windows NT/2000 makes available support for lightweight threads, called *fibers*. Certain high-volume symmetric multiprocessing (SMP) systems can gain considerable performance benefits by using fibers instead of using threads, and Microsoft wanted to make this functionality possible with SQL Server.

> **NOTE** A more complete description of the Windows NT/2000 process and thread model is beyond the scope of this book. For more information, see *Inside Microsoft Windows 2000*, Third Edition, by David Solomon and Mark Russinovich (Microsoft Press, 2000) or *Programming Server-Side Applications for Microsoft Windows 2000* by Jeffrey Richter (Microsoft Press, 2000).

To make the best use of fibers, SQL Server takes control of their scheduling; it does so by using one or more operating system threads as its own schedulers. These threads are called *UMS threads,* or *User Mode Schedulers.* Whether it's running in thread mode or fiber mode, SQL Server uses only one UMS thread per CPU. Each SQL Server fiber is associated with exactly one UMS thread, and the fiber remains with that UMS thread for its lifetime. Windows NT/2000 can schedule each of the UMS threads on any of the available processors. Each UMS thread determines which of the SQL Server processes associated with that UMS thread should run at any given time. Chapter 17 examines in detail how to control whether SQL Server processes run on threads or fibers, and the benefits and drawbacks of each option.

SQL Server processes that execute non–SQL Server code aren't scheduled by the UMS. These processes include those that run extended stored procedures and those that run distributed queries. These processes are scheduled on normal operating system threads and managed by Windows NT/2000's own scheduler. In addition, when SQL Server is executing a backup or restore operation, additional UMS threads control the progress of the operation.

Multiuser Performance

The efficiency of the SQL Server threading model is borne out by its multiuser performance. SQL Server can efficiently handle hundreds, even thousands, of simultaneous active users. Built-in thread pooling allows workloads of this magnitude without the need for an external Transaction Processing (TP) Monitor, which adds cost and complexity to a system.

> **NOTE** Of course, questions such as "How many users can SQL Server handle?" and "How big a database can it handle?" never have simple answers. The answers depend on the application and its design, required response times and throughput, and the hardware on which the system is running.

Most systems that just a couple of years ago required a mainframe or large minicomputer-based solution can now be efficiently built, deployed, and managed using SQL Server. Such industry-standard benchmarks as TPC-C can be illuminating. Today's SQL Server can perform workloads that surpass those submitted by the largest mainframe systems of a few years ago. As computer resources continue to grow, SQL Server will extend its reach into systems that have traditionally required a mainframe solution.

SECURITY

SQL Server 2000 security provides two basic methods for authenticating logins: Windows Authentication and SQL Server Authentication. In Windows Authentication, SQL Server login security is integrated directly with Windows NT/2000 security, allowing the operating system to authenticate SQL Server users. Windows Authentication allows SQL Server to take advantage of the security features of the operating system, such as password encryption, password aging, and minimum and maximum length restrictions on passwords. In SQL Server Authentication, an administrator creates SQL Server login accounts within SQL Server, and any user connecting to SQL Server must supply a valid SQL Server login name and password.

Windows Authentication makes use of *trusted connections,* which rely on the impersonation feature of Windows NT/2000. Through impersonation, SQL Server can take on the security context of the Windows NT/2000 user account initiating the connection and test whether the security identifier (SID) has a valid privilege level. Windows NT/2000 impersonation and trusted connections are supported by any of the available network libraries (Net-Libraries) when connecting to SQL Server running under Windows NT/2000.

Under Windows 2000 only, SQL Server 2000 can use Kerberos to support mutual authentication between the client and the server, as well as the ability to pass a client's security credentials between computers so that work on a remote server can proceed using the credentials of the impersonated client. With Windows 2000, SQL Server 2000 uses Kerberos and delegation to support Windows Authentication as well as SQL Server Authentication.

The authentication method (or methods) used by SQL Server is determined by its security mode. SQL Server can run in one of two different security modes: Windows Authentication Mode (which uses Windows Authentication) and Mixed Mode (which uses both Windows Authentication and SQL Server Authentication). Windows Authentication Mode is available only for instances of SQL Server running on Windows NT/2000. When you connect to an instance of SQL Server configured for Windows Authentication Mode, you cannot supply a SQL Server login name and your Windows NT/2000 username determines your level of access to SQL Server.

Under Mixed Mode, Windows NT/2000–based clients can connect using Windows Authentication, and connections that don't come from Windows NT/2000 clients or that come across the Internet can connect using SQL Server Authentication. In addition, when a user connects to an instance of SQL Server that has been installed in Mixed Mode, the connection can always explicitly supply a SQL Server login name. This allows a connection to be made using a login name distinct from the username in Windows NT/2000. Because Windows 98 doesn't support Windows Authentication, SQL Server on Windows 98 runs only in Mixed Mode and only supports SQL Server Authentication.

Monitoring and Managing Security

SQL Server makes it easy to monitor logon successes and failures. Using SQL Enterprise Manager, administrators can simply select the appropriate Audit Level option on the Security tab of the Properties dialog box for a particular installation of SQL Server. When logon monitoring is enabled in this way, each time a user successfully or unsuccessfully attempts to log on to SQL Server, a message is written to the Windows NT/2000 event log, the SQL Server error log, or both, indicating the time, date, and user who tried to log on.

SQL Server has a number of facilities for managing data security. You can grant or deny access privileges (select, insert, update, and delete) to users or groups of users for objects such as tables and views. You can grant execute privileges for normal and extended stored procedures. For example, to prevent a user from directly updating a specific table, you can write a stored procedure that updates the table and then cascades those updates to other tables as necessary. You can grant the user access to execute the stored procedure, thereby ensuring that all updates take place through the stored procedure, eliminating the possibility of integrity problems arising from ad hoc updates to the base table.

HIGH AVAILABILITY

In many mission-critical environments, the application must be available at all times—24 hours a day, seven days a week. SQL Server helps ensure availability by providing online backup, online maintenance, automatic recovery, and the ability to install SQL Server on a cluster for failover support. SQL Server's dynamic online backup allows databases to be backed up while users are actively querying and updating the database. The SQL Server Agent service provides a built-in scheduling engine that enables backups to occur automatically, without administrator involvement. You can also accomplish other maintenance tasks, such as diagnostics, design changes (for example, adding a column to a table), and integrity changes without having to shut down SQL Server or restrict user access.

Only a few systemwide configuration modifications, such as changing the maximum number of user connections, require that SQL Server be restarted. Although reconfiguration doesn't commonly occur in a well-planned and well-deployed production system, it can typically be completed with less than a minute of system downtime if it's necessary.

In the event of a system failure, such as a power outage, SQL Server ensures rapid database recovery when services are restored. By using the transaction logs associated with each database, SQL Server quickly recovers each database upon startup, rolling back transactions that weren't completed and rolling forward transactions that were committed but not yet written to disk. In addition, you can set the SQL Server Agent service to continually monitor the state of SQL Server. If an error occurs that causes SQL Server to stop unexpectedly, the service detects this and can automatically restart SQL Server with minimal interruption.

In cooperation with shared-disk cluster hardware, SQL Server Enterprise Edition provides failover support when you install one or more instances of SQL Server 2000 on a node that's part of a Microsoft Cluster Service (MSCS) cluster. Up to four nodes can be part of a cluster. The applications communicating with SQL Server don't need to know that the server they're connecting to is actually a virtual server, which can be running on any member of a cluster. If the server on which SQL Server is running fails, one of the other servers in the cluster immediately takes ownership of the disks that hold the SQL Server data and takes over the failed server's workload. The other servers in the cluster don't need to be inactive when the first server is working—they can run SQL Server while it performs other activities.

DISTRIBUTED DATA PROCESSING

SQL Server provides features such as linked servers, remote procedure calls, and a two-phase commit protocol that enable you to easily manage and use data in distributed environments. Microsoft Distributed Transaction Coordinator (MS DTC) is the vote collector and coordinator of transactions, and it allows many types of systems to participate, laying the foundation for ACID transactions among heterogeneous systems.

A system participating in a transaction coordinated by MS DTC manages its own work and is called a *resource manager*. This resource manager system communicates with MS DTC, which coordinates all the resource managers participating in the transaction to implement the two-phase commit protocol. Distributed transactions honoring the ACID properties are supported as a whole: the entire distributed transaction at all sites either commits or aborts.

In the first phase of the two-phase commit protocol, all participating resource managers (that is, those that have enlisted in the transaction) *prepare to commit*. This means that they have acquired all the locks and resources they need to complete the transaction. MS DTC then acts as a vote collector. If it gets confirmation that all participants are prepared to commit, it signals to go ahead and commit.

The actual COMMIT is the second phase of the protocol. If one or more participants notify the system that they can't successfully prepare the transaction, MS DTC automatically sends a message to all participants indicating that they must abort the transaction. (In this case, an *abort,* rather than a commit, is the protocol's second phase.) If one or more participants don't report back to MS DTC in phase one, the resource managers that have indicated they're prepared to commit (but haven't committed because they haven't yet received the instruction to do so) are said to be *in doubt*. Resource managers that have transactions in doubt hold the necessary locks and resources until the transaction either commits or aborts, thereby maintaining the ACID properties. (SQL Server provides a way to force in-doubt transactions to abort.)

Another important distributed capability allows SQL Server to issue a *remote procedure call (RPC)* to another server running SQL Server. RPCs are stored procedures that can be invoked from a remote server, allowing server-to-server communication. This communication can be transparent to the client application because the client can execute a procedure on one server and that procedure can then invoke a procedure on a different server.

By using RPCs, you can easily extend the capacity of an application without the added cost of reengineering the client application. RPCs can also be coordinated by the MS DTC service to ensure that the transactions maintain their ACID properties. The default behavior is to *not* execute the RPC in the context of a transaction so that if the local transaction is rolled back, work done by the RPC will still be committed. You can override this behavior by using the command BEGIN DISTRIBUTED TRANSACTION or by setting the configuration option *remote proc trans* to 1.

You can also manage distributed data by defining and accessing *linked servers*. A linked server can be any data source for which an OLE DB provider exists. The most commonly used OLE DB providers are the SQL Server OLE DB provider; the Jet provider, which allows you to connect to Microsoft Access databases, Excel spreadsheets, and text files; and the Open Database Connectivity (ODBC) provider, which allows you to connect to any ODBC data source.

A linked server is a logical name defined using the *sp_addlinkedserver* stored procedure. The information you provide when you define the linked server includes the name and location of the data source to connect to. Once you've defined the name, you can use that name as the first part of a four-part name for any object, such as a table, a view, or a stored procedure. Objects on the linked server can be queried as well as modified, and they can be used in joins with local objects. The types of queries possible on the linked server depend on the capabilities of the particular OLE DB providers. Some providers, such as the one for SQL Server, allow all data modification operations and full transaction control across linked servers. Others, such as the OLE DB provider for text files, allow only querying of data.

DATA REPLICATION

Replication allows you to automatically distribute copies of data from one server to one or more destination servers at one or more remote locations. *Data integrity* is a key design point of SQL Server's replication capabilities. The data at replicating sites might be slightly outdated, but it will accurately reflect the state of the data at a recent point in time and is guaranteed to reflect any changes made soon after they occur (or soon after a reliable network connection is established).

SQL Server 2000 supports three modes of replication, which are detailed on the companion CD in a whitepaper titled "Understanding SQL Server 7.0 Replication."

- **Transactional replication**   In this mode of replication, one site is considered the owner, or publisher, of a published article (a table or a subset of a table), and other sites subscribe to that article. All changes made to the article must be made at the publisher and then replicated to the subscribers.

- **Merge replication**   Although the publisher defines the articles to be published, any participating sites can make changes. System tables keep track of the changes, which are then propagated to all participants, including the original publisher. You can define which type of conflict resolution to use in the event of conflicting updates made by multiple sites.

- **Snapshot replication**   All data from the publishing site is periodically copied to all the subscribing sites. Individual changes aren't propagated. This method was formerly called *scheduled table refresh*.

Distributed transactions that use the two-phase commit protocol guarantee that the ACID properties are maintained, but replication doesn't. Replication isn't strongly consistent (the *C* in ACID). Instead, it provides *loosely consistent* data. With the two-phase commit protocol, a transaction is an all-or-nothing proposition, and the data is guaranteed to be *strongly consistent*. But inherent in the two-phase commit algorithm is the fact that a failure at any one site makes the entire transaction fail or can keep the transaction in doubt for a long period of time, during which all participants must hold locks, thereby crippling concurrency. SQL Server does provide an option to transactional replication called Immediate Updating Subscribers that uses distributed transactions between one subscriber and the publisher. Other subscribers to the same publication will not be updated as part of the transaction, however.

At first glance, you might think a system should require that updates be made at all sites in *real time*. In fact, when the costs of two-phase commit are realized (chiefly, the vulnerability that can result from a failure at just one node), the most pragmatic solution might be to make changes in *real-enough time*.

For example, suppose you run a car rental agency with 500 rental counters worldwide and you maintain a customer profile table containing 500,000 renters who belong to your Gold Card program. You want to store this customer profile table locally at all 500 rental counters so that even if a communication failure occurs, the profiles will be available wherever a Gold Card member might walk up to do business. Although all sites should have up-to-date records of all customers, it would be disastrous to insist that an update of the Gold Card profile must occur as part of a two-phase transaction for all 500 sites or not at all. If you were to do that, because of the vagaries of worldwide communication or because a storm might knock out the power at one site, you wouldn't be able to perform a simple update to the customer profile very often.

Replication is a much better solution in this case. The master customer profile table is maintained at your corporate headquarters. Replication publishes this data, and the rental counters subscribe to this information. When customer data is changed or when a customer is added or removed, these changes (and *only* these changes) are propagated to all the subscribing sites. In a well-connected network, the time delay might be just a few seconds. If a particular site is unavailable, no other sites are affected—they still get their changes. When the unavailable site is back online, the changes are automatically propagated and the subscriber is brought up to date. At any time, a given rental counter might have information that's slightly out of date— that is, it might reflect the state of the data at the corporate headquarters at some earlier time. This is considered loosely consistent, as opposed to the strongly consistent model of two-phase commit, in which all sites (or none) immediately reflect the change.

Although a time delay can occur in loosely consistent systems, maintaining transactional consistency is one of the chief design points of SQL Server replication. If multiple updates occur as a single atomic transaction to data being replicated, the entire transaction is also replicated. At the subscribing site, the transaction either entirely commits or is again replicated until it commits.

With SQL Server, data can be replicated continuously or at specified intervals. It can be replicated in its entirety or as filtered subsets (known as *horizontal* and *vertical partitions*). In addition to replicating to other SQL Servers, SQL Server 2000 can replicate to heterogeneous data sources that have an appropriate ODBC driver or OLE DB provider available. These include Access databases, Oracle databases, and other ODBC data sources. SQL Server 2000 can also replicate *from* other data sources, using ODBC drivers or OLE DB providers. These sources include Oracle 8, Microsoft Jet version 4, and IBM DB/2.

Unlike SQL Server, some products on the market promote replication as an "update anywhere, anytime, any way" model. However, this model has inherently unstable behavior if many nodes participate and update activity is moderate to heavy.[1]

---

1. Gray, Helland, O'Neil, and Shasha, "The Dangers of Replication and a Solution," SIGMOD (1996). SIGMOD (Special Interest Group on Management of Data) is a yearly database-oriented conference for developers. For more information, see http://www.acm.org/sigmod/.

Updates made at multiple sites will conflict with one another and will have to be reconciled. SQL Server 2000's merge replication does allow multiple site updates, but it's not a true "update anywhere, anytime, any way" solution. (See the whitepaper on the companion CD for more details on exactly what SQL Server merge replication can do.)

SYSTEMS MANAGEMENT

The difficulty of systems management is probably the single biggest obstacle to mass deployment of client/server solutions. Far from being a downsized version of the mainframe, today's distributed client/server system can be deployed on dozens or even hundreds of distributed servers, all of which must be controlled to the same exacting standards as mainframe production software systems. The issues here reside both inside and outside the database environment. SQL Server provides a comprehensive architecture and tools for managing the database and related activities.

SQL Server Enterprise Manager

SQL Server Enterprise Manager is a major advancement in making client/server deployments manageable. In SQL Server 2000, SQL Server Enterprise Manager is a snap-in to Microsoft Management Console (MMC), a tool that provides a common interface for managing various server applications in a Windows network. (Another snap-in that's provided on your SQL Server 2000 CD for use with MMC is the SQL Server OLAP Services snap-in.)

The easy-to-use SQL Server Enterprise Manager supports centralized management of all aspects of multiple installations of SQL Server, including security, events, alerts, scheduling, backup, server configuration, tuning, and replication. SQL Server Enterprise Manager allows you to create, modify, and copy SQL Server database schemas and objects such as tables, views, and triggers. Because multiple installations of SQL Server can be organized into groups and treated as a unit, SQL Server Enterprise Manager can manage hundreds of servers simultaneously.

Although it can run on the same computer as the SQL Server engine, SQL Server Enterprise Manager offers the same management capabilities while running on any Windows NT/2000–based machine. SQL Server Enterprise Manager also runs on Windows 98, although a few capabilities aren't available in this environment (most notably the ability to use the Service Control Manager, a feature of Windows NT/2000, to remotely start and stop SQL Server). In addition, the efficient client/server architecture of SQL Server makes it practical to use the remote access (dial-up networking) capabilities of Windows NT/2000 as well as Windows 98 for administration and management.

Enterprise Manager's easy-to-use interface is shown in Figure 2-2. You can perform even complex tasks with just a few mouse clicks.

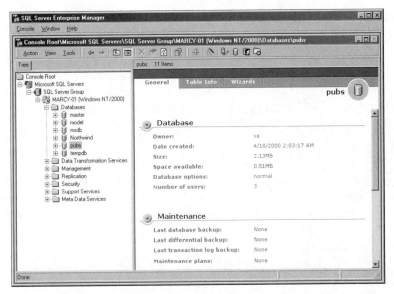

Figure 2-2. *The SQL Server Enterprise Manager interface.*

SQL Server Enterprise Manager relieves you from having to know the specific steps and syntax to complete a job. It provides more than 20 wizards to guide you through the process of setting up and maintaining your installation of SQL Server. A partial list is shown in Figure 2-3.

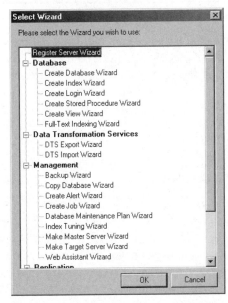

Figure 2-3. *Some of the wizards available for setting up and maintaining your server.*

Distributed Management Objects

Microsoft SQL Server Distributed Management Objects (SQL-DMO) is the SQL Server Automation object model. You can use the SQL-DMO objects, properties, methods, and collections to write scripts and programs that administer multiple servers running SQL Server distributed across a network. SQL Server Enterprise Manager is built entirely with SQL-DMO. You can customize your own specific management needs using SQL-DMO, or you can integrate management of SQL Server into other tools you use or provide.

All SQL Server functions are exposed through the SQL-DMO object model. The primary object is SQLServer, which contains a collection of Database objects. Each Database object contains a collection of Table, View, and StoredProcedure objects. You can control SQL Server by changing SQL-DMO object properties (*SQLServer.Name = "MARKETING_SVR"*) and by invoking SQL-DMO object methods (SQLServer.Start or SQLServer.Shutdown).

Table 2-1 provides some examples of SQL-DMO objects and methods.

Object.Method	*Action*
SQLServer.Shutdown	Stops SQL Server
SQLServer.Start	Starts SQL Server
Index.UpdateStatistics	Updates optimizer information for indexes
Database.Tables.Add	Adds a table to a database

Table 2-1. *SQL-DMO objects and methods.*

The SQL-DMO object model is comprehensive, consisting of dozens of distinct objects and hundreds of Component Object Model (COM) interfaces. The organization of these objects greatly simplifies the task of learning and fully using SQL Server management components.

Any Automation-controlling application can harness the power and services of SQL-DMO. Probably the most common such Automation controller is Microsoft Visual Basic.

Windows Management Instrumentation

The SQL Server 2000 CD contains a technology preview of a new API for supporting your SQL Server installations called Windows Management Instrumentation (WMI). WMI, which is similar to SQL-DMO and in fact maps directly to SQL-DMO methods and objects, lets you access and manipulate not only your SQL Server objects but also other components in your Windows network. These other components can include servers, printers, registry keys, performance monitor counters (system monitor counters in Windows 2000), and events from Windows NT/2000's application log, system log, and security log.

WMI is not installed by the SQL Server 2000 installation program but is available in the \x86\other\wmi folder on the same CD. Unlike SQL-DMO, the WMI components are installed on the server instead of on the client machines. In future releases, WMI will communicate directly with SQL Server rather than going through an SQL-DMO layer.

SQL-DMO and Visual Basic Scripting

The power of using the SQL-DMO object model for SQL Server management becomes clear when you consider the potential of using a rapid application development (RAD) language such as Visual Basic as a scripting environment for administrative tasks. The following sample code lists the name of and space available on all databases on a server. This code is simple, compact, and easy to write and read, yet it's powerful. (Traditionally, programming such a task would have required several pages of much more complex C code.)

```
Dim MyServer As New SQLServer     ' Declare the SQLServer object
Dim MyDB As Database

MyServer.Name = "MARKETING_SVR"
MyServer.Login = "sa"
MyServer.Password = "password"
MyServer.Connect              ' Connect to the SQL Server

' List the name and space available for all databases
For Each MyDB In MyServer.Databases
    Debug.Print MyDB.Name, MyDB.SpaceAvailable
Next MyDB

MyServer.DisConnect           ' Disconnect
```

SQL Server Agent

SQL Server Agent is an active, intelligent agent that plays an integral role in the management of the SQL Server environment. It provides a full-function scheduling engine that supports regular tasks for the management and administration of SQL Server, and it allows you to schedule your own jobs and programs.

SQL Server Agent is a Windows NT/2000–based service that can be started when the operating system starts. You can also control and configure it from within SQL Server Enterprise Manager or SQL Server Service Manager. SQL Server Agent is entirely driven by entries in SQL Server tables that act as its control block. Clients never directly communicate with or connect to SQL Server Agent to add or modify scheduled jobs. Instead, they simply make the appropriate entries in the SQL Server tables (although this typically occurs through SQL Server Enterprise Manager via a simple dialog box that's similar to a typical calendar program). At startup, SQL Server Agent connects to an installation of SQL Server that contains its job table and then loads the list of jobs, the steps that make up each job, and the possible alerts that can be fired.

SQL Server Agent, like the SQL Server engine, is a single multithreaded process. It runs in its own process space and manages the creation of operating system threads to execute scheduled jobs. Its discrete managed subsystems (for replication, task management, and event alerting) are responsible for all aspects of processing specific jobs. When jobs are completed (successfully or not), the subsystem returns a result status (with optional messages) to SQL Server Agent. SQL Server Agent then records the completion status in both the operating system's application log and the job history table in SQL Server and optionally sends an e-mail report of the job status to the designated operator.

In SQL Server 2000, scheduled jobs can be made up of multiple steps; each step defines the action to take if it succeeds and the action to take if it fails. Thus, you can control the execution of subsequent steps when a step fails.

SQL Server 2000 allows you to define a server as a *master* server for the purpose of scheduling jobs that will be carried out by one or more *target* servers. These target servers periodically poll their master server to determine whether any new jobs have been defined. If so, the master server downloads the job definitions to the target server. After the jobs are run on the target server, the success or failure status is reported back to the master server. The master server keeps the complete job history for all its target servers.

The event/alert subsystem gives SQL Server its ability to support proactive management. The primary role of the event/alert subsystem is to respond to events by raising alerts and invoking responses. As triggering activities (or user-defined activities) occur in the system, an event is posted to the operating system application log. SQL Server Agent monitors the application log to detect when an event has occurred.

SQL Server Agent determines whether any alerts have been defined for this event by examining the event's error number, severity, database of origin, and message text. If an alert has been defined (in the alert table), the operator(s) can be alerted via e-mail or pager or with a *net send* message. Alternatively, a SQL Server Agent job can be invoked when the alert is fired and can take corrective action. (For example, SQL Server Agent might automatically expand a full database.)

If no alerts have been defined locally, the event can be forwarded to another server for processing. This feature allows groups of servers to be monitored centrally so that alerts and operators can be defined once and then applied to multiple servers. Beyond the database environment, Microsoft Systems Management Server (SMS)—a BackOffice component—is available to provide key services to manage the overall software configuration of all the desktops and servers in the environment.

Alerts can also be fired in response to System Monitor (or Performance Monitor) thresholds being crossed. Normally, the crossing of a threshold isn't considered an error, and no event is written to the application log. However, the alert system in SQL Server 2000 is integrated with the performance counters available through System Monitor (discussed later in this chapter), and SQL Server can take action when a counter rises above or falls below a specified value. The kinds of actions possible are the same actions described on the previous page: the operator(s) can be alerted via e-mail or pager or with a *net send* message. Alternatively, a SQL Server Agent job can be invoked to take corrective action when the alert is fired.

For example, SQL Server Agent might automatically expand a database that's *almost* full. Note that being almost full is technically not an error: no error number or severity level is associated with this situation. However, because Performance Monitor can detect the condition of a database file reaching a certain percentage of its capacity, an alert can be raised. Figure 2-4 shows the definition of an alert based on a Performance Monitor threshold. This alert is fired when the log file for the *Northwind* database exceeds 80 percent of its capacity.

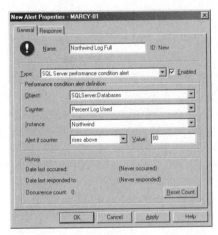

Figure 2-4. *Alert definition for a greater-than-80-percent-full condition in the* Northwind *database log file.*

SQL SERVER UTILITIES AND EXTENSIONS

SQL Server also includes utilities and extensions that provide increased functionality, such as Internet enabling, monitoring capability, easy setup, and easy data importing. (For in-depth information on any of the following utilities and extensions, see SQL Server Books Online.)

Web Assistant Wizard and Internet Enabling

SQL Server provides dynamic ways to work with the Internet using Web Assistant Wizard and interoperability with Microsoft Internet Information Services (IIS). Although both Web Assistant Wizard and IIS enable SQL Server data to be used with Web pages, they satisfy different needs.

Web Assistant Wizard generates HTML files from the result sets of SQL Server queries, making it simple to publish SQL Server data on the Internet. Let's say, for example, that a parts supplier keeps its inventory list in SQL Server. The supplier can publish its current parts inventory as a Web page (an HTML file) using Web Assistant Wizard. The wizard lets you submit an ad hoc query or stored procedure, do some simple formatting, include links to other Web pages, and use a template for more advanced formatting. The output of the query is written as an HTML table, and a Web page is created. You can also use Web Assistant Wizard to automatically update the Web page at regular intervals or whenever the data changes (via a trigger).

Web Assistant Wizard is distinct from but complementary to IIS in BackOffice. With the wizard, users browsing the Web page work separately from SQL Server because the data on the Web page has been extracted from the database beforehand. The wizard doesn't use or require IIS, and pages that the wizard generates can be viewed using any Internet browser.

IIS uses SQL Server's high-performance native ODBC interface to allow SQL queries to be fired from a Web page when a user accesses a particular region on the page. The results are then dynamically retrieved and combined with the HTML file for up-to-date viewing. In addition to Web Assistant Wizard and the dynamic query capabilities enabled with IIS, SQL Server is Internet-enabled in several other important ways. By minimizing network traffic and handshaking, SQL Server is inherently designed for efficient client/server computing. Extremely rich requests can be packaged via stored procedures or Transact-SQL batches for resolution entirely at the server, with only the results sent back to the initiating client application.

This capability has been a hallmark of SQL Server's client/server architecture from the outset, but nowhere is it more important than on the Internet, where network speed and bandwidth are often quite limited. In addition, SQL Server's networking architecture allows for ease of use and security on the Internet, including network name resolution. For example, Internet users can connect to SQL Server via a friendly name such as www.microsoft.com instead of via an arcane IP address such as 200.154.54.678. Secure encryption of data over the Internet is also possible.

SQL Server 2000 also provides XML support that enables querying and updating of XML documents in a SQL Server 2000 database. Standard SQL statements with the FOR XML clause can be issued from a Web-based client, and the results are returned to the client in XML format.

SQL Profiler

SQL Profiler is a graphical utility that allows database administrators and application developers to monitor and record database activity. SQL Profiler can display all server activity in real time, or it can create filters that focus on the actions of particular users, applications, or types of commands. SQL Profiler can display any SQL statement or stored procedure sent to any instance of SQL Server (if your security privileges allow it) as well as the output or response sent back to the initiating client.

SQL Profiler allows you to drill down even deeper into SQL Server and see every statement executed as part of a stored procedure, every data modification operation, every lock acquired or released, or every occurrence of a database file growing automatically. And that's just for starters. Dozens of different events can be captured, and dozens of data items can be captured for each event.

SQL Profiler is an important tool for tuning and debugging applications and for auditing and profiling the use of SQL Server. I'll discuss SQL Profiler in more detail in Chapter 17.

SQL Server Service Manager

SQL Server Service Manager (Figure 2-5) manages all instances of SQL Server, SQL Server Agent and MS DTC, as well as Microsoft Search and MSSQLServerOLAPService services. It provides a simple way to start, stop, or check the state of any of these services. Once you've used this application after booting the operating system, the application places an icon on the taskbar in the area of the taskbar clock. You can right-click on this icon to retrieve a menu of all the tasks that SQL Server Service Manager supports.

> **NOTE**   On machines running Windows 98, SQL Server Service Manager looks as shown in Figure 2-5. However, the components that can be started aren't services. Machines running Windows 98 don't support services, so SQL Server Service Manager actually starts separate executable programs. (The Microsoft Search service isn't available at all on Windows 98.)

Figure 2-5. *SQL Server Service Manager.*

System Monitor Integration

SQL Server provides an extension DLL (SQLCTR80.DLL) that integrates with the Windows NT/2000 Performance tool and graphically displays many important performance statistics such as memory use, number of users, transactions per second, and CPU use. Integrating with the Performance tool is advantageous because it allows you to use a single tool to measure all aspects of a system's performance. If SQL Server simply provided its own performance-monitoring tool, you'd still have to check the performance of the operating system and network. Integration with the operating system's Performance tool provides one-stop shopping. A Windows 2000 Performance tool System Monitor graph is shown in Figure 2-6.

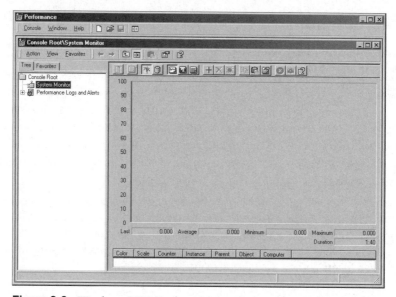

Figure 2-6. *Windows 2000 Performance tool.*

Using the Performance tool, you can set an alert on any statistic that's being monitored; when a predefined threshold is reached, the operating system automatically executes a predefined command. As previously mentioned, you can allow SQL Server Agent to respond directly to Performance tool thresholds being crossed.

Client Network Utility

The Client Network utility is used to configure DB-Library and the Net-Libraries that clients use when connecting to various SQL Servers. If you don't use DB-Library or you don't do any customization of network connections, you might not need to use this tool. However, if you want to examine or change the TCP/IP port that your named instance of SQL Server is listening on, you can do that using the Client Network utility. Also, if you want client tools to communicate with any local SQL Server instance using the Shared Memory Net-Library, you must make sure that feature is enabled using the Client Network utility. The Client Network utility also allows you to set up aliases for your server names. You can set up a simple one-word name to use instead of the two-part name normally required to access a named instance of SQL Server. I'll show an example of how to do this when I discuss named instances in detail in Chapter 4.

Server Network Utility

The Server Network utility is used to manage the Net-Libraries on the server machine. Because the Net-Libraries on which SQL Server listens for client requests are specified during installation, most administrators never need to use this utility.

SQL Server Installation

SQL Server's graphical installation program allows you to set up SQL Server with a degree of ease and speed unprecedented for a full-featured DBMS. If you select the defaults, you can install SQL Server in 5 to 10 minutes, depending on the speed of the computer. A custom installation will typically take well under 30 minutes. You can easily specify options so that the installation program is fully automated for numerous machines, or you can encapsulate the installation of SQL Server in the rest of an application's installation process.

OSQL and ISQL

A simple interactive window in which to submit basic SQL commands and get results is a crucial tool for a database developer—as a hammer is to a carpenter. Even though other, more sophisticated power tools are useful, the basic tools are essential. SQL Server provides the basic tools in two styles: OSQL and ISQL.

Both OSQL (OSQL.EXE) and ISQL (ISQL.EXE) are character-based command-line utilities. ISQL is based on the DB-Library interface, and OSQL is ODBC-based. Many parameters, including the SQL statement or the name of the file containing the statement, can be passed to these character-based utilities. Upon exit, they can return status values to the Windows client that can be checked within a command file (CMD or BAT). Consequently, programs commonly launch scripts of SQL commands by spawning one of these character-based utilities and passing the appropriate parameters and filenames. The SQL Server installation program itself spawns OSQL.EXE numerous times with scripts that install various database objects and permissions.

SQL Query Analyzer

SQL Query Analyzer (ISQLW.EXE) provides a clean, simple, graphical user interface (GUI) for running SQL queries and viewing the results. SQL Query Analyzer allows for multiple windows so that simultaneous database connections (to one or more installations of SQL Server) can exist and be separately sized, tiled, or minimized. You can choose to have your query results displayed in a text window or in a grid. SQL Query Analyzer provides a graphical representation of SHOWPLAN, the steps chosen by the optimizer for query execution. It also provides optional reports of the actual commands processed by SQL Server (a server-side trace) and of the work done by the client. SQL Server 2000 Query Analyzer comes with an Object Browser that lets you drag and drop object or table names into your query window and helps you build SELECT, INSERT, UPDATE, or DELETE statements for any table. SQL Query Analyzer also comes with a T-SQL Debugger tool that I'll describe in more detail in Chapter 16.

SQL Query Analyzer is a wonderfully versatile tool for development and for testing batches and stored procedures that you'll incorporate into your SQL Server applications. Take some time to just play with the terrific interface so that you get very comfortable with it. You can use SQL Query Analyzer to:

- Format your SQL queries

- Use templates for your stored procedures, functions, and basic SQL statements

- Drag object names from the Object Browser to the Query window to see their definition

- Define your own hotkeys

Bulk Copy and Data Transformation Services

SQL Server provides a character-based utility called *bcp*, or bulk copy (BCP.EXE), for flexible importing and exporting of SQL Server data. Similar in format to ISQL and OSQL, *bcp* allows parameters to be passed to it and is often called from command files. A special set of functions exists in ODBC that lets you easily create a custom data loader for your application; the *bcp* utility is a generalized wrapper application that calls these functions.

SQL Enterprise Manager provides facilities to simplify the transfer of data into or out of SQL Server, and this functionality is incorporated into the Data Transformation Services (DTS) tool. Unlike the command-line *bcp* utility, DTS allows you to create a new table as you copy data to your SQL Server as well as to easily change column datatypes or formats. DTS goes far beyond just simple import and export of data to or from SQL Server, however. You can also use it to move data to or from any OLE DB data source, applying all kinds of data transformations along the way. Multiple transfers can be defined and stored in a DTS package, which can then be run from a command line using the *dtsrun* utility (DTSRUN.EXE).

SNMP Integration

SQL Server provides support for Simple Network Management Protocol (SNMP), a standard protocol within TCP/IP environments, via SQL Server Management Information Base (MIB), another standard of the SNMP and TCP/IP environment. A group of database vendors, including Microsoft, cooperated to define a standard MIB that reports certain status data about a database environment for monitoring purposes.

> **NOTE** This group of database vendors was a subcommittee of the Internet Engineering Task Force (IETF). The draft specification is known as IETF SNMP RDBMS-MIB (RFC 1697). SQL Server MIB is generally based on this proposal but provides additional data beyond that called for in the specification.

For example, status information (such as whether SQL Server is currently running, when it was last started, and how many users are connected) is reported to SNMP via this MIB. A variety of SNMP management and monitoring tools exist and can access this data. If, for example, you use Hewlett-Packard's OpenView in managing your network, SQL Server MIB enables those tools to also monitor multiple statistics regarding SQL Server.

SQL Server Books Online

All SQL Server documentation is available on line as well as in printed form. A powerful viewer for the online documentation makes it easy to search for topics. Even if you favor printed books, you'll appreciate the speed and convenience of the SQL Server Books Online search capabilities. Also, because of the lead time required in the production of the printed manuals that ship with SQL Server, SQL Server Books Online is more complete and accurate than the manuals. Because this book can't hope to and doesn't try to replace the complete documentation set, the SQL Server evaluation CD that accompanies this book also contains the complete SQL Server Books Online documentation. Although you need to install SQL Server to view the complete Books Online, you can view all the SQL Server Setup documentation right from the initial screen of the installation CD.

CLIENT DEVELOPMENT INTERFACES

SQL Server provides several interfaces that support client application development—ODBC, Remote Data Objects (RDO), OLE DB, ActiveX Data Objects (ADO), and the legacy interfaces DB-Library and Embedded SQL for C (ESQL/C). The book's companion CD includes a whitepaper titled "Designing Efficient Applications for SQL Server" that compares all the interfaces described in this section—and a few more besides.

ODBC

ODBC is an API for database access that's both a formal and a de facto industry standard. Besides being one of the most popular database interfaces used by applications today, ODBC has gained status as the formal call-level interface standard by American National Standards Institute (ANSI) and International Organization for Standardization (ISO). SQL Server provides a high-performance ODBC interface for all Windows-based programming environments, and it can be distributed royalty-free with any application. The SQL Server ODBC driver implements every function in the ODBC 3 specification. In ODBC-speak, this makes it fully Level 2 (the highest level) conformant.

RDO is an object interface that's closely tied to ODBC, which means that it exposes all the functionality in the ODBC driver and is easily available to Visual Basic programs. RDO supports building visual controls tied directly to SQL Server data, which greatly reduces the amount of code that must be written to display data on the screen.

OLE DB

OLE DB was first released by Microsoft in 1996 to provide a COM interface to any tabular data source (that is, data that can be represented with rows and columns). This includes data in spreadsheets and even text files. OLE DB can be considered an object version of ODBC but is more powerful in that it can access data from data sources beyond those that ODBC can access. Unlike other object interfaces to SQL Server such as RDO, OLE DB doesn't make programming a call-level interface like ODBC any easier. Also, because OLE DB uses pointer data types extensively, it's only accessible from C and C++.

ADO

ADO is a higher-level object interface on top of OLE DB that provides much of the same functionality and performance. Because ADO is pointerless, it can be accessed from scripting languages such as JScript and development software such as Visual Basic, as well as from C and C++.

ADO is the recommended and supported interface for Internet applications written using the Microsoft Visual InterDev development tool. Applications written with Visual InterDev can call ADO from Active Server Pages (ASP) and incorporate code written in VBScript or JScript.

DB-Library

DB-Library is a SQL Server–specific API that provides all the necessary macros and functions for an application to open connections, format queries, send them to the server, and process the results. You can write custom DB-Library applications using C, C++, or Visual Basic (or any programming language capable of calling a C function).

DB-Library is the original SQL Server programming interface. Libraries are provided for MS-DOS, Windows 3.1, Windows 98, and Windows NT/2000. Developers are granted licensed rights to redistribute the DB-Library runtimes royalty-free. Although DB-Library continues to be officially supported for SQL Server 2000, it's not guaranteed to support the full-feature set.

ESQL/C

SQL Server provides an ESQL/C precompiler that allows developers to write SQL Server applications by embedding the SQL queries directly in their C source code. Many minicomputer and mainframe developers are already accustomed to this style of programming, and ESQL/C might be a natural choice for that reason. In addition, Microsoft has licensed some of the ESQL/C run-time environment to MERANT Micro Focus, the leading provider of COBOL compilers and tools. MERANT Micro Focus offers an embedded SQL interface for SQL Server directly in its COBOL development environment.

Server Development Interface

SQL Server offers an open API for developing server-based applications that work in conjunction with SQL Server. ODS is an event-driven API that is primarily used for developing extended stored procedures. ODS is actually a core part of the SQL Server architecture and benefits from the high-performance architecture. It provides all the network, connection, and thread management that SQL Server uses.

Formerly ODS was frequently used to develop custom database gateways, data-driven event alerters, external program triggers, and request auditing in addition to extended stored procedure DLLs. However, with the advent of SQL Server distributed queries and newer technologies such as Windows Component Services, the need for ODS in developing applications of this type of gateway has largely been eliminated. I strongly recommend that you investigate other methods of developing the types of applications just mentioned and use ODS only for developing extended stored procedures.

SUMMARY

The SQL Server component and product family—including the SQL Server RDBMS, visual systems management tools, distributed systems components, open client/server interfaces, and visual development tools—provides a complete and robust platform for developing and deploying large-scale database applications.

This chapter has provided an overview of the various tools available. The remainder of this book concentrates on the capabilities and uses of the SQL Server 2000 engine, which is the foundation of the product.

Part II

Architectural Overview

Chapter 3

SQL Server Architecture

Throughout this book, I'll be telling you about specific features of the Microsoft SQL Server engine. In this chapter, I'll describe what makes up that engine and how it works. If you're interested only in the functional operations of SQL Server and want to consider everything as a black box operation, you can safely skip this chapter. Or if you're new to databases and don't have a clear idea of what makes up an RDBMS, you can come back to this chapter after you become more familiar with SQL Server's external capabilities. This chapter will focus on what happens inside the engine. I'll also point out system behavior that might affect application development and suggest ways to deal with it.

THE SQL SERVER ENGINE

Figure 3-1 on page 71 shows the general architecture of SQL Server. For simplicity, I've made some minor omissions and simplifications and ignored certain "helper" modules. Now let's look in detail at the major modules.

The Net-Library

The Net-Library (often called Net-Lib, but in this book I'll use Net-Library) abstraction layer enables SQL Server to read from and write to many different network protocols, and each such protocol (such as TCP/IP sockets) can have a specific driver. The Net-Library layer makes it relatively easy to support many different network protocols without having to change the core server code.

A Net-Library is basically a driver that's specific to a particular network interprocess communication (IPC) mechanism. (Be careful not to confuse *driver* with *device driver.*) All code in SQL Server, including Net-Library code, makes calls only to the Microsoft Win32 subsystem. SQL Server uses a common internal interface between Microsoft Open Data Services (ODS)—which manages its use of the network—and each Net-Library. If your development project needs to support a new and different network protocol, you can handle all network-specific issues by simply writing a new Net-Library. In addition, you can load multiple Net-Libraries simultaneously, one for each network IPC mechanism in use.

SQL Server uses the Net-Library abstraction layer on both the server and client machines, making it possible to support several clients simultaneously on different networks. Microsoft Windows NT/2000 and Windows 98 support the simultaneous use of multiple protocol stacks. Net-Libraries are paired. For example, if a client application is using a Named Pipes Net-Library, SQL Server must also be listening on a Named Pipes Net-Library. The client application determines which Net-Library is actually used for the communication, and you can control the client application's choice by using a tool called the Client Network utility. You can easily configure SQL Server to listen on multiple Net-Libraries by using the Server Network utility, which is available under Programs\Microsoft SQL Server on the Start menu.

SQL Server 2000 has two primary Net-Libraries: Super Socket and Shared Memory. TCP/IP, Named Pipes, IPX/SPX, and so on are referred to as secondary Net-Libraries. The OLE DB Provider for SQL Server, SQL Server ODBC driver, DB-Library, and the database engine communicate directly with these two primary network libraries. Intercomputer connections communicate through the Super Socket Net-Library. Local connections between an application and a SQL Server instance on the same computer use the Shared Memory Net-Library if Shared Memory support has been enabled (which it is, by default). SQL Server 2000 supports the Shared Memory Net-Library on all Windows platforms.

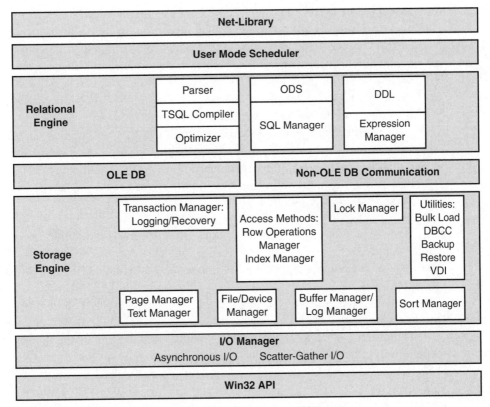

Figure 3-1. *The major components of the SQL Server architecture.*

The Super Socket Net-Library has two components:

■ **Communication path** If the client is configured to communicate over TCP/IP Sockets or NWLink IPX/SPX connection, the Super Socket Net-Library directly calls the Windows Socket 2 API for the communication between the application and the SQL Server instance.

If the client is configured to communicate over a Named Pipes, Multiprotocol, AppleTalk, or Banyan VINES connection, a subcomponent of the Super Socket Net-Library called the Net-Library router loads the secondary Net-Library for the chosen protocol and routes all Net-Library calls to it.

- **Encryption layer**   The encryption is implemented using the Secure Sockets Layer (SSL) API. The level of encryption, 40-bit or 128-bit, depends on the Windows version on the application and SQL Server–based computers. Enabling encryption can slow network performance not only because of the extra work of encrypting and decrypting communication between the client and the server but also because an extra roundtrip is required between the client and the server every time a connection is made.

  Shared Memory Net-Library communication is inherently secure without the need for encryption. The Shared Memory Net-Library never participates in intercomputer communication. The area of memory shared between the application process and the database engine process cannot be accessed from any other Windows process.

For compatibility with earlier versions of SQL Server, the Multiprotocol Net-Library continues to support its own encryption. This encryption is specified independently of the SSL encryption and is implemented by calling the Windows RPC encryption API.

Figure 3-2 (taken from SQL Server Books Online) shows SQL Server 2000's Net-Library architecture.

The distinction between the IPC mechanisms and the underlying network protocols is important. IPC mechanisms used by SQL Server include Named Pipes, RPC, SPX, and Windows Sockets. Network protocols used include TCP/IP, NetBEUI, Shared Memory, NWLink IPX/SPX, Banyan VINES SPP, and AppleTalk ADSP. Two Net-Libraries, Multiprotocol and Named Pipes, can be used simultaneously over multiple network protocols (NetBEUI, NWLink IPX/SPX, and TCP/IP). You can have multiple network protocols in your environment and still use only one Net-Library.

SQL Server 2000 running on Windows NT/2000 supports impersonation of security contexts to provide an integrated logon authentication capability called Windows Authentication. Windows Authentication operates over network protocols that support authenticated connections between clients and servers. Such connections are referred to as *trusted connections* and are supported by SQL Server 2000 using any available Net-Library. Instead of requiring a separate user ID/password logon each time a connection to SQL Server is requested, SQL Server can impersonate the security context of the user running the application that requests the connection. If that user has sufficient privileges (or is part of a Windows NT/2000 domain group that does), the connection is established. Note that Windows Authentication is not available when SQL Server is running on Windows 98. When you connect to SQL Server running on Windows 98, you must specify a SQL Server logon ID and password.

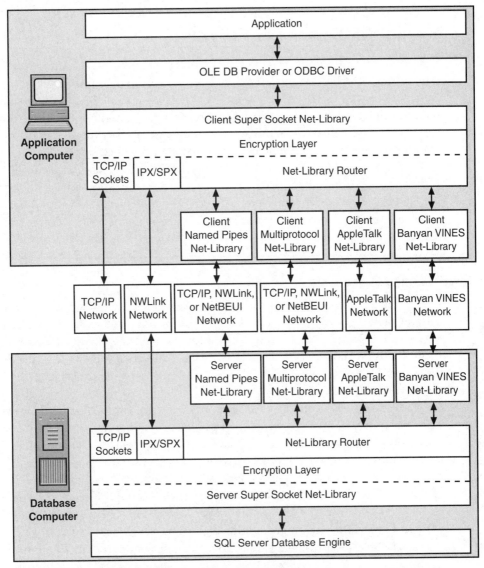

Figure 3-2. *SQL Server 2000's Net-Library architecture.*

WHICH NET-LIBRARY IS FASTEST?

Strictly speaking, the TCP/IP Sockets Net-Library is the fastest Net-Library. In a pure network test that does nothing except throw packets back and forth between Net-Library pairs, the TCP/IP Sockets Net-Library is perhaps 30 percent faster than the slowest Net-Library. But in LAN environments and applications, the speed of the Net-Library probably makes little difference because the network interface is generally not a limiting factor in a well-designed application.

On a LAN, however, turning on encryption does cause a performance hit. But again, most applications probably wouldn't notice the difference. Your best bet is to choose the Net-Library that matches your network protocols and provides the services you need in terms of unified logon, encryption, and dynamic name resolution. (I'll explain these choices further in Chapter 4.)

Open Data Services

Open Data Services (ODS) functions as the client manager for SQL Server; it's basically an interface between server Net-Libraries and server-based applications, including SQL Server. ODS manages the network: it listens for new connections, cleans up failed connections, acknowledges "attentions" (cancellations of commands), coordinates threading services to SQL Server, and returns result sets, messages, and status values back to the client.

SQL Server clients and the server speak a private protocol known as *Tabular Data Stream (TDS)*. TDS is a self-describing data stream. In other words, it contains tokens that describe column names, datatypes, events (such as cancellations), and status values in the "conversation" between client and server. The server notifies the client that it is sending a result set, indicates the number of columns and datatypes of the result set, and so on—all encoded in TDS. Neither clients nor servers write directly to TDS. Instead, the open interfaces of OLE-DB, ODBC, and DB-Library at the client emit TDS using a client implementation of the Net-Library.

ODS accepts new connections, and if a client unexpectedly disconnects (for example, if a user reboots the client computer instead of cleanly terminating the application), ODS automatically frees resources such as locks held by that client.

You can use the ODS open interface to extend the functionality of SQL Server by writing extended stored procedures. The code for the ODS API itself was formerly stored outside of SQL Server as part of the DLL opends60.dll. In SQL Server 2000, to enhance the performance of SQL Server's own internal mechanisms that need to use presupplied extended procedures, the code that makes up ODS is internal to the SQL Server engine. Any extended stored procedure DLLs that you create must link against opends60.dll, which contains stubs to access the real ODS routines internal to SQL Server.

ODS Input and Output Buffers

After SQL Server puts result sets into a network output buffer (write buffer) that's equal in size to the configured packet size, the Net-Library dispatches the buffer to the client. The first packet is sent as soon as the network output buffer is full or, if an entire result set fits in one packet, when the batch is completed. (A *batch* is one or more commands sent to SQL Server to be parsed and executed together. For example, if you're using OSQL.EXE, a batch is the collection of all the commands that appear before a specific GO command.) In some exceptional operations (such as one that provides progress information for database dumping or provides DBCC messages), the output buffer is flushed and sent even before it is full or before the batch completes.

SQL Server has two input buffers (read buffers) and one output buffer per client. Double-buffering is needed for the reads because while SQL Server reads a stream of data from the client connection, it must also look for a possible attention. (This allows that "Query That Ate Cleveland" to be canceled directly from the issuer. Although the ability to cancel a request is extremely important, it's relatively unusual among client/server products.) Attentions can be thought of as "out-of-band" data, although they can be sent with network protocols that do not explicitly have an out-of-band channel. The SQL Server development team experimented with double-buffering and asynchronous techniques for the output buffers, but these didn't improve performance substantially. The single network output buffer works nicely. Even though the writes are not posted asynchronously, SQL Server doesn't need to bypass the operating system caching for these as it does for writes to disk.

Because the operating system provides caching of network writes, write operations appear to complete immediately with no significant latency. If, however, several writes are issued to the same client and the client is not currently reading data from the network, the network cache eventually becomes full and the write blocks. This is essentially a throttle. As long as the client application is processing results, SQL Server has a few buffers queued up and ready for the client connection to process. But if the client's queue is already stacked up with results and is not processing them, SQL Server stalls sending them and the network write operation to that connection has to wait. Since the server has only one output buffer per client, data cannot be sent to that client connection until it reads information off the network to free up room for the write to complete. (Writes to other client connections are not held up, however; only those for the laggard client are affected.)

Stalled network writes can also affect locks. For example, if READ COMMITTED isolation is in effect (the default), a share lock can normally be released after SQL Server has completed its scan of that page of data. (Exclusive locks used for changing data must always be held until the end of the transaction to ensure that the changes can be rolled back.) However, if the scan finds more qualifying data and the output buffer is not free, the scan stalls. When the previous network write completes, the output buffer becomes available and the scan resumes. But as I stated earlier, that write won't complete until the client connection "drains" (reads) some data to free up some room in the pipe (the virtual circuit between SQL Server and the client connection).

If a client connection delays processing results that are sent to it, concurrency issues can result because locks are held longer than they otherwise would be. A kind of chain reaction occurs: if the client connection has not read several outstanding network packets, further writing of the output buffer at the SQL Server side must wait because the pipe is full. Since the output buffer is not available, the scan for data might also be suspended because no space is available to add qualifying rows. Since the scan is held up, any lock on the data cannot be released. In short, if a client application does not process results in a timely manner, database concurrency can suffer.

The size of the network output buffer can also affect the speed at which the client receives the first result set. As mentioned earlier, the output buffer is sent when the batch, not simply the command, is done, even if the buffer is not full. If two queries exist in the same batch and the first query has only a small amount of data, its results are not sent back to the client until the second query is done or has supplied enough data to fill the output buffer. If both queries are fast, waiting for both queries to finish is not a problem. But suppose the first query is fast and the second is slow. And suppose the first query returns 1000 bytes of data. If the network packet size is 4096 bytes, the first result set must wait in the output buffer for the second query to fill it. The obvious solution here is to either make the first command its own batch or make the network packet size smaller. The first solution is probably best in this case, since it is typically difficult to fine-tune your application to determine the best buffer size for each command. But this doesn't mean that each command should be its own batch. Quite the contrary. In fact, under normal circumstances, grouping multiple commands into a single batch is most efficient and is recommended because it reduces the amount of handshaking that must occur between client and server.

ODS Default Net-Libraries

On the server side, ODS provides functionality that mirrors that of ODBC, OLE DB, or DB-Library at the client. Calls exist for an ODS server application to describe and send result sets, to convert values between datatypes, to assume the security context associated with the specific connection being managed, and to raise errors and messages to the client application.

ODS uses an event-driven programming model. Requests from servers and clients trigger events that your server application must respond to. Using the ODS API, you create a custom routine, called an *event handler,* for each possible type of event. Essentially, the ODS library drives a server application by calling its custom event handlers in response to incoming requests.

ODS server applications respond to the following events:

- **Connect events** When a connect event occurs, SQL Server initiates a security check to determine whether a connection is allowed. Other ODS applications, such as a gateway to DB/2, have their own logon handlers that determine whether connections are allowed. Events also exist that close a connection, allowing the proper connection cleanup to occur.

- **Language events** When a client sends a command string, such as an SQL statement, SQL Server passes this command along to the command parser. A different ODS application, such as a gateway, would install its own handler that accepts and is responsible for execution of the command.

- **Remote stored procedure events** These events occur each time a client or SQL Server directs a remote stored procedure request to ODS for processing.

ODS also generates events based on certain client activities and application activities. These events allow an ODS server application to respond to changes to the status of the client connection or of the ODS server application.

In addition to handling connections, ODS manages threads (and fibers) for SQL Server. It takes care of thread creation and termination and makes the threads available to the User Mode Scheduler (UMS). Since ODS is an open interface with a full programming API and toolkit, independent software vendors (ISVs) writing server applications with ODS get the same benefits that SQL Server derives from this component, including SMP-capable thread management and pooling, as well as network handling for multiple simultaneous networks. This multithreaded operation enables ODS server applications to maintain a high level of performance and availability and to transparently use multiple processors under Windows NT/2000 because the operating system can schedule any thread on any available processor.

The Relational Engine and the Storage Engine

The SQL Server database engine is made up of two main components, the relational engine and the storage engine. These two pieces are clearly separated, and their primary method of communication with each other is through OLE DB. The relational engine comprises all the components necessary to parse and optimize any query. It also manages the execution of queries as it requests data from the storage engine in terms of OLE DB row sets and then processes the row sets returned. (*Row set* is the OLE DB term for a result set.) The storage engine comprises the components needed to actually access and modify data on disk.

The Command Parser

The command parser handles language events raised by ODS. It checks for proper syntax and translates Transact-SQL commands into an internal format that can be operated on. This internal format is known as a *query tree*. If the parser doesn't recognize the syntax, a syntax error is immediately raised and identifies where the error occurred. However, non-syntax error messages cannot be explicit about the exact source line that caused the error. Because only the command parser can access the source of the statement, the statement is no longer available in source format when the command is actually executed.

The Optimizer

The optimizer takes the query tree from the command parser and prepares it for execution. This module compiles an entire command batch, optimizes queries, and checks security. The query optimization and compilation result in an execution plan.

The first step in producing such a plan is to *normalize* each query, which potentially breaks down a single query into multiple, fine-grained queries. After the optimizer normalizes a query, it *optimizes* it, which means that the optimizer determines a plan for executing that query. Query optimization is cost-based; the optimizer chooses the plan that it determines would cost the least based on internal metrics that include estimated memory requirements, estimated CPU utilization, and the estimated number of required I/Os. The optimizer considers the type of statement requested, checks the amount of data in the various tables affected, looks at the indexes available for each table, and then looks at a sampling of the data values kept for each index or column referenced in the query. The sampling of the data values is called *distribution statistics* and will be discussed in detail in Chapter 15. Based on the available information, the optimizer considers the various access methods and join strategies it could use to resolve a query and chooses the most cost-effective plan. The optimizer also decides which indexes, if any, should be used for each table in the query, and, in the case of a multitable query, the order in which the tables should be accessed and the join strategy to use.

The optimizer also uses pruning heuristics to ensure that more time isn't spent optimizing a query than it would take to simply choose a plan and execute it. The optimizer doesn't necessarily do exhaustive optimization. Some products consider every possible plan and then choose the most cost-effective one. The advantage of this exhaustive optimization is that the syntax chosen for a query would theoretically never cause a performance difference, no matter what syntax the user employed. But if you deal with an involved query, it could take much longer to estimate the cost of every conceivable plan than it would to accept a good plan, even if not the best one, and execute it.

After normalization and optimization are completed, the normalized tree produced by those processes is compiled into the execution plan, which is actually a data structure. Each command included in it specifies exactly which table will be affected, which indexes will be used (if any), which security checks must be made, and which criteria (such as equality to a specified value) must evaluate to TRUE for selection. This execution plan might be considerably more complex than is immediately apparent. In addition to the actual commands, the execution plan includes all the steps necessary to ensure that constraints are checked. Steps for calling a trigger are a bit different from those for verifying constraints. If a trigger is included for the action being taken, a call to the procedure that comprises the trigger is appended. If the trigger is an *instead-of* trigger, the call to the trigger's plan replaces the actual data modification command. For *after* triggers, the trigger's plan is branched to right after the plan for the modification statement that fired the trigger, before that modification is committed. The specific steps for the trigger are not compiled into the execution plan, unlike those for constraint verification.

A simple request to insert one row into a table with multiple constraints can result in an execution plan that requires many other tables to also be accessed or expressions to be evaluated. The existence of a trigger can also cause many additional steps to be executed. The step that carries out the actual INSERT statement might be just a small part of the total execution plan necessary to ensure that all actions and constraints associated with adding a row are carried out.

For more details on query processing and optimization, see Chapter 15.

The SQL Manager

The SQL manager is responsible for everything having to do with managing stored procedures and their plans. It determines when a stored procedure needs recompilation based on changes in the underlying objects' schemas, and it manages the caching of procedure plans so that other processes can reuse them.

The SQL manager also handles autoparameterization of queries. In SQL Server 2000, certain kinds of ad hoc queries are treated as if they were parameterized stored procedures, and query plans are generated and saved for them. This can happen if a query uses a simple equality comparison against a constant, as in the following statement:

```
SELECT * FROM pubs.dbo.titles
WHERE type = 'business'
```

This query can be parameterized as if it were a stored procedure with a parameter for the value of *type*:

```
SELECT * FROM pubs.dbo.titles
WHERE type = @param
```

A subsequent query, differing only in the actual value used for the value of *type*, can use the same query plan that was generated for the original query. I'll discuss the details of autoparameterization in Chapter 15.

The Expression Manager

The expression manager handles computation, comparison, and data movement. Suppose your query contains an expression like this one:

```
SELECT @myqty = qty * 10 FROM mytable
```

The expression manager copies the value of *qty* from the row set returned by the storage engine, multiplies it by 10, and stores the result in *@myqty*.

The Query Executor

The query executor runs the execution plan that the optimizer produced, acting as a dispatcher for all the commands in the execution plan. This module loops through each command step of the execution plan until the batch is complete. Most of the commands require interaction with the storage engine to modify or retrieve data and to manage transactions and locking.

Communication Between the Relational Engine and the Storage Engine

The relational engine uses OLE DB for most of its communication with the storage engine. The following description of that communication is adapted from the section titled "Database Engine Components" in SQL Server Books Online. It describes how a SELECT statement that processes data from local tables only is processed:

1. The relational engine compiles the SELECT statement into an optimized execution plan. The execution plan defines a series of operations against simple OLE DB row sets from the individual tables or indexes referenced in the SELECT statement. The row sets requested by the relational engine return the amount of data needed from a table or index to perform one of the operations used to build the SELECT result set. For example, this SELECT statement requires a table scan if it references a table with no indexes:

    ```
    SELECT * FROM Northwind.dbo.ScanTable
    ```

    The relational engine implements the table scan by requesting one row set containing all the rows from *ScanTable*. This next SELECT statement needs only information available in an index:

    ```
    SELECT DISTINCT LastName
    FROM Northwind.dbo.Employees
    ```

    The relational engine implements the index scan by requesting one row set containing the leaf rows from the index that was built on the *LastName* column. The following SELECT statement needs information from two indexes:

```
SELECT CompanyName, OrderID, ShippedDate
FROM Northwind.dbo.Customers AS Cst
JOIN Northwind.dbo.Orders AS Ord
ON (Cst.CustomerID = Ord.CustomerID)
```

    The relational engine requests two row sets: one for the nonclustered index on *Customers* and the other for one of the clustered indexes on *Orders*.

2. The relational engine uses the OLE DB API to request that the storage engine open the row sets.

3. As the relational engine works through the steps of the execution plan and needs data, it uses OLE DB to fetch the individual rows from the row sets it asked the storage engine to open. The storage engine transfers the data from the data buffers to the relational engine.

4. The relational engine combines the data from the storage engine row sets into the final result set transmitted back to the user.

    Not all communication between the relational engine and the storage engine uses OLE DB. Some commands cannot be expressed in terms of OLE DB row sets. The most obvious and common example is when the relational engine processes data definition language (DDL) requests to create a table or other SQL Server object.

The Access Methods Manager

When SQL Server needs to locate data, it calls the access methods manager. The access methods manager sets up and requests scans of data pages and index pages and prepares the OLE DB row sets to return to the relational engine. It contains services to open a table, retrieve qualified data, and update data. The access methods manager doesn't actually retrieve the pages; it makes the request to the buffer manager, which ultimately serves up the page already in its cache or reads it to cache from disk. When the scan is started, a look-ahead mechanism qualifies the rows or index entries on a page. The retrieving of rows that meet specified criteria is known as a *qualified retrieval*. The access methods manager is employed not only for queries (selects) but also for qualified updates and deletes (for example, UPDATE with a WHERE clause).

    A session opens a table, requests and evaluates a range of rows against the conditions in the WHERE clause, and then closes the table. A session descriptor data structure (SDES) keeps track of the current row and the search conditions for the object being operated on (which is identified by the object descriptor data structure, or DES).

The Row Operations Manager and the Index Manager

You can consider the row operations manager and the index manager as components of the access methods manager because they carry out the actual method of access. Each is responsible for manipulating and maintaining its respective on-disk data structures, namely rows of data or B-tree indexes. They understand and manipulate information on data and index pages.

The Row Operations Manager

The row operations manager retrieves, modifies, and performs operations on individual rows. (For more information about on-disk structures, see Chapter 5; for more on data page and row format, see Chapter 6.) It performs an operation within a row, such as "retrieve column 2" or "write this value to column 3." As a result of the work performed by the access methods manager, as well as by the lock manager and transaction manager, which will be discussed shortly, the row will have been found and will be appropriately locked and part of a transaction. After formatting or modifying a row in memory, the row operations manager inserts or deletes a row.

The row operations manager also handles updates. SQL Server 2000 offers three methods for handling updates. All three are direct, which means that there's no need for two passes through the transaction log, as was the case with deferred updates in versions of SQL Server prior to SQL Server 7. SQL Server 2000 has no concept of a deferred data modification operation.

SQL Server 2000 has three update modes:

- **In-place mode**   This mode is used to update a heap or clustered index when none of the clustering keys change. The update can be done in place, and the new data is written to the same slot on the data page.

- **Split mode**   This mode is used to update nonunique indexes when the index keys change. The update is split into two operations—a delete followed by an insert—and these operations are performed independently of each other.

- **Split with collapse mode**   This mode is used to update a unique index when the index keys change. After the update is rewritten as delete and insert operations, if the same index key is both deleted and then reinserted with a new value, the delete and insert are "collapsed" into a single update operation.

In Chapter 9, we'll look at examples of each type of update.

The Index Manager

The index manager maintains and supports searches on B-trees, which are used for SQL Server indexes. An index is structured as a tree, with a root page and intermediate-level and lower-level pages (or branches). A B-tree groups records that have similar index keys, thereby allowing fast access to data by searching on a key value. The B-tree's core feature is its ability to balance the index tree. (*B* stands for *balanced*.) Branches of the index tree are spliced together or split apart as necessary so that the search for any given record always traverses the same number of levels and thus requires the same number of page accesses.

The traversal begins at the root page, progresses to intermediate index levels, and finally moves to bottom-level pages called *leaf pages*. The index is used to find the correct leaf page. On a qualified retrieval or delete, the correct leaf page is the lowest page of the tree at which one or more rows with the specified key or keys reside. SQL Server supports both clustered and nonclustered indexes. In a nonclustered index, shown in Figure 3-3, the leaf level of the tree (the leaf pages of the index) contains every key value in the index along with a bookmark for each key value. The bookmark indicates where to find the referenced data and can have one of two forms, depending on whether the base table has a clustered index. If the base table has no clustered index, the table is referred to as a *heap*. The bookmarks in nonclustered index leaf pages for a heap are pointers to the actual records in which the data can be found, and these pointers consist of a row ID (RID), which is a file number, a page number, and a row number on the page. If the base table has a clustered index, the bookmark in any nonclustered index leaf page contains the clustered index key value for the row.

After reaching the leaf level in a nonclustered index, you can find the exact location of the data, although you still must separately retrieve the page on which that data resides. Because you can access the data directly, you don't need to scan all the data pages to find a qualifying row. Better yet, in a clustered index, shown in Figure 3-4 on page 85, the leaf level actually contains the full data rows, not simply the index keys. A clustered index keeps the data in a table logically ordered around the key of the clustered index, and the leaf pages of a clustered index are in fact the data pages of the table. All the data pages of a table with a clustered index are linked together in a doubly linked list. Following the pages, and the rows on those pages, from the first page to the last page provides the logical order to the data.

Because data can be ordered in only one way, only one clustered index can exist per table. This makes the selection of the appropriate key value on which to cluster data an important performance consideration.

You can also use indexes to ensure the uniqueness of a particular key value. In fact, the PRIMARY KEY and UNIQUE constraints on a column work by creating a unique index on the column's values. The optimizer can use the knowledge that an index is unique in formulating an effective query plan. Internally, SQL Server always ensures that clustered indexes are unique by adding a 4-byte *uniqueifier* to clustered index key values that occur more than once. This uniqueifier becomes part of the key and is used in all levels of the clustered index and in references to the clustered index key through all nonclustered indexes.

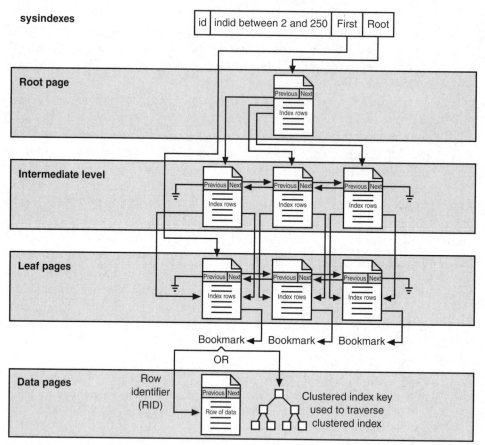

Figure 3-3. *A nonclustered index with the leaf level containing bookmarks—either a RID or a clustered index key value.*

Since SQL Server maintains ordering in index leaf levels, you do not need to unload and reload data to maintain clustering properties as data is added and moved. SQL Server always inserts rows into the correct page in clustered sequence. For a clustered index, the correct leaf page is the data page in which a row is inserted. For a nonclustered index, the correct leaf page is the one into which SQL Server inserts a row containing the key value (and bookmark) for the newly inserted row. If data is updated and the key values of an index change, or if the row is moved to a different page, SQL Server's transaction control ensures that all affected indexes are modified to reflect these changes. With transaction control, index operations are performed as atomic operations. The operations are logged and fully recovered in the event of a system failure.

For more details on index structures and maintenance, see Chapter 7.

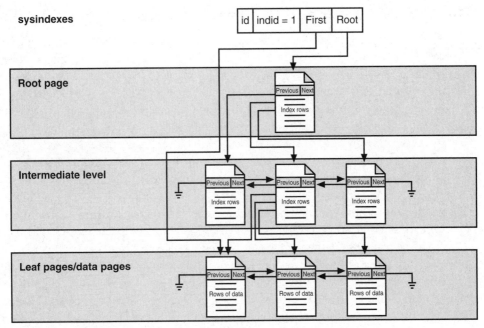

Figure 3-4. *A clustered index with the data located at the leaf level.*

LOCKING AND INDEX PAGES

As you'll see later, in the section on the lock manager, pages of an index use a slightly different locking mechanism than regular data pages. A lightweight lock called a *latch* is used to lock upper levels of indexes. Latches are not involved in deadlock detection because SQL Server 2000 uses "deadlock-proof" algorithms for index maintenance.

You can customize the locking strategy for indexes on a table basis or index basis. You can use the system stored procedure *sp_indexoption* to enable or disable page or row locks with any particular index or, by specifying a table name, for every index on that table. The settable options are *DisAllowPageLocks* and *DisAllowRowLocks*. If both of these options are set to TRUE for a particular index, only table level locks are applied.

The Page Manager and the Text Manager

The page manager and the text manager cooperate to manage a collection of pages as named databases. Each database is a collection of 8-KB disk pages, which are spread across one or more physical files. (In Chapter 5, you'll find more details about the physical organization of databases.)

SQL Server uses eight types of disk pages: data pages, text/image pages, index pages, Page Free Space (PFS) pages, Global Allocation Map (GAM and SGAM) pages, Index Allocation Map (IAM) pages, Bulk Changed Map pages, and Differential Changed Map pages. All user data, except for the *text*, *ntext*, and *image* datatypes, are stored on data pages. These three datatypes, which are used for storing large objects (up to 2 GB each of text or binary data), can use a separate collection of pages, so the data is not typically stored on regular data pages with the rest of the rows. Instead, a pointer on the regular data page identifies the starting page and offset of the text/image data. However, in SQL Server 2000, large object data that contains only a few bytes can optionally be stored in the data row itself. Index pages store the B-trees that allow fast access to data. PFS pages keep track of which pages in a database are available to hold new data. Allocation pages (GAMs, SGAMs, and IAMs) keep track of the other pages. They contain no database rows and are used only internally. Bulk Changed Map pages and Differential Changed Map pages are used to make backup and recovery more efficient. I'll cover all the types of pages extensively in Chapters 5, 6, and 8.

The page manager allocates and deallocates all types of disk pages, organizing extents of eight pages each. An extent can be either a uniform extent, for which all eight pages are allocated to the same object (table or index), or a mixed extent, which can contain pages from multiple objects. If an object uses fewer than eight pages, the page manager allocates new pages for that object from mixed extents. When the size of the object exceeds eight pages, the page manager allocates new space for that object in units of entire uniform extents. This optimization prevents the overhead of allocation from being incurred every time a new page is required for a large table; this overhead is incurred only every eighth time. Perhaps most important, this optimization forces data of the same table to be contiguous, for the most part. At the same time, the ability to use mixed extents keeps SQL Server from wasting too much space if a database contains many small tables.

To determine how contiguous a table's data is, you use the DBCC SHOWCONTIG command. A table with a lot of allocation and deallocation can get fairly fragmented, and rebuilding the clustered index (which also rebuilds the table) or running DBCC INDEXDEFRAG can improve performance, especially when a table is accessed frequently using ordered index scans. I'll discuss these two commands in detail in Chapter 8.

The Transaction Manager

A core feature of SQL Server is its ability to ensure that transactions follow the ACID properties (discussed in Chapter 2). Transactions must be *atomic*—that is, all or nothing. If a transaction has been committed, it must be recoverable by SQL Server no matter what—even if a total system failure occurs one millisecond after the commit was acknowledged. In SQL Server, if work was in progress and a system failure occurred before the transaction was committed, all the work is rolled back to the state that existed before the transaction began. Write-ahead logging makes it possible to always roll back work in progress or roll forward committed work that has not yet been applied to the data pages. Write-ahead logging ensures that a transaction's changes—the "before and after" images of data—are captured on disk in the transaction log before a transaction is acknowledged as committed. Writes to the transaction log are always synchronous—that is, SQL Server must wait for them to complete. Writes to the data pages can be asynchronous because all the effects can be reconstructed from the log if necessary. The transaction manager coordinates logging, recovery, and buffer management. These topics are discussed later in this chapter; at this point, we'll just look at transactions themselves.

The transaction manager delineates the boundaries of statements that must be grouped together to form an operation. It handles transactions that cross databases within the same SQL Server, and it allows nested transaction sequences. (However, nested transactions simply execute in the context of the first-level transaction; no special action occurs when they are committed. And a rollback specified in a lower level of a nested transaction undoes the entire transaction.) For a distributed transaction to another SQL Server (or to any other resource manager), the transaction manager coordinates with the Microsoft Distributed Transaction Coordinator (MS DTC) service using operating system remote procedure calls. The transaction manager marks *savepoints,* which let you designate points within a transaction at which work can be partially rolled back or undone.

The transaction manager also coordinates with the lock manager regarding when locks can be released, based on the isolation level in effect. The isolation level in which your transaction runs determines how sensitive your application is to changes made by others and consequently how long your transaction must hold locks to protect against those changes. Four isolation-level semantics are available in SQL Server 2000: Uncommitted Read (also called "dirty read"), Committed Read, Repeatable Read, and Serializable.

The behavior of your transactions depends on the isolation level. We'll look at these levels now, but a complete understanding of isolation levels also requires an understanding of locking because the topics are so closely related. The next section gives an overview of locking; you'll find more detailed information in Chapter 14.

Uncommitted Read

Uncommitted Read, or dirty read (not to be confused with "dirty page," which I'll discuss later) lets your transaction read any data that is currently on a data page, whether or not that data has been committed. For example, another user might have a transaction in progress that has updated data, and even though it's holding exclusive locks on the data, your transaction can read it anyway. The other user might then decide to roll back his or her transaction, so logically those changes were never made. If the system is a single-user system and everyone is queued up to access it, the changes will not have been visible to other users. In a multiuser system, however, you read the changes and take action based on them. Although this scenario isn't desirable, with Uncommitted Read you can't get stuck waiting for a lock, nor do your reads issue share locks (described in the next section) that might affect others.

When using Uncommitted Read, you give up the assurance of strongly consistent data in favor of high concurrency in the system without users locking each other out. So when should you choose Uncommitted Read? Clearly, you don't want to use it for financial transactions in which every number must balance. But it might be fine for certain decision-support analyses—for example, when you look at sales trends—for which complete precision isn't necessary and the tradeoff in higher concurrency makes it worthwhile.

Committed Read

Committed Read is SQL Server's default isolation level. It ensures that an operation never reads data that another application has changed but not yet committed. (That is, it never reads data that logically never existed.) With Committed Read, if a transaction is updating data and consequently has exclusive locks on data rows, your transaction must wait for those locks to be released before you can use that data (whether you're reading or modifying). Also, your transaction must put share locks (at a minimum) on the data that will be visited, which means that data might be unavailable to others to use. A share lock doesn't prevent others from reading the data, but it makes them wait to update the data. Share locks can be released after the data has been sent to the calling client—they don't have to be held for the duration of the transaction.

> **NOTE**   Although a transaction can never read uncommitted data when running with Committed Read isolation, if the transaction subsequently revisits the same data, that data might have changed or new rows might suddenly appear that meet the criteria of the original query. If data values have changed, we call that a *non-repeatable read*. New rows that appear are called *phantoms*.

Repeatable Read

The Repeatable Read isolation level adds to the properties of Committed Read by ensuring that if a transaction revisits data or if a query is reissued, the data will not have changed. In other words, issuing the same query twice within a transaction will not pick up any changes to data values made by another user's transaction. However, Repeatable Read isolation level does allow phantom rows to appear.

Preventing nonrepeatable reads from appearing is a desirable safeguard. But there's no free lunch. The cost of this extra safeguard is that all the shared locks in a transaction must be held until the completion (COMMIT or ROLLBACK) of the transaction. (Exclusive locks must always be held until the end of a transaction, no matter what the isolation level, so that a transaction can be rolled back if necessary. If the locks were released sooner, it might be impossible to undo the work.) No other user can modify the data visited by your transaction as long as your transaction is outstanding. Obviously, this can seriously reduce concurrency and degrade performance. If transactions are not kept short or if applications are not written to be aware of such potential lock contention issues, SQL Server can appear to "hang" when it's simply waiting for locks to be released.

> **NOTE** You can control how long SQL Server waits for a lock to be released by using the session option LOCK_TIMEOUT. I'll discuss this option, as well as many other ways of customizing locking behavior, in Chapter 16.

Serializable

The Serializable isolation level adds to the properties of Repeatable Read by ensuring that if a query is reissued, rows will not have been added in the interim. In other words, phantoms will not appear if the same query is issued twice within a transaction. More precisely, Repeatable Read and Serializable affect sensitivity to another connection's changes, whether or not the user ID of the other connection is the same. Every connection within SQL Server has its own transaction and lock space. I use the term "user" loosely so as not to obscure the central concept.

Preventing phantoms from appearing is another desirable safeguard. But once again, there's no free lunch. The cost of this extra safeguard is similar to that of Repeatable Read—all the shared locks in a transaction must be held until completion of the transaction. In addition, enforcing the Serializable isolation level requires that you not only lock data that has been read, but also lock data *that does not exist!* For example, suppose that within a transaction we issue a SELECT statement to read all the customers whose zip code is between 98000 and 98100, and on first execution no rows satisfy that condition. To enforce the Serializable isolation level, we must lock that "range" of *potential* rows with zip codes between 98000 and 98100 so that if the same query is reissued, there will still be no rows that satisfy the condition. SQL Server handles this by using a special kind of lock called a *key-range lock,* which I'll discuss in Chapter 14. The Serializable level gets its name from the fact that running multiple serializable transactions at the same time is the equivalent of running them one at a time—that is, serially. For example, suppose transactions A, B, and C run simultaneously at the Serializable level and each tries to update the same range of data. If the order in which the transactions acquire locks on the range of data is B,

C, and A, the result obtained by running all three simultaneously is the same as if they were run one at a time in the order B, C, and A. Serializable does not imply that the order is known in advance. The order is considered a chance event. Even on a single-user system, the order of transactions hitting the queue would be essentially random. If the batch order is important to your application, you should implement it as a pure batch system.

> **SEE ALSO**   For an interesting critique of the formal definitions of the ANSI isolation levels, see the companion CD, which contains a technical report called "A Critique of ANSI SQL Isolation Levels," published by the Microsoft Research Center.

The tough part of transaction management, of course, is dealing with rollback/rollforward and recovery operations. I'll return to the topic of transaction management and recovery a bit later. But first I'll discuss locking and logging further.

The Lock Manager

Locking is a crucial function of a multiuser database system such as SQL Server. Recall from Chapter 2 that SQL Server lets you manage multiple users simultaneously and ensures that the transactions observe the properties of the chosen isolation level. At the highest level, Serializable, SQL Server must make the multiuser system perform like a single-user system—as though every user is queued up to use the system alone with no other user activity. Locking guards data and the internal resources that make it possible for many users to simultaneously access the database and not be severely affected by others' use.

The lock manager acquires and releases various types of locks, such as share locks for reading, exclusive locks for writing, intent locks to signal a potential "plan" to perform some operation, extent locks for space allocation, and so on. It manages compatibility between the lock types, resolves deadlocks, and escalates locks if needed. The lock manager controls table, page, and row locks as well as system data locks. (System data, such as page headers and indexes, are private to the database system.)

The lock manager provides two separate locking systems. The first enables row locks, page locks, and table locks for all fully shared data tables, data pages and rows, text pages, and leaf-level index pages and index rows. The second locking system is used internally only for restricted system data; it protects root and intermediate index pages while indexes are being traversed. This internal mechanism uses *latches,* a lightweight, short-term variation of a lock for protecting data that does not need to be locked for the duration of a transaction. Full-blown locks would slow the system down. In addition to protecting upper levels of indexes, latches protect rows while they are being transferred from the storage engine to the relational engine. If you examine locks by using the *sp_lock* stored procedure or a similar mechanism that gets its information from the *syslockinfo* system table, you won't see or be aware of latches; you'll see only the locks for fully shared data. However, counters are available in the System Monitor to monitor latch requests, acquisitions, and releases. These will be discussed in Chapter 17.

Locking is an important aspect of SQL Server. Many developers are keenly interested in locking because of its potential effect on application performance. Chapter 14 is devoted to the subject, so I won't go into it further here.

Other Managers

Also included in the storage engine are managers for controlling utilities such as bulk load, DBCC commands, backup and restore operations, and the Virtual Device Interface (VDI). VDI allows ISVs to write their own backup and restore utilities and to access the SQL Server data structures directly, without going through the relational engine. There is a manager to control sorting operations and one to physically manage the files and backup devices on disk.

MANAGING MEMORY

One of the major goals of SQL Server 2000 was to scale easily from a laptop installation on Windows 98 to an SMP server running on Windows 2000 DataCenter Server. This ability to scale requires a robust policy for managing memory. By default, SQL Server 2000 adjusts its use of system memory to balance the needs of other applications running on the machine and the needs of its own internal components. These other applications can include other instances of SQL Server running on the same machine.

When determining the optimal amount of memory to dynamically allocate to SQL Server, the memory manager strives to keep at least 4 MB of memory completely free and available for the operating system, but it might try to keep more available. The amount of free space reserved for the operating system is partially determined by the average life expectancy of a page in cache. The memory manager determines a Life Expectancy value that indicates how many seconds, on average, a page stays in cache if it isn't referenced at all. The Performance tool has a counter that allows you to view the current Life Expectancy value. That value is of course only an estimate, and it's based on the speed at which the lazywriter checks for referenced pages and the total amount of memory available. (I'll talk about the lazywriter later in this section.) If the average Life Expectancy of a page is small, the memory manager tries to keep the reserve memory at about 4 MB to increase the amount of memory available to SQL Server. If the average Life Expectancy increases, the space reserved for the operating system increases to up to 10 MB and the total memory for SQL Server decreases. All instances of SQL Server on a single machine tend to work toward the same reserve value and a similar Life Expectancy value.

As an alternative to dynamically computing the total amount of memory, you can configure SQL Server to use a fixed amount of memory. Whether memory allocation is fixed or dynamically adjusted, the total memory space for each instance is considered one unified cache and is managed as a collection of various pools with their own policies and purposes. Memory can be requested by and granted to any of several internal components.

The Buffer Manager and Memory Pools

The main memory component in SQL Server is the buffer pool; all memory not used by another memory component remains in the buffer pool. The buffer manager manages disk I/O functions for bringing data and index pages into the buffer pool so that data can be shared among users. When other components require memory, they can request a buffer from the buffer pool. A buffer is a page in memory that's the same size as a data or index page. You can think of it as a page frame that can hold one page from a database.

Another memory pool is the operating system itself. Occasionally, SQL Server must request contiguous memory in larger blocks than the 8-KB pages that the buffer pool can provide. Typically, use of large memory blocks is kept to a minimum, so direct calls to the operating system account for a small fraction of SQL Server's memory usage.

You can think of the procedure cache as another memory pool, in which query trees and plans from stored procedures, triggers, user-defined functions or ad hoc queries can be stored. Other pools are used by memory-intensive queries that use sorting or hashing, and by special memory objects that need less than one 8-KB page.

Access to In-Memory Pages

Access to pages in the buffer pool must be fast. Even with real memory, it would be ridiculously inefficient to have to scan the whole cache for a page when you have hundreds of megabytes, or even gigabytes, of data. To avoid this inefficiency, pages in the buffer pool are hashed for fast access. *Hashing* is a technique that uniformly maps a key via a hash function across a set of hash buckets. A *hash bucket* is a structure in memory that contains an array of pointers (implemented as a linked list) to the buffer pages. If all the pointers to buffer pages do not fit on a single hash page, a *linked list* chains to additional hash pages.

Given a dbid-fileno-pageno identifier (a combination of the database ID, file number, and page number), the hash function converts that key to the hash bucket that should be checked; in essence, the hash bucket serves as an index to the specific page needed. By using hashing, even when large amounts of memory are present, SQL Server can find a specific data page in cache with only a few memory reads. Similarly, it takes only a few memory reads for SQL Server to determine that a desired page is not in cache and that it must be read in from disk.

NOTE   Finding a data page might require that multiple hash buckets be accessed via the chain (linked list). The hash function attempts to uniformly distribute the dbid-fileno-pageno values throughout the available hash buckets. The number of hash buckets is set internally by SQL Server and depends on the total size of the buffer pool.

Access to Free Pages (Lazywriter)

You can use a data page or an index page only if it exists in memory. Therefore, a buffer in the buffer pool must be available for the page to be read into. Keeping a supply of buffers available for immediate use is an important performance optimization. If a buffer isn't readily available, many memory pages might have to be searched simply to locate a buffer to free up for use as a workspace.

The buffer pool is managed by a process called the lazywriter that uses a clock algorithm to sweep through the buffer pool. Basically, a lazywriter thread maintains a pointer into the buffer pool that "sweeps" sequentially through it (like the hand on a clock). As the lazywriter visits each buffer, it determines whether that buffer has been referenced since the last sweep by examining a reference count value in the buffer header. If the reference count is not 0, the buffer stays in the pool and its reference count is adjusted downward in preparation for the next sweep; otherwise, the buffer is made available for reuse: it is written to disk if dirty, removed from the hash lists, and put on a special list of buffers called the free list.

NOTE   The set of buffers that the lazywriter sweeps through is sometimes called the LRU (for least recently used list). However, it doesn't function as a traditional LRU because the buffers do not move within the list according to their use or lack of use; the lazywriter clock hand does all the moving. Also note that the set of buffers that the lazywriter inspects actually includes more than pages in the buffer pool. The buffers also include pages from compiled plans for procedures, triggers, or ad hoc queries.

The reference count of a buffer is incremented each time the buffer's contents are accessed by any process. For data or index pages, this is a simple increment by one. But objects that are expensive to create, such as stored procedure plans, get a higher reference count that reflects their "replacement cost." When the lazywriter clock hand sweeps through and checks which pages have been referenced, it does not use a simple decrement. It divides the reference count by 4. This means that frequently referenced pages (those with a high reference count) and those with a high replacement cost are "favored" and their count will not reach 0 any time soon, keeping them in the pool for further use. The lazywriter hand sweeps through the buffer pool when the number of pages on the free list falls below its minimum size. The minimum size is computed as a percentage of the overall buffer pool size but is always between 128 KB and 4 MB. SQL Server 2000 estimates the need for free pages based on the load on the system and the number of stalls occurring. A stall occurs when a process needs a free page and none is available; the process goes to sleep and waits for the lazywriter to free some pages. If a lot of stalls occur—say, more than three or four per second—SQL Server increases the minimum size of the free list. If the load on the system is light and few stalls occur, the minimum free list size is reduced and the excess pages can be used for hashing additional data and index pages or query plans. The Performance Monitor has counters that let you examine not only the number of free pages but also the number of stalls occurring.

User threads also perform the same function of searching for pages that can be placed on a free list. This happens when a user process needs to read a page from disk into a buffer. Once the read has been initiated, the user thread checks to see whether the free list is too small. (Note that this process consumes one page of the list for its own read.) If so, the user thread performs the same function as the lazywriter: it advances the clock hand and searches for buffers to free. Currently, it advances the clock hand through 16 buffers, regardless of how many it actually finds to free in that group of 16. The reason for having user threads share in the work of the lazywriter is to distribute the cost across all of the CPUs in an SMP environment. In fact, SQL Server 2000 actually has a separate free list for each CPU to help further distribute the cost and improve scalability. A user thread that needs a free page first checks the free list for the CPU it is running on; only if no pages are available will the user thread check the free lists for other CPUs.

Keeping Pages in the Cache Permanently

You can specially mark tables so that their pages are never put on the free list and are therefore kept in memory indefinitely. This process is called *pinning* a table. Any page (data, index, or text) belonging to a pinned table is never marked as free and never reused unless it is unpinned. Pinning and unpinning is accomplished using the *pintable* option of the *sp_tableoption* stored procedure. Setting this option to TRUE for a table doesn't cause the table to be brought into cache, nor does it mark pages of the table as "favored" in any way; instead, it avoids the unnecessary overhead and simply doesn't allow any pages belonging to that table to be put on the free list for possible replacement.

Because mechanisms such as write-ahead logging and checkpointing are completely unaffected, such an operation in no way impairs recovery. Still, pinning too many tables can result in few or even no pages being available when a new buffer is needed. In general, you should pin tables only if you've carefully tuned your system, plenty of memory is available, and you have a good feel for which tables constitute hot spots.

Pages that are "very hot" (accessed repeatedly) are never placed on the free list. A page in the buffer pool that has a nonzero use count, such as a newly read or newly created page, is not added to the free list until its use count falls to 0. Before that point, the page is clearly hot and isn't a good candidate for reuse. Very hot pages might never get on the free list, even if their objects aren't pinned—which is as it should be.

Checkpoints

Checkpoint operations minimize the amount of work that SQL Server must do when databases are recovered during system startup. Checkpoints are run on a database-by-database basis. They flush dirty pages from the current database out to disk so that those changes don't have to be redone during database recovery. A *dirty page* is one that has been modified since it was brought from disk into the buffer pool. When a checkpoint occurs, SQL Server writes a checkpoint record to the transaction log, which lists all the transactions that are active. This allows the recovery process to build a table containing a list of all the potentially dirty pages.

Checkpoints are triggered when

- A database owner explicitly issues a checkpoint command to perform a checkpoint in that database.

- The log is getting full (more than 70 percent of capacity) and the database is in SIMPLE recovery mode, or the option *trunc. log on chkpt.* is set. (I'll tell you about recovery modes in Chapter 5.) A checkpoint is triggered to truncate the transaction log and free up space. However, if no space can be freed up, perhaps because of a long running transaction, no checkpoint occurs.

- A long recovery time is estimated. When recovery time is predicted to be longer than the *recovery interval* configuration option, a checkpoint is triggered. SQL Server 2000 uses a simple metric to predict recovery time because it can recover, or redo, in less time than it took the original operations to run. Thus, if checkpoints are taken at least as often as the recovery interval frequency, recovery completes within the interval. A recovery interval setting of 1 means that checkpoints occur at least every minute as long as transactions are being processed in the database. A minimum amount of work must be done for the automatic checkpoint to fire; this is currently 10 MB of log per minute. In this way, SQL Server doesn't waste time taking checkpoints on idle databases. A default recovery interval of 0 means that SQL Server chooses an appropriate value automatically; for the current version, this is one minute.

In a system with a large amount of memory, checkpoints can potentially generate lots of write operations to force all the dirty pages out to disk. To limit the amount of resources checkpoints can consume, SQL Server limits checkpoint operations to a maximum of 100 concurrent write operations. That might seem like a large number of writes, but on a huge system, even 100 concurrent writes can take a long time to write out all the dirty pages. To optimize checkpoints and to make sure that checkpoints don't need to do any more work than necessary, the checkpoint algorithm keeps track of a generation number for each buffer in the cache. Without this number to help keep track of the work that's been done, checkpoint operations could potentially write the same pages to disk multiple times.

CHECKPOINTS AND PERFORMANCE ISSUES

A checkpoint is issued as part of an orderly shutdown, so a typical recovery upon restart takes only seconds. (An orderly shutdown occurs when you explicitly shut down SQL Server, unless you do so via the SHUTDOWN WITH NOWAIT command. An orderly shutdown also occurs when the SQL Server service is stopped through Service Control Manager or the net stop command from an operating system prompt.) Although a checkpoint speeds up recovery, it does slightly degrade run-time performance.

Unless your system is being pushed with high transactional activity, the run-time impact of a checkpoint probably won't be noticeable. You can also use the *sp_configure* recovery interval option to influence checkpointing frequency, balancing the time to recover vs. any impact on run-time performance. If you're interested in tracing how often checkpoints actually occur, you can start your SQL Server with trace flag 3502, which writes information to SQL Server's error log every time a checkpoint occurs.

The checkpoint process goes through the buffer pool, scanning the pages in buffer number order, and when it finds a dirty page, it looks to see whether any physically contiguous (on the disk) pages are also dirty so that it can do a large block write. But this means that it might, for example, write pages 14, 200, 260, and 1000 at the time that it sees page 14 is dirty. (Those pages might have contiguous physical locations even though they're far apart in the buffer pool. In this case, the noncontiguous pages in the buffer pool can be written as a single operation called a gather-write. I'll define gather-writes in more detail later in this chapter.) As the process continues to scan the buffer pool, it then gets to page 1000. Potentially, this page could be dirty *again,* and it might be written out a second time. The larger the buffer pool, the greater the chance that a buffer that's already been written will get dirty again before the checkpoint is done. To avoid this, each buffer has an associated bit called a *generation number.* At the beginning of a checkpoint, all the bits are toggled to the same value, either all 0's or all 1's. As a checkpoint checks a page, it toggles the generation bit to the opposite value. When the checkpoint comes across a page whose bit has already been toggled, it doesn't write that page. Also, any new pages brought into cache during the checkpoint get the new generation number, so they won't be written during that checkpoint cycle. Any pages already written because they're in proximity to other pages (and are written together in a gather write) aren't written a second time.

Accessing Pages Using the Buffer Manager

The buffer manager handles the in-memory version of each physical disk page and provides all other modules access to it (with appropriate safety measures). The memory image in the buffer pool, if one exists, takes precedence over the disk image. If the page is dirty, the copy of the data page in memory includes updates that have not yet been written to disk. When a page is needed for a process, it must exist in memory in the buffer pool. If the page isn't there, a physical I/O is performed to get it. Obviously, because physical I/Os are expensive, the fewer physical I/Os you have to perform the better. The more memory there is (the bigger the buffer pool), the more pages can reside there and the more likely a page can be found there.

A database appears as a simple sequence of numbered pages. The dbid-fileno-pageno identifier uniquely specifies a page for the entire SQL Server environment. When another module (such as the access methods manager, row manager, index manager, or text manager) needs to access a page, it requests access from the buffer manager by specifying the dbid-fileno-pageno identifier.

The buffer manager responds to the calling module with a pointer to the memory buffer holding that page. The response might be immediate if the page is already in the cache, or it might take an instant for a disk I/O to complete and bring the page into memory. Typically, the calling module also requests that the lock manager perform the appropriate level of locking on the page. The calling module notifies the buffer manager if and when it is finished dirtying, or making updates to, the page. The buffer manager is responsible for writing these updates to disk in a way that coordinates with logging and transaction management.

Large Memory Issues

Systems with hundreds of megabytes of RAM are not uncommon. In fact, for benchmark activities, Microsoft runs with a memory configuration of as much as 2 GB of physical RAM. Using the Enterprise Edition of SQL Server allows the use of even more memory. The reason to run with more memory is, of course, to reduce the need for physical I/O by increasing your cache-hit ratio.

MEMORY: HOW MUCH IS TOO MUCH?

Some systems cannot benefit from huge amounts of memory. For example, if you have 2 GB of RAM and your entire database is 1 GB, you won't even be able to fill the available memory, let alone benefit from its size. A pretty small portion of most databases is "hot," so a memory size that's only a small percentage of the entire database size can often yield a high cache-hit ratio. If you find that SQL Server is doing a lot of memory-intensive processing, such as internal sorts and hashing, you can add additional memory. Adding memory beyond what's needed for a high cache-hit ratio and internal sorts and hashes might bring only marginal improvement.

The Enterprise Edition of SQL Server 2000 running on Windows 2000 can use as much memory as Windows 2000 Advanced Server or Windows 2000 DataCenter Server allows by using the Windows 2000 Address Windowing Extensions (AWE) API to support extra large address spaces. You must specifically configure an instance of SQL Server to use the AWE extensions; the instance can then access up to 8 GB of physical memory on Advanced Server and up to 64 GB on DataCenter Server. Although standard 32-bit addressing supports only 4 GB of physical memory, the AWE extensions allow the additional memory to be acquired as nonpaged memory. The memory manager can then dynamically map views of the nonpaged memory to the 32-bit address space.

You must be very careful when using this extension because nonpaged memory cannot be swapped out. Other applications or other instances of SQL Server on the same machine might not be able to get the memory they need. You should consider manually configuring the maximum amount of physical memory that SQL Server can use if you're also going to enable it to use AWE. I'll talk more about configuring memory in Chapter 17.

Read Ahead

SQL Server supports a mechanism called read ahead, whereby the need for data and index pages can be anticipated and pages can be brought into the buffer pool before they're actually read. This performance optimization allows large amounts of data to be processed effectively. Read ahead is managed completely internally, and no configuration adjustments are necessary. In addition, read ahead doesn't use separate operating system threads. This ensures that read ahead stays far enough—but not too far—ahead of the scan of the actual data.

There are two kinds of read ahead: one for table scans on heaps and one for index ranges. For table scans, the table's allocation structures are consulted to read the table in disk order. Up to 32 extents (32 * 8 pages/extent * 8192 bytes/page = 2

MB) of read ahead are outstanding at a time. Four extents (32 pages) at a time are read with a single 256-KB scatter read. (Scatter-gather I/O was introduced in Windows NT 4, Service Pack 2, with the Win32 functions *ReadFileScatter* and *WriteFileGather*.) If the table is spread across multiple files in a file group, SQL Server has one read ahead thread per file. In SQL Server Standard Edition, each thread can still read up to 4 extents at a time from a file, and up to 32 files can be processed concurrently. This means that the read ahead threads can process up to 128 pages of data. In SQL Server Enterprise Edition, more extents can be read from each file, and more files can be processed concurrently. In fact there is no set upper limit to number of extents or number of files; SQL Server Enterprise Edition can read ahead enough data to fill 1 percent of the buffer pool.

For index ranges, the scan uses level one of the index structure (the level immediately above the leaf) to determine which pages to read ahead. When the index scan starts, read ahead is invoked on the initial descent of the index to minimize the number of reads performed. For instance, for a scan of *WHERE state* = *'WA'*, read ahead searches the index for *key* = *'WA'*, and it can tell from the level one nodes how many pages have to be examined to satisfy the scan. If the anticipated number of pages is small, all the pages are requested by the initial read ahead; if the pages are contiguous, they're fetched in scatter reads. If the range contains a large number of pages, the initial read ahead is performed and thereafter every time another 16 pages are consumed by the scan, the index is consulted to read in another 16 pages. This has several interesting effects:

- Small ranges can be processed in a single read at the data page level whenever the index is contiguous.

- The scan range (for example, *state* = *'WA'*) can be used to prevent reading ahead of pages that won't be used since this information is available in the index.

- Read ahead is not slowed by having to follow page linkages at the data page level. (Read ahead can be done on both clustered indexes and nonclustered indexes.)

> **NOTE** Scatter-gather I/O and asynchronous I/O are available only to SQL Server running on Windows 2000 or Windows NT. This includes the Personal Edition of SQL Server if it has been installed on Windows 2000 Professional or Windows NT Workstation.

Merry-Go-Round Scans

The Enterprise Edition of SQL Server 2000 includes another optimization to improve the performance of nonordered scans (a scan that isn't requested to be in any particular order), particularly if multiple nonordered scans of the same table are requested simultaneously by different processes. Without this optimization, one process can start scanning and get perhaps 20 percent of the way through the table before another process requests the same data. If the cache is small, or is used by other processes for completely unrelated data, the pages scanned by the original process might have been swapped out, which means that the buffer manager has to go back to disk to get the first pages of this table again. When the original scanning process resumes, any pages that were read in ahead might be gone, and more disk reads have to be done. This can cause some serious disk thrashing. A new optimization called Merry-Go-Round scans allows SQL Server 2000 Enterprise Edition to avoid this thrashing by allowing the second process to start at the same point the original process already reached. Both processes can then read the same data, and each page can be read from disk only once and be used by both scans. When the first process finishes, the second process can read the initial 20 percent of the table. Figure 3-5 illustrates a Merry-Go-Round scan.

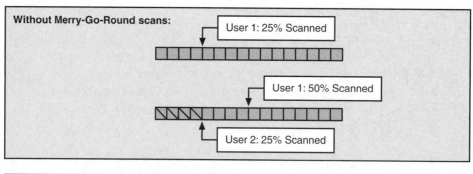

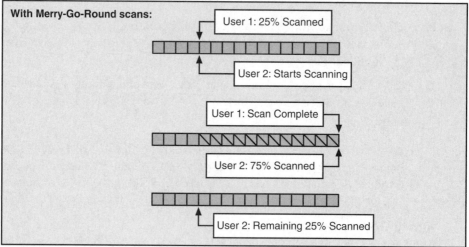

Figure 3-5. *SQL Server Enterprise Edition's Merry-Go-Round scan.*

The Log Manager

All changes are "written ahead" by the buffer manager to the transaction log. This means that the log records for a transaction are always written to disk before the changed data pages are written. Write-ahead logging ensures that all databases can be recovered to a consistent state, even in the event of a complete server failure, as long as the physical medium (hard disk) survives. A process never receives acknowledgment that a transaction has been committed unless it is on disk in the transaction log. For this reason, all writes to the transaction log are synchronous—SQL Server must wait for acknowledgment of completion. Writes to data pages can be made asynchronously, without waiting for acknowledgment, because if a failure occurs the transactions can be undone or redone from the information in the transaction log.

The log manager formats transaction log records in memory before writing them to disk. To format these log records, the log manager maintains regions of contiguous memory called *log caches*. In SQL Server 2000, log records do not share the buffer pool with data and index pages. Log records are maintained only in the log caches.

To achieve maximum throughput, the log manager maintains two or more log caches. One is the current log cache, in which new log records are added. In addition, there are one or more log caches available to be used when the current log cache is filled. The log manager also has two queues of log caches: a flushQueue, which contains filled log caches waiting to be flushed, and a freeQueue, which contains log caches that have no data (because they have been flushed) and can be reused.

When a user process requires that a particular log cache be flushed (for example, when a transaction commits), the log cache is placed into the flushQueue (if it isn't already there). Then the thread (or fiber) is put into the list of connections waiting for the log cache to be flushed. The connection does not do further work until its log records have been flushed.

The *log writer* is a dedicated thread that goes through the flushQueue in order and flushes the log caches out to disk. The log caches are written one at a time. The log writer first checks to see whether the log cache is the current log cache. If it is, the log writer pads the log cache to sector alignment and updates some header information. It then issues an I/O event for that log cache. When the flush for a particular log cache is completed, any processes waiting on that log cache are woken up and can resume work.

TRANSACTION LOGGING AND RECOVERY

The transaction log records all changes made to the database and stores enough information to allow any changes to be undone (rolled back) or redone (rolled forward) in the event of a system failure or if it is told to do so by the application (in the case of a rollback command). Physically, the transaction log is a set of files associated with a database at the time the database is created or altered. Modules that perform database updates write log entries that exactly describe the changes made. Each log entry is labeled with a log sequence number (LSN) that is guaranteed to be unique. All log entries that are part of the same transaction are linked together so that all parts of a transaction can be easily located for both undo activities (as with a rollback) and redo activities (during system recovery).

The buffer manager guarantees that the transaction log is written before the changes to the database are written (write-ahead logging). This is possible because SQL Server keeps track of its current position in the log by means of the LSN. Every time a page is changed, the LSN corresponding to the log entry for that change is written into the header of the data page. Dirty pages can be written to disk only when the LSN on the page is less than the LSN for the last page written to the log. The buffer manager also guarantees that log pages are written in a specific order, making it clear which log pages must be processed after a system failure, regardless of when the failure occurred. The log records for a transaction are written to disk before the commit acknowledgement is sent to the client process, but the actual changed data might not have been physically written out to the data pages. Therefore, although the writes to the log must be synchronous (SQL Server must wait for them to complete so it knows that they're safely on disk), writes to data pages can be asynchronous. That is, writes to data pages need only be posted to the operating system, and SQL Server can check later to see that they were completed. They don't have to complete immediately because the log contains all the information needed to redo the work, even in the event of a power failure or system crash before the write completes. The system would be much slower if it had to wait for every I/O request to complete before proceeding.

Logging involves demarcation of the beginning and end of each transaction (and savepoints, if a transaction uses them). Between the beginning and ending demarcations, information exists about the changes made to the data. This information can take the form of the actual "before and after" data values, or it can refer to the operation that was performed so that those values can be derived. The end of a typical transaction is marked with a Commit record, which indicates that the transaction must be reflected in the database or redone if necessary. A transaction aborted during normal runtime (not system restart) due to an explicit rollback or something like a resource error (for example, out of memory) actually undoes the operation by applying changes that undo the original data modifications. The records of these changes are written to the log and marked as "compensation log records." If the system crashes after a transaction commits but before the data is written out to the data pages, the transaction must be recovered. The recovery process runs automatically at system startup. I'll continue to refer to recovery as a system startup function, which is its most common role by far. However, recovery is also run during the final step of restoring a database from backup and also can be forced manually.

There are some special issues regarding media recovery during a database restore that I won't discuss here. These include the three recovery modes that you can set using the ALTER DATABASE statement and the ability to place a named marker in the log to indicate a specific point to recover to. I'll talk about these issues in Chapter 5. The discussion that follows deals with recovery in general, whether it's performed when the SQL Server Service is restarted or when a database is being restored from a backup.

Recovery performs both redo (rollforward) and undo (rollback) operations. In a redo operation, the log is examined and each change is verified as being already reflected in the database. (After a redo, every change made by the transaction is guaranteed to have been applied.) If the change doesn't appear in the database, it is again performed from the information in the log. Undo requires the removal of partial changes made by a transaction if the transaction did not entirely complete.

During recovery, only changes that occurred or were still open (in progress) since the last checkpoint are redone or undone. There are three phases to the recovery algorithm, and they are centered around the last checkpoint record in the transaction log. The three phases are illustrated in Figure 3-6. The descriptions refer to a crash of SQL Server, but these same recovery plans take place if SQL Server is intentionally stopped.

- **Phase 1: Analysis** The first phase is a forward pass starting at the last checkpoint record in the transaction log. This pass determines and constructs a dirty page table (DPT) consisting of pages that might have been dirty at the time of the crash (or when SQL Server stopped). An active transaction table is built that consists of uncommitted transactions at the time of the crash.

- **Phase 2: Redo** This phase repeats history by returning the database to the state it was in at the time of the crash. The starting point for this forward pass is the minimum of all the LSNs in the DPT. The DPT is used to avoid reading pages that don't need recovering and to avoid overwriting nonlogged changes.

- **Phase 3: Undo** This phase moves backward from the end of the log, following the links between entries in the transaction log for each transaction. Any transaction that was not committed at the time of the crash is undone so that none of its changes are actually reflected in the database.

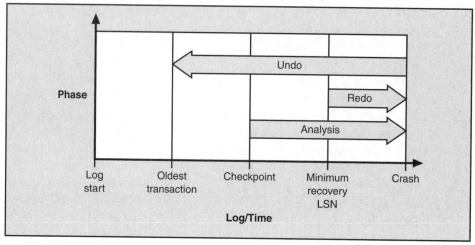

Figure 3-6. *The three phases of the SQL Server recovery process.*

Locking and Recovery

Locking, transaction management (rollback and rollforward), and recovery are all closely related. A transaction can be rolled back only if all affected data was locked exclusively so that no other process could have seen changes in progress (which might still be rolled back) or could have made changes to resources used by the transaction that would prevent its being rolled back. Only one active transaction can modify a row at a time. This is why exclusive locks must be held until a transaction is either committed or aborted. Until the moment it is committed, the transaction logically does not exist. A transaction operating with Read Uncommitted isolation (dirty read) can sometimes read data that logically never existed because it doesn't honor the existence of exclusive locks. But any other transaction operating with a higher level of isolation (which occurs by default—operating with Read Uncommitted isolation must be requested) would never allow such a phenomenon.

Page LSNs and Recovery

Every database page has an LSN in the page header that uniquely identifies it, by version, as rows on the page are changed over time. This page LSN reflects the location in the transaction log of the last log entry that modified a row on this page. During a redo operation of transactions, the LSN of each log record is compared to the page LSN of the data page that the log entry modified; if the page LSN is less than the log LSN, the operation indicated in the log entry is redone, as shown in Figure 3-7.

Because recovery finds the last checkpoint record in the log (plus transactions that were still active at the time of the checkpoint) and proceeds from there, recovery time is short and all changes committed before the checkpoint can be purged from the log or archived. Otherwise, recovery can take a long time and transaction logs become unreasonably large. A transaction log cannot be purged beyond the point of the earliest transaction that is still open, no matter how many checkpoints might have occurred subsequently. If a transaction remains open, the log must be preserved because it's still not clear whether the transaction is done or ever will be done. The transaction might ultimately need to be rolled back or rolled forward.

Some SQL Server administrators have noted that the transaction log seems unable to be purged to free up space, even after the log has been archived. This problem often results from some process having opened a transaction, which it then forgets about. For this reason, from an application development standpoint, you should ensure that transactions are kept short. Another possible reason for this problem relates to a table being replicated using transactional replication when the replication log reader hasn't processed it yet. This situation is less common, though, because typically a latency of only a few seconds occurs while the log reader does its work. You can use DBCC OPENTRAN to look for the earliest open transaction, or oldest replicated transaction not yet processed, and then take corrective measures (such as killing the offending process or running the *sp_repldone* stored procedure to allow the replicated transactions to be purged).

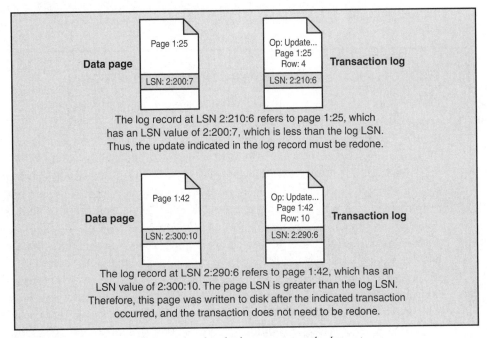

Figure 3-7. *Comparing LSNs to decide whether to process the log entry.*

THE SQL SERVER KERNEL AND INTERACTION WITH THE OPERATING SYSTEM

The SQL Server kernel is responsible for interacting with the operating system. It's a bit of a simplification to suggest that SQL Server has one module for all operating system calls, but for ease of understanding, you can think of it in this way. All requests to operating system services are made via the Win32 API and C run-time libraries. When SQL Server runs on Windows NT/2000, it runs entirely in the Win32 protected subsystem. Absolutely no calls are made in Windows NT/2000 Privileged Mode; the calls are made in User Mode. This means that SQL Server cannot crash the entire system, it cannot crash another process running in User Mode, and other such processes cannot crash SQL Server. SQL Server has no device driver–level calls, nor does it use any undocumented calls to the operating system. If the entire system crashes (giving you the so-called "Blue Screen of Death") and SQL Server happens to have been running there, one thing is certain: SQL Server did not crash the system. Such a crash must be the result of faulty or incompatible hardware, a buggy device driver operating in Privileged Mode, or a critical bug in the Windows NT/2000 operating system code (which is doubtful).

> **NOTE**   The Blue Screen of Death—a blue "bug check" screen with some diagnostic information—appears if a crash of Windows NT/2000 occurs. It looks similar to the screen that appears when Windows NT initially boots up.

EXPLOITING THE WINDOWS NT/2000 PLATFORM

Competitors have occasionally, and falsely, claimed that SQL Server must have special, secret hooks into the operating system. Such claims are likely the result of SQL Server's astonishing level of performance. Yes, it is tightly integrated with the operating systems on which it runs. But this integration is accomplished via completely public interfaces—there are no secret "hooks" into the operating system. Yes, the product is optimized for Windows NT/2000. That's SQL Server's primary platform. But other products could also achieve this level of optimization and integration if they made it a chief design goal. Instead, they tend to abstract away the differences between operating systems. Of course, there's nothing wrong with that. If Microsoft had to make sure that SQL Server could run on 44 different operating systems, it might also take a lowest-common-denominator approach to engineering. To do anything else would be almost impossible. So although such an approach is quite rational, it is in direct conflict with the goal of fully exploiting all services of a specific operating system. Since SQL Server runs exclusively on Microsoft operating systems, it intentionally uses every service in the smartest way possible.

A key design goal of both SQL Server and Windows NT is scalability. The same binary executable files that run on notebook computer systems run on symmetric multiprocessor super servers with loads of processors. Windows NT/2000 is an ideal platform for a database server because it provides a fully protected, secure, 32-bit environment. The foundations of a great database server platform are preemptive scheduling, virtual paged memory management, symmetric multiprocessing, and asynchronous I/O. The operating system provides these, and SQL Server uses them fully. The SQL Server engine runs as a single process on Windows NT/2000. Within that process are multiple threads of execution. The operating system schedules each thread to the next processor available to run one.

Threading and Symmetric Multiprocessing

SQL Server approaches multiprocessor scalability differently than most other symmetric multiprocessing (SMP) database systems. Two characteristics separate this approach from other implementations:

- **Single-process architecture**   SQL Server maintains a single-process, multithreaded architecture that reduces system overhead and memory use. This is called the Symmetric Server Architecture.

- **Native thread-level multiprocessing**   SQL Server supports multiprocessing at the thread level rather than at the process level, which allows for preemptive operation and dynamic load balancing across multiple CPUs. Using multiple threads is significantly more efficient than using multiple processes.

To understand how SQL Server works, it's useful to compare its strategies to strategies generally used by other products. On a nonthreaded operating system such as some UNIX variants, a typical SMP database server has multiple DBMS processes, each bound to a specific CPU. Some implementations even have one process per user, which results in a high memory cost. These processes communicate using Shared Memory, which maintains the cache, locks, task queues, and user context information. The DBMS must include complex logic that takes on the role of an operating system: it schedules user tasks, simulates threads, coordinates multiple processes, and so on. Because processes are bound to specific CPUs, dynamic load balancing can be difficult or impossible. For the sake of portability, products often take this approach even if they run on an operating system that offers native threading services, such as Windows NT.

SQL Server, on the other hand, has a clean design with a single process and multiple operating system threads. The threads are scheduled onto a CPU by a User Mode Scheduler, as discussed in Chapter 2. Figure 3-8 shows the difference between SQL Server's threading architecture and that of other typical SMP database systems.

SQL Server always uses multiple threads, even on a single-processor system. Threads are created and destroyed depending on system activity, so thread count is not constant. Typically, the number of active threads in SQL Server ranges from 16 to 100, depending on system activity and configuration. A pool of threads handles each of the Net-Libraries that SQL Server simultaneously supports, another thread handles database checkpoints, another handles the lazywriter process, and another handles the log writer. A separate thread is also available for general database cleanup tasks, such as periodically shrinking a database that is in autoshrink mode. Finally, a pool of threads handles all user commands.

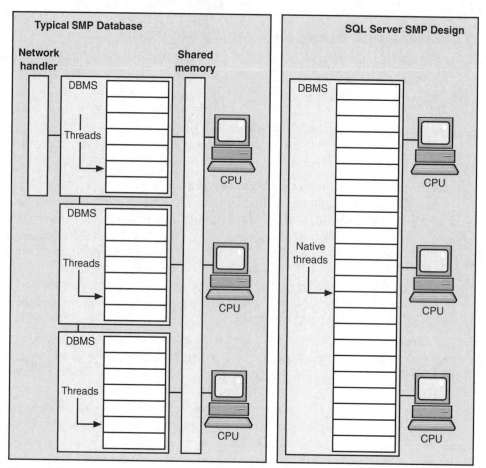

Figure 3-8. *SQL Server's single-process, multiple-thread design.*

The Worker Thread Pool

Although SQL Server might seem to offer each user a separate operating system thread, the system is actually a bit more sophisticated than that. Because it's inefficient to use hundreds of separate operating system threads to support hundreds of users, SQL Server establishes a pool of worker threads.

When a client issues a command, the SQL Server network handler places the command in a "completion queue" and the next available thread from the worker thread pool takes the request. Technically, this queue is an operating system facility called an IOCompletion port. The SQL Server worker thread waits in the completion queue for incoming network requests to be posted to the IOCompletion port. If no idle worker thread is available to wait for the next incoming request, SQL Server dynamically creates a new thread until the maximum configured worker thread limit has been reached. The client's command must wait for a worker thread to be freed.

Even in a system with thousands of connected users, most are typically idle at any given time. As the workload decreases, SQL Server gradually eliminates idle threads to improve resource and memory use.

The worker thread pool design is efficient for handling thousands of active connections without the need for a transaction monitor. Most competing products, including those on the largest mainframe systems, need to use a transaction monitor to achieve the level of active users that SQL Server can handle without such an extra component. If you support a large number of connections, this is an important capability.

> **NOTE** In many cases, you should allow users to stay connected—even if they will be idle for periods of, say, an hour—rather than have them continually connect and disconnect. Repeatedly incurring the overhead of the logon process is more expensive than simply allowing the connection to remain live but idle.

A thread from the worker thread pool services each command to allow multiple processors to be fully utilized as long as multiple user commands are outstanding. In addition, with SQL Server 2000, a single user command with no other activity on the system can benefit from multiple processors if the query is complex. SQL Server can break complex queries into component parts that can be executed in parallel on multiple CPUs. Note that this intraquery parallelism occurs only if there are processors to spare—that is, if the number of processors is greater than the number of connections. In addition, intraquery parallelism is not considered if the query is not expensive to run, and the threshold for what constitutes "expensive" can be controlled with a configuration option called *cost threshold for parallelism*.

ACTIVE VS. IDLE

SQL Server may consider many database connections idle, even though the associated human end user might be quite active, filling in the data entry screen, getting information from customers, and so forth. But those activities don't require any server interaction until a command is actually sent. So from the SQL Server engine perspective, the connection is idle.

When you think of an active user vs. an idle user, be sure to consider the user in the context of the back-end database server. In practically all types of applications that have many end users, at any given time the number of users who have an active request with the database is relatively small. A system with 1000 active connections might reasonably be configured with 150 or so worker threads. But this doesn't mean that all 150 worker threads are created at the start—they're created only as needed, and 150 is only a high-water mark. In fact, fewer than 100 worker threads might be active at a time, even if end users all think that they're actively using the system all the time.

Under the normal pooling scheme, a worker thread runs each user request to completion. If a given thread performs an operation that causes a page fault, only that thread, and hence only that one client, is blocked. (A page fault occurs if the thread makes a request for a memory page that isn't yet in RAM, so the virtual memory manager of the operating system must swap that page in from disk. Such a request for memory must wait a long time relative to the normal memory access time because a physical I/O is thousands of times more expensive than reading real memory.)

Now consider something more serious than a page fault. Suppose that while a user request is being carried out, a bug is exposed in SQL Server that results in an illegal operation that causes an access violation (for example, the thread tries to read some memory outside the SQL Server address space). The operating system immediately terminates the offending thread—an important feature of a truly protected operating system. Because SQL Server makes use of structured exception handling in Windows NT/2000, only the specific SQL Server user who made the request is affected. All other users of SQL Server or other applications on the system are unaffected and the system at large will not crash. Of course, such a bug should never occur and in reality is rare. But this is software, and software is never perfect. Having this important reliability feature is like wearing a seat belt—you hope you never need it, but you're glad it's there if a crash occurs.

> **NOTE** Since Windows 98 does not support SMP systems or thread pooling, the previous discussion is relevant only to SQL Server running on Windows NT/2000. The following discussion of disk I/O is also relevant only to SQL Server on Windows NT/2000.

Disk I/O in Windows NT/2000

SQL Server 2000 uses two Windows NT/2000 features to improve its disk I/O performance: scatter-gather I/O and asynchronous I/O. The following descriptions were adapted from SQL Server Books Online:

Scatter-gather I/O   As mentioned earlier, scatter-gather I/O was introduced in Windows NT 4, Service Pack 2. Previously, all the data for a disk read or write on Windows NT had to be in a contiguous area of memory. If a read transferred in 64 KB of data, the read request had to specify the address of a contiguous area of 64 KB of memory. Scatter-gather I/O allows a read or write to transfer data into or out of discontiguous areas of memory.

If SQL Server 2000 reads in a 64-KB extent, it doesn't have to allocate a single 64-KB area and then copy the individual pages to buffer cache pages. It can locate eight buffer pages and then do a single scatter-gather I/O that specifies the address of the eight buffer pages. Windows NT/2000 places the eight pages directly into the buffer pages, eliminating the need for SQL Server to do a separate memory copy.

Asynchronous I/O   In an asynchronous I/O, after an application requests a read or write operation, Windows NT/2000 immediately returns control to the application. The application can then perform additional work, and it can later test to see whether the read or write has completed. By contrast, in a synchronous I/O, the operating system doesn't return control to the application until the read or write completes. SQL Server supports multiple concurrent asynchronous I/O operations against each file in a database. The maximum number of I/O operations for any file is determined by the resources of the system, and SQL Server issues as many asynchronous, concurrent I/O requests as possible.

SUMMARY

In this chapter, we've looked at the general workings of the SQL Server engine, including the key modules and functional areas that make up the engine. I've also covered issues dealing with integration with Windows NT/2000. By necessity, I've made some simplifications throughout the chapter, but the information should provide some insight into the roles and responsibilities of the major subsystems in SQL Server, the general flow of the system, and the interrelationships among subsystems.

Part III

Using Microsoft SQL Server

Chapter 4

Planning for and Installing SQL Server

If you have appropriate hardware that's running Microsoft Windows, installing Microsoft SQL Server 2000 is a snap. It requires little more than inserting the CD into the drive and answering a few questions. Even a novice can comfortably install SQL Server in less than 15 minutes. The installation program doesn't ask a lot of questions about how to configure your system because SQL Server 2000 is primarily self-configuring. I won't spend much time discussing the mechanics of the installation program. You can consult the online Help and the documentation's step-by-step guide if you need to. In fact, you can read the complete documentation on installation and upgrading right from the CD before you take the first step in the installation process. The first splash screen that appears when you load the CD into the drive contains an option to "Browse Setup/Upgrade Help." Installing SQL Server is so easy that you might be tempted to dive in a bit too soon. That's OK if you're in "learning mode," but an installation that will be part of a production system deserves some thoughtful planning.

SQL SERVER EDITIONS

SQL Server is available in seven editions. Most are available on their own CD. The following descriptions are taken from SQL Server Books Online:

- **Enterprise Edition**   Used as a production database server. Supports all features available in SQL Server 2000 and scales to the performance levels required to support the largest Web sites and enterprise online transaction processing (OLTP) and data warehousing systems.

- **Standard Edition**   Used as a database server for a small workgroup or department.

- **Personal Edition**   Used by mobile users who spend some of their time disconnected from the network but run applications that require SQL Server data storage. Also used for stand-alone applications that require local SQL Server data storage on a client computer.

- **Developer Edition**   Used by programmers who develop applications that use SQL Server 2000 as their data store. This edition supports all the features of the Enterprise Edition, but it is licensed for use only as a development and test system, not a production server.

- **Desktop Engine**   The redistributable version of the SQL Server 2000 database engine, which independent software vendors can package with their applications.

- **Windows CE Edition** Used as the data store on Microsoft Windows CE devices. Capable of replicating data with SQL Server 2000 Enterprise and Standard editions to keep Windows CE data synchronized with the primary database.

- **Enterprise Evaluation Edition**   A full-featured version available for free downloading from the Web. Intended only for use in evaluating the features of SQL Server; stops running 120 days after installation.

Table 4-1, taken from SQL Server Books Online, summarizes the main differences between the editions and indicates the database engine features that they support. You can read about other differences between the versions (in areas such as replication, analysis services, and data transformation services) in SQL Server Books Online. Most of this book will deal specifically with the Enterprise and Standard editions. Also, because the Developer Edition has the same feature support as the Enterprise Edition (only the license agreement is different), most of the discussion will also be relevant to the Developer Edition.

Any edition lets you install the full server and tools suite or just the tools. In fact, if you try to install an edition of SQL Server on an OS for which it is not supported, all you will be able to install are the client tools. (For example, if you try to install SQL Server Enterprise Edition on Windows 2000 Professional, you will get only the tools.)

Feature	Personal	Standard	Enterprise
Runs on Microsoft Windows NT 4 Server or Windows 2000 Server	Yes	Yes	Yes
Runs on Windows NT 4 Server, Enterprise Edition or Windows 2000 Advanced Server	Yes	Yes	Yes
AWE Support (Windows 2000 only)	No	No	Yes
SQL Server failover support	No	No	Yes
Supports Microsoft Search Service, full-text catalogs, and full-text indexes	Yes, except on Windows 98	Yes	Yes
Maximum database size	2 GB	1,048,516 TB	1,048,516 TB
Number of symmetric multiprocessing (SMP) CPUs	2 on all platforms except Windows 98, which supports only 1	4 on all platforms except Windows NT 4 Server, Enterprise Edition, which supports 8	32 on Windows 2000 Datacenter Server 8 on Windows NT 4 Server Enterprise Edition and Windows 2000 Advanced Server 4 on Windows NT 4 Server and Windows 2000 Server
Physical memory supported	2 GB	2 GB	64 GB on Windows 2000 Datacenter Server 8 GB on Windows 2000 Advanced Server 4 GB on Windows 2000 Server 3 GB on Windows NT 4 Server, Enterprise Edition 2 GB on Windows NT 4 Server

Table 4-1. *Features of the SQL Server editions.*

The Personal Edition has the same features as the Standard Edition, with only the following differences:

- The Personal Edition cannot support more than two processors; the Standard Edition supports four processors on Windows 2000 Datacenter Server, Advanced Server and Server zand on Microsoft Windows NT 4 Server. It supports up to eight processors on Windows NT 4 Server, Enterprise Edition.

- In the Personal Edition, the maximum size of a database is 2 GB. The maximum size in the Standard Edition is 1,048,516 TB.

- The Personal Edition can run on Microsoft Windows 98; the Standard Edition cannot.

- The Personal Edition is optimized for up to five concurrent users; the Standard Edition has practically no limit on users.

Because of the limitations of the operating system, if the Personal Edition is installed on a machine running Windows 98, it also does not support:

- The Named Pipes and Banyan VINES server-side Net-Libraries. (The Windows 98 computer cannot accept incoming connections using these protocols, but the client tools on such a computer can connect to other SQL Servers on Windows NT and Windows 2000 using these protocols.)

- AppleTalk Net-Libraries.

- Windows Authentication for incoming server connections.

- The server side of Multiprotocol Net-Library encryption.

- Asynchronous I/O or scatter-gather I/O. (This includes true read-ahead scans. SQL Server issues what it thinks are read-ahead requests, but these must be translated to synchronous calls because Windows 98 doesn't support asynchronous I/O. You get the benefit of the larger I/Os that read-ahead provides, but they are synchronous.)

- Any component that corresponds to Windows NT and Windows 2000 Services. (The SQL Server database engine and SQL Server Agent run as executable programs on Windows 98.)

- Event logs. (SQL Server uses a SQL Server Profiler–based mechanism to launch alerts on Windows 98.)

- SQL Server Performance Monitor.

- The SQL Server Version Upgrade utility.

I'll discuss most of these capabilities and tools in more detail later in the book.

Embedded SQL Server

If you want a version of SQL Server that you can embed in your own applications and redistribute, take a look at Desktop Engine. Desktop Engine is the server component of SQL Server and includes basically the relational engine and the storage engine. This edition of SQL Server 2000 is available on any of the CDs for the other editions in the MSDE folder and also is available with Microsoft Office 10. Office 2000 users can download Desktop Engine, but you need a Service Release version of Office 2000 to access Desktop Engine data from an Office 2000 product.

None of the usual SQL Server tools is installed with Desktop Engine; you're expected to use the visual tools that come with Microsoft Visual Studio for creating objects. In addition, you can use all the usual tools that come with a full SQL Server installation, such as SQL Server Enterprise Manager and SQL Query Analyzer, to access the data stored in Desktop Engine.

Desktop Engine is also available as a set of Windows Installer merge modules, which independent software vendors (ISVs) can use to install Desktop Engine during their own setup process. These modules can be merged into the ISV setup program using available Windows Installer setup development tools. I won't discuss Desktop Engine further in this book; see the documentation for additional details.

> **NOTE** When you install Microsoft Access 2000, you have the option of installing Desktop Engine or the JET database engine for query processing. A whitepaper on the companion CD in the file Access Data Engine Options.doc describes the differences between these two choices.

HARDWARE GUIDELINES

Because SQL Server runs on any hardware that runs Windows NT or Windows 2000, you can choose from among thousands of hardware options. Although SQL Server Personal Edition runs on any hardware that runs Windows 98, your production applications probably will be deployed on Windows NT or Windows 2000. Therefore, the following discussion of hardware focuses on the needs of SQL Server running on Windows NT and Windows 2000 only.

Use Hardware on the Windows Hardware Compatibility List

If you cobble together a system from spare parts, Windows NT and Windows 2000 will run just fine, but your system might be unreliable. Unless you're a hobbyist and you like to tinker, this method isn't suitable for a production system. Support is another issue. Many people buy motherboards, chassis, processors, hard drives, memory, video cards, and assorted other peripherals separately and put together terrific systems, but the support options are limited.

Keep in mind that even name-brand systems occasionally fail. If you're using hardware that's on the Windows Hardware Compatibility List (HCL) and you get a "blue screen" (Windows NT and Windows 2000 system crash), you're more likely to be able to identify the problem as a hardware failure or find out, for example, that some known device driver problem occurs with that platform (and that you can get an update for the driver). With a homegrown system, such a problem can be nearly impossible to isolate. If you plan to use SQL Server, data integrity is probably a key concern for you. Most cases of corrupt data in SQL Server can be traced to hardware or device driver failure. (These device drivers are often supplied by the hardware vendor.)

> **NOTE**   Over the life of a system, hardware costs are a relatively small portion of the overall cost. Using no-name or homegrown hardware is penny-wise and pound-foolish. You can definitely get a good and cost-effective HCL-approved system without cutting corners.

Performance = Fn (Processor Cycles, Memory, I/O Throughput)

System throughput is only as fast as the slowest component: A bottleneck in one area reduces the rest of the system to the speed of the slowest part. The performance of your hardware is a function of the processing power available, the amount of physical memory (RAM) in the system, and the number of I/Os per second that the system can support.

Of course, the most important aspect of performance is the application's design and implementation. You should choose your hardware carefully, but there's no substitute for efficient applications. Although SQL Server can be a brilliantly fast system, you can easily write an application that performs poorly—one that's impossible to "fix" simply by "tuning" the server or by "killing it with hardware." You might double performance by upgrading your hardware or fine-tuning your system, but application changes can often yield a hundredfold increase.

Unfortunately, there's no simple formula for coming up with an appropriately sized system. Many people ask for such a formula, and minicomputer and mainframe vendors often provide "configuration programs" that claim to serve this purpose. But the goal of those programs often seems to be to sell more hardware.

Once again, your application is the key. In reality, your hardware needs are dependent on your application. How CPU-intensive is the application? How much data will you store? How random are the requests for data? Can you expect to get numerous "cache hits" with the most frequently requested data often being found in memory, without having to perform physical I/Os? How many users will simultaneously and actively use the system?

Invest in Benchmarking

If you're planning a large system, it's worthwhile to invest up front in some benchmarking. SQL Server has numerous published benchmarks, most of them Transaction Processing Council (TPC) benchmarks. Although such benchmarks are useful for comparing systems and hardware, they offer only broad guidelines and the benchmark workload is unlikely to compare directly to yours. It's probably best to do some custom benchmarking for your own system.

Benchmarking can be a difficult, never-ending job, so keep the process in perspective. Remember that what counts is how fast your application runs, not how fast your benchmark performs. And sometimes significant benchmarking efforts are unnecessary—the system might perform clearly within parameters or similarly enough to other systems. Experience is the best guide. But if you're testing a new application that will be widely deployed, the up-front cost of a benchmark can pay big dividends in terms of a successful system rollout. Benchmarking is the developer's equivalent of following the carpenter's adage "Measure twice, cut once."

> **SEE ALSO** For information on TPC benchmarks and a summary of results, see the TPC home page at http://www.tpc.org.

Nothing beats a real-world system test, but that's not always practical. You might need to make hardware decisions before or while the application is being developed. In that case, you should develop a proxy test. Much of the work in benchmarking comes from developing the appropriate *test harness*—the framework used to dispatch multiple clients that can run the test programs simultaneously, to run the test programs for an allotted time, and to gather the results.

HARDWARE COMPONENTS

The following general guidelines are no substitute for your own experience with your application, but they can help you at the outset. For simplicity, the following sections assume that your server is basically dedicated to running SQL Server, with little else going on. You can certainly combine SQL Server with other applications on the same machine, and you can administer SQL Server locally using SQL Enterprise Manager. You can support multiple databases from one SQL Server installation, and in SQL Server 2000, you can have multiple installations of SQL Server on the same machine.

Table 4-2 (adapted from the SQL Server Books Online) shows the hardware requirements for installing SQL Server 2000.

Hardware	Minimum Requirements
Computer	Intel or compatible.
	Pentium 166 MHz or higher.
Memory (RAM)[1]	Enterprise Edition: 64 MB minimum; 128 MB or more recommended.
	Standard Edition: 64 MB minimum.
	Personal Edition: 64 MB minimum on Windows 2000; 32 MB minimum on all other operating systems.
	Developer Edition: 64 MB minimum.
	Desktop Engine: 64 MB minimum on Windows 2000; 32 MB minimum on all other operating systems.
Hard disk space[2]	SQL Server database components: 95 to 270 MB; 250 MB typical.
	Analysis Services: 50 MB minimum; 130 MB typical.
	English Query: 80 MB.
	Desktop Engine only: 44 MB.
Monitor	VGA or higher resolution.
	800 x 600 or higher resolution required for the SQL Server graphical tools.
Pointing device	Microsoft Mouse or compatible.
CD-ROM drive	Required.

Table 4-2. *SQL Server 2000 hardware requirements.*

1   Additional memory might be required, depending on operating system requirements.

2   Actual requirements will vary based on your system configuration and the applications and features you choose to install.

The Processor

SQL Server is CPU-intensive—more so than you might think if you assume that it is mostly I/O-constrained. Plenty of processing capacity is a good investment. Your system uses a lot of processing cycles to manage many connections, manage the data cache effectively, optimize and execute queries, check constraints, execute stored procedures, lock tables and indexes, and enforce security. Because SQL Server typically performs few floating-point operations, a processor that is fabulous with such operations but mediocre with integer operations is not the ideal choice. Before you choose a processor, you should check benchmarks such as SPECint (integer)—not SPECfp (floating-point) or any benchmark that's a combination of floating-point and integer performance. Performance on SPECint correlates to the relative performance of SQL Server among different processor architectures, given sufficient memory and I/O capacity. The correlation is a bit loose, of course, because other factors (such as the size of the processor cache, the system bus efficiency, and the efficiency of the optimizing compiler used to build the system when comparing processor architectures) also play an important role. But integer-processing performance is a key metric for SQL Server.

SQL Server is built for SMP, but if your system is dedicated to SQL Server and supports fewer than 100 simultaneous users, a single CPU system will likely meet your needs. If you work with large data-warehousing applications, you can use an SMP system effectively with a small number of users. SQL Server 2000 can run complex queries in parallel, which means that the same query is processed simultaneously by multiple processors, each doing a subset of the computations. SQL Server executes queries on multiple processors if sufficient processors are available at the time of execution. (Chapter 15 has more details about how to choose the number of processors.) If you're uncertain about your needs or you expect them to grow, get a single-processor system that can be upgraded to a dual (or even a quad) system.

For your server platform, you should buy the fastest single-processor system in its class. Buy tomorrow's technology, not yesterday's. With many other applications, the extra processing power doesn't make much difference, but SQL Server is CPU-intensive.

> **TIP** Remember that the processor's cache affects its performance. A big L2 (level 2, or secondary) cache is a good investment. You might see a difference of 20 percent or more simply by using a 512 KB L2 cache instead of a 256 KB L2 cache in a given system. The cost difference is perhaps $100, so this is money well spent.

If your application is already available or you can conduct a fairly realistic system test, you can be much more exacting in evaluating your hardware needs. Using the Windows Performance Monitor, simply profile the CPU usage of your system during a specified period of time. (Use the Processor object and the % Processor Time counter.) Watch all processors if you're using an SMP system. If your system is consistently above 70 percent usage or can be expected to grow to that level soon, or if it frequently spikes to greater than 90 percent for 10 seconds or more, you should consider getting a faster processor or an additional processor. You can use the SPECint95 guidelines to determine the relative additional processing power that would be available by upgrading to a different or an additional processor.

Memory

Memory is used for many purposes in SQL Server 2000; I mentioned some of those purposes in Chapter 3, and I'll discuss memory usage further in Chapter 17. By default, SQL Server 2000 automatically configures the amount of memory it uses based on its needs and the needs of the operating system and other running applications.

If the SQL Server buffer manager can find data in the cache (memory), it can avoid physical I/Os. As discussed earlier, retrieving data from memory is tens of thousands of times faster than the mechanical operation of performing a physical I/O. (Physical I/O operations also consume thousands more CPU clock cycles than simply addressing real memory.) As a rule, you should add physical memory to the system until you stop getting significant increases in cache hits—or until you run out of money. You can easily monitor cache hits by using Performance Monitor. (For more information, see Chapter 17.) Using the SQLServer:Buffer Manager object, watch the Buffer Cache Hit Ratio counter. If adding physical memory makes the buffer cache-hit ratio increase significantly, the memory is a good investment.

As mentioned earlier, by default SQL Server automatically adjusts its memory use to meet its needs and the needs of the rest of the system. However, an administrator can override this and configure SQL Server to use a fixed amount of memory. You should be extremely cautious if you decide to do this. Configuring memory appropriately is crucial to good performance; configuring too little or too much memory can drastically impair performance. Too little memory gives you a poor buffer cache-hit ratio. Too much memory means that the combined working sets of the operating system and all applications (including SQL Server) will exceed the amount of real memory, requiring memory to be paged to and from disk. You can monitor paging in Performance Monitor using statistics such as the Memory object's counter for Pages/Sec.

Fortunately, adding physical memory to systems is usually quite simple (you pop in some SIMMs) and economical. You should start conservatively and add memory based on empirical evidence as you test your application. SQL Server needs no single correct amount of memory, so it's pointless to try to establish a uniform memory configuration for all SQL Server applications that you might ever deploy.

SQL Server can run with a minimum 32 MB system (64 MB for SQL Server Enterprise Edition), but as is typically the case with a minimum requirement, this is not ideal. If your budget isn't constrained, you should consider starting with at least 128 MB of RAM. (If your budget is flexible or you believe that your application will be more demanding, you might want to bump up memory to 256 MB. But it's probably best not to go higher than this initially without some evidence that your SQL Server application will use it.)

When you buy your initial system, give some consideration to the configuration of the memory SIMMs, not only to the total number of megabytes, so that you can later expand in the most effective way. If you're not careful, you can get a memory configuration that makes it difficult to upgrade. For example, suppose your machine allows four memory banks for SIMMs and you want 64 MB of memory that you might upgrade in the future. If your initial configuration of 64 MB was done with four 16-MB SIMMs, you're in trouble. If you want to upgrade, you have to remove some or all of the 16-MB SIMMs and buy new memory. But if you configure your 64 MB as two 32-MB SIMMs, you can add another one or two such SIMMs to get to 96 MB or 128 MB without replacing any of the initial memory. Starting with one 64-MB SIMM gives you even more flexibility in upgrading.

When deciding on the initial amount of memory, you should also consider whether your system will be more query-intensive or more transaction-intensive. Although more memory can help either way, it typically benefits query-intensive systems most, especially if part of the data is "hot" and often queried. That data tends to remain cached, and more memory allows more of the data to be accessed from the cache instead of necessitating physical I/Os. If you have a query-intensive system, you might want to start with more memory than 128 MB. You can use the memory not only to keep more of the needed data in cache, but also for some of the SQL Server 2000 query processing techniques, such as hash joins, that work best with large amounts of memory. In contrast, a transaction-intensive system might get relatively few cache hits, especially if the transactions are randomly dispersed or don't rely much on preexisting data. In addition, the query processing techniques used for transaction processing are typically much simpler and can't take advantage of extra memory for the actual processing. In such a system, the amount of memory needed might be low and adding a faster I/O subsystem might make more sense than adding more memory.

Disk Drives, Controllers, and Disk Arrays

Obviously, you need to acquire enough disk space to store all your data, plus more for working space and system files. But you shouldn't simply buy storage capacity—you should buy I/O throughput and fault tolerance as well. A single 8-GB drive stores as much as eight 1-GB drives, but its maximum I/O throughput is likely to be only about one-eighth as much as the combined power of eight smaller drives (assuming that the drives have the same speed). Even relatively small SQL Server installations should have at least two or three physical disk drives rather than a single large drive. Microsoft has benchmarked systems that can do, say, 1000 transactions per second (tps) (in a Debit-Credit scenario) using more than 40 physical disk drives and multiple controllers to achieve the I/O rates necessary to sustain that level of throughput.

If you know your transaction level or can perform a system test to determine it, you might be able to produce a good estimate of the number of I/Os per second you need to support during peak use. Then you should procure a combination of drives and controllers that can deliver that number.

Typically, you should buy a system with SCSI drives, not IDE or EIDE drives. An IDE channel supports only two devices. An EIDE setup consists of two IDE channels and can support four (2 × 2) devices. But more important, an IDE channel can work with only a single device at a time—and even relatively small SQL Server installations usually have at least two or three disk drives. If multiple disks are connected on an IDE channel, only one disk at a time can do I/O. This is especially problematic if the channel also supports a slow device such as a CD-ROM drive. Since the average access time for data on CDs is many times slower than for data on disk, your disk I/O would be delayed while the CD is accessed.

SCSI is also a lot smarter than IDE or EIDE. A SCSI controller hands off commands to a SCSI drive and then logically disconnects and issues commands to other drives. If multiple commands are outstanding, the SCSI controller queues the commands inside the associated device (if the device supports command queuing) so that the device can start on the next request as soon as the current request finishes. When a request finishes, the device notifies the controller. A SCSI channel can support multiple fast drives and allow them to work at full speed. Slow devices such as CD-ROM drives and tape drives do not hog the SCSI channel because the controller logically disconnects. A single SCSI channel can support many drives, but from a practical standpoint, you shouldn't go beyond a 5:1 ratio if you need to push the drives close to capacity. (That is, you should add an additional channel for every five drives or so.) If you're not pushing the drives to capacity, you might be able to use as many as eight to ten drives per channel—even more with some high-end controllers or random I/O patterns.

In TPC benchmarks (which are I/O-intensive, and in which the I/O is deliberately random), Microsoft generally follows a 6:1 ratio of drives per SCSI channel. (Since most of the standard benchmarks measure both performance and cost, Microsoft must balance the cost and benefits, just as they would for a real application.) Most real applications don't have such perfectly random I/O characteristics, however. When the I/O is perfectly random, a significant amount of the I/O time is spent with the disk drives seeking data rather than transferring data, which consumes the SCSI channel. Seeking is taxing only on the drive itself, not on the SCSI channel, so the ratio of drives per channel can be higher in the benchmark.

Note that this discussion is in terms of channels, not controllers. Most controllers have a single SCSI channel, so you can think of the two terms as synonymous. Some high-end cards (typically RAID controllers, not just standard SCSI) are dual-channel cards.

SOME HISTORY

The original acronym *RAID* apparently stood for "redundant array of *inexpensive* disks," as evidenced in the paper presented to the 1988 ACM SIGMOD by Patterson, Gibson, and Katz called "A Case for Redundant Arrays of Inexpensive Disks (RAID)." However, the current *RAID*book, published by the RAID Advisory Board, uses *independent,* which seems like a better description because the key function of RAID is to make separate, physically independent drives function logically as one drive.

RAID Solutions

Simply put, RAID solutions are usually the best choice for SQL Server for these reasons:

- RAID makes multiple physical disk drives appear logically as one drive.

- Different levels of RAID provide different performance and redundancy features.

- RAID provides different ways of distributing physical data across multiple disk drives.

- RAID can be provided as a hardware solution (with a special RAID disk controller card), but it doesn't necessarily imply special hardware. RAID can also be implemented via software.

- Windows NT and Windows 2000 Server provides RAID levels 0 (striping), 1 (mirroring), and 5 (striping with parity) for implementation with SQL Server.

Some RAID levels provide increased I/O bandwidth (striping), and others provide fault-tolerant storage (mirroring or parity). With a hardware RAID controller, you can employ a combination of striping and mirroring, often referred to as RAID-10 (and sometimes as RAID-1+0 or RAID-1&0). RAID solutions vary in how much additional disk space is required to protect the data and how long it takes to recover from a system outage. The type and level of RAID you choose depends on your I/O throughput and fault tolerance needs.

RAID-0

RAID-0, or striping, offers pure performance but no fault tolerance. I/O is done in "stripes" and is distributed among all drives in the array. Instead of the I/O capacity of one drive, you get the benefit of all the drives. A table's hot spots are dissipated, and the data transfer rates go up cumulatively with the number of drives in the array.

So although an 18-GB disk might do 100 random I/Os per second, an array of eight 2.1-GB disks striped with Windows NT Server or Windows 2000 Server's RAID-0 might perform more than 400 I/Os per second.

CHOOSING AN APPROPRIATE BACKUP STRATEGY

Although you can use RAID for fault tolerance, it's no substitute for regular backups. RAID solutions can protect against a pure disk-drive failure, such as a head crash, but that's far from the only case in which you would need a backup. If the controller fails, garbage data might appear on both your primary and redundant disks. Even more likely, an administrator could accidentally clobber a table, a disaster (such as a fire, flood, or earthquake) could occur at the site, or a simple software failure (in a device driver, the operating system, or SQL Server) could threaten your data. RAID doesn't protect your data against any of those problems, but backups do. I'll talk about SQL Server's options for backing up your data in Chapter 5.

NOTE   You could argue that RAID-0 shouldn't be considered RAID at all because it provides no redundancy. That might be why it's classified as level 0.

Windows NT and Windows 2000 provides RAID-0; a hardware RAID controller can also provide it. RAID-0 requires little processing overhead, so a hardware implementation of RAID-0 offers at best a marginal performance advantage over the built-in Windows NT and Windows 2000 capability. One possible advantage is that RAID-0 in hardware often lets you adjust the stripe size, while the size is fixed at 64 KB in Windows NT and Windows 2000 and cannot be changed.

RAID-1

RAID-1, or mirroring, is conceptually simple: a mirror copy exists for every disk drive. Writes are made to the primary disk drive and to the mirrored copy. Because writes can be made concurrently, the elapsed time for a write is usually not much greater than it would be for a single, unmirrored device. The write I/O performance to a given logical drive is only as fast as that of a single physical drive.

Therefore, you can at best get I/O rates of perhaps 100 I/Os per second to a given logical RAID-1 drive, as opposed to the much higher I/O rates to a logical drive that can be achieved with RAID-0. You can, of course, use multiple RAID-1 drives. But if a single table is the hot spot in your database, even multiple RAID-1 drives won't be of much help from a performance perspective. (SQL Server 2000 lets you create filegroups within a database for, among other purposes, placing a table on a specific drive or drives. But no range partitioning capability is available for data within a table, so this option doesn't really give you the control you need to eliminate hot spots.) If you need fault tolerance, RAID-1 is normally the best choice for the transaction log. Because transaction log writes are synchronous and sequential, unlike writes to the data pages, they're ideally suited to RAID-1.

HARDWARE-BASED VS. SOFTWARE-BASED RAID

If price and performance are your only criteria, you might find that software-based RAID is perfectly adequate. If you have a fixed budget, the money you save on hardware RAID controllers might be better spent elsewhere, such as on a faster processor, more disks, more memory, or an uninterruptible power supply.

Purely in terms of performance, it might not be wise to spend extra money on low-end hardware RAID (if you have sufficient CPU capacity in the server), but mid-level to high-end RAID offers many other benefits, including hot swappability of drives and intelligent controllers that are well worth the extra money—especially for systems that need to run 24 hours a day, 7 days a week.

You might also combine hardware-based and software-based RAID to great advantage. For example, if you have three hardware-based RAID units, each with seven 9-GB disks, with RAID-5 you'd have 6 x 9 = 54 GB in each, and Windows NT and Windows 2000 would see three 54-GB disks. You can then use software-based RAID on Windows NT and Windows 2000 to define a RAID-0 striped volume to get a single 162-GB partition on which to create SQL Server databases.

RAID-1 can significantly increase read performance because a read can be obtained from either the primary device or the mirror device. (A single read isn't performed faster, but multiple reads will have a faster overall time because they can be performed simultaneously.) If one of the drives fails, the other continues and SQL Server uses the surviving drive. Until the failed drive is replaced, fault tolerance is not available unless multiple mirror copies were used.

> **NOTE** The Windows NT and Windows 2000 RAID software doesn't allow you to keep multiple mirror copies; it allows only one copy. But some RAID hardware controllers offer this feature. You can keep one or more mirror copies of a drive to ensure that even if a drive fails, a mirror still exists. If a crucial system is difficult to access in a timely way to replace a failed drive, this option might make sense.

Windows NT Server and Windows 2000 Server provide RAID-1, and some hardware RAID controllers also provide it. RAID-1 requires little processing overhead, so a hardware implementation of RAID-1 offers at best a marginal performance advantage over the built-in Windows NT and Windows 2000 capability (although the hardware solution might provide the ability to mirror more than one copy of the drive).

RAID-5

RAID-5, or striping with parity, is a common choice for SQL Server use. RAID-5 not only logically combines multiple disks to act like one disk, but it also records extra parity information on every drive in the array (thereby requiring only one extra drive). If any drive fails, the others can reconstruct the data and continue without any data loss or immediate down time. By doing an Exclusive OR (XOR) between the surviving drives and the parity information, the bit patterns for a failed drive can be derived on the fly.

RAID-5 is less costly to implement than mirroring all the drives because only one additional drive is needed rather than the double drives that mirroring requires. Although RAID-5 is commonly used, it's often not the best choice for SQL Server because it imposes a significant I/O hit on write performance. RAID-5 turns one write into two reads and two writes to keep the parity information updated. This doesn't mean that a single write takes four or five times as long, because the operations are done in parallel. It does mean, however, that many more I/Os occur in the system, so many more drives and controllers are required to reach the I/O levels that RAID-0 can achieve. So although RAID-5 certainly is less costly than mirroring all the drives, the performance overhead for writes is significant. Read performance, on the other hand, is excellent—it's almost equivalent to that of RAID-0.

RAID-5 makes sense, then, for the data portion of a database that needs fault tolerance, that is heavily read, and that does not demand high write performance. Typically, you shouldn't place the transaction log on a RAID-5 device unless the system has a low rate of changes to the data. (As mentioned before, RAID-1 is a better choice for the transaction log because of the sequential nature of I/O to the log.)

RAID-5 requires more overhead for writes than RAID-0 and RAID-1 do, so the incremental advantage provided by a hardware RAID-5 solution over the Windows NT and Windows 2000 software solution can be somewhat higher because more work must be offloaded to the hardware. However, such a difference would be noticeable only if the system were nearly at I/O capacity. If this is the case in your system, you probably shouldn't use RAID-5 in the first place because of the write performance penalty. You're probably better served by the combination of RAID-0 and RAID-1, known as RAID-10.

RAID-10

RAID-10, or mirroring and striping, is the ultimate choice for performance and recoverability. This capability is really not a separate type of RAID, but rather a combination of RAID-1 and RAID-0. It is sometimes also referred to as RAID-1+0 or RAID-1&0. A set of disks is striped to provide the performance advantages of RAID-0, and the stripe is mirrored to provide the fault-tolerance features and increased read performance of RAID-1. Performance for both writes and reads is excellent.

The most serious drawback to RAID-10 is cost. Like RAID-1, it demands duplicate drives. In addition, the built-in RAID software in the operating system doesn't provide this solution, so RAID-10 requires a hardware RAID controller. Some hardware RAID controllers explicitly support RAID-10, but you can achieve this support using virtually any RAID controller by combining its capabilities with those of Windows NT and Windows 2000. For example, you can set up two stripe sets of the same size and number of disks using hardware RAID. Then you can use Windows NT and Windows 2000 mirroring on the two stripe sets, which Windows NT and Windows 2000 see as two drives of equal size. If you need high read and write performance and fault tolerance and you cannot afford an outage or decreased performance if a drive fails, RAID-10 is the best choice.

A separate RAID-10 array is usually not an appropriate choice for the transaction log. Because the write activity tends to be sequential and is synchronous, the benefits of multiple disks are not realized. A RAID-1 mirroring of the transaction log is preferable and cheaper. With internal Debit-Credit benchmarks, Microsoft has shown that the transaction log on a simple RAID-1 device is sufficient to sustain thousands of transactions per second—which is likely more than you need. Log records are packed, and a single log write can commit multiple transactions (known as *group commit*). In the Debit-Credit benchmarks, 40 transactions can be packed into a log record. At a rate of 100 writes per second (writes/second), the log on a RAID-1 mirror would not become a bottleneck until around 4000 tps.

In fact, this threshold is probably even higher than 4000 tps. For pure sequential I/O, 100 writes/second is a conservative estimate. Although a typical disk drive is capable of doing 100 random I/Os per second, the rate for pure sequential I/O—largely eliminating the seek time of the I/Os—is probably better than 200 writes/second.

In a few cases, a physically separate RAID-10 array for the log might make sense—for example, if your system requires high online transaction processing (OLTP) performance but you also use replication of transactions. Besides performing sequential writes to the log, the system also does many simultaneous reads of the log for replication and might benefit from having the multiple disks available. (In most cases, however, the log pages are in cache, so RAID-10 probably won't provide a significant benefit. However, if replication is in a "catch-up" mode because the distribution database isn't available or for some other reason, some significant benefit might exist.)

RAID-01

Most of the discussion in the SQL Server documentation that concerns combining RAID-0 and RAID-1 assumes that two stripes will be created first, and then one of the stripes will be defined as the mirror of the other. However, there is another possibility, which is to create multiple mirrored sets of disks first and then create a stripe from the mirrors. The first solution is referred to as *mirrored stripes*, and is the RAID 10 solution I discussed in the previous section. The second solution is referred to as striped mirrors and can be called RAID-01.

NOTE   Both RAID-10 and RAID-01 refer to combining the capabilities of RAID-0 (striping) with RAID-1 (mirroring) so that speed and fault tolerance are achieved, without the overhead of computing a parity value. However, the terminology is not standard. As mentioned previously, some sources will refer to RAID-1&0, or RAID-1+0. Some use the term RAID-10 to refer to striping a set of mirrored volumes, and use RAID-01 to refer to mirroring a striped volume, which is the opposite of the terminology I've been using. In many cases it might not matter which is done first, striping or mirroring, at least for the discussion at hand. I hope that in situations where it does matter, the authors of whatever sources you read will define the terms they use.

Choosing the Best RAID Solution

Table 4-3 summarizes the characteristics of various RAID configurations commonly used with SQL Server. Obviously, innumerable configurations are possible, but this chart will help you predict the characteristics for additional configurations as well as typical ones. You should reject Option 1 for all but the smallest environments because with this option the entire system runs with one disk drive. This is not efficient even for a low-end system, unless you have little write performance and enough memory to get a high cache-hit ratio. Unless you're running SQL Server on a laptop, there's little excuse for using only one drive.

Option 2, two physical drives and no use of RAID, represents an entry-level or development system. It offers far-from-ideal performance and no fault tolerance. But it is significantly better than having only a single drive. Because you should separate your data from your log before you even think about RAID, putting your data on one drive and your log on the other is the best you can do.

If you don't need fault tolerance and limited recovery ability is sufficient, Option 3—using RAID-0 for the data and placing the transaction log on a separate physical device (without mirroring)—is an excellent configuration. It offers peak performance and low cost. One significant downside, however, is that if the drive with the log fails, you can recover the data only to the point of your last transaction log or database backup. Because of this, Option 3 is not appropriate for many environments. On the other hand, if you lose the drive with the data, you can back up the log to the point of failure using the NO_TRUNCATE option and then restore that last log backup as the last step in restoring the whole database.

Option 4 is the entry level for environments in which it is essential that no data be lost if a drive fails. This option uses RAID-0 (striping, without parity) for the devices holding the data and uses RAID-1 (mirroring) for the transaction log, so data can always be recovered from the log. However, any failed drive in the RAID-0 array renders SQL Server unable to continue operation on that database until the drive is replaced. You can recover all the data from the transaction logs, but you experience an outage while you replace the drive and load your transaction logs. If a drive fails on either a transaction log or its mirrored copy, the system continues unaffected, using the surviving drive for the log. However, until the failed log drive is replaced, fault tolerance is disabled and you're back to the equivalent of Option 3. If that surviving drive also fails, you must revert to your last backup and you'll lose changes that occurred since the last transaction log or database backup.

Option	Description	Relative read performance	Relative write performance	Eases I/O hot spots and does not require handcrafting physical layout	Relative cost	Up-to-the-minute data protection (for failure of one drive)	Any single drive failure does not cause immediate outage of SQL Server	Can sustain multiple drive failures without an outage of SQL Server	Supported with Windows NT Server software, without need for special hardware controller
1	1 physical drive	Very Low	Very Low	No	Very Low	No	No	No	Yes
2	2 physical drives: DATA: Separate LOG: Separate No RAID	Low	Low	No	Low	No	No	No	Yes
3	Multiple drives: (3+) DATA: RAID-0 LOG: Separate, physical non-RAID drive	High[1]	High	Yes	Low-Moderate	No	No	No	Yes
4	Multiple drives: DATA: RAID-0 LOG: Separate, physical mirrored, RAID-1 devices	High	High	Yes	Moderate	Yes	No[2]	No	Yes
5	Multiple drives: DATA: RAID-1 LOG: Separate, physical RAID-1 devices	Varies widely[3]	Varies widely[3]	No	High	Yes	Yes	Partial[4]	Yes
6	Multiple drives: DATA: RAID-5 LOG: Separate, physical RAID-1 devices	High	Low-Moderate	Yes	Moderate	Yes	Yes	No	Yes
7	Multiple drives: DATA: RAID-10 or RAID-01 LOG: Separate, physical RAID-1 devices	Very High	High	Yes	High	Yes	Yes	Partial[4]	No
8	Multiple drives: DATA: RAID-10 or RAID-01 with multiple, mirrored copies LOG: Separate, physical RAID-1 devices with multiple, mirrored copies	Very High	High	Yes	Very High	Yes	Yes	Yes	No

[1] Additional memory might be required, depending on operating system requirements.

[2] Actual requirements will vary based on your system configuration and the applications and features you choose to install.

[3] This is case-by-case dependent. The degree to which I/Os can be balanced by carefully laying out the database will determine if this is a good performing option. This is a difficult proposition to get right and one we typically try to avoid.

[4] If a primary is lost and then its mirror is also lost, drive failures cannot be sustained. With the loss of two different primaries (or mirrors), drive failures can be sustained.

Table 4-3. *Characteristics of RAID configurations used with SQL Server.*

Option 4 offers excellent performance—almost as good as Option 3. This might come as a surprise to those concerned with the mirroring of the log. RAID-1, of course, turns a single write into two. However, since the writes are done in parallel, the elapsed time for the I/O is about the same as it would be for a single drive, assuming that both the primary and mirrored drives are physically separate and are used only for log operations. If you need to protect all data but recovery time is not a major concern and an outage while you recover is acceptable (that is, if loading transaction logs or database backups is acceptable), Option 4 is ideal.

If you cannot tolerate an interruption of operations because of a failed drive, you should consider some form of RAID-1 or RAID-5 for your database (as well as for the *master* database and *tempdb*, the internal workspace area), as described in the following discussion of Options 5 through 8.

Option 5 uses basic RAID-1, a one-for-one mirroring of drives for the data as well as the log. I don't recommend this option because RAID-1 doesn't provide the performance characteristics of RAID-0. Recall that RAID-0 enables multiple drives to operate logically as one, with additive I/O performance capabilities. Although RAID-1 can theoretically work well if you handcraft your data layout, in practice this approach has the same drawbacks as using filegroups instead of RAID-0. (See the following sidebar regarding filegroups.) This high-cost option is usually not a high-performing option, at least if the database has significant hot spots. It's appropriate only for specialized purposes in which I/O patterns can be carefully balanced.

DATA PLACEMENT USING FILEGROUPS

Are you better off simply putting all your data on one big RAID-0 striped set, or should you use filegroups to carefully place your data on specific disk drives? Unless you're an expert at performance tuning and really understand your data access patterns, I don't recommend using filegroups as an alternative to RAID. To use filegroups to handcraft your physical layout, you must understand and identify the hot spots in the database. And although filegroups do allow you to place tables on certain drives, doing so is tricky. It's currently not possible to partition certain ranges of a table to different disks, so hot spots often occur no matter how cleverly you designed your data distribution. If you have three or more physical disk drives, you should probably use some level of RAID, not filegroups. I'll discuss filegroups in detail in Chapter 5.

Option 6, using RAID-5 for the data and RAID-1 for the log, is appropriate if the write activity for the data is moderate at most and the update activity can be sustained. Remember that RAID-5 imposes a significant penalty on writes because it must maintain parity information so that the data of a failed drive can be reconstructed on the fly. Although the system does remain usable while operating with a failed drive, I/O performance is terrible: each read of the failed disk must read each of the other disks in the array and reconstruct the value from the failed drives, and each write becomes a similar read from each of the other disks, plus a write, so throughput drops precipitously when a drive fails. With RAID-5, if you lose another drive in the system before you replace the first failed drive, you can't recover because the parity information can't continue to be maintained after the first drive is lost. Until the failed drive is replaced and regenerated, continued fault-tolerance capability is lost. RAID-5 uses fewer bytes for storage overhead than are used by mirroring all drives, but because disk drives are inexpensive and disks are rarely full, the performance tradeoff is often simply not worth it. Finally, RAID-5 has more exposure to operational error than mirroring. If the person replacing the failed drive in a RAID-5 set makes a mistake and pulls a good drive instead of the failed drive, the failed drive might be unrecoverable.

If you need high read and write performance, cannot lose any data, and cannot suffer an unplanned system outage when a drive fails, Option 7—RAID-10 or RAID-01 and a simple RAID-1 mirror for your log—is the way to go. As mentioned earlier, RAID-10 offers the ultimate combination of performance and fault tolerance. Its obvious disadvantage is cost. Option 7 requires not only a doubling of disk drives but also special hardware array controllers, which command a premium price.

Options 7 and 8 differ in whether additional mirrored copies are kept. Option 7 presents the typical case using either RAID-10 or RAID-01. Although both RAID-10 and RAID-01 exhibit the same behavior when all the disks are functional, there is a significant difference when things start to break, both in terms of the fault tolerance provided and in terms of performance.

Fault tolerance comparison of RAID-10 and RAID-01   I can best describe the difference in fault tolerance between RAID-10 and RAID-01 with an example. Suppose we have 20 disk drives. For RAID-10, we could first form two stripes of ten disks each and then mirror one stripe on the other. For RAID-01, we could first define ten mirrored volumes and then create a stripe from those ten volumes. Either system can survive a failure of a single disk. But what about a second disk failure? What are the chances that a second drive failure will bring down the whole system?

Using RAID-10, if one disk in each stripe fails, the entire system will fail. You can compare this to having ten red balls and ten black balls in a bucket, and asking what the chances are of pulling out two balls with different colors in the first two pulls. After you pull out the first ball, statistically you have a 10/19 chance to pull out a ball with the opposite color in the second pull. In other words, there's a 52.6 percent chance that a second failure will bring the system down.

Using RAID-01 and a stripe of ten mirrors, the system would break down only if two disks from the same mirror crash. In our bucket of balls analogy, we have ten pairs of balls, each pair with a different color. What are the chances of pulling out two balls with the same color in our first two pulls? After pulling out the first ball, statistically, we have a 1/19 chance to pull out a ball with the same color in our second pull, or a 5.3 percent chance that a second failure will bring the system down. So we can conclude that the latter configuration, using a stripe of mirrors, is much safer in terms of fault tolerance—about ten times safer.

Performance comparison of RAID-10 and RAID-01   If one of the disks in a mirrored stripe (RAID-10) fails, the whole failed stripe is unusable, leaving ten operational disks; therefore, we potentially lose 50 percent read performance when performing asynchronous I/O. On the other hand, if one of the disks in a striped mirror (RAID-01) fails, only one disk is unusable, leaving 19 operational disks; therefore, we potentially lose only 5 percent read performance when performing asynchronous I/O.

Option 7, using the combined capabilities of striping and mirroring (RAID-10 or RAID-01), is probably a better choice for many sites that currently use RAID-5. The performance and fault-tolerance capabilities are significantly better, and with today's low-priced hardware, the cost isn't prohibitive.

If you need the utmost in fault tolerance of drive failures and your application is extremely mission critical, you can consider more than a single mirrored copy of the data and log. Option 8 is overkill for most environments, but hard drive prices are low enough that this option isn't necessarily prohibitively expensive. If you have a server in a remote offsite location and it's difficult to get a technician to the site in a timely manner, building in expensive fault-tolerance capabilities might make sense.

The Bottom Line: Buy the Right System

By now, you should know there's no one correct answer to the RAID-level question. The appropriate decision depends on your performance characteristics and fault tolerance needs. A complete discussion of RAID and storage systems is beyond the scope of this book. But the most important point is that you shouldn't simply buy storage space—you should buy the system that gives you the appropriate level of redundancy and fault tolerance for your data.

> SEE ALSO   For a detailed, authoritative discussion of RAID, consult the *RAID*book produced by the RAID Advisory Board. For more information about the RAID Advisory Board, see its home page at http://www.raid-advisory.com.

Hardware or Software RAID?

After choosing a RAID level, you must decide whether to use the RAID capabilities of your operating system or those of a hardware controller. If you decide to use

RAID-10, the choice is simple. Windows NT Server RAID does not currently allow you to keep more than one mirror copy of a drive, so you must use hardware array controllers. Windows 98 doesn't support software-based RAID at all, and Windows NT Workstation and Windows 2000 Professional provide only RAID-0 support.

As for solutions using RAID-0 and RAID-1, the performance advantage of a hardware array controller over the capabilities of the operating system might be minimal. If price and performance are your main criteria, you can use standard fast-wide SCSI controllers and use the money you save to buy more drives or more memory. Several of the formal TPC benchmarks submitted using SQL Server used only the Windows NT versions of RAID-0 and RAID-1 solutions (Option 4) and standard SCSI controllers and drives, with no special hardware RAID support. Hardware RAID solutions provide the largest relative performance difference over the equivalent Windows NT and Windows 2000 software solution if you use RAID-5, but even in this case, the difference is usually marginal at best. Each hardware RAID controller can cost thousands of dollars, and a big system still needs multiple controllers. Using hardware controllers makes the most sense when you need the additional capabilities they provide, such as hot swappability (discussed in the following section).

More About Drives and Controllers

No matter what RAID level you use, you should replace a failed drive as soon as possible. For this reason, you should consider a system that offers *hot swappable drives*. These drives let you quickly replace the faulty drive without shutting down the system. If the drive is part of a RAID-1 or RAID-5 set, SQL Server can continue to run without error or interruption when the drive fails and even while it is being physically replaced. If you use the Windows NT or Windows 2000 version of RAID-1 or RAID-5, you must shut down SQL Server only briefly to reestablish the fault tolerance for the drive because that process requires an exclusive lock on the disk drive by the operating system. (For RAID-1 you'll need to break and re-establish the mirror, and for RAID-5 you'll need to regenerate the striped set with parity.) When you restart SQL Server, the server computer won't even need to be rebooted. (Some hardware RAID solutions might also be able to regenerate or remirror the drive "below" the level of the operating system and hence not require SQL Server to be shut down.) Some systems also offer *hot-standby drives,* which are simply extra drives that are already installed, waiting to take over. Either of these approaches can get you back in business quickly.

Your disk controller must guarantee that any write operation reported to the operating system as successful will actually be completed. You should never use a write-back caching controller that can "lie" (report a write as completed without guaranteeing that it will actually perform the write) because your databases can become corrupted. In a write-back cache scheme, performance is increased because the bits are simply written to the cache (memory) and the I/O completion is immediately acknowledged. The controller writes the bits to the actual media a moment later. This introduces a timing window that makes the system vulnerable unless the controller designer has protected the cache with a battery backup and has provided correct recovery logic.

Let's say, for example, that a power failure occurs immediately after the controller reports that a write operation has completed but before the cache is actually written to disk. With write-ahead logging, SQL Server assumes that any change is physically written to its transaction log before it acknowledges the commit to the client. If the controller has just cached the write and then fails and never completes it, the system's integrity is broken. If a controller provides write-back caching as a feature, it must also guarantee that the writes will be completed and that they will be properly sequenced if they are reported to the operating system as successful. To be reliable, the caching controller also must guarantee that once it reports that an I/O has completed, the I/O will actually be carried out, no matter what. Such a controller typically employs a built-in battery backup and has solutions that guarantee that any write reported as completed will in fact be completed. If the system fails before a write operation has been completed, the operation is maintained in the controller's memory and is performed immediately after the system restarts, before any other I/O operations occur.

If a controller cannot guarantee that the write will ultimately be completed, you should disable the write-back caching feature of the controller or use a different controller. Disabling write-back caching in an I/O-intensive environment (more than 250 I/Os per second) might result in a SQL Server performance penalty of less than 5 percent. (After all, those writes must be performed eventually. The caching reduces the latency, but ultimately just as much I/O must be carried out.) In a less I/O-intensive test, the effect would likely be negligible. Realistically, the amount of the penalty doesn't matter much if the write isn't guaranteed to complete. Write-back caching must be disabled, or you run the risk of corrupting your data.

Uninterruptible Power Supply

If you're not using a write-back caching controller, you don't need UPS hardware to protect the integrity of your data from a power outage. SQL Server recovers your system to a consistent state after any sudden loss of power. However, you should definitely consider using a UPS; support for UPS hardware is built into Windows NT Server and Windows 2000 Server. Most hardware failures, such as memory failures and hardware crashes, result from power spikes that a UPS would prevent. Adding a UPS is probably the single most important thing you can do from a hardware perspective to maximize the availability and reliability of your system.

Without a UPS, the machine reboots and perhaps does a CHKDSK of the file system after a power flicker or power spike. This can take several minutes. During this time, your SQL Server is unavailable. A UPS can prevent these interruptions. Even if a power outage lasts longer than the life of your UPS, you have time to do an orderly shutdown of SQL Server and checkpoint all the databases. The subsequent restart will be much faster because no transactions will need to be rolled back or rolled forward.

BATTERY BACKUP, UPS, AND CACHING

A UPS is not the same as the battery backup of the on-board controller RAM. The job of a UPS is to bridge power failures and to give you time to do an orderly shutdown of the system. The computer continues to run for a while from the power supplied by the UPS, and it can be shut down in an orderly way (which the UPS software will do) if power isn't restored within the expected battery life.

The battery backup on a caching controller card ensures that the contents of the controller's volatile memory survive; the memory is not lost, so when the system restarts, the write completes. But it doesn't provide the power to actually ensure that a write succeeds. Some cards even allow the battery backed-up RAM to be moved to a different controller if the initial controller fails. Some provide two sets of batteries so that one can be replaced while the other maintains the RAM's contents, theoretically allowing you to keep adding new batteries indefinitely.

You might expect that using a caching controller that doesn't have a battery backup in combination with a UPS is generally OK if you do an orderly shutdown of SQL Server during the life of the UPS's power. However, this isn't always the case. SQL Server support engineers who get customers' servers back up and running can tell horror stories about customers who use write-caching controllers that were not designed around transactional integrity. The caching controller must take into account issues besides power. For example, how does the controller respond to the user pressing the Reset button on the computer? A couple of years ago, a well-known caching controller would have dumped its cache if you hit the Reset button—those writes were never carried out even though the calling application (SQL Server) was notified that they had been carried out. This situation often led to corrupt databases.

The Disk Subsystem

The reliability of the disk subsystem (including device drivers) is vital to the integrity of your SQL Server data. To help you uncover faulty disk systems, the SQL Server support team created a stand-alone, I/O-intensive, multithreaded file system stress test application. This application exercises the Win32 overlapped (asynchronous) I/O services, opens its files with the same write-through cache flags used by SQL Server, and performs similar types of I/O patterns. But the test is totally distinct from SQL Server. If this non–SQL Server I/O test cannot run without I/O errors, you do not have a reliable platform on which to run SQL Server, period. Of course, like any diagnostic program, the test might miss some subtle errors. But your confidence should certainly be higher than it would be without testing. You can download the test program for free from the Microsoft Support site at http://support.microsoft.com. On the Knowledge Base Search page, select All Microsoft Products in Step 1. In Step 2, select Specific Article ID Number. In Step 3, enter Q231619. Click Go. Open the Knowledge Base article that's returned ("INF: SQL70IOStress Utility to Stress Disk Subsystem") and download the file called SQL70IOStress.exe. SQL70IOStress.exe is also included on the companion CD.

Fallback Server Capability

SQL Server Enterprise Edition can take advantage of Microsoft Cluster Server (MSCS), which is available on Windows NT 4 Server, Enterprise Edition, Windows 2000 Advanced Server, and Windows 2000 Datacenter Server. You can install SQL Server 2000 on multiple nodes in a cluster, and all nodes are seen as having a single name on the network. Applications do not have to be aware that SQL Server is installed on a cluster, and MSCS handles the failover completely invisibly to users of SQL Server. For more details, see the operating system documentation.

MSCS requires specialized hardware. By using various RAID options, you can protect your data without clustering. But without clustering, you are not protected against an application outage if the machine fails. MSCS can automatically shift the control of a "switchable" hard-drive array from a damaged node in the cluster to another node. SQL Server 2000 supports two-node clustering on Windows NT Server 4, Enterprise Edition and Windows 2000 Advanced Server, and up to four-node clustering on Windows 2000 Datacenter Server. Only one of the connections to the hard-drive array is active at any time. One of the other hard-drive connections becomes active only if the system detects that the computer currently in control of the hard drive has shut down because of a hardware failure.

The SQL Server installation on the other nodes in the cluster can perform useful work while the first installation of SQL Server operates normally and accesses the data on the shared disk. The other servers can run SQL Server (using different databases than those used by the primary server), they can act as file and print servers, or they can run some other application. If another server needs to take over the work of the first server, that second server must have enough resources to add the primary server's workload to its existing workload.

> **NOTE**   Keep in mind that even with clustering, you need RAID to protect against media failure. The log, at the very least, must be mirrored to protect against a disk failure. The second server can run the disk drives of the failed first server, but those drives must also be protected against media failure.

Most applications probably do not need clustering because today's hardware is highly reliable. The most common hardware failure occurs in a disk drive, which can be protected without clustering by using RAID. As with RAID, clustering does not reduce the need for comprehensive and rigorous backup procedures. You'll probably need backups to recover from an occasional administrator mistake (human error), a catastrophe such as a fire or flood at the site, or a software anomaly. But some applications are so critical that the redundancy of clustering is necessary.

Other Hardware Considerations

If the server is mostly a "lights-out" operation and you won't be administering it locally or running other applications from the actual server machine, it doesn't make much sense to buy a first-class monitor or video card. Consider using an electronic switch box and sharing a monitor, keyboard, and mouse among multiple servers. If you don't use multiple servers, use a basic VGA monitor and video card.

From a performance perspective, a single high-quality network card is sufficient to handle virtually every SQL Server installation. Windows NT and Windows 2000 Server can support multiple network cards simultaneously, and sometimes your network topology will compel you to use this configuration with SQL Server as well. (Perhaps you're supporting both Ethernet and token ring clients on the same server.) However, one network card usually is more than enough—some sites support hundreds or thousands of users with a single 10-Mbit Ethernet card.

When you plan your hardware configuration, be sure to plan for your backup needs. You can back up to either tape or disk devices. As with regular I/O, you'll frequently need multiple backup devices to sustain the I/O rates required for backup. SQL Server can stripe its backup to multiple devices, including tape devices, for higher performance. For the same reasons mentioned earlier when I discussed disk devices, a SCSI tape device is typically preferable to an IDE/EIDE device.

> **NOTE** Not long ago, backup meant tape. Today, with disk space being the least expensive component of the entire system, many sites configure their hardware with additional disk devices purely for backup use because they prefer the extra speed and ease that backup to disk offers over tape backup. Some sites even use hot swappable drives for their backup; they rotate between a few sets of such drives, keeping a set off site in case of disaster.

THE OPERATING SYSTEM

The SQL Server engine runs best on Windows NT Server and Windows 2000 Server, and your production applications are meant to run on SQL Server on Windows NT 4 Server, Enterprise Edition, Windows NT and Windows 2000 Server, Windows 2000 Advanced Server, or Windows 2000 Datacenter Server. Although you can install the Personal

Edition of SQL Server on Windows NT 4 Workstation, Windows 2000 Professional, or Windows 98, many SQL Server capabilities are not supported on the Personal Edition. (I discussed these limitations earlier in the chapter.) Memory management and the process scheduling behavior on Windows NT and Windows 2000 Server are optimized for running services such as SQL Server. Windows NT and Windows 2000 Workstation and Windows 98, on the other hand, are more suited to running desktop applications. The simple fact is that SQL Server runs better with medium to large workloads on Windows NT Server and Windows 2000 Server than on any other platform.

Although you might get SQL Server to work on a platform other than its supported ones, you should stick with the supported platforms for the following reasons:

■ Only supported platforms get significant test coverage. An unsupported platform might seem to work, but a subtle problem might occur later.

■ Authorized SQL Server support providers and Microsoft SQL Server Product Support Services (PSS) focus on the supported platforms. If your problem is specific to an unsupported platform, you might not be able to get enough help.

■ Typically, a new release of SQL Server is targeted at the most recent (or an impending) release of Microsoft's Server operating system and also supports the prior major release. As of this writing, Windows 2000 has been released, so SQL Server 2000 runs on Windows NT 4 (with Service Pack 5) and Windows 2000. It is not supported on Windows NT Server 3.51 or earlier. If you try to run Setup on a Windows NT version earlier than version 4 with Service Pack 5, you'll get an error and will be prevented from continuing.

You can install SQL Server on any Windows NT Server or Windows 2000 Server in your domain, but for the best performance, do not install it on any of your domain controllers. Although SQL Server will run fine on a domain controller, the controller's tasks of maintaining and replicating the Windows NT and Windows 2000 accounts database take up processing cycles and memory. In less resource-intensive environments, this usually doesn't make much difference, but if your system is part of a large domain, it's better to separate SQL Server processing from those activities.

THE FILE SYSTEM

The performance difference between running SQL Server on the two major Windows NT and Windows 2000 file systems—NTFS and FAT—is minimal. This isn't surprising because SQL Server manages the structures within its database files without much use of the operating system.

I recommend NTFS as the file system of choice for SQL Server. It's more robust than FAT, and it's better able to recover fully and quickly from an ungraceful system shutdown. The integrity of the file system is vital to the integrity of your data, so this fact alone should drive most SQL Server users to NTFS. Also, the security features of NTFS are vital if security is important to you. Unlike FAT, NTFS allows security and auditing on all files; these are important ways to protect your data when SQL Server is not running. (SQL Server provides its own robust security.) When SQL Server is not running, the operating system is your prime protection. If you have a legitimate need to dual-boot your system to MS-DOS or to Windows 98, or if you need to use some disk utilities that work only with FAT, you might choose FAT. (You can, of course, make the partition the system boots from a FAT partition and format the other partitions with NTFS.)

Although it is physically possible to create SQL Server databases on NTFS compressed volumes, Microsoft does not support this, so I can't recommend that you ever consider it. Other reasons for avoiding compressed drives, in addition to Microsoft's lack of support, include performance degradation (over 50 percent in some conditions) and the inability to provide reliable transaction recovery of your databases. Transactional recovery requires sector-aligned write, and compressed volumes do not support this feature.

With previous versions of SQL Server, you could run SQL Server on a new partition that was not formatted with any file system. Such a partition is commonly referred to as a *raw partition*. Although you cannot run SQL Server 2000 from a raw partition, you still have the option of creating database files on raw partitions. Storing data on raw partitions is common for UNIX database products, and users who have UNIX DBMS backgrounds sometimes do this with SQL Server as well. Under heavy workloads, raw partitions can provide a small (about two percent) performance benefit. If the I/O system is not at capacity, you'll probably notice no performance difference at all.

For most installations, using raw partitions is not appropriate. Even if you gain some performance benefits by forgoing a file system, you also forgo benefits that a file system provides, such as basic file operations and utilities (copy, delete, rename, and dir) and important operations such as detecting and resolving bad disk sectors. If there's no file system to perform bad sector operations, you must be sure that your hardware will take care of this. (This type of hardware is available but costly.)

SECURITY AND THE USER CONTEXT

To install SQL Server on a machine, you need not be an administrator of the domain, but you must have administrator privileges on the machine. Users can install most of the SQL Server client utilities without administrator privileges.

Before you set up your system, give some thought to the user context in which SQL Server and SQL Server Agent will run. A new SQL Server environment can set up the SQL Server engine to run in the context of the special system (LocalSystem) account if it is not being installed on a Windows 2000 domain controller. This account is typically used to run services, but it has no privileges on other machines, nor can it be granted such privileges. However, the default is to have the SQL Server service and the SQL Server Agent service run in the context of a domain administrator account. This allows SQL Server to more easily perform tasks that require an external security context, such as backing up to another machine or using replication. If you don't have access to a domain administrator account, you might want to set up SQL Server to run in the context of a local administrator. This will still give SQL Server sufficient privileges to run on the local machine.

If you're not going to use the LocalSystem account, it's a good idea to change the account under which SQL Server runs to a user account that you've created just for this purpose rather than use an actual local or domain administrator account. The account must be in the local Administrators group if you're installing SQL Server on Windows NT or Windows 2000. You can create this account before you begin installing SQL Server, or you can change the account under which SQL Server runs at a later time. Changing the account is easy: you use the Services applet in the Windows NT Control Panel. In Windows 2000, you can use the Microsoft Management Console, which is accessible from Start/Programs/Administrative Tools/Computer Management. When you choose or create a user account for running SQL Server, make sure you configure the account so that the password never expires; if the password expires, SQL Server won't start until the information for the service is updated. (This is why I don't recommend using the real Administrator account for SQL Server; that account will probably have its password changed regularly.)

If you plan to use the mail integration features (SQL Mail), you should be aware of one additional issue: if you're using Microsoft Exchange on the same machine as SQL Server, you should run SQL Server in the context of the user account for which your Exchange client is configured. SQL Server can then pick up the Exchange configuration for that user automatically.

By default, the installation program chooses to use the same account for both the SQL Server and the SQL Server Agent services. SQL Server Agent needs a domain-level security context to connect to other computers in more situations than does SQL Server. For example, if you plan to publish data for replication, SQL Server Agent needs a security context to connect to the subscribing machines. If you won't be publishing data for replication or scheduling tasks on SQL Server that require access to other computers, you can have SQL Server Agent run in the LocalSystem account. If you specify a domain account but the domain controller cannot validate the account (because the domain controller is temporarily unavailable, for example), go ahead and install using the LocalSystem account and change it later using the Services applet (in Windows NT) or the Microsoft Management Console (in Windows 2000).

The accounts under which the SQL Server service and the SQL Server Agent service run can also be changed from SQL Enterprise Manager. For the SQL Server service, right-click on the name of your SQL Server, choose Properties, and then go to the Security tab. For the SQL Server Agent service, open the Management folder, right-click on SQL Server Agent, choose Properties, and stay on the General tab.

LICENSING

When you install SQL Server, you'll see a dialog box asking which licensing option you want to use: per-processor or per-seat.

> **NOTE** The license agreement in the SQL Server box is a legal document that you should read and understand. This section explains the licensing schemes but does not represent the official licensing policy of the product. Packaging and licensing periodically change. Consult the licensing agreement to be sure you're in compliance and have chosen the best options for your needs.

SQL Server Processor License

A Processor License includes access for an unlimited number of users to connect from inside the corporate LAN or WAN or outside the firewall. Under the per-processor licensing model, a Processor License is required for each processor running the SQL Server 2000 software. Processor Licenses can be used in any Internet, extranet, or intranet scenario. No additional Server Licenses, Client Access Licenses, or Internet Connector Licenses will need to be purchased.

Server Licenses and CALs

A Server License (for either Standard or Enterprise Edition) is required for every server on which that edition of SQL Server software is installed. The only exception is a Passive machine in an Active-Passive cluster. Each client needing access to any of the SQL Servers needs a Client Access License (CAL). You can think of a client as any device (for example, a PC, workstation, terminal, or pager) utilizing the services of either SQL Server 2000 Standard Edition or SQL Server 2000 Enterprise Edition. A client with a per-seat CAL can access any instance of SQL Server in the environment. You can deploy additional installations of SQL Server with minimal expense, and you don't have to buy additional client licenses. You simply acquire as many additional server licenses as you need, and your users are already licensed to use them. Figure 4-1 illustrates a scenario requiring two SQL Server licenses and three CALs deployed in the per-seat mode.

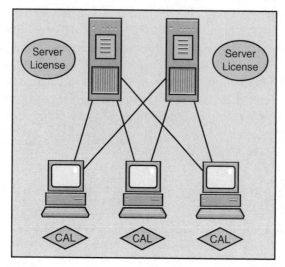

Figure 4-1. *A scenario requiring two Server Licenses and three CALs.*

You should consider you licensing agreement carefully before installation as the licensing mode cannot be changed without reinstalling SQL Server. In addition to the two licensing modes discussed above, there are some additional considerations.

Multiplexing: Use of Middleware, Transaction Servers, and Multitiered Architectures

Sometimes organizations develop network scenarios that use various forms of hardware and software that reduce the number of devices that directly access or utilize the software on a particular server, often called *multiplexing* or *pooling* hardware or software. For example, let's say a client PC is using a server application that calls the Microsoft Transaction Service (MTS) component of Microsoft Windows 2000 Server on one server, which in turn pulls data from a Microsoft SQL Server database on another server. In this case, the only *direct* connection to Microsoft SQL Server comes from the server running MTS. The client PC has a *direct* connection to the server running MTS, but also has an *indirect* connection to SQL Server because it is ultimately retrieving and using the SQL Server data through MTS. Use of such multiplexing or pooling hardware and software does not reduce the number of CALs required to access or utilize SQL Server software. A CAL is required for each distinct input to the multiplexing or pooling software or hardware front end. If, in the preceding example, 50 PCs were connected to the MTS server, 50 SQL Server CALs would be required. This is true no matter how many tiers of hardware or software exist between the SQL Server and the client devices that ultimately use its data, services, or functionality.

Multiple Instances

SQL Server 2000 includes a multi-instancing feature that allows customers to install SQL Server more than once on a server. If you're using SQL Server Standard Edition, you must fully license each instance server (whether in per-seat or per-processor mode). If you're using SQL Server Enterprise Edition, you can install an unlimited number of instances on each machine without requiring any additional licensing.

There are additional issues when determining licensing requirements for SQL Server Personal Edition and for SQL Server Desktop Engine. And if you are running SQL Server on MSCS, there are different licensing issues depending on whether the SQL Servers are configured on the cluster as active-active or as active-passive. The Microsoft Web site has full details on the licensing requirements in these, and all other, situations. Please refer to http://www.microsoft.com/sql for any of the following:

- End User License Agreement
- Upgrade roadmaps to SQL Server 2000
- Additional Questions and Answers

NETWORK PROTOCOLS

If you accept the default installation option during setup, SQL Server on Windows NT and Windows 2000 installs named pipes, shared memory, and TCP/IP sockets as its interprocess communication (IPC) mechanisms for communication with clients. SQL Server can simultaneously use many IPC mechanisms and networking protocols, but any specific client connection uses only one for its connection. You learned in Chapter 3 that each SQL Server networking interface is known as a Net-Library and represents a specific IPC mechanism. In addition to the Named Pipes, Shared Memory, and TCP/IP Sockets Net-Libraries, you can install one or more of the following:

- Multiprotocol
- NWLink IPX/SPX
- AppleTalk ADSP
- Banyan VINES

Although the Named Pipes Net-Library remains a good choice, its use as a default is mostly historical. Named pipes was the first, and for a while the only, IPC mechanism used by the early versions of SQL Server. Later, even when TCP/IP sockets and

IPX/SPX were supported, those protocols were more difficult to configure than named pipes, requiring configuration at each client. For example, using TCP/IP required that the administrator configure an arcane IP address at every client workstation for every installation of SQL Server it might access. Now, with the sophisticated network naming services provided by Windows NT and Windows 2000 (such as WINS, DHCP, and DNS), TCP/IP sockets are almost as easy to use as named pipes.

In addition, SQL Server 2000 allows the Shared Memory Net-Library to be used to communicate between SQL Server and local clients. The Network Libraries dialog box that appears during a custom installation of SQL Server 2000 does not give you the option of specifying or not specifying this library. SQL Server always enables it. You can determine whether you actually want shared memory to be used by local clients by using the Client Network Utility. Figure 4-2 shows the dialog box for determining which protocols will be used by a client and in which order the protocols will be tried. A check box at the lower left allows you to specify whether to use shared memory when communicating with local SQL Server instances.

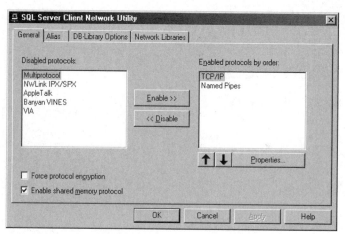

Figure 4-2. *Using the Client Network Utility to determine which protocols the local clients will use.*

Unless you have a compelling reason to choose a different network interface (the most compelling, of course, is if your existing network or network standards dictate some other network choice), use the defaults because they provide the most functionality. They are protocol-independent and allow the use of Windows Authentication Mode when you connect to SQL Server; you can thus provide a single logon name to your users so they don't have to log on to both the Windows NT or Windows 2000 domain and SQL Server. Windows Authentication Mode is an important feature for convenience and ease of administration as well as for making your system more secure. Windows Authentication Mode is also assumed with SQL Server replication services and when Performance Monitor connects to SQL Server.

The Multiprotocol Net-Library is built using the operating system's remote procedure call (RPC) services. Prior to SQL Server 2000, it was one of the only ways to get encryption over your network connection. Now, you should use Multiprotocol only for compatibility with existing systems. Secure Sockets Layer (SSL) encryption can be enabled over any Net-Library in SQL Server 2000 using the Server Network Utility. Multiprotocol is not supported on machines running Windows 98 or for named instances of SQL Server.

Microsoft internal testing has found the TCP/IP Sockets Net-Library to be the fastest networking choice, although in a typical LAN you rarely see the network as a performance bottleneck. In a low-speed WAN, however, this can be an important issue. Some network administrators have also been concerned about potentially routing NetBIOS traffic across their LANs and WANs. However, if SQL Server is not using the Named Pipes Net-Library and the Multiprotocol Net-Library is not using named pipes under the covers for IPC, SQL Server is not using NetBIOS at all and this is not a concern.

The NWLink IPX/SPX Net-Library is of most interest to those running Novell networking software on their clients that access SQL Server. If you are using a Novell NetWare–based network and file server but your SQL Server clients use Windows 98 or Windows NT and Windows 2000, using the NWLink IPX/SPX Net-Library is unnecessary. If your clients use networking software provided by Novell, NWLink IPX/SPX is probably your best choice. Server enumeration is available with NWLink IPX/SPX using the NetWare Bindery services.

Choose Banyan VINES if you interoperate with that environment. The Banyan VINES Net-Library uses StreetTalk naming services for server enumeration and name resolution. Use the AppleTalk ADSP Net-Library if you will support Apple Macintosh clients (using the Inprise—formerly Visigenic—ODBC driver for Macintosh) that run only AppleTalk, not TCP/IP.

During installation, you must supply additional information for any of the network options you have selected—for example, the port number or network name on which the server running SQL Server will "listen" for new connections or broadcast its existence to a network naming service. In most cases, you should accept the default unless you have a compelling reason not to. In the case of TCP/IP Sockets, you should accept the default port number of 1433 for the default instance only. This number is reserved for use with SQL Server by the Internet Assigned Numbers Authority (IANA), and as such it should not conflict with a port used by any other server application on your computer. (This assumes that the developers of other applications also follow the proper protocol of getting assigned numbers.) Additional named instances of SQL Server installed on the same machine will need to use a different port number, which can be dynamically assigned. We'll discuss named instances in detail later in this chapter.

SQL Server on Windows 98 doesn't support the server Named Pipes, Multiprotocol, Banyan VINES, and AppleTalk Net-Libraries. SQL Server does support the client side of Named Pipes and Banyan VINES Net-Libraries on Windows 98, so Windows 98 clients can use them to connect to SQL Server installations on Windows NT and Windows 2000.

> **TIP**   If you're new to networking and don't know your IP from your DHCP, don't fret. Accept the defaults, and configure your networking later as your understanding improves (or get your network administrator to help you). Although it's a good idea to understand your networking choices before installing SQL Server, you can easily change the networking options later without disturbing your SQL Server environment.

COLLATION

The term *collation* refers to a set of rules that determine how data is compared and sorted. Character data is sorted using rules that define the correct sequence of characters and options that specify case-sensitivity, accent-sensitivity, and kana/width-sensitivity. During installation, you must decide which collation will be the default for your server. The value you choose determines the default code page for non-Unicode characters, the default sort order for non-Unicode characters, and the Unicode collation for your server. The collation you choose during setup determines the collation of the system databases (*master, model, tempdb, msdb,* and *distribution*).

Earlier versions of SQL Server required that you make three separate decisions regarding collation during the installation process. These decisions applied to all the data stored in all the databases on a single SQL Server and were irrevocable. To change your decision, you had to rebuild your server and completely reload all your data. The three decisions were:

- The character set to use for non-Unicode characters, which was determined by the code page

- The sort order to use for non-Unicode characters, which included information on case sensitivity and accent sensitivity

- The sort order to use for Unicode characters, which was called the "Unicode Collation"

For SQL Server 2000, you must make these same three decisions, but you need to choose only one collation value, which includes all three of your choices. I'll talk about how to specify your choice after I discuss the issues with each of the three decisions.

Character Sets

Most non-Unicode characters are stored in SQL Server as a single byte (8 bits), which means that 256 (2^8) different characters can be represented. But the combined total of characters in all the world's languages is more than 256. So if you don't want to store all your data as Unicode, which takes twice as much storage space, you must choose a character set that contains all the characters (referred to as the *repertoire*) that you need to work with. For installations in the Western Hemisphere and Western Europe, the ISO character set (also often referred to as Windows Characters, ISO 8859-1, Latin-1, or ANSI) is the default and is compatible with the character set used by all versions of Windows in those regions. (Technically, there is a slight difference between the Windows character set and ISO 8859-1.) If you choose ISO, you might want to skip the rest of this section on character sets, but you should still familiarize yourself with sort order issues.

You should also ensure that all your client workstations use a character set that is consistent with the characters used by your installation of SQL Server. If, for example, the character ¥, the symbol for the Japanese yen, is entered by a client application using the standard Windows character set, internally SQL Server stores a byte value (also known as a *code point*) of 165 (0xA5). If an MS-DOS–based application using code page 437 retrieves that value, that application displays the character Ñ. (MS-DOS uses the term *code pages* to mean character sets; you can think of the terms as interchangeable.) In both cases, the internal value of 165 is stored, but the Windows character set and the MS-DOS code page 437 render it differently. You must consider whether the ordering of characters is what is semantically expected (discussed later in the "Sort Orders" section) and whether the character is rendered on the application monitor (or other output device) as expected.

SQL Server provides services in the OLE DB provider and the ODBC driver that use Windows services to perform character set conversions. Conversions cannot always be exact, however, because by definition each character set has a somewhat different repertoire of characters. For example, there is no exact match in code page 437 for the Windows character Õ, so the conversion must give a close, but different, character.

Windows NT and Windows 2000 and SQL Server 2000 also support 2-byte characters that allow representation of virtually every character used in any language. This is known as Unicode, and it provides many benefits—with some costs. The principal cost is that 2 bytes instead of 1 are needed to store a character. SQL Server allows storage of Unicode data by using the three datatypes *nchar*, *nvarchar*, and *ntext*. I'll discuss these in more detail when I talk about datatypes in Chapter 7. The use of Unicode characters for certain data does not affect the character set chosen for storing the non-Unicode data, which is stored using the datatypes *char*, *varchar*, and *text*.

THE ASCII CHARACTER SET

It is worth pointing out that the first 128 characters are the same for the character sets ISO, code page 437, and code page 850. These 128 characters make up the ASCII character set. (Standard ASCII is only a 7-bit character set. ASCII was simple and efficient to use in telecommunications because the character and a "stop bit" for synchronization could all be expressed in a single byte.) If your application uses ASCII characters but not the so-called *extended characters* (typically characters with diacritical marks, such as à, Å, and ä) that differentiate the upper 128 characters among these three character sets, it probably doesn't matter which character set you choose. In this situation (only), whether you choose one of these three character sets or use different character sets on your client and server machines doesn't matter because the rendering and sorting of every important character uses the same byte value in all cases.

Earlier versions of SQL Server did not support Unicode, but they did support double-byte character sets (DBCS). DBCS is a hybrid approach and is the most common way for applications to support Asian languages such as Japanese and Chinese. With DBCS encoding, some characters are 1 byte and others are 2 bytes. The first bit in the character indicates whether the character is a 1-byte or a 2-byte character. (In non-Unicode datatypes, each character is considered 1 byte for storage; in Unicode datatypes, every character is 2 bytes.) To store two DBCS characters, a field would need to be declared as *char(4)* instead of *char(2)*. SQL Server correctly parses and understands DBCS characters in its string functions. The DBCSs are still available for backward compatibility, but for new applications that need more flexibility in character representation, you should consider using the Unicode datatypes exclusively.

Sort Orders

The specific character set used might not be important in many sites where most of the available character sets can represent the full range of English and Western European characters. However, in nearly every site, whether you realize it or not, the basics of sort order (which is more properly called *collating sequence*) is important. Sort order determines how characters compare and assign their values. It determines whether your SQL operations are case sensitive. For example, is an uppercase *A* considered identical to a lowercase *a*? If your sort order is case sensitive, these two characters are not equivalent, and SQL Server will sort *A* before *a* because the byte value for *A* is less than that for *a*. If your sort order is case insensitive, whether *A* sorts before or after *a* is unpredictable unless you also specify a preference value.

Uppercase preference can be specified only with a case-insensitive sort order, and it means that although *A* and *a* are treated as equivalent for comparisons, *A* is sorted before *a*.

If your data will include extended characters, you must also decide whether your data will be accent insensitive. For our purposes, accents refer to any diacritical marks. So an accent-insensitive sort order treats *a* and *ä* as equivalent.

For certain character sets, you also need to specify two other options. Double-byte character sets can specify width insensitivity, which means that equivalent characters represented in either 1 or 2 bytes are treated the same. For a Japanese sort order, you can specify kana insensitive, which means that katakana characters are always unequal to hiragana characters. If you use only ASCII characters and no extended characters, you should simply decide whether you need case sensitivity and choose your collation settings accordingly.

Sort order affects not only the ordering of a result set but also which rows of data qualify for that result set. If a query's search condition is

```
WHERE name='SMITH'
```

the case sensitivity determines whether a row with the name *Smith* qualifies.

Character matching, string functions, and aggregate functions (MIN, MAX, COUNT (DISTINCT), GROUP BY, UNION, CUBE, LIKE, and ORDER BY) all behave differently with character data depending on the sort order specified.

Sort Order Semantics

You can think of characters as having primary, secondary, and tertiary sort values, which are different for different sort order choices. A character's primary sort value is used to distinguish it from other characters, without regard to case and diacritical marks. It is essentially an optimization: if two characters do not have the same primary sort value, they cannot be considered identical for either comparison or sorting and there is no reason to look further. The secondary sort value distinguishes two characters that share the same primary value. If the characters share the same primary and secondary values (for example *A* = *a*), they are treated as identical for comparisons. The tertiary value allows the characters to compare identically but sort differently. Hence, based on *A* = *a*, *apple* and *Apple* are considered equal. However, *Apple* sorts before *apple* when a sort order with uppercase preference is used. If there is no uppercase preference, whether *Apple* or *apple* sorts first is simply a random event based on the order in which the data is encountered when retrieved.

For example, a sort order specification of "case insensitive, accent sensitive, uppercase preference" defines all *A*-like values as having the same primary sort value. *A* and *a* not only have the same primary sort value, they also have the same secondary sort value because they are defined as equal (case insensitive). The character *à* has the same primary value as *A* and *a* but is not declared equal to them (accent sensitive), so *à* has a different secondary value. And although *A* and *a* have the same primary and secondary sort values, with an uppercase preference sort order, each has a different tertiary sort value, which allows it to compare identically but sort differently. If the sort order didn't have uppercase preference, *A* and *a* would have the same primary, secondary, and tertiary sort values.

Some sort order choices allow for accent insensitivity. This means that extended characters with diacritics are defined with primary and secondary values equivalent to those without. If you want a search of *name = 'Jose'* to find both *Jose* and *José*, you should choose accent insensitivity. Such a sort order defines all *E*-like characters as equal:

E=e=è=É=é=ê=ë

> **NOTE** When deciding on the case sensitivity for your SQL Server databases, you should be aware that the case sensitivity applies to object names as well as user data because object names (the metadata) are stored in tables just like user data. So if you have a case-insensitive sort order, the table *CustomerList* is seen as identical to a table called *CUSTOMERLIST* and to one called *customerlist*. If your server is case sensitive and you have a table called *CustomerList*, SQL Server will not find the table if you refer to it as *customerlist*.

Binary Sorting

As an alternative to specifying case or accent sensitivity, you can choose a binary sorting option, in which characters are sorted based on their internal byte representation. If you look at a chart for the character set, you see the characters ordered by this numeric value. In a binary sort, the characters sort according to their position by value, just as they do in the chart. Hence, by definition, a binary sort is always case sensitive and accent sensitive and every character has a unique byte value.

Binary sorting is the fastest sorting option because all that is required internally is a simple byte-by-byte comparison of the values. But if you use extended characters, binary sorting is not always semantically desirable. Characters that are *A*-like, such as *Ä*, *ä*, *Å*, and *å*, all sort after *Z* because the extended character *A*'s are in the top 128 characters and *Z* is a standard ASCII character in the lower 128. If you deal with only ASCII characters (or otherwise don't care about the sort order of extended characters), you want case sensitivity, and you don't care about "dictionary" sorting, binary sorting is an ideal choice. In case-sensitive dictionary sorting, the letters *abcxyzABCXYZ* sort as *AaBbCcXxYyZz*. In binary sorting, all uppercase letters appear before any lowercase letters—for example, *ABCXYZabcxyz*.

Specifying a Collation

During the installation of SQL Server 2000, you are asked to specify a default collation for your server. This is the collation that your system databases will use, and any new database you create will use this collation by default. In Chapter 5, I'll describe how you can create a database with a different collation than the one chosen during installation. Two types of collation are available; the documentation calls them SQL Collation and Windows Collation. Figure 4-3 shows the installation dialog box in which you choose your collation. The two choices are described during installation as Windows Locale Collation Designator and SQL Collation.

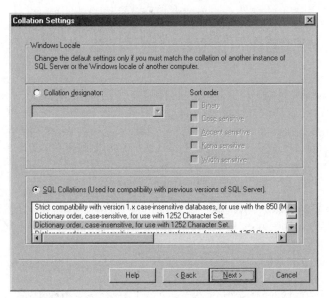

Figure 4-3. *The dialog box for selecting the default collation.*

SQL Collation is intended for backward compatibility and basically addresses all three collation issues in a single description string: the code page for non-Unicode data, the sort order for non-Unicode data, and the sort order for Unicode data. Figure 4-3 shows the default for an installation on a US English SQL Server, and the description of the SQL Collation is "Dictionary Order, Case-Insensitive, For Use With 1252 Character Set". The code page for non-Unicode data is 1252, the sort order for non-Unicode data is case insensitive, and the sort order for Unicode is Dictionary Order. The actual name of this collation is *SQL_Latin1_General_CP1_CI_AS*, and you can use this name when referring to this collation using SQL statements, as we'll see in later chapters. The prefix *SQL* indicates that this is a SQL Collation as opposed to a Windows Collation. The *Latin1_General* part indicates that the Unicode sort order corresponds to dictionary order, *CP1* indicates the default code page 1252, and *CI_AS* indicates case insensitive, accent sensitive. Other collation names use the full code page number; only 1252 has the special abbreviation *CP1*. For example, *SQL_Scandinavian_CP850_CS_AS* is the SQL Collation using Scandinavian sort order for Unicode data, code page 850 for non-Unicode data, and a case-sensitive, accent-sensitive sort order.

The SQL Collations are intended only for backward compatibility with previous SQL Server versions. There is a fixed list of possible values for SQL Collations, and not every combination of sort orders, Unicode collations, and code pages is possible. Some combinations don't make any sense, and others are omitted just to keep the list of possible values manageable.

As an alternative to a SQL Collation for compatibility with a previous installation, you can define a collation based on a Windows locale. In Windows Collation, the Unicode data types always have the same sorting behavior as non-Unicode data types. A Windows Collation is the default for non-English SQL Server installations, with the specific default value for the collation taken from your Windows operating system configuration. You can choose to always sort by byte values for a binary sort, or you can choose case sensitivity and accent sensitivity. When using SQL code to specify a Windows collation for a database, a column, or an expression, you can also specify a case preference for sorts, and, where applicable, the sensitivity of the collation to width and kana. I'll talk about the SQL statements for specifying collations when I discuss character datatypes in Chapter 7.

Performance Considerations

Binary sorting uses significantly fewer CPU instructions than sort orders with defined sort values. So binary sorting is ideal if it fulfills your semantic needs. However, you won't pay a noticeable penalty for using either a simple case-insensitive sort order (for example, Dictionary Order, Case Insensitive) or a case-sensitive choice that offers better support than binary sorting for extended characters. Most large sorts in SQL Server tend to be I/O-bound, not CPU-bound, so the fact that fewer CPU instructions are used by binary sorting doesn't typically translate to a significant performance difference. When you sort a small amount of data that is not I/O-bound, the difference is minimal; the sort will be fast in both cases.

A more significant performance difference results if you choose a sort order of Case Insensitive, Uppercase Preference. Recall that this choice considers all values as equal for comparisons, which also includes indexing. Characters retain a unique tertiary sort order, however, so they might be treated differently by an ORDER BY clause. Uppercase Preference, therefore, can often require an additional sort operation in queries.

Consider a query that specifies *WHERE last_name >= 'Jackson' ORDER BY last_name*. If an index exists on the *last_name* field, the query optimizer will likely use it to find rows whose *last_name* value is greater than or equal to *Jackson*. If there is no need to use Uppercase Preference, the optimizer knows that because it is retrieving records based on the order of *last_name*, there is also no need to physically sort the rows because they were extracted in that order already. *Jackson*, *jackson*, and *JACKSON* are all qualifying rows. All are indexed and treated identically, and they simply appear in the result set in the order in which they were encountered. If Uppercase Preference is required for sorting, a subsequent sort of the qualifying rows is required to differentiate the rows even though the index can still be used for selecting qualifying rows. If many qualifying rows are present, the performance difference between the two cases (one needs an additional sort operation) can be dramatic. This doesn't mean that you shouldn't choose Uppercase Preference. If you require those semantics, performance might well be a secondary concern. But you should be aware of the trade-off and decide which is most important to you.

Another performance issue arises when you decide between SQL Collation and Windows Collation. Because any character data defined using a Windows Collation is sorted based on the Unicode sort table for the collation, all non-Unicode data must be converted to Unicode during the sort. I ran some simple tests with two 10,000-row tables. The only difference between the tables was in a column called *last_name*. In one table, *last_name* was defined using a SQL Collation, and in the other, it was defined using an equivalent Windows Collation. Repeated sorts of the column in both tables showed a 15 to 30 percent increase in CPU time for the sort on the Unicode column.

MULTIPLE INSTANCES

SQL Server 2000 allows you to install multiple instances of SQL Server on a single computer. One instance of SQL Server can be referred to as the *default* instance, and all others must have names and are referred to as *named instances*. Each instance is installed separately and has its own default collation, its own system administrator password, and its own set of databases and valid users.

The ability to install multiple instances on a single machine provides benefits in several different areas. First is the area of application hosting. One site can provide machine resources and administration services for multiple companies. These might be small companies that don't have the time or resources (human or machine) to manage and maintain their own SQL Servers. They might want to hire another company to "host" their SQL Server private or public applications. Each company will need full administrative privileges over its own data. However, if each company's data were stored in a separate database on a single SQL Server, any SQL Server system administrator (sa) would be able to access any of the databases. Installing each company's data on a separate SQL Server allows each company to have full sa privileges for its own data but no access at all to any other company's data. In fact, each company might be totally unaware that other companies are using the same application server.

A second area in which multiple instances provide great benefits is server consolidation. Instead of having 10 separate machines to run 10 separate applications within a company, all the applications can be combined on one machine. With separate instances, each application can still have its own administrator and its own set of users and permissions. For the company, this means fewer boxes to administer and fewer operating system licenses required. For example, one Windows NT 4 Server, Enterprise Edition (or Windows 2000 Advanced Server) with 10 SQL Server instances costs less than 10 separate server boxes.

An added benefit to running multiple instances on one big computer is that you are more likely to take care of a more powerful computer, which will lead to greater reliability. For example, if you decide to purchase an eight-way Compaq ProLiant with 4 GB of RAM, it might cost you about $100,000. With that kind of investment, you'll probably want to set it up in its own climate-controlled data center instead of next to someone's desk. You'll meticulously maintain both the hardware and the software and only let trained engineers get near it. This means that reliability and availability will be greatly enhanced.

The third area in which multiple instances are beneficial is testing and support. Because the separate instances can be different versions of SQL Server or even the same version with different service packs installed, you can use one box for reproducing problem reports or testing bug fixes. You can verify which versions the problems can be reproduced on and which versions they can't. A support center can similarly use multiple instances to make sure that it can use the same exact version that the customer has installed.

Installing Named Instances

When you install multiple SQL Server instances on a single machine, only one instance is the "default" instance. This is the SQL Server that is accessed in the same way that SQL Servers in previous versions were accessed—by supplying the machine name as the name of the SQL Server. For example, to use the Query Analyzer to access the SQL Server on my machine called KALESSIN, I just type *KALESSIN* in the SQL Server text box in the Connect To SQL Server dialog box. Any other instances on the same machine will have an additional name, which must be specified along with the machine name. I can install a second SQL Server instance with its own name—for example, SQL2000. Then I must enter *KALESSIN\SQL2000* in the initial text box to connect using Query Analyzer.

Your default instance can be SQL Server 6.5, SQL Server 7, or SQL Server 2000. In fact, if you're using the version switch capability (discussed shortly) to switch between SQL Server 6.5 and SQL Server 7 or between SQL Server 6.5 and SQL Server 2000, your default instance can be this switched instance. Your default instance cannot be SQL Server 6 even if it is being version-switched with a later version. If you have SQL Server 6 or an older SQL Server 4.2 installation on your machine, you cannot install SQL Server 2000 at all.

Named instances can only be SQL Server 2000. Microsoft documents that you can have a maximum of 16 instances on a single machine, but this is only the supported limit. There is nothing hardcoded into the system to prevent you from installing additional instances, as long as you have the resources on the machine to support them.

Each instance has its own separate directory for storing the server executables, and each instance's data files can be placed wherever you choose. During installation, you can specify the desired path for the program files and the data files. Each instance also has its own SQL Server Agent service. The service names for the default instance do not change—they are MSSQLServer and SQLServerAgent. For an instance named SQL2000, the services are named MSSQL$SQL2000 and SQLAGENT$SQL2000.

However, only one installation of the tools is used for all instances of SQL Server 7 and SQL Server 2000. However, you will still have your SQL Server 7 Books Online, as well as your SQL Server 7 Server Network Utility available. In addition, there is only one Search Service, one Distributed Transaction Coordinator (DTC) service, one copy of English Query, one copy of the development libraries, and one copy of Microsoft SQL Server 2000 Analysis Services (formerly OLAP Services).

Named Instance Server Connectivity

I mentioned earlier in this chapter that the default Net-Libraries for SQL Server 2000 are Named Pipes, Shared Memory, and TCP/IP. Of the additional protocols that can be added, Multiprotocol, Banyan VINES, and AppleTalk are not supported for named instances. The default instance listens on a pipe named \\.\pipe\sql\query and on TCP port number 1433. A named instance listens on a pipe named \\.\pipe\MSSQL$<instance name>\sql\query, so for my SQL2000 instance, it is \\.\pipe\MSSQL$SQL2000\sql\query.

Determining which TCP port to use for a named instance is a little more problematic. Microsoft reserved port number 1433 but was unable to reserve additional ports. During setup, you can choose any port number, but you should be aware that other services from other vendors might conflict with the port number you choose. To avoid problems, the setup program allows you to specify 0 for the port number, which means that every time the SQL Server starts, it finds an unused port number to use. You can see what port has been chosen by using the Server Network Utility, selecting the name of the instance, and then displaying the properties for TCP/IP.

Allowing multiple instances of SQL Server to run on a single machine requires a Listener service to determine what instances are actually running on a machine. The new Listener service runs on UDP port 1434 but doesn't have an actual service name on the machine. This service exposes which SQL Server instances are installed, their network addresses, and so forth, for use by SQL Server client tools. At server startup, a component of every SQL Server instance checks whether anyone is listening on UDP port 1434. If no other instance is listening, it starts listening and becomes the listener service for the machine.

When a client asks to connect to a machine, the tool being used communicates with the Listener service server, asking for information about all the instances installed, their addresses, whether they are a cluster, and so forth. For each instance, the Listener service tells the client computer which server Net-Libraries and network addresses the instance is listening on. After the client computer receives this report, it chooses a Net-Library that is enabled on both the application computer and on the instance of SQL Server, and it makes a connection to the address listed for that Net-Library in the packet.

> CAUTION   Because you can only have one set of client tools installed on a machine, as soon as you install an instance of SQL Server 2000, you lose any SQL Server 7 tools you had on your machine, except for Books Online and the Server Network Utility. If one of the reasons you're using multiple instances is to have multiple versions available for testing purposes, you will only be able to test the SQL Servers. If you're doing troubleshooting and think the problem might be with the tools themselves, you're out of luck. You can't test using a different version of the tools on the same machine.

INSTALLING SQL SERVER

Now that you understand all the preliminary considerations of installing and using SQL Server, you're ready to install the software. The actual mechanics of installation are simple—the installation program starts automatically when you insert the CD into the drive; if it doesn't, you can initiate the installation by executing the autorun.exe program at the root of the SQL Server CD.

SQL Server 2000 is installed using the InstallShield program, which is common to many Microsoft products. One advantage of using InstallShield instead of a specific SQL Server Setup program is that you can use the Add/Remove Programs options in Control Panel to add SQL Server components or to completely remove a SQL Server instance. In addition, InstallShield makes the process of running an unattended installation much easier than in previous versions.

The lengthiest part of installation, along with the mechanics of copying the files, is building and configuring SQL Server's *master* database, which stores configuration information and information about all other databases as well as many system stored procedures. If you accept the default collation, the installation program simply copies a mostly prebuilt *master* database from the files master.mdf and mastlog.ldf on the CD. These files are in a subfolder called Data in the x86 folder. Then the installation program does a small amount of additional configuration. A new installation using the default character set can typically take less than 15 minutes from start to finish (sometimes as little as 5 minutes, depending on the speed of your hardware and how much "think time" you need for the questions). If you do not accept the default collation, the installation program must reindex the entire *master* database. This reindexing is a totally automatic operation, but it can add 5 to 10 minutes to the installation time. The total installation time is still usually under 30 minutes.

Upgrading from a Previous Version

The installation program will detect if a version of SQL Server is already installed on your machine. Depending on whether the previous installation is SQL Server 6 or SQL Server 7, you will be presented with some choices to make when installing SQL Server 2000.

Upgrading from SQL Server 7

If your machine has SQL Server 7 installed, you will be given a choice of installing a new, named instance or upgrading the existing SQL Server 7 to SQL Server 2000. If you choose to upgrade the previous installation, the installation program rebuilds all the system stored procedures to ensure that the most recent versions are installed. The database files for each database are modified slightly to conform to the structure of SQL Server 2000 database files (which I'll discuss in detail in Chapter 5). The actual table data isn't touched, and after the upgrade is complete, all your SQL Server 7 databases will be available on your SQL Server 2000 server.

Alternatively, you can upgrade an individual database from SQL Server 7 to SQL Server 2000 if you install a separate named instance of SQL Server 2000 alongside your original SQL Server 7 server. You can load database backups from SQL Server 7 into SQL Server 2000, you can use the *sp_attach_db* procedure to connect database files from a SQL Server 7 database to your SQL Server 2000, or you can use a feature called the Copy Database Wizard. This wizard is based on the *sp_attach_db* functionality but is available as a GUI wizard to make the process a bit more painless. Moving a database from SQL Server 7 to SQL Server 2000 is a one-way operation, partly because of the change to the database files that takes place. You cannot load a SQL Server 2000 backup into a SQL Server 7 database, and you cannot use *sp_attach_db* with SQL Server 7 to connect to files from a SQL Server 2000 database.

Upgrading from SQL Server 6.5

If the installation process detects that you have SQL Server 6.5 installed (and you don't have SQL Server 7 available for version switching), you are given the choice of making the new SQL Server 2000 server a separate named instance or setting up a version switch with your SQL Server 6.5 server. In either case, your SQL Server 6.5 is not affected and the installation is treated as a new installation rather than as an upgrade. Because of tremendous structural changes between versions 6.5 and 7, all your version 6.5 data must be completely rebuilt in order to be used with SQL Server 2000. The rebuilding process is called a *database upgrade* and can be accomplished using the SQL Server Upgrade Wizard, which is available from a program group called Microsoft SQL Server - Switch. You can run this wizard while the installation of SQL Server 2000 is taking place, or you can run it at a later time. The only way to accomplish the upgrade is by using the wizard.

If you choose not to install SQL Server 2000 as a separate named instance, your new SQL Server 2000 will be the default instance. Since your SQL Server 6.5 can only be a default instance and you can only have one default instance running, you must decide whether you want to run SQL Server 6.5 or the new SQL Server 2000 instance at any given time. You can version-switch between the two by choosing Programs/ Microsoft SQL Server - Switch from the Start menu and then choosing the option to switch to the desired version. Only the default instance of SQL Server can be involved in a version switch.

For more details on installation, see the online documentation and the whitepaper titled "Installing Microsoft SQL Server 2000"on the companion CD.

BASIC CONFIGURATION AFTER INSTALLATION

After the installation, you should verify the basic operation of SQL Server. SQL Server 2000 is mostly self-configuring. Many options are available for fine-tuning the configuration, but these are necessary for specialized purposes only. I'll discuss configuration in detail in Chapter 17. Initially, you should leave the default configuration alone unless you have a particular reason to change it.

Starting the SQL Server Service

After a successful installation, start SQL Server. The most common way to do this is to use the SQL Server Service Manager. From the Start menu, choose Programs, Microsoft SQL Server, and then Service Manager. The installation program also puts the SQL Server Service Manager in the startup group for the operating system, so after you reboot your machine, an icon for the SQL Server Service Manager will appear on the taskbar, in the corner near the clock. You can also use the Services applet in Windows NT and Windows 2000. In Windows NT, you can get to the applet from Control Panel. In Windows 2000, you choose Programs/Administrative Tools/Services from the Start menu. From the Microsoft Management Console, you can then find the service name for any SQL Server instance in the right pane. You can use SQL Enterprise Manager to start a SQL Server instance, or you can issue a NET START MSSQLSERVER command from a Windows NT or Windows 2000 console (command prompt). If you're starting a named instance, you must supply the instance name. You can also configure any instance of SQL Server to start automatically, either by using the Services applet or by editing the properties of SQL Server in Enterprise Manager.

After SQL Server is running, you can use one of the most basic applications, SQL Query Analyzer, to make sure that you can connect. Initially, the only available SQL Server login name (sa) has a null password, so you can leave *sa* in the Login Name text box and leave the Password text box blank. Or you can choose the Windows Authentication option so that no login name or password is required. Then you change your database to the *pubs* sample database, and run a couple of simple queries (for example, *SELECT * FROM authors ORDER BY au_lname*) to make sure that SQL Server is running correctly.

Changing the System Administrator Password

During installation, you are given the option of setting up Windows Authentication Mode only or using Mixed Mode security. If you choose Mixed Mode security, you are asked to specify a password for the SQL Server login sa. If you want the password to be blank, you must specify this by using a check box, and the installation screen lets you know that this is not recommended. If you did choose a blank password during installation, after you verify that SQL Server is running and responding to queries, you should change the password for the sa account. From the Query Analyzer, use *sp_password* to change the sa password. Be sure to pick a password you'll remember, because by design there is no way to read a password (it is stored in encrypted form)—it can only be changed to something else.

Using Query Analyzer from the *master* database to change the password to *Banks_14*, you'd issue the following command:

```
sp_password NULL, 'Banks_14', sa
```

Using Enterprise Manager, you can change the password from the server's Security folder. Choose Logins, and then double-click sa in the right pane.

Note that the actual password is stored in a table as SQL Server data. So if you've chosen a case-sensitive sort order, passwords will also be case sensitive and must be entered exactly as defined.

SQL ENTERPRISE MANAGER VS. SQL STATEMENTS

You can do nearly any task with SQL Server by directly executing SQL Server statements (including stored procedure calls) using tools such as SQL Query Analyzer. However, in some cases it is simpler to use Enterprise Manager, which provides a front end for these commands and frees you from needing to know exact steps and syntax. Administrators who are proficient with Microsoft Visual Basic for Applications (VBA) might choose to use simple VBA scripts that use the SQL Server database administration object model, known as SQL-DMO (SQL Distributed Management Objects), or the Windows Management Instrumentation (WMI) interface.

Since this book is geared toward database developers and administrators, I'll typically show the SQL statements and stored procedures that are used to accomplish a task and simply reference the easier methods. I'll also tell you what to do without providing step-by-step directions. You can consult the SQL Server documentation for the exact syntax of all options. This book is meant to complement, but not replace, the product documentation.

Configuring SQL Server's Error Log

A new error log is created each time the SQL Server service is started. If you want to start a new error log without stopping and restarting SQL Server, you can use the *sp_cycle_errorlog* system stored procedure. Keep in mind that the new error log created when you execute this procedure will not contain all the normal boot messages that are put in the error log when SQL Server starts up. You'll have to refer to an older copy of the error log to see these messages. However, if you execute *sp_cycle_errorlog* too many times, you might not have any copies that contain the boot messages. By default, SQL Server retains copies of the previous six error logs and gives the most recent copy (prior to the currently active error log) the extension .1, the second most recent copy the extension .2, and so on. The current error log has no extension. You can change the number of error logs maintained by editing the Registry for any instance. For the default instance, find the key HKEY_LOCAL_MACHINE\SOFTWARE\Microsoft\MSSQLServer\MSSQLServer and edit it by adding a new value. Define the value with the name *NumErrorLogs*, and the type REG_DWORD. Supply any initial value desired, but keep in mind that the value you enter when editing the Registry will be in hexadecimal format.

For a named instance, you need to find the key HKEY_LOCAL_MACHINE\SOFTWARE\Microsoft\Microsoft SQL Server\<SQL Server Instance Name>\MSSQLServer. Again, use the Edit feature of the Registry to add a new value with the name *NumErrorLogs* of type REG_DWORD, and supply an initial value in hexadecimal format.

Working with Multiple Instances

As mentioned earlier, in order to connect to a named instance, you must specify both the server name and the instance name. To use the OSQL command line utility to connect to an instance named SQL2000, you use this command:

```
osql /U sa /S KALESSIN\SQL2000
```

SQL Server 2000 includes a property function called SERVERPROPERTY that allows you to programmatically find out information about your SQL Server instance. SQL Server Books Online lists all the parameters of the function, but the ones relevant to multiple instances are *InstanceName*, *MachineName*, and *ServerName*. I can run the following three commands:

```
SELECT SERVERPROPERTY('InstanceName')
SELECT SERVERPROPERTY('MachineName')
SELECT SERVERPROPERTY('ServerName')
```

On my machine called RAKAM, with my instance named SQL2000, I get the following results:

```
SQL2000
RAKAM
RAKAM\SQL2000
```

Other parameters of SERVERPROPERTY allow you to determine which licensing mode you're running under, what service pack you're using, and what the operating system process ID is. The latter can be very important if you need to access one instance through the Windows Task Manager. The process image name will be sqlservr.exe for all instances, but the column labeled PID (process ID) will allow you to distinguish between multiple instances.

As mentioned earlier, each SQL Server instance has its own path for the executable program files and its own default location of data files. If you have more than a couple of instances, it can become quite a chore to remember the location of each instance. Fortunately, there is a tool in the Windows NT 4 Resource Kit and the Windows 2000 Support Tools that can help you. You need to know the name of the Registry key where the information about each instance is stored, but if you know that, you can use the utility called reg.exe to find out the file paths used. To find the program file path for a named instance, you can type the following in a command window, all on a single line:

```
REG QUERY "HKLM\Software\Microsoft\Microsoft SQL Server\<InstanceName>\
    Setup\SQLPath"
```

To find the default data file path, change *SQLPath* at the end of the key name to *SQLDataRoot:*

```
REG QUERY "HKLM\Software\Microsoft\Microsoft SQL Server\<InstanceName>\
    Setup\SQLDataRoot"
```

The old DB-Library API doesn't work with named instances because the code that looks for your server name does not recognize the Servername\InstanceName specification. Microsoft has been saying for years that DB-Library will not continue to be supported, and now they're showing us that they meant it. This means that you cannot use the ISQL command line tool to connect to a named instance. At least, by default you cannot connect, but as is frequently the case, there's a way around it. For those of you who refuse to give up your DB-Library, you can use the Client Network Utility to alias your named instance to a one-part server name that ISQL will recognize. When specifying the properties of this alias, you must specify the TCP port number. If this instance has its port number dynamically determined, you can check the box that says to dynamically determine the port for the alias as well, as shown in Figure 4-4.

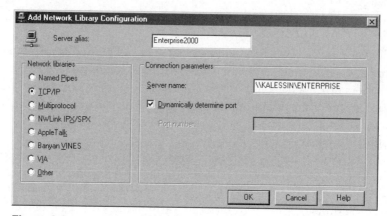

Figure 4-4. *Using the Client Network Utility to alias a named instance of SQL Server.*

REMOTE AND UNATTENDED INSTALLATION

SQL Server can be installed on a remote computer, and it can be totally scripted, requiring no user intervention. With SQL Server 2000, the InstallShield-based installation, remote setup, and unattended setup are almost the same thing. The remote installation option can be useful when you are responsible for many SQL Server installations. In fact, the feature was added (in the days predating Microsoft Systems Management Server) at the behest of Microsoft's own MIS organization, which manages more than 200 machines running SQL Server (and thousands of databases). Installing and upgrading those 200 servers remotely from one computer greatly simplified MIS's work.

Other sites script their installations by using the unattended installation feature to deploy many servers instead of using the remote installation option, which is still an interactive process. Microsoft Systems Management Server uses this capability and can be used to install SQL Server at multiple sites. (In fact, unattended installation scripts and a PDF file, used by Systems Management Server, are provided on the root directory of the SQL Server CD.)

The unattended installation option is also useful if you're embedding SQL Server in a turnkey solution and want to provide a single, unified installation. As should be apparent by now, the SQL Server installation program makes multiple entries to the Registry, changes system paths and various system settings, creates program groups and user accounts, and performs basic initial configuration for its operation. The installation program is far from a glorified file-copy program. It would not be realistic for solution providers to create their own programs to install SQL Server as part of their services or products. But they can easily achieve the same results by simply creating a script that can drive the SQL Server installation program without any user intervention.

Remote Installation

Remote installation is similar to a normal, local installation. After you choose the remote installation option (by clicking Remote in the first dialog box of the installation program), you are prompted to answer a few questions in addition to those a local installation needs. Along with providing the machine name of the anticipated SQL Server, you must do the following:

- Run the installation program from an account with administrator privileges on the remote (target) server

- Be aware that drive paths should be relative to the remote server

After specifying that you want a remote installation, the information that you provide in the rest of the dialog boxes is collected into a file called setup.iss. Then a program is started on the remote computer, and the local installation program exits. The remote program (remsetup.exe) copies files to the \admin$ share directory and runs an unattended installation on the remote computer using the options specified in the setup.iss file.

Unattended Installation

Unattended installation creates a file using the options you selected in the SQL Server installation program. To invoke an unattended installation, you must first generate an InstallShield ISS file using one of the three methods described in the following list. All the methods require that you run the SQL Server installation program from a command prompt instead of using the autorun.exe program. The program is in the x86\Setup folder on the SQL Server installation CD.

- **Normal Installation**   The normal installation creates a file called setup.iss. This file is saved in the Install folder in the MSSQL7 directory (for the default instance) or in program directory for the named instance. The setup.iss file contains your answers to all the questions in the installation dialog boxes.

■ **Advanced Installation** During installation, you are presented with a dialog box that allows you to choose to create a named instance, upgrade an existing instance (if one exists), or choose advanced options. If you choose Advanced, you can choose the option to record an Unattended ISS file. You then go through the rest of the dialog boxes, providing answers to questions, and your answers are saved in a setup.iss file in the root directory of your operating system. SQL Server isn't actually installed.

■ **Manual File Creation** The installation CD contains a sample setup file called sqlins.iss. You can use a text editor to modify this file to correspond to the installation options you want. For details of the format of this file, see the online documentation.

After the setup ISS file is created, you can move or copy it to another location for use on other servers. For subsequent automated installations, start Setupsql and specify a previously generated setup ISS file as input by using the *-f1* command-line option. The syntax for this command is:

```
START Setupsql.exe -f1 <full path to iss file> -SMS -s
```

The *-s* switch causes setup to run in a silent mode with no user interface. If the *-SMS* switch is not specified, the setup program launches InstallShield to perform the installation and then exits. Control immediately returns to the user. If the *-SMS* switch is specified, the setup program waits until the installation is complete before terminating. This allows an automated process or a user-created batch file to launch the setup program, wait for setup to complete, and then perform additional actions. Without the *-SMS* switch, the additional actions might be initiated before the installation of SQL Server completes.

NOTE For remote or unattended installation, you might choose to copy all the files from the CD to a network share. Normally, you should not notice any difference between network installation and installation from the CD.

Changing Installation Options

All the decisions you make during installation can be changed at a later time. As mentioned earlier, you can change your decisions about the account under which the SQL Server service runs and whether SQL Server should start automatically when the system starts. You do this either using the Services applet or by editing the properties of your SQL Server through SQL Enterprise Manager. You can also change the Security options for SQL Server by using SQL Enterprise Manager to specify whether SQL Server should use Windows Authentication only or also use standard SQL Server Authentication. You can change the network interface options by using the Server

Network Utility. The collation cannot be changed on the system databases, but new databases can be built with any collation, and you can change an existing user database to a new collation.

SQL Server 2000 provides the following additional utilities to carry out these special operations:

■ **Rebuilding the master database** The Rebuild master utility rebuildm.exe in the Program Files\Microsoft SQL Server\80\Tools\Binn directory rebuilds the *master* database completely. You might have to restore backups of the *msdb* and *model* system databases after you rebuild the *master* database.

■ **Rebuilding the Registry entries** You can use the setup program to restore the SQL Server Registry entries if they become corrupted. The same Advanced Options dialog box that allows you to build an unattended installation file gives you the option of rebuilding the Registry. You might have to rebuild the Registry if the Windows NT and Windows 2000 Registry was partially corrupted (for example, if it was inadvertently deleted using the Registry editing program) or if Windows NT and Windows 2000 was reinstalled (not upgraded) on a machine and the new Registry is not aware of the previous SQL Server installation.

Adding Additional Components

If you want to add components, you can rerun the SQL Server installation program from the original CD. The program detects and displays components that you already have installed and lets you select additional components. The main dialog box is very specific about the actions it will perform: "Selecting components already installed will not reinstall them and unselecting components already installed will not remove them." The components you might want to install after the initial installation include:

■ **Server components** You can install replication support, the performance counters, and full-text search capabilities.

■ **Management tools** You can install SQL Enterprise Manager, SQL Query Analyzer, SQL Server Profiler, and DTC Client Support.

Two other tools are available with SQL Server 2000 that are not part of the standard installation. The initial installation screen gives you the choice of installing SQL Server (Personal or one of the full server editions), SQL Server 2000 Analysis Services, or English Query. If you choose either of the latter two options, SQL Server itself is not installed and any existing SQL Server 2000 instances are not affected.

SUMMARY

SQL Server offers unprecedented ease of installation for a database server of its caliber. But you should understand your choices in terms of hardware, licensing, and sort orders before you proceed too far down the path of a major application rollout. Installing SQL Server is also fast and reliable. You need to do very little custom configuration because SQL Server 2000 automatically configures itself as needed.

The SQL Server installation process offers options for unattended and remote installation, for installing multiple instances of SQL Server on the same machine, for installing a Desktop version, and for client-tools–only installation. Utilities are provided for changing many of the options chosen during the initial installation, but to add new components, you must keep your original CD handy (if you haven't copied its contents to a network share).

Chapter 5

Databases and Database Files

Simply put, a Microsoft SQL Server database is a collection of objects that hold and manipulate data. A typical SQL Server installation has only a handful of databases, but it's not unusual for a single installation to contain several dozen databases. (Theoretically, one SQL Server installation can have as many as 32,767 databases. But practically speaking, this limit would never be reached.)

A SQL Server database:

■ Is a collection of many objects, such as tables, views, stored procedures, and constraints. The theoretical limit is $2^{31} -1$ (more than 2 billion) objects. Typically, the number of objects ranges from hundreds to tens of thousands.

■ Is owned by a single user account but can contain objects owned by other users.

■ Has its own set of system tables that catalog the definition of the database.

■ Maintains its own set of user accounts and security.

■ Is the primary unit of recovery and maintains logical consistency among objects in the database. (For example, primary and foreign key relationships always refer to other tables within the same database, not to other databases.)

- Has its own transaction log and manages the transactions within the database.

- Can participate in two-phase commit transactions with other SQL Server databases on the same server or different servers.

- Can span multiple disk drives and operating system files.

- Can range in size from 1 MB to a theoretical limit of 1,048,516 TB.

- Can grow and shrink, either automatically or by command.

- Can have objects joined in queries with objects from other databases in the same SQL Server installation or on linked servers.

- Can have specific options set or disabled. (For example, you can set a database to be read-only or to be a source of published data in replication.)

- Is conceptually similar to but richer than the ANSI SQL-schema concept (discussed later in this chapter).

A SQL Server database is *not*:

- Synonymous with an entire SQL Server installation.

- A single SQL Server table.

- A specific operating system file.

A database itself isn't synonymous with an operating system file, but a database always exists in two or more such files. These files are known as SQL Server *database files* and are specified either at the time the database is created, using the CREATE DATABASE command, or afterwards, using the ALTER DATABASE command.

SPECIAL SYSTEM DATABASES

A new SQL Server 2000 installation automatically includes six databases: *master, model, tempdb, pubs, Northwind,* and *msdb*.

master

The *master* database is composed of system tables that keep track of the server installation as a whole and all other databases that are subsequently created. Although every database has a set of system catalogs that maintain information about objects it contains, the *master* database has system catalogs that keep information about disk space, file allocations, usage, systemwide configuration settings, login accounts, the existence of other databases, and the existence of other SQL servers (for distributed operations). The *master* database is absolutely critical to your system, so be sure to always keep a current backup copy of it. Operations such as creating another database, changing configuration values, and modifying login accounts all make modifications to *master*, so after performing such activities, you should back up *master*.

model

The *model* database is simply a template database. Every time you create a new database, SQL Server makes a copy of *model* to form the basis of the new database. If you'd like every new database to start out with certain objects or permissions, you can put them in *model*, and all new databases will inherit them.

tempdb

The temporary database, *tempdb*, is a workspace. SQL Server's *tempdb* database is unique among all other databases because it's re-created—not recovered—every time SQL Server is restarted. It's used for temporary tables explicitly created by users, for worktables to hold intermediate results created internally by SQL Server during query processing and sorting, and for the materialization of static cursors and the keys of keyset cursors. Operations within *tempdb* are logged so that transactions on temporary tables can be rolled back, but the records in the log contain only enough information to roll back a transaction, not to recover (or redo) it. No recovery information is needed because every time SQL Server is started, *tempdb* is completely re-created; any previous user-created temporary objects (that is, all your tables and data) will be gone. Logging only enough information for rolling back transactions in *tempdb* was a new feature in SQL Server 7 and can potentially increase the performance of INSERT statements to make them up to four times faster than inserts in other (fully logged) databases.

All users have the privileges to create and use private and global temporary tables that reside in *tempdb*. (Private and global table names have # and ## prefixes, respectively, which I'll discuss in more detail in Chapter 6.) However, by default, users don't have the privileges to USE *tempdb* and then create a table there (unless the table name is prefaced with # or ##). But you can easily add such privileges to *model*, from which *tempdb* is copied every time SQL Server is restarted, or you can grant the privileges in an autostart procedure that runs each time SQL Server is restarted. If you choose to add those privileges to the *model* database, you must remember to revoke them on any other new databases that you subsequently create if you don't want them to appear there as well.

pubs

The *pubs* database is a sample database used extensively by much of the SQL Server documentation and in this book. You can safely delete it if you like, but it consumes only 2 MB of space, so unless you're scrounging for a few more megabytes of disk space, I recommend leaving it. This database is admittedly fairly simple, but that's a feature, not a drawback. The *pubs* database provides good examples without out a lot of peripheral issues to obscure the central points. Another nice feature of *pubs* is that it's available to everyone in the SQL Server community, which makes it easy to use to illustrate examples without requiring the audience to understand the underlying tables or install some new database to try out your examples. As you become more skilled with SQL Server, chances are you'll find yourself using this database in examples for developers or users.

You shouldn't worry about making modifications in the *pubs* database as you experiment with SQL Server features. You can completely rebuild the *pubs* database from scratch by running a script in the \Install subdirectory (located right under the SQL Server installation directory). In SQL Query Analyzer, open the file named Instpubs.sql and execute it. You do need to make sure that there are no current connections to *pubs*, because the current *pubs* database is dropped before the new one is created.

Northwind

The *Northwind* database is a sample database that was originally developed for use with Microsoft Access. Much of the documentation dealing with APIs uses *Northwind*, as do some of the newer examples in the SQL Server documentation. It's a bit more complex than *pubs*, and at almost 4 MB, slightly larger. I'll be using it in this book to illustrate some concepts that aren't easily demonstrated using *pubs*. As with *pubs*, you can safely delete *Northwind* if you like, although the disk space it takes up is extremely small compared to what you'll be using for your real data. I recommend leaving *Northwind* there.

The *Northwind* database can be rebuilt just like the *pubs* database, by running a script located in the \Install subdirectory. The file is called Instnwnd.sql.

msdb

The *msdb* database is used by the SQL Server Agent service, which performs scheduled activities such as backups and replication tasks. In general, other than performing backups and maintenance on this database, you should ignore *msdb*. (But you might take a peek at the backup history and other information kept there.) All the information in *msdb* is accessible from the SQL Server Enterprise Manager tools, so you usually don't need to access these tables directly. Think of the *msdb* tables as another form of system tables: just as you should never directly modify system tables, you shouldn't directly add data to or delete data from tables in *msdb* unless you really know what you're doing or are instructed to do so by a Microsoft SQL Server technical support engineer.

DATABASE FILES

A database file is nothing more than an operating system file. (In addition to database files, SQL Server also has *backup devices,* which are logical devices that map to operating system files, to physical devices such as tape drives, or even to named pipes. I won't be discussing files that are used to store backups.) A database spans at least two, and possibly several, database files, and these files are specified when a database is created or altered. Every database must span at least two files, one for the data (as well as indexes and allocation pages), and one for the transaction log. SQL Server 2000 allows the following three types of database files:

- **Primary data files**   Every database has one primary data file that keeps track of all the rest of the files in the database, in addition to storing data. By convention, the name of a primary data file has the extension MDF.

- **Secondary data files**   A database can have zero or more secondary data files. By convention, the name of a secondary data file has the extension NDF.

- **Log files**   Every database has at least one log file that contains the information necessary to recover all transactions in a database. By convention, a log file has the extension LDF.

Each database file has five properties: a logical filename, a physical filename, an initial size, a maximum size, and a growth increment. The properties of each file, along with other information about the file, are noted in the *sysfiles* table (shown in Table 5-1), which contains one row for each file used by a database.

Column Name	Description
fileid	The file identification number (unique for each database).
groupid	The filegroup identification number.
size	The size of the file (in 8-KB pages).
maxsize	The maximum file size (in 8-KB pages). A value of 0 indicates no growth, and a value of −1 indicates that the file should grow until the disk is full.
growth	The growth size of the database. A value of 0 indicates no growth. Can be either the number of pages or a percentage of the file size, depending on the value of *status*.
status	0x1 = Default device (unused in SQL Server 2000). 0x2 = Disk file.
	0x40 = Log device.
	0x80 = File has been written to since last backup. 0x4000 = Device created implicitly by CREATE DATABASE 0x8000 = Device created during database creation.
	0x100000 = Growth is in percentage, not pages.
name	The logical name of the file.
filename	The name of the physical device, including the full path of the file.

Table 5-1. *The* sysfiles *table.*

CREATING A DATABASE

The easiest way to create a database is to use SQL Server Enterprise Manager, which provides a graphical front end to Transact-SQL commands and stored procedures that actually create the database and set its properties. Figure 5-1 shows the SQL Server Enterprise Manager Database Properties dialog box, which represents the Transact-SQL CREATE DATABASE command for creating a new user database. Only someone with the *sysadmin* role or a user who's been granted CREATE DATABASE permission by someone with the *sysadmin* role can issue the CREATE DATABASE command.

When you create a new user database, SQL Server copies the *model* database, which—as you just learned—is simply a template database. For example, if you have an object that you would like created in every subsequent user database, create that object in *model* first. (You can also use *model* to set default database options in all subsequently created databases.) The *model* database also includes 19 system tables and 2 system views, which means that every new database also includes these 21 system objects. SQL Server uses these objects for the definition and maintenance of each database. The two system views are provided for backward compatibility and have no current functionality. They mimic information that was available in earlier versions of SQL Server.

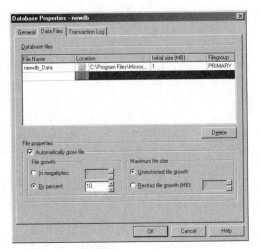

Figure 5-1. *The Database Properties dialog box, which creates a new database called* newdb.

The system objects have names starting with *sys*. If you haven't added any other objects to *model*, these 21 system objects will be the entire contents of a newly created database. Every Transact-SQL command or system stored procedure that creates, alters, or drops a SQL Server object will result in entries being made to system tables.

WARNING Do not directly modify the system tables. You might render your database unusable by doing so. Direct modification is prevented by default: a system administrator must take deliberate action via the *sp_configure* stored procedure to allow system tables to be modified directly. I'll discuss system tables in more detail in Chapter 6.

A new user database must be 1 MB or greater in size, and the primary data file size must be at least as large as the primary data file of the *model* database. Almost all the possible arguments to the CREATE DATABASE command have default values so that it's possible to create a database using a simple form of CREATE DATABASE, such as this:

```
CREATE DATABASE newdb
```

This command creates the *newdb* database, with a default size, on two files whose logical names—*newdb* and *newdb_log*—are derived from the name of the database. The corresponding physical files, newdb.mdf and newdb_log.ldf, are created in the default data directory (as determined at the time SQL Server was installed).

NOTE If you use Enterprise Manager to create a database called *newdb*, the default logical and physical names will be different than if you use the CREATE DATABASE command. Enterprise Manager will give the data file the logical name of *newdb_Data* (instead of just *newdb*), and the physical file will have the name newdb_data.mdf.

The SQL Server login account that created the database is known as the *database owner*, and has the user name DBO when using this database. The default size of the data file is the size of the primary data file of the *model* database, and the default size of the log file is half a megabyte. Whether the database name, *newdb*, is case sensitive depends on the sort order you chose during setup. If you accepted the default, the name is case insensitive. (Note that the actual command CREATE DATABASE is case insensitive, regardless of the case sensitivity chosen for data.)

Other default property values apply to the new database and its files. For example, if the LOG ON clause is not specified but data files are specified, a log file is automatically created with a size that is 25 percent of the sum of the sizes of all data files.

For the files, if the MAXSIZE clause isn't specified, the file will grow until the disk is full. (In other words, the file size is considered unlimited.) The values supplied for SIZE, MAXSIZE, and FILEGROWTH can be specified in units of TB, GB, MB (the default), or KB. The FILEGROWTH property can also be specified as a percentage. A value of 0 for FILEGROWTH indicates no growth. If no FILEGROWTH value is specified at all, the default value is 10 percent, and the minimum value is 64 KB.

A CREATE DATABASE Example

The following is a complete example of the CREATE DATABASE command, specifying three files and all the properties of each file:

```
CREATE DATABASE Archive
ON
PRIMARY
( NAME = Arch1,
FILENAME =
    'c:\program files\microsoft sql server\mssql\data\archdat1.mdf',
SIZE = 100MB,
MAXSIZE = 200,
FILEGROWTH = 20),
( NAME = Arch2,
FILENAME =
    'c:\program files\microsoft sql server\mssql\data\archdat2.ndf',
SIZE = 100MB,
MAXSIZE = 200,
FILEGROWTH = 20)
```

```
LOG ON
( NAME = Archlog1,
FILENAME =
    'c:\program files\microsoft sql server\mssql\data\archlog1.ldf',
SIZE = 100MB,
MAXSIZE = 200,
FILEGROWTH = 20)
```

EXPANDING AND SHRINKING A DATABASE

Databases can be expanded and shrunk either automatically or manually. The mechanism for automatic expansion is completely different from the mechanism for automatic shrinkage. Manual expansion is also handled differently than manual shrinkage. Log files have their own rules for growing and shrinking, so I'll discuss changes in log file size in a separate section.

Automatic File Expansion

Expansion of a database can happen automatically to any one of the database's files when that particular file becomes full. The file property FILEGROWTH determines how that automatic expansion happens. The FILEGROWTH specified when the file is first defined can be qualified using the suffix MB, KB, or % and is always rounded up to the nearest 64 KB. If the value is specified as a percent, the growth increment is the specified percentage of the size of the file when the expansion occurs. The file property MAXSIZE sets an upper limit on the size.

Manual File Expansion

Manual expansion of a database file is accomplished using the ALTER DATABASE command to change the SIZE property of one or more of the files. When you alter a database, the new size of a file must be larger than the current size. To decrease the size of files, you use the DBCC SHRINKFILE command, which I'll tell you about shortly.

Automatic File Shrinkage

The database property *autoshrink* allows a database to shrink automatically. The effect is the same as doing a DBCC SHRINKDATABASE *(dbname, 25)*. This option leaves 25 percent free space in a database after the shrink, and any free space beyond that is returned to the operating system. The thread that performs autoshrink—which always has server process ID (spid) 6—shrinks databases at 30-minute intervals. I'll discuss the DBCC SHRINKDATABASE command in more detail momentarily.

Manual File Shrinkage

You can manually shrink a database using the following two DBCC commands:

```
DBCC SHRINKFILE ( {file_name | file_id }
[, target_size][, {EMPTYFILE | NOTRUNCATE | TRUNCATEONLY} ]  )

DBCC SHRINKDATABASE (database_name [, target_percent]
[, {NOTRUNCATE | TRUNCATEONLY} ]  )
```

DBCC SHRINKFILE

DBCC SHRINKFILE allows you to shrink files in the current database. When *target_size* is specified, DBCC SHRINKFILE attempts to shrink the specified file to the specified size in megabytes. Used pages in the part of the file to be freed are relocated to available free space in the part of the file retained. For example, for a 15-MB data file, a DBCC SHRINKFILE with a *target_size* of 12 causes all used pages in the last 3 MB of the file to be reallocated into any free slots in the first 12 MB of the file. DBCC SHRINKFILE doesn't shrink a file past the size needed to store the data. For example, if 70 percent of the pages in a 10-MB data file are used, a DBCC SHRINKFILE statement with a *target_size* of 5 shrinks the file to only 7 MB, not 5 MB.

DBCC SHRINKDATABASE

The DBCC SHRINKDATABASE command shrinks all files in a database. The database can't be made smaller than the *model* database. In addition, the DBCC SHRINKDATABASE command does not allow any file to be shrunk to a size smaller than its minimum size. The minimum size of a database file is the initial size of the file (specified when the database was created) or the size to which the file has been explicitly extended or reduced, using either the ALTER DATABASE or DBCC SHRINKFILE command. If you need to shrink a database smaller than this minimum size, you should use the DBCC SHRINKFILE command to shrink individual database files to a specific size. The size to which a file is shrunk becomes the new minimum size.

The numeric *target_percent* argument passed to the DBCC SHRINKDATABASE command is a percentage of free space to leave in each file of the database. For example, if you've used 60 MB of a 100-MB database file, you can specify a shrink percentage of 25 percent. SQL Server will then shrink the file to a size of 80 MB, and you'll have 20 MB of free space in addition to the original 60 MB of data. In other words, the 80-MB file will have 25 percent of its space free. If, on the other hand, you've used 80 MB or more of a 100-MB database file, there is no way that SQL Server can shrink this file to leave 25 percent free space. In that case, the file size remains unchanged.

Because DBCC SHRINKDATABASE shrinks the database on a file-by-file basis, the mechanism used to perform the actual shrinking is the same as that used with

DBCC SHRINKFILE. SQL Server first moves pages to the front of files to free up space at the end, and then it releases the appropriate number of freed pages to the operating system. Two options for the DBCC SHRINKDATABASE and DBCC SHRINKFILE commands can force SQL Server to do either of the two steps just mentioned, while a third option is available only to DBCC SHRINKFILE:

■ The NOTRUNCATE option causes all the freed file space to be retained in the database files. SQL Server only compacts the data by moving it to the front of the file. The default is to release the freed file space to the operating system.

■ The TRUNCATEONLY option causes any unused space in the data files to be released to the operating system. No attempt is made to relocate rows to unallocated pages. When TRUNCATEONLY is used, *target_size* and *target_percent* are ignored.

■ The EMPTYFILE option, available only with DBCC SHRINKFILE, empties the contents of a data file and moves them to other files in the filegroup.

> **NOTE** DBCC SHRINKFILE specifies a target *size* in megabytes. DBCC SHRINKDATABASE specifies a target *percentage* of free space to leave in the database.

Both the DBCC SHRINKFILE and DBCC SHRINKDATABASE commands give a report for each file that can be shrunk. For example, if my *pubs* database currently has an 8-MB data file and a log file of about the same size, I get the following report when I issue this DBCC SHRINKDATABASE command:

```
DBCC SHRINKDATABASE(pubs, 10)
RESULTS:
DbId    FileId  CurrentSize  MinimumSize  UsedPages   EstimatedPages
------  ------  -----------  -----------  ----------- --------------
5       1       256          80           152         152
5       2       1152         63           1152        56
```

The current size is the size in pages after any shrinking takes place. In this case, the database file (FileId = 1) was able to be shrunk to 256 pages of 8 KB each, which is 2 MB. But only 152 pages are used. There could be several reasons for the difference between used pages and current pages:

■ If I asked to leave a certain percentage free, the current size will be bigger than the used pages because of that free space.

- If the minimum size to which I can shrink a file is bigger than the used pages, the current size cannot become smaller than the minimum size. (The minimum size of a file is the smaller of the initial creation size and the size the file has been increased to using the ALTER DATABASE command.)

- If the size of the data file for the *model* database is bigger than the used pages, the current size cannot become smaller than the size of *model*'s data file.

For the log file (FileId = 2), the only values that really matter are the current size and the minimum size. The other two values are basically meaningless for log files because the current size is always the same as the used pages, and because there is really no simple way to estimate how small a log file can be shrunk down.

CHANGES IN LOG SIZE

No matter how many physical files have been defined for the transaction log, SQL Server always treats the log as one contiguous file. For example, when the DBCC SHRINKDATABASE command determines how much the log can be shrunk, it does not consider the log files separately but determines the shrinkable size based on the entire log.

The transaction log for any database is managed as a set of virtual log files (VLFs) whose size is determined internally by SQL Server based on the total size of all the log files and the growth increment used when enlarging the log. A log always grows in units of entire VLFs and can be shrunk only to a VLF boundary. (Figure 5-2 illustrates a physical log file along with several VLFs.)

A VLF can exist in one of the following three states:

- **Active** The active portion of the log begins at the minimum log sequence number (LSN) representing an active (uncommitted) transaction. The active portion of the log ends at the last LSN written. Any VLFs that contain any part of the active log are considered active VLFs. (Unused space in the physical log is not part of any VLF.)

- **Recoverable** The portion of the log preceding the oldest active transaction is needed only to maintain a sequence of log backups for restoring the database to a former state.

- **Reusable** If transaction log backups are not being maintained or if you have already backed up the log, VLFs prior to the oldest active transaction are not needed and can be reused.

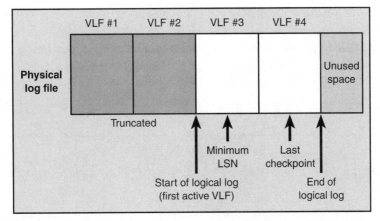

Figure 5-2. *The VLFs that make up a physical log file.*

SQL Server will assume you're not maintaining a sequence of log backups if any of the following are true:

- You have truncated the log using BACKUP LOG WITH NO_LOG or BACKUP LOG WITH TRUNCATE_ONLY.

- You have set the database to truncate the log automatically on a regular basis with the database option *trunc. log on chkpt.* or by setting the recovery mode to SIMPLE.

- You have never taken a full database backup.

In any of these situations, when SQL Server reaches the end of the physical log file, it starts reusing that space in the physical file by circling back to the file's beginning. In effect, SQL Server recycles the space in the log file that is no longer needed for recovery or backup purposes. If a log backup sequence *is* being maintained, the part of the log before the minimum LSN cannot be overwritten until those log records have actually been backed up. After the log backup, SQL Server can circle back to the beginning of the file. Once it has circled back to start writing log records earlier in the log file, the reusable portion of the log is then between the end of the logical log and the active portion of the log. Figure 5-3 depicts this cycle.

You can actually observe this behavior in one of the sample databases, such as *pubs*, as long as you have never made a full backup of the database. If you have never made any modifications to *pubs*, the size of its transaction log file will be just about 0.75 MB. The script on the following page creates a new table in the *pubs* database, inserts three records, and then updates those records 1000 times. Each update is an individual transaction, and each one is written to the transaction log. However, you should note that the log does not grow at all, even after 3000 update records are written. (If you've already taken a backup of *pubs*, you might want to re-create the database before trying this example. You can do that by running the script *instpubs.sql* in the folder \Program Files\Microsoft SQL Server\MSSQL\install. If your SQL Server is a named instance, you'll need to replace MSSQL with the string MSSQL$<instance_name>.)

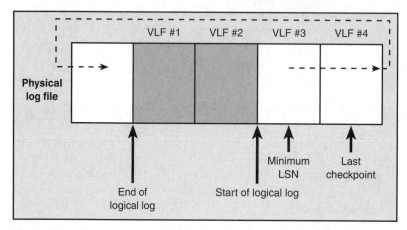

Figure 5-3. *The active portion of the log circling back to the beginning of the physical log file.*

```
CREATE TABLE newtable (a int)
GO
INSERT INTO newtable VALUES (10)
INSERT INTO newtable VALUES (20)
INSERT INTO newtable VALUES (30)
GO
DECLARE @counter int
SET @counter = 1
WHILE @counter < 1000 BEGIN
    UPDATE newtable SET a = a + 1
    SET @counter = @counter + 1
END
```

Now make a backup of the *pubs* database after making sure that the database is not in the SIMPLE recovery mode. I'll discuss recovery modes later in this chapter, but for now, you can just make sure that *pubs* is in the appropriate recovery mode by executing the following command:

```
ALTER DATABASE pubs SET RECOVERY FULL
```

You can use the following statement to make the backup, substituting the path shown with the path to your SQL Server installation:

```
BACKUP DATABASE pubs to disk =
    'c:\Program Files\Microsoft SQL Server\MSSQL\backup\pubs.bak'
```

Run the update script again, starting with the DECLARE statement. You should see that the physical log file has grown to accommodate the log records added. The initial space in the log could not be reused because SQL Server assumed that you were saving that information for backups.

Now you can try to shrink the log back down again. If you issue the following command or if you issue the DBCC SHRINKFILE command for the log file, SQL Server will mark a shrinkpoint in the log but no actual shrinking will take place until log records are freed by either backing up or truncating the log.

```
DBCC SHRINKDATABASE (pubs)
```

You can truncate the log with this statement:

```
BACKUP LOG pubs WITH TRUNCATE_ONLY
```

At this point, you should notice that the physical size of the log file has been reduced. If a log is truncated without any prior shrink command issued, SQL Server marks the space used by the truncated records as available for reuse but it does not change the size of the physical file.

In the previous version of SQL Server, running the preceding commands exactly as specified did not always shrink the physical log file. The cases in which the log file did not shrink happened when the active part of the log was located at the end of the physical file. Physical shrinking can take place only from the end of the log, and the active portion is never shrinkable. To remedy this situation, you had to enter some "dummy" transactions after truncating the log, to force the active part of the log to move around to the beginning of the file. In SQL Server 2000, this process is unnecessary. If a shrink command has already been issued, truncating the log internally generates a series of NO-OP log records that force the active log to move from the physical end of the file. Shrinking happens as soon as the log is no longer needed.

Log Truncation

If a database log backup sequence is not being maintained for a database, you can set the database into log truncate mode by setting the recovery mode to SIMPLE or by using the older mechanism of setting the database option *trunc. log on chkpt.* to TRUE. The log is thus truncated every time it gets "full enough." (I'll explain this in a moment.)

Truncation means that all log records prior to the oldest active transaction are removed. It does not necessarily imply shrinking of the physical log file. In addition, if your database is a publisher in a replication scenario, the oldest open transaction could be a transaction marked for replication that has not yet been replicated.

"Full enough" means that there are more log records than can be redone during system startup in a reasonable amount of time, which is referred to as the "recovery interval." You can manually change the recovery interval by using the *sp_configure* stored procedure or by using SQL Server Enterprise Manager (right-click the server, select Properties, click the Database Settings tab, and set the value in the Recovery Interval box), but it is recommend that you let SQL Server autotune this value. In most cases, this recovery interval value is set to 1 minute. (SQL Server Enterprise Manager shows zero minutes by default, meaning SQL Server will autotune the value.) SQL Server bases its recovery interval on the estimation that 10 MB worth of transactions can be recovered in 1 minute.

The actual log truncation is invoked by the checkpoint process, which is usually sleeping and is only woken up on demand. Each time a user thread calls the log manager, the log manager checks the size of the log. If the size exceeds the amount of work that can be recovered during the recovery interval, the checkpoint thread is woken up. The checkpoint thread checkpoints the database and then truncates the inactive portion.

In addition, if the log ever gets to 70 percent full, the log manager wakes up the checkpoint thread to force a checkpoint. Growing the log is much more expensive than truncating it, so SQL Server truncates the log whenever it can.

> **NOTE**   If the log is in auto truncate mode and the autoshrink option is set, the log will be physically shrunk at regular intervals.

If a database has the autoshrink option on, an autoshrink process kicks in every 30 minutes and determines the size to which the log should be shrunk. The log manager accumulates statistics on the maximum amount of log space used in the 30-minute interval between shrinks. The autoshrink process marks the shrinkpoint of the log as 125 percent of the maximum log space used or the minimum size of the log, whichever is larger. (Minimum size is the creation size of the log or the size to which it has been manually increased or decreased.) The log then shrinks to that size whenever it gets the chance, which is when the log gets truncated or backed up. It's possible to have autoshrink without having the database in auto truncate mode, although there's no way to guarantee that the log will actually shrink. For example, if the log is never backed up, it will never be cleared.

USING DATABASE FILEGROUPS

You can group data files for a database into filegroups for allocation and administration purposes. In some cases, you can improve performance by controlling the placement of data and indexes into specific filegroups on specific disk drives. The filegroup containing the primary data file is called the primary filegroup. There is only one primary filegroup, and if you don't specifically ask to place files in other filegroups when you create your database, *all* your data files will be in the primary filegroup.

In addition to the primary filegroup, a database can have one or more user-defined filegroups. You can create user-defined filegroups by using the FILEGROUP keyword in the CREATE DATABASE or ALTER DATABASE statement.

Don't confuse the primary filegroup and the primary file:

■ The primary file is always the first file listed when you create a database, and it typically has the file extension MDF. The one special feature of the primary file is that its header contains information about all the other files in the database.

■ The primary filegroup is always the filegroup that contains the primary file. This filegroup contains the primary data file and any files not put into another specific filegroup. All pages from system tables are always allocated from files in the primary filegroup.

The Default Filegroup

One filegroup always has the property of DEFAULT. Note that DEFAULT is a property of a filegroup and not a name. Only one filegroup in each database can be the default filegroup. By default, the primary filegroup is the also the default filegroup. A database owner can change which filegroup is the default by using the ALTER DATABASE statement. The default filegroup contains the pages for all tables and indexes that aren't placed in a specific filegroup.

Most SQL Server databases have a single data file in one (default) filegroup. In fact, most users will probably never know enough about how SQL Server works to know what a filegroup is. As a user acquires greater database sophistication, she might decide to use multiple devices to spread out the I/O for a database. The easiest way to accomplish this is to create a database file on a RAID device. Still, there would be no need to use filegroups. At the next level up the sophistication and complexity scale, the user might decide that she really wants multiple files—perhaps to create a database that uses more space than is available on a single drive. In this case, she still doesn't need filegroups—she can accomplish her goals using CREATE DATABASE with a list of files on separate drives.

More sophisticated database administrators (DBAs) might decide that they want to have different tables assigned to different drives. Only then will they need to use filegroups. The easiest way to accomplish this goal is to use SQL Server Enterprise Manager to create the database. SQL Server Enterprise Manager will create the necessary filegroups, and the user still doesn't have to learn anything about filegroup syntax. Only the most sophisticated users who want to write scripts that set up databases with multiple filegroups will need to know the underlying details.

WHY USE MULTIPLE FILES?

You might wonder what the reason would be for creating a database on multiple files located on one physical drive. There's no performance benefit in doing so, but it gives you added flexibility in two important ways.

First, if you need to restore a database from a backup because of a disk crash, the new database must contain the same number of files as the original. For example, if your original database consisted of one large 12-GB file, you would need to restore it to a database with one file of that size. If you don't have another 12-GB drive immediately available, you cannot restore the database! If, however, you originally created the database on several smaller files, you have added flexibility during a restoration. You might be more likely to have several 4-GB drives available than one large 12-GB drive.

Second, spreading the database onto multiple files, even on the same drive, gives you the flexibility of easily moving the database onto separate drives if you modify your hardware configuration in the future. Microsoft's internal SAP system uses a SQL Server database created on 12 files. Microsoft has found that this provides the ultimate flexibility. They could separate the files into two groups of six, six groups of two, four groups of three, and so on, which would allow them to experiment with performance enhancements gained as files are spread over different numbers of physical drives.

You can also use filegroups to allow backups of only parts of the database at one time. However, if you create an index in a filegroup that's different from the filegroup the table resides in, you must back up both filegroups (the filegroup containing the table and the filegroup containing the index). If you create more than one index in a filegroup that's different from the filegroups in which the corresponding tables reside, you must immediately back up all filegroups to accommodate these differing filegroups. The BACKUP statement detects all these filegroup situations and communicates to the user the minimum filegroups that must be backed up.

When you add space to objects stored in a particular filegroup, the data is stored in a *proportional fill* manner, which means that if you have one file in a filegroup with twice as much free space as another, the first file will have two extents (or units of space) allocated from it for each extent allocated from the second file. I'll discuss extents in more detail later in this chapter.

A FILEGROUP CREATION Example

This example creates a database named *sales* with three filegroups:

■ The primary filegroup with the files Spri1_dat and Spri2_dat. The FILEGROWTH increment for these files is specified as 15 percent.

■ A filegroup named SalesGroup1 with the files SGrp1Fi1 and SGrp1Fi2.

■ A filegroup named SalesGroup2 with the files SGrp2Fi1 and SGrp2Fi2.

```
CREATE DATABASE Sales
ON PRIMARY
( NAME = SPri1_dat,
FILENAME =
    'c:\program files\microsoft sql server\mssql\data\SPri1dat.mdf',
SIZE = 10,
MAXSIZE = 50,
FILEGROWTH = 15% ),
( NAME = SPri2_dat,
FILENAME =
    'c:\program files\microsoft sql server\mssql\data\SPri2dat.ndf',
SIZE = 10,
MAXSIZE = 50,
FILEGROWTH = 15% ),
FILEGROUP SalesGroup1
( NAME = SGrp1Fi1_dat,
FILENAME =
    'c:\program files\microsoft sql server\mssql\data\SG1Fi1dt.ndf',
SIZE = 10,
MAXSIZE = 50,
FILEGROWTH = 5 ),
( NAME = SGrp1Fi2_dat,
FILENAME =
    'c:\program files\microsoft sql server\mssql\data\SG1Fi2dt.ndf',
SIZE = 10,
MAXSIZE = 50,
FILEGROWTH = 5 ),
FILEGROUP SalesGroup2
( NAME = SGrp2Fi1_dat,
FILENAME =
    'c:\program files\microsoft sql server\mssql\data\SG2Fi1dt.ndf',
SIZE = 10,
MAXSIZE = 50,
FILEGROWTH = 5 ),
```

(continued)

```
( NAME = SGrp2Fi2_dat,
FILENAME =
    'c:\program files\microsoft sql server\mssql\data\SG2Fi2dt.ndf',
SIZE = 10,
MAXSIZE = 50,
FILEGROWTH = 5 )
LOG ON
( NAME = 'Sales_log',
FILENAME =
    'c:\program files\microsoft sql server\mssql\data\saleslog.ldf',
SIZE = 5MB,
MAXSIZE = 25MB,
FILEGROWTH = 5MB )
```

ALTERING A DATABASE

You can use the ALTER DATABASE statement to change a database's definition in one of the following ways:

- Change the name of the database.

- Add one or more new data files to the database, which you can option-ally put in a user-defined filegroup. You must put all files added in a single ALTER DATABASE statement in the same filegroup.

- Add one or more new log files to the database.

- Remove a file or a filegroup from the database. You can do this only if the file or filegroup is completely empty. Removing a filegroup removes all the files in it.

- Add a new filegroup to a database.

- Modify an existing file in one of the following ways:

   ❑ Increase the value of the SIZE property.

   ❑ Change the MAXSIZE or FILEGROWTH properties.

   ❑ Change the name of a file by specifying a NEWNAME property. The value given for NEWNAME is then used as the NAME property for all future references to this file.

   ❑ Change the FILENAME property for files only in the *tempdb* database; this change doesn't go into effect until you stop and restart SQL Server. You can change the FILENAME in order to move the *tempdb* files to a new physical location.

■ Modify an existing filegroup in one of the following ways:

❑ Mark the filegroup as READONLY so that updates to objects in the filegroup aren't allowed. The primary filegroup cannot be made READONLY.

❑ Mark the filegroup as READWRITE, which reverses the READONLY property.

❑ Mark the filegroup as the default filegroup for the database.

❑ Change the name of the filegroup.

❑ Change one or more database options. (I'll discuss database options later in the chapter.)

The ALTER DATABASE statement can make only one of the changes described each time it is executed. Note that you cannot move a file from one filegroup to another.

ALTER DATABASE Examples

The following examples demonstrate some of the changes you can make using the statement ALTER DATABASE.

This example increases the size of a database file:

```
USE master
GO
ALTER DATABASE Test1
MODIFY FILE
( NAME = 'test1dat3',
SIZE = 20MB)
```

The following example creates a new filegroup in a database, adds two 5-MB files to the filegroup, and makes the new filegroup the default filegroup. We need three ALTER DATABASE statements.

```
ALTER DATABASE Test1
ADD FILEGROUP Test1FG1
GO
ALTER DATABASE Test1
ADD FILE
( NAME = 'test1dat3',
FILENAME =
    'c:\program files\microsoft sql server\mssql\data\t1dat3.ndf',
SIZE = 5MB,
MAXSIZE = 100MB,
FILEGROWTH = 5MB),
```

(continued)

```
( NAME = 'test1dat4',
FILENAME =
    'c:\program files\microsoft sql server\mssql\data\t1dat4.ndf',
SIZE = 5MB,
MAXSIZE = 100MB,
FILEGROWTH = 5MB)
TO FILEGROUP Test1FG1
GO
ALTER DATABASE Test1
MODIFY FILEGROUP Test1FG1 DEFAULT
GO
```

DATABASES UNDER THE HOOD

A database consists of user-defined space for the permanent storage of user objects such as tables and indexes. This space is allocated in one or more operating system files.

Databases are divided into logical pages (of 8 KB each), and within each file the pages are numbered contiguously from 0 to x, with the upper value x being defined by the size of the file. You can refer to any page by specifying a database ID, a file ID, and a page number. When you use the ALTER DATABASE command to enlarge a file, the new space is added to the end of the file. That is, the first page of the newly allocated space is page $x + 1$ on the file you're enlarging. When you shrink a database by using either the DBCC SHRINKDATABASE or DBCC SHRINKFILE command, pages are removed starting at the highest page in the database (at the end) and moving toward lower-numbered pages. This ensures that page numbers within a file are always contiguous.

The *master* database contains 50 system tables: the same 19 tables found in user databases, plus 31 tables that are found only in *master*. Many of these tables—including *syslockinfo*, *sysperfinfo*, *syscurconfigs*, and *sysprocesses*—don't physically exist in the *master* database; rather, they're built dynamically each time a user queries them. Twelve of these tables contain information about remote servers; they don't contain any data until you define other servers with which you'll be communicating. The *master* database also contains 26 system views. Twenty of these are INFORMATION_SCHEMA views; I'll discuss them in Chapter 6. Except for the INFORMATION_SCHEMA views, all these system objects, in both the *master* and *user* databases, have names that begin with *sys*. To see a list of the system tables and views that are found in only the *master* database, you can execute the following query:

```
SELECT type, name FROM master..sysobjects
WHERE type IN ('s', 'v') AND name NOT IN
    (SELECT name FROM model..sysobjects)
GO
```

The *master* database also contains nine tables that can be referred to as *pseudo-system tables*. These table names begin with *spt_* and are used as lookup tables by various system procedures, but they aren't true system tables. You should never modify them directly because that might break some of the system procedures. However, deleting them doesn't invalidate the basic integrity of the database, which is what happens if true system tables are altered.

When you create a new database using the CREATE DATABASE statement, it is given a unique database ID, or *dbid*, and a new row is inserted in the table *master..sysdatabases* for that database. Only the *master* database contains a *sysdatabases* table. Figure 5-4 on the following page depicts a sample *sysdatabases* table, and Table 5-2 shows its columns.

The rows in *sysdatabases* are updated when a database's ownership or name is changed or when database options are changed. (I'll discuss this in more detail later in the chapter.)

Column	*Information*
name	Name of the database.
dbid	Unique database ID; can be reused when the database is dropped.
sid	System ID of the database creator.
mode	Locking mode; used internally while a database is being created.
status	Bit mask that shows whether a database is read-only, off line, designated for use by a single user only, and so on. Some of the bits can be set by a database owner using the ALTER DATABASE command; others are set internally. (The SQL Server documentation shows most of the possible bit-mask values.)
status2	Another bit mask–like status, with bits indicating additional database options.
crdate	For user databases, the date when the database was created. For *tempdb*, this is the date and time that SQL Server was last started. For other system databases, this date is not really useful. Depending on decisions made during installation, it could be the date Microsoft originally created the database prior to shipping the code, or it could be the date that you installed SQL Server.
reserved	Reserved for future use.
category	Another bit mask–like status. Contains information about whether the database is involved with replication.
cmptlevel	Compatibility level for the database. (I'll discuss this concept briefly at the end of the chapter.)
filename	Operating system path and name of the primary file.
version	Internal version of SQL Server that was used to create the database.

Table 5-2. *Columns of the* sysdatabases *table.*

```
name        dbid  sid   status      crdate                   cmptlevel filename
--------    ----- ----- ----------  -----------------------  --------- -------------------
master      1     0x01  24          2000-04-18 01:51:58.363  80        C:\...\master.mdf
model       3     0x01  1073741840  2000-04-18 02:03:11.240  80        C:\...\model.mdf
msdb        4     0x01  24          2000-04-18 02:03:15.613  80        C:\...\msdbdata.mdf
newdb       7     0x01  16          2000-05-10 13:26:42.013  80        C:\...\newdb.mdf
Northwind   6     0x01  28          2000-04-18 02:03:19.113  80        C:\...\northwind.mdf
pubs        5     0x01  24          2000-05-29 13:18:54.380  80        C:\...\pubs.mdf
tempdb      2     0x01  8           2000-05-28 10:53:39.620  80        C:\...\tempdb.mdf
```

Figure 5-4. *A partial listing of a* sysdatabases *table.*

Space Allocation

The space in a database is used for storing tables and indexes. The space is managed in units called *extents*. An extent is made up of eight logically contiguous pages (or 64 KB of space). To make space allocation more efficient, SQL Server 2000 doesn't allocate entire extents to tables with small amounts of data. SQL Server 2000 has two types of extents:

■ **Uniform extents** These are owned by a single object; all eight pages in the extent can be used only by the owning object.

■ **Mixed extents** These are shared by up to eight objects.

SQL Server allocates pages for a new table or index from mixed extents. When the table or index grows to eight pages, all future allocations use uniform extents.

When a table or index needs more space, SQL Server needs to find space that's available to be allocated. If the table or index is still less than eight pages total, SQL Server must find a mixed extent with space available. If the table or index is eight pages or larger, SQL Server must find a free uniform extent.

SQL Server uses two special types of pages to record which extents have been allocated and which type of use (mixed or uniform) the extent is available for:

■ **Global Allocation Map (GAM) pages** These pages record which extents have been allocated for any type of use. A GAM has a bit for each extent in the interval it covers. If the bit is 0, the corresponding extent is in use; if the bit is 1, the extent is free. Since there are almost 8000 bytes, or 64,000 bits, available on the page after the header and other overhead are accounted for, each GAM can cover about 64,000 extents, or almost 4 GB of data. This means that one GAM page exists in a file for every 4 GB of size.

■ **Shared Global Allocation Map (SGAM) pages** These pages record which extents are currently used as mixed extents and have at least one unused page. Just like a GAM, each SGAM covers about 64,000 extents, or almost 4 GB of data. The SGAM has a bit for each extent in the interval it covers. If the bit is 1, the extent is being used as a mixed extent and has free pages; if the bit is 0, the extent isn't being used as a mixed extent, or it's a mixed extent whose pages are all in use.

Table 5-3 shows the bit patterns that each extent has set in the GAM and SGAM based on its current use.

Current Use of Extent	*GAM Bit Setting*	*SGAM Bit Setting*
Free, not in use	1	0
Uniform extent, or full mixed extent	0	0
Mixed extent with free pages	0	1

Table 5-3. *Bit settings in GAM and SGAM pages.*

If SQL Server needs to find a new, completely unused extent, it can use any extent with a corresponding bit value of 1 in the GAM page. If it needs to find a mixed extent with available space (one or more free pages), it finds an extent with a value in the GAM of 0 and a value in the SGAM of 1.

SQL Server can quickly locate the GAMs in a file because a GAM is always the third page in any database file (page 2). An SGAM is the fourth page (page 3). Another GAM appears every 511,230 pages after the first GAM on page 2, and another SGAM every 511,230 pages after the first SGAM on page 3. Page 0 in any file is the File Header page, and only one exists per file. Page 1 is a Page Free Space (PFS) page (which I'll discuss shortly). In Chapter 6, I'll say more about how individual pages within a table look. For now, because I'm talking about space allocation, I'll examine how to keep track of which pages belong to which tables.

Index Allocation Map (IAM) pages map the extents in a database file used by a heap or index. Recall from Chapter 3 that a heap is a table without a clustered index. Each heap or index has one or more IAM pages that record all the extents allocated to the object. A heap or index has at least one IAM for each file on which it has extents. A heap or index can have more than one IAM on a file if the range of the extents exceeds the range that an IAM can record.

An IAM contains a small header, eight page-pointer slots, and a set of bits that map a range of extents onto a file. The header has the address of the first extent in the range mapped by the IAM. The eight page-pointer slots might contain pointers to pages belonging to the relevant objects that are contained in mixed extents; only the first IAM for an object has values in these pointers. Once an object takes up more than eight pages, all its extents are uniform extents—which means that an object will never need more than eight pointers to pages in mixed extents. If rows have been deleted from a table, the table can actually use fewer than eight of these pointers. Each bit of the bitmap represents an extent in the range, regardless of whether the extent is allocated to the object owning the IAM. If a bit is on, the relative extent in the range is allocated to the object owning the IAM; if a bit is off, the relative extent isn't allocated to the object owning the IAM.

For example, if the bit pattern in the first byte of the IAM is 1100 0000, the first and second extents in the range covered by the IAM are allocated to the object owning the IAM and extents 3 through 8 aren't allocated to the object owning the IAM.

IAM pages are allocated as needed for each object and are located randomly in the database file. Each IAM covers a possible range of about 512,000 pages. *Sysindexes.FirstIAM* points to the first IAM page for an object. All the IAM pages for that object are linked in a chain.

> **NOTE**   In a heap, the data pages and the rows within them aren't in any specific order and aren't linked together. The only logical connection between data pages is recorded in the IAM pages.

Once extents have been allocated to an object, SQL Server can use pages in those extents to insert new data. If the data is to be inserted into a B-tree, the location of the new data is based on the ordering within the B-tree. If the data is to be inserted into a heap, the data can be inserted into any available space. PFS pages within a file record whether an individual page has been allocated and the amount of space free on each page. Each PFS page covers 8088 contiguous pages (almost 64 MB). For each page, the PFS has 1 byte recording whether the page is empty, 1–50 percent full, 51–80 percent full, 81–95 percent full, or 96–100 percent full. SQL Server uses this information when it needs to find a page with free space available to hold a newly inserted row. The second page (page 1) of a file is a PFS page, as is every 8088th page thereafter.

There are also two other kinds of special pages within a data file. The seventh page (page 6) is called a DCM (Differential Changed Map) page and keeps track of which extents in a file have been modified since the last full database backup. The eighth page (page 7) of a file is called a BCM (Bulk Changed Map) page and is used when an extent in the file is used in a minimally or bulk-logged operation. I'll tell you more about these two kinds of pages in the "Backing Up and Restoring a Database" section later in this chapter. Like GAM and SGAM pages, DCM and BCM pages have one bit for each extent in the section of the file they represent. They occur at regular intervals, every 511,230 pages.

SETTING DATABASE OPTIONS

Twenty options can be set for a database to control certain behavior within that database. Most of the options must be set to ON or OFF. By default, all the options that allow only these two values have an initial value of OFF unless they were set to ON in the *model* database. All databases created after an option is changed in *model* will have the same values as *model*. You can easily change the value of some of these options by using SQL Server Enterprise Manager. You can set all of them directly by using the ALTER DATABASE command. You can also use the *sp_dboption* system stored procedure to set some, but that procedure is provided for backward compatibility only. All the options correspond to bits in the *status* and *status2* columns of *sysdatabases*, although those bits can also show states that the database owner can't set directly (such as when the database is in the process of being recovered).

Executing the *sp_helpdb* stored procedure for a database shows you all the values for the non-Boolean options. For the Boolean options, the procedure lists the options that are ON. The option values are all listed in the status column of the output. In addition, the status column of the *sp_helpdb* output provides the database collation and sort order. The procedure also returns other useful information, such as database size, creation date, and database owner. Executing *sp_helpdb* with no parameters shows information about all the databases in that installation. The following databases exist on a new default installation of SQL Server, and *sp_helpdb* produces this output (although the created dates and sizes can vary):

```
> EXEC sp_helpdb
name        db_size  owner dbid created     status
---------   -------- ----- ---- ----------- ----------------------------------
master      11.94 MB sa    1    Jul 31 2000 Status=ONLINE, Updateability=R...
model        1.13 MB sa    3    Jul 31 2000 Status=ONLINE, Updateability=R...
msdb        13.00 MB sa    4    Jul 31 2000 Status=ONLINE, Updateability=R...
Northwind    3.63 MB sa    6    Jul 31 2000 Status=ONLINE, Updateability=R...
pubs         2.00 MB sa    5    Jul 31 2000 Status=ONLINE, Updateability=R...
tempdb       8.50 MB sa    2    Aug 21 2000 Status=ONLINE, Updateability=R...
```

The database options are divided into five categories: state options, cursor options, auto option, SQL options, and recovery options. Some of the options, in particular the SQL options, have corresponding SET options that you can turn on or off for a particular connection. Be aware that the ODBC or OLE DB drivers turn a number of these SET options on by default, so applications will act as though the corresponding database option has already been set. (Chapter 6 goes into more detail about the SET options that are set by the ODBC and OLE DB drivers and the interaction with the database options.)

Here is a list of all 20 options, by category. Options listed on a single line are mutually exclusive.

- State options

  SINGLE_USER | RESTRICTED_USER | MULTI_USER
  OFFLINE | ONLINE
  READ_ONLY | READ_WRITE

- Cursor options

  CURSOR_CLOSE_ON_COMMIT { ON | OFF }
  CURSOR_DEFAULT { LOCAL | GLOBAL }

- Auto options

  AUTO_CLOSE {ON | OFF }
  AUTO_CREATE_STATISTICS {ON | OFF }
  AUTO_SHRINK {ON | OFF }
  AUTO_UPDATE_STATISTICS {ON | OFF }

- SQL options

  ANSI_NULL_DEFAULT { ON | OFF }
  ANSI_NULLS { ON | OFF }
  ANSI_PADDING { ON | OFF }
  ANSI_WARNINGS { ON | OFF }
  ARITHABORT { ON | OFF }
  CONCAT_NULL_YIELDS_NULL { ON | OFF }
  NUMERIC_ROUNDABORT { ON | OFF }
  QUOTED_IDENTIFIER { ON | OFF }
  RECURSIVE_TRIGGERS { ON | OFF }

- Recovery options

  RECOVERY { FULL | BULK_LOGGED | SIMPLE }
  TORN_PAGE_DETECTION { ON | OFF }

The following sections describe all the options except RECOVERY, which I'll discuss in detail later, in the section titled "Backing Up and Restoring a Database."

State Options

The state options control the usability of the database, in terms of who can use the database and for what operations. There are three aspects to usability: the user access state option determines which users can use the database, the status state option determines whether the database is available to anybody for use, and the updateability state option determines what operations can be performed on the database. You control each of these aspects by using the ALTER DATABASE command to enable an option for the database. None of the state options uses the keywords ON and OFF to control the state value.

SINGLE_USER | RESTRICTED_USER | MULTI_USER

These three options describe the user access property of a database. They are mutually exclusive; setting any one of them unsets the others. To set one of these options for your database, you just use the option name. For example, to set the *pubs* database to single user mode, you use the following code:

```
ALTER DATABASE pubs SINGLE_USER
```

A database in SINGLE_USER mode can have only one connection at a time. A database in RESTRICTED_USER mode can have connections only from users who are considered "qualified." A qualified user is any member of the dbcreator or sysadmin server roles or any member of the db_owner role for that database. The default for a database is MULTI_USER mode, which means anyone with a valid user name in the database can connect to it. If you attempt to change a database's state to a mode that is incompatible with the current conditions—for example, if you try to change the database to SINGLE_USER mode when other connections exist—SQL Server's behavior is determined by the TERMINATION option you specify. I'll discuss termination options shortly.

To determine which user access value is set for a database, you can use the DATABASEPROPERTYEX() function, as shown here:

```
SELECT DATABASEPROPERTYEX('<name of database>', 'UserAccess')
```

In previous versions of SQL Server, database access was controlled using the procedure *sp_dboption* and setting the value of the options *dbo use only* or *single user*. If both of these options had a value of *false*, the database was in MULTI_USER mode. If the option *single user* was set to *true*, the database was in SINGLE_USER mode, and if the option *dbo use only* was set to *true* and *single user* was set to *false*, the database was in a state similar to RESTRICTED_USER. In SQL Server 2000, the user access value is still determined by the same bits in the *sysdatabases.status* field that were used in previous versions to determine *single user* or *dbo use only* mode. If the 12 bit is set (with a value of 4096), the database is in SINGLE_USER mode, and if the 11 bit is set (with a value of 2048), the database is in RESTRICTED_USER mode. In SQL Server 2000, you cannot have both of these bits set at the same time.

OFFLINE | ONLINE

These two options are the status options; the status property of a database is described using one of these option names. They are mutually exclusive. The default is for a database to be ONLINE. As with the user access options, when you use ALTER DATABASE to put the database in one of these modes, you don't specify a value of ON or OFF—you just use the name of the option. When a database is set to OFFLINE, the database is closed and shut down cleanly and marked as off line. The database cannot be modified while the database is off line. A database cannot be put into OFFLINE mode if there are any connections in the database. Whether SQL Server waits for the other connections to terminate or generates an error message is determined by the TERMINATION option specified.

The following code examples show how to set a database's status value to OFFLINE and how to determine the status of a database:

```
ALTER DATABASE pubs SET OFFLINE
SELECT DATABASEPROPERTYEX('pubs', 'status')
```

DATABASEPROPERTYEX() could return status values other than OFFLINE and ONLINE, but those values are not directly settable using ALTER DATABASE. A database can have the status value RESTORING while it is in the process of being restored from a backup. It can have the status value RECOVERING during a restart of SQL Server. The restore process is done on one database at a time, and until SQL Server has finished restoring a database, the database has a status of RECOVERING. It can have a status of SUSPECT if the recovery process could not be completed for some reason—the most common ones being that one or more of the log files for the database is unavailable or unreadable. Each of the five status values corresponds to a different bit set in the *sysdatabases.status* column.

READ_ONLY | READ_WRITE

These two options are the updateability options; they describe the updateability property of a database. They are mutually exclusive. The default is for a database to be READ_WRITE. As with the user access options, when you use ALTER DATABASE to put the database in one of these modes, you don't specify a value of ON or OFF, you just use name of the option. When the database is in READ_WRITE mode, any user with the appropriate permissions can carry out data modification operations. In READ_ONLY mode, no INSERT, UPDATE, or DELETE operations can be executed. In addition, because no modifications are done when a database is in READ_ONLY mode, automatic recovery is not run on this database when SQL Server is restarted and no locks need to be acquired during any SELECT operations. Shrinking a database in READ_ONLY mode is not possible.

A database cannot be put into READ_ONLY mode if there are any connections to the database. Whether SQL Server waits for the other connections to terminate or generates an error message is determined by the TERMINATION option specified.

The following code examples show how to set a database's updatability value to READ_ONLY and how to determine the updatability of a database:

```
ALTER DATABASE pubs SET READ_ONLY
SELECT DATABASEPROPERTYEX('pubs', 'updateability')
```

Termination Options

As I just mentioned, several of the state options cannot be set when a database is in use or when it is in use by an unqualified user. You can specify how SQL Server should handle this situation by indicating a termination option in the ALTER DATA-BASE command. You can specify that SQL Server wait for the situation to change, that it generate an error message, or that it terminate the connections of nonqualified users. The termination option determines SQL Server's behavior in the following situations:

- When you attempt to change a database to SINGLE_USER and it has more than one current connection

- When you attempt to change a database to RESTRICTED_USER and un-qualified users are currently connected to it

- When you attempt to change a database to OFFLINE and there are cur-rent connections to it

- When you attempt to change a database to READ_ONLY and there are current connections to it

SQL Server's default behavior in any of these situations is to wait indefinitely. The following TERMINATION options change this behavior:

ROLLBACK AFTER *integer* [SECONDS] This option causes SQL Server to wait for the specified number of seconds and then break unqualified connections. Incomplete transactions are rolled back. When the transition is to SINGLE_USER mode, unqualified connections are all connections except the one issuing the ALTER DATABASE statement. When the transition is to RESTRICTED_USER mode, unqualified connections are connections of users who are not members of the *db_owner* fixed database role or the *dbcreator* and *sysadmin* fixed server roles.

ROLLBACK IMMEDIATE This option breaks unqualified connections immediately. All incomplete transactions are rolled back. Unqualified connections are the same as those described earlier.

NO_WAIT This option causes SQL Server to check for connections before attempting to change the database state and causes the ALTER DATABASE statement to fail if certain connections exist. If the database is being set to SINGLE_USER mode, the ALTER DATABASE statement fails if any other connections exist. If the transition is to RESTRICTED_USER mode, the ALTER DATABASE statement fails if any unqualified connections exist.

The following command changes the user access option of the *pubs* database to SINGLE_USER and generates an error if any other connections to the *pubs* database exist:

```
ALTER DATABASE pubs SET SINGLE_USER WITH NO_WAIT
```

Cursor Options

All of the cursor options control the behavior of server-side cursors that were defined using one of the following Transact-SQL commands for defining and manipulating cursors: DECLARE, OPEN, FETCH, CLOSE, and DEALLOCATE. In Chapter 13, I'll discuss Transact-SQL cursors in detail.

CURSOR_CLOSE_ON_COMMIT {ON | OFF}

When this option is set to ON, any open cursors are automatically closed (in compliance with SQL-92) when a transaction is committed or rolled back. If OFF (the default) is specified, cursors remain open after a transaction is committed. Rolling back a transaction closes any cursors except those defined as INSENSITIVE or STATIC.

CURSOR_DEFAULT {LOCAL | GLOBAL}

When this option is set to LOCAL and cursors aren't specified as GLOBAL when created, the scope of any cursor is local to the batch, stored procedure, or trigger in which it was created. The cursor name is valid only within this scope. The cursor can be referenced by local cursor variables in the batch, stored procedure, or trigger, or by a stored procedure output parameter. When this option is set to GLOBAL and cursors aren't specified as LOCAL when created, the scope of the cursor is global to the connection. The cursor name can be referenced in any stored procedure or batch executed by the connection.

Auto Options

The auto options affect actions that SQL Server might take automatically. All these options are Boolean options, with values of either ON or OFF.

AUTO_CLOSE

When this option is set to ON (the default when SQL Server runs on Windows 98), the database is closed and shut down cleanly when the last user of the database exits, thereby freeing any resources. When a user tries to use the database again, it automatically reopens. If the database was shut down cleanly, the database isn't initialized (reopened) until a user tries to use the database the next time SQL Server is restarted. The AUTO_CLOSE option is handy for personal SQL Server databases because it allows you to manage database files as normal files. You can move them, copy them to make backups, or even e-mail them to other users. However, you shouldn't use this option for databases accessed by an application that repeatedly makes and breaks connections to SQL Server. The overhead of closing and reopening the database between each connection will hurt performance.

AUTO_CREATE_STATISTICS

When this option is set to ON (the default), statistics are automatically created by the SQL Server query optimizer on columns referenced in a query's WHERE clause.

Adding statistics improves query performance because the SQL Server query optimizer can better determine how to evaluate a query.

AUTO_SHRINK

When this option is set to ON, all of a database's files are candidates for periodic shrinking. Both data files and log files can be automatically shrunk by SQL Server. The only way to free space in the log files so that they can be shrunk is to back up the transaction log or set the recovery mode to SIMPLE. The log files shrink at the point that the log is backed up or truncated.

AUTO_UPDATE_STATISTICS

When this option is set to ON (the default), existing statistics are automatically updated if the data in the tables has changed. SQL Server keeps a counter of the modifications that have been made to a table and uses it to determine when statistics are outdated. When this option is set to OFF, existing statistics are not automatically updated. (They can be updated manually.) I'll discuss statistics in much more detail in Chapter 15.

SQL Options

The SQL options control how various SQL statements are interpreted. All of these are Boolean options. Although the default for all of these options is OFF for SQL Server itself, many tools, such as the SQL Query Analyzer, and many programming interfaces, such as ODBC, enable certain session-level options that override the database options and make it appear as if the ON behavior is the default. I'll discuss the interaction of the SET options with the database options in Chapter 7.

ANSI_NULL_DEFAULT

When this option is set to ON, columns comply with the ANSI-92 rules for column nullability. That is, if you don't specifically indicate whether a column in a table allows NULL values, NULLs are allowed. When this option is set to OFF, newly created columns do not allow NULLs if no nullability constraint is specified.

ANSI_NULLS

When this option is set to ON, any comparisons with a NULL value result in UNKNOWN, as specified by the ANSI-92 standard. If this option is set to OFF, comparisons of non-Unicode values to NULL result in a value of TRUE if both values being compared are NULL.

ANSI_PADDING

When this option is set to ON, strings being compared to each other are set to the same length before the comparison takes place. When this option is OFF, no padding takes place.

ANSI_WARNINGS

When this option is set to ON, errors or warnings are issued when conditions such as division by zero or arithmetic overflow occur.

ARITHABORT

When this option is set to ON, a query is terminated when an arithmetic overflow or division-by-zero error is encountered during the execution of a query. When this option is OFF, the query returns NULL as the result of the operation.

CONCAT_NULL_YIELDS_NULL

When this option is set to ON, concatenating two strings results in a NULL string if either of the strings is NULL. When this option is set to OFF, a NULL string is treated as an empty (zero-length) string for the purposes of concatenation.

NUMERIC_ROUNDABORT

When this option is set to ON, an error is generated if an expression will result in loss of precision. When this option is OFF, the result is simply rounded. The setting of ARITHABORT determines the severity of the error. If ARITHABORT is OFF, only a warning is issued and the expression returns a NULL. If ARITHABORT is ON, an error is generated and no result is returned.

QUOTED_IDENTIFIER

When this option is set to ON, identifiers such as table and column names can be delimited by double quotation marks and literals must then be delimited by single quotation marks. All strings delimited by double quotation marks are interpreted as object identifiers. Quoted identifiers don't have to follow the Transact-SQL rules for identifiers when QUOTED_IDENTIFIER is ON. They can be keywords and can include characters not normally allowed in Transact-SQL identifiers, such as spaces and dashes. You can't use double quotation marks to delimit literal string expressions; you must use single quotation marks. If a single quotation mark is part of the literal string, it can be represented by two single quotation marks ("). This option must be set to ON if reserved keywords are used for object names in the database. When it is OFF, identifiers can't be in quotation marks and must follow all Transact-SQL rules for identifiers.

RECURSIVE_TRIGGERS

When this option is set to ON, triggers can fire recursively, either directly or indirectly. Indirect recursion occurs when a trigger fires and performs an action that causes a trigger on another table to fire, thereby causing an update to occur on the original table, which causes the original trigger to fire again. For example, an application updates table *T1*, which causes trigger *Trig1* to fire. *Trig1* updates table *T2*, which causes trigger *Trig2* to fire. *Trig2* in turn updates table *T1*, which causes *Trig1* to fire again. Direct recursion occurs when a trigger fires and performs an action that causes the same trigger to fire again. For example, an application updates table *T3*, which causes trigger *Trig3* to fire. *Trig3* updates table *T3* again, which causes trigger *Trig3* to fire again. When this option is OFF (the default), triggers can't be fired recursively.

Recovery Options

Recovery options control how much recovery can be done on a SQL Server database. The RECOVERY option itself also controls how much information is logged and how much of the log is available for backups. I'll cover this option in more detail in the section titled "Backing Up and Restoring a Database" later in this chapter.

TORN_PAGE_DETECTION

When this option is set to ON (the default), it causes a bit to be flipped for each 512-byte sector in a database page (8 KB) whenever the page is written to disk. It allows SQL Server to detect incomplete I/O operations caused by power failures or other system outages. If a bit is in the wrong state when the page is later read by SQL Server, the page was written incorrectly. (A torn page has been detected.) Although SQL Server database pages are 8 KB, disks perform I/O operations using 512-byte sectors. Therefore, 16 sectors are written per database page. A torn page can occur if the system crashes (for example, because of power failure) between the time the operating system writes the first 512-byte sector to disk and the completion of the 8-KB I/O operation. If the first sector of a database page is successfully written before the crash, it will appear that the database page on disk was updated even though the operation might not have succeeded. Using battery-backed disk caches can ensure that the data is successfully written to disk or not written at all. In this case, you can set TORN_PAGE_DETECTION to OFF because it isn't needed. If a torn page is detected, the database must be restored from backup because it will be physically inconsistent.

OTHER DATABASE CONSIDERATIONS

Keep these additional points in mind about databases in SQL Server.

Databases vs. Schemas

The ANSI SQL-92 standard includes the notion of a *schema*—or, more precisely, an *SQL-schema,* which in many ways is similar to SQL Server's database concept. Per the ANSI standard, an SQL-schema is a collection of *descriptors,* each of which is described in the documentation as "a coded description of an SQL object." Basically, a schema is a collection of SQL objects, such as tables, views, and constraints. ANSI SQL-schemas are similar to SQL Server databases.

SQL Server 6.5 introduced support for the ANSI SQL-schema. However, the concept of a database in SQL Server is longstanding and much richer than that of a schema. SQL Server provides more extensive facilities for working with a database than for working with a schema. SQL Server includes commands, stored procedures, and powerful tools such as SQL Server Enterprise Manager that are designed around the fundamental concept of a database. These tools control backup, restoring, security, enumeration of objects, and configuration; counterparts of these tools don't exist for schemas. The SQL Server implementation of a schema is essentially a check box feature that provides conformance with the ANSI standard; it's not the preferred choice. Generally speaking, you should use databases, not schemas.

Using Removable Media

After you've created a database, you can package it so that you can distribute it via removable media such as CD. This can be useful for distributing large datasets. For example, you might want to put a detailed sales history database on a CD and send a copy to each of your branch offices. Typically, such a database is read-only (because CDs are read-only), although this isn't mandatory.

To create a removable media database, you create the database using the stored procedure *sp_create_removable* instead of the CREATE DATABASE statement. When calling the procedure, you must specify three or more files (one for the system catalog tables, one for the transaction log, and one or more for the user data tables). You must have a separate file for the system tables because when the removable media database is distributed and installed, the system tables will be installed to a writable device so that users can be added, permissions can be granted, and so on. The data itself is likely to remain on the read-only device.

Because removable media devices such as CDs are typically slower than hard drives, you can distribute on removable media a database that will be moved to a hard disk. If you're using a writable removable device, such as an optical drive, be sure that the device and controller are both on the Hardware Compatibility List (HCL). (You can find the HCL at www.microsoft.com/hcl.) I also recommend that you run the hard-disk test discussed in Chapter 4 on any such device. The failure rates of removable media devices are typically higher than those of standard hard disks.

A database can use multiple CDs or removable media devices. However, all media must be available simultaneously. For example, if a database uses three CDs, the system must have three CD drives so that all discs can be available when the database is used.

You can use the *sp_certify_removable* stored procedure to ensure that a database created with the intention of being burned onto a CD or other removable media meets certain restrictions. The main restriction is that the login sa must own the database and all the objects must be owned by the user dbo. There can be no users in the database other than dbo and guest. You can, however, have roles defined in the database, and permissions can be assigned to those roles. The stored procedure *sp_certify_removable* ensures that the database was created properly with the system tables separate from any user tables.

The first time you use a database sent on removable media, you use the *sp_attach_db* stored procedure to see the location of each file. You'll probably want to move the file containing the system tables to a writable disk so that you can create users, stored procedures, and additional permissions. You can keep the data on the removable media if you won't be modifying it. You can subsequently set the OFFLINE database option using ALTER DATABASE to toggle the database's availability. This book's companion CD contains a sample script that creates a database, ensures that it's appropriate for removable media use, and then installs it on your system. However, a database with no tables or data is pretty useless, so in the next chapter you'll learn how to create tables.

Detaching and Reattaching a Database

The ability to detach and reattach databases offers much broader benefits than just allowing the creation of removable databases. You can use the procedures *sp_detach_db* and *sp_attach_db* to move a database to a new physical drive—for example, if you're upgrading your hardware. You can use these stored procedures to make a copy of the database for testing or development purposes or as an alternative to the backup and restore commands.

Detaching a database requires that no one is using the database. If you find existing connections that you can't terminate, you can use the ALTER DATABASE command and set the database to SINGLE_USER mode using one of the termination options that automatically breaks existing connections. Detaching a database ensures that there are no incomplete transactions in the database and that there are no dirty pages for this database in memory. If these conditions cannot be met, the detach operation will not succeed. Once the database is detached, the entry for it is removed from the *sysdatabases* table in the *master* database, and from SQL Server's perspective, it's as if you had dropped the database. The command to detach a database is shown here:

```
EXEC sp_detach_db <name of database>
```

> **NOTE** You can also drop the database with the DROP DATABASE command, but using this command is a little more severe. SQL Server makes sure that no one is connected to the database before dropping it, but no check of dirty pages or open transactions is made. Dropping a database also removes the physical files from the operating system, so unless you have a backup, the database is really gone.

The files for a detached database still exist, but the operating system considers them closed files, so they can be copied, moved, or even deleted like any other operating system files. A database that has been detached can be reattached using the stored procedure *sp_attach_db*. This procedure has a few more options than its detaching counterpart. If all the files still exist in their original locations, which would be the case if you detached the database just so you could copy the files to another server, all you need to specify is the location of the primary file. Remember that the primary file's header information contains the location of all the files belonging to the database. In fact, if some of the files exist in the original locations and only some of them have moved, you must specify only the moved files' locations when you execute the *sp_attach_db* procedure.

Although the documentation says that you should use *sp_attach_db* only on databases that were previously detached using *sp_detach_db,* sometimes following this recommendation isn't necessary. If you shut down the SQL server, the files will be closed, just as if you had detached the database. However, you will not be guaranteed that all dirty pages from the database were written to disk before the shutdown. This should not cause a problem when you attach such a database if the log file is available. The log file will have a record of all completed transactions, and a full recovery will be done when the database is attached to make sure that the database is consistent. One benefit of using the *sp_detach_db* procedure is that SQL Server will know that the database was cleanly shut down, and the log file does not have to be available to attach the database. SQL will build a new log file for you. This can be a quick way to shrink a log file that has become much larger than you would like, because the new log file that *sp_attach_db* creates for you will be the minimum size— less than 1 MB. Note that this trick for shrinking the log will not work if the database has more than one log file.

Here is the syntax for the *sp_attach_db* procedure:

```
sp_attach_db [ @dbname = ] 'dbname' ,
  [ @filename1 = ] 'filename_n'
  [ ,...16 ]
```

Note that all you need to specify is the current filenames, regardless of whether the current names are the same as the original names. SQL Server will find the specified files and use them when attaching the database. You can even supply a new database name as you're attaching the files. You are limited to specifying up to 16 files for the database. Remember that you have to specify the filenames only if they are not in the original location stored in the header of the primary file. If you have a database for which you must specify more than 16 files, you can use the CREATE DATABASE command and specify the FOR ATTACH option.

Compatibility Levels

SQL Server 7 included a tremendous amount of new functionality and changed certain behaviors that existed in earlier versions. SQL Server 2000 has added even more new features. To provide the most complete level of backward compatibility, Microsoft allows you to set the compatibility level of a database to one of four modes: 80, 70,

65, or 60. All newly created databases in SQL Server 2000 have a compatibility level of 80 unless you change the level for the *model* database. A database that has been upgraded (using the Upgrade Wizard) from SQL Server version 6.0 or 6.5 will have its compatibility level set to the SQL Server version under which the database was last used (either 60 or 65). If you upgrade a server for SQL Server 7 to SQL Server 2000, all the databases on that server will have their compatibility level set to 80, although you can force SQL Server 2000 to behave like SQL Server 7 by setting this level to 70.

All the examples and explanations in this book assume that you're using a database that's in 80 compatibility mode unless otherwise noted. If you find that your SQL statements behave differently than the ones in the book, you should first verify that your database is in 80 compatibility mode by executing this procedure:

```
EXEC sp_dbcmptlevel 'database name'
```

To change to a different compatibility level, run the procedure using a second argument of one of the three modes:

```
EXEC sp_dbcmptlevel 'database name', compatibility-mode
```

> **NOTE** Not all changes in behavior from older versions of SQL Server can be duplicated by changing the compatibility level. For the most part, the differences have to do with whether new keywords and new syntax are recognized and have no effect on how your queries are processed internally. For a complete list of the behavioral differences between the four modes, see the online documentation for the *sp_dbcmptlevel* procedure.

The compatibility-level options merely provide a transition period while you're upgrading a database or an application to SQL Server 2000. I strongly suggest that you carefully consider your use of this option and make every effort to change your applications so that compatibility options are no longer needed. Microsoft doesn't guarantee that these options will continue to work in future versions of SQL Server.

BACKING UP AND RESTORING A DATABASE

As you're probably aware by now, this book is not intended as a how-to book for database administrators. The Bibliography lists several excellent books that can teach you the mechanics of actually making database backups and restoring and can suggest best practices for setting up a backup-and-restore plan for your organization. Nevertheless, I'd like to discuss some important issues relating to backup and restore processes to help you understand why one backup plan might be better suited to your needs than another.

Types of Backups

No matter how much fault tolerance you have implemented on your database system, it is no replacement for regular backups. Backups can provide a solution to accidental or malicious data modifications, programming errors, and natural disasters (if you store backups in a remote location). If you choose to provide the fastest possible speed for your data files at the cost of fault tolerance, backups provide insurance in case your data files are damaged.

The process of re-creating a database from backups is called restoring. The degree to which you can restore the lost data depends on the type of backup. There are three main types of backups in SQL Server 2000, and a couple of additional variations on those types:

- **Full backup**   A full database backup basically copies all the pages from a database onto a backup device, which can be a local or network disk file, a local tape drive, or even a named pipe.

- **Differential backup**   A differential backup copies only the extents that were changed since the last full backup was made. The extents are copied onto a specified backup device. SQL Server can quickly tell which extents need to be backed up by examining the bits on the DCM pages for each data file in the database. Each time a full backup is made, all the bits are cleared to 0. When any page in an extent is changed, its corresponding bit in the DCM page is changed to 1.

- **Log backup**   In most cases, a log backup copies all the log records that have been written to the transaction log since the last full or log backup was made. However, the exact behavior of the BACKUP LOG command depends on your database's recovery mode setting. I'll discuss recovery modes shortly.

> **NOTE**   For full details on the mechanics of defining backup devices, making backups, or scheduling backups to occur at regular intervals, consult SQL Server Books Online or one of the SQL Server administration books listed in the Bibliography.

A full backup can be made while your SQL Server is in use. This is considered a "fuzzy" backup—that is, it is not an exact image of the state of the database at any particular point in time. The backup threads just copy extents, and if other processes need to make changes to those extents while the backup is in progress, they can do so.

To maintain consistency for either a full or a differential backup, SQL Server records the current log sequence number (LSN) at the time the backup starts and then again at the time the backup ends. This allows the backup to also capture the relevant parts of the log. The relevant part starts with the oldest open transaction at the time of the first recorded LSN and ends with the second recorded LSN.

As mentioned previously, what gets recorded with a log backup depends on the recovery model you are using. So before I talk about log backup in detail, I'll tell you about recovery models.

Recovery Models

As I told you in the section on database options, three values can be set for the RECOVERY option: FULL, BULK_LOGGED, or SIMPLE. The value you choose determines the speed and size of your transaction log backups as well as the degree to which you are at risk for loss of committed transactions in case of media failure.

FULL Recovery Model

The FULL recovery model provides the least risk of losing work in the case of a damaged data file. If a database is in this mode, all operations are fully logged, which means that in addition to logging every row added with the INSERT operation, removed with the DELETE operation, or changed with the UPDATE operation, SQL Server also writes to the transaction log in its entirety every row inserted using a *bcp* or BULK INSERT operation. If you experience a media failure for a database file and need to recover a database that was in FULL recovery mode, and you've been making regular transaction log backups preceded by a full database backup, you can restore to any specified point in time up to the time of the last log backup. In addition, if your log file is available after the failure of a data file, you can restore up to the last transaction committed before the failure. SQL Server 2000 also supports a feature called log marks, which allows you to place reference points in the transaction log. If your database is in FULL recovery mode, you can choose to recover to one of these log marks. I'll talk a bit more about log marks in Chapter 12.

In FULL recovery mode, SQL Server will also fully log CREATE INDEX operations. In SQL Server 2000, when you restore from a transaction log backup that includes index creations, the recovery operation is much faster because the index does not have to be rebuilt—all the index pages have been captured as part of the database backup. In previous versions, SQL Server logged only the fact that an index had been built, so when you restored from a log backup, the entire index would have to be built all over again!

So, FULL recovery mode sounds great, right? As always, there's a tradeoff. The biggest tradeoff is that the size of your transaction log files can be enormous, and therefore it can take substantially longer to make log backups than with any previous release.

BULK_LOGGED Recovery Model

The BULK_LOGGED recovery model allows you to completely restore a database in case of media failure and also gives you the best performance and least log space usage for certain bulk operations. These bulk operations include BULK INSERT, *bcp*, CREATE INDEX, SELECT INTO, WRITETEXT, and UPDATETEXT. In FULL recovery mode, these operations are fully logged, but in BULK_LOGGED recovery mode, they are only minimally logged.

When you execute one of these bulk operations, SQL Server logs only the fact that the operation occurred. However, the operation is fully recoverable because SQL Server keeps track of what extents were actually modified by the bulk operation. Every data file in a SQL Server 2000 database now has an additional allocation page called a BCM page, which is managed much like the GAM and SGAM pages that I discussed earlier in the chapter. Each bit on a BCM page represents an extent, and if the bit is 1 it means that this extent has been changed by a minimally logged bulk operation since the last full database backup. A BCM page is located at the 8th page of every data file, and every 511,230 pages thereafter. All the bits on a BCM page are reset to 0 every time a full database backup or a log backup occurs.

Because of the ability to minimally log bulk operations, the operations themselves can be carried out much faster than in FULL recovery mode. There is a little overhead to setting the bits in the appropriate BCM page, but compared to the cost of logging each individual change to a data or index row, the cost of flipping bits is almost negligible.

If your database is in BULK_LOGGED mode and you have not actually performed any bulk operations, you can restore your database to any point in time or to a named log mark because the log will contain a full sequential record of all changes to your database.

The tradeoff comes during the backing up of the log. In addition to copying the contents of the transaction log to the backup media, SQL Server scans the BCM pages and backs up all the modified extents along with the transaction log itself. The log file itself stays small, but the backup of the log can be many times larger. So the log backup takes more time and might take up a lot more space than in FULL recovery mode. The time it takes to restore a log backup made in BULK_LOGGED recovery mode is similar to the time it takes to restore a log backup made in FULL recovery mode. The operations don't have to be redone; all the information necessary to recover all data and index structures is available in the log backup.

SIMPLE Recovery Model

The SIMPLE recovery model offers the simplest backup-and-restore strategy. Your transaction log is truncated at regular, frequent intervals. Therefore, only full database backups and differential backups are allowed. You get an error if you try to back up the log while in SIMPLE recovery mode. Because the log is not needed for backup purposes, sections of it can be reused as soon as all the transactions it contains are committed or rolled back, and the transactions are no longer needed for recovery from server or transaction failure.

Converting from SQL Server 7

Microsoft intended these recovery models to replace the *select into/bulkcopy* and *trunc. log on chkpt.* database options. Earlier versions of SQL Server required that the *select into/bulkcopy* option be set in order to perform a SELECT INTO or bulk copy operation. The *trunc. log on chkpt.* option forced your transaction log to be truncated every time a checkpoint occurred in the database. This option was recommended only for test or development systems, not for production servers. You can still set these options using the *sp_dboption* procedure, but not using the ALTER DATABASE command. However, in SQL Server 2000, changing either of these options using *sp_dboption* also changes your recovery mode, and changing your recovery mode changes the value of one or both of these options, as you'll see below. The recommended method for changing your database recovery mode is to use the ALTER DATABASE command:

```
ALTER DATABASE <database_name>
    SET RECOVERY [FULL | BULK_LOGGED | SIMPLE]
```

To see what mode your database is in, you can use the DATABASEPROPERTYEX() property function:

```
SELECT DATABASEPROPERTYEX('<database_name>', 'recovery')
```

As I just mentioned, you can change the recovery mode by changing the database options. For example, if your database is in FULL recovery mode and you change the *select into/bulkcopy* option to *true*, your database recovery mode automatically changes to BULK_LOGGED. Conversely, if you force the database back into FULL mode using ALTER DATABASE, the value of the *select into/bulkcopy* option changes automatically. In fact, *sysdatabases* doesn't record any special information for the recovery mode. The recovery mode is determined by the status bits for these two database options. If bit 3 in *sysdatabases.status* is set, the database has *select into/bulkcopy* enabled, and if bit 4 is set, the database has *trunc. log on chkpt.* enabled. Table 5-4 shows the relationship between the database options and the new recovery modes.

If trunc. log on chkpt. is:	And select into/bulkcopy is:	The recovery mode is:
FALSE	FALSE	FULL
FALSE	TRUE	BULK_LOGGED
TRUE	FALSE	SIMPLE
TRUE	TRUE	SIMPLE

Table 5-4. *The relationship between SQL Server 7 database options and recovery modes.*

If you're using SQL Server 2000 Standard or Enterprise Edition, the *model* database starts in FULL recovery mode, so all your new databases will also be in FULL mode. If you're using SQL Server Personal Edition or the Microsoft SQL Server Desktop Engine, the *model* database starts in SIMPLE recovery mode. You can change the mode of the *model* database or any other user database by using the ALTER DATABASE command.

The new recovery model offers you two major benefits over previous versions. First, you can always perform a SELECT INTO operation without having to worry about what options you've set. Prior to SQL Server 2000, you could only run the SELECT INTO or minimally logged bulk copy operation if you had set the specific database option to true, and only a database owner could change that option. That sometimes meant a restriction on what non-DBO developers could accomplish.

Second, you can freely switch between the FULL and BULK_LOGGED modes without worrying about your backup scripts failing. Prior to SQL Server 2000, once you performed a SELECT INTO or a bulk copy, you could no longer back up your transaction log. So if you had automatic log backup scripts scheduled to run at regular intervals, these would break and generate an error. This can no longer happen. You can run SELECT INTO or bulk copy in any recovery mode, and you can back up the log in either FULL or BULK_LOGGED mode.

In addition, you can easily switch between FULL and BULK_LOGGED modes if you usually operate in FULL mode but occasionally need to perform a bulk operation quickly. You can change to BULK_LOGGED and pay the price later when you back up the log; the backup will simply take longer and be larger.

You can't easily switch to and from SIMPLE mode. When you use the ALTER DATABASE command to change from SIMPLE to FULL or BULK_LOGGED, you must first make a complete database backup in order for the change in behavior to be complete. Remember that SIMPLE recovery mode is comparable to the database option that truncates the log at regular intervals. The truncation option isn't recommended for production databases, where you need maximum transaction recoverability. The only time that SIMPLE mode is really useful is in test and development situations or for small databases that are primarily read-only. I suggest that you use FULL or BULK_LOGGED for your production databases and that you switch between those modes whenever you need to.

Choosing a Backup Type

If you're responsible for creating the backup plan for your data, you'll not only need to choose a recovery mode but also decide what kind of backup to make. I mentioned the three main types: full, differential, and log. In fact, you can use all three types together. To accomplish any type of full restoration of a database, you must occasionally make a full database backup. In addition, you can also make differential or log backups. Here are some facts to help you decide between these last two:

A differential backup:

- Is faster if your environment includes a lot of changes to the same data. It will back up only the most recent change, whereas a log backup will capture every individual update.

- Captures the entire B-tree structures for new indexes, whereas a log backup captures each individual step in building the index.

- Is cumulative. When you recover from a media failure, only the most recent differential backup needs to be restored because it will contain all the changes since the last full database backup.

A log backup:

- Allows you to restore to any point in time because it is a sequential record of all changes.

- Can be made after a failure of the database media, as long as the log is available. This will allow you to recover right up to the point of the failure. The last log backup (called the tail of the log) must specify the WITH NO_TRUNCATE option in the BACKUP LOG command if the database itself is unavailable.

- Is sequential and discrete. Each log backup contains completely different log records. When you use a log backup to restore a database after a media failure, all log backups must be applied in the order that they were made.

Restoring a Database

How often you make each type of backup determines two things: how fast you can restore a database and how much control you have over which transactions are restored. Consider the schedule in Figure 5-5, which shows a database fully backed up on Sunday. The log is backed up daily, and a differential backup is made on Tuesday and Thursday. A drive failure occurs on Friday. If the failure does not include the log files or if you have mirrored them using RAID 1, you should back up the tail of the log with the NO_TRUNCATE option.

> **WARNING** If you are operating in BULK_LOGGED recovery mode, backing up the log also backs up any data that was changed with a BULK_LOGGED operation, so you might need to have more than just the log file available to back up the tail of the log. You'll also need to have available any filegroups containing data inserted with a bulk copy or SELECT INTO command.

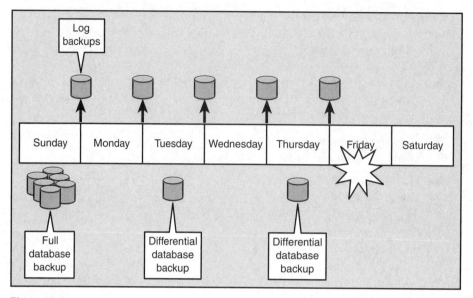

Figure 5-5. *Combined usage of log and differential backups reduces total restore time.*

To restore this database after a failure, you must start by restoring the full backup made on Sunday. This does two things: it copies all the data, log, and index pages from the backup media to the database files, and it applies all the transactions in the log. You must determine whether incomplete transactions are rolled back. You can opt to recover the database by using the WITH RECOVERY option of the RESTORE command. This will roll back any incomplete transactions and open the database for use. No further restoring can be done. If you choose not to roll back incomplete transactions by specifying the WITH NORECOVERY option, the database will be left in an inconsistent state and will not be usable.

If you choose WITH NORECOVERY, you can then apply the next backup. In the scenario depicted in Figure 5-5, you would restore the differential backup made on Thursday, which would copy all the changed extents back into the data files. The differential backup also contains the log records spanning the time the differential backup was being made, so again you have to decide whether to recover the database. Complete transactions are always rolled forward, but you determine whether incomplete transactions are rolled back.

After the last differential backup is restored, you must restore, in sequence, all the log backups made after the last differential backup was made. This includes the tail of the log backed up after the failure if you were able to make this last backup.

NOTE The recovery done during a restore operation works almost exactly the same way as restart recovery, which I described in Chapter 3. There is an analysis pass to determine how much work might need to be done, a roll-forward pass to redo completed transactions and return the database to the state it was in when the backup was complete, and a rollback pass to undo incomplete transactions. The big difference between restore recovery and restart recovery is that with restore recovery you have control over when the rollback pass is done. It should not be done until all the rolling forward from all the backups has been applied. Only then should you roll back any transactions that are still not complete.

Backing Up and Restoring Files and Filegroups

SQL Server 2000 allows you to back up individual files or filegroups. This can be useful in environments with extremely large databases. You can choose to back up just one file or filegroup each day, so the entire database does not have to be backed up as often. It also can be useful when you have an isolated media failure on just a single drive and you think that restoring the entire database would take too long.

Here are a few details you should keep in mind when backing up and restoring files and filegroups:

- Individual files and filegroups can be backed up only when your database is in FULL or BULK_LOGGED recovery mode because you must apply log backups after you restore a file or filegroup and you can't make log backups in SIMPLE mode.

- Unlike differential and full database backups, a backup of a file or filegroup does not back up any portion of the transaction log.

- You can restore individual file or filegroup backups from a full database backup.

- Immediately before restoring an individual file or filegroup, you must back up the transaction log. You must have an unbroken chain of log backups from the time the file or filegroup backup was made.

- After restoring a file or filegroup backup, you must restore all the transaction logs made between the time you backed up the file or filegroup and the time you restored it. This guarantees that the restored files are in sync with the rest of the database.

  For example, suppose you backed up Filegroup FG1 at 10 A.M. Monday. The database is still in use, and changes happen to data on FG1 and transactions are processed that change data in both FG1 and other filegroups. You back up the log at 4 P.M. More transactions are processed that change data in both FG1 and other filegroups. At 6 P.M., a media failure occurs and you lose one or more of the files making up FG1.

To restore, you must first back up the tail of the log containing all changes that occurred between 4 P.M. and 6 P.M. You can then restore FG1 using the RESTORE DATABASE command, specifying just filegroup FG1. Your database will not be in a consistent state because the restored FG1 will have changes only through 10 A.M. but the rest of the database will have changes through 6 P.M. However, SQL Server knows when the last change was made to the database because each page in a database stores the LSN of the last log record that changed that page. When restoring a filegroup, SQL Server makes a note of the maximum LSN in the database. You must restore log backups until the log reaches at least the maximum LSN in the database, and you will not reach that point until you apply the 6 P.M. log backup.

Partial Restore

SQL Server 2000 lets you do a partial restore of a database in emergency situations. Although the description and the syntax seem similar to file and filegroup backups, there is a big difference. With file and filegroup backups, you start with a complete database and replace one or more files or filegroups with previously backed up versions. With a partial database restore, you don't start with a full database. You restore individual filegroups, which must include the primary filegroup containing all the system tables, to a new location. Any filegroups you don't restore no longer exist and are treated as OFFLINE when you attempt to reference data stored on them. You can then restore log backups or differential backups to bring the data in those filegroups to a later point in time. This allows you the option of recovering the data from a subset of tables after an accidental deletion or modification of table data. You can use the partially restored database to extract the data from the lost tables and copy it back into your original database.

Restoring with Standby

In normal recovery operations, you have the choice of either running recovery to roll back incomplete transactions or not running recovery. If you run recovery, no further log backups can be restored and the database is fully usable. If you don't run recovery, the database is inconsistent and SQL Server won't let you use it at all. You have to choose one or the other because of the way log backups are made.

For example, in SQL Server 2000, log backups do not overlap—each log backup starts where the previous one ended. Consider a transaction that makes hundreds of updates to a single table. If you back up the log in the middle of the updating and again after the updating is finished, the first log backup will have the beginning of the transaction and some of the updates and the second log backup will have the remainder of the updates and the commit. Suppose you then need to restore these log backups after restoring the full database. If, after restoring the first log backup, you run recovery, the first part of the transaction is rolled back. If you then try to restore the second log backup, it will start in the middle of a transaction and SQL Server won't know what the beginning of the transaction did. You certainly can't recover transactions from this point because their operations might depend on this update that you've lost part of. So, SQL Server will not allow any more restoring to be done. The alternative is to not run recovery to roll back the first part of the transaction, but instead to leave the transaction incomplete. SQL Server will know that the database is inconsistent and will not allow any users into the database until you finally run recovery on it.

What if you want to combine the two approaches? It would be nice to be able to restore one log backup and look at the data before restoring more log backups, particularly if you're trying to do a point-in-time recovery, but you won't know what the right point is. SQL Server provides an option called STANDBY that allows you to recover the database and still restore more log backups. If you restore a log backup and specify WITH STANDBY = '*<some filename>*', SQL Server will roll back incomplete transactions but keep track of the rolled-back work in the specified file, which is known as a standby file. The next restore operation will first read the contents of the standby file and redo the operations that were rolled back, and then it will restore the next log. If that restore also specifies WITH STANDBY, incomplete transactions will again be rolled back but a record of those rolled back transactions will be saved. Keep in mind that you can't modify any data if you've restored WITH STANDBY (SQL Server will generate an error message if you try), but you can read the data and continue to restore more logs. The final log must be restored WITH RECOVERY (and no standby file will be kept) to make the database fully usable.

SUMMARY

A database is a collection of objects such as tables, views, and stored procedures. Although a typical SQL Server installation has many databases, it always includes the following three: *master*, *model*, and *tempdb*. (An installation usually also includes *pubs*, *Northwind*, and *msdb*.) Every database has its own transaction log; integrity constraints among objects keep a database logically consistent.

Databases are stored in operating system files in a one-to-many relationship. Each database has at least one file for the data and one file for the transaction log. You can easily increase and decrease the size of databases and their files either manually or automatically.

Now that you understand database basics, it's time to move on to tables, the fundamental data structures you'll work with.

Chapter 6

Tables

In this chapter, I'll look at some in-depth implementation examples. But let's start with a basic introduction to tables. Simply put, a *table* is a collection of data about a specific *entity* (person, place, or thing) that has a discrete number of named *attributes* (for example, quantity or type). Tables are at the heart of Microsoft SQL Server and the relational model in general. Tables are easy to understand—they're just like the everyday lists that you make for yourself. In SQL Server, a table is often referred to as a *base table* to emphasize where data is stored. Calling it a base table also distinguishes the table from a <u>*view*</u>, a virtual table that's an internal query referencing one or more base tables.

Attributes of a table's data (such as color, size, quantity, order date, and supplier's name) take the form of named *columns* in the table. Each instance of data in a table is represented as a single entry, or *row* (formally called a *tuple*). In a true relational database, every row in a table is unique and each row has a unique identifier called the *primary key*. (SQL Server, in accordance with the ANSI SQL standard, doesn't require you to make a row unique or declare a primary key. However, because both of these concepts are central to the relational model, you should always implement them.)

Most tables will have some relationship to other tables. For example, in an order-entry system, the *orders* table likely has a *customer_number* column in which it keeps track of the customer number for an order; *customer_number* also appears in the *customer* table. Assuming that *customer_number* is a unique identifier, or primary key, of the *customer* table, a foreign key relationship is established by which the *orders* and *customer* tables can subsequently be joined.

So much for the 30-second database design primer. You can find plenty of books that discuss logical database and table design, but this isn't one of them. I'll assume that you understand basic database theory and design and that you generally know what your tables will look like. The rest of this chapter discusses the internals of tables in SQL Server and implementation considerations.

CREATING TABLES

To create a table, SQL Server uses the ANSI SQL standard CREATE TABLE syntax. SQL Enterprise Manager provides a front-end, fill-in-the-blanks table designer that can make your job easier. Ultimately, the SQL syntax is always sent to SQL Server to create a table. You can create a table directly using a tool such as OSQL, ISQL, or SQL Query Analyzer; from SQL Enterprise Manager; or using a third-party data-modeling tool (such as ER*win* or Microsoft Visual InterDev) that transmits the SQL syntax under the cover of a friendly interface.

In this chapter, I'll emphasize direct use of the data definition language (DDL) rather than discuss the interface tools. You should keep all DDL commands in a script so that you can run them easily at a later time to re-create the table. (Even if you use one of the friendly front-end tools, it's critical that you be able to re-create the table later.) SQL Enterprise Manager and other front-end tools can create and save operating system files with the SQL DDL commands necessary to create the object. This DDL is essentially source code, and you should treat it as such. Keep a backup copy. You should also consider keeping these files under version control using a source control product such as Microsoft Visual SourceSafe or PVCS from MERANT (formerly INTERSOLV).

At the basic level, creating a table requires little more than knowing what you want to name it, what columns it will contain, and what range of values (domain) each column will be able to store. Here's the basic syntax for creating the *customer* table, with three fixed-length character (*char*) columns. (Note that this table definition isn't necessarily the most efficient way to store data because it always requires 46 bytes per entry plus a few bytes of overhead, regardless of the actual length of the data.)

```
CREATE TABLE customer
(
name        char(30),
phone       char(12),
emp_id      char(4)
)
```

This example shows each column on a separate line, for readability. As far as the SQL Server parser is concerned, white spaces created by tabs, carriage returns, and the spacebar are identical. From the system's standpoint, the following CREATE TABLE example is identical to the one above, but it's harder to read from a user's standpoint:

```
CREATE TABLE customer (name char(30), phone char(12), emp_id char(4))
```

We'll see many more detailed examples of tables later in the chapter.

Naming Tables and Columns

A table is always created within a database and is owned by one particular user. Normally, the owner is the user who created the table, but anyone with the *sysadmin, db_ddladmin,* or *db_owner* role can create a table that is owned by another user. A database can contain multiple tables with the same name, as long as the tables have different owners. The full name of a table has three parts, in the following form:

database.owner.tablename

For example, say that a user (with the username *Kalen*) creates a sample *customer* table in the *pubs* sample database. This user's table will have the *pubs.kalen.customer* three-part name. (If this user is also the database owner, *pubs.dbo.customer* will be her table's name because *dbo* is the special username for the database owner in every database.)

The first two parts of the three-part name specification have default values. The default for the name of the database is whatever database context you're currently working in. The table owner actually has two possible defaults. If no table owner name is specified when you reference a table, SQL Server assumes that either you or the owner of the database owns the table. For example, if our hypothetical user owns the *customer* table and her database context is *pubs*, she can refer to the table simply as *customer*.

> **NOTE**   To access a table owned by anyone other than yourself or the database owner, you must include the owner name along with the table name.

You should make column names descriptive, and because you'll use them repeatedly, you should avoid wordiness. The name of the column (or any object in SQL Server, such as a table or a view) can be whatever you choose, as long as it conforms to the SQL Server rule for identifiers: it must consist of a combination of 1 through 128 letters, digits, or the symbols #, $, @, or _. (For more on identifier rules, see "Using Identifiers" in *SQL Server Books Online*. The discussions there apply to all SQL Server object names, not just column names.)

In some cases, a table can be addressed using a four-part name, in which the first part is the name of the SQL Server. However, you can refer to a table using a four-part name only if the SQL Server has been defined as a linked server. You can read more about linked servers in *SQL Server Books Online*; I won't discuss them further here.

Reserved Keywords

Certain reserved keywords, such as *table*, *create*, *select*, and *update*, have special meaning to the SQL Server parser, and collectively they make up the SQL language implementation. You should avoid using reserved keywords for your object names. In addition to the SQL Server reserved keywords, the SQL-92 standard has its own list of reserved keywords. In some cases, this list is more restrictive than SQL Server's list; in other cases, it's less restrictive. *SQL Server Books Online* includes both lists.

Watch out for SQL-92's reserved keywords. Some of the words aren't reserved keywords in SQL Server yet, but they might become reserved keywords in a future SQL Server version. If you use a SQL-92 reserved keyword, you might end up having to alter your application before upgrading it if the word has become a SQL Server reserved keyword.

Delimited Identifiers

You can't use keywords in your object names unless you use a delimited identifier. In fact, if you use a delimited identifier, not only can you use keywords as identifiers but you can also use any other string as an object name—whether or not it follows the rules for identifiers. This includes spaces and other nonalphanumeric characters that are normally not allowed. Two types of delimited identifiers exist:

- Bracketed identifiers are delimited by square brackets ([*object name*]).

- Quoted identifiers are delimited by double quotation marks ("*object name*").

You can use bracketed identifiers in any environment, but to use quoted identifiers, you must enable a special option using SET QUOTED_IDENTIFIER ON. If you turn on QUOTED_IDENTIFIER, double quotes are interpreted as referencing an object. To delimit string or date constants, you must use single quotes.

Let's look at some examples. Because *column* is a reserved keyword, the first statement that follows is illegal in all circumstances. The second statement is illegal unless QUOTED_IDENTIFIER is on. The third statement is legal in any circumstance.

```
CREATE TABLE customer(name char(30), column char(12), emp_id char(4))

CREATE TABLE customer(name char(30), "column" char(12), emp_id char(4))

CREATE TABLE customer(name char(30), [column] char(12), emp_id char(4))
```

The ODBC driver that comes with SQL Server sets the QUOTED_IDENTIFIER option to ON by default, but some of the SQL Server–specific tools set it to OFF. You can determine whether this option is on or off for your session by executing the following command:

```
DBCC USEROPTIONS
```

If you're using SQL Query Analyzer, you can check the setting by running the preceding command or by choosing Options from the Tools menu and examining the Connection Properties tab.

Theoretically, you can always use delimited identifiers with all object and column names, so you never have to worry about reserved keywords. However, I don't recommend this. Many third-party tools for SQL Server don't handle quoted identifiers well. Using quoted identifiers might make upgrading to future versions of SQL Server more difficult. For example, if you're using the SQL Server Upgrade Wizard to upgrade a database directly to SQL Server 2000 from SQL Server 6.5, objects such as views and stored procedures are automatically dropped and re-created so that they include the structures of the latest version. If your tables have names that were reserved keywords, they have to be re-created using quoted identifiers.

When you use quoted identifiers, upgrading can't be fully automated and you must tell the SQL Server Upgrade Wizard whether it should assume that QUOTED_IDENTIFIER is on. If you don't know, or if you have a mixture of objects, you can tell the wizard to use a mixed mode. It will then try to interpret all objects with double quotes as if the option is on; if that's unsuccessful, it will assume that the option is off for that object. This interpretation might not always result in the stored procedure or view having the same meaning as was intended.

Rather than using delimited identifiers to protect against reserved keyword problems, you should simply adopt some simple naming conventions. For example, you can precede column names with the first few letters of the table name and an underscore. This naming style makes the column or object name more readable and also greatly reduces your chances of encountering a keyword or reserved word conflict.

Naming Conventions

Many organizations and multiuser development projects adopt standard naming conventions. This is generally a good practice. For example, assigning a standard moniker of *cust_id* to represent a customer number in every table clearly shows that all the tables share common data. If an organization instead uses several monikers in the tables to represent a customer number, such as *cust_id*, *cust_num*, *customer_number*, and *customer_#*, it won't be as obvious that these monikers represent common data.

One naming convention is the Hungarian-style notation for column names. Hungarian-style notation is a widely used practice in C programming, whereby variable names include information about their datatypes. This notation uses names such as *sint_nn_custnum* to indicate that the *custnum* column is a small integer (*smallint* of 2 bytes) and is NOT NULL (doesn't allow nulls). Although this practice makes good sense in C programming, it defeats the datatype independence that SQL Server provides; therefore, I recommend against using it.

Suppose, for example, that after the table is built and applications have been written, you discover that the *custnum* column requires a 4-byte integer (*int*) instead of a 2-byte small integer. You can use the ALTER TABLE command to modify the datatype of the existing table to *int* instead of *smallint*. SQL Server stored procedures handle the different datatypes automatically. Applications using ODBC, OLE DB, or DB-Library that bind the retrieved column to a *character* or *integer* datatype will be unaffected. The applications would need to change if they bound the column to a *small integer* variable because the variable's type would need to be larger. Therefore, you should try not to be overly conservative with variable datatypes, especially in your client applications. You should be most concerned with the type on the server side; the type in the application can be larger and will automatically accommodate smaller values. By overloading the column name with datatype information, which is readily available from the system catalogs, the insulation from the underlying datatype is compromised. If you changed the datatype from a *smallint* to an *int*, the Hungarian-style name would no longer accurately reflect the column definition. Changing the column name would then result in the need to change application code, stored procedures, or both.

Datatypes

SQL Server provides many datatypes, most of which I'll discuss in this section. Choosing the appropriate datatype is simply a matter of mapping the domain of values you need to store to the corresponding datatype. In choosing datatypes, you want to avoid wasting storage space while allowing enough space for a sufficient range of possible values over the life of your application.

Datatype Synonyms

SQL Server syntactically accepts as datatypes both the words listed as synonyms and the base datatypes shown in Table 6-1, but it uses only the type listed as the datatype. For example, you can define a column as *character(1)*, *character*, or *char(1)* and SQL Server will accept any of them as valid syntax. Internally, however, the expression is considered *char(1)*, and subsequent querying of the SQL Server system catalogs for the datatype will show it as *char(1)* regardless of the syntax that you used when you created it.

Synonym	Mapped to System Datatype
binary varying	varbinary
char varying	varchar
character	char(1)
character(n)	char(n)
character varying(n)	varchar(n)
dec	decimal
double precision	float
float[(n)] for n = 1 to 7	real
float[(n)] for n = 8 to 15	float
integer	int
national character(n)	nchar(n)
national char(n)	nchar(n)
national character varying(n)	nvarchar(n)
national char varying(n)	nvarchar(n)
national text	ntext
numeric	decimal

Table 6-1. *SQL Server datatype synonyms.*

Choosing a Datatype

The decision about what datatype to use for each column depends primarily on the nature of the data the column will hold. There are five basic datatype categories in SQL Server 2000: numeric, character, date and time, LOB (large object), and miscellaneous. SQL Server 2000 also supports a variant datatype called *sql_variant*. Values stored in a *sql_variant* column can be of any datatype. I'll discuss LOB and *sql_variant* columns later in this chapter when I discuss the internal storage of data on a page. I'll also provide more details about several of the datatypes later in the book when I illustrate programming techniques using the various datatypes. In this section, I'll examine some of the issues related to storing data of different datatypes.

Numeric Datatypes

You should use numeric datatypes for data on which you want to perform numeric comparisons or arithmetic operations. Your main decisions are the maximum range of possible values you want to be able to store and the accuracy you need. The trade-off is that datatypes that can store a greater range of values take up more space.

Numeric datatypes can also be classified as either exact or approximate. Exact numeric values are guaranteed to store exact representations of your numbers. Approximate numeric values have a far greater range of values, but the values are not guaranteed to be stored precisely. Exact numeric values can store data in the range $-10^{38} + 1$ to $10^{38} -1$. Unless you need numbers with greater magnitude, I recommend that you don't use the approximate numeric datatypes.

The exact numeric datatypes can be divided into two groups: integers and decimals. Integer types range in size from 1 to 8 bytes, with a corresponding increase in the range of possible values. The *money* and *smallmoney* datatypes are frequently included among the integer types because internally they are stored in the same way. For the *money* and *smallmoney* datatypes, it is just understood that the rightmost four digits are after the decimal point. For the other integer types, no digits come after the decimal point. Table 6-2 lists the integer datatypes along with their storage size and range of values.

Datatype	Range	Storage (bytes)
bigint	-2^{63} to $2^{63}-1$	8
int	-2^{31} to $2^{31}-1$	4
smallint	-2^{15} to $2^{15}-1$	2
tinyint	0 to 255	1
money	−922,337,203,685,477.5808 to 922,337,203,685,477.5807, with accuracy of one ten-thousandth of a monetary unit	8
smallmoney	−214,748.3648 to 214,748.3647, with accuracy of one ten-thousandth of a monetary unit	4

Table 6-2. *SQL Server integer datatypes.*

The decimal and numeric datatypes allow quite a high degree of accuracy as well as a large range of values For these two synonymous datatypes, you can specify a *precision* (the total number of digits stored) and a *scale* (the maximum number of digits to the right of the decimal point). The maximum number of digits that can be stored to the left of the decimal point is (precision − scale). Two different decimal values can have the same precision and very different ranges. For example, a column defined as decimal (8,4) can store values from −9999.9999 to 9999.9999 and a column defined as decimal (8,0) can store values from −99,999,999 to 99,999,999.

Table 6-3 shows the storage space required for decimal and numeric data based on the defined precision.

Precision	Storage (bytes)
1 to 9	5
10 to 19	9
20 to 28	13
29 to 38	17

Table 6-3. *SQL Server decimal and numeric datatype storage requirements.*

Date and Time Datatypes

SQL Server supports two datatypes for storing date and time information: *datetime* and *smalldatetime*. Again, the difference between these types is the range of possible dates and the number of bytes needed for storage. Both types have both a date and a time component. The range and storage requirements are shown in Table 6-4. If no date is supplied, the default of January 1, 1900 is assumed; if no time is supplied, the default of 00:00:00.000 (midnight) is assumed. In Chapter 7, I'll address many issues dealing with how SQL Server interprets datetime values entered by an application and how you can control the formatting of the displayed datetime value.

Internally, *datetime* and *smalldatetime* values are stored completely differently from how you enter them or how they are displayed. They are stored as two separate components, a date component and a time component. The date is stored as the number of days before or after the base date of January 1, 1900. For *datetime* values, the time is stored as the number of clock ticks after midnight, with each tick representing 3.33 milliseconds, or 1/300 of a second. For *smalldatetime* values, the time is stored as the number of minutes after midnight. You can actually see these two parts if you convert a *datetime* value to a binary string of 8 hexadecimal bytes. The first four hexadecimal bytes are the number of days before or after the base date, and the second four bytes are the number of clock ticks after midnight. You can then convert these four-byte hexadecimal strings to integers. I'll provide more details about hexadecimal strings later in the chapter.

The following example shows how to see the component parts of the current date and time by using the parameterless system function *current_timestamp*. The example stores the current date and time in a local variable so we can know we're using the same value for both computations. I'll talk about local variables in detail in Chapter 10.

```
DECLARE @today datetime
SELECT @today = current_timestamp
SELECT @today
SELECT CONVERT (varbinary(8), @today)
SELECT CONVERT (int, SUBSTRING (CONVERT (varbinary(8), @today), 1, 4))
SELECT CONVERT (int, SUBSTRING (CONVERT (varbinary(8), @today), 5, 4))
```

Datatype (bytes)	Range	Storage
datetime	January 1, 1753, through December 31, 9999, with an accuracy of three-hundredths of a second	8
smalldatetime	January 1, 1900, through June 6, 2079, with an accuracy of one minute	4

Table 6-4. *SQL Server* date *and* time *datatypes.*

Character Datatypes

Character datatypes come in four varieties. They can be fixed-length or variable-length single-byte character strings (*char* and *varchar*) or fixed-length or variable-length Unicode character strings (*nchar* and *nvarchar*). Unicode character strings need two bytes for each stored character; use them when you need to represent characters that can't be stored in the single-byte characters that are sufficient for storing most of the characters in the English and European alphabets. Single-byte character strings can store up to 8000 characters, and Unicode character strings can store up to 4000 characters. You should know the type of data you'll be dealing with in order to decide between single-byte and double-byte character strings.

Deciding whether to use a variable-length or a fixed-length datatype is a more difficult decision, and it isn't always straightforward or obvious. As a general rule, variable-length datatypes are most appropriate when you expect significant variation in the size of the data for a column and when the data in the column won't be frequently changed.

Using variable-length datatypes can yield important storage savings. They can sometimes result in a minor performance loss, and at other times they can result in improved performance. A row with variable-length columns requires special offset entries in order to be internally maintained. These entries keep track of the actual length of the column. Calculating and maintaining the offsets requires slightly more overhead than does a pure fixed-length row, which needs no such offsets. This task requires a few addition and subtraction operations to maintain the offset value. However, the extra overhead of maintaining these offsets is generally inconsequential, and this alone would not make a significant difference on most systems, if any.

Another potential performance issue with variable-length fields is the cost of increasing the size of a row on an almost full page. If a row with variable-length columns uses only part of its maximum length and is later updated to a longer length, the enlarged row might no longer fit on the same page. If the table has a clustered index, the row must stay in the same position relative to the other rows, so the solution is to split the page and move some of the rows from the page with the enlarged row onto a newly linked page. This can be an expensive operation. If the table has no clustered index, the row can move to a new location and leave a forwarding pointer in the original location. I'll talk about the details of page splitting and moving rows when I discuss data modification operations in Chapter 9.

On the other hand, using variable-length columns can sometimes improve performance because they can allow more rows to fit on a page. But the efficiency results from more than simply requiring less disk space. A data page for SQL Server is 8 KB (8192 bytes), of which 8096 bytes are available to store data. (The rest is for internal use to keep track of structural information about the page and the object to which it belongs.) One I/O operation brings back the entire page. If you can fit 80 rows on a page, a single I/O operation brings back 80 rows. But if you can fit 160 rows on a page, one I/O operation is essentially twice as efficient. In operations that scan for data and return lots of adjacent rows, this can amount to a significant performance improvement. The more rows you can fit per page, the better your I/O and cache-hit efficiency will be.

For example, consider a simple customer table. Suppose you could define it in two ways, fixed length and variable length, as shown in Figures 6-1 and 6-2.

```
CREATE TABLE customer
(
cust_id          smallint  NOT NULL,
cust_name        char(50)  NOT NULL,
cust_addr1       char(50)  NOT NULL,
cust_addr2       char(50)  NOT NULL,
cust_city        char(50)  NOT NULL,
cust_state       char(2)   NOT NULL,
cust_zip         char(10)  NOT NULL,
cust_phone       char(20)  NOT NULL,
cust_fax         char(20)  NOT NULL,
cust_email       char(30)  NOT NULL,
cust_web_url     char(20)  NOT NULL
)
```

Figure 6-1. *A customer table with all fixed-length columns.*

```
CREATE TABLE customer
(
cust_id          smallint      NOT NULL,
cust_name        varchar(50)   NOT NULL,
cust_addr1       varchar(50)   NOT NULL,
cust_addr2       varchar(50)   NOT NULL,
cust_city        varchar(50)   NOT NULL,
cust_state       char(2)       NOT NULL,
cust_zip         varchar(10)   NOT NULL,
cust_phone       varchar(20)   NOT NULL,
cust_fax         varchar(20)   NOT NULL,
cust_email       varchar(30)   NOT NULL,
cust_web_url     varchar(20)   NOT NULL
)
```

Figure 6-2. *A customer table with variable-length columns.*

Columns that contain addresses, names, or URLs all have data that varies significantly in length. Let's look at the differences between choosing fixed-length columns vs. choosing variable-length columns. In Figure 6-1, which uses all fixed-length columns, every row uses 304 bytes for data regardless of the number of characters actually inserted in the row. SQL Server also needs an additional 10 bytes of overhead for every row in this table, so each row needs a total of 314 bytes for storage. But let's say that even though the table must accommodate addresses and names up to the specified size, the average entry is only half the maximum size.

In Figure 6-2, assume that for all the variable-length (*varchar*) columns, the average entry is actually only about half the maximum. Instead of a row length of 304 bytes, the average length is 184 bytes. This length is computed as follows: the *smallint* and *char(2)* columns total 4 bytes. The *varchar* columns' maximum total length is 300, half of which is 150 bytes. And a 2-byte overhead exists for each of nine *varchar* columns, for 18 bytes. Add 2 more bytes for any row that has one or more variable-length columns. In addition, such rows require another 10 bytes of overhead, regardless of the presence of variable-length fields. (This is the same 10 bytes of overhead needed in the case of all fixed-length columns; in other words, all rows have these same 10 bytes of constant overhead.) So the total is 4 + 150 + 18 + 2 + 10, or 184. (I'll discuss the actual meaning of each of these bytes of overhead later in this chapter.)

In the fixed-length example in Figure 6-1, you always fit 25 rows on a data page (8096/314, discarding the remainder). In the variable-length example in Figure 6-2, you can fit an average of 44 rows per page (8096/184). The table using variable-length columns will consume about half as many pages in storage, a single I/O operation will retrieve almost twice as many rows, and a page cached in memory is twice as likely to contain the row you're looking for.

When choosing lengths for columns, don't be wasteful—but don't be cheap, either. Allow for future needs, and realize that if the additional length doesn't change how many rows will fit on a page, the additional size is free anyway. Consider again the examples in Figures 6-1 and 6-2. The *cust_id* was declared as a *smallint*, meaning that its maximum positive value is 32,767 (unfortunately, SQL Server doesn't provide any unsigned *int* or unsigned *smallint* datatypes), and it consumes 2 bytes of storage. Although 32,767 customers might seem like a lot to a new company, the company might be surprised by its own success and, in a couple of years, find out that 32,767 is too limited.

The database designers might regret that they tried to save 2 bytes and didn't simply make the datatype an *int*, using 4 bytes but with a maximum positive value of 2,147,483,647. They'll be especially disappointed if they realize they didn't really save any space. If you compute the rows-per-page calculations just discussed, increasing the row size by 2 bytes, you'll see that the same number of rows still fit on a page.

The additional 2 bytes are free—they were simply wasted space before. They never cause fewer rows per page in the fixed-length example, and they'll rarely cause fewer rows per page even in the variable-length case.

So which strategy wins? Potentially better update performance? Or more rows per page? Like most questions of this nature, no one answer is right. It depends on your application. If you understand the tradeoffs, you'll be able to make the best choice. Now that you know the issues, this general rule merits repeating: variable-length datatypes are most appropriate when you expect significant variation in the size of the data for that column and when the column won't be updated frequently.

Miscellaneous datatypes

I'll end this part of the discussion by showing you a few additional datatypes that you might have use for.

Binary   These datatypes are *binary* and *varbinary*. They are used to store strings of bits, and the values are entered and displayed using their hexadecimal (hex) representation, which is indicated by a prefix of 0x. So a hex value of 0x270F corresponds to a decimal value of 9999 and a bit string of 10011100001111. In hex, each two displayed characters represent a byte, so the value of 0x270F represents 2 bytes. You need to decide whether you want your data to be fixed or variable length, and you can use some of the same considerations I discussed for deciding between *char* and *varchar* to make your decision. The maximum length of *binary* or *varbinary* data is 8000 bytes.

Bit   The *bit* datatype can store a 0 or a 1 and can consume only a single bit of storage space. However, if there is only one *bit* column in a table, it will take up a whole byte. Up to 8 *bit* columns are stored in a single byte.

Large object   These datatypes are *text*, *ntext*, and *image*. The *text* datatype can store up to $2^{31} - 1$ non-Unicode characters, *ntext* can store up to $2^{30} - 1$ (half as many) Unicode characters, and *image* can store up to $2^{31} - 1$ bytes of binary data. We'll look at the storage mechanisms used for these large object (LOB) datatypes later in the chapter.

Cursor   The *cursor* datatype can hold a reference to a cursor. Although you can't declare a column in a table to be of type *cursor*, I've included *cursor* in this list for completeness. I'll talk about cursors and cursor variables in detail in Chapter 13.

Rowversion   The *rowversion* datatype is a synonym in SQL Server 2000 for what was formerly called a *timestamp*. I like the new name because people always assumed that the *timestamp* datatype had something to do with dates or times, and it doesn't. A column of type *rowversion* holds an internal sequence number that SQL Server automatically updates every time the row is modified. The value of any *rowversion* column is actually unique within an entire database, and a table can have only one column of type *rowversion*. Any operation that modifies any *rowversion* column in the database generates the next sequential value. The actual value stored in a *rowversion* column is seldom important by itself. The column is used to detect whether a row has been modified since the last time it was accessed by finding out whether the *rowversion* value has changed.

Sql_variant The *sql_variant* datatype allows a column to hold values of any other datatype except *text*, *ntext*, *image*, or *rowversion* (*timestamp*). I'll describe the internal storage of *sql_variant* data later in this chapter, and I'll show you some examples of using *sql_variant* data in Chapter 7.

Table The *table* datatype can be used to store the result of a function and can be used as the datatype of local variables. Columns in tables cannot be of type *table*. I'll talk about the *table* datatype in more detail in Chapter 11 when I discuss user-defined functions.

Uniqueidentifier The *uniqueidentifier* datatype is sometimes referred to as a globally unique identifier (GUID) or universal unique identifier (UUID). A GUID or UUID is a 128-bit (16-byte) value generated in a way that, for all practical purposes, guarantees uniqueness worldwide, even among unconnected computers. It is becoming an important way to identify data, objects, software applications, and applets in distributed systems. Since I won't be talking about *uniqueidentifier* data anywhere else in the book, I'll give you a bit more detail about it here.

The Transact-SQL language supports the system function NEWID, which can be used to generate a *uniqueidentifier* value. A column or variable of datatype *uniqueidentifier* can be initialized to a value in one of the following two ways:

- Using the system-supplied function NEWID.

- Using a string constant in the following form (32 hexadecimal digits separated by hyphens): xxxxxxxx-xxxx-xxxx-xxxx-xxxxxxxxxxxx. (Each *x* is a hexadecimal digit in the range 0 through 9 or *a* through *f*.)

This datatype can be quite cumbersome to work with, and the only operations that are allowed against a *uniqueidentifier* value are comparisons (=, <>, <, >, <=, >=) and checking for NULL. However, using this datatype internally can offer several advantages.

One advantage is that the values are guaranteed to be globally unique for any machine on a network because the last six bytes of a *uniqueidentifier* value make up the node number for the machine. On a machine without a Network Interface Card

(NIC) (such as a home computer that connects to the Internet via modem), the node is a pseudorandom 48-bit value that isn't guaranteed to be unique now but is highly likely to be unique in the near future.

Another advantage is that the list of *uniqueidentifier* values can't be exhausted. This is not the case with other datatypes frequently used as unique identifiers. In fact, SQL Server uses this datatype internally for row-level merge replication. A *uniqueidentifier* column can have a special property called the ROWGUIDCOL property; at most, one *uniqueidentifier* column can have this property per table. The ROWGUIDCOL property can be specified as part of the column definition in CREATE TABLE and ALTER TABLE ADD *column* or can be added or dropped for an existing column using ALTER TABLE ALTER COLUMN.

You can reference a *uniqueidentifier* column with the ROWGUIDCOL property using the keyword ROWGUIDCOL in a query. This is similar to referencing an identity column using the IDENTITYCOL keyword. The ROWGUIDCOL property does not imply any automatic value generation, and if automatic value generation is needed, the NEWID function should be defined as the default value of the column. You can have multiple *uniqueidentifier* columns per table, but only one of them can have the ROWGUIDCOL property. You can use the *uniqueidentifier* datatype for whatever reason you come up with, but if you're using one to identify the current row, an application must have a generic way to ask for it without needing to know the column name. That's what the ROWGUIDCOL property does.

Much Ado About NULL

The issue of whether to allow NULL has become an almost religious one for many in the industry, and no doubt the discussion here will outrage a few people. However, my intention isn't to engage in a philosophical debate. Pragmatically, dealing with NULL brings added complexity to the storage engine because SQL Server keeps a special bitmap in every row to indicate which nullable columns actually *are* NULL. If NULLs are allowed, SQL Server must decode this bitmap for every row accessed. Allowing NULL also adds complexity in application code, which can often lead to bugs. You must always add special logic to account for the case of NULL.

As the database designer, you might understand the nuances of NULL and three-valued logic in aggregate functions, when doing joins, and when searching by values. However, you must consider whether your development staff also understands. I recommend, if possible, that you use all NOT NULL columns and define *default* values (discussed later in this chapter) for missing or unknown entries (and possibly make such character columns *varchar* if the default value is significantly different in size from the typical entered value).

In any case, it's good practice to explicitly declare NOT NULL or NULL when creating a table. If no such declaration exists, SQL Server assumes NOT NULL. (In other words, no NULLs are allowed.) However, you can set the default to allow NULLs by using a session setting or a database option. The ANSI SQL standard says that if neither is specified, NULL should be assumed, but as I mentioned, this isn't SQL Server's default. If you script your DDL and then run it against another server that has a different default setting, you'll get different results if you don't explicitly declare NULL or NOT NULL in the column definition.

Several database options and session settings can control SQL Server's behavior regarding NULL values. You can set database options using the ALTER DATABASE command, as I showed you in Chapter 5. And you can enable session settings for one connection at a time using the SET command.

NOTE   The database option *ANSI null default* corresponds to the two session settings ANSI_NULL_DFLT_ON or ANSI_NULL_DFLT_OFF. When the *ANSI null default* database option is false (the default setting for SQL Server), new columns created with the ALTER TABLE and CREATE TABLE statements are, by default, NOT NULL if the nullability status of the column isn't explicitly specified. SET ANSI_NULL_DFLT_OFF and SET ANSI_NULL_DFLT_ON are mutually exclusive options that indicate whether the database option should be overridden. When on, each option forces the opposite option off. Neither option, when set off, turns the opposite option on—it only discontinues the current on setting.

You use the function GETANSINULL to determine the default nullability for your current session. This function returns 1 when new columns allow null values and the column or datatype nullability wasn't explicitly defined when the table was created or altered. I strongly recommend declaring NULL or NOT NULL explicitly when you create a column. This removes all ambiguity and ensures that you're in control of how the table will be built, regardless of the default nullability setting.

WARNING   Although internally SQL Server's default behavior is to *not* allow NULLs unless they are specifically declared in the CREATE TABLE statement, you might never see this behavior in action. Because SQL Query Analyzer—the basic tool for submitting SQL code to SQL Server—is ODBC-based, it automatically turns on the ANSI_NULL_DFLT_ON option. This setting means that all your new columns will allow NULLs by default. I can't overemphasize that your best bet for avoiding confusion is to always state explicitly in your table definition whether NULLs should be allowed.

The database option *concat null yields null* corresponds to the session setting SET CONCAT_NULL_YIELDS_NULL. When CONCAT_NULL_YIELDS_NULL is on, concatenating a NULL value with a string yields a NULL result. For example, SELECT 'abc' + NULL yields NULL. When SET CONCAT_NULL_YIELDS_NULL is off, concatenating a NULL value with a string yields the string itself. In other words, the NULL value is treated as an empty string. For example, SELECT 'abc' + NULL yields *abc*. If the session level setting isn't specified, the value of the database option *concat null yields null* applies.

The database option *ANSI nulls* corresponds to the session setting SET ANSI_NULLS. When true, all comparisons to a null value evaluate to FALSE. When this option is set to false, comparisons of non-Unicode values to a null value evaluate to TRUE if both values are NULL. In addition, when this option is set to true, your code must use the condition IS NULL to determine whether a column has a NULL value. When this option is set to false, SQL Server allows "= NULL" as a synonym for "IS NULL" and "<> NULL" as a synonym for "IS NOT NULL."

You can see this behavior yourself by looking at the *titles* table in the *pubs* database. The *titles* table has two rows with a NULL price. The first batch of statements that follows, when executed from SQL Query Analyzer, should return two rows, and the second batch should return no rows.

```
-- First batch will return 2 rows
USE pubs
SET ANSI_NULLS OFF
GO
SELECT * FROM titles WHERE price = NULL
GO

-- Second batch will return no rows
USE pubs
SET ANSI_NULLS ON
GO
SELECT * FROM titles WHERE price = NULL
GO
```

A fourth session setting is ANSI_DEFAULTS. Setting this to ON is a shortcut for enabling both ANSI_NULLS and ANSI_NULL_DFLT_ON as well as other session settings not related to NULL handling. SQL Server's ODBC driver and the SQL Server OLE DB provider automatically set ANSI_DEFAULTS to ON. You can change the ANSI_NULLS setting when you define your data source name (DSN). Two of the client tools supplied with SQL Server (SQL Query Analyzer and the text-based OSQL) use the SQL Server ODBC driver but then internally turn off some of these options. To see which options are enabled for the tool you're using, you can run the following command:

```
DBCC USEROPTIONS
```

Here's a sample of the output it might return:

```
Set Option                      Value
------------------------------  ------------------------
textsize                        64512
language                        us_english
dateformat                      mdy
datefirst                       7
ansi_null_dflt_on               SET
ansi_warnings                   SET
ansi_padding                    SET
ansi_nulls                      SET
concat_null_yields_null         SET
```

> **WARNING**   The relationship between the database options and the corresponding session level SET options is not clearly documented for the *concat null yields null* and *ANSI nulls* options. The SET option always overrides the database option, whether the SET option has been turned ON or OFF. The only time the database option applies is when the SET option has not been touched. So you can think of the ANSI_NULLS and CONCAT_NULL_YIELDS_NULL options as having three possible values: ON, OFF, and "never been set." If the SET option is either ON or OFF, the database option is ignored. Since the ODBC driver (used by both SQL Query Analyzer and the OSQL command tool) as well as the OLE DB provider for SQL Server set both of these options to ON, the database option is never taken into account.
>
> In addition, the command DBCC USEROPTIONS shows you which options have been set to ON, but it doesn't show you which options have been explicitly set to OFF. I recommend that you try to write your queries so that it doesn't matter which option is in effect. When that is impossible, you should rely on the session-level option only and not the database-level option.

The database compatibility level controls two additional aspects of how SQL Server handles NULL values, as determined by the system procedure *sp_dbcmptlevel*. If the compatibility level is set to 70 or 80, the nullability of *bit* columns without explicit nullability is determined by either the session setting of SET ANSI_NULL_DFLT_ON or SET ANSI_NULL_DFLT_OFF or the database setting of *ANSI null default*. In 60 or 65 compatibility mode, *bit* columns created without an explicit NULL or NOT NULL option in CREATE TABLE or ALTER TABLE are created as NOT NULL.

The database compatibility level also controls whether SQL Server interprets an empty string (two single quotes with nothing between them) as either a single space or a true empty string. In compatibility level 60 or 65, SQL Server interprets empty strings as single spaces. If the compatibility level is 70 or 80, SQL Server interprets empty strings as truly empty—that is, a character string with no characters in it. Sometimes this empty string is referred to as a NULL, but SQL Server doesn't treat it like a NULL. SQL Server marks NULLs internally as NULLs, but an empty string is actually stored as a variable-length character field of 0 length.

In 60 or 65 compatibility mode, the empty string is interpreted as a single space in INSERT or assignment statements on *varchar* data. When you are concatenating *varchar*, *char*, or *text* data, the empty string is interpreted as a single space. This means that you can never have a truly empty string. The only alternative in 60 or 65 compatibility mode is to define the field as allowing NULLs and to use a NULL in place of an empty string.

As you can see, you can configure and control the treatment and behavior of NULL values in several ways, and you might think it would be impossible to keep track of all the variations. If you try to control every aspect of NULL handling separately within each individual session, you can cause immeasurable confusion and even grief. However, most of the issues become moot if you follow a few basic recommendations:

■   Never allow NULL values in your tables.

■   Include a specific NOT NULL qualification in your table definitions.

■   Make sure all your databases are running in 80 compatibility mode.

If you must use NULLs in some cases, you can minimize problems by always following the same rules, and the easiest rules to follow are the ones that ANSI already specifies.

USER-DEFINED DATATYPES

A user-defined datatype (UDDT) provides a convenient way for you to guarantee consistent use of underlying native datatypes for columns known to have the same domain of possible values. For example, perhaps your database will store various phone numbers in many tables. Although no single, definitive way exists to store phone numbers, in this database consistency is important. You can create a *phone_number* UDDT and use it consistently for any column in any table that keeps track of phone numbers to ensure that they all use the same datatype. Here's how to create this UDDT:

```
EXEC sp_addtype phone_number, 'varchar(20)', 'NOT NULL'
```

And here's how to use the new UDDT when you create a table:

```
CREATE TABLE customer
(
cust_id        smallint        NOT NULL,
cust_name      varchar(50)     NOT NULL,
cust_addr1     varchar(50)     NOT NULL,
cust_addr2     varchar(50)     NOT NULL,
cust_city      varchar(50)     NOT NULL,
cust_state     char(2)         NOT NULL,
cust_zip       varchar(10)     NOT NULL,
cust_phone     phone_number,
cust_fax       varchar(20)     NOT NULL,
cust_email     varchar(30)     NOT NULL,
cust_web_url   varchar(20)     NOT NULL
)
```

When the table is created, internally the *cust_phone* datatype is known to be *varchar(20)*. Notice that both *cust_phone* and *cust_fax* are *varchar(20)*, although *cust_phone* has that declaration through its definition as a UDDT.

Here's how the *customer* table appears in the entries in the *syscolumns* table for this table:

```
SELECT colid, name, xtype, length, xusertype, offset
FROM syscolumns WHERE id=object_id('customer')
```

colid	name	xtype	length	xusertype	offset
1	cust_id	52	2	52	2
2	cust_name	167	50	167	-1
3	cust_addr1	167	50	167	-2
4	cust_addr2	167	50	167	-3
5	cust_city	167	50	167	-4
6	cust_state	175	2	175	4
7	cust_zip	167	10	167	-5
8	cust_phone	167	20	261	-6
9	cust_fax	167	20	167	-7
10	cust_email	167	30	167	-8
11	cust_web_url	167	20	167	-9

You can see that both the *cust_phone* and *cust_fax* columns have the same *xtype* (datatype), although the *cust_phone* column shows that the datatype is a UDDT (*xusertype* = 261). The type is resolved when the table is created, and the UDDT can't be dropped or changed as long as one or more tables are currently using it. Once declared, a UDDT is static and immutable, so no inherent performance penalty occurs in using a UDDT instead of the native datatype.

The use of UDDTs can make your database more consistent and clear. SQL Server implicitly converts between compatible columns of different types (either native types or UDDTs of different types).

Currently, UDDTs don't support the notion of subtyping or inheritance, nor do they allow a DEFAULT value or CHECK constraint to be declared as part of the UDDT itself. These powerful object-oriented concepts will likely make their way into future versions of SQL Server. These limitations notwithstanding, UDDT functionality is a dynamic and often underused feature of SQL Server.

IDENTITY PROPERTY

It is common to provide simple counter-type values for tables that don't have a natural or efficient primary key. Columns such as *cust_id* are usually simple counter fields. The IDENTITY property makes generating unique numeric values easy. IDENTITY isn't a datatype; it's a *column property* that you can declare on a whole-number datatype such as *tinyint, smallint, int,* or *numeric/decimal* (having a scale of zero). Each table can have only one column with the IDENTITY property. The table's creator can specify the starting number (seed) and the amount that this value increments or decrements. If not otherwise specified, the seed value starts at 1 and increments by 1, as shown in this example:

```
CREATE TABLE customer
(
cust_id        smallint        IDENTITY   NOT NULL,
cust_name      varchar(50)     NOT NULL
)
```

To find out which seed and increment values were defined for a table, you can use the IDENT_SEED(*tablename*) and IDENT_INCR(*tablename*) functions. The following statement:

```
SELECT IDENT_SEED('customer'), IDENT_INCR('customer')
```

produces

```
1    1
```

for the *customer* table because values weren't explicitly declared and the default values were used.

This next example explicitly starts the numbering at 100 (seed) and increments the value by 20:

```
CREATE TABLE customer
(
cust_id        smallint        IDENTITY(100, 20)  NOT NULL,
cust_name      varchar(50)     NOT NULL
)
```

The value automatically produced with the IDENTITY property is normally unique, but that isn't guaranteed by the IDENTITY property itself. Nor is it guaranteed to be consecutive. For efficiency, a value is considered used as soon as it is presented to a client doing an INSERT operation. If that client doesn't ultimately commit the INSERT, the value never appears, so a break occurs in the consecutive numbers. An unacceptable level of serialization would exist if the next number couldn't be parceled out until the previous one was actually committed or rolled back. (And even then, as soon as a row was deleted, the values would no longer be consecutive. Gaps are inevitable.)

> **NOTE** If you need exact sequential values without gaps, IDENTITY isn't the appropriate feature to use. Instead, you should implement a *next_number*-type table in which you can make the operation of bumping the number contained within it part of the larger transaction (and incur the serialization of queuing for this value).

To temporarily disable the automatic generation of values in an identity column, you use the SET IDENTITY_INSERT *tablename* ON option. In addition to filling in gaps in the identity sequence, this option is useful for tasks such as bulk-loading data in which the previous values already exist. For example, perhaps you're loading a new database with customer data from your previous system. You might want to preserve the previous customer numbers but have new ones automatically assigned using IDENTITY. The SET option was created exactly for cases like this.

Because of the SET option's ability to allow you to determine your own values for an IDENTITY column, the IDENTITY property alone doesn't enforce uniqueness of a value within the table. Although IDENTITY will generate a unique number if IDENTITY_INSERT has never been enabled, the uniqueness is not guaranteed once you have used the SET option. To enforce uniqueness (which you'll almost always want to do when using IDENTITY), you should also declare a UNIQUE or PRIMARY KEY constraint on the column. If you insert your own values for an identity column (using SET IDENTITY_INSERT), when automatic generation resumes, the next value is the next incremented value (or decremented value) of the highest value that exists in the table, whether it was generated previously or explicitly inserted.

> **TIP** If you use the *bcp* utility for bulk loading data, be aware of the -E (uppercase) parameter if your data already has assigned values that you want to keep for a column that has the IDENTITY property. You can also use the Transact-SQL BULK INSERT command with the KEEPIDENTITY option. For more information, see the SQL Server documentation for *bcp* and BULK INSERT.

The keyword IDENTITYCOL automatically refers to the specific column in a table that has the IDENTITY property, whatever its name. If that column is *cust_id*, you can refer to the column as IDENTITYCOL without knowing or using the column name or you can refer to it explicitly as *cust_id*. For example, the following two statements work identically and return the same data:

```
SELECT IDENTITYCOL FROM customer
SELECT cust_id FROM customer
```

The column name returned to the caller is *cust_id*, not IDENTITYCOL, in both of these cases.

When inserting rows, you must omit an identity column from the column list and VALUES section. (The only exception is when the IDENTITY_INSERT option is on.) If you do supply a column list, you must omit the column for which the value will be automatically supplied. Here are two valid INSERT statements for the *customer* table shown earlier:

```
INSERT customer VALUES ('ACME Widgets')
INSERT customer (cust_name) VALUES ('AAA Gadgets')
```

Selecting these two rows produces this output:

```
cust_id     cust_name
-------     ---------
1           ACME Widgets
2           AAA Gadgets

(2 row(s) affected)
```

Sometimes in applications, it's desirable to immediately know the value produced by IDENTITY for subsequent use. For example, a transaction might first add a new customer and then add an order for that customer. To add the order, you probably need to use the *cust_id*. Rather than selecting the value from the *customer* table, you can simply select the special system function @@IDENTITY, which contains the last identity value used by that connection. It doesn't necessarily provide the last value inserted in the table, however, because another user might have subsequently inserted data. If multiple INSERT statements are carried out in a batch on the same or different tables, the variable has the value for the last statement only. In addition, if there is an INSERT trigger that fires after you insert the new row and if that trigger inserts rows into a table with an identity column, @@IDENTITY will not have the value inserted by the original INSERT statement. To you, it might look like you're inserting and then immediately checking the value:

```
INSERT customer (cust_name) VALUES ('AAA Gadgets')
SELECT @@IDENTITY
```

However, if a trigger was fired for the INSERT, the value of @@IDENTITY might have changed.

There are two other functions that you might find useful when working with identity columns. SCOPE_IDENTITY returns the last identity value inserted into a table in the same scope, which could be a stored procedure, trigger, or batch. So if we replace @@IDENTITY with the SCOPE_IDENTITY function in the code snippet above, we can see the identity value inserted into the customer table. If an INSERT trigger also inserted a row that contained an identity column, it would be in a different scope:

```
INSERT customer (cust_name) VALUES ('AAA Gadgets')
SELECT SCOPE_IDENTITY()
```

In other cases, you might want to know the last identity value inserted in a specific table from any application or user. You can get this value using the IDENT_CURRENT function, which takes a table name as an argument:

```
SELECT IDENT_CURRENT('customer')
```

This doesn't always guarantee that you can predict the next identity value to be inserted because another process could insert a row between the time you check the value of IDENT_CURRENT and the time you execute your INSERT statement.

You can't define the IDENTITY property as part of a UDDT, but you can declare the IDENTITY property on a column that uses a UDDT. A column that has the IDENTITY property must always be declared NOT NULL (either explicitly or implicitly); otherwise, error number 8147 will result from the CREATE TABLE statement and CREATE won't succeed. Likewise, you can't declare the IDENTITY property and a DEFAULT on the same column. To check that the current identity value is valid based on the current maximum values in the table, and to reset it if an invalid value is found (which should never be the case), use the DBCC CHECKIDENT(*tablename*) statement.

Identity values are fully recoverable. If a system outage occurs while insert activity is taking place with tables that have identity columns, the correct value will be recovered when SQL Server is restarted. SQL Server accomplishes this during the checkpoint processing by flushing the current identity value for all tables. For activity beyond the last checkpoint, subsequent values are reconstructed from the transaction log during the standard database recovery process. Any inserts into a table that have the IDENTITY property are known to have changed the value, and the current value is retrieved from the last INSERT statement (post-checkpoint) for each table in the transaction log. The net result is that when the database is recovered, the correct current identity value is also recovered.

In rare cases, the identity value can get out of sync. If this happens, you can use the DBCC CHECKIDENT command to reset the identity value to the appropriate number. In addition, the RESEED option to this command allows you to set a new starting value for the identity sequence. See the online documentation for complete details.

INTERNAL STORAGE

This section covers system catalogs and the internal data storage of tables. Although you can use SQL Server effectively without understanding the internals, understanding the details of how SQL Server stores data will help you develop efficient applications. (If you don't need this in-depth information, you can skip this discussion and proceed to the section on constraints.)

When you create a table, one or more rows are inserted into a number of system catalogs to manage that table. At a minimum, rows are added to the *sysobjects*, *sysindexes*, and *syscolumns* system catalogs (tables). When you define the new table with one or more foreign key constraints, rows are added to the *sysreferences* system table.

For every table created, a single row that contains—among other things—the name, object ID, and owner of the new table is added to the *sysobjects* table. The *syscolumns* table gains one row for each column in the new table, and each row will contain information such as the column name, datatype, and length. Each column receives a column ID, which directly corresponds to the order in which you specified the columns when you created the table—that is, the first column listed in the CREATE TABLE statement will have a column ID of 1, the second column will have a column ID of 2, and so on. Figure 6-3 shows the rows added to the *sysobjects* and *syscolumns* system tables when you create a table. (Not all columns are shown for each table.)

```
CREATE TABLE employee
(
emp_lname   varchar(15)   NOT NULL,
emp_fname   varchar(10)   NOT NULL,
address     varchar(30)   NOT NULL,
phone       char(12)      NULL,
)

sysobjects    id          name        uid    xtype
              ----------- ----------- ------ -----
              1977058079  employee    1      U


syscolumns    id          colid  name        xtype length xoffset
              ----------- ------ ----------- ----- ------ -------
              1977058079  1      emp_lname   167   15     -1
              1977058079  2      emp_fname   167   10     -2
              1977058079  3      address     167   30     -3
              1977058079  4      phone       175   12     4
              1977058079  5      job_level   52    2      16
```

Figure 6-3. *Catalog information stored after a table is created.*

Notice in the *syscolumns* output in the figure that the *xoffset* column contains negative numbers in some rows. Any column that contains variable-length data will have a negative *xoffset* value in *syscolumns*. Successive variable-length columns in the CREATE TABLE statement are given decreasing *xoffset* values (−1, −2, −3, and so on). You can see in Figure 6-3 that the employee last name (*emp_lname*) is the first variable-length column in the table.

The *sysindexes* table will have at least one row that will eventually contain pointers to the storage space that the new table uses and information about the table's size. However, when the table is first created, no space is allocated to it, so the columns in *sysindexes* that indicate page addresses and storage space reserved will all be 0. Note that this is a change from all previous versions of SQL Server, in which at least two pages were allocated to the table as soon as it was created—one page for the data, one root page for each index, one Index Allocation Map (IAM) page for each index, and one IAM page for the table itself.

In SQL Server 2000, no space is allocated until the first row is inserted. If the table is defined without any primary key or unique constraints, *sysindexes* will have only one row, with an *indid* (index ID) value of 0, which means that the table is a heap. If a primary key or unique constraint is defined on the table, specifying that it is to be supported by a clustered index, the *indid* value for the table's row in *sysindexes* will be 1. Any additional constraints supported by nonclustered indexes will require that additional rows be added to *sysindexes*. Each nonclustered index will have a row with an *indid* value between 2 and 250. In addition, if there is text or image data in the row, there will be a row in sysindexes for the text or image data. The name for that row will be the name of the table prefixed by the character *t*, and the *indid* will always be 255. *indid* values of 251 through 254 are reserved for future needs.

Data Pages

Data pages are the structures that contain all data that is not text or image. As with all other types of pages in SQL Server, data pages have a fixed size of 8 KB, or 8192 bytes. They consist of three major components: the page header, data rows, and the row offset array, as shown in Figure 6-4.

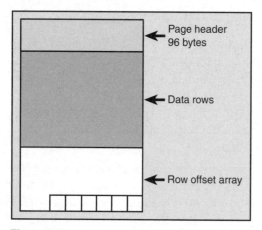

Figure 6-4. *The structure of a data page.*

Page Header

As you can see in Figure 6-4, the page header occupies the first 96 bytes of each data page (leaving 8096 bytes for data and row offsets). Table 6-5 shows the information contained in the page header.

Data Rows

Following the page header is the area in which the table's actual data rows are stored. The maximum size of a single data row is 8060 bytes. A data row can't span multiple pages (except for text or image columns, which can be stored in their own separate pages). The number of rows stored on a given page will vary depending on the structure of the table and on the data being stored. A table that has all fixed-length columns will always store the same number of rows per page; variable-length rows will store as many rows as will fit based on the actual length of the data entered. Keeping row length shorter allows more rows to fit on a page, thus reducing I/O and improving the cache-hit ratio.

Field	*What It Contains*
pageID	File number and page number of this page in the database
nextPage	File number and page number of the next page if this page is in a page chain
prevPage	File number and page number of the previous page if this page is in a page chain
objID	ID of the object to which this page belongs
lsn	Log sequence number (LSN) value used for changes and updates to this page
slotCnt	Total number of slots (rows) used on this page
level	Level of this page in an index (always 0 for leaf pages)
indexId	Index ID of this page (always 0 for data pages)
freeData	Byte offset of the first free space on this page
pminlen	Number of bytes in fixed-length portion of rows
freeCnt	Number of free bytes on page
reservedCnt	Number of bytes reserved by all transactions
xactreserved	Number of bytes reserved by the most recently started transaction
tornBits	1 bit per sector for detecting torn page writes (discussed in Chapter 5)
flagBits	2-byte bitmap that contains additional information about the page

Table 6-5. *Information contained in the page header.*

Row Offset Array

The row offset array is a block of 2-byte entries, each of which indicates the offset on the page on which the corresponding data row begins. Every row has a 2-byte entry in this array (as discussed on page 232, where I mentioned the 10 overhead bytes needed by every row). Although these bytes aren't stored in the row with the data, they do affect the number of rows that will fit on a page.

The row offset array indicates the logical order of rows on a page. For example, if a table has a clustered index, SQL Server will store the rows in the order of the clustered index key. This doesn't mean that the rows will be physically stored on the page in the order of the clustered index key. Rather, slot 0 in the offset array will refer to the first row in the order, slot 1 will refer to the second row, and so forth. As we'll see shortly when we examine an actual page, the offset of these rows can be anywhere on the page.

There's no internal global row number for every row in a table. SQL Server uses the combination of file number, page number, and slot number on the page to uniquely identify each row in a table.

Examining Data Pages

You can view the contents of a data page by using the DBCC PAGE statement, which allows you to view the page header, data rows, and row offset table for any given page in a database. Only a system administrator can use DBCC PAGE. But because you typically won't need to view the content of a data page, you won't find much about DBCC PAGE in the SQL Server documentation. Nevertheless, in case you want to use it, here's the syntax:

```
DBCC PAGE ({dbid | dbname}, filenum, pagenum[, printopt])
```

The DBCC PAGE command includes the parameters shown in Table 6-6. Figure 6-5 shows sample output from DBCC PAGE. Note that DBCC TRACEON(3604) instructs SQL Server to return the results to the client instead of to the error log, as is the default for many of the DBCC commands that deal with internals issues.

Parameter	Description
dbid	ID of the database containing the page
dbname	Name of the database containing the page
filenum	File number containing the page
pagenum	Page number within the file

Table 6-6. *Parameters of the DBCC PAGE command.*

Parameter	Description
printopt	Optional print option; takes one of these values:
	0: Default; prints the buffer header and page header
	1: Prints the buffer header, page header, each row separately, and the row offset table
	2: Prints the buffer and page headers, the page as a whole, and the offset table
	3: Prints the buffer header, page header, each row separately, and the row offset table; each row is followed by each of its column values listed separately

```
DBCC TRACEON(3604)
GO
DBCC PAGE (5, 1, 88, 1)
GO


PAGE: (1:88)
------------

BUFFER:
-------

BUF @0x10EC4E80
---------------
bpage = 0x1B8A4000        bhash = 0x00000000        bpageno = (1:88)
bdbid = 5                 breferences = 0           bstat = 0x9
bspin = 0                 bnext = 0x00000000

PAGE HEADER:
------------

Page @0x1B8A4000
----------------
m_pageId = (1:88)         m_headerVersion = 1       m_type = 1
m_typeFlagBits = 0x0      m_level = 0               m_flagBits = 0x0
m_objId = 1977058079      m_indexId = 0             m_prevPage = (0:0)
m_nextPage = (0:0)        pminlen = 24              m_slotCnt = 23
m_freeCnt = 6010          m_freeData = 2136         m_reservedCnt = 0
m_lsn = (3:243:2)         m_xactReserved = 0        m_xdesId = (0:0)
m_ghostRecCnt = 0         m_tornBits = -2147483591
```

Figure 6-5. *Sample output from DBCC PAGE.*   *(continued)*

Figure 6-5 *continued*

```
Allocation Status
-----------------
GAM (1:2) = ALLOCATED     SGAM (1:3) = NOT ALLOCATED
PFS (1:1) = 0x60 MIXED_EXT ALLOCATED   0_PCT_FULL  DIFF (1:6) = CHANGED
ML (1:7) = NOT MIN_LOGGED


DATA:
-----


Slot 0, Offset 0x631
--------------------
Record Type = PRIMARY_RECORD
Record Attributes =  NULL_BITMAP VARIABLE_COLUMNS
1b8a4631:  00180030  20383034  2d363934  33323237 0...408 496-7223
1b8a4641:  34394143  01353230  00000009  00330005 CA94025.......3.
1b8a4651:  003f0038  0058004e  2d323731  312d3233 8.?.N.X.172-32-1
1b8a4661:  57363731  65746968  6e686f4a  316e6f73 176WhiteJohnson1
1b8a4671:  32333930  67694220  52206567  654d2e64 0932 Bigge Rd.Me
1b8a4681:  206f6c6e  6b726150                       nlo Park

Slot 1, Offset 0xb8
-------------------
Record Type = PRIMARY_RECORD
Record Attributes =  NULL_BITMAP VARIABLE_COLUMNS
1b8a40b8:  00180030  20353134  2d363839  30323037 0...415 986-7020
1b8a40c8:  34394143  01383136  00000009  00330005 CA94618.......3.
1b8a40d8:  00400038  00580051  2d333132  382d3634 8.@.Q.X.213-46-8
1b8a40e8:  47353139  6e656572  6a72614d  6569726f 915GreenMarjorie
1b8a40f8:  20393033  64723336  2e745320  31342320 309 63rd St. #41
1b8a4108:  6b614f31  646e616c                       10akland

Slot 2, Offset 0x110
--------------------
Record Type = PRIMARY_RECORD
Record Attributes =  NULL_BITMAP VARIABLE_COLUMNS
1b8a4110:  00180030  20353134  2d383435  33323737 0...415 548-7723
1b8a4120:  34394143  01353037  00000009  00330005 CA94705.......3.
1b8a4130:  003f0039  0055004d  2d383332  372d3539 9.?.M.U.238-95-7
1b8a4140:  43363637  6f737261  6568436e  356c7972 766CarsonCheryl5
1b8a4150:  44203938  69777261  6e4c206e  7265422e 89 Darwin Ln.Ber
1b8a4160:  656c656b      79                        keley


/* Data for slots 3 through 20 not shown */
```

```
Slot 21, Offset 0x1c0
---------------------
Record Type = PRIMARY_RECORD
Record Attributes =  NULL_BITMAP VARIABLE_COLUMNS
1b8a41c0:  00180030  20313038  2d363238  32353730 0...801 826-0752
1b8a41d0:  34385455  01323531  00000009  00330005 UT84152.......3.
1b8a41e0:  003d0039  0059004b  2d393938  322d3634 9.=.K.Y.899-46-2
1b8a41f0:  52353330  65676e69  6e6e4172  20373665 035RingerAnne67
1b8a4200:  65766553  2068746e  532e7641  20746c61 SeventhAv.Salt
1b8a4210:  656b614c  74694320        79           Lake City

Slot 22, Offset 0x165
---------------------
Record Type = PRIMARY_RECORD
Record Attributes =  NULL_BITMAP VARIABLE_COLUMNS
1b8a4165:  00180030  20313038  2d363238  32353730 0...801 826-0752
1b8a4175:  34385455  01323531  00000009  00330005 UT84152.......3.
1b8a4185:  003f0039  005b004d  2d383939  332d3237 9.?.M.[.998-72-3
1b8a4195:  52373635  65676e69  626c4172  36747265 567RingerAlbert6
1b8a41a5:  65552037  746e6576  76412068  6c61532e 7 Seventh Av.Sal
1b8a41b5:  614c2074  4320656b  797469          t Lake City

OFFSET TABLE:
-------------
Row - Offset
22 (0x16) - 357 (0x165)
21 (0x15) - 448 (0x1c0)
20 (0x14) - 711 (0x2c7)
19 (0x13) - 1767 (0x6e7)
18 (0x12) - 619 (0x26b)
17 (0x11) - 970 (0x3ca)
16 (0x10) - 1055 (0x41f)
15 (0xf) - 796 (0x31c)
14 (0xe) - 537 (0x219)
13 (0xd) - 1673 (0x689)
12 (0xc) - 1226 (0x4ca)
11 (0xb) - 1949 (0x79d)
10 (0xa) - 1488 (0x5d0)
9 (0x9) - 1854 (0x73e)
8 (0x8) - 1407 (0x57f)
7 (0x7) - 1144 (0x478)
6 (0x6) - 96 (0x60)
5 (0x5) - 2047 (0x7ff)
4 (0x4) - 884 (0x374)
3 (0x3) - 1314 (0x522)
2 (0x2) - 272 (0x110)
1 (0x1) - 184 (0xb8)
0 (0x0) - 1585 (0x631)
```

As you can see, the output from DBCC PAGE is divided into four main sections: BUFFER, PAGE HEADER, DATA, and OFFSET TABLE (really the offset array). The BUFFER section shows information about the buffer for the given page. (A *buffer* in this context is an in-memory structure that manages a page.)

The PAGE HEADER section in Figure 6-5 displays the data for all the header fields on the page. (Table 6-5 shows the meaning of most of these fields.) The DATA section contains information for each row. For each row, DBCC PAGE indicates the slot position of the row and the offset of the row on the page. The page data is then divided into three parts. The left column indicates the byte position within the row where the displayed data occurs. The next four columns contain the actual data stored on the page, displayed in hexadecimal. The right column contains a character representation of the data. Only character data is readable in this column, although some of the other data might be displayed.

The OFFSET TABLE section shows the contents of the row offset array at the end of the page. In the figure, you can see that this page contains 23 rows, with the first row (indicated by slot 0) beginning at offset 1585 (0x631). The first row physically stored on the page is actually row 6, with an offset in the row offset array of 96. DBCC PAGE displays the rows in slot number order, even though, as you can see by the offset of each of the slots, that isn't the order in which the rows physically exist on the page.

The Structure of Data Rows

A table's data rows have the general structure shown in Figure 6-6. The data for all fixed-length columns is stored first, followed by the data for all variable-length columns. Table 6-7 shows the information stored in each row.

Status Bits A contains a bitmap indicating properties of the row. The bits have the following meaning:

- **Bit 0**   Versioning information; in SQL Server 2000, it's always 0.

- **Bits 1 through 3**   Taken as a 3-bit value, 0 indicates a primary record, 1 indicates a forwarded record, 2 indicates a forwarded stub, 3 indicates an index record, 4 indicates a blob fragment, 5 indicates a ghost index record, and 6 indicates a ghost data record. (I'll discuss forwarding and ghost records in Chapter 9.)

- **Bit 4**   Indicates that a NULL bitmap exists; in SQL Server 2000, a NULL bitmap is always present, even if no NULLs are allowed in any column.

- **Bit 5**   Indicates that variable-length columns exist in the row.

- **Bits 6 and 7**   Not used in SQL Server 2000.

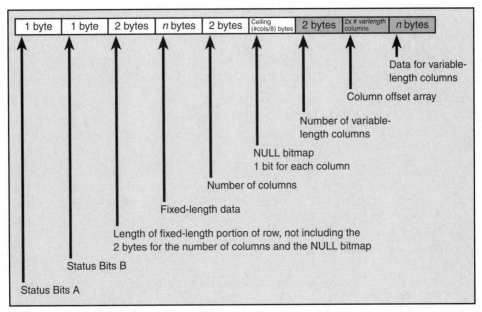

Figure 6-6. *The structure of data rows.*

Information	Mnemonic	Size
Status Bits A	TagA	1 byte
Status Bits B (not used in SQL Server 2000)	TagB	1 byte
Fixed-length size	Fsize	2 bytes
Fixed-length data	Fdata	Fsize − 4
Number of columns	Ncol	2 bytes
NULL bitmap (1 bit for each column in table; a 1 indicates that the corresponding column is NULL.)	Nullbits	Ceiling (Ncol / 8)
Number of variable-length columns	VarCount	2 bytes
Variable column offset array	VarOffset	2 * VarCount
Variable-length data	VarData	VarOff[VarCount] − (Fsize + 4 + Ceiling (Ncol / 8) + 2 * VarCount)

Table 6-7. *Information stored in a table's data rows.*

Within each block of fixed-length or variable-length data, the data is stored in the column order in which the table was created. For example, suppose a table is created with the following statement:

```
CREATE TABLE Test1
(
Col1 int          NOT NULL,
Col2 char(25)     NOT NULL,
Col3 varchar(60)  NULL,
Col4 money        NOT NULL,
Col5 varchar(20)  NOT NULL
)
```

The fixed-length data portion of this row would contain the data for *Col1*, followed by the data for *Col2*, followed by the data for *Col4*. The variable-length data portion would contain the data for *Col3*, followed by the data for *Col5*. For rows that contain only fixed-length data, the following is true:

■ The first hexadecimal digit of the first byte of the data row will be 1, indicating that no variable-length columns exist. (The first hexadecimal digit is comprised of bits 4 through 7; bits 6 and 7 are always 0, and if there are no variable-length columns, bit 5 is also 0. Bit 4 is always 1, so the value of the four bits is displayed as 1.)

■ The data row ends after the NULL bitmap, which follows the fixed-length data. (That is, the shaded portion shown in Figure 6-6 won't exist in rows with only fixed-length data.)

■ The total length of every data row will be the same.

Column Offset Arrays

A data row that has all fixed-length columns has no variable column count or column offset array. A data row that has variable-length columns has a column offset array in the data row with a 2-byte entry for each variable-length column, indicating the position within the row where each column ends. (The terms *offset* and *position* aren't exactly interchangeable. *Offset* is 0-based, and *position* is 1-based. A byte at an offset of 7 is in the eighth byte position in the row.)

Storage of Fixed-Length and Variable-Length Rows

The two examples that follow illustrate how fixed-length and variable-length data rows are stored. First, the simpler case of an all fixed-length row:

```
CREATE TABLE Fixed
(
Col1 char(5)      NOT NULL,
Col2 int          NOT NULL,
Col3 char(3)      NULL,
Col4 char(6)      NOT NULL,
Col5 float        NOT NULL
)
```

When this table is created, the following row (or one very much like it) is inserted into the *sysindexes* system table:

```
id           name  indid  first           minlen
-----------  ----- ------ --------------- ------
1797581442   Fixed 0      0xC70000000100  30
```

And these rows are inserted into the *syscolumns* system table:

```
name  colid  xtype  length  xoffset
----  -----  -----  ------  -------
Col1  1      175    5       4
Col2  2      56     4       9
Col3  3      175    3       13
Col4  4      175    6       16
Col5  5      62     8       22
```

For tables containing only fixed-length columns, the *minlen* value in *sysindexes* will be equal to the sum of the column lengths (from *syscolumns.length*), plus 4 bytes. It won't include the 2 bytes for the number of columns or the bytes for the NULL bitmap.

To look at a specific data row in this table, you first insert a new row:

```
INSERT Fixed VALUES ('ABCDE', 123, NULL, 'CCCC', 4567.8)
```

Figure 6-7 shows this row's actual contents on the data page. To run the DBCC PAGE command, I had to take the value of *first* from the *syindexes* output above (0xC70000000100) and convert it to a file and page address. In hexadecimal notation, each set of two hexadecimal digits represents a byte. I first had to swap the bytes to get 00 01 00 00 00 C7. The first two groups represent the 2-byte file number; the last four groups represent the page number. So the file is 0x0001, which is 1, and the page number is 0x000000C7, which is 199 in decimal.

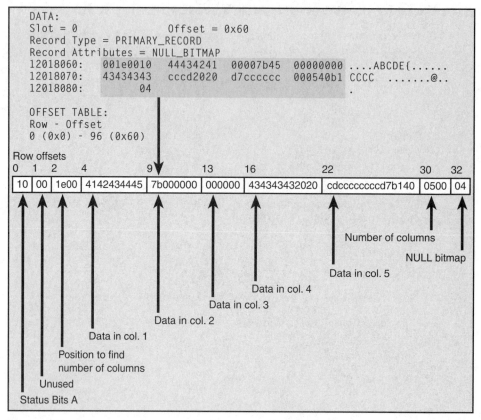

```
DATA:
Slot = 0                    Offset = 0x60
Record Type = PRIMARY_RECORD
Record Attributes = NULL_BITMAP
12018060:    001e0010    44434241    00007b45    00000000 ....ABCDE{......
12018070:    43434343    cccd2020    d7cccccc    000540b1 CCCC   .......@..
12018080:         04                                    .

OFFSET TABLE:
Row - Offset
0 (0x0) - 96 (0x60)
```

Figure 6-7. *A data row containing all fixed-length columns.*

NOTE   The *sysindexes* table contains three columns that represent page numbers within a database: *first*, *firstIAM*, and *root*. Each is stored in a byte-swapped format. To convert to a decimal file number and page number, you must first swap the bytes and then convert the values from hexadecimal to decimal. You could use the Microsoft Windows calculator to do the conversion, but a script has been provided on the companion CD to create a stored procedure called *ConvertPageNums*, which converts all these columns in the *sysindexes* table for you.

WARNING   SQL Server does not guarantee that the *sysindexes.first* column will also indicate the first page of a table. I've found that *first* is reliable until you begin to perform deletes and updates on the data in the table.

Reading the output takes a bit of practice. DBCC PAGE displays the data rows in groups of 4 bytes at a time. Within each group of four, the bytes are listed in reverse order. So the first group of four bytes is byte 3, byte 2, byte 1, and byte 0. The shaded area in Figure 6-7 has been expanded to show the bytes in the actual byte-number sequence.

The first byte is Status Bits A, and its value (0x10) indicates that only bit 3 is on, so the row has no variable-length columns. The second byte in the row remains unused. The third and fourth bytes (1e00) indicate the length of the fixed-length fields, which is also the column offset in which the *Ncol* value can be found. (The byte-swapped value is 0x001e, which translates to 30.) You can identify the data in the row for each column simply by using the offset value in the *syscolumns* table: the data for column *Col1* begins at offset 4, the data for column *Col2* begins at offset 9, and so on. As an *int*, the data in *Col2* (7b000000) must be byte-swapped to give us the value 0x0000007b, which is equivalent to 123 in decimal.

Note that the 3 bytes of data for *Col3* are all zeros, representing an actual NULL in the column. Because the row has no variable-length columns, the row ends 3 bytes after the data for column *Col5*. The 2 bytes starting right after the fixed-length data at offset 30 (0500, which is byte-swapped to yield 0x0005) indicate that five columns are in the row. The last byte is the NULL bitmap. The value of 4 means that only the third bit is on, because in our row, the third column was indeed a NULL.

> **WARNING** Fixed-length columns always use the full number of bytes defined for the table, even if the column holds a NULL value. If you're just upgrading from version 6.5 of SQL Server, this might take you by surprise. I know of at least one large database at a manufacturing company that expanded to three or four times its size when it was upgraded from version 6.5. This is because they had fields in many tables that were defined as *char(255)* and allowed NULLs. Some tables had 10 or more such columns, and the vast majority of the data was actually NULL. In version 6.5, the only space that these NULL columns needed was the 2 bytes in the variable column offset array; the actual NULL data took no space at all. In SQL Server 2000, every one of these columns needed a full 255 bytes of storage and the database ballooned in size!

Here's the somewhat more complex case of a table with variable-length data. Each row has three *varchar* columns:

```
CREATE TABLE Variable
(
Col1 char(3)       NOT NULL,
Col2 varchar(250)  NOT NULL,
Col3 varchar(5)    NULL,
Col4 varchar(20)   NOT NULL,
Col5 smallint      NULL
)
```

When you create this table, the following row is inserted into the *sysindexes* system table:

```
id          name     indid  first          minlen
----------- -------- ------ -------------- ------
1333579789  Variable 0      0xC90000000100 9
```

And these rows are inserted into the *syscolumns* system table:

```
name colid  xtype length xoffset
---- ------ ----- ------ -------
Col1 1      175   3      4
Col2 2      167   250    -1
Col3 3      167   5      -2
Col4 4      167   20     -3
Col5 5      52    2      7
```

Now you insert a row into the table:

```
INSERT Variable VALUES
    ('AAA', REPLICATE('X', 250), NULL, 'ABC', 123)
```

The REPLICATE function is used here to simplify populating a column; this function builds a string of 250 *X*s to be inserted into *Col2*.

As shown in Figure 6-8, the data for the fixed-length columns is located using the offset value in *syscolumns*. In this case, *Col1* begins at offset 4, and *Col5* begins at offset 7.

To find the variable-length columns, you first locate the column offset array in the row. Right after the 2-byte field indicating the total number of columns (0x0500) and the NULL bitmap with the value 0x04, a 2-byte field exists with the value 0x0300 (or 3, decimal) indicating that three variable-length fields exist. Next comes the column offset array. Three 2-byte values indicate the ending position of each of the three variable-length columns: 0x0e01 is byte-swapped to 0x010e, so the first variable byte column ends at position 270. The next 2-byte offset is also 0x0e01, so that column has no length and has nothing stored in the variable data area. Unlike with fixed-length fields, if a variable-length field has a NULL value, it takes no room in the data row. SQL Server distinguishes between a *varchar* containing NULL and an empty string by determining whether the bit for the field is 0 or 1 in the NULL bitmap. The third 2-byte offset is 0x1101, which, when byte-swapped, gives us 0x0111. This means that the row ends at position 273 (and is a total of 273 bytes in length).

The total storage space needed for a row depends on a number of factors. Variable-length fields add additional overhead to a row, and their actual size is probably unpredictable. Even for fixed-length fields, the number of bytes of overhead can change depending on the number of columns in the table. In the earlier example illustrated in Figure 6-1, I mentioned that 10 bytes of overhead will exist if a row contains all fixed-length columns. For that row, 10 is the correct number. The size of the NULL bitmap needs to be long enough to store a bit for every column in the row. In the Figure 6-1 example, the table has 11 columns, so the NULL bitmap needs to be 2 bytes. In the examples illustrated by Figures 6-7 and 6-8, the table has only 5 columns, so the NULL bitmaps need only a single byte. Don't forget that the total row overhead also needs to include the 2 bytes for each row in the offset table at the bottom of the page.

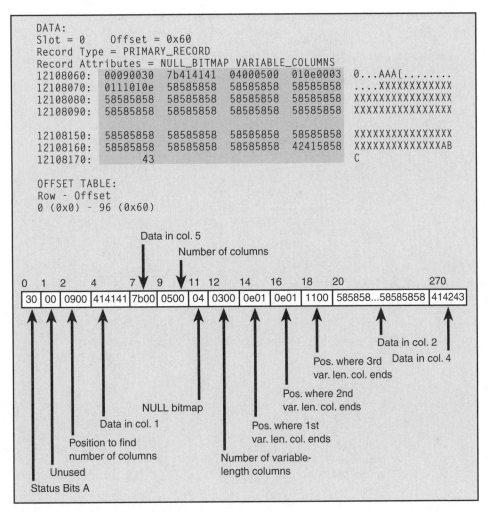

Figure 6-8. *A data row with variable-length columns.*

Page Linkage

SQL Server 2000 doesn't connect the individual data pages of a table in a doubly linked list unless the table has a clustered index. Pages at each level of an index are linked together, and since the data is considered the leaf level of a clustered index, SQL Server does maintain the linkage. However, for a heap, there is no such linked list connecting the pages to each other. The only way that SQL Server determines which pages belong to a table is by inspecting the IAMs for the table.

If the table has a clustered index, you can use the *M_nextPage* and *M_prevPage* values in the page header information to determine the ordering of pages in the list. Alternatively, you can use the DBCC EXTENTINFO command to get a list of all the extents that belong to an object. This example uses the *Orders* table in the *Northwind* database:

```
DBCC EXTENTINFO ('Northwind', 'Orders', 1)
```

The last argument indicates only extents for index 1, which is the clustered index (and includes the data). Here is the output:

```
file_id      page_id     pg_alloc     ext_size     obj_id
----------   ---------   ----------   ----------   ----------
1            203         1            1            21575115
1            205         1            1            21575115
1            230         1            1            21575115
1            231         1            1            21575115
1            232         1            1            21575115
1            233         1            1            21575115
1            234         1            1            21575115
1            235         1            1            21575115
1            240         8            8            21575115
1            264         5            8            21575115
```

```
index_id   pfs_bytes
--------   --------
1          0x60000000…
1          0x60000000…
1          0x60000000…
1          0x60000000…
1          0x60000000…
1          0x60000000…
1          0x60000000…
1          0x60000000…
1          0x40404040…
1          0x40404040…
```

Notice that the first eight rows indicate an extent size (*ext_size*) of 1. As discussed in Chapter 5, the first eight pages of a table are allocated from mixed extents. Only after the table has reached eight pages does SQL Server allocate uniform extents of eight pages each. The last two rows in the table show this situation, and the page number (*page_id*) column gives the page number of the first page of the extent. Note that the last extent (starting on page 264) has used only five of its pages so far.

Text and Image Data

As mentioned earlier, if a table contains LOB data (*text*, *ntext*, or *image* data), the actual data might not be stored on the data pages with the rest of the data for a row. In versions prior to SQL Server 2000, SQL Server always stored a 16-byte pointer in the data row that indicated where the actual data could be found. In SQL Server 2000, the default behavior is identical to that in SQL Server 7, but you have the option of changing the storage mechanism by setting a table option to allow LOB data to be stored in the data row itself. First I'll tell you about the default storage of LOB data.

LOB Data Stored Outside the Table

As stated earlier, by default no LOB data is stored in the data row. Instead, the data row contains only a 16-byte pointer to a page where the data can be found. These pages are 8 KB in size, like any other page in SQL Server, and individual *text*, *ntext*, and *image* pages aren't limited to holding data for only one occurrence of a *text*, *ntext*, or *image* column. A *text*, *ntext*, or *image* page can hold data from multiple columns and from multiple rows; the page can even have a mix of *text*, *ntext*, and *image* data. However, one text or image page can hold only *text* or *image* data from a single table.

The collection of 8-KB pages that make up a LOB field aren't necessarily located next to each other. The pages are logically organized in a B-tree structure so that operations starting in the middle of the string are very efficient. SQL Server 2000 can quickly navigate the tree; earlier versions of SQL Server had to scan through the page chain. The structure of the B-tree differs slightly depending on whether the amount of data is less than or more than 32 KB. (See Figure 6-9 for the general structure.) I'll discuss B-trees in more detail when I talk about index internals in Chapter 8.

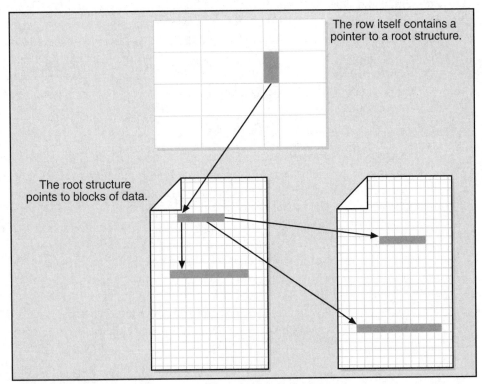

The row itself contains a pointer to a root structure.

The root structure points to blocks of data.

Figure 6-9. *A text column pointing to a B-tree that contains the blocks of data.*

If the amount of data is less than 32 KB, the text pointer in the data row points to an 84-byte text root structure. This forms the root node of the B-tree structure. The root node points to the blocks of *text, ntext,* or *image* data. While the data for LOB columns is arranged logically in a B-tree, physically both the root node and the individual blocks of data are spread throughout LOB pages for the table. They're placed wherever space is available. The size of each block of data is determined by the size written by an application. Small blocks of data are combined to fill a page. If the amount of data is less than 64 bytes, it's all stored in the root structure.

If the amount of data for one occurrence of a LOB column exceeds 32 KB, SQL Server starts building intermediate nodes between the data blocks and the root node. The root structure and the data blocks are interleaved throughout the *text* and *image* pages in the same manner as described earlier. The intermediate nodes, however, are stored in pages that aren't shared between occurrences of *text* or *image* columns. Each page storing intermediate nodes contains only intermediate nodes for one *text* or *image* column in one data row.

LOB Data Stored in the Data Row

If you store all your LOB data outside of your data pages, every time you access that data SQL Server will need to perform additional page reads. If you need the LOB data frequently, and if some of your data is small enough to fit within a SQL Server data page, you might notice a performance improvement by allowing some of the LOB data to be stored in the data row. You can enable a table option called *text in row* for a particular table by either setting the option 'ON' or by specifying a maximum number of bytes to be stored in the data row. The following command enables up to 500 bytes of LOB data to be stored on the data pages of the *Employees* table in the *Northwind* database:

```
sp_tableoption Employees, 'text in row', 500
```

Instead of a number, you can specify the option 'ON' (including the quotes), which sets the maximum size to 256 bytes. Note that in the *employees* table, the only LOB column is *notes*, which is defined as *ntext*. This means that 500 bytes allows only 250 characters. Once you enable the *text in row* option, you never get just the 16-byte pointer for the LOB data in the row, as is the case when the option is not on. If the data in the LOB field is more than the specified maximum, the row will hold the root structure containing pointers to the separate chunks of LOB data. The minimum size of a root structure is 24 bytes, and the possible range of values that *text in row* can be set to is 24 to 7000 bytes.

To disable the *text in row* option, you can set the value to either 'OFF' or 0. To determine whether a table has the *text in row* property enabled, you can use the OBJECTPROPERTY function, as shown here:

```
SELECT OBJECTPROPERTY (object_id('Employees'), 'TableTextInRowLimit')
```

This function returns the maximum number of bytes allowed for storing LOBs in a data row. If a 0 is returned, the *text in row* option is disabled.

Let's create a table very similar to the one we created to look at row structures, but we'll change the *varchar(250)* column to the *text* datatype. We'll use almost the same insert statement to insert one row into the table.

```
CREATE TABLE HasText
(
Col1 char(3)      NOT NULL,
Col2 text         NOT NULL,
Col3 varchar(5)   NULL,
Col4 varchar(20)  NOT NULL,
Col5 smallint     NULL
)

INSERT HasText VALUES
    ('AAA', REPLICATE('X', 250), NULL, 'ABC', 123)
```

Now let's find the necessary information for this table from the *sysindexes* table and note the results:

```
SELECT indid, first, name FROM sysindexes
    WHERE id = object_id('HasText')
```

Results:

```
indid   first            name
------  ---------------  --------------
0       0xBF0000000100   HasText
255     0xBD0000000100   tHasText
```

Even though there are no indexes on this table, there are two rows in *sysindexes*. *Sysindexes* keeps track of all objects that take up space, and since a LOB field takes space separate from the table, it has its own row in *sysindexes*. The index ID for LOB data is always 255, and the "name" of the structure is the name of the table prefixed by the letter *t*. The first page of the table is page 0xBF, which is 191 decimal, and the LOB data is at 0xBD, which is 189 decimal. Figure 6-10 shows the output from running DBCC PAGE. The row structure is very similar to the row structure in Figure 6-8, except for the text field itself. Bytes 20 to 35 are the 16-byte text pointer, and you can see the value *bd* (or 0xBD) at offset 31. This is the pointer to the page where the text data starts, and as we saw from the row in *sysindexes*, that is indeed the location of the LOB data for this table.

```
DATA:
-----

Slot 0, Offset 0x60
---------------------
Record Type = PRIMARY_RECORD
Record Attributes =    NULL_BITMAP VARIABLE_COLUMNS
1c0a8060:   00090030   7b414141   04000500   80240003    0...AAA{......$.
1c0a8070:   00270024   02be0000   00000000   000000bd    $.'............
1c0a8080:   00010001   434241                            ....ABC
```

Figure 6-10. *A row containing a text pointer.*

Now let's enable text data in the row, for up to 500 bytes:

```
EXEC sp_tableoption HasText, 'text in row', 500
```

Enabling this option does not force the text data to be moved into the row. We have to update the text value to actually force the data movement:

```
UPDATE HasText
SET col2 = REPLICATE('Z', 250)
```

Figure 6-11 shows the output from running DBCC PAGE after the text has been moved into the row. Note that the row is practically identical to the row containing *varchar* data, as shown in Figure 6-8.

```
DATA:
-----

Slot 0, Offset 0x60
---------------------
Record Type = PRIMARY_RECORD
Record Attributes =    NULL_BITMAP VARIABLE_COLUMNS
1c0a8060:   00090030   7b414141   04000500   010e0003    0...AAA{........
1c0a8070:   0111010e   5a5a5a5a   5a5a5a5a   5a5a5a5a    ....ZZZZZZZZZZZZ
1c0a8080:   5a5a5a5a   5a5a5a5a   5a5a5a5a   5a5a5a5a    ZZZZZZZZZZZZZZZZ
1c0a8090:   5a5a5a5a   5a5a5a5a   5a5a5a5a   5a5a5a5a    ZZZZZZZZZZZZZZZZ
1c0a80a0:   5a5a5a5a   5a5a5a5a   5a5a5a5a   5a5a5a5a    ZZZZZZZZZZZZZZZZ
1c0a80b0:   5a5a5a5a   5a5a5a5a   5a5a5a5a   5a5a5a5a    ZZZZZZZZZZZZZZZZ
1c0a80c0:   5a5a5a5a   5a5a5a5a   5a5a5a5a   5a5a5a5a    ZZZZZZZZZZZZZZZZ
1c0a80d0:   5a5a5a5a   5a5a5a5a   5a5a5a5a   5a5a5a5a    ZZZZZZZZZZZZZZZZ
1c0a80e0:   5a5a5a5a   5a5a5a5a   5a5a5a5a   5a5a5a5a    ZZZZZZZZZZZZZZZZ
1c0a80f0:   5a5a5a5a   5a5a5a5a   5a5a5a5a   5a5a5a5a    ZZZZZZZZZZZZZZZZ
1c0a8100:   5a5a5a5a   5a5a5a5a   5a5a5a5a   5a5a5a5a    ZZZZZZZZZZZZZZZZ
1c0a8110:   5a5a5a5a   5a5a5a5a   5a5a5a5a   5a5a5a5a    ZZZZZZZZZZZZZZZZ
1c0a8120:   5a5a5a5a   5a5a5a5a   5a5a5a5a   5a5a5a5a    ZZZZZZZZZZZZZZZZ
1c0a8130:   5a5a5a5a   5a5a5a5a   5a5a5a5a   5a5a5a5a    ZZZZZZZZZZZZZZZZ
1c0a8140:   5a5a5a5a   5a5a5a5a   5a5a5a5a   5a5a5a5a    ZZZZZZZZZZZZZZZZ
1c0a8150:   5a5a5a5a   5a5a5a5a   5a5a5a5a   5a5a5a5a    ZZZZZZZZZZZZZZZZ
1c0a8160:   5a5a5a5a   5a5a5a5a   5a5a5a5a   42415a5a    ZZZZZZZZZZZZZZAB
1c0a8170:      43                                       C
```

Figure 6-11. *A row containing text data.*

Finally let's change the maximum size of in-row text data to only 50 bytes. This will force the text data to be moved off the page, and the root of the text structure will be stored in the row. As long as the *text in row* option is not OFF (or 0), SQL Server will never store the simple 16-byte LOB pointer in the row. It will store either the LOB data itself, if it fits, or the root structure for the LOB data B-tree.

```
EXEC sp_tableoption HasText, 'text in row', 50
```

Figure 6-12 shows the output from running DBCC PAGE after the text pointer root has been stored on the page. A root structure is at least 24 bytes long (which is why 24 is the minimum size for setting the text-in-row limit.) Again, you can see the page number 0xBD at offset 40, indicating the location of the actual text data. Other information in the root includes:

- Bytes 0 through 1: The type of column; 1 indicates a LOB root.

- Byte 2: Level in the B-tree.

- Byte 3: Unused.

- Bytes 4 through 7: A value used by optimistic concurrency control for cursors that increases every time a LOB is updated.

- Bytes 8 through 11: A random value used by DBCC CHECKTABLE that remains unchanged during the lifetime of each LOB.

- Bytes 12 through 23 and each succeeding group of 12 bytes in the column: Links to LOB data on a separate page.

```
DATA:
-----

Slot 0, Offset 0x60
-------------------
Record Type = PRIMARY_RECORD
Record Attributes =  NULL_BITMAP VARIABLE_COLUMNS
1c0a8060:  00090030  7b414141  04000500  802c0003    0...AAA{........,.
1c0a8070:  002f002c  00000001  00000001  00002cd6    ,./...........,..
1c0a8080:  000000fa  000000bd  00000001    434241    ............ABC
```

Figure 6-12. *A row containing a text pointer root.*

As indicated above, when you first enable *text in row*, no data movement occurs until text data is actually updated. The same is true if the limit is increased—that is, even if the new limit is large enough to accommodate LOB data that had been stored outside the row, the LOB data will not be moved onto the row automatically. You must update the actual LOB data first.

However, if the *text in row* option is turned OFF or the limit is reduced, all LOB data must adjust to comply with the new specifications. If the option is set to OFF, all LOB data is moved off the rows and replaced by a 16-byte text pointer. If the option limit is decreased, all LOB data larger than the new limit is moved off the rows and replaced by a LOB root pointer. You should be aware that SQL Server will log all movement of LOB data, which means that reducing the limit of or turning OFF the *text in row* option can be a very time-consuming operation for a large table.

Another point to keep in mind is that just because the amount of LOB data is less than the limit, that does not always mean the data will be stored in the row. You're still limited to a maximum row size of 8060 bytes for a single row on a data page. In addition, if a variable-length column needs to grow, it might push LOB data off of the page so as not to exceed the 8060-byte limit. Growth of variable-length columns always has priority over storing LOB data in the row because the non-LOB data must be stored on the data page. If no variable-length *char* fields need to grow during an update operation, SQL Server will check for growth of in-row LOB data, in column offset order. If one LOB needs to grow, others might be pushed off the row.

sql_variant Datatype

The new *sql_variant* datatype provides support for columns that contain any or all of SQL Server's base datatypes except LOBs, *rowversion* (*timestamp*), and the types that can't be defined for a column in a table, namely *cursor* and *table*. For instance, a column can contain a *smallint* value in some rows, a *float* value in others, and a *char* value in the remainder.

This feature was designed to support what appears to be semistructured data in products sitting above SQL Server. This semistructured data exists in conceptual tables that have a fixed number of columns of known datatypes and one or more optional columns whose type might not be known in advance. An example is e-mail messages in Microsoft Outlook and Microsoft Exchange. With the *sql_variant* datatype, you can pivot a conceptual table into a real, more compact table with sets of property-value pairs. Here is a graphical example: The conceptual table shown in Table 6-8 has three rows of data. The fixed columns are the ones that exist in every row. Each row can also have values for one or more of the three different properties, which have different datatypes.

	fixed-columns	*property-1*	*property-2*	*property-3*
row-1	XXXXXX	value-11		value-13
row-2	YYYYYY	value-22		
row-3	ZZZZZZ	value-31	value-32	

Table 6-8. *Conceptual table with an arbitrary number of columns and datatypes.*

This can be pivoted into Table 6-9, where the fixed columns are repeated for each different property that appears with those columns. The column called *value* can be represented by *sql_variant* data and be of a different datatype for each different property.

fixed-columns	property	value
XXXXXX	property-1	value-11
XXXXXX	property-3	value-13
YYYYYY	property-2	value-22
ZZZZZZ	property-1	value-31
ZZZZZZ	property-2	value-32

Table 6-9. *Semi-structured data stored using the* sql_variant *datatype.*

Internally, columns of type *sql_variant* are always considered variable length. Their storage structure depends on the type of data, but the first byte of every *sql_variant* field always indicates the actual datatype being used in that row.

I'll create a simple table with a *sql_variant* column and insert a few rows into it so we can observe the structure of the *sql_variant* storage.

```
USE pubs
GO
CREATE TABLE var (a int, b sql_variant)
GO
INSERT INTO var VALUES (1, 3)
INSERT INTO var VALUES (2, 3000000000)
INSERT INTO var VALUES (3, 'abc')
INSERT INTO var VALUES (4, current_timestamp)
```

SQL Server decides what datatype to use in each row based on the data supplied. For example, the 3 in the first INSERT is assumed to be an integer. In the second INSERT, the 3000000000 is larger than the biggest possible integer, so SQL Server assumes a decimal with a precision of 10 and a scale of 0. (It could have used a *bigint*, but that would need more storage space.) We can now find the first page of the table and use DBCC PAGE to see its contents:

```
SELECT first FROM sysindexes WHERE name = 'var'
-- (I got a value of 0x8E0000000100 for first, so that can be
-- converted to a value of 142 decimal.)
GO
DBCC TRACEON (3604)
GO
DBCC PAGE (5, 1, 142, 1)
```

Figure 6-13 shows the contents of the four rows. I won't go into the details of every single byte because most are the same as what we've already examined.

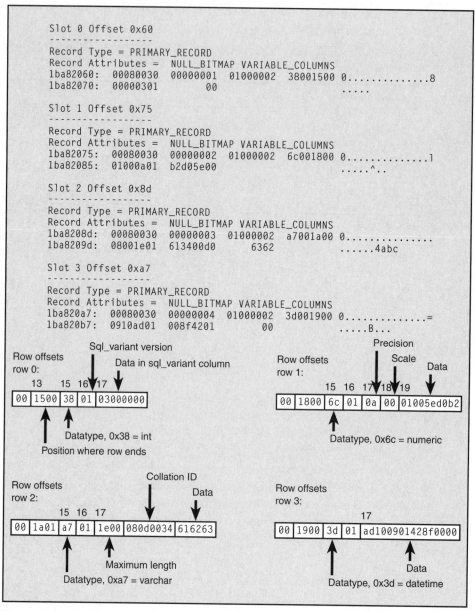

```
Slot 0 Offset 0x60
------------------
Record Type = PRIMARY_RECORD
Record Attributes =  NULL_BITMAP VARIABLE_COLUMNS
1ba82060:  00080030  00000001  01000002  38001500 0..............8
1ba82070:  00000301      00                         .....

Slot 1 Offset 0x75
------------------
Record Type = PRIMARY_RECORD
Record Attributes =  NULL_BITMAP VARIABLE_COLUMNS
1ba82075:  00080030  00000002  01000002  6c001800 0..............1
1ba82085:  01000a01  b2d05e00                       .....^..

Slot 2 Offset 0x8d
------------------
Record Type = PRIMARY_RECORD
Record Attributes =  NULL_BITMAP VARIABLE_COLUMNS
1ba8208d:  00080030  00000003  01000002  a7001a00 0...............
1ba8209d:  08001e01  613400d0      6362            ......4abc

Slot 3 Offset 0xa7
------------------
Record Type = PRIMARY_RECORD
Record Attributes =  NULL_BITMAP VARIABLE_COLUMNS
1ba820a7:  00080030  00000004  01000002  3d001900 0..............=
1ba820b7:  0910ad01  008f4201      00              .....B...
```

Figure 6-13. *Rows containing* sql_variant *data.*

The difference between the three rows starts at bytes 13-14, which indicate the position where the first variable-length column ends. Since there is only one variable-length column, this is also the length of the row. The *sql_variant* data begins at byte

15. Byte 15 is the code for the datatype. You can find the codes in the *xtype* column of the *systypes* system table. I've reproduced the relevant part of that table here:

```
xtype  name
-----  ----------------
34     image
35     text
36     uniqueidentifier
48     tinyint
52     smallint
56     int
58     smalldatetime
59     real
60     money
61     datetime
62     float
98     sql_variant
99     ntext
104    bit
106    decimal
108    numeric
122    smallmoney
127    bigint
165    varbinary
167    varchar
167    tid
167    id
173    binary
175    char
175    empid
189    timestamp
231    sysname
231    nvarchar
239    nchar
```

In our table, we have the datatypes 38 hex (which is 56 decimal, which is *int*), 6C hex (which is 108 decimal, which is *numeric*), A7 hex (which is 167 decimal, which is *varchar*) and 3D hex (which is 61 decimal, which is *datetime*). Following the byte for datatype is a byte representing the version of the *sql_variant* format, and that is always 1 in SQL Server 2000. Following the version, there can be one of the following four sets of bytes:

- For *numeric* and *decimal*: 1 byte for the precision and 1 byte for the scale

- For strings: 2 bytes for the maximum length and 4 bytes for the collation ID

- For *binary* and *varbinary*: 2 bytes for the maximum length

- For all other types: no extra bytes

These bytes are then followed by the actual data in the *sql_variant* column. There are many other issues related to working with *sql_variant* data and comparing data of different types. I'll cover these when we look at data retrieval and manipulation in Chapter 7.

CONSTRAINTS

Constraints provide a powerful yet easy way to enforce the data integrity in your database. As described in Chapter 2, data integrity comes in three forms:

- Entity integrity ensures that a table has a primary key. In SQL Server 2000, you can guarantee entity integrity by defining PRIMARY KEY or UNIQUE constraints or by building unique indexes. Alternatively, you can write a trigger to enforce entity integrity, but this is usually far less efficient.

- Domain integrity ensures that data values meet certain criteria. In SQL Server 2000, domain integrity can be guaranteed in several ways. Choosing appropriate datatypes can ensure that a data value meets certain conditions—for example, that the data represents a valid date. Other approaches include defining CHECK constraints or FOREIGN KEY constraints or writing a trigger. You might also consider DEFAULT constraints as an aspect of enforcing domain integrity.

- Referential integrity enforces relationships between two tables, a referenced table, and a referencing table. SQL Server 2000 allows you to define FOREIGN KEY constraints to enforce referential integrity, and you can also write triggers for enforcement. It's crucial to note that there are always two sides to referential integrity enforcement. If data is updated or deleted from the referenced table, referential integrity ensures that any data in the referencing table that refers to the changed or deleted data is handled in some way. On the other side, if data is updated or inserted into the referencing table, referential integrity ensures that the new data matches a value in the referenced table.

In this section, I'll discuss the use of constraints for enforcing your data integrity requirements. Constraints are also called *declarative data integrity* because they are part of the actual table definition. This is in contrast to *programmatic data integrity enforcement*, which uses stored procedures or triggers. Here are the five types of constraints:

- PRIMARY KEY
- UNIQUE

- FOREIGN KEY

- CHECK

- DEFAULT

You might also sometimes see the IDENTITY property and the nullability of a column described as constraints. I typically don't consider these attributes to be constraints; instead, I think of them as properties of a column, for two reasons. First, as we'll see, each constraint has its own row in the *sysobjects* system table, but IDENTITY and nullability information is not stored in *sysobjects*, only in *syscolumns*. This makes me think that these properties are more like datatypes, which are also stored in *syscolumns*. Second, when you use the special command SELECT INTO, a new table can be created that is a copy of an existing table. All column names and datatypes are copied, as well as IDENTITY information and column nullability. However, constraints are *not* copied to the new table. This makes me think that IDENTITY and nullability are more a part of the actual table structure than constraints are.

PRIMARY KEY and UNIQUE Constraints

A central tenet of the relational model is that every row in a table is in some way unique and can be distinguished in some way from every other row in the table. You could use the combination of all columns in a table as this unique identifier, but the identifier is usually at most the combination of a handful of columns, and often it's just one column: the primary key. Although some tables might have multiple unique identifiers, each table can have only one primary key. For example, perhaps the *employee* table maintains both an *Emp_ID* column and an *SSN* (social security number) column, both of which can be considered unique. Such column pairs are often referred to as *alternate keys* or *candidate keys,* although both terms are design terms and aren't used by the ANSI SQL standard or by SQL Server. In practice, one of the two columns is logically promoted to primary key using the PRIMARY KEY constraint, and the other is usually declared by a UNIQUE constraint. Although neither the ANSI SQL standard nor SQL Server require it, it's good practice to declare a PRIMARY KEY constraint on every table. Furthermore, you must designate a primary key for a table that will be published for transaction-based replication.

Internally, PRIMARY KEY and UNIQUE constraints are handled almost identically, so I'll discuss them together here. Declaring a PRIMARY KEY or UNIQUE constraint simply results in a unique index being created on the specified column or columns, and this index enforces the column's uniqueness in the same way that a unique index created manually on a column would. The query optimizer makes decisions based on the presence of the unique index rather than on the fact that a column was declared as a primary key. How the index got there in the first place is irrelevant to the optimizer.

Nullability

All columns that are part of a primary key must be declared (either explicitly or implicitly) as NOT NULL. Columns that are part of a UNIQUE constraint can be declared to allow NULL. However, for the purposes of unique indexes, all NULLs are considered equal. So if the unique index is on a single column, only one NULL value can be stored (another good reason to try to avoid NULL whenever possible). If the unique index is on a composite key, one of the columns can have many NULLs as long as the value in the other column is unique. For example, if the constraint contains two *int* columns, exactly one row of each of these combinations will be allowed:

NULL	NULL
0	NULL
NULL	0
1	NULL
NULL	1

This behavior is questionable: NULL represents an unknown, but using it this way clearly implies that NULL is equal to NULL. As you'll recall, I recommend that you avoid using NULLs, especially in key columns.

Index Attributes

You can explicitly specify the index attributes CLUSTERED or NONCLUSTERED when you declare a constraint. If you don't, the index for a UNIQUE constraint will be nonclustered and the index for a PRIMARY KEY constraint will be clustered (unless CLUSTERED has already been explicitly stated for a unique index, because only one clustered index can exist per table). You can specify the index FILLFACTOR attribute if a PRIMARY KEY or UNIQUE constraint is added to an existing table using the ALTER TABLE command. FILLFACTOR doesn't make sense in a CREATE TABLE statement because the table has no existing data, and FILLFACTOR on an index affects how full pages are only when the index is initially created. FILLFACTOR isn't maintained when data is added.

Choosing Keys

Try to keep the key lengths as compact as possible. Columns that are the primary key or that are unique are most likely to be joined and frequently queried. Compact key lengths allow more index entries to fit on a given 8-KB page, thereby reducing I/O, increasing cache hits, and speeding up character matching. Clustered index keys are used as bookmarks in all your nonclustered indexes, so a long clustered key will increase the size and decrease the I/O efficiency of all your indexes. So if your primary key has a clustered index, you've got plenty of good reasons to keep it short. When no naturally efficient compact key exists, it's often useful to manufacture a surrogate key using the IDENTITY property on an *int* column. If *int* doesn't provide enough range, a good second choice is a *numeric* column with the required precision and with scale 0. Alternatively, you can consider a *bigint* for an identity column. You might use this surrogate as the primary key, use it for most join and retrieval operations, and declare a UNIQUE constraint on the natural but inefficient columns that provide the logical unique identifier in your data. Or you might dispense with the UNIQUE constraint altogether if you don't need to have SQL Server enforce the uniqueness. Indexes slow performance of data modification statements because the index as well as the data must be maintained.

Although it's permissible to do so, don't create a PRIMARY KEY constraint on a column of type *float* or *real*. Because these are approximate datatypes, the uniqueness of such columns is also approximate, and the results can sometimes be unexpected.

Removing PRIMARY KEY or UNIQUE Constraints

You can't directly drop a unique index created as a result of a PRIMARY KEY or UNIQUE constraint by using the DROP INDEX statement. Instead, you must drop the constraint by using ALTER TABLE DROP CONSTRAINT (or you must drop the table itself). This feature was designed so that a constraint can't be compromised accidentally by someone who doesn't realize that the index is being used to enforce the constraint.

There is no way to temporarily disable a PRIMARY KEY or UNIQUE constraint. If disabling is required, use ALTER TABLE DROP CONSTRAINT and then later restore the constraint by using ALTER TABLE ADD CONSTRAINT. If the index you use to enforce uniqueness is clustered, when you add the constraint to an existing table, the entire table and all nonclustered indexes will be internally rebuilt to establish the cluster order. This can be a time-consuming task, and it requires about 1.2 times the existing table space as a temporary work area in the database would require (2.2 times total, counting the permanent space needed) so that the operation can be rolled back if necessary. However, you can rebuild an index that is enforcing a constraint by using the DROP_EXISTING option of the CREATE INDEX statement. This drops and re-creates the index behind the scenes as a single operation. I'll discuss the CREATE INDEX command in detail, including the DROP_EXISTING option, in Chapter 8.

Creating PRIMARY KEY and UNIQUE Constraints

Typically, you declare PRIMARY KEY and UNIQUE constraints when you create the table (CREATE TABLE). However, you can add or drop both by subsequently using the ALTER TABLE command. To simplify matters, you can declare a PRIMARY KEY or UNIQUE constraint that includes only a single column on the same line that you define that column in the CREATE TABLE statement. Or you can declare the constraint as a separate line in your CREATE TABLE statement. I'll show you examples of both methods shortly. The approach you use is largely a matter of personal preference unless your constraint involves multiple columns. Constraints defined along with a column definition can refer only to that column.

Following are examples of four ways to declare a PRIMARY KEY constraint on a single column. They all cause a unique, clustered index to be created. Note the (abridged) output of the *sp_helpconstraint* procedure for each—especially the constraint name.

EXAMPLE 1

```
CREATE TABLE customer
(
cust_id      int          IDENTITY  NOT NULL  PRIMARY KEY,
cust_name    varchar(30)  NOT NULL
)
GO

EXEC sp_helpconstraint customer
GO

>>>>

Object Name
-----------
customer

constraint_type              constraint_name
----------------------       -------------------------------
PRIMARY KEY (clustered)      PK__customer__68E79C55
```

EXAMPLE 2

```
CREATE TABLE customer
(
cust_id      int          IDENTITY  NOT NULL
                          CONSTRAINT cust_pk PRIMARY KEY,
cust_name    varchar(30)  NOT NULL
)
GO

EXEC sp_helpconstraint customer
GO

>>>>

Object Name
-----------
customer

constraint_type              constraint_name
----------------------       ----------------
PRIMARY KEY (clustered)      cust_pk
```

No foreign keys reference this table.

EXAMPLE 3

```
CREATE TABLE customer
(
cust_id      int          IDENTITY  NOT NULL,
cust_name    varchar(30)  NOT NULL,
                          PRIMARY KEY (cust_id)
)
GO

EXEC sp_helpconstraint customer
GO
```

>>>>

```
Object Name
-----------
customer


constraint_type              constraint_name
---------------              ---------------
PRIMARY KEY (clustered)      PK__customer__59063A47
```

No foreign keys reference this table.

EXAMPLE 4

```
CREATE TABLE customer
(
cust_id      int          IDENTITY  NOT NULL,
cust_name    varchar(30)  NOT NULL,
CONSTRAINT customer_PK PRIMARY KEY (cust_id)
)
GO

EXEC sp_helpconstraint customer
GO
```

>>>>

```
Object Name
-----------
customer


constraint_type              constraint_name
---------------              ---------------
PRIMARY KEY (clustered)      customer_PK
```

No foreign keys reference this table.

In Examples 1 and 3, I did not provide an explicit name for the constraint, so SQL Server came up with the names. The names, *PK__customer__68E79C55 and PK__customer__59063A47,* seem cryptic, but there is some method to this apparent madness. All types of single-column constraints use this same naming scheme, which I'll discuss later in the chapter, and multi-column constraints use a similar scheme. Whether you choose a more intuitive name, such as *cust_pk* in Example 2 or *customer_PK* in Example 4, or the less intuitive (but information-packed), system-generated name is up to you. Here's an example of creating a multi-column, UNIQUE constraint on the combination of multiple columns. (The primary key case is essentially identical.)

```
CREATE TABLE customer_location
(
cust_id                  int     NOT NULL,
cust_location_number     int     NOT NULL,
CONSTRAINT customer_location_unique UNIQUE
    (cust_id, cust_location_number)
)
GO

EXEC sp_helpconstraint customer_location
GO

>>>
Object Name
-----------------
customer_location


constraint_type  constraint_name                 constraint_keys
--------------   ------------------------------  ---------------
UNIQUE           customer_location_unique        cust_id,
(non-clustered)                                  cust_location_number
```

No foreign keys reference this table.

As noted earlier, a unique index is created to enforce either a PRIMARY KEY or a UNIQUE constraint. The name of the index is the same as the constraint name, whether the name was explicitly defined or system-generated. The index used to enforce the CUSTOMER_LOCATION_UNIQUE constraint in the above example is also named *customer_location_unique*. The index used to enforce the column-level, PRIMARY KEY constraint of the *customer* table in Example 1 is named *PK__customer__68E79C55*, which is the system-generated name of the constraint. You can use the *sp_helpindex* stored procedure to see information for all indexes of a given table. For example:

```
EXEC sp_helpindex customer

>>>
index_name                         index_description    index_keys
-----------------------------      ------------------   ----------
PK__customer__68E79C55             clustered, unique,   cust_id
                                   primary key
                                   located on default
```

FOREIGN KEY Constraints

One of the fundamental concepts of the relational model is the logical relationships between tables. In most databases, certain relationships must exist (that is, the data must have referential integrity) or else the data will be logically corrupt.

SQL Server automatically enforces referential integrity through the use of FOREIGN KEY constraints. This feature is sometimes referred to as *declarative referential integrity*, or DRI, to distinguish it from other features, such as triggers, that you can also use to enforce the existence of the relationships.

Referential Actions

The full ANSI SQL-92 standard contains the notion of the *referential action,* sometimes (incompletely) referred to as a *cascading delete*. SQL Server 7 doesn't provide this feature as part of FOREIGN KEY constraints, but this notion warrants some discussion here because the capability exists via triggers.

The idea behind referential actions is this: sometimes, instead of just preventing an update of data that would violate a foreign key reference, you might be able to perform an additional, compensating action that will still enable the constraint to be honored. For example, if you were to delete a *customer* table that has references to *orders*, you can have SQL Server automatically delete all those related *order* records (that is, cascade the delete to *orders*), in which case the constraint won't be violated and the *customer* table can be deleted. This feature is intended for both UPDATE and DELETE statements, and four possible actions are defined: NO ACTION, CASCADE, SET DEFAULT, and SET NULL.

- **NO ACTION**   The delete is prevented. This default mode, per the ANSI standard, occurs if no other action is specified. NO ACTION is often referred to as RESTRICT, but this usage is slightly incorrect in terms of how ANSI defines RESTRICT and NO ACTION. ANSI uses RESTRICT in DDL statements such as DROP TABLE, and it uses NO ACTION for FOREIGN KEY constraints. (The difference is subtle and unimportant. It's common to refer to the FOREIGN KEY constraint as having an action of RESTRICT.)

- **CASCADE**   A delete of all matching rows in the referencing table occurs.

- ■ **SET DEFAULT**   The delete is performed, and all foreign key values in the referencing table are set to a default value.

- ■ **SET NULL**   The delete is performed, and all foreign key values in the referencing table are set to NULL.

SQL Server 2000 allows you to specify either NO ACTION or CASCADE when you define your foreign key constraints. I'll give you some examples shortly. If you want to implement either SET DEFAULT or SET NULL, you can use a trigger. Implementing the SET NULL action is very straightforward, as you'll see in Chapter 12, which discusses triggers in detail. One reason it's so straightforward is that while a FOREIGN KEY requires any value in the referencing table to match a value in the referenced table, NULLs are not considered to be a value and having a NULL in the referencing table doesn't break any relationships. Implementing the SET DEFAULT action is just a little more involved. Suppose you want to remove a row from the referenced table and set the foreign key value in all referencing rows to −9999. If you want to maintain referential integrity, you have to have a "dummy" row in the referenced table with the primary key value of −9999.

Keep in mind that enforcing a foreign key implies that SQL Server will check data in both the referenced and the referencing tables. The referential actions just discussed apply only to actions that are taken on the referenced table. On the referencing table, the only action allowed is to not allow an update or an insert if the relationship will be broken as a result.

> **NOTE**   Because a constraint is checked before a trigger fires, you can't have both a FOREIGN KEY constraint to enforce the relationship when a new key is inserted into the referencing table and a trigger that performs an operation such as SET NULL on the referenced table. If you do have both, the constraint will fail and the statement will be aborted before the trigger to cascade the delete fires. If you want to allow the SET NULL action, you have to write two triggers. You have to have a trigger for delete and update on the referenced table to perform the SET NULL action and a trigger for insert and update on the referencing table that disallows new data that would violate the referential integrity.
>
> If you do decide to enforce your referential integrity with triggers, you might still want to declare the foreign key relationship largely for readability so that the relationship between the tables is clear. You can then use the NOCHECK option of ALTER TABLE to disable the constraint, and then the trigger will fire.
>
> This note is just referring to AFTER triggers. SQL Server 2000 provides an additional type of trigger called an INSTEAD OF trigger, which I'll talk about in Chapter 12.

Here's a simple way to declare a primary key/foreign key relationship:

```
CREATE TABLE customer
(
cust_id       int            NOT NULL  IDENTITY  PRIMARY KEY,
cust_name     varchar(50)    NOT NULL
)


CREATE TABLE orders
(
order_id      int      NOT NULL  IDENTITY  PRIMARY KEY,
cust_id       int      NOT NULL  REFERENCES customer(cust_id)
)
```

Since the default referential action is NO ACTION, the orders table could also have been written in this way:

```
CREATE TABLE orders
(
order_id      int      NOT NULL  IDENTITY  PRIMARY KEY,
cust_id       int      NOT NULL  REFERENCES customer(cust_id)
                       ON UPDATE NO ACTION ON DELETE NO ACTION
)
```

The *orders* table contains the column *cust_id*, which references the primary key of the *customer* table. An order (*order_id*) must not exist unless it relates to an existing customer (*cust_id*). With this definition, you can't delete a row from the *customer* table if a row that references it currently exists in the *orders* table, and you can't modify the *cust_id* column in a way that would destroy the relationship.

Note that a referential action can be specified for both DELETE and UPDATE operations on the referenced table, and the two operations can have different actions. For example, you can choose to CASCADE any updates to the *cust_id* in *customer* but not allow (NO ACTION) any deletes of referenced rows in *customer*.

Here's an example of adding a FOREIGN KEY constraint to the *orders* table that does just that. It cascades any updates to the *cust_id* in *customer* but does not allow any deletes of referenced rows in *customer*:

```
CREATE TABLE orders
(
order_id      int      NOT NULL  IDENTITY  PRIMARY KEY,
cust_id       int      NOT NULL  REFERENCES customer(cust_id)
                       ON UPDATE CASCADE ON DELETE NO ACTION
)
```

The previous examples show the syntax for a single-column constraint—both the primary key and foreign key are single columns. This syntax uses the keyword REFERENCES, and the term "foreign key" is implied but not explicitly stated. The name of the FOREIGN KEY constraint is generated internally, following the same general form described earlier for PRIMARY KEY and UNIQUE constraints. Here's a portion of the output of *sp_helpconstraint* for both the *customer* and *orders* tables. (The tables were created in the *pubs* sample database.)

```
EXEC sp_helpconstraint customer
>>>

Object Name
------------
customer

constraint_type     constraint_name              constraint_keys
---------------     ----------------------       ---------------
PRIMARY KEY         PK__customer__07F6335A       cust_id
(clustered)

Table is referenced by
----------------------------------------------
pubs.dbo.orders: FK__orders__cust_id__0AD2A005


EXEC sp_helpconstraint orders
>>>

Object Name
-----------
orders


constraint_type     constraint_name              delete_    update_
                                                 action     action
---------------     ----------------------       ---------  ------
FOREIGN KEY         FK__orders__cust_id__0AD2A005 no action no action
PRIMARY KEY         PK__orders__09DE7BCC
(clustered)


constraint_keys

---------------
cust_id REFERENCES pubs.dbo.customer(cust_id)
order_id



No foreign keys reference this table.
```

Constraints defined inline with the column declaration can reference only a single column. This is also true for PRIMARY KEY and UNIQUE constraints. You must declare a multi-column constraint as a separate table element. The following example shows a multi-column FOREIGN KEY constraint:

```
CREATE TABLE customer
(
cust_id          int           NOT NULL,
location_num     smallint      NULL,
cust_name        varchar(50)   NOT NULL,
CONSTRAINT CUSTOMER_UNQ UNIQUE CLUSTERED (location_num, cust_id)
)

CREATE TABLE orders
(
order_id    int       NOT NULL  IDENTITY CONSTRAINT ORDER_PK
                                 PRIMARY KEY NONCLUSTERED,
cust_num    int       NOT NULL,
cust_loc    smallint  NULL,
CONSTRAINT FK_ORDER_CUSTOMER FOREIGN KEY (cust_loc, cust_num)
REFERENCES customer (location_num, cust_id)
)
GO

EXEC sp_helpconstraint customer
EXEC sp_helpconstraint orders
GO

>>>
Object Name
-----------
customer


constraint_type        constraint_name         constraint_keys
------------------     -----------------       --------------------
UNIQUE (clustered)     CUSTOMER_UNQ            location_num, cust_id



Table is referenced by
---------------------------
pubs.dbo.orders: FK_ORDER_CUSTOMER



Object Name
-----------
orders
```

(continued)

```
constraint_type        constraint_name       constraint_keys
----------------       ----------------      ------------------
FOREIGN KEY            FK_ORDER_CUSTOMER     cust_loc, cust_num
                                             REFERENCES pubs.dbo.customer
                                             (location_num, cust_id)


PRIMARY KEY            ORDER_PK                order_id
(non-clustered)
No foreign keys reference this table.
```

The preceding example also shows the following variations on how you can create constraints:

- You can use a FOREIGN KEY constraint to reference a UNIQUE constraint (an alternate key) instead of a PRIMARY KEY constraint. (Note, however, that referencing a PRIMARY KEY is much more typical and is generally better practice.)

- You don't have to use identical column names in tables involved in a foreign key reference, but doing so is often good practice. The *cust_id* and *location_num* column names are defined in the *customer* table. The *orders* table, which references the *customer* table, uses the names *cust_num* and *cust_loc*.

- The datatypes of the related columns must be identical, except for nullability and variable-length attributes. (For example, a column of *char(10) NOT NULL* can reference one of *varchar(10) NULL*, but it can't reference a column of *char(12) NOT NULL*. A column of type *smallint* can't reference a column of type *int*.) Notice in the preceding example that *cust_id* and *cust_num* are both *int NOT NULL* and that *location_num* and *cust_loc* are both *smallint NULL*.

Unlike a PRIMARY KEY or UNIQUE constraint, an index isn't automatically built for the column or columns declared as FOREIGN KEY. However, in many cases, you'll want to build indexes on these columns because they're often used for joining to other tables. To enforce foreign key relationships, SQL Server must add additional steps to the execution plan of every insert, delete, and update (if the update affects columns that are part of the relationship) that affects either the table referencing another table or the table being referenced. The execution plan, determined by the SQL Server optimizer, is simply the collection of steps that carries out the operation. (In Chapter 16, you'll see the actual execution plan by using the SHOWPLAN options.)

If no FOREIGN KEY constraints exist, a statement specifying the update of a single row of the *orders* table might have an execution plan such as the following:

1. Find a qualifying *order* record using a clustered index.

2. Update the *order* record.

When a FOREIGN KEY constraint exists on the *orders* table, the same operation has more steps in the execution plan:

1. Check for the existence of a related record in the *customer* table (based on the updated *order* record) using a clustered index.

2. If no related record is found, raise an exception and terminate operation.

3. Find a qualifying *order* record using a clustered index.

4. Update the *order* record.

The execution plan is more complex if the *orders* table has many FOREIGN KEY constraints declared. Internally, a simple update or insert operation might no longer be possible. Any such operation requires checking many other tables for matching entries. Because a seemingly simple operation might require checking as many as 253 other tables (see the next paragraph) and possibly creating multiple worktables, the operation might be much more complicated than it looks and much slower than expected.

A table can have a maximum of 253 FOREIGN KEY references. This limit is derived from the internal limit of 256 tables in a single query. In practice, an operation on a table with 253 or fewer FOREIGN KEY constraints might still fail with an error because of the 256-table query limit if worktables you require for the operation.

A database designed for excellent performance doesn't reach anything close to this limit of 253 FOREIGN KEY references. For best performance results, use FOREIGN KEY constraints judiciously. Some sites unnecessarily use too many FOREIGN KEY constraints because the constraints they declare are logically redundant. Take the following example. The *orders* table declares a FOREIGN KEY constraint to both the *master_customer* and *customer_location* tables:

```
CREATE TABLE master_customer
(
cust_id       int            NOT NULL   IDENTITY   PRIMARY KEY,
cust_name     varchar(50)    NOT NULL
)

CREATE TABLE customer_location
(
cust_id     int            NOT NULL,
cust_loc    smallint       NOT NULL,
CONSTRAINT PK_CUSTOMER_LOCATION PRIMARY KEY (cust_id,cust_loc),
CONSTRAINT FK_CUSTOMER_LOCATION FOREIGN KEY (cust_id)
    REFERENCES master_customer (cust_id)
)
```

(continued)

```
CREATE TABLE orders
(
order_id    int             NOT NULL  IDENTITY  PRIMARY KEY,
cust_id     int             NOT NULL,
cust_loc    smallint        NOT NULL,
CONSTRAINT FK_ORDER_MASTER_CUST FOREIGN KEY (cust_id)
    REFERENCES master_customer (cust_id),
CONSTRAINT FK_ORDER_CUST_LOC FOREIGN KEY (cust_id, cust_loc)
    REFERENCES customer_location (cust_id, cust_loc)
)
```

Although logically the relationship between the *orders* and *master_customer* tables exists, the relationship is redundant to and subsumed by the fact that *orders* is related to *customer_location*, which has its own FOREIGN KEY constraint to *master_customer*. Declaring a foreign key for *master_customer* adds unnecessary overhead without adding any further integrity protection.

> **NOTE** In the case just described, declaring a foreign key improves the readability of the table definition, but you can achieve the same result by simply adding comments to the CREATE TABLE command. It's perfectly legal to add a comment practically anywhere—even in the middle of a CREATE TABLE statement. A more subtle way to achieve this result is to declare the constraint so that it appears in *sp_helpconstraint* and in the system catalogs but then disable the constraint by using the ALTER TABLE NOCHECK option. Because the constraint will then be unenforced, an additional table isn't added to the execution plan.

The CREATE TABLE statement shown in the following example for the *orders* table omits the redundant foreign key and, for illustrative purposes, includes a comment. Despite the lack of a FOREIGN KEY constraint in the *master_customer* table, you still can't insert a *cust_id* that doesn't exist in the *master_customer* table because the reference to the *customer_location* table will prevent it.

```
CREATE TABLE orders
(
order_id    int             NOT NULL  IDENTITY  PRIMARY KEY,
cust_id     int             NOT NULL,
cust_loc    smallint        NOT NULL,
-- Implied Foreign Key Reference of:
-- (cust_id) REFERENCES master_customer (cust_id)
CONSTRAINT FK_ORDER_CUST_LOC FOREIGN KEY (cust_id, cust_loc)
    REFERENCES customer_location (cust_id, cust_loc)
)
```

Note that the table on which the foreign key is declared (the referencing table, which in this example is *orders*) isn't the only table that requires additional execution steps. When being updated, the table being referenced (in this case *customer_location*) must also have additional steps in its execution plan to ensure that an update of the columns being referenced won't break a relationship and create an orphan entry in the *orders* table. Without making any changes directly to the *customer_location* table, you can see a significant decrease in update or delete performance because of foreign key references added to other tables.

Practical Considerations for FOREIGN KEY Constraints

When using constraints, you should consider triggers, performance, and indexing. Let's take a look at the ramifications of each.

Triggers   I won't discuss triggers in detail until Chapter 12, but for now, you should simply note that constraints are enforced before an AFTER triggered action is performed. If the constraint is violated, the statement will abort before the trigger fires.

> **NOTE**   The owner of a table isn't allowed to declare a foreign key reference to another table unless the owner of the other table has granted REFERENCES permission to the first table owner. Even if the owner of the first table is allowed to select from the table to be referenced, that owner must have REFERENCES permission. This prevents another user from changing the performance of operations on your table without your knowledge or consent. You can grant any user REFERENCES permission even if you don't also grant SELECT permission, and vice-versa. The only exception is that the DBA, or any user who is a member of the *db_owner* role, has full default permissions on all objects in the database.

Performance   When deciding on the use of foreign key relationships, you must weigh the protection provided against the corresponding performance overhead. Be careful not to add constraints that form logically redundant relationships. Excessive use of FOREIGN KEY constraints can severely degrade the performance of seemingly simple operations.

Indexing   The columns specified in FOREIGN KEY constraints are often strong candidates for index creation. You should build the index with the same key order used in the PRIMARY KEY or UNIQUE constraint of the table that it references so that joins can be performed efficiently. Also be aware that a foreign key is often a subset of the table's primary key. In the *customer_location* table used in the preceding two examples, *cust_id* is part of the primary key as well as a foreign key in its own right. Given that *cust_id* is part of a primary key, it's already part of an index. In this example, *cust_id* is the lead column of the index, and building a separate index on it alone probably isn't warranted. However, if *cust_id* is *not* the lead column of the index B-tree, it might make sense to build an index on it.

Constraint-Checking Solutions

Sometimes two tables reference one another, which creates a bootstrap problem. Suppose *Table1* has a foreign key reference to *Table2*, but *Table2* has a foreign key reference to *Table1*. Even before either table contains any data, you'll be prevented from inserting a row into *Table1* because the reference to *Table2* will fail. Similarly, you can't insert a row into *Table2* because the reference to *Table1* will fail.

ANSI SQL has a solution: *deferred constraints,* in which you can instruct the system to postpone constraint checking until the entire transaction is committed. Using this elegant remedy puts both INSERT statements into a single transaction that results in the two tables having correct references by the time COMMIT occurs. Unfortunately, no mainstream product currently provides the deferred option for constraints. The deferred option is part of the complete SQL-92 specification, which no product has yet fully implemented.

SQL Server 2000 provides *immediate* constraint checking; it has no deferred option. SQL Server offers three options for dealing with constraint checking: it allows you to add constraints after adding data, it lets you temporarily disable checking of foreign key references, and it allows you to use the *bcp* (bulk copy) program or BULK INSERT command to initially load data and avoid checking FOREIGN KEY constraints. (You can override this default option with *bcp* or the BULK INSERT command and force FOREIGN KEY constraints to be validated.) To add constraints after adding data, don't create constraints via the CREATE TABLE command. After adding the initial data, you can add constraints by using the ALTER TABLE command.

With the second option, the table owner can temporarily disable checking of foreign key references by using the ALTER TABLE *table* NOCHECK CONSTRAINT statement. Once data exists, you can reestablish the FOREIGN KEY constraint by using ALTER TABLE *table* CHECK CONSTRAINT. Note that when an existing constraint is reenabled using this method, SQL Server doesn't automatically check to see that all rows still satisfy the constraint. To do this, you can simply issue a *dummy update* by setting a column to itself for all rows, determining whether any constraint violations are raised, and then fixing them. (For example, you can issue UPDATE orders SET cust_id = cust_id.)

Finally you can use the *bcp* program or the BULK INSERT command to initially load data. The BULK INSERT command and the *bcp* program don't check any FOREIGN KEY constraints by default. You can use the CHECK_CONSTRAINTS option to override this behavior. BULK INSERT and *bcp* are faster than regular INSERT commands because they usually bypass normal integrity checks and most logging.

When you use ALTER TABLE to add (instead of reenable) a new FOREIGN KEY constraint for a table in which data already exists, the existing data is checked by default. If constraint violations occur, the constraint isn't added. With large tables, such a check can be quite time-consuming. You do have an alternative—you can add a

FOREIGN KEY constraint and omit the check. To do this, you specify the WITH NOCHECK option with ALTER TABLE. All subsequent operations will be checked, but existing data won't be checked. As in the case of reenabling a constraint, you can then perform a dummy update to flag any violations in the existing data. If you use this option, you should do the dummy update as soon as possible to ensure that all the data is clean. Otherwise, your users might see constraint error messages when they perform update operations on the preexisting data even if they haven't changed any values.

Restrictions on Dropping Tables

If you're dropping tables, you must drop all the referencing tables or drop the referencing FOREIGN KEY constraints before dropping the referenced table. For example, in the preceding example's *orders*, *customer_location*, and *master_customer* tables, the following sequence of DROP statements fails because a table being dropped is referenced by a table that still exists—that is, *customer_location* can't be dropped because the *orders* table references it, and *orders* isn't dropped until later:

```
DROP TABLE customer_location
DROP TABLE master_customer
DROP TABLE orders
```

Changing the sequence to the following works fine because *orders* is dropped first:

```
DROP TABLE orders
DROP TABLE customer_location
DROP TABLE master_customer
```

When two tables reference each other, you must first drop the constraints or set them to NOCHECK (both operations use ALTER TABLE) before the tables can be dropped. Similarly, a table that's being referenced can't be part of a TRUNCATE TABLE command. You must drop or disable the constraint or else simply drop and rebuild the table.

Self-Referencing Tables

A table can be self-referencing—that is, the foreign key can reference one or more columns in the same table. The following example shows an employee table in which a column for managers references another *employee* entry:

```
CREATE TABLE employee
(
emp_id      int           NOT NULL PRIMARY KEY,
emp_name    varchar(30)   NOT NULL,
mgr_id      int           NOT NULL REFERENCES employee(emp_id)
)
```

The *employee* table is a perfectly reasonable table. It illustrates most of the issues I've discussed. However, in this case, a single INSERT command that satisfies the reference is legal. For example, if the CEO of the company has an *emp_id* of 1 and is also his own manager, the following INSERT will be allowed and can be a useful way to insert the first row in a self-referencing table:

```
INSERT employee VALUES (1, 'Chris Smith', 1)
```

Although SQL Server doesn't currently provide a deferred option for constraints, self-referencing tables add a twist that sometimes makes SQL Server use deferred operations internally. Consider the case of a nonqualified DELETE statement that deletes many rows in the table. After all rows are ultimately deleted, you can assume that no constraint violation will occur. However, violations might occur *during* the DELETE operation because some of the remaining referencing rows might be orphaned before they are actually deleted. SQL Server handles such *interim violations* automatically and without any user intervention. As long as the self-referencing constraints are valid at the end of the data modification statement, no errors are raised during processing.

To gracefully handle these interim violations, however, additional processing and worktables are required to hold the work-in-progress. This adds substantial overhead and can also limit the actual number of foreign keys that can be used. An UPDATE statement can also cause an interim violation. For example, if all employee numbers are to be changed by multiplying each by 1000, the following UPDATE statement would require worktables to avoid the possibility of raising an error on an interim violation:

```
UPDATE employee SET emp_id=emp_id * 1000, mgr_id=mgr_id * 1000
```

The additional worktables and the processing needed to handle the worktables are made part of the execution plan. Therefore, if the optimizer sees that a data modification statement *could* cause an interim violation, the additional temporary worktables will be created even if no such interim violations ever actually occur. These extra steps are needed only in the following situations:

- A table is self-referencing (it has a FOREIGN KEY constraint that refers back to itself).

- A single data modification statement (UPDATE, DELETE, or INSERT based on a SELECT) is performed and can affect more than one row. (The optimizer can't determine *a priori,* based on the WHERE clause and unique indexes, whether more than one row could be affected.) Multiple data modification statements within the transaction don't apply—this condition must be a single statement that affects multiple rows.

■ Both the referencing and referenced columns are affected (which is always the case for DELETE and INSERT operations, but might or might not be the case for UPDATE).

If a data modification statement in your application meets the preceding criteria, you can be sure that SQL Server is automatically using a limited and special-purpose form of deferred constraints to protect against interim violations.

CHECK Constraints

Enforcing *domain integrity* (that is, ensuring that only entries of expected types, values, or ranges can exist for a given column) is also important. SQL Server provides two ways to enforce domain integrity: CHECK constraints and rules. CHECK constraints allow you to define an expression for a table that must not evaluate to FALSE for a data modification statement to succeed. (Note that I didn't say that the constraint must evaluate to TRUE. The constraint will allow the row if it evaluates to TRUE or to unknown. The constraint evaluates to unknown when NULL values are present, and this introduces three-value logic. The issues of NULLs and three-value logic are discussed in depth in Chapter 7.) SQL Server provides a similar mechanism to CHECK constraints, called *rules*, which are provided basically for backward-compatibility reasons. Rules perform almost the same function as CHECK constraints, but they use different syntax and have fewer capabilities. Rules have existed in SQL Server since its initial release in 1989, well before CHECK constraints, which are part of the ANSI SQL-92 standard and were added in SQL Server 6 in 1995.

CHECK constraints make a table's definition more readable by including the domain checks in the DDL. Rules have a potential advantage in that they can be defined once and then bound to multiple columns and tables (using *sp_bindrule* each time), while you must respecify a CHECK constraint for each column and table. But the extra binding step can also be a hassle, so this capability for rules is beneficial only if a rule will be used in many places. Although performance between the two approaches is identical, CHECK constraints are generally preferred over rules because they're a direct part of the table's DDL, they're ANSI-standard SQL, they provide a few more capabilities than rules (such as the ability to reference other columns in the same row or to call a system function), and perhaps most important, they're more likely than rules to be further enhanced in future releases of SQL Server. For these reasons, I'm not going to talk about rules any more.

CHECK constraints add additional steps to the execution plan to ensure that the expression doesn't evaluate to FALSE (which would result in the operation being aborted). Although steps are added to the execution plan for data modifications, these are typically much less expensive than the extra steps discussed earlier for FOREIGN KEY constraints. For foreign key checking, another table must be searched, requiring additional I/O. CHECK constraints deal only with some logical expression for the specific row already being operated on, so no additional I/O is required. Because additional processing cycles are used to evaluate the expressions, the system requires more CPU use. But if there's plenty of CPU power to spare, the effect might well be negligible. You can watch this by using Performance Monitor.

As with other constraint types, you can declare CHECK constraints on a single column or on multiple columns. You must declare a CHECK constraint that refers to more than one column as a separate element in the CREATE TABLE statement. Only single-column CHECK constraints can be defined right along with the column definition, and only one CHECK constraint can be defined with the column. All other CHECK constraints have to be defined as separate elements. However, keep in mind that one constraint can have multiple logical expressions that can be AND'ed or OR'ed together.

Some CHECK constraint features have often been underutilized by SQL Server database designers, including the ability to reference other columns in the same row, use system and niladic functions (which are evaluated at runtime), use combinations of expressions combined with AND or OR, and use CASE expressions. The following example shows a table with multiple CHECK constraints (as well as a PRIMARY KEY constraint and a FOREIGN KEY constraint) and showcases some of these features:

```
CREATE TABLE employee
(
emp_id          int         NOT NULL PRIMARY KEY
                            CHECK (emp_id BETWEEN 0 AND 1000),

emp_name        varchar(30) NOT NULL CONSTRAINT no_nums
                            CHECK (emp_name NOT LIKE '%[0-9]%'),

mgr_id          int         NOT NULL REFERENCES employee(emp_id),

entered_date    datetime    NULL CHECK (entered_date >=
                                CURRENT_TIMESTAMP),

entered_by      int         CHECK (entered_by IS NOT NULL),
                            CONSTRAINT valid_entered_by CHECK
                                (entered_by = SUSER_ID(NULL) AND
                                entered_by <> emp_id),

CONSTRAINT valid_mgr CHECK (mgr_id <> emp_id OR emp_id=1),

CONSTRAINT end_of_month CHECK (DATEPART(DAY, GETDATE()) < 28)
)
GO

EXEC sp_helpconstraint employee
GO
>>>>
```

```
Object Name
---------------
employee
```

constraint_type	constraint_name	constraint_keys
CHECK on column emp_id	CK__employee__emp_id__2C3393D0	([emp_id] >= 0 [emp_id] <= 1000)
CHECK on column entered_by	CK__employee__entered_by__300424B4	(((not([entered_by] is null))))
CHECK on column entered_date	CK__employee__entered_date__2F10007B	([entered_date] >= getdate())
CHECK Table Level	end_of_month	(datepart(day, getdate()) < 28)
FOREIGN KEY	FK__employee__mgr_id__2E1BDC42	mgr_id
CHECK on column emp_name	no_nums	([emp_name] not like '%[0-9]%')
PRIMARY KEY (clustered)	PK__employee__2B3F6F97	emp_id
CHECK Table Level	valid_entered_by	([entered_by] = suser_id(null) and [entered_by] <> [emp_id])
CHECK Table Level	valid_mgr	([mgr_id] <> [emp_id] or [emp_id] = 1)

```
Table is referenced by
-----------------------------------
pubs.dbo.employee: FK__employee__mgr_id__2E1BDC42
```

This example illustrates the following points:

- CHECK constraints can be expressed at the column level with abbreviated syntax (leaving naming to SQL Server), such as the check on *entered_date*; at the column level with an explicit name, such as the NO_NUMS constraint on *emp_name*; or as a table-level constraint, such as the VALID_MGR constraint.

- CHECK constraints can use regular expressions—for example, NO_NUMS ensures that a digit can never be entered as a character in a person's name.

- Expressions can be AND'ed and OR'ed together to represent more complex situations—for example, VALID_MGR. However, SQL Server won't check for logical correctness at the time a constraint is added to the table. Suppose you want to restrict the values in a *department_id* column to either negative numbers or values greater than 100. (Perhaps numbers between 0 and 100 are reserved.) You can add this column and constraint to the table using ALTER TABLE.

  ```
  ALTER TABLE employee
  add department_no int CHECK
      (department_no < 0 AND department_no > 100)
  ```

  However, once the preceding command executes successfully and the new column and constraint are added to the table, you can't add another row to the table. I accidentally typed *AND* in the ALTER TABLE statement instead of *OR*, but that isn't considered an illegal CHECK constraint. Each time I try to insert a row, SQL Server will try to validate that the value in the *department_no* column is both less than 0 and more than 100! Any value for *department_no* that doesn't meet that requirement will cause the insert to fail. It could take a long time to come up with a value to satisfy this constraint. In this case, I'd have to drop the constraint and add a new one with the correct definition before I could insert any rows.

- Table-level CHECK constraints can refer to more than one column in the same row. For example, VALID_MGR means that no employee can be his own boss, except employee number 1, who is assumed to be the CEO. SQL Server currently has no provision that allows you to check a value from another row or from a different table.

- You can make a CHECK constraint prevent NULL values—for example, CHECK (*entered_by* IS NOT NULL). Generally, you simply declare the column NOT NULL.

- A NULL column might make the expression logically unknown. For example, a NULL value for *entered_date* gives CHECK *entered_date* >= CURRENT_TIMESTAMP an unknown value. This doesn't reject the row, however. The constraint rejects the row only if the expression is clearly false, even if it isn't necessarily true.

- You can use system functions, such as GETDATE, APP_NAME, DATALENGTH, and SUSER_ID, as well as niladic functions, such as SYSTEM_USER, CURRENT_TIMESTAMP, and USER, in CHECK constraints. This subtle feature is powerful and can be useful, for example, to ensure that a user can change only records that she has entered by comparing *entered_by* to the user's system ID, as generated by SUSER_ID (or by comparing *emp_name* to SYSTEM_USER). Note that niladic functions such as CURRENT_TIMESTAMP are provided for ANSI SQL conformance and simply map to an underlying SQL Server function, in this case GETDATE. So while the DDL to create the constraint on *entered_date* uses CURRENT_TIMESTAMP, *sp_helpconstraint* shows it as GETDATE, which is the underlying function. Either expression is valid, and they are equivalent in the CHECK constraint. The VALID_ENTERED_BY constraint ensures that the *entered_by* column can be set only to the currently connected user's ID, and it ensures that users can't update their own records.

- A constraint defined as a separate table element can call a system function without referencing a column in the table. In the example preceding this list, the END_OF_MONTH CHECK constraint calls two date functions, DATEPART and GETDATE, to ensure that updates can't be made after day 27 of the month (which is when the business's payroll is assumed to be processed). The constraint never references a column in the table. Similarly, a CHECK constraint might call the APP_NAME function to ensure that updates can be made only from an application of a certain name, instead of from an ad hoc tool such as SQL Query Analyzer.

As with FOREIGN KEY constraints, you can add or drop CHECK constraints by using ALTER TABLE. When adding a constraint, by default the existing data is checked for compliance; you can override this default by using the WITH NOCHECK syntax. You can later do a dummy update to check for any violations. The table or database owner can also temporarily disable CHECK constraints by using NOCHECK in the ALTER TABLE statement.

Default Constraints

A default allows you to specify a constant value, NULL, or the run-time value of a system function if no known value exists or if the column is missing in an INSERT statement. Although you could argue that a default isn't truly a constraint (because a default doesn't enforce anything), you can create defaults in a CREATE TABLE statement using the CONSTRAINT keyword; therefore, I'll refer to defaults as constraints. Defaults add little overhead, and you can use them liberally without too much concern about performance degradation.

SQL Server provides two ways of creating defaults. First, you can create a default (CREATE DEFAULT) and then bind the default to a column (*sp_bindefault*). This has been the case since the original SQL Server release. Second, you can use default constraints. These were introduced in 1995 with SQL Server 6 as part of the CREATE TABLE and ALTER TABLE statements, and they're based on the ANSI SQL standard (which includes such niceties as being able to use system functions). Using defaults is pretty intuitive. The type of default you use is a matter of preference; both perform the same function internally. Future enhancements are likely to be made to the ANSI-style implementation. Having the default within the table DDL seems a cleaner approach. I recommend that you use defaults within CREATE TABLE and ALTER TABLE rather than within CREATE DEFAULT, so I'll focus on that style here.

Here's the example from the previous CHECK constraint discussion, now modified to include several defaults:

```
CREATE TABLE employee
(
emp_id        int          NOT NULL  PRIMARY KEY  DEFAULT 1000
                           CHECK (emp_id BETWEEN 0 AND 1000),

emp_name      varchar(30)  NULL  DEFAULT NULL  CONSTRAINT no_nums
                           CHECK (emp_name NOT LIKE '%[0-9]%'),

mgr_id        int          NOT NULL  DEFAULT (1)  REFERENCES
                           employee(emp_id),

entered_date  datetime     NOT NULL  CHECK (entered_date >=
                           CONVERT(char(10), CURRENT_TIMESTAMP, 102))
                           CONSTRAINT def_today DEFAULT
                           (CONVERT(char(10), GETDATE(), 102)),

entered_by    int          NOT NULL  DEFAULT SUSER_ID()
                           CHECK (entered_by IS NOT NULL),

CONSTRAINT valid_entered_by CHECK (entered_by=SUSER_ID() AND
entered_by <> emp_id),
```

```
CONSTRAINT valid_mgr CHECK (mgr_id <> emp_id OR emp_id=1),

CONSTRAINT end_of_month CHECK (DATEPART(DAY, GETDATE()) < 28)
)
GO


EXEC sp_helpconstraint employee
GO

>>>


Object Name
---------------
employee
```

constraint_type	constraint_name	constraint_keys
CHECK on column emp_id	CK__employee__emp_id__2C3393D0	([emp_id] >= 0 [emp_id] <= 1000)
CHECK on column entered_by	CK__employee__entered_by__300424B4	(((not([entered_by] is null))))
DEFAULT on column entered_date	def_today	convert(char(10), getdate(), 102))
DEFAULT on column emp_id	DF__employee__emp_id__35BCFE0A	(1000)
DEFAULT on column emp_name	DF__employee__emp_name__37A5467C	(null)
DEFAULT on column entered_by	DF__employee__entered_by__3D5E1FD2	(suser_id())
DEFAULT on column mgr_id	DF__employee__mgr_id__398D8EEE	(1)
CHECK on column entered_date	CK__employee__entered_date__2F10007B	([entered_date] >= getdate())

(continued)

CHECK Table Level	end_of_month	(datepart(day, getdate()) < 28)
FOREIGN KEY	FK__employee__mgr_id__2E1BDC42	mgr_id
CHECK on column emp_name	no_nums	([emp_name] not like '%[0-9]%')
PRIMARY KEY (clustered)	PK__employee__2B3F6F97	emp_id
CHECK Table Level	valid_entered_by	([entered_by] = suser_id(null) and [entered_by] <> [emp_id])
CHECK Table Level	valid_mgr	([mgr_id] <> [emp_id] or [emp_id] = 1)

```
Table is referenced by
-----------------------------------
pubs.dbo.employee: FK__employee__mgr_id__2E1BDC42
```

The preceding code demonstrates the following about defaults:

- A default constraint is always a single-column constraint because it pertains only to one column and can be defined only along with the column definition; you cannot define a default constraint as a separate table element. You can use the abbreviated syntax that omits the keyword CONSTRAINT and the specified name, letting SQL Server generate the name, or you can specify the name by using the more verbose CONSTRAINT *name* DEFAULT syntax.

- A default value can clash with a CHECK constraint. This problem appears only at runtime, not when you create the table or when you add the default using ALTER TABLE. For example, a column with a default of 0 and a CHECK constraint that states that the value must be greater than 0 can never insert or update the default value.

■ Although you can assign a default to a column that has a PRIMARY KEY or a UNIQUE constraint, it doesn't make much sense to do so. Such columns must have unique values, so only one row could exist with the default value in that column. The preceding example sets a DEFAULT on a primary key column for illustration, but in general, this practice is unwise.

■ You can write a constant value within parentheses, as in DEFAULT (1), or without them, as in DEFAULT 1. A character or date constant must be enclosed in either single or double quotation marks.

■ One tricky concept is knowing when a NULL is inserted into a column as opposed to a default value. A column declared NOT NULL with a default defined uses the default only under one of the following conditions:

❑ The INSERT statement specifies its column list and omits the column with the default.

❑ The INSERT statement specifies the keyword DEFAULT in the values list (whether the column is explicitly specified as part of the column list or implicitly specified in the values list and the column list is omitted, meaning "All columns in the order in which they were created"). If the values list explicitly specifies NULL, an error is raised and the statement fails; the default value isn't used. If the INSERT statement omits the column entirely, the default is used and no error occurs. (This behavior is in accordance with ANSI SQL.) The keyword DEFAULT can be used in the values list, and this is the only way the default value will be used if a NOT NULL column is specified in the column list of an INSERT statement (either, as in the following example, by omitting the column list—which means all columns—or by explicitly including the NOT NULL column in the columns list).

```
INSERT EMPLOYEE VALUES (1, 'The Big Guy', 1, DEFAULT, DEFAULT)
```

Table 6-10 summarizes the behavior of INSERT statements based on whether a column is declared NULL or NOT NULL and whether it has a default specified. It shows the result for the column for three cases:

■ Omitting the column entirely (no entry)

■ Having the INSERT statement use NULL in the values list

■ Specifying the column and using DEFAULT in the values list

	No Entry		Enter NULL		Enter DEFAULT	
	No Default	Default	No Default	Default	No Default	Default
NULL	NULL	default	NULL	NULL	NULL	default
NOT NULL	error	default	error	error	error	default

Table 6-10. *INSERT behavior with defaults.*

Declaring a default on a column that has the IDENTITY property doesn't make sense, and SQL Server will raise an error if you try it. The IDENTITY property acts as a default for the column. But the DEFAULT keyword cannot be used as a placeholder for an identity column in the values list of an INSERT statement. You can use a special form of INSERT statement if a table has a default value for every column (an identity column does meet this criteria) or allows NULL. The following statement uses the DEFAULT VALUES clause instead of a column list and values list:

```
INSERT employee DEFAULT VALUES
```

> **TIP**   You can generate some test data by putting the IDENTITY property on a primary key column and declaring default values for all other columns and then repeatedly issuing an INSERT statement of this form within a Transact-SQL loop.

More About Constraints

This section offers some advice on working with constraints. I'll look at constraint names and system catalog entries, the *status* field, constraint failures and multiple-row data modifications, and integrity checks.

Constraint Names and System Catalog Entries

Earlier in this chapter, you learned about the cryptic-looking constraint names that SQL Server generates. Now I'll explain the naming. Consider again the following simple CREATE TABLE statement:

```
CREATE TABLE customer
(
cust_id      int           IDENTITY   NOT NULL   PRIMARY KEY,
cust_name    varchar(30) NOT NULL
)
```

The constraint produced from this simple statement bears the nonintuitive name *PK__customer__68E79C55*. All types of single-column constraints use this naming scheme, which I'll explain shortly. The advantage of explicitly naming your constraint rather than using the system-generated name is greater clarity. The constraint name is used in the error message for any constraint violation, so creating a name such as CUSTOMER_PK probably makes more sense to users than a name such as

PK__customer__cust_i__0677FF3C. You should choose your own constraint names if such error messages are visible to your users. The first two characters (PK) show the constraint type—PK for PRIMARY KEY, UQ for UNIQUE, FK for FOREIGN KEY, and DF for DEFAULT. Next are two underscore characters, which are used as a separator. (You might be tempted to use one underscore to conserve characters and to avoid having to truncate as much. However, it's common to use a single underscore in a table name or a column name, both of which appear in the constraint name. Using two underscore characters distinguishes the kind of a name it is and where the separation occurs.)

Next comes the table name (*customer*), which is limited to 116 characters for a PRIMARY KEY constraint and slightly fewer characters for all other constraint names. For all constraints other than PRIMARY KEY, there are two more underscore characters for separation followed by the next sequence of characters, which is the column name. The column name is truncated to five characters if necessary. If the column name has fewer than five characters in it, the length of the table name portion can be slightly longer.

And finally, the hexadecimal representation of the object ID for the constraint (*68E79C55*) comes after another separator. (This value is used as the *id* column of the *sysobjects* system table and the *constid* column of the *sysconstraints* system table.) Object names are limited to 128 characters in SQL Server 2000, so the total length of all portions of the constraint name must also be less than or equal to 128.

Note the queries and output using this value that are shown in Figure 6-14.

```
Query:
SELECT OBJECT_NAME(0x68E79C55), OBJECT_ID('customer')

Results:
PK_customer_68E79C55      1463580359


Query:
SELECT * FROM sysconstraints WHERE constid = 0x68E79C55

Results:
constid       id             collid  sparel  status  actions  error
-----------   -----------    ------- ------- ------- -------- ------
1760009301    1493580359     0       0       133665  4096     0


Query:
SELECT name, id, type FROM sysobjects WHERE id = 0x59FA5E80

Results:
name                       id             type
---------------------      -----------    -----
PK_CUSTOMER_59FA5E80       1509580416     K
```

Figure 6-14. *Querying the system tables using the hexadecimal ID value.*

TIP The hexadecimal value 0x68E79C55 is equal to the decimal value 1760009301, which is the value of *constid* in *sysconstraints* and of *id* in *sysobjects*.

These sample queries of system tables show the following:

- **A constraint is an object.** A constraint has an entry in the *sysobjects* table in the *xtype* column of C, D, F, PK, or UQ for CHECK, DEFAULT, FOREIGN KEY, PRIMARY KEY, and UNIQUE, respectively.

- *Sysconstraints* **relates to** *sysobjects*. The *sysconstraints* table is just a view of the *sysobjects* system table. The *constid* column in the view is the object ID of the constraint, and the *id* column of *sysconstraints* is the object ID of the base table on which the constraint is declared.

- *Colid* **values in** *sysconstraints* **indicate the column the constraint applies to.** If the constraint is a column-level CHECK, FOREIGN KEY, or DEFAULT constraint, *sysconstraints.colid* has the column ID of the column. This *colid* in *sysconstraints* is related to the *colid* of *syscolumns* for the base table represented by *id*. A table-level constraint or any PRIMARY KEY/UNIQUE constraint (even if column level) always has 0 in this column.

TIP To see the names and order of the columns in a PRIMARY KEY or UNIQUE constraint, you can query the *sysindexes* and *syscolumns* tables for the index being used to enforce the constraint. The name of the constraint and that of the index enforcing the constraint are the same, whether the name was user-specified or system-generated. The columns in the index key are somewhat cryptically encoded in the *keys1* and *keys2* fields of *sysindexes*. The easiest way to decode these values is to simply use the *sp_helpindex* system stored procedure; alternatively, you can use the code of that procedure as a template if you need to decode them in your own procedure.

Decoding the *status* Field

The *status* field of the *sysconstraints* view is a pseudo–bit-mask field packed with information. We could also call it a bitmap, because each bit has a particular meaning. If you know how to crack this column, you can essentially write your own *sp_helpconstraint*-like procedure. Note that the documentation is incomplete regarding the values of this column. One way to start decoding this column is to look at the definition of the *sysconstraints* view using the *sp_helptext* system procedure.

The lowest four bits, obtained by AND'ing *status* with 0xF (*status* & *0xF*), contain the constraint type. A value of 1 is PRIMARY KEY, 2 is UNIQUE, 3 is FOREIGN KEY, 4 is CHECK, and 5 is DEFAULT. The fifth bit is on (*status* & *0x10 <> 0*) when the constraint is a nonkey constraint on a single column. The sixth bit is on (*status* & *0x20 <> 0*) when the constraint is on multiple columns or is a PRIMARY KEY or UNIQUE constraint.

NOTE Some of the documentation classifies constraints as either table-level or column-level. This implies that any constraint defined on the line with a column is a column-level constraint and any constraint defined as a separate line in the table or added to the table with the ALTER TABLE command is a table-level constraint. However, this distinction does not hold true when you look at *sysconstraints*. Although it is further documented that the fifth bit is for a column-level constraint, you can see for yourself that this bit is on for any single column constraint except PRIMARY KEY and UNIQUE and that the sixth bit, which is documented as indicating a table-level constraint, is on for all multi-column constraints, as well as PRIMARY KEY and UNIQUE constraints.

Some of the higher bits are used for internal status purposes, such as noting whether a nonclustered index is being rebuilt, and for other internal states. Table 6-11 shows some of the other bit-mask values you might be interested in.

Bitmap Value	Description
16	The constraint is a "column-level" constraint, which means that it's a single column constraint and isn't enforcing entity integrity.
32	The constraint is a "table-level" constraint, which means that it's either a multi-column constraint, a PRIMARY KEY, or a UNIQUE constraint.
512	The constraint is enforced by a clustered index.
1024	The constraint is enforced by a nonclustered index.
16384	The constraint has been disabled.
32767	The constraint has been enabled.
131072	SQL Server has generated a name for the constraint.

Table 6-11. *Bitmap values in the* status *column of* sysconstraints.

Using this information, and not worrying about the higher bits used for internal status, you could use the following query to show constraint information for the *employee* table:

```
SELECT
    OBJECT_NAME(constid) 'Constraint Name',
    constid 'Constraint ID',
    CASE (status & 0xF)
        WHEN 1 THEN 'Primary Key'
        WHEN 2 THEN 'Unique'
        WHEN 3 THEN 'Foreign Key'
        WHEN 4 THEN 'Check'
        WHEN 5 THEN 'Default'
        ELSE 'Undefined'
    END 'Constraint Type',
```

(continued)

```
    CASE (status & 0x30)
        WHEN 0x10 THEN 'Column'
        WHEN 0x20 THEN 'Table'
        ELSE 'NA'
    END 'Level'
FROM sysconstraints
WHERE id=OBJECT_ID('employee')
```

>>>

Constraint Name	Constraint ID	Constraint Type	Level
PK__employee__49C3F6B7	1237579447	Primary Key	Table
DF__employee__emp_id__4AB81AF0	1253579504	Default	Column
CK__employee__emp_id__4BAC3F29	1269579561	Check	Column
DF__employee__emp_name__4CA06362	1285579618	Default	Column
no_nums	1301579675	Check	Column
DF__employee__mgr_id__4E88ABD4	1317579732	Default	Column
FK__employee__mgr_id__4F7CD00D	1333579789	Foreign Key	Column
CK__employee__entered_date__5070F446	1349579846	Check	Column
def_today	1365579903	Default	Column
DF__employee__entered_by__52593CB8	1381579960	Default	Column
CK__employee__entered_by__534D60F1	1397580017	Check	Column
valid_entered_by	1413580074	Check	Table
valid_mgr	1429580131	Check	Table
end_of_month	1445580188	Check	Table

Constraint Failures in Transactions and Multiple-Row Data Modifications

Many bugs occur in application code because developers don't understand how failure of a constraint affects a multiple-statement transaction declared by the user. The biggest misconception is that any error, such as a constraint failure, automatically aborts and rolls back the entire transaction. On the contrary, after an error is raised, it's up to the transaction to either proceed and ultimately commit or to roll back. This feature provides the developer with the flexibility to decide how to handle errors. (The semantics are also in accordance with the ANSI SQL-92 standard for COMMIT behavior.)

Following is an example of a simple transaction that tries to insert three rows of data. The second row contains a duplicate key and violates the PRIMARY KEY constraint. Some developers believe that this example wouldn't insert *any* rows because of the error that occurs in one of the statements; they think that this error will cause the entire transaction to be aborted. However, this doesn't happen—

instead, the statement inserts two rows and then commits that change. Although the second INSERT fails, the third INSERT is processed because no error checking has occurred between the statements, and then the transaction does a COMMIT. Because no instructions were provided to take some other action after the error other than to proceed, SQL Server does just that. It adds the first and third INSERT statements to the table and ignores the second statement.

```
IF EXISTS (SELECT * FROM sysobjects WHERE name='show_error' AND
    type='U')
    DROP TABLE show_error
GO

CREATE TABLE show_error
(
col1    smallint NOT NULL PRIMARY KEY,
col2    smallint NOT NULL
)
GO

BEGIN TRANSACTION

INSERT show_error VALUES (1, 1)
INSERT show_error VALUES (1, 2)
INSERT show_error VALUES (2, 2)

COMMIT TRANSACTION
GO

SELECT * FROM show_error
GO

Server: Msg 2627, Level 14, State 1, Line 1
Violation of PRIMARY KEY constraint 'PK__show_error__6EF57B66'.
    Cannot insert duplicate key in object 'show_error'.
The statement has been terminated.

col1    col2
----    ----
1       1
2       2
```

Following is a modified version of the transaction. This example does some simple error checking using the system function @@ERROR and rolls back the transaction if any statement results in an error. In this example, no rows are inserted because the transaction is rolled back.

```
IF EXISTS (SELECT * FROM sysobjects WHERE name='show_error'
    AND type='U')
    DROP TABLE show_error
GO

CREATE TABLE show_error
(
col1    smallint NOT NULL PRIMARY KEY,
col2    smallint NOT NULL
)
GO

BEGIN TRANSACTION
INSERT show_error VALUES (1, 1)
IF @@ERROR <> 0 GOTO TRAN_ABORT
INSERT show_error VALUES (1, 2)
if @@ERROR <> 0 GOTO TRAN_ABORT
INSERT show_error VALUES (2, 2)
if @@ERROR <> 0 GOTO TRAN_ABORT
COMMIT TRANSACTION
GOTO FINISH

TRAN_ABORT:
ROLLBACK TRANSACTION

FINISH:
GO

SELECT * FROM show_error
GO

Server: Msg 2627, Level 14, State 1, Line 1
Violation of PRIMARY KEY constraint 'PK__show_error__70DDC3D8'.
Cannot insert duplicate key in object 'show_error'.
The statement has been terminated.

col1    col2
----    ----
(0 row(s) affected)
```

Because many developers have handled transaction errors incorrectly and because it can be tedious to add an error check after every command, SQL Server includes a SET statement that aborts a transaction if it encounters any error during the transaction. (Transact-SQL has no WHENEVER statement, although such a feature would be useful for situations like this.) Using SET XACT_ABORT ON causes the entire transaction to be aborted and rolled back if any error is encountered. The default setting is OFF, which is consistent with ANSI-standard behavior. By setting the option XACT_ABORT ON, we can now rerun the example that does no error checking, and no rows will be inserted:

```
IF EXISTS (SELECT * FROM sysobjects WHERE name='show_error'
    AND type='U')
    DROP TABLE show_error
GO

CREATE TABLE show_error
(
col1    smallint NOT NULL PRIMARY KEY,
col2    smallint NOT NULL
)
GO

SET XACT_ABORT ON
BEGIN TRANSACTION

INSERT show_error VALUES (1, 1)
INSERT show_error VALUES (1, 2)
INSERT show_error VALUES (2, 2)

COMMIT TRANSACTION
GO

SELECT * FROM show_error
GO


Server: Msg 2627, Level 14, State 1, Line 1
Violation of PRIMARY KEY constraint 'PK__show_error__72C60C4A'.
Cannot insert duplicate key in object 'show_error'.

col1    col2
----    ----
(0 row(s) affected)
```

A final comment about constraint errors and transactions: a single data modification statement (such as an UPDATE statement) that affects multiple rows is automatically an atomic operation, even if it's not part of an explicit transaction. If such an UPDATE statement finds 100 rows that meet the criteria of the WHERE clause but one row fails because of a constraint violation, no rows will be updated.

The Order of Integrity Checks

The modification of a given row will fail if any constraint is violated or if a trigger aborts the operation. As soon as a failure in a constraint occurs, the operation is aborted, subsequent checks for that row aren't performed, and no trigger fires for the row. Hence, the order of these checks can be important, as the following list shows.

1. Defaults are applied as appropriate.

2. NOT NULL violations are raised.

3. CHECK constraints are evaluated.

4. FOREIGN KEY checks of *referencing* tables are applied.

5. FOREIGN KEY checks of *referenced* tables are applied.

6. UNIQUE/PRIMARY KEY is checked for correctness.

7. Triggers fire.

ALTERING A TABLE

SQL Server 2000 allows existing tables to be modified in several ways, and you've seen some of these methods already. You can use ALTER TABLE to add or drop constraints from a table. You've seen that some types of constraints have the option of not being applied to existing data by using the WITH NOCHECK option. Using the ALTER table command, you can make the following types of changes to an existing table:

- Change the datatype or NULL property of a single column.

- Add one or more new columns, with or without defining constraints for those columns.

- Add one or more constraints.

- Drop one or more constraints.

- Drop one or more columns.

- Enable or disable one or more constraints (only applies to CHECK and FOREIGN KEY constraints).

- Enable or disable one or more triggers.

Changing a Datatype

By using the ALTER COLUMN clause of ALTER TABLE, you can modify the datatype or NULL property of an existing column. But be aware of the following restrictions:

- The modified column can't be a *text*, *image*, *ntext*, or *rowversion* (*timestamp*) column.

- If the modified column is the ROWGUIDCOL for the table, only DROP ROWGUIDCOL is allowed; no datatype changes are allowed.

- The modified column can't be a computed or replicated column.

- The modified column can't have a PRIMARY KEY or FOREIGN KEY constraint defined on it.

- The modified column can't be referenced in a computed column.

- The modified column can't have the type changed to *timestamp*.

- If the modified column participates in an index, the only type changes that are allowed are increasing the length of a variable-length type (for example, VARCHAR(10) to VARCHAR(20)), changing nullability of the column, or both.

- If the modified column has a UNIQUE OR CHECK constraint defined on it, the only change allowed is altering the length of a variable-length column. For a UNIQUE constraint, the new length must be greater than the old length.

- If the modified column has a default defined on it, the only changes that are allowed are increasing or decreasing the length of a variable-length type, changing nullability, or changing the precision or scale.

- The old type of the column should have an allowed implicit conversion to the new type.

- The new type always has ANSI_PADDING semantics if applicable, regardless of the current setting.

- If conversion of an old type to a new type causes an overflow (arithmetic or size), the ALTER TABLE statement is aborted.

Here's the syntax and an example of using the ALTER COLUMN clause of the ALTER TABLE statement:

SYNTAX
```
ALTER TABLE table-name ALTER COLUMN column-name
        { type_name [ ( prec [, scale] ) ] [COLLATE <collation name> ]
        [ NULL | NOT NULL ]
        | {ADD | DROP} ROWGUIDCOL }
```

EXAMPLE
```
/* Change the length of the emp_name column in the employee
   table from varchar(30) to varchar(50) */
ALTER TABLE employee
ALTER COLUMN emp_name varchar(50)
```

Adding a New Column

You can add a new column, with or without specifying column-level constraints. You can add only one column for each ALTER TABLE statement. If the new column doesn't allow NULLs and isn't an identity column, the new column must have a default constraint defined. SQL Server populates the new column in every row with a NULL, the appropriate identity value, or the specified default. If the newly added column is nullable and has a default constraint, the existing rows of the table are not filled with the default value, but rather with NULL values. You can override this restriction by using the WITH VALUES clause so that the existing rows of the table are filled with the specified default value.

Adding, Dropping, Disabling, or Enabling a Constraint

I covered constraint modifications earlier in the discussion about constraints. The trickiest part of using ALTER TABLE to manipulate constraints is that the word CHECK can be used in three different ways:

- To specify a CHECK constraint.

- To defer checking of a newly added constraint. In the following example, we're adding a constraint to validate that *cust_id* in *orders* matches a *cust_id* in *customer*, but we don't want the constraint applied to existing data:

  ```
  ALTER TABLE orders
  WITH NOCHECK
  ADD FOREIGN KEY (cust_id) REFERENCES customer (cust_id)
  ```

  NOTE   I could also use WITH CHECK to force the constraint to be applied to existing data, but that's unnecessary because it's the default behavior.

- To enable or disable a constraint. In the next example, we're enabling all the constraints on the employee table:

  ```
  ALTER TABLE EMPLOYEE
  CHECK CONSTRAINT ALL
  ```

You need to be aware when using ALTER TABLE to drop constraints that dropping a PRIMARY KEY or UNIQUE constraint automatically drops the associated index. In fact, the only way to drop those indexes is by altering the table to remove the constraint.

NOTE   You can't use ALTER TABLE to modify a constraint definition. You must use ALTER TABLE to drop the constraint and then use ALTER TABLE to add a new constraint with the new definition.

Dropping a Column

You can use ALTER TABLE to remove one or more columns from a table. However, you can't drop the following columns:

- A replicated column

- A column used in an index

- A column used in a CHECK, FOREIGN KEY, UNIQUE, or PRIMARY KEY constraint

- A column associated with a default defined with the DEFAULT keyword or bound to a default object

- A column to which a rule is bound

Dropping a column is accomplished using the following syntax:

```
ALTER TABLE table-name
    DROP COLUMN column-name [, next-column-name]...
```

> **NOTE** Notice the syntax difference between dropping a column and adding a new column: the word COLUMN is required when dropping a column, but not when adding a new column to a table.

Enabling or Disabling a Trigger

You can enable or disable one or more (or all) triggers on a table using the ALTER TABLE command. I'll look at this topic in more detail in Chapter 12.

Note that not all the ALTER TABLE variations require SQL Server to change every row when the ALTER TABLE is issued. In many cases, SQL Server can just change the metadata (in *syscolumns*) to reflect the new structure. In particular, the data isn't touched when a column is dropped, when a new column is added and NULL is assumed as the new value for all rows, when the length of a variable-length column is changed, or when a non-nullable column is changed to allow NULLs. All other changes to a table's structure require SQL Server to physically update every row and to write the appropriate records to the transaction log.

TEMPORARY TABLES

Temporary tables are useful workspaces, like scratch pads, that you can use to try out intermediate data processing or to share work-in-progress with other connections. You can create temporary tables from within any database, but they exist in only the *tempdb* database, which is created every time the server is restarted. Don't assume that temporary tables aren't logged: temporary tables, and actions on those tables, are logged in *tempdb* so that transactions can be rolled back as necessary. However, the log isn't used for recovery of the database at system restart because the database is entirely re-created. Likewise, *tempdb* is never restored from a backup, so the log in *tempdb* is never needed for restoring the database.

SQL Server 2000 can log just enough information to allow rollback of transactions without logging the additional information that would be necessary to recover those transactions, either at system startup or when recovering from a backup. This reduced logging means that data modification operations on tables in *tempdb* can be up to four times faster than the same operations in other databases. You can use temporary tables in three ways in SQL Server: privately, globally, and directly.

Private Temporary Tables (#)

By prefixing a table name with a single pound sign (#)—as in CREATE TABLE *#my_table*—you can create it (from within any database) as a private temporary table. Only the connection that created the table can access the table, making it truly private. Privileges can't be granted to another connection. As a temporary table, it exists for the life of that connection only; that connection can drop the table using DROP TABLE.

Because the scoping of a private temporary table is specific to the connection that created it, you won't encounter a name collision should you choose a table name that's used in another connection. Private temporary tables are analogous to local variables—each connection has its own private version, and private temporary tables that are held by other connections are irrelevant. (However, temporary tables do differ from local variables in one crucial way: temporary tables exist for the life of the session, while local variables exist only for a single batch.)

Global Temporary Tables (##)

By prefixing a table name with double pound signs (##)—as in CREATE TABLE *##our_table*—you can create a global temporary table (from within any database and any connection). Any connection can subsequently access the table for retrieval or data modification, even without specific permission. Unlike with private temporary tables, all connections can use the single copy of a global temporary table. Therefore, you might encounter a name collision if another connection has created a global temporary table of the same name, and the CREATE TABLE statement will fail.

A global temporary table exists until the creating connection terminates and all current use of the table completes. After the creating connection terminates, however, only those connections already accessing it are allowed to finish, and no further use of the table is allowed. If you want a global temporary table to exist per-manently, you can create the table in a stored procedure that's marked to autostart whenever SQL Server is started. That procedure can be put to sleep using WAITFOR, and it will never terminate, so the table will never be dropped. Or you can choose to use *tempdb* directly, which I'll discuss next.

Direct Use of *tempdb*

Realizing that *tempdb* is re-created every time SQL Server is started, you can use *tempdb* to create a table or you can fully qualify the table name to include the data-base name *tempdb* in the CREATE TABLE statement issued from another database. To do this, you need to establish *create table* privileges in *tempdb*.

You can set up privileges in *tempdb* in one of two ways every time SQL Server starts: you can set the privileges in *model* (the template database) so that they are copied to *tempdb* when it's created at system restart, or you can have an *autostart* procedure set the *tempdb* privileges every time SQL Server is started. One reason to consider not setting the privileges for *tempdb* in the *model* database is because *tempdb* isn't the only database that will be affected. Any new database you create will inherit those permissions as well.

Tables created directly in *tempdb* can exist even after the creating connection is terminated, and the creator can specifically grant and revoke access permissions to specific users:

```
-- Creating a table in tempdb from pubs. Another method would be
-- to first do a 'use tempdb' instead of fully qualifying
-- the name.
CREATE TABLE tempdb.dbo.testtemp
(
col1 int
)
```

Constraints on Temporary Tables

A few articles about SQL Server erroneously state that constraints don't work on temporary tables. However, all constraints work on temporary tables explicitly built in *tempdb* (not using the # or ## prefixes). All constraints except FOREIGN KEY constraints work with tables using the # (private) and ## (global) prefixes. FOREIGN KEY references on private and global temporary tables are designed to not be en-forced because such a reference could prevent the temporary table from being dropped at close-connection time (for private temporary tables) or when a table goes out of scope (for global temporary tables) if the referencing table wasn't dropped first.

SYSTEM TABLES

As I've mentioned, SQL Server maintains a set of tables that store information about all the objects, datatypes, constraints, configuration options, and resources available to SQL Server. This set of tables is sometimes called the *system catalog*. We've looked at a few such tables already, in particular *sysconstraints* and *sysobjects*. Some of the system tables exist only in the *master* database and contain systemwide information, and others exist in every database (including *master*) and contain information about the objects and resources belonging to that particular database.

The most common way of identifying a system table is by its name. All system tables start with the three characters *sys*, but that doesn't mean that everything that starts with *sys* is a system table. Another way of identifying system tables is by their *object_id*, which is always less than 100. A third way of identifying system tables is to look at the *type* column in *sysobjects*; system tables have a type of *S*. In SQL Server 2000, some of the objects that were system tables in previous versions have become views. You can get a list of these views by querying the *sysobjects* table directly, as follows:

```
SELECT name FROM sysobjects
WHERE type = 'V'
AND name LIKE 'sys%'
```

If you run this query in the *master* database, you'll see six tables returned, and in all user databases you'll see only two. The views *syslogins*, *sysremotelogins*, *sysopentapes*, and *sysoledbusers* do not exist in the user databases.

Another type of system table isn't really a table at all, but a pseudotable. These tables take no space and are not stored permanently on disk. Rather, SQL Server builds them dynamically every time you query them. In most cases, it doesn't make sense to store these tables on disk because their values change constantly and exist only while the server is running.

For example, storing *syslockinfo* on disk would be meaningless because locks do not exist unless SQL Server is running. In addition, lock information needs to be accessed so often and so quickly that storing it in a table would be much too slow. The information is actually stored in internal memory structures and is displayed as a table only when requested. You can select from *syslockinfo* as if it were a table, using the following statement:

```
SELECT * FROM master..syslockinfo
```

In addition, the stored procedure *sp_lock* retrieves information from *syslockinfo*, treating it just like any other system table. You can select from any of the tables that are really pseudotables, and most of them have one or more associated stored procedures for accessing their information.

Prior to SQL Server 2000, you could find out which tables were pseudotables by looking in the *sysindexes* table, which is where actual storage information is kept. There is a separate *sysindexes* table in every database, and every table and every index has a row in *sysindexes*. The rows in this table indicate where the data for the table or index is stored and how much space it takes up. Every table has a row in *sysindexes* with an *indid* (index ID) value of either 0 or 1. If the *indid* value is 0, the table has no clustered index and is called a *heap*. The value in the *name* column is the name of the table. If the *indid* value is 1, the table has a clustered index and the name of the clustered index is stored in the *name* column. The value in the *id* column is the ID of the table itself. Every nonclustered index on a table has a row in *sysindexes* with an *indid* value between 2 and 250. To see how much space the table is using, all you need to do is look at the value in the column called *dpages* in the row for the table. Any value greater than 0 means the table is actually taking some space.

The following query returns space usage information for all the tables with an object ID of less than 100, which generally means that it is a system table:

```
SELECT name = CONVERT(CHAR(30), o.name), rows, dpages, o.id, type
FROM sysindexes i JOIN sysobjects o ON o.id = i.id
WHERE o.id < 100 AND (indid = 0 OR indid = 1)
```

A system pseudotable is one that doesn't take any space. You might be tempted to look at the number of rows to determine whether a table takes up any space, but that might not give you the right answer. In the *master* database on my SQL server, both *sysreferences* and *sysfulltextcatalogs* have 0 rows just because I haven't used those tables yet. In earlier versions of SQL Server, you could tell that a table was a real table by looking at the value in the *dpages* column. As soon as a table was created, SQL Server would allocate at least two pages for it, even without inserting any rows. In SQL Server 2000, as you saw earlier in this chapter, that just doesn't happen. The only way to tell whether a table is a pseudotable is to look at the 11th bit (with a value of 1024) in the *sysstat* column of *sysobjects*. You can perform a bit-wise AND operation of *sysobjects.sysstat* & 1024, which in binary would be all zeros except for the 11th bit. Since 0 and anything is 0, all the bits except the 11th will be zero in the output. If the 11th bit is also zero, the result will be 0, but if the 11th bit is 1, it will stay 1 in the output and the result will be 1024. The following query shows this:

```
SELECT name = CONVERT(CHAR(30), o.name), rows,
    PseudoTable = o.sysstat & 1024, o.type
FROM sysindexes i JOIN sysobjects o ON o.id = i.id
WHERE o.id < 100 AND (indid = 0 OR indid = 1)
```

The result rows that come back from the query that have a value of 1024 for the column labeled *PseudoTable* are the pseudotables. Here are the pseudotables tables in my *master* database:

```
sysindexkeys
sysforeignkeys
sysmembers
sysprotects
sysperfinfo
sysprocesses
syslocks
syscurconfigs
syslockinfo
syscursorrefs
syscursors
syscursorcolumns
syscursortables
syscacheobjects
sysfiles
```

In the *pubs* database, there are only five pseudotables:

```
sysindexkeys
sysforeignkeys
sysmembers
sysprotects
sysfiles
```

There's actually a much easier way to find out if a table is a pseudotable, without doing all this fancy bit arithmetic. SQL Server provides a whole suite of property functions, many of which I'll tell you about in relevant places throughout this book. The function OBJECTPROPERTY has a parameter *TableIsFake*. The first parameter of this function is an object ID, which you can get by using the OBJECT_ID function. The following statement returns the *TableIsFake* value for the *syslockinfo* and *sysobjects* tables in the *master* database:

```
USE master
SELECT OBJECTPROPERTY(OBJECT_ID('syslockinfo'), 'TableIsFake'),
    OBJECTPROPERTY(OBJECT_ID('sysobjects'), 'TableIsFake')

RESULTS:

----------- -----------
0
```

The return value of 1 means that the table is a pseudotable, and the return value of 0 means that it is not. The function will return a NULL value if the table doesn't exist or if you misspell the name of the property.

Microsoft does not recommend that you directly query the system tables at all. The online documentation states:

> The structure of the system catalog tables is dependent on the underlying architecture of SQL Server and changes from one version to another. Even an application that only issues SELECT statements may have to be at least partially rewritten when migrating to a new version of SQL Server if it directly queries system tables that change or are not present in the new version.

So, if you aren't supposed to directly access the system tables, how are you supposed to find out information about your system? SQL Server 2000 provides a number of tools for accomplishing this. We took a look in the preceding section at one of many possible property functions. There are also system stored procedures, such as *sp_help* and *sp_helpconstraint*. I'll tell you more about system procedures in Chapter 11. Finally, in compliance with the ANSI SQL Standard, there is a set of INFORMATION SCHEMA VIEWS, some of which we'll look at later in the book.

SUMMARY

Tables are the heart of relational databases in general and SQL Server in particular. In this chapter, we've looked at datatype issues, including size and performance tradeoffs. SQL Server provides a datatype for almost every use. We also looked at variable-length datatype issues and saw that it's simplistic to think that variable-length datatypes are either always good or always bad to use. You've also seen how data is physically stored in data pages, and we discussed some of the system table entries that are made to support tables.

SQL Server provides user-defined datatypes for support of domains, and it provides the IDENTITY property to make a column produce autosequenced numeric values. It also provides constraints, which offer a powerful way to ensure your data's logical integrity. In addition to the NULL/NOT NULL designation, SQL Server provides PRIMARY KEY, UNIQUE, FOREIGN KEY, CHECK, and DEFAULT constraints. Our discussion of these features also touched on a number of pragmatic issues, such as performance implications, conflicts between different constraints and triggers, and transaction semantics when a constraint fails.

Chapter 7

Querying Data

You wouldn't have any reason to store data if you didn't want to retrieve it. Relational databases gained wide acceptance principally because they enabled users to query, or access, data easily, without using predefined, rigid navigational paths. Indeed, the acronym *SQL* stands for Structured *Query* Language. Microsoft SQL Server provides rich and powerful query capabilities.

In this chapter, I'll examine the SELECT statement and concentrate on features beyond the basics, including NULL, OUTER JOIN, correlated subqueries, aggregates, UNION, and the special CUBE operator. In Chapter 9, we'll see how to modify data. Then, in Chapter 10, I'll build on these topics and explore the constructs and techniques that make Transact-SQL more than simply a query language.

THE SELECT STATEMENT

The SELECT statement is the most frequently used SQL command and is the fundamental way to query data. The SQL syntax for the SELECT statement is intuitive—at least in its simplest forms—and resembles how you might state a request in English. As its name implies, it is also *structured* and precise. However, a SELECT statement can be obscure or even tricky. Brainteasers about writing a SELECT statement to perform some tricky task often appear in database publications. As long as you write a query that's syntactically correct, you get a result. However, it might not be the result you really want—you might get the answer to a different question than the one you thought you posed! Queries with incorrect semantics commonly cause bugs in applications, so you should understand proper query formulation.

The basic form of SELECT, which uses brackets ([]) to identify optional items, is shown here.

```
SELECT [DISTINCT][TOP n] <columns to be chosen, optionally eliminating
                         duplicate rows from result set or limiting
                         number of rows to be returned>
[FROM] <table names>
[WHERE] <criteria that must be true for a row to be chosen>
[GROUP BY] <columns for grouping aggregate functions>
[HAVING] <criteria that must be met for aggregate functions>
[ORDER BY] <optional specification of how the results should be
           sorted>
```

Notice that the only clause that must always be present is the verb SELECT; the other clauses are optional. For example, if the entire table is needed, you don't need to restrict data using certain criteria, so you can omit the WHERE clause.

Here's a simple query that retrieves all columns of all rows from the *authors* table in the *pubs* sample database:

```
SELECT * FROM authors
```

Figure 7-1 shows the output.

Using tools such as OSQL and SQL Query Analyzer, you can issue queries interactively. You can also, of course, build queries into applications. The calling application determines the formatting of the data output. SQL Server returns the data back to the calling application, which then works with the data. In the case of an ad hoc query tool, it displays the output on a monitor.

```
au_id       au_lname        au_fname   phone        address                city           state zip    contract
----------- --------------- ---------- ------------ ---------------------- -------------- ----- -----  --------
172-32-1176 White           Johnson    408 496-7223 10932 Bigge Rd.        Menlo Park      CA   94025  1
213-46-8915 Green           Marjorie   415 986-7020 309 63rd St. #411      Oakland         CA   94618  1
238-95-7766 Carson          Cheryl     415 548-7723 589 Darwin Ln.         Berkeley        CA   94705  1
267-41-2394 O'Leary         Michael    408 286-2428 22 Cleveland Av. #14   San Jose        CA   95128  1
274-80-9391 Straight        Dean       415 834-2919 5420 College Av.       Oakland         CA   94609  1
341-22-1782 Smith           Meander    913 843-0462 10 Mississippi Dr.     Lawrence        KS   66044  0
409-56-7008 Bennet          Abraham    415 658-9932 6223 Bateman St.       Berkeley        CA   94705  1
427-17-2319 Dull            Ann        415 836-7128 3410 Blonde St.        Palo Alto       CA   94301  1
472-27-2349 Gringlesby      Burt       707 938-6445 PO Box 792             Covelo          CA   95428  1
486-29-1786 Locksley        Charlene   415 585-4620 18 Broadway Av.        San Francisc    CA   94130  1
527-72-3246 Greene          Morningstar 615 297-2723 22 Graybar House Rd.  Nashville       TN   37215  0
648-92-1872 Blotchet-Halls  Reginald   503 745-6402 55 Hillsdale Bl.       Corvallis       OR   97330  1
672-71-3249 Yokomoto        Akiko      415 935-4228 3 Silver Ct.           Walnut Creek    CA   94595  1
712-45-1867 del Castillo    Innes      615 996-8275 2286 Cram Pl. #86      Ann Arbor       MI   48105  1
722-51-5454 DeFrance        Michel     219 547-9982 3 Balding Pl.          Gary            IN   46403  1
724-08-9931 Stringer        Dirk       415 843-2991 5420 Telegraph Av.     Oakland         CA   94609  0
724-80-9391 MacFeather      Stearns    415 354-7128 44 Upland Hts.         Oakland         CA   94612  1
756-30-7391 Karsen          Livia      415 534-9219 5720 McAuley St.       Oakland         CA   94609  1
807-91-6654 Panteley        Sylvia     301 946-8853 1956 Arlington Pl.     Rockville       MD   20853  1
846-92-7186 Hunter          Sheryl     415 836-7128 3410 Blonde St.        Palo Alto       CA   94301  1
893-72-1158 McBadden        Heather    707 448-4982 301 Putnam             Vacaville       CA   95688  0
899-46-2035 Ringer          Anne       801 826-0752 67 Seventh Av.         Salt Lake Ci    UT   84152  1
998-72-3567 Ringer          Albert     801 826-0752 67 Seventh Av.         Salt Lake Ci    UT   84152  1
```

Figure 7-1. *The* authors *table in the* pubs *database.*

NOTE In general, this book concentrates on topics specific to Microsoft SQL Server, but it wouldn't be complete without some discussion of the SQL language. Because the treatment of generic SQL in this book is, by design, far from complete, please see Appendix D for suggestions on further reading, including books on ANSI Standard SQL-92 and SQL-99 as well as books on the nuances of Microsoft Transact-SQL.

The power of the SQL language begins to reveal itself when you limit the information to be returned to specified ranges. For example, you can specify that a query from one table return only certain columns or rows that meet your stated criteria. In the select list, you specify the exact columns you want, and then in the WHERE clause, you specify the criteria that determine whether a row should be included in the answer set. Still using the *pubs* sample database, suppose we want to find the first name and the city, state, and zip code of residence for authors whose last name is *Ringer*:

```
SELECT au_lname, au_fname, city, state, zip
FROM authors
WHERE au_lname='Ringer'
```

Here's the output:

```
au_lname    au_fname    city              state    zip
--------    --------    --------------    -----    -----
Ringer      Albert      Salt Lake City    UT       84152
Ringer      Anne        Salt Lake City    UT       84152
```

The results of this query tell us that two authors are named Ringer. But we're interested only in Anne. Retrieving only Anne Ringer's data requires an additional expression that is combined (AND'ed) with the original. In addition, we'd like the output to have more intuitive names for some columns, so we respecify the query:

```
SELECT 'Last Name'=au_lname, 'First'=au_fname, city, state, zip
FROM authors
WHERE au_lname='Ringer' AND au_fname='Anne'
```

Here's the output, just as we want it:

```
Last Name    First    city              state    zip
---------    -----    --------------    -----    -----
Ringer       Anne     Salt Lake City    UT       84152
```

JOINS

You gain much more power when you join tables, which typically results in combining columns of matching rows to project and return a *virtual table*. Usually, joins are based on the primary and foreign keys of the tables involved, although the tables aren't required to explicitly declare keys. The *pubs* database contains a table of authors (*authors*) and a table of book titles (*titles*). An obvious query would be, "Show me the titles that each author has written and sort the results alphabetically by author. I'm interested only in authors who live outside California." Neither the *authors* table nor the *titles* table alone has all this information. Furthermore, a many-to-many relationship exists between authors and titles; an author might have written several books, and a book might have been written by multiple authors. So an intermediate table, *titleauthor*, exists expressly to associate authors and titles, and this table is necessary to correctly join the information from *authors* and *titles*. To join these tables, you must include all three tables in the FROM clause of the SELECT statement, specifying that the columns that make up the keys have the same values:

```
SELECT
'Author'=RTRIM(au_lname) + ', ' + au_fname,
'Title'=title
FROM authors AS A JOIN titleauthor AS TA
    ON A.au_id=TA.au_id          -- JOIN CONDITION
JOIN titles AS T
    ON T.title_id=TA.title_id    -- JOIN CONDITION
WHERE A.state <> 'CA'
ORDER BY 1
```

Here's the output:

```
Author                          Title
-----------------------         ---------------------------------
Blotchet-Halls, Reginald        Fifty Years in Buckingham Palace
                                Kitchens
DeFrance, Michel                The Gourmet Microwave
del Castillo, Innes             Silicon Valley Gastronomic Treats
Panteley, Sylvia                Onions, Leeks, and Garlic: Cooking
                                Secrets of the Mediterranean
Ringer, Albert                  Is Anger the Enemy?
Ringer, Albert                  Life Without Fear
Ringer, Anne                    The Gourmet Microwave
Ringer, Anne                    Is Anger the Enemy?
```

Before discussing join operations further, let's study the preceding example. The author's last and first names have been concatenated into one field. The RTRIM (right trim) function is used to strip off any trailing whitespace from the *au_lname* column.

Then we add a comma and a space and concatenate on the *au_fname* column. This column is then *aliased* as simply *Author* and is returned to the calling application as a single column.

> **NOTE** The RTRIM function isn't needed for this example. Because the column is of type *varchar*, trailing blanks won't be present. RTRIM is shown for illustration purposes only.

Another important point is that the ORDER BY 1 clause indicates that the results should be sorted by the first column in the result set. It's more typical to use the column name rather than its number, but using the column number provides a convenient shorthand when the column is an expression and hence isn't present in the base table or view (virtual table) being queried.

Instead of using ORDER BY 1, you can repeat the same expression used in the select list and specify *ORDER BY RTRIM(au_lname) + ', ' + au_fname* instead. Alternatively, SQL Server provides a feature supported by the ANSI SQL-99 standard that allows sorting by columns not included in the select list. So even though you don't individually select the columns *au_lname* or, *au_fname*, you can nonetheless choose to order the query based on these columns by specifying columns *ORDER BY au_lname, au_fname*. We'll see this in the next example. Notice also that the query contains comments (*-- JOIN CONDITION*). A double hyphen (--) signifies that the rest of the line is a comment (similar to *//* in C++). You can also use the C-style */* comment block */*, which allows blocks of comment lines.

> **TIP** Comments can be nested, but you should generally try to avoid this. You can easily introduce a bug by not realizing that a comment is nested within another comment and misreading the code.

Now let's examine the join in the example above. The ON clauses specify how the tables relate and set the join criteria, stating that *au_id* in *authors* must equal *au_id* in *titleauthor*, and *title_id* in *titles* must equal *title_id* in *titleauthor*. This type of join is referred to as an *equijoin,* and it's the most common type of join operation. To remove ambiguity, you must qualify the columns. You can do this by specifying the columns in the form *table.column*, as in *authors.au_id = titleauthor.au_id*. The more compact and common way to do this, however, is by specifying a *table alias* in the FROM clause, as was done in this example. By following the *titles* table with the word *AS* and the letter *T,* the *titles* table will be referred to as *T* anywhere else in the query where the table is referenced. Typically, such an alias consists of one or two letters, although it can be much longer (following the same rules as identifiers).

After a table is aliased, it must be referred to by the alias, so now we can't refer to *authors.au_id* because the *authors* table has been aliased as *A*. We must use *A.au_id*. Note also that the *state* column of *authors* is referred to as *A.state*. The other two tables don't contain a *state* column, so qualifying it with the *A.* prefix isn't necessary; however, doing so makes the query more readable—and less prone to subsequent bugs.

The join is accomplished using the ANSI JOIN SQL syntax, which was introduced in SQL Server version 6.5. Many examples and applications continue to use an old-style JOIN syntax, which is shown below. (The term "old-style JOIN" is actually used by the SQL-92 specification.) The ANSI JOIN syntax is based on ANSI SQL-92. The main differences between the two types of join formulations are

- The ANSI JOIN actually uses the keyword JOIN.

- The ANSI JOIN segregates join conditions from search conditions.

The ANSI JOIN syntax specifies the JOIN conditions in the ON clauses (one for each pair of tables), and the search conditions are specified in the WHERE clause—for example, WHERE *state* <> *'CA'*. Although slightly more verbose, the explicit JOIN syntax is more readable. There's no difference in performance; behind the scenes, the operations are the same. Here's how you can respecify the query using the old-style JOIN syntax:

```
SELECT
'Author'=RTRIM(au_lname) + ', ' + au_fname,
'Title'=title
FROM authors A, titles T, titleauthor TA
WHERE
A.au_id=TA.au_id AND T.title_id=TA.title_id  -- JOIN CONDITIONS
AND A.state <> 'CA'
ORDER BY 1
```

This query produces the same output and the same execution plan as the previous query.

One of the most common errors that new SQL users make when using the old-style JOIN syntax is not specifying the join condition. Omitting the WHERE clause is still a valid SQL request and causes a result set to be returned. However, that result set is likely not what the user wanted. In the query above, omitting the WHERE clause would return the Cartesian product of the three tables: it would generate every possible combination of rows between them. Although in a few unusual cases you might want all permutations, usually this is just a user error. The number of rows returned can be huge and typically doesn't represent anything meaningful. For example, the Cartesian product of the three small tables here (*authors*, *titles*, and *titleauthor* each have less than 26 rows) generates 10,350 rows of (probably) meaningless output.

Using the ANSI JOIN syntax, it's impossible to accidentally return a Cartesian product of the tables—and that's one reason to use ANSI JOINs almost exclusively.

The ANSI JOIN syntax requires an ON clause for specifying how the tables are related. In cases where you actually do want a Cartesian product, the ANSI JOIN syntax allows you to use a CROSS JOIN operator, which we'll examine in more detail later in this chapter.

> **NOTE** This book uses the ANSI JOIN syntax almost exclusively. You might want to try translating some of them into queries using old-style JOIN syntax, because you should be able to recognize both forms. If you have to read SQL code written earlier than version 7, you're bound to come across queries using this older syntax.

The most common form of join is an *equijoin,* which means that the condition linking the two tables is based on equality. An equijoin is sometimes referred to as an *inner join* to differentiate it from an *outer join,* which I'll discuss shortly. Strictly speaking, an inner join isn't quite the same as an equijoin; an inner join can use an operator such as less than (<) or greater than (>). So all equijoins are inner joins but not all inner joins are equijoins. I'll use the term inner join because it is the broader term. To make this distinction clear in your code, you can use the INNER JOIN syntax in place of JOIN, as in this example:

```
FROM authors AS A INNER JOIN titleauthor TA ON A.au_id=TA.au_id
```

Other than making the syntax more explicit, there's no difference in the semantics or the execution. By convention, the modifier INNER generally isn't used.

> **NOTE** ANSI SQL-92 also specifies the natural join operation, in which you don't have to specify the tables' column names. By specifying syntax such as *FROM authors NATURAL JOIN titleauthor,* the system automatically knows how to join the tables without your specifying the column names to match. SQL Server doesn't yet support this feature.
>
> The ANSI specification calls for the natural join to be resolved based on identical column names between the tables. Perhaps a better way to do this would be based on a declared primary key–foreign key relationship, *if it exists.* Admittedly, declared key relationships have issues, too, because there's no restriction that only one such foreign key relationship be set up. Also, if the natural join were limited to only such relationships, all joins would have to be known in advance—as in the old CODASYL days.

The FROM clause in this example shows an alternative way to specify a table alias—by omitting the AS. The use of AS preceding the table alias, as used in the previous example, conforms to ANSI SQL-92. From SQL Server's standpoint, the two methods are equivalent (stating *FROM authors AS A* is identical to stating *FROM authors A*). Commonly, the AS formulation is used in ANSI SQL-92 join operations and the formulation that omits AS is used with the old-style join formulation. However, you can use either formulation—it's strictly a matter of preference.

Outer Joins

Inner joins return only rows from the respective tables that meet the conditions specified in the ON clause. In other words, if a row in the first table doesn't match any rows in the second table, that row isn't returned in the result set. In contrast, outer joins preserve some or all of the unmatched rows. To illustrate how easily subtle semantic errors can be introduced, let's refer back to the previous two query examples, in which we want to see the titles written by all authors not living in California. The result omits two writers who do not, in fact, live in California. Are the queries wrong? No! They perform exactly as written—we didn't specify that authors who currently have no titles in the database should be included. The results of the query are as we requested. In fact, the *authors* table has four rows that have no related row in the *titleauthor* table, which means these "authors" actually haven't written any books. Two of these authors don't contain the value CA in the *state* column, as the following result set shows.

```
au_id          Author               state
-----------    -------------------  -----
341-22-1782    Smith, Meander       KS
527-72-3246    Greene, Morningstar  TN
724-08-9931    Stringer, Dirk       CA
893-72-1158    McBadden, Heather    CA
```

The *titles* table has one row for which there is no author in our database, as shown here. (Later in this chapter, you'll see the types of queries used to produce these two result sets.)

```
title_id    title
--------    ----------------------------------
MC3026      The Psychology of Computer Cooking
```

If our queries were meant to be "Show me the titles that each author has written; include authors for whom there's no title currently in our database; if there's a title with no author, show me that as well; sort the results alphabetically by the author; I'm interested only in authors who live outside of California," the query would use an outer join so that authors with no matching titles would be selected:

```
SELECT
'Author'=RTRIM(au_lname) + ', ' + au_fname,
'Title'=title
FROM
    (                   -- JOIN CONDITIONS
    -- FIRST join authors and titleauthor
        (authors AS A
        FULL OUTER JOIN titleauthor AS TA ON A.au_id=TA.au_id
        )
    -- The result of the previous join is then joined to titles
```

```
        FULL OUTER JOIN titles AS T ON TA.title_id=T.title_id
    )
WHERE
state <> 'CA' OR state IS NULL
ORDER BY 1
```

Here's the output:

```
Author                          Title
----------------------          ----------------------------------
NULL                            The Psychology of Computer Cooking
Blotchet-Halls, Reginald        Fifty Years in Buckingham Palace
                                Kitchens
DeFrance, Michel                The Gourmet Microwave
del Castillo, Innes             Silicon Valley Gastronomic Treats
Greene, Morningstar             NULL
Panteley, Sylvia                Onions, Leeks, and Garlic: Cooking
                                Secrets of the Mediterranean
Ringer, Albert                  Is Anger the Enemy?
Ringer, Albert                  Life Without Fear
Ringer, Anne                    The Gourmet Microwave
Ringer, Anne                    Is Anger the Enemy?
Smith, Meander                  NULL
```

The query demonstrates a *full outer join*. Rows in the *authors* and *titles* tables that don't have a corresponding entry in *titleauthor* are still presented, but with a NULL entry for the *title* or *author* column. (The data from the *authors* table is requested as a comma between the last names and the first names. Because we have the option CONCAT_NULL_YIELDS_NULL set to ON, the result is NULL for the *author* column. If we didn't have that option set to ON, SQL Server would have returned the single comma between the nonexistent last and first names.) A full outer join preserves nonmatching rows from both the lefthand and righthand tables. In the example above, the *authors* table is presented first, so it is the lefthand table when joining to *titleauthor*. The result of that join is the lefthand table when joining to *titles*.

ANSI OUTER JOINS

At the beginning of this chapter, I promised not to go into much detail about generic SQL operations. The outer join formulations here are standard ANSI SQL-92. However, this is one area in which there aren't enough good examples. Using OUTER JOIN with more than two tables introduces some obscure issues; in fact, few products provide support for full outer joins. Because you must understand outer joins thoroughly if you are to use OUTER JOIN, I'll go into a bit more detail in this section.

You can generate missing rows from one or more of the tables by using either a *left outer join* or a *right outer join*. So if we want to preserve all authors and generate a row for all authors who have a missing title, but we don't want to preserve titles that have no author, we can reformulate the query using LEFT OUTER JOIN, as shown below. This join preserves entries only on the lefthand side of the join. Note that the left outer join of the *authors* and *titleauthor* columns generates two such rows (for Greene and Smith). The result of the join is the lefthand side of the join to *titles*; therefore, the LEFT OUTER JOIN must be specified again to preserve these rows with no matching *titles* rows.

```
⋮
FROM
    (
        (authors as A
        LEFT OUTER JOIN titleauthor AS TA ON A.au_id=TA.au_id
        )
        LEFT OUTER JOIN titles AS T ON TA.title_id=T.title_id
    )
⋮
```

Here's the output:

Author	Title
Blotchet-Halls, Reginald	Fifty Years in Buckingham Palace Kitchens
DeFrance, Michel	The Gourmet Microwave
del Castillo, Innes	Silicon Valley Gastronomic Treats
Greene, Morningstar	NULL
Panteley, Sylvia	Onions, Leeks, and Garlic: Cooking Secrets of the Mediterranean
Ringer, Albert	Is Anger the Enemy?
Ringer, Albert	Life Without Fear
Ringer, Anne	The Gourmet Microwave
Ringer, Anne	Is Anger the Enemy?
Smith, Meander	NULL

The query produces the same rows as the full outer join, except for the row for *The Psychology of Computer Cooking*. Because we specified only LEFT OUTER JOIN, there was no request to preserve *titles* (righthand) rows with no matching rows in the result of the join of *authors* and *titleauthor*.

You must use care with OUTER JOIN operations because the order in which tables are joined affects which rows are preserved and which aren't. In an inner join, the symmetric property holds (if A equals B, then B equals A) and no difference results, whether something is on the left or the right side of the equation, and no difference results in the order in which joins are specified. This is definitely *not* the case for OUTER JOIN operations. For example, consider the following two queries and their results:

QUERY 1

```
SELECT
'Author'= RTRIM(au_lname) + ', ' + au_fname,
'Title'=title
FROM (titleauthor AS TA
RIGHT OUTER JOIN authors AS A ON (A.au_id=TA.au_id))
FULL OUTER JOIN titles AS T ON (TA.title_id=T.title_id)
WHERE
A.state <> 'CA' or A.state is NULL
ORDER BY 1
```

Author	Title
NULL	The Psychology of Computer Cooking
Blotchet-Halls, Reginald	Fifty Years in Buckingham Palace Kitchens
DeFrance, Michel	The Gourmet Microwave
del Castillo, Innes	Silicon Valley Gastronomic Treats
Greene, Morningstar	NULL
Panteley, Sylvia	Onions, Leeks, and Garlic: Cooking Secrets of the Mediterranean
Ringer, Albert	Is Anger the Enemy?
Ringer, Albert	Life Without Fear
Ringer, Anne	The Gourmet Microwave
Ringer, Anne	Is Anger the Enemy?
Smith, Meander	NULL

This query produces results semantically equivalent to the previous FULL OUTER JOIN formulation, although we've switched the order of the *authors* and *titleauthor* tables. This query and the previous one preserve both authors with no matching titles and titles with no matching authors. This might not be obvious because RIGHT OUTER JOIN is clearly different than FULL OUTER JOIN. However, in this case we know it's true because a FOREIGN KEY constraint exists on the *titleauthor* table to ensure that there can never be a row in the *titleauthor* table that doesn't match a row in the *authors* table, and the FOREIGN KEY columns in *titleauthor* are defined to not allow NULL values. So we can be confident that the *titleauthor* RIGHT OUTER JOIN to *authors* can't produce any fewer rows than would a FULL OUTER JOIN.

But if we modify the query ever so slightly by changing the join order again, look what happens:

QUERY 2

```
SELECT
'Author'=RTRIM(au_lname) + ', ' + au_fname,
'Title'=title
FROM (titleauthor AS TA
FULL OUTER JOIN titles AS T ON TA.title_id=T.title_id)
RIGHT OUTER JOIN authors AS A ON A.au_id=TA.au_id
WHERE
A.state <> 'CA' or A.state is NULL
ORDER BY 1
```

```
Author                        Title
----------------------        ---------------------------------
Blotchet-Halls, Reginald      Fifty Years in Buckingham Palace
                              Kitchens
DeFrance, Michel              The Gourmet Microwave
del Castillo, Innes           Silicon Valley Gastronomic Treats
Greene, Morningstar           NULL
Panteley, Sylvia              Onions, Leeks, and Garlic: Cooking
                              Secrets of the Mediterranean
Ringer, Albert                Is Anger the Enemy?
Ringer, Albert                Life Without Fear
Ringer, Anne                  The Gourmet Microwave
Ringer, Anne                  Is Anger the Enemy?
Smith, Meander                NULL
```

At a glance, Query 2 looks equivalent to Query 1, although the join order is slightly different. But notice how the results differ. Query 2 didn't achieve the goal of preserving the *titles* rows without corresponding *authors*, and the row for *The Psychology of Computer Cooking* is again excluded. This row would have been preserved in the first join operation:

```
FULL OUTER JOIN titles AS T ON TA.title_id=T.title_id
```

But then the row is discarded because the second join operation preserves only authors without matching titles:

```
RIGHT OUTER JOIN authors AS A ON A.au_id=TA.au_id
```

Because the title row for *The Psychology of Computer Cooking* is on the lefthand side of this join operation and only a RIGHT OUTER JOIN operation is specified, this title is discarded.

> **NOTE** Just as INNER is an optional modifier, so is OUTER. Hence, LEFT OUTER JOIN can be equivalently specified as LEFT JOIN, and FULL OUTER JOIN can be equivalently expressed as FULL JOIN. However, although INNER is seldom used by convention and is usually only implied, OUTER is almost always used by convention when specifying any type of outer join.

Because join order matters, I urge you to use parentheses and indentation carefully when specifying OUTER JOIN operations. Indentation, of course, is always optional, and use of parentheses is often optional. But as this example shows, it's easy to make mistakes that result in your queries returning the wrong answers. As is true with almost all programming, simply getting into the habit of using comments, parentheses, and indentation often results in such bugs being noticed and fixed by a developer or database administrator before they make their way into your applications.

The Obsolete *= OUTER JOIN Operator

Prior to version 6.5, SQL Server had limited outer-join support in the form of the special operators *= and =*. Many people assume that the LEFT OUTER JOIN syntax is simply a synonym for *=, but this isn't the case. LEFT OUTER JOIN is semantically different from and superior to *=.

For inner joins, the symmetric property holds, so the issues with old-style JOIN syntax don't exist. You can use either new-style or old-style syntax with inner joins. For outer joins, you should consider the *= operator obsolete and move to the OUTER JOIN syntax as quickly as possible—the *= operator might be dropped entirely in future releases of SQL Server.

ANSI's OUTER JOIN syntax, which was adopted in SQL Server version 6.5, recognizes that for outer joins, the conditions of the join must be evaluated separately from the criteria applied to the rows that are joined. ANSI gets it right by separating the JOIN criteria from the WHERE criteria. The old SQL Server *= and =* operators are prone to ambiguities, especially when three or more tables, views, or subqueries are involved. Often the results aren't what you'd expect, even though you might be able to explain them. But sometimes you simply can't get the result you want. These aren't implementation bugs; more accurately, these are inherent limitations in trying to apply the outer-join criteria in the WHERE clause.

WHO'S WRITING THE QUERIES?

Notice that I use the terms "developer" and "database administrator," not "end user." SQL is often regarded as a language suitable for end users as well as database professionals. This is true to some extent, such as with straightforward single table queries. But if you expect end users to understand the semantics of outer joins or deal correctly with NULL, you might as well just give them a random data generator. These concepts are tricky, and it's your job to insulate your users from them. Later in this chapter, you'll see how you can use views to accomplish this.

When *= was introduced, no ANSI specification existed for OUTER JOIN or even for INNER JOIN. Just the old-style join existed, with operators such as =* in the WHERE clause. So the designers quite reasonably tried to fit an outer-join operator into the WHERE clause, which was the only place where joins were ever stated. However, efforts to resolve this situation helped spur the ANSI SQL committee's specification of proper OUTER JOIN syntax and semantics. Implementing outer joins correctly is difficult, and SQL Server is one of the few mainstream products that has done so.

To illustrate the semantic differences and problems with the old *= syntax, I'll walk through a series of examples using both new and old outer-join syntax. The following is essentially the same outer-join query shown earlier, but this one returns only a count. It correctly finds the 11 rows, preserving both authors with no titles and titles with no authors.

```
-- New style OUTER JOIN correctly finds 11 rows
SELECT COUNT(*)
FROM
    (
    -- FIRST join authors and titleauthor
        (authors AS A
        LEFT OUTER JOIN titleauthor AS TA ON A.au_id=TA.au_id
        )

        -- The result of the previous join is then joined to titles
        FULL OUTER JOIN titles AS T ON TA.title_id=T.title_id
    )
WHERE
state <> 'CA' OR state IS NULL
```

There's really no way to write this query—which does a full outer join—using the old syntax, because the old syntax simply isn't expressive enough. Here's what looks to be a reasonable try—but it generates several rows that you wouldn't expect:

```
-- Attempt with old-style join. Really no way to do FULL OUTER
-- JOIN. This query finds 144 rows--WRONG!!
SELECT COUNT(*)
FROM
    authors A, titleauthor TA, titles T
WHERE
A.au_id *= TA.au_id
AND
TA.title_id =* T.title_id
AND
(state <> 'CA' OR state IS NULL)
```

Now let's examine some issues with the old-style outer join using a simple example of only two tables, *Customers* and *Orders*:

```
CREATE TABLE Customers
(
Cust_ID        int   PRIMARY KEY,
Cust_Name      char(20)
)

CREATE TABLE Orders
(
OrderID    int      PRIMARY KEY,
Cust_ID    int      REFERENCES Customers(Cust_ID)
)
GO

INSERT Customers VALUES (1, 'Cust 1')
INSERT Customers VALUES (2, 'Cust 2')
INSERT Customers VALUES (3, 'Cust 3')
INSERT Orders VALUES (10001, 1)
INSERT Orders VALUES (20001, 2)
GO
```

At a glance, in the simplest case, the new-style and old-style syntax appear to work the same. Here's the new syntax:

```
SELECT
'Customers.Cust_ID'=Customers.Cust_ID, Customers.Cust_Name,
    'Orders.Cust_ID'=Orders.Cust_ID
FROM Customers LEFT JOIN Orders
    ON Customers.Cust_ID=Orders.Cust_ID
```

Here's the output:

Customers.Cust_ID	Cust_Name	Orders.Cust_ID
1	Cust 1	1
2	Cust 2	2
3	Cust 3	NULL

And here's the old-style syntax:

```
SELECT 'Customers.Cust_ID'=Customers.Cust_ID, Customers.Cust_Name,
    'Orders.Cust_ID'=Orders.Cust_ID
FROM Customers, Orders WHERE Customers.Cust_ID *= Orders.Cust_ID
```

Here's the output:

Customers.Cust_ID	Cust_Name	Orders.Cust_ID
1	Cust 1	1
2	Cust 2	2
3	Cust 3	NULL

But as soon as you begin to add restrictions, things get tricky. What if you want to filter out *Cust 2*? With the new syntax it's easy, but remember not to filter out the row with NULL that the outer join just preserved!

```
SELECT 'Customers.Cust_ID'=Customers.Cust_ID, Customers.Cust_Name,
'Orders.Cust_ID'=Orders.Cust_ID
FROM Customers LEFT JOIN Orders
    ON Customers.Cust_ID=Orders.Cust_ID
WHERE Orders.Cust_ID <> 2 OR Orders.Cust_ID IS NULL
```

Here's the output:

Customers.Cust_ID	Cust_Name	Orders.Cust_ID
1	Cust 1	1
3	Cust 3	NULL

Now try to do this query using the old-style syntax and filter out *Cust 2*:

```
SELECT 'Customers.Cust_ID'=Customers.Cust_ID, Customers.Cust_Name,
'Orders.Cust_ID'=Orders.Cust_ID
FROM Customers, Orders
WHERE Customers.Cust_ID *= Orders.Cust_ID
AND (Orders.Cust_ID <> 2 OR Orders.Cust_ID IS NULL)
```

Here's the output:

Customers.Cust_ID	Cust_Name	Orders.Cust_ID
1	Cust 1	1
2	Cust 2	NULL
3	Cust 3	NULL

Notice that this time, we don't get rid of *Cust 2*. The check for NULL occurs before the JOIN, so the outer-join operation puts *Cust 2* back. This result might be less than intuitive, but at least we can explain and defend it. That's not always the case, as you'll see in a moment.

If you look at the preceding query, you might think that we should have filtered out *Customers.Cust_ID* rather than *Orders.Cust_ID*. How did we miss that? Surely this query will fix the problem:

```
SELECT 'Customers.Cust_ID'=Customers.Cust_ID, Customers.Cust_Name,
'Orders.Cust_ID'=Orders.Cust_ID
FROM Customers, Orders
WHERE Customers.Cust_ID *= Orders.Cust_ID
AND (Customers.Cust_ID <> 2 OR Orders.Cust_ID IS NULL)
```

Here's the output:

Customers.Cust_ID	Cust_Name	Orders.Cust_ID
1	Cust 1	1
2	Cust 2	NULL
3	Cust 3	NULL

Oops! Same result. The problem here is that *Orders.Cust_ID IS NULL* is now being applied *after* the outer join, so the row is presented again. If we're careful and understand exactly how the old outer join is processed, we can get the results we want with the old-style syntax for this query. We need to understand that the *OR Orders.Cust_ID IS NULL* puts back *Cust_ID 2*, so just take that out. Here is the code:

```
SELECT 'Customers.Cust_ID'=Customers.Cust_ID, Customers.Cust_Name,
    'Orders.Cust_ID'=Orders.Cust_ID
FROM Customers, Orders
WHERE Customers.Cust_ID *= Orders.Cust_ID
AND Customers.Cust_ID <> 2
```

Here's the output:

Customers.Cust_ID	Cust_Name	Orders.Cust_ID
1	Cust 1	1
3	Cust 3	NULL

Finally! This is the result we want. And if you really think about it, the semantics are even understandable (although different from the new style). So maybe this is much ado about nothing; all we have to do is understand how it works, right? Wrong. Besides the issues of joins with more than two tables and the lack of a full outer join, we also can't effectively deal with subqueries and views (virtual tables). For example, let's try creating a view with the old-style outer join:

```
CREATE VIEW Cust_old_OJ AS
(SELECT Orders.Cust_ID, Customers.Cust_Name
FROM Customers, Orders
WHERE Customers.Cust_ID *= Orders.Cust_ID)
```

A simple select from the view looks fine:

```
SELECT * FROM Cust_old_OJ
```

And it gives this output:

Cust_ID	Cust_Name
1	Cust 1
2	Cust 2
NULL	Cust 3

But restricting from this view doesn't seem to make sense:

```
SELECT * FROM Cust_old_OJ WHERE Cust_ID <> 2
    AND Cust_ID IS NOT NULL
```

The output shows NULLs in the *Cust_ID* column, even though we tried to filter them out:

```
Cust_ID        Cust_Name
-------        ---------
1              Cust 1
NULL           Cust 2
NULL           Cust 3
```

If we expand the view to the full select and we realize that *Cust_ID* is *Orders.Cust_ID*, not *Customers.Cust_ID*, perhaps we can understand why this happened. But we still can't filter out those rows!

In contrast, if we create the view with the new syntax and correct semantics, it works exactly as expected:

```
CREATE VIEW Cust_new_OJ AS
(SELECT Orders.Cust_ID, Customers.Cust_Name
FROM Customers LEFT JOIN Orders
    ON Customers.Cust_ID=Orders.Cust_ID )
GO

SELECT * FROM Cust_new_OJ WHERE Cust_ID <> 2 AND Cust_ID IS NOT NULL
```

Here's what was expected:

```
Cust_ID        Cust_Name
-------        ---------
1              Cust 1
```

In the preceding examples, the new syntax performed the outer join and then applied the restrictions in the WHERE clause to the result. In contrast, the old style applied the WHERE clause to the tables being joined and then performed the outer join, which can reintroduce NULL rows. This is why the results often seemed bizarre. However, if that behavior is what you want, you could apply the criteria in the JOIN clause instead of in the WHERE clause.

The following example uses the new syntax to mimic the old behavior. The WHERE clause is shown here simply as a placeholder to make clear that the statement *Cust_ID <> 2* is in the JOIN section, not in the WHERE section.

```
SELECT 'Customers.Cust_ID'=Customers.Cust_ID, Customers.Cust_Name,
    'Orders.Cust_ID'=Orders.Cust_ID
FROM Customers LEFT JOIN Orders
    ON Customers.Cust_ID=Orders.Cust_ID
    AND Orders.Cust_ID <> 2
WHERE 1=1
```

Here's the output:

```
Customers.Cust_ID       Cust_Name        Orders.Cust_ID
-----------------       ---------        --------------
1                       Cust 1           1
2                       Cust 2           NULL
3                       Cust 3           NULL
```

As you can see, the row for *Cust 2* was filtered out from the *Orders* table before the join, but because it was NULL, it was reintroduced by the OUTER JOIN operation.

With the improvements in outer-join support, you can now use outer joins where you couldn't previously. A bit later, you'll see how to use an outer join instead of a correlated subquery in a common type of query.

Cross Joins

In addition to INNER JOIN, OUTER JOIN, and FULL JOIN, the ANSI JOIN syntax allows a CROSS JOIN. Earlier, you saw that the advantage of using the ANSI JOIN syntax was that you wouldn't *accidentally* create a Cartesian product. However, in some cases, creating a Cartesian product might be exactly what you want to do. SQL Server allows you to specify a CROSS JOIN with no ON clause to produce a Cartesian product.

For example, one use for CROSS JOINs is to generate sample or test data. For example, to generate 10,000 names for a sample *employees* table, you don't have to come up with 10,000 individual INSERT statements. All you need to do is build a *first_names* table and a *last_names* table with 26 names each (perhaps one starting with each letter of the English alphabet), and a *middle_initials* table with the 26 letters. When these three small tables are joined using the CROSS JOIN operator, the result is well over 10,000 unique names to insert into the *employees* table. The SELECT statement used to generate these names looks like this:

```
SELECT first_name, middle_initial, last_name
FROM first_names CROSS JOIN middle_initials
    CROSS JOIN last_names
```

To summarize the five types of ANSI JOIN operations, consider two tables, *TableA* and *TableB*:

INNER JOIN (default)

```
TableA INNER JOIN TableB ON join_condition
```

The INNER JOIN returns rows from either table only if they have a corresponding row in the other table. In other words, the INNER JOIN disregards any rows in which the specific join condition, as specified in the ON clause, isn't met.

LEFT OUTER JOIN

```
TableA LEFT OUTER JOIN TableB ON join_condition
```

The LEFT OUTER JOIN returns all rows for which a connection exists between *TableA* and *TableB*; in addition, it returns all rows from *TableA* for which no corresponding row exists in *TableB*. In other words, it preserves unmatched rows from *TableA*. *TableA* is sometimes called the *preserved* table. In result rows containing unmatched rows from *TableA*, any columns selected from *TableB* are returned as NULL.

RIGHT OUTER JOIN

```
TableA RIGHT OUTER JOIN TableB ON join_condition
```

The RIGHT OUTER JOIN returns all rows for which a connection exists between *TableA* and *TableB*; in addition, it returns all rows from *TableB* for which no corresponding row exists in *TableA*. In other words, it preserves unmatched rows from *TableB*, and in this case *TableB* is the preserved table. In result rows containing unmatched rows from *TableB*, any columns selected from *TableA* are returned as NULL.

FULL OUTER JOIN

```
TableA FULL OUTER JOIN TableB ON join_condition
```

The FULL OUTER JOIN returns all rows for which a connection exists between *TableA* and *TableB*. In addition, it returns all rows from *TableA* for which no corresponding row exists in *TableB*, with any values selected from *TableB* returned as NULL. In addition, it returns all rows from *TableB* for which no corresponding row exists in *TableA*, with any values selected from *TableA* returned as NULL. In other words, FULL OUTER JOIN acts as a combination of LEFT OUTER JOIN and RIGHT OUTER JOIN.

CROSS JOIN

```
TableA CROSS JOIN TableB
```

The CROSS JOIN returns all rows from *TableA* combined with all rows from *TableB*. No ON clause exists to indicate any connecting column between the tables. A CROSS JOIN returns a Cartesian product of the two tables.

DEALING WITH NULL

The full outer join example shown on page 330 has a necessary twist because of the NULL value that's generated for the missing author *state* column. Note the WHERE clause:

```
WHERE state <> 'CA' OR state IS NULL
```

Without the following statement

```
OR state IS NULL
```

our favorite row, which contains the title *The Psychology of Computer Cooking,* wouldn't have been selected. Because this title is missing a corresponding author, the *state* column for the query is NULL.

The expression

```
state <> 'CA'
```

doesn't evaluate to TRUE for a NULL value. NULL is considered unknown. If you were to omit the expression

```
OR state IS NULL
```

and execute the query once with the predicate

```
state = 'CA'
```

and once with the predicate

```
state <> 'CA'
```

it might seem intuitive that, between the two queries, all rows will have been selected. But this isn't the case. A NULL *state* satisfies neither condition, and the row with the title *The Psychology of Computer Cooking* won't be part of either result.

This example illustrates the essence of *three-valued logic,* which is so named because a comparison can evaluate to one of three conditions: TRUE, FALSE, or Unknown. Dealing with NULL entries requires three-valued logic. If you allow NULL entries or have cases in which outer joins are necessary, correctly applying three-valued logic is necessary to avoid introducing bugs into your application.

Assume that the table *Truth_Table* has columns *X* and *Y.* We have only one row in the table, as follows, with *X* being *NULL* and *Y* being *1*:

```
X      Y
----   -
NULL   1
```

Without looking ahead, test yourself to see which of the following queries returns *1*:

```
SELECT 1 FROM Truth_Table WHERE X <> Y -- NOT EQUAL
SELECT 1 FROM Truth_Table WHERE X = Y  -- EQUAL
SELECT 1 FROM Truth_Table WHERE X != Y -- NOT EQUAL
                                       -- (alternative formulation)
SELECT 1 FROM Truth_Table WHERE X < Y  -- LESS THAN
SELECT 1 FROM Truth_Table WHERE X !< Y -- NOT LESS THAN
SELECT 1 FROM Truth_Table WHERE X > Y  -- GREATER THAN
SELECT 1 FROM Truth_Table WHERE X !> Y -- NOT GREATER THAN
```

In fact, none of them returns *1* because none of the comparison operations against *X*, which is NULL, evaluate to TRUE. All evaluate to Unknown. Did you get this right? If so, are you confident that all your developers would, too? If you allow NULL, your answer had better be yes.

Further complexity arises when you use expressions that can be Unknown with the logical operations of AND, OR, and NOT. Given that an expression can be TRUE, FALSE, or Unknown, the truth tables in Table 7-1 summarize the result of logically combining expressions.

These truth tables can reveal some situations that might not be obvious otherwise. For example, you might assume that the condition *(X >= 0 OR X <= 0)* must be TRUE because *X* for any number always evaluates to TRUE; it must be either 0 or greater, or 0 or less. However, if *X* is NULL, then *X >= 0* is Unknown, and *X <= 0* is also Unknown. Therefore, the expression evaluates as *Unknown OR Unknown*. As the OR truth table shows, this evaluates to Unknown. To further illustrate, the following SELECT statement doesn't return a *1*:

```
SELECT 1 FROM Truth_Table WHERE (X >= 0 OR X <= 0)
```

AND with Value	True	Unknown	False
TRUE	TRUE	Unknown	FALSE
Unknown	Unknown	Unknown	FALSE
FALSE	FALSE	FALSE	FALSE

OR with Value	True	Unknown	False
TRUE	TRUE	TRUE	TRUE
Unknown	TRUE	Unknown	Unknown
FALSE	TRUE	Unknown	FALSE

NOT	Evaluates to
TRUE	FALSE
Unknown	Unknown
FALSE	TRUE

Table 7-1. *Truth tables showing results of logically combining expressions.*

And because *(X >= 0 OR X <= 0)* is Unknown, the condition:

```
WHERE NOT (X >= 0 OR X <= 0)
```

is equivalent (in pseudocode) to:

```
WHERE NOT (Unknown)
```

The NOT truth table shows that *NOT (Unknown)* is Unknown, so the following negation of the previous SELECT statement also returns nothing:

```
SELECT 1 FROM Truth_Table WHERE NOT (X >= 0 OR X <= 0)
```

And, at the risk of belaboring the point, since neither expression evaluates to TRUE, OR'ing them makes no difference either; consequently, this SELECT also returns nothing:

```
SELECT 1 FROM TRUTH_TABLE
    WHERE (X >= 0 OR X <= 0) OR NOT (X >= 0 OR X <= 0)
```

The fact that none of these SELECT statements evaluates to TRUE, even when negating the expression, illustrates that *not* evaluating to TRUE doesn't imply evaluating to FALSE. Rather, it means either evaluating to FALSE or evaluating to Unknown.

Two special operators, IS NULL and IS NOT NULL, exist to deal with NULL. Checking an expression with one of these operators always evaluates to either TRUE or FALSE. The result returned by IS NULL depends on whether the original expression is a known or unknown value. No Unknown condition is produced when you use IS NULL or IS NOT NULL, as shown in Table 7-2.

IS NULL	*Evaluates to*	*IS NOT NULL*	*Evaluates to*
Known Value	FALSE	Known Value	TRUE
Unknown Value (NULL)	TRUE	Unknown Value (NULL)	FALSE

Table 7-2. *Truth tables for IS NULL and IS NOT NULL.*

In the full outer-join query example, the search criteria were

```
WHERE state <> 'CA' OR state IS NULL
```

For the row with the title *The Psychology of Computer Cooking* (which was produced by the outer join operation preserving the *titles* row with an unmatched *authors* entry), the *authors.state* column is NULL. Hence, the expression

```
state <> 'CA'
```

is Unknown for that row, but the expression

```
state IS NULL
```

is TRUE for that row. The full expression evaluates to *(Unknown OR TRUE)*, which is TRUE, and the row qualifies. Without

```
OR state IS NULL
```

the expression is only *(Unknown)*, so the row doesn't qualify.

NULL in the Real World

As you know, I strongly recommend that you minimize the use of NULL. In outer-join operations, you should carefully account for NULL values that are generated to preserve rows that don't have a match in the table being joined. And even if you're comfortable with three-valued logic, your developers and anyone querying the data using the SQL language typically won't be; therefore, introducing NULL will be a source of bugs just waiting to happen. You can, of course, make all column definitions NOT NULL and declare default values if no value is specified.

You can often avoid the problems of having no matching rows—without the need for outer-join operations—by providing *placeholder,* or *dummy,* rows. For example, you can easily create a dummy *titles* row and a dummy *authors* row. By using constraints or triggers, you can insist that every row in *authors* must have a matching entry in *titleauthor,* even if the ultimate matching row in *titles* is simply the dummy row. Likewise, every row in *titles* can be made to reference *titleauthor,* even if the matching row in *authors* is just the dummy row. In this way, a standard inner join returns all rows because no unmatched rows exist. There's no outer join or NULL complication.

Here's an example: after you add a dummy row for *authors,* one for *titles,* and one for each unmatched row to the *titleauthor* table, you use a standard inner join (with INNER specified purely to emphasize the point) to produce essentially the same results as the full outer join. The only difference in the results is that the placeholder values ***No Current Author**** and ***No Current Title**** are returned instead of NULL.

```
BEGIN TRAN -- Transaction will be rolled back so as to avoid
           -- permanent changes

-- Dummy authors row
INSERT authors
(au_id, au_lname, au_fname, phone, address, city, state, zip, contract)
VALUES
('000-00-0000', '***No Current Author***',
'', 'NONE', 'NONE', 'NONE', 'XX', '99999', 0)


-- Dummy titles row
INSERT titles
(title_id, title, type, pub_id, price, advance, royalty, ytd_sales,
notes, pubdate)
VALUES
('ZZ9999', '***No Current Title***',
'NONE', '9999', 0.00, 0, 0, 0, 'NONE', '1900.01.01')
```

```
-- Associate authors with no current titles to dummy title
INSERT titleauthor VALUES ('341-22-1782', 'ZZ9999', 0, 0)
INSERT titleauthor VALUES ('527-72-3246', 'ZZ9999', 0, 0)
INSERT titleauthor VALUES ('724-08-9931', 'ZZ9999', 0, 0)
INSERT titleauthor VALUES ('893-72-1158', 'ZZ9999', 0, 0)

-- Associate titles with no current author to dummy author
INSERT titleauthor VALUES ('000-00-0000', 'MC3026', 0, 0)

-- Now do a standard INNER JOIN
SELECT
'Author'=RTRIM(au_lname) + ', ' + au_fname,
'Title'=title
FROM
    authors AS A              -- JOIN conditions
    INNER JOIN titleauthor AS TA ON A.au_id=TA.au_id
    INNER JOIN titles AS T ON t.title_id=TA.title_id
WHERE
A.state <> 'CA'
ORDER BY 1

ROLLBACK TRAN     -- Undo changes
```

This is the result:

```
Author                       Title
-------------                ------------------
***No Current Author***,     The Psychology of Computer Cooking
Blotchet-Halls, Reginald     Fifty Years in Buckingham Palace
                             Kitchens
DeFrance, Michel             The Gourmet Microwave
del Castillo, Innes          Silicon Valley Gastronomic Treats
Greene, Morningstar          ***No Current Title***
Panteley, Sylvia             Onions, Leeks, and Garlic: Cooking
                             Secrets of the Mediterranean
Ringer, Albert               Is Anger the Enemy?
Ringer, Albert               Life Without Fear
Ringer, Anne                 The Gourmet Microwave
Ringer, Anne                 Is Anger the Enemy?
Smith, Meander               ***No Current Title***
```

Earlier, you saw how OUTER JOIN became complicated and prone to mistakes. It's comforting to know that, regardless of the order in which you specify the tables for the join operation using dummy rows, the semantics and results are the same because now this operation is simply an INNER JOIN.

However, dummy values won't solve all the woes created by using NULL. First, using dummy values demands more work in your application to ensure that relationships to the placeholder values are maintained. Even more important, many queries still need to be able to discern that the placeholders are special values, or else the results of the query might be suspect. For example, if you use the placeholder value of 0 (zero) instead of NULL for a *salary* field in an *employee* table, you have to be careful not to use such a value in a query that looks for average values or minimum salaries because a salary of 0 would alter your average or minimum calculations inappropriately. If the placeholder is simply another designation for "unknown," you must write your queries with that in mind. Placeholder values usually solve the issues that arise in joining tables, and they can be an effective alternative to using OUTER JOIN. With placeholder values, developers—especially those with only basic SQL knowledge—are less likely to write incorrect queries.

In the previous example, the naïve query returns the same result set as the query with an OUTER JOIN and the criteria *OR state IS NULL*. It took careful work to construct the placeholder data and maintain the relationships for this to be the case. But the group database expert (probably you!) can do that work, and once it is done, individuals with less SQL or database knowledge won't be as likely to introduce bugs in their queries simply because they're unfamiliar with the issues of OUTER JOINS and three-valued logic. Sometimes you might feel you have to use NULL values; however, if you can minimize or avoid these cases, you're wise to do so.

If dummy entries aren't practical for you to use, try a few other tricks. A handy and underused function is ISNULL. Using ISNULL(*expression, value*) substitutes the specified value for the expression when the expression evaluates to NULL. In the earlier outer-join example, the WHERE clause was specified as

```
WHERE state <> 'CA' OR state IS NULL
```

By using the ISNULL function, you can assign a special value (in this case, *XX*) to any NULL *state* values. Then the expression <> *'CA'* will always evaluate to TRUE or FALSE rather than to Unknown. The clause *OR state IS NULL* isn't needed.

The following query produces the full outer-join result, without using IS NULL:

```
SELECT
'Author'=RTRIM(au_lname) + ', ' + au_fname,
'Title'=title
FROM
    authors AS A              -- JOIN CONDITIONS
    FULL OUTER JOIN titleauthor AS TA ON A.au_id=TA.au_id
    FULL OUTER JOIN titles AS T ON t.title_id=TA.title_id
WHERE
ISNULL(state, 'XX') <> 'CA'
ORDER BY 1
```

IS NULL and = NULL

You've seen how the IS NULL operator exists to handle the special case of looking for NULL. Because NULL is considered Unknown, ANSI-standard SQL doesn't provide for an equality expression of NULL—that is, there's no *WHERE value = NULL*. Instead, you must use the IS NULL operator *WHERE value IS NULL*. This can make queries more awkward to write and less intuitive to non-SQL experts. And it's somewhat curious, or at least nonorthogonal, that ANSI SQL doesn't force an UPDATE statement to set a value TO NULL but instead uses the = NULL formulation. (See Table 7-3 for a summary of this state of affairs.)

> **NOTE** *Orthogonal* is a somewhat jargony adjective that's often applied to programming languages and APIs. It's a mathematical term meaning that the sum of the products of corresponding elements in a system equals 0. Thus, a system is orthogonal if all of its primitive operations fully describe the base capabilities of the system and those primitives are independent and mutually exclusive of one another. In a broader sense, the term denotes a certain symmetry and consistency. For example, an API that has a *GetData* call also has a *PutData* call, each taking arguments that are as consistent as possible between the two. The two APIs make up a mutually exclusive domain of operations that you can perform on data, and they are named and invoked in a consistent manner. Such a pair of APIs is considered orthogonal. SQL Server 2000 has a BULK INSERT command but no BULK EXPORT command, so this is an example of *nonorthogonal* behavior.

ANSI SQL Doesn't Provide for This	*And Provides Only for This*
SELECT… WHERE salary = NULL	SELECT… WHERE salary IS NULL

Yet ANSI SQL Uses Only This	*And Not Something Like This*
UPDATE employee SET salary = NULL	UPDATE employee SET salary TO NULL

Table 7-3. *ANSI SQL's treatment of NULLs.*

SQL Server provides an extension to ANSI SQL that allows queries to use = NULL as an alternative to IS NULL. However, this alternative is available only when the ANSI_NULLS session option is OFF. When the ANSI_NULLS option is ON, a condition testing for = NULL is always UNKNOWN.

Note that the formulation is not = *'NULL'*— the quotation marks would have the effect of searching for a character string containing the word *NULL*, as opposed to searching for the special meaning of NULL. The = NULL formulation is simply a shorthand for IS NULL and in some cases provides a more convenient formulation of queries, particularly by allowing NULL within an IN clause. The IN clause is a standard SQL shorthand notation for an expression that checks multiple values, as illustrated here:

Multiple OR Conditions	Equivalent Shorthand Formulation
WHERE state = 'CA' OR state = 'WA' OR state = 'IL'	WHERE state IN ('CA', 'WA', 'IL')

If you want to find states that are either one of the three values depicted in the previous example or NULL, ANSI SQL prescribes that the condition be stated using both an IN clause and an *OR state IS NULL* expression; SQL Server also allows all the conditions to be specified using the IN clause, as shown here:

ANSI SQL Prescribes	SQL Server Also Allows
WHERE state IN ('CA', 'WA', 'IL') OR state IS NULL	WHERE state IN ('CA', 'WA', 'IL', NULL)

The = NULL shorthand can be particularly handy when you're dealing with parameters passed to a stored procedure, and this is the main reason it exists. Here's an example:

```
CREATE PROCEDURE get_employees (@dept char(8), @class char(5))
AS
    SELECT * FROM employee WHERE employee.dept=@dept
        AND employee.class=@class
```

By default, you can pass NULL to this procedure for either parameter; no special treatment is necessary. But without the = NULL shorthand, you need to put in extensive special handling even for this simple procedure:

```
CREATE PROCEDURE get_employees (@dept char(8), @class char(5))
AS
    IF (@dept IS NULL AND @class IS NOT NULL)
        SELECT * FROM employee WHERE employee.dept IS NULL
        AND employee.class=@class
    ELSE IF (@dept IS NULL AND @class IS NULL)
        SELECT * FROM employee WHERE employee.dept IS NULL
        AND employee.class IS NULL
    ELSE IF (@dept IS NOT NULL AND @class IS NULL)
        SELECT * FROM employee WHERE employee.dept=@dept
        AND employee.class IS NULL
    ELSE
        SELECT * FROM employee WHERE employee.dept=@dept
        AND employee.class=@class
```

This example is pretty trivial; the situation becomes much more complex if you have multiple parameters and any one of them might be NULL. You then need a SELECT statement for every combination of parameters that might be NULL or NOT NULL. It can get ugly quickly.

Because your ODBC driver or OLE DB provider can enable the ANSI_NULLS option for you, in effect disallowing the = NULL syntax, I recommend that you write your applications using only IS NULL. If you do have situations in which you might pass NULLs as parameters to a procedure, you have another solution besides the multiple SELECTs described above for every condition of NULL and NOT NULL parameter values. Stored procedures keep track of what the ANSI_NULLS setting was at the time the procedure was created. You can open a Query Analyzer session and explicitly SET ANSI_NULLS OFF. Then you can create all your procedures that might otherwise require separate SELECTs to check for NULL parameters and NOT NULL parameters. Once created, those procedures can be run in any connection, whether ANSI_NULLS is ON or OFF, and they will always be able to compare a column to a parameter, whether the parameter is NULL or not.

SUBQUERIES

SQL Server has an extremely powerful capability for nesting queries that provides a natural and efficient way to express WHERE clause criteria in terms of the results of other queries. You can express most joins as *subqueries,* although this method is often less efficient than performing a join operation. For example, to use the *pubs* database to find all employees of the New Moon Books publishing company, you can write the query as either a join (using ANSI join syntax) or as a subquery.

Here's the query as a join (equijoin, or inner join):

```
SELECT emp_id, lname
FROM employee JOIN publishers ON employee.pub_id=publishers.pub_id
WHERE pub_name='New Moon Books'
```

This is the query as a subquery:

```
SELECT emp_id, lname
FROM employee
WHERE employee.pub_id IN
    (SELECT publishers.pub_id
     FROM publishers WHERE pub_name='New Moon Books')
```

You can write a join (equijoin) as a subquery (subselect), but the converse isn't necessarily true. The equijoin offers an advantage in that the two sides of the equation equal each other and the order doesn't matter. In certain types of subqueries, it does matter which query is the nested query. However, if the query with the subquery can be rephrased as a semantically equivalent JOIN query, the optimizer will do the conversion internally and the performance will be the same whether you write your queries as joins or with subqueries.

Relatively complex operations are simple to perform when you use subqueries. For example, earlier you saw that the *pubs* sample database has four rows in the *authors* table that have no related row in the *titleauthor* table (which prompted our outer-join discussion). The following simple subquery returns those four *author* rows:

```
SELECT 'Author ID'=A.au_id,
    'Author'=CONVERT(varchar(20), RTRIM(au_lname) +  ', '
    + RTRIM(au_fname)), state
FROM authors A
WHERE A.au_id NOT IN
    (SELECT B.au_id FROM titleauthor B)
```

Here's the output:

```
Author ID          Author                   state
---------          -------------------      -----
341-22-1782        Smith, Meander           KS
527-72-3246        Greene, Morningstar      TN
724-08-9931        Stringer, Dirk           CA
893-72-1158        McBadden, Heather        CA
```

The IN operation is commonly used for subqueries, either to find matching values (similar to a join) or to find nonmatching values by negating it (NOT IN), as shown above. Using the IN predicate is actually equivalent to = ANY. If you wanted to find every row in *authors* that had at least one entry in the *titleauthor* table, you could use either of these queries.

Here's the query using IN:

```
SELECT 'Author ID'=A.au_id,
    'Author'=CONVERT(varchar(20), RTRIM(au_lname) + ', '
    + RTRIM(au_fname)), state
FROM authors A
WHERE A.au_id IN
    (SELECT B.au_id FROM titleauthor B)
```

This is the query using equivalent formulation with = ANY:

```
SELECT 'Author ID'=A.au_id,
    'Author'=CONVERT(varchar(20), RTRIM(au_lname) + ', '
    + RTRIM(au_fname)), state
FROM authors A
WHERE A.au_id=ANY
    (SELECT B.au_id FROM titleauthor B)
```

Here's the output:

Author ID	Author	state
172-32-1176	White, Johnson	CA
213-46-8915	Green, Marjorie	CA
238-95-7766	Carson, Cheryl	CA
267-41-2394	O'Leary, Michael	CA
274-80-9391	Straight, Dean	CA
409-56-7008	Bennet, Abraham	CA
427-17-2319	Dull, Ann	CA
472-27-2349	Gringlesby, Burt	CA
486-29-1786	Locksley, Charlene	CA
648-92-1872	Blotchet-Halls, Regi	OR
672-71-3249	Yokomoto, Akiko	CA
712-45-1867	del Castillo, Innes	MI
722-51-5454	DeFrance, Michel	IN
724-80-9391	MacFeather, Stearns	CA
756-30-7391	Karsen, Livia	CA
807-91-6654	Panteley, Sylvia	MD
846-92-7186	Hunter, Sheryl	CA
899-46-2035	Ringer, Anne	UT
998-72-3567	Ringer, Albert	UT

Each of these formulations is equivalent to testing the value of *au_id* in the *authors* table to the *au_id* value in the first row in the *titleauthor* table, and then OR'ing it to a test of the *au_id* value of the second row, and then OR'ing it to a test of the value of the third row, and so on. As soon as one row evaluates to TRUE, the expression is TRUE, and further checking can stop because the row in *authors* qualifies. However, it's an easy mistake to conclude that NOT IN must be equivalent to <> ANY, and some otherwise good discussions of the SQL language have made this exact mistake. More significantly, some products have also erroneously implemented it as such. Although IN is equivalent to = ANY, NOT IN is instead equivalent to <> ALL, not to <> ANY.

> **NOTE** Careful reading of the ANSI SQL-92 specifications also reveals that NOT IN is equivalent to <> ALL but is not equivalent to <> ANY. Section 8.4 of the specifications shows that R NOT IN T is equivalent to NOT (R = ANY T). Furthermore, careful study of section 8.7 <quantified comparison predicate> reveals that NOT (R = ANY T) is TRUE if and only if R <> ALL T is TRUE. In other words, NOT IN is equivalent to <> ALL.

By using NOT IN, you're stating that *none* of the corresponding values can match. In other words, *all* of the values must not match (<> ALL), and if even one does match, it's FALSE. With <> ANY, as soon as one value is found to be not equivalent, the expression is TRUE. This, of course, is also the case for every row of *authors*: rows in *titleauthor* will always exist for other *au_id* values, and hence all *authors* rows will have at least one nonmatching row in *titleauthor*. That is, every row in *authors* will evaluate to TRUE for a test of <> ANY row in *titleauthor*.

The following query using <> ALL returns the same four rows as the earlier one that used NOT IN:

```
SELECT 'Author ID'=A.au_id,
    'Author'=CONVERT(varchar(20), RTRIM(au_lname) + ', '
    + RTRIM(au_fname)), state
FROM authors A
WHERE A.au_id <> ALL
    (SELECT B.au_id FROM titleauthor B)
```

Here is the output:

```
Author ID            Author                 state
---------            -------------------    -----
341-22-1782          Smith, Meander         KS
527-72-3246          Greene, Morningstar    TN
724-08-9931          Stringer, Dirk         CA
893-72-1158          McBadden, Heather      CA
```

If you had made the mistake of thinking that because IN is equivalent to = ANY, then NOT IN is equivalent to <> ANY, you would have written the query as follows. This returns all 23 rows in the *authors* table!

```
SELECT 'Author ID'=A.au_id,
    'Author'=CONVERT(varchar(20), RTRIM(au_lname) + ', '
    + RTRIM(au_fname)), state
FROM authors A
WHERE A.au_id <> ANY
    (SELECT B.au_id FROM titleauthor B)
```

Here's the output:

```
Author ID            Author                 state
---------            -------------------    -----
172-32-1176          White, Johnson         CA
213-46-8915          Green, Marjorie        CA
238-95-7766          Carson, Cheryl         CA
267-41-2394          O'Leary, Michael       CA
274-80-9391          Straight, Dean         CA
341-22-1782          Smith, Meander         KS
409-56-7008          Bennet, Abraham        CA
427-17-2319          Dull, Ann              CA
472-27-2349          Gringlesby, Burt       CA
486-29-1786          Locksley, Charlene     CA
527-72-3246          Greene, Morningstar    TN
648-92-1872          Blotchet-Halls, Regi   OR
672-71-3249          Yokomoto, Akiko        CA
712-45-1867          del Castillo, Innes    MI
```

722-51-5454	DeFrance, Michel	IN
724-08-9931	Stringer, Dirk	CA
724-80-9391	MacFeather, Stearns	CA
756-30-7391	Karsen, Livia	CA
807-91-6654	Panteley, Sylvia	MD
846-92-7186	Hunter, Sheryl	CA
893-72-1158	McBadden, Heather	CA
899-46-2035	Ringer, Anne	UT
998-72-3567	Ringer, Albert	UT

The examples just shown use IN, NOT IN, ANY, and ALL to compare values to a set of values from a subquery. This is common. However, it's also common to use expressions and compare a set of values to a single, scalar value. For example, to find *titles* whose royalties exceed the average of all royalty values in the *roysched* table by 25 percent or more, you can use this simple query:

```
SELECT titles.title_id, title, royalty
FROM titles
WHERE titles.royalty >=
    (SELECT 1.25 * AVG(roysched.royalty) FROM roysched)
```

This query is perfectly good because the aggregate function AVG (*expression*) stipulates that the subquery must return exactly one value and no more. Without using IN, ANY, or ALL (or their negations), a subquery that returns more than one row will result in an error. If you incorrectly rewrote the query as follows, without the AVG function, you'd get run-time error 512:

```
SELECT titles.title_id, title, royalty
FROM titles
WHERE titles.royalty >=
    (SELECT 1.25 * roysched.royalty FROM roysched)
```

Here is the output:

```
Server: Msg 512, Level 16, State 1, Line 1
Subquery returned more than 1 value. This is not permitted when the
subquery follows =, !=, <, <= , >, >= or when the subquery is used
as an expression.
```

It is significant that this error is a run-time error and not a syntax error: in the SQL Server implementation, if that subquery didn't produce more than one row, the query would be considered valid and would execute. For example, the subquery in the following code returns only one row, so the query is valid and returns four rows:

```
SELECT titles.title_id, royalty, title
FROM titles
WHERE titles.royalty >=
    (SELECT 1.25*roysched.royalty FROM roysched
     WHERE roysched.title_id='MC3021' AND lorange=0)
```

Here is the output:

```
title_id royalty    title
-------- ---------- ---------------------------------------------
BU2075   24         You Can Combat Computer Stress!
MC3021   24         The Gourmet Microwave
PC1035   16         But Is It User Friendly?
TC4203   14         Fifty Years in Buckingham Palace Kitchens
```

However, this sort of query can be dangerous, and you should avoid it or use it only when you know that a PRIMARY KEY or UNIQUE constraint will ensure that the subquery returns only one value. The query here appears to work, but it's a bug waiting to happen. As soon as another row is added to the *roysched* table—say, with a *title_id* of MC3021 and a *lorange* of 0—the query returns an error. No constraint exists to prevent such a row from being added.

You might argue that SQL Server should determine whether a query formation could conceivably return more than one row regardless of the data at the time and then disallow such a subquery formulation. The reason it doesn't is that such a query might be quite valid when the database relationships are properly understood, so the power shouldn't be limited to try to protect naïve users. Whether you agree with this philosophy or not, it's consistent with SQL in general—and you should know by now that you can easily write a perfectly legal, syntactically correct query that answers a question in a way that's entirely different from what you thought you were asking!

Correlated Subqueries

You can use powerful correlated subqueries to compare specific rows of one table to a condition in a matching table. For each row otherwise qualifying in the main (or top) query, the subquery is evaluated. Conceptually, a correlated subquery is similar to a loop in programming, although it's entirely without procedural constructs such as *do-while* or *for*. The results of each execution of the subquery must be correlated to a row of the main query. In the next example, for every row in the *titles* table that has a price of $19.99 or less, the row is compared with each *sales row* for stores in California for which the revenue (*price* × *qty*) is greater than $250. In other words, "Show me titles with prices of under $20 for which any single sale in California was more than $250."

```
SELECT T.title_id, title
FROM titles T
WHERE price <= 19.99
AND T.title_id IN (
    SELECT S.title_id FROM sales S, stores ST
    WHERE S.stor_id=ST.stor_id
    AND ST.state='CA' AND S.qty*T.price > 250
    AND T.title_id=S.title_id)
```

Here's the result:

```
title_id        title
--------        -----------------------------
BU7832          Straight Talk About Computers
PS2091          Is Anger the Enemy?
TC7777          Sushi, Anyone?
```

Notice that this correlated subquery, like many subqueries, could have been written as a join (here using the old-style JOIN syntax):

```
SELECT T.title_id, T.title
FROM sales S, stores ST, titles T
WHERE S.stor_id=ST.stor_id
AND T.title_id=S.title_id
AND ST.state='CA'
AND T.price <= 19.99
AND S.qty*T.price > 250
```

It becomes nearly impossible to create alternative joins when the subquery isn't doing a simple IN or when it uses aggregate functions. For example, suppose we want to find titles that lag in sales for each store. This could be defined as "Find any title for every store in which the title's sales in that store are below 80 percent of the average of sales for all stores that carry that title and ignore titles that have no price established (that is, the price is NULL)." An intuitive way to do this is to first think of the main query that will give us the gross sales for each title and store, and then for each such result, do a subquery that finds the average gross sales for the title for all stores. Then we correlate the subquery and the main query, keeping only rows that fall below the 80 percent standard.

Such an example follows. For clarity, notice the two distinct queries, each of which answers a separate question. Then notice how they can be combined into a single correlated query to answer the specific question posed here. All three queries use the old-style JOIN syntax.

```
-- This query computes gross revenues by
-- title for every title and store
SELECT T.title_id, S.stor_id, ST.stor_name, city, state,
    T.price*S.qty
FROM titles AS T, sales AS S, stores AS ST
WHERE T.title_id=S.title_id AND S.stor_id=ST.stor_id

-- This query computes 80% of the average gross revenue for each
-- title for all stores carrying that title:
SELECT T2.title_id, .80*AVG(price*qty)
FROM titles AS T2, sales AS S2
WHERE T2.title_id=S2.title_id
GROUP BY T2.title_id
```

(continued)

```
-- Correlated subquery that finds store-title combinations whose
-- revenues are less than 80% of the average of revenues for that
-- title for all stores selling that title
SELECT T.title_id, S.stor_id, ST.stor_name, city, state,
    Revenue=T.price*S.qty
FROM titles AS T, sales AS S, stores AS ST
WHERE T.title_id=S.title_id AND S.stor_id=ST.stor_id
AND T.price*S.qty <
    (SELECT 0.80*AVG(price*qty)
    FROM titles T2, sales S2
    WHERE T2.title_id=S2.title_id
    AND T.title_id=T2.title_id )
```

And the answer is (from the third query):

title_id	stor_id	stor_name	city	state	Revenue
BU1032	6380	Eric the Read Books	Seattle	WA	99.95
MC3021	8042	Bookbeat	Portland	OR	44.85
PS2091	6380	Eric the Read Books	Seattle	WA	32.85
PS2091	7067	News & Brews	Los Gatos	CA	109.50
PS2091	7131	Doc-U-Mat: Quality Laundry and Books	Remulade	WA	219.00

When the newer ANSI JOIN syntax was first introduced, it wasn't obvious how to use it to write a correlated subquery. It could be that the creators of the syntax forgot about the correlated subquery case, because using the syntax seems like a hybrid of the old and the new: the correlation is still done in the WHERE clause rather than in the JOIN clause. For illustration, examine the two equivalent formulations of the above query using the ANSI JOIN syntax:

```
 SELECT T.title_id, S.stor_id, ST.stor_name, city, state,
    Revenue=T.price*S.qty
FROM titles AS T JOIN sales AS S ON T.title_id=S.title_id
    JOIN stores AS ST ON S.stor_id=ST.stor_id
WHERE T.price*S.qty <
    (SELECT 0.80*AVG(price*qty)
    FROM titles T2 JOIN sales S2 ON T2.title_id=S2.title_id
    WHERE T.title_id=T2.title_id )

SELECT T.title_id, S.stor_id, ST.stor_name, city, state,
    Revenue=T.price*S.qty
FROM titles AS T JOIN sales AS S
    ON T.title_id=S.title_id
    AND T.price*S.qty <
        (SELECT 0.80*AVG(T2.price*S2.qty)
        FROM sales AS S2 JOIN titles AS T2
            ON T2.title_id=S2.title_id
        WHERE T.title_id=T2.title_id)
    JOIN stores AS ST ON S.stor_id=ST.stor_id
```

To completely avoid the old-style syntax with the join condition in the WHERE clause, we could write this using a subquery with a GROUP BY in the FROM clause (creating a derived table, which I'll describe in more detail later in this section). However, although this gets around having to use the old syntax, it might not be worth it. The query is much less intuitive than either of the preceding two formulations, and it takes twice as many logical reads to execute it.

```
SELECT T.title_id, S.stor_id, ST.stor_name, city, state,
    Revenue = T.price * S.qty
FROM
    titles AS T JOIN  sales AS S
        ON T.title_id = S.title_id
  JOIN stores AS ST
        ON S.stor_id  = ST.stor_id
  JOIN
     (SELECT T2.title_id, .80 * AVG(price * qty) AS avg_val
      FROM titles AS T2 JOIN sales AS S2
      ON T2.title_id = S2.title_id
      GROUP BY T2.title_id) AS AV ON  T.title_id = AV.title_id
                              AND T.price * S.qty < avg_val
```

Often, correlated subqueries use the EXISTS statement, which is the most convenient syntax to use when multiple fields of the main query are to be correlated to the subquery. (In practice, EXISTS is seldom used other than with correlated subqueries.) EXISTS simply checks for a nonempty set. It returns (internally) either TRUE or NOT TRUE (which we won't refer to as FALSE, given the issues of three-valued logic and NULL). Because no column value is returned and the only thing that matters is whether any rows are returned, convention dictates that a column list isn't specified. You can either use the * to indicate all columns or a constant such as the number 1 to indicate that the column list is really ignored

A common use for EXISTS is to answer a query such as "Show me the titles for which no stores have sales."

```
SELECT T.title_id, title FROM titles T
WHERE NOT EXISTS
(SELECT  1
FROM sales S
WHERE T.title_id=S.title_id )
```

Here is the output:

```
title_id    title
--------    -----------------------------------
MC3026      The Psychology of Computer Cooking
PC9999      Net Etiquette
```

Conceptually, this query is pretty straightforward. The subquery, a simple equijoin, finds all matches of *titles* and *sales*. Then NOT EXISTS correlates *titles* to those matches, looking for *titles* that don't have even a single row returned in the subquery.

Another common use of EXISTS is to determine whether a table is empty. The optimizer knows that as soon as it gets a single hit using EXISTS, the operation is TRUE and further processing is unnecessary. For example, here's how you determine whether the *authors* table is empty:

```
SELECT 'Not Empty' WHERE EXISTS (SELECT * FROM authors)
```

Earlier, when discussing outer joins, I mentioned that you can now use an outer-join formulation to address what was traditionally a problem in need of a correlated subquery solution. Here's an outer-join formulation for the problem described earlier: "Show me the titles for which no stores have sales."

```
SELECT T1.title_id, title FROM titles T1
    LEFT OUTER JOIN sales S ON T1.title_id=S.title_id
WHERE S.title_id IS NULL
```

> **TIP** Depending on your data and indexes, the outer-join formulation might be faster or slower than a correlated subquery. But before deciding to write your query one way or the other, you might want to come up with a couple of alternative formulations and then choose the one that's fastest in your situation.
>
> In this example, for which little data exists, both solutions run in subsecond elapsed time. But the outer-join query requires fewer than half the number of logical I/Os than does the correlated subquery. With more data, that difference would be significant.

This query works by joining the *stores* and *titles* tables and by preserving the titles for which no store exists. Then, in the WHERE clause, it specifically chooses *only* the rows that it preserved in the outer join. Those rows are the ones for which a title had no matching store.

At other times, a correlated subquery might be preferable to a join, especially if it's a self-join back to the same table or some other exotic join. Here's an example. Given the following table (and assuming that the *row_num* column is guaranteed unique), suppose we want to identify the rows for which *col2* and *col3* are duplicates of another row:

```
row_num          col2          col3
-------          ----          ----
1                C             D
2                A             A
4                C             B
5                C             C
6                B             C
7                C             A
8                C             B
9                C             D
10               D             D
```

We can do this in two standard ways. The first way uses a self-join. In a self-join, the table (or view) is used multiple times in the FROM clause and is aliased at least once. Then it can be treated as an entirely different table and you can compare columns between two "instances" of the same table. A self-join to find the rows having duplicate values for *col2* and *col3* is easy to understand:

```
SELECT DISTINCT A.row_num, A.col2, A.col3
FROM match_cols AS A, match_cols AS B
WHERE A.col2=B.col2 AND A.col3=B.col3 AND A.row_num <> B.row_num
ORDER BY A.col2, A.col3
```

```
row_num      col2      col3
-------      ----      ----
4            C         B
8            C         B
1            C         D
9            C         D
```

But in this case, a correlated subquery using aggregate functions provides a considerably more efficient solution, especially if many duplicates exist:

```
SELECT A.row_num, A.col2, A.col3 FROM match_cols AS A
WHERE EXISTS (SELECT B.col2, B.col3 FROM match_cols AS B
              WHERE B.col2=A.col2
              AND B.col3=A.col3
              GROUP BY B.col2, B.col3 HAVING COUNT(*) > 1)
ORDER BY A.col2, A.col3
```

This correlated subquery has another advantage over the self-join example—the *row_num* column doesn't need to be unique to solve the problem at hand.

You can take a correlated subquery a step further to ask a seemingly simple question that's surprisingly tricky to answer in SQL: "Show me the stores that have sold every title." Even though it seems like a reasonable request, relatively few people can come up with the correct SQL query, especially if I throw in the restrictions that you aren't allowed to use an aggregate function like COUNT(*) and that the solution must be a single SELECT statement (that is, you're not allowed to create temporary tables or the like).

The previous query already revealed two titles that no store has sold, so we know that with the existing dataset, no stores can have sales for all titles. For illustrative purposes, let's add sales records for a hypothetical store that does, in fact, have sales for every title. Following that, we'll see the query that finds all stores that have sold every title (which we know ahead of time is only the phony one we're entering here):

```
-- The phony store
INSERT stores (stor_id, stor_name, stor_address, city, state, zip)
```

(continued)

```
VALUES ('9999', 'WE SUPPLY IT ALL', 'One Main St', 'Poulsbo',
    'WA', '98370')

-- By using a combination of hard-coded values and selecting every
-- title, generate a sales row for every title
INSERT sales (stor_id, title_id, ord_num, ord_date, qty, payterms)
SELECT '9999', title_id, 'PHONY1', GETDATE(), 10, 'Net 60'
FROM titles

-- Find stores that supply every title
SELECT ST.stor_id, ST.stor_name, ST.city, ST.state
FROM stores ST
WHERE NOT EXISTS
    (SELECT * FROM titles T1
    WHERE NOT EXISTS
        (SELECT * FROM sales S
        WHERE S.title_id=T1.title_id AND ST.stor_id=S.stor_id)
    )
```

Here's the result:

```
stor_id        stor_name          city       state
-------        ---------          ----       -----
9999           WE SUPPLY IT ALL   Poulsbo    WA
```

Although this query might be difficult to think of immediately, you can easily understand why it works. In English, it says, "Show me the store(s) such that no titles exist that the store doesn't sell." This query consists of the two subqueries that are applied to each store. The bottommost subquery produces all the titles that the store has sold. The upper subquery is then correlated to that bottom one to look for any titles that are *not* in the list of those that the store has sold. The top query returns any stores that aren't in this list. This type of query is known as a *relational division,* and unfortunately, it isn't as easy to express as we'd like. Although the query shown is quite understandable, once you have a solid foundation in SQL, it's hardly intuitive. As is almost always the case, you could probably use other formulations to write this query.

I've already alluded to writing this query without using an aggregate function like COUNT. There's nothing wrong with using an aggregate function—I imposed this restriction only to make writing the query more of a challenge. If you think of the query in English as "Find the stores that have sold as many unique titles as there are total unique titles," you'll find the following formulation somewhat more intuitive:

```
SELECT ST.stor_id, ST.stor_name
FROM stores ST, sales SA, titles T
WHERE SA.stor_id=ST.stor_id AND SA.title_id=T.title_id
GROUP BY ST.stor_id,ST.stor_name
HAVING COUNT(DISTINCT SA.title_id)=(SELECT COUNT(*) FROM titles T1)
```

The following formulation runs much more efficiently than either of the previous two. The syntax is similar to the preceding one but its approach is novel because it's just a standard subquery, not a join or a correlated subquery. You might think it's an illegal query, since it does a GROUP BY and a HAVING without an aggregate in the select list of the first subquery. But that's OK, both in terms of what SQL Server allows and in terms of the ANSI specification. What isn't allowed is having an item in the select list that isn't an aggregate function but then omitting it from the GROUP BY clause, if there is a GROUP BY clause.

```
-- Find stores that have sold every title
SELECT stor_id, stor_name FROM stores WHERE stores.stor_id IN
(SELECT stor_id FROM sales GROUP BY stor_id
    HAVING COUNT(DISTINCT title_id)=(SELECT COUNT(*) FROM titles)
)
```

And as a lead-in to the next topic, here's a formulation that uses a derived table—a feature that allows you to use a subquery in a FROM clause. This capability lets you alias a virtual table returned as the result set of a SELECT statement, and then lets you use this result set as if it were a real table. This query also runs efficiently.

```
SELECT ST.stor_id, ST.stor_name
FROM stores ST,
    (SELECT stor_id, COUNT(DISTINCT title_id) AS title_count
        FROM sales
        GROUP BY stor_id
    ) as SA
WHERE ST.stor_id=SA.stor_id AND SA.title_count=
    (SELECT COUNT(*) FROM titles)
```

VIEWS AND DERIVED TABLES

Think of a view as a virtual table. Simply put, a view is a named SELECT statement that dynamically produces a result set that you can further operate on. A view doesn't actually store any data. It acts as a filter for underlying tables in which the data is stored. The SELECT statement that defines the view can be from one or more underlying tables or from other views. To relieve users of the complexity of having to know how to write an outer join properly, we can turn the previous outer-join query into a view:

```
CREATE VIEW outer_view AS
(
SELECT
    'Author'=RTRIM(au_lname) + ', ' + au_fname, 'Title'=title
FROM (titleauthor AS TA
FULL OUTER JOIN titles AS T ON (TA.title_id=T.title_id))
RIGHT OUTER JOIN authors AS A ON (A.au_id=TA.au_id)
```

(continued)

```
WHERE
A.state <> 'CA' OR A.state IS NULL
)
```

Now, instead of formulating the outer join, we can simply query the outer-join view, *outer_view*. Then we can do a search for author names starting with *Ri*.

```
SELECT * FROM outer_view WHERE Author LIKE 'Ri%' ORDER BY Author
```

Here's the output:

```
Author          Title
-------------   --------------------
Ringer, Albert  Is Anger the Enemy?
Ringer, Albert  Life Without Fear
Ringer, Anne    The Gourmet Microwave
Ringer, Anne    Is Anger the Enemy?
```

Notice that the view defines the set of rows that are included, but it doesn't define their order. If we want a specific order, we must specify the ORDER BY clause in the SELECT statement on the view rather than on the SELECT statement that defines the view.

A *derived table* is a fancy name for the result of using another SELECT statement in the FROM clause of a SELECT statement. This works because the result of a SELECT statement is a table, which is exactly what the FROM clause requires. You can think of a view as a named derived table. A view is named, and its definition is persistent and reusable; a derived table is a completely dynamic, temporal concept. To show the difference, here's an equivalent *LIKE 'Ri%'* query using a derived table instead of a view:

```
SELECT *
FROM
    (SELECT
    'Author'=RTRIM(au_lname) + ',' + au_fname, 'Title'=title
    FROM (titleauthor AS TA
    FULL OUTER JOIN titles AS T ON (TA.title_id=T.title_id))
    RIGHT OUTER JOIN authors AS A ON (A.au_id=TA.au_id)
    WHERE A.state <> 'CA' OR A.state IS NULL
    ) AS T
WHERE T.Author LIKE 'Ri%'
```

You can insert, update, and delete rows in a view but not in a derived table. Keep in mind that you're always modifying rows in the tables on which a view is based, because the view has no data of its own. The definition of the view is persistent, but the data is not. The data exists only in the view's base tables. Think of it as modifying data *through* a view rather than modifying data *in* a view. Some limitations to modifying data through a view exist; the SQL Server documentation explains them, but they bear repeating here with a bit more comment.

The ability to modify data through a view is determined by the characteristics of the view, the properties of the base tables, and the actual change being made. If the view has INSTEAD-OF triggers, then none of the following rules for modification apply because the INSTEAD-OF trigger replaces the modification operations with other actions. (I'll discuss INSTEAD-OF triggers in Chapter 12.) If the view is a partitioned view, it has its own rules for modification (as discussed in the next section). If the view does not have relevant INSTEAD-OF triggers and is not a partitioned view, it is considered updateable if it does not contain TOP, GROUP BY, UNION, or DISTINCT. You can use aggregate functions only in a subquery in the view. So if the view is considered updateable by these rules, the following restrictions apply to the actual modification statements:

Modifications restricted to one base table   Data modification statements (INSERT and UPDATE only) are allowed on multiple-table views if the data modification statement affects only one base table. DELETE statements are never allowed on multiple-table views.

INSERT statements and NOT NULL columns   INSERT statements aren't accepted unless all the NOT NULL columns without defaults in the underlying table or view are included in the view through which you're inserting new rows and values for those columns are included in the INSERT statement. SQL Server has no way to supply values for NOT NULL columns in the underlying table or view if no default value has been defined.

Data restrictions   All columns being modified must adhere to all restrictions for the data modification statement as if they were executed directly against the base table. This applies to column nullability, constraints, identity columns, and columns with rules and/or defaults and base table triggers.

Limitations on INSERT and UPDATE statements   INSERT and UPDATE statements can't add or change any column in a view that's a computation or the result of an aggregate function.

READTEXT or WRITETEXT   You can't use READTEXT or WRITETEXT on text or image columns in views.

Modifications and view criteria   By default, data modification statements through views aren't checked to determine whether the rows affected are within the scope of the view. For example, you can issue an INSERT statement for a view that adds a row to the underlying base table, but that doesn't add the row to the view. This behavior occurs because the column values are all valid to the table, so they can be added; however, if the column values don't meet the view's criteria, they aren't represented in the selection for the view. Similarly, you can issue an UPDATE statement that changes a row in such a way that the row no longer meets the criteria for the view. If you want all modifications to be checked, use the WITH CHECK OPTION option when you create the view.

For the most part, these restrictions are logical and understandable, except for WITH CHECK OPTION. For instance, if you use a view that defines some select criteria and allows the rows produced by the view to be modified, you must use WITH CHECK OPTION or you might experience the bizarre results of inserting a row that you can never see or updating rows in such a way that they disappear from the view.

Here's an example:

```
CREATE VIEW CA_authors AS
(
SELECT * FROM authors
WHERE state='CA'
)
GO

SELECT * FROM CA_authors

-- (returns 15 rows)
BEGIN TRAN
UPDATE CA_authors SET state='IL'
SELECT * FROM CA_authors

-- (returns 0 rows)

ROLLBACK TRAN
```

Should you be able to update rows in a way that causes them to disappear from the view or add rows and never see them again? It's a matter of opinion. But because the SQL Server behavior is as ANSI SQL specifies, and such disappearing rows are as specified, you should consider *always* using WITH CHECK OPTION if a view is to be updated and the criteria are such that WITH CHECK OPTION might be violated.

If we rewrite the view as follows

```
CREATE VIEW CA_authors AS
(
SELECT * FROM authors
WHERE state='CA'
)
WITH CHECK OPTION
```

when we attempt to update the state column to *IL*, the command fails and we get this error message:

```
Server: Msg 550, Level 16, State 1, Line 1
The attempted insert or update failed because the target view either
specifies WITH CHECK OPTION or spans a view that specifies WITH CHECK
OPTION and one or more rows resulting from the operation did not
qualify under the CHECK OPTION constraint.
The statement has been terminated.
```

Views also have an often-overlooked ability to use a system function in the view definition, making it dynamic for the connection. Suppose we keep a personnel table that has a column called *sqldb_name*, which is the person's login name to SQL Server. The function SUSER_SNAME (*server_user_id*) returns the login name for the current connection. We can create a view using the SUSER_SNAME system function to limit that user to only his or her specific row in the table:

```
CREATE VIEW My_personnel AS
(
SELECT * FROM personnel WHERE sqldb_name = SUSER_SNAME()
)
WITH CHECK OPTION
```

SQL Server provides system functions that return the application name, database username (which might be different from the server login name), and workstation name, and you can use these functions in similar ways. You can see from the previous example that a view can also be important in dealing with security. For details on the system functions, see the SQL Server documentation.

Altering Views

SQL Server 2000 allows you to alter the definition of a view. The syntax is almost identical to the syntax for creating the view initially:

```
ALTER VIEW view_name [(column [,...n])]
[WITH ENCRYPTION]
AS
select_statement
[WITH CHECK OPTION]
```

The big difference is that *view_name* must already exist and the definition specified replaces whatever definition the view had before ALTER VIEW was executed. You might wonder why this is a useful command, since the entire definition must be reentered in the ALTER VIEW. Why don't we just drop the view and re-create it? The benefit comes from the fact that the view's *object_id* won't change, which means that all the internal references to this view remain intact. If other views reference this one, they'll be unaffected. If you've assigned permissions on this view to various users and roles, dropping the view means that all permission information is lost. Altering the view keeps the permissions intact.

There is one gotcha when you deal with permissions on views if the permissions have been assigned on individual columns. Internally, SQL Server keeps track of permissions by the column ID number. If you alter a view and change the order of the columns, the permissions might no longer be what you expect. Suppose you've created a view on the *authors* table to select the authors' names and phone numbers. You want all users to be able to see the authors' names, but you want the phone numbers to be unavailable.

```
CREATE VIEW authorlist (first, last, phone)
AS
SELECT au_fname, au_lname, phone
FROM authors
GO
GRANT SELECT ON authorlist (first, last) TO PUBLIC
GO
```

All users in the *pubs* database can now execute this command:

```
SELECT first, last FROM authorlist
```

You can then alter the view to put the phone number column in the first position:

```
ALTER VIEW authorlist (phone, first, last)
AS
SELECT phone, au_fname, au_lname
FROM authors
```

Because the permissions have been granted on the first two columns, users will get an error message when they run this query:

```
Server: Msg 230, Level 14, State 1
SELECT permission denied on column 'last' of object 'authorlist',
database 'pubs', owner 'dbo'.
```

However, all users can now select the values in the *phone* column, which you're trying to keep hidden.

Partitioned Views

Views in SQL Server can contain the UNION ALL clause, and if these UNION views meet certain conditions, they are called *partitioned views*. Partitioned views let you separate disjoint sets of similar data into separate tables, but through the view, all the tables can be accessed simultaneously. For example, if you were to separate your sales data by quarter so that each quarter was in its own table, you could create a view for the year's sales that unioned the data from all the quarterly tables. Alternatively, you could have sales data for each region of the country in a separate table and use UNION ALL to combine all the regional tables into a view for the whole country.

A view can be considered a partitioned view if it meets all the following criteria:

- The columns in the corresponding positions in each SELECT list are of the same exact type, including having the same collation.

- One column in each table, in the same position, must have a CHECK constraint defined on it that is mutually exclusive with the corresponding constraints in the other tables. This column is called the partitioning column. For example, one table could have the constraint (region = 'East'), one table could have the constraint (region = 'North'), one could have (region = 'West'), and another could have (region = 'South'). No row could satisfy more than one of these constraints.

■   The partitioning column cannot be a computed column.

■   If any of the underlying tables exists on servers other than the local SQL Server on which the view is defined, the view is called a *distributed partitioned view* and is subject to additional restrictions. You can find out more about distributed partitioned views in SQL Server Books Online.

■   The same underlying table cannot appear more than once in the view.

■   The underlying tables cannot have indexes on computed columns.

Here's an example of a partitioned view:

```
-- Create the tables and insert the values
CREATE TABLE Sales_West (
    Ordernum INT,
    total money,
    region char(5) check (region = 'West'),
    primary key (Ordernum, region)
    )
CREATE TABLE Sales_North (
    Ordernum INT,
    total money,
    region char(5) check (region = 'North'),
    primary key (Ordernum, region)
    )
CREATE TABLE Sales_East (
    Ordernum INT,
    total money,
    region char(5) check (region = 'East'),
    primary key (Ordernum, region)
    )
CREATE TABLE Sales_South (
    Ordernum INT,
    total money,
    region char(5) check (region = 'South'),
    primary key (Ordernum, region)
    )
GO

INSERT Sales_West VALUES (16544, 2465, 'West')
INSERT Sales_West VALUES (32123, 4309, 'West')
INSERT Sales_North VALUES (16544, 3229, 'North')
INSERT Sales_North VALUES (26544, 4000, 'North')
INSERT Sales_East VALUES ( 22222, 43332, 'East')
```

(continued)

```
INSERT Sales_East VALUES ( 77777, 10301, 'East')
INSERT Sales_South VALUES (23456, 4320, 'South')
INSERT Sales_South VALUES (16544, 9999, 'South')
GO

-- Create the view that combines all sales tables
CREATE VIEW Sales_National
AS
SELECT *
FROM Sales_West
    UNION ALL
SELECT *
FROM Sales_North
    UNION ALL
SELECT *
FROM Sales_East
    UNION ALL
SELECT *
FROM Sales_South
```

- Partitioned views are updateable under certain conditions. In addition to meeting all the above criteria for the view to be partitioned, the view must meet these restrictions: the primary key column of each table should be included in the select list and must include the partitioning column.

- All columns in the underlying tables not included in the SELECT list should allow NULLs. Default constraints cannot be defined on these columns.

To INSERT into a partitioned view, you must supply a value for all non-nullable columns in the view, even if the column has a default defined in the underlying table. In addition, the value being inserted into the partitioning column must satisfy one of the CHECK constraints in one of the underlying tables; otherwise, you'll get an error message stating that a constraint violation has occurred.

The SQL Server optimizer can be quite clever about processing queries that access partitioned views. In particular, it can determine that it does not need to look at every table in the view, but only the table that contains the rows that match the value of the partitioning column. Here's an example:

```
SELECT *
FROM Sales_National
WHERE region = 'South'
```

For this query, the optimizer can determine that the only table that needs to be accessed is the *Sales_South* table. You can see that this is the case by inspecting the query plan produced when you execute this query. We'll look at the details of examining query plans in Chapter 16.

OTHER SEARCH EXPRESSIONS

In addition to the SELECT statement and joins, SQL Server provides other useful search expressions that enable you to tailor your queries. These expressions include LIKE and BETWEEN, along with aggregate functions such as AVG, COUNT, and MAX.

LIKE

In an earlier example, we used LIKE to find authors whose names start with *Ri*. LIKE allows you to search using the simple pattern matching that is standard with ANSI SQL, but SQL Server adds capability by introducing wildcard characters that allow the use of regular expressions. Table 7-4 shows how wildcard characters are used in searches.

Wildcard	Searches for
%	Any string of zero or more characters.
_	Any single character.
[ ]	Any single character within the specified range (for example, [a-f]) or the specified set (for example, [abcdef]).
[^]	Any single character not within the specified range (for example, [^a-f]) or the specified set (for example, [^abcdef]).

Table 7-4. *Wildcard characters recognized by SQL Server for use in regular expressions.*

Table 7-5 shows examples from the SQL Server documentation of how LIKE can be used.

Form	Searches for
LIKE 'Mc%'	All names that begin with the letters *Mc* (such as McBadden).
LIKE '%inger'	All names that end with *inger* (such as Ringer and Stringer).
LIKE '%en%'	All names that include the letters *en* (such as Bennet, Green, and McBadden).
LIKE '_heryl'	All six-letter names ending with *heryl* (such as Cheryl and Sheryl).
LIKE '[CK]ars[eo]n'	All names that begin with *C* or *K*, then *ars*, then *e* or *o*, and end with *n* (such as Carsen, Karsen, Carson, and Karson).
LIKE '[M-Z]inger'	All names ending with *inger* that begin with any single letter from *M* through *Z* (such as Ringer).
LIKE 'M[^c]%'	All names beginning with the letter *M* that don't have the letter *c* as the second letter (such as MacFeather).

Table 7-5. *Using LIKE in searches.*

Trailing Blanks

Trailing blanks (blank spaces) can cause considerable confusion and errors. In SQL Server, when you use trailing blanks you must be aware of differences in how *varchar* and *char* data is stored and of how the SET ANSI_PADDING option is used.

Suppose that I create a table with five columns and insert data as follows:

```
SET ANSI_PADDING OFF

DROP TABLE checkpad
GO

CREATE TABLE checkpad
(
rowid          smallint      NOT NULL PRIMARY KEY,
c10not         char(10)      NOT NULL,
c10nul         char(10)      NULL,
v10not         varchar(10)   NOT NULL,
v10nul         varchar(10)   NULL
)

-- Row 1 has names with no trailing blanks
INSERT checkpad VALUES (1, 'John', 'John', 'John', 'John')

-- Row 2 has each name inserted with three trailing blanks
INSERT checkpad VALUES
    (2, 'John   ', 'John   ', 'John   ', 'John   ')

-- Row 3 has each name inserted with a full six trailing blanks
INSERT checkpad VALUES
    (3, 'John      ', 'John      ', 'John      ', 'John      ')

-- Row 4 has each name inserted with seven trailing blanks (too many)
INSERT checkpad VALUES
    (4, 'John       ', 'John       ', 'John       ', 'John       ')
```

I can then use the following query to analyze the contents of the table. I use the DATALENGTH(*expression*) function to determine the actual length of the data and then convert to VARBINARY to display the hexadecimal values of the characters stored. (For those of you who don't have the ASCII chart memorized, a blank space is 0x20.) I then use a LIKE to try to match each column, once with one trailing blank and once with six trailing blanks.

```
SELECT ROWID,
"0xC10NOT"=CONVERT(VARBINARY(10), c10not), L1=DATALENGTH(c10not),
"LIKE 'John %'"=CASE WHEN (c10not LIKE 'John %') THEN 1 ELSE 0 END,
"LIKE 'John      %'"=CASE WHEN (c10not LIKE 'John      %')
    THEN 1 ELSE 0 END,
"0xC10NUL"=CONVERT(VARBINARY(10), c10nul), L2=DATALENGTH(c10nul),
"LIKE 'John %'"=CASE WHEN (c10nul LIKE 'John %') THEN 1 ELSE 0 END,
"LIKE 'John      %'"=CASE WHEN (c10nul LIKE 'John      %')
    THEN 1 ELSE 0 END,
```

```
"0xV10NOT"=CONVERT(VARBINARY(10), v10not), L3=DATALENGTH(v10not),
"LIKE 'John %'"=CASE WHEN (v10not LIKE 'John %') THEN 1 ELSE 0 END,
"LIKE 'John      %'"=CASE WHEN (v10not LIKE 'John        %')
    THEN 1 ELSE 0 END,
"0xV10NUL"=CONVERT(VARBINARY(10), v10nul), L4=DATALENGTH(v10nul),
"LIKE 'John %'"=CASE WHEN (v10nul LIKE 'John %') THEN 1 ELSE 0 END,
"LIKE 'John      %'"=CASE WHEN (v10nul LIKE 'John        %')
    THEN 1 ELSE 0 END
FROM checkpad
```

Figure 7-2 shows the results of this query from the *checkpad* table.

Figure 7-2. *The results of the query using SET ANSI_PADDING OFF.*

If you don't enable SET ANSI_PADDING ON, SQL Server trims trailing blanks for variable-length columns and for fixed-length columns that allow NULLs. Notice that only column *c10not* has a length of 10. The other three columns are treated identically and end up with a length of 4 and no padding. For these columns, even trailing blanks explicitly entered within the quotation marks are trimmed. All the variable-length columns as well as the fixed-length column that allows NULLs have only the 4 bytes J-O-H-N (4A-6F-68-6E) stored. The true fixed-length column, *c10not*, is automatically padded with six blank spaces (0x20) to fill the entire 10 bytes.

All four columns match LIKE 'John%' (no trailing blanks), but only the fixed-length column *c10not* matches LIKE 'John ?' (one trailing blank) and LIKE 'JOHN %'?' (six trailing blanks). The reason is apparent when you realize that those trailing blanks are truncated and aren't part of the stored values for the other columns. A column query gets a hit with LIKE and trailing blanks only when the trailing blanks are stored. In this example, only the *c10not* column stores trailing blanks, so that's where the hit occurs.

SQL Server has dealt with trailing blanks in this way for a long time. However, when the developers began working to pass the National Institute of Standards and Technology (NIST) test suite for ANSI SQL conformance, they realized that this behavior was inconsistent with the ANSI specification. The specification requires that you always pad *char* datatypes and that you don't truncate trailing blanks entered by the user, even for *varchar*. I could argue for either side—both the long-standing SQL Server behavior and the ANSI specification behavior can be desirable, depending on the circumstances. However, if SQL Server had changed its behavior to conform to ANSI, it would have broken many deployed SQL Server applications. So, to satisfy both sides, the ANSI_PADDING option was added in version 6.5. If you enable SET ANSI_PADDING ON, re-create the table, reinsert the rows, and then issue the same query, you get the results shown in Figure 7-3, which are different from those shown in Figure 7-2.

If you set ANSI_PADDING ON, the *char(10)* columns *c10not* and *c10nul*, whether declared NOT NULL or NULL, are always padded out to 10 characters regardless of how many trailing blanks were entered. In addition, the variable-length columns *v10not* and *v10nul* contain the number of trailing blanks that were inserted. Trailing blanks are not truncated. Because the variable-length columns now store any trailing blanks that were part of the INSERT (or UPDATE) statement, the columns get hits in queries with LIKE and trailing blanks if the query finds that number of trailing blanks (or more) in the columns' contents. Notice that no error occurs as a result of inserting a column with seven (instead of six) trailing blanks. The final trailing blank simply gets truncated. If you want a warning message to appear in such cases, you can use SET ANSI_WARNINGS ON.

ROWID	0xC10NOT	L1	LIKE 'John %'	LIKE 'John'	0xC10NUL	L2	LIKE 'John %'	LIKE 'John'	0xV10NOT	L3	LIKE 'John %'	LIKE 'John'	0xV10NUL	L4	LIKE 'John %'	LIKE 'John'
1	0x4A6F686E2020 20202020	10	1	1	0x4A6F686E20 2020202020	10	1	1	0x4A6F686E	4	0	0	0x4A6F686E	4	0	0
2	0x4A6F686E2020 20202020	10	1	1	0x4A6F686E20 2020202020	10	1	1	0x4A6F686E 202020	7	1	0	0x4A6F686E 202020	7	1	0
3	0x4A6F686E2020 20202020	10	1	1	0x4A6F686E20 2020202020	10	1	1	0x4A6F686E 2020202020 20	10	1	1	0x4A6F686E 2020202020 20	10	1	1
4	0x4A6F686E2020 20202020	10	1	1	0x4A6F686E20 2020202020	10	1	1	0x4A6F686E 2020202020 20	10	1	1	0x4A6F686E 2020202020 20	10	1	1

Figure 7-3. *The results of the query using SET ANSI_PADDING ON.*

Note that the SET ANSI_PADDING ON option applies to a table only if the option was enabled at the time the table was created. (SET ANSI_PADDING ON also applies to a column if the option was enabled at the time the column was added via ALTER TABLE.) Enabling this option for an existing table does nothing. To determine whether a column has ANSI_PADDING set to ON, examine the status field of the *syscolumns* table and do a bitwise AND 20 (decimal). If the bit is on, you know the column was created with the option enabled. For example:

```
SELECT name, 'Padding On'=CASE WHEN status & 20 <> 0
    THEN 'YES' ELSE 'NO' END
FROM syscolumns WHERE id=OBJECT_ID('checkpad') AND name='v10not'
GO
```

SET ANSI_PADDING ON also affects the behavior of *binary* and *varbinary* fields, but the padding is done with zeros instead of spaces. Table 7-6 shows the effects of the SET ANSI_PADDING setting when values are inserted into columns with *char*, *varchar*, *binary*, and *varbinary* data types.

Note that when a fixed-length column allows NULLs, it mimics the behavior of variable-length columns if ANSI_PADDING is off. If ANSI_PADDING is on, fixed-length columns that allow NULLs behave the same as fixed-length columns that don't allow NULLs.

The fact that a fixed-length character column that allows NULLs is treated as a variable-length column does not affect how the data is actually stored on the page. If you use the DBCC PAGE command (as discussed in Chapter 6) to look at the column *c10nul*, you'll see that it always holds a full 10 characters, including the 6 trailing spaces in our example above. When you manipulate the column using SQL statements, the query processor checks the status of the bit in *syscolumns.status*, and if the column is marked with ANSI_PADDING set to ON, the query processor ignores trailing blanks.

You should also be aware that comparing these strings using LIKE is quite a bit different than comparing the strings for equality. The following query returns only rows in which the query processor recognizes at least one trailing space after the 'John':

```
SELECT * FROM checkpad
WHERE c10nul LIKE 'John %'
```

On the other hand, a comparison that looks for equality always ignores any trailing spaces and finds a match whenever all the leading, nonspace characters are the same. The following query returns all the rows in the *checkpad* table, whether ANSI_PADDING is ON or OFF, and in addition, it returns all the rows in the table if you replace the *c10nul* column with any of the columns in the table:

```
SELECT * from checkpad
WHERE c10nul = 'John'
```

The SQL Server ODBC driver and OLE DB Provider for SQL Server automatically set ANSI_PADDING to ON when they connect. When you write your own applications, the ANSI_PADDING setting can be changed in the ODBC connection attributes or the OLE DB connection properties before your application makes its connection to the SQL Server. In addition, the ANSI_PADDING setting can be changed in the ODBC Data Sources dialog box, available through the Control Panel.

Setting of ANSI_PADDING	char(n) NOT NULL or binary(n) NOT NULL	char(n) NULL or binary(n) NULL	varchar(n) or varbinary(n)
ON	Pad original value to the length of the column.	Follows same rules as for char(n) or binary(n) NOT NULL.	Trailing blanks (for varchar) or zeros (for varbinary) in values inserted aren't trimmed. Values are not padded to the length of the column.
OFF	Pad original value to the length of the column.	Follows same rules as for varchar or varbinary.	Trailing blanks (for varchar) or trailing zeros (for varbinary) are trimmed.

Table 7-6. *The effects of the ANSI_PADDING setting.*

Regardless of how the column was created, SQL Server provides functions that can help you deal effectively with trailing blanks. The RTRIM(*char_expression*) function removes trailing blanks if they exist. You can add trailing blanks to your output by concatenating with the SPACE(*integer_expression*) function. An easier way is to use the CONVERT function to convert to a fixed-length *char* of whatever length you want. Then variable-length columns will be returned as fully padded, regardless of the ANSI_PADDING setting and regardless of the columns' actual storage, by converting them to *char(10)* or whatever size you want. The following SELECT statement against the *checkpad* table illustrates this:

```
SELECT CONVERT(VARBINARY(10), CONVERT(char(10), v10nul))
FROM checkpad
```

Here's the result:

```
0x4a6f686e202020202020
0x4a6f686e202020202020
0x4a6f686e202020202020
0x4a6f686e202020202020
```

BETWEEN

BETWEEN is shorthand for greater-than-or-equal-to AND less-than-or-equal-to. The *clause WHERE C BETWEEN B AND D* is equivalent to *WHERE C >= B AND C <= D.* The order of the values to be checked is important when you use *BETWEEN*. If *B, C,* and *D* are increasing values, for example, *WHERE C BETWEEN D AND B* isn't true because it evaluates *to WHERE C >= D AND C <= B.*

Aggregate Functions

Aggregate functions (sometimes referred to as *set functions*) allow you to summarize a column of output. SQL Server provides six general aggregate functions that are standard ANSI SQL-92 fare. I won't go into much detail about their general use; instead, I'll focus on some aspects specific to SQL Server. Table 7-7 summarizes SQL Server's ANSI SQL aggregate functions.

Consider the following table, *automobile_sales_detail.* I'll use this table to demonstrate how aggregate functions simplify finding the answers to complex questions:

rowid	model	year	color	units_sold
1	Chevy	1990	Red	5
2	Chevy	1990	White	87
3	Chevy	1990	Blue	62
4	Chevy	1991	Red	54
5	Chevy	1991	White	95
6	Chevy	1991	Blue	49
7	Chevy	1992	Red	31
8	Chevy	1992	White	54
9	Chevy	1992	Blue	71
10	Ford	1990	Red	64
11	Ford	1990	White	62
12	Ford	1990	Blue	63
13	Ford	1991	Red	52
14	Ford	1991	White	9
15	Ford	1991	Blue	55
16	Ford	1992	Red	27
17	Ford	1992	White	62
18	Ford	1992	Blue	39

Aggregate Function	Description
AVG(*expression*)	Returns the average (mean) of all the values, or only the DISTINCT values, in the expression. You can use AVG with numeric columns only.* Null values are ignored.
COUNT(*expression*)	Returns the number of non-null values in the expression. When DISTINCT is specified, COUNT finds the number of unique non-null values. You can use COUNT with both numeric and character columns. Null values are ignored.
COUNT(*)	Returns the number of rows. COUNT(*) takes no parameters and can't be used with DISTINCT. All rows are counted, even those with null values.
MAX(*expression*)	Returns the maximum value in the expression. You can use MAX with numeric, character, and datetime columns but not with *bit* columns. With character columns, MAX finds the highest value in the collating sequence. MAX ignores any null values. DISTINCT is available for ANSI compatibility, but it's not meaningful with MAX.
MIN(*expression*)	Returns the minimum value in the expression. You can use MIN with numeric, character, and datetime columns, but not with *bit* columns. With character columns, MIN finds the value that is lowest in the sort sequence. MIN ignores any null values. DISTINCT is available for ANSI compatibility, but it's not meaningful with MIN.
SUM(*expression*)	Returns the sum of all the values, or only the DISTINCT values, in the expression. You can use SUM with numeric columns only. Null values are ignored.

* As used here, numeric columns refers to decimal, float, int, money, numeric, real, smallint, smallmoney, bigint, and tinyint datatypes.

Table 7-7. *SQL Server's ANSI aggregate functions.*

You can increase the power of aggregate functions by allowing them to be grouped and by allowing the groups to have criteria established for inclusion via the HAVING clause. The following queries provide some examples.

EXAMPLE 1

Show the oldest and newest model years for sale, and show the average sales of all the entries in the table:

```
SELECT 'Oldest'=MIN(year), 'Newest'=MAX(year),
    'Avg Sales'=AVG(units_sold)
FROM automobile_sales_detail
```

Here's the output:

```
Oldest   Newest   Avg Sales
------   ------   ---------
1990     1992     52
```

EXAMPLE 2

Do the Example 1 query, but show the values only for autos that are Chevys:

```
SELECT 'Oldest'=MIN(year), 'Newest'=MAX(year),
    'Avg Sales'=AVG(units_sold)
FROM automobile_sales_detail
WHERE model='Chevy'
```

Here's the result:

```
Oldest   Newest   Avg Sales
------   ------   ---------
1990     1992     56
```

EXAMPLE 3

Show the same values as in Example 1, but group them based on the model and color of the cars:

```
SELECT model, color, 'Oldest'=MIN(year), 'Newest'=MAX(year),
    'Avg Sales'=AVG(units_sold)
FROM automobile_sales_detail
GROUP BY model, color
ORDER BY model, color
```

Here's the output:

```
model   color   Oldest   Newest   Avg Sales
-----   -----   ------   ------   ---------
Chevy   Blue    1990     1992     60
Chevy   Red     1990     1992     30
Chevy   White   1990     1992     78
Ford    Blue    1990     1992     52
Ford    Red     1990     1992     47
Ford    White   1990     1992     44
```

EXAMPLE 4

Show the same values for only those model-year rows with average sales of 65 or fewer. Also, order and group the output first by color and then by model, but keep the columns in the same order:

```
SELECT model, color, 'Oldest'=MIN(year), 'Newest'=MAX(year),
    'Avg Sales'=AVG(units_sold)
FROM automobile_sales_detail
GROUP BY color, model HAVING AVG(units_sold) <= 65
ORDER BY color, model
```

Here's the output:

model	color	Oldest	Newest	Avg Sales
Chevy	Blue	1990	1992	60
Ford	Blue	1990	1992	52
Chevy	Red	1990	1992	30
Ford	Red	1990	1992	47
Ford	White	1990	1992	44

NOTE   I included an ORDER BY clause in these queries even though I speci-fied that the criteria of the ORDER BY be the same as for the GROUP BY clause. SQL Server has several alternative strategies for handling GROUP BY that don't require sorting of the results, so the order in which the results are returned is unpredictable. If you want the results in a particular order, you must specify ORDER BY.

An Alternative to Using COUNT(*)

You can use COUNT(*) to find the count of all the rows in the table, but a consider-ably faster way exists. The *rows* column in the *sysindexes* table keeps the current rowcount dynamically for the clustered index. If one exists, *indid* = 1. If no clustered index exists, *sysindexes* keeps the count for the table (*indid* = 0). A faster query looks something like this:

```
SELECT rows
FROM sysindexes
WHERE id=OBJECT_ID ('authors')
    AND indid < 2
```

This query works only for base tables, not views, and it works only if you apply no selection criteria via a WHERE clause. If you want to respond to a query such as "Show me the count of all rows for which the author lives in California," you'd still need to use COUNT(*). In addition, there's no guarantee that this number will be accurate 100 percent of the time. In previous versions of SQL Server, certain op-erations (such as SELECT INTO), didn't always correctly update the *rows* column in *sysindexes*. SQL Server 2000 is much more likely to keep *sysindexes* up to date, but there's still no guarantee. In addition, you can execute the command DBCC UPDATEUSAGE to force the values in *sysindexes* to be updated. However, there will be some nonzero lag time between running this command and looking at the con-tents of *sysindexes*, and if the table is modified during that time, your result will still not be 100 percent guaranteed. If you absolutely must know exactly how many rows are in a table in your application, use the COUNT(*) aggregate.

Aggregates and *bigint*

As the footnote to Table 7-7 indicates, numeric columns used in aggregate function can include the 8-byte integer type *bigint*. However, you should keep in mind some special considerations when you work with *bigint* values. First of all, Microsoft considers the 4-byte integer as the primary integer type; the 8-byte integer is something specialized. Automatic promotions to *bigint* do not occur. When you use the aggregates AVG, SUM, MIN, and MAX on *int*, *smallint*, or *tinyint* data, the result of the function is *int*. Only when the datatype of the expression operated upon by these functions is *bigint* is the result of the function *bigint*. However, to avoid overflow of the internal counters, internally SQL Server uses *bigint* values to process the AVG aggregate. Both the counter accumulating the total number of rows and the counter accumulating the sum are stored internally as *bigint*.

With SUM, if there is a possibility that the result will be too large to fit into a 4-byte *int,* you should use the CONVERT function to avoid an overflow error:

```
SELECT col1, SUM(CONVERT(bigint, col2))
FROM mytable
GROUP BY col1
```

COUNT always returns an *int*. If there is a possibility that the number of rows will exceed the maximum value of an *int* (2^31-1), you can use the new aggregate function COUNT_BIG, which always returns a *bigint*.

Aggregate Functions and NULLs

As usual, you must understand the effect of using NULLs to use them appropriately with aggregate functions. Unfortunately, these effects aren't necessarily intuitive or even consistent. Because NULL is considered Unknown, one could certainly argue that using SUM, MAX, MIN, or AVG on a table containing one or more NULL values should also produce NULL. Obviously, if we have three employees and we don't know the salaries of two of them, it's totally inaccurate to state that the SUM of the salaries for the three employees is equal to the one known salary. Yet this is exactly how SUM, MIN, MAX, AVG, and COUNT work (but not COUNT(*)). Implicitly, these functions seem to tack on the criterion of "for only those values that are not NULL."

You'll probably want these operations to work this way most of the time, and pragmatically, it's good that they do because that means they're simpler to use in common situations. But if you don't understand exactly how these functions will affect your code, you might introduce bugs. For example, if you divide SUM by the result of COUNT(*) as a way to compute the mean value, the result probably won't be what you intended—SUM disregards the NULL values, but COUNT(*) counts the rows that include those NULL values.

I've suggested a few times that using default or dummy values can be a good alternative to using NULL. But I've also tried to make clear that while these alternatives solve some issues, they introduce other problems. You must account for aggregates, and you might want to get back to exactly the semantics that aggregates such as SUM use with defaults, ignoring the default or dummy values. Aggregating on only one column is pretty straightforward, and your WHERE clause can simply exclude those values you want to disregard. But if you're aggregating on multiple columns, eliminating rows in the WHERE clause might be a poor solution.

For example, suppose that in our *employee* table, we have both an *emp_age* column and an *emp_salary* column. To avoid using NULL, we use 0.00 when we don't know the actual value. We want one query to do aggregations of each column. Yet we don't want to disregard a row's value for *emp_age* if we don't have an actual value for *emp_salary*, or vice-versa.

Here's our *employee* table:

```
emp_id    emp_name    emp_age    emp_salary
------    --------    -------    ----------
1         Smith       34         26000.00
2         Doe         30         35000.00
3         Jones       45         0.00
4         Clark       0          65000.00
5         Kent        63         0.00
```

Now suppose we want to write a simple query to get the count of all employees, the average and lowest salaries, and the average and lowest ages. Here's our first simplistic query:

```
SELECT
'Num Employees'=COUNT(*),
'Avg Salary'=AVG(emp_salary),
'Low Salary'=MIN(emp_salary),
'Avg Age'=AVG(emp_age),
'Youngest'=MIN(emp_age)
FROM employee
```

Here's the result:

```
Num Employees    Avg Salary    Low Salary    Avg Age    Youngest
-------------    ----------    ----------    -------    --------
5                25200.00      0.00          34         0
```

Obviously, this query doesn't correctly answer our question because the dummy values of 0 have distorted the results for the AVG and MIN columns. So we decide to exclude those rows by stating in the WHERE clause that the salary should not be the default value:

```
SELECT
'Num Employees'=COUNT(*),
'Avg Salary'=AVG(emp_salary),
'Low Salary'=MIN(emp_salary),
'Avg Age'=AVG(emp_age),
'Youngest'=MIN(emp_age)
FROM employee
WHERE emp_salary > 0 AND emp_age > 0
```

Here's what we get:

```
Num Employees    Avg Salary    Low Salary    Avg Age    Youngest
-------------    ----------    ----------    -------    --------
2                30500.00      26000.00      32         30
```

This query is marginally better because at least the average salary is no longer lower than any actually known salary. The values are based on only the first two employees, Smith and Doe—we have *five* employees, not just *two,* as this result claims. Two other employees, Jones and Kent, are significantly older than the two who were used to compute the average age. And had Clark's salary been considered, the average salary would be much higher. We are seemingly stuck. It looks as if we can't write a single query to answer the question and might have to write separate queries to get the count, the salary information, and the age information.

Fortunately, the NULLIF function comes to the rescue. This function is one of many handy Transact-SQL functions. NULLIF takes two expressions, NULLIF(*expression1, expression2*), and it returns NULL if the two expressions are equivalent and *expression1* if they aren't equivalent. The NULLIF function is roughly the mirror image of another function, ISNULL, which produces a value if a NULL is encountered (as discussed earlier in this chapter). The NULLIF function is actually a special-purpose shorthand of the ANSI SQL-92 CASE expression (discussed in detail in Chapter 10). Using NULLIF is equivalent to the following:

```
CASE
    WHEN expression1=expression2 THEN NULL
    ELSE expression1
END
```

Hence, NULLIF(*emp_salary, 0)* produces NULL for rows in which the salary equals 0. By converting the 0 values to NULL, we can use the aggregate functions just as we'd use them with NULL so that SUM and MIN disregard the NULL entries.

```
SELECT
'Num Employees'=COUNT(*),
'Avg Salary'=AVG(NULLIF(emp_salary, 0)),
'Low Salary'=MIN(NULLIF(emp_salary, 0)),
'Avg Age'=AVG(NULLIF(emp_age, 0)),
'Youngest'=MIN(NULLIF(emp_age, 0))
FROM employee
```

Here's the more accurate result:

```
Num Employees    Avg Salary    Low Salary    Avg Age    Youngest
-------------    ----------    ----------    -------    --------
5                42000.00      26000.00      43         30
```

Finally! This result is exactly what we want, and all five employees are represented. Of the three whose salaries we know, the average salary is $42,000.00 and the low salary is $26,000.00. Of the four whose ages we know, the average age is 43 and the youngest is 30.

Datacube—Aggregate Variations

The previous aggregate examples in this chapter, which all use standard SQL-92 syntax, show that by formulating a specific query on the sample table with one of the aggregate functions, we can answer almost any question regarding aggregate sales for some combination of model, year, and color of car. However, answering any of these questions requires a separate, specific query. Of course, it's common to look at data and keep formulating and posing new and different questions. Such questions are the hallmark of data mining, decision-support systems (DSSs), online analytic processing (OLAP), or whatever other name is used these days for this age-old need to examine data.

To address this inherent weakness in standard SQL, developers have created several front-end tools that maintain a set of data that allow you to easily query changes in aggregation, thereby eliminating the need to sweep through data for every new aggregation request. One such tool is Microsoft Analysis Services, which you can install from the same CD that contains your SQL Server 2000 software. Analysis Services tools can add a lot of value, and they make it easy to slice and dice the values pertaining to any "cut" of the data groupings. But even these tools can perform better with help from the database engine.

SQL Server has two extensions to GROUP BY—CUBE and ROLLUP—that allow SQL Server to optionally generate all the aggregate groupings in a single query.

CUBE

CUBE explodes data to produce a result set containing a superset of groups, with a cross-tabulation of every column to the value of every other column, as well as a special super-aggregate value that can be thought of as meaning ALL VALUES. Here's the CUBE for the 18 rows of the *automobile_sales_detail* table. Notice that these 18 rows generate 48 rows in the datacube.

```
units   model   year   color
-----   -----   ----   -----
62      Chevy   1990   Blue
5       Chevy   1990   Red
87      Chevy   1990   White
154     Chevy   1990   ALL
49      Chevy   1991   Blue
54      Chevy   1991   Red
95      Chevy   1991   White
198     Chevy   1991   ALL
```

71	Chevy	1992	Blue
31	Chevy	1992	Red
54	Chevy	1992	White
156	Chevy	1992	ALL
508	Chevy	ALL	ALL
63	Ford	1990	Blue
64	Ford	1990	Red
62	Ford	1990	White
189	Ford	1990	ALL
55	Ford	1991	Blue
52	Ford	1991	Red
9	Ford	1991	White
116	Ford	1991	ALL
39	Ford	1992	Blue
27	Ford	1992	Red
62	Ford	1992	White
128	Ford	1992	ALL
433	Ford	ALL	ALL
941	ALL	ALL	ALL
125	ALL	1990	Blue
69	ALL	1990	Red
149	ALL	1990	White
343	ALL	1990	ALL
104	ALL	1991	Blue
106	ALL	1991	Red
104	ALL	1991	White
314	ALL	1991	ALL
110	ALL	1992	Blue
58	ALL	1992	Red
116	ALL	1992	White
284	ALL	1992	ALL
182	Chevy	ALL	Blue
157	Ford	ALL	Blue
339	ALL	ALL	Blue
90	Chevy	ALL	Red
143	Ford	ALL	Red
233	ALL	ALL	Red
236	Chevy	ALL	White
133	Ford	ALL	White
369	ALL	ALL	White

The results of the CUBE make it simple to answer just about any sales aggregation question that you can think of. If you want to get sales information for all 1992 automobiles, regardless of model or color, you can find the corresponding row and see that 284 cars were sold. To find all Chevy sales for all years and colors, it's equally easy to find 508. Such a result set might be used as is for a reference chart or in coordination with a Data Mining tool.

SOME HISTORY

The motivation for inventing CUBE came from a paper written by Jim Gray and others soon after Jim joined Microsoft as a researcher. After reading his paper, a few of the developers got excited about adding the feature to SQL Server 6.5, and Don Reichart did a masterful job of implementing this important feature in record time. Subsequently, this feature was submitted to the ANSI SQL committee as a proposed addition to the standard. For more details about CUBE, you can read the paper that Jim Gray submitted to the ACM on the companion CD.

The number of rows exploded by a CUBE operation can be surprisingly large. In the example above, 18 rows generated 48 rows of output. However, the result of a CUBE operation won't necessarily produce more rows of output than what appears in the underlying data. The number of rows generated will depend on the number of attributes being grouped and the actual combinations in your data. Without detailed knowledge of the data, you can't predict the number of rows produced by a CUBE operation. However, the upper bound can be easily predicted. The upper bound will be equal to the cross-product of the (number of distinct values + 1) value for each attribute. The addition of 1 is for the case of "ALL." The *automobile_sales_detail* example has three attributes: model, year, and color.

Upper bound of number of rows
*= (Number of models + 1) * (Number of years + 1) ***
  (Number of colors + 1)
*= (2 + 1) * (3 + 1) * (3 + 1)*
= 48

This example should make clear that the upper bound of the number of rows depends not on the number of data rows, but rather on the number of attributes being grouped and the number of distinct values for each attribute. For example, if the table had 18 million instead of 18 data rows but still had no more than two models, three years, and three colors (there's no stated UNIQUE or PRIMARY KEY constraint on the model, year, or color fields), the CUBE operation will again return at most only 48 rows.

The actual number of rows might be considerably less than the upper bound, however, because CUBE doesn't try to force a 0 or a NULL aggregate for combinations for which no values exist. In the carefully constructed example you just saw, there's complete coverage across every attribute. Each of the two models has an entry for each of the three years and for each of the three colors. But suppose that no sales data appears for the 1990 Chevy and that no red Fords exist for any year. The raw data would look like this:

Rowid	Model	Year	Color	Units_Sold
1	Chevy	1991	Red	54
2	Chevy	1991	White	95
3	Chevy	1991	Blue	49
4	Chevy	1992	Red	31
5	Chevy	1992	White	54
6	Chevy	1992	Blue	71
7	Ford	1990	White	62
8	Ford	1990	Blue	63
9	Ford	1991	White	9
10	Ford	1991	Blue	55
11	Ford	1992	White	62
12	Ford	1992	Blue	39

Here's the new cube:

Units	Model	Year	Color
49	Chevy	1991	Blue
54	Chevy	1991	Red
95	Chevy	1991	White
198	Chevy	1991	ALL
71	Chevy	1992	Blue
31	Chevy	1992	Red
54	Chevy	1992	White
156	Chevy	1992	ALL
354	Chevy	ALL	ALL
63	Ford	1990	Blue
62	Ford	1990	White
125	Ford	1990	ALL
55	Ford	1991	Blue
9	Ford	1991	White
64	Ford	1991	ALL
39	Ford	1992	Blue
62	Ford	1992	White
101	Ford	1992	ALL
290	Ford	ALL	ALL
644	ALL	ALL	ALL
63	ALL	1990	Blue
62	ALL	1990	White
125	ALL	1990	ALL
104	ALL	1991	Blue
54	ALL	1991	Red
104	ALL	1991	White
262	ALL	1991	ALL
110	ALL	1992	Blue
31	ALL	1992	Red
116	ALL	1992	White

(continued)

```
257      ALL      1992     ALL
120      Chevy    ALL      Blue
157      Ford     ALL      Blue
277      ALL      ALL      Blue
85       Chevy    ALL      Red
85       ALL      ALL      Red
149      Chevy    ALL      White
133      Ford     ALL      White
282      ALL      ALL      White
```

We now have 12 data rows but still three attributes and the same number of distinct values for each attribute. But instead of 48 rows for the result of the CUBE, we have only 39 rows because some combinations of attributes have no data. For example, no row exists for all models of red cars for 1990 because no data met that specific criterion.

If you would benefit from always having the full cube populated when you use CUBE, you might want to add a placeholder row with dummy values for the columns being aggregated so that every combination is represented. Or you can run a query that produces the cross-product of all combinations that do not exist, and then UNION the result with the cube. (I'll show you an example of this later when I discuss UNION.) Be careful: as the number of attributes and the cardinality between the values increases, the cube can quickly get large. The full cube based on five attributes, each having 50 distinct values, with at least one matching entry for each combination, generates $(50 + 1)^5$, or 345,025,251, rows in the cube. If coverage of all these combinations is nowhere near full, the cube might generate "only" a few thousand rows instead of more than 345 million!

We haven't seen the actual query used to produce the cube because you need to understand the basic concepts before yet again dealing with issues of NULL. A simple GROUP BY *column* WITH CUBE does not, by default, produce super-aggregate rows with a value that outputs as "ALL." The ALL value is really a nonvalue, like NULL (gasp!). In fact, the ALL column is represented by (gulp!) a special kind of NULL, referred to as a *grouping NULL*.

While implementing this new feature, the developers debated whether to use NULL or invent a new marker value similar in some ways to NULL but clearly still separate from data. The decision wasn't easy. A new data value would be more theoretically pure. The meaning of "ALL" is really different from "unknown" or "missing"— that is, it's different from NULL. However, had they introduced another special-meaning marker, it would have required the same level of complexity as NULL—when working with special operators like IS ALL, for example—and the truth tables would be all the more difficult to work with in expressions such as =, <, IN, and so on. And the developers did have some precedents that they wanted to avoid.

In many ways, the longtime SQL Server feature COMPUTE BY is quite similar to CUBE. (Actually, it's more similar to a derivative of CUBE called ROLLUP, which we'll see shortly.) COMPUTE BY, although helpful, is rarely used, largely because it doesn't generate a standard row format for the result set but rather returns a special *alternate result set*. Applications must go to significant lengths to handle this special-purpose result, which is nonrelational in that the output itself isn't a table. Most applications haven't been able or willing to go the distance and have therefore not supported COMPUTE BY. Because of this, the SQL Server development team chose to overload NULL, which applications already have to deal with to some extent. (This presents a few wrinkles of its own, which I'll come back to.)

The following query performs a basic CUBE operation on the *automobile_sales_detail* table:

```
SELECT SUM(units_sold), model, year, color
FROM automobile_sales_detail
GROUP BY model, year, color WITH CUBE
```

Here's the output:

	model	year	color
62	Chevy	1990	Blue
5	Chevy	1990	Red
87	Chevy	1990	White
154	Chevy	1990	NULL
49	Chevy	1991	Blue
54	Chevy	1991	Red
95	Chevy	1991	White
198	Chevy	1991	NULL
71	Chevy	1992	Blue
31	Chevy	1992	Red
54	Chevy	1992	White
156	Chevy	1992	NULL
508	Chevy	NULL	NULL
63	Ford	1990	Blue
64	Ford	1990	Red
62	Ford	1990	White
189	Ford	1990	NULL
55	Ford	1991	Blue
52	Ford	1991	Red
9	Ford	1991	White
116	Ford	1991	NULL
39	Ford	1992	Blue
27	Ford	1992	Red
62	Ford	1992	White
128	Ford	1992	NULL
433	Ford	NULL	NULL
941	NULL	NULL	NULL
125	NULL	1990	Blue

(continued)

69	NULL	1990	Red
149	NULL	1990	White
343	NULL	1990	NULL
104	NULL	1991	Blue
106	NULL	1991	Red
104	NULL	1991	White
314	NULL	1991	NULL
110	NULL	1992	Blue
58	NULL	1992	Red
116	NULL	1992	White
284	NULL	1992	NULL
182	Chevy	NULL	Blue
157	Ford	NULL	Blue
339	NULL	NULL	Blue
90	Chevy	NULL	Red
143	Ford	NULL	Red
233	NULL	NULL	Red
236	Chevy	NULL	White
133	Ford	NULL	White
369	NULL	NULL	White

Notice that rather than ALL, which we had constructed earlier to be a place-holder, the super-aggregate values are represented by NULL—here formatted as *NULL* as in SQL Query Analyzer, although the actual display of a NULL is application specific. The data in this case has no NULL values, so we can easily tell the difference between NULL meaning "unknown" and NULL meaning "ALL."

If your data uses some NULL values, however, you won't be so lucky. Suppose we add one row of data that has NULL for both model and year (assuming that these columns allow NULL):

```
INSERT automobile_sales_detail values (NULL, NULL, 'White', 10)
```

The last row in the CUBE above (which has 369 as total sales for all white cars) would be seemingly indistinguishable from this new data row. Fortunately, the GROUPING function comes to the rescue to differentiate between the two. It returns 1 (TRUE) if the element is an ALL value and 0 (FALSE) otherwise. Here is a modified query to show the CUBE with the inclusion of the row that has NULL values and with the addition of the GROUPING function to designate ALL values:

```
SELECT 'Units Sold'=SUM(units_sold),
model, 'ALL Models'=GROUPING(model),
year, 'ALL Years'=GROUPING(year),
color, 'ALL Colors'=GROUPING(color)
FROM automobile_sales_detail
GROUP BY model, year, color WITH CUBE
```

Here's the result set:

Units Sold	model	ALL Models	year	ALL Years	color	ALL Colors
10	NULL	0	NULL	0	White	0
10	NULL	0	NULL	0	NULL	1
10	NULL	0	NULL	1	NULL	1
62	Chevy	0	1990	0	Blue	0
5	Chevy	0	1990	0	Red	0
87	Chevy	0	1990	0	White	0
154	Chevy	0	1990	0	NULL	1
49	Chevy	0	1991	0	Blue	0
54	Chevy	0	1991	0	Red	0
95	Chevy	0	1991	0	White	0
198	Chevy	0	1991	0	NULL	1
71	Chevy	0	1992	0	Blue	0
31	Chevy	0	1992	0	Red	0
54	Chevy	0	1992	0	White	0
156	Chevy	0	1992	0	NULL	1
508	Chevy	0	NULL	1	NULL	1
63	Ford	0	1990	0	Blue	0
64	Ford	0	1990	0	Red	0
62	Ford	0	1990	0	White	0
189	Ford	0	1990	0	NULL	1
55	Ford	0	1991	0	Blue	0
52	Ford	0	1991	0	Red	0
9	Ford	0	1991	0	White	0
116	Ford	0	1991	0	NULL	1
39	Ford	0	1992	0	Blue	0
27	Ford	0	1992	0	Red	0
62	Ford	0	1992	0	White	0
128	Ford	0	1992	0	NULL	1
433	Ford	0	NULL	1	NULL	1
951	NULL	1	NULL	1	NULL	1
10	NULL	1	NULL	0	White	0
10	NULL	1	NULL	0	NULL	1
125	NULL	1	1990	0	Blue	0
69	NULL	1	1990	0	Red	0
149	NULL	1	1990	0	White	0
343	NULL	1	1990	0	NULL	1
104	NULL	1	1991	0	Blue	0
106	NULL	1	1991	0	Red	0
104	NULL	1	1991	0	White	0
314	NULL	1	1991	0	NULL	1
110	NULL	1	1992	0	Blue	0

(continued)

58	NULL	1	1992	0	Red	0
116	NULL	1	1992	0	White	0
284	NULL	1	1992	0	NULL	1
182	Chevy	0	NULL	1	Blue	0
157	Ford	0	NULL	1	Blue	0
339	NULL	1	NULL	1	Blue	0
90	Chevy	0	NULL	1	Red	0
143	Ford	0	NULL	1	Red	0
233	NULL	1	NULL	1	Red	0
10	NULL	0	NULL	1	White	0
236	Chevy	0	NULL	1	White	0
133	Ford	0	NULL	1	White	0
379	NULL	1	NULL	1	White	0

Note that the GROUPING function takes a column name as an argument. A 0 returned for GROUPING(*column_name*) means that the value returned for that column is a *real* value. A 1 returned for GROUPING(*column_name*) means that the value returned for that column is not real—it was returned only because of the use of the CUBE or ROLLUP option.

The GROUPING function enables you to differentiate between a GROUPING NULL value and a NULL value, but it hardly makes reading and analyzing the results returned by CUBE and ROLLUP as intuitive as when you use ALL. An alternative is to write a view that outputs a grouping value as ALL. You might be more comfortable turning your programmers and power users loose on such a view rather than relying on them understanding GROUPING NULL vs. NULL. This example uses the CASE expression, which is discussed in detail in Chapter 10:

```
CREATE VIEW auto_cube (units, model, year, color) AS
SELECT SUM(units_sold),
CASE    WHEN (GROUPING(model)=1) THEN 'ALL'
    ELSE ISNULL(model, '????')
    END,
CASE    WHEN (GROUPING(year)=1) THEN 'ALL'
    ELSE ISNULL(CONVERT(char(6), year), '????')
    END,
CASE    WHEN (GROUPING(color)=1) THEN 'ALL'
    ELSE ISNULL(color, '????')
    END
FROM automobile_sales_detail
GROUP BY model, year, color WITH CUBE
```

With this view, it's simple for someone to understand the difference between grouping values (represented by "ALL") and NULL data values (represented by "????"), and to easily refine the query if necessary to look for certain data. Here's a simple query:

```
SELECT * FROM auto_cube
```

Here's the result:

units	model	year	color
10	????	????	White
10	????	????	ALL
10	????	ALL	ALL
62	Chevy	1990	Blue
5	Chevy	1990	Red
87	Chevy	1990	White
154	Chevy	1990	ALL
49	Chevy	1991	Blue
54	Chevy	1991	Red
95	Chevy	1991	White
198	Chevy	1991	ALL
71	Chevy	1992	Blue
31	Chevy	1992	Red
54	Chevy	1992	White
156	Chevy	1992	ALL
508	Chevy	ALL	ALL
63	Ford	1990	Blue
64	Ford	1990	Red
62	Ford	1990	White
189	Ford	1990	ALL
55	Ford	1991	Blue
52	Ford	1991	Red
9	Ford	1991	White
116	Ford	1991	ALL
39	Ford	1992	Blue
27	Ford	1992	Red
62	Ford	1992	White
128	Ford	1992	ALL
433	Ford	ALL	ALL
951	ALL	ALL	ALL
10	ALL	????	White
10	ALL	????	ALL
125	ALL	1990	Blue
69	ALL	1990	Red
149	ALL	1990	White
343	ALL	1990	ALL
104	ALL	1991	Blue
106	ALL	1991	Red
104	ALL	1991	White
314	ALL	1991	ALL
110	ALL	1992	Blue
58	ALL	1992	Red
116	ALL	1992	White

(continued)

```
284      ALL      1992     ALL
182      Chevy    ALL      Blue
157      Ford     ALL      Blue
339      ALL      ALL      Blue
90       Chevy    ALL      Red
143      Ford     ALL      Red
233      ALL      ALL      Red
10       ????     ALL      White
236      Chevy    ALL      White
133      Ford     ALL      White
379      ALL      ALL      White
```

Working with this view is easy. Grouping values appear as "ALL." Actual NULL values are represented by question marks, which is appropriate because they're unknown. You can easily further select from the view to drill into any dimension of the cube. For example, this query finds all Chevy sales, regardless of the year and color:

```
SELECT * FROM auto_cube
WHERE model='Chevy' AND year='ALL' AND color='ALL'
```

Here's the result:

```
units    model    year     color
-----    -----    ----     -----
508      Chevy    ALL      ALL
```

In this view, I elected to output everything as character data; thus, "ALL" was a reasonable choice. If keeping the data numeric had been important, I could've chosen some special value, such as -999999.

ROLLUP

If you're looking for a hierarchy or a *drill-down report* (what you might know as a *control-break report* if you've ever programmed in COBOL), CUBE can be overkill. It generates many more result rows than you want, and it obscures the requested information with more data. (Don't be confused into thinking that data and information are equivalent.) When you use CUBE, you get all permutations, including super-aggregates, for all attributes for which corresponding data exists. SQL Server provides the ROLLUP operator to extract statistics and summary information from result sets. ROLLUP returns only the values for a hierarchy of the attributes that you specify.

This behavior is best explained with an example. If we change the CUBE query to use ROLLUP instead, the results are more compact and easier to interpret when we drill into progressive levels of detail for sales by model. However, with ROLLUP, we don't get one-stop shopping to answer a question like "How many white cars of any model were sold?"

```
SELECT 'units sold'=SUM(units_sold),
'model'=CASE WHEN (GROUPING(model)=1) THEN 'ALL'
    ELSE ISNULL(model, '????')
    END,
'year'=CASE WHEN (GROUPING(year)=1) THEN 'ALL'
    ELSE ISNULL(CONVERT(char(6), year), '????')
    END,
'color'=CASE WHEN (GROUPING(color)=1) THEN 'ALL'
    ELSE ISNULL(color, '????')
    END
FROM automobile_sales_detail
GROUP BY model, year, color WITH ROLLUP
```

The results:

```
units sold    model    year    color
----------    -----    ----    -----
10            ????     ????    White
10            ????     ????    ALL
10            ????     ALL     ALL
62            Chevy    1990    Blue
5             Chevy    1990    Red
87            Chevy    1990    White
154           Chevy    1990    ALL
49            Chevy    1991    Blue
54            Chevy    1991    Red
95            Chevy    1991    White
198           Chevy    1991    ALL
71            Chevy    1992    Blue
31            Chevy    1992    Red
54            Chevy    1992    White
156           Chevy    1992    ALL
508           Chevy    ALL     ALL
63            Ford     1990    Blue
64            Ford     1990    Red
62            Ford     1990    White
189           Ford     1990    ALL
55            Ford     1991    Blue
52            Ford     1991    Red
9             Ford     1991    White
116           Ford     1991    ALL
39            Ford     1992    Blue
27            Ford     1992    Red
62            Ford     1992    White
128           Ford     1992    ALL
433           Ford     ALL     ALL
951           ALL      ALL     ALL
```

ROLLUP is similar to COMPUTE BY, which has nice functionality. However, COMPUTE BY is not as relational as ROLLUP—it doesn't simply produce results as an ordinary table of values. COMPUTE BY always requires special application programming to deal with its alternate result sets, which are essentially equivalent to super-aggregates. Recall that CUBE and ROLLUP simply use ordinary result sets and that the super-aggregates are represented as a GROUPING NULL. Generally speaking, CUBE and ROLLUP are preferable to COMPUTE BY because they're easier to fit into applications; you can use them with views, CASE, subselects, and column aliases; and they're internally better optimized. But for completeness, here's an example that uses COMPUTE BY as functionally equivalent to ROLLUP:

```
SELECT units_sold, model, year, color
FROM automobile_sales_detail
ORDER BY model, year, color
COMPUTE SUM(units_sold) BY model, year
COMPUTE SUM(units_sold) BY model
COMPUTE SUM(units_sold)
```

Here's the result:

units_sold	model	year	color
10	NULL	NULL	White

Sum
10

Sum
10

units_sold	model	year	color
62	Chevy	1990	Blue
5	Chevy	1990	Red
87	Chevy	1990	White

Sum
154

units_sold	model	year	color
49	Chevy	1991	Blue
54	Chevy	1991	Red
95	Chevy	1991	White

Sum
198

```
units_sold    model    year    color
----------    -----    ----    -----
71            Chevy    1992    Blue
31            Chevy    1992    Red
54            Chevy    1992    White

Sum
===========
156
Sum
===========
508

units_sold    model    year    color
----------    -----    ----    -----
63            Ford     1990    Blue
64            Ford     1990    Red
62            Ford     1990    White

Sum
===========
189

units_sold    model    year    color
----------    -----    ----    -----
55            Ford     1991    Blue
52            Ford     1991    Red
9             Ford     1991    White

Sum
===========
116

units_sold    model    year    color
----------    -----    ----    -----
39            Ford     1992    Blue
27            Ford     1992    Red
62            Ford     1992    White

Sum
===========
128
Sum
===========
433
Sum
===========
951
```

Statistical Aggregates

SQL Server 2000 includes four statistical aggregate functions in addition to the standard six, plus COUNT_BIG, described earlier. These functions are for statistical applications and are considered aggregate functions because they operate on a set of values instead of on a single value. Table 7-8 describes the four statistical aggregate functions.

You can find the standard deviation and variance of the prices in the *titles* table with this query, for example:

```
SELECT STDEV(price), VAR(price)
FROM titles
```

Alternatively, you can calculate the standard deviation and variance of the prices for each different type of book:

```
SELECT type, STDEV(price), VAR(price)
FROM titles
GROUP BY type
```

Aggregate Function	Description
STDEV(*expression*)	Returns the statistical standard deviation of all values in the given expression.
STDEVP(*expression*)	Returns the statistical standard deviation for the population for all values in the given expression.
VAR(*expression*)	Returns the statistical variance of all values in the given expression.
VARP(*expression*)	Returns the statistical variance for the population for all values in the given expression.

Table 7-8. *Statistical aggregate functions.*

TOP

You've already seen that the WHERE clause allows you to limit the number of rows that a SELECT statement will return. But the WHERE clause assumes that you have knowledge of the actual data values present. What if you want to see only a screenful of rows from a table but you have no idea which range of values are present in the table? Prior to SQL Server version 7, you could use the option SET ROWCOUNT *n* to limit SQL Server to sending only *n* rows to the client. Every SELECT statement would just stop sending rows back to the client after *n* rows had been sent.

For example, the following query returns only 10 rows from the *authors* table:

```
SET ROWCOUNT 10
GO
SELECT * FROM authors
GO
```

This is useful in some situations, but it's quite limited in functionality. Using the TOP keyword in the SELECT list allows much greater control over the quantity of data you want to see. Here's the syntax for using TOP:

```
SELECT [ TOP n [PERCENT] [ WITH TIES] ] select_list
FROM table_list
WHERE conditions
...rest of query
```

When the query includes an ORDER BY clause, TOP causes the first *n* rows ordered by the ORDER BY clause to be output. When the query has no ORDER BY clause, you can't predict which rows will be returned. Compare the output of the following two queries:

QUERY 1

```
SELECT TOP 5 title_id, price, type
FROM titles
```

title_id	price	type
BU1032	19.9900	business
BU1111	11.9500	business
BU2075	2.9900	business
BU7832	19.9900	business
MC2222	19.9900	mod_cook

QUERY 2

```
SELECT TOP 5 title_id, price, type
FROM titles
ORDER BY price DESC
```

title_id	price	type
PC1035	22.9500	popular_comp
PS1372	21.5900	psychology
TC3218	20.9500	trad_cook
PC8888	20.0000	popular_comp
BU1032	19.9900	business

Notice that simply including TOP 5 in the SELECT list is functionally equivalent to setting ROWCOUNT to 5. SQL Server just stops returning rows after the first five. I say "functionally equivalent" because you get the same rows back using either method. However, the SQL Server query processor can optimize queries using TOP, and in many cases chooses a more efficient query plan if it knows during optimization that only a few rows are needed.

In the example above, other books exist with a price of $19.99, but because we wanted only five, we didn't see them. Does this output really answer the question "What are the five highest priced books?" If not, and you really want to see all the books with the same price as the ones listed, you can use the WITH TIES option. This option is allowed only if your SELECT statement includes an ORDER BY:

```
SELECT TOP 5 WITH TIES title_id, price, type
FROM titles
ORDER BY price DESC
```

The query returns the following eight rows:

```
title_id price                     type
-------- ---------------------     ------------
PC1035   22.9500                   popular_comp
PS1372   21.5900                   psychology
TC3218   20.9500                   trad_cook
PC8888   20.0000                   popular_comp
BU1032   19.9900                   business
BU7832   19.9900                   business
MC2222   19.9900                   mod_cook
PS3333   19.9900                   psychology
```

You can think of SQL Server carrying out this operation by first counting out the number of rows specified by TOP—in this case, five. Only after the first five are returned does SQL Server check to see whether any other rows have a value equivalent to the last one returned.

This doesn't necessarily return the books with the five highest prices. If we change TOP 5 to TOP 8, we get the same eight rows back, which represent only five different prices. I compare this to a race in which ribbons are awarded to the first five finishers. If four participants tie for fifth place, coming in at exactly the same time, we have to award more than five ribbons. Note that only ties at the end cause extra rows to come back. In the race analogy, if we have four racers tied for first place and the fifth-fastest racer comes in alone, we can still award just five ribbons. There are only two different times for the five winners.

If you really want to see the eight highest prices (or eight fastest times), you can use DISTINCT with TOP. You can't select *title_id* at the same time because DISTINCT applies to the whole result row and every *title_id* and *price* combination is distinct in itself. However, you can use a subquery to determine which rows have one of the eight highest prices:

```
SELECT title_id, price, type
FROM titles
WHERE price in (SELECT DISTINCT TOP 8 price
    FROM titles
    ORDER BY price DESC)
```

In this case, the rows won't come back in descending order of price because the order is controlled by the outer query. To get this, you have to add another ORDER BY at the end.

If you want to see a certain fraction of the rows, you can use TOP with PER-CENT, which rounds up to the nearest integer number of rows:

```
SELECT TOP 30 Percent title_id, price, type
FROM titles
ORDER BY price DESC
```

The *titles* table contains 18 rows, and 30 percent of 18 is 5.6. This is rounded up to return these six rows:

```
title_id price                    type
-------- --------------------     ------------
PC1035   22.9500                  popular_comp
PS1372   21.5900                  psychology
TC3218   20.9500                  trad_cook
PC8888   20.0000                  popular_comp
BU1032   19.9900                  business
BU7832   19.9900                  business
```

You can also use the WITH TIES option with PERCENT. If you use it in the above query, you get the additional two rows that also have a price of $19.99.

UNION

UNION is conceptually easy to understand. Given the same number of columns and compatible datatypes, UNION combines two or more result sets into a single result set. By default, duplicate rows are eliminated, although you can include them by specifying UNION ALL. The datatypes of the result sets to be combined with UNION don't have to be identical, but they must be able to be *implicitly* converted. If this isn't the case, you can *explicitly* convert them to identical or compatible types using the handy CONVERT function.

The following example shows UNION at its most basic level. It also demonstrates that a SELECT statement in SQL Server doesn't need to be from a table or a view but can be a constant or a variable:

```
SELECT col1=2, col2=1
UNION
SELECT xxx=1, yyy=2
UNION
SELECT '3', '0'
UNION
SELECT TAN(0), 3*1000/10/100  -- Tangent of 0 is 0.
                              -- So this row produces 0.0, 3
UNION
SELECT 1, 2
```

The output follows:

```
col1    col2
----    ----
0.0     3
3.0     0
1.0     2
2.0     1
```

Versions of SQL Server prior to SQL Server 7 always returned the result of a UNION in sorted order unless you specified UNION ALL. This occurred because UNION eliminated duplicate rows using a sorting strategy. The ordering was simply a by-product of the sorting to eliminate duplicates. However, SQL Server 2000 has several alternative strategies available for removing duplicates, so there's no guarantee of any particular order when you use UNION. If order is important to you, you should explicitly use ORDER BY at the end of the last SELECT statement.

In the example above, the datatypes are compatible but not identical. Because TAN(0) returns a float datatype, *col1* is automatically cast to float (since using an integer would lose precision), and the other values are implicitly converted. In addition, the one duplicate row (1.0, 2) is eliminated, and the columns take their monikers from the first result set.

If you use UNION ALL instead of UNION, no extra work is needed to find and eliminate any duplicate rows. If there's no need to eliminate duplicates, or if you know that there won't be any duplicates, you can achieve a noticeable performance improvement by using UNION ALL. The following query illustrates the use of UNION ALL and uses ORDER BY to present the results in a particular order. It also converts the result of the tangent operation to a *tinyint* so that *col1* is then implicitly converted to an *int*.

```
SELECT col1=2, col2=1
UNION ALL
SELECT xxx=1, yyy=2
UNION ALL
SELECT '3', '0'
UNION ALL
SELECT CONVERT(smallint, TAN(0)), 3*1000/10/100
-- Tangent of 0 is 0. So this row produces 0.0, 3
UNION ALL
SELECT 1, 2
ORDER BY col2
```

Here's the output:

```
col1    col2
----    ----
3       0
2       1
1       2
1       2
0       3
```

Earlier you saw that the CUBE operation doesn't generate missing rows with the value 0. However, you might occasionally want the full cube, with 0 as the SUM value for missing combinations. I promised you an example of how this can be accomplished using UNION, so here's the example. And here's the key: the table can be cross-joined to itself to produce a 0 row for every combination possible given the non-NULL data. This query uses the existing data to produce a list of every possible combination of model, color, and year:

```
SELECT DISTINCT units_sold=0, A.model, B.color, C.year
FROM
automobile_sales_detail A
CROSS JOIN
automobile_sales_detail B
CROSS JOIN
automobile_sales_detail C
```

Here's the output:

```
units_sold    model    color    year
----------    -----    -----    ----
0             Chevy    Blue     1990
0             Chevy    Blue     1991
0             Chevy    Blue     1992
0             Chevy    Red      1990
0             Chevy    Red      1991
0             Chevy    Red      1992
0             Chevy    White    1990
0             Chevy    White    1991
0             Chevy    White    1992
0             Ford     Blue     1990
0             Ford     Blue     1991
0             Ford     Blue     1992
0             Ford     Red      1990
0             Ford     Red      1991
0             Ford     Red      1992
0             Ford     White    1990
0             Ford     White    1991
0             Ford     White    1992
```

The real underlying data is the set of 12 rows shown earlier and shown again here. Recall that six combinations have no value—that is, there are no Chevys for 1990 and no red Fords:

```
model   year   color   units_sold
-----   ----   -----   ----------
Chevy   1991   Red     54
Chevy   1991   White   95
Chevy   1991   Blue    49
Chevy   1992   Red     31
Chevy   1992   White   54
Chevy   1992   Blue    71
Ford    1990   White   62
Ford    1990   Blue    63
Ford    1991   White   9
Ford    1991   Blue    55
Ford    1992   White   62
Ford    1992   Blue    39
```

Having generated all the dummy rows as such, we can then easily UNION the cross-joined dummy results with the output of the CUBE. But that still won't do because we get both a real row and a dummy row whenever a real combination exists. SQL Server provides several good ways to solve this dilemma. We can use NOT EXISTS to produce the dummy rows only for combinations that don't exist. Another approach, and perhaps the most intuitive one, is to make a view of the cross-joined dummy rows and the actual data, and then perform the CUBE on the view. The 0 values, of course, don't affect the SUM, so this works nicely:

```
CREATE VIEW fullcube
    (
    units_sold,
    model,
    year,
    color
    )
    AS
    (
    SELECT D.units_sold, D.model, D.year, D.color
    FROM automobile_sales_detail D
    UNION ALL
    SELECT DISTINCT 0,
    A.model, C.year, B.color
    FROM
    automobile_sales_detail A
    CROSS JOIN
    automobile_sales_detail B
    CROSS JOIN
    automobile_sales_detail C
    )
```

Having constructed the view, we can then issue our CUBE query against it, just as we did previously against the base table:

```
SELECT units_sold=SUM(units_sold), model, year, color
FROM fullcube
GROUP BY model, year, color WITH CUBE
```

Here's the output:

units_sold	model	year	color
0	Chevy	1990	Blue
0	Chevy	1990	Red
0	Chevy	1990	White
0	Chevy	1990	NULL
49	Chevy	1991	Blue
54	Chevy	1991	Red
95	Chevy	1991	White
198	Chevy	1991	NULL
71	Chevy	1992	Blue
31	Chevy	1992	Red
54	Chevy	1992	White
156	Chevy	1992	NULL
354	Chevy	NULL	NULL
63	Ford	1990	Blue
0	Ford	1990	Red
62	Ford	1990	White
125	Ford	1990	NULL
55	Ford	1991	Blue
0	Ford	1991	Red
9	Ford	1991	White
64	Ford	1991	NULL
39	Ford	1992	Blue
0	Ford	1992	Red
62	Ford	1992	White
101	Ford	1992	NULL
290	Ford	NULL	NULL
644	NULL	NULL	NULL
63	NULL	1990	Blue
0	NULL	1990	Red
62	NULL	1990	White
125	NULL	1990	NULL
104	NULL	1991	Blue
54	NULL	1991	Red
104	NULL	1991	White
262	NULL	1991	NULL
110	NULL	1992	Blue
31	NULL	1992	Red
116	NULL	1992	White

(continued)

257	NULL	1992	NULL
120	Chevy	NULL	Blue
157	Ford	NULL	Blue
277	NULL	NULL	Blue
85	Chevy	NULL	Red
0	Ford	NULL	Red
85	NULL	NULL	Red
149	Chevy	NULL	White
133	Ford	NULL	White
282	NULL	NULL	White

We can then define yet another view on top to generate the "ALL" and "????" placeholders. No NULL data exists in this example, so I'll look at only the "ALL" case:

```
CREATE VIEW auto_cube (units, model, year, color) AS
SELECT SUM(units_sold),
ISNULL(model, 'ALL'), ISNULL(CONVERT(char(4), year), 'ALL'),
ISNULL(color, 'ALL')
FROM fullcube
GROUP BY model, year, color WITH CUBE
```

One advantage of filling out the cube with placeholder rows is that no matter what combination you formulate, you get an answer. There are no unknowns and there's no need to use the GROUPING function. Had we not constructed the cube, this query would return no rows found instead of a row with 0 units:

```
SELECT * FROM auto_cube WHERE model='Chevy' AND color='ALL'
AND year='1990'
```

units	model	year	color
0	Chevy	1990	ALL

Just for fun, here's the equivalent of the *fullcube* view as a derived table:

```
SELECT units_sold=SUM(T1.units_sold), T1.model, T1.year, T1.color
FROM (
    SELECT D.units_sold, D.model, D.year, D.color
    FROM automobile_sales_detail D
    UNION ALL
    SELECT DISTINCT 0,
    A.model, C.year, B.color
    FROM
    automobile_sales_detail A
    CROSS JOIN
    automobile_sales_detail B
    CROSS JOIN
    automobile_sales_detail C
    )
```

```
      AS T1
GROUP BY T1.model, T1.year, T1.color WITH CUBE
GO
```

Now that you've seen these somewhat exotic uses of CROSS JOIN and views to fill out the cube, be aware that if you had wanted the whole cube to be generated, you might have inserted some placeholder rows with a value of 0 in the base table itself (assuming you had access to do so). That way, every combination would be accounted for in the base table itself.

SUMMARY

This chapter examined the SELECT statement, the hallmark of the SQL language. Although I presented a fairly well-rounded treatment of SELECT, instead of focusing on basic queries I looked at more subtle issues and SQL Server–specific capabilities.

We discussed the issues of NULL and three-valued logic, and you learned why you must always consider these issues when you're formulating queries. In three-valued logic, an answer is TRUE, FALSE, or Unknown. If you must work with NULL values but you don't understand three-valued logic, you'll introduce bugs. You must fully understand three-valued logic or structure the database to avoid the use of NULL.

You must also understand NULL for doing JOIN operations, and I discussed issues concerning OUTER JOIN with several examples. Unlike a JOIN based on equality, the JOIN order for an OUTER JOIN is vitally important. We looked at search expressions such as LIKE and the issues of trailing blanks. We examined aggregate functions, again with a discussion of how you must understand NULL for proper use of these functions.

Finally, we looked at the CUBE and ROLLUP extensions to the standard GROUP BY clause for use with aggregate functions, and we discussed some tips and techniques for using these capabilities.

Although this chapter is far from a complete treatise on the SQL language or SQL Server's capabilities, it demonstrates how to use SQL Server facilities and extensions to help you solve real-world problems and write better applications.

Chapter 8

Indexes

Indexes are the other significant user-defined, on-disk data structure besides tables. An index provides fast access to data when the data can be searched by the value that is the index key. You learned basic information about indexes in Chapter 3, but to really understand the benefit that indexes can provide and how to determine the best indexes for your environment, you need to take a deeper look into the organization of Microsoft SQL Server indexes.

In this chapter, I'll show you the physical organization of index pages for both types of SQL Server indexes, clustered and nonclustered. I'll discuss the various options available when you create and re-create indexes, and I'll tell you how, when, and why to rebuild your indexes. I'll tell you about SQL Server 2000's online index defragmentation utility and about a tool you can use to determine whether your indexes need defragmenting.

Indexes allow data to be organized in a way that allows optimum performance when you access or modify it. SQL Server does not *need* indexes to successfully retrieve results for your SELECT statements or to find and modify the specified rows in your data modification statements. Most of the examples you saw in Chapter 6 could be executed just fine without any indexes at all. However, as your tables get larger, the value of using proper indexes becomes obvious. You can use indexes to quickly find data rows that satisfy conditions in your WHERE clauses, to find matching rows in your JOIN clauses, or to efficiently maintain uniqueness of your key columns during INSERT and UPDATE operations. In some cases, you can use indexes to help SQL Server sort, aggregate, or group your data or to find the first few rows as indicated in a TOP clause.

It is the job of the query optimizer to determine which indexes, if any, are most useful in processing a specific query. The final choice of which indexes to use is one of the most important components of the query optimizer's execution plan. I'll tell you a lot more about the query optimizer in Chapters 15 and 16, including the factors that determine whether the query optimizer actually chooses to use indexes at all. In this chapter, I'll focus on what indexes look like and how they can speed up your queries.

INDEX ORGANIZATION

Think of the indexes that you see in your everyday life—those in books and other documents. Suppose you're trying to write a SELECT statement in SQL Server using the CASE expression, and you're using two SQL Server documents to find out how to write the statement. One document is the *Microsoft SQL Server 2000 Transact-SQL Language Reference Manual*. The other is this book *Inside Microsoft SQL Server 2000*. You can quickly find information in either book about CASE, even though the two books are organized differently.

In the Transact-SQL language reference, all the information is organized alphabetically. You know that CASE will be near the front, so you can just ignore the last 80 percent of the book. Keywords are shown at the top of each page to tell you what topics are on that page. So you can quickly flip through just a few pages and end up at a page that has BREAK as the first keyword and CEILING as the last keyword, and you know that CASE will be on this page. If CASE is not on this page, it's not in the book. And once you find the entry for CASE, right between BULK INSERT and CAST, you'll find all the information you need, including lots of helpful examples.

Next you try to find CASE in this book. There are no helpful keywords at the top of each page, but there's an index at the back of the book and all the index entries are organized alphabetically. So again, you can make use of the fact that CASE is near the front of the alphabet and quickly find it between "cascading updates" and "case-insensitive searches." However, unlike in the reference manual, once you find the word CASE, there are no nice neat examples right in front of you. Instead, the index gives you pointers. It tells you what pages to look at—it might list two or three pages that point you to various places in the book. If you look up SELECT in the back of the book, however, there might be dozens of pages listed, and if you look up SQL Server, there might be hundreds.

These searches through the two books are analogous to using clustered and nonclustered indexes. In a clustered index, the data is actually stored in order, just as the reference manual has all the main topics in order. Once you find the data you're looking for, you're done with the search. In a nonclustered index, the index is a completely separate structure from the data itself. Once you find what you're looking for in the index, you have to follow pointers to the actual data. A nonclustered index in SQL Server is very much like the index in the back of this book. If there is only one page reference listed in the index, you can quickly find the information. If a dozen pages are listed, it's quite a bit slower. If hundreds of pages are listed, you might think there's no point in using the index at all. Unless you can narrow down your topic of interest to something more specific, the index might not be of much help.

In Chapter 3, I explained that both clustered and nonclustered indexes in SQL Server store their information using standard B-trees, as shown in Figure 8-1. A B-tree provides fast access to data by searching on a key value of the index. B-trees cluster records with similar keys. The *B* stands for *balanced,* and balancing the tree is a core feature of a B-tree's usefulness. The trees are managed, and branches are grafted as necessary, so that navigating down the tree to find a value and locate a specific record takes only a few page accesses. Because the trees are balanced, finding any record requires about the same amount of resources, and retrieval speed is consistent because the index has the same depth throughout.

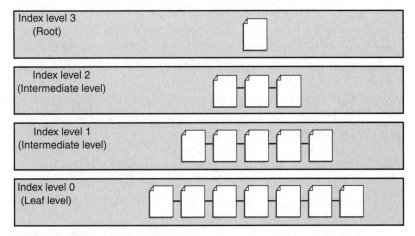

Figure 8-1. *A B-tree for a SQL Server index.*

An index consists of a tree with a root from which the navigation begins, possible intermediate index levels, and bottom-level leaf pages. You use the index to find the correct leaf page. The number of levels in an index will vary depending on the number of rows in the table and the size of the key column or columns for the index. If you create an index using a large key, fewer entries will fit on a page, so more pages (and possibly more levels) will be needed for the index. On a qualified select, update, or delete, the correct leaf page will be the lowest page of the tree in which one or more rows with the specified key or keys reside. A qualified operation is one that affects only specific rows that satisfy the conditions of a WHERE clause, as opposed to one that accesses the whole table. In any index, whether clustered or nonclustered, the leaf level contains every key value, in key sequence.

Clustered Indexes

The leaf level of a clustered index contains the data pages, not just the index keys. Another way to say this is that the data itself is part of the clustered index. A clustered index keeps the data in a table ordered around the key. The data pages in the table are kept in a doubly linked list called the *page chain*. The order of pages in the page chain, and the order of rows on the data pages, is the order of the index key or keys. Deciding which key to cluster on is an important performance consideration. When the index is traversed to the leaf level, the data itself has been *retrieved,* not simply *pointed to.*

Because the actual page chain for the data pages can be ordered in only one way, a table can have only one clustered index. The query optimizer strongly favors a clustered index because such an index allows the data to be found directly at the leaf level. Because it defines the actual order of the data, a clustered index allows especially fast access for queries looking for a range of values. The query optimizer detects that only a certain range of data pages must be scanned.

Most tables should have a clustered index. If your table will have only one index, it generally should be clustered. Many documents describing SQL Server indexes will tell you that the clustered index physically stores the data in sorted order. This can be misleading if you think of physical storage as the disk itself. If a clustered index had to keep the data on the actual disk in a particular order, it could be prohibitively expensive to make changes. If a page got too full and had to be split in two, all the data on all the succeeding pages would have to be moved down. Sorted order in a clustered index simply means that the data page chain is in order. If SQL Server follows the page chain, it can access each row in clustered index order, but new pages can be added by simply adjusting the links in the page chain. I'll tell you more about page splitting and moving rows in Chapter 9 when I discuss data modification.

In SQL Server 2000, all clustered indexes are unique. If you build a clustered index without specifying the UNIQUE keyword, SQL Server forces uniqueness by adding a *uniqueifier* to the rows when necessary. This uniqueifier is a 4-byte value added as an additional sort key to only the rows that have duplicates of their primary sort key. You'll be able to see this extra value when we look at the actual structure of index rows later in this chapter.

Nonclustered Indexes

In a nonclustered index, the lowest level of the tree (the leaf level) contains a bookmark that tells SQL Server where to find the data row corresponding to the key in the index. As you saw in Chapter 3, a bookmark can take one of two forms. If the table has a clustered index, the bookmark is the clustered index key for the corresponding data row. If the table is a heap (in other words, it has no clustered index), the bookmark is a row identifier (RID), which is an actual row locator in the form File#:Page#:Slot#. (In contrast, in a clustered index, the leaf page *is* the data page.)

The presence or absence of a nonclustered index doesn't affect how the data pages are organized, so you're not restricted to having only one nonclustered index per table, as is the case with clustered indexes. Each table can include as many as 249 nonclustered indexes, but you'll usually want to have far fewer than that.

When you search for data using a nonclustered index, the index is traversed and then SQL Server retrieves the record or records pointed to by the leaf-level indexes. For example, if you're looking for a data page using an index with a depth of three—a root page, one intermediate page, and the leaf page—all three index pages must be traversed. If the leaf level contains a clustered index key, all the levels of the clustered index then have to be traversed to locate the specific row. The clustered index will probably also have three levels, but in this case remember that the leaf level is the data itself. There are two additional index levels separate from the data, typically one less than the number of levels needed for a nonclustered index. The data page still must be retrieved, but because it has been exactly identified, there's no need to scan the entire table. Still, it takes six logical I/O operations to get one data page. You can see that a nonclustered index is a win only if it's highly selective.

Figure 8-2 illustrates this process without showing you the individual levels of the B-trees. I want to find the first name for the employee named Anson, and I have a nonclustered index on the last name and a clustered index on the employee ID. The nonclustered index uses the clustered keys as its bookmarks. Searching the index for Anson, SQL Server finds that the associated clustered index key is 7. It then traverses the clustered index looking for the row with a key of 7, and it finds Kim as the first name in the row I'm looking for.

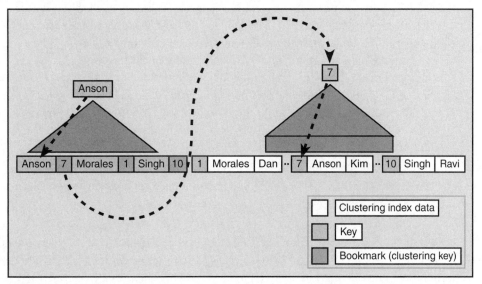

Figure 8-2. *SQL Server traverses both the clustered and nonclustered indexes to find the first name for the employee named Anson.*

CREATING AN INDEX

The typical syntax for creating an index is straightforward:

```
CREATE [UNIQUE] [CLUSTERED | NONCLUSTERED] INDEX index_name
  ON table_name (column_name [ASC | DESC][,...n])
```

When you create an index, you must specify a name for it. You must also specify the table on which the index will be built and one or more columns. For each column, you can specify that the leaf level will store the key values sorted in either ascending (ASC) or descending (DESC) order. The default is ascending. You can specify that SQL Server must enforce uniqueness of the key values by using the keyword UNIQUE. If you don't specify UNIQUE, duplicate key values will be allowed. You can specify that the index be either clustered or nonclustered. Nonclustered is the default.

CREATE INDEX has some additional options available for specialized purposes. You can add a WITH clause to the CREATE INDEX command:

```
[WITH
[FILLFACTOR = fillfactor]
[[,] [PAD_INDEX]
[[,] IGNORE_DUP_KEY]
[[,] DROP_EXISTING]
[[,] STATISTICS_NORECOMPUTE]
[[,] SORT_IN_TEMPDB]
]
```

FILLFACTOR is probably the most commonly used of these options. FILLFACTOR lets you reserve some space on each leaf page of an index. In a clustered index, since the leaf level contains the data, you can use FILLFACTOR to control how much space to leave in the table itself. By reserving free space, you can later avoid the need to split pages to make room for a new entry. Chapter 3 includes some discussion of index management and page splitting, and you'll find more details in Chapter 9. But remember that FILLFACTOR is not maintained; it indicates only how much space is reserved with the existing data at the time the index is built. If you need to, you can use the DBCC DBREINDEX command to rebuild the index and reestablish the original FILLFACTOR specified.

TIP   If you plan to rebuild all of a table's indexes, simply specify the clustered index with DBCC DBREINDEX. Doing so internally rebuilds the entire table and all nonclustered indexes.

FILLFACTOR isn't usually specified on an index-by-index basis, but you can specify it this way for fine-tuning. If FILLFACTOR isn't specified, the serverwide default is used. The value is set for the server via *sp_configure, fillfactor*. This value is 0 by default, which means that leaf pages of indexes are made as full as possible.

FILLFACTOR generally applies only to the index's leaf page (the data page for a clustered index). In specialized and high-use situations, you might want to reserve space in the intermediate index pages to avoid page splits there, too. You can do this by specifying the PAD_INDEX option, which uses the same value as FILLFACTOR.

The DROP_EXISTING option specifies that a given index should be dropped and rebuilt as a single transaction. This option is particularly useful when you rebuild clustered indexes. Normally, when a clustered index is dropped, every nonclustered index has to be rebuilt to change its bookmarks to RIDs instead of the clustering keys. Then, if a clustered index is built (or rebuilt), all nonclustered indexes need to be rebuilt again to update the bookmarks. The DROP_EXISTING option of the CREATE INDEX command allows a clustered index to be rebuilt without having to rebuild the nonclustered indexes twice. If you are creating the index on the exact same keys that it had previously, the nonclustered indexes do not need to be rebuilt at all. If you are changing the key definition, the nonclustered indexes are rebuilt only once, after the clustered index is rebuilt.

You can ensure the uniqueness of an index key by defining the index as UNIQUE or by defining a PRIMARY KEY or UNIQUE constraint. If an UPDATE or INSERT statement would affect multiple rows, and if even one row is found that would cause duplicate keys defined as unique, the entire statement is aborted and no rows are affected. Alternatively, when you create the unique index, you can use the IGNORE_DUP_KEY option so that a duplicate key error on a multiple-row INSERT won't cause the entire statement to be rolled back. The nonunique row will be discarded, and all other rows will be inserted or updated. IGNORE_DUP_KEY doesn't allow the uniqueness of the index to be violated; instead, it makes a violation in a multiple-row data modification nonfatal to all the nonviolating rows.

I'll discuss the STATISTICS_NORECOMPUTE option in Chapter 15 when I discuss statistics maintenance.

The SORT_IN_TEMPDB option allows you to control where SQL Server performs the sort operation on the key values needed to build an index. The default is that SQL Server uses space from the filegroup on which the index is to be created. While the index is being built, SQL Server scans the data pages to find the key values and then builds leaf-level index rows in internal sort buffers. When these sort buffers are filled, they are written to disk. The disk heads for the database can then move back and forth between the base table pages and the work area where the sort buffers are being stored. If, instead, your CREATE INDEX command includes the option SORT_IN_TEMPDB, performance can be greatly improved, particularly if your *tempdb* database is on a separate physical disk from the database you're working with, with its own controller. You can optimize head movement because two separate heads read the base table pages and manage the sort buffers. You can get even more improvement in index creation speed if your *tempdb* database is on a faster disk than your user database and you use the SORT_IN_TEMPDB option. As an alternative to using the SORT_IN_TEMPDB option, you can create separate filegroups for a table and its indexes—that is, the table is on one filegroup and its indexes are on another. If the two filegroups are on different disks with their own controllers, you can also minimize the disk head movement.

Constraints and Indexes

As I mentioned in Chapter 6, when you declare a PRIMARY KEY or UNIQUE constraint, a unique index is created on one or more columns, just as if you had used the CREATE INDEX command. The names of indexes that are built to support these constraints are the same as the constraint names. In terms of internal storage and maintenance of indexes, there is no difference between unique indexes created using the CREATE INDEX command and indexes created to support constraints. The query optimizer makes decisions based on the presence of the unique index rather than on the fact that a column was declared as a primary key. How the index got there in the first place is irrelevant to the query optimizer.

When you create a table that includes PRIMARY KEY or UNIQUE constraints, you can specify whether the associated index will be clustered or nonclustered and you can also specify the fillfactor. Since the fillfactor applies only at the time the index is created, and since there is no data when you first create the table, it might seem that specifying the fillfactor at that time is completely useless. However, if after the table is populated you decide to use DBCC DBREINDEX to rebuild all your indexes, you can specify a fillfactor of 0 to indicate that SQL Server should use the fillfactor that was specified when the index was created. You can also specify a fillfactor when you use ALTER TABLE to add a PRIMARY KEY or UNIQUE constraint to a table, and if the table already had data in it, the fillfactor value is applied when you build the index to support the new constraint.

If you check the documentation for CREATE TABLE and ALTER TABLE, you'll see that the SORT_IN_TEMPDB option is not available for either command. It really doesn't make sense to specify a sort location when you first create the table because there's nothing to sort. However, the fact that you can't specify this alternate location when you add a PRIMARY KEY or UNIQUE constraint to a table with existing data seems like an oversight. Also note that SORT_IN_TEMPDB is not an option when you use DBCC DBREINDEX. Again, there's no reason why it couldn't have been included, but it isn't available in this release.

The biggest difference between indexes created using the CREATE INDEX command and indexes that support constraints is in how you can drop the index. The DROP INDEX command allows you to drop only indexes that were built with the CREATE INDEX command. To drop indexes that support constraints, you must use ALTER TABLE to drop the constraint. In addition, to drop a PRIMARY KEY or UNIQUE constraint that has any FOREIGN KEY constraints referencing it, you must first drop the FOREIGN KEY constraint. This can leave you with a window of vulnerability while you redefine your constraints and rebuild your indexes. While the FOREIGN KEY constraint is gone, an INSERT statement can add a row to the table that violates your referential integrity.

One way to avoid this problem is to use DBCC DBREINDEX, which drops and rebuilds all your indexes on a table in a single transaction, without requiring the auxiliary step of removing FOREIGN KEY constraints. Alternatively, you can use the CREATE INDEX command with the DROP_EXISTING option. In most cases, you cannot use this command on an index that supports a constraint. However, there is an exception. For example, I used the following command to attempt to rebuild the index on the *title_id* column of the *titles* table in the *pubs* database:

```
CREATE CLUSTERED INDEX UPKCL_titleidind ON titles(title_id)
    WITH DROP_EXISTING
```

SQL Server returned this error message to me:

```
Server: Msg 1907, Level 16, State 1, Line 1
Cannot re-create index 'UPKCL_titleidind'. The new index definition
does not match the constraint being enforced by the existing index.
```

How could I have known that this index supported a constraint? First of all, the name includes *UPKCL*, which is a big clue. However, the output of *sp_helpindex* tells us only the names of the indexes, the property (clustered or unique), and the columns the index is on. It doesn't tell us if the index supports a constraint. However, if we execute *sp_help* on a table, the output will tell us that *UPKCL_titleidind* is a PRIMARY KEY constraint. The error message indicates that we can't use the DROP_EXISTING clause to rebuild this index because the new definition doesn't match the current index. We can use this command as long as the properties of the new index are exactly the same as the old. In this case, I didn't specify that the index was to be UNIQUE. We can rephrase the command as follows so that the CREATE INDEX is successful:

```
CREATE UNIQUE CLUSTERED INDEX UPKCL_titleidind ON titles(title_id)
    WITH DROP_EXISTING
```

THE STRUCTURE OF INDEX PAGES

Index pages are structured much like data pages. As with all other types of pages in SQL Server, index pages have a fixed size of 8 KB, or 8192 bytes. Index pages also have a 96-byte header, but just like in data pages, there is an offset array at the end of the page with two bytes for each row to indicate the offset of that row on the page. However, if you use DBCC PAGE with style 1 to print out the individual rows on an index page, the slot array is not shown. If you use style 2, it will only print out all the bytes on a page with no attempt to separate the bytes into individual rows. You can then look at the bottom of the page and notice that each set of 2 bytes does refer to a byte offset on the page. Each index has a row in the *sysindexes* table, with an *indid* value of either 1, for a clustered index, or a number between 2 and 250, indicating a nonclustered index. An *indid* value of 255 indicates LOB data (*text*, *ntext* or *image* information). The *root* column value contains a file number and page number where the root of the index can be found. You can then use DBCC PAGE to examine index pages, just as you do for data pages.

The header information for index pages is almost identical to the header information for data pages. The only difference is the value for *type*, which is 1 for data and 2 for index. The header of an index page also has nonzero values for *level* and *indexId*. For data pages, these values are both always 0.

There are basically three different kinds of index pages: leaf level for nonclustered indexes, node (nonleaf) level for clustered indexes, and node level for nonclustered indexes. There isn't really a separate structure for leaf level pages of a clustered index because those are the data pages, which we've already seen in detail. There is, however, one special case for leaf-level clustered index pages.

Clustered Index Rows with a Uniqueifier

If your clustered index was not created with the UNIQUE property, SQL Server adds a 4-byte field when necessary to make each key unique. Since clustered index keys are used as bookmarks to identify the base rows being referenced by nonclustered indexes, there needs to be a unique way to refer to each row in a clustered index. SQL Server adds the uniqueifier only when necessary—that is, when duplicate keys are added to the table. As an example, I'll use the same table I initially used in Chapter 6 to illustrate the row structure of a table with all fixed-length columns. I'll create an identical table with a different name, and then I'll add a clustered (nonunique) index to the table:

```
USE pubs
GO
CREATE TABLE Clustered_Dupes
  (Col1 char(5)   NOT NULL,
   Col2 int      NOT NULL,
   Col3 char(3)   NULL,
   Col4 char(6)   NOT NULL,
   Col5 float    NOT NULL)
GO
CREATE CLUSTERED INDEX Cl_dupes_col1 ON Clustered_Dupes(col1)
```

The rows in *syscolumns* look identical to the ones for the table in Chapter 6, without the clustered index. However, if you look at the *sysindexes* row for this table, you'll notice something different.

```
SELECT first, indid, keycnt, name FROM sysindexes
WHERE id = object_id ('Clustered_Dupes')
RESULT:
first           indid  keycnt name
-------------- ------ ------ ---------------
0x000000000000 1      2      Cl_dupes_col1
```

The column called *keycnt*, which indicates the number of keys an index has, is 2. If I had created this index using the UNIQUE qualifier, the *keycnt* value would be 1. If I had looked at the *sysindexes* row before adding a clustered index, when the table was still a heap, the row for the table would have had a *keycnt* value of 0. I'll now add the same initial row that I added to the table in Chapter 6, and then I'll look at *sysindexes* to find the first page of the table:

```
INSERT Clustered_Dupes VALUES ('ABCDE', 123, null, 'CCCC', 4567.8)
GO
SELECT first, root, id,indid FROM sysindexes
WHERE id = object_id('Clustered_Dupes')

RESULT:
first          root           id          indid
-------------- -------------- ----------- ------
0xB50500000100 0xB30500000100 1426104121  1
```

The *first* column tells me that the first page of the table is 1461 (0x05B5), so I can use DBCC PAGE to examine that page. Remember to turn on trace flag 3604 prior to executing this undocumented DBCC command.

```
DBCC TRACEON (3604)
GO
DBCC PAGE (5,1,1461, 1)
```

The only row on the page looks exactly as it was shown in Figure 6-7, but I'll reproduce it again here, in Figure 8-3. When you read the row output from DBCC PAGE, remember that each two displayed characters represents a byte and that the bytes are displayed from right to left within each group of 4 bytes in the output. For character fields, you can just treat each byte as an ASCII code and convert that to the associated character. Numeric fields are stored with the low-order byte first, so within each numeric field, we must swap bytes to determine what value is being stored. Right now, there are no duplicates of the clustered key, so no extra information has to be provided. However, if I add two additional rows, with duplicate values in *col1*, the row structure changes:

```
INSERT Clustered_Dupes VALUES ('ABCDE', 456, null, 'DDDD', 4567.8)
INSERT Clustered_Dupes VALUES ('ABCDE', 64, null, 'EEEE', 4567.8)
```

Figure 8-4 shows the three rows that are now on the page.

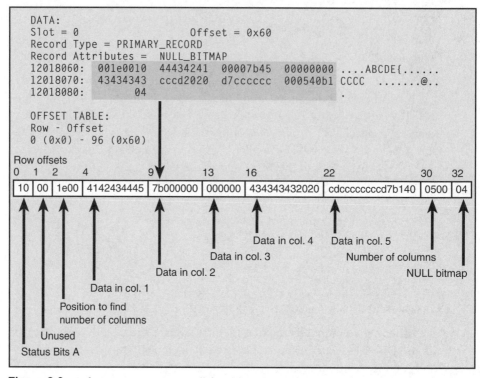

```
DATA:
Slot = 0                    Offset = 0x60
Record Type = PRIMARY_RECORD
Record Attributes = NULL_BITMAP
12018060:   001e0010  44434241  00007b45  00000000 ....ABCDE{......
12018070:   43434343  cccd2020  d7cccccc  000540b1 CCCC   .......@..
12018080:        04                                 .

OFFSET TABLE:
Row - Offset
0 (0x0) - 96 (0x60)
```

Figure 8-3. *A data row containing all fixed-length columns, and a unique value in the clustered key column.*

The first difference in the second two rows is that the bits in the first byte (TagA) are different. Bit 5 is on, giving TagA a value of 0x30, which means the variable block is present in the row. Without this bit on, TagA would have a value of 0x10. The "extra" variable-length portions of the second two rows are shaded in the figure. You can see that 8 extra bytes are added when we have a duplicate row. In this case, the first 4 extra bytes are added because the uniqueifier is considered a variable-length column. Since there were no variable-length columns before, SQL Server adds 2 bytes to indicate the number of variable-length columns present. These bytes are at offsets 33-34 in these rows with the duplicate keys and have the value of 1. The next 2 bytes (offsets 35-36) indicate the position where the first variable-length column ends. In both these rows, the value is 0x29, which converts to 41 decimal. The last 4 bytes (offsets 37-40) are the actual uniqueifier. In the second row, which has the first duplicate, the uniqueifier is 1. The third row has a uniqueifier of 2.

```
Slot 0, Offset 0x60
-------------------
Record Type = PRIMARY_RECORD
Record Attributes =  NULL_BITMAP
1bb0a060:   001e0010  44434241  00007b45  00000000     ....ABCDE{......
1bb0a070:   43434343  cccd2020  d7cccccc  000540b1     CCCC  .......@..
1bb0a080:        04                                       .

Slot 1, Offset 0x81
-------------------
Record Type = PRIMARY_RECORD
Record Attributes =  NULL_BITMAP VARIABLE_COLUMNS
1bb0a081:   001e0030  44434241  0001c845  00000000     0...ABCDE.......
1bb0a091:   44444444  cccd2020  d7cccccc  000540b1     DDDD  .......@..
1bb0a0a1:   29000104  00000100       00               ...)......

Slot 2, Offset 0xaa
-------------------
Record Type = PRIMARY_RECORD
Record Attributes =  NULL_BITMAP VARIABLE_COLUMNS
1bb0a0aa:   001e0030  44434241  00004045  00000000     0...ABCDE@......
1bb0a0ba:   45454545  cccd2020  d7cccccc  000540b1     EEEE  .......@..
1bb0a0ca:   29000104  00000200       00               ...)......
```

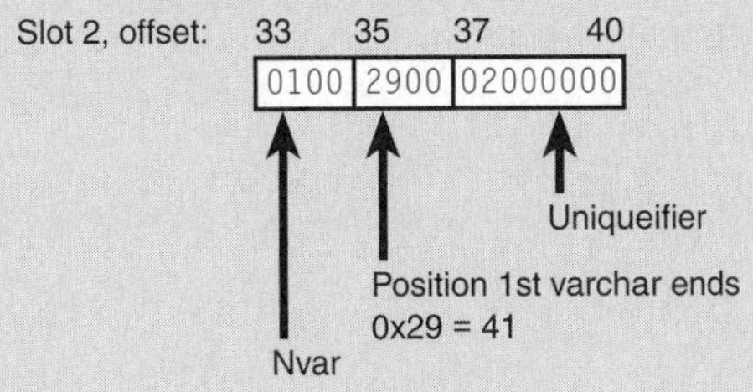

```
Slot 2, offset:    33    35    37      40
                  0100  2900  02000000
                   ↑     ↑       ↑
                   │     │       │  Uniqueifier
                   │     │
                   │     └── Position 1st varchar ends
                   │         0x29 = 41
                   │
                   └── Nvar
```

Figure 8-4. *Three data rows containing duplicate values in the clustered key column.*

Index Row Formats

The row structure of an index entry is very similar to the structure of a data row. An index row does not use the TagB or Fsize row header values. In place of the Fsize field, which indicates where the fixed-length portion of a row ends, the page header *pminlen* value is used to decode an index row. The *pminlen* value indicates the offset at which the fixed-length data portion of the row ends. If there are no variable-length or nullable columns in the index row, that is the end of the row. Only if the index row has nullable columns are the field called *Ncol* and the null bitmap both present. The *Ncol* field contains a value indicating how many columns are in the index row; this value is needed to determine how many bits are in the null bitmap. Data rows have an *Ncol* field and null bitmap whether or not any columns allow NULL, but index rows have only a null bitmap and an *Ncol* field if any NULLs are allowed in an index column. Table 8-1 shows the general format of an index row.

Information	Mnemonic	Size
Status Bits A	TagA	1 byte
	Some of the relevant bits are: ■ Bits 1 through 3: Taken as a 3-bit value, 0 indicates a primary record, 3 indicates an index record, and 5 indicates a ghost index record. (I'll discuss ghost records in Chapter 9.) ■ Bit 4: Indicates that a NULL bitmap exists. ■ Bit 5: Indicates that variable-length columns exist in the row.	
Fixed-length data	Fdata	*pminlen* − 1
Number of columns	Ncol	2 bytes
NULL bitmap (1 bit for each column in the table; a 1 indicates that the corresponding column is NULL.)	Nullbits	Ceiling (Ncol / 8)
Number of variable-length columns; only present if > 0	VarCount	2 bytes
Variable column offset array; only present if VarCount > 0	VarOffset	2 * VarCount
Variable-length data, if any	VarData	

Table 8-1. *Information stored in an index row.*

The data contents of an index row depend on the level of the index. All rows except those in the leaf level contain a 6-byte down-page pointer in addition to the key values and bookmarks. The down-page pointer is the last column in the fixed-data portion of the row. In nonclustered indexes, the nonclustered keys and bookmarks are treated as normal columns. They can reside in either the fixed or variable portion of the row, depending on how each of the key columns was defined. A bookmark that is a RID, however, is always part of the fixed-length data.

If the bookmark is a clustered key value and the clustered and nonclustered indexes share columns, the actual data is stored only once. For example, if your clustered index key is *lastname* and you have a nonclustered index on (*firstname, lastname*), the index rows will not store the value of *lastname* twice. I'll show you an example of this shortly.

Clustered Index Node Rows

The node levels of a clustered index contain pointers to pages at the next level down in the index, along with the first key value on each page pointed to. Page pointers are 6 bytes: 2 bytes for the file number and 4 bytes for the page number in the file. The following code creates and populates a table that I'll use to show you the structure of clustered index node rows.

```
CREATE TABLE clustered_nodupes (
  id int NOT NULL ,
  str1 char (5) NOT NULL ,
  str2 char (600) NULL
)
GO
CREATE CLUSTERED INDEX idxCL ON clustered_nodupes(str1)
GO
SET NOCOUNT ON
GO
DECLARE @i int
SET @i = 1240
WHILE @i < 13000 BEGIN
  INSERT INTO clustered_nodupes
    SELECT @i, cast(@i AS char), cast(@i AS char)
  SET @i = @i + 1
 END
GO
SELECT first, root, id, indid FROM sysindexes
WHERE id = object_id('clustered_nodupes')

RESULT:
first          root            id          indid
-------------- --------------- ----------- ------
0xB80500000100 0xB60500000100 1458104235  1

DBCC TRACEON (3604)
GO
DBCC PAGE (5,1,1462, 1)
```

The root of this index is at 0x05B6, which is 1462 decimal. Using DBCC PAGE to look at the root, we can see two index entries, as shown in Figure 8-5. When you examine index pages, you need to be aware that the first index key entry on each page is frequently either meaningless or empty. The down-page pointer is valid, but the data for the index key might not be a valid value. When SQL Server traverses the index, it starts looking for a value by comparing the search key with the second key value on the page. If the value being sought is less than the second entry on the page, SQL Server follows the page pointer indicated in the first index entry. In this example, the down-page pointer is at byte offsets 6 through 9, with a hex value of 0x0839. In decimal, this is 2105.

We can then use DBCC PAGE again to look at page 2105, part of which is shown in Figure 8-6. The row structure is identical to the rows on page 1462, the root page.

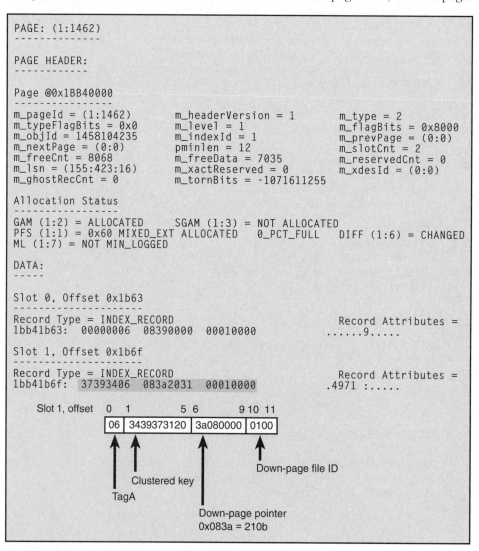

```
PAGE: (1:1462)
--------------

PAGE HEADER:
------------

Page @0x1BB40000
----------------
m_pageId = (1:1462)       m_headerVersion = 1        m_type = 2
m_typeFlagBits = 0x0      m_level = 1                m_flagBits = 0x8000
m_objId = 1458104235      m_indexId = 1              m_prevPage = (0:0)
m_nextPage = (0:0)        pminlen = 12               m_slotCnt = 2
m_freeCnt = 8068          m_freeData = 7035          m_reservedCnt = 0
m_lsn = (155:423:16)      m_xactReserved = 0         m_xdesId = (0:0)
m_ghostRecCnt = 0         m_tornBits = -1071611255

Allocation Status
-----------------
GAM (1:2) = ALLOCATED      SGAM (1:3) = NOT ALLOCATED
PFS (1:1) = 0x60 MIXED_EXT ALLOCATED   0_PCT_FULL    DIFF (1:6) = CHANGED
ML (1:7) = NOT MIN_LOGGED

DATA:
-----

Slot 0, Offset 0x1b63
---------------------
Record Type = INDEX_RECORD                           Record Attributes =
1bb41b63:  00000006  08390000  00010000              ......9.....

Slot 1, Offset 0x1b6f
---------------------
Record Type = INDEX_RECORD                           Record Attributes =
1bb41b6f:  37393406  083a2031  00010000              .4971 :.....
```

Slot 1, offset   0 1   5 6   9 10 11

06 | 3439373120 | 3a080000 | 0100

Down-page file ID

Clustered key

TagA

Down-page pointer
0x083a = 210b

Figure 8-5. *The root page of a clustered index.*

```
PAGE: (1:2105)
--------------

PAGE HEADER:
------------

Page @0x1C034000
----------------
m_pageId = (1:2105)        m_headerVersion = 1        m_type = 2
m_typeFlagBits = 0x0       m_level = 0                m_flagBits = 0x0
m_objId = 1458104235       m_indexId = 1              m_prevPage = (0:0)
m_nextPage = (1:2106)      pminlen = 12               m_slotCnt = 537
m_freeCnt = 575            m_freeData = 6543          m_reservedCnt = 0
m_lsn = (175:101:9)        m_xactReserved = 0         m_xdesId = (0:0)
m_ghostRecCnt = 0          m_tornBits = 337945226

Allocation Status
-----------------
GAM (1:2) = ALLOCATED      SGAM (1:3) = NOT ALLOCATED
PFS (1:1) = 0x40 ALLOCATED   0_PCT_FULL                    DIFF (1:6) = CHANGED
ML (1:7) = NOT MIN_LOGGED

DATA:
-----

Slot 0, Offset 0x60
-------------------
Record Type = INDEX_RECORD
Record Attributes =  NULL_BITMAP
1c034060:  00000016  07dd0000  00010000     000002 ...............

Slot 1, Offset 0xdef
--------------------
Record Type = INDEX_RECORD                             Record Attributes =
1c034def:  30303106  07df3331  00010000              .10013......

/* Slots 2 - 534 not shown */

Slot 535, Offset 0xdbf
----------------------
Record Type = INDEX_RECORD                             Record Attributes =
1c034dbf:  34393406  09662035  00010000              .4945 f.....

Slot 536, Offset 0xdcb
----------------------
Record Type = INDEX_RECORD                             Record Attributes =
1c034dcb:  35393406  09672038  00010000              .4958 g.....
```

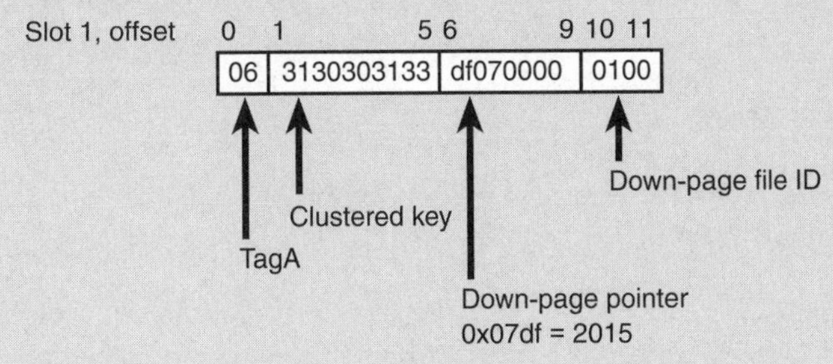

Figure 8-6. *An intermediate index-level page for a clustered index.*

The first row has a meaningless key value, but the page-down pointer should be the first page in clustered index order. The hex value for the page-down pointer is 0x07df, which is 2015 decimal. That page is the leaf level page, and it has a structure of a normal data page. If we use DBCC PAGE to look at that page, we'll see that the first row has the value of '10000', which is the minimum value of the *str1* column in the table. We can verify this with the following query:

```
SELECT min(str1)
FROM clustered_nodupes
```

Remember that the clustered index column is a *char*(5) column. Although the first number I entered was 1240, when converted to a *char*(5), that's '1240 '. When sorted alphabetically, '10000' comes well before '1240 '.

Nonclustered Index Leaf Rows

Index node rows in a clustered index contain only the first key value of the page they are pointing to in the next level and page-down pointers to guide SQL Server in traversing the index. Nonclustered index rows can contain much more information. The rows in the leaf level of a nonclustered index contain every key value and a bookmark. I'll show you three different examples of nonclustered index leaf rows. First we'll look at the leaf level of a nonclustered index built on a heap. I'll use the same code I used to build the clustered index with no duplicates in the previous example, but the index I build on the *str1* column will be nonclustered. I'll also put only a few rows in the table so that the root page will be the entire index.

```
CREATE TABLE nc_heap_nodupes (
  id int NOT NULL ,
  str1 char (5) NOT NULL ,
  str2 char (600) NULL
)
GO
CREATE UNIQUE INDEX idxNC_heap ON nc_heap_nodupes (str1)
GO
SET NOCOUNT ON
GO
DECLARE @i int
SET @i = 1240
WHILE @i < 1300 BEGIN
  INSERT INTO nc_heap_nodupes
    SELECT @i, cast(@i AS char), cast(@i AS char)
  SET @i = @i + 1
 END
GO
SELECT first, root, id, indid FROM sysindexes
WHERE id = object_id('nc_heap_nodupes')
 AND indid > 1
```

```
RESULT:
first           root            id          indid
--------------  --------------  ----------  ------
0xC10500000100  0xC10500000100  1506104406  2


DBCC TRACEON (3604)
GO
DBCC PAGE (5,1,1473, 1)
```

Since this index is built on a heap, the bookmark is an 8-byte RID. As you can see in Figure 8-7, this RID is fixed-length and is located in the index row immediately after the index key value of '1240 '. The first 4 bytes are the page address, the next 2 bytes are the file ID, and the last 2 bytes are the slot number.

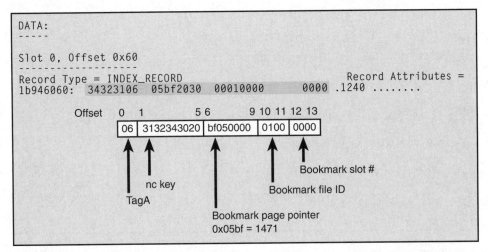

Figure 8-7. *An index row on a leaf-level page from a nonclustered index on a heap.*

I'll now build a nonclustered index on a similar table, but before building the nonclustered index, I'll build a clustered index on a *varchar* column so we can see what an index looks like when a bookmark is a clustered index key. Also, in order not to have the same values in the same sequence in both the *str1* and *str2* columns, I'll introduce a bit of randomness into the generation of the values for *str2*. If you run this script, the randomness might end up generating some duplicate values for the unique clustered index column *str2*. Since each row is inserted in its own INSERT statement, a violation of uniqueness will cause only that one row to be rejected. If you get error messages about PRIMARY KEY violation, just ignore them. You'll still end up with enough rows.

```
CREATE TABLE nc_nodupes (
  id int NOT NULL ,
  str1 char (5) NOT NULL ,
  str2 varchar (10) NULL
```

(continued)

```
)
GO
CREATE UNIQUE CLUSTERED INDEX idxcl_str2 on nc_nodupes (str2)
CREATE UNIQUE INDEX idxNC ON nc_nodupes (str1)
GO
SET NOCOUNT ON
GO
DECLARE @i int
SET @i = 1240
WHILE @i < 1300 BEGIN
  INSERT INTO nc_nodupes
   SELECT @i, cast(@i AS char),
       cast(cast(@i * rand() AS int) as char)
  SET @i = @i + 1
 END
GO
SELECT first, root, id, indid FROM sysindexes
WHERE id = object_id('nc_nodupes')
 AND indid > 1


RESULT:
first           root            id           indid
-------------- --------------- ----------- ------
0xD00500000100 0xD00500000100 1586104691  2


DBCC TRACEON (3604)
GO
DBCC PAGE (5,1,1488, 1)
```

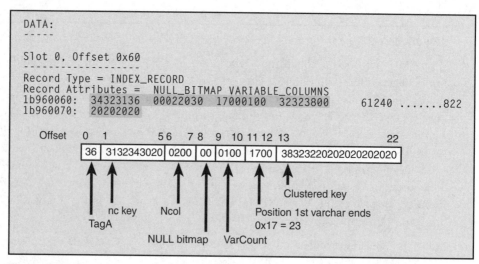

Figure 8-8. *An index row on a leaf-level page from a nonclustered index built on a clustered table.*

The index row contains the nonclustered key value of '1240 ', and the book-mark is the clustered key '822'. Because the clustered key is variable length, it comes at the end of the row after the *Ncol* value and null bitmap. A variable-length key column in an index uses only the number of bytes needed to store the value inserted. In the script to create this table, an *int* is converted to a *char* to get the value for the field. Since no length is supplied for the *char*, SQL Server by default allows 30 characters. However, since the table was defined to allow a maximum of 10 characters in that column, that is all that was stored in the row. If the script to create the table had actually converted to *char*(3), the clustered key bookmark in the index row would use only 3 bytes.

The third example will show a composite nonclustered index on *str1* and *str2* and an overlapping clustered index on *str2*. I'll just show you the code to create the table and indexes; the code to populate the table and to find the root of the index is identical to the code in the previous example.

```
CREATE TABLE nc_overlap (
  id int NOT NULL ,
  str1 char (5) NOT NULL ,
  str2 char (10) NULL
)
GO
CREATE UNIQUE CLUSTERED INDEX idxCL_overlap ON nc_overlap(str2)
CREATE UNIQUE INDEX idxNC_overlap ON nc_overlap (str1, str2)
GO
```

Figure 8-9 shows a leaf-level index row from the nonclustered composite in-dex on the table *nc_overlap*.

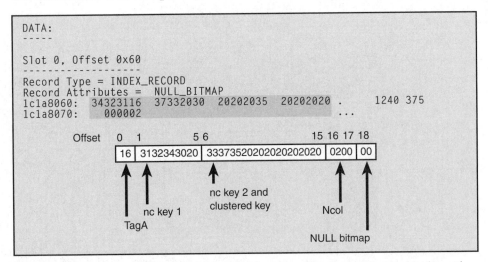

Figure 8-9. *An index row on a leaf-level page from a composite nonclustered index with an overlapping clustered key.*

Note that the value in column *str2* ('375' in this row) is part of the index key for the nonclustered index as well as the bookmark because it is the clustered index key. Although it serves two purposes in the row, its value is not duplicated. The value '375' occurs only once, taking the maximum allowed space of 10 bytes. Because this is a leaf-level row, there is no page-down pointer, and because the index is built on a clustered table, there is no RID, only the clustered key to be used as a bookmark.

Nonclustered Index Node Rows

You now know that the leaf level of a nonclustered index must have a bookmark because from the leaf level you want to be able to find the actual row of data. The nonleaf levels of a nonclustered index only need to help us traverse down to pages at the lower levels. If the nonclustered index is unique, the node rows need to have only the nonclustered key and the page-down pointer. If the index is *not* unique, the row contains key values, a down-page pointer, and a bookmark.

Let's say I need to create a table that will have enough rows for more than a single nonclustered index level. I can use a script similar to the ones shown previously and change the upper limit of the WHILE loop to 13000. I'll do this twice: I'll create one table with a nonunique nonclustered index on *str1* and a clustered index on *str2* and another table with a unique nonclustered index on *str1* and a clustered index on *str2*. For the purposes of creating the index rows, SQL Server doesn't care whether the keys in the nonunique index actually contain duplicates. If the index is not defined to be unique, even if all the values are unique, the nonleaf index rows will contain bookmarks. You can see this is in the index row in Figure 8-10. Figure 8-11 shows an index row for a nonclustered index row for a unique index.

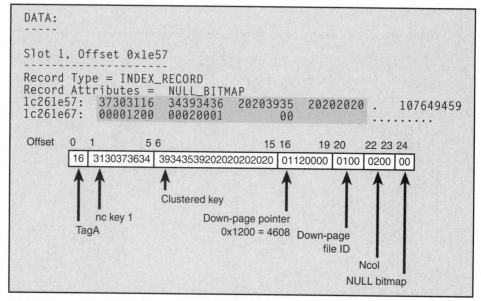

Figure 8-10. *A nonleaf index row for a nonunique, nonclustered index.*

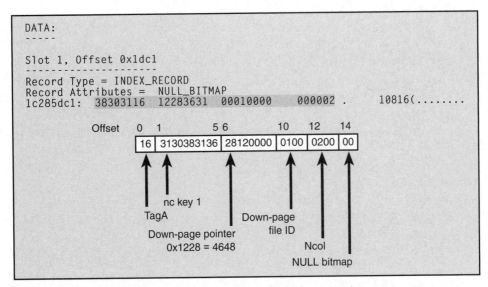

Figure 8-11. *A nonleaf index row for a unique, nonclustered index.*

As you've seen, once you've found the root page of an index in the *sysindexes* table, you can decode down-page pointers in every row to find all the pages that belong to the index. The header information of an index page also has *level*, *prevPage*, and *nextPage* values, so you can ascertain the order of pages at a particular level of the index. As much as I enjoy decoding strings of bytes and converting hex values to decimal, I don't mind an occasional shortcut. You can use an undocumented DBCC command that lists all the pages that belong to a particular index. Keep in mind that Microsoft doesn't support this command and that it isn't guaranteed to maintain the same behavior from release to release. The command DBCC IND has three parameters.

```
DBCC IND ({'dbname' | dbid }, { 'objname' | objid },
{ indid | 0 | -1 | -2 })
```

The first parameter is the database name or the database ID. The second parameter is an object name or object ID within the database. The third parameter is a specific index ID or one of the values 0, −1, or −2. The values for this parameter have the following meanings:

0	Displays the page numbers for all Index Allocation Maps (IAMs) and data pages.
−1	Displays the page numbers for all IAMs, data pages, and index pages.
−2	Displays the page numbers for all IAMs.
Index ID	Displays the page numbers for all IAMs and index pages for this index. If the index ID is 1 (meaning the clustered index), the data pages are also displayed.

If we run this command on the table I created for Figure 8-10, which is called *nc_nonunique_big*, with a third parameter of 2 (for the nonclustered index), we get the following results:

```
DBCC IND(5, nc_nonunique_big, 2)
RESULTS:
```

PageFID	PagePID	IAMFID	IAMPID	IndexLevel	NextPageFID Page FID	Next Page PID	Prev Page FID	Prev Page PID
1	1594	NULL	NULL	0	0	0	0	0
1	1593	1	1594	1	0	0	0	0
1	1596	1	1594	0	1	4608	0	0
1	1597	1	1594	0	1	1599	1	4611
1	1599	1	1594	0	1	1602	1	1597
1	1602	1	1594	0	1	1604	1	1599
1	1604	1	1594	0	1	1606	1	1602
1	1606	1	1594	0	1	1607	1	1604
1	1607	1	1594	0	1	4584	1	1606
1	4584	1	1594	0	1	4585	1	1607
1	4585	1	1594	0	1	4586	1	4584
1	4586	1	1594	0	1	4587	1	4585
1	4587	1	1594	0	1	4588	1	4586
1	4588	1	1594	0	1	4589	1	4587
1	4589	1	1594	0	1	4590	1	4588
1	4590	1	1594	0	0	0	1	4589
1	4591	1	1594	0	1	4611	1	4610
1	4608	1	1594	0	1	4609	1	1596
1	4609	1	1594	0	1	4610	1	4608
1	4610	1	1594	0	1	4591	1	4609
1	4611	1	1594	0	1	1597	1	4591

The columns in the result set are described in Table 8-2. Note that all page references have the file and page component conveniently split between two columns, so you don't have to do any conversion.

Column	*Meaning*
PageFID	Index file ID
PagePID	Index page ID
IAMFID	File ID of the IAM managing this page
IAMPID	Page ID of the IAM managing this page
ObjectID (not shown in output)	Object ID
IndexID (not shown in output)	Index ID

Table 8-2. *Column descriptions for DBCC IND output.*   *(continued)*

Column	Meaning
PageType (not shown in output)	Page type: 1 = Data page, 2 = Index page, 10 = IAM page
IndexLevel	Level of index; 0 is leaf
NextPageFID	File ID for next page at this level
NextPagePID	Page ID for next page at this level
PrevPageFID	File ID for previous page at this level
PrevPagePID	Page ID for previous page at this level

INDEX SPACE REQUIREMENTS

I've shown you the structure and number of bytes in individual index rows, but you really need to be able to translate that into overall index size. In general, the size of an index is based on the size of the index keys, which determines how many index rows can fit on an index page and the number of rows in the table.

B-Tree Size

When we talk about index size, we usually mean the size of the index tree. The clustered index does include the data, but since you still have the data even if you drop the clustered index, we're usually just interested in how much additional space the nonleaf levels require. A clustered index's node levels typically take up very little space. You have one index row for each page of table data, so the number of index pages at the level above the leaf (level 1) is the bytes available per page divided by the index key row size, and this quotient divided *into* the number of data pages. You can do a similar computation to determine the pages at level 2. Once you reach a level with only one page, you can stop your computations because that level is the root.

For example, consider a table of 10,000 pages and 500,000 rows with a clustered key of a 5-byte fixed-length character. As you saw in Figure 8-5, the index key row size is 12 bytes, so we can fit 674 rows (8096 bytes available on a page / 12 bytes per row) on an index page. Since we need index rows to point to all 10,000 pages, we'll need 15 index pages (10000 / 674) at level 1. Now, all these index pages need pointers at level 2, and since one page can contain 15 index rows to point to these 15 pages, level 2 is the root. If our 10,000-page table also has a 5-byte fixed-length character nonclustered index, the leaf-level rows (level 0) will be 11 bytes long, as they will each contain a clustered index key (5 bytes), a nonclustered index key (5 bytes) and 1 byte for the status bits. The leaf level will contain every single nonclustered key value along with the corresponding clustered key values. An index page can hold 736 index rows at this leaf level. We need 500,000 index rows, one for each row of data, so we need 680 leaf pages. If this nonclustered index is unique, the index rows at the higher levels will be 12 bytes each, so 674 index rows will fit per page, and we'll need two pages at level 1, with level 2 as the one root page.

So how big are these indexes compared to the table? For the clustered index, we had 16 index pages for a 10,000-page table, which is less than 1 percent of the size of the table. I frequently use 1 percent as a ballpark estimate for the space requirement of a clustered index, even though you can see that in this case it's an overly large estimate. On the other hand, our nonclustered index needed 683 pages for the 10,000-page table, which is about 6 percent additional space. For nonclustered indexes, it is much harder to give a good ballpark figure. My example used a very short key. Nonclustered index keys are frequently much larger, or even composite, so it's not unusual to have key sizes of over $100n$ bytes. In that case, we'd need a lot more leaf level pages, and the total nonclustered index size could be 30 or 40 percent of the size of the table. I've even seen nonclustered indexes that are as big or bigger than the table itself. Once you have two or three nonclustered indexes, you need to double the space to support these indexes. Remember that SQL Server allows you to have up to 249 nonclustered indexes! Disk space is cheap, but is it that cheap? You still need to plan your indexes carefully.

Actual vs. Estimated Size

The actual space used for tables or indexes, as opposed to the ballpark estimates I just described, is stored in the *sysindexes* table. A column called *rowcnt* contains the number of data rows in the table. A column called *dpages* contains, for a clustered index or a heap, the number of data pages used; for all other indexes, *dpages* contains the number of index pages used. For LOB data (*text, ntext,* or *image*), with an *indid* value of 255, *dpages* is 0. *Sysindexes* also has a column called *reserved*, which, for a clustered index or a heap, contains the number of data pages reserved; for a nonclustered index, it contains the number of pages reserved for the index itself; and for LOB data, *reserved* is a count of the pages allocated. I'll tell you more about what "reserved" means later in this section.

Finally, there is a column in *sysindexes* called *used*. For clustered indexes or heaps, it contains the total number of pages used for all index and table data. For LOB data, *used* is the number of LOB pages. For nonclustered indexes, *used* is the count of index pages. Because no specific value is just the number of nonleaf, or nondata, pages in a clustered index, you must do additional computations to determine the total number of index pages for a table, not including the data.

The stored procedure *sp_spaceused* examines these values and reports the total size used by a table. Keep in mind that these values in *sysindexes* are not updated every time a table or index is modified. In particular, immediately after you create a table and after some bulk operations, *sp_spaceused* might not accurately reflect the total space because the values in *sysindexes* are not accurate.

You can force SQL Server to update the *sysindexes* data in two ways. The simplest way to force the space used values to be updated is to ask for this when you execute the *sp_spaceused* procedure. The procedure takes two optional parameters: the first is called *@objname* and is a table name in the current database, and the second is called *@updateusage*, which can have a value of TRUE or FALSE. If you specify TRUE, the data in *sysindexes* will be updated. The default is FALSE.

Here's an example of forcing SQL Server to update the space used data for a table called *charge*:

```
exec sp_spaceused charge, true
```

Here's the result:

name	rows	reserved	data	index_size	unused
charge	100000	10328 KB	5384 KB	4696 KB	248 KB

Remember that after the first 8 pages are allocated to a table, SQL Server grants all future allocations in units of 8 pages, called *extents*. The sum of all the allocations is the value of *reserved*. It might be that only a few of the 8 pages in some of the extents actually have data in them and are counted as used, so that the *reserved* value is frequently higher than the *used* value. The *data* value is computed by looking at the *data* column in *sysindexes* for the clustered index or heap and adding any LOB pages. The *index_size* value is computed by taking the *used* value from *sysindexes* for the clustered index or heap, which includes all index pages for all indexes. Because this value includes the number of data pages, which are at the leaf level of the clustered index, we must subtract the number of data pages from used pages to get the total number of index pages. The procedure *sp_spaceused* does all of its space reporting in KB, which we can divide by 8 to get the number of pages. The *unused* value is then the leftover amount after we subtract the *data* value and the *index_size* value from the *reserved* value.

You can also use the DBCC UPDATEUSAGE command to update the space information for every table and index in *sysindexes*. Or, by supplying additional arguments, you can have the values updated for only a single table, view, or index. In addition, DBCC UPDATEUSAGE gives you a report of the changes it made. You might want to limit the command to only one table because the command works by actually counting all the rows and all the pages in each table it's interested in. For a huge database, this can take a lot of time. In fact, *sp_spaceused* with the *@updateusage* argument set to TRUE actually calls DBCC UPDATEUSAGE and suppresses the report of changes made. The following command updates the space used information for every table in the current database:

```
DBCC UPDATEUSAGE (0)
```

Here's some of the output I received when I ran this in the *Northwind* database:

```
DBCC UPDATEUSAGE: sysindexes row updated for table 'syscolumns' (index ID 2):
    USED pages: Changed from (2) to (5) pages.
    RSVD pages: Changed from (2) to (5) pages.
DBCC UPDATEUSAGE: sysindexes row updated for table 'Orders' (index ID 2):
    USED pages: Changed from (2) to (5) pages.
    RSVD pages: Changed from (2) to (5) pages.
DBCC UPDATEUSAGE: sysindexes row updated for table 'Orders' (index ID 3):
    USED pages: Changed from (2) to (5) pages.
    RSVD pages: Changed from (2) to (5) pages.
:
DBCC UPDATEUSAGE: sysindexes row updated for table
'Order Details' (index ID 3):
    USED pages: Changed from (2) to (6) pages.
    RSVD pages: Changed from (2) to (6) pages.
```

Note that you can use this command to update both the *used* and *reserved* values in *sysindexes*.

It's great to have a way to see how much space is being used by a particular table or index, but what if we're getting ready to build a database and we want to know how much space our data and indexes will need? For planning purposes, it would be nice to know this information ahead of time.

If you've already created your tables and indexes, even if they're empty, SQL Server can get column and datatype information from the *syscolumns* system table, and it should be able to see any indexes you've defined in the *sysindexes* table. There shouldn't be a need for you to type all this information into a spreadsheet. The companion CD also includes a set of stored procedures you can use to calculate estimated space requirements when the table and indexes have already been built. The main procedure is called *sp_EstTableSize*, and it requires only two parameters: the table name and the anticipated number of rows. The procedure calculates the storage requirements for the table and all indexes by extracting information from the *sysindexes, syscolumns,* and *systypes* tables. The result is only an estimate when you have variable-length fields. The procedure has no way of knowing whether a variable-length field will be completely filled, half filled, or mostly empty in every row, so it assumes that variable-length columns will be filled to the maximum size. If you know that this won't be the case with your data, you can create a second table that more closely matches the expected data. For example, if you have a *varchar(1000)* field that you must set to the maximum because a few rare entries might need it but 99 percent of your rows will use only about 100 bytes, you can create a second table with a *varchar(100)* field and run *sp_EstTableSize* on that table.

NOTE The procedures for calculating estimated storage space were developed primarily by SQL Server MVP B.P. Margolin and are included on the companion CD with his permission.

MANAGING AN INDEX

SQL Server maintains your indexes automatically. As you add new rows, it automatically inserts them into the correct position in a table with a clustered index, and it adds new leaf-level rows to your nonclustered indexes that will point to the new rows. When you remove rows, SQL Server automatically deletes the corresponding leaf-level rows from your nonclustered indexes. In Chapter 9, you'll see some specific examples of the changes that take place within an index as data modification operations take place.

Types of Fragmentation

In general, you need to do very little in terms of index maintenance. However, indexes can become fragmented. The fragmentation can be of two types. Internal fragmentation occurs when space is available within your index pages—that is, when the indexes are not making the most efficient use of space. External fragmentation occurs when the logical order of pages does not match the physical order, or when the extents belonging to a table are not contiguous.

Internal fragmentation means that the index is taking up more space than it needs to. Scanning the entire table involves more read operations than if no free space were available on your pages. However, internal fragmentation is sometimes desirable. In fact, you can request internal fragmentation by specifying a low fillfactor value when you create an index. Having room on a page means that there is space to insert more rows without having to split a page. Splitting is a relatively expensive operation and can lead to external fragmentation because when a page is split, a new page must be linked into the indexes page chain, and usually the new page is not contiguous to the page being split.

External fragmentation is truly bad only when SQL Server is doing an ordered scan of all or part of a table or an index. If you're seeking individual rows through an index, it doesn't matter where those rows are physically located—SQL Server can find them easily. If SQL Server is doing an unordered scan, it can use the IAM pages to determine which extents need to be fetched, and the IAM pages list the extents in disk order, so the fetching can be very efficient. Only if the pages need to be fetched in logical order, according to their index key values, do you need to follow the page chain. If the pages are heavily fragmented, this operation is more expensive than if there were no fragmentation.

Detecting Fragmentation

You can use the DBCC SHOWCONTIG command to report on the fragmentation of an index. Here's the syntax:

```
DBCC SHOWCONTIG
    [ ( { table_name | table_id | view_name | view_id }
        [ , index_name | index_id ]
      )
    ]
    [ WITH { ALL_INDEXES
           | FAST [ , ALL_INDEXES ]
           | TABLERESULTS [ , { ALL_INDEXES } ]
           [ , { FAST | ALL_LEVELS } ]
        }
    ]
```

You can ask to see the information for all the indexes on a table or view or just one index. You can specify the object and index by name or by ID number. Alternatively, you can use the ALL_INDEXES option, which provides an individual report for each index on the object, regardless of whether a specific index is specified.

Here's some sample output from running a basic DBCC SHOWCONTIG on the *order details* table in the *Northwind* database:

```
DBCC SHOWCONTIG scanning 'Order Details' table...
Table: 'Order Details' (325576198); index ID: 1, database ID: 6
TABLE level scan performed.
- Pages Scanned................................: 9
- Extents Scanned..............................: 6
- Extent Switches..............................: 5
- Avg. Pages per Extent........................: 1.5
- Scan Density [Best Count:Actual Count].......: 33.33% [2:6]
- Logical Scan Fragmentation ..................: 0.00%
- Extent Scan Fragmentation ...................: 16.67%
- Avg. Bytes Free per Page.....................: 673.2
- Avg. Page Density (full).....................: 91.68%
```

By default, DBCC SHOWCONTIG scans the page chain at the leaf level of the specified index and keeps track of the following values:

■ Average number of bytes free on each page (*Avg. Bytes Free per Page*)

■ Number of pages accessed (*Pages Scanned*)

■ Number of extents accessed (*Extents Scanned*)

- Number of times a page had a lower page number than the previous page in the scan (This value for *Out of order pages* is not displayed, but it is used for additional computations.)

- Number of times a page in the scan was on a different extent than the previous page in the scan (*Extent Switches*)

SQL Server also keeps track of all the extents that have been accessed, and then it determines how many gaps are in the used extents. An extent is identified by the page number of its first page. So, if extents 8, 16, 24, 32, and 40 make up an index, there are no gaps. If the extents are 8, 16, 24, and 40, there is one gap. The value in DBCC SHOWCONTIG's output called *Extent Scan Fragmentation* is computed by dividing the number of gaps by the number of extents, so in this example the *Extent Scan Fragmentation* is ¼, or 25 percent. A table using extents 8, 24, 40, and 56 has 3 gaps, and its *Extent Scan Fragmentation* is ¾, or 75 percent. The maximum number of gaps is the number of extents − 1, so *Extent Scan Fragmentation* can never be 100 percent.

The value in DBCC SHOWCONTIG's output called *Logical Scan Fragmentation* is computed by dividing the number of *Out Of Order Pages* by the number of pages in the table. This value is meaningless in a heap.

You can use either the *Extent Scan Fragmentation* value or the *Logical Scan Fragmentation* value to determine the general level of fragmentation in a table. The lower the value, the less fragmentation there is. Alternatively, you can use the value called *Scan Density*, which is computed by dividing the optimum number of extent switches by the actual number of extent switches. A high value means that there is little fragmentation. *Scan Density* is not valid if the table spans multiple files, so all in all it is less useful than the other values.

You can use DBCC SHOWCONTIG to have the report returned in a format that can be easily inserted into a table. If you have a table with the appropriate columns and datatypes, you can execute the following:

```
INSERT INTO CONTIG_TABLE
  EXEC ('dbcc showcontig ([order details])
  with all_indexes, tableresults')
```

Here's a subset of the results:

ObjectName	IndexId	Level	Pages	Rows
Order Details	1	0	9	2155
Order Details	2	0	4	2155
Order Details	3	0	4	2155

Many more columns are returned if you specify TABLERESULTS. In addition to the values that the nontabular output returns, you also get the values listed in Table 8-3.

Column	Meaning
ObjectName	Name of the table or view processed.
ObjectId	ID of the object processed.
IndexName	Name of the index processed (NULL for a heap).
IndexId	ID of the index (0 for a heap).
Level	Level of the index. Level 0 is the leaf (or data) level of the index. The level number increases moving up the tree toward the index root. The level is 0 for a heap. By default, only level 0 is reported. If you specify ALL_LEVELS along with TABLERESULTS, you get a row for each level of the index.
Pages	Number of pages composing that level of the index or the entire heap.
Rows	Number of data or index records at that level of the index. For a heap, this is the number of data records in the entire heap.
MinimumRecordSize	Minimum record size in that level of the index or the entire heap.
MaximumRecordSize	Maximum record size in that level of the index or the entire heap.
AverageRecordSize	Average record size in that level of the index or the entire heap.
ForwardedRecords	Number of forwarded records in that level of the index or the entire heap.
Extents	Number of extents in that level of the index or the entire heap.

Table 8-3. *Additional columns returned when TABLERESULTS is specified.*

One last option available to DBCC SHOWCONTIG is the FAST option. The command takes less time to run when you specify this option, as you might imagine, because it gathers only data that is available from the IAM pages and the nonleaf levels of the index, and it returns only these values:

- *Pages Scanned*
- *Extent Switches*

- *Scan Density*

- *Logical Scan Fragmentation*

Since the level above the leaf has pointers to every page, SQL Server can determine all the page numbers and determine the *Logical Scan Fragmentation*. In fact, it can also use the IAM pages to determine the *Extent Scan Fragmentation*. However, the purpose of the FAST option is to determine whether a table would benefit from online defragmenting, and since online defragmenting cannot change the *Extent Scan Fragmentation*, there is little benefit in reporting it. I'll talk about online defragmenting in the next section.

Removing Fragmentation

Several methods are available for removing fragmentation from an index. First, you can rebuild the index and have SQL Server allocate all new contiguous pages for you. You can do this by using a simple DROP INDEX and CREATE INDEX, but I've already discussed some reasons why this is not optimal. In particular, if the index supports a constraint, you can't use the DROP INDEX command. Alternatively, you can use DBCC DBREINDEX, which can rebuild all the indexes on a table in a single operation, or you can use the *drop_existing* clause along with CREATE INDEX.

The drawback of these methods is that the table is unavailable while the index is being rebuilt. If you are rebuilding only nonclustered indexes, there is a shared lock on the table, which means that no modifications can be made, but other processes can SELECT from the table. Of course, they cannot take advantage of the index you're rebuilding, so the query might not perform as well as it should. If you're rebuilding the clustered index, SQL Server takes an exclusive lock and no access is allowed at all.

SQL Server 2000 allows you to defragment an index without completely rebuilding it. In this release, DBCC INDEXDEFRAG reorders the leaf level pages into physical order as well as logical order, but using only the pages that are already allocated to the leaf level. It basically does an in-place ordering, similar to a sorting technique called *bubble-sort*. This can reduce the logical fragmentation to 0 to 2 percent, which means that an ordered scan through the leaf level will be much faster. In addition, DBCC INDEXDEFRAG compacts the pages of an index, based on the original fillfactor, which is stored in the *sysindexes* table. This doesn't mean that the pages always end up with the original fillfactor, but SQL Server uses that as a goal. The process does try to leave at least enough space for one average-size row after the defragmentation takes place. In addition, if a lock cannot be obtained on a page during the compaction phase of DBCC INDEXDEFRAG, SQL Server skips the page and doesn't go back to it. Any empty pages created as a result of this compaction are removed. Here's an example:

```
DBCC INDEXDEFRAG(0, 'charge', 1)
```

Here's the output:

```
Pages Scanned Pages Moved Pages Removed
------------- ----------- -------------
673              668          12
```

The algorithm SQL Server uses for DBCC INDEXDEFRAG finds the next physical page in a file belonging to the leaf level and the next logical page in the leaf level with which to swap it. It finds the next physical page by scanning the IAM pages for that index. The single-page allocations are not included in this release. Pages on different files are handled separately. The algorithm finds the next logical page by scanning the leaf level of the index. After each page move, all locks and latches are dropped and the key of the last page moved is saved. The next iteration of the algorithm uses the key to find the next logical page. This allows other users to update the table and index while DBCC INDEXDEFRAG is running.

For example, suppose the leaf level of an index consists of these pages, in this order:

47 22 83 32 12 90 64

The first step is to find the first physical page, which is 12, and the first logical page, which is 47. These pages are then swapped, using a temporary buffer as a holding area. After the first swap, the leaf level looks like this:

12 22 83 32 47 90 64

The next physical page is 22, which is the same as the next logical page, so no work is done. The next physical page is 32, which is swapped with the next logical page, 83, to look like this:

12 22 32 83 47 90 64

After the next swap of 47 with 83, the leaf level looks like this:

12 22 32 47 83 90 64

The 64 is swapped with 83:

12 22 32 47 64 90 83

And finally, 83 and 90 are swapped:

12 22 32 47 64 83 90

Keep in mind that DBCC INDEXDEFRAG uses only pages that are already part of the index leaf level. No new pages are allocated. In addition, the defragmenting can take quite a while on a large table. You get a report every five minutes on the estimated percentage completed.

SPECIAL INDEXES

SQL Server 2000 allows you to create two special kinds of indexes: indexes on computed columns and indexes on views. Without indexes, both of these constructs are purely logical. There is no physical storage for the data involved. A computed column is not stored with the table data; it is recomputed every time a row is accessed. A view does not save any data; it basically saves a SELECT statement that is reexecuted every time the data in the view is accessed. With the new special indexes, SQL Server actually materializes what was only logical data into the physical leaf level of an index.

Prerequisites

Before you can create indexes on either computed columns or views, certain prerequisites must be met. The biggest issue is that SQL Server needs to be able to guarantee that given the identical base table data, the same values will always be returned for any computed columns or for the rows in a view. To guarantee that the same values will always be generated, these special indexes have certain requirements, which fall into three categories. First, a number of session-level options must be set to a specific value. Second, there are some restrictions on the functions that can be used within the column or view definition. The third requirement, which applies only to indexed views, is that the tables that the view is based on must meet certain criteria.

SET Options

The following seven SET options can affect the result value of an expression or predicate, so you must set them as shown to create indexed views or indexes on computed columns:

```
SET ARITHABORT ON
SET CONCAT_NULL_YIELDS_NULL ON
SET QUOTED_IDENTIFIER ON
SET ANSI_NULLS ON
SET ANSI_PADDING ON
SET ANSI_WARNINGS ON
SET NUMERIC_ROUNDABORT OFF
```

Note that all the options have to be ON except the NUMERIC_ROUNDABORT option, which has to be OFF. If any of these options are not set as specified, you'll get an error message when you create a special index. In addition, if you've already created one of these indexes and then you attempt to modify the column or view on which the index is based, you'll get an error. If you issue a SELECT that normally should use the index, and if the seven SET options do not have the values indicated, the index will be ignored but no error will be generated.

You can also use the property function SESSIONPROPERTY to test whether you have each option appropriately set. A returned value of 1 means that the setting is ON, and a 0 means OFF. The following example checks the current session setting for the option NUMERIC_ROUNDABORT:

```
SELECT SessionProperty('NUMERIC_ROUNDABORT')
```

Permissible Functions

A function is either *deterministic* or *nondeterministic*. If the function returns the same result every time it is called with the same set of input values, it is deterministic. If it can return different results when called with the same set of input values, it is nondeterministic. For the purposes of indexes, a function is considered deterministic if it always returns the same values for the same input values when the seven SET options have the required settings. Any function used in a computed column's definition or used in the SELECT list or WHERE clause of an indexable view must be deterministic.

Table 8-4 lists the deterministic and nondeterministic functions in SQL Server 2000. Where it might not be obvious, I have included an indication of why a particular function is nondeterministic—that is, why you might not always get the same result when the function is called with the same input values.

Function	Deterministic or Nondeterministic Attribute
Aggregate functions (SUM, AVG, and so on) (Note that you cannot use aggregate functions in computed columns—as I'll discuss shortly—but you can use some of them in indexed views.)	Deterministic
Configuration Functions	All are nondeterministic
Cursor Functions	All are nondeterministic

Table 8-4. *SQL Server 2000 deterministic and nondeterministic functions.*   *(continued)*

Function	Deterministic or Nondeterministic Attribute
Date and Time Functions:	
DATEADD(datepart, number, date)	Deterministic
DATEDIFF(datepart, startdate, enddate)	Deterministic
DATENAME	Nondeterministic (The result is language dependent, particularly for the value returned when you're looking for the names of months or days of the week.)
DATEPART	Deterministic (except for DATEPART(dw,date) because the value depends on the current setting of DATEFIRST)
DAY (date)	Deterministic
GETDATE	Nondeterministic
GETUTCDATE	Nondeterministic
MONTH (date)	Deterministic
YEAR (date)	Deterministic
Mathematical Functions:	
RAND()	Nondeterministic
The rest of mathematical functions, including RAND(SEED)	Deterministic
Metadata functions (object info)	All are Nondeterministic
Security functions (such as IS_MEMBER)	All are Nondeterministic
String functions (such as ASCII and STR)	All are Deterministic except CHARINDEX and PATINDEX
System Functions:	
APP_NAME	Nondeterministic
CAST	Nondeterministic if the datatype is *datetime, smalldatetime*, or *sql_variant*. Deterministic otherwise.
CONVERT (data_type[(length)], pression)	Nondeterministic if the datatype is ex-*datetime, smalldatetime*, or *sql_variant*. Deterministic otherwise.
CONVERT (data_type[(length)], expression, style)	Deterministic
COALESCE	Deterministic

(continued)

Table 8-4 *continued*

Function	Deterministic or Nondeterministic Attribute
System Functions *(continued)*:	
CURRENT_TIMESTAMP	Nondeterministic
CURRENT_USER	Nondeterministic
DATALENGTH	Deterministic
@@ERROR	Nondeterministic
FORMATMESSAGE	Nondeterministic
GETANSINULL	Nondeterministic
HOST_ID	Nondeterministic
HOST_NAME	Nondeterministic
IDENT_INCR	Nondeterministic
IDENT_SEED	Nondeterministic
@@IDENTITY	Nondeterministic
IDENTITY (function)	Nondeterministic
ISDATE (expression)	Nondeterministic (because it depends on DATEFORMAT)
	(Note that this function can be deterministic if used with the CONVERT function, with CONVERT style parameter specified, and style not equal to 0, 100, 9, or 109.)
ISNULL	Deterministic
ISNUMERIC	Deterministic
NEWID	Nondeterministic
NULLIF	Deterministic
PARSENAME	Deterministic
PERMISSIONS	Nondeterministic
@@ROWCOUNT	Nondeterministic
SESSION_USER	Nondeterministic
STATS_DATE	Nondeterministic
SYSTEM_USER	Nondeterministic
@@TRANCOUNT	Nondeterministic
USER_NAME	Nondeterministic
CHECKSUM(select list)	Deterministic except for CHECKSUM(*)
System statistical functions such as @@cpu_busy, @@idle	Nondeterministic

(continued)

Function	Deterministic or Nondeterministic Attribute
Text and Image Functions:	
PATINDEX	Nondeterministic
TEXTPTR	Nondeterministic
TEXTVALID	Nondeterministic
OPERATORS (such as +, −, /, *, string +, − neg)	Deterministic
Implicit Date Conversion Functions:	
String -> date	Nondeterministic (because it depends on DATEFORMAT)

This might seem like quite a restrictive list, but the same restrictions apply to functions you use in your own user-defined functions (UDFs)—that is, your own functions cannot be based on any nondeterministic built-in function. I'll talk about UDFs in Chapter 11.

Schema Binding

To create an indexed view, a requirement on the table itself is that you don't want the definition of any underlying object's schema to change. To prevent a change in schema definition, SQL Server 2000's CREATE VIEW statement allows the WITH SCHEMABINDING option. When you specify WITH SCHEMABINDING, the SELECT statement that defines the view must include the two-part names (owner.object) of all referenced tables. You can't drop or alter tables participating in a view created with the SCHEMABINDING clause unless you've dropped that view or changed the view so that it no longer has schema binding. Otherwise, SQL Server raises an error. If any of the tables on which the view is based is owned by someone other than the user creating the view, the view creator doesn't automatically have the right to create the view with schema binding because that would restrict the table's owner from making changes to her own table. The table owner must grant another user REFERENCES permission in order for that user to create a view with schema binding on that table. We'll see an example of schema binding in a moment.

Indexes on Computed Columns

SQL Server 2000 allows you to build indexes on deterministic computed columns where the resulting data type is otherwise indexable. This means that the column's datatype cannot be *text*, *ntext*, or *image*. Such a computed column can participate at any position of an index or in a PRIMARY KEY or UNIQUE constraint. You cannot define a FOREIGN KEY, CHECK, or DEFAULT constraint on a computed column, and computed columns are always considered nullable, unless you enclose the expression in the ISNULL function.. You cannot create indexes on any computed columns in system tables. When you create an index on computed columns, the seven SET options must first have the correct values set.

Here's an example:

```
CREATE TABLE t1 (a int, b as 2*a)
GO
CREATE INDEX i1 on t1 (b)
GO
```

If any of your seven SET options don't have the correct values when you create the table, you get this message when you try to create the index:

```
Server: Msg 1934, Level 16, State 1, Line 2
CREATE INDEX failed because the following SET options have
incorrect settings: '<OPTION NAME>'.
```

If more than one option has an incorrect value, the error message reports only one incorrectly set option.

Here's an example that creates a table with a nondeterministic computed column:

```
CREATE TABLE t2 (a int, b datetime, c AS datename(mm, b))
GO
CREATE INDEX i2 on t2 (c)
GO
```

When you try to create the index on the computed column c, you get this error:

```
Server: Msg 1933, Level 16, State 1, Line 1
Cannot create index because the key column 'c' is
non-deterministic or imprecise.
```

Column c is nondeterministic because the month value of *datename* can have different values depending on the language you're using.

Using the COLUMNPROPERTY Function

You can use the new IsDeterministic property to determine before you create an index on a computed column whether that column is deterministic. If you specify this property, the COLUMNPROPERTY function returns 1 if the column is deterministic and 0 otherwise. The result is undefined for noncomputed columns, so you should consider checking the IsComputed property before you check the IsDeterministic property. The following example detects that column c in table t2 in the previous example is nondeterministic:

```
SELECT COLUMNPROPERTY(object_id('t2'), 'c', 'IsDeterministic')
```

The value 0 is returned, which means that column c is nondeterministic. Note that the COLUMNPROPERTY function requires an object ID for the first argument and a column name for the second argument.

Implementation of a Computed Column

If you create a clustered index on a computed column, the computed column is no longer a virtual column in the table. Its computed value will physically exist in the rows of the table, which is the leaf level of the clustered index. Updates to the columns that the computed column is based on will also update the computed column in the table itself. For example, in the t1 table created previously, if we insert a row with the value 10 in column a, the row will be created with both the values 10 and 20 in the actual data row. If we then update the 10 to 15, the second column will be automatically updated to 30.

In Chapter 16, I'll revisit indexes on computed columns and show you some situations where you can make good use of them.

Indexed Views

Indexed views in SQL Server 2000 are similar to what other products call materialized views. The first index you must build on a view is a clustered index, and since the clustered index contains all the data at its leaf level, this index actually does materialize the view. The view's data is physically stored at the leaf level of the clustered index.

Additional Requirements

In addition to the requirement that all functions used in the view be deterministic and that the seven SET options be set to the appropriate values, the view definition can't contain any of the following:

- TOP
- *text*, *ntext*, or *image* columns
- DISTINCT
- MIN, MAX, COUNT(*), COUNT(<expression>), STDEV, VARIANCE, AVG
- SUM on a nullable expression
- A derived table
- The ROWSET function
- Another view (you can reference only base tables)
- UNION
- Subqueries, OUTER joins, or self-joins

■ Full-text predicates (CONTAINS, FREETEXT)

■ COMPUTE, COMPUTE BY

■ ORDER BY

Also, if the view definition contains GROUP BY, you must include the aggregate COUNT_BIG(*) in the SELECT list. COUNT_BIG returns a value of the datatype BIGINT, which is an 8-byte integer. A view that contains GROUP BY can't contain HAVING, CUBE, ROLLUP, or GROUP BY ALL. Also, all GROUP BY columns must appear in the SELECT list. Note that if your view contains both SUM and COUNT_BIG(*), you can compute the equivalent of the AVG function even though AVG is not allowed in indexed views. Although these restrictions might seem severe, remember that they apply to the view definitions, not to the queries that might use the indexed views.

To verify that you've met all the requirements, you can use the OBJECTPROPERTY function's IsIndexable property. The following query tells you whether you can build an index on a view called Product Totals:

```
SELECT ObjectProperty(object_id('Product_Totals'), 'IsIndexable')
```

A return value of 1 means you've met all requirements and can build an index on the view.

Creating an Indexed View

The first step to building an index on a view is to create the view itself. Here's an example from the *Northwind* database:

```
USE northwind
GO
CREATE VIEW Product_Totals
WITH SCHEMABINDING
AS
select productid, total_volume = sum(unitPrice * Quantity),
total_qty = sum(Quantity) , number = count_big(*)
from dbo."order details"
group by productid
```

Note the WITH SCHEMABINDING clause and the specification of the owner name (dbo) for the table. At this point, we have a normal view—a stored SELECT statement that uses no storage space. In fact, if we run the system stored procedure *sp_spaceused* on this view, we'll get this error message:

```
Server: Msg 15235, Level 16, State 1, Procedure sp_spaceused, Line 91
Views do not have space allocated.
```

To create an indexed view, you need to create an index. The first index you create on a view must be a *unique clustered index*. Clustered indexes are the only type of SQL Server index that contains data; the clustered index on a view contains all the data that makes up the view definition. This statement defines a unique clustered index, *PV_IDX*, for the view:

```
CREATE UNIQUE CLUSTERED INDEX PV_IDX on Product_Totals(productid)
```

After you create the index, you can rerun *sp_spaceused*. My output looks like this:

```
Name                rows    reserved    data   index_size unused
----------------    -----   ----------  -----  ---------- ------
Product_Totals      77      24 KB       8 KB   16 KB      0 KB
```

Data that composes the indexed view is persistent, with the indexed view storing the data in the clustered index's leaf level. You could construct something similar by using temporary tables to store the data you're interested in. But a temporary table is static and doesn't reflect changes to underlying data. In contrast, SQL Server automatically maintains indexed views, updating information stored in the clustered index whenever anyone changes data that affects the view.

After you create the unique clustered index, you can create multiple nonclustered indexes on the view. You can determine whether a view is indexed by using the OBJECTPROPERTY function's IsIndexed property. For the *Total_Products* indexed view, the following statement returns a 1, which means that the view is indexed:

```
SELECT ObjectProperty(object_id('Product_Totals'), 'IsIndexed')
```

Executing the system stored procedure *sp_help* or *sp_helpindex* returns complete information about any indexes on the view.

Using an Indexed View

One of the most valuable benefits of indexed views is that your queries don't have to directly reference a view to use the index on the view. Consider the *Product_Totals* indexed view. Suppose you issue the following SELECT statement:

```
SELECT productid, total_qty = sum(Quantity)
FROM dbo."order details"
GROUP BY productid
```

SQL Server's query optimizer will realize that the precomputed sums of all the Quantity values for each *productid* are already available in the index for the *Product_Totals* view. The query optimizer will evaluate the cost of using that indexed view in processing the query. But just because you have an indexed view doesn't mean that the query optimizer will always choose it for the query's execution plan. In fact, even if you reference the indexed view directly in the FROM clause, the query optimizer might decide to directly access the base table instead. In Chapters 15 and 16, I'll tell you more about how the query optimizer decides whether to use indexed views and how you can tell if indexed views are being used for a query.

USING AN INDEX

This chapter has primarily been concerned with the structure of indexes and the nuances of creating and managing them. Hopefully, you're aware of at least some of the places that indexes can be useful in your SQL Server applications. I will list a few of the situations in which you can benefit greatly from indexes; I'll also revisit most of these situations in Chapters 15 and 16 when I discuss SQL Server query processing and tuning in detail.

Looking for Rows

The most straightforward use of an index is to help SQL Server find one or more rows in a table that satisfy a certain condition. For example, if you're looking for all the customers who live in a particular state (for example, your WHERE clause is WHERE state = 'WI'), you can use an index on the *state* column to find those rows more quickly. SQL Server can traverse the index from the root, comparing index key values to 'WI', to determine whether 'WI' exists in the table and then find the data associated with that value.

Joining

A typical join tries to find all the rows in one table that match rows in anther table. Of course, you can have joins that aren't looking for exact matching, but you're looking for some sort of relationship between tables, and equality is by far the most common relationship. A query plan for a join frequently starts with one of the tables, finds the rows that match the search conditions, and then uses the join key in the qualifying rows to find matches in the other table. An index on the join column in the second table can be used to quickly find the rows that match.

Sorting

A clustered index stores the data logically in sorted order. The data pages are linked together in order of the clustering keys. If you have a query to ORDER BY the clustered keys or by the first column of a composite clustered key, SQL Server does not have to perform a sort operation to return the data in sorted order.

If you have a nonclustered index on the column you're sorting by, the sort keys themselves are in order at the leaf level. For example, consider the following query:

```
SELECT firstname, lastname, state, zipcode
FROM customers
ORDER BY zipcode
```

The nonclustered index will have all the zip codes in sorted order. However, we want the data pages themselves to be accessed to find the *firstname* and *lastname* values associated with the *zipcode*. The query optimizer will decide if it's faster to traverse the nonclustered index leaf level and from there access each data row or to just perform a sort on the data. If you're more concerned with getting the first few rows of data as soon as possible and less concerned with the overall time to return all the results, you can force SQL Server to use the nonclustered index with the FAST hint. I'll tell you all about hints in Chapter 16.

Inverse Indexes

SQL Server allows you to sort in either ascending or descending order, and if you have a clustered index on the sort column, SQL Server can use that index and avoid the actual sorting. The pages at the leaf level of the clustered index are doubly linked, so SQL Server can use a clustered index on *lastname* to satisfy this query

```
SELECT * FROM customers ORDER BY lastname DESC
```

as easily as it can use the same index for this query:

```
SELECT * FROM customers ORDER BY lastname
```

Earlier in the chapter, I mentioned that SQL Server 2000 allows you to create descending indexes. Why would you need them if an ascending index can be scanned in reverse order? The real benefit is when you want to sort with a combination of ascending and descending order. For example, take a look at this query:

```
SELECT * FROM employees
ORDER BY lastname, salary DESC
```

The default sort order is ascending, so the query wants the names ordered alphabetically by last name, and within duplicate last names, the rows should be sorted with the highest salary first and lowest salary last. The only kind of index that can help SQL Server avoid actually sorting the data is one with the *lastname* and *salary* columns sorted in opposite orders, such as this one:

```
CREATE CLUSTERED INDEX name_salary_indx
ON employees (lastname, salary DESC)
```

If you execute *sp_help* or *sp_helpindex* on a table, SQL Server will indicate whether the index is descending by placing a minus (–) after the index key. Here's a subset of some *sp_helpindex* output:

```
index_name            index_description                  index_keys
--------------------  ---------------------------------  -------------------
lastname_salary_indx  nonclustered located on PRIMARY    LastName, Salary(-)
```

Grouping

One way that SQL Server can perform a GROUP BY operation is by first sorting the data by the grouping column. For example, if you want to find out how many customers live in each state, you can write a query with a GROUP BY state clause. A clustered index on state will have all the rows with the same value for state in logical sequence, so the sorting and grouping operations will be very fast.

Maintaining Uniqueness

Creating a unique index (or defining a PRIMARY KEY or UNIQUE constraint that builds a unique index) is by far the most efficient method of guaranteeing that no duplicate values are entered into a column. By traversing an index tree to determine where a new row should go, SQL Server can detect within a few page reads that a row already has that value. Unlike all the other uses of indexes described in this section, using unique indexes to maintain uniqueness isn't just one option among others. Although SQL Server might not always traverse a particular unique index to determine where to try to insert a new row, SQL Server will always use the existence of a unique index to verify whether a new set of data is acceptable.

SUMMARY

In this chapter, I showed you how SQL Server indexes organize the data on disk and help you access your data more quickly than if no indexes existed. Indexes are organized as B-trees, which means that you will always traverse through the same number of index levels when you traverse from the root to any leaf page. To use an index to find a single row of data, SQL Server never has to read more pages than there are levels in an appropriate index.

You also learned about all the options available when you create an index, how to determine the amount of space an index takes up, and how to predict the size of an index that doesn't have any data yet.

Indexes can become fragmented in SQL Server 2000, but the performance penalty for fragmentation is usually much less than in earlier versions of SQL Server. When you want to defragment your indexes, you have several methods to choose from, one of which allows the index to continue to be used by other operations while the defragmentation operation is going on.

Finally you learned about some of the situations in which you can get the greatest performance gains by having the appropriate indexes on your tables.

Modifying Data

In Chapter 7, we looked at how to query data. In this chapter, we'll look at inserting, updating, and deleting data in tables. We'll cover the basic SQL commands for these operations but focus on Microsoft SQL Server–specific behaviors. This chapter considers each statement as an independent, atomic operation. Chapter 12 discusses combining multiple statements into an all-or-nothing atomic operation (that is, a *transaction*). The use of constraints (covered in Chapter 6) is closely related to the topic of modifying data, but this chapter will assume that the modifications being performed satisfy any constraints on a table.

BASIC MODIFICATION OPERATIONS

SQL has three basic data modification statements: INSERT, UPDATE, and DELETE. I used these in some examples in previous chapters, assuming that you were already familiar with them. Here, I'll quickly review the most typical operations. Along with SELECT, the INSERT, UPDATE, and DELETE statements are referred to as *DML*, or *data manipulation language*. (DML is sometimes mistakenly referred to as *data modification language*, in which case SELECT couldn't be included, because it doesn't modify anything.) SELECT can manipulate data as the data is returned by using functions, aggregates, grouping, or the like. (Creation operations such as CREATE TABLE are *DDL—data definition language*—whereas security operations such as GRANT, DENY, and REVOKE are *DCL—data control language*.)

INSERT

You generally use INSERT to add one row to a table. Here's the most common form of INSERT:

```
INSERT [INTO] {table_name|view_name} [(column_list)]
VALUES value_list
```

In SQL Server, the use of INTO is always optional, but ANSI SQL specifies using INTO. If you're providing a value for every column in the table and the values appear in the exact order in which the columns were defined, the column list is optional. The one exception to this is when the table has an identity column, which you must not include in the list of values. Later in this chapter, you'll learn more about inserting rows into a table that contains an identity column. If you omit a value for one or more columns or if the order of your values differs from the order in which the columns were defined for the table, you must use a named columns list. If you don't provide a value for a particular column, that column must allow NULL or must have a default declared for it. You can use the keyword DEFAULT as a placeholder. You can explicitly enter NULL for a column, or SQL Server will implicitly enter NULL for an omitted column for which no default value exists.

You can issue an INSERT statement for a view, but the row is always added to only one underlying table. If the view is an indexed view, all indexes will be updated to reflect the new data. You can insert data into a view as long as values (or defaults) are provided for all the columns of the underlying table into which the new row is being added. Partitioned views have a few additional restrictions, some of which I discussed in Chapter 6. I'll tell you more about partitioned views when I discuss query tuning in Chapter 16.

Following are some simple examples of using INSERT statements in a table that's similar to *publishers* in the *pubs* sample database. The CREATE TABLE statement is shown so that you can easily see column order and you can see which columns allow NULL and which have defaults declared.

```
CREATE TABLE publishers2
(
    pub_id        int            NOT NULL PRIMARY KEY IDENTITY,
    pub_name      varchar(40)    NULL DEFAULT ('Anonymous'),
    city          varchar(20)    NULL,
    state         char(2)        NULL,
    country       varchar(30)    NOT NULL DEFAULT('USA')
)
GO
```

```
INSERT publishers2 VALUES ('AAA Publishing', 'Vancouver', 'BC',
    'Canada')

INSERT INTO publishers2 VALUES ('Best Publishing', 'Mexico City',
    NULL, 'Mexico')

INSERT INTO publishers2 (pub_name, city, state, country)
VALUES ('Complete Publishing', 'Washington', 'DC', 'United States')

INSERT publishers2 (state, city) VALUES ('WA', 'Poulsbo')

INSERT publishers2 VALUES (NULL, NULL, NULL, DEFAULT)

INSERT publishers2 VALUES (DEFAULT, NULL, 'WA', DEFAULT)

INSERT publishers2 VALUES (NULL, DEFAULT, DEFAULT, DEFAULT)

INSERT publishers2 DEFAULT VALUES
GO
```

The table has these values:

pub_id	pub_name	city	state	country
0001	AAA Publishing	Vancouver	BC	Canada
0002	Best Publishing	Mexico City	NULL	Mexico
0003	Complete Publishing	Washington	DC	United States
0004	Anonymous	Poulsbo	WA	USA
0005	NULL	NULL	NULL	USA
0006	Anonymous	NULL	WA	USA
0007	NULL	NULL	NULL	USA
0008	Anonymous	NULL	NULL	USA

These INSERT examples are pretty self-explanatory, but you should be careful of the following:

■ If a column is declared to allow NULL and it also has a default bound to it, omitting the column entirely from the INSERT statement results in the default value being inserted, not the NULL value. This is also true if the column is declared NOT NULL.

■ Other than for quick-and-dirty, one-time use, you're better off providing the column list to explicitly name the columns. Your INSERT statement will then still work even if you add a column via ALTER TABLE.

■   If one of the INSERT statements in this example had failed, the others would have continued and succeeded. Even if I had wrapped multiple INSERT statements in a BEGIN TRAN/COMMIT TRAN block (and did nothing more than that), a failure of one INSERT (because of an error such as a constraint violation or duplicate value) wouldn't cause the others to fail. This behavior is expected and proper. If you want all the statements to fail when one statement fails, you must add error handling. (Chapter 12 covers error handling in more detail.)

■   The special form of the INSERT statement that uses DEFAULT VALUES and no column list is a shorthand method that enables you to avoid supplying the keyword DEFAULT for each column.

■   You can't specify the column name for a column that has the IDENTITY property, and you can't use the DEFAULT placeholder for a column with the IDENTITY property. (This would be nice, but SQL Server doesn't currently work this way.) You must completely omit a reference to the identity column. To explicitly provide a value for the column, you must use SET IDENTITY_INSERT ON. You can use the DEFAULT VALUES clause, however.

DEFAULT and NULL Precedence

You should understand the general behavior of INSERT in relation to NULL and DEFAULT precedence. If you omit a column from the column list and the values list, the column takes on the default value, if one exists. If a default value doesn't exist, SQL Server tries a null value. An error results if the column has been declared NOT NULL. If NULL is explicitly specified in the values list, a column is set to NULL (assuming it allows NULL) even if a default exists. When you use the DEFAULT placeholder on a column allowing NULL and no default has been declared, NULL is inserted for that column. An error results in a column declared NOT NULL without a default if you specify NULL or DEFAULT or if you omit the value entirely.

Table 9-1 summarizes the results of an INSERT statement that omits columns, specifies NULL, or specifies DEFAULT, depending on whether the column is declared NULL or NOT NULL and whether it has a default declared.

	Column default status			
	Default exists		No default exists	
	Nullability of Column			
Entry description	Null	Not null	Null	Not null
Value entered for column satisfies all constraints	Value entered	Value entered	Value entered	Value entered
Value entered for column fails some constraint on table	ERROR Default not used even if it exists	ERROR Default not used even if it exists	ERROR Default not used even if it exists	ERROR Default not used even if it exists
Column omitted	DEFAULT	DEFAULT	NULL	ERROR
Explicitly entered NULL	NULL	ERROR	NULL	ERROR
Explicitly entered DEFAULT	DEFAULT	DEFAULT	NULL	ERROR

Table 9-1. *The effects of an INSERT statement that omits columns, specifies NULL, or specifies DEFAULT.*

Expressions in the VALUES Clause

So far, the INSERT examples have used only constant values in the VALUES clause of INSERT. In fact, you can use a scalar expression such as a function or a local variable in the VALUES clause. (I'll show you functions and variables in Chapter 10; you can take a quick look ahead if you need to.) You can't use an entire SELECT statement as a scalar value even if you're certain that it returns only one row and one column. However, you can take the result of that SELECT statement and assign it to a variable, and then you can use that variable in the VALUES clause. In the next section, you'll see how a SELECT statement can completely replace the VALUES clause.

The example at the top of the following page demonstrates how functions, expressions, arithmetic operations, string concatenation, and local variables are used in the VALUES clause of an INSERT statement.

```
CREATE TABLE mytable
(
    int_val         int,
    smallint_val    smallint,
    numeric_val     numeric(8, 2),
    tiny_const      tinyint,
    float_val       float,
    date_val        datetime,
    char_strng      char(10)
)
GO

DECLARE @myvar1 numeric(8, 2)
SELECT @myvar1=65.45

INSERT mytable (int_val, smallint_val, numeric_val, tiny_const,
    float_val, date_val, char_strng)
VALUES
(OBJECT_ID('mytable'), @@spid, @myvar1 / 10.0, 5,
SQRT(144), GETDATE(), REPLICATE('A', 3) + REPLICATE('B', 3))
GO

SELECT * FROM mytable
GO
```

The results will look something like this:

```
int_val      smallint_val    Numeric_val    tiny_const    float_val
----------   ------------    -----------    ----------    ---------
2082106458   56              6.55           5             12.0

date_val                     char_string
---------------------        -------------------
2000-06-27 12:22:55.040      AAABBB
```

If you run this query, your values will be slightly different because your table will have a different *object_id* value, your process ID (*spid*) might be different, and you'll be executing this query at a different date and time.

Multiple-Row INSERT Statements

The most typical use of INSERT is to add one row to a table. However, two special forms of INSERT (INSERT/SELECT and INSERT/EXEC) and a special SELECT statement (SELECT INTO) allow you to add multiple rows of data at once. Note that you can use the system function @@ROWCOUNT after all these statements to find out the number of rows affected.

INSERT/SELECT   As mentioned earlier, you can use a SELECT statement instead of a VALUES clause with INSERT. You get the full power of SELECT, including joins, subqueries, UNION, and all the other goodies. The table you're inserting into must already exist; it can be a permanent table or a temporary table. The operation is atomic, so a failure of one row, such as from a constraint violation, causes all rows chosen by the SELECT statement to be thrown away. An exception to this occurs if a duplicate key is found on a unique index created with the IGNORE_DUP_KEY option. In this case, the duplicate row is thrown out but the entire statement continues and isn't aborted. You can, of course, also use expressions in the SELECT statement, and using the CONVERT function is common if the target table has a datatype that's different from that of the source table.

For example, suppose I want to copy the *authors* table (in the *pubs* sample database) to a temporary table. But rather than show the author ID as a *char* field in Social Security–number format with hyphens, I want to strip out the hyphens and store the ID as an *int*. I want to use a single name field with the concatenation of the last and first name. I also want to record the current date but strip off the time so that the internal time is considered midnight. If you're working only with dates and want to ignore the time portion of *datetime* values, this is a good idea because it avoids issues that occur when the time portions of columns aren't equal. I'll also record each author's area code—the first three digits of the phone number. I need the author's state, but if it's NULL, I'll use WA instead.

```
CREATE TABLE #authors
(
    au_id           int                 PRIMARY KEY,
    au_fullname     varchar(60)         NOT NULL,
    date_entered    smalldatetime       NOT NULL,
    area_code       char(3)             NOT NULL,
    state           char(2)             NOT NULL
)
GO

INSERT INTO #authors
SELECT
CONVERT(int, SUBSTRING(au_id, 1, 3) + SUBSTRING(au_id, 5, 2)
    + SUBSTRING(au_id, 8, 4)),
au_lname + ', ' + au_fname,
CONVERT(varchar, GETDATE(), 102),
CONVERT(char(3), phone),
ISNULL(state, 'WA')
FROM authors

SELECT * FROM #authors
```

Here's the result:

```
au_id       au_fullname          date_entered           area_code   state
---------   ------------------   --------------------   ---------   -----
172321176   White, Johnson       1998-08-19 00:00:00    408         CA
213468915   Green, Marjorie      1998-08-19 00:00:00    415         CA
238957766   Carson, Cheryl       1998-08-19 00:00:00    415         CA
267412394   O'Leary, Michael     1998-08-19 00:00:00    408         CA
274809391   Straight, Dean       1998-08-19 00:00:00    415         CA
341221782   Smith, Meander       1998-08-19 00:00:00    913         KS
409567008   Bennet, Abraham      1998-08-19 00:00:00    415         CA
427172319   Dull, Ann            1998-08-19 00:00:00    415         CA
472272349   Gringlesby, Burt     1998-08-19 00:00:00    707         CA
486291786   Locksley, Charlene   1998-08-19 00:00:00    415         CA
527723246   Greene, Morningstar  1998-08-19 00:00:00    615         TN
648921872   Blotchet-Halls,      1998-08-19 00:00:00    503         OR
            Reginald
672713249   Yokomoto, Akiko      1998-08-19 00:00:00    415         CA
712451867   del Castillo, Innes  1998-08-19 00:00:00    615         MI
722515454   DeFrance, Michel     1998-08-19 00:00:00    219         IN
724089931   Stringer, Dirk       1998-08-19 00:00:00    415         CA
724809391   MacFeather, Stearns  1998-08-19 00:00:00    415         CA
756307391   Karsen, Livia        1998-08-19 00:00:00    415         CA
807916654   Panteley, Sylvia     1998-08-19 00:00:00    301         MD
846927186   Hunter, Sheryl       1998-08-19 00:00:00    415         CA
893721158   McBadden, Heather    1998-08-19 00:00:00    707         CA
899462035   Ringer, Anne         1998-08-19 00:00:00    801         UT
998723567   Ringer, Albert       1998-08-19 00:00:00    801         UT
```

I find that using INSERT/SELECT is typically the most convenient way to quickly get some sample data into a table because the SELECT statement can simply select constants. For example, to create a table with an *int* and a *varchar*(10) column and then insert two rows into the table, I can use the following code:

```
CREATE TABLE demo (col1 int, col2 varchar(10))
GO


INSERT INTO demo SELECT 1, 'hello'
INSERT INTO demo SELECT 10, 'good-bye'
GO
```

INSERT/EXEC   You can use INSERT with the results of a stored procedure or a dynamic EXECUTE statement taking the place of the VALUES clause. This procedure is similar to INSERT/SELECT except that EXEC is used instead. EXEC should return exactly one result set with types that match the table you've set up for it. You can pass parameters if you're executing a stored procedure, use EXEC('*string*'), or even call out to extended procedures (your own custom DLLs) or to remote procedures on other servers. By calling to a remote procedure on another server, putting the data into a temporary table, and then joining on it, you get the capabilities of a distributed join.

For example, suppose I want to store the results of executing the *sp_configure* stored procedure in a temporary table. (You can also do this with a permanent table.)

```
CREATE TABLE #config_out
(
    name_col      varchar(50),
    minval        int,
    maxval        int,
    configval     int,
    runval        int
)

INSERT #config_out
    EXEC sp_configure

SELECT * FROM #config_out
```

Here's the result:

name_col	minval	maxval	configval	runval
allow updates	0	1	0	0
default language	0	9999	0	0
max text repl size (B)	0	2147483647	65536	65536
nested triggers	0	1	1	1
remote access	0	1	1	1
remote login timeout	0	2147483647	20	20
remote proc trans	0	1	0	0
remote query timeout	0	2147483647	600	600
show advanced options	0	1	0	0
user options	0	4095	0	0

If I want to execute the procedure against the remote server named *dogfood*, that's almost as easy (assuming that the same table *#config_out* exists):

```
INSERT #config_out
    EXEC dogfood.master.dbo.sp_configure
```

NOTE Before executing a procedure on another server, you must perform several administrative steps to enable the servers to communicate with each other. See the SQL Server documentation for details on linked servers. After you carry out these simple steps, you can execute procedures on the remote server by simply including the name of the server as part of the procedure name, as shown in the previous example.

SELECT INTO   SELECT INTO is in many ways similar to INSERT/SELECT, but it directly builds the table rather than requiring that the table already exist. In addition, SELECT INTO can operate as a minimally logged operation, depending on your recovery model. When you're running in SIMPLE or BULK_LOGGED recovery mode, the SELECT INTO operation can be a lot faster than an INSERT that adds the same data. (Chapter 5 discussed recovery models.)

You can also use SELECT INTO with temporary tables (which are prefixed with # or ##). A user executing SELECT INTO—whether to create a temporary or a permanent table—must have permission to select from the source table and must also have CREATE TABLE permission because the SELECT INTO statement does both actions.

SELECT INTO is handy. It's commonly used to copy a table, modify the datatype of a column, or switch the order of columns. To illustrate the SELECT INTO statement, here's an equivalent operation to the earlier INSERT/SELECT example. The results, including the column names of the new temporary table, appear identical to those produced using INSERT/SELECT.

```
SELECT
CONVERT(int, SUBSTRING(au_id, 1, 3) + SUBSTRING(au_id, 5, 2)
    + SUBSTRING(au_id, 8, 4)) AS au_id,
    au_lname + ', ' + au_fname AS au_fullname,
CONVERT(varchar, GETDATE(), 102) AS date_entered,
CONVERT(char(3), phone) AS area_code,
ISNULL(state, 'WA') AS state

INTO #authors
FROM authors
```

However, there's one important difference between the two procedures: the datatypes of the table created automatically are slightly different from the datatypes declared explicitly using INSERT/SELECT. If the exact datatypes are important, you can use CONVERT to cast them to the types you want in all cases or you can create the table separately and then use INSERT/SELECT. However, if you want to specify a particular nullability value, there is no way to do that. If a column is copied directly from the source to the destination, it keeps the same NULL or NOT NULL property; if any conversion is done on the column, the new column will have the default nullability of the connection. To force a nullability different from these defaults, you have to create the table before you copy the data into it and specify NULL or NOT NULL for each column.

Another feature of SELECT INTO is that you can add an identity column to the new table by using the function IDENTITY in the SELECT clause. The function takes up to three parameters. The first is the datatype, the second is the seed, and the third is the increment. SQL Server automatically populates the rows with the appropriate identity values if the table already has data in it. The following script creates a copy of the *sales* table in the *pubs* database, adding an additional identity column to be the order ID for each row:

```
SELECT IDENTITY(int, 1, 1) AS OrderID, *
INTO NewSales
FROM Sales
```

BULK INSERT

SQL Server 2000 provides the BULK INSERT command for loading a flat file of data into a SQL Server table. However, it offers no corresponding command for copying data out to a file. The file to be copied in must be either local or available via a UNC name. Here's the general syntax for BULK INSERT:

```
BULK INSERT [['database_name'.]['owner'].]{'table_name' FROM data_file}
    [WITH
        (
            [ BATCHSIZE [ = batch_size]]
            [[,] CODEPAGE [ = ACP | OEM | RAW | code_page]]
            [[,] CHECK_CONSTRAINTS]
            [[,] DATAFILETYPE [ =
                {'char' | 'native' | 'widechar' | 'widenative'}]]
            [[,] FIELDTERMINATOR [ = 'field_terminator']]
            [[,] FIRETRIGGERS]
            [[,] FIRSTROW [ = first_row]]
            [[,] FORMATFILE [ = 'format_file_path']]
            [[,] KEEPIDENTITY]
            [[,] KILOBYTES_PER_BATCH [ = kilobytes_per_batch]]
            [[,] KEEPNULLS]
            [[,] LASTROW [ = last_row]]
            [[,] MAXERRORS [ = max_errors]]
            [[,] ORDER ({column [ASC | DESC]} [, ...n])]
            [[,] ROWTERMINATOR [ = 'row_terminator']]
            [[,] TABLOCK]
        )
```

To use the BULK INSERT command, the table must already exist. The number and datatypes of the columns must be compatible with the data in the file that you plan to copy in.

Here's a simple example to give you a feel for what this command can do:

Create a simple table in the *pubs* database using the batch at the top of the next page.

```
USE pubs
CREATE TABLE mybcp
(
    col1 char(3),
    col2 INT
)
```

Use your favorite editor (such as Notepad) to save a text file named mydata.txt to the root directory of drive C. Include the following text:

```
abc,1;def,2;ghi,3;
```

Load the file into the table using the following Transact-SQL statement:

```
BULK INSERT pubs.dbo.mybcp
FROM 'c:\mydata.txt'
WITH
(DATAFILETYPE = 'char',
FIELDTERMINATOR = ',', ROWTERMINATOR = ';')
```

> **NOTE**   The data file must specify a valid path from the machine on which SQL Server is running. If the file is a remote file, you must specify a UNC name.

As the syntax specification shows, the BULK INSERT command has quite a few possible arguments. These arguments are described in the online documentation, but because some of their descriptions might be unclear, I'll give you the highlights in Table 9-2.

Argument	*Description*
BATCHSIZE	Each batch is copied to the server as a single transaction. If an entire batch is successfully loaded, the data is immediately written to disk. If a server failure occurs in the middle of a batch, all rows in that batch will be lost but all rows up to the end of the previous batch will still be available. By default, all data in the specified data file is one batch.
ORDER (*column_list*) where *column_list* = {*column* [ASC | DESC] [,...*n*]}	The data file is already sorted by the same columns in *column_list* as the destination table. A clustered index on the same columns, in the same order as the columns in *column_list*, must already exist in the table. Using a sorted data file can improve the performance of the BULK INSERT command. By default, BULK INSERT assumes that the data file is unordered.

Table 9-2. *Some of the BULK INSERT command arguments.*   *(continued)*

Argument	Description
TABLOCK	A table-level lock is acquired for the duration of the bulk copy. It improves performance because of reduced lock contention on the table. This special kind of BulkUpdate lock is primarily compatible only with other BulkUpdate locks, so a table can be loaded quickly using multiple clients running BULK INSERT in parallel. By default, no table-level lock is acquired. You can still run parallel BULK INSERTs, but their performance will be much slower, similar to running individual INSERT statements. (Chapter 14 covers locking in detail.)
CHECK_CONSTRAINTS	Any constraints on the table are applied during the bulk copy. By default, constraints aren't enforced, except for PRIMARY KEY and UNIQUE constraints. Applying constraints can have several benefits and is the recommended approach. By checking the constraints on the data, you know that the data you load will be valid. In addition, SQL Server might be able to better optimize the entire operation because it has advance knowledge of the kind of data that will be loaded.
FIRE_TRIGGERS	Any INSERT triggers on the destination table will execute during the bulk copy operations. By default, no triggers will execute. If FIRE_TRIGGERS is specified, any bulk load will be fully logged no matter what recovery mode your SQL Server is in. (I'll discuss why triggers require fully logged INSERTs in Chapter 12.)

Unlike for previous versions of SQL Server, I don't always recommend that you drop all your indexes before running the BULK INSERT operation (or the BCP command, described in the next section). In many cases, the copy operation doesn't perform noticeably better if a table has no indexes, so you should usually leave your indexes on a table while copying data into it. The only exception is when you want to have multiple clients load data into the same table simultaneously; in that case, you should drop indexes before loading the data.

When SQL Server executes a BULK INSERT operation, the rows of data go straight into the server as an OLE DB row set. The functionality of a BULK INSERT operation is quite similar to that of the command-line utility BCP. In contrast to the BULK INSERT operation, BCP data is sent to SQL Server as a tabular data stream (TDS) result set and flows through network protocols and Microsoft Open Data Services (ODS). This can generate a lot of additional overhead, and you might find that BULK INSERT is up to twice as fast as BCP for copying data into a table from a local file.

Tools and Utilities Related to Multiple-Row Inserts

INSERT and BULK INSERT aren't the only ways to get data into SQL Server tables. SQL Server also provides some tools and utilities for loading tables from external sources. I'll mention them briefly here.

Bulk copy libraries, SQL-DMO objects, and BCP.EXE   The ODBC standard doesn't directly support SQL Server bulk copy operations. When it runs against SQL Server 2000, however, the SQL Server 2000 ODBC driver supports a set of older DB-Library functions that perform SQL Server bulk copy operations. The specialized bulk copy support requires that the following files be available: *odbcss.h*, *odbcbcp.lib*, and *odbcbcp.dll*.

The BCP.EXE command-line utility for SQL Server 2000 is written using the ODBC bulk copy interface. This utility has little code other than the code that accepts various command-line parameters and then invokes the functions of the *bcp* library. I won't go into the details of BCP.EXE except to say that it was built for function, not form. It's totally command-line driven. If you're a fan of UNIX utilities, you'll love it. The possible arguments are similar to those for the BULK INSERT command, and you can find a complete description in the online documentation.

The SQL-DMO BulkCopy object ultimately invokes these same *bcp* functions, but it provides some higher-level methods and ease of use within the world of COM (Component Object Model) objects. The BulkCopy object represents the parameters of a single bulk copy command issued against SQL Server.

The BulkCopy object doesn't have a place in the SQL-DMO object tree. Instead, it is used as a parameter to the ImportData method of the Table object and the ExportData method of the Table and View objects.

Data Transformation Services   One of the most exciting tools available with SQL Server 2000 is Data Transformation Services (DTS). Using this tool, you can import and export data to and from any OLE DB or ODBC data source. You can do a straight copy of the data, or you can transform the data using simple SQL statements or procedures. Alternatively, you can execute a Microsoft ActiveX script that modifies (transforms) the data when it is copied from the source to the destination, or you can perform any operation supported by the Microsoft JScript, PerlScript, or Microsoft Visual Basic Script (VBScript) languages.

Unlike the BCP and BULK INSERT operations, DTS creates the destination table for you as part of the copying operation and allows you to specify the exact column names and datatypes (depending on what the destination data store allows). DTS is installed by default with a standard SQL Server setup, and complete documentation is available in SQL Server Books Online.

Copy SQL Server Objects   SQL Server Enterprise Manager puts an easy-to-use graphical interface on top of the SQL-DMO BulkCopy object to make it easy to transfer data between two SQL Server installations. This provides the same functionality as the SQL Transfer Manager utility or the transfer management interface in earlier versions of SQL Server. The tool allows you to transfer all objects—not just data, but stored procedures, rules, constraints, and so on—but only when moving from one SQL Server database to another. The Copy SQL Server Objects tool is accessible as a task from the DTS Package Designer.

UPDATE

UPDATE, the next data modification statement, changes existing rows. Usually, UPDATE contains a WHERE clause that limits the update to only a subset of rows in the table. (The subset can be a single row, as would be the case when testing for equality with the primary key values in the WHERE clause.) If no WHERE clause is provided, UPDATE changes every row in the table. You can use the @@ROWCOUNT system function to determine the number of rows that were updated.

Here's the basic UPDATE syntax:

```
UPDATE {table_name | view_name}
SET column_name1 = {expression1 | NULL | DEFAULT | (SELECT)}
    [, column_name2 = {expression2 | NULL | DEFAULT | (SELECT)}
    [ ,...n ]
WHERE {search_conditions}
```

Columns are set to an expression. The expression can be almost anything that returns a scalar value—a constant, another column, an arithmetic expression, a bunch of nested functions that end up returning one value, a local variable, or a system function. You can set a column to a value conditionally determined using the CASE expression or to a value returned from a subquery. You can also set columns to NULL (if the column allows it) or to DEFAULT (if a default is declared or if the column allows NULL), much like you can with the INSERT statement.

You can set multiple columns in a single UPDATE statement. Like a multiple-row INSERT, an UPDATE that affects multiple rows is an atomic operation: if a single UPDATE statement affects multiple rows and one row fails a constraint, all the changes made by that statement are rolled back.

The following simple UPDATE statements should be self-explanatory. Later in this chapter, I'll show you some that aren't this simple and intuitive.

```
-- Change a specific employee's last name after his marriage
UPDATE employee
    SET lname='Thomas-Kemper'
WHERE emp_id='GHT50241M'

-- Raise the price of every title by 12%
-- No WHERE clause, so it affects every row in the table
UPDATE titles
    SET price=price * 1.12
```

(continued)

```
-- Publisher 1389 was sold, changing its name and location.
-- All the data in other tables relating to pub_id 1389 is
-- still valid; only the name of the publisher and its
-- location have changed.
UPDATE publishers
    SET pub_name='O Canada Publications',
        city='Victoria',
        state='BC',
        country='Canada'
WHERE pub_id='1389'

-- Change the phone number of authors living in Gary, IN,
-- back to the DEFAULT value
UPDATE authors
    SET phone=DEFAULT
WHERE city='Gary' AND state='IN'
```

Advanced UPDATE Examples

You can go well beyond these UPDATE examples, however, and use subqueries, the CASE expression, and even joins in specifying search criteria. (Chapter 10 covers CASE in depth.) For example, the following UPDATE statement is like a correlated subquery. It sets the *ytd_sales* field of the *titles* table to the sum of all *qty* fields for matching titles:

```
UPDATE titles
SET titles.ytd_sales=(SELECT SUM(sales.qty) FROM sales
    WHERE titles.title_id=sales.title_id)
```

In the next example, you can use the CASE expression with UPDATE to selectively give pay raises based on an employee's review rating. Assume that reviews have been turned in and big salary adjustments are due. A review rating of 4 doubles the employee's salary. A rating of 3 increases the salary by 60 percent. A rating of 2 increases the salary by 20 percent, and a rating lower than 2 doesn't change the salary.

```
UPDATE employee_salaries
    SET salary =
        CASE review
            WHEN 4 THEN salary * 2.0
            WHEN 3 THEN salary * 1.6
            WHEN 2 THEN salary * 1.2
            ELSE salary
        END
```

FORCING THE USE OF DEFAULTS

Notice the use of the keyword DEFAULT in the last example. Sometimes you'll want to stamp a table with the name of the user who last modified the row or with the time it was last modified. You could use system functions, such as SUSER_SNAME or GETDATE, as the DEFAULT value, and then specify that data modification be done only via stored procedures that explicitly update such columns to the DEFAULT keyword. Or you can make it policy that such columns must always be set to the DEFAULT keyword in the UPDATE statement, and then you can monitor this by also having a CHECK constraint on the same column that insists that the value be equal to that which the function returns. (If you use GETDATE, you'll probably want to use it in conjunction with other string and date functions to strip off the milliseconds and avoid the possibility that the value from the DEFAULT might be slightly different than that in the CHECK.) Here's a sample using SUSER_SNAME:

```
CREATE TABLE update_def
(
    up_id       int           PRIMARY KEY,
    up_byname   varchar(30)   NOT NULL DEFAULT SUSER_SNAME()
    CHECK (up_byname=SUSER_SNAME())
    -- Assume other columns would be here
)
GO

UPDATE update_def
SET
-- SET other columns to their value here, and then append the
-- following:
up_byname=DEFAULT
WHERE up_id=1
GO
```

DELETE

DELETE, the last data manipulation statement, removes rows from a table. Once the action is committed, no undelete action is available. (If the statement is not wrapped in a BEGIN TRAN/COMMIT TRAN block, the COMMIT, of course, occurs by default as soon as the statement completes.) Because you delete only rows, not columns, you never specify column names in a DELETE statement as you do with INSERT or

UPDATE. But in many other ways, DELETE acts much like UPDATE does—you specify a WHERE clause to limit the DELETE to certain rows. If you omit the WHERE clause, every row in the table will be deleted. The system function @@ROWCOUNT keeps track of the number of rows deleted. You can delete through a view but only if the view is based on a single table. If you delete through a view, all the underlying FOREIGN KEY constraints on the table must still be satisfied in order for the delete to succeed.

Here's the general form of DELETE:

```
DELETE [FROM] {table_name | view_name} WHERE {search_conditions}
```

The FROM preposition is ANSI standard, but its inclusion is always optional in SQL Server (similar to INTO with INSERT). The preposition must be specified per ANSI SQL. If the preposition is always needed, it is logically redundant, which is why SQL Server doesn't require it.

Here are some simple examples:

```
DELETE discounts
-- Deletes every row from the discounts table but does not
-- delete the table itself. An empty table remains.

DELETE FROM sales WHERE qty > 5
-- Deletes those rows from the sales table that have a value for
-- qty of 6 or more

DELETE FROM WA_stores
-- Attempts to delete all rows qualified by the WA_stores view,
-- which would delete those rows from the stores table that have
-- state of WA. This delete is correctly stated but would fail
-- because of a foreign key reference.
```

TRUNCATE TABLE

In the first example, *DELETE discounts* deletes every row of that table. Every row is fully logged. SQL Server provides a much faster way to purge all the rows from the table. TRUNCATE TABLE empties the whole table by deallocating all the table's data pages and index pages. TRUNCATE TABLE is orders of magnitude faster than an unqualified DELETE against the whole table. Delete triggers on the table won't fire because the rows deleted aren't individually logged. If a foreign key references the table to be truncated, however, TRUNCATE TABLE won't work. And if the table is publishing data for replication, which requires the log records, TRUNCATE TABLE won't work.

Despite contrary information, TRUNCATE TABLE isn't really an unlogged operation. The deletions of rows aren't logged because they don't really occur. Rather, entire pages are deallocated. But the page deallocations *are* logged. If TRUNCATE TABLE were not logged, you couldn't use it inside transactions, which must have the capacity to be rolled back. Here's a simple example that shows that the action can indeed be rolled back:

```
BEGIN TRAN
-- Get the initial count of rows
SELECT COUNT(*) FROM titleauthor
    25

TRUNCATE TABLE titleauthor

-- Verify that all rows are now gone
SELECT COUNT(*) FROM titleauthor
    0

-- Undo the truncate operation
ROLLBACK TRAN

-- Verify that rows are still there after the undo
SELECT COUNT(*) FROM titleauthor
    25
```

Modifying Data Through Views

You can specify INSERT, UPDATE, and DELETE statements on views as well as on tables, although you should be aware of some restrictions and other issues. Modifications through a view end up affecting the data in an underlying base table (and only one such table) because views don't store data. All three types of data modifications work easily for single-table views, especially in the simplest case, in which the view exposes all the columns of the base table. But a single-table view doesn't necessarily have to expose every column of the base table—it can restrict the view to a subset of columns only.

If your views or your desired data modification statements don't meet the requirements for actually updating through the view, you can create INSTEAD OF triggers on a view. The code in an INSTEAD OF trigger is executed instead of a specified modification operation, and this is the only kind of trigger you can place on a view. (The other kind of trigger is an AFTER trigger.) For example, suppose you have a view based on a join between two tables and you want to update columns in both tables. An INSTEAD OF trigger on UPDATE of your view can issue two separate UPDATE statements so that both tables can actually be updated. I'll discuss INSTEAD OF triggers along with AFTER triggers in Chapter 12. The remaining discussion in this section will assume there are no INSTEAD OF triggers on your views and that you want to modify the base table data directly through the view.

For any direct modification, all the underlying constraints of the base table must still be satisfied. For example, if a column in the base table is defined as NOT NULL and doesn't have a DEFAULT declared for it, the column must be visible to the view and the insert must supply a value for it. If the column weren't part of the view, an insert through that view could never work because the NOT NULL constraint could never be satisfied. And, of course, you can't modify or insert a value for a column that's derived by the view, such as an arithmetic calculation or concatenation of two strings of the base table. (You can still modify the nonderived columns in the view, however.)

Basing a view on multiple tables is far less straightforward. You can issue an UPDATE statement against a view that is a join of multiple tables, but only if all columns being modified (that is, the columns in the SET clause) are part of the same base table. An INSERT statement can also be performed against a view that does a join only if columns from a single table are specified in the INSERT statement's column list. Only the table whose columns are specified will have a row inserted: any other tables in the view will be unaffected. A DELETE statement can't be executed against a view that's a join because entire rows are deleted and modifications through a view can affect only one base table. Because no columns are specified in a delete, which table would the rows be deleted from?

In the real world, you would probably have little use for an INSERT statement against a view with a join because all but one table in the underlying query would be totally ignored. But the insert is possible. The following simple example illustrates this:

```
CREATE TABLE one
(
    col11    int    NOT NULL,
    col12    int    NOT NULL
)

CREATE TABLE two
(
    col21    int    NOT NULL,
    col22    int    NOT NULL
)
GO

CREATE VIEW one_two
AS
(SELECT col11, col12, col21, col22
FROM one LEFT JOIN two ON (col11=col21))
GO

INSERT one_two (col11, col12)
VALUES (1, 2)

SELECT * FROM one_two
```

Here's the result:

```
col11    col12    col21    col22
-----    -----    -----    -----
1        2        NULL     NULL
```

Notice that this insert specifies values only for columns from table *one*, and only table *one* gets a new row. Selecting from the view produces the row only because LEFT OUTER JOIN is specified in the view. Because table *two* contains no actual rows, a simple equijoin would have found no matches. Although the row would still have been inserted into table *one,* it would have seemingly vanished from the view. You could specify the view as an equijoin and use WITH CHECK OPTION to prevent an insert that wouldn't find a match. But the insert must still affect only one of the tables, so matching rows would have to already exist in the other table. I'll come back to WITH CHECK OPTION in the next section; for now, here's how it would be specified:

```
CREATE VIEW one_two_equijoin
AS
(SELECT col11, col12, col21, col22
FROM one JOIN two ON (col11=col21))
WITH CHECK OPTION
GO
```

If you try to specify all columns with either view formulation, even if you simply try to insert null values into the columns of table *two,* an error results because the single INSERT operation can't be performed on both tables. Admittedly, the error message is slightly misleading.

```
INSERT one_two (col11, col12, col21, col22)
VALUES (1, 2, NULL, NULL)

Server: Msg 4405, Level 16, State 2, Line 1
View or function 'one_two' is not updatable because the modification
affects multiple base tables.
```

Similarly, a DELETE against this view with a join would be disallowed and results in the same message:

```
DELETE one_two

Server: Msg 4405, Level 16, State 1, Line 1
View or function 'one_two' is not updatable because the modification
affects multiple base tables referenced.
```

The UPDATE case isn't common, but it's somewhat more realistic. You'll probably want to avoid allowing updates through views that do joins (unless you have INSTEAD OF triggers), and the next example shows why.

Given the following view,

```
CREATE VIEW titles_and_authors
AS
(
SELECT A.au_id, A.au_lname, T.title_id, T.title
FROM
authors AS A
FULL OUTER JOIN titleauthor AS TA ON (A.au_id=TA.au_id)
FULL OUTER JOIN titles AS T ON (TA.title_id=T.title_id)
)
```

selecting from the view

```
SELECT * FROM titles_and_authors
```

yields this:

```
au_id           au_lname          title_id    title
-----------     --------------    --------    --------------------------------
172-32-1176     White             PS3333      Prolonged Data Deprivation:
                                              Four Case Studies
213-46-8915     Green             BU1032      The Busy Executive's Database
                                              Guide
213-46-8915     Green             BU2075      You Can Combat Computer
                                              Stress!
238-95-7766     Carson            PC1035      But Is It User Friendly?
267-41-2394     O'Leary           BU1111      Cooking with Computers:
                                              Surreptitious Balance Sheets
267-41-2394     O'Leary           TC7777      Sushi, Anyone?
274-80-9391     Straight          BU7832      Straight Talk About Computers
409-56-7008     Bennet            BU1032      The Busy Executive's Database
                                              Guide
427-17-2319     Dull              PC8888      Secrets of Silicon Valley
472-27-2349     Gringlesby        TC7777      Sushi, Anyone?
486-29-1786     Locksley          PC9999      Net Etiquette
486-29-1786     Locksley          PS7777      Emotional Security: A New
                                              Algorithm
648-92-1872     Blotchet-Halls    TC4203      Fifty Years in Buckingham
                                              Palace Kitchens
672-71-3249     Yokomoto          TC7777      Sushi, Anyone?
712-45-1867     del Castillo      MC2222      Silicon Valley Gastronomic
                                              Treats
722-51-5454     DeFrance          MC3021      The Gourmet Microwave
724-80-9391     MacFeather        BU1111      Cooking with Computers:
                                              Surreptitious Balance Sheets
724-80-9391     MacFeather        PS1372      Computer Phobic AND Non-Phobic
                                              Individuals: Behavior
                                              Variations
```

756-30-7391	Karsen	PS1372	Computer Phobic AND Non-Phobic Individuals: Behavior Variations
807-91-6654	Panteley	TC3218	Onions, Leeks, and Garlic: Cooking Secrets of the Mediterranean
846-92-7186	Hunter	PC8888	Secrets of Silicon Valley
899-46-2035	Ringer	MC3021	The Gourmet Microwave
899-46-2035	Ringer	PS2091	Is Anger the Enemy?
998-72-3567	Ringer	PS2091	Is Anger the Enemy?
998-72-3567	Ringer	PS2106	Life Without Fear
341-22-1782	Smith	NULL	NULL
527-72-3246	Greene	NULL	NULL
724-08-9931	Stringer	NULL	NULL
893-72-1158	McBadden	NULL	NULL
NULL	NULL	MC3026	The Psychology of Computer Cooking

```
(30 rows affected)
```

The following UPDATE statement works fine because only one underlying table, *authors,* is affected. This example changes the author's name from *DeFrance* to *DeFrance-Macy*.

```
UPDATE TITLES_AND_AUTHORS
SET au_lname='DeFrance-Macy'
WHERE au_id='722-51-5454'
(1 row(s) affected)
```

This UPDATE statement yields an error, however, because two tables from a view can't be updated in the same statement:

```
UPDATE TITLES_AND_AUTHORS
SET au_lname='DeFrance-Macy', title='The Gourmet Microwave Cookbook'
WHERE au_id='722-51-5454' and title_id='MC3021'

Server: Msg 4405, Level 16, State 2, Line 1
View or function 'TITLES_AND_AUTHORS' is not updatable because the
modification affects multiple base tables referenced.
```

If you created the view, it might seem obvious that the UPDATE statement above won't be allowed. But if the person doing the update isn't aware of the underlying tables—which a view does a great job of hiding—it will *not* be obvious why one UPDATE statement works and the other one doesn't.

Views that join multiple tables can be extremely useful for querying and are wonderful constructs that make querying simpler and less prone to bugs from misstated joins. But modifications against them are problematic. Even if you have created INSTEAD OF triggers, you still need to carefully plan exactly what the INSTEAD OF trigger will do. If you do allow an update through a view that's a join, be sure that the relationships are properly protected via FOREIGN KEY constraints or triggers; otherwise, you'll run into bigger problems.

Suppose we want to change only the *au_id* column in the example view above. If the existing value in the underlying *authors* table is referenced by a row in *titleauthor,* such an update won't be allowed because it would orphan the row in *titleauthor*. The FOREIGN KEY constraint protects against the modification. But here, we'll temporarily disable the FOREIGN KEY constraint between *titleauthor* and *titles*:

```
ALTER TABLE titleauthor    -- This disables the constraint
    NOCHECK CONSTRAINT ALL
```

Notice that although we'll be updating the *authors* table, the constraint we're disabling (the constraint that would otherwise be violated) is on the *titleauthor* table. New users often forget that a FOREIGN KEY constraint on one table is essentially a constraint on *both* the referencing table (here, *titleauthor*) and the referenced table (here, *titles*). With the constraint now disabled, we'll change the value of *au_id* through the view for the author Anne Ringer:

```
-- With constraint now disabled, the following update succeeds:
UPDATE titles_and_authors
SET au_id='111-22-3333'
WHERE au_id='899-46-2035'
```

But look at the effect on the same SELECT of all rows in the view:

au_id	au_lname	title_id	title
172-32-1176	White	PS3333	Prolonged Data Deprivation: Four Case Studies
213-46-8915	Green	BU1032	The Busy Executive's Database Guide
213-46-8915	Green	BU2075	You Can Combat Computer Stress!
238-95-7766	Carson	PC1035	But Is It User Friendly?
267-41-2394	O'Leary	BU1111	Cooking with Computers: Surreptitious Balance Sheets
267-41-2394	O'Leary	TC7777	Sushi, Anyone?
274-80-9391	Straight	BU7832	Straight Talk About Computers
409-56-7008	Bennet	BU1032	The Busy Executive's Database Guide
427-17-2319	Dull	PC8888	Secrets of Silicon Valley
472-27-2349	Gringlesby	TC7777	Sushi, Anyone?
486-29-1786	Locksley	PC9999	Net Etiquette
486-29-1786	Locksley	PS7777	Emotional Security: A New Algorithm
648-92-1872	Blotchet-Halls	TC4203	Fifty Years in Buckingham Palace Kitchens

672-71-3249	Yokomoto	TC7777	Sushi, Anyone?
712-45-1867	del Castillo	MC2222	Silicon Valley Gastronomic Treats
722-51-5454	DeFrance-Macy	MC3021	The Gourmet Microwave
724-80-9391	MacFeather	BU1111	Cooking with Computers: Surreptitious Balance Sheets
724-80-9391	MacFeather	PS1372	Computer Phobic AND Non-Phobic Individuals: Behavior Variations
756-30-7391	Karsen	PS1372	Computer Phobic AND Non-Phobic Individuals: Behavior Variations
807-91-6654	Panteley	TC3218	Onions, Leeks, and Garlic: Cooking Secrets of the Mediterranean
846-92-7186	Hunter	PC8888	Secrets of Silicon Valley
NULL	NULL	MC3021	The Gourmet Microwave
NULL	NULL	PS2091	Is Anger the Enemy?
998-72-3567	Ringer	PS2091	Is Anger the Enemy?
998-72-3567	Ringer	PS2106	Life Without Fear
111-22-3333	Ringer	NULL	NULL
341-22-1782	Smith	NULL	NULL
527-72-3246	Greene	NULL	NULL
724-08-9931	Stringer	NULL	NULL
893-72-1158	McBadden	NULL	NULL
NULL	NULL	MC3026	The Psychology of Computer Cooking

(31 rows affected)

Although we haven't added or deleted any rows, the view now produces 31 rows instead of 30 rows, as was the case earlier, because the outer join fabricates a row for the new *au_id* that has no match in the *titles* table. (It appears with NULLs in the title fields.) Also notice that the two titles that matched the old *au_id* now have NULLs in their author fields. This might be comprehensible to someone who has a detailed understanding of the tables, but if the view is the only window for updating the table, it will be extremely confusing.

Even if your FOREIGN KEY constraint specifies that any updates are to be cascaded to the referencing tables, you'll still have the problem of affecting columns from more than one table without knowing which is which. In the example above, both the *authors* and *titleauthor* table have an *au_id* column, so we would have to make sure we knew which table was actually being updated through the view.

WITH CHECK OPTION

Earlier, you saw that modifying data with views based on one table is pretty straightforward. However, there's one "gotcha" to think about: disappearing rows. By default, a view can allow an UPDATE or an INSERT even if the result is that the row no longer qualifies for the view. Consider the following view, which qualifies only stores in the state of Washington:

```
CREATE VIEW WA_stores AS
SELECT * FROM stores
WHERE state='WA'
GO

SELECT stor_id, stor_name, state
FROM WA_stores
```

Here's the result:

```
stor_id    stor_name                                   state
-------    -----------------------------------------   -----
6380       Eric the Read Books                         WA
7131       Doc-U-Mat: Quality Laundry and Books        WA
(2 rows affected)
```

The following UPDATE statement changes both qualifying rows so that they no longer satisfy the view's criteria and have seemingly disappeared:

```
UPDATE WA_stores
SET state='CA'
SELECT stor_id, stor_name, state
FROM WA_stores
```

Here's the result:

```
stor_id    stor_name    state
-------    ---------    -----

(0 rows affected)
```

Modifications you make against a view without WITH CHECK OPTION can result in rows being added or modified in the base table, but the rows can't be selected from the view because they don't meet the view's criteria. The rows seem to disappear, as the example above illustrates. For users who realize that *WA_stores* is a view and who understand exactly how views work, this might not be a big problem. But if your environment attempts to have users treat views as if they were actually tables, having an UPDATE statement cause rows to disappear can be very disconcerting.

If you allow data to be modified through a view that uses a WHERE clause and you want your views to act exactly as if they were tables, you should consider using WITH CHECK OPTION when you define the view. In fact, I think it would be better if WITH CHECK OPTION were the default behavior. But the behavior described above is in accordance with the ANSI and ISO SQL standards, and the expected result is that the disappearing row phenomenon can occur unless WITH CHECK OPTION is specified.

Of course, any modifications you make through the view must also satisfy the constraints of the underlying table or else the statement will be aborted. This is true whether or not WITH CHECK OPTION is declared.

The following example shows how WITH CHECK OPTION protects against the disappearing rows phenomenon:

```
CREATE VIEW WA_stores AS
SELECT * FROM stores
WHERE state='WA'
WITH CHECK OPTION
GO

UPDATE WA_stores
SET state='CA'
```

Here's the result:

```
Server: Msg 550, Level 16, State 1, Line 1
The attempted insert or update failed because the target view either
specifies WITH CHECK OPTION or spans a view that specifies WITH CHECK
OPTION and one or more rows resulting from the operation did not
qualify under the CHECK OPTION constraint.

The statement has been terminated.

SELECT stor_id, stor_name, state
FROM WA_stores
```

And here's the final result:

```
stor_id    stor_name                                    state
-------    ----------------------------------------     -----
6380       Eric the Read Books                          WA
7131       Doc-U-Mat: Quality Laundry and Books         WA
(2 rows affected)
```

Reenabling Integrity Constraints

To demonstrate a point in the preceding section, we disabled foreign key checks on the *titleauthor* table. When you're reenabling constraints, make sure that no rows violate the constraints. By default, when you add a new constraint, SQL Server automatically checks for violations, and the constraint won't be added until the data is cleaned up and such violations are eliminated. You can suppress this check by using the NOCHECK option. With this option, when you reenable an existing constraint that has just been disabled, SQL Server doesn't recheck the constraint's relationships.

After reenabling a disabled constraint, adding a new constraint with the NOCHECK option, or performing a bulk load operation without specifying the CHECK CONSTRAINTS option, you should check to see that constraints have been satisfied.

You can query for constraint violations using subqueries of the type discussed in Chapter 7. You must formulate a separate query to check for every constraint, which can be tedious if you have many constraints. Alternatively, you can execute DBCC CHECKCONSTRAINTS, as you'll see shortly.

In an earlier example, we disabled the constraints on the *titleauthor* table and updated one row in such a way that the FOREIGN KEY constraint was violated. Here's an example that reenables the constraints on *titleauthor* and then runs DBCC CHECKCONSTRAINTS, which reveals the constraint failure:

```
-- Reenable constraints. Note that this does not check the validity
-- of the constraints.
ALTER TABLE titleauthor
    CHECK CONSTRAINT ALL
GO

DBCC CHECKCONSTRAINTS (titleauthor)
```

RESULT:

```
Table        Constraint                        Where
-----------  --------------------------------  ---------------------
titleauthor  FK__titleauth__au_id__07020F21  au_id = '899-46-2035'
```

The constraint failure occurred because of the foreign key reference to the *authors* table. The output shows which value(s) in *titleauthor* has no matching value in *authors*. In earlier versions of SQL Server, you could actually issue a dummy UPDATE statement that set the column with the constraint to itself, as in this example:

```
UPDATE titleauthor
SET au_id = au_id
```

This would cause SQL Server to verify constraints on the *au_id* column and detect that there was an unmatched foreign key. However, in SQL Server 2000, the optimizer will detect that this operation is really not doing anything, so no plan is generated, no UPDATE is carried out, and no constraints are checked. DBCC CHECKCONSTRAINTS performs all the validation you need.

DATA MODIFICATION INTERNALS

In Chapter 6, we examined how SQL Server stores data. Now we'll look at what SQL Server actually does internally when data is modified. We've already discussed (in Chapters 3 and 8) clustered indexes and how they control space usage in SQL Server. As a rule of thumb, you should always have a clustered index on a table. Only a couple of cases exist in which you would not have one. In Chapter 15, when we look at the query optimizer, we'll examine the benefits and tradeoffs of clustered and nonclustered indexes and review some guidelines for their use. In this chapter, we'll look only at how SQL Server deals with the existence of indexes when processing data modification statements.

Inserting Rows

When inserting a new row into a table, SQL Server must determine where to put it. When a table has no clustered index—that is, when the table is a heap—a new row is always inserted wherever room is available in the table. In Chapter 5, I showed you how IAMs and the PFS pages keep track of which extents in a file already belong to a table and which of the pages in those extents have space available. Even without a clustered index, space management is quite efficient. If no pages with space are available, SQL Server must allocate a whole new extent to the table. Chapter 5 also discussed how the GAMs and SGAMs were used to find extents available to be allocated to an object.

A clustered index directs an insert to a specific page based on the value the new row has for the clustered index key columns. The insert occurs when the new row is the direct result of an INSERT statement or when it's the result of an UPDATE statement executed via a delete-followed-by-insert (delete/insert) strategy. New rows are inserted into their clustered position, splicing in a page via a page split if the current page has no room. You saw in Chapters 3 and 6 that if a clustered index isn't declared as unique and duplicate values are inserted for a key, an automatic uniqueifier is generated for all subsequent rows with the same key. Internally, SQL Server treats all clustered index keys as unique.

Because the clustered index dictates a particular ordering for the rows in a table, every new row has a specific location where it belongs. If there's no room for the new row on the page where it belongs, you must allocate a new page and link it into the list of pages. If possible, this new page is allocated from the same extent as the other pages to which it will be linked. If the extent is full, a new extent (eight pages, or 64 KB) is allocated to the object. As described in Chapter 5, SQL Server uses the GAM pages to find an available extent.

Splitting Pages

After SQL Server finds the new page, the original page must be split; half the rows are left on the original page, and half are moved to the new page. In some cases, SQL Server finds that even after the split, there's no room for the new row, which, because of variable-length fields, could potentially be much larger than any of the existing rows on the pages. After the split, one or two rows are promoted to the parent page.

An index tree is always searched from the root down, so during an insert operation it is split on the way down. This means that while the index is being searched on an insert, the index is being protected in anticipation of possibly being updated.

A parent node (not a leaf node) is latched until the child node is known to be available for its own latch. Then the parent latch can be released safely.

Before the latch on a parent node is released, SQL Server determines whether the page will accommodate another two rows; if not, it splits the page. This occurs only if the page is being searched with the objective of adding a row to the index. The goal is to ensure that the parent page always has room for the row or rows that result from a child page splitting. (Occasionally, this results in pages being split that don't need to be—at least not yet. In the long run, it's a performance optimization.) The type of split depends on the type of page being split: a root page of an index, an intermediate index page, or a data page.

Splitting the Root Page of an Index

If the root page of an index needs to be split in order for a new index row to be inserted, two new pages are allocated to the index. All the rows from the root are split between these two new pages, and the new index row is inserted into the appropriate place on one of these pages. The original root page is still the root, but now it has only two rows on it, pointing to each of the newly allocated pages. A root page split creates a new level in the index. Because indexes are usually only a few levels deep, this type of split doesn't occur often.

Splitting the Intermediate Index Page

An intermediate index page split is accomplished simply by locating the midpoint of the index keys on the page, allocating a new page, and then copying the lower half of the old index page into the new page. Again, this doesn't occur often, although it's more common than splitting the root page.

Splitting the Data Page

A data page split is the most interesting and potentially common case, and it's probably the only split that you, as a developer, should be concerned with. Data pages split only under insert activity and only when a clustered index exists on the table. If no clustered index exists, the insert goes on any page that has room for the new row, according to the PFS pages. Although splits are caused only by insert activity, that activity can be a result of an UPDATE statement, not just an INSERT statement. As you're about to learn, if the row can't be updated in place or at least on the same page, the update is performed as a delete of the original row followed by an insert of the new version of the row. The insertion of the new row can, of course, cause a page split.

Splitting a data page is a complicated operation. Much like an intermediate index page split, it's accomplished by locating the midpoint of the index keys on the data page, allocating a new page, and then copying half of the old page into the new page. It requires that the index manager determine the page on which to locate the new row and then handle large rows that don't fit on either the old page or the new page. When a data page is split, the clustered index key values don't change, so the nonclustered indexes aren't affected.

Let's look at what happens to a page when it splits. The following script creates a table with large rows—so large, in fact, that only five rows will fit on a page. Once the table is created and populated with five rows, we'll find its first page by looking at the *sysindexes.first* column. As discussed in Chapter 6, I'll convert the address of the first page of the table to a decimal value and then use DBCC PAGE to look at the contents of the page. Because we don't need to see all 8020 bytes of data on the page, we'll look at only the row offset array at the end of the page and then see what happens to those rows when we insert a sixth row.

```
/* First create the table */
USE pubs
GO

DROP TABLE bigrows
GO

CREATE TABLE bigrows
(
    a int  primary key,
    b varchar(1600)
)
GO

/* Insert five rows into the table */
INSERT INTO bigrows
    VALUES (5, REPLICATE('a', 1600))

INSERT INTO bigrows
    VALUES (10, replicate('b', 1600))

INSERT INTO bigrows
    VALUES (15, replicate('c', 1600))

INSERT INTO bigrows
    VALUES (20, replicate('d', 1600))

INSERT INTO bigrows
    VALUES (25, replicate('e', 1600))
GO

SELECT first FROM sysindexes WHERE id = OBJECT_ID ('bigrows')
GO
```

(continued)

```
/* Convert the value returned to a decimal by byte-swapping
   and then doing a hex-to-decimal conversion on the last four
   bytes. See Chapter 6 for details. For our example,
   we'll assume the converted value is decimal 249. */

DBCC TRACEON(3604)
GO

DBCC PAGE(pubs, 1, 249, 1, 1)
GO
```

Here is the row offset array from the results:

```
Row - Offset
4 (0x4) - 6556 (0x199c)
3 (0x3) - 4941 (0x134d)
2 (0x2) - 3326 (0xcfe)
1 (0x1) - 1711 (0x6af)
0 (0x0) - 96 (0x60)
```

Now we'll insert one more row and look at the row offset array again:

```
INSERT INTO bigrows
    VALUES (22, REPLICATE('x', 1600))
GO

DBCC PAGE(pubs, 1, 249, 1, 1)
GO
```

When you inspect the original page after the split, you might find that it contains either the first half of the rows from the original page or the second half. SQL Server normally moves the rows so that the new row to be inserted goes on the new page. Since the rows are moving anyway, it makes more sense to adjust their positions to accommodate the new inserted row. In this example, the new row, with a clustered key value of 22, would have been inserted in the second half of the page. So when the page split occurs, the first three rows stay on the original page, 249. You need to inspect the page header to find the location of the next page, which contains the new row.

The page number is indicated by the *m_nextPage* field. This value is expressed as a *file number:page number* pair, in decimal, so you can easily use it with the DBCC PAGE command. When I ran this query, I got an *m_nextPage* of 1:2592, so I ran the following command:

```
DBCC PAGE(pubs, 1, 2592, 1, 1)
```

Here's the row offset array after the insert for the second page:

```
Row - Offset
2 (0x2) - 1711 (0x6af)
1 (0x1) - 3326 (0xcfe)
0 (0x0) - 96 (0x60)
```

Note that after the page split, three rows are on the page: the last two original rows with keys of 20 and 25, and the new row with a key of 22. If you examine the actual data on the page, you'll notice that the new row is at slot position 1, even though the row itself is the last one on the page. Slot 1 (with value 22) starts at offset 3326, and slot 2 (with value 25) starts at offset 1711. The clustered key ordering of the rows is indicated by the slot number of the row, not by the physical position on the page. If a clustered index is on the table, the row at slot 1 will always have a key value less than the row at slot 2 and greater than the row at slot 0.

Although the typical page split isn't too expensive, you'll want to minimize the frequency of page splits in your production system, at least during peak usage times. You can avoid system disruption during busy times by reserving some space on pages using the FILLFACTOR clause when you're creating the clustered index on existing data. You can use this clause to your advantage during your least busy operational hours by periodically re-creating the clustered index with the desired FILLFACTOR. That way, the extra space is available during peak usage times, and you'll save the overhead of splitting then. If there are no "slow" times, you can use DBCC INDEXDEFRAG to reorganize an index's pages and readjust the FILLFACTOR without having to make the entire table unavailable. Using SQL Server Agent, you can easily schedule the rebuilding of indexes or the execution of DBCC INDEXDEFRAG to occur at times when activity is lowest.

> **NOTE** The FILLFACTOR setting is helpful only when you're creating the index on existing data; the FILLFACTOR value isn't maintained when you insert new data. Trying to maintain extra space on the page would actually defeat the purpose because you'd need to split pages anyway to keep that amount of space available.

Deleting Rows

When you delete rows from a table, you have to consider what happens both to the data pages and the index pages. Remember that the data is actually the leaf level of a clustered index, and deleting rows from a table with a clustered index happens the same way as deleting rows from the leaf level of a nonclustered index. Deleting rows from a heap is managed in a different way, as is deleting from node pages of an index.

Deleting Rows from a Heap

SQL Server 2000 doesn't automatically compress space on a page when a row is deleted. As a performance optimization, the compaction doesn't occur until a page needs additional contiguous space for inserting a new row. You can see this in the following example, which deletes a row from the middle of a page and then inspects that page using DBCC PAGE. Figure 9-1 shows the output from DBCC PAGE.

```
USE pubs
GO

DROP TABLE smallrows
GO

CREATE TABLE smallrows
(
    a int identity,
    b char(10)
)
GO

INSERT INTO smallrows
    VALUES ('row 1')
INSERT INTO smallrows
    VALUES ('row 2')
INSERT INTO smallrows
    VALUES ('row 3')
INSERT INTO smallrows
    VALUES ('row 4')
INSERT INTO smallrows
    VALUES ('row 5')
GO

SELECT first FROM sysindexes WHERE id = OBJECT_ID ('smallrows')
GO

DBCC TRACEON(3604)
GO

DBCC PAGE(pubs, 1, 248, 1, 1)
GO
```

```
DATA:
-----


Slot 0, Offset 0x60
-------------------
Record Type = PRIMARY_RECORD
Record Attributes =  NULL_BITMAP
1d200060:  00120010  00000001  20776f72  20202031 ........row 1
1d200070:  00022020      00                         ...

Slot 1, Offset 0x75
-------------------
Record Type = PRIMARY_RECORD
Record Attributes =  NULL_BITMAP
1d200075:  00120010  00000002  20776f72  20202032 ........row 2
1d200085:  00022020      00                         ...

Slot 2, Offset 0x8a
-------------------
Record Type = PRIMARY_RECORD
Record Attributes =  NULL_BITMAP
1d20008a:  00120010  00000003  20776f72  20202033 ........row 3
1d20009a:  00022020      00                         ...

Slot 3, Offset 0x9f
-------------------
Record Type = PRIMARY_RECORD
Record Attributes =  NULL_BITMAP
1d20009f:  00120010  00000004  20776f72  20202034 ........row 4
1d2000af:  00022020      00                         ...

Slot 4, Offset 0xb4
-------------------
Record Type = PRIMARY_RECORD
Record Attributes =  NULL_BITMAP
1d2000b4:  00120010  00000005  20776f72  20202035 ........row 5
1d2000c4:  00022020      00                         ...

OFFSET TABLE:
-------------
Row - Offset
4 (0x4) - 180 (0xb4)
3 (0x3) - 159 (0x9f)
2 (0x2) - 138 (0x8a)
1 (0x1) - 117 (0x75)
0 (0x0) - 96 (0x60)
```

Figure 9-1. *Page contents before a delete.*

Now we'll delete the middle row (WHERE a = 3) and look at the page again. Figure 9-2 contains the output from the second execution of DBCC PAGE.

```
DELETE FROM smallrows
WHERE a = 3
GO

DBCC PAGE(pubs, 1, 248, 1, 1)
GO
```

```
DATA:
-----

Slot 0, Offset 0x60
-------------------
Record Type = PRIMARY_RECORD
Record Attributes =  NULL_BITMAP
1d200060:  00120010  00000001  20776f72  20202031 ........row 1
1d200070:  00022020      00                        ...

Slot 1, Offset 0x75
-------------------
Record Type = PRIMARY_RECORD
Record Attributes =  NULL_BITMAP
1d200075:  00120010  00000002  20776f72  20202032 ........row 2
1d200085:  00022020      00                        ...

Slot 3, Offset 0x9f
-------------------
Record Type = PRIMARY_RECORD
Record Attributes =  NULL_BITMAP
1d20009f:  00120010  00000004  20776f72  20202034 ........row 4
1d2000af:  00022020      00                        ...

Slot 4, Offset 0xb4
-------------------
Record Type = PRIMARY_RECORD
Record Attributes =  NULL_BITMAP
1d2000b4:  00120010  00000005  20776f72  20202035 ........row 5
1d2000c4:  00022020      00                        ...

OFFSET TABLE:
------------
Row - Offset
4 (0x4) - 180 (0xb4)
3 (0x3) - 159 (0x9f)
2 (0x2) - 0 (0x0)
1 (0x1) - 117 (0x75)
0 (0x0) - 96 (0x60)
```

Figure 9-2. *Page contents after the delete from a heap.*

Note that in the heap in Figure 9-2, the row doesn't show up in the page itself. The row offset array at the bottom of the page shows that row 3 (at slot 2) is now at offset 0 (which means there really is no row using slot 2), and the row using slot 3 is at its same offset as before the delete. The data on the page is *not* compressed.

Deleting Rows from a B-Tree

In the leaf level of an index, when rows are deleted, they're marked as *ghost records*. This means that the row stays on the page but a bit is changed in the row header to indicate that the row is really a ghost. The page header also reflects the number of ghost records on a page. Ghost records are primarily a concurrency optimization for key-range locking. I'll discuss the details of key-range locking, as well as all other locking modes, in Chapter 14, but a short explanation is in order here, just for completeness.

Ghost records are present only in the index leaf nodes. If ghost records weren't used, the entire range surrounding a deleted key would have to be locked. So suppose you have a unique index on an integer and the index contains the values 1, 30, and 100. If you delete 30, SQL Server will need to lock (and prevent inserts into) the entire range between 1 and 100. With ghosted records, the 30 is still visible to be used as an endpoint of a key-range lock so that during the delete transaction, SQL Server can allow inserts for any value other than 30 to proceed.

SQL Server provides a special housekeeping thread that periodically checks B-trees for ghosted records and asynchronously removes them from the leaf level of the index. This same thread carries out the automatic shrinking of databases if you have that option set. When this thread is active, the Current Activity window in SQL Server Enterprise Manager or the *sp_who* command will show you an active process with a *spid* value of 6.

The following example builds the same table used in the previous DELETE example, but this time the table has a primary key declared, which means a clustered index will be built. The data is the leaf level of the clustered index, so when the row is removed, it will be marked as a ghost. (Figure 9-3 shows the output from DBCC PAGE.)

```
USE pubs
GO

DROP TABLE smallrows
GO

CREATE TABLE smallrows
(
    a int IDENTITY PRIMARY KEY,
    b char(10)
)
GO
```

(continued)

```
INSERT INTO smallrows
    VALUES ('row 1')
INSERT INTO smallrows
    VALUES ('row 2')
INSERT INTO smallrows
    VALUES ('row 3')
INSERT INTO smallrows
    VALUES ('row 4')
INSERT INTO smallrows
    VALUES ('row 5')
GO

SELECT first FROM sysindexes WHERE id = OBJECT_ID ('smallrows')
GO


DELETE FROM smallrows
WHERE a = 3
GO

DBCC PAGE(pubs, 1, 253, 1, 1)
GO
```

```
PAGE HEADER:
------------


Page @0x1F026000
----------------
m_pageId = (1:144)        m_headerVersion = 1       m_type = 1
m_typeFlagBits = 0x0      m_level = 0               m_flagBits = 0x8000
m_objId = 821577965       m_indexId = 0             m_prevPage = (0:0)
m_nextPage = (0:0)        pminlen = 18              m_slotCnt = 5
m_freeCnt = 7981          m_freeData = 201          m_reservedCnt = 0
m_lsn = (59:353:2)        m_xactReserved = 0        m_xdesId = (0:13461)
m_ghostRecCnt = 1         m_tornBits = 0


Allocation Status
-----------------
GAM (1:2) = ALLOCATED     SGAM (1:3) = ALLOCATED
PFS (1:1) = 0x68 MIXED_EXT ALLOCATED    0_PCT_FULL    DIFF (1:6) = CHANGED
ML (1:7) = NOT MIN_LOGGED
```

Figure 9-3. *Page contents after the delete from a table with a clustered index.*

```
DATA:
-----


Slot 0, Offset 0x60
-------------------
Record Type = PRIMARY_RECORD
Record Attributes =  NULL_BITMAP
1f026060:  00120010  00000001  20776f72  20202031 ........row 1
1f026070:  00022020      00                         ...


Slot 1, Offset 0x75
-------------------
Record Type = PRIMARY_RECORD
Record Attributes =  NULL_BITMAP
1f026075:  00120010  00000002  20776f72  20202032 ........row 2
1f026085:  00022020      00                         ...


Slot 2, Offset 0x8a
-------------------
Record Type = GHOST_DATA_RECORD
Record Attributes =  NULL_BITMAP
1f02608a:  0012001c  00000003  20776f72  20202033 ........row 3
1f02609a:  00022020      00                         ...


Slot 3, Offset 0x9f
-------------------
Record Type = PRIMARY_RECORD
Record Attributes =  NULL_BITMAP
1f02609f:  00120010  00000004  20776f72  20202034 ........row 4
1f0260af:  00022020      00                         ...


Slot 4, Offset 0xb4
-------------------
Record Type = PRIMARY_RECORD
Record Attributes =  NULL_BITMAP
1f0260b4:  00120010  00000005  20776f72  20202035 ........row 5
1f0260c4:  00022020      00                         ...


OFFSET TABLE:
-------------
Row - Offset
4 (0x4) - 180 (0xb4)
3 (0x3) - 159 (0x9f)
2 (0x2) - 138 (0x8a)
1 (0x1) - 117 (0x75)
0 (0x0) - 96 (0x60)
```

Note that in the figure, the row still shows up in the page itself because the table has a clustered index. The header information for the row shows that this is really a ghosted record. The row offset array at the bottom of the page shows that the row at slot 2 is still at the same offset and that all rows are in the same location as before the deletion. In addition, the page header gives us a value (*m_ghostRecCnt*) for the number of ghosted records in the page. To see the total count of ghost records in a table, you can enable trace flag 2514. If you then execute the DBCC CHECKTABLE command, you'll see the number of ghost records in that table.

```
DBCC TRACEON (2514)
GO

DBCC CHECKTABLE (smallrows)
```

You'll see results that look like this:

```
DBCC results for 'smallrows'.
There are 4 rows in 1 page for object 'smallrows'.
Ghost Record count = 1
DBCC execution completed. If DBCC printed error messages, contact your
system administrator.
```

Note that the trace flag setting applies only to the current connection. You can apply the setting to all connections by enabling the trace flag along with a −1:

```
DBCC TRACEON (2514, -1)
```

Also note that I put the DELETE statement inside a user transaction. The house-keeping thread that cleans up ghost records is fast and efficient, and there is a chance that the ghost record will be cleaned up between the time that I issue the DELETE operation and the time I execute DBCC PAGE to look at the rows. To guarantee that the ghost will not be cleaned up, I put the DELETE into a transaction, and I don't commit or roll back the transaction before examining the page or running DBCC CHECKTABLE. The housekeeping thread will not clean up ghost records that are part of an active transaction.

Deleting Rows in the Node Levels of an Index

When you delete a row from a table, all nonclustered indexes need to be maintained because every nonclustered index has a pointer to the row that's now gone. Rows in index node pages aren't ghosted when deleted, but just as with heap pages, the space isn't compressed until new index rows need space in that page.

Reclaiming Pages

When the last row is deleted from a data page, the entire page is deallocated. (If the page is the only one remaining in the table, it isn't deallocated. A table always contains at least one page, even if it's empty.) This also results in the deletion of the row in the index page that pointed to the old data page. Index pages are deallocated if an index row is deleted (which, again, might occur as part of a delete/insert update strategy), leaving only one entry in the index page. That entry is moved to its neighboring page, and then the empty page is deallocated.

The discussion so far has focused on the page manipulation necessary for deleting a single row. If multiple rows are deleted in a single delete operation, you need to be aware of some other issues. Because the issues of modifying multiple rows in a single query are the same for inserts, updates, and deletes, we'll discuss this issue near the end of the chapter.

Updating Rows

SQL Server updates rows in multiple ways, automatically and invisibly choosing the fastest update strategy for the specific operation. In determining the strategy, SQL Server evaluates the number of rows affected, how the rows will be accessed (via a scan or an index retrieval, and via which index), and whether changes to the index keys will occur. Updates can happen either in place or as a delete followed by an insert. In addition, updates can be managed by the query processor or by the storage engine. In this section, we'll examine only whether the update happens in place. The question of whether the update is controlled by the query processor or the storage engine is actually relevant to all data modification operations (not just updates), so we'll look at that in a separate section.

Prior to version 7, SQL Server could perform either a direct or a deferred update. "Deferred" meant that the update occurred in two complete passes. The first pass would use the transaction log as a holding area, in which SQL Server recorded all the changes that were going to be made and marked them as NO-OP because they weren't actually executed at that time. The second pass would then reread the log and apply the changes. Because all changes—including changes to every nonclustered index—must be recorded twice, this was log-intensive. In addition, any time a row moved, every nonclustered index had to be updated to hold the new location of the row. Deferred updates were by far the slowest kind of update.

SQL Server 2000 doesn't have deferred updates. All updates are done in a direct mode, without using the transaction log as an intermediate holding area. In addition, because of the way SQL Server 2000 maintains nonclustered indexes, the overhead of moving rows, even if the table has multiple nonclustered indexes, is an inexpensive operation.

Moving Rows

What happens if a table row has to move to a new location? In SQL Server 2000, this can happen because a row with variable-length columns is updated to a new, larger size so that it no longer fits on the original page. It can also happen when the clustered index column is changing, because rows are stored in order of the clustering key. For example, if we have a clustered index on *lastname*, a row with a *lastname* value of *Abbot* will be stored near the beginning of the table. If the *lastname* value is then updated to *Zappa*, this row will have to move to near the end of the table.

In Chapter 8, we looked at the structure of indexes and saw that the leaf level of nonclustered indexes contains a row locator for every single row in the table. If the table has a clustered index, that row locator is the clustering key for that row. So if—and only if—the clustered index key is being updated, modifications are required in every nonclustered index. Keep this in mind when you decide which columns to build your clustered index on. It's a great idea to cluster on a nonvolatile column.

If a row moves because it no longer fits on the original page, it will still have the same row locator (in other words, the clustering key for the row stays the same), and no nonclustered indexes will have to be modified.

In Chapter 8, you also saw that if a table has no clustered index (in other words, it's a heap), the row locator stored in the nonclustered index is actually the physical location of the row. In SQL Server 2000, if a row in a heap moves to a new page, the row will leave a forwarding pointer in the original location. The nonclustered indexes won't need to be changed; they'll still refer to the original location, and from there they'll be directed to the new location.

Let's look at an example. I'll create a table a lot like the one we created for doing inserts, but this table will have a third column of variable length. After I populate the table with five rows, which will fill the page, I'll update one of the rows to make its third column much longer. The row will no longer fit on the original page and will have to move. Remember that I need to select the *first* column from *sysindexes* to know the address of the page. The value you actually supply to DBCC PAGE depends on the value that *first* returns.

```
USE pubs
GO

DROP TABLE bigrows
GO

CREATE TABLE bigrows
(
    a int IDENTITY ,
    b varchar(1600),
    c varchar(1600))
GO

INSERT INTO bigrows
    VALUES (REPLICATE('a', 1600), '')
INSERT INTO bigrows
    VALUES (REPLICATE('b', 1600), '')
INSERT INTO bigrows
    VALUES (REPLICATE('c', 1600), '')
```

```
INSERT INTO bigrows
    VALUES (REPLICATE('d', 1600), '')
INSERT INTO bigrows
    VALUES (REPLICATE('e', 1600), '')
GO

SELECT first FROM sysindexes WHERE id = OBJECT_ID ('bigrows')
GO

UPDATE bigrows
SET c = REPLICATE('x', 1600)
WHERE a = 3
GO

DBCC TRACEON(3604)
GO

DBCC PAGE(pubs, 1, 138, 1, 1)
GO
```

I won't show you the entire output from the DBCC PAGE command, but I'll show you what appears in the slot where the row with $a = 3$ formerly appeared:

```
Slot 2, Offset 0x1feb
---------------------
Record Type = FORWARDING_STUB           Record Attributes =
1d9cdfeb:  00008c04  00000100      00   .........
```

The value of 4 in the first byte means that this is just a forwarding stub. The 00008c in the next 3 bytes is the page number to which the row has been moved. Because this is a hexadecimal value, we need to convert it to 138 decimal. The next group of 4 bytes tells us that the page is at slot 0, file 1. If you then use DBCC PAGE to look at that page 138, you can see what the forwarded record looks like.

Managing Forward Pointers

Forward pointers allow you to modify data in a heap without worrying about having to make drastic changes to the nonclustered indexes. If a row that has been forwarded must move again, the original forwarding pointer is updated to point to the new location. You'll never end up with a forwarding pointer pointing to another forwarding pointer. In addition, if the forwarded row shrinks enough to fit in its original place, the forward pointer is eliminated and the record moves back to its place.

A future version of SQL Server might include some mechanism for performing a physical reorganization of the data in a heap, which will get rid of forward pointers. Note that forward pointers exist only in heaps, and that DBCC INDEXDEFRAG will not work on heap tables. You can defragment a nonclustered index on a heap but not the table itself. Currently, when a forward pointer is created, it stays there forever—with only two exceptions. The first exception is the case I already mentioned, in which a row shrinks enough to return to its original location. The second exception is when the entire database shrinks. The bookmarks are actually reassigned when a file is shrunk. The shrink process never generates forwarding pointers. For pages that were removed because of the shrink process, any forwarded rows or stubs they contain are effectively "unforwarded."

There are two ways to see the total count of forwarded records in a table. First, you can enable trace flag 2509 and then execute the DBCC CHECKTABLE command:

```
DBCC TRACEON (2509)
GO

DBCC CHECKTABLE (bigrows)
```

You'll see results like this:

```
DBCC results for 'bigrows'.
There are 5 rows in 2 pages for object 'bigrows'.
Forwarded Record count = 1
DBCC execution completed. If DBCC printed error messages, contact your
system administrator.
```

The second way to see a count of forwarding pointers is to execute DBCC SHOWCONTIG with the TABLERESULTS option. As I mentioned in Chapter 8, one of the extra columns returned with this option is the number of forwarded records in the table.

Updating in Place

In SQL Server 2000, updating a row in place is the rule rather than the exception. This means that the row stays in exactly the same location on the same page and only the bytes affected are changed. In addition, the log will contain a single record for each such updated row unless the table has an update trigger on it or is marked for replication. In these cases, the update still happens in place, but the log will contain a delete record followed by an insert record.

In cases where a row can't be updated in place, the cost of a not-in-place update is minimal because of the way the nonclustered indexes are stored and because of the use of forwarding pointers. Updates will happen in place if a heap is being updated or if a table with a clustered index is updated without any change to the clustering keys. You can also get an update in place if the clustering key changes but the row does not need to move. For example, if you have a clustered index on a last name column containing consecutive key values of 'Able', 'Becker', and 'Charlie', you might want to update 'Becker' to 'Baker'. Since the row would stay in the same location even after changing the clustered index key, SQL Server will perform this as an update in place.

Updating Not in Place

If your update can't happen in place because you're updating clustering keys, it will occur as a delete followed by an insert. In some cases, you'll get a hybrid update: Some of the rows will be updated in place and some won't. If you're updating index keys, SQL Server builds a list of all the rows that need to change as both a delete and an insert operation. This list is stored in memory, if it's small enough, and is written to *tempdb* if necessary. This list is then sorted by key value and operator (delete or insert). If the index whose keys are changing isn't unique, the delete and insert steps are then applied to the table. If the index is unique, an additional step is carried out to collapse delete and insert operations on the same key into a single update operation.

Let's look at a simple example. The following code builds a table with a unique clustered index on column *X* and then updates that column in both rows:

```
USE pubs
GO

DROP TABLE T1
GO

CREATE TABLE T1(X int PRIMARY KEY, Y int)
INSERT T1 VALUES(1, 10)
INSERT T1 VALUES(2, 20)
GO

UPDATE T1 SET X = 3 - X
GO
```

Table 9-3 shows the operations that SQL Server generates internally for the above update statement. This list of operations is called the *input stream* and consists of both the old and new values of every column and an identifier for each row that is to be changed.

Operation	Original X	Original Y	New X	New Y	Row ID
update	1	10	2	10	ROW1
update	2	20	1	20	ROW2

Table 9-3. *A SQL Server input stream for an update operation.*

However, in this case the updates must be split into delete and insert operations. If they aren't, the update to the first row, changing *X* from 1 to 2, will fail with a duplicate-key violation. A converted input stream is generated, as shown in Table 9-4.

Operation	Original X	Original Y	Row ID
delete	1	10	ROW1
insert	2	10	<null>
delete	2	20	ROW2
insert	1	20	<null>

Table 9-4. *Converted input stream for an update operation.*

Note that for insert operations, the Row ID isn't relevant in the input stream of operations to be performed. Before a row is inserted, it has no Row ID. This input stream is then sorted by index key and operation, as in Table 9-5.

Operation	X	Y	Row ID
delete	1	10	ROW1
insert	1	20	<null>
delete	2	20	ROW2
insert	2	10	<null>

Table 9-5. *Input stream sorted by index key and operation.*

Finally, if the same key value has both a delete and an insert, the two rows in the input stream are collapsed into an update operation. The final input stream looks like Table 9-6.

Operation	Original X	Original Y	New X	New Y	Row ID
update	1	10	1	20	ROW1
update	2	20	2	10	ROW2

Table 9-6. *The final input stream for an update operation.*

Note that, although the original query was an update to column X, after the split, sort, and collapse of the input stream the final set of actions looks like we're updating column Y! This method of actually carrying out the update ensures that no intermediate violations of the index's unique key occur.

Part of the graphical query plan for this update (see Figure 9-4) shows you the split, sort, and collapse phases. We'll look at query plans and the mechanisms for examining query plans in Chapter 15.

Updates to any nonclustered index keys also affect the leaf level of the index by splitting the operation into deletes and inserts. Think of the leaf level of a nonclustered index as a mini–clustered index, so any modification of the key can potentially affect the sequence of values in the leaf level. Just like for the data in a clustered index, the actual type of update is determined by whether the index is unique. If the nonclustered index is not unique, the update is split into delete and insert operators. If the nonclustered index is unique, the split is followed by a sort and an attempt to collapse any deletes and inserts on the same key back into an update operation.

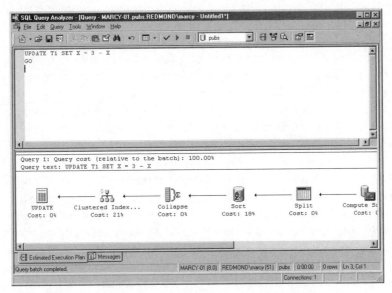

Figure 9-4. *The update query plan displayed graphically.*

Table-Level vs. Index-Level Data Modification

I've been discussing only the placement and index manipulation necessary for modifying either a single row or a few rows with no more than a single index. If you are modifying multiple rows in a single insertion operation (insert, update, or delete) or by using BCP or the BULK INSERT command and the table has multiple indexes, you must be aware of some other issues. SQL Server 2000 offers two strategies for maintaining all the indexes that belong to a table: table-level modification and index-level modification. The query optimizer chooses between them based on its estimate of the anticipated execution costs for each strategy.

Table-level modification is sometimes called *row-at-a-time,* and index-level modification is sometimes called *index-at-a-time*. In table-level modification, all indexes are maintained for each row as that row is modified. If the update stream isn't sorted in any way, SQL Server has to do a lot of random index accesses, one access per index per update row. If the update stream is sorted, it can't be sorted in more than one order, so there might be nonrandom index accesses for at most one index.

In index-level modifications, SQL Server gathers all the rows to be modified and sorts them for each index. In other words, there are as many sort operations as there are indexes. Then, for each index, the updates are merged into the index, and each index page is never accessed more than once, even if multiple updates pertain to a single index leaf page.

Clearly, if the update is small, say less than a handful of rows, and the table and its indexes are sizable, the query optimizer usually considers table-level modification the best choice. Most OLTP operations use table-level modification. On the other hand, if the update is relatively large, table-level modifications require a lot of random I/O operations and might even read and write each leaf page in each index multiple times. In that case, index-level modification offers much better performance. The amount of logging required is the same for both strategies.

Let's look at a specific example with some actual numbers. Suppose you use BULK INSERT to increase the size of a table by 1 percent (which could correspond to one week in a two-year sales history table). The table is stored in a heap (no clustered index), and the rows are simply appended because there is not much available space on other pages in the table. There's nothing to sort on for insertion into the heap, and the rows (and the required new heap pages and extents) are simply appended to the heap. Assume also that there are two nonclustered indexes on columns a and b. The insert stream is sorted on column a and merged into the index on a.

If an index entry is 20 bytes long, an 8-KB page filled at 70 percent (which is the natural, self-stabilizing value in a B-tree after lots of random insertions and deletions) would contain 8 KB * 70% / 20 bytes = 280 entries. Eight pages (one extent) would then contain 2240 entries, assuming that the leaf pages are nicely laid out in extents. Table growth of 1 percent would mean an average of 2.8 new entries per page, or 22.4 new entries per extent.

Table-level (row-at-a-time) insertion would touch each page an average of 2.8 times. Unless the buffer pool is large, row-at-a-time insertion reads, updates, and writes each page 2.8 times. That's 5.6 I/O operations per page, or 44.8 I/O operations per extent. Index-level (index-at-a-time) insertion would read, update, and write each page (and extent, again presuming a nice contiguous layout) exactly once. In the best case, about 45 page I/O operations are replaced by 2 extent I/O operations for each extent. Of course, the cost of doing the insert this way also includes the cost of sorting the inputs for each index. But the cost savings of the index-level insertion strategy can easily offset the cost of sorting.

NOTE Earlier versions of SQL Server recommended that you drop all your indexes if you were going to import a lot of rows into a table using a bulkcopy interface because they offered no index-level strategy for maintaining all the indexes.

You can determine whether your updates were done at the table level or the index level by inspecting the SHOWPLAN output. (I'll discuss query plans and SHOWPLAN in more detail in Chapter 15.) If SQL Server performs the update at the index level, you'll see a plan produced that contains an update operator for each of the affected indexes. If SQL Server performs the update at the table level, you'll see only a single update operator in the plan.

Logging

Standard INSERT, UPDATE, and DELETE statements are always logged to ensure atomicity, and you can't disable logging of these operations. The modification must be known to be safely on disk in the transaction log (write-ahead logging) before the commit of the statement or transaction can be acknowledged to the calling application. Page allocations and deallocations, including those done by TRUNCATE TABLE, are also logged. Certain operations can be minimally logged when your database is in the BULK_LOGGED recovery mode, but even then, information on allocations and deallocations is written to the log, along with the fact that a minimally logged operation has been executed.

Locking

Any data modification must always be protected with some form of exclusive lock. For the most part, SQL Server makes all the locking decisions internally; a user or programmer doesn't need to request a particular kind of lock. Chapter 14 explains the different types of locks and their compatibility. Chapter 15 discusses techniques for overriding SQL Server's default locking behavior. However, because locking is closely tied to data modification, you should always be aware of the following:

- Every type of data modification performed in SQL Server requires some form of exclusive lock. For most data modification operations, SQL Server considers row locking as the default, but if many locks are required, this could escalate to page locks or even a full table lock.

- Update locks can be used to signal the intention to do an update, and they are important for avoiding deadlock conditions. But ultimately, the UPDATE operation requires that an exclusive lock be performed. The update lock serializes access to ensure that an exclusive lock can be acquired, but the update lock isn't sufficient by itself.

- Exclusive locks must always be held until the end of a transaction in case the transaction needs to be undone (unlike shared locks, which can be released as soon as the scan moves off the page, assuming that READ COMMITTED isolation is in effect).

- If a full table scan must be employed to find qualifying rows for an update or a delete, SQL Server has to inspect every row to determine the row to modify. Other processes that need to find individual rows will be blocked even if they will ultimately modify different rows. Without inspecting the row, SQL Server has no way of knowing whether the row qualifies for the modification. If you're modifying only a subset of rows in the table, as determined by a WHERE clause, be sure that you have indexes available to allow SQL Server to access the needed rows directly so it doesn't have to scan every row in the table. (I'll talk about how to choose the best indexes for your tables in Chapters 15 and 16.) Doing full table scans to modify rows won't result in a high-concurrency environment.

SUMMARY

This chapter covered data modification within SQL Server. You modify most data using the three SQL DML statements: INSERT, UPDATE, and DELETE. Although you can typically think of INSERT as affecting only one row, SQL Server provides several forms of INSERT that can insert an entire result set at once. In addition, SQL Server offers utilities and interfaces for fast bulk loading of data. UPDATE and DELETE operations can include search operations to find the rows to modify, bringing to bear all the power of the SQL query language to specify the rows.

Programming with Transact-SQL

Microsoft Transact-SQL allows you to use standard SQL as a programming language to write logic that can execute within the database engine. This powerful capability is one of the keys to the success and growth of Microsoft SQL Server. Transact-SQL simplifies application development and reduces the amount of conversation necessary between the client application and the server by allowing more code to be processed at the server.

In this book, I won't delve into all the available syntax of the Transact-SQL language. I'll leave that to the SQL Server documentation. Instead, we'll see the significant programming constructs available, along with some comments and examples. In Chapter 7, I examined the SELECT statement, which is the foundation for effective use of Transact-SQL. Before reading any further, be sure you have a good understanding of the concepts presented in that chapter.

This chapter focuses on the Transact-SQL programming extensions, such as control of flow, looping, error handling, and environment-specific options. These extensions allow you to easily write complex routines entirely in SQL, and they provide the basis for the additional power of Transact-SQL over standard SQL. Later in this chapter, I'll show you some extensive examples that sometimes use Transact-SQL in nonintuitive ways, but it will be far from exhaustive coverage of what is possible using the Transact-SQL language. In the last year, several books dealing specifically with programming in SQL Server have been published, and another one is due out about the same time as this book. Those books are described in the bibliography, and I strongly suggest you take a look at one or more of them if you want to see the full range of possibilities with SQL Server programming. In Chapter 11, we'll look at batches, stored procedures, and functions. In Chapter 12, we'll look at transactions and triggers. Chapter 13 deals with cursors, which bridge the set-based world of SQL with sequential processing. If you're interested in developing applications using SQL Server, the information in all of these chapters will be important to you.

TRANSACT-SQL AS A PROGRAMMING LANGUAGE

Is Transact-SQL really a programming language? On the one hand, Microsoft doesn't claim that Transact-SQL is an alternative to C, C++, Microsoft Visual Basic, COBOL, Fortran, or such 4GL development environments as Sybase PowerBuilder or Borland Inprise Delphi. You'd be hard-pressed to think of a substantial application that you could write entirely in Transact-SQL, and every one of those other languages or tools exists to do exactly that. Also, Transact-SQL offers no user interface and no file or device I/O, and the programming constructs are simple and limited.

On the other hand, you can argue that Transact-SQL is a specialized language that is best used in addition to one of those other languages or tools. It allows SQL Server to be programmed to execute complex tasks such as declaring and setting variables, branching, looping, and error checking, without the need for code to be written in another language. You can write reusable routines that you subsequently invoke and pass variables to. You can introduce bugs if you make an error in logic or syntax. Your Transact-SQL code can quickly get so complicated that you'll be glad you can use the same debugger to debug Transact-SQL routines that you use for C, C++, and Java development.

With Transact-SQL routines, conditional logic executes within the SQL Server engine and even within an executing SQL statement. This can improve performance greatly—the alternative would be message passing between the client process and the server. In today's increasingly networked world, reducing round-trip conversations is a key to developing and deploying efficient applications. Some might claim that the emergence of the Internet makes client/server computing irrelevant. But in fact, the typically slow network conditions found in Internet applications make client/server computing *more important*—operations should be written so that the client/server conversation is minimized. The best way to do this is to use the programming aspects of Transact-SQL to let whole routines execute remotely, without the need for intermediate processing at the client. The corresponding performance gains are phenomenal.

In addition, by having SQL Server, rather than the application, handle the database logic, applications can often better insulate themselves from change. An application can execute a procedure simply by calling it and passing some parameters, and then the database structure or the procedure can change radically while the application remains entirely unaffected. As long as the inputs and outputs of the procedure are unchanged, the application is shielded from underlying changes to the database. The ability to encapsulate the database routines can result in a more efficient development environment for large projects in which the application programmers are often distinct from the database experts.

Programming at Multiple Levels

In the early days of database management systems, a single computer handled all processing—what we now call the *one-tier model*. The advent of client/server computing introduced the classic *two-tier model*: a server receiving requests from and providing data to a separate client. The newest approach, the *three-tier model,* places an intermediate layer between the database server and the client application.

Figure 10-1 shows the two-tier client/server model, and Figure 10-2 shows the three-tier model, which some programmers find preferable for some applications.

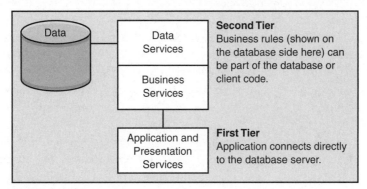

Figure 10-1. *The two-tier model.*

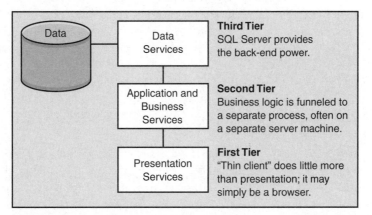

Figure 10-2. *The three-tier model.*

The two-tier model has a client (first tier) and a server (second tier). The client handles application and presentation logic, and the server handles data services and business services. The two-tier model uses the so-called *fat client*—the client does a large amount of application processing locally. Many solutions are deployed using this topology; certainly the lion's share of today's non-Internet client/server solutions are two-tier.

In the three-tier model, a *thin client* handles mostly presentation tasks. Supporters of the three-tier approach point out that this model allows the client computer to be less powerful; allows a variety of client operating environments (obviously the case with Internet browsers); and reduces the complexity of installing, configuring, and maintaining software at the client. The client connects to an application server that handles the application process. The application server then connects to the database server, handling data services. The application server is typically a more powerful machine than the client, and it handles all the issues of application code maintenance, configuration, operations, and so on.

Presumably, far fewer application servers exist than clients; therefore, server costs and issues should be reduced in the three-tier model. (The three tiers are logical concepts; the actual number of computers involved might be more or less than three.) Typically, you're part of a three-tier model when you use the Internet with a browser and access a Web page residing on an Internet server that performs database work. An example of a three-tier application is a mail-order company's Web page that checks current availability by using ODBC calls to access its inventory in SQL Server.

Both two-tier and three-tier solutions have advantages and disadvantages, and each can be viewed as a potential solution to a given problem. The specifics of the problem and the constraints imposed by the environment (including costs, hardware, and expertise of both the development staff and the user community) should drive the solution's overall design. However, some people claim that a three-tier solution means that such capabilities as stored procedures, rules, constraints, or triggers are no longer important or shouldn't be used. In a three-tier solution, the middle tier doing application logic is still a client from the perspective of the database services—that is, SQL Server. Consequently, for that tier, it's still preferable that remote work be done close to the data. If the data can be accessed by servers other than the application server, integrity checking must be done at the database server as well as in the application. Otherwise, you've left a gaping hole through which the integrity checks in the application can be circumvented.

Throughout the remainder of this book, unless otherwise noted, I'll use the term *client* from the perspective of SQL Server. The client sends the commands and processes the results, and it makes no difference to SQL Server whether an application server process does this or whether the process that the end user is running directly does it. The benefits of the programmable server provide much more efficient network use and better abstraction of data services from the application and application server.

A THREE-TIER SOLUTION THAT WORKS

Perhaps the single most successful three-tier solution available today is R/3 from SAP. The financial and operations capabilities that R/3 provides use a three-tier model, with a terminal-like interface connected to the R/3 application server that then accesses SQL Server. The R/3 application server wisely and heavily uses stored procedures that provide both performance gains and development efficiency.

TRANSACT-SQL PROGRAMMING CONSTRUCTS

Transact-SQL extends standard SQL by adding many useful programming constructs. These constructs will look familiar to developers experienced with C/C++, Basic, Visual Basic, Fortran, Java, Pascal, and similar languages. The Transact-SQL extensions are wonderful additions to the original SQL standard. Before the extensions were available, requests to the database were always simple, single statements. Any conditional logic had to be provided by the calling application. With a slow network or via the Internet, this would be disastrous, requiring many trips across the network—more than are needed by simply letting conditions be evaluated at the server and allowing subsequent branching of execution.

Variables

Without variables, a programming language wouldn't be very useful. Transact-SQL is no exception. Variables that you declare are *local variables,* which have scope and visibility only within the batch or stored procedure in which you declare them. (The next chapter discusses the details of batches and stored procedures.) In code, the single @ character designates a local variable. SQL Server 2000 introduces the ability to store and retrieve session context information, which allows information to be available throughout a connection; in any stored procedure, function, or trigger; and across batches. You can use this session context information as you would use a session variable, with a scope broader than that of SQL Server's local variables but not as broad as that of a true global variable.

Transact-SQL has no true global variables that allow information to be shared across connections. Older documentation refers to certain parameterless system functions as *global variables* because they're designated by @@, which is similar to the designation for local variables. We'll look at these in more detail in Chapter 12 in the section on system functions.

User-declared global variables would be a nice enhancement that we might see in a future release. Until then, temporary tables provide a decent alternative for sharing values among connections.

Local Variables

You declare local variables at the beginning of a batch or a stored procedure. You can subsequently assign values to local variables with the SELECT statement or the SET statement, using an equal (=) operator. The values you assign using the SET statement can be constants, other variables, or expressions. When you assign values to a variable using a SELECT statement, you typically select the values from a column in a table. The syntax for declaring and using the variables is identical, regardless of the method you use to assign the values to the variable. In the following example, I declare a variable, assign it a value using the SET statement, and then use that variable in a WHERE clause:

```
DECLARE @limit money
SET @limit = $10
SELECT * FROM titles
WHERE price <= @limit
```

I could have written the same code using only the SELECT statement instead of the SET statement. However, you typically use SELECT when the values to be assigned are found in a column of a table. A SELECT statement used to assign values to one or more variables is called an *assignment SELECT*. You can't combine the functionality of the assignment SELECT and a "regular" SELECT in the same statement—that is, if a SELECT statement is used to assign values to variables, it can't also return values to the client as a result set. In the following simple example, I declare two variables, assign values to them from the *roysched* table, and then select their values as a result set:

```
DECLARE @min_range int, @hi_range int          -- Variables declared
SELECT  @min_range=MIN(lorange),
        @hi_range=MAX(hirange) FROM roysched    -- Variables assigned
SELECT  @min_range, @hi_range                   -- Values of variables
                                                --   returned as result
```

Note that a single DECLARE statement can declare multiple variables. When you use a SELECT statement for assigning values, you can assign more than one value at a time. When you use SET to assign values to variables, you must use a separate SET statement for each variable. For example, the following SET statement returns an error:

```
SET @min_range = 0, @hi_range = 100
```

Be careful when you assign variables by selecting a value from the database—you want to ensure that the SELECT statement will return only one row. It's perfectly legal to assign a value to a variable in a SELECT statement that will return multiple rows, but the variable's value might not be what you expect: no error message is returned, and the variable has the value of the last row returned.

For example, suppose that the following *stor_name* values exist in the *stores* table of the *pubs* database:

```
stor_name
---------
Eric the Read Books
Barnum's
News & Brews
Doc-U-Mat: Quality Laundry and Books
Fricative Bookshop
Bookbeat
```

The following assignment runs without error but is probably a mistake:

```
DECLARE @stor_name varchar(30)
SELECT @stor_name=stor_name FROM stores
```

The resulting value of *@stor_name* is the last row, *Bookbeat*. But consider the order returned, without an ORDER BY clause, as a chance occurrence. Assigning a variable to a SELECT statement that returns more than one row usually isn't intended, and it's probably a bug introduced by the developer. To avoid this situation, you should qualify the SELECT statement with an appropriate WHERE clause to limit the result set to the one row that meets your criteria.

Alternatively, you can use an aggregate function, such as MAX, MIN, or SUM, to limit the number of rows returned. Then you can select only the value you want. If you want the assignment to be to only one row of a SELECT statement that might return many rows (and it's not important which row that is), you should at least use SELECT TOP 1 to avoid the effort of gathering many rows, with all but one row thrown out. (In this case, the first row would be returned, not the last. You could use ORDER BY to explicitly indicate which row should be first.) You might also consider checking the value of @@ROWCOUNT immediately after the assignment and, if it's greater than 1, branch off to an error routine.

Also be aware that if the SELECT statement assigning a value to a variable doesn't return any rows, nothing will be assigned. The variable will keep whatever value it had before the assignment SELECT statement was run. For example, suppose we use the same variable twice to find the first names of authors with a particular last name:

```
DECLARE @firstname varchar(20)
SELECT @firstname = au_fname
FROM authors
WHERE au_lname = 'Greene'
SELECT @firstname  -- Return the first name as a result
SELECT @firstname = au_fname
FROM authors
WHERE au_lname = 'Ben-Gan'
SELECT @firstname  -- Return the first name as a result
```

If you run the previous code, you'll see the same first name returned both times because no authors with the last name of Ben-Gan exist, at least not in the *pubs* database!

You can also assign a value to a variable in an UPDATE statement. This approach can be useful and more efficient than using separate statements to store the old value of a column and assign it a new value. The following UPDATE will reduce the price of one book by 20 percent and save the original price in a variable:

```
DECLARE @old_price money

UPDATE title
SET @old_price = price = price * 0.8
WHERE title_id = 'PC2091'
```

A variable can be assigned a value from a subquery, and in some cases it might look like there's no difference between using a subquery and a straight SELECT. For example, the following two batches return exactly the same result set:

```
-- First batch using a straight SELECT:
DECLARE @firstname varchar(20)
SELECT @firstname = au_fname
FROM authors
WHERE au_lname = 'Greene'
SELECT @firstname

-- Second batch using a subquery:
DECLARE @firstname varchar(20)
SELECT @firstname = ( SELECT au_fname
FROM authors
WHERE au_lname = 'Greene')
SELECT @firstname
```

However, if we leave off the WHERE clause, these two batches will behave very differently. As we saw earlier in the example selecting from the *stores* table, the first batch will leave the variable with the value that the last row supplied.

```
DECLARE @firstname varchar(20)
SELECT @firstname = au_fname
FROM authors
SELECT @firstname
```

RESULT:

Akiko

This one row is returned because the assignment to the variable is happening for every row that the query would return. With no WHERE clause, every row in the table is returned, and for every row, the first name value is assigned to the variable, overriding whatever value was assigned by the previous row returned. We are left with the value from the last row because there are no more values to override that one.

However, when I use a subquery and leave off the WHERE clause, the result is very different:

```
DECLARE @firstname varchar(20)
SELECT @firstname = (SELECT au_fname
FROM authors)
SELECT @firstname
```

RESULT:
Server: Msg 512, Level 16, State 1, Line 0
Subquery returned more than 1 value. This is not permitted when the
subquery follows =, !=, <, <= , >, >= or when the subquery is used
as an expression.

```
--------------------
```
NULL

In this case, the query returns an error. When you use a subquery, the entire subquery is processed before any assignment to the variable is made. The subquery's result set contains 23 rows, and then all 23 rows are used in the assignment to the variable. Since we can assign only a single value to a variable, the error message is generated.

Session Variables

SQL Server 2000 allows you to store and retrieve session-level context information by directly querying the *sysprocesses* table in the *master* database. As I mentioned in Chapter 6, normally it is recommended that you never access the system tables directly, but for this release, direct access of *sysprocesses* is the only way to retrieve this information. A construct is supplied for setting this information, but you have nothing other than direct system table access for retrieving it.

The *sysprocesses* table in the *master* database in SQL Server 2000 has a 128-byte field called *context_info* of type *binary*, which means you have to manipulate the data using hexadecimal values. You can use the entire column to store a single value or, if you're comfortable with manipulating binary values, you can use different groups of bytes for different purposes. The following statements store the price of one particular book in the *context_info* column:

```
DECLARE @cost money
SELECT @cost = price FROM titles
WHERE title_id = 'bu1032'
SET context_info @cost
```

If we stored this value in a local variable, it would have the scope of only a single query batch and we wouldn't be able to come back after executing several more batches and check the value. But storing it in the *sysprocesses* table means that the value will be available as long as my connection is active. The *sysprocesses* table has one row for each active process in SQL Server, and each row is assigned a unique Server Process ID (spid) value. A system function, @@spid, returns the process ID for the current connection. Using @@spid, I can find the row in *sysprocesses* that contains my *context_info* value.

Using *SET context_info*, I assigned a money value to the binary column. If you check the documentation for the CONVERT function, you'll see that money is implicitly convertible to binary. For convenience, in Figure 10-3 I have reproduced the chart that shows which datatypes are implicitly and explicitly convertible.

If, instead, I had tried to assign a character value to CONTEXT_INFO, I would have received an error message because the chart in Figure 10-3 tells me that conversion from character to binary must be done explicitly. The SET CONTEXT_INFO statement stores the assigned value in the fewest number of bytes, starting with the first byte. So I can use the SUBSTRING function to extract a value from the *context_info* column, and since the *money* datatype is stored in 8 bytes, I need to get the first 8 bytes of the column. I can then convert those first 8 bytes to *money*:

```
SELECT convert(money, substring(context_info, 1, 8))
FROM master..sysprocesses
WHERE spid = @@spid
```

Note that if I hadn't taken only the first 8 bytes of the *context_info* field, as shown below, and tried to convert that directly to *money*, SQL Server would have assumed that the *money* value was in the last 8 bytes of the 128-byte field and would have returned a 0.

```
SELECT convert(money, context_info)
FROM master..sysprocesses
WHERE spid = @@spid
```

From: \ To:	binary	varbinary	char	varchar	nchar	nvarchar	datetime	smalldatetime	decimal	numeric	float	real	bigint	int(INT4)	smallint(INT2)	tinyint(INT1)	money	smallmoney	bit	timestamp	uniqueidentifier	image	ntext	text	sql_variant
binary		◐	◐	◐	◐	◐	◐	◐	◐	◐	○	○	◐	◐	◐	◐	◐	◐	◐	◐	◐	◐	○	○	◐
varbinary	◐		◐	◐	◐	◐	◐	◐	◐	◐	○	○	◐	◐	◐	◐	◐	◐	◐	◐	◐	◐	○	○	◐
char	●	●		◐	◐	◐	◐	◐	◐	◐	◐	◐	◐	◐	◐	◐	●	●	◐	◐	●	◐	◐	◐	◐
varchar	●	●	◐		◐	◐	◐	◐	◐	◐	◐	◐	◐	◐	◐	◐	●	●	◐	◐	●	◐	◐	◐	◐
nchar	●	●	◐	◐		◐	◐	◐	◐	◐	◐	◐	◐	◐	◐	◐	●	●	◐	◐	●	○	◐	◐	◐
nvarchar	●	●	◐	◐	◐		◐	◐	◐	◐	◐	◐	◐	◐	◐	◐	●	●	◐	◐	●	○	◐	◐	◐
datetime	●	●	◐	◐	◐	◐		◐	●	●	●	●	●	●	●	●	●	●	●	◐	○	○	○	○	◐
smalldatetime	●	●	◐	◐	◐	◐	◐		●	●	●	●	●	●	●	●	●	●	●	◐	○	○	○	○	◐
decimal	◐	◐	◐	◐	◐	◐	◐	◐		★	◐	◐	◐	◐	◐	◐	◐	◐	◐	◐	○	○	○	○	◐
numeric	◐	◐	◐	◐	◐	◐	◐	◐	★		◐	◐	◐	◐	◐	◐	◐	◐	◐	◐	○	○	○	○	◐
float	◐	◐	◐	◐	◐	◐	◐	◐	◐	◐		◐	◐	◐	◐	◐	◐	◐	◐	◐	○	○	○	○	◐
real	◐	◐	◐	◐	◐	◐	◐	◐	◐	◐	◐		◐	◐	◐	◐	◐	◐	◐	◐	○	○	○	○	◐
bigint	◐	◐	◐	◐	◐	◐	◐	◐	◐	◐	◐	◐		◐	◐	◐	◐	◐	◐	◐	○	○	○	○	◐
int(INT4)	◐	◐	◐	◐	◐	◐	◐	◐	◐	◐	◐	◐	◐		◐	◐	◐	◐	◐	◐	○	○	○	○	◐
smallint(INT2)	◐	◐	◐	◐	◐	◐	◐	◐	◐	◐	◐	◐	◐	◐		◐	◐	◐	◐	◐	○	○	○	○	◐
tinyint(INT1)	◐	◐	◐	◐	◐	◐	◐	◐	◐	◐	◐	◐	◐	◐	◐		◐	◐	◐	◐	○	○	○	○	◐
money	◐	◐	●	●	●	●	◐	◐	◐	◐	◐	◐	◐	◐	◐	◐		◐	◐	◐	○	○	○	○	◐
smallmoney	◐	◐	●	●	●	●	◐	◐	◐	◐	◐	◐	◐	◐	◐	◐	◐		◐	◐	○	○	○	○	◐
bit	◐	◐	◐	◐	◐	◐	◐	◐	◐	◐	◐	◐	◐	◐	◐	◐	◐	◐		◐	○	○	○	○	◐
timestamp	◐	◐	◐	◐	○	○	◐	◐	◐	◐	○	○	◐	◐	◐	◐	◐	◐	◐		○	◐	○	○	○
uniqueidentifier	◐	◐	◐	◐	◐	◐	○	○	○	○	○	○	○	○	○	○	○	○	○	○		○	○	○	◐
image	◐	◐	○	○	○	○	○	○	○	○	○	○	○	○	○	○	○	○	○	◐	○		○	○	○
ntext	○	○	●	●	◐	◐	○	○	○	○	○	○	○	○	○	○	○	○	○	○	○	○		◐	○
text	○	○	◐	◐	●	●	○	○	○	○	○	○	○	○	○	○	○	○	○	○	○	○	◐		○
sql_variant	●	●	●	●	●	●	●	●	●	●	●	●	●	●	●	●	●	●	●	○	●	○	○	○	

● Explicit conversion
◐ Implicit conversion
○ Conversion not allowed
★ Requires explicit CAST to prevent the loss of precision or scale that might occur in an implicit conversion

Figure 10-3. *Conversion table from the SQL Server documentation.*

Since the *context_info* column is 128 bytes long, there's lot of room to work with. I can store another price in the second set of 8 bytes if I'm careful. I need to take the first 8 bytes and concatenate them to the second price value after converting it to hexadecimal. Concatenation works for hexadecimal values the same way as it does for character strings, and the operator is the plus sign (+):

```
DECLARE @cost money, @context binary(128)
SELECT @cost = price FROM titles
WHERE title_id = 'ps2091'
```

(continued)

```
SELECT @context =
    convert(binary(8),context_info) + convert(binary(8), @cost)
FROM master..sysprocesses
WHERE spid = @@spid
SET context_info @context
```

Now the second 8 bytes contains the second price, and if I use the SUBSTRING function appropriately, I can extract either price value from the *context_info* column:

```
SELECT First_price = convert(money, substring(context_info, 1, 8))
FROM master..sysprocesses
WHERE spid = @@spid

SELECT Second_price = convert(money, substring(context_info, 9, 8))
FROM master..sysprocesses
WHERE spid = @@spid
```

Control-of-Flow Tools

Like any programming language worth its salt, Transact-SQL provides a decent set of control-of-flow tools. (True, Transact-SQL has only a handful of tools—perhaps not as many as you'd like—but they're enough to make it dramatically more powerful than standard SQL.) The control-of-flow tools include conditional logic (IF...ELSE and CASE), loops (only WHILE, but it comes with CONTINUE and BREAK options), unconditional branching (GOTO), and the ability to return a status value to a calling routine (RETURN). Table 10-1 presents a quick summary of these control-of-flow constructs, which you'll see used at various times in this book.

Construct	Description
BEGIN...END	Defines a statement block. Using BEGIN...END allows a group of statements to be executed. Typically, BEGIN immediately follows IF, ELSE, or WHILE. (Otherwise, only the next statement will be executed.) For C programmers, BEGIN...END is similar to using a {..} block.
GOTO label	Continues processing at the statement following the specified label.
IF...ELSE	Defines conditional and, optionally, alternate execution when a condition is false.
RETURN [*n*]	Exits unconditionally. Typically used in a stored procedure or trigger (although it can also be used in a batch). Optionally, a whole number *n* (positive or negative) can be set as the return status, which can be assigned to a variable when you execute the stored procedure.

Table 10-1. *Control-of-flow constructs in Transact-SQL.* *(continued)*

Construct	Description
WAITFOR	Sets a time for statement execution. The time can be a delay interval (up to 24 hours) or a specific time of day. The time can be supplied as a literal or with a variable.
WHILE	The basic looping construct for SQL Server. Repeats a statement (or block) while a specific condition is true.
...BREAK	Exits the innermost WHILE loop.
...CONTINUE	Restarts a WHILE loop.

CASE

The CASE expression is enormously powerful. Although CASE is part of the ANSI SQL-92 specification, it's not required for ANSI compliance certification, and few database products other than Microsoft SQL Server have implemented it. If you have experience with an SQL database system other than Microsoft SQL Server, chances are you haven't used CASE. If that's the case (pun intended), you should get familiar with it now. It will be time well spent. CASE was added in version 6, and once you get used to using it, you'll wonder how SQL programmers ever managed without it.

CASE is a conceptually simpler way to do IF-ELSE IF-ELSE IF-ELSE IF-ELSE–type operations. It's roughly equivalent to a *switch* statement in C. However, CASE is far more than shorthand for IF—in fact, it's not really even that. CASE is an expression, not a control-of-flow keyword, which means that it can be used *only* inside other statements. You can use CASE in a SELECT statement in the SELECT list, in a GROUP BY clause, or in an ORDER BY clause. You can use it in the SET clause of an UPDATE statement. You can include CASE in the values list for an INSERT statement. You can also use CASE in a WHERE clause in any SELECT, UPDATE, or DELETE statement. Anywhere that Transact-SQL expects an expression, you can use CASE to determine the value of that expression.

Here's a simple example of CASE. Suppose we want to classify books in the *pubs* database by price. We want to segregate them as low-priced, moderately priced, or expensive. And we'd like to do this with a single SELECT statement and not use UNION. Without CASE, we can't do it. With CASE, it's a snap:

```
SELECT
title,
price,
'classification'=CASE
    WHEN price < 10.00 THEN 'Low Priced'
    WHEN price BETWEEN 10.00 AND 20.00 THEN 'Moderately Priced'
    WHEN price > 20.00 THEN 'Expensive'
    ELSE 'Unknown'
    END
FROM titles
```

Notice that even in this example, we have to worry about NULL because a NULL price won't fit into any of the category buckets.

Here are the abbreviated results:

```
title                                    price   classification
-------------------------------------    ------  -----------------
The Busy Executive's Database Guide       19.99   Moderately Priced
Cooking with Computers: Surreptitious     11.95   Moderately Priced
Balance Sheets
You Can Combat Computer Stress!            2.99   Low Priced
Straight Talk About Computers             19.99   Moderately Priced
Silicon Valley Gastronomic Treats         19.99   Moderately Priced
The Gourmet Microwave                      2.99   Low Priced
The Psychology of Computer Cooking        NULL    Unknown
But Is It User Friendly?                  22.95   Expensive
```

If all the conditions after your WHEN clauses are equality comparisons against the same value, you can use an even simpler form so that you don't have to keep repeating the expression. Suppose we want to print the type of each book in the *titles* table in a slightly more user-friendly fashion—for example, *Modern Cooking* instead of *mod_cook*. We could use the following SELECT statement:

```
SELECT
title,
price,
'Type' =  CASE
    WHEN type = 'mod_cook' THEN 'Modern Cooking'
    WHEN type = 'trad_cook' THEN 'Traditional Cooking'
    WHEN type = 'psychology' THEN 'Psychology'
    WHEN type = 'business' THEN 'Business'
    WHEN type = 'popular_comp' THEN 'Popular Computing'
    ELSE 'Not yet decided'
    END
FROM titles
```

In this example, because every condition after WHEN is testing for equality with the value in the *type* column, we can use an even simpler form. You can think of this simplification as factoring out the *type* = from every WHEN clause, and you can place the *type* column at the top of the CASE expression:

```
SELECT
title,
price,
'Type' = CASE type
    WHEN 'mod_cook' THEN 'Modern Cooking'
    WHEN 'trad_cook' THEN 'Traditional Cooking'
    WHEN 'psychology' THEN 'Psychology'
    WHEN 'business' THEN 'Business'
```

```
    ELSE 'Not yet decided'
    END
FROM titles
```

You can use CASE in some unusual places; because it's an expression, you can use it anywhere that an expression is legal. Using CASE in a view is a nice technique that can make your database more usable to others. For example, in Chapter 7, we saw CASE in a view using CUBE to shield users from the complexity of "grouping NULL" values. Using CASE in an UPDATE statement can make the update easier. More important, CASE can allow you to make changes in a single pass of the data that would otherwise require you to do multiple UPDATE statements, each of which would have to scan the data.

Cousins of CASE

SQL Server provides three nice shorthand derivatives of CASE: COALESCE, NULLIF, and ISNULL. COALESCE and NULLIF are both part of the ANSI SQL-92 specification; they were added to version 6 at the same time that CASE was added. ISNULL is a longtime SQL Server function.

COALESCE   This function is equivalent to a CASE expression that returns the first NOT NULL expression in a list of expressions.

```
COALESCE(expression1, expression2, ... expressionN)
```

If no non-null values are found, COALESCE returns NULL (which is what *expressionN* was, given that there were no non-null values). Written as a CASE expression, COALESCE looks like this:

```
CASE
    WHEN expression1 IS NOT NULL THEN expression1
    WHEN expression2 IS NOT NULL THEN expression2
    ⋮
ELSE expressionN
END
```

NULLIF   This function is equivalent to a CASE expression in which NULL is returned if *expression1* = *expression2*.

```
NULLIF(expression1, expression2)
```

If the expressions aren't equal, *expression1* is returned. In Chapter 7, you saw that NULLIF can be handy if you use dummy values instead of NULL, but you don't want those dummy values to skew the results produced by aggregate functions. Written using CASE, NULLIF looks like this:

```
CASE
    WHEN expression1=expression2 THEN NULL
    ELSE expression1
END
```

ISNULL   This function is almost the mirror image of NULLIF:

```
ISNULL(expression1, expression2)
```

ISNULL allows you to easily substitute an alternative expression or value for an expression that's NULL. In Chapter 7, you saw the use of ISNULL to substitute the string *'ALL'* for a GROUPING NULL when using CUBE and to substitute a string of question marks (*'????'*) for a NULL value. The results were more clear and intuitive to users. The functionality of ISNULL written instead using CASE looks like this:

```
CASE
    WHEN expression1 IS NULL THEN expression2
    ELSE expression1
END
```

The second argument to ISNULL (the value to be returned if the first argument is NULL) can be an expression or even a SELECT statement. Say, for example, that we want to query the *titles* table. If a title has NULL for *price,* we want to instead use the lowest price that exists for any book. Without CASE or ISNULL, this isn't an easy query to write. With ISNULL, it is easy:

```
SELECT title, pub_id, ISNULL(price, (SELECT MIN(price)
    FROM titles)) FROM titles
```

For comparison, here's an equivalent SELECT statement written with the long-hand CASE formulation:

```
SELECT title, pub_id,
    CASE WHEN price IS NULL THEN (SELECT MIN(price) FROM titles)
    ELSE price
    END
FROM titles
```

PRINT

Transact-SQL, like other programming languages, provides printing capability through the PRINT and RAISERROR statements. I'll discuss RAISERROR momentarily, but first I'll take a look at the PRINT statement.

PRINT is the most basic way to display any character string of up to 8000 characters. You can display a literal character string or a variable of type *char, varchar, nchar, nvarchar, datetime,* or *smalldatetime.* You can concatenate strings and use functions that return string or date values. In addition, PRINT can print any expression or function that is implicitly convertible to a character datatype. (Refer to Figure 10-3 on page 509 to determine which datatypes are implicitly convertible.)

It seems like every time you learn a new programming language, the first assignment is to write the "Hello World" program. Using Transact-SQL, it couldn't be easier:

```
PRINT 'Hello World'
```

Even before you saw PRINT, you could've produced the same output in your SQL Query Analyzer screen with the following:

```
SELECT 'Hello World'
```

So what's the difference between the two? The PRINT statement returns a message, nothing more. The SELECT statement returns output like this:

```
-----------
Hello World

(1 row(s) affected)
```

The SELECT statement returns the string as a result set. That's why we get the *(1 row(s) affected)* message. When you use SQL Query Analyzer to submit your queries and view your results, you might not see much difference between the PRINT and the SELECT statements. But for other client tools (besides ISQL, OSQL, and SQL Query Analyzer), there could be a big difference. PRINT returns a message of severity 0, and you need to check the documentation for the client API that you're using to determine how messages are handled. For example, if you're writing an ODBC program, the results of a PRINT statement are handled by *SQLError*.

On the other hand, a SELECT statement returns a set of data, just like selecting prices from a table does. Your client interface might expect you to bind data to local (client-side) variables before you can use them in your client programs. Again, you'll have to check your documentation to know for sure. The important distinction to remember here is that PRINT returns a message and SELECT returns data.

PRINT is extremely simple, both in its use and in its capabilities. It's not nearly as powerful as, say, *printf* in C. You can't give positional parameters or control formatting. For example, you can't do this:

```
PRINT 'Today is %s', GETDATE()
```

Part of the problem here is that *%s* is meaningless. In addition, the built-in function GETDATE returns a value of type *datetime*, which can't be concatenated to the string constant. So, you can do this instead:

```
PRINT 'Today is ' + CONVERT(char(30), GETDATE())
```

RAISERROR

RAISERROR is similar to PRINT but can be much more powerful. RAISERROR also sends a message (not a result set) to the client; however, RAISERROR allows you to specify the specific error number and severity of the message. It also allows you to reference an error number, the text of which you can add to the *sysmessages* table.

RAISERROR makes it easy for you to develop international versions of your software. Rather than using multiple versions of your SQL code when you want to change the language of the text, you need only one version. You can simply add the text of the message in multiple languages. The user will see the message in the language used by the particular connection.

Unlike PRINT, RAISERROR accepts *printf*-like parameter substitution as well as formatting control. RAISERROR can also allow messages to be logged to the Microsoft Windows NT or Microsoft Windows 2000 event service, making the messages visible to the Windows NT or Windows 2000 Event Viewer, and it allows SQL Server Agent alerts to be configured for these events. In many cases, RAISERROR is preferable to PRINT, and you might choose PRINT only for quick-and-dirty situations. For production-caliber code, RAISERROR is usually a better choice. Here's the syntax:

```
RAISERROR ({msg_id | msg_str}, severity, state[, argument1
[, argumentn]])
[WITH LOG]|[WITH NOWAIT]
```

After you call RAISERROR, the system function @@ERROR returns the value passed as *msg_id*. If no ID is passed, the error is raised with error number 50000 and @@ERROR is set to that number. Error numbers lower than 50000 are reserved for SQL Server use, so choose a higher number for your own messages.

You can also set the severity level; an informational message should be considered severity 0 (or severity 10; 0 and 10 are used interchangeably for a historical reason that's not important). Only someone with the system administrator (SA) role can raise an error with a severity of 19 or higher. Errors of severity 20 and higher are considered fatal, and the connection to the client is automatically terminated.

By default, if a batch includes a WAITFOR statement, results or messages are not returned to the client until the WAITFOR has completed. If you want the messages generated by your RAISERROR statement to be returned to the client immediately, even if the batch contains a subsequent WAITFOR, you can use the WITH NOWAIT option

You must use the WITH LOG option for all errors of severity 19 or higher. For errors of severity 20 or higher, the message text isn't returned to the client. Instead, it's sent to the SQL Server error log, and the error number, text, severity, and state are written to the operating system event log. A SQL Server system administrator can use the WITH LOG option with any error number or any severity level.

Errors written to the operating system event log from RAISERROR go to the application event log, with *MSSQLServer* as the source if the server is the default server, and *MSSQL$InstanceName* as the source if your server is a named instance. These errors have event ID 17060. (Errors that SQL Server raises can have different event IDs, depending on which component they come from.) The type of message in the event log depends on the severity used in the RAISERROR statement. Messages with severity 14 and lower are recorded as *informational messages,* severity 15 messages are *warnings,* and severity 16 and higher messages are *errors.* Note that the severity used by the event log is the number that's passed to RAISERROR, regardless of the stated severity in *sysmessages.* So, although I don't recommend it, you can raise a serious message as informational or a noncritical message as an error. If you look at the data section of the event log for a message raised from RAISERROR, or if you're reading from the event log in a program, you can choose to display the data as bytes or words. I find that when I display the error data as words, it's easy to see that the first word is the error number, and the second word is the severity (in hexadecimal, of course!).

You can use any number from 1 through 127 as the *state* parameter. You might pass a line number that tells where the error was raised. In a user-defined error message, however, *state* has no real relevance to SQL Server. For internally generated error messages, the value of *state* is an indication of where in the code the error came from. It can sometimes be of use to Microsoft Product Support personnel to know the value of *state* that was returned with an error message.

> **TIP** There's a little-known way to cause ISQL.EXE or OSQL.EXE (command-line query tools) to terminate. Raising any error with *state* 127 causes ISQL or OSQL to immediately exit, with a return code equal to the error number. (You can determine the error number from a batch command file by inspecting the system ERRORLEVEL value.) You could write your application so that it does something similar—it's a simple change to the error-handling logic. This trick can be a useful way to terminate a set of scripts that would be run through ISQL or OSQL. You could get a similar result by raising a high-severity error to terminate the connection. But using a *state* of 127 is actually simpler, and no scary message will be written to the error log or event log for what is a planned, routine action.

You can add your own messages and text for a message in multiple languages by using the *sp_addmessage* stored procedure. By default, SQL Server uses U.S. English, but you can add languages. SQL Server distinguishes U.S. English from British English because of locale settings, such as currency. The text of messages is the same. The procedure *sp_helplanguage* shows you what languages are available on your SQL Server instance. If a language you are interested in doesn't appear in the list returned by *sp_helplanguage,* take a look at the script INSTLANG.SQL, which can be found in the INSTALL subdirectory of your SQL Server instance installation files. This script adds locale settings for additional languages but does not add the actual translated error messages. Suppose we want to rewrite "Hello World" to use RAISERROR, and we want the text of the message to be able to appear in both U.S. English and German (language ID of 1). Here's how:

```
EXEC sp_addmessage 50001, 10, 'Hello World', @replace='REPLACE'
-- New message 50001 for U.S. English
```

(continued)

```
EXEC sp_addmessage 50001, 10, 'Hallo Welt' , @lang='Deutsch',
    @replace='REPLACE'
-- New message 50001 for German
```

When RAISERROR is executed, the text of the message becomes dependent on the SET LANGUAGE setting of the connection. If the connection does a *SET LANGUAGE Deutsch*, the text returned for *RAISERROR (50001, 10, 1)* will be *Hallo Welt*. If the text for a language doesn't exist, the U.S. English text (by default) is returned. For this reason, the U.S. English message must be added before the text for another language is added. If no entry exists, even in U.S. English, error 2758 results:

```
Msg 2758, Level 16, State 1
RAISERROR could not locate entry for error n in Sysmessages.
```

We could easily enhance the message to say whom the "Hello" is from by providing a parameter marker and passing it when calling RAISERROR. (For illustration, we'll use some *printf*-style formatting, *#6x*, to display the process number in hexadecimal format.)

```
EXEC sp_addmessage 50001, 10,
    'Hello World, from: %s, process id: %#6x', @replace='REPLACE'
```

When user *kalend* executes

```
DECLARE @parm1 varchar(30), @parm2 int
SELECT @parm1=USER_NAME(), @parm2=@@spid
RAISERROR (50001, 15, -1, @parm1, @parm2)
```

this error is raised:

```
Msg 50001, Level 15, State 1
Hello, World, from: kalend, process id: 0xc
```

FORMATMESSAGE

If you have created your own error messages with parameter markers, you might need to inspect the entire message with the parameters replaced by actual values. RAISERROR makes the message string available to the client but not to your SQL Server application. To construct a full message string from a parameterized message in the *sysmessages* table, you can use the function FORMATMESSAGE.

If we consider the last example from the preceding RAISERROR section, we can use FORMATMESSAGE to build the entire message string and save it in a local variable for further processing. Here's an example of the use of FORMATMESSAGE:

```
DECLARE @parm1 varchar(30), @parm2 int, @message varchar(100)
SELECT @parm1=USER_NAME(), @parm2=@@spid
SELECT @message = FORMATMESSAGE(50001, @parm1, @parm2)
PRINT 'The message is: ' + @message
```

This returns the following:

```
The message is: Hello World, from: kalend, process id:    0xc
```

Note that no error number or state information is returned.

Operators

Transact-SQL provides a large collection of operators for doing arithmetic, comparing values, doing bit operations, and concatenating strings. These operators are similar to those you might be familiar with in other programming languages. You can use Transact-SQL operators in any expression, including in the select list of a query, in the WHERE or HAVING clauses of queries, in UPDATE and IF statements, and in CASE expressions.

Arithmetic Operators

We won't go into much detail here because arithmetic operators are pretty standard stuff. If you need more information, please refer to the online documentation. Table 10-2 shows the arithmetic operators.

Symbol	*Operation*	*Used with These Datatypes*
+	Addition	*int, smallint, tinyint, bigint, numeric, decimal, float, real, money, smallmoney, datetime,* and *smalldatetime*
−	Subtraction	*int, smallint, tinyint, bigint, numeric, decimal, float, real, money, smallmoney, datetime,* and *smalldatetime*
*	Multiplication	*int, smallint, tinyint, bigint, numeric, decimal, float, real, money,* and *smallmoney*
/	Division	*int, smallint, tinyint, bigint, numeric, decimal, float, real, money,* and *smallmoney*
%	Modulo	*int, smallint, tinyint,* and *bigint*

Table 10-2. *Arithmetic operators in Transact-SQL.*

As with other programming languages, in Transact-SQL you need to consider the datatypes you're using when you perform arithmetic operations. Otherwise, you might not get the results you expect. For example, which of the following is correct?

```
1 / 2 = 0
1 / 2 = 0.5
```

If the underlying datatypes are both integers (including *bigint, tinyint,* and *smallint*), the correct answer is 0. If one or both of the datatypes are *float* (including *real*) or *numeric/decimal*, the correct answer is 0.5 (or 0.50000, depending on the precision and scale of the datatype). When an operator combines two expressions of different datatypes, the datatype precedence rules specify which datatype is converted to the other. The datatype with the lower precedence is converted to the datatype with the higher precedence.

Here's the precedence order for SQL Server datatypes:

```
sql_variant (highest)
datetime
smalldatetime
float
real
decimal
money
smallmoney
bigint
int
smallint
tinyint
bit
ntext
text
image
timestamp (rowversion)
uniqueidentifier
nvarchar
nchar
varchar
char
varbinary
binary (lowest)
```

As you can see from the precedence list, an *int* multiplied by a *float* produces a *float*. If you need to use data of type *sql_variant* in an arithmetic operation, you must first convert the *sql_variant* data to its base datatype. You can explicitly convert to a given datatype by using the CAST function or its predecessor, CONVERT. I'll discuss these conversion functions later in this chapter.

The addition (+) operator is also used to concatenate character strings. In this example, we want to concatenate last names, followed by a comma and a space, followed by first names from the *authors* table (in *pubs*), and then we want to return the result as a single column:

```
SELECT 'author'=au_lname + ', ' + au_fname FROM authors
```

Here's the abbreviated result:

```
author
------
White, Johnson
Green, Marjorie
Carson, Cheryl
O'Leary, Michael
```

Bit Operators

Table 10-3 shows the SQL Server bit operators.

Symbol	Meaning
&	Bitwise AND (two operands)
|	Bitwise OR (two operands)
^	Bitwise exclusive OR (two operands)
~	Bitwise NOT (one operand)

Table 10-3. *SQL Server bit operators.*

The operands for the two-operand bitwise operators can be any of the datatypes of the integer or binary string datatype categories (except for the *image* datatype), with the exception that both operands cannot be a type of binary string. So, one of the operands can be *binary* or *varbinary*, but they can't both be *binary* or *varbinary*. In addition, the right operand can be of the *bit* datatype only if the left operand is of type *bit*. Table 10-4 shows the supported operand datatypes.

Left Operand	Right Operand
binary	*int, smallint, tinyint,* or *bigint*
bit	*int, smallint, tinyint, bigint,* or *bit*
int	*int, smallint, tinyint, bigint, binary,* or *varbinary*
smallint	*int, smallint, tinyint, bigint, binary,* or *varbinary*
tinyint	*int, smallint, tinyint, bigint, binary,* or *varbinary*
bigint	*int, smallint, tinyint, bigint, binary,* or *varbinary*
varbinary	*int, smallint, tinyint,* or *bigint*

Table 10-4. *Datatypes supported for two-operand bitwise operators.*

The single operand for the bitwise NOT operator must be one of the integer datatypes.

Often, you must keep a lot of indicator-type values in a database, and bit operators make it easy to set up bit masks with a single column to do this. The SQL Server system tables use bit masks. For example, the *status* field in the *sysdatabases* table is a bit mask. If we wanted to see all databases marked as read-only, which is the 11th bit or decimal 1024 (2^{10}), we could use this query:

```
SELECT 'read only databases'=name FROM master..sysdatabases
WHERE status & 1024 > 0
```

This example is for illustrative purposes only. As I mentioned in Chapter 6, in general, you shouldn't query the system catalogs directly. Sometimes the catalogs need to change between product releases, and if you query directly, your applications can break because of these required changes. Instead, you should use the provided system catalog stored procedures and object property functions, which return catalog information in a standard way. If the underlying catalogs change in subsequent releases, the property functions are also updated, insulating your application from unexpected changes.

So, for this example, to see whether a particular database was marked read-only, we could use the DATABASEPROPERTY function:

```
SELECT DATABASEPROPERTY('mydb', 'IsReadOnly')
```

A return value of 1 would mean that *mydb* was set to read-only status.

Note that keeping such indicators as *bit* datatype columns can be a better approach than using an *int* as a bit mask. It's more straightforward—you don't always need to look up your bit-mask values for each indicator. To write the "read only databases" query we just looked at, you'd need to check the documentation for the bit-mask value for "read only." And many developers, not to mention end users, aren't that comfortable using bit operators and are likely to use them incorrectly. From a storage perspective, *bit* columns don't require more space than equivalent bit-mask columns require. (Eight *bit* fields can share the same byte of storage.)

But you wouldn't typically want to do that with a "yes/no" indicator field anyway. If you have a huge number of indicator fields, using bit-mask columns of integers instead of *bit* columns might be a better alternative than dealing with hundreds of individual *bit* columns. However, there's nothing to stop you from having hundreds of *bit* columns. You'd have to have an awful lot of *bit* fields to actually exceed the column limit because a table in SQL Server can have up to 1024 columns. If you frequently add new indicators, using a bit mask on an integer might be better. To add a new indicator, you can make use of an unused bit of an integer status field rather than do an ALTER TABLE and add a new column (which you must do if you use a *bit* column). The case for using a *bit* column boils down to clarity.

Comparison Operators

Table 10-5 shows the SQL Server comparison operators.

Symbol	Meaning
=	Equal to
>	Greater than
<	Less than
>=	Greater than or equal to
<=	Less than or equal to

Table 10-5. *SQL Server comparison operators.*

(continued)

Symbol	Meaning
<>	Not equal to (ANSI standard)
!=	Not equal to (not ANSI standard)
!>	Not greater than (not ANSI standard)
!<	Not less than (not ANSI standard)

Comparison operators are straightforward. Only a few related issues might be confusing to a novice SQL Server developer:

■ When you deal with NULL, remember the issues with three-value logic and the truth tables that were discussed in Chapter 7. Also understand that NULL is an unknown.

■ Comparisons of *char* and *varchar* data (and their Unicode counterparts) depend on the collation value associated with the column. Whether comparisons evaluate to TRUE depends on the sort order installed. You can review the discussion of collation in Chapter 4.

■ Comparison of *sql_variant* values involves special rules that break down the SQL Server datatype hierarchy shown previously into datatype families, as shown in Table 10-6. The following script creates a table that I can use to illustrate some of the issues involved in comparing values of type *sql_variant*:

```
CREATE TABLE variant2
(a sql_variant, b sql_variant )
GO
INSERT INTO variant2
    VALUES (CAST (111 as int), CAST(222 as money ))
GO
INSERT INTO variant2
    VALUES (CAST (333 as int), CAST(444 as char(3) ))
GO
```

Here are the special rules governing comparison of *sql_variant* values:

■ When *sql_variant* values of different base datatypes are compared and the base datatypes are in different datatype families, the value whose datatype family is higher in the hierarchy chart is considered the higher of the two values.

You can see this behavior by executing the following query:

```
SELECT *
FROM variant2
WHERE a > b
```

(continued)

```
Result:
a     b
----- -----
333   444
```

The second row inserted had a value of base type *int* and a value of base type *char*. Even though you would normally think that 333 is not greater than 444 because 333 is of datatype *int* and the family *exact numeric*, it is considered higher than 444, of datatype *char*, and of the family *Unicode*.

- When *sql_variant* values of different base datatypes are compared and the base datatypes are in the same datatype family, the value whose base datatype is lower in the hierarchy chart is implicitly converted to the other datatype and the comparison is then made.

  You can see this behavior by executing the following query:

  ```
  SELECT *
  FROM variant2
  WHERE a < b

  Result:
  a                       b
  ---------------------   -----------------
  111                     222.0000
  ```

  In this case, the two base types are *int* and *money*, which are in the same family, so 111 is considered less than 222.0000.

- When *sql_variant* values of the *char*, *varchar*, *nchar*, or *varchar* datatypes are compared, they are evaluated based on additional criteria, including the locale code ID (LCID), the LCID version, the comparison flags use for the column's collation, and the sort ID.

Datatype Hierarchy	*Datatype Family*
sql_variant	*sql_variant*
datetime	*datetime*
smalldatetime	*datetime*
float	*approximate numeric*
real	*approximate numeric*
decimal	*exact numeric*

Table 10-6. *Datatype families for use when comparing* sql_variant *values.*   (continued)

Datatype Hierarchy	*Datatype Family*
money	*exact numeric*
smallmoney	*exact numeric*
bigint	*exact numeric*
int	*exact numeric*
smallint	*exact numeric*
tinyint	*exact numeric*
bit	*exact numeric*
nvarchar	*Unicode*
nchar	*Unicode*
varchar	*Unicode*
char	*Unicode*
varbinary	*binary*
binary	*binary*
uniqueidentifier	*uniqueidentifier*

Logical and Grouping Operators (Parentheses)

The three logical operators (AND, OR, and NOT) are vitally important in expressions, especially in the WHERE clause. You can use parentheses to group expressions and then apply logical operations to the group. In many cases, it's impossible to correctly formulate a query without using parentheses. In other cases, you might be able to avoid them, but your expression won't be very intuitive and the absence of parentheses could result in bugs. You could construct a convoluted expression using some combination of string concatenations or functions, bit operations, or arithmetic operations instead of using parentheses, but there's no good reason to do this.

Using parentheses can make your code clearer, less prone to bugs, and easier to maintain. Because there's no performance penalty beyond parsing, you should use parentheses liberally. Below is a query that you couldn't readily write without using parentheses. This query is simple, and in English the request is well understood. But you're also likely to get this query wrong in Transact-SQL if you're not careful, and it clearly illustrates just how easy it is to make a mistake.

```
Find authors who do not live in either Salt Lake City, UT, or Oakland, CA.
```

Following are four examples that attempt to formulate this query. Three of them are wrong. Test yourself: which one is correctly stated? (As usual, multiple correct formulations are possible—not just the one presented here.)

EXAMPLE 1

```
SELECT au_lname, au_fname, city, state FROM authors
WHERE
city <> 'OAKLAND' AND state <> 'CA'
OR
city <> 'Salt Lake City' AND state <> 'UT'
```

EXAMPLE 2

```
SELECT au_lname, au_fname, city, state FROM authors
WHERE
(city <> 'OAKLAND' AND state <> 'CA')
OR
(city <> 'Salt Lake City' AND state <> 'UT')
```

EXAMPLE 3

```
SELECT au_lname, au_fname, city, state FROM authors
WHERE
(city <> 'OAKLAND' AND state <> 'CA')
AND
(city <> 'Salt Lake City' AND state <> 'UT')
```

EXAMPLE 4

```
SELECT au_lname, au_fname, city, state FROM authors
WHERE
NOT
(
(city='OAKLAND' AND state='CA')
OR
(city='Salt Lake City' AND state='UT')
)
```

I hope you can see that only Example 4 operates correctly. This query would be much more difficult to write without some combination of parentheses, NOT, OR (including IN, a shorthand for OR), and AND.

You can also use parentheses to change the order of precedence in mathematical and logical operations. These two statements return different results:

```
SELECT 1.0 + 3.0 / 4.0      -- Returns 1.75
SELECT (1.0 + 3.0) / 4.0    -- Returns 1.00
```

The order of precedence is similar to what you learned back in algebra class (except for the bit operators). Operators of the same level are evaluated left to right. You use parentheses to change precedence levels to suit your needs, when you're unsure, or when you simply want to make your code more readable. Groupings with parentheses are evaluated from the innermost grouping outward. Table 10-7 shows the order of precedence.

Operation	Operators
Bitwise NOT	~
Multiplication/division/modulo	* / %
Addition/subtraction	+ / −
Bitwise exclusive OR	^
Bitwise AND	&
Bitwise OR	|
Logical NOT	NOT
Logical AND	AND
Logical OR	OR

Table 10-7. *Order of precedence in mathematical and logical operations, from highest to lowest.*

If you didn't pick the correct example, you can easily see the flaw in Examples 1, 2, and 3 by examining the output. Examples 1 and 2 both return every row. Every row is either not in CA or not in UT because a row can be in only one or the other. A row in CA isn't in UT, so the expression returns TRUE. Example 3 is too restrictive—for example, what about the rows in San Francisco, CA? The condition *(city <> 'OAKLAND' AND state <> 'CA')* would evaluate to *(TRUE and FALSE)* for San Francisco, CA, which, of course, is FALSE, so the row would be rejected when it should be selected, according to the desired semantics.

Scalar Functions

In Chapter 7, we looked at aggregate functions, such as MAX, SUM, and COUNT. These functions operate on a set of values to produce a single aggregated value. In addition to aggregate functions, SQL Server provides *scalar functions,* which operate on a single value. *Scalar* is just a fancy term for *single value.* You can also think of the value in a single column of a single row as *scalar.* Scalar functions are enormously useful—the Swiss army knife of SQL Server. You've probably noticed that scalar functions have been used in several examples already—we'd all be lost without them.

You can use scalar functions in any legal expression, such as:

- In the select list
- In a WHERE clause, including one that defines a view
- Inside a CASE expression

- In a CHECK constraint

- In the VALUES clause of an INSERT statement

- In an UPDATE statement to the right of the equals sign in the SET clause

- With a variable assignment

- As a parameter inside another scalar function

SQL Server provides too many scalar functions to remember. The best you can do is to familiarize yourself with those that exist, and then, when you encounter a problem and a light bulb goes on in your head to remind you of a function that will help, you can look at the online documentation for details. Even with so many functions available, you'll probably find yourself wanting some functions that don't exist. You might have a specialized need that would benefit from a specific function, so in Chapter 11 I'll show you how to create functions of your own.

The following sections describe the scalar functions that are supplied with SQL Server 2000. We'll first look at the CAST function because it's especially important.

Conversion Functions

SQL Server provides three functions for converting datatypes: the generalized CAST function, the CONVERT function—which is analogous to CAST but has a slightly different syntax—and the more specialized STR function.

> **NOTE** The CAST function is a synonym for CONVERT and was added to the product to comply with ANSI-92 specifications. You'll see CONVERT used in older documentation and older code.

CAST is possibly the most useful function in all of SQL Server. It allows you to change the datatype when you select a field, which can be essential for concatenating strings, joining columns that weren't initially envisioned as related, performing mathematical operations on columns that were defined as character but which actually contain numbers, and other similar operations. Like C, SQL is a fairly strongly typed language.

Some languages, such as Visual Basic or PL/1 (Programming Language 1), allow you to almost indiscriminately mix datatypes. If you mix datatypes in SQL, however, you'll often get an error. Some conversions are implicit, so, for example, you can add or join a *smallint* and an *int* without any such error; trying to do the same between an *int* and a *char,* however, produces an error. Without a way to convert datatypes in SQL, you would have to return the values back to the client application, convert them there, and then send them back to the server. You might need to create temporary tables just to hold the intermediate converted values. All of this would be cumbersome and inefficient.

Recognizing this inefficiency, the ANSI committee added the CAST operator to SQL-92. SQL Server's CAST—and the older CONVERT—provides a superset of ANSI CAST functionality. The CAST syntax is simple:

```
CAST (original_expression AS desired_datatype)
```

Suppose I want to concatenate the *job_id* (*smallint*) column of the *employee* table with the *lname* (*varchar*) column. Without CAST, this would be impossible (unless it was done in the application). With CAST, it's trivial:

```
SELECT lname + '-' + CAST(job_id AS varchar(2)) FROM employee
```

Here's the abbreviated output:

```
Accorti-13
Afonso-14
Ashworth-6
Bennett-12
Brown-7
Chang-4
Cramer-2
Cruz-10
Devon-3
⋮
```

Specifying a length shorter than the column or expression in your call to CAST is a useful way to truncate the column. You could use the SUBSTRING function for this with equal results, but you might find it more intuitive to use CAST. Specifying a length when you convert to *char, varchar, decimal,* or *numeric* isn't required, but it's recommended. Specifying a length shields you better from possible behavioral changes in newer releases of the product.

> **NOTE** Although behavioral changes generally don't occur by design, it's difficult to ensure 100 percent consistency of subtle behavioral changes between releases. The development team strives for such consistency, but it's nearly impossible to ensure that no behavioral side effects result when new features and capabilities are added. There's little point in relying on the current default behavior when you can just as easily be explicit about what you expect.

You might want to avoid CAST when you convert *float* or *numeric/decimal* values to character strings if you expect to see a certain number of decimal places. CAST doesn't currently provide formatting capabilities for numbers. The older CONVERT function has some limited formatting capabilities, which we'll see shortly. Formatting floating-point numbers and such when converting to character strings is another area that's ripe for subtle behavior differences. So if you need to transform a floating-point number to a character string in which you expect a specific format, you can use the other conversion function, STR. STR is a specialized conversion function that always converts from a number (*float, numeric,* and so on) to a character datatype, but it allows you to explicitly specify the length and number of decimal places that should be formatted for the character string. Here's the syntax:

```
STR(float_expression, character_length, number_of_decimal_places)
```

Remember that *character_length* must include room for a decimal point and a negative sign if they might exist. Also be aware that STR rounds the value to the number of decimal places requested, while CAST simply truncates the value if the character length is smaller than the size required for full display. Here's an example of STR:

```
SELECT discounttype, 'Discount'=STR(discount, 7, 3) FROM discounts
```

And here's the output:

```
discounttype       Discount
------------       --------
Initial Customer    10.500
Volume Discount      6.700
Customer Discount    5.000
```

You can think of the ASCII and CHAR functions as special type-conversion functions, but I'll discuss them later in this chapter along with string functions.

If all you're doing is converting an expression to a specific datatype, you can actually use either CAST or the older CONVERT. However, the syntax of CONVERT is slightly different and allows for a third, optional argument. Here's the syntax for CONVERT:

```
CONVERT (desired_datatype[(length)], original_expression
  [, style])
```

CONVERT has an optional third parameter, *style*. This parameter is most commonly used when you convert an expression of type *datetime* or *smalldatetime* to type *char* or *varchar*. You can also use it when you convert *float, real, money,* or *smallmoney* to a character datatype.

When you convert a *datetime* expression to a character datatype, if the *style* argument isn't specified, the conversion will format the date with the default SQL Server date format (for example, Oct 3 1999 2:25PM). By specifying a *style* type, you can format the output as you want. You can also specify a shorter length for the character buffer being converted to, in order to perhaps eliminate the time portion or for other reasons. Table 10-8 shows the various values you can use as the *style* argument.

Style Number without Century (yy)	Style Number with Century (yyyy)	Output Type	Style
–	0 or 100	Default	mon dd yyyy hh:miAM (or PM)
1	101	USA	mm/dd/yyyy
2	102	ANSI	yyyy.mm.dd
3	103	British/French	dd/mm/yyyy
4	104	German	dd.mm.yyyy
5	105	Italian	dd-mm-yyyy
6	106	–	dd mon yyyy
7	107	–	mon dd, yyyy
–	8 or 108	–	hh:mm:ss
–	9 or 109	Default + milliseconds (or PM)	mon dd yyyy hh:mi:ss:mmmAM
10	110	USA	mm-dd-yy
11	111	JAPAN	yy/mm/dd
12	112	ISO	yymmdd
–	13 or 113	Europe default + milliseconds	dd mon yyyy hh:mi:ss:mmm (24h)
14	114	–	hh:mi:ss:mmm (24h)
	20 or 120	ODBC canonical	yyyy-mm-dd hh:mi:ss(24h)
	21 or 121	ODBC canonical + milliseconds	yyyy-mm-dd hh:mi:ss.mmm(24h)

Table 10-8. *Values for the* style *argument of the CONVERT function when you convert a* datetime *expression to a character expression.*

NOTE Although SQL Server uses style 0 as the default when converting a *datetime* value to a character string, SQL Query Analyzer (and OSQL) use style 121 when displaying a *datetime* value.

Since we just passed a change in the century, using two-character formats for the year could be a bug in your application just waiting to happen! Unless you have a compelling reason not to, you should always use the full year (*yyyy*) for both the input and output formatting of dates to prevent any ambiguity.

SQL Server has no problem dealing with the year 2000—in fact, the change in century isn't even a boundary condition in SQL Server's internal representation of dates. But if you represent a year by specifying only the last two digits, the inherent ambiguity might cause your application to make an incorrect assumption. When a date formatted that way is entered, SQL Server's default behavior is to interpret the year as 19*yy* if the value is greater than or equal to 50 and as 20*yy* if the value is less than 50. That might be OK now, but by the year 2050 you won't want a two-digit year of 50 to be interpreted as 1950 instead of 2050. (If you simply assume that your application will have been long since retired, think again. A lot of COBOL programmers in the 1960s didn't worry about the year 2000.)

SQL Server 2000 allows you to change the cutoff year that determines how a two-digit year is interpreted. A two-digit year that is less than or equal to the last two digits of the cutoff year is in the same century as the cutoff year. A two-digit year that is greater than the last two digits of the cutoff year is in the century that precedes the cutoff year. You can change the cutoff year by using the Properties dialog box for your SQL server in SQL Server Enterprise Manager and selecting the Server Settings tab. Or you can use the *sp_configure* stored procedure:

```
EXEC sp_configure 'two digit year cutoff', '2000'
```

In this example, since *two digit year cutoff* is 2000, all two-digit years other than 00 are interpreted as occurring in the 20th century. With the default *two digit year cutoff* value of 2049, the two-digit year 49 is interpreted as 2049 and the two-digit year 50 is interpreted as 1950. You should be aware that although SQL Server uses 2049 as the cutoff year for interpreting dates, OLE Automation objects use 2030. You can use the *two digit year cutoff* option to provide consistency in date values between SQL Server and client applications. However, to avoid ambiguity with dates, you should always use four-digit years in your data.

You don't need to worry about how changing the *two digit year cutoff* value will affect your existing data. If data is stored using the *datetime* or *smalldatetime* datatypes, the full four-digit year is part of the internal storage. The *two digit year cutoff* value controls only how SQL Server interprets date constants such as *10/12/99*.

Day First or Month First   The *two digit year cutoff* value determines how SQL Server interprets the *99* in *10/12/99*, but this date constant has another ambiguity. Are we talking about October 12 or December 10? The SET option DATEFORMAT determines whether SQL Server interprets a numeric three-part date as month followed by day, day followed by month, or even year followed by month. The default value of DATEFORMAT is controlled by the language you're using, but you can change it using the SET DATEFORMAT command. There are six possible values for DATEFORMAT, which should be self-explanatory: *mdy, dmy, ymd, ydm, dym,* and *myd*. Only the first three are commonly used. Note that DATEFORMAT controls only how SQL Server interprets date constants that are entered by you or your program. It does not control how date values are displayed. As I've mentioned, output format is controlled by the client or by having SQL Server convert the *datetime* value to a character string and using a style option.

Here's an example that shows how changing the DATEFORMAT value can change how input dates are interpreted:

```
SET DATEFORMAT mdy
SELECT 'FORMAT is mdy' = CONVERT(datetime, '7/4/2000')
SET DATEFORMAT dmy
SELECT 'FORMAT is dmy' = CONVERT(datetime, '7/4/2000')

RESULTS:
FORMAT is mdy
---------------------------
2000-07-04 00:00:00.000

FORMAT is dmy
---------------------------
2000-04-07 00:00:00.000
```

You might consider using ISO style when you insert dates. This format has the year followed by month and then the day, with no punctuation. This style is always recognizable, no matter what the SQL Server default language and no matter what the DATEFORMAT setting. Here's the above conversion command with dates supplied in ISO format:

```
SET DATEFORMAT mdy
SELECT 'FORMAT is mdy' = CONVERT(datetime, '20000704')
SET DATEFORMAT dmy
SELECT 'FORMAT is mdy' = CONVERT(datetime, '20000704')

RESULTS:
FORMAT is mdy
---------------------------
2000-07-04 00:00:00.000

FORMAT is mdy
---------------------------
2000-07-04 00:00:00.000
```

Be sure to always put your dates in quotes. If we had left off the quotes, SQL Server would assume we meant the number 20,000,704 and would interpret that as the number of days after January 1, 1900. It would try to figure out the date that was that many days after the base date, which is out of the range of possible *datetime* values that SQL Server can store.

One other date format can override your default language or DATEFORMAT setting, but it behaves a little inconsistently. If you enter a date in all numeric format with the year first but you include punctuation (as in 1999.05.02), SQL Server will assume that the first part is the year even if your DATEFORMAT is *dmy*. However, which number is the month and which is the day? SQL Server will still use your DATEFORMAT setting to determine the order of the month and the day values. So if your DATEFORMAT is *mdy*, *SELECT CONVERT(datetime, '1999.5.2')* will return *1999-05-02 00:00:00.000*, and if your DATEFORMAT is *dmy*, *SELECT CONVERT(datetime, '1999.5.2')* will return *1999-02-05 00:00:00.000* and *SELECT CONVERT(datetime, '1999.5.22')* will return an out-of-range error. To me, this seems quite inconsistent. SQL Server is partially ignoring the DATEFORMAT, but not completely. I suggest that you avoid this format for inputting dates, and if you're going to use all numbers, leave out the punctuation.

Instead of setting the DATEFORMAT value, you can use the *style* argument when you convert from a *character* string to a *datetime* value. You must be sure to enter the date in the format that the style requires, as indicated in Table 10-8 (shown earlier). These two statements return different values:

```
SELECT CONVERT(datetime, '10.12.99',1)
SELECT CONVERT(datetime, '10.12.99',4)
```

The first statement assumes that the date is style 1, *mm.dd.yy*, so the string can be converted to the corresponding *datetime* value and returned to the client. The client then returns the *datetime* value according to its own display conventions. The second statement assumes that the date is represented as *dd.mm.yy*. If I had tried to use style 102 or 104, both of which require a four-digit year, I would have received a conversion error because I specified only a two-digit year.

CONVERT can also be useful if you insert the current date using the GETDATE function but don't consider the time elements of the *datetime* datatype to be meaningful. (Remember that SQL Server doesn't currently have separate date and time datatypes.) You can use CONVERT to format and insert *datetime* data with only a date element. Without the time specification in the GETDATE value, the time will consistently be stored as 12:00AM for any given date. That eliminates problems that can occur when you search among columns or join columns of *datetime*. For example, if the date elements are equal between columns but the time element is not, an equality search will fail.

You can eliminate this equality problem by making the time portion consistent. Consider this:

```
CREATE TABLE my_date (Col1 datetime)
INSERT INTO my_date VALUES (CONVERT(char(10), GETDATE(), 112))
```

In this example, the CONVERT function converts the current date and time value to a character string that doesn't include the time. However, because the table we're inserting into expects a *datetime* value, the new character string is converted back to a *datetime* datatype using the default time of midnight.

You can also use the optional *style* argument when you convert *float*, *real*, *money*, or *smallmoney* to a character datatype. When you convert from *float* or *real*, the style allows you to force the output to appear in scientific notation and also allows you to specify either 8 or 16 digits. When you convert from a *money* type to a character type, the style allows you to specify whether you want a comma to appear every three digits and whether you want two digits to the right of the decimal point or four.

In Table 10-9, the column on the left represents the *style* values for *float* or *real* conversion to character data.

Style Value	Output
0 (the default)	Six digits maximum. In scientific notation when appropriate.
1	Always 8 digits. Always scientific notation.
2	Always 16 digits. Always scientific notation.

Table 10-9. *Values for the* style *argument of the CONVERT function when you convert a floating-point expression to a character datatype.*

In Table 10-10, the column on the left represents the *style* value for *money* or *smallmoney* conversion to character data.

Style Value	Output
0 (the default)	No commas to the left of the decimal point. Two digits appear to the right of the decimal point. Example: 4235.98.
1	Commas every three digits to the left of the decimal point. Two digits appear to the right of the decimal point. Example: 3,510.92.
2	No commas to the left of the decimal point. Four digits appear to the right of the decimal point. Example: 4235.9819.

Table 10-10. *Values for the* style *argument of the CONVERT function when you convert a money expression to a character datatype.*

Here's an example from the *pubs* database. The *advance* column in the *titles* table lists the advance paid by the publisher for each book, and most of the amounts are greater than $1000. In the *titles* table, the value is stored as a *money* datatype. The following query returns the value of *advance* as a *money* value, a *varchar* value with the default style, and as *varchar* with each of the two optional styles:

```
SELECT "Money" = advance,
       "Varchar" = CONVERT(varchar(10), advance),
```

(continued)

```
        "Varchar-1" = CONVERT(varchar(10), advance, 1),
        "Varchar-2" = CONVERT(varchar(10), advance, 2)
FROM titles
```

Here's the abbreviated output:

```
Money                   Varchar     Varchar-1   Varchar-2
--------------------    ----------  ----------  ----------
5000.0000               5000.00     5,000.00    5000.0000
5000.0000               5000.00     5,000.00    5000.0000
10125.0000              10125.00    10,125.00   10125.0000
5000.0000               5000.00     5,000.00    5000.0000
.0000                   0.00        0.00        0.0000
15000.0000              15000.00    15,000.00   15000.0000
NULL                    NULL        NULL        NULL
7000.0000               7000.00     7,000.00    7000.0000
8000.0000               8000.00     8,000.00    8000.0000
```

Be aware that when you use CONVERT, the conversion occurs on the server and the value is sent to the client application in the converted datatype. Of course, it's also common for applications to convert between datatypes, but conversion at the server is completely separate from conversion at the client. It's the client that determines how to display the value returned. In the previous example, the results in the first column have no comma and four decimal digits. This is how SQL Query Analyzer displays values of type *money* that it receives from SQL Server. If we run this same query using the command-line ISQL tool, the (abbreviated) results look like this:

```
Money                       Varchar     Varchar-1   Varchar-2
--------------------------  ----------  ----------  ----------
         5,000.00 5000.00    5,000.00    5000.0000
         5,000.00 5000.00    5,000.00    5000.0000
        10,125.00 10125.00   10,125.00   10125.0000
         5,000.00 5000.00    5,000.00    5000.0000
             0.00 0.00       0.00        0.0000
        15,000.00 15000.00   15,000.00   15000.0000
          (null) (null)      (null)      (null)
         7,000.00 7000.00    7,000.00    7000.0000
         8,000.00 8000.00    8,000.00    8000.0000
```

NOTE   In addition to determining how to display a value of a particular datatype, the client program determines whether the output should be left-justified or right-justified and how NULLs are displayed. I'm frequently asked how to change this default output to, for example, print *money* values with four decimal digits in SQL Query Analyzer. Unfortunately, SQL Query Analyzer has its own set of predefined formatting specifications, and, for the most part, you can't change them. Other client programs, such as report writers, might give you a full range of capabilities for specifying the output format, but SQL Query Analyzer isn't a report writer.

Here's another example of how the display can be affected by the client. If we use the GETDATE function to select the current date, it is returned to the client application as a *datetime* datatype. The client application will likely convert that internal date representation to a string for display. On the other hand, if we use GETDATE but also explicitly use CONVERT to change the *datetime* to character data, the column is sent to the calling application already as a character string.

So let's see what one particular client will do with that returned data. The command-line program ISQL is a DB-Library program and uses functions in DB-Library for binding columns to character strings. DB-Library allows such bindings to automatically pick up locale styles based on the settings of the workstation running the application. (You must select the Use International Settings option in the SQL Server Client Network Utility in order for this to occur by default.) So a column returned internally as a *datetime* datatype is converted by ISQL.EXE into the same format as the locale setting of Windows. A column containing a date representation as a character string is not reformatted, of course.

When we issue the following SELECT statement with SQL Server configured for U.S. English as the default language and with Windows NT and Windows 2000 on the client configured as English (United States), the date and string look alike:

```
SELECT
'returned as date'=GETDATE(),
'returned as string'=CONVERT(varchar(20), GETDATE())

returned as date      returned as string
------------------    -------------------
Dec 3 2000  3:10PM    Dec  3 2000  3:10PM
```

However, if we change the locale in the Regional Options application of the Windows 2000 Control Panel to French (Standard), the same SELECT statement returns the following:

```
returned as date      returned as string
------------------    -------------------
3 déc. 2000 15:10     Dec  3 2000  3:10PM
```

You can see that the value returned to the client in internal date format was converted at the client workstation in the format chosen by the application. The conversion that uses CONVERT was formatted at the server.

> **NOTE** Although I've used dates in these examples, this discussion is also relevant to formatting numbers and currency with different regional settings.

I cannot use the command-line OSQL program to illustrate the same behavior. OSQL, like SQL Query Analyzer, is an ODBC-based program, and *datetime* values are converted to ODBC Canonical format, which is independent of any regional settings. Using OSQL, the previous query would return this result:

```
returned as date            returned as string
--------------------------  --------------------
2000-12-03 15:10:24.793     Dec  3 2000  3:10PM
```

The rest of the book primarily uses CAST instead of CONVERT when converting between datatypes. CONVERT is used only when the *style* argument is needed.

Some conversions are automatic and implicit, so using CAST is unnecessary (but OK). For example, converting between numbers with types *int, smallint, tinyint, float, numeric*, and so on happens automatically and implicitly as long as an overflow doesn't occur, in which case you'd get an error for arithmetic overflow. Converting numbers with decimal places to integer datatypes results in the truncation of the values to the right of the decimal point—without warning. (If you're converting between decimal or numeric datatypes, you must explicitly use CAST if a loss of precision is possible.)

Even though Figure 10-3 on page 509 indicates that conversion from character strings to *datetime* values can happen implicitly, this conversion is possible only when SQL Server can figure out what the *datetime* value needs to be. If you use wildcards in your character strings, SQL Server might not be able to do a proper conversion.

Suppose I use the following query to find all orders placed in August 1996 and stored in the *orders* table in the *Northwind* database:

```
USE Northwind
SELECT  * FROM orders WHERE OrderDate BETWEEN '8/1/96' and '8/31/96'
```

Because all the dates have a time of midnight in the *orders* table, SQL Server will correctly interpret this query and return 25 rows. It converts the two string constants to *datetime* values, and then it can do a proper chronological comparison. However, if your string has a wildcard in it, SQL Server cannot convert it to a *datetime*, so instead it converts the *datetime* into a string. To do this, it uses its default date format, which, as you've seen, is *mon dd yyyy hh:miAM* (or *PM*). So this is the format you have to match in the character string with wildcards. Obviously, *%1996%* will match but '*8/1/%*' won't. Although SQL Server is usually very flexible in how dates can be entered, once you compare a *datetime* to a string with wildcards, you can assume only the default format.

Note that in the default format, there are two spaces before a single-digit day. So if I want to find all rows in the *orders* table with an *OrderDate* of July 8, 1996, at any time, I have to use the following and be sure to put two spaces between *Jul* and *8*:

```
WHERE OrderDate LIKE 'Jul  8 1996%'
```

Other conversions, such as between character and integer data, can be performed explicitly only by using CAST or CONVERT. Conversions between certain datatypes are nonsensical—for example, between a *float* and a *datetime*—and attempting such an operation results in error 529, which states that the conversion is impossible.

Figure 10-3 on page 509, reprinted from the SQL Server documentation, is one that you'll want to refer to periodically for conversion issues.

Date and Time Functions

Operations on *datetime* values are common, such as "get current date and time," "do date arithmetic—50 days from today is what date," or "find out what day of the week falls on a specific date." Programming languages such as C or Visual Basic are loaded with functions for operations like these. Transact-SQL also provides a nice assortment to choose from, as shown in Table 10-11.

The *datetime* parameter is any expression with a SQL Server *datetime* datatype or one that can be implicitly converted, such as an appropriately formatted character string like *1999.10.31*. The *datepart* parameter uses the encodings shown in Table 10-12. Either the full name or the abbreviation can be passed as an argument.

Date Function	Return Type	Description
DATEADD (*datepart, number, datetime*)	*datetime*	Produces a date by adding an interval to a specified date
DATEDIFF (*datepart, datetime1, datetime2*)	*int*	Returns the number of *datepart* "boundaries" crossed between two specified dates
DATENAME (*datepart, datetime*)	*varchar*	Returns a character string representing the specified *datepart* of the specified date
DATEPART (*datepart, datetime*)	*int*	Returns an integer representing the specified *datepart* of the specified date
DAY (*datetime*)	*int*	Returns an integer representing the day *datepart* of the specified date
MONTH (*datetime*)	*int*	Returns an integer representing the month *datepart* of the specified date
YEAR (*datetime*)	*int*	Returns an integer representing the year *datepart* of the specified date

Table 10-11. *Date and time functions in Transact-SQL.* (continued)

Table 10-11. *continued*

Date Function	Return Type	Description
GETDATE	*datetime*	Returns the current system date and time in the SQL Server standard internal format for *datetime* values
GETUTCDATE	*datetime*	Returns the current Universal Time Coordinate (Greenwich Mean Time), which is derived from the current local time and the time zone setting in the operating system of the machine SQL Server is running on

datepart *(Full Name)*	Abbreviation	Values
year	Yy	1753–9999
quarter	Qq	1–4
month	Mm	1–12
dayofyear	Dy	1–366
day	Dd	1–31
week	Wk	1–53
weekday	Dw	1–7 (Sunday–Saturday)
hour	Hh	0–23
minute	Mi	0–59
second	Ss	0–59
millisecond	Ms	0–999

Table 10-12. *Values for the* datepart *parameter.*

Like other functions, the date functions provide more than simple convenience. Suppose we need to find all records entered on the second Tuesday of every month and all records entered within 48 weeks of today. Without SQL Server date functions, the only way we could accomplish such a query would be to select all the rows and return them to the application and then filter them there. With a lot of data and a slow network, this can get ugly. With the date functions, the process is simple and efficient, and only the rows that meet these criteria are selected. For this example, let's assume that the *records* table includes these columns:

```
Record_number    int
Entered_on       datetime
```

This query returns the desired rows:

```
SELECT Record_number, Entered_on
FROM records
WHERE
DATEPART(WEEKDAY, Entered_on) = 3
-- Tuesday is 3rd day of week (in USA)
AND
DATEPART(DAY, Entered_on) BETWEEN 8 AND 14
-- The 2nd week is from the 8th to 14th
AND
DATEDIFF(WEEK, Entered_on, GETDATE()) <= 48
-- Within 48 weeks of today
```

> **NOTE** The day of the week considered "first" is locale-specific and depends on the DATEFIRST setting.

SQL Server 2000 also allows you to add or subtract an integer to or from a *datetime* value. This is actually just a shortcut for the DATEADD function, with a *datepart* of *day*. For example, the following two queries are equivalent. They each return the date 14 days from today:

```
SELECT DATEADD(day, 14, GETDATE())

SELECT GETDATE() + 14
```

The date functions don't do any rounding. The DATEDIFF function just subtracts the components from each date that correspond to the *datepart* specified. For example, to find the number of years between New Year's Day and New Year's Eve of the same year, this query would return a value of 0. Because the *datepart* specifies years, SQL Server subtracts the year part of the two dates, and because they're the same, the result of subtracting them is 0:

```
SELECT DATEDIFF(yy, 'Jan 1, 1998', 'Dec 31, 1998')
```

However, if we want to find the difference in years between New Year's Eve of one year and New Year's Day (the next day), the following query would return a value of 1 because the difference in the year part is 1:

```
SELECT DATEDIFF(yy, 'Dec 31, 1998', 'Jan 1, 1999')
```

There's no built-in mechanism for determining whether two date values are actually the same day unless you've forced all *datetime* values to use the default time of midnight. (We saw a technique for doing this earlier.) If you want to compare two *datetime* values (@date1 and @date2) to determine whether they're on the same day, regardless of the time, one technique is to use a three-part condition like this:

```
IF (DATEPART(mm, @date1) = DATEPART(mm, @date2)) AND
   (DATEPART(dd, @date1) = DATEPART(dd, @date2)) AND
```

(continued)

```
(DATEPART(yy, @date1) = DATEPART(yy, @date2))
PRINT 'The dates are the same'
```

But there is a much simpler way. Even though these two queries both return the same *dd* value, if we try to find the difference in days between these two dates, SQL Server is smart enough to know that they are different dates:

```
SELECT DATEPART(dd, '7/5/99')
SELECT DATEPART(dd, '7/5/00')
```

So, the following query returns the message that the dates are different:

```
IF DATEDIFF(dd, '7/5/99','7/5/00') = 0
    PRINT 'The dates are the same'
ELSE PRINT 'The dates are different'
```

And the following general form allows us to indicate whether two dates are really the same date, irrespective of the time:

```
IF DATEDIFF(day, @date1, @date2) = 0
    PRINT 'The dates are the same'
```

Math Functions

Transact-SQL math functions are straightforward and typical. Many are specialized and of the type you learned about in trigonometry class. If you don't have an engineering or mathematical application, you probably won't use those. A handful of math functions are useful in general types of queries in applications that aren't mathematical in nature. ABS, CEILING, FLOOR, and ROUND are the most useful functions for general queries to find values within a certain range.

The random number function, RAND, is useful for generating test data or conditions. You'll see examples of RAND later in this chapter.

Table 10-13 shows the complete list of math functions and a few simple examples. Some of the examples use other functions in addition to the math ones to illustrate how to use functions within functions.

Function	*Parameters*	*Result*
ABS	(*numeric_expr*)	Absolute value of the numeric expression. Results returned are of the same type as *numeric_expr*.
ACOS	(*float_expr*)	Angle (in radians) whose cosine is the specified approximate numeric (*float*) expression.
ASIN	(*float_expr*)	Angle (in radians) whose sine is the specified approximate numeric (*float*) expression.

Table 10-13. *Math functions in Transact-SQL.*

(continued)

Function	Parameters	Result
ATAN	(*float_expr*)	Angle (in radians) whose tangent is the specified approximate numeric (*float*) expression.
ATN2	(*float_expr1*, *float_expr2*)	Angle (in radians) whose tangent is (*float_expr1/float_expr2*) between two approximate numeric (*float*) expressions.
CEILING	(*numeric_expr*)	Smallest integer greater than or equal to the numeric expression. Result returned is the integer portion of the same type as *numeric_expr*.
COS	(*float_expr*)	Trigonometric cosine of the specified angle (in radians) in an approximate numeric (*float*) expression.
COT	(*float_expr*)	Trigonometric cotangent of the specified angle (in radians) in an approximate numeric (*float*) expression.
DEGREES	(*numeric_expr*)	Degrees converted from radians of the numeric expression. Results are of the same type as *numeric_expr*.
EXP	(*float_expr*)	Exponential value of the specified approximate numeric (*float*) expression.
FLOOR	(*numeric_expr*)	Largest integer less than or equal to the specified numeric expression. Result is the integer portion of the same type as *numeric_expr*.
LOG	(*float_expr*)	Natural logarithm of the specified approximate numeric (*float*) expression.
LOG10	(*float_expr*)	Base-10 logarithm of the specified approximate numeric (*float*) expression.
PI	( )	Constant value of 3.141592653589793.
POWER	(*numeric_expr*, *y*)	Value of numeric expression to the power of *y*, where *y* is a numeric datatype (*bigint, decimal, float, int, money, numeric, real, smallint, smallmoney,* or *tinyint*). Result is of the same type as *numeric_expr*.
RADIANS	(*numeric_expr*)	Radians converted from degrees of the numeric expression. Result is of the same type as *numeric_expr*.
RAND	([*seed*])	Random approximate numeric (*float*) value between 0 and 1, optionally specifying an integer expression as the seed.

(continued)

Table 10-13. *continued*

Function	Parameters	Result
ROUND	(*numeric_expr, length*)	Numeric expression rounded off to the length (or precision) specified as an integer expression (*bigint, tinyint, smallint,* or *int*). Result is of the same type as *numeric_expr*. ROUND always returns a value even if *length* is illegal. If the specified length is positive and longer than the digits after the decimal point, 0 is added after the fraction digits. If the length is negative and larger than or equal to the digits before the decimal point, ROUND returns 0.00.
SIGN	(*numeric_expr*)	Returns the positive (+1), zero (0), or negative (−1) sign of the numeric expression. Result is of the same type as *numeric_expr*.
SIN	(*float_expr*)	Trigonometric sine of the specified angle (measured in radians) in an approximate numeric (*float*) expression.
SQRT	(*float_expr*)	Square root of the specified approximate numeric (*float*) expression.
SQUARE	(*float_expr*)	Square of the specified approximate numeric (*float*) expression.
TAN	(*float_expr*)	Trigonometric tangent of the specified angle (measured in radians) in an approximate numeric (*float*) expression.

The following examples show some of the math functions at work.

EXAMPLE 1

Produce a table with the sine, cosine, and tangent of all angles in multiples of 10, from 0 through 180. Format the return value as a string of eight characters, with the value rounded to five decimal places. (We need one character for the decimal point and one for a negative sign, if needed.)

```
DECLARE @degrees smallint
DECLARE @radians float
SELECT @degrees=0
SELECT @radians=0
WHILE (@degrees <= 180)
BEGIN
    SELECT
```

```
       DEGREES=@degrees,
       RADIANS=STR(@radians, 8, 5),
       SINE=STR(SIN(@radians), 8, 5),
       COSINE=STR(COS(@radians), 8, 5),
       TANGENT=STR(TAN(@radians), 8, 5)
       SELECT @degrees=@degrees + 10
       SELECT @radians=RADIANS(CONVERT(float, @degrees))
END
```

NOTE This example actually produces 19 different result sets because the SELECT statement is issued once for each iteration of the loop. These separate result sets are concatenated and appear as one result set in this example. That works fine for illustrative purposes, but you should avoid doing an operation like this in the real world, especially on a slow network. Each result set carries with it metadata to describe itself to the client application. I'll show you a better technique later in the chapter.

And here are the results concatenated as a single table:

```
DEGREES RADIANS SINE    COSINE  TANGENT
------- ------- ------- ------- -------
0       0.00000 0.00000 1.00000 0.00000

10      0.17453 0.17365 0.98481 0.17633

20      0.34907 0.34202 0.93969 0.36397

30      0.52360 0.50000 0.86603 0.57735

40      0.69813 0.64279 0.76604 0.83910

50      0.87266 0.76604 0.64279 1.19175

60      1.04720 0.86603 0.50000 1.73205

70      1.22173 0.93969 0.34202 2.74748

80      1.39626 0.98481 0.17365 5.67128

90      1.57080 1.00000 0.00000 *******

100     1.74533 0.98481 -0.1736 -5.6713

110     1.91986 0.93969 -0.3420 -2.7475

120     2.09440 0.86603 -0.5000 -1.7321

130     2.26893 0.76604 -0.6428 -1.1918
```

(continued)

```
140      2.44346 0.64279 -0.7660 -0.8391

150      2.61799 0.50000 -0.8660 -0.5774

160      2.79253 0.34202 -0.9397 -0.3640

170      2.96706 0.17365 -0.9848 -0.1763

3.14159 0.00000 -1.0000 -0.0000
```

EXAMPLE 2

Express in whole-dollar terms the range of prices (non-null) of all books in the *titles* table. This example combines the scalar functions FLOOR and CEILING inside the aggregate functions MIN and MAX:

```
SELECT 'Low End'=MIN(FLOOR(price)),
    'High End'=MAX(CEILING(price))
FROM titles
```

And the result:

```
Low End    High End
-------    --------
2.00       23.00
```

EXAMPLE 3

Use the same *records* table that was used in the earlier date functions example. Find all records within 150 days of September 30, 1997. Without the absolute value function ABS, you would have to use BETWEEN or provide two search conditions and AND them to account for both 150 days before and 150 days after that date. ABS lets you easily reduce that to a single search condition.

```
SELECT Record_number, Entered_on
FROM records
WHERE
ABS(DATEDIFF(DAY, Entered_on, '1997.09.30')) <= 150
-- Plus or minus 150 days
```

String Functions

String functions make it easier to work with character data. They let you slice and dice character data, search it, format it, and alter it. Like other scalar functions, string functions allow you to perform functions directly in your search conditions and SQL batches that would otherwise need to be returned to the calling application for further processing. (Also, remember the concatenation operator, +, for concatenating strings. You'll use this operator often in conjunction with the string functions.)

The string functions appear in Table 10-14. For more detailed information, consult the online documentation.

Function	Parameters	Result
ASCII	(*char_expr*)	Indicates the numeric code value of the leftmost character of a character expression.
CHAR	(*integer_expr*)	Returns the character represented by the ASCII code. The ASCII code should be a value from 0 through 255; otherwise, NULL is returned.
CHARINDEX	('*pattern*', *expression*)	Returns the starting position of the specified exact pattern. A *pattern* is a *char_expr*. The second parameter is an *expression*, usually a column name, in which SQL Server searches for *pattern*.
DIFFERENCE	(*char_expr1*, *char_expr2*)	Shows the difference between the values of two character expressions as returned by the SOUNDEX function. DIFFERENCE compares two strings and evaluates the similarity between them, returning a value 0 through 4. The value 4 is the best match.
LEFT	(*char_expression*, *int_expression*)	Returns *int_expression* characters from the left of the *char_expression*.
LEN	(*char_expression*)	Returns the number of characters, rather than the number of bytes, of *char_expression*, excluding trailing blanks.
LOWER	(*char_expr*)	Converts uppercase character data to lowercase.
LTRIM	(*char_expr*)	Removes leading blanks.
NCHAR	(*int_expression*)	Returns the Unicode character with code *int_expression*, as defined by the Unicode standard.
PATINDEX	('*%pattern%*', *expression*)	Returns the starting position of the first occurrence of *pattern* in the specified expression or 0 if the pattern isn't found.
QUOTENAME	QUOTENAME ('*char_string*' [,'*quote_character*'])	Returns a Unicode string with *quote_character* used as the delimiter to make the input string a valid SQL Server delimited identifier.
REPLACE	('*char_expression1*', '*char_expression2*', '*char_expression3*')	Replaces all occurrences of *char_expression2* in *char_expression1* with *char_expression3*.

Table 10-14. *String functions in Transact-SQL.*   *(continued)*

Table 10-14. *continued*

Function	Parameters	Result
REPLICATE	(*char_expr*, *integer_expr*)	Repeats a character expression a specified number of times. If *integer_expr* is negative, NULL is returned.
REVERSE	(*char_expr*)	Returns the *char_expr* backwards. This function takes a constant, variable, or column as its parameter.
RIGHT	(*char_expr*, *integer_expr*)	Returns part of a character string starting *integer_expr* characters from the right. If *integer_expr* is negative, NULL is returned.
RTRIM	(*char_expr*)	Removes trailing blanks.
SOUNDEX	(*char_expr*)	Returns a four-character (SOUNDEX) of two strings. The SOUNDEX function converts an alpha string to a four-digit code used to find similar-sounding words or names.
SPACE	(*integer_expr*)	Returns a string of repeated spaces. The number of spaces is equal to *integer_expr*. If *integer_expr* is negative, NULL is returned.
STR	(*float_expr* [, *length* [,*decimal*]])	Returns character data converted from numeric data. The *length* is the total length, including decimal point, sign, digits, and spaces. The *decimal* value is the number of spaces to the right of the decimal point.
STUFF	(*char_expr1*, *start*, *length*, *char_expr2*)	Deletes *length* characters from *char_expr1* at *start* and then inserts *char_expr2* into *char_expr1* at *start*.
SUBSTRING	(*expression*, *start*, *length*)	Returns part of a character or binary string. The first parameter can be a character or binary string, a column name, or an expression that includes a column name. The second parameter specifies where the substring begins. The third parameter specifies the number of characters in the substring.
UNICODE	('*nchar_expression*')	Returns the integer value, as defined by the Unicode standard, for the first character of *nchar_expression*.
UPPER	(*char_expr*)	Converts lowercase character data to uppercase.

ASCII and CHAR functions   The function name ASCII is really a bit of a misnomer. ASCII is only a 7-bit character set and hence can deal with only 128 characters. The character parameter to this function doesn't need to be an ASCII character. The ASCII function returns the code point for the character set associated with the database or the column if the argument to the function is a column from a table. The return value can be from 0 through 255. For example, if the current database is using a Latin-1 character set, the following statement returns 196, even though the character *Ä* isn't an ASCII character:

```
SELECT ASCII('Ä')
```

The CHAR function is handy for generating test data, especially when combined with RAND and REPLICATE. CHAR is also commonly used for inserting control characters such as tabs and carriage returns into your character string. Suppose, for example, that we want to return authors' last names and first names concatenated as a single field, but with a carriage return (0x0D, or decimal 13) separating them so that without further manipulation in our application, the names occupy two lines when displayed. The CHAR function makes this simple:

```
SELECT 'NAME'=au_fname + CHAR(13) + au_lname
FROM authors
```

Here's the abbreviated result:

```
NAME
--------
Johnson
White
Marjorie
Green
Cheryl
Carson
Michael
O'Leary
Dean
Straight
Meander
Smith
Abraham
Bennet
Ann
Dull
```

UPPER and LOWER functions   These functions are useful if you must perform case-insensitive searches on data that is case sensitive. The following example copies the *authors* table from the *pubs* database into a new table, using a case-sensitive collation for the authors' name fields.

```
SELECT au_id,
       au_lname = au_lname  collate Latin1_General_CS_AS,
       au_fname = au_fname  collate Latin1_General_CS_AS,
      phone, address, city, state, zip, contract
INTO authors_CS
FROM authors
```

This query finds no rows in the new table even though author name Cheryl Carson is included in that table:

```
SELECT COUNT(*) FROM authors_CS WHERE au_lname='CARSON'
```

If we change the query to the following, the row will be found:

```
SELECT COUNT(*) FROM authors_CS WHERE UPPER(au_lname)='CARSON'
```

If the value to be searched might be of mixed case, you need to use the function on both sides of the equation. This query will find the row in the case-sensitive table:

```
DECLARE @name_param varchar(30)
SELECT @name_param='cArSoN'
SELECT COUNT(*) FROM authors_CS WHERE UPPER(au_lname)=UPPER(@name_param)
```

In these examples, even though we might have an index on *au_lname,* it won't be useful because the index keys aren't uppercase. However, we could create a computed column on *UPPER(au_lname)* and build an index on the computed column, as described in Chapter 8. In Chapter 15, I'll show you how you can tell if such an index is being used.

You'll also often want to use UPPER or LOWER in stored procedures in which character parameters are used. For example, in a procedure that expects *Y* or *N* as a parameter, you'll likely want to use one of these functions in case *y* is entered instead of *Y*.

TRIM functions   The functions LTRIM and RTRIM are handy for dealing with leading or trailing blanks. Recall that by default (and if you don't enable the ANSI_PADDING setting) a *varchar* datatype is automatically right-trimmed of blanks, but a fixed-length *char* isn't. Suppose that we want to concatenate the *type* column and the *title_id* column from the *titles* table, with a colon separating them but with no blanks. The following query doesn't work because the trailing blanks are retained from the *type* column:

```
SELECT type + ':' + title_id FROM titles
```

Here's the result (in part):

```
business    :BU1032
business    :BU1111
business    :BU2075
```

```
business    :BU7832
mod_cook    :MC2222
mod_cook    :MC3021
UNDECIDED   :MC3026
popular_comp:PC1035
popular_comp:PC8888
popular_comp:PC9999
```

But RTRIM returns what we want:

```
SELECT RTRIM(type) + ':' + title_id FROM titles
```

And here's the result (in part):

```
business:BU1032
business:BU1111
business:BU2075
business:BU7832
mod_cook:MC2222
mod_cook:MC3021
UNDECIDED:MC3026
popular_comp:PC1035
popular_comp:PC8888
popular_comp:PC9999
```

String manipulation functions Functions are useful for searching and manipulating partial strings that include SUBSTRING, CHARINDEX, PATINDEX, STUFF, REPLACE, REVERSE, and REPLICATE. CHARINDEX and PATINDEX are similar, but CHARINDEX demands an exact match and PATINDEX works with a regular expression search.

> **NOTE** You can also use CHARINDEX or PATINDEX as a replacement for LIKE. For example, instead of saying *WHERE name LIKE '%Smith%'*, you can say *WHERE CHARINDEX('Smith', name) > 0*.

Suppose I want to change occurrences of the word "computer" within the *notes* field of the *titles* table and replace it with "Hi-Tech Computers." Assume that SQL Server is case sensitive and, for simplicity, that I know that "computer" won't appear more than once per column. I want to be careful that the plural form, "computers," isn't also changed. I can't just rely on searching on "computer" with a trailing blank because the word might fall at the end of the sentence followed by a period or be followed by a comma. The regular expression *computer[^s]* always finds the word "computer" and ignores "computers," so it'll work perfectly with PATINDEX.

Here's the data before the change:

```
SELECT title_id, notes
FROM titles
WHERE notes LIKE '%[Cc]omputer%'
```

(continued)

title_id	notes
BU7832	Annotated analysis of what computers can do for you: a no-hype guide for the critical user.
PC8888	Muckraking reporting on the world's largest computer hardware and software manufacturers.
PC9999	A must-read for computer conferencing.
PS1372	A must for the specialist, this book examines the difference between those who hate and fear computers and those who don't.
PS7777	Protecting yourself and your loved ones from undue emotional stress in the modern world. Use of computer and nutritional aids emphasized.

You might consider using the REPLACE function to make the substitution. However, REPLACE requires that we search for a specific string that can't include wildcards like *[^s]*. Instead, we can use the older STUFF function, which has a slightly more complex syntax. STUFF requires that we specify the starting location within the string to make a substitution. We can use PATINDEX to find the correct starting location, and PATINDEX allows wildcards:

```
UPDATE titles
SET notes=STUFF(notes, PATINDEX('%computer[^s]%', notes),
    DATALENGTH('computer'), 'Hi-Tech Computers')
WHERE PATINDEX('%computer[^s]%', notes) > 0
```

Here's the data after the change:

```
SELECT title_id, notes
FROM titles
WHERE notes LIKE '%[Cc]omputer%'
```

title_id	notes
BU7832	Annotated analysis of what computers can do for you: a no-hype guide for the critical user.
PC8888	Muckraking reporting on the world's largest Hi-Tech Computers hardware and software manufacturers.
PC9999	A must-read for Hi-Tech Computers conferencing.
PS1372	A must for the specialist, this book examines the difference between those who hate and fear computers and those who don't.
PS7777	Protecting yourself and your loved ones from undue emotional stress in the modern world. Use of Hi-Tech Computers and nutritional aids emphasized.

Of course, we could have simply provided 8 as the *length* parameter of the string "computer" to be replaced. But we used yet another function, LEN, which would be more realistic if we were creating a general-purpose, search-and-replace procedure.

Note that DATALENGTH returns NULL if the expression is NULL, so in your applications, you might go one step further and use DATALENGTH inside the ISNULL function to return 0 in the case of NULL.

The REPLICATE function is useful for adding filler characters—such as for test data. (In fact, generating test data seems to be about the only practical use for this function.) The SPACE function is a special-purpose version of REPLICATE: it's identical to using REPLICATE with the space character. REVERSE reverses a character string. You can use REVERSE in a few cases to store and, more importantly, to index a character column backward to get more selectivity from the index. But in general, these three functions are rarely used.

SOUNDEX and DIFFERENCE Functions

If you've ever wondered how telephone operators are able to give you telephone numbers so quickly when you call directory assistance, chances are they're using a SOUNDEX algorithm. The SOUNDEX and DIFFERENCE functions let you search on character strings that sound similar when spoken. SOUNDEX converts each string to a four-character code. DIFFERENCE can then be used to evaluate the level of similarity between the SOUNDEX values for two strings as returned by SOUNDEX. For example, you could use these functions to look at all rows that sound like "Erickson," and they would find "Erickson," "Erikson," "Ericson," "Ericksen," "Ericsen," and so on.

SOUNDEX algorithms are commonplace in the database business, but the exact implementation can vary from vendor to vendor. For SQL Server's SOUNDEX function, the first character of the four-character SOUNDEX code is the first letter of the word, and the remaining three characters are single digits that describe the phonetic value of the first three consonants of the word with the underlying assumption that there's one consonant per syllable. Identical consonants right next to each other are treated as a single consonant. Only nine phonetic values are possible in this scheme because only nine possible digits exist. SOUNDEX relies on phonetic similarities between sounds to group consonants together. In fact, SQL Server's SOUNDEX algorithm uses only seven of the possible nine digits. No SOUNDEX code uses the digits 8 or 9.

Vowels are ignored, as are the characters *h* and *y*, so "Zastrak" would have the same code as "Zasituryk." If no second or subsequent consonant exists, the phonetic value for it is 0. In addition, SQL Server's SOUNDEX algorithm stops evaluating the string as soon as the first nonalphabetic character is found. So if you have a hyphenated or two-word name (with a space in between), SOUNDEX ignores the second part of the name. More seriously, SOUNDEX stops processing names as soon as it finds an apostrophe. So "O'Flaherty," "O'Leary," and "O'Hara" all have the same SOUNDEX code, namely O000.

DIFFERENCE internally compares two SOUNDEX values and returns a score from 0 through 4 to indicate how close the match is. A score of 4 is the best match, and 0 means no matches were found. Executing *DIFFERENCE(a1, a2)* first generates the four-character SOUNDEX values for a1 (call it *sx_a1*) and a2 (call it *sx_a2*). Then, if all four values of the SOUNDEX value *sx_a2* match the values of *sx_a1*, the match is perfect and the level is 4. Note that this compares the SOUNDEX values by character position, not by actual characters.

For example, the names "Smythe" and "Smith" both have a SOUNDEX value of S530, so their difference level is 4, even though the spellings differ. If the first character (a letter, not a number) of the SOUNDEX value *sx_a1* is the same as the first character of *sx_a2*, the starting level is 1. If the first character is different, the starting level is 0. Then each character in *sx_a2* is successively compared to all characters in *sx_a1*. When a match is found, the level is incremented and the next scan on *sx_a1* starts from the location of the match. If no match is found, the next *sx_a2* character is compared to the entire four-character list of *sx_a1*.

The preceding description of the algorithms should make it clear that SOUNDEX at best provides an approximation. Even so, sometimes it works extremely well. Suppose we want to query the *authors* table for names that sound similar to "Larsen." We'll define *similar* to mean "having a SOUNDEX value of 3 or 4":

```
SELECT au_lname,
Soundex=SOUNDEX(au_lname),
Diff_Larsen=DIFFERENCE(au_lname, 'Larson')
FROM authors
WHERE
DIFFERENCE(au_lname, 'Larson') >= 3
```

Here's the result:

```
au_lname    Soundex    Diff_Larsen
--------    -------    -----------
Carson      C625       3
Karsen      K625       3
```

In this case, we found two names that rhyme with "Larsen" and didn't get any bad hits of names that don't seem close. Sometimes you'll get odd results, but if you follow the algorithms I've described, you'll understand how these oddities occur. For example, do you think "Bennet" and "Smith" sound similar? Well, SOUNDEX does. When you investigate, you can see why the two names have a similar SOUNDEX value. The SOUNDEX values have a different first letter, but the *m* and *n* sounds are converted to the same digit, and both names include a *t*, which is converted to a digit for the third position. "Bennet" has nothing to put in the fourth position, so it gets a 0. For Smith, the *h* becomes a 0. So, except for the initial letter, the rest of the SOUNDEX strings are the same. Hence, the match.

This type of situation happens often with SOUNDEX—you get hits on values that don't seem close, although usually you won't miss the ones that are similar. So if you query the *authors* table for similar values (with a DIFFERENCE value of 3 or

4) as "Smythe," you get a perfect hit on "Smith" as you'd expect, but you also get a close match for "Bennet," which is far from obvious:

```
SELECT au_lname,
Soundex=SOUNDEX(au_lname),
Diff_Smythe=DIFFERENCE(au_lname, 'Smythe')
FROM authors
WHERE
DIFFERENCE(au_lname, 'Smythe') >= 3
```

```
au_lname    Soundex    Diff_Smythe
--------    -------    -----------
Smith       S530       4
Bennet      B530       3
```

Sometimes SOUNDEX misses close matches altogether. This happens when consonant blends are present. For example, you might expect to get a close match between "Knight" and "Nite." But you get a low value of 1 in the DIFFERENCE between the two:

```
SELECT
"SX_KNIGHT"=SOUNDEX('Knight'),
"SX_NITE"=SOUNDEX('Nite'),
"DIFFERENCE"=DIFFERENCE('Nite', 'Knight')
```

```
SX_KNIGHT    SX_NITE    DIFFERENCE
---------    -------    ----------
K523         N300       1
```

System Functions

System functions are most useful for returning certain metadata, security, or configuration settings. Table 10-15 lists of some of the more commonly used system functions, and it's followed by a brief discussion of the interesting features of a few of them. For complete details, see the SQL Server online documentation.

Function	Parameters	Description
APP_NAME	NONE	Returns the program name for the current connection if one has been set by the program before you log on.
COALESCE	(*expression1, expression2, ... expressionN*)	A specialized form of the CASE statement. Returns the first non-null expression.
COL_LENGTH	('*table_name*', '*column_name*')	The defined (maximum) storage length of a column.

Table 10-15. *System functions in Transact-SQL.*   *(continued)*

Table 10-15. *continued*

Function	Parameters	Description
COL_NAME	(*table_id, column_id*)	The name of the column.
DATALENGTH	('*expression*')	The length of an expression of any datatype.
DB_ID	(['*database_name*'])	The database identification number.
DB_NAME	([*database_id*])	The database name.
GETANSINULL	(['*database_name*'])	The default nullability for the database. Returns 1 when the nullability is the ANSI NULL default.
HOST_ID	NONE	The process ID of the application calling SQL Server on the workstation. (If you look at the PID column on the Processes tab in Windows Task Manager, you will see this number associated with the client application.)
HOST_NAME	NONE	The workstation name.
IDENT_INCR	('*table_or_view*')	The increment value specified during creation of an identity column of a table or view that includes an identity column.
IDENT_SEED	('*table_or_view*')	The seed value specified during creation of an identity column of a table or view that includes an identity column.
INDEX_COL	('*table_name*', *index_id, key_id*)	The indexed column names.
ISDATE	(*expression_of_possible_date*)	Checks whether an expression is a *datetime* datatype or a string in a recognizable *datetime* format. Returns 1 when the expression is compatible with the *datetime* type; otherwise, returns 0.
ISNULL	(*expression, value*)	Replaces NULL entries with the specified value.

(continued)

Function	Parameters	Description
ISNUMERIC	(*expression_of_possible_ number*)	Checks whether an expression is a numeric datatype or a string in a recognizable number format. Returns 1 when the expression is compatible with arithmetic operations; otherwise, returns 0.
NULLIF	(*expression1, expression2*)	A specialized form of CASE. The resulting expression is NULL when *expression1* is equivalent to *expression2*.
OBJECT_ID	('*object_name*')	The database object identification number.
OBJECT_NAME	(*object_id*)	The database object name.
STATS_DATE	(*table_id, index_id*)	The date when statistics for the specified index (*index_id*) were last updated.
SUSER_SID	(['*login_name*'])	The security identification number (SID) for the user's login name.
SUSER_SNAME	([*server_user_sid*])	The login identification name from a user's security identification number (SID).
USER_ID	(['*user_name*'])	The user's database ID number.
USER_NAME	([*user_id*])	The user's database username.

The DATALENGTH function is most often used with variable-length data, especially character strings, and it tells you the actual storage length of the expression (typically a column name). A fixed-length datatype always returns the storage size of its defined type (which is also its actual storage size), which makes it identical to COL_LENGTH for such a column. The DATALENGTH of any NULL expression returns NULL. The OBJECT_ID, OBJECT_NAME, SUSER_SNAME, SUSER_SID, USER_ID, USER_NAME, COL_NAME, DB_ID, and DB_NAME functions are commonly used to more easily eliminate the need for joins between system catalogs and to get run-time information dynamically.

For example, recognizing that an object name is unique within a database for a specific user, we can use the following statement to determine whether an object by the name "foo" exists for our current user ID; if so, we can drop the object (assuming that we know it's a table).

```
IF (SELECT id FROM sysobjects WHERE id=OBJECT_ID('foo')
    AND uid=USER_ID() AND type='U') > 0
    DROP TABLE foo
```

System functions can be handy with constraints and views. Recall that a view can benefit from the use of system functions. For example, if the *accounts* table includes a column that is the system login ID of the user to whom the account belongs, we can create a view of the table that allows the user to work only with his or her own accounts. We do this simply by making the WHERE clause of the view something like this:

```
WHERE system_login_id=SUSER_SID()
```

Or if we want to ensure that updates on a table occur only from an application named CS_UPDATE.EXE, we can use a CHECK constraint in the following way:

```
CONSTRAINT APP_CHECK(APP_NAME()='CS_UPDATE.EXE')
```

For this particular example, the check is by no means foolproof because the application must set the *app_name* in its login record. A rogue application could simply lie. To prevent casual use by someone running an application like ISQL.EXE, the preceding constraint might be just fine for your needs. But if you're worried about hackers, this formulation isn't appropriate. Other functions, such as SUSER_SID, have no analogous way to be explicitly set, so they're better for security operations such as this.

The ISDATE and ISNUMERIC functions can be useful for determining whether data is appropriate for an operation. For example, suppose your predecessor didn't know much about using a relational database and defined a column as type *char* and then stored values in it that were naturally of type *money*. Then she compounded the problem by sometimes encoding letter codes in the same field as notes. You're trying to work with the data as is (eventually you'll clean it up, but you have a deadline to meet), and you need to get a sum and average of all the values whenever a value that makes sense to use is present. (If you think this example is contrived, talk to a programmer in an MIS shop of a Fortune 1000 company with legacy applications.) Suppose the table has a *varchar(20)* column named *acct_bal* with these values:

```
acct_bal
--------
205.45
E
(NULL)
B
605.78
32.45
```

```
8
98.45
64.23
8456.3
```

If you try to simply use the aggregate functions directly, you'll get error 409:

```
SELECT SUM(acct_bal). AVG(acct_bal)
FROM bad_column_for_money

MSG 235, Level 16, State 0
Cannot covert CHAR value to MONEY. The CHAR value has incorrect
syntax.
```

But if you use both CONVERT in the select list and ISNUMERIC in the WHERE clause to choose only those values for which a conversion would be possible, everything works great:

```
SELECT
"SUM"=SUM(CONVERT(money, acct_bal)),
"AVG"=AVG(CONVERT(money, acct_bal))
FROM bad_column_for_money
WHERE ISNUMERIC(acct_bal)=1

SUM        AVG
--------   --------
9,470      1.352.95
```

Metadata Functions

In earlier versions of SQL Server, the only way to determine which options or properties an object had was to actually query a system table and possibly even decode a bitmap *status* column. SQL Server 2000 provides a set of functions that return information about databases, files, filegroups, indexes, objects, and datatypes.

For example, to determine what recovery model a database is using, you can use the DATABASEPROPERTYEX function:

```
IF DATABASEPROPERTYEX('pubs', 'Recovery') <> 'SIMPLE'
    /*run a command to backup the transaction log */
```

Many of the properties that you can check for using either of the functions DATABASEPROPERTY and DATABASEPROPERTYEX correspond to database options that you can set using the *sp_dboption* stored procedure. One example is the AUTO_CLOSE option, which determines the value of the IsAutoClose property. Other properties, such as IsInStandBy, are set internally by SQL Server. For a complete list of all the possible database properties and their possible values, please see the SQL Server documentation. The documentation also provides the complete list of properties and possible values for use with the functions on the following page.

- COLUMNPROPERTY
- FILEGROUPPROPERTY
- FILEPROPERTY
- INDEXPROPERTY
- OBJECTPROPERTY
- TYPEPROPERTY

Niladic Functions

ANSI SQL-92 has a handful of what it calls *niladic* functions—a fancy name for functions that don't accept any parameters. Niladic functions were first implemented in version 6, and each one maps directly to one of SQL Server's system functions. They were actually added to SQL Server 6 for conformance with the ANSI SQL-92 standard; all of their functionality was already provided, however. Table 10-16 lists the niladic functions and their equivalent SQL Server system functions.

Niladic Function	Equivalent SQL Server System Function
CURRENT_TIMESTAMP	GETDATE
SYSTEM_USER	SUSER_SNAME
CURRENT_USER	USER_NAME
SESSION_USER	USER_NAME
USER	USER_NAME

Table 10-16. *Niladic functions and their equivalent SQL Server functions.*

If you execute the following two SELECT statements, you'll see that they return identical results:

```
SELECT CURRENT_TIMESTAMP, USER, SYSTEM_USER, CURRENT_USER,
SESSION_USER

SELECT GETDATE(), USER_NAME(), SUSER_SNAME(),
USER_NAME(), USER_NAME()
```

Other Parameterless Functions

As I mentioned earlier in the chapter, the older SQL Server documentation refers to a set of parameterless system functions as *global variables* because they're designated by @@, which is similar to the designation for local variables. However, these values aren't variables because you can't declare them and you can't assign them values.

These functions are global only in the sense that any connection can access their values. However, in many cases, the value returned by these functions is specific to the connection. For example, @@ERROR represents the last error number generated for a specific connection, not the last error number in the entire system. @@ROWCOUNT represents the number of rows selected or affected by the last statement for the current connection.

Many of these parameterless system functions keep track of performance-monitoring information for your SQL Server. These functions include @@CPU_BUSY, @@IO_BUSY, @@PACK_SENT, and @@PACK_RECEIVED.

Some of these functions are extremely static, and others are extremely volatile. For example, @@VERSION represents the build number and code freeze date of the SQL Server executable (Sqlservr.exe) that you're running. It will change only when you upgrade or apply a service pack. Functions like @@ROWCOUNT are extremely volatile. Take a look at the following code and its results.

```
USE pubs
SELECT * FROM publishers
SELECT @@ROWCOUNT
SELECT @@ROWCOUNT
```

Here are the results:

```
pub_id  pub_name                 city                    state country
------  ------------------------ ----------------------- ----- ----------
0736    New Moon Books           Boston                  MA    USA
0877    Binnet & Hardley         Washington              DC    USA
1389    Algodata Infosystems     Berkeley                CA    USA
1622    Five Lakes Publishing    Chicago                 IL    USA
1756    Ramona Publishers        Dallas                  TX    USA
9901    GGG&G                    München                 NULL  Germany
9952    Scootney Books           New York                NY    USA
9999    Lucerne Publishing       Paris                   NULL  France

(8 row(s) affected)


-----------
8

(1 row(s) affected)


-----------
1

(1 row(s) affected)
```

Note that the first time @@ROWCOUNT was selected, it returned the number of rows in the *publishers* table (8). The second time @@ROWCOUNT was selected, it returned the number of rows returned by the previous SELECT @@ROWCOUNT (1). Any query you execute that affects rows will change the value of @@ROWCOUNT. For the complete list of parameterless functions, refer to the SQL Server documentation.

Table-Valued Functions

SQL Server 2000 provides a set of system functions that return tables; because of this, the functions can appear in the FROM clause of a query. To invoke these functions, you must use the special signifier `::` as a prefix to the function name and then omit any database or owner name. Several of these table-valued functions return information about traces you have defined, and I'll talk about those functions in Chapter 17 when I discuss SQL Profiler. Another one of the functions can also be useful during monitoring and tuning, as shown in this example:

```
SELECT *
FROM ::fn_virtualfilestats(5,1)
```

The function *fn_virtualfilestats* takes two parameters, a database ID and a file ID, and it returns statistical information about the I/O on the file. Here is some sample output from running this query on the *pubs* database:

```
                         Number Number Bytes   Bytes
DbId FileId TimeStamp    Reads  Writes Read    Written IoStallMS
---- ------ ---------    ------ ------ ------- ------- ---------

5    1      38140863     44     0      360448  0       3164
```

Because the function returns a table, you can control the result set by limiting it to only certain columns or to rows that meet certain conditions. As another example, the function *fn_helpcollations* lists all the collations supported by SQL Server 2000. An unqualified SELECT from this function would return 753 rows in two columns. If I just want the names of all the SQL Collations that are case insensitive, have no preference, and are based on the Latin1 character set, I can issue the following query, which returns only 14 rows:

```
SELECT name
FROM ::fn_helpcollations()
WHERE name LIKE 'SQL%latin%CI%'
    AND name NOT LIKE '%pref%'

RESULT:
name
----------------------------------------
SQL_Latin1_General_CP1_CI_AI
SQL_Latin1_General_CP1_CI_AS
SQL_Latin1_General_CP1250_CI_AS
SQL_Latin1_General_CP1251_CI_AS
SQL_Latin1_General_CP1253_CI_AI
SQL_Latin1_General_CP1253_CI_AS
SQL_Latin1_General_CP1254_CI_AS
SQL_Latin1_General_CP1255_CI_AS
SQL_Latin1_General_CP1256_CI_AS
SQL_Latin1_General_CP1257_CI_AS
```

```
SQL_Latin1_General_CP437_CI_AI
SQL_Latin1_General_CP437_CI_AS
SQL_Latin1_General_CP850_CI_AI
SQL_Latin1_General_CP850_CI_AS
```

TRANSACT-SQL
EXAMPLES AND BRAINTEASERS

In this section, we'll look at some relatively common programming tasks that aren't as simple as you might think. If you find a solution here for something you need to do, that's great. But the real goal is to give you some insight into the power and flexibility of Transact-SQL. For some examples, I'll offer multiple solutions, often with different performance characteristics. Keep in mind that there are often many ways to solve a problem, and you can find more examples similar to the ones I present here in some of the SQL programming books listed in the bibliography.

Generating Test Data

There is actually nothing particularly tricky to generating test data, but because generating test data is a common need and some of the later solutions depend on test data, we'll look at a few simple techniques. Of course, it's preferable to use an actual dataset of representative values for testing rather than generated test data before you deploy a production application. But sometimes it's more practical to generate test data when you need something quick and dirty.

If you need a bunch of rows and you don't care about the distribution of values, you can easily create a table using default values for every column and the Identity property on a column that will act as the primary key. You can then set a counter to loop as many times as necessary to achieve the number of rows you want and execute the special INSERT...DEFAULT VALUES statement. This example creates 1000 rows in table *xyz*:

```
-- Method 1.  Simple DEFAULT values on table.
CREATE TABLE xyz
(
col1    int         PRIMARY KEY IDENTITY(1, 1) NOT NULL,
col2    int         NOT NULL DEFAULT 999,
col3    char(10)    NOT NULL DEFAULT 'ABCEFGHIJK'
)
GO
SET NOCOUNT ON
DECLARE @counter int
SET @counter=1
```

(continued)

```
WHILE (@counter <= 1000)
    BEGIN
    INSERT xyz DEFAULT VALUES
    SET @counter=@counter+1
    END

SELECT * FROM xyz

col1    col2    col3
----    ----    -----------
1       999     ABCEFGHIJK
2       999     ABCEFGHIJK
3       999     ABCEFGHIJK
4       999     ABCEFGHIJK
5       999     ABCEFGHIJK
:
999     999     ABCEFGHIJK
1000    999     ABCEFGHIJK
```

Usually, you want some distribution in the data values; the RAND function, the modulo operator, and the functions CONVERT, CHAR, and REPLICATE come in handy for this purpose. RAND is a standard random number generator that's just like the function used in C, which RAND calls. Because RAND returns a *float* with a value between 0 and 1, you typically multiply it and convert the result to an integer so that you can use the modulo operator to indicate the range of values. For example, if you want a random integer from 0 through 9999, the following expression works nicely:

```
(CONVERT(int, RAND() * 100000) % 10000)
```

If you want to include negative numbers (for example, a range from -9999 through 9999), you can use RAND to flip a coin and generate 0 or 1 (by doing modulo 2) and then use CASE to multiply half of the numbers by −1:

```
CASE
WHEN CONVERT(int, RAND() * 1000) % 2 = 1 THEN
    (CONVERT(int, RAND() * 100000) % 10000 * -1)
ELSE CONVERT(int, RAND() * 100000) % 10000
END
```

To produce character data, you can generate a random number from 0 through 25 (since the English alphabet has 26 letters) and add that number to 65, which is the ASCII value for *A*. The result is the ASCII value for a character from *A* through *Z*. You can perform this operation a specified number of times or in a loop to generate as many characters as you want. Usually, after you indicate a few lead characters, you can use filler characters for the rest of a field. The REPLICATE function is a nice tool to use for creating the filler. If you want to be sure that different executions of the routine return different random numbers, you should seed the RAND function by including an integer value between the parentheses. You can use *@@spid*, the *object_id* of the newly created table, or any other "almost random" integer value.

The most common way to generate character data is to use local variables for the generated data inside a WHILE loop that does INSERT statements using the variables. Here's an example:

```
-- Method 2.    Generate random data in a loop.
IF (ISNULL(OBJECT_ID('random_data'), 0)) > 0
    DROP TABLE random_data
GO

CREATE TABLE random_data
(
col1        int PRIMARY KEY,
col2        int,
col3        char(15)
)
GO

DECLARE @counter int, @col2 int, @col3 char(15)
/* Insert 100 rows of data  */
-- Seed random generator
SELECT @counter=0, @col2=RAND(@@spid + cpu + physical_io)
FROM master..sysprocesses where spid=@@spid

WHILE (@counter < 1000)
    BEGIN
    SELECT @counter=@counter + 10,    -- Sequence numbers by 10
    @col2=
        CASE        -- Random integer between -9999 and 9999
            WHEN CONVERT(int, RAND() * 1000) % 2 = 1
            THEN (CONVERT(int, RAND() * 100000) % 10000 * -1)
            ELSE CONVERT(int, RAND() * 100000) % 10000
        END,
    @col3=        -- Four random letters followed by random fill letter
        CHAR((CONVERT(int, RAND() * 1000) % 26 ) + 65) -- 65 is 'A'
            + CHAR((CONVERT(int, RAND() * 1000) % 26 ) + 65)
            + CHAR((CONVERT(int, RAND() * 1000) % 26 ) + 65)
            + CHAR((CONVERT(int, RAND() * 1000) % 26 ) + 65)
            + REPLICATE(CHAR((CONVERT(int, RAND() * 1000) % 26 )
            + 65), 11)

    INSERT random_data VALUES (@counter, @col2, @col3)
    END
GO

SELECT * FROM random_data WHERE COL1 < 200
```

(continued)

```
col1    col2     col3
----    -----    ----------------
10      -5240    LXDSGGGGGGGGGGGG
20      9814     TTPDOOOOOOOOOOOO
30      3004     IEYXEEEEEEEEEEEE
40      -9377    MITDAAAAAAAAAAAA
50      -3823    ISGMUUUUUUUUUUUU
60      -4249    DHZQQQQQQQQQQQQQ
70      2335     XBJKEEEEEEEEEEEE
80      -4570    ILYWNNNNNNNNNNNN
90      4223     DHISDDDDDDDDDDDD
100     -3332    THXLWWWWWWWWWWWW
110     -9959    ALHFLLLLLLLLLLLL
120     4580     BCZNGGGGGGGGGGGG
130     6072     HRTJOOOOOOOOOOOO
140     -8274    QPTKWWWWWWWWWWWW
150     8212     FBQABBBBBBBBBBBB
160     8223     YXAPLLLLLLLLLLLL
170     -9469    LIHCAAAAAAAAAAAA
180     -2959    GYKRZZZZZZZZZZZZ
190     7677     KWWBJJJJJJJJJJJJ
```

You can also set up the table with a DEFAULT that includes the random data expression and then use the DEFAULT VALUES statement. This method is a combination of the previous two methods. All the complexity of the random values is segregated to the CREATE TABLE command, and the INSERT is again a simple loop that uses DEFAULT VALUES. In the following example, we use a CASE statement in a DEFAULT clause of a CREATE TABLE command:

```
-- Method 3.   Generate random values for DEFAULT.
CREATE TABLE random_data
(
col1    int      PRIMARY KEY IDENTITY(10,10) NOT NULL,
col2    int      NOT NULL DEFAULT CASE
                 -- Random integer between -9999 and 9999
                 WHEN CONVERT(int, RAND() * 1000) % 2 = 1
                 THEN (CONVERT(int, RAND() * 100000) % 10000 * -1 )
                 ELSE CONVERT(int, RAND() * 100000) % 10000
                 END,
col3    char(15) NOT NULL DEFAULT
                  CHAR((CONVERT(int, RAND() * 1000) % 26 ) + 65)
                 -- 65 is 'A'
                 + CHAR((CONVERT(int, RAND() * 1000) % 26 ) + 65)
                 + CHAR((CONVERT(int, RAND() * 1000) % 26 ) + 65)
                 + CHAR((CONVERT(int, RAND() * 1000) % 26 ) + 65)
                 + REPLICATE(CHAR((CONVERT(int, RAND() * 1000)
                    % 26) + 65), 11)
)
```

```
GO

DECLARE @counter int
SET @counter=1
WHILE (@counter <= 1000)
    BEGIN
    INSERT random_data DEFAULT VALUES
    SET @counter=@counter + 1
    END

-- Limit number of rows for illustration only
SELECT * FROM random_data WHERE col1 <= 200
```

col1	col2	col3
10	-6358	LCNLMMMMMMMMMMM
20	-2284	SSAITTTTTTTTTTT
30	-1498	NARJAAAAAAAAAAA
40	-1908	EINLZZZZZZZZZZZ
50	-716	KNIOFFFFFFFFFFF
60	-8331	WZPRYYYYYYYYYYY
70	-2571	TMUBEEEEEEEEEEE
80	-7965	LILNCCCCCCCCCCC
90	9728	IXLOBBBBBBBBBBB
100	878	IPMPPPPPPPPPPPP
110	-2649	QXPAPPPPPPPPPPP
120	-4443	EBVHKKKKKKKKKKK
130	6133	VRJWXXXXXXXXXXX
140	-5154	HMHXLLLLLLLLLLL
150	-480	RNLVQQQQQQQQQQQ
160	-2655	SEHXTTTTTTTTTTT
170	-8204	JVLHZZZZZZZZZZZ
180	-3201	PTWGBBBBBBBBBBB
190	-7529	TDCJXXXXXXXXXXX
200	2622	ANLDHHHHHHHHHHH

Getting Rankings

To get the five highest or five lowest values in a dataset, you use the TOP clause in a SQL Server SELECT statement. (I discussed TOP in Chapter 7.) The TOP clause also lets you specify WITH TIES. It's not always clear what that means, so an example might help. The following SELECT statement returns the rows with the five highest values for the *ytd_sales* column, including any ties:

```
SELECT TOP 5 WITH TIES title_id, ytd_sales, title
FROM titles
ORDER BY ytd_sales DESC
```

Here's the result:

```
title_id ytd_sales    title
-------- ----------   -----
MC3021   22246        The Gourmet Microwave
BU2075   18722        You Can Combat Computer Stress!
TC4203   15096        Fifty Years in Buckingham Palace Kitchens
PC1035   8780         But Is It User Friendly?
BU1032   4095         The Busy Executive's Database Guide
BU7832   4095         Straight Talk About Computers
PC8888   4095         Secrets of Silicon Valley
TC7777   4095         Sushi, Anyone?
(8 row(s) affected)
```

You end up with more than the five rows you requested. SQL Server returned the first five rows after sorting the data, and because additional rows had the same value as the fifth row returned (4095), it kept returning rows as long as there were equivalent *ytd_sales* values. The WITH TIES clause requires that the data be sorted using ORDER BY. A more formal definition of TOP *n* WITH TIES and ORDER BY *c* DESC is "return all rows that have a value of *c* for which there are at most *n*−1 greater values of *c*." So, in the dataset above, *n* is 5 and *c* is *ytd_sales*. The value 22246 has 0 rows with a greater value of *ytd_sales*, and 18722 has only one value greater. The last value returned, 4095, has only four values that are greater.

Another way to think of this concept of "the number of distinct values greater than a given value" is as the rank of the value. A value for which there are no greater values has a rank of 1, and a value for which there are two greater values has a rank of 3. The previous query returns all the rows with a rank of 5 or less, using the TOP clause. However, it's not so simple to get a list of the rows with a rank of 5 or less along with an integer indicating the actual rank value. Let's look at several possible solutions to this problem.

Approach 1: The Standard SQL Approach Using a View

First, let's look again at the *titles* table. Suppose you want to assign a rank value to all rows in the table based on their *ytd_sales* values (with the highest value getting the top rank). You can do this by performing a ranking of the values by nesting a SELECT inside the select list. For each row in the outer SELECT, the inner SELECT returns the number of values in the table that are equal to or greater than the value being ranked. This "rows rank" value is then correlated back to the main query. You can query the view to obtain any rank.

Performance suffers on large tables because a table must be scanned for every row. Ties are assigned equal rank; unique numbers are not guaranteed unless the columns are known to be unique. In the next example, the next nontie value's rank is one higher, not lower. Notice that we completely disregard rows with NULL values for *ytd_sales*.

```
CREATE VIEW ranked_sales (rank, title_id, ytd_sales, title)
AS
SELECT
(SELECT COUNT(DISTINCT T2.ytd_sales) FROM titles AS T2
    WHERE T2.ytd_sales >= T1.ytd_sales ) AS rank,
title_id,
ytd_sales,
title
FROM titles AS T1 WHERE ytd_sales IS NOT NULL
GO

SELECT * FROM ranked_sales WHERE rank <= 10 ORDER BY rank

rank  title_id  ytd_sales  title
----  --------  ---------  --------------------------------------------
1     MC3021    22246      The Gourmet Microwave
2     BU2075    18722      You Can Combat Computer Stress!
3     TC4203    15096      Fifty Years in Buckingham Palace Kitchens
4     PC1035    8780       But Is It User Friendly?
5     BU1032    4095       The Busy Executive's Database Guide
5     BU7832    4095       Straight Talk About Computers
5     PC8888    4095       Secrets of Silicon Valley
5     TC7777    4095       Sushi, Anyone?
6     PS3333    4072       Prolonged Data Deprivation: Four Case Studies
7     BU1111    3876       Cooking with Computers: Surreptitious Balance
                           Sheets
8     PS7777    3336       Emotional Security: A New Algorithm
9     PS2091    2045       Is Anger the Enemy?
10    MC2222    2032       Silicon Valley Gastronomic Treats
```

Approach 2: The Standard SQL Approach Without Using a View

This approach is basically the same as the first one, but it saves you the step of creating the view, at the possible cost of being a bit harder to understand. Instead of using a view, you use a derived table (by adding a SELECT in the FROM clause). Performance is identical to that of the view approach, however—that is, it's not too good. The results are also identical, so I won't show them here.

```
SELECT rank, title_id, ytd_sales, title
FROM (SELECT
    T1.title_id,
    ytd_sales,
    T1.title,
        (SELECT COUNT(DISTINCT T2.ytd_sales) FROM titles AS T2
        WHERE T1.ytd_sales <= T2.ytd_sales) AS rank
        FROM titles AS T1) AS X
    WHERE (ytd_sales IS NOT NULL) AND (rank <= 10)
    ORDER BY rank
```

Approach 3: Using a Temporary Table with an *identity* Column and No Ties

If you want to assign a unique number even in the case of ties, or if you know that ties will not occur, you can create a temporary table with an *identity* column and then SELECT into the temporary table in an ordered fashion. This gives you a material-ized table with rankings. This approach is conceptually easy to understand, and it's fast. Its only downside is that it doesn't recognize tied values. It's not ANSI-standard SQL, but this approach takes advantage of SQL Server–specific features. This approach can be useful with other sequential operations, as you'll see later.

```
CREATE TABLE #ranked_order
(
rank        int         IDENTITY NOT NULL PRIMARY KEY,
title_id    char(6)     NOT NULL,
ytd_sales   int         NOT NULL,
title       varchar(80) NOT NULL
)
GO

INSERT #ranked_order
    SELECT title_id, ytd_sales, title FROM titles WHERE ytd_sales
    IS NOT NULL ORDER BY ytd_sales DESC

SELECT * FROM #ranked_order

DROP TABLE #ranked_order
```

rank	title_id	ytd_sales	title
1	MC3021	22246	The Gourmet Microwave
2	BU2075	18722	You Can Combat Computer Stress!
3	TC4203	15096	Fifty Years in Buckingham Palace Kitchens
4	PC1035	8780	But Is It User Friendly?
5	BU1032	4095	The Busy Executive's Database Guide
6	BU7832	4095	Straight Talk About Computers
7	PC8888	4095	Secrets of Silicon Valley
8	TC7777	4095	Sushi, Anyone?
9	PS3333	4072	Prolonged Data Deprivation: Four Case Studies
10	BU1111	3876	Cooking with Computers: Surreptitious Balance Sheets
11	PS7777	3336	Emotional Security: A New Algorithm
12	PS2091	2045	Is Anger the Enemy?
13	MC2222	2032	Silicon Valley Gastronomic Treats
14	PS1372	375	Computer Phobic AND Non-Phobic Individuals
15	TC3218	375	Onions, Leeks, and Garlic: Cooking Secrets of the Med
16	PS2106	111	Life Without Fear

Approach 4: Using a Temporary Table with an *identity* Column and Ties

With standard SQL solutions, if the query focuses on four rows with two rows tied for second rank, then one row has the rank of first, two rows are second, and one row is third. No row is ranked fourth. An alternative way to rank them is to make one row first, two rows second, no row third, and one row fourth. (This is how standings in a race are posted if two swimmers tie for second place.) After populating the temporary table, you can query the table for the lowest rank for a given value and correlate that value back to the main query with a nested SELECT.

```
-- Approach 4A. Create a temp table with an identity, and then do
-- an ordered select to populate it.
-- Do a nested select correlated back to itself to find the lowest
-- rank for a given value.
CREATE TABLE #ranked_order
(
rank        int         IDENTITY NOT NULL,
title_id    char(6)     NOT NULL,
ytd_sales   int         NOT NULL,
title       varchar(80) NOT NULL
)
GO

INSERT #ranked_order
    SELECT title_id, ytd_sales, title FROM titles WHERE ytd_sales
        IS NOT NULL ORDER BY ytd_sales DESC

SELECT B.rank, A.title_id, B.ytd_sales , A.title
FROM
(SELECT MIN(T2.rank) AS rank, T2.ytd_sales FROM #ranked_order AS T2
    GROUP BY T2.ytd_sales) AS B,
#ranked_order AS A
WHERE A.ytd_sales=B.ytd_sales
ORDER BY B.rank

DROP TABLE #ranked_order
```

```
rank  title_id  ytd_sales  title
----  --------  ---------  -------------------------------------------
1     MC3021    22246      The Gourmet Microwave
2     BU2075    18722      You Can Combat Computer Stress!
3     TC4203    15096      Fifty Years in Buckingham Palace Kitchens
4     PC1035    8780       But Is It User Friendly?
5     BU1032    4095       The Busy Executive's Database Guide
5     BU7832    4095       Straight Talk About Computers
5     PC8888    4095       Secrets of Silicon Valley
```

(continued)

5	TC7777	4095	Sushi, Anyone?
9	PS3333	4072	Prolonged Data Deprivation: Four Case Studies
10	BU1111	3876	Cooking with Computers: Surreptitious Balance Sheets
11	PS7777	3336	Emotional Security: A New Algorithm
12	PS2091	2045	Is Anger the Enemy?
13	MC2222	2032	Silicon Valley Gastronomic Treats
14	PS1372	375	Computer Phobic AND Non-Phobic Individuals
14	TC3218	375	Onions, Leeks, and Garlic: Cooking Secrets of the Med
16	PS2106	111	Life Without Fear

You can slightly modify the SELECT on the temporary table and explicitly indicate where ties exist and how many values were tied. The creation and population of the temporary table are identical, so I'll show just the SELECT statement:

```
-- Approach 4B. Same as 4A, explicitly noting the ties.
CREATE TABLE #ranked_order
(
rank        int           IDENTITY NOT NULL,
title_id    char(6)       NOT NULL,
ytd_sales   int           NOT NULL,
title       varchar(80)   NOT NULL
)
GO

INSERT #ranked_order
    SELECT title_id, ytd_sales, title FROM titles WHERE ytd_sales
        IS NOT NULL ORDER BY ytd_sales DESC

SELECT B.rank,
CASE B.number_tied
    WHEN 1 THEN ' '
    ELSE '('+ CONVERT(varchar, number_tied) + ' Way Tie)'
    END AS tie,
A.title_id,
B.ytd_sales,
A.title
FROM
(SELECT MIN(T2.rank) AS rank, COUNT(*) AS number_tied, T2.ytd_sales
FROM #ranked_order AS T2 GROUP BY T2.ytd_sales) AS B,
#ranked_order AS A
WHERE A.ytd_sales=B.ytd_sales
ORDER BY B.rank

DROP TABLE #ranked_order
```

```
rank tie            title_id ytd_sales title
---- -----------    -------- --------- -----------------------------------------
1                   MC3021   22246     The Gourmet Microwave
2                   BU2075   18722     You Can Combat Computer Stress!
3                   TC4203   15096     Fifty Years in Buckingham Palace Kitchens
4                   PC1035   8780      But Is It User Friendly?
5    (4 Way Tie)    BU1032   4095      The Busy Executive's Database Guide
5    (4 Way Tie)    BU7832   4095      Straight Talk About Computers
5    (4 Way Tie)    PC8888   4095      Secrets of Silicon Valley
5    (4 Way Tie)    TC7777   4095      Sushi, Anyone?
9                   PS3333   4072      Prolonged Data Deprivation
10                  BU1111   3876      Cooking with Computers
11                  PS7777   3336      Emotional Security: A New Algorithm
12                  PS2091   2045      Is Anger the Enemy?
13                  MC2222   2032      Silicon Valley Gastronomic Treats
14   (2 Way Tie)    PS1372   375       Computer Phobic AND Non-Phobic Individuals
14   (2 Way Tie)    TC3218   375       Onions, Leeks, and Garlic
16                  PS2106   111       Life Without Fear
```

Finding Differences Between Intervals

Suppose we have a table with two columns that records data for measured temperatures. The first column is the *datetime* at which the measurement was taken, and the second column is the temperature. We want to find the change in temperature between one interval and the next, and we want it expressed as the absolute value of the number of degrees that changed per minute. There is no preexisting primary key, such as *measurement_id*. It's unlikely that duplicate measurements exist for any single time—that is, the *datetime* field is probably unique—but we don't know this for sure. And the intervals between data measurements are not consistent. In fact, the data was not inserted in order. Like the rankings problem, this problem can be solved using standard (but tricky) SQL. In fact, you can think of this as another type of ranking problem—but here, you want to see the differences between adjacent ranks.

First, I'll set up the table with some fairly random data. I really don't care whether the temperature values are realistic or how much they might fluctuate in even a few minutes. So if you run this example and see temperatures of −100° F or a 40-degree change in temperature in five minutes, don't worry. These readings might not be from Earth!

> **NOTE** It's worthwhile to set up the routine to generate test data even though in this case it would be quicker to manually insert 20 rows of data. Once the routine is working and you've checked your solution on the small table, you can easily change the constant in the WHILE loop to add much more data. This is important because many solutions perform well with small amounts of data but can degrade badly with large amounts of data. This can be especially true if a solution uses correlated subqueries or self-joins or if it does table scans.

```sql
-- diff_intervals.sql
IF NULLIF(OBJECT_ID('measurements'), 0) > 0
    DROP TABLE measurements
GO

CREATE TABLE measurements
(
when_taken      datetime      NOT NULL,
temperature     numeric(4, 1)   -- (Fahrenheit)
)
CREATE CLUSTERED INDEX measurements_idx01
    ON measurements (when_taken)
GO

DECLARE @counter int, @whendate datetime, @val numeric(4, 1),
    @randdiff smallint, @randmins smallint
SELECT @counter=1, @whendate=GETDATE(), @val=50.0
/* Insert 20 rows of data.  Change constant if you want more.   */
WHILE (@counter <= 20)
    BEGIN
    INSERT measurements VALUES (@whendate, @val)
    -- Get a random number between -20 and 20 for change in
    -- temperature. This will be added to the previous value,
    -- plus RAND again to give a fractional component.
      SELECT
      @randdiff=CASE
      WHEN CONVERT(int, RAND() * 100) % 2 = 1 THEN
          CONVERT(int, RAND() * 1000) % 21 * -1
      ELSE CONVERT(int, RAND() * 1000) % 21
      END,
    -- Get a random number between 0 and 10080 (the number of minutes
    -- in a week). This will be added to the current GETDATE
    -- value. Since GETDATE returns a value to the millisecond,
    -- it's unlikely there will ever be a duplicate, although it
    -- is possible if the result of the addition and the current
    -- GETDATE() value happen to collide with the addition in
    -- another row. (That's intentional; we are not assuming
    -- that duplicates are automatically prevented.)
        @randmins=CONVERT(int, RAND() * 100000) % 10080
    SELECT @counter=@counter + 1,
    @whendate=DATEADD(mi, @randmins, GETDATE()),
     @val=@val + @randdiff + RAND()
    END

SELECT * FROM measurements
```

```
when_taken                temperature
-------------------------   -----------
2000-07-17 12:31:41.203    50.0
2000-07-17 16:07:41.243    48.0
2000-07-17 23:56:41.233    55.7
2000-07-18 00:13:41.243    32.8
2000-07-18 13:40:41.273    -18.2
2000-07-18 20:35:41.283    27.2
2000-07-18 21:53:41.243    34.6
2000-07-19 01:21:41.283    -34.6
2000-07-19 22:52:41.253    16.8
2000-07-20 03:56:41.283    -27.8
2000-07-20 06:56:41.283    38.1
2000-07-21 08:28:41.243    67.6
2000-07-21 20:43:41.283    -7.0
2000-07-22 19:12:41.293    20.9
2000-07-23 05:59:41.273    .4
2000-07-23 07:33:41.243    58.1
2000-07-23 09:25:41.243    65.6
2000-07-23 16:04:41.283    7.0
2000-07-23 16:05:41.253    2.2
2000-07-23 20:59:41.253    30.9
```

Approach 1: Using Standard SQL

This approach is similar to the rankings solution. I assign a ranking to each row and then join the table back to itself on the ranking value minus 1. If duplicate *datetime* values exist, this approach still computes the differential to the previous (nonduplicate) measurement, which might or might not be how you'd want to deal with it. As with the rankings solution, you can use this approach either as a view or as a derived table. Since a view is easier for most people to understand, I'll write it that way.

As in the top *n* and rankings problems, this approach is a good brainteaser, but it's not a good performer if the table is anything but very small. In addition, this approach is problematic if duplicate *datetime* values might exist.

```
CREATE VIEW rankdates (when_taken, temperature, daterank)
AS
SELECT when_taken, temperature,
    (SELECT COUNT(DISTINCT when_taken) FROM measurements AS T1
    WHERE T1.when_taken <= T0.when_taken) AS rank
FROM measurements AS T0
GO
SELECT * FROM rankdates ORDER BY daterank
GO
```

(continued)

```
when_taken                    temperature   daterank
--------------------------    -----------   --------
2000-07-17 12:31:41.203       50.0          1
2000-07-17 16:07:41.243       48.0          2
2000-07-17 23:56:41.233       55.7          3
2000-07-18 00:13:41.243       32.8          4
2000-07-18 13:40:41.273       -18.2         5
2000-07-18 20:35:41.283       27.2          6
2000-07-18 21:53:41.243       34.6          7
2000-07-19 01:21:41.283       -34.6         8
2000-07-19 22:52:41.253       16.8          9
2000-07-20 03:56:41.283       -27.8         10
2000-07-20 06:56:41.283       38.1          11
2000-07-21 08:28:41.243       67.6          12
2000-07-21 20:43:41.283       -7.0          13
2000-07-22 19:12:41.293       20.9          14
2000-07-23 05:59:41.273       .4            15
2000-07-23 07:33:41.243       58.1          16
2000-07-23 09:25:41.243       65.6          17
2000-07-23 16:04:41.283       7.0           18
2000-07-23 16:05:41.253       2.2           19
2000-07-23 20:59:41.253       30.9          20

-- Correlate each value with the one right before it
SELECT
P1_WHEN=V1.when_taken, P2_WHEN=V2.when_taken,
P1=V1.temperature, P2=V2.temperature,
DIFF=(V2.temperature - V1.temperature)
FROM rankdates AS V1 LEFT OUTER JOIN rankdates AS V2
ON (V2.daterank=V1.daterank + 1)
GO

P1_WHEN                    P2_WHEN                    P1      P2      DIFF
----------------------     ----------------------     -----   -----   ----
2000-07-17 12:31:41.203    2000-07-17 16:07:41.243    50.0    48.0    -2.0
2000-07-17 16:07:41.243    2000-07-17 23:56:41.233    48.0    55.7    7.7
2000-07-17 23:56:41.233    2000-07-18 00:13:41.243    55.7    32.8    -22.9
2000-07-18 00:13:41.243    2000-07-18 13:40:41.273    32.8    -18.2   -51.0
2000-07-18 13:40:41.273    2000-07-18 20:35:41.283    -18.2   27.2    45.4
2000-07-18 20:35:41.283    2000-07-18 21:53:41.243    27.2    34.6    7.4
2000-07-18 21:53:41.243    2000-07-19 01:21:41.283    34.6    -34.6   -69.2
2000-07-19 01:21:41.283    2000-07-19 22:52:41.253    -34.6   16.8    51.4
2000-07-19 22:52:41.253    2000-07-20 03:56:41.283    16.8    -27.8   -44.6
2000-07-20 03:56:41.283    2000-07-20 06:56:41.283    -27.8   38.1    65.9
2000-07-20 06:56:41.283    2000-07-21 08:28:41.243    38.1    67.6    29.5
2000-07-21 08:28:41.243    2000-07-21 20:43:41.283    67.6    -7.0    -74.6
2000-07-21 20:43:41.283    2000-07-22 19:12:41.293    -7.0    20.9    27.9
2000-07-22 19:12:41.293    2000-07-23 05:59:41.273    20.9    .4      -20.5
```

```
2000-07-23 05:59:41.273    2000-07-23 07:33:41.243    .4     58.1   57.7
2000-07-23 07:33:41.243    2000-07-23 09:25:41.243    58.1   65.6   7.5
2000-07-23 09:25:41.243    2000-07-23 16:04:41.283    65.6   7.0    -58.6
2000-07-23 16:04:41.283    2000-07-23 16:05:41.253    7.0    2.2    -4.8
2000-07-23 16:05:41.253    2000-07-23 20:59:41.253    2.2    30.9   28.7
2000-07-23 20:59:41.253    NULL                       30.9   NULL   NULL
```

NOTE If you're interested in the derived table solution, go back to the rankings problem and note the difference between a view and a derived table; it should be easy to see how the derived table solution can be done here as well.

Approach 2: Materializing Rankings and Using a Self-Join

Conceptually, this solution is similar to the standard SQL approach. But rather than using a true view, we'll materialize the rankings as a temporary table, similar to the approach in one of the rankings solutions. Then we'll do the self-join with the temporary table. The advantage, of course, is that we create the rankings only once instead of many times. This is faster because the identity value simply assigns the rank in the order that the rows are presented.

In SQL Server 2000, this solution performs about 33 percent faster than the standard SQL solution. The results are the same, so I won't repeat the output. The standard SQL approach takes 122 logical reads with this dataset; the temporary table approach here takes 44 logical reads to create the *temp* table and 42 logical reads to access it. Because so little data is involved, no more than two physical reads occur in either of these solutions.

```
CREATE TABLE #rankdates (
when_taken datetime,
temperature numeric(4, 1),
daterank int IDENTITY PRIMARY KEY)
GO
INSERT #rankdates (when_taken, temperature)
    SELECT when_taken, temperature
    FROM measurements
    ORDER BY when_taken ASC
GO

SELECT
P1_WHEN=V1.when_taken, P2_WHEN=V2.when_taken,
P1=V1.temperature, P2=V2.temperature,
DIFF=(V2.temperature - V1.temperature)
FROM #rankdates AS V1 LEFT OUTER JOIN #rankdates AS V2
ON (V2.daterank=V1.daterank + 1)
GO

DROP TABLE #rankdates
```

Selecting Instead of Iterating

One common need is to perform some operation for every value, from 1 to *n*. Earlier in this chapter, I used the trigonometry functions to produce a listing of sine/cosine/tangent for every 10 degrees between 0 and 180. I took the obvious route and wrote a simple loop. However, that approach results in every row being its own result set. As I've mentioned many times, sending many result sets when one will do is inefficient, and it is also more cumbersome to process in the client application. To refresh your memory, here's the solution I used earlier:

```
DECLARE @degrees smallint
DECLARE @radians float
SELECT @degrees=0
SELECT @radians=0
WHILE (@degrees <= 180)
BEGIN
    SELECT
    DEGREES=@degrees,
    RADIANS=STR(@radians, 8, 5),
    SINE=STR(SIN(@radians), 8, 5),
    COSINE=STR(COS(@radians), 8, 5),
    TANGENT=STR(TAN(@radians), 8, 5)
    SELECT @degrees=@degrees + 10
    SELECT @radians=RADIANS(CONVERT(float, @degrees))
END
```

Since it's common to iterate in this way, a simple table of ordered numbers can come in handy:

```
-- Create the seq_num table
CREATE TABLE seq_num
(seq_num INT PRIMARY KEY NOT NULL)

-- Populate the seq_num table with values from -500 through 500
DECLARE @counter int
SELECT @counter= -500
WHILE (@counter <= 500)
    BEGIN
    INSERT seq_num VALUES (@counter)
    SELECT @counter=@counter + 1
    END

-- If doing this for real, you might as well set FILLFACTOR to 100
```

I can select or join to this handy *seq_num* table rather than iterating. The following solution runs much faster than the earlier solution. It returns a single result set, and it's easier to write:

```
SELECT
    ANGLE=seq_num * 10,
    SINE=STR(SIN(seq_num * 10), 7, 4),
    COSINE=STR(COS(seq_num * 10), 7, 4),
    TANGENT=STR(TAN(seq_num * 10), 7, 4)
FROM seq_num
WHERE seq_num BETWEEN 0 AND 18
```

ANGLE	SINE	COSINE	TANGENT
0	0.0000	1.0000	0.0000
10	-0.5440	-0.8391	0.6484
20	0.9129	0.4081	2.2372
30	-0.9880	0.1543	-6.4053
40	0.7451	-0.6669	-1.1172
50	-0.2624	0.9650	-0.2719
60	-0.3048	-0.9524	0.3200
70	0.7739	0.6333	1.2220
80	-0.9939	-0.1104	9.0037
90	0.8940	-0.4481	-1.9952
100	-0.5064	0.8623	-0.5872
110	-0.0442	-0.9990	0.0443
120	0.5806	0.8142	0.7131
130	-0.9301	-0.3673	2.5323
140	0.9802	-0.1978	-4.9554
150	-0.7149	0.6993	-1.0223
160	0.2194	-0.9756	-0.2249
170	0.3466	0.9380	0.3696
180	-0.8012	-0.5985	1.3387

FULL-TEXT SEARCHING

The Transact-SQL language in SQL Server 2000 includes several programming extensions that allow you to access SQL Server data that is maintained and accessed by the Microsoft Search service. These extensions allow you to use special indexes to perform powerful, flexible searches that are beyond the capacity of normal SQL statements. The searching that you can do with SQL Server full-text searching is similar to the searching you can do in *SQL Server Books Online* or online resources such as MSDN and TechNet, where you supply any combination of keywords and the application returns a list of "hits," ranked in order by how closely they match your keyword list. Although these tools do not use the Microsoft Search service, they can give you an idea of the type of searching that is possible. For an example of a real site using Microsoft full-text search technology, you can take a look at the MSN E-Shop at www.eshop.com.

You're aware by now that you can do searches with normal SQL, using a LIKE operator. For example, we can use the following query to find all the employees in the *Northwind* database who mention French in their *notes* field:

```
USE Northwind
SELECT LastName, FirstName, Notes
FROM EMPLOYEES
WHERE notes like '%french%'
```

This should return five rows. But what if we then want to find all the employees who list both German and French? We could try executing the following query:

```
SELECT LastName, FirstName, Notes
FROM EMPLOYEES
WHERE notes like '%german%french%'
```

However, this query does not return any rows because the pattern matching of LIKE looks for parts of the string in the order listed: SQL Server returns only rows in which the *notes* field contains some (or no) characters, followed by the string *german* followed by some (or no) characters, followed by the string *french* followed by some (or no) characters. If the string *french* comes before the string *german*, SQL Server does not return the row. However, this query returns two rows:

```
SELECT LastName, FirstName, Notes
FROM EMPLOYEES
WHERE notes like '%french%german%'
```

Using the full-text search capability, we could write a similar query to the above and list German and French in any order. Of course, we could write this query with two separate conditions in order to find either order of *french* and *german*. However, having the flexibility to write our query with the search strings in any order is only one of the advantages of using SQL Server's full-text search features.

The biggest advantage of using the full-text search functionality is that each word in your textual data is indexed, so queries looking for parts of strings can be amazingly fast. When using its own internal indexes, SQL Server considers all the data stored in the key field as a single value. Consider an index on the *notes* field in the *Northwind* database's *employees* table. The index would help us quickly find how many *notes* fields start with the word *I* but would be of no use at all in finding which rows have the word *french* in their *notes* field because the entire *notes* field is sorted starting with the first character. A full-text index, on the other hand, could be a big help because it keeps track of each word in the *notes* field independently.

The full-text searching feature in SQL Server 2000 actually consists of two basic components: full-text indexing, which lets you create and populate full-text catalogs that are maintained outside of SQL Server and managed by the Microsoft Search service, and full-text searching, which uses four new Transact-SQL operations—CONTAINS, FREETEXT, CONTAINSTABLE, and FREETEXTTABLE. The CONTAINS and

FREETEXT operators are predicates used in a WHERE clause, and CONTAINSTABLE and FREETEXTTABLE are rowset functions used in a FROM clause. These operations allow you to query your full-text catalogs.

Full-Text Indexes

SQL Server 2000 allows you to create full-text indexes with support from Microsoft Search service. The Microsoft Search service creates and manages full-text indexes and can work in conjunction with other products in addition to SQL Server 2000, such as Windows 2000 and Microsoft Exchange Server 2000. The indexing components of the Search service use a word-breaking algorithm to take specified columns of textual data and break them into individual words. These words are then stored in a full-text index, which is external to SQL Server's data storage.

Figure 10-4 shows the relationship of the Search service to SQL Server's relational and storage engines. The SQL Server handler is a driver that contains the logic to extract the textual data from the appropriate SQL Server columns and pass them to the indexing components of the Search service. The handler can also pass values from the Search service to the SQL Server engine to indicate how to repopulate the indexes. I'll tell you about population techniques shortly.

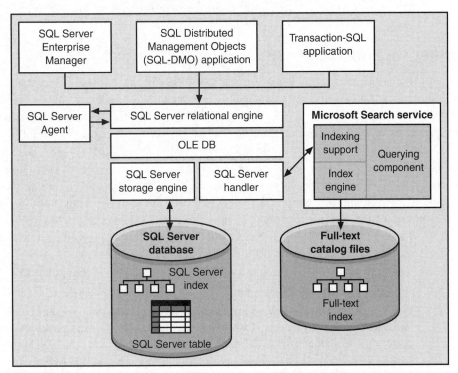

Figure 10-4. *Full-text indexing support, reproduced from SQL Server documentation.*

In the most general sense, you can think of full-text indexes as similar to SQL Server indexes in that they organize your data so you can find information very quickly. But the similarity stops there. I'll list the most important differences here and elaborate on most of them in the sections that follow.

- SQL Server indexes are stored in your database files; full-text indexes are stored externally in operating system files.

- You can have several (actually, up to 250) SQL Server indexes per table; you can only have one full-text index per table.

- There is only one entry in each SQL Server index for each row of data; there can be many entries in a full-text index for each row because each row is broken into its separate words.

- SQL Server indexes are maintained individually; full-text indexes are grouped together in catalogs for ease of maintenance.

- SQL Server indexes are automatically updated as you modify your data; full-text indexes are updated asynchronously. This is called *repopulation* of full-text indexes, and you can schedule repopulation to occur at regular times, or you can manually request a repopulation to take place.

Setting Up Full-Text Indexes

You need only take a few basic steps to get your data set up for full-text searching. An important prerequisite is to make sure that the full-text indexing feature has been installed with SQL Server. In SQL Server 7, the tools for full-text indexing were not installed by default; if you've upgraded a SQL Server 7 server on which the full-text indexing was not installed, your SQL Server 2000 server also will not install full-text indexing. A new installation of SQL Server 2000 will have full-text indexing installed by default if you choose the Typical installation option. (One exception is if you are installing SQL Server 2000 on Windows 2000 Professional or Windows NT 4 Workstation; in these cases, you must choose a custom installation in order to have full-text indexing installed.) To choose not to install full-text indexing, you have to choose the Custom installation and uncheck the box for full-text indexing. To install full-text indexing after installation, you can rerun the setup program from your SQL Server 2000 CD and choose the option to add new components to an existing installation.

> NOTE There are several ways to determine whether full-text indexing has been installed for your SQL Server. The easiest way is probably to expand any user database in the left pane in SQL Server Enterprise Manager and see if you have a folder called Full-Text Catalogs. Alternatively, you can examine the DATABASEPROPERTYEX metadata function and check the value of the option 'IsFullTextEnabled'.

You can set up full-text indexing through wizards and dialog boxes in SQL Server Enterprise Manger or by using stored procedures. (The full-text wizard is not available if you haven't installed full-text indexing). In this section, I'll describe the general process of setting up full-text searching using system stored procedures. Once you understand what's involved, the graphical user interface (GUI) should be completely self-explanatory. I'll show examples of most of the stored procedures, which of course are called behind the scenes by SQL Server Enterprise Manager. The examples that follow set up full-text indexing on the *products* table in the *Northwind* database. If you execute these examples for setting up full-text indexing, you'll be able to run the full-text querying examples later in this section.

The first step in setting up full-text indexing is to enable a database to allow this feature. From the command line in SQL Query Analyzer, you can run this procedure:

```
USE Northwind
EXEC sp_fulltext_database 'enable'
```

Note that the name of the database is not an argument in the procedure; this procedure enables the current database for full-text indexing and searching.

> **WARNING** You should enable a database for full-text indexing only once. If you run this procedure a second time, any catalogs that you have already created will have to be completely repopulated.

The second step is to create a catalog in the operating system to store the full-text indexes. A catalog can contain the indexes from one or more tables, and it is treated as a unit for maintenance purposes. In general, you shouldn't need more than one catalog per database. You may find that a huge table of more than 10 million rows will benefit from being in its own catalog, but it would really depend on how often that table is being updated and how often the full-text index needs repopulating.

From SQL Query Analyzer, you can build a catalog that specifies a full path for the directory in which to store the catalog, as shown here:

```
EXEC sp_fulltext_catalog 'Northwind_data', 'create', 'D:\FTcatalogs'
```

Specifying the directory path is optional, and the default is NULL. A NULL for the path indicates that the default location should be used. This is the FTDATA subdirectory in the install directory for your SQL Server instance; for example, C:\Program Files\Microsoft SQL Server\MSSQL$<instance name>\Ftdata. The specified root directory must reside on a drive on the same computer as your SQL Server instance. The drive on which you're building the catalog must have at least 50 MB of free space; otherwise, you'll get an error and will have to free up space or choose another location. If you're using the full-text index wizard, you will actually specify the tables and columns first and then choose whether to store the full-text indexes in a new or existing catalog.

Any table that will have a full-text index must already have a unique index. If the table has more than one unique index, you will need to choose one of them to be the index used by full-text indexing. In the full-text index, the individual words are stored along with an indication of where in the original table those words can be found. The location is indicated by a key value for the unique index. For example, suppose we have a full-text index on the *notes* field in the *titles* table in the *pubs* database. The unique key for the *titles* table is the *title_id* column. A subset of the full-text index might look something like this:

```
business BU1032
computer:    BU7832 PC8888 PC9999 PS1372 PS7777
software    PC1035 PC8888
```

Each keyword is followed by a list of all the *title_id* values that have the indicated keyword in the row for that *title_id*. Note that this is just an abstraction of the way the full-text index would really look. The individual keys are actually encoded before they are stored, and the keys are found by using a hashing algorithm. Also, each keyword stores more than just a unique index key; it also stores information about what table the key is in and the position within the row where the word can be found.

To specify which tables to index, which column will be the full-text index key, and what catalog the index should be stored in, you can use the following procedure:

```
EXEC sp_fulltext_table 'products', 'create', 'Northwind_data',
    'PK_Products'
```

As I mentioned, you can have at most one full-text index on a table, but any number of columns can be included in that index. The columns must be character based, or of type *image*: *char, varchar, nchar, nvarchar, text, image* or *ntext*. The columns can be different datatypes—for example, there can be one *char* column and one *text* column—and the columns can even be based on different languages. Remember that the language used to determine the word-breaking algorithm and the inflectional forms allowed for words in a particular column does not have to explicitly defined. The default is determined by the configuration option 'default full-text language'. On my SQL Server, this option has the value 1033, which is equivalent to 0x0409. The Books Online description for the *sp_fulltext_column* procedure gives you the locale ID values for all the languages supported for full-text indexing, and you can see that 0x0409 is the ID for US English. When defining a column to add to a full-text index, the fourth parameter is the locale ID. Leaving this value out or supplying an explicit NULL means that the default locale ID will be used. You can specify a 0 to mean that neutral word-breaking and inflectional algorithms should be used—for example, if the column contains data in multiple languages or in an unsupported language.

If using stored procedures, each column must be added separately.

```
EXEC sp_fulltext_column 'products', 'ProductName', 'add', 0
EXEC sp_fulltext_column 'products', 'QuantityPerUnit', 'add', 0
```

That's all that you need to do to create full-text indexes. However, the information that the index stores is not collected automatically. You must manually maintain the indexes by determining when they should be populated.

Maintaining Full-Text Indexes

Populating a full-text index simply means building it. The process of building a full-text index is quite different from creating a SQL Server index because the external Search service is involved. To create the original index, you do a full population and SQL Server takes every row from the indexed table and passes it to the Search service. The Search service applies an algorithm called word-breaking to each row of each indexed column in order to generate the individual words that will be part of the index. The word-breaking algorithm is unique for each supported language and determines what is considered the end of one word and the beginning of another. For example, not all languages break words with spaces. The full-text index keeps track of each word in each field, what unique keys each word is associated with, and where in each column the words appears. When I tell you about querying your full-text indexes, you'll see that you can ask for words that are "near" other words, and in order to determine "nearness," the full-text index must know whether a word occurs as the 2nd word in a column or the 222nd word.

The index-building procedure ignores certain words that are considered unimportant. These are called *noise words*, and the list is different for each language. There is a predefined list of noise words for each language supported, and these lists are stored as ASCII files that you can edit using any text editor. The noise words typically include pronouns, prepositions, conjunctions, numbers, and individual letters. You can take a look at the noise word files to see what else is ignored. You can add words to be ignored or remove words from the list that you want to have in your full-text indexes. The Search service has its own set of noise word files that are separate from SQL Server noise word files. If there is no SQL Server file for a particular language, the one for the Search service is used. The Search service noise word files are stored on the partition with your operating system files, in the directory \Program Files\Common Files\System\MSSearch\Data\Config.

The SQL Server full-text index noise words files are in the same directory that your catalogs are stored in, which by default is \Program Files\Microsoft SQL Server\MSSQL$<instance name>\Ftdata. The noise word files are in a subdirectory under Ftdata called SQLServer$<instance name>\Config. The file containing the US English language noise words is called noise.enu, the file containing the UK English noise words is noise.eng, the file containing the French noise words is noise.fra, and the Spanish file is noise.esn. Each language has its own suffix.

Full Population of Full-Text Indexes

Full population can take a long time for a large table or a catalog—up to many hours for a catalog involving a million rows. Obviously, you won't want to have to do a full population more often than is necessary. However, if most of your data is changing on a regular basis—for example, if 90 percent of your keys are changing every day—you might find it necessary to fully repopulate your full-text index. From SQL Query Analyzer, you can start a full population with this command:

```
EXEC sp_fulltext_catalog 'Northwind_data', 'start_full'
```

Note that populating or repopulating is done on a catalog, whether the catalog contains data from one table or from several. All the words from all the tables in the catalog are stored together, and the index keeps track of which table each word came from.

The population is done asynchronously, and the preceding command only starts the process. The property function FULLTEXTCATALOGPROPERTY tells you the current status of a full-text catalog, including whether the full population has finished. This function also tells you the number of keys for all indexes in the catalog and the elapsed time since the last population. To find out if a full population has completed, you can execute the following:

```
SELECT FULLTEXTCATALOGPROPERTY ( 'Northwind_data', 'PopulateStatus' )
```

A return value of 0 means there is no current population activity, a value of 1 means a full population is in progress, and a value of 6 means an incremental population is in progress. You can use the FULLTEXTCATALOGPROPERTY function and look for the value of the property PopulateCompletionAge to see when the population finished. The value is returned in number of seconds since a base date of January 1, 1990. We can then use the SQL Server *dateadd* function to find out the actual date that is being referenced:

```
SELECT dateadd(ss, FULLTEXTCATALOGPROPERTY ( 'Northwind_data',
    'PopulateCompletionAge' ), '1/1/1990' )
```

NOTE Keep in mind that if a property function returns NULL, it means you've typed something in incorrectly or the function call has failed for some reason. The FULLTEXTCATALOGPROPERTY function returns 0 if no activity is in progress. Since this is an asynchronous activity, you might need to pause while you wait for the population to complete. You can check the status of the population in a loop, but since the population could take hours, I recommend that you avoid continuously checking and looping. You should probably pause between checks. For a full population, you might want to check the status every 10 minutes, and for an incremental population, you might want to check every 2 minutes. A simple loop looks like this:

```
WHILE FULLTEXTCATALOGPROPERTY ( 'Northwind_data',
              'PopulateStatus' ) = 1
    WAITFOR DELAY '0:10:00'  -- pause for 10 minutes
-- Now you can use your full-text index!
```

You have two alternatives to full population to keep your full-text indexes up to date: incremental population and change tracking. Both require that you first do a full population of your catalog.

Incremental Population

Incremental population affects only rows that have changed since the last full or incremental population. When you start an incremental population, the Search service sends a request to SQL Server, along with the timestamp of the last population, and SQL Server returns all the rows that have changed. Only those rows are processed, and only the words in those rows are used to update the full-text index. If a table does not have a timestamp column, an incremental population will automatically revert to a full population with no warning. Since a full population can take many times longer than an incremental population, you should be very sure that your tables have a timestamp field before you request an incremental population.

You can start an incremental population manually using this command:

```
EXEC sp_fulltext_catalog 'Northwind_data', 'start_incremental'
```

In addition, you can use SQL Server Agent to schedule population of the full-text indexes at whatever interval you need. Remember that no automatic updating of full-text indexes is done; if new data has been added to a table with a full-text index, your full-text search queries won't find that data until the full-text index has been updated. In SQL Server Enterprise Manager, you can right-click the name of the catalog or the table in the right pane and choose to start a population or create a schedule for a population.

Change Tracking

You can also have changes automatically tracked in a table with a full-text index. You can do this in SQL Server Enterprise Manager by right-clicking on the table name in the right pane after expanding the Tables folder. Note that you don't enable change tracking for a catalog, only for an individual table. From SQL Query Analyzer, you can use this command:

```
EXEC sp_fulltext_table 'products', 'Start_change_tracking'
```

If no full population has been done, SQL Server will do a full population when this procedure is called. If the full population is in progress already, calling this procedure will restart the full population. If a full population has already been done, an incremental update will be done so that when change tracking begins, the full-text index is known to be completely up-to-date. Once change tracking is enabled, the system table *sysfulltextnotify* is updated every time any of the columns in the full-text index is modified. This table basically just keeps track of the table ID and the value of the unique index key for the rows that have been modified.

You can apply these tracked changes in two ways. This procedure updates all the appropriate full-text index rows based on the changes in the *sysfulltextnotify* table:

```
EXEC sp_fulltext_table 'products', 'Update_index'
```

As with incremental population, you can schedule this update at whatever interval you choose. Alternatively, you can choose to have the updating of the full-text index be an ongoing activity, using this command:

```
EXEC sp_fulltext_table 'products', 'Start_background_updateindex'
```

Once the background updating has started, the maintenance of the full-text index will be close to real time. Depending on the load on your system, there might still be a lag between the time you update the table and the time the modified data shows up in the full-text index, but in many cases the change to the index will seem to be immediate.

I recommend that you use change tracking whenever possible. If most of the data in the table is changing on a regular basis, you might need to do repeated full populations. But as an alternative to incremental population, change tracking is a clear performance winner. Two aspects of incremental population make it very time consuming. First, the timestamp in a row can tell you only that an existing row has changed or that it is a new row. Inserts and updates can be handled by this mechanism, but what happens if a row is deleted? How can the Search service know to remove an entry from the full-text index? After all the rows in the base table are compared to the previous timestamp in order to check for new or updated rows, the Search service compares all keys in the full-text index with all keys in the base table to determine which ones might have been deleted. Admittedly, this is not nearly as time consuming as full population, in which each word in each column must be isolated, but it can take quite a long time for a large table. The second shortcoming of incremental population is that the timestamp is changed when any change is made to a row, even if the change did not involve any of the full-text indexed columns. So if you update all the prices in the *products* table, the timestamp in every row will change. When it comes time to do the incremental population, SQL Server will send every single row to the Search service to be completely reindexed. This activity could take about as long as the initial population and is very undesirable.

The use of change tracking avoids both of these problems. The *sysfulltextnotify* table gets a simple entry only when a change is made to a full-text indexed column, and each row contains only three values: the ID of the table that was changed, the key value corresponding to the changed row, and a field indicating the operation that took place (insert, update, or delete). This simple structure contains all the information that is needed to make the necessary changes to update the full-text index.

Querying Full-Text Indexes

As I mentioned earlier, there are four predicates you can use to search data that has been full-text indexed. I won't go into great detail on the nuances of these predicates because the SQL Server 2000 documentation, as well as some of the SQL Server programming books listed in the bibliography, adequately illustrate the types of queries you can run. I'll just give you some of the basics and some simple examples.

To see some interesting results, you might need some data beyond what comes with the *pubs* or *Northwind* sample databases. On the companion CD, I put a script named ModifyProductNames.sql that modifies the data in the *products* table in the *Northwind* database, and it illustrates some of the basic full-text searching techniques. The *products* table contains the names of all the products sold by the Northwind Traders Company, and I modified these product names by adding "Hot and Spicy," "Spicy Hot," "Extra Hot," and "Supreme" at the beginning or end of various product names. This script contains five UPDATE statements to make the changes, but first it increases the size of the *ProductName* column to allow for these new names. The sample queries below will run against a *Northwind* database that includes these changes.

CONTAINS and CONTAINSTABLE Predicates

The most general purpose of the four full-text predicates is CONTAINS. It takes two arguments: the first is the column you want to search in the table, and the second is the word or words you want to search for. Single quotes enclose the complete search value that will be sent to the Search service, and that search value can contain multiple words as well as the conjunctions AND, OR, and NOT. You can also use the conjunctions & (for AND), | (for OR) and || (for NOT). You can use the wildcard character (*) only at the end of a search word. Here are a few examples:

```
--USE Northwind
-- This query returns 25 rows
SELECT * FROM products
WHERE CONTAINS(*, 'hot')

-- This query returns rows that have both hot and spicy anywhere
-- in the row: 24 rows
SELECT * FROM products
WHERE CONTAINS(*, 'hot and spicy')

-- This query returns rows that have hot but not spicy: 1 row
SELECT * FROM products
WHERE CONTAINS(*, 'hot and not spicy')
```

(continued)

```
-- This query returns rows that contain any words that start with
-- "ch." Note that the double quotes are needed; otherwise,
-- the "*" will not be interpreted as a wildcard. The result set is
-- 9 rows, containing products that include "chocolate," "chowder,"
-- "chai," and "chinois."
SELECT * FROM products
WHERE CONTAINS(*, '"ch*"')
```

```
-- This query returns rows that contain the string "hot and spicy";
-- note the double quotes inside the single quotes:
-- 15 rows
SELECT * FROM products
WHERE CONTAINS(*, '"hot and spicy"')
```

The last query is different from one that has this condition: *WHERE CONTAINS(*, 'hot and spicy')*. If SQL Server sends only the string *hot and spicy* to the Search service, the Search service will recognize it as two words conjoined by the AND operator. However, when the whole string is in double quotes, it becomes one search string and the AND is no longer an operator, it is part of the search string. The problem is that the Search service doesn't keep track of the word *and* because it is a noise word, so it has no idea which rows in the *products* table have *hot and spicy*. All it can do is find rows that have *hot* separated by one noise word from *spicy*. So the following query will return exactly the same rows:

```
SELECT * FROM products
WHERE CONTAINS(*, '"hot or spicy"')
```

The following query will not return any rows because no rows have *hot* right next to *spicy,* in that order:

```
SELECT * FROM products
WHERE CONTAINS(*, '"hot spicy"')
```

And this query will also return no rows. *Sweet* is not a noise word, so it must actually appear in the data, and it doesn't—at least not between *hot* and *spicy.*

```
SELECT * FROM products
WHERE CONTAINS(*, '"hot sweet spicy"')
```

The CONTAINS predicate can also look for inflectional forms of words—the plural, singular, gender, and neutral forms of nouns, verbs, and adjectives will match the search criteria. The data in the *products* table doesn't give us too many inflectional forms of the same word, but here's one example:

```
-- Find all rows containing any form of the word "season."
-- One row, with "seasoning," will be returned.
SELECT * FROM products
WHERE CONTAINS(*, 'FORMSOF( INFLECTIONAL,season)' )
```

Note that the syntax is quite awkward here because you need the nested predicate FORMSOF with the argument of INFLECTIONAL. Remember that everything inside the single quotes is sent to the Search service, which requires this syntax. In future versions of the product, you'll be able to expand FORMSOF to look for other forms besides inflectional—for example, synonyms (THESAURUS), words that might be misspelled, or words that sound the same.

You can use full-text searching to look for words that appear near each other, using either the word NEAR or the tilde (~). The meaning of *near* is imprecise by design, which allows the Search service to return rows containing words of various degrees of nearness. NEAR has to take into account numerous factors, including:

- Distance between words. If I'm looking for *hot* near *spicy*, the string *spicy hot* has the words at a distance of 0 and the string *hot and very spicy* has the words at a distance of 2.

- Minimum distance between words. If the search words occur multiple times within the same row, what is the minimum distance apart?

- Size of columns. If the data columns are 200 words long, a distance of 5 between *hot* and *spicy* is considered nearer than a distance of 2 in a column with only 10 words.

Here's a simple example that uses NEAR

```
-- This query returns rows that have hot near spicy
SELECT * FROM products
WHERE CONTAINS(*, 'hot near spicy')
```

The query above returns the same results as the query that looks for *hot and spicy*. In my small data set, all occurrences of *hot* and *spicy* are near each other.

Each row that meets the conditions of a full-text search is given a ranking value that indicates how "strongly" it meets the criteria. If our search string includes NEAR, rows that have the search words nearer will be ranked higher. Rows that contain the search words more often will also be ranked higher. We can also supply our own weighing with an argument called ISABOUT and assign a weight to certain words. Here's an example:

```
SELECT *
FROM Products
WHERE CONTAINS(*,'ISABOUT(spicy weight(.8), supreme weight(.2),
hot weight(.1))')
```

The query asks for rows that contain *spicy*, *supreme*, or *hot*. The word *spicy* will have four times the weight of the word *supreme*, which in turn will have twice the weight of *hot*. The results don't mean much in terms of the rank. To see the internal ranking that the Search service has assigned to each qualifying row, we need to use the predicate CONTAINSTABLE. Here's a similar query with the same search string:

```
SELECT *
FROM CONTAINSTABLE(Products, *,
    'ISABOUT(spicy weight(.8), supreme weight(.1),hot weight(.2))')
```

The output here is even less meaningful. Here are the first few rows:

```
KEY         RANK
----------- -----------
5           130
3           4
4
```

The results returned by CONTAINSTABLE report *only* the internal ranking and the unique index key associated with each row. However, since we know which column has the unique index, we can join the result of CONTAINSTABLE with the original table and order by the *RANK* column. For the *products* table, the unique key is *ProductID*. Here's the query:

```
SELECT [KEY], RANK, ProductID, ProductName
FROM CONTAINSTABLE(Products, *,
    'ISABOUT(spicy weight(.8), supreme weight(.1), hot weight(.2))') C
JOIN Products P
    ON P.productID = C.[KEY]
ORDER BY RANK DESC
```

Here are the complete results:

```
KEY   RANK   ProductID   ProductName
----  ------ ----------- -------------------------------------------------
65    58         65      Hot and Spicy Louisiana Fiery Hot Pepper Sauce
15    53         15      Hot and Spicy Genen Shouyu Supreme
63    53         63      Spicy Hot Vegie-spread Supreme
20    53         20      Supreme Hot and Spicy Sir Rodney's Marmalade
21    53         21      Spicy Hot Sir Rodney's Scones Supreme
28    53         28      Supreme Spicy Hot Rössle Sauerkraut
75    53         75      Hot and Spicy Rhönbräu Klosterbier Supreme
30    53         30      Hot and Spicy Nord-Ost Matjeshering Supreme
40    53         40      Supreme Hot and Spicy Boston Crab Meat
42    53         42      Spicy Hot Singaporean Hokkien Fried Mee Supreme
45    53         45      Hot and Spicy Rogede sild Supreme
56    53         56      Supreme Spicy Hot Gnocchi di nonna Alice
60    53         60      Hot and Spicy Camembert Pierrot Supreme
55    48         55      Hot and Spicy Pâté chinois
49    48         49      Spicy Hot Maxilaku
```

50	48	50	Hot and Spicy Valkoinen suklaa
35	48	35	Hot and Spicy Steeleye Stout
77	48	77	Spicy Hot Original Frankfurter grüne Soße
25	48	25	Hot and Spicy NuNuCa Nuß-Nougat-Creme
70	48	70	Hot and Spicy Outback Lager
10	48	10	Hot and Spicy Ikura
7	48	7	Spicy Hot Uncle Bob's Organic Dried Pears
14	48	14	Spicy Hot Tofu
5	48	5	Hot and Spicy Chef Anton's Gumbo Mix
9	43	9	Mishi Kobe Niku Supreme Extra Spicy
18	43	18	Carnarvon Tigers Supreme Extra Spicy
27	43	27	Schoggi Schokolade Supreme Extra Spicy
72	43	72	Mozzarella di Giovanni Supreme Extra Spicy
36	43	36	Inlagd Sill Supreme Extra Spicy
54	43	54	Tourtière Supreme Extra Spicy
66	14	66	Louisiana Hot Spiced Okra Supreme
8	4	8	Supreme Northwoods Cranberry Sauce
3	4	3	Aniseed Syrup Supreme
4	4	4	Supreme Chef Anton's Cajun Seasoning
6	4	6	Grandma's Boysenberry Spread Supreme
16	4	16	Supreme Pavlova
12	4	12	Queso Manchego La Pastora Supreme
32	4	32	Supreme Mascarpone Fabioli
33	4	33	Geitost Supreme
69	4	69	Gudbrandsdalsost Supreme
64	4	64	Supreme Wimmers gute Semmelknödel
24	4	24	Guaraná Fantástica Supreme
68	4	68	Supreme Scottish Longbreads
52	4	52	Supreme Filo Mix
76	4	76	Supreme Lakkalikööri
51	4	51	Manjimup Dried Apples Supreme
39	4	39	Chartreuse verte Supreme
48	4	48	Chocolade Supreme
44	4	44	Supreme Gula Malacca
57	4	57	Ravioli Angelo Supreme

(50 row(s) affected)

Note that the rows containing multiple occurrences of some of the words are returned first, followed by rows containing all three search words, rows containing only *spicy*, and then rows containing only *supreme*.

Rank can be a value between 0 and 1000, but because of the complex algorithm used to determine rank, you'll never get a rank of 1000. In addition to the complex rules for determining what NEAR means, other rules come into play during a search for a simple word. If a word occurs in every row in a table, it carries less weight internally than a word that only occurs a few times, as you can see in the example on the next page.

```
SELECT [KEY], RANK, ProductID, ProductName
FROM CONTAINSTABLE(Products, *,'hot or tofu ') C
JOIN Products P
    ON P.productID = C.[KEY]
ORDER BY RANK DESC
```

Because *hot* occurs in many of the rows of the *products* table, it is given less weight than *tofu*, which occurs only in two rows. This is the Search service's own weighting, which is applied even if you don't use the ISABOUT function to specify a weight. Rows that contain both *hot* and *tofu* are ranked highest, followed by rows containing just *tofu*, rows that contain just *hot*, and then rows that contain *hot* more than once!

FREETEXT and FREETEXTTABLE Predicates

The FREETEXT and FREETEXTTABLE predicates allow you to compare one text value with another to determine how similar they are. You can enter just a string of individual words, or you can grab a value from another table to use for comparison. Here's a simple example:

```
SELECT *
FROM Products
WHERE FREETEXT (*, 'I love hot and spicy scones')
```

The Search service breaks the FREETEXT argument apart into meaningful words and compares those words to the words in the full-text index. FREETEXT includes an implied "inflectional" function, but you cannot add an explicit function to FREETEXT. So this query will find the row with *seasoning*:

```
SELECT *
FROM Products
WHERE FREETEXT (*, 'Highly seasoned foods')
```

Again, by default the rows don't come back in any order. However, the FREETEXTTABLE predicate, which functions analogously to the CONTAINSTABLE predicate, allows us to obtain the ranks and join back to the base table:

```
SELECT [Key], Rank, ProductID, ProductName
FROM FREETEXTTABLE (Products, *,'I love hot and spicy scones') F
JOIN Products P
    ON P.productID = F.[KEY]
ORDER BY RANK DESC
```

Here are the first few rows of the result:

```
Key   Rank  ProductID   ProductName
----- ----- ----------- -------------------------------------------------
21    56    21          Spicy Hot Sir Rodney's Scones Supreme
65    18    65          Hot and Spicy Louisiana Fiery Hot Pepper Sauce
```

5	12	5	Hot and Spicy Chef Anton's Gumbo Mix
10	12	10	Hot and Spicy Ikura
7	12	7	Spicy Hot Uncle Bob's Organic Dried Pears
14	12	14	Spicy Hot Tofu

Sometimes hundreds or even thousands of rows will meet your criteria to some degree. SQL Server 2000 lets you ask the Search service to give you only a few rows, based on the internal ranking. You can use a fourth argument to the CONTAINSTABLE or FREETEXTTABLE predicates, which is an integer described as TOP *n* BY RANK. Here is the CONTAINSTABLE query, with the addition of an argument to ask for only the TOP 10 rows:

```
SELECT [KEY], RANK, ProductID, ProductName
FROM CONTAINSTABLE(Products, *,'
    ISABOUT(spicy weight(.8), supreme weight(.1), hot weight(.2))', 10) C
JOIN Products P
    ON P.productID = C.[KEY]
ORDER BY RANK DESC
```

Be very careful with this TOP *n* BY RANK argument if you're applying other search conditions to your CONTAINSTABLE or FREETEXTTABLE queries. The full-text search is done first, the limited rows are returned to SQL Server, and only then is your own WHERE condition applied. Suppose I want to see the names of products that contain *spicy*, *supreme*, or *hot*, as weighted in the preceding query, but I'm interested only in products in category 6. A lookup in the *category* table tells me that this is meat and poultry. It turns out that none of the top 10 ranking rows is in category 6, so this query will find no rows:

```
SELECT [KEY], RANK, ProductID, ProductName
FROM CONTAINSTABLE(Products, *,'
    ISABOUT(spicy weight(.8), supreme weight(.1), hot weight(.2))', 10) C
JOIN Products P
    ON P.productID = c.[KEY]
WHERE categoryID = 6
ORDER BY RANK DESC
```

If we want our condition to be applied first, and then get the top 10 rows, we have to use SQL Server's own TOP function:

```
SELECT TOP 10 [KEY], RANK, ProductID, ProductName
FROM CONTAINSTABLE(Products, *,'
    ISABOUT(spicy weight(.8), supreme weight(.1), hot weight(.2))') C
JOIN Products P
    ON P.productID = C.[KEY]
WHERE categoryID = 6
ORDER BY RANK DESC
```

More About Full-Text Indexes

I've already told you about the FULLTEXTCATALOGPROPERTY function, which gives you some important information about the status of your catalog population. The OBJECTPROPERTY function also has some arguments that allow you to get full-text index information from individual tables. In some cases, you might find these more useful than FULLTEXTCATALOGPROPERTY, and I recommend that you use them when possible. Future versions of full-text indexes might minimize or hide the catalogs, so you'll work only with the individual tables. Table 10-17 lists the OBJECTPROPERTY arguments that deal with full-text indexes.

OBJECTPROPERTY Argument	Description
TableFullTextBackgroundUpdateIndexOn	The table has full-text back ground update index enabled. 1 = TRUE 0 = FALSE
TableFulltextCatalogId	The ID of the full-text catalog in which the full-text index data for the table resides. Nonzero = Full-text catalog ID, associated with the unique index that identifies the rows in a full-text indexed table. 0 = Table is not full-text indexed.
TableFullTextChangeTrackingOn	The table has full-text change tracking enabled. 1 = TRUE 0 = FALSE
TableFulltextKeyColumn	The ID of the column associated with the single-column unique index that is participating in the full-text index definition. 0 = Table is not full-text indexed.
TableFullTextPopulateStatus	0 = No population 1 = Full population 2 = Incremental population
TableHasActiveFulltextIndex	The table has an active full-text index. 1 = True 0 = False

Table 10-17. *Arguments of OBJECTPROPERTY.*

So, to find out if my *products* table has background index updating enabled, I can execute the following query:

```
SELECT OBJECTPROPERTY ( object_id('products'),
    'TableFullTextBackgroundUpdateIndexOn')
```

A returned value of 1 means that background index updating is enabled, a value of 0 means no, and a NULL means that I typed something wrong.

Performance Considerations for Full-Text Indexes

If you are full-text indexing on tables that have less than a million rows, you have little performance tuning to do. If you create full-text indexes on SQL Server tables that contain millions of rows, you need to be aware that this will sustain heavy read and write activity. You should consider configuring your SQL Server and the directory where your catalogs are stored to maximize disk I/O performance by load balancing across multiple disk drives.

Hardware and Operating System Configuration

For your hardware, you should consider multiple fast processors and lots of additional memory. If you'll be doing a lot of full-text indexing and searching, 1 GB should be the minimum memory. You'll also want multiple disk controllers with several channels each, if possible, or, at a minimum, multiple channels on a single controller. Consider using a very fast disk system with striping and no fault tolerance to maximize read and write performance.

If you're installing SQL Server on a server running Windows NT, your page file will need to be 1.5 to 2 times the amount of available physical RAM. This amount can be reduced on Windows 2000 if you have larger amounts of RAM. The page file should be placed on its own drive with its own controller.

SQL Server Configuration

After a full population of a table with more than a million rows, the fastest, most efficient method of maintaining your indexes is to use the change-tracking feature with the background update option. If you must do a full or incremental population or update the changes in a single operation rather than in the background, the population should be done during (or scheduled for) periods of low system activity, typically during database maintenance windows, if you have them.

When you determine whether to use one or multiple full-text catalogs, you must take into account both maintenance and searching considerations. There is a trade-off between performance and maintenance when considering this design question with large SQL tables, and I suggest that you test both options for your environment.

If you choose to have multiple tables in one catalog, you'll incur some overhead because of longer running full-text search queries, but the main penalty will be that any population will take longer because all tables in the catalog will need to be updated. If you choose to have a single SQL table per catalog, you'll have the overhead of maintaining separate catalogs. You also should be aware that there is a limit of 256 full-text catalogs per machine. The Search service imposes this limit, and there is only one Search service per machine. The limit is not related to the number of SQL Server instances you might have.

> **NOTE** You should also be aware that because the Search service is a component external to SQL Server, it can change when you upgrade other components. For example, Windows NT 4 and Windows 2000 have slightly different Search service implementations, with different word-breaking algorithms. You might occasionally see slightly different results when you run on these different platforms. You'll need to check the documentation to see if products you install on your server after installing SQL Server 2000 use the Microsoft Search service.

SUMMARY

This chapter discussed the programming extensions beyond typical implementations of SQL that make Transact-SQL a specialized programming language. These extensions include control of flow, conditional branching, looping, variables, logical operations, bitwise operations, and a variety of scalar functions. The extensions let you write sophisticated routines directly in Transact-SQL and execute them directly in the SQL Server engine. Without them, you would have to write much more logic into client applications, which would hurt performance because more conversation would need to take place across the network. We also looked at how to use SQL Server 2000 in conjunction with the Search service to maintain and query full-text indexes on your data.

From here, we'll move on to using the Transact-SQL extensions in stored procedures and triggers.

Chapter 11

Batches, Stored Procedures, and Functions

In this chapter, we'll use Transact-SQL for more than interactive queries. When you send a query to the server, you're sending a command batch to SQL Server. But we can do even more. For example, we can wrap up commands in a module that can be stored and cached at the server for later reuse. Modules that contain data modification operations can be created as stored procedures; modules that return a value or a result set without affecting other data in your database can be created as user-defined functions.

I'll describe the creation, use, and internal storage of stored procedures and user-defined functions. The ANSI SQL Standard refers to both stored procedures and user-defined functions as "routines"; I'll use that term when I need to refer to both of these types of objects together. SQL Server allows us to create another type of stored module that is automatically executed when a request is made to modify data; this type of object is called a trigger. However, the SQL Standard does not consider triggers in its definition of "routines," so I won't either. I'll cover the details of trigger creation and use in Chapter 12.

BATCHES

A batch is one or more SQL Server commands that are dispatched and executed together. Because every batch sent from the client to the server requires handshaking between the two, sending a batch instead of sending separate commands can be more efficient. Even a batch that doesn't return a result set (for example, a single INSERT statement) requires at least an acknowledgment that the command was processed and a status code for its level of success. At the server, the batch must be received, queued for execution, and so on.

Although commands are grouped and dispatched together for execution, each command is distinct from the others. Let's look at an example. Suppose you need to execute 150 INSERT statements. Executing all 150 statements in one batch requires the processing overhead to be incurred once rather than 150 times. In one real-world situation, an application that took 5 to 6 seconds to complete 150 individual INSERT statements was changed so that all 150 statements were sent as one batch. The processing time decreased to well under 0.5 second, more than a tenfold improvement. And this was on a LAN, not on a slow network such as a WAN or the Internet, where the improvement would have been even more pronounced. Try running an application with 150 batches to insert 150 rows over the Internet, and you'll be really sorry!

Using a batch is a huge win. By using the Transact-SQL constructs presented in Chapter 10, such as conditional logic and looping, you can often perform sophisticated operations within a single batch and eliminate the need for an extensive conversation between the client and the server. Those operations can also be saved on the server as a stored procedure, which allows them to execute even more efficiently. If your operations are returning values rather than modifying them, you can also save the code as a user-defined function. Using batches and stored modules to minimize client/server conversations is crucial for achieving high performance. And now that more applications are being deployed on slower networks—such as WANs, the Internet, and dial-up systems—instead of on LANs only, using batches and stored modules is crucial.

Every SELECT statement (except those used for assigning a value to a variable) generates a result set. Even a SELECT statement that finds zero rows returns a result set that describes the columns selected. Every time the server sends a result set back to the client application, it must send *metadata* as well as the actual data. The metadata describes the result set to the client. You can think of metadata in this way: "Here's a result set with eight columns. The first column is named *last_name* and is of type *char(30)*. The second column is..."

Obviously, then, executing a single SELECT statement with a WHERE clause formulated to find, in one fell swoop, all 247 rows that meet your criteria is much more efficient than separately executing 247 SELECT statements that each return one row of data. In the former case, one result set is returned. In the latter case, 247 result sets are returned. The performance difference is striking.

Although batches seem like an obvious necessity, many programmers still write applications that perform poorly because they don't use batches. This problem is especially common among developers who have worked on ISAM or similar sequential files that do row-at-a-time processing. Unlike ISAM, SQL Server works best with sets of data, not individual rows of data, so that you can minimize conversations between the server and the client application.

There's actually a middle ground between using one SELECT statement that returns all your rows and using an individual batch to return each row. Batches can contain multiple statements, each one returning its own metadata, so the ideal solution is to minimize your total number of statements. Multiple SELECTs within a single batch are still better than having each statement in its own batch because each batch has the overhead of handshaking between the client and server.

Here is a simple batch, issued from SQL Query Analyzer. Even though three unrelated operations are being performed, we can package them in a single batch to conserve bandwidth:

```
INSERT authors VALUES (etc.)
SELECT * FROM authors
UPDATE publishers SET pub_id= (etc.)
<click the Execute Query button>
```

All statements within a single batch are parsed as a unit. This means that if you have a syntax error in any of the statements, none of the statements will execute. For example, consider this batch of two statements, which you can try to execute from SQL Query Analyzer:

```
SELECT * FROM sales
SELECT * FOM titleauthor
<click the Execute Query button>
```

When you execute this batch, you get the following error:

```
Server: Msg 170, Level 15, State 1, Line 2
Line 2: Incorrect syntax near 'FOM'.
```

Even though the first SELECT statement is perfectly legal, no data is returned because of the error in the second statement. If we separated this into two different batches, the first one would return a result set and the second one would return an error.

Now suppose that instead of mistyping the keyword FROM as *FOM*, we had mistyped the name of the table:

```
SELECT * FROM sales
SELECT * FROM titleautor
<click the Execute Query button>
```

SQL Server 2000 provides delayed name resolution, in which object names aren't resolved until execution time. In this example, SQL Server returns the data from the first SELECT, followed by this error message:

```
Server: Msg 208, Level 16, State 1, Line 1
Invalid object name 'titleautor'.
```

However, if we had mistyped the object name in the first statement, execution of the batch would stop when the error was encountered. No data would be returned by any subsequent valid queries.

Note that delayed object resolution does not apply to column names. If you changed the second query to one that used a valid table name but specified an invalid column in that table, the error would be detected at compile time and none of the statements in the batch would be executed. Here's an example:

```
SELECT * FROM sales
SELECT lastname FROM titleauthor
<click the Execute Query button>
```

Normally, everything in SQL Query Analyzer's query window is considered a single batch and is sent to SQL Server for parsing, compiling, and execution when you click the green EXECUTE button. However, SQL Query Analyzer provides two ways around this. First, you can highlight a section of code in the query window so that when you click the EXECUTE button, only the highlighted text is sent as a batch to SQL Server. Alternatively, you can include the word GO between your queries.

If you use either of the text-based query tools (OSQL or ISQL), there's no green Execute Query button to click. When you use these tools, you must type *GO* on a line by itself to indicate that everything you've typed up to that point is a batch. The tool will then send that batch to SQL Server for processing.

GO isn't an SQL command or keyword. It's the end-of-batch signal understood only by certain client tools. The client interprets it to mean that everything since the last GO should be sent to the server for execution. SQL Server never sees the GO command and has no idea what it means. With a custom application, a batch is executed with a single *SQLExecute* from ODBC (or *dbsqlexec* from DB-Library).

If you include the GO command in the query window, SQL Query Analyzer breaks up your statement into the indicated batches behind the scenes. Each batch (as marked by the GO command) is sent individually to SQL Server.

A collection of batches that are frequently executed together is sometimes called a *script*. Most of the client tools provide a mechanism for loading a script that you've saved to a text file and for executing it. In SQL Query Analyzer, you can use the File/Open command to load a script. From the command-line OSQL or ISQL programs, we can specify the */i* flag followed by a filename to indicate that the SQL Server batches to execute should come from the specified file. Alternatively, if we're using OSQL or ISQL interactively, we can read in a file containing one or more SQL statement by typing *:r* followed by the filename. (See *SQL Server Books Online* for details about using OSQL and ISQL.)

The fact that the client tool and not SQL Server processes GO can lead to some unexpected behavior. Suppose you have a script containing several batches. During testing, you want to comment out a couple of the batches to ignore them for the time being. Your commented script might look something like this:

```
SELECT * FROM authors
/*
GO
SELECT * FROM sales
GO
SELECT * FROM publishers
GO
*/
SELECT * FROM titles
GO
```

The intention here was to comment out the SELECT from the *sales* and *publishers* tables and to run the SELECT from *authors* and *titles* as a single batch. However, if you run this script from SQL Query Analyzer, you'll get exactly the opposite behavior! That is, you'll see the data from the *sales* and *publishers* tables but not from *authors* or *titles*. If you look at this script from the perspective of the client tool, the behavior makes sense. The tool doesn't try to interpret any of your SQL statements; it just breaks the statements into batches to be sent to SQL Server. A batch is marked by a GO command at the beginning of a line.

So the above script contains four batches. The first batch (everything before the first GO) is as follows:

```
SELECT * FROM authors
/*
```

SQL Server generates an error message because there's an open comment with no corresponding close comment.

The second and third batches are as follows:

```
SELECT * FROM sales
```

and

```
SELECT * FROM publishers
```

Both of these batches are perfectly legal, and SQL Server can process them and return results.

The fourth batch is as follows:

```
*/
SELECT * FROM titles
```

SQL Server also generates an error for this last one because it has a close comment without an open comment marker, and no data is returned.

If you want to comment out statements within a script that can contain the end-of-batch GO command, you should use the alternative comment marker—the double dash—in front of every GO. Alternatively, you can just use the double dash in front of every line you want to comment out. Your script would then look like this:

```
SELECT * FROM authors
-- GO
-- SELECT * FROM sales
-- GO
-- SELECT * FROM publishers
-- GO
SELECT * FROM titles
GO
```

SQL Query Analyzer makes it easy to comment out a group of lines as in the code above. You can highlight all the lines to be commented out, and from the Edit menu, choose Advanced/Comment Out. The keystroke combination to perform the same action is Ctrl-Shift-C. With this revised script, the client tool won't recognize the GO as the end-of-batch marker because it's not the first thing on a line. The client will consider this script to be one single batch and send it to SQL Server as such.

ROUTINES

In SQL Server 2000, stored procedures and user-defined functions are considered routines. The ANSI SCHEMA VIEW called ROUTINES contains information about all your procedures and user-defined functions, including the text that makes up the routine's definition. You can inspect this view and get information about all the routines in a database by selecting from this ANSI SCHEMA VIEW. I ran the following in the *master* database:

```
SELECT routine_type, routine_name FROM INFORMATION_SCHEMA.ROUTINES
```

Here are the partial results:

```
routine_type           routine_name
--------------------   -------------------------------
PROCEDURE              sp_MSgetrowmetadata
PROCEDURE              sp_MSindexspace
FUNCTION               fn_sqlvarbasetostr
FUNCTION               fn_helpcollations
PROCEDURE              sp_describe_cursor_tables
PROCEDURE              sp_MSIfExistsRemoteLogin
FUNCTION               fn_trace_getinfo
PROCEDURE              sp_MSmakedynsnapshotvws
```

```
FUNCTION            fn_chariswhitespace
FUNCTION            fn_generateparameterpattern
FUNCTION            fn_skipparameterargument
PROCEDURE           sp_MSmakeexpandproc
FUNCTION            fn_removeparameterwithargument
```

As you'll see in more detail later, stored procedures and functions are invoked in different ways. Simply put, stored procedures can be invoked anywhere a statement can be executed, while a function is invoked inside another statement. You can use scalar functions anywhere that your SQL command expects a single value, and you can use table-valued functions in the FROM clause to indicate the rowset to be processed.

STORED PROCEDURES

Understanding batches is a crucial prerequisite to understanding stored procedures, but you shouldn't confuse the two. Batches involve communication between a client program and SQL Server, and stored procedures are objects that exist only on the server. A stored procedure always executes within context of a single batch, but a single batch can contain calls to multiple stored procedures as well as other commands that are not part of stored procedures.

We've actually seen stored procedures in use quite a few times already. For example, we've looked at the output to the system stored procedures *sp_help*, *sp_helpconstraint,* and *sp_helpindex*. The stored procedures that you can create are not too different from the system-supplied procedures. After I tell you a bit more about stored procedures, you'll be able to see exactly what the similarities and differences are between the procedures you write and the ones Microsoft supplies with SQL Server.

To create a stored procedure, you take a batch and wrap it inside a CREATE PROCEDURE statement. The procedure's definition can consist of any Transact-SQL commands, with nothing special except for declaring which parameters are passed to the procedure.

To demonstrate how easy it is to create a stored procedure, I've written a simple procedure called *get_author* that takes one parameter, the author ID, and returns the names of any authors that have IDs equal to whatever character string is passed to the procedure:

```
CREATE PROC get_author @au_id varchar(11)
AS
SELECT au_lname, au_fname
FROM authors
WHERE au_id=@au_id
```

This procedure can be subsequently executed with syntax like the following:

```
EXEC get_author '172-32-1176'
```

or

```
EXEC get_author @au_id='172-32-1176'
```

As you can see, you can pass the parameters anonymously by including specific values for them. If the procedure is expecting more than one parameter and you want to pass them anonymously, you must specify their values in the order that the parameters were listed in the CREATE PROCEDURE statement. Alternatively, you can explicitly name the parameters so that the order in which they're passed isn't important.

If executing the procedure is the first statement in the batch, using the keyword EXEC is optional. However, it's probably best to use EXEC (or EXECUTE) so that you won't wind up wondering why your procedure wouldn't execute (only to realize later that it's no longer the first statement of the batch).

In practice, you'll probably want a procedure like the one above to be a bit more sophisticated. Perhaps you'll want to search for author names that begin with a partial ID that you pass. If you choose not to pass anything, the procedure should show all authors rather than return an error message stating that the parameter is missing.

Or maybe you'd like to return some value as a variable (distinct from the result set returned and from the return code) that you can use to check for successful execution. You can do this by passing an output parameter, which has a pass-by-reference capability. Passing an output parameter to a stored procedure is similar to passing a pointer when you call a function in C. Rather than passing a value, you pass the address of a storage area in which the procedure will cache a value. That value is subsequently available to the SQL batch after the stored procedure has executed.

For example, you might want an output parameter to tell you the number of rows returned by a SELECT statement. While the @@ROWCOUNT system function provides this information, it's available for only the last statement executed. If the stored procedure has executed many statements, you must put this value away for safekeeping. An output parameter provides an easy way to do this.

Here's a simple procedure that selects all the rows from the *authors* table and all the rows from the *titles* table. It also sets an output parameter for each table based on @@ROWCOUNT. The calling batch retrieves the @@ROWCOUNT values through the variables passed as the output parameters.

```
CREATE PROC count_tables @authorcount int OUTPUT,
@titlecount int OUTPUT
AS
SELECT * FROM authors
SET @authorcount=@@ROWCOUNT
SELECT * FROM titles
```

```
SET @titlecount=@@ROWCOUNT
RETURN(0)
```

The procedure would then be executed like this:

```
DECLARE @a_count int, @t_count int
EXEC count_tables @a_count OUTPUT, @t_count OUTPUT
```

> **TIP** Parameters passed to a routine are treated much like local variables. Variables declared in a stored procedure are always local, so we could have used the same names for both the variables in the procedure and those passed by the batch as output parameters. In fact, this is probably the most common way to invoke them. However, the variables passed into a routine don't need to have the same name as the associated parameters. Even with the same name, they are in fact different variables because their scoping is different.

This procedure returns all the rows from both tables. In addition, the variables *@a_count* and *@t_count* retain the row counts from the *authors* and *titles* tables, respectively. After the EXEC statement inside the batch, we can look at the values in the two variables passed to procedure to see what values they ended up with:

```
SELECT authorcount=@a_count, titlecount=@t_count
```

Here's the output for this SELECT:

```
authorcount    titlecount
-----------    ----------
23             18
```

When you create a stored procedure, you can reference a table, a view, or another stored procedure that doesn't currently exist. In the latter case, you'll get a warning message informing you that a referenced object doesn't exist. As long as the object exists at the time the procedure is executed, all will be fine.

Nested Stored Procedures

Stored procedures can be nested and can call other procedures. A procedure invoked from another procedure can also invoke yet another procedure. In such a transaction, the top-level procedure has a nesting level of 1. The first subordinate procedure has a nesting level of 2. If that subordinate procedure subsequently invokes another stored procedure, the nesting level is 3, and so on, to a limit of 32 nesting levels. If the 32-level limit is reached, a fatal error occurs, the batch is aborted, and any open transaction is rolled back.

The nesting-level limit prevents stack overflows that can result from procedures recursively calling themselves infinitely. The limit allows a procedure to recursively call itself only 31 subsequent times (for a total of 32 procedure calls). To determine how deeply a procedure is nested at runtime, you can select the value of the system function @@NESTLEVEL.

Unlike with nesting levels, SQL Server has no practical limit on the number of stored procedures that can be invoked from a given stored procedure. For example, a main stored procedure can invoke hundreds of subordinate stored procedures. If the subordinate procedures don't invoke other subordinate procedures, the nesting level never reaches a depth greater than 2.

An error in a nested (subordinate) stored procedure isn't necessarily fatal to the calling stored procedure. When you invoke a stored procedure from another stored procedure, it's smart to use a RETURN statement and check the return value in the calling procedure. In this way, you can work conditionally with error situations (as shown in the upcoming factorial example).

Recursion in Stored Procedures

Stored procedures can perform nested calls to themselves, also known as *recursion*. Recursion is a technique by which the solution to a problem can be expressed by applying the solution to subsets of the problem. Programming instructors usually demonstrate recursion by having students write a factorial program using recursion to display a table of factorial values for *0!* through *10!*. Recall that a factorial of a positive integer n, written as $n!$, is the product of all integers from 1 through n. The following is an example:

```
8!    = 8 x 7 x 6 x 5 x 4 x 3 x 2 x 1 = 40320
```

(Zero is a special case—*0!* is defined as equal to 1.)

We can write a stored procedure that computes factorials, and we can do the recursive programming assignment in Transact-SQL:

```
-- Use Transact-SQL to recursively calculate factorial
-- of numbers between 0 and 12.
-- Parameters greater than 12 are disallowed because the
-- result overflows the bounds of an int.

CREATE PROC factorial @param1 int
AS
DECLARE @one_less int, @answer int
IF (@param1 < 0 OR @param1 > 12)
    BEGIN
        -- Illegal parameter value. Must be between 0 and 12.
        RETURN -1
    END

IF (@param1=0 or @param1=1)
    SELECT @answer=1
ELSE
    BEGIN
        SET @one_less=@param1 - 1
```

```
    EXEC @answer=factorial @one_less -- Recursively call itself
    IF (@answer= -1)
        BEGIN
            RETURN -1
        END

    SET @answer=@answer * @param1
    IF (@@ERROR <> 0)
        RETURN -1
END
```

```
RETURN(@answer)
```

Note that when the procedure is initially created, a warning message like the one shown here will indicate that the procedure references a procedure that doesn't currently exist (which is itself in this case):

```
Cannot add rows to sysdepends for the current stored procedure
because it depends on the missing object 'factorial'. The stored
procedure will still be created.
```

Once the procedure exists, we can use it to display a standard factorial:

```
DECLARE @answer int, @param int
SET @param=0
WHILE (@param <= 12) BEGIN
    EXEC @answer = factorial @param
        IF (@answer= -1) BEGIN
        RAISERROR('Error executing factorial procedure.', 16, -1)
        RETURN
    END
PRINT CONVERT(varchar, @param) + '! = ' + CONVERT(varchar(50), @answer)
SET @param=@param + 1
END
```

Here's the output table:

```
0! = 1
1! = 1
2! = 2
3! = 6
4! = 24
5! = 120
6! = 720
7! = 5040
8! = 40320
9! = 362880
10! = 3628800
11! = 39916800
12! = 479001600
```

We stopped at *12!* in the *factorial* procedure because *13!* is 6,227,020,800, which exceeds the range of a 32-bit (4-byte) integer. Even if we changed the parameter *@answer* to be type *decimal*, we would still be limited to *12!* because the value included in a RETURN statement must be type *int*.

Here's another version of the procedure that uses an output parameter for the answer and introduces a new variable to hold the returned status of the procedure. You can use a *decimal* datatype with a scale of 0 as an alternative to *int* for integer operations that require values larger than the 4-byte *int* can handle.

```
CREATE PROC factorial @param1 decimal(38,0), @answer decimal(38,0) output
AS
DECLARE @one_less decimal(38,0), @status int

IF (@param1 < 0 OR @param1 > 32)
    BEGIN
        -- Illegal parameter value. Must be between 0 and 32.
        RETURN -1
    END

IF (@param1=0 or @param1=1)
    SET @answer=1
ELSE
    BEGIN
        SET @one_less=@param1 - 1
        EXEC @status=factorial @one_less, @answer output
        -- Recursively call itself
        IF (@status= -1)
            BEGIN
                RETURN -1
            END

        SET @answer=@answer * @param1

        IF (@@ERROR <> 0)
            RETURN -1
    END

RETURN  0
```

To call this procedure, we can use the following code:

```
DECLARE @answer decimal(38,0), @param int
SET @param=0
WHILE (@param <= 32) BEGIN
    EXEC factorial  @param, @answer output
    IF (@answer= -1)
        BEGIN
            RAISERROR('Error executing factorial procedure.', 16, -1)
```

```
        RETURN
    END
PRINT CONVERT(varchar, @param) + '! = ' + CONVERT(varchar(50), @answer)
SET @param=@param + 1
END
```

Even though this procedure has removed the range limit on the result by using a *decimal* datatype to hold the answer, we can only go to *32!* because we'd reach the maximum nesting depth of 32, which includes recursive calls. If we took out the condition *OR @param1 > 32*, this would allow an initial parameter > *32*, which would result in a nesting level that exceeded the maximum. We would then get this error:

```
Server: Msg 217, Level 16, State 1, Procedure factorial, Line 17
Maximum stored procedure, function, trigger, or view-nesting level
exceeded (limit 32).
```

In C, you need to be sure that you don't overflow your stack when you use recursion. Using Transact-SQL shields you from that concern, but it does so by steadfastly refusing to nest calls more than 32 levels deep. You can also watch @@NESTLEVEL and take appropriate action before reaching the hard limit. As is often the case with a recursion problem, you can perform an iterative solution without the restriction of nesting or worries about the stack.

Here's an iterative approach. To illustrate that there's no restriction of 32 levels because it's simple iteration, we'll go one step further, to *33!*. We'll stop at *33!* because *34!* would overflow the precision of a *numeric(38,0)* variable. So even though the iterative approach removes the nesting level limit, we can only go one step further because of the range limitations of SQL Server's exact numeric datatypes:

```
-- Alternative iterative solution does not have the restriction
-- of 32 nesting levels
CREATE PROC factorial2 @param1 int, @answer NUMERIC(38,0) OUTPUT
AS
DECLARE @counter int
IF (@param1 < 0 OR @param1 > 33)
    BEGIN
        RAISERROR ('Illegal Parameter Value. Must be between 0 and 33',
            16, -1)
        RETURN -1
    END

SET @counter=1 SET @answer=1

WHILE (@counter < @param1 AND @param1 <> 0 )
    BEGIN
        SET @answer=@answer * (@counter + 1)
        SET @counter=@counter + 1
    END
```

(continued)

```
RETURN
GO

DECLARE @answer numeric(38, 0), @param int
SET @param=0
WHILE (@param <= 32)
    BEGIN
        EXEC factorial2 @param, @answer OUTPUT
        PRINT CONVERT(varchar(50), @param) + '! = '
            + CONVERT(varchar(50), @answer)
        SET @param=@param + 1
    END
```

And here's the output :

```
0!  = 1
1!  = 1
2!  = 2
3!  = 6
4!  = 24
5!  = 120
6!  = 720
7!  = 5040
8!  = 40320
9!  = 362880
10! = 3628800
11! = 39916800
12! = 479001600
13! = 6227020800
14! = 87178291200
15! = 1307674368000
16! = 20922789888000
17! = 355687428096000
18! = 6402373705728000
19! = 121645100408832000
20! = 2432902008176640000
21! = 51090942171709440000
22! = 1124000727777607680000
23! = 25852016738884976640000
24! = 620448401733239439360000
25! = 15511210043330985984000000
26! = 403291461126605635584000000
27! = 10888869450418352160768000000
28! = 304888344611713860501504000000
29! = 8841761993739701954543616000000
30! = 265252859812191058636308480000000
31! = 8222838654177922817725562880000000
32! = 263130836933693530167218012160000000
33! = 8683317618811886495518194401280000000
```

Because this factorial procedure is really producing a single valued result, we could have created it as a user-defined function. I'll show you how to do that a little later in this chapter.

Stored Procedure Parameters

Stored procedures take parameters, and you can give parameters default values. If you don't supply a default value when you create the procedure, an actual parameter will be required when the procedure is executed. If you don't pass a required parameter, you'll get an error like the following, which occurs when I try to call the factorial procedure without a parameter:

```
Server: Msg 201, Level 16, State 3, Procedure factorial, Line 0
Procedure 'factorial' expects parameter '@param1', which was not supplied.
```

You can pass values by explicitly naming the parameters or by furnishing all the parameter values anonymously but in correct positional order. You can also use the keyword DEFAULT as a placeholder when you pass parameters. You can also pass NULL as a parameter (or define it as the default). Here's a simple example with results in bold:

```
CREATE PROCEDURE pass_params
@param0 int=NULL,    -- Defaults to NULL
@param1 int=1,       -- Defaults to 1
@param2 int=2        -- Defaults to 2
AS
SELECT @param0, @param1, @param2
GO

EXEC pass_params              -- PASS NOTHING - ALL Defaults
(null)    1    2

EXEC pass_params 0, 10, 20    -- PASS ALL, IN ORDER
0    10    20

EXEC pass_params @param2=200, @param1=NULL
-- Explicitly identify last two params (out of order)
(null)    (null)    200

EXEC pass_params 0, DEFAULT, 20
-- Let param1 default. Others by position.
0    1    20
```

Note that if you pass parameters by value, you can't leave any gaps. That is, you can't pass only the first and third, using syntax such as this:

```
EXEC pass_params 0,, 20
-- You'll get a syntax error here
```

Also, be aware of the differences between leaving a parameter value unspecified, using the keyword DEFAULT, and passing in an explicit NULL. In the first two cases, the procedure must have a default defined for the parameter in order to avoid an error. If you pass an explicit NULL, you will not get an error, but if there is a default value for the parameter, it will not be used. NULL will be the "value" used by the procedure.

Wildcards in Parameters

If you have a parameter that is of type *character*, you might want to pass an incomplete string as a parameter and use it for pattern matching. Consider this procedure that accepts an input parameter of type *varchar* and returns the title of any book from the *titles* table in the *pubs* database for which the *title_id* matches the input string:

```
CREATE PROC gettitles
@tid varchar(6) = '%'
--    The parameter default means that if no parameter
--    is specified, the procedure will return all the
--    titles
AS

SELECT title
FROM titles
WHERE title_id LIKE @tid

IF @@rowcount = 0
    PRINT 'There are no titles matching your input'

RETURN
```

We can call this procedure in a number of different ways. You should be aware that in many cases, SQL Server is very smart about datatype conversion, and the following is an acceptable statement, even without quotes around the character parameter:

```
EXEC gettitles bu1032
```

The parser breaks the command into individual units of meaning, called *tokens*, by using spaces and other nonalphanumeric characters as separators. Since the parameter here is completely alphanumeric, the parser recognizes it as a single token and can then assume that it is a parameter of the procedure. The procedure expects a parameter of type *varchar*, so it just interprets the value it receives as a *varchar*.

If your parameter includes any nonalphanumeric characters, such as dashes or spaces, the parser will not be able to deal with it appropriately and you'll need to help it by enclosing such parameters in quotes or square brackets. So note what happens if we call the *gettitles* procedure with a % in the parameter:

```
EXEC gettitles  bu%
```

```
RESULT:
Server: Msg 170, Level 15, State 1, Line 1
Line 1: Incorrect syntax near '%'.
```

This error is not generated by the stored procedure but by the parser before the procedure is ever called. The parser is unable to determine that the *bu%* needs to be treated as a single token. If there are quotes around the parameter, the parser is satisfied and the procedure can be executed. Because the query inside the procedure uses LIKE instead of =, the pattern matching can be done and we get back all the titles for which the *title_id* starts with *bu*:

```
EXEC gettitles  'bu%'
```

```
RESULTS:
title
-----------------------------------------------------------
The Busy Executive's Database Guide
Cooking with Computers: Surreptitious Balance Sheets
You Can Combat Computer Stress!
Straight Talk About Computers
```

```
(4 row(s) affected)
```

If you want your procedure to handle wildcards in parameters, you need to make sure not only that the search condition uses LIKE, but also that the type of parameter is *varchar* instead of *char*. You might not think that this would be necessary here because all of the *title_id* values are exactly six characters long. But suppose that in this *gettitles* example we had declared *@tid* to be *char(6)*. This would mean that the procedure would need a parameter of exactly six characters. If we had passed in the three characters *bu%*, SQL Server would have had to pad the parameter with spaces (*'bu% '*) to get the full six characters. Then, when the comparison was made in the WHERE clause of the procedure's SELECT statement, SQL Server would look for *title_id* values that start with *bu*, are followed by anything (because of the %), and end with three spaces! Because none of the *title_id* values in the *titles* table end with three spaces, no rows would be returned.

The default of % in the procedure means that if no parameter is specified, the procedure will compare the *title_id* with % and return all the rows in the table. This is a useful technique to make the procedure more versatile. Many of our system procedures work this way; for example, if you execute *sp_helpdb* with a parameter, that parameter is considered the name of a database and you'll get back details about that database. With no parameter, *sp_helpdb* will return information about *all* your databases.

However, this technique works only for character string parameters because that is the only datatype that allows wildcards. What if I wanted to write a procedure to find all books with a particular value for *price*? If no price is specified, I want the procedure to return the names of all the books.

One solution is to define a parameter with a default of NULL. I could write the procedure as two completely separate SELECT statements, one for when the parameter has a non-null value and one without a WHERE clause for when the parameter is NULL. However, there is another way to do this in a single SELECT statement:

```
CREATE PROC gettitle_by_price
@cost money = NULL
AS
SELECT price, title
FROM titles
WHERE price = ISNULL(@cost, price)
RETURN
```

This procedure assigns a default value of NULL to the parameter, which prevents an error from being generated if no parameter is actually passed in. However, only a single SELECT statement is needed. The ISNULL function will end up comparing a price to itself if the parameter is NULL, and all values for price will be equal to themselves.

There is one little gotcha here, which is that the result from executing this procedure with no parameter is not exactly the same as executing a SELECT without a WHERE clause. A SELECT with no WHERE clause will return all the rows. The SELECT with the ISNULL in the WHERE clause will return all rows in which the value of *price* is equal to the parameter or equal to the same value for *price*. But what if *price* has no value? In the *titles* table, two rows have a nonvalue, in other words NULL, for the *price*, and will not be returned from the above procedure. In this situation, even setting ANSI_NULLS to OFF will not help. We'll try to find the rows WHERE price = price, and because NULL is never considered equal to NULL, the rows with NULL for price will not be returned. One alternative would be to write the WHERE clause like this:

```
WHERE ISNULL(price, 0) = ISNULL(@cost, ISNULL(price, 0))
```

If we write the procedure with this condition, the results we will get from executing the procedure with no parameter will be the same as executing a SELECT without a WHERE clause; that is, all the rows will be returned. However, the drawback to this solution is that SQL Server might not be able to optimize this query and find a good execution plan. As we'll see in Chapter 16, if a column is embedded in a function call or other expression, the optimizer is very unlikely to consider using any indexes on that column. That means if our table has an index on the *price* column and we actually do pass in a value for *price*, SQL Server probably won't choose to use that index to find the rows in the table with the requested price.

USER-DEFINED FUNCTIONS

Just as I've showed you stored procedure examples (using *sp_help* and so on) in earlier chapters, I've also used functions. You've seen parameterized functions such as CONVERT, RTRIM, and ISNULL as well as parameterless functions such as @@SPID. SQL Server 2000 lets you create functions of your own. However, whereas user-defined procedures are managed similarly to system stored procedures, the functions you create are managed very differently from the supplied functions. As I've mentioned, the ANSI SCHEMA VIEW called ROUTINES allows you to see all the procedures and functions in a database. This view shows system-defined stored procedures but not built-in functions such as the ones you've seen in earlier chapters. You should think of the built-in functions as almost like built-in commands in the SQL language; they are not listed in any system table, and there is no way for you to see how they are defined.

Table Variables

To make full use of user-defined functions, it's useful to understand a special type of variable that SQL Server 2000 provides. You can declare a local variable as a table or use a table value as the result set of a user-defined function. You can think of *table* as a special kind of datatype. Note that you cannot use table variables as stored procedure or function parameters, nor can a column in a table be of type *table*.

Like the other kinds of local variables I told you about in Chapter 10, table variables have a well-defined scope, which is limited to the procedure, function, or batch in which they are declared. Here's a simple example:

```
DECLARE @pricelist TABLE(tid varchar(6), price money)
INSERT @pricelist SELECT title_id, price FROM titles
SELECT * FROM @pricelist
```

The definition of a table variable looks almost like the definition of a normal table, except that you use the word DECLARE instead of CREATE, and the name of the table variable comes before the word TABLE.

The definition of a table variable can include the following:

- A column list defining the datatypes for each column and specifying the NULL or NOT NULL property

- PRIMARY KEY, UNIQUE, CHECK, or DEFAULT constraints

The definition of a table variable cannot include the following:

- Foreign key references to other tables

- Columns referenced by a FOREIGN KEY constraint in another table

Within their scope, table variables can be treated like any other table. All data manipulation statements (SELECT, INSERT, UPDATE, and DELETE) can be performed on the data in a table variable, with two exceptions:

- You cannot use SELECT INTO to add data to a table variable. This is because SELECT INTO creates a table, and table variables must be created using DECLARE. For example, you cannot do the following:

  ```
  SELECT select_list INTO table_variable statements
  ```

- You cannot directly INSERT the result set of a stored procedure into a table variable. For example, you cannot do the following:

  ```
  INSERT INTO table_variable EXEC stored_procedure
  ```

In addition, you need to be aware of the following facts:

- A table variable is not part of a transaction. A ROLLBACK TRANSACTION command will not affect data added to a table variable. (The same is true of any other nontable variables.)

- You cannot use the CREATE INDEX command to build an index on a table variable.

Scalar-Valued Functions

You can use a scalar-valued function anywhere that your Transact-SQL command is expecting a value. It can take up to 1024 input parameters but no output parameters. The function can return a value of any datatype except *rowversion* (or *timestamp)*, *cursor*, or *table*.

Unlike a stored procedure, a function must include the RETURN statement. (In stored procedures, the RETURN is optional.) You can declare a scalar local variable to hold the return value of the function and then use this variable with the RETURN statement, or the RETURN statement can include the computation of the return value. The following two function definitions are equivalent; both will return the average price for books in the titles table for which the type is the same as the type specified as the input parameter:

```
CREATE FUNCTION AveragePrice(@booktype varchar(12))
RETURNS money
AS
BEGIN
    DECLARE @avg money
    SELECT @avg = avg(price)
    FROM titles
    WHERE type = @booktype
```

```
    RETURN @avg
END

CREATE FUNCTION AveragePrice2(@booktype varchar(12))
RETURNS money
AS
BEGIN

    RETURN ( SELECT avg(price)
             FROM titles
             WHERE type = @booktype)
END
```

Invoking a Scalar Function

To invoke a user-defined scalar function, you must specify the owner name. The following query will return an error:

```
SELECT title_id, price
FROM titles
WHERE price > AveragePrice('business')
AND type = 'business'

RESULT:
Server: Msg 195, Level 15, State 10, Line 3
'AveragePrice' is not a recognized function name.
```

Here's the correct invocation:

```
SELECT title_id, price
FROM titles
WHERE price > dbo.AveragePrice('business')
AND type = 'business'

RESULT:
title_id price
-------- ---------------------
BU1032   19.9900
BU7832   19.9900
```

You can invoke user-defined scalar functions by simply SELECTing their value:

```
SELECT dbo.AveragePrice ('business')
```

You can also use the keyword EXECUTE to invoke a user-defined function as if it were a stored procedure. You might want to do this to assign the return value to a variable. In this case, though, the syntax is different. You must not specify the parameter list in parentheses, as in the examples above. Instead, you should just list them after the name of the function:

```
DECLARE @avg money
EXEC @avg = dbo.AveragePrice 'business'
SELECT @avg
```

Additional Restrictions

The SQL statements inside your scalar-valued functions cannot include any non-deterministic system functions. I talked about determinism in Chapter 8 when I discussed the requirements for creating Indexed Views and indexes on computed columns. You can refer to page 438 to see which system-supplied functions are deterministic and which are not.

For example, suppose I want a function that will format today's date using any separator that I supply. I might try to write the function like this:

```
CREATE FUNCTION MyDateFormat
              (@Separator char(1)='-')
RETURNS nchar(20)
AS
BEGIN
DECLARE @indate datetime
    SELECT @indate = GETDATE()
    RETURN
        CONVERT(nvarchar(20), DATEPART(dd, @indate))
        + @Separator
        + CONVERT(nvarchar(20), DATEPART(mm, @indate))
        + @Separator
        + CONVERT(nvarchar(20), DATEPART(yy, @indate))
    END
```

However, because GETDATE is nondeterministic, I get this error:

```
Server: Msg 443, Level 16, State 1, Procedure MyDateFormat, Line 7
Invalid use of 'getdate' within a function.
```

I can change the function definition to accept a *datetime* value as an input parameter and then call the function with GETDATE as an argument. Not only does this allow me to accomplish my goal, but also it makes my function much more versatile. Here's the function:

```
CREATE FUNCTION MyDateFormat
        (@indate datetime,
         @Separator char(1)='-')
RETURNS nchar(20)
AS
BEGIN
    RETURN
        CONVERT(nvarchar(20), DATEPART(dd, @indate))
        + @Separator
        + CONVERT(nvarchar(20), DATEPART(mm, @indate))
        + @Separator
        + CONVERT(nvarchar(20), DATEPART(yy, @indate))
    END
```

And here's an example of its invocation:

```
SELECT dbo.MyDateFormat(GETDATE(), '*')
```

```
RESULT:
-------------------
18*7*2000
```

As a final example, I'll rewrite the factorial routine as a function. As you've seen, we can go only one value higher using the iterative solution instead of the recursive solution. Since functions work very nicely recursively, I'll rewrite it as a recursive function. The function will call itself by multiplying the input parameter by the factorial of the number one less than the parameter. So 10 is computed by finding the factorial of 9 and multiplying by 10. To avoid overflow problems, the function simply returns a 0 for the result of any input value that is out of range. Here's the function:

```
CREATE FUNCTION fn_factorial (@param decimal(38, 0) )
RETURNS decimal(38, 0)

AS
BEGIN
    IF (@param < 0 OR @param > 32) RETURN (0)
    RETURN (CASE
        WHEN @param > 1 THEN @param  * dbo.fn_factorial(@param - 1)
        ELSE 1
        END)
END
```

Unlike the factorial procedure, which lists all the factorial values up to and including the factorial of the input parameter, the function *fn_factorial* simply returns the value that is the factorial for the argument. Remember that you must always specify a two-part name when you call a user-defined scalar function:

```
SELECT factorial = dbo.fn_factorial(10)
```

```
RESULT:
factorial
----------------------------------------
3628800
```

Table-Valued Functions

Table-valued functions return a rowset. You can invoke them in the FROM clause of a SELECT statement, just as you would a view. In fact, think of a table-valued function as if it were a parameterized (or parameterizable) view. A table-valued function is indicated in its definition using the word TABLE in the RETURNS clause. There are two ways to write table-valued functions: as inline functions or as multistatement functions. This difference is relevant only to the way the function is written; all table-valued functions are invoked in the same way. You'll also see in Chapter 15 that there is a difference in the way that the query plans for how inline and multistatement functions are cached.

Inline Functions

If the RETURNS clause specifies TABLE with no additional table definition information, the function is an inline function and there should be a single SELECT statement as the body of the function. Here's a function that will return the names and quantities of all the books sold by a particular store for which the store ID is passed as an input parameter:

```
CREATE FUNCTION SalesByStore(@storid varchar(30))
RETURNS TABLE
AS
RETURN (SELECT title, qty
        FROM sales s, titles t
        WHERE s.stor_id = @storid AND t.title_id = s.title_id)
```

We can execute this function by invoking it in a FROM clause:

```
SELECT * FROM SalesByStore ('8042')

RESULT:
title                                                         qty
------------------------------------------------------------ ------
The Gourmet Microwave                                         15
The Busy Executive's Database Guide                          10
Cooking with Computers: Surreptitious Balance Sheets         25
But Is It User Friendly?                                      30
```

Note that for a table-valued function, you don't have to include the owner name.

Multistatement Table-Valued Functions

If the RETURNS clause specifies that it's returning a TABLE and specifying a table variable name, the function is a multistatement table-valued function. The RETURNS clause also lists the columns and datatypes for the table. The body of the function populates the table using INSERT and possibly UPDATE statements. When the RETURN is executed, it simply returns the table variable specified earlier in the RETURNS clause.

Here's an example of the previous inline function rewritten as a multistatement function:

```
CREATE FUNCTION SalesByStore_MS(@storid varchar(30))
RETURNS @sales TABLE(title varchar(80), qty int)
AS
```

```
BEGIN
    INSERT @sales
        SELECT title, qty
        FROM sales s, titles t
        WHERE s.stor_id = @storid AND t.title_id = s.title_id
    RETURN
END
```

The function is invoked exactly as the inline table-valued function is invoked. The following statements are the only ones allowed in a multistatement table-valued function:

- Assignment statements.

- Control-of-flow statements.

- DECLARE statements that define data variables and cursors that are local to the function.

- SELECT statements containing select lists with expressions that assign values to variables that are local to the function.

- Cursor operations referencing local cursors that are declared, opened, closed, and deallocated in the function. Only FETCH statements that assign values to local variables using the INTO clause are allowed; FETCH statements that return data to the client are not allowed. (For more details on cursors, see Chapter 13.)

- INSERT, UPDATE, and DELETE statements that modify table variables that are local to the function.

Also, as with scalar functions, table-valued functions cannot contain any built-in nondeterministic functions.

Side Effects

Basically, the statements that aren't allowed are ones that return data other than the function's return value and the ones that product side effects. A side effect is a change to some persisted state that is not local to the function. Invoking a function should not change your database in any way; it should only return a value (scalar or table-valued) to the client. Thus, the following are not allowed:

- Updates to tables

- Global cursor statements

- Creation of objects

- Transaction control statements

System Table-Valued Functions

SQL Server 2000 includes a set of systemwide table-valued functions that can be invoked from any database. Normally, the table-valued functions you create will be objects in one particular database, and to invoke them from another database, you must specify the database name. System table-valued functions do not have this restriction. However, to invoke one of these functions, you must use a special syntax and precede the function name with *::*. In fact, you cannot specify an owner or database name; you can only use this special syntax.

Here are the documented system table-valued functions:

```
fn_helpcollations
fn_listextendedproperty
fn_servershareddrives
fn_trace_geteventinfo
fn_trace_getfilterinfo
fn_trace_getinfo
fn_trace_gettable
fn_virtualfilestats
fn_virtualservernodes
```

The function *fn_virtualfilestats* returns I/O statistics for a database file and requires a database ID and a file ID as parameters. The following example calls this function for the data file of the *pubs* database. We'll discuss the meaning of some of the return values in Chapter 17.

```
SELECT * FROM ::fn_virtualfilestats(5, 1)

RESULT:
DbId    FileId  TimeStamp     NumberReads   NumberWrites  BytesRead
------  ------  -----------   ------------  ------------  ------------
5       1       34138899      115           9             942080


BytesWritten   IoStallMS
-------------  -----------------
90112          4585
```

Managing User-Defined Functions

Just like a view, a function can be created using WITH SCHEMABINDING. This option means that any object referenced by the function cannot be dropped or altered. Any attempt to alter such a referenced object will result in an error. Let's use the inline table-value function I created above and re-create it using WITH SCHEMABINDING. Note that we can use ALTER FUNCTION to change the function's definition without dropping and re-creating it. However, we cannot use ALTER to change a table-valued function to a scalar function or to change an inline function to a multi-statement function.

```
ALTER FUNCTION SalesByStore(@storid varchar(30))
RETURNS TABLE
WITH SCHEMABINDING
AS
RETURN (SELECT title, qty
        FROM dbo.sales s, dbo.titles t
        WHERE s.stor_id = @storid AND t.title_id = s.title_id)
```

A function can be schema-bound only if the following conditions are true:

- The user-defined functions and views referenced by the function are also schema-bound.

- All objects referenced by the function are referred to by a two-part name.

- The function is in the same database as all the referenced objects.

- Any user referencing the function has REFERENCES permission on all the database objects that the function references.

SQL Server keeps track of objects that are dependent on other objects in the *sysdepends* table. The data in the table looks very cryptic—it's all numbers. To get meaningful information from the *sysdepends* table, you have to get the names of the objects stored in the *id* column, which are the dependent objects, and the names of the objects stored in the *depid* column, which are the referenced objects.

For example, in my *SalesByStore* function above, the function itself is the dependent object, and the objects it depends on are the *titles* and *sales* tables. The *depnumber* column refers to a column in the referenced object that the dependent object depends on. My *SalesByStore* functions depend on the *qty*, *stor_id*, and *title_id* columns from *sales* and the *title_id* and *title* columns from *titles*. Finally, the column *deptype* indicates whether the dependency is schema-bound—that is, whether a change to the referenced column should be prevented. By accessing the *syscolumns* and *sysdepends* tables and using the OBJECT_NAME function to extract the name from *sysobjects*, we can see what columns are schema-bound in the *SalesByStore* functions:

```
SELECT obj_name = SUBSTRING(OBJECT_NAME(d.id), 1, 20),
       dep_obj  = SUBSTRING(OBJECT_NAME(d.depid), 1, 20),
       col_name = SUBSTRING(name, 1, 15),
       IsSchemaBound = CASE deptype
           WHEN 1 THEN 'Schema Bound'
           ELSE 'Free'
       END
FROM
    sysdepends d
    JOIN syscolumns c ON d.depid = c.id
    AND d.depnumber = c.colid
WHERE object_name(d.id) LIKE 'SalesByStore%'
```

(continued)

```
RESULTS:
obj_name                dep_obj              col_name          IsSchemaBound
-------------------     ------------------   ----------------  -------------
SalesByStore            sales                stor_id           Schema Bound
SalesByStore            sales                qty               Schema Bound
SalesByStore            sales                title_id          Schema Bound
SalesByStore            titles               title_id          Schema Bound
SalesByStore            titles               title             Schema Bound
SalesByStore_MS         sales                stor_id           Free
SalesByStore_MS         sales                qty               Free
SalesByStore_MS         sales                title_id          Free
SalesByStore_MS         titles               title_id          Free
SalesByStore_MS         titles               title             Free
```

To see the impact of schema binding, I'll try to change one of the referenced columns. The following ALTER will attempt to change the datatype of *qty* from *smallint* to *int*:

```
ALTER TABLE sales
ALTER COLUMN qty int
```

I get these error messages:

```
Server: Msg 5074, Level 16, State 3, Line 1
The object 'SalesByStore' is dependent on column 'qty'.
Server: Msg 4922, Level 16, State 1, Line 1
ALTER TABLE ALTER COLUMN qty failed because one or more objects
access this column.
```

On the other hand, changing the datatype of the *ord_date* column from *datetime* to *smalldatetime* will succeed because the *ord_date* column is not referenced by a schema-bound object.

Getting Information About Your Functions

SQL Server 2000 provides many utilities for getting information about your functions. To see the definition of a function, you can use the system procedure *sp_helptext* or look in the ANSI SCHEMA VIEW called ROUTINES. Both commands shown below will return the definition of my *SalesByStore* function:

```
EXEC sp_helptext SalesByStore

SELECT routine_definition
FROM INFORMATION_SCHEMA.routines
WHERE routine_name = 'SalesByStore'
```

Although you can use either *sp_helptext* or ROUTINES to get information about your own functions, you can't get the definition of the system table-valued functions using *sp_helptext*. You must use the *master* database and look in the ROUTINES view.

In fact, for some of the supplied system table-valued functions, you won't get the entire definition. You'll get only the declaration section because the rest of the code is hidden. The query below shows the complete definition of a system function:

```
USE master
SELECT routine_definition
FROM INFORMATION_SCHEMA.ROUTINES
WHERE routine_name = 'fn_helpcollations'
```

You can also get information about your functions from the ANSI SCHEMA VIEWS called ROUTINE_COLUMNS and PARAMETERS. For details about using these views, see *SQL Server Books Online*.

The metadata function OBJECTPROPERTY also has quite a few property values that are relevant to user-defined functions. For example, I mentioned earlier that you can tell whether a function is a table-valued function by looking at its definition and checking to see whether the RESULTS clause contains the word TABLE. Alternatively, you can use the OBJECTPROPERTY function with the 'IsTableFunction' or 'IsInlineFunction' argument:

```
SELECT OBJECTPROPERTY(object_id('SalesByStore'), 'IsInlineFunction')
```

Calling the OBJECTPROPERTY function with the 'IsInlineFunction' property parameter returns one of three values. The value 1 means TRUE, the function is an inline table-valued function, and 0 means FALSE, the function isn't an inline table-valued function. A NULL will be returned if you typed something wrong—for example, if you supplied an invalid object ID, supplied the ID of an object that is not a function, or misspelled the property name. If you call the OBJECTPROPERTY function with the 'IsTableFunction' property parameter, it returns a 1 if the function is a table-valued function that is not also an inline function. Here are the other parameters of OBJECTPROPERTY that can give you useful information about your functions:

```
IsScalarFunction
IsSchemaBound
IsDeterministic
```

REWRITING STORED PROCEDURES AS FUNCTIONS

User-defined functions are new in SQL Server 2000. In previous releases, many applications had stored procedures to perform tasks that could have been more naturally coded as functions, but because there was no facility for writing user-defined functions, stored procedures had to be used. If you've upgraded to SQL Server 2000 from an earlier release, you might be wondering which of your existing stored procedures you should rewrite as functions.

The following list of criteria for creating functions from stored procedures mostly duplicates what you'll find in *SQL Server Books Online*, but I've included it here for convenience. Your main consideration should be whether you want to be able to invoke an existing stored procedure directly from within a query. If so, you should consider re-creating the procedures as a function.

In general, if the stored procedure returns a (single) result set, you should define a table-valued function. If the stored procedure computes a scalar value, you should define a scalar function.

If a stored procedure meets the following criteria, it's a good candidate for being rewritten as a table-valued function:

■   The logic is expressible in a single SELECT statement but is a stored procedure, rather than a view, only because of the need for parameters. You can handle this scenario using an inline table-valued function.

■   The stored procedure does not perform update operations (except to table variables).

■   There is no need for dynamic EXECUTE statements (discussed later in this chapter).

■   The stored procedure returns one result set.

■   The primary purpose of the stored procedure is to build intermediate results that are to be loaded into a temporary table, which is then queried in a SELECT statement.

ROLLING YOUR OWN SYSTEM ROUTINES

You've seen that SQL Server 2000 provides both system-level stored procedures and system-level table-valued functions. The two types of objects are similar in that they can be invoked from any database even though they are stored only in the *master* database.

Your Own System Procedures

All the system stored procedure names begin with *sp_*. This is more than just a convention. Any procedure created in the *master* database that begins with *sp_* can be called from any other database without having to be fully referenced with the database name. This can also be useful for procedures you create. The *sp_* magic works even for extended stored procedures, which are user-written calls to DLLs. By convention, extended stored procedure names begin with *xp_*, but the *sp_* prefix and its special property can be applied to them as well (but only when added to the *master* database). In fact, some extended procedures that are supplied as part of the product, such as those used to create Automation objects (for example, *sp_OACreate*), use the *sp_* prefix so that they can be called from anywhere, even though they're actually functions in a DLL, not a Transact-SQL stored procedure.

The *sp_* prefix actually makes a procedure special in two ways. First, as I've mentioned, a procedure whose name starts with *sp_* can be called directly from any database, without a fully qualified name. Second, system tables referenced in your special procedures will always refer to the tables in the database from which the procedure was called. For example, the *sp_help* stored procedure lists all the objects from the *sysobjects* system table. But every database has its own *sysobjects* table, so which one is used? If you execute *sp_help* from the *pubs* database, you get a list of the objects in *pubs*; if you call *sp_help* from *msdb*, you get a list of objects in *msdb*, and so on. Two tables are exceptions to this rule. For some undetermined reason, if your system stored procedure references the *sysfiles* or *sysfilegroups* table, the procedure will always access the table from the *master* database even though there is a *sysfiles* and *sysfilegroups* table in every database.

The following example illustrates this behavior:

```
CREATE PROC sp_list_files_and_objects
AS
SELECT filename FROM sysfiles
SELECT name from sysobjects
RETURN
```

I won't show you the output from executing the procedure because the list of objects will probably be quite long no matter what database you run this procedure from. But you can try it yourself:

```
USE pubs
EXEC sp_list_files_and_objects
USE northwind
EXEC sp_list_files_and_objects
```

You'll always see the same list of filenames, which are the ones for the *master* database, but the list of objects will change depending on your current database.

Of course, if the *sp_* procedure references a table that exists only in the *master* database, such as *sysconfigures*, the table in *master* will be referenced no matter where you are when you call the procedure. This trick works only for system tables, however. If you create a user table called *MasterLookup* and reference it in an *sp_* stored procedure, SQL Server will look only in the *master* database to try to find the *MasterLookup* table. If it doesn't exist in *master*, you'll get an error message when executing your procedure, even if you call the procedure from the database where the table is located.

> **WARNING** Microsoft strongly discourages any direct references to the system tables and suggests that you instead use only the presupplied stored procedures and the object property functions to get any system information you need. It's not guaranteed that the structures of the system tables will remain the same from one release to the next, or even between service packs. In fact, the Upgrade Wizard for converting SQL Server 6 to SQL Server 2000 doesn't even attempt to upgrade any procedures that modify system tables.

I don't recommend that you use *sp_* as a prefix for your own local stored procedures. The *sp_* prefix has a special meaning, and unless you intend your procedure to have this special meaning and exist in the master database, it can be confusing for users who are aware of the special meaning.

Your Own System Functions

SQL Server 2000 also provides system functions that are treated in some ways just like the user-defined functions that you can write. These are the functions that are listed in the *sysobjects* table and that are listed when you select from the ROUTINES view. These system functions are different from the ones that you would normally create because they are available from any database. You saw the list of these functions on page 624, but I'll repeat it here:

```
fn_helpcollations
fn_listextendedproperty
fn_servershareddrives
fn_trace_geteventinfo
fn_trace_getinfo
fn_virtualfilestats
fn_virtualservernodes
```

Unlike the prefix for system stored procedures, the prefix *fn_* by itself has no special meaning. In fact, I used it when creating my factorial function to distinguish my function from my procedure. In addition, it's not nearly as easy to create system functions of your own. Although it is possible, it is not supported at all, and you need to be aware that any system functions you write in one release might not work in a subsequent release.

The supplied system functions listed above all have the following characteristics:

- They are objects in the *master* database.

- Their names start with *fn_*.

- They are owned by the user *system_function_schema*.

- Their names use only lowercase letters.

If you want your function to be available from any database, it must have the characteristics in the list. However, it's not easy to create a function owned by *system_function_schema*. If you try, you get an error that there is no such user, even though that value is listed as a name in the *sysusers* table.

In order to create objects owned by the user name *system_function_schema*, you must enable updates to the system tables, which is why this technique is unsupported and undocumented. In addition, you cannot create a recursive system function. So, to create our factorial function as a system function, you have to use the iterative approach. Here's a complete example of creating my own system function:

```
USE master
GO

EXEC sp_configure 'allow updates', 1
GO

RECONFIGURE WITH OVERRIDE
GO

CREATE FUNCTION system_function_schema.fn_factorial (@param1 int)
    RETURNS NUMERIC(38, 0)
AS
BEGIN
    DECLARE @counter int, @result NUMERIC(38, 0)
    IF (@param1 < 0 OR @param1 > 33) RETURN (0)

    SET @counter=1 SET @result=1

    WHILE (@counter < @param1 AND @param1 <> 0 )
        BEGIN
            SET @result=@result * (@counter + 1)
            SET @counter=@counter + 1
        END
    RETURN (@result)
END
GO

EXEC sp_configure 'allow updates', 0
GO

RECONFIGURE WITH OVERRIDE
GO
```

Now invoke it:

```
USE <some_other_db>
GO

SELECT fn_factorial(5)
```

EXECUTING BATCHES, OR WHAT'S STORED ABOUT STORED PROCEDURES (AND FUNCTIONS)?

Typically, when a batch of Transact-SQL commands is received from a client connection, the following high-level steps are performed.

Step One: Parse Commands and Create the Sequence Tree

The command parser checks for proper syntax and translates the Transact-SQL commands into an internal format that can be operated on. The internal format is known as a *sequence tree* or *query tree*. The command parser handles these language events.

Step Two: Compile the Batch

An execution plan is generated from the sequence tree. The entire batch is compiled, queries are optimized, and security is checked. The execution plan contains the necessary steps to check any constraints that exist. If an after trigger exists for any data modification statement, the call to that trigger is appended to the execution plan for the statement. If an instead-of trigger exists, the call to that trigger replaces the execution plan for the data modification statement. Recall that a trigger is really a specialized type of stored procedure. Its plan is cached, and the trigger doesn't need to be recompiled every time it is invoked.

The execution plan includes the following:

- All the necessary steps to carry out the commands in the batch or stored procedure.

- The steps needed to enforce constraints. (For example, for a foreign key, this would involve checking values in another table.)

- A branch to the stored procedure plan for a trigger, if one exists.

Step Three: Execute

During execution, each step of the execution plan is dispatched serially to a manager that's responsible for carrying out that type of command. For example, a data definition command (in DDL), such as CREATE TABLE, is dispatched to the DDL manager. DML statements, such as SELECT, UPDATE, INSERT, and DELETE, go to the DML manager. Miscellaneous commands, such as DBCC and WAITFOR, go to the utility manager. Calls to stored procedures (for example, EXEC *sp_who*) are dispatched to the stored procedure manager. A statement with an explicit BEGIN TRAN interacts directly with the transaction manager.

Contrary to what you might think, the execution plans for stored procedures and functions are not permanently stored on disk. (This is a feature—the execution plan is relatively dynamic.) Think for a moment about why it's important for the execution plan to be dynamic. As new indexes are added, preexisting indexes are dropped, constraints are added or changed, and triggers are added or changed; or as the amount of data changes, the plan can easily become obsolete.

So, what's stored about a stored procedure or function?

The SQL statements that were used to create the routine are stored in the system table *syscomments*. The first time a routine is executed after SQL Server was last restarted, the SQL text is retrieved and an execution plan is compiled. The execution plan is then cached in SQL Server's memory, and it remains there for possible reuse until it's forced out in a least recently used (LRU) manner. We'll look at more details about the SQL Server's caching mechanism and when plans are forced out of cache in Chapter 15.

Hence, a subsequent execution of the routine can skip not only step 1, *parsing,* but also step 2, *compiling,* and go directly to step 3, *execution.* Steps 1 and 2 always add some overhead and can sometimes be as costly as actually executing the commands. Obviously, if you can eliminate the first two steps in a three-step process, you've done well. That's what the stored routines let you do. Note that most of this discussion of routines applies to triggers as well as to stored procedures and functions, even though triggers are not listed in the SCHEMA VIEW called ROUTINES.

When you execute a routine, if a valid execution plan exists in the procedure cache, it will be used (eliminating the parsing and compiling steps). When the server is restarted, no execution plans will be in the cache; so the first time the server is restarted, routines will all be compiled the first time they are executed.

> **TIP** You can preload your procedure cache with execution plans for routines by defining a startup stored procedure that executes the routines you want to have compiled and cached.

After a routine executes, its plan remains in the cache and is reused the next time any connection executes the same routine. In addition, because multiple connections might try to execute the same plan concurrently, a part of the plan (called the shareable portion) is reentrant. Each concurrent user of that plan also requires an execution context. If you think of this in traditional programming terms, this execution context is needed to contain the dirty data.

The execution context tends to be fairly small compared to the plans. The execution contexts are themselves serially reusable for certain plans that don't contain special operators. Figures 11-1 and 11-2 show execution with and without a stored routine.

EXECUTE Stored Procedure

Figure 11-1. *Efficient execution using a stored routine.*

EXECUTE Batch (Without Stored Procedure)

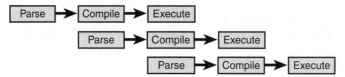

Figure 11-2. *Less efficient execution with an ad hoc query.*

In Chapter 15, you'll see that even ad hoc queries do not need to be recompiled every time they're run. But when and how their plans are stored and reused is not nearly as predictable as with stored routines. In addition, you have little explicit control over the recompilation of ad hoc queries.

Step Four: Recompile Execution Plans

By now, it should be clear that the SQL code for routines persists in the database but execution plans don't. Execution plans are cached in memory. But sometimes they can be invalidated and a new plan generated.

So, when is a new execution plan compiled?

The short answer is: whenever SQL Server needs to! This can include the following cases:

- When a copy of the execution plan isn't available in memory.

- When an index on a referenced object is dropped.

- When updated statistics are available for any table used by the routine. (Chapter 15 covers statistics in detail.)

- When an object referenced in the routine is altered using ALTER TABLE.

■ When the object has been named as the argument to *sp_recompile*. If the object is a routine, the routine will be marked so that it is recompiled the next time it is run. If the object is a table or view, all the routines that reference that object will be recompiled the next time they are run. The system procedure *sp_recompile* increments the schema column of *sysobjects* for a given object. This invalidates any plans for the object as well as any plans that reference the object, as described in the previous examples.

■ When a stored procedure has been created using the WITH RECOMPILE option. A stored procedure can be created using WITH RECOMPILE to ensure that its execution plan will be recompiled for every call and will never be reused. Note that the WITH RECOMPILE option is available only when you create stored procedures and is not available for function creation. Creating a stored procedure using WITH RECOMPILE can be useful if procedures take parameters and the values of the parameters differ widely, resulting in a need for different execution plans to be formulated. For example, if a procedure is passed a value to be matched in the WHERE clause of a query, the best way to carry out that query can depend on the value passed. SQL Server maintains statistics for each index as a histogram to help it decide whether the index is selective enough to be useful.

For one given value, an index might be highly selective, and the distribution statistics might indicate that only 5 percent of the rows have that value. SQL Server might decide to use that index because it would exclude many pages of data from having to be visited. Using the index would be a good strategy, and the cached plan for the procedure might include the instructions to use the index. However, using another value, the index might not be so selective. Rather than use only the index to visit most of the data pages (ultimately doing more I/O because you're reading both the index and the data), you'd be better off simply scanning the data and not reading the index.

For example, suppose we have a nonclustered index on the *color* column of our *automobile* table. Forty percent of the cars are blue, 40 percent are red, and 5 percent each are yellow, orange, green, and purple. It's likely that a query based on color should scan the table if the color being searched on is blue or red, but it should use the index for the other colors. Without using the WITH RECOMPILE option, the execution plan created and saved would be based on the color value the first time the procedure was executed.

So if we passed *yellow* to the procedure the first time it executed, we'd get a plan that used an index. Subsequently, if we passed *blue*, we might be able to use the previous plan that was created for *yellow*. In this case, however, we'd be traversing a nonclustered index to access a large percentage of rows in the table. This could end up being far more expensive than simply scanning the entire table. In such a case, when there's a lot of variance in the distribution of data and execution plans are based on the parameters passed, it makes sense to use the WITH RECOMPILE option.

This example also shows that two execution plans for the same procedure can be different. Suppose we're not using WITH RECOMPILE, and we execute the procedure for both *blue* and *green* simultaneously from two different connections. Assume for a moment that no plan is cached. Each will generate a new plan, but one plan will use the index and the other won't. When a subsequent request for *red* arrives, the plan it uses will be a matter of chance. And if two simultaneous calls come in for *red* and each plan is available, the two equivalent requests will execute differently because they'll use different plans. If, as you're processing queries, you see significant deviations in the execution times of apparently identical procedures, think back to this example.

- When the stored procedure or function is executed using the WITH RE-COMPILE option. This case is similar to the preceding one, except that the routine isn't created with the option; rather, the option is specified when the routine is invoked. The WITH RECOMPILE option can always be added upon execution, forcing a new execution plan to be generated. Note that you can use this option with user-defined scalar functions, but only if you invoke the function with the EXEC keyword.

Storage of Routines

With each new routine, a row is created in the *sysobjects* table, as happens for all database objects. The text of a routine (including comments) is stored in *syscomments,* which is typically useful. Storing the text allows procedures such as *sp_helptext* to display the source code of a routine so that you can understand what's going on, and it allows function editors and debuggers to exist.

Most users and developers find it helpful to have the full text of a routine stored in clear text. There is a limit on the size of the text for a routine due to the amount of text that *syscomments* can store for a given routine, but you're not likely to run up against that limit soon. The *syscomments.text* field can hold up to 8000 bytes, and you can have multiple rows in *syscomments* for each routine. The sequence of the rows for a given routine is tracked in the *colid* column. Since *colid* is a *smallint,* there can be up to 32,767 rows for any routine. Any one routine should then be able hold 8000 × 32,767 bytes, or 250 MB. There's one additional limiting factor, however: the maximum size of a batch. To create the routine, the client must send the complete definition to SQL Server in the CREATE statement, and this must be sent as a single batch. SQL Server has a limit on the batch size, which is 65,536 times the network packet size. Because the default value for network packet size is 4096 bytes, we get a batch size of 256 MB. So the limit on the size of your routines text isn't worth worrying about right away.

Encrypting Routines

With the rollout of version 6, the SQL Server developers at Microsoft learned somewhat painfully that some users didn't appreciate that the text of certain programmable objects was available in the *syscomments* system table. Several ISVs had built integrated solutions or tools that created stored procedures to use with earlier versions of SQL Server. In most cases, these solutions were sophisticated applications, and the ISVs viewed the source code as their proprietary intellectual property. They noticed that the text of the procedure in *syscomments* didn't seem to do anything, so they set the text field to NULL and the procedure still ran fine. In this way, they avoided publishing their procedure source code with their applications.

Unfortunately, when it came time to upgrade a database to version 6, this approach created a significant problem. The internal data structures for the sequence plans had changed between versions 4.2 and 6. The ISVs had to re-create procedures, triggers, and views to generate the new structure. Although SQL Server's Setup program was designed to do this automatically, it accomplished the tasks by simply extracting the text of the procedure from *syscomments* and then dropping and re-creating the procedure using the extracted text. Obviously, this automatic approach failed for procedures in which the creator had deleted the text.

When the SQL Server developers at Microsoft learned of this problem after the release of the version 6 beta, they immediately understood why developers had felt compelled to delete the text. Nonetheless, they couldn't undo the work that they had already done. Developers with these ISVs had to dig out their original stored procedure creation scripts and manually drop and re-create all their procedures. It might have been possible to create a converter program that would operate purely on the internal data structures used to represent procedures and views, but it wasn't practical. Attempting this would have been like developing a utility to run against an executable program and have it reverse-engineer the precise source code (more than a disassembly) that was used to create the binary. The SQL source code compilation process is designed to be a descriptive process that produces the executable, not an equation that can be solved for either side.

After the beta release but before the final release of version 6, the developers added the ability to encrypt the text stored in *syscomments* for stored procedures, triggers, and views. This allowed programmers to protect their source code without making it impossible for the upgrade process to re-create stored procedures, triggers, and views in the future. You can now protect your source code by simply adding the modifier WITH ENCRYPTION to CREATE PROCEDURE. No decrypt function is exposed (which would defeat the purpose of hiding the textlike source code). Internally, SQL Server can read this encrypted text and upgrade the sequence trees when necessary. Because the text isn't used at runtime, no performance penalty is associated with executing procedures created using WITH ENCRYPTION.

> **NOTE**   You give up some capabilities when you use WITH ENCRYPTION. For example, you can no longer use the *sp_helptext* stored procedure or object editors that display and edit the text of the stored procedure, and you can't use a source-level debugger for Transact-SQL. Unless you're concerned about someone seeing your procedures, you shouldn't use the WITH ENCRYPTION option.

With SQL Server 2000, if you create a procedure, function, trigger, or view using WITH ENCRYPTION, the status column of *syscomments* will have a value of 1 (it's first bit will be set) and if it's not encrypted, the status column will be 2 (the second bit will be set). The *encrypted* and *texttype* columns of *syscomments* will also reflect the encryption status, but these columns are both computed columns based on the value that is in the *status* column. The value of *texttype* is 6 for an encrypted routine and 2 otherwise. If you want to programmatically determine whether a routine is encrypted, it's safer to check the *encrypted* column for a value of 0 or 1. Also, the SCHEMA VIEW called ROUTINES will have NULL in the *routine_definition* column if the routine is encrypted.

I created two procedures—one encrypted and one not—to illustrate the effects on *syscomments*:

```
CREATE PROCEDURE cleartext
AS
SELECT * FROM authors
GO
```

```
CREATE PROCEDURE hidetext WITH ENCRYPTION
AS
SELECT * FROM authors
GO


SELECT o.name, o.id,
       number, colid, c.status, texttype, encrypted, text
FROM syscomments c JOIN sysobjects o
ON  o.id=c.id
WHERE o.id=OBJECT_ID('hidetext') OR o.id=OBJECT_ID('cleartext')
```

Here's the output:

```
name           id          number colid  status texttype encrypted
-------------  ----------- ------ ------ ------ -------- ---------
cleartext      1189579276  1      1      2      2        0

hidetext       1205579333  1      1      1      6        1


text
---------------------------------
CREATE PROCEDURE cleartext
AS
SELECT * FROM authors

????????????????????????????????
```

To find created objects that have encrypted text, you can use a simple query:

```
-- Find the names and types of objects that have encrypted text
SELECT name, type FROM syscomments c JOIN sysobjects o
ON o.id=c.id
WHERE encrypted = 1
```

Here's the output:

```
name                  type
--------------------- ----
hidetext              P
```

The values that you might see in the *type* column are P (procedure), TR (trigger), V (view), FN (scalar function), and TN (table function). If you try to run *sp_helptext* against an encrypted procedure, it will return a message stating that the text is encrypted and can't be displayed:

```
EXEC sp_helptext 'hidetext'
The object's comments have been encrypted.
```

Altering a Routine

SQL Server allows you to alter the definition of a routine. The syntax is almost identical to the syntax for creating the routine initially, except that the keyword CREATE is replaced by the keyword ALTER.

The big difference is that the *routine name* used with ALTER must already exist, and the definition specified replaces whatever definition the routine had before. Just like when you use the ALTER VIEW command, the benefit of ALTER PROCEDURE or ALTER FUNCTION comes from the fact that the routine's *object_id* won't change, so all the internal references to this routine will stay intact. If other routines reference this one, they'll be unaffected. If you've assigned permissions on this routine to various users and roles, dropping the routine removes all permission information. Altering the routine keeps the permissions intact.

TEMPORARY STORED PROCEDURES

Temporary stored procedures allow an execution plan to be cached, but the object's metadata and the text of the procedure are stored in the system tables of the *tempdb* database—in *sysobjects* and *syscomments*. Recall that *tempdb* is re-created every time SQL Server is restarted, so these objects no longer exist after SQL Server is shut down. During a given SQL Server session, you can reuse the procedure without permanently storing it.

Typically, you use a temporary stored procedure when you want to regularly execute the same task several times in a session, although you might use different parameter values and you don't want to permanently store the task. You could conceivably use a permanent stored procedure and drop it when you're finished, but you'd inevitably run into cleanup issues if a stored procedure were still hanging around and the client application terminated without dropping the procedure. Because temporary stored procedures are deleted automatically when SQL Server is shut down (and *tempdb* is created anew at startup), cleanup isn't an issue.

Just as SQL Server has three types of temporary tables, it also has three types of temporary stored procedures: *private*, *global*, and those created from direct use of *tempdb*.

Private Temporary Stored Procedures

By adding a single pound sign (#) to the beginning of the stored procedure name (as in *CREATE PROC #get_author AS...*), you can create the procedure from within any database as a private temporary stored procedure. Only the connection that created the procedure can execute it, and you can't grant privileges on it to another connection. The procedure exists for the life of the creating connection only; that connection can explicitly use DROP PROCEDURE on it to clean up sooner. Because the scoping of a private temporary procedure is specific only to the connection that created it, you won't encounter a name collision if you choose a procedure name that's used by another connection. As with temporary tables, you use your private version, and what occurs in other connections is irrelevant.

Global Temporary Stored Procedures

By adding two pound signs (##) to the beginning of the stored procedure name (as in *CREATE PROC ##get_author AS...*), you can create the procedure from within any database as a global temporary stored procedure. Any connection can subsequently execute that procedure without EXECUTE permission being specifically granted. Unlike with private temporary stored procedures, only one copy of a global temporary stored procedure exists for all connections. If another connection has created a procedure with the same name, the two names will collide and the CREATE PROCEDURE statement will fail. Permission to execute global temporary procedures defaults to public and can't be changed. You can issue a command to deny other users permission, but it will have no effect. Any user, on any connection, can execute a global temporary stored procedure.

A global temporary stored procedure exists until the creating connection terminates and all current execution of the procedure completes. Once the creating connection terminates, however; no further execution is allowed. Only the connections that have already started executing are allowed to finish.

Procedures Created from Direct Use of *tempdb*

Realizing that *tempdb* is re-created every time SQL Server is started, you can create a procedure in *tempdb* that fully qualifies objects in other databases. Procedures created in *tempdb* in this way can exist even after the creating connection is terminated, and the creator can specifically grant and deny execute permissions to specific users. To do this, the creator of the procedure must have CREATE PROCEDURE privileges in *tempdb*. You can set up privileges in *tempdb* in one of two ways: you can set privileges in *model* (the template database) so that they will be copied to *tempdb* when it is created at system restart, or you can set up an autostart procedure to set the *tempdb* privileges every time SQL Server is started.

Here's an example of creating a procedure in *tempdb* and then executing it from the *pubs* database:

```
USE tempdb
GO

CREATE PROC testit AS
SELECT * FROM pubs.dbo.authors
GO
```

(continued)

```
-- Executing the procedure created above from the pubs database
USE pubs
EXEC tempdb..testit
```

While we're on the subject of temporary objects, keep in mind that a private temporary table created within a stored procedure isn't visible to the connection after the creating procedure completes. You can, however, create a local temporary table before executing a stored procedure and make the table visible to the stored procedure. The scoping of the temporary table extends to the current statement block and all subordinate levels.

> **NOTE**   You can use the @@NESTLEVEL system function to check for the visibility of temporary tables. A temporary table created at nest level 0 will be visible to all further levels on that connection. A table created within a procedure at nest level 1, for example, won't be visible when execution returns to the calling block at nest level 0. A global temporary table, or a table directly created in *tempdb* without using either # or ##, will be visible no matter what the nesting level.

AUTOSTART STORED PROCEDURES

SQL Server has the ability to mark a stored procedure as *autostart*. Autostart stored procedures are useful if you want to perform housekeeping functions regularly or if you have a background daemon procedure that's always expected to be running. Another handy use for an autostart procedure is to have it assign some privileges in *tempdb*. Or the procedure can create a global temporary table and then sleep indefinitely using WAITFOR. This will ensure that such a temporary table will always exist, because the calling process is the first thing executed and it never terminates.

You can use the system stored procedure *sp_procoption* to make a stored procedure start automatically. This procedure allows you to turn options for stored procedures on or off. In SQL Server 2000, the only available option is *startup*. Here's the syntax of the command to enable a procedure to automatically execute on SQL Server startup:

```
sp_procoption procedure_name, startup, true
```

You can remove the *startup* option by executing the same procedure and changing the value to FALSE. A procedure that's autostarted runs in the context of a system administrator account. (The procedure can use SETUSER to impersonate another account.) A procedure with the *startup* option set to TRUE must be in the *master* database and must be owned by the database owner (dbo) in *master*. You can, of course, reference objects in other databases from within the startup procedure or even call procedures that exist in other databases. A startup procedure is launched asynchronously, and it can execute in a loop for the entire duration of the SQL Server process. This allows several such procedures to be launched simultaneously at startup. When a startup procedure is running, it's seen as an active user connection.

A single startup procedure can nest calls to other stored procedures, consuming only a single user connection. Such execution of the nested procedures is synchronous, as would normally be the case. (That is, execution in the calling procedure doesn't continue until the procedure being called completes.) Typically, a stored procedure that's autostarted won't generate a lot of output. Errors, including those raised with RAISERROR, will be written to the SQL Server error log. Any result sets generated will seemingly vanish. If you need the stored procedure to return result sets, you should use a stored procedure that calls the main stored procedure with INSERT/EXEC to insert the results into a table.

If you want to prevent a procedure with the *startup* option from executing, you can start the server using trace flag 4022 or as a minimally configured server using the *-f* switch to SQLSERVR.EXE. You can set the *-T4022* flag by using the SQL Server Properties dialog box in SQL Server Enterprise Manager. (Right-click on the name of your server and choose Properties to get to this dialog box.) These safeguards allow you to recover from problems. Consider the illustrative but perhaps absurd example of someone including a procedure that executes the SHUTDOWN command. If you had given such a procedure the *autostart* option, SQL Server would immediately shut itself down before you could do anything about it!

SYSTEM STORED PROCEDURES

SQL Server installs a large number of system stored procedures that are used mostly for administrative and informational purposes. In many cases, these are called behind the scenes by the SQL-DMO objects used by SQL Server Enterprise Manager and other applications. But the system stored procedures can also be called directly; only a few years ago, doing so was the primary mechanism by which SQL Server was administered. Old-time SQL Server users were indoctrinated into using system stored procedures.

With the great tools and interfaces that are a core part of SQL Server today, there's no longer much reason to work with these system stored procedures directly. But it's good to be familiar with them—understanding them can help you understand the operations that occur on the system tables and can take much of the mystery out of what's going on behind the scenes with the graphical tools. If you look carefully through the *sysobjects* system table (particularly in the *master* database), you'll find system procedures and system functions that are not among the documented system routines. Typically, these routines exist to be called by some other system routine that is exposed; to support some SQL Server utility, such as Enterprise Manager; or to provide statistics to the Microsoft System Monitor. These procedures aren't documented for direct use because they exist only to support functionality exposed elsewhere—they don't provide that functionality independently.

There's nothing secret about these routines. For the most part, their text is exposed clearly in *syscomments*. You're welcome to explore them to see what they do and use them if you want. But unlike with the documented system routines, Microsoft has no commitment to maintaining the undocumented system routines or making them exhibit exactly consistent behavior in future releases. Of course, if your applications were to become dependent on one of these routines, you could certainly maintain your own version of it to perform exactly as you specify, or you could use one of them as a starting point and customize it to suit your needs. You'll probably want to use a different name for your own replacement routines so that they won't be overwritten during a service pack upgrade.

The SQL Server online documentation explains the specifics of each system routine, so I won't go into detail on each and every routine here. Since there are many more system stored procedures than system functions, the following sections discuss the broad categories for grouping stored procedures: General, Catalog, SQL Server Agent, Replication, and Extended.

General System Procedures

System stored procedures aid in the administration of your system, and they sometimes modify the system tables. You shouldn't configure the system to allow direct modification of the system tables because a mistake can render your database useless. That's why direct modification of system tables is prohibited by default. If modification is necessary, you can use a system stored procedure that is known to do the job correctly.

The following are some of the SQL Server system stored procedures, divided into four categories: basic, security, cursor, and distributed query procedures. Each procedure's name gives you a clue about its function.

Some basic system procedures:

```
sp_helptext
sp_helptrigger
sp_attach_db
sp_lock
sp_help
sp_helpconstraint
sp_recompile
sp_helpindex
sp_who
```

Some of the security stored procedures:

```
sp_addapprole
sp_defaultlanguage
sp_helplogins
sp_helpntgroup
sp_addlogin
sp_addrolemember
sp_changedbowner
sp_grantdbaccess
sp_changeobjectowner
sp_grantlogin
```

The following *cursor procedures* are used to find information about existing cursors:

```
sp_describe_cursor
sp_describe_cursor_columns
sp_describe_cursor_tables
sp_cursor_list
```

Finally, here are some of the stored procedures available for managing distributed queries. Distributed queries access data from multiple heterogeneous data sources. You can store this data in the same computer or different computers, and you can access it by using OLE DB.

```
sp_addlinkedserver
sp_addlinkedsrvlogin
sp_serveroption
```

Catalog Stored Procedures

Applications and development tools commonly need access to information about table names, column types, datatypes, constraints, privileges, and configuration options. All this information is stored in the system tables, which are also known as the system catalogs. But system tables might require changes between releases to support new features, so directly accessing the system tables could result in your application breaking from a new SQL Server release.

For this reason, SQL Server provides *catalog stored procedures,* a series of stored procedures that extract the information from the system tables, providing an abstraction layer that insulates your application. If the system tables are changed, the stored procedures that extract and provide the information will also be changed to ensure that they operate consistently (from an external perspective) from one release to another. Many of these procedures also map nearly identically to ODBC calls. The SQL Server ODBC driver calls these procedures in response to those function calls.

While it's fine to directly query the system catalogs for ad hoc use, if you're deploying an application that needs to get information from the system tables, you should use these catalog stored procedures. Here's a partial list:

```
sp_column_privileges
sp_columns
sp_stored_procedures
sp_databases
sp_table_privileges
sp_tables
```

SQL Server Agent Stored Procedures

SQL Server Enterprise Manager uses SQL Server Agent stored procedures to set up alerts and schedule tasks for execution. If your application needs to carry out tasks such as these, you can call the following procedures directly. They must be called from or qualified by the *msdb* database. Here are some of the SQL Server Agent stored procedures:

```
sp_add_alert
sp_add_job
sp_add_jobstep
sp_helptask
sp_delete_alert
sp_start_job
sp_stop_job
sp_help_alert
```

Web Assistant Procedures

SQL Server provides a number of procedures for creating and managing Web pages. These procedures are typically called from within the Web Assistant Wizard, but they're documented and you can call them directly. You can consider them a sub-category of the SQL Server Agent procedures because SQL Server Agent handles much of the automatic updating of Web pages. Here are the Web assistant procedures:

```
sp_dropwebtask
sp_enumcodepages
sp_makewebtask
sp_runwebtask
```

Replication Stored Procedures

You use replication stored procedures to set up and manage publication and sub-scription tasks. SQL Server Enterprise Manager typically provides a front end to these procedures, but you can also call them directly. SQL Server has many replication stored procedures; frankly, it's hard to manually use replication with these procedures. You can do it, though, if you're determined. Everything SQL Server Enterprise Manager does ultimately uses these system stored procedures. I urge you to use SQL Server Enterprise Manager or SQL-DMO if you need to add customized replication administration to your application.

Extended Stored Procedures

You can use extended stored procedures to create your own external routines in a language such as C and have SQL Server automatically load and execute those routines just like a regular stored procedure. As with stored procedures, you can pass parameters to extended stored procedures, and they can return result sets, status values, or both. This allows you to extend SQL Server capabilities in powerful ways. Many SQL Server features introduced in the last few years have been implemented using extended stored procedures. These features include additions to SQL Server Enterprise Manager, login integration with Windows NT and Windows 2000 domain security, the ability to send and receive e-mail messages, and the ability to create a Web page based on a query.

Extended stored procedures are DLLs that SQL Server can dynamically load and execute. They aren't separate processes spawned by SQL Server—they run directly in the address space of SQL Server. The DLLs are created using the Open Data Services (ODS) API, which SQL Server also uses.

Writing an extended stored procedure sounds harder than it really is, which is probably why these procedures are somewhat underused. But writing one can be as simple as writing a wrapper around a C function. For example, consider the formatting capabilities in SQL Server's PRINT statement, which are limited and don't allow parameter substitution. The C language provides the *sprintf* function, which is powerful for formatting a string buffer and includes parameter substitution. It's easy to wrap the C *sprintf* function and create an extended stored procedure that calls it, resulting in the procedure *xp_sprintf*. To show you how easy this is, the following is the entire source code for the procedure *xp_sprintf*. Note that most of this code is setup code, and at the heart is the call to the C run-time function *sprintf*:

```
// XP_SPRINTF
//
// Format and store a series of characters and values into an
// output string using sprintf
//
// Parameters:
//      srvproc - the handle to the client connection
//
```

(continued)

```
// Returns:
//      XP_NOERROR or XP_ERROR
//
// Side Effects:
//
//
SRVRETCODE xp_sprintf( SRV_PROC * srvproc )
{
    int numparams;
    int paramtype;
    int i;
    char string[MAXSTRLEN];
    char format[MAXSTRLEN];
    char values[MAXARGUMENTS][MAXSTRLEN];
    char szBuffer[MAXSTRLEN];

    // Get number of parameters
    //
    numparams=srv_rpcparams(srvproc);

    // Check number of parameters
    //
    if (numparams < 3)
    {
        // Send error message and return
        //
        LoadString(hModule, IDS_ERROR_PARAM, szBuffer,
                sizeof(szBuffer));
        goto ErrorExit;
    }

    if (paramtype != SRVVARCHAR)
    {
        // Send error message and return
        //
        LoadString(hModule, IDS_ERROR_PARAM_TYPE, szBuffer,
                sizeof(szBuffer));
        goto ErrorExit;
    }

    if (!srv_paramstatus(srvproc, 1))
    {
        // Send error message and return
        //
        LoadString(hModule, IDS_ERROR_PARAM_STATUS, szBuffer,
                sizeof(szBuffer));
        goto ErrorExit;
    }
```

```
for (i = 2; i <= numparams; i++)
{
    paramtype=srv_paramtype(srvproc, i);

    if (paramtype != SRVVARCHAR)
    {
        // Send error message and return
        //
        LoadString(hModule, IDS_ERROR_PARAM_TYPE, szBuffer,
                    sizeof(szBuffer));
        goto ErrorExit;
    }
}

for (i = 0; i < MAXARGUMENTS; i++)
{
    memset(values[i], 0, MAXSTRLEN);

    srv_bmove(srv_paramdata(srvproc, i + 3),
                values[i],
                srv_paramlen(srvproc, i + 3));
}

memset(string, 0, MAXSTRLEN);
srv_bmove(srv_paramdata(srvproc, 2), format,
            srv_paramlen(srvproc, 2));
format[srv_paramlen(srvproc, 2)]='\0';

// This is the heart of the function -- it simply wraps sprintf
// and passes back the string
sprintf(string, format,
    values[0],  values[1],  values[2],  values[3],  values[4],
    values[5],  values[6],  values[7],  values[8],  values[9],
    values[10], values[11], values[12], values[13], values[14],
    values[15], values[16], values[17], values[18], values[19],
    values[20], values[21], values[22], values[23], values[24],
    values[25], values[26], values[27], values[28], values[29],
    values[30], values[31], values[32], values[33], values[34],
    values[35], values[36], values[37], values[38], values[39],
    values[40], values[41], values[42], values[43], values[44],
    values[45], values[46], values[47], values[48], values[49]);

srv_paramset(srvproc, 1, string, strlen(string));

return XP_NOERROR;
```

(continued)

```
ErrorExit:
    srv_sendmsg(srvproc,
                SRV_MSG_ERROR,
                SPRINTF_ERROR,
                SRV_INFO,
                (DBTINYINT) 0,
                NULL,
                0,
                0,
                szBuffer,
                SRV_NULLTERM);

    return XP_ERROR;
}
```

Because extended stored procedures run in the same address space as SQL Server, they can be efficient; however, a badly behaved extended stored procedure can crash SQL Server, although this is unlikely. A server crash is more likely to result from someone's maliciousness rather than carelessness. But this is a definite area for concern, and you should understand the issues that are covered in the rest of this section.

An extended stored procedure runs on the thread that called it. Each calling thread executes using the operating system's structured exception handling constructs (most notably *try-except*). When a thread is poorly written and performs a bad operation, such as trying to reference memory outside its address space, it is terminated. But only that single connection is terminated, and SQL Server remains unaffected. Any resources held by the thread, such as locks, are automatically released.

In actual use, extended stored procedures don't introduce significant stability problems into the environment. Nonetheless, it's certainly possible for an extended stored procedure to twiddle some data structure within SQL Server (to which it would have access because the procedure is part of SQL Server's address space) that could disrupt SQL Server's operation or even corrupt data. If you're unlucky, this could happen as the result of a bug in the extended stored procedure; however, it's more likely that the procedure would cause an access violation and have its thread terminated with no ill effects.

A procedure could conceivably cause data corruption, but such data structures aren't exposed publicly, so it would be hard to write a malicious procedure. It is possible, however, and given the propensity of some malicious people to create viruses, we can't rule this problem out (although no such cases have been documented). The ultimate responsibility for protecting your data has to rest with your system administrator, who has control over which, if any, extended stored procedures can be added to the system.

A WORD OF WARNING

Although extended stored procedures can be terrific additions to your applications and in most cases do not negatively impact your system's behavior, exceptions do exist. You can save yourself hours of grief if you keep the following points in mind:

- Be sure to include full error checking and exception handling. An unhandled exception will usually bring down SQL Server and generate a Dr. Watson dump.

- Be sure to stress test your extended procedures thoroughly. Even though they're not running on SQL Server itself, don't assume that you don't have to be concerned about how SQL Server will behave with hundreds or thousands of users accessing it.

- Read and follow the guidelines in Microsoft Knowledge Base article Q190987, entitled "Extended Stored Procedures: What Everyone Should Know," which is included on the companion CD.

Only someone with the *sysadmin* role can register an extended stored procedure with the system (using *sp_addextendedproc*), and only a system administrator can grant others permission to execute the procedure. Extended stored procedures can be added only to the *master* database (eliminating their ability to be easily transferred to other systems via a backup and restore of databases, for example). Administrators should allow use of only the procedures that have been thoroughly tested and proven to be safe and nondestructive.

Ideally, administrators could also have access to the source code and build environment of the extended stored procedure to verify that it bears no malicious intent. (Some people say they don't even want their SQL Server administrator to be able to do this, because that person might not be trustworthy. If that's the case, you have bigger problems. If you can't trust your system administrator, you'd better get a new one!)

Even without extended stored procedures, an administrator can disrupt a SQL Server environment in many ways. (Munging the system tables would be a good start.) Of course, you can decide that no one will ever add extended stored procedures to your system. That's certainly a safe approach, but you give up a powerful capability by taking this route. (It's kind of like deciding never to ride in a car in order to avoid an accident.)

Even if you prohibit foreign extended stored procedures from your system, don't go overboard with a sweeping rule that prevents the use of even the procedures provided by Microsoft to implement new features. Could one of these procedures have a bug that could disrupt SQL Server? Sure, but a bug is no more likely to occur than if the code for these procedures had simply been statically linked into the SQLSERVR.EXE file rather than implemented as a DLL and loaded on demand. Of course, Microsoft procedures are thoroughly tested before their release. The chance of a catastrophic bug occurring is pretty low. The fact that these are *extended* stored procedures in no way increases the risk of bugs. It's an engineering decision—and a smart one—that allows Microsoft to add more features to the product in a way that doesn't require extra change to the core product or additional resource use by environments that don't call these features.

By convention, most of the extended stored procedures provided with the product begin with *xp_*. Unlike the *sp_* prefix, no special properties are associated with *xp_*. In fact, several extended stored procedures begin with *sp_* (for example, *sp_getbindtoken*), which allows them to be called from any database without being fully qualified, so we could just call it with *EXEC sp_getbindtoken* instead of *EXEC master.dbo.xp_getbindtoken*. To ascertain whether a procedure is a regular stored procedure or an extended stored procedure, you shouldn't rely on the prefix of the name. Use the function OBJECTPROPERTY. For example, the following should return 1, indicating that *sp_getbindtoken* is an extended procedure:

```
USE master
SELECT OBJECTPROPERTY(OBJECT_ID('sp_getbindtoken'), 'IsExtendedProc')
```

If you substitute a "real" stored procedure name for *sp_getbindtoken*, such as *sp_help*, the function will return a 0.

As with stored procedures, some extended stored procedures that come with the product are not documented for direct use. These procedures exist to support functionality elsewhere—especially for SQL Server Enterprise Manager, SQL-DMO, and replication—rather than to provide features directly themselves.

The following extended stored procedures are provided and documented for direct use. First, here are the general extended stored procedures:

```
xp_cmdshell
xp_sprintf
xp_sscanf
```

Here are some of the administration and monitoring extended stored procedures:

```
xp_logevent
xp_msver
xp_sqlmaint
```

These are the integrated security-related extended stored procedures:

```
xp_enumgroups
xp_grantlogin
xp_loginconfig
xp_logininfo
xp_revokelogin
```

And finally, here are the SQL mail–related extended stored procedures:

```
xp_deletemail
xp_findnextmsg
xp_readmail
xp_sendmail
xp_startmail
xp_stopmail
```

SQL Profiler Extended Procedures

SQL Profiler provides a graphical user interface to a set of extended stored procedures for monitoring dozens of aspects of SQL Server's internal behavior and for creating traces. You can also use extended stored procedures to create your own applications that monitor SQL Server. In Chapter 17, I'll discuss SQL Profiler and describe many of the extended procedures available for working with traces.

EXECUTE(*"ANY STRING"*)

The ability to formulate and then execute a string dynamically in SQL Server is a subtle but powerful capability. Using this capability, you can avoid additional round-trips to the client application by formulating a new statement to be executed directly on the server. You can pass a string directly, or you can pass a local variable of type *char* or *varchar*. This capability is especially useful if you need to pass an object name to a procedure or if you want to build an SQL statement from the result of another SQL statement.

For example, suppose that we had partitioned our database to have multiple tables similar to the *authors* table. We could write a procedure like the one shown below to pass the name of the table we want to insert into. The procedure would then formulate the INSERT statement by concatenating strings, and then it would execute the string it formulated:

```
CREATE PROC add_author
@au_id char(11),
@au_lname varchar(20),
@au_fname varchar(20),
@tabname varchar(30) AS
```

(continued)

```
BEGIN
    DECLARE @insert_stmt varchar(255)
    SELECT @insert_stmt='INSERT ' + @tabname + ' (au_id,
        au_lname, au_fname, contract) VALUES ('' + @au_id +
        '','' + @au_lname + '','' + @au_fname + '', 1)'
    -- PRINT @insert_stmt
    EXECUTE (@insert_stmt)
END

EXEC add_author '999-99-1234', 'Pike', 'Neil', 'authors'
```

Note that the procedure uses lots of single quotes. I didn't want to use double quotes because the option QUOTED_IDENTIFIER is ON by default in SQL Query Analyzer, and that means you can use double quotes only to indicate object names. Two single quotes together, inside of a string, will be interpreted as a single quote. It's the way to "quote the quote." In addition, you might notice that I included a simple debugging technique. I commented a statement that will actually show me the value I built in the string *@insert_stmt*. If SQL Server complains of syntax errors when the procedure is executed and I just can't figure out where the error is, I can ALTER the procedure, uncomment the PRINT statement, and put the comment marks in front of the EXECUTE statement.

If you make use of this dynamic EXECUTE inside a routine, there are a few additional issues that you need to be aware of:

■ The plan for the SQL statement constructed from the string is not saved as part of the routine's plan. If the values of any of the variables or parameters used to build the SQL string change, the SQL statement will need to be recompiled. This means you won't always get the full benefit of having the plans for routines precompiled.

■ Although SQL Server can use variables from outside the EXEC string to construct the SQL statement, any variables assigned a value in the constructed string will not be available outside the EXEC.

■ A USE statement issued to change your database context is in effect only for the EXEC string's execution. The following example illustrates this behavior:

```
SET NOCOUNT ON
USE pubs
PRINT db_name()
EXEC ('USE Northwind PRINT db_name() SELECT count(*) FROM products')
PRINT db_name()
GO
```

```
RESULTS:
pubs
Northwind


- - - - - - - - - - -
77

pubs
```

■ Normally, if a user has permission to execute a stored procedure or function, that user will also have implied permission to access all objects in the routine owned by the routine's owner. This does not apply to objects accessed inside an EXEC string. Even if a user has permission to execute a procedure, if the user doesn't have permission to perform all the actions specified in the EXEC string, a run-time error will occur.

■ The only operation that you can use to build the string inside the EXEC is the concatenation operator. You cannot use functions. For example, if you want to select from a table that has the name of the user plus the day of the month for its name (for example: *kalen20*), you must build the string to be executed outside of the EXEC. Here's an example:

```
DECLARE @sqlstring varchar(100)
SELECT @sqlstring = 'SELECT * FROM ' + LTRIM(user_name()) +
                    CONVERT(char(2),DATEPART(dd, GETDATE()))
EXEC (@sqlstring)
```

SUMMARY

Transact-SQL statements can be grouped together in batches, they can persist in the database, and they can repeatedly execute as stored procedures or return values within a statement as functions. It is essential that you understand the differences between these programming constructs and that you understand that their actions are not mutually exclusive.

Transact-SQL routines can be quite complex, and they can become a significant portion of your application's source code. However, the hardest part of writing routines is writing the SQL code that they are composed of.

Chapter 12

Transactions
and Triggers

In this chapter, we'll continue looking at the use of Transact-SQL for creating programmable modules. In particular, we'll look at modules that automatically execute when a data modification statement is issued. This type of module is called a *trigger*. You can define a trigger to execute as an alternative to the requested data modification or to execute after the modification takes place. To thoroughly understand how triggers behave, you need to have a fuller understanding of transactions and transaction boundaries. This chapter will go into more detail about transactions and how they affect changes made by multiple users.

TRANSACTIONS

Like a batch (discussed in Chapter 11), a user-declared transaction typically consists of several SQL commands that read and update the database. However, a batch is basically a client-side concept; it controls how many statements are sent to SQL Server for processing at once. A transaction, on the other hand, is a server-side concept. It deals with how much work SQL Server will do before it considers the changes committed. A multistatement transaction doesn't make any permanent changes in a database until a COMMIT TRANSACTION statement is issued. In addition, a multistatement transaction can undo its changes when a ROLLBACK TRANSACTION statement is issued.

Both batches and transactions can contain multiple commands. In fact, transactions and batches can have a many-to-many relationship. A single transaction can span several batches (although that's a bad idea from a performance perspective), and a batch can contain multiple transactions. The following examples illustrate these possibilities. Note that you can use TRAN as an abbreviation for TRANSACTION.

The first script is one transaction spread across four batches:

```
BEGIN TRAN
INSERT authors VALUES (etc.)
GO
SELECT * FROM authors
GO
UPDATE publishers SET pub_id = (etc.)
GO
COMMIT TRAN
GO
```

This second script is one batch that contains two transactions:

```
BEGIN TRAN
INSERT authors VALUES (etc.)
SELECT * FROM authors
COMMIT TRAN
BEGIN TRAN
UPDATE publishers SET pub_id = (etc.)
INSERT publishers VALUES (etc.)
COMMIT TRAN
GO
```

Now let's look at a simple transaction in a little more detail. The BEGIN TRAN and COMMIT TRAN statements cause the commands between them to be performed as a unit:

```
BEGIN TRAN
INSERT authors VALUES (etc.)
SELECT * FROM authors
UPDATE publishers SET pub_id = (etc.)
COMMIT TRAN
GO
```

Transaction processing in SQL Server ensures that all commands within a transaction are performed as a unit of work—even in the presence of a hardware or general system failure. Such transactions are considered to have the ACID properties (atomicity, consistency, isolation, and durability). (For more information about the ACID properties, see Chapter 2.)

Explicit and Implicit Transactions

By default, SQL Server treats each statement—whether it's dispatched individually or as part of a batch—as independent and immediately commits it. Logically, the only kind of statement that can be committed is a statement that changes something in the database, so talking about committing a SELECT statement is really meaningless. When we look at transaction isolation levels later in this section, you'll see that it's important in some cases to include SELECTs inside larger transactions. However, when we talk about transactions, we're generally talking about data modification statements (INSERT, UPDATE, and DELETE). So any individual data modification statement by itself is an *implicit transaction*. No matter how many rows are modified, either they will all be modified or none of them will be. If a system failure occurs while a million-row table is being updated, when SQL Server recovers, it will roll back the part of the update that's already been written to disk, and the state of the database will be as if the update never happened.

If you want a transaction to include multiple statements, you must wrap the group of statements within BEGIN TRANSACTION and COMMIT TRANSACTION or ROLLBACK TRANSACTION statements. Most of the examples in this section will deal with transactions containing multiple statements, which are called *explicit transactions*.

You can also configure SQL Server to implicitly start a transaction by using SET IMPLICIT_TRANSACTIONS ON or by turning on the option globally using *sp_configure 'user options', 2*. More precisely, you take the previous value for the *user options* setting and OR it with (decimal) 2, which is the mask for IMPLICIT_TRANSACTIONS.

For example, if the previous value were (decimal) 8, you'd set it to 10 because 8|2 is 10. (The symbol used here is the vertical bar, not a forward or backward slash.) If bit operations such as 8|2 are somewhat foreign to you, let SQL Server do the work. You can issue a SELECT 8|2 in SQL Query Analyzer, and the value returned will be 10. (But be careful not to assume that you just add 2 to whatever is already there—for example, 10|2 is 10, not 12.)

If implicit transactions are enabled, all statements are considered part of a transaction and no work is committed until and unless an explicit COMMIT TRAN (or synonymously, COMMIT WORK) is issued. This is true even if all the statements in the batch have executed: you must issue a COMMIT TRANSACTION in a subsequent batch before any changes are considered permanent. The examples in this book assume that you have not set IMPLICIT_TRANSACTIONS on and that any multistatement transaction must begin with BEGIN TRAN.

Error Checking in Transactions

One of the most common mistakes that developers make with SQL Server is to assume that *any* error within a transaction will cause the transaction to automatically roll back. This is an understandable misconception because we're always talking about transactions being atomic. However, when we talk about a failure causing a transaction to be rolled back, it usually means a system failure. If the whole system stops functioning, SQL Server must be restarted and the automatic recovery process will roll back any incomplete transactions. However, for many errors encountered in a transaction, only the current statement will be aborted—the rest of the statements in the transaction can continue to be processed and even committed. Here's an example:

```
USE PUBS
BEGIN TRAN
UPDATE authors
SET state = 'FL'
WHERE state = 'KS'

UPDATE jobs
SET min_lvl = min_lvl - 10

COMMIT TRAN

SELECT * FROM authors
WHERE state = 'FL'
```

The transaction contains two UPDATE statements. The first UPDATE changes the *state* value in one row to 'FL'. The second UPDATE attempts to subtract 10 from all the *min_lvl* values in the *jobs* table, but there is a CHECK constraint on the *min_lvl* column that specifies that *min_lvl* must be greater than or equal to 10. Most of the values in the *jobs* table are greater than 20, so subtracting 10 would not violate the constraint. However, there is one row with a value of 10, and subtracting 10 would cause a constraint violation. Because of that one conflicting row, the entire statement is aborted and no rows in *jobs* are updated, but the transaction is not rolled back. The SELECT statement after the COMMIT shows that we still have one author with a value for *state* of 'FL'.

Your multistatement transactions should check for errors by selecting the value of @@ERROR after each statement. If a nonfatal error is encountered and you don't take action on it, processing moves to the next statement. Only fatal errors cause the batch to be automatically aborted and the transaction rolled back. Here's what the preceding batch would look like with the appropriate error checking:

```
USE PUBS
BEGIN TRAN
UPDATE authors
```

```
SET state = 'FL'
WHERE state = 'KS'

IF @@ERROR <> 0 BEGIN
    ROLLBACK TRAN
    GOTO ON_ERROR
 END
UPDATE jobs
SET  min_lvl = min_lvl - 10
IF @@ERROR <> 0 BEGIN
    ROLLBACK TRAN
    GOTO ON_ERROR
 END

COMMIT TRAN
ON_ERROR:

SELECT * FROM authors
WHERE state = 'FL'
```

In this batch, we're checking for errors after each of the data modification statements. Just rolling back the transaction if an error is found is not sufficient, however, because in most cases a ROLLBACK TRAN does not change the flow of control in the execution of your statements. The ROLLBACK TRAN would undo any completed modifications in the current transaction and make the appropriate entries in the transaction log. However, program flow would continue to the next line. In this case, with no GOTO, if the first UPDATE had an error we would still continue to the second UPDATE; if the second UPDATE had an error, we would still continue and try to execute the COMMIT TRAN. Since we would have already executed a ROLLBACK TRAN, there would no longer be an open transaction to commit and we would get an error for the COMMIT TRAN statement.

> **TIP** A query that finds no rows meeting the criteria of the WHERE clause is not an error. Nor is a searched UPDATE statement that affects no rows. @@ERROR returns a 0 (meaning no error) in either case. If you want to check for "no rows affected," use @@ROWCOUNT, not @@ERROR.

Syntax errors always cause the entire batch to be aborted before execution even begins, and references to objects that don't exist (for example, a SELECT from a table that doesn't exist) cause a batch to stop execution at that point. However, just because a batch has been aborted doesn't mean that the transaction has been rolled back. You've seen that transactions can span batches. If you receive an error and you're not sure whether your transaction has been rolled back, you can check the status of the transaction using the system function @@TRANCOUNT. If @@TRANCOUNT is greater than 0, there is an active transaction and you can execute a ROLLBACK TRAN.

I'll discuss @@TRANCOUNT in more detail later in this section. Typically, you'll work out syntax errors and correct references to objects before you put an application into production, so these won't be much of an issue.

A syntax error on a batch dynamically built and executed using EXECUTE('*string*') can never be caught until execution. You can think of this EXECUTE('*string*') construct as a way of nesting batches. If the *string* consists of multiple statements, a syntax or object reference error will abort the inner batch only. Processing proceeds to the next statement in the outer batch. For example, consider the following script:

```
DECLARE @tablename sysname
SET @tablename = 'authours'
EXECUTE ('USE pubs SELECT * FROM ' + @tablename +
' PRINT ''Inner Batch Done'' ')
PRINT 'Outer Batch Done'
```

This batch won't have an error detected at parse time, so SQL Server will attempt to execute it. The DECLARE and the SET will be executed successfully, but the nested batch inside the EXECUTE will have a problem. There's an error in the SELECT because the table name *authours* doesn't exist in the *pubs* database. The inner batch will generate an error during its name resolution phase, so the third statement in the inner batch (PRINT) will not be executed. However, the outer batch will continue and the message "Outer Batch Done" will be printed.

Errors that occur in a production environment are typically resource errors. You probably won't encounter these much, especially if you've done sufficient testing to make sure that your configuration settings and environment are appropriate. Out-of-resource errors occur when a database file fills up, when there isn't enough memory to run a procedure, when a database is off line and unavailable, and so on. For these types of fatal errors, conditional action based on @@ERROR is moot because the batch will automatically be aborted.

The following are among the most common errors that you need to be concerned about:

- Lack of permissions on an object

- Constraint violations

- Duplicates encountered while trying to update or insert a row

- Deadlocks with another user

- NOT NULL violations

- Illegal values for the current datatype

Here's an example that creates three tables, two of which have a primary/foreign key relationship. Table *b* has a foreign key reference to table *a*; any INSERT into *b* should fail if the value inserted doesn't already exist in table *a*. A procedure then tries to insert into two of the tables. The procedure is written to perform error checking, with a branch to perform a rollback if any error is encountered. Since no inserts have been done into table *a*, any insert into *b* should fail:

```
CREATE TABLE a (
a char(1) primary key)

CREATE TABLE b (
b char(1) references a)

CREATE TABLE c (
c char(1))
GO

CREATE PROC test as
BEGIN TRANSACTION
INSERT c VALUES ('X')
    IF (@@ERROR <> 0) GOTO on_error
INSERT b VALUES ('X')  -- Fails reference
    IF (@@ERROR <> 0) GOTO on_error
COMMIT TRANSACTION
RETURN(0)

on_error:
ROLLBACK TRANSACTION
RETURN(1)
```

This simple procedure illustrates the power of Transact-SQL. The system function @@ERROR can return a value for the connection after each statement. A value of 0 for @@ERROR means that no error occurred. Given the data the user provided, when the procedure *test* is executed, the INSERT statement on table *b* will fail with a foreign key violation. The error message for that type of failure is error 547, with text such as this:

```
INSERT statement conflicted with COLUMN FOREIGN KEY constraint
'FK__b__b__723BFC65'. The conflict occurred in database 'pubs',
table 'a', column 'a'
```

Consequently, @@ERROR would be set to 547 following that INSERT statement. Therefore, the statement *IF (@@ERROR <> 0)* evaluates as TRUE, and execution follows the *GOTO* to the *on_error:* label. Here the transaction is rolled back. The procedure terminates with a return code of 1 because the RETURN(1) statement was used.

Had the branch to *on_error:* not been followed (by virtue of @@ERROR not being 0), the procedure would have continued line-by-line execution. It would have reached COMMIT TRANSACTION, and then it would have returned value 0 and never made it all the way to the *on_error:* section.

As with most programming languages, with Transact-SQL you can return a status code from a procedure to indicate success or failure (or other possible outcomes); those return status codes are checked from the calling routines. However, you have to remember to check the status after executing the procedures. Merely using *EXEC test* won't directly provide information about whether the procedure performed as expected. A better method is to use a local variable to examine the return code from that procedure:

```
DECLARE @retcode int
EXEC @retcode=test
```

Following execution of the test procedure, the local variable *@retcode* has the value 0 (if no errors occurred in the procedure) or 1 (if execution branched to the *on_error:* section).

The SET XACT_ABORT option was added to SQL Server to force any error—not just a fatal error—to terminate the batch. Here's another way to ensure that nothing is committed if any error is encountered:

```
CREATE PROC test AS
SET XACT_ABORT ON
BEGIN TRANSACTION
INSERT c VALUES ('X')
INSERT b VALUES ('X')  -- Fails reference
COMMIT TRANSACTION
GO

EXEC test
GO

SELECT * FROM c
```

Here's the output:

```
(0 rows affected)
```

Note that the name of the XACT_ABORT option is a bit of a misnomer because the current batch, not simply the transaction, is immediately aborted if an error occurs, just as it is when a fatal resource error is encountered. This has consequences that might not be immediately apparent. For example, if you issued two transactions within one batch, the second transaction would never be executed because the batch would be aborted before the second transaction got a chance to execute. More subtly, suppose we want to use good programming practice and check the return status of the previous procedure. (Note that even though it doesn't explicitly do a RETURN, every procedure has a return status by default, with 0 indicating SUCCESS.)

We could write a batch like this:

```
DECLARE @retcode int
EXEC @retcode=test
SELECT @retcode
```

Yet there's a subtle but important problem here. If the procedure has an error, the SELECT @RETCODE statement will never be executed: the entire batch will be aborted by virtue of the SET XACT_ABORT statement. This is why I recommend checking @@ERROR instead of using SET XACT_ABORT. Checking @@ERROR after each statement is a bit more tedious, but it gives you finer control of execution in your procedures.

Unfortunately, error handling in SQL Server 2000 can be somewhat messy and inconsistent. For example, there's no way to install a routine that means "Do this on any error" (other than SET XACT_ABORT, which aborts but doesn't let you specify the actions to be performed). Instead, you must use something similar to the preceding examples that check @@ERROR and then do a GOTO.

In addition, there's currently no easy way to determine in advance which errors might be considered fatal so that the batch can be aborted and which errors are nonfatal so that the next statement can be executed. In most cases, an error with a severity level of 16 or higher is fatal and the batch will be aborted. Syntax that refers to nonexistent functions is a level-15 error, yet the batch is still aborted. Although you can use @@ERROR to return the specific error number, no function such as @@SEVERITY is available to indicate the error's severity level. Instead, you must subsequently select from the *sysmessages* table to see the severity level of the last error. To further complicate matters, some level-16 errors aren't fatal, including the constraint violation error encountered in the first error-checking example. Table 12-1 lists the most common nonfatal level-16 errors. Note the %.*s placeholders in the error messages: SQL Server substitutes the actual names being referenced when it issues the error message.

Admittedly, the rules are hardly consistent, and this area is ripe for some attention in future releases. As you write your procedures, keep in mind that they might be automatically aborted because of an unexpected fatal error, or you can cause them to abort with a nonfatal error.

Level-16 Error	Error Message
515	Attempt to insert the value NULL into column %.*s', table %.*s'; column doesn't allow nulls. %s fails.
544	Attempt to insert explicit value for *identity* column in table %.*s' when IDENTITY_INSERT is set to OFF.
547	Attempt to execute %s statement conflicted with %s %s constraint %.*s'. The conflict occurred in database %.*s', table %.*s %s%.*s%s.
550	Attempt to insert or update failed because the target view either specifies WITH CHECK OPTION or spans a view that specifies WITH CHECK OPTION, and one or more rows resulting from the operation didn't qualify under the CHECK OPTION constraint.

Table 12-1. *Common nonfatal level-16 errors.*

Transaction Isolation Levels

The isolation level at which your transaction runs determines your application's sensitivity to changes made by others; consequently, it also determines how long your transaction needs to hold locks to potentially protect against changes made by others. SQL Server 2000 offers four isolation levels:

- READ UNCOMMITTED (dirty read)
- READ COMMITTED (default—READ COMMITTED is equivalent to the term CURSOR STABILITY, which is used by several other products, such as IBM DB2)
- REPEATABLE READ
- SERIALIZABLE

Your transactions will behave differently depending on which isolation level is set. The saying "Not to decide *is* to decide" applies here because every transaction has an isolation level, whether you've specified it or not. You should understand the levels and choose the one that best fits your needs.

NOTE The syntactical options listed above correspond to the SQL standard isolation levels, which I discussed in detail in Chapter 3. In this section, we'll look at information that wasn't covered earlier. See Chapter 3 if you need a refresher.

When you use the READ UNCOMMITTED option, keep in mind that you should deal with inconsistencies that might result from dirty reads. Because share locks aren't issued and exclusive locks of other connections aren't honored (that is, the data pages can be read even though they're supposedly locked), it's possible to get some spurious errors during execution when you use READ UNCOMMITTED. A moment later, reexecuting the same command is likely to work without error.

Nothing illustrates the differences and effects of isolation levels like seeing them for yourself with some simple examples. To run the following examples, you'll need to establish two connections to SQL Server. Remember that each connection is *logically* a different user, even if both connections use the same login ID. Locks held by one connection affect the other connection, even if both are logged in as the same user. In case you can't run these examples, the SQL scripts and output are shown here.

EXAMPLE 1

This example shows a dirty read. To test these examples yourself, you have to run the commands for connection 1 in one SQL Query Analyzer window and the commands for connection 2 in a second window. The commands for each connection will be listed side by side, and it is important to execute the batches for each connection at the appropriate time relative to the batches for the other connection. That is, the batches should be executed in the order of the "batch number" listed in the leftmost column. Following is the code and the output (in bold):

Batch	Connection 1	Connection 2
1		USE PUBS GO
2		USE PUBS GO
3		-- First verify there's only -- one author named 'Smith' SELECT au_lname FROM authors WHERE au_lname='Smith' GO **RESULTS** **au_lname** **-------------------------** **Smith** **(1 row affected)** SET TRANSACTION ISOLATION LEVEL READ UNCOMMITTED GO

(continued)

continued

Batch	Connection 1	Connection 2
| 4 | ```
BEGIN TRAN
  UPDATE authors
    SET au_lname='Smith'
-- Give other connection chance to
-- read uncommitted data
GO
(23 rows affected)
``` | |
| 5 | | ```
SELECT au_lname FROM authors
WHERE au_lname='Smith'

au_lname
-------------------------
Smith
Smith
Smith
Smith
Smith
Smith
Smith
Smith
Smith
Smith
Smith
Smith
Smith
Smith
Smith
Smith
Smith
Smith
Smith
Smith
Smith
Smith
Smith

(23 rows affected)

IF (@@ROWCOUNT > 1)
    PRINT 'Just read uncommitted
    data !!'

Just read uncommitted data !!
``` |

(continued)

Batch	Connection 1	Connection 2

6	`-- UNDO the changes`
	`-- to the authors table`
	`ROLLBACK TRAN`
	`GO`	

7		`-- Now check again for authors`
		`-- of name 'Smith'.`
		`-- Find only one now because`
		`-- other connection did a rollback.`
		`SELECT au_lname FROM authors`
		`WHERE au_lname='Smith'`
		
		`au_lname`
		`-------------------------`
		`Smith`
		
		`(1 row affected)`

These batches, running simultaneously, illustrate that by setting the isolation level to READ UNCOMMITTED, you can read data that logically never existed (a dirty read). The update to *Smith* was never committed by connection 1, yet the other connection read it. Not only did the connection read the updated data, but it did so immediately and didn't have to wait for the exclusive lock of the first connection updating the data to be released.

In this example, concurrency is high; however, consistency of the data isn't maintained. By changing the isolation level back to the default (READ COMMITTED), the same batches would never see more than one row containing *Smith*. But with READ COMMITTED, the connection reading the data must wait until the updating transaction is done. This is the trade-off: higher consistency is achieved (the uncommitted rows aren't seen by others), but concurrency is reduced.

EXAMPLE 2

This example illustrates the semantic differences between selecting data under the default isolation level of READ COMMITTED (cursor stability) and under the isolation level of REPEATABLE READ.

Batch	Connection 1	Connection 2
1	`USE PUBS` `GO`	
2		`USE PUBS` `GO`

(continued)

continued

Batch	Connection 1	Connection 2
| 3 | | ```
UPDATE authors SET au_lname='Doe'
-- Make sure no Smith or Jones
(23 rows affected)

-- Change the transaction isolation
-- level, and then verify there
-- are no authors named 'Smith'
SET TRANSACTION ISOLATION LEVEL
    READ COMMITTED
GO
BEGIN TRAN
SELECT au_lname FROM authors
WHERE au_lname='Smith'
GO
(0 rows affected)
``` |
| 4 | ```
UPDATE authors
SET au_lname='Smith'
GO
(23 rows affected)
``` | |
| 5 | | ```
SELECT au_lname FROM authors
WHERE au_lname='Smith'
GO

au_lname
------------------------
Smith
Smith
Smith
  :
Smith
Smith

(23 rows affected)

COMMIT TRAN
GO

-- Now do the same thing,
-- but with REPEATABLE READ
    isolation

SET TRANSACTION ISOLATION LEVEL
    REPEATABLE READ
``` |

(continued)
```

Batch	Connection 1	Connection 2
5		GO BEGIN TRAN SELECT au_lname FROM authors WHERE au_lname='Smith' GO au_lname ------------------------ Smith Smith Smith ⋮ Smith Smith (23 rows affected)
6	UPDATE authors SET au_lname='Jones' GO **(query will block)**	
7		SELECT au_lname FROM authors WHERE au_lname='Smith' GO au_lname ------------------------ Smith Smith Smith ⋮ Smith Smith (23 rows affected) COMMIT TRAN GO
8	-- Now notice that query -- has completed **(23 rows affected)**	

(continued)

continued

Batch	Connection 1	Connection 2
| 9 | | ```
-- Now notice that Jones updates
-- have been done
SELECT au_lname FROM authors
GO

au_lname
Jones
Jones
Jones
Jones
Jones
Jones
Jones
Jones
Jones
Jones
Jones
Jones
Jones
Jones
Jones
Jones
Jones
Jones
Jones
Jones
Jones
Jones
Jones

(23 rows affected)
``` |

As you can see, when the isolation level was set to READ COMMITTED, selecting the same data twice within a transaction yielded totally different results: first no Smiths were found, and then 23 of them appeared. If this were a banking transaction, these results would be unacceptable. For applications that are less sensitive to minor changes, or when business functions guard against such inconsistencies in other ways, this behavior might be acceptable.

After changing the isolation level to REPEATABLE READ, we got the same result (no Joneses) with both SELECT statements. Immediately after the transaction was committed, the other connection updated all the names to *Jones*. So when we again selected for *Jones* (immediately after the transaction was committed), the update took
```

place—but at some cost. In the first case, the other connection was able to do the update as soon as the first SELECT was processed. It didn't have to wait for the second query and subsequent transaction to complete. In the second case, that second connection had to wait until the first connection completed the transaction in its entirety. In this example, concurrency was significantly reduced but consistency was perfect.

EXAMPLE 3

This example illustrates the semantic differences between selecting data under the isolation level of REPEATABLE READ and under the isolation level of SERIALIZABLE.

Batch	Connection 1	Connection 2
1	USE PUBS GO	
2		USE PUBS GO
3		SET TRANSACTION ISOLATION LEVEL REPEATABLE READ GO BEGIN TRAN SELECT title FROM titles WHERE title_id LIKE 'BU%' GO **title** -- The Busy Executive's Database Guide Cooking with Computers: Surreptitious Balance Sheets You Can Combat Computer Stress! Straight Talk About Computers
4	INSERT titles VALUES ('BU2000', 'Inside SQL Server 2000', 'popular_comp', '0877', 59.95, 5000, 10, 0, null, 'Sep 10, 2000') GO (1 row(s) affected)	

(continued)

continued

Batch	Connection 1	Connection 2

5		`-- execute the same SELECT again`
		`SELECT title FROM titles`
		`WHERE title_id LIKE 'BU%'`
		`GO`
		`title`
		`-----------------------------------`
		
		`Inside SQL Server 2000`
		`The Busy Executive's Database Guide`
		`Cooking with Computers:`
		`    Surreptitious Balance Sheets`
		`You Can Combat Computer Stress!`
		`Straight Talk About Computers`
		
		`COMMIT TRAN`
		
		`-- Now do the same thing,`
		`-- but with SERIALIZABLE isolation`
		
		`SET TRANSACTION ISOLATION LEVEL`
		`      SERIALIZABLE`
		`GO`
		
		`BEGIN TRAN`
		`SELECT title FROM titles`
		`WHERE title_id LIKE 'BU%'`
		`GO`
		
		`title`
		`-----------------------------------`
		
		`Inside SQL Server 2000`
		`The Busy Executive's Database Guide`
		`Cooking with Computers:`
		`    Surreptitious Balance Sheets`
		`You Can Combat Computer Stress!`
		`Straight Talk About Computers`

6	`INSERT titles VALUES ('BU3000',`
	`'Itzik and His Black Belt SQL Tricks',`
	`'popular_comp', '0877', 39.95,`
	` 10000, 12, 15000, null,`
	`'Sep 15 2000')`
	`GO`
	`(query will block)`	

(continued)

Batch	Connection 1	Connection 2
| 7 | | ```
SELECT title FROM titles
WHERE title_id LIKE 'BU%'
GO


title
-----------------------------------
Inside SQL Server 2000
The Busy Executive's Database Guide
Cooking with Computers:
    Surreptitious Balance Sheets
You Can Combat Computer Stress!
Straight Talk About Computers

COMMIT TRAN
GO
``` |
| 8 | ```
-- Now notice that query
-- has completed
(1 row affected)
``` | |
| 9 | | ```
-- Now notice that the second
-- new title has been inserted
-- after the COMMIT TRAN
SELECT title FROM titles
WHERE title_id LIKE 'BU%'
GO


title
-----------------------------------
Inside SQL Server 2000
Itzik and His Black Belt SQL Tricks
The Busy Executive's Database Guide
Cooking with Computers:
    Surreptitious Balance Sheets
You Can Combat Computer Stress!
Straight Talk About Computers
``` |

As you can see, when the isolation level was set to REPEATABLE READ, phantoms were possible. Another connection could add new data so that reissuing the same SELECT within a transaction would return more rows the second time. In this case, *Inside SQL Server 2000* just mysteriously appeared; it's the phantom row.

After changing the isolation level to SERIALIZABLE, we got the same result (five titles) with both SELECT statements in the second connection. Immediately after the
```

transaction committed, the first connection could complete the insert of a new book with the title *Itzik and His Black Belt SQL Tricks*. So when we again selected all the titles (immediately after the transaction was committed), the INSERT had taken place—but again, at some cost. In the first case, the first connection was able to do the INSERT as soon as the second connection's first SELECT was processed. It didn't have to wait for the second SELECT and for the transaction to commit. In the second case, that first connection had to wait until the second connection completed the transaction in its entirety. Just as in Example 2, concurrency was significantly reduced but consistency was perfect.

Another way to look at the difference between these isolation levels is to see what modification operations are possible once you've selected data within a transaction. In ISOLATION LEVEL REPEATABLE READ, the actual rows read can't be modified or deleted. However, new rows can be added to the range of data specified in the WHERE clause of the SELECT statement. All data read is locked so that no modifications can occur. However, since INSERT is adding new data, the locks on the existing data do not interfere. In ISOLATION LEVEL SERIALIZABLE, once you have selected data within a transaction, no modifications are possible to that data, or to the covered range of data, by any other connection. SERIALIZABLE locks ranges of data, including data that didn't actually exist, so that INSERTs are not allowed.

Other Characteristics of Transactions

In addition to isolation levels, it's important to understand the following characteristics of transactions.

First, a single UPDATE, DELETE, or INSERT/SELECT statement that affects multiple rows is always an atomic operation; it must complete without error, or else it will be automatically rolled back. For example, if you performed a single UPDATE statement that updated all rows but one row failed a constraint, the operation would be terminated with no rows updated. Because there's no way to do error checking for each row within such a statement, any error rolls back the statement. However, the batch isn't aborted. Execution proceeds to the next available statement in the batch. This will occur even in INSERT operations that are based on a SELECT statement (INSERT/SELECT or SELECT INTO).

Alternatively, a single UPDATE statement that updates hundreds of rows could fail to complete because of a system failure, possibly unrelated to SQL Server. (For example, the power might go out and your UPS system might not arrive until next Tuesday.) Because SQL Server considers the single UPDATE to be an atomic unit of work, when SQL Server comes back up and runs recovery on the database, it will be as if the UPDATE had never happened. If SQL Server doesn't know for sure that a transaction committed, the transaction will be rolled back. Even if 999,999 rows out of a million had been updated before the failure, we're left with nothing because the transaction is an all-or-nothing operation.

Like the statements mentioned earlier, modifications made by a trigger are always atomic with the underlying data modification statement. For example, if an update trigger attempts to update data but fails, the underlying data modification operation is rolled back. Both operations must succeed, or neither will.

It might not be obvious, but Example 2 (the REPEATABLE READ example) shows that a transaction can affect pure SELECT operations in which no data is modified. The transaction boundaries define the statements between which a specified isolation level will be assured. Two identical SELECT statements might behave differently if they were executed while wrapped by BEGIN TRAN/COMMIT TRAN with an isolation level of REPEATABLE READ than they would behave if they were executed together in the same batch but not within a transaction.

Nested Transaction Blocks

It's syntactically acceptable for blocks of BEGIN TRANSACTION followed by COMMIT TRAN or ROLLBACK TRAN to be nested within other such blocks. You can also do this kind of nesting with calls to nested stored procedures. However, the semantics of such a formulation might not be what you'd expect if you think that the transactions are truly nested: they aren't. But the behavior is reasonable and predictable. A ROLLBACK TRAN rolls back all levels of the transaction, not only its inner block. A COMMIT TRAN does nothing to commit the transaction if the statement isn't part of the outermost block. If the COMMIT TRAN is part of the outermost block, it commits all levels of the transaction.

So the behavior of a COMMIT or a ROLLBACK isn't too orthogonal when the transaction blocks are nested. Only the outermost COMMIT is able to commit the transaction, but any ROLLBACK will roll back the entire transaction at all levels. If this weren't true, a ROLLBACK in an outer transaction wouldn't be able to perform its job because the data would have already been committed. This behavior allows stored procedures (and triggers) to be executed automatically and in a predictable way without your needing to check the transaction state. A nested stored procedure that does a ROLLBACK TRAN will roll back the entire transaction, including work done by the top-level procedure.

In addition, the blocks of BEGIN TRAN and COMMIT TRAN or ROLLBACK TRAN are determined only by what actually executes, not by what's present in the batch. If conditional branching occurs (via IF statements, for example) and one of the statements doesn't execute, the statement isn't part of a block.

A common misconception about ROLLBACK TRAN, which I briefly discussed earlier, is that it changes the flow of control, causing, for example, an immediate return from a stored procedure or a batch. However, flow of control continues to the next statement, which, of course, could be an explicit RETURN. ROLLBACK affects only the actual data; it doesn't affect local variables or SET statements. If local variables are changed during a transaction or if SET statements are issued, those variables and options *do not* revert to the values they had before the transaction started. Variables, including table variables, and SET options aren't part of transaction control.

The system function @@TRANCOUNT will return the depth of executed BEGIN TRAN blocks. You can think of the behavior of COMMIT TRAN and ROLLBACK TRAN in this way: ROLLBACK TRAN performs its job for all levels of transaction blocks whenever @@TRANCOUNT is 1 or greater. A COMMIT TRAN commits changes *only* when @@TRANCOUNT is 1.

NOTE Beginning on the next page, you'll see several examples of nesting transaction blocks. For illustration, the value of @ @TRANCOUNT is shown in the comments. If this discussion isn't totally clear to you, you should work through these examples by hand to understand why the value of @ @TRANCOUNT is what it is, why it changes, and why the behavior of COMMIT TRAN or ROLL-BACK TRAN acts in a way that depends on the @ @TRANCOUNT value.

Executing a BEGIN TRAN statement always increments the value of @@TRANCOUNT. If no transaction is active, @@TRANCOUNT is 0. Executing a COMMIT TRAN decrements the value of @@TRANCOUNT. Executing a ROLLBACK TRAN rolls back the entire transaction and sets @@TRANCOUNT to 0. Executing either a COMMIT TRAN or a ROLLBACK TRAN when there's no open transaction (@@TRANCOUNT is 0) results in error 3902 or 3903, which states that the COMMIT or ROLLBACK request has no corresponding BEGIN TRANSACTION. In this case, @@TRANCOUNT is not decremented, so it can never go below 0.

Other errors, not of your making, can be fatal as well—for example, running out of memory, filling up the transaction log (if you don't have it set to *autogrow*), or terminating because of a deadlock. Such errors cause an open transaction to automatically roll back. If that occurs, @@TRANCOUNT will return 0, signaling that no open transaction exists.

The following incidents cause fatal errors:

- The system runs out of resources.

- The log runs out of space.

- Deadlock conditions exist.

- Protection exceptions occur (that is, sufficient permissions are unavailable on an object).

- A stored procedure can't run (for example, it's not present or you don't have privileges).

- The maximum nesting level of stored procedure executions has been reached.

You can't plan precisely for all of these situations, and even if you could, a new release could likely add another one. In a production environment, fatal errors should be few and far between. But as is true in nearly all programming, it's up to you to decide whether to try to plan for every conceivable problem and then deal with each one specifically or whether to accept the system default behavior. In SQL Server, the default behavior would typically be to raise an error for the condition encountered and then, when the COMMIT TRAN or ROLLBACK TRAN is executed, raise another error that says it has no corresponding BEGIN TRANSACTION.

One possibility is to write some retry logic in your client application to deal with a possible deadlock condition. For the other error conditions, you might decide to go with the default error behavior. If your applications are deployed with proper system management, such errors should be nonexistent or rare. You could also easily check @@TRANCOUNT before executing a ROLLBACK TRAN or COMMIT TRAN to ensure that a transaction to operate on is open.

The nesting of transaction blocks provides a good reason to *not* name the transaction in a ROLLBACK statement. If, in a rollback, any transaction other than the top-level transaction is named, error 6401 will result:

```
Cannot roll back XXX. No transaction or savepoint of that name was found.
```

It's fine to name the transaction in the BEGIN TRAN block, however. A COMMIT can also be named, and it won't prompt an error if it's not paired in the top-level branch because it's basically a NO-OP in that case anyway (except that it decrements the value returned by @@TRANCOUNT).

One reason for naming your BEGIN TRAN statements is to allow your COMMIT and ROLLBACK statements to be self-documenting. ROLLBACK TRAN doesn't require a transaction name, but you can include one as a way of emphasizing that you are rolling back the entire transaction.

The following batch will result in an error. The statement ROLLBACK TRAN B will fail with error 6401. The subsequent ROLLBACK TRAN A will succeed because it's the top-level transaction block. Remember, though, that we'd get the same behavior if we simply used ROLLBACK TRAN instead of ROLLBACK TRAN A.

```
-- To start with, verify @@TRANCOUNT is 0
SELECT @@TRANCOUNT
BEGIN TRAN A
    -- Verify @@TRANCOUNT is 1
    SELECT @@TRANCOUNT
    -- Assume some real work happens here
    BEGIN TRAN B
        -- Verify @@TRANCOUNT is 2
        SELECT @@TRANCOUNT
        -- Assume some real work happens here
    ROLLBACK TRAN B
-- @@TRANCOUNT is still 2 because the previous ROLLBACK
-- failed because of error 6401
SELECT @@TRANCOUNT -- Assume some real work happens here
```

(continued)

```
ROLLBACK TRAN A
-- This ROLLBACK succeeds, so @@TRANCOUNT is back to 0
SELECT @@TRANCOUNT
```

The following example is arguably an improvement over the previous attempt. The first ROLLBACK will execute, and the second ROLLBACK will fail with error 3903:

```
Server: Msg 3903, Level 16, State 1
The ROLLBACK TRANSACTION request has no corresponding BEGIN TRANSACTION.
```

The first ROLLBACK did its job, and there is no open transaction:

```
-- To start with, verify @@TRANCOUNT is 0
SELECT @@TRANCOUNT
BEGIN TRAN A
    -- Verify @@TRANCOUNT is 1
    SELECT @@TRANCOUNT
    -- Assume some real work happens here
    BEGIN TRAN B
        -- Verify @@TRANCOUNT is 2
        SELECT @@TRANCOUNT
        -- Assume some real work happens here
    ROLLBACK TRAN -- Notice the tran is unnamed but works
    -- That ROLLBACK terminates transaction. @@TRANCOUNT is now 0.
    SELECT @@TRANCOUNT
-- The following ROLLBACK will fail because there is no open
-- transaction (that is, @@TRANCOUNT is 0)
ROLLBACK TRAN
-- @@TRANCOUNT does not go negative. It remains at 0.
SELECT @@TRANCOUNT
```

If you syntactically nest transactions, be careful not to nest multiple ROLLBACK statements in a way that would allow more than one to execute. To illustrate that COMMIT behaves differently than ROLLBACK, note that the following example will run without error. However, the statement COMMIT TRAN B doesn't commit any changes. It does have the effect of decrementing @@TRANCOUNT, however.

```
-- To start with, verify @@TRANCOUNT is 0
SELECT @@TRANCOUNT
BEGIN TRAN A
    -- Verify @@TRANCOUNT is 1
    SELECT @@TRANCOUNT
    -- Assume some real work happens here
        BEGIN TRAN B
            -- Verify @@TRANCOUNT is 2
            SELECT @@TRANCOUNT
            -- Assume some real work happens here
        COMMIT TRAN B
-- The COMMIT didn't COMMIT anything, but does decrement
-- @@TRANCOUNT
    -- Verify @@TRANCOUNT is back down to 1
```

```
    SELECT @@TRANCOUNT
    -- Assume some real work happens here
COMMIT TRAN A
-- closes the transaction.
-- Since there's no open transaction, @@TRANCOUNT is again 0.
SELECT @@TRANCOUNT
```

In summary, nesting transaction blocks is perfectly valid, but you must understand the semantics. If you understand when @@TRANCOUNT is incremented, decremented, and set to 0 and you know the simple rules for COMMIT TRAN and ROLLBACK TRAN, you can pretty easily produce the effect you want.

Savepoints

Often users will nest transaction blocks only to find that the resulting behavior isn't what they want. What they *really* want is for a *savepoint* to occur in a transaction. A savepoint provides a point up to which a transaction can be undone—it might have been more accurately named a "rollback point." A savepoint doesn't "save" or commit any changes to the database—only a COMMIT statement can do that.

SQL Server allows you to use savepoints via the SAVE TRAN statement, which doesn't affect the @@TRANCOUNT value. A rollback to a savepoint (not a transaction) doesn't affect the value returned by @@TRANCOUNT either. However, the rollback must explicitly name the savepoint: using ROLLBACK TRAN without a specific name will always roll back the entire transaction.

In the first nested transaction block example shown on the preceding pages, a rollback to a transaction name failed with error 6401 because the name wasn't the top-level transaction. Had the name been a savepoint instead of a transaction, no error would have resulted, as this example shows:

```
-- To start with, verify @@TRANCOUNT is 0
SELECT @@TRANCOUNT
BEGIN TRAN A
    -- Verify @@TRANCOUNT is 1
    SELECT @@TRANCOUNT
    -- Assume some real work happens here
    SAVE TRAN B
-- Verify @@TRANCOUNT is still 1. A savepoint does not affect it.
        SELECT @@TRANCOUNT
        -- Assume some real work happens here
    ROLLBACK TRAN B
-- @@TRANCOUNT is still 1 because the previous ROLLBACK
-- affects just the savepoint, not the transaction
SELECT @@TRANCOUNT
-- Assume some real work happens here
 ROLLBACK TRAN A
-- This ROLLBACK succeeds, so @@TRANCOUNT is back to 0
SELECT @@TRANCOUNT
```

TRIGGERS

A trigger is a special type of stored procedure that is fired on an event-driven basis rather than by a direct call. Here are some common uses for triggers:

- To maintain data integrity rules that extend beyond simple referential integrity

- To implement a referential action, such as cascading deletes

- To maintain an audit record of changes

- To invoke an external action, such as beginning a reorder process if inventory falls below a certain level or sending e-mail or a pager notification to someone who needs to perform an action because of data changes

You can set up a trigger to fire when a data modification statement is issued—that is, an INSERT, UPDATE, or DELETE statement. SQL Server 2000 provides two types of triggers: *after triggers* and *instead-of triggers*.

After Triggers

After triggers are the default type of trigger in SQL Server 2000, so you don't have to use the word AFTER in the CREATE TRIGGER statement. In addition, if any documentation discusses "triggers" without specifying after or instead-of triggers, you can assume that the discussion is referring to after triggers.

You can define multiple after triggers on a table for each event, and each trigger can invoke many stored procedures as well as carry out many different actions based on the values of a given column of data. However, you have only a minimum amount of control over the order in which triggers are fired on the same table.

For example, if you have four INSERT triggers on the *inventory* table, you can determine which trigger will be the first and which will be the last, but the other two triggers will fire in an unpredictable order. Controlling trigger order is a feature that is needed for some of SQL Server's own internal functionality. For example, when you set up merge replication, you can designate a trigger as the first trigger to fire. In general, I recommend that you don't create multiple triggers with any expectation of a certain execution order. If it's crucial that certain steps happen in a prescribed order, you should reconsider whether you really need to split the steps into multiple triggers.

You can create a single after trigger to execute for any or all the INSERT, UPDATE, and DELETE actions that modify data. Currently SQL Server offers no trigger on a SELECT statement because SELECT does not modify data. In addition, after triggers can exist only on base tables, not on views. Of course, data modified through a view does cause an after trigger on the underlying base table to fire. As you'll see, you can define instead-of triggers on views.

An after trigger is executed once for each UPDATE, INSERT, or DELETE statement, regardless of the number of rows it affects. Although some people assume that a trigger is executed once per row or once per transaction, these assumptions are incorrect, strictly speaking. Let's see a simple example of this. The script below creates and populates a small table with three rows. It then builds a trigger on the table to be fired when a DELETE statement is executed for this table.

```
CREATE TABLE test_trigger
(col1 int,
 col2 char(6) )
GO
INSERT INTO test_trigger VALUES (1, 'First')
INSERT INTO test_trigger VALUES (2, 'Second')
INSERT INTO test_trigger VALUES (3, 'Third')
INSERT INTO test_trigger VALUES (4, 'Fourth')
INSERT INTO test_trigger VALUES (5, 'Fifth')
GO
CREATE TRIGGER delete_test
ON test_trigger AFTER DELETE
AS
PRINT 'You just deleted a row!'
GO
```

Now let's put the trigger to the test. What do you think will happen when the following statement is executed?

```
DELETE test_trigger
WHERE col1 = 0
```

If you execute this statement, you'll see the following message:

```
You just deleted a row!
(0 row(s) affected)
```

The message appears because the DELETE statement is a legal DELETE from the *test_trigger* table. The trigger is fired once no matter how many rows are affected, even if the number of rows is 0! To avoid executing code that is meaningless, it is not uncommon to have the first statement in a trigger check to see how many rows were affected. We have access to the @@ROWCOUNT function, and if the first thing the trigger does is check its value, it will reflect the number of rows affected by the data modification statement that caused the trigger to be fired. So we can change the trigger to something like this:

```
ALTER TRIGGER delete_test
ON test_trigger AFTER DELETE
AS
IF @@ROWCOUNT = 0 RETURN
PRINT 'You just deleted a row!'
```

The trigger will still fire, but it will end almost as soon as it begins. You can also inspect the trigger's behavior if many rows are affected. What do you think will happen when the following statement is executed?

```
DELETE test_trigger
```

A DELETE without a WHERE clause means that all the rows will be removed, and we get the following message:

```
You just deleted a row!
```

```
(5 row(s) affected)
```

Again, the trigger was fired only once, even though more than one row was affected.

If a statement affects only one row or is a transaction unto itself, the trigger will exhibit the characteristics of per-row or per-transaction execution. For example, if you set up a WHILE loop to perform an UPDATE statement repeatedly, an update trigger would execute each time the UPDATE statement was executed in the loop.

An after trigger fires after the data modification statement has performed its work but before that work is committed to the database. Both the statement and any modifications made in the trigger are implicitly a transaction (whether or not an explicit BEGIN TRANSACTION was declared). Therefore, the trigger can roll back the data modifications that caused the trigger to fire. A trigger has access to the before image and after image of the data via the special pseudotables *inserted* and *deleted*. These two tables have the same set of columns as the underlying table being changed. You can check the before and after values of specific columns and take action depending on what you encounter. These tables are not physical structures—SQL Server constructs them from the transaction log. In fact, you can think of the *inserted* and *deleted* tables as views of the transaction log. For regular logged operations, a trigger will always fire if it exists and has not been disabled. You can disable a trigger by using the DISABLE TRIGGER clause of the ALTER TABLE statement.

You cannot modify the *inserted* and *deleted* pseudotables directly because they don't actually exist. As I mentioned earlier, the data from these tables can only be queried. The data they appear to contain is based entirely on modifications made to data in an actual underlying base table. The *inserted* and *deleted* pseudotables will contain as many rows as the INSERT, UPDATE, or DELETE statement affected. Sometimes it is necessary to work on a row-by-row basis within the pseudotables, although, as usual, a set-based operation is generally preferable to row-by-row operations. You can perform row-by-row operations by executing the underlying INSERT, UPDATE, or DELETE in a loop so that any single execution affects only one row, or you can perform the operations by opening a cursor on one of the *inserted* or *deleted* tables within the trigger.

Specifying Trigger Firing Order

As I mentioned earlier, in most cases you shouldn't manipulate the trigger firing order. However, if you do want a particular trigger to fire first or fire last, you can use the *sp_settriggerorder* procedure to indicate this ordering. This procedure takes a trigger name, an order value (FIRST, LAST, or NONE), and an action (INSERT, UPDATE, or DELETE) as arguments. Setting a trigger's order value to NONE removes the ordering from a particular trigger. Here's an example:

```
sp_settriggerorder delete_test, first, 'delete'
```

Note that you'll get an error if you specify an action that is not associated with the particular trigger—for example, if the above statement had tried to make *delete_test* the first "update" trigger. You'll also get an error if you attempt any of the following:

- Setting a trigger order for an instead-of trigger.

- Specifying an order for a trigger when a trigger already exists for that action in that position. (For example, if there is already a first delete trigger for a table, you must set the order value of that trigger to NONE before you can define a different trigger as the first delete trigger.)

- Attempting to give the same trigger both the first and last order value for the same action. One trigger can have two different order values, but only if the trigger is defined for two different actions. You must execute *sp_settriggerorder* multiple times to accomplish this. Here's an example:

```
CREATE TRIGGER delete_update_test
ON test_trigger AFTER DELETE, UPDATE
AS
PRINT 'You just deleted or updated a row!'
GO
EXEC sp_settriggerorder delete_update_test, first, 'delete'
EXEC sp_settriggerorder delete_update_test, last, 'update'
```

Information about trigger type and firing order is stored in the *status* column of the *sysobjects* table. Nine of the bits are needed to keep track of this information. Three bits are used to indicate whether the trigger is an insert, update, or delete trigger, three are used for the first triggers for each action, and three are used for the last triggers for each action. Table 12-2 shows which bits correspond to which properties.

Bit	Decimal Value	Meaning
8	256	Delete Trigger
9	512	Update Trigger
10	1024	Insert Trigger
14	16384	First Delete Trigger
15	32768	Last Delete Trigger
16	65536	First Update Trigger
17	131072	Last Update Trigger
18	262144	First Insert Trigger
19	524288	Last Insert Trigger

Table 12-2. *Bits in* sysobjects.status *that indicate a trigger's functionality.*

To check to see whether a trigger has a particular functionality, you can decode the *sysobjects.status* value or use the OBJECTPROPERTY function. There are nine property functions, which correspond to the nine bits indicated in Table 12-2. For example, to check to see whether a trigger is the last update trigger for its table, you would execute this:

```
SELECT OBJECTPROPERTY(object_id('delete_update_test'),
'ExecIsLastUpdateTrigger')
```

A value of 1 means that the trigger has this property, a value of 0 means it doesn't, and a value of NULL means you typed something wrong or the object is not a trigger. However, to find all the properties that a trigger has would mean executing this statement nine times, checking nine different property values. To simplify the process, I created a new version of the *sp_helptrigger* procedure named *sp_helptrigger2* (available on the companion CD), which provides ordering information for each of the triggers. Here's an example of its use:

```
EXEC sp_helptrigger2 test_trigger
PARTIAL RESULTS:
trigger_name       IsUpdate UpdateOrd IsDelete DeleteOrd   IsInsert InsertOrd
------------------ -------- --------- -------- ----------- -------- ---------
delete_test        0        n/a       1        Unspecified 0        n/a
delete_update_test 1        Last      1        First       0        n/a
```

The *IsUpdate* column has a 1 if the trigger is an update trigger, and it has a 0 otherwise. If the trigger is not an update trigger, the order of the update trigger is *n/a*. If the trigger is an update trigger, values for the trigger order are *First*, *Last*, and *Unspecified*. You can interpret the *IsDelete* and *DeleteOrd* columns in the same way, as well as the *IsInsert* and *InsertOrd* columns. This procedure is available on the companion CD.

Rolling Back a Trigger

Executing a ROLLBACK from within a trigger is different from executing a ROLLBACK from within a nested stored procedure. In a nested stored procedure, a ROLLBACK will cause the outermost transaction to abort, but the flow of control continues. However, if a trigger results in a ROLLBACK (because of a fatal error or an explicit ROLLBACK command), the entire batch is aborted.

Suppose the following pseudocode batch is issued from SQL Query Analyzer:

```
begin tran
delete....
update....
insert.... -- This starts some chain of events that fires a trigger
           -- that rolls back the current transaction
update.... -- Execution never gets to here - entire batch is
           -- aborted because of the rollback in the trigger
if....commit  -- Neither this statement nor any of the following
           -- will be executed
else....rollback
begin tran....
insert....
if....commit
else....rollback

GO              -- batch terminator only

select...   -- Next statement that will be executed is here
```

As you can see, once the trigger in the first INSERT statement aborts the batch, SQL Server not only rolls back the first transaction but skips the second transaction completely and continues execution following the GO.

Misconceptions about triggers include the belief that the trigger cannot do a SELECT statement that returns rows and that it cannot execute a PRINT statement. Although you can use SELECT and PRINT in a trigger, doing these operations is usually a dangerous practice unless you control all the applications that will work with the table that includes the trigger. Otherwise, applications not written to expect a result set or a print message following a change in data might fail because that unexpected behavior occurs anyway. For the most part, you should assume that the trigger will execute invisibly and that if all goes well, users and application programmers will never even know that a trigger was fired.

Be aware that if a trigger modifies data in the same table on which the trigger exists, using the same operation (INSERT, UPDATE, or DELETE) won't, by default, fire that trigger again. That is, if you have an UPDATE trigger for the *inventory* table that updates the *inventory* table within the trigger, the trigger will not be fired a second time. You can change this behavior by allowing triggers to be recursive. You control this on a database-by-database basis by setting the option *recursive triggers* to TRUE.

It's up to the developer to control the recursion and make sure that it terminates appropriately. However, it will not cause an infinite loop if the recursion isn't terminated because, just like stored procedures, triggers can be nested only to a maximum level of 32. Even if recursive triggers have not been enabled, if separate triggers exist for INSERT, UPDATE, and DELETE statements, one trigger on a table could cause other triggers on the same table to fire (but only if *sp_configure 'nested triggers'* is set to 1, as you'll see in a moment).

A trigger can also modify data on some other table. If that other table has a trigger, whether that trigger also fires depends on the current *sp_configure* value for the *nested triggers* option. If that option is set to 1 (TRUE), which is the default, triggers will cascade to a maximum chain of 32. If an operation would cause more than 32 triggers to fire, the batch will be aborted and any transaction will be rolled back. This prevents an infinite cycle from occurring. If your operation is hitting the limit of 32 firing triggers, you should probably look at your design—you've reached a point at which there are no longer any simple operations, so you're probably not going to be ecstatic with the performance of your system. If your operation truly is so complex that you need to perform further operations on 32 or more tables to modify any data, you could call stored procedures to perform the actions directly rather than enabling and using cascading triggers. Although cascading triggers can be of value, overusing them can make your system a nightmare to maintain.

Instead-of Triggers

SQL Server 2000 allows you create a second kind of trigger, called an instead-of trigger. An instead-of trigger, rather than the data modification operation that fires the triggers, specifies the action to take. Instead-of triggers are different from after triggers in several ways:

- You can have only one instead-of trigger for each action (INSERT, UPDATE, and DELETE).

- You cannot combine instead-of triggers and foreign keys that have been defined with CASCADE on a table. For example, if Table2 has a FOREIGN KEY constraint that references Table1 and specifies CASCADE as the response to DELETE operations, you will get an error message if you try to create an instead-of trigger for DELETE on Table2. However, you can have instead-of triggers for INSERT or UPDATE. Similarly, if you already have an instead-of trigger on Table2, you cannot alter the table to add a foreign key constraint with the CASCADE action for the same data modification operation.

■ Instead-of triggers can never be recursive, regardless of the setting of the *recursive triggers* database option. For example, if an instead-of trigger is executed for INSERT into Table1 and the trigger does an INSERT into Table1, the instead-of trigger is not processed. Instead, the INSERT is processed as if there were no instead-of trigger for INSERT, and any constraints and after triggers will take effect.

Instead-of triggers are intended to allow updates to views that are not normally updateable. For example, a view that is based on a join normally cannot have DELETE operations executed on it. However, you can write an instead-of DELETE trigger. The trigger has access to the rows of the view that would have been deleted had the view been a real table. The deleted rows are available in a worktable, which is accessed with the name *deleted*, just like for after triggers. Similarly, in an UPDATE or INSERT instead-of trigger, you can access the new rows in the *inserted* table.

Here's a simple example that uses a Table1 and Table2 and builds a view on a join of these tables:

```
USE pubs
SET NOCOUNT ON
-- drop table Table1
CREATE TABLE Table1
(a int  PRIMARY KEY,
 b datetime default getdate(),
 c varchar(10))


--drop table Table2
CREATE TABLE Table2
 (a int
   ,message varchar(100))
GO

/* Insert 4 rows into Table1 */
INSERT INTO Table1(a) VALUES (1)
INSERT INTO Table1(a) VALUES (2)
INSERT INTO Table1(a) VALUES (3)
INSERT INTO Table1(a) VALUES (4)

/* Insert 6 rows into Table2 */
INSERT INTO Table2 VALUES (1, 'first row')
INSERT INTO Table2 VALUES (1, 'second row')
INSERT INTO Table2 VALUES (2, 'first row')
INSERT INTO Table2 VALUES (2, 'second row')
INSERT INTO Table2 VALUES (2, 'third row')
INSERT INTO Table2 VALUES (3, 'first row')
GO
```

(continued)

```
/* Create a view based on a join of the tables
   and then an instead-of trigger on the view
*/

CREATE VIEW join_view AS
SELECT Table1.a as a1, b, c,
       Table2.a as a2, message
FROM Table1 join Table2
ON Table1.a = Table2.a
GO

CREATE TRIGGER DEL_JOIN
ON join_view
INSTEAD OF DELETE

AS
  DELETE Table1
    WHERE a IN (SELECT a1 FROM deleted)
  DELETE Table2
    WHERE a IN (SELECT a2 FROM deleted)
```

In this case, the view contained values from each table that could be used to determine which rows in the base table needed to be removed.

In addition to views based on joins, another kind of view that has severe limitations on its updateability is a view based on a UNION. Some UNION views are updateable, and I'll discuss them in Chapter 16 when we look at partitioned views. But for views that don't meet the conditions for partitioning, direct updates might not be possible.

In the following example, I'll create a contacts list view in the *pubs* database consisting of the name, city, state, and country of all authors, stores, and publishers:

```
USE pubs
GO
CREATE VIEW contact_list
AS
SELECT ID = au_id, name = au_fname + ' ' + au_lname,
     city, state, country = 'USA'
     FROM authors
UNION ALL
SELECT stor_id, stor_name, city, state, 'USA'
     FROM stores
UNION ALL
SELECT pub_id, pub_name, city, state, country
     FROM publishers
```

I want to be able to insert a new contact into this list, and to do that I'll use an instead-of INSERT trigger. The inserted table in the trigger will have values only for the columns included in the view, so all other columns in all three tables will have to have default values or allow NULLS. The only column not meeting this requirement is the *contract* column of the *authors* table, which is a bit column. I'll alter the column to give it a default value:

```
ALTER TABLE authors
  ADD CONSTRAINT contract_dflt DEFAULT 0 FOR contract
```

The trigger must determine which base table should accept the row inserted into the *contacts_list* view. Author ID values look very different from store or publisher ID values, so by looking for a hyphen, I can determine that the new row is an author. To distinguish stores from publishers, I can notice that there is a CHECK constraint on the underlying *publishers* table that requires new publisher ID values to start with the digits *99*. (You can execute *sp_helpconstraint* on the *publishers* table to see this constraint.) This means that I can't allow any stores to have an ID that starts with *99*, and if you can't limit yourself to this restriction, you might need a different solution than this instead-of trigger.

The trickiest part of this instead-of trigger is that the view has concatenated the authors' first and last names into a single *name* column, so the instead-of trigger must separate a single name into a two-part name. It uses the simplest approach of looking for the first space in the name. Everything before the first space is considered the first name, and everything after the first space is considered the last name.

```
CREATE TRIGGER Insert_Contact
ON contact_list
INSTEAD OF INSERT
AS
IF @@ROWCOUNT = 0 RETURN
IF (SELECT COUNT(*) FROM inserted) > 1 BEGIN
    PRINT 'Only one row at a time can be inserted'
    RETURN
END
-- check for a hyphen in the fourth position in the ID
IF (SELECT substring(ID,4,1) FROM inserted) = '-'
-- Inserting an author
        INSERT into authors(au_id, au_fname, au_lname, city, state)
        SELECT id, rtrim(substring(name, 1, charindex(' ',name) - 1)),
               rtrim(substring(name, charindex(' ',name) + 1,
            datalength(name) - charindex(' ',name))), city, state
    FROM inserted
ELSE
-- Check for two nines at the beginning of the ID
```

(continued)

```
IF (SELECT ID FROM inserted) like '99[0-9][0-9]'
-- Inserting a publisher
    INSERT INTO publishers (pub_id, pub_name, city, state, country)
        SELECT * FROM inserted
ELSE
-- Inserting a store
    INSERT INTO stores(stor_id, stor_name, city, state)
        SELECT id, name, city, state from inserted
RETURN
```

You can write similar instead-of triggers for updates and deletes.

Managing Triggers

The options available for managing triggers are similar to those for managing stored procedures. Here are some of the options:

- You can see the definition of a trigger by executing *sp_helptext <trigger name>*.

- You can create a trigger WITH ENCRYPTION so that its text cannot be exposed.

- You can change a trigger's definition using ALTER TRIGGER so that it keeps its same internal ID number.

    WARNING   If you ALTER a trigger that has had any firing order properties set, all such order values will be lost when the ALTER is done. You must reexecute *sp_settriggerorder* procedures to reestablish the firing order.

In addition, a special procedure named *sp_helptrigger* is available. It takes the name of a table as an argument, and optionally the name of a data modification action, and gives you the name and some of the properties for each trigger on that table. However, as I mentioned earlier, *sp_helptrigger* does not tell you what order the trigger will be fired in, so I created the *sp_helptrigger2* procedure to do that.

Using Triggers to Implement Referential Actions

As I discussed in Chapter 6, SQL Server implements FOREIGN KEY (or REFERENCES) constraints. You can define the constraint to either not allow changes that would break the relationship (NO ACTION) or cascade any changes in the referenced table into the referencing table. The NO ACTION option is the default; with this option specified for your foreign key, if you attempt a data modification that would break a relationship—for example, if you attempt to delete the primary key row while foreign key references exist—the data modification is disallowed and the command is aborted. In other words, no action is taken—in fact, ANSI SQL-92 calls this the NO ACTION referential action. Colloquially, NO ACTION is often referred to as RESTRICT, but technically this is incorrect. ANSI uses RESTRICT for security and permissions purposes.

> **NOTE** A FOREIGN KEY constraint can of course be directed toward a UNIQUE constraint, not just a PRIMARY KEY constraint. But there is no performance difference if the referenced table is declared using UNIQUE. In this section, we'll refer only to PRIMARY KEY in the referenced table for simplicity.

Keep in mind that a FOREIGN KEY constraint affects two tables, not just one. It affects the *referenced* table as well as the *referencing* table. While the constraint is declared on the referencing table, a modification that affects the primary key of the referenced table checks to see whether the constraint has been violated. The change to the referenced table will be either disallowed or cascaded to the referencing table, depending on how the FOREIGN KEY constraint was defined.

As described in Chapter 6, the SQL-92 standard specifies four referential actions for modifying the primary key side of a relationship: NO ACTION, SET NULL, SET DEFAULT, and CASCADE. The four referential actions have the following characteristics. (These descriptions were given in Chapter 6, but I'll repeat them here for your convenience.)

- **NO ACTION** Disallows the action if the FOREIGN KEY constraint would be violated. This is the only referential action implemented by SQL Server 7 for a declared FOREIGN KEY constraint, and it's the only one that must be implemented in order for a product to claim to be "SQL-92 conformant."

- **SET NULL** Updates the referencing table so that the foreign key columns are set to NULL. Obviously, this requires that the columns be defined to allow NULL.

- **SET DEFAULT** Updates the referencing table so that the foreign key columns are set to their DEFAULT values. The columns must have DEFAULT values defined.

- **CASCADE** Updates the referencing table so that the foreign key columns are set to the same values that the primary key was changed to, or deletes the referencing rows entirely if the primary key row is deleted.

A declared FOREIGN KEY constraint, rather than a trigger, is generally the best choice for implementing NO ACTION. The constraint is easy to use and eliminates the possibility of writing a trigger that introduces a bug. In SQL Server 2000, you can also use FOREIGN KEY constraints for the CASCADE action if you want to simply cascade any changes. You can use triggers to implement either of the other referential actions not currently available with declared FOREIGN KEY constraints.

You can also use a trigger to customize the referential actions in other ways. For example, you can customize error messages to make them more informative than the generic messages sent with a violation of a declared constraint. Also, since you cannot use the CASCADE option for FOREIGN KEY constraints that reference the same table, you can use a trigger to implement a cascading action on a self-referencing table.

Recall that constraint violations are tested before triggers fire. If a constraint violation is detected, the statement is aborted and execution never gets to the trigger (and the trigger never fires). Therefore, you cannot use a declared FOREIGN KEY constraint to ensure that a relationship is never violated by the update of a foreign key and then also use a trigger to perform a SET NULL or SET DEFAULT action when the primary key side of the same relationship is changed. If you use triggers to implement SET NULL or SET DEFAULT behavior for changes to the referenced table, you must also use triggers to restrict invalid inserts and updates to the referencing table. You can and should still declare PRIMARY KEY or UNIQUE constraints on the table to be referenced, however. It's relatively easy to write triggers to perform referential actions, as you'll see in the upcoming examples. For the sake of readability, you can still declare the FOREIGN KEY constraint in your CREATE TABLE scripts but then disable the constraint using ALTER TABLE NOCHECK so that it is not enforced. In this way, you ensure that the constraint still appears in the output of *sp_help <table>* and similar procedures.

> **NOTE** Although you're about to see triggers that perform referential actions, you might want to consider another option entirely. If you want to define constraints and still have update and delete capability beyond NO ACTION and CASCADE, a good alternative is using stored procedures that exclusively perform the update and delete operations. A stored procedure can easily perform the referential action (within the scope of a transaction) before the constraint would be violated. No violation occurs because the corresponding "fix-up" operation is already performed in the stored procedure. If an INSERT or UPDATE statement is issued directly (and you can prevent that in the first place by not granting such permissions), the FOREIGN KEY constraint still ensures that the relationship is not violated.

Here's an example of using triggers to implement a referential action. Rather than simply implementing NO ACTION, we want to implement ON DELETE SET NULL and ON UPDATE SET DEFAULT for the foreign key relationship between *titleauthor* and *titles*. We must create the following three triggers (or suitable alternatives):

```
-- 1. INSERT and UPDATE trigger on referencing table.
-- Disallow any insert or update if the foreign key title_id
-- in the referencing table titleauthor does not match
-- the primary key title_id in the referenced table titles.
```

```
CREATE TRIGGER INS_UPD_titleauthor
    ON titleauthor
    FOR INSERT, UPDATE
AS
-- Do any rows exist in the inserted table that do not have
-- a matching ID in titles?
IF EXISTS
    (SELECT * FROM inserted WHERE inserted.title_id NOT IN
        (SELECT titles.title_id FROM titles) )
    BEGIN
    RAISERROR('No matching title found. Statement will be aborted.',
            16, 1)
    ROLLBACK TRAN
    END
GO


-- 2. If primary key in referenced table titles is changed,
-- update any rows in titleauthor to the DEFAULT value.
-- This implements ON UPDATE SET DEFAULT. Notice that this trigger could
-- be easily changed to set the column to NULL instead of DEFAULT,
-- which would implement ON UPDATE SET NULL.
CREATE TRIGGER UPD_titles
    ON titles
    FOR UPDATE
AS
    DECLARE @counter int
    IF UPDATE(title_id)
        BEGIN
        UPDATE titleauthor
        SET titleauthor.title_id=DEFAULT
        FROM titleauthor, deleted
        WHERE titleauthor.title_id=deleted.title_id

        SET @COUNTER=@@ROWCOUNT
        -- If the trigger resulted in modifying rows of
         -- titleauthor, raise an informational message
        IF (@counter > 0)
            RAISERROR('%d rows of titleauthor were updated to
            DEFAULT title_id as a result of an update to titles table',
            10, 1, @counter)
        END
GO


-- 3. DELETE of the referenced table titles will set to NULL the
--   referencing titleauthor rows
CREATE TRIGGER DelCascadeTrig
    ON titles
    FOR DELETE
```

(continued)

```
AS
    DECLARE @counter int
    UPDATE titleauthor
    SET title_id = NULL
    FROM titleauthor, deleted
    WHERE titleauthor.title_id=deleted.title_id
    SET @counter=@@ROWCOUNT

    IF (@counter > 0)
        RAISERROR('%d rows of titleauthor were set to a
        NULL title_id as a result of a delete to the titles table',
        10, 1, @counter)
GO
```

> **NOTE** In order for these examples to run, you must drop or suspend the existing FOREIGN KEY constraints on *titleauthor* that reference *titles* as well as FOREIGN KEY constraints on two other tables (*sales* and *roysched*) that reference *titles*. In addition, you must modify the *title_id* column of *titleauthor* to allow NULLS, and you must re-create the PRIMARY KEY constraint on the *titleauthor* table as a UNIQUE constraint so that NULLs in the *title_id* column are allowed. (The code on the companion CD that corresponds to these examples does this.)

The following trigger is just an example of how you can use triggers to implement a cascade action. This trigger is actually unnecessary because you can define a FOREIGN KEY constraint to cascade any changes. It is a cascading update trigger on the *titles* (referenced) table that updates all rows in the *titleauthor* table with matching foreign key values. The cascading update is tricky, which is why I'm presenting it. It requires that you associate both the before and after values (from the *inserted* and *deleted* pseudotables) to the referencing table. In a cascading update, you by definition change that primary key or unique value. This means that typically the cascading update works only if one row of the referenced table is updated. If you change the values of multiple primary keys in the same update statement, you lose the ability to correctly associate the referencing table. You can easily restrict an update of a primary key to not affect more than one row by checking the value of the @@ROWCOUNT function, as follows:

```
CREATE TRIGGER UpdCascadeTrig1
    ON titles
    AFTER UPDATE
AS
    DECLARE @num_affected int, @title_id varchar(11),
        @old_title_id varchar(11)
    SET @num_affected=@@ROWCOUNT
    IF (@num_affected=0)      -- No rows affected, so nothing to do
        RETURN
```

```
IF UPDATE(title_id)
    BEGIN
    IF (@num_affected=1)
        BEGIN
        SELECT @title_id=title_id FROM inserted
        SELECT @old_title_id=title_id FROM deleted
        UPDATE titleauthor
        SET title_id=@title_id
        FROM titleauthor
        WHERE titleauthor.title_id=@old_title_id
        SELECT @num_affected=@@ROWCOUNT
        RAISERROR ('Cascaded update in titles of Primary Key
            from %s to %s to %d rows in titleauthor', 10, 1,
            @old_title_id, @title_id, @num_affected)
        END
    ELSE
        BEGIN
        RAISERROR ('Cannot update multiple Primary Key values
            in a single statement due to Cascading Update
            trigger in existence.', 16, 1)
        ROLLBACK TRANSACTION
        END
    END
```

Again, this trigger is shown just as an example. If you define a FOREIGN KEY constraint to cascade updates, you can update multiple primary key values in a single update. But you should carefully evaluate whether this is something you really want to do. The inability to update more than one primary key value at a time might save you from making a mistake. You typically won't want to make mass updates to a primary key. If you declare a PRIMARY KEY or UNIQUE constraint (as you should), mass updates usually won't work because of the constraint's need for uniqueness. Although such an update is rare, you might want to set the value to some expression, such as multiplying all Customer ID values by 1000 to renumber them. In a situation like this, the ability to cascade updates can be useful.

Another situation in which you might want to update multiple primary keys in a single statement is if you have a mail-order customer list that uses the customer phone number as the primary key. As phone companies add numbers to accommodate fax machines, server remote access, and cellular phones, some area codes run out of possible numbers, which leads to the creation of new area codes. If a mail-order company needs to keep up with such changes, it must update the primary key for all customers who get new area codes. If you assume that the phone number is stored as a character string of 10 digits, you must update the first three characters only. If the new area code is 425, for example, your UPDATE statement would look something like the top of the following page.

```
UPDATE customer_list
    SET phone = '425' +  substring(phone, 4, 7)
    WHERE zip IN (list of affected zip codes)
```

This UPDATE would affect the primary key of multiple rows, and it would be difficult to write a trigger to implement a cascade operation (perhaps into an *orders* table).

You might think that you can write a trigger to handle multiple updates to the primary key by using two cursors to step through the *inserted* and *deleted* tables at the same time. However, this won't work. There's no guarantee that the first row in the *deleted* table will correspond to the first row in the *inserted* table, so you cannot determine which old foreign key values in the referencing tables should be updated to which new values.

Although it is logically the correct thing to do, you are not required to create a PRIMARY KEY or UNIQUE constraint on a referenced table. (Unless, of course, you are going to actually declare a FOREIGN KEY constraint to reference a column in the referenced table.) And there is no hard-and-fast requirement that the constraint be unique. (However, not making it unique violates the logical relationship.) In fact, the "one row only" restriction in the previous cascading trigger is a tad more restrictive than necessary. If uniqueness were not required on *title_id*, the restriction could be eased a bit to allow the update to affect more than one row in the *titles* table as long as all affected rows were updated to the same value for *title_id*. When uniqueness on *titles.title_id* is required (as should usually be the case), the two restrictions are actually redundant. Since all affected rows are updated to the same value for *title_id*, you no longer have to worry about associating the new value in the referencing table, *titleauthor*—there is only one value. The trigger looks like this:

```
CREATE TRIGGER UpdCascadeTrig2
    ON titles
    FOR UPDATE
AS
    DECLARE @num_distinct int, @num_affected int,
        @title_id varchar(11)
    SET @num_affected=@@ROWCOUNT
    IF (@num_affected=0)      -- No rows affected, so nothing to do
        RETURN

    IF UPDATE(title_id)
        BEGIN
        SELECT @num_distinct=COUNT(DISTINCT title_id) FROM inserted
        IF (@num_distinct=1)
            BEGIN
            -- Temporarily make it return just one row
            SET ROWCOUNT 1
            SELECT @title_id=title_id FROM inserted
```

```
        SET ROWCOUNT 0      -- Revert ROWCOUNT back
        UPDATE titleauthor
        SET titleauthor.title_id=@title_id
        FROM titleauthor, deleted
        WHERE titleauthor.title_id=deleted.title_id
        SELECT @num_affected=@@ROWCOUNT
        RAISERROR ('Cascaded update of Primary Key to value in
            titles to %d rows in titleauthor', 10, 1,
            @title_id, @num_affected)
        END
    ELSE
        BEGIN
        RAISERROR ('Cannot cascade a multirow update that
            changes title_id to multiple different values.', 16, 1)
        ROLLBACK TRANSACTION
        END
    END
```

Using *COUNT(DISTINCT title_id) FROM inserted* ensures that even if multiple rows are affected, they are all set to the same value. So *@title_id* can pick up the value of *title_id* for any row in the inserted table. You use the *SET ROWCOUNT 1* statement to limit the subsequent SELECT to only the first row. This is not required, but it's good practice and a small optimization. If you don't use *SET ROWCOUNT 1*, the assignment still works correctly but every inserted row is selected and you end up with the value of the last row (which, of course, is the same value as any other row). Note that you can't use the TOP clause in a SELECT statement that assigns to a variable unless the assignment is done by a subquery. For example, you can do this:

```
DECLARE @v1 varchar(11)
SET @v1 = (SELECT TOP 1 au_id FROM authors)
PRINT @v1
```

but you can't do this:

```
DECLARE @v1 varchar(11)
SET @v1 = TOP 1 au_id FROM authors
PRINT @v1
```

It's not good practice to do a SELECT or a variable assignment that assumes that just one row is returned unless you're sure that only one row *can* be returned. You can also ensure a single returned row by doing the assignment like this:

```
SELECT @title_id=title_id FROM titles GROUP BY title_id HAVING
    COUNT(DISTINCT title_id)=1
```

Because the previous IF allows only one distinct *title_id* value, you are assured that the preceding SELECT statement returns only one row.

In the previous two triggers, you first determine whether any rows were up-dated; if none were, you do a RETURN. This illustrates something that might not be obvious: a trigger fires even if no rows were affected by the update. Recall that the plan for the trigger is appended to the rest of the statements' execution plan. You don't know the number of rows affected until execution. This is a feature, not a bug; it allows you to take action when you expect some rows to be affected but none are. Having no rows affected is not an error in this case. However, you can use a trigger to return an error when this occurs. The previous two triggers use RAISERROR to provide either a message that indicates the number of rows cascaded or an error message. If no rows are affected, we don't want any messages to be raised, so we return from the trigger immediately.

Recursive Triggers

SQL Server allows triggers to recursively call themselves if the database option *recursive triggers* is set to TRUE. This means that if a trigger modifies the table on which the trigger is based, the trigger might fire a second time. But then, of course, the trigger modifies the table and fires the trigger again, which modifies the table and fires the trigger again…and so on. This process does not result in an infinite loop because SQL Server has a maximum nesting depth of 32 levels; after the 32nd call to the trigger, SQL Server generates the following error. The batch stops executing, and all data modifications since the original one that caused the trigger to be fired are rolled back.

```
Server: Msg 217, Level 16, State 1, Procedure up_rt1, Line 4
Maximum stored procedure, function, trigger, or view nesting level
exceeded (limit 32).
```

Writing recursive routines is not for the faint of heart. You must be able to determine what further actions to take based on what has already happened, and you must make sure that the recursion stops before the nesting reaches its limit. Let's look at a simple example. Suppose we have a table that keeps track of budgets for various departments. Departments are members (or children) of other departments, so the budget for a parent department includes the budgets for all its child departments. If a child department's budget increases or decreases, the change must be propagated to the parent department, the parent's parent, and so forth. The following code creates a small budget table and inserts three rows into it:

```
CREATE TABLE BUDGET
    (dept_name      varchar(30)     not null,
     parent_name    varchar(30)     null,
     budget_amt     money           not null)
GO
INSERT INTO budget values ('Internal Training', 'Training', $10)
INSERT INTO budget values ('Training', 'Services', $100)
INSERT INTO budget values ('Services', NULL, $500)
GO
```

The following trigger is fired if a single row in the budget table is updated. If the department is not the highest-level department, its parent name is not NULL, so you can adjust the budget for the parent department by the same amount that the current row was just updated. (The amount of the change is equal to the new amount in the *inserted* table minus the old amount in the *deleted* table.) That new update causes the trigger to fire again. If the next department has a non-null parent, the update is applied again. The recursion stops when you get to the highest level and the parent department is NULL. In that case, the trigger simply returns and all work is done.

```
CREATE TRIGGER update_budget
ON budget FOR update AS
DECLARE @rows int
SELECT @rows = @@ROWCOUNT
IF (@rows=0) RETURN
IF (@rows > 1) BEGIN
    PRINT 'Only one row can be updated at a time'
    ROLLBACK TRAN
    RETURN
END
IF (SELECT parent_name FROM inserted) IS NULL RETURN
UPDATE budget
    SET budget_amt = budget_amt + (SELECT budget_amt FROM inserted) -
                                  (SELECT budget_amt FROM deleted)
WHERE dept_name = (SELECT parent_name FROM inserted)
```

SUMMARY

SQL Server allows you to group statements together in a program unit that will execute automatically whenever a data modification statement occurs. This code, stored on the server as a trigger, can be defined as either an after trigger or an instead-of trigger. Triggers can maintain referential integrity in ways that constraints cannot, and you can write triggers to enforce other business rules that you can't specify using constraints.

To fully understand how triggers affect the work done in your database, you also need to understand how transactions work. SQL Server provides four different modes of transaction behavior, called isolation levels, which control what data is available to other processes while you're working with that data. Programming effectively with Transact-SQL requires that you understand transactional topics, such as when transactions will be committed and when they can be rolled back. Since you'll likely be working in a multiuser environment, it is vital that you make the appropriate concurrency and consistency choices to suit the isolation level of your environment.

Chapter 13

Special Transact-SQL Operations: Working with Cursors and Large Objects

A relational database such as Microsoft SQL Server is naturally set oriented. This means that a given statement, such as SELECT, returns a set of results—often more than one row of data. On the other hand, most programming languages and many applications tend to be ultimately record based. For example, in an application that displays a list of customers, users scroll through the list and periodically drill down to get more detail about a customer and perhaps make some modifications. Then they might proceed to the next customer and do the operation again, and so on, one record at a time.

The incongruity between the set-oriented approach and the record-based approach is sometimes referred to as an *impedance mismatch*. To deal with this mismatch, SQL Server provides a significant bridge between the two models: cursors.

You can think of a cursor as a named result set in which a current position is always maintained as you move through the result set. For example, as you visually scan names in a printed phone book, you probably run your finger down the entries. Your finger acts like a cursor—it maintains a pointer to the current entry. You can think of the entries on the current page of the phone book as the result set from your query. The action of moving your finger through the listings on that page is similar to the action of a *scrollable cursor*—it moves forward and backward or up and down at different times, but it always maintains a current position on a particular row.

SQL Server has different types of cursors that you can choose based on your scrolling requirements and on how insulated you want the cursor to be from data changes made by other users. Special cursor libraries in ODBC, OLE DB, and DB-Library have network optimizations that prevent each row fetched in a cursor from incurring the overhead of its own network conversation. Figure 13-1 shows how a cursor works.

CURSOR BASICS

To work with a cursor, you take the following steps:

1. Declare the cursor using the DECLARE statement. You choose a cursor based on how sensitive you want it to be to the changes of other users and on the level of scrolling you want. Then you specify the SELECT statement that will produce the cursor's result set. Often, the rows in the result set will be explicitly sorted using the ORDER BY clause. Most database systems that provide cursors allow you to move only forward through the result set. SQL Server's scrollable cursors allow you to reposition the cursor to any row. They are also fully updateable.

2. Open the cursor. You can think of this step as executing the DECLARE statement from step 1.

3. Fetch rows in the cursor. The cursor position moves within the result set to get the next row or the previous row, to go back five rows, to get the last row, and so on. Typically, the FETCH statement is executed many times—at least once for every row in the result set. (The other cursor

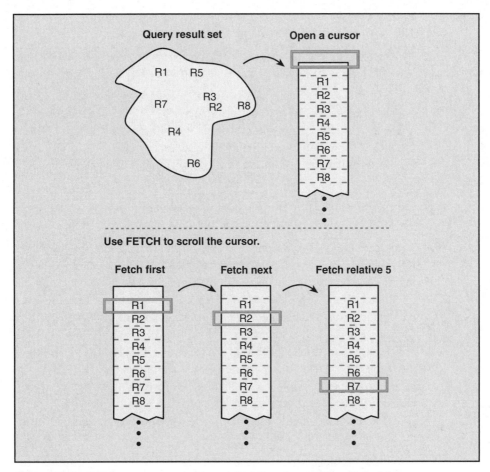

Figure 13-1. *SQL Server cursors bridge set-based and record-based models.*

control statements tend to be executed only once per cursor.) In SQL Server, you typically check the system function @@FETCH_STATUS after each fetch. A 0 value indicates that the fetch was successful. A –1 value indicates that there are no more rows—that is, the fetch would move the cursor beyond the result set, either past the last row or before the first row. A value of –2 indicates that the row no longer exists in the cursor—it was deleted from the base table after the cursor was opened, or it was updated in a way that no longer meets the criteria of the SELECT statement that generated the result set.

4. Update or delete the row of the table in which the cursor is positioned. This step is optional. Here's the syntax:

```
UPDATE table SET column = value WHERE CURRENT OF cursor_name
DELETE table WHERE CURRENT OF cursor_name
```

After the cursor is positioned at a specific row, that row is usually updated or deleted. Instead of supplying a WHERE clause that identifies a row in the table using values such as the primary key for the UPDATE or DELETE statement, you identify the row to be operated on by specifying CURRENT, which is the row the cursor points to. This type of operation is known as a *positioned update* (or a *positioned delete*).

5. Close the cursor. This ends the active cursor operation. The cursor is still declared, so you can reopen it without having to declare it again.

6. Deallocate the cursor to remove a cursor reference. When the last cursor reference is deallocated, SQL Server releases the data structures composing the cursor. (We'll see later in this chapter that you can have multiple references to the same cursor by using cursor variables.) Because internal data structures consume memory in the procedure cache, you should use the DEALLOCATE statement to clean up after you're done with the cursor. You can think of DEALLOCATE as essentially "UNDECLARE"— the opposite of DECLARE, just as CLOSE is the opposite of OPEN. Below is an example of a simple cursor that fetches forward through the *authors* table and retrieves rows one by one. (For now, note that this is partly pseudocode—and highly inefficient—because we don't want to get immersed in the details quite yet.)

```
DECLARE au_cursor CURSOR FOR
SELECT * FROM authors ORDER by au_lname

OPEN au_cursor

WHILE (more rows)
FETCH NEXT FROM au_cursor     -- Do until end
CLOSE au_cursor
DEALLOCATE au_cursor
```

Of course, to get all the rows from the *authors* table, it would be a lot easier to issue the SELECT statement directly, which would return all the rows in one set. Using a cursor to return a simple result set is inappropriate, and this example serves only to illustrate the basic flow of cursor operations. We'll talk about uses for cursors next.

CURSORS AND ISAMS

Before you proceed, you must understand something crucial about using cursors: you should never let cursors turn SQL Server into a network indexed sequential access method (ISAM).

You might recall from Chapter 1 that the initial grand plan for SQL Server called for it to be a higher-performance back end for Ashton-Tate's dBASE IV. dBASE was really a record-oriented, ISAM-like data management system—that is, it did sequential, row-by-row processing. It was not set based. At the time, SQL Server didn't use cursors, which made a difficult task even more difficult. The original plan to make the two record-oriented and set-based systems totally compatible and seamlessly interchangeable was doomed from the outset because of inherent differences in the models. If the original SQL Server had featured the rich cursor model it has now, cursors would have been heavily used to build the dBASE IV front end from the start. But it was probably better that the impedance mismatch became obvious. It forced the SQL Server development team to reexamine its basic goals and dramatically improve its plans. It also highlighted the importance of orienting yourself to work with sets of data, not individual records as you would do with an ISAM. Had cursors existed then, they probably would have been misused, with the result being a bad SQL Server front end.

Cursors can be an important tool when used prudently. However, because cursors are record oriented, developers who are familiar with ISAM systems (such as IMS, dBASE, VSAM, or the Microsoft Jet database engine used in Microsoft Access) are often tempted to use cursors to port an application from an ISAM system to SQL Server. Such a port can be done quickly, but this is also one of the fastest ways to produce a truly bad SQL Server application. In the basic cursor example shown previously, the operation to fetch each row of the *authors* table is much like an ISAM operation on the *authors* file. Using that cursor is an order of magnitude less efficient than simply using a single SELECT statement to get all authors. This type of cursor misuse is more common than you'd think. If you need to port an ISAM application to SQL Server, do a *deep port*—that is, go back and look at the basic design of the application and the data structures before you do the port. A *shallow port*—making SQL Server mimic an ISAM—is appropriate only if you're one of those programmers who believes that there's never time to do the port right but there's always time to do it over.

For example, even a modestly experienced SQL Server programmer who wants to show authors and their corresponding book titles would write a single SELECT statement similar to the one below that joins the appropriate tables. This SELECT statement is likely to yield subsecond response time even if all the tables are large, assuming that appropriate indexes exist on the tables.

```
SELECT A.au_id, au_lname, title
FROM authors A
JOIN titleauthor TA ON (A.au_id=TA.au_id)
JOIN titles T ON (T.title_id=TA.title_id)
ORDER BY A.au_id, title
```

> **NOTE** When I refer to response time, I mean the time it takes to begin sending results back to the client application—in other words, how long it takes until the first row is returned.

In the preceding example, all the join processing is done at the back end and a single result set is returned. Minimal conversation occurs between the client application and the server—only the single request is received, and all the qualifying rows are returned as one result set. SQL Server decides on the most efficient order in which to work with the tables and returns a single result set to satisfy the request.

An ISAM programmer who doesn't know about an operation such as a join would approach this problem by opening the *authors* "file" (as an ISAM programmer would think of it) and then iterating for each author by scanning the *titleauthor* "connecting file." The programmer would then traverse into the *titles* file to retrieve the appropriate records. So rather than write the simple and efficient SQL join described above, the programmer might see cursors as the natural solution and write the code shown below. This solution works in a sense: it produces the correct results. But it is truly horrific in terms of its relative complexity to write and its performance compared to the set-based join operation. The join would be more than 100 times faster than this batch:

```
DECLARE @au_id char(11), @au_lname varchar(40), @title_id char(6),
    @au_id2 char(11), @title_id2 char(6), @title varchar(80)

DECLARE au_cursor CURSOR FOR
    SELECT au_id, au_lname FROM authors ORDER BY au_id

DECLARE au_titles CURSOR FOR
    SELECT au_id, title_id FROM titleauthor ORDER BY au_id

DECLARE titles_cursor CURSOR FOR
    SELECT title_id, title FROM titles ORDER BY title

OPEN au_cursor
FETCH NEXT FROM au_cursor INTO @au_id, @au_lname
```

```
WHILE (@@FETCH_STATUS=0)
    BEGIN
    OPEN au_titles
    FETCH NEXT FROM au_titles INTO @au_id2, @title_id


    WHILE (@@FETCH_STATUS=0)
        BEGIN
        -- If this is for the current author, get
        -- titles too
        IF (@au_id=@au_id2)
            BEGIN
            OPEN titles_cursor
            FETCH NEXT FROM titles_cursor INTO
                @title_id2, @title

            WHILE (@@FETCH_STATUS=0)
                BEGIN
                -- If right title_id, display the values
                IF (@title_id=@title_id2)
                    SELECT @au_id, @au_lname, @title

                FETCH NEXT FROM titles_cursor INTO
                    @title_id2, @title
                END
                CLOSE titles_cursor
            END
        FETCH NEXT FROM au_titles INTO @au_id2, @title_id
        END

    CLOSE au_titles
    FETCH NEXT FROM au_cursor INTO @au_id, @au_lname
    END
CLOSE au_cursor

DEALLOCATE titles_cursor
DEALLOCATE au_titles
DEALLOCATE au_cursor
```

Although this cursor solution is technically correct and is similar to the way ISAM processing would be written, if your developers are writing SQL Server applications like this, *stop them immediately* and educate them. It might be easy for a developer who is familiar with SQL to see that the join is much better, but a developer who is steeped in ISAM operations might see the cursor solution as more straightforward even though it is more verbose. This is much more than just a style issue. Even for this trivial example from *pubs* with only 25 rows of output, the join solution is orders of magnitude faster. SQL Server is designed for set operations, so whenever possible you should perform set operations instead of sequential row-by-row operations. In addition to the huge performance gain, join operations are simpler to write and are far less likely to introduce a bug.

Programmers familiar with the ISAM model do positioned updates. That is, they seek (or position) to a specific row, modify it, seek to another row, update it, and so forth. Cursors also offer positioned updates, but performance is far slower than what you can achieve using a single UPDATE statement that simultaneously affects multiple rows. Although the previous example showed a SELECT operation, you can also accomplish updates and deletes using subquery and join operations. (For details, see Chapter 9.)

Problems with ISAM-Style Applications

The main problems with the ISAM style of writing applications for SQL Server are as follows:

- The ISAM-style operation makes excessive requests to the SQL server. When cursor operations are done in the client application, a huge increase in network traffic results. In the join solution example we just examined, one request was made to the server: the SQL query doing the join. But in ISAM-style code, if every OPEN and FETCH presents a command to the server, this simple example that produces fewer than 30 rows of output results in more than 1000 commands being sent to the SQL server!

  For the sake of illustration, the procedure on page 708 is written entirely with Transact-SQL cursors. But cursors are typically written from a client application, and almost every OPEN and every FETCH would indeed be a separate command and a separate network conversation. The number of commands grows large because of all the nested iteration that happens with the series of inner loops, as you'll see if you trace through the commands. Although this procedure is admittedly convoluted, it's not unlike ones that exist in real applications.

- It is almost always more expensive to use a cursor than it is to use set-oriented SQL to accomplish a given task. ISAM's only form of update is the positioned update, but this requires at least two round-trips to the server—one to position on the row and another to change it. In set-oriented SQL, the client application tells the server that it wants to update the set of records that meet specified criteria. Then the server figures out how to accomplish the update as a single unit of work. When you use a cursor, the client doesn't allow the server to manage retrieving and updating records.

In addition, using a cursor implies that the server is maintaining client "state" information—such as the user's current result set at the server, usually in *tempdb*—as well as consumption of memory for the cursor itself. Maintaining this state unnecessarily for a large number of clients is a waste of server resources. A better strategy for using SQL Server (or any server resource, in fact) is for the client application to get a request in and out as quickly as possible, minimizing the client state at the server between requests. Set-oriented SQL supports this strategy, which makes it ideal for the client/server model.

■ The ISAM-style application example uses a conversational style of communicating with the server, which often involves many network round-trips within the scope of a single transaction. The effect is that transactions take longer. Transactions handled in this way can require seconds or minutes between the BEGIN TRANSACTION and COMMIT TRANSACTION statements. These long-running transactions might work fine for a single user, but they scale much too poorly for multiple users if any update activity occurs.

To support transactional consistency, the database must hold locks on shared resources from the time the resources are first acquired within the transaction until the commit time. Other users must wait to access the same resources. If one user holds these locks longer, that user will affect other users more and increase the possibility of a deadlock. (For more on locking, see Chapter 14.)

CURSOR MODELS

The subject of cursors confuses many people, at least in part because several cursor models are available and those models have different options and capabilities. We can group these models into three categories: Transact-SQL cursors, API server cursors, and client cursors.

Transact-SQL Cursors

You use Transact-SQL cursors within SQL typically in a stored procedure or in a batch that needs to do row-by-row processing. Transact-SQL cursors use the familiar statements DECLARE CURSOR, OPEN *cursor*, and FETCH. At times, Transact-SQL cursors have been referred to as "ANSI cursors" because their syntax and capabilities fully implement—and go well beyond—the scrollable cursor functionality specified by ANSI SQL-92. The ANSI specification states that scrollable cursors are read-only. This isn't the way applications work, of course, so fortunately SQL Server allows scrollable cursors that can be updated. SQL Server provides backward scrolling, relative and absolute positioning within the result set, and many options regarding sensitivity to changes made by other users, as well as positioned updates and deletes. Few other products implement even the ANSI specification for scrollable, read-only cursors, let alone a cursor model as rich as SQL Server's. The cursor functionality of SQL Server is without question the richest in the industry. The term "ANSI cursor" is rarely used anymore because it implies a feature that is commonplace in the industry; the extensive cursor functionality is unique to SQL Server and greatly exceeds that specified by ANSI.

API Server Cursors

The OLE DB provider for SQL Server, the ODBC driver for SQL Server, and the DB-Library programming libraries have special cursor functions that are optimized for cursor operations and better network use between a client application and a server application. For a high-performance application, it is important that there be no excessive conversation between the client and the server. The hallmark of high-quality client/server computing is to have the client issue a single, brief command and then have the server respond. If every row fetched in a cursor had to be individually requested over the network and had to provide all the metadata to describe the row fetched, performance would be abysmal.

The OLE DB provider and the ODBC driver that Microsoft provides for SQL Server fully implement these special cursor commands, as does the DB-Library programming interface. Higher-level interfaces, such as RDO and ADO, also implement these functions. These capabilities have the cumbersome names "ODBC server cursors," "DB-Library server cursors," and "OLE DB server cursors," so they're all generally referred to in the documentation as "API server cursors."

API server cursors enable smarter communication between the calling client application and the SQL Server back end. Central to this is the interface's ability to specify a "fat" cursor. That is, instead of thinking of a cursor as pointing to a single row, imagine the cursor pointing to multiple rows. Take, for example, an application that displays a list box of 20 customers at a time. As the user scrolls through the list box, a FETCH requests the next 20 rows. Or perhaps it fetches the previous 20 rows, the last 20 rows, or the 20 rows thought to be about three-fourths of the way through the result set. The interface is provided by such function calls as SQLFetchScroll for ODBC and IRowset::GetNextRows for OLE DB. These functions make sense within those programming environments, and they are used instead of SQL statements such as DECLARE CURSOR and FETCH. These API functions allow options and capabilities, such as defining the "width" of the cursor (the number of rows), that cannot be expressed using Transact-SQL cursor syntax. Another important performance optimization of API server cursors is that metadata is sent only once for the cursor and not with every FETCH operation, as is the case with a Transact-SQL cursor statement.

Besides offering performance advantages (especially for operations across a network), API server cursors have other capabilities that Transact-SQL cursors do not have. You can declare API server cursors on a stored procedure if the procedure contains only one SELECT statement. You use API server cursors mostly in application code.

> **NOTE** Many APIs provide access to API server cursors, but in this chapter I'll look at them primarily in the context of Transact-SQL cursor syntax, which is the most widely readable syntax. But when a capability is available only via API server cursors, I'll point that out. The information on Transact-SQL cursors is also relevant to all forms of API server cursors. After reading the information here, you should consult the programming reference for the specific API you use to better understand the capabilities offered.

Client Cursors

If you consider that the job of a cursor is to set a position within a result set, it should be clear to you that this task can be performed (although possibly less efficiently) within the client application with no assistance from the server. SQL Server originally had no cursor support, and many application designers wrote their own client-side cursor libraries to do this type of operation. While SQL Server 4.2 did not have cursor support in the engine, it offered a rich set of cursor functions for DB-Library so that application programmers would not have to reinvent the wheel. These functions were implemented entirely on the client. No magic was performed, and these functions did nothing that other independent software vendors (ISVs) couldn't do. But the designers knew from the outset that they eventually wanted cursor support in the engine. They designed the API so that the bulk of the work could eventually be executed remotely at the server and so that a new API or substantial changes to applications using the API would not be necessary.

Version 6 introduced scrollable cursor support directly in the engine. With this support, applications written using the DB-Library version 4.2 cursor library typically worked without any changes. In fact, they worked quite a bit better because of the server-side assistance that they got. Version 6 added an optimized ODBC driver that fully exploited SQL Server's support for scrollable cursors. With database management systems other than SQL Server (most of which do not have scrollable cursors), it's not unusual for an ODBC driver to take on these cursor functions, as DB-Library used to for SQL Server. But with the ODBC driver that ships with SQL Server, cursor operations use the back-end engine's capabilities.

With SQL Server, you tend to make use of cursors on the server. Because client cursors are more of a programming convenience, we won't cover them in much depth. Instead, we'll focus on the server. But be aware that you can still use the OLE DB or ODBC cursor library to do the cursor operations for you (using client cursors) instead of having them processed at the server.

Some people consider client cursors obsolete now that server cursors are available. But client cursors can make a lot of sense when properly used. For example, if you want your user interface to provide forward and backward scrolling but you want to use the more efficient default result set rather than a server cursor, you need a local buffering mechanism to cache the entire result set and provide the scrolling operations. You can write this mechanism yourself, but client cursors already provide it. Also, the Internet has brought new issues and challenges for "stateless" management of data. (That is, the connection to SQL Server is not persistent.) Client cursors can play a major part in these solutions. Although the introduction of server cursors in version 6 might have made client cursors obsolete, the Internet will probably drive future work into new and more sophisticated client-cursor solutions.

Default Result Sets

Do not fall into the habit of thinking that every result set is a cursor, at least of the type previously discussed, or you'll inch toward the dark side—always using cursors. Earlier we said that you can think of a cursor as a named result set. You can think of rows not returned in a cursor as the *default result set* or as just a result set. A default result set is really not a cursor. You can think of it as a fourth type of cursor if you remember that no cursor functionality at the server is involved.

A default result set is frequently referred to as a *firehose cursor* in discussions of the cursor capabilities of ODBC. Within the SQL Server ODBC driver, you use the same function call, SQLFetchScroll, to process rows from SQL Server whether they emanate from a cursor operation or simply from a default result set. With ODBC, if you request a cursor that is forward-only and read-only, with a row set size of 1, the driver doesn't ask for a cursor at all. Instead, it asks for a default result set, which is much more efficient than a cursor. The term "firehose" reflects the way that the server blasts rows to the client as long as the client keeps processing them so that there is room in the network buffer to send more results. In Chapter 3, we saw how results are sent from the server to the client, and this is exactly what happens with a firehose cursor. The fact that the same ODBC functions work for both cursor and noncursor results is a nice programming convenience, so I'll continue to use the term "firehose cursor." Just remember that from the SQL Server engine's perspective, it is not a cursor.

API Server Cursors vs. Transact-SQL Cursors

Although this book is not about OLE DB or ODBC programming, cursors are intrinsically related to those programming interfaces. This shouldn't be too surprising, since you know that a key motivation for including cursors in SQL Server was to bridge the impedance mismatch between the set operations of SQL Server and the ISAM operations of traditional programming languages. And traditional programming languages use ODBC or OLE DB (or higher-level interfaces that build on them, such as ADO). For more details about API server cursors, along with programming examples, see *Hitchhiker's Guide to Visual Basic and SQL Server, 6th Edition* (Microsoft Press, 1998) by William (Bill) Vaughn. Bill's discussion is obviously centered on Microsoft Visual Basic, but he covers cursor options thoroughly enough that you can apply your understanding to programming in Microsoft Visual C++. If you program with Visual Basic, Bill's book is a must-read.

SQL Server provides some specialized cursor functions that are called only internally by the OLE DB provider, the ODBC driver, or DB-Library. These functions look like stored procedures and have stubs in the *sysobjects* table, so you might see their names there (for example, *sp_cursor*). If you trace the functions going to SQL Server (using SQL Profiler or perhaps a network sniffer), you'll see these functions flowing from the client application. In fact, you can execute them directly from ad hoc tools such as SQL Query Analyzer, although you should not call them directly from your applications.

These functions are not really stored procedures; they are capabilities implemented directly in SQL Server. The code is compiled into SQLSERVR.EXE—it is not a stored procedure or an extended stored procedure. I'll refer to such functions as "pseudo–stored procedures." The stubs in *sysobjects* make cursor execution mimic the execution of a stored procedure so that there is no need for major changes to the tabular data stream (TDS) between client and server. Remember that when server cursor support was implemented in version 6, a major goal was to have SQL Server work seamlessly with applications that had been written to use the client cursor functions of DB-Library version 4.2, so implementing cursors without changing the TDS was a clever idea. These functions are not intended, or supported, for direct use by an application. They are invoked directly by the ODBC driver, the DB-Library programming libraries, and the native OLE DB provider for SQL Server.

Transact-SQL cursors and API server cursors use the same code within SQL Server, although the Transact-SQL cursors do not directly call the pseudo–stored procedures. Because the procedures exist only for the sake of remoting the work from OLE DB, ODBC, and DB-Library, an SQL statement, which is already executing inside the engine, has no need to call the routines in that way. While Transact-SQL and API server cursors execute the same code and have many similarities, you should not think of them as alternative ways to do the same thing.

APPROPRIATE USE OF CURSORS

When should you use cursors? A somewhat simplistic answer is, "Only when you have to." This is not a totally facetious answer because if you can think of a set-based solution to a problem and avoid using a cursor, you should do that. Ordinarily, cursors should be near the bottom of your list of possible solutions. Remember that SQL Server is a relational database, so it is inherently set based. As I mentioned earlier, if you overuse cursors, you turn SQL Server into an ISAM-like product and severely cripple its power.

You should not interpret this warning as a blanket statement that you should never use cursors. Scrollable cursors were, in fact, near the top of the new features wish list of many members of the SQL Server development team. More important, cursors were near the top of the developer community's wish list. Cursors are extremely powerful and provide SQL Server with capabilities that cannot be achieved with other products. So let's look at some situations in which cursors provide a great benefit.

Row-by-Row Operations

Transact-SQL cursors are great for row-by-row operations with a stored procedure or a single batch. For example, suppose a table has some financial data, and for each row of that data, we want to perform one of several sets of conversions on the data. Each set of conversions is written as a separate stored procedure, so we want to send the data values from each row as parameters to the appropriate stored procedure. So, for example, if the value in the *balance* column is less than 1000, we want to call a procedure called *BasicConversions*; if the balance value is between 1000 and 10,000, we want to call a procedure called *ExtendedConversions*; and if the balance value is greater than 10,000, we want to call *AdvancedConversions*. You might think you could process this operation with CASE, but remember that in Transact-SQL, CASE is an expression that returns a value; CASE doesn't allow you to choose completely different actions to perform. With Transact-SQL cursors, we can step through each row of the table, and depending on the value in the *balance* column for each row, we can conditionally determine which of the three stored procedures to execute.

Transact-SQL's FETCH command is almost always done in a loop, and the cursor is used to perform row-by-row processing on the entire result set. But you should not use Transact-SQL cursors across multiple batches. For example, you shouldn't issue singular FETCH commands as their own batches. If your application fetches rows, does some work, fetches more rows, and so on, you should use API server cursors, not Transact-SQL cursors.

Query Operations

Transact-SQL cursors are often used in conjunction with EXECUTE('*string*') to write and execute SQL statements based on the results of some query. For example, suppose we want to GRANT permission to UPDATE data in every table in a database to a particular group of users. SQL Server provides a built-in role in every database called *db_datawriter*, but this allows all three data modification operations: INSERT, UPDATE, and DELETE. To allow only UPDATE permission, we want to create a user-defined role called *db_dataupdaters* and GRANT UPDATE to this role on all user tables. Using Transact-SQL cursors, we can use the following generic batch to do the entire operation—without having to return the names of the tables to the calling client application, reformat them into the correct commands, and send them back to the server. Instead, the entire operation is done at the server; only the initial request is sent from the client application.

```
EXEC sp_addrole 'db_dataupdaters'
GO
DECLARE tables_curs CURSOR FOR
    SELECT name FROM sysobjects
    WHERE type='U' -- user table, not system table
OPEN tables_curs
DECLARE @tablename varchar(30), @output_msg varchar(80)
FETCH NEXT FROM tables_curs INTO @tablename
WHILE (@@FETCH_STATUS=0 )
    BEGIN
    EXEC ('GRANT UPDATE ON ' + @tablename
        + ' TO db_dataupdaters')
        IF (@@ERROR=0)
            SELECT @output_msg=
                'UPDATE permission granted on table '
                + @tablename
        ELSE
            SELECT @output_msg=
                'Failed to grant UPDATE permission on table '
                + @tablename + ' @@ERROR=' +
                CONVERT(varchar, @@ERROR)
    PRINT @output_msg
    FETCH NEXT FROM tables_curs INTO @tablename
    END
CLOSE tables_curs
DEALLOCATE tables_curs
```

Scrolling Applications

The need for Transact-SQL cursors was not the biggest motivation for adding cursors to SQL Server. Rather, the crying need was for API server cursors to support "scrolling applications." Many of these applications originated from ISAM applications or started out as single-user Microsoft FoxPro or dBASE applications (or they followed that paradigm—you know the type).

For example, think of an address book of the type used in your e-mail program. The user opens the address book and scrolls up or down to view the list of names. The user drags the scroll bar slider to the bottom and expects to be positioned at the last record. Dragging the slider to the beginning of the list, the user expects to be repositioned at the first record. Is this an appropriate use for a cursor? It depends on what you want to do with the information in the list. On the following page are some examples of how you might think about the problem.

EXAMPLE 1

A cursor is unnecessary if the address book includes only a few hundred entries, if it will be read-only, or if you're not concerned with sensitivity to changes in data—that is, you don't care whether the most up-to-date copy of the data is available. After the user's list box is initially populated, a few new names might be added or the information might change in some way. But for our purposes, it is unnecessary for the list box to exhibit dynamic behavior such as names appearing, disappearing, or changing as the user scrolls through the list. In this case and with these requirements, you can simply issue the query and get the results. You can easily buffer a few hundred rows of information on the client, so there is no need for cursors.

EXAMPLE 2

An API server cursor is appropriate if the address book has 100,000 entries. The user will probably look at only a few dozen entries and then quit. Should you select all 100,000 rows to populate the list box so that the user can see only a few dozen? In most cases, the answer is no. Using a cursor is reasonable in this situation; you can use an API server cursor.

Suppose the list box can display 20 names at a time. You can set the cursor width to 20 (a fat cursor) so that with any fetch forward or backward you get one list box worth of data. Or you can fetch 60 or 80 rows at a time so that the user can scroll by a few screenfuls within the application without having to ask the server for more rows. If the user moves the scroll bar slider to the bottom of the list, you fetch the bottom 20 rows by using LAST. If the user moves the slider to the top, you fetch the top 20 rows by using FIRST. And if the slider moves three-fourths of the way down the list, you can do some quick division and scroll to that point by using ABSOLUTE n. (For example, you can easily determine the total number of qualifying rows. If 100,000 rows are available and you want to scroll approximately three-fourths of the way down, you can do a FETCH ABSOLUTE 75000 statement.)

If you have to provide this type of application with a large amount of data, using a cursor makes sense. Of course, it might be better if the user is required to type in a few characters—that would allow the application to qualify the result set of the cursor. If you know that the user is interested only in names starting with S, for example, you can significantly reduce the size of the cursor by adding the appropriate criteria (for example, *name LIKE ('S%')* in the cursor SELECT statement.

Choosing a Cursor

Although it might seem as if you have an overabundance of choices for your cursor model, the decision-making process is fairly straightforward. Follow these guidelines to choose the appropriate cursor for your situation:

■ If you can do the operation with a good set-oriented solution, do so and avoid using a cursor. (In ODBC parlance, use a firehose cursor.)

■ If you've decided that a cursor is appropriate and you'll be doing multiple fetches over the network (such as to support a scrolling application), use an API server cursor. You'll use OLE DB, ODBC, RDO, DB-Library, ADO, or another API, depending on your application needs.

■ For the most part, avoid using client-side cursors and products or libraries that perform many cursor operations in the client application. Such applications tend to make excessive requests to the server and use the server inefficiently—the multitude of network round-trips makes for a slow, sluggish application.

Table 13-1 compares the ways cursors are declared and opened and how operations are performed in Transact-SQL cursor statements; their rough equivalents among the pseudo–stored procedures used by the ODBC driver and DB-Library; and the ODBC and OLE DB cursor methods.

Transact-SQL Cursor Statement	*Pseudo– Stored Procedure*	*ODBC Cursor Function*	*OLE DB Cursors*
DECLARE/ OPEN	*sp_cursoropen*	SQLSetStmtAttr (SQL_ATTR_ CURSOR_TYPE) SQLSetStmtAttr (SQL_ATTR_ CONCURRENCY) SQLExecDirect or SQLExecute	Set row set properties OPEN such as DBPROP_OTHERINSERT, DBPROP_ OTHERUPDATEDELETE, DBPROP_OWNINSERT, or DBPROP_ OWNUPDATEDELETE to control cursor behaviors
FETCH	*sp_cursorfetch*	SQLFetch or SQLExtendedFetch	IRowset::GetNextRows
UPDATE/ DELETE (positioned)	*sp_cursor*	SQLSetPos	IRowsetChange::SetData or IRowsetChange::DeleteRows
CLOSE/ DEALLOCATE	*sp_cursorclose*	SQLCloseCursor	IRowset::Release

Table 13-1. *Equivalent Transact-SQL cursor statements, pseudo–stored procedures, ODBC cursor functions, and OLE DB cursor methods.*

Cursor Membership, Scrolling, and Sensitivity to Change

In addition to understanding the cursor model (that is, Transact-SQL or API server cursors), you must understand some other key options that deal with the "membership" of the cursor and the behavior the cursor exhibits as you scroll through the result set. We can divide these options into two categories:

- **Cursor types** The API server cursors usually specify cursor behavior by dividing them into four types: static, keyset, dynamic, and forward-only.

- **Cursor behaviors** The ANSI SQL-92 standard defines the keywords SCROLL and INSENSITIVE to specify the behavior of cursors. Some of the APIs also support defining a cursor's behavior using these terms. SQL Server 2000 lets you specify many more aspects of the cursor's behavior.

Transact-SQL cursors can use either the ANSI-specified syntax with INSENSITIVE and SCROLL options or the full range of cursor types, which we call Transact-SQL Extended Syntax. Prior to SQL Server 7, only the ANSI syntax was available. However, because Transact-SQL Extended Syntax, which allows all the various options available through API cursors, provides much greater control and flexibility, I'll use that syntax in most of my examples. The ANSI specification does not define standards for several semantic issues related to sensitivity to changes made by other users. The issue of sensitivity to changes is further complicated in the client/server environment because using a FETCH statement means fetching across the network. When you use the ANSI specification to declare a cursor, the behavior characteristics are specified before the word *CURSOR*:

```
DECLARE cursor_name [INSENSITIVE] [SCROLL] CURSOR
FOR select_statement
[FOR {READ ONLY | UPDATE [OF column_list]}]
```

When implementing cursors, Microsoft engineers had to make a lot of decisions about subtle behavioral issues. They wanted efficient scrollable cursors that could be used for updating in a networked client/server environment. However, according to the ANSI specification, scrollable cursors are read-only! Fortunately, they were able to go way beyond the specification when they implemented scrollable, updateable cursors. In fact, Microsoft's original cursor specification went so far beyond the original ANSI specification that they started using the terminology of the four cursor types (static, keyset, dynamic, and forward-only) even though the syntax allowed only the words INSENSITIVE and SCROLL. Since the new API-based syntax for declaring cursors actually uses these types in the declaration, that is the syntax I'll mainly use.

Here's how to declare a cursor using Transact-SQL Extended Syntax:

```
DECLARE cursor_name CURSOR
[LOCAL | GLOBAL]
[FORWARD_ONLY | SCROLL]
[STATIC | KEYSET | DYNAMIC | FAST_FORWARD]
[READ_ONLY | SCROLL_LOCKS | OPTIMISTIC]
[TYPE_WARNING]
FOR select_statement
[FOR UPDATE [OF column_list]]
```

The keywords describe how membership in the cursor is maintained (that is, which rows qualify), the available scrolling capabilities, and the cursor's sensitivity to change. Notice that the keywords appear after the word *CURSOR* in the DECLARE statement. That is how the parser distinguishes the older ANSI cursor syntax from the new Transact-SQL Extended Syntax for cursors. In the former, the cursor qualifiers come before the word *CURSOR*; in the latter, the qualifiers come after.

Static Cursors

A static cursor is attached to a snapshot of the data that qualifies for the cursor. The snapshot is stored in *tempdb*. A static cursor is read-only, and the rows in the cursor and the data values of the rows never change when you fetch anywhere in the cursor because you operate on a private, temporary copy of the data. Membership in a static cursor is fixed—that is, as you fetch in any direction, new rows cannot qualify and old rows cannot change in such a way that they no longer qualify.

Before you use a static cursor, consider whether you need to use a cursor at all. If the data is static and read-only, it probably makes more sense to process it all in the client application as a default result set and not use a cursor. If the number of rows is too large to reasonably process on the client, creating this temporary table on the server can also prove to be an expensive undertaking.

If you use ANSI-style cursors and specify the modifier INSENSITIVE, the cursor will be static. Using Transact-SQL Extended Syntax, you can actually specify the keyword STATIC. A private temporary table is created for the SELECT statement you specify. Note that the cursor cannot do positioned updates or deletes on this snapshot of data in the temporary table. For comparison, here are two cursor definitions for the same query, using the two syntax possibilities:

```
-- ANSI-style syntax for declaring static cursor
DECLARE my_cursor1 INSENSITIVE CURSOR
FOR SELECT au_id, au_lname
FROM authors
WHERE state != 'CA'

-- Transact-SQL Extended Syntax for declaring static cursor
DECLARE my_cursor1 CURSOR STATIC
```

(continued)

```
FOR SELECT au_id, au_lname
FROM authors
WHERE state != 'CA'
```

The result rows returned from the two cursors above are identical, with one minor behavioral difference. A static cursor defined using the ANSI syntax and the keyword INSENSITIVE is not scrollable—that is, you can fetch rows only in the forward direction. If you want the cursor to be scrollable, you must specify the SCROLL keyword. The Transact-SQL Extended Syntax creates static cursors that are scrollable by default.

You might want to use a static cursor for some "what if"–type operations on the data when you know that the changes will never be reflected in the base tables. If you want to carry out this type of operation, you can do a SELECT INTO in a temporary table and then declare a cursor on that table without specifying STATIC. If you specify a query that performs an aggregate function (such as SUM, MIN, MAX, GROUP BY, or UNION), the cursor might also have to be materialized in a temporary table and therefore will automatically be a static cursor.

Keyset Cursors

With a keyset cursor, a list of all the key values for the rows that meet the SELECT statement criteria is kept in *tempdb*. For example, if you declare a scrollable cursor on the *customer* table, the keyset is a list of those *cust_id* values that qualified for membership in the SELECT statement when the cursor was opened. Suppose that when the cursor was opened, the SELECT statement used to declare the cursor had a WHERE clause in this form:

```
WHERE cust_balance > 100000
```

Suppose also that customers 7, 12, 18, 24, and 56 (that is, rows with *cust_id* of those values) qualified. These keys are used whenever fetching is performed. Conceptually, further selection for the cursor takes this form

```
WHERE cust_id IN (7, 12, 18, 24, 56)
```

rather than this form:

```
WHERE cust_balance > 100000
```

(Internally, the SELECT statement is not issued again. This is for purposes of illustration only.) Membership in the keyset cursor is fixed. That is, these five identified rows are part of the cursor and no other rows are seen in subsequent fetching. Even if other rows that meet the SELECT statement criteria are subsequently inserted or updated, they are not seen by this cursor after it is opened.

In a keyset cursor as opposed to a static cursor, you can see changes to the data in the rows that meet the SELECT criteria when the cursor is opened. For example, if another user modifies the customer balance while you hold the cursor open and then fetch the row again, you see those changes (unless you hold locks to prevent such changes). In fact, even if the modification causes the row to no longer satisfy the criteria of *cust_balance > 100000*, you still see the row in a subsequent fetch. The row disappears only if it is actually deleted. The key value still exists because it was squirreled away in *tempdb,* but the row is gone. Default values, NULL values, blank spaces, or zeros (as appropriate) are supplied for the column values. But more important, the @@FETCH_STATUS system function returns a value of –2 in this case, indicating that the row no longer exists.

Because the keys are stored in *tempdb* when the cursor is open and membership is fixed, keyset cursors can fetch to an absolute position within the result set. For example, it is reasonable to fetch to row 4 of the cursor:

```
FETCH ABSOLUTE 4 FROM cursor_name
```

It shouldn't come as a surprise that a keyset cursor demands that a unique index exist on every table used in the SELECT statement for the cursor. The unique index is necessary to identify the keys. The index can be created directly (with CREATE INDEX), or it can exist as a result of a PRIMARY KEY or UNIQUE constraint.

> **NOTE**   In SQL Server 2000, every clustered index is treated as unique internally, even if you didn't specifically define the index to be unique. For this reason, you can always define a keyset cursor on a table that has a clustered index.

If you declare a keyset cursor using Transact-SQL Extended Syntax on a table that doesn't have a unique index, you do not receive an error message or any warning unless the cursor was declared with the option TYPE_WARNING. Without that option specified, you just don't get a keyset cursor. Instead, the cursor is created as STATIC. Later in this chapter, we'll see the stored procedures that provide information about your currently available cursors.

Dynamic Cursors

You can think of a dynamic cursor as a cursor in which the SELECT statement is applied again in subsequent FETCH operations. That is, the cursor does not refetch specific rows, as in this statement:

```
WHERE cust_id IN (12, 18, 24, 56, 7)
```

Instead, conceptually, the WHERE clause is reapplied. For example:

```
WHERE cust_balance > 100000
```

This means that membership is *not* fixed—subsequent fetches might include newly qualifying rows, or previously qualifying rows might disappear. This can occur because of changes you have made within the cursor or because of changes made by others. If the cursor has not locked the rows of the result set (which is dependent on the concurrency options selected, as we'll see in a moment), the changes made by others are seen in your cursor when you do a subsequent fetch on the cursor. You see such changes only on a subsequent fetch. The image of data in the buffer from the last fetch is just that—a copy in memory of what the row or rows looked like when the last fetch was performed.

Since membership in a dynamic cursor is not fixed, there is no guarantee that subsequent fetches will always bring up the same information. For this reason, FETCH ABSOLUTE is not supported for cursors declared using the DYNAMIC keyword, even if you declare the cursor through the API. It doesn't make sense, for example, to simply fetch to row 104 if every subsequent fetch brings up a row 104 that contains different information. However, FETCH RELATIVE is supported with dynamic cursors, which sometimes surprises people. When used with a dynamic cursor, FETCH RELATIVE *n* starts fetching from the first row in the current cursor set and skips the first *n* rows from that point.

A cursor declared with an ORDER BY clause can be dynamic only if an index contains keys that match the ORDER BY clause. If no such index exists, the cursor automatically converts to either a keyset or a static cursor. As previously mentioned, you need a unique index on some column in the table to get a keyset cursor. So if you have a unique index that just doesn't happen to be on the columns in the ORDER BY, you get a keyset cursor. If there is no index that matches the ORDER BY and no unique index on any column, the cursor reverts to a static cursor.

Forward-Only Cursors

Forward-only cursors are dynamic cursors that allow only a FETCH type of NEXT. It's OK for you to think of SQL Server as having only three types of cursors (static, keyset, and dynamic). Forward-only is treated here as its own type because the Transact-SQL Extended Syntax, as well as API server cursors, specify forward-only at the same level as KEYSET and DYNAMIC.

Forward-only scrolling is consistent with the recommended use of Transact-SQL cursors to provide row-by-row processing within a stored procedure or batch. Such processing is usually from start to end—one way—so that rows are never refetched. If you use Transact-SQL cursors appropriately, you typically scroll forward-only to do a row-by-row operation and you do not revisit rows. Forward-only cursors are usually the fastest type of cursor, but a standard SELECT statement (not a cursor) is still significantly faster.

Fast Forward–Only Cursors

Transact-SQL Extended Syntax allows for a special type of forward-only cursor called a fast forward–only cursor. This type of cursor is always read-only, in addition to being forward-only. You can also specify fast forward–only cursors through the ODBC driver, and in fact this is the environment in which they provide the most benefit. Applications using the SQL Server ODBC driver can set the driver-specific statement attribute SQL_SOPT_SS_CURSOR_OPTIONS to SQL_CO_FFO or SQL_CO_FFO_AF. The

SQL_CO_FFO_AF option specifies that an autofetch option also be enabled. Autofetch enables two optimizations that can significantly reduce network traffic:

■ When the cursor is opened, the first row or batch of rows is automatically fetched from the cursor. This saves you from having to send a separate fetch request across the network.

■ When a fetch hits the end of the cursor, the cursor is automatically closed. This saves you from having to send a separate close request across the network.

The most dramatic improvement comes when you process cursors with relatively small result sets that can be cached in the memory of an application. The fast forward–only cursor with autofetch enabled is the most efficient way to get a result set into an ODBC application.

The autofetch option is not available when you use Transact-SQL Extended Syntax. It is meant as an optimization when you declare and manage cursors through your client application.

Implicit conversion of fast forward–only cursors   Fast forward–only cursors are implicitly converted to other cursor types in certain situations. If the SELECT statement joins one or more tables with triggers to tables without triggers, the cursor is converted to a static cursor. If a fast forward–only cursor is not read-only, it is converted to a dynamic cursor. If the SELECT statement is a distributed query that references one or more remote tables on linked servers, the cursor is converted to a keyset-driven cursor.

Other implicit conversions are also carried out when you work with Transact-SQL Extended Syntax cursors, depending on the structure of the underlying tables and the keywords used in the cursor's SELECT statement. We saw previously that a cursor declared as a keyset is implicitly converted to a static cursor if any of the underlying tables don't have a unique index. A cursor based on a SELECT statement that needs to build a *temp* table is implicitly converted to a static cursor. If you have any doubt whether SQL Server actually created the type of cursor you requested, you can use the cursor procedures described in the following sections to verify all of the cursor's properties.

WORKING WITH TRANSACT-SQL CURSORS

In the following sections, I'll discuss the cursor syntax for each of the cursor manipulation statements and then look at issues of locking and concurrency control. Throughout this discussion, we'll look at cursor functionality that is present in the server, which in some cases is available only through API server cursors.

DECLARE

Here again is the Transact-SQL Extended Syntax for declaring a cursor with a given name:

```
DECLARE cursor_name CURSOR
[LOCAL | GLOBAL]
[FORWARD_ONLY | SCROLL]
[STATIC | KEYSET | DYNAMIC | FAST_FORWARD]
[READ_ONLY | SCROLL_LOCKS | OPTIMISTIC]
[TYPE_WARNING]
FOR select_statement
[FOR UPDATE [OF column_list]]
```

A cursor is always limited in scope to the connection that declares it. Although the cursor is named, it is not visible to other connections and other connections can have cursors of the same name. This is true whether the cursor is declared as GLOBAL or LOCAL; it is always private to the connection.

Global and Local Cursors

By default, Transact-SQL cursors are global for the connection in which they are declared. This means that you can declare a cursor in one batch and use it in subsequent batches or fetch each row in its own batch. It also means that you can declare a cursor in a stored procedure and have access to the cursor outside of the stored procedure. This is not necessarily a good thing: if the stored procedure is then called a second or subsequent time, it can get an error message when it tries to declare a cursor that already exists (from a previous execution using the same connection).

You can use the syntax for declaring a cursor to specify whether the cursor is global or local. As mentioned earlier, *global* means global to the connection for which the cursor was declared. A *local* cursor is local to the batch, stored procedure, or trigger in which it is declared, and no reference can be made to the cursor outside of that scope. If you need access to a cursor declared as local inside a stored procedure, you can pass the cursor as an output parameter to the batch that called the procedure. (You'll see the details when we look at cursor variables and parameters.)

Transact-SQL cursors are global by default in SQL Server. You can override this at the database level by setting the database option *default to local cursor* to TRUE or by using the ALTER DATABASE command to set the CURSOR_DEFAULT option to LOCAL. Local cursors are implicitly deallocated when the batch, stored procedure, or trigger terminates unless it was passed back in an output parameter. If it is passed back in an output parameter, the cursor is deallocated when the last variable referencing it is deallocated or goes out of scope.

Specifying the Cursor's Result Set

A Transact-SQL cursor always has its result set generated from a SELECT statement. The SELECT statement can be ordered (ORDER BY), and it often is. An API server cursor can also be declared; the result set is the result of a stored procedure. This powerful capability, which is important for scrolling applications, is not available using the Transact-SQL syntax.

Specifying the Cursor's Behavior

In addition to specifying whether the cursor is local or global, the DECLARE statement also specifies what kind of directional movement is possible, using the keywords SCROLL and FORWARD_ONLY. When neither of these is specified, FORWARD_ONLY is the default, unless a STATIC, KEYSET, or DYNAMIC keyword is specified. STATIC, KEYSET, and DYNAMIC cursors default to SCROLL.

The DECLARE statement also controls how much of the cursor's result set is stored in *tempdb* and how subject to change the cursor's result set is. These behaviors are specified using the STATIC, KEYSET, and DYNAMIC keywords, which I discussed earlier. The DECLARE statement uses the READ_ONLY option to prevent updates from being made through this cursor by the connection that opened the cursor. A READ_ONLY cursor cannot be referenced in a WHERE CURRENT OF clause in an UPDATE or DELETE statement. This option overrides the cursor's default ability to be updated.

The READ_ONLY option controls only whether the connection that opened the cursor can update the data through the cursor. It has no affect on what changes can be made to the cursor's data from other connections. Such changes are controlled by the STATIC, KEYSET, and DYNAMIC options. The READ_ONLY option also controls the locks that are taken when rows are fetched through the cursor. The locking (or concurrency) options are discussed later.

It is worth pointing out that if the DECLARE statement includes a local variable, the variable's value is captured at declare time, not at open time. In the following example, the cursor uses a WHERE clause of *qty > 30*, not *qty > 5*:

```
DECLARE @t smallint
SELECT @t=30

DECLARE c1 CURSOR SCROLL FOR SELECT ord_num, qty FROM sales
    WHERE qty > @t

DECLARE @ordnum varchar(20), @qty smallint

SELECT @t=5
OPEN c1
```

OPEN

The OPEN statement opens the cursor, generating and populating temporary tables if needed:

```
OPEN cursor_name
```

If the cursor is keyset based, the keys are also retrieved when the cursor is opened. Subsequent update or fetch operations on a cursor are illegal unless the cursor opens successfully. You can call the system function @@CURSOR_ROWS after the OPEN statement to retrieve the number of qualifying rows in the last opened cursor. Depending on the number of rows expected in the result set, SQL Server might populate the keyset cursor asynchronously on a separate thread. This allows fetches to proceed immediately, even if the keyset cursor is not fully populated. Table 13-2 shows the values returned by using @@CURSOR_ROWS and a description of each value.

Value	Description
−1	The cursor is dynamic. @@CURSOR_ROWS is not applicable.
−m	A keyset cursor is still in the process of being populated asynchronously. This value refers to the number of rows in the keyset so far. The negative value indicates that the keyset is still being retrieved. A negative value (asynchronous population) can be returned only with a keyset cursor.
n	This value refers to the number of rows in the cursor.
0	No cursors have been opened, the last opened cursor has been closed, or the cursor has no rows.

Table 13-2. *Possible values returned by @@CURSOR_ROWS.*

To set the threshold at which SQL Server generates keysets asynchronously (and potentially returns a negative value), you use the *cursor threshold* configuration option with *sp_configure*. Note that this is an "advanced option" and is not visible unless Show Advanced Options is also enabled with *sp_configure*. By default, the setting for this cursor threshold is −1, which means that the keyset is fully populated before the OPEN statement completes. (That is, the keyset generation is synchronous.) With asynchronous keyset generation, OPEN completes almost immediately and you can begin fetching rows while other keys are still being gathered. However, this can lead to some puzzling behaviors. For example, you can't really FETCH LAST until the keyset is fully populated. Unless you are generating large cursors, it's usually not necessary to set this option—synchronous keyset generation works fine and the behavior is more predictable. If you need to open a large cursor, however, this is an important capability for maintaining good response times.

FETCH

The FETCH statement fetches a row from the cursor in the specified direction:

```
FETCH [row_selector FROM] cursor_name [INTO @v1, @v2, ...]
```

A successful fetch results in the system function @@FETCH_STATUS returning the value 0. If the cursor is scrollable, *row_selector* can be NEXT, PRIOR, FIRST, LAST, ABSOLUTE *n*, or RELATIVE *n*. (We've seen one exception: a DYNAMIC cursor cannot FETCH ABSOLUTE.) If no *row_selector* is specified, the default is NEXT. FETCH NEXT operations are the most common type of fetch for Transact-SQL cursors. This is consistent with their recommended use when row-by-row processing is needed with a stored procedure or batch. Such processing is nearly always from start to finish.

More exotic forms of FETCH are also supported. ABSOLUTE *n* returns the *n*th row in the result set, with a negative value representing a row number counting backward from the end of the result set. RELATIVE *n* returns the *n*th row relative to the last row fetched, and a negative value indicates the row number is counted backward starting from the last row fetched. Fetches using NEXT, PRIOR, or RELATIVE operations are done with respect to the current cursor position.

RELATIVE 0 means "refetch the current row." This can be useful to "freshen" a "stale" row. The row number *n* specified in RELATIVE and ABSOLUTE fetch types can be a local variable or a parameter of type *integer, smallint,* or *tinyint.*

When a cursor is opened, the current row position in the cursor is logically before the first row. This causes the fetch options to have slightly different behaviors if they are the first fetch performed after the cursor is opened:

- FETCH NEXT is equivalent to FETCH FIRST.

- FETCH PRIOR does not return a row.

- FETCH RELATIVE is equivalent to FETCH ABSOLUTE if *n* is positive. If *n* is negative or 0, no row is returned.

The ANSI SQL-92 specification states that scrollable cursors must be read-only. There really isn't any rational reason for this, except that updateable scrollable cursors were considered too hard to implement to put into the standard. Fortunately, SQL Server scrollable cursors are indeed updateable—a quantum leap beyond what the standard specifies!

If the cursor is not scrollable, only NEXT (or no explicit parameter, which amounts to the same thing) is legal. When the cursor is opened and no fetch is done, the cursor is positioned before the first row—that is, FETCH NEXT returns the first row. When some rows are fetched successfully, the cursor is positioned on the last row fetched. When a FETCH request causes the cursor position to exceed the given result set, the cursor is positioned after the last row—that is, a FETCH PRIOR returns the last row. A fetch that causes the position to go outside the cursor range (before the first row or after the last row) causes the system function @@FETCH_STATUS to return the value −1.

> **TIP**   Probably the most common and appropriate use of Transact-SQL cursors is to FETCH NEXT within a loop while @@FETCH_STATUS equals 0 (or <> −1). However, you must issue the first FETCH before checking the value of @@FETCH_STATUS and then reissue your FETCH within the loop. If your cursor is a keyset cursor, you must also check for a @@FETCH_STATUS of −2 after every row is read to verify that the row is still available. If a row is fetched but no longer exists with a keyset cursor, the row is considered "missing" and @@FETCH_STATUS returns −2. The row might have been deleted by some other user or by an operation within the cursor. A missing row has been deleted, not simply updated so that it no longer meets the criteria of the SELECT statement. (If that's the semantic you want, you should use a dynamic cursor.)

Missing rows apply to keyset cursors only. A static cursor, of course, never changes—it is merely a snapshot of the data stored in a temporary table and cannot be updated. A dynamic cursor does not have fixed membership. The row is not expected to be part of a dynamic cursor because rows come and go as the cursor is fetched, depending on what rows currently meet the query criteria. So there is no concept of a missing row for a dynamic cursor.

If an INTO clause is provided, the data from each column in the SELECT list is inserted into the specified local variable; otherwise, the data is sent to the client as a normal result set with full metadata using TDS. In other words, the result set of a Transact-SQL cursor is the same as any other result set. But doing 50 fetches back to the application in this way produces 50 result sets, which is inefficient. An error occurs from the fetch if the datatypes of the column being retrieved and the local variable being assigned are incompatible or if the length of the local variable is less than the maximum length of the column. Also, the number of variables and their order must exactly match those of the selected columns in the SELECT statement that defines the cursor.

UPDATE

The UPDATE statement updates the table row corresponding to the given row in the cursor:

```
UPDATE table_name SET assignment_list WHERE CURRENT OF cursor_name
```

This is referred to as a *positioned update*. Using Transact-SQL cursors, a positioned update (or a *positioned delete*) operates only on the last row fetched and can affect only one row. (API server cursors can update multiple rows in a single operation. You can think of this capability as an array of structures that can all be applied in one operation. This is a significant capability, but it makes sense to use it only from an application programming language.)

An update involving a column that is used as a key value is treated internally as a delete/insert—as though the row with the original key values was deleted and a new row with the modified key values was inserted into the table.

DELETE

The following is a positioned delete:

```
DELETE FROM table_name WHERE CURRENT OF cursor_name
```

This statement deletes from the given table the row corresponding to the current position of the cursor. This is similar to a positioned update. Using Transact-SQL cursors, however, you can't perform positioned inserts. Since a cursor can be thought of as a named result set, it should be clear that you insert not into a cursor but into the table (or view) that the cursor is selecting from.

CLOSE

The CLOSE statement closes the cursor:

```
CLOSE cursor_name
```

After the cursor is closed, it can no longer be fetched from or updated/deleted. Closing the cursor deletes its keyset while leaving the definition of the cursor intact. (That is, a closed cursor can be reopened without being redeclared.) The keyset is regenerated during the next OPEN. Similarly, closing a static cursor deletes the temporary table of results, which can be regenerated when the cursor is reopened. Closing a dynamic cursor doesn't have much effect because neither the data nor the keys are materialized.

ANSI specifies that cursors are closed when a COMMIT TRAN or ROLLBACK TRAN statement is issued, but this is not SQL Server's default behavior. In the types of applications in which cursors are most appropriate (what you might call scrolling applications), it is common to make a change and want to both commit it and keep working within the cursor. Having the cursor close whenever a COMMIT is issued seems inefficient and rather pointless. But if you want to be consistent with ANSI on this, you can use the following SET option, which provides this "feature" by closing all open cursors when a COMMIT or a ROLLBACK occurs:

```
SET CURSOR_CLOSE_ON_COMMIT ON
```

Note that when you use API server cursors with ODBC, the default is to close the cursor on COMMIT; ODBC followed the ANSI lead here. But the SQL Server ODBC driver and the SQL Server OLE DB provider both set the CURSOR_CLOSE_ON_COMMIT option to OFF. You can also control this behavior at the database level with the database option *close cursor on commit* or by using the ALTER DATABASE command to set the CURSOR_CLOSE_ON_COMMIT option to ON or OFF.

DEALLOCATE

DEALLOCATE, which is not part of the ANSI specification, is a cleanup command:

```
DEALLOCATE cursor_name
```

When the last cursor reference is deallocated, SQL Server releases the data structures comprising the cursor. As you'll see shortly, with cursor variables you can have additional references to a cursor besides the original cursor name specified in the DECLARE statement. You can deallocate one of the references, but if other references to the same cursor exist, you can still access the cursor's rows using those other references.

Once the last reference to a cursor is deallocated, the cursor cannot be opened until a new DECLARE statement is issued. Although it's considered standard practice to close a cursor, if you DEALLOCATE the last reference to an open cursor it is automatically closed. The existence of DEALLOCATE is basically a performance optimization. Without it, when would a cursor's resources be cleaned up? How would SQL Server know that you are really done using the cursor? Probably the only alternative would be to do the cleanup anytime a CLOSE is issued. But then all the overhead of a new DECLARE would be necessary before a cursor could be opened again. Although it is yet another command to issue, providing a separate DEALLOCATE command lets you close and reopen a cursor without redeclaring it.

The Simplest Cursor Syntax

In its simplest form, with no other options declared, this example cursor is forward-only (a dynamic cursor subtype):

```
DECLARE my_curs CURSOR FOR SELECT au_id, au_lname FROM authors
```

If you try any FETCH operation other than FETCH NEXT (or simply FETCH, since NEXT is the default if no modifier is specified), you get an error like this:

```
Msg 16911, Level 16, State 1
fetch: The fetch type LAST cannot be used with forward only cursors
```

Transact-SQL cursors can scroll only to the NEXT row (forward-only) unless the SCROLL option is explicitly stated or the type of cursor is specified as STATIC, KEYSET, or DYNAMIC, in which case any FETCH operation is legal.

Fully Scrollable Transact-SQL Cursors

Here's a an example of a fully scrollable Transact-SQL cursor:

```
DECLARE my_curs CURSOR SCROLL FOR SELECT au_id, au_lname
    FROM authors
OPEN my_curs
FETCH ABSOLUTE 6 FROM my_curs
```

Since the ordering of the rows in the cursor cannot be controlled or predicted without an ORDER BY, everyone running the preceding code could get different results. Here's the output I got:

```
au_id            au_lname
------------     --------------
427-17-2319      Dull
```

> **NOTE** To keep the focus on the central point, my examples don't check @@FETCH_STATUS or @@ERROR. Real production-caliber code, of course, would check.

If the cursor is scrollable but not every table listed in the SELECT statement has a unique index, the cursor is created as a static (read-only) cursor, although it is still scrollable. The results of the SELECT statement are copied into a temporary table when the cursor is opened. Unless the FOR UPDATE OF clause is used (or the cursor is declared with the option TYPE_WARNING), you receive no indication that this will occur. An error results after the DECLARE cursor statement is issued:

```
CREATE TABLE foo
(
    col1    int,
    col2    int
)
-- No indexes on this table
GO

DECLARE my_curs2 SCROLL CURSOR FOR SELECT col1, col2 FROM foo
FOR UPDATE OF col1
```

This returns:

```
Server: Msg 16957, Level 16, State 4, Line 2
FOR UPDATE cannot be specified on a READ ONLY cursor.
```

> **WARNING** The error above is a compile-time error, which means that the cursor is not created at all. A subsequent attempt to open this cursor will yield an error message that the cursor does not exist.

Some options don't make sense when used together. For example, you can't declare a cursor using FOR UPDATE OF and combine that with either STATIC or READ_ONLY. This generates an error message when the cursor is declared. Remember that the STATIC option and READ_ONLY are not quite equivalent. When STATIC is specified, the results are copied into a temporary table when the cursor is opened. From then on, the results are returned from this temporary table in the server and the updates done by other users are not reflected in the cursor rows. A dynamic or keyset cursor can be READ_ONLY but not STATIC. As you scroll, you might see values that have been changed by other users since the cursor was opened. A cursor declared with these characteristics doesn't allow positioned updates or deletes via the cursor, but it doesn't prevent updates or deletes made by others from being visible.

BEWARE THE DYNAMIC CURSOR

Because a dynamic cursor has no guaranteed way of keeping track of which rows are part of the cursor's result set, you can end up with badly behaving dynamic cursors. For example, suppose you have a nonunique clustered index on a table for which you have declared a dynamic cursor. Internally, SQL Server makes the clustered index keys unique if necessary by adding a unique suffix to each duplicate value. If you use a positioned update to update the clustered keys to a value that already exists, SQL Server adds the next unique suffix in sequence. (That is, the second occurrence of any value gets a suffix of 1, the next occurrence gets a 2, and so on.) That means that the row has to move to a place in the table after the last row with that key in order to maintain the clustered ordering sequence. If you fetch through the cursor one row at a time and update the keys to values that already exist, you can end up revisiting the same row, or rows, over and over. In fact, you could end up in an infinite loop. This code does just that:

```
CREATE TABLE bad_cursor_table
(
    a char(3),
    b int IDENTITY
)
GO

CREATE CLUSTERED INDEX idx ON bad_cursor_table (a)
GO

INSERT INTO bad_cursor_table (a)   VALUES ('1')
INSERT INTO bad_cursor_table (a)   VALUES ('2')
INSERT INTO bad_cursor_table (a)   VALUES ('3')
INSERT INTO bad_cursor_table (a)   VALUES ('4')
GO

SET NOCOUNT ON
GO

DECLARE bad_cursor CURSOR DYNAMIC FOR SELECT * FROM bad_cursor_table
OPEN bad_cursor
FETCH bad_cursor
WHILE (@@fetch_status = 0)
BEGIN
    UPDATE bad_cursor_table
        SET a = 'new'
        WHERE CURRENT OF bad_cursor
    FETCH bad_cursor
END
```

> If you execute this code, you'll see the value of column *b*, which you are not changing, cycle through the values 1 to 4 over and over as each update moves the updated row to the end of the table. The solution to this problem is to always create a clustered index on a truly unique column or to not create dynamic cursors on tables without a declared unique index.

Concurrency Control with Transact-SQL Cursors

If you use a cursor that's not in the scope of a transaction, locks are not held for long durations by default. A shared lock is briefly requested for the fetch operation and then immediately released. If you subsequently attempt to update through the cursor, optimistic concurrency control is used to ensure that the row being updated is still consistent with the row you fetched into the cursor. (Locking is discussed in detail in Chapters 14 and 16.)

```
DECLARE my_curs SCROLL CURSOR FOR SELECT au_id, au_lname
FROM authors
OPEN my_curs
FETCH ABSOLUTE 8 FROM my_curs

-- Assume some other user modifies this row between this and
-- the next statement:
UPDATE authors SET au_lname='Kronenthal' WHERE CURRENT OF my_curs
```

This returns:

```
Server: Msg 16934, Level 10, State 1, Line 1
Optimistic concurrency check failed. The row was modified outside of
this cursor.

Server: Msg 16947, Level 10, State 1, Line 1
No rows were updated or deleted.
```

With optimistic concurrency control, locks are not held on the selected data, so concurrency increases. At the time of the update, the current row in the table is compared to the row that was fetched into the cursor. If nothing has changed, the update occurs. If a change is detected, the update does not occur and error message 16934 is returned. The term "optimistic" is meant to convey that the update is attempted with the hope that nothing has changed. A check is made at the time of the update to ensure that, in fact, nothing has changed. (It's not so optimistic that it forgoes the check.) In this case, although a change is detected and the update is refused, no locks are issued to prevent such a change. You could decide to go ahead and update the row even though it failed the optimistic concurrency check. To do so, you would fully qualify the update with a normal WHERE clause specifying the unique key instead of issuing a positioned update (*WHERE CURRENT OF my_curs*). See the example on the following page.

```
UPDATE authors
SET au_lname='Kronenthal'
WHERE au_id='427-17-2319'
```

Although here we are looking at this situation via the Transact-SQL syntax, in the real world you're much more likely to encounter this situation using API server cursors. In such a case, you might use optimistic concurrency control. If a conflict is encountered, you can display a message to your end user—something like: "The row has subsequently changed. Here is the new value [which you could refetch to get]. Do you still want to go ahead with your update?"

There are actually two types of optimistic concurrency. With Transact-SQL cursors, if the table has a *rowversion* (or *timestamp)* column defined, a cursor update uses it to determine whether the row has been changed since it was fetched. (Recall that a *rowversion* column is an automatically increasing value that is updated for any change to the row. It is unique within the database, but it bears no relationship to the system or calendar's date and time.) When the update is attempted, the current *rowversion* on the row is compared to the *rowversion* that was present when the row was fetched. The *rowversion* is automatically and invisibly fetched into the cursor even though it was not declared in the select list. Be aware that an update will fail the optimistic concurrency check even if a column not in the cursor has been updated since the row was fetched. The update to that column (not in the cursor) will increase the *rowversion*, making the comparison fail. But this happens only if a *rowversion* column exists on the table being updated.

If there is no *rowversion* column, optimistic concurrency control silently reverts to a "by-value" mode. Since no *rowversion* exists to indicate whether the row has been updated, the values for *all* columns in the row are compared to the current values in the row at the time of the update. If the values are identical, the update is allowed. Notice that an attempt to update a column in a row that is not part of the cursor causes optimistic concurrency control to fail, whether it is *rowversion* based or value based. You can also use traditional locking in conjunction with a cursor to prevent other users from changing the data that you fetch.

Although optimistic concurrency is the default for updateable cursors, you can designate this kind of locking explicitly by using the keyword OPTIMISTIC in your DECLARE statement.

Optimistic concurrency control works quite well in environments with relatively low update contention. With high update activity, optimistic concurrency control might not be appropriate; for example, you might not be able to get an update to succeed because the row is being modified by some other user. Whether optimistic or pessimistic (locking) concurrency control is more appropriate depends on the nature of your application. An address book application with few updates is probably well suited to optimistic concurrency control. An application used to sell a product and keep track of inventory is probably not.

As another example, if you write an application to sell reserved tickets for a flight and sales are brisk, optimistic concurrency control is probably not appropriate. Here's what the telephone conversation between the ticket agent and the customer might sound like if you use optimistic concurrency control:

Caller: "I'd like two tickets to Honolulu for January 15."

Ticket agent: "OK, I have two seats on flight number 1 leaving at 10 A.M."

Caller: "Great, I'll take them."

Ticket agent: "Oops. I just tried to reserve them, and they've been sold by another agent. Nothing else seems to be available on that date."

If you want to make sure that no other users have changed the data that you've fetched, you can force SQL Server to hold update locks on data that is fetched while the cursor is open or until the next fetch. You can do this by specifying the SCROLL_LOCKS option in the cursor's DECLARE statement. These update locks prevent other users from updating the cursor's row or reading the row through another cursor using SCROLL_LOCKS, but they do not prevent other users from reading the data. Update locks are held until the next row is fetched or until the cursor is closed, whichever occurs first. If you need full pessimistic concurrency control, you should read the cursor row inside a transaction; these locks are held until the transaction is either committed or rolled back.

Here's an example of a cursor that holds scroll locks while the cursor is open, ensuring that another user cannot update the fetched row:

```
DECLARE my_curs CURSOR SCROLL SCROLL_LOCKS FOR SELECT au_id, au_lname
    FROM authors
OPEN my_curs
FETCH ABSOLUTE 12 FROM my_curs
-- Pause to create window for other connection.
-- From other connection, try to update the row. E.g.,
-- UPDATE authors SET au_lname='Newest val' WHERE au_id='486-29-1786'.
-- The update will be blocked by a KEY UPDATE lock until this cursor is
-- closed. Refetch the row next and see that it has not changed.
-- The CLOSE cursor will release the SH_PAGE lock.

FETCH RELATIVE 0 FROM my_curs
-- RELATIVE 0 = "freshen" current row
CLOSE my_curs
DEALLOCATE my_curs
```

In this example, we're only reading data, not modifying it. When you do positioned updates or deletes, you might want to group all the cursor operations as a single transaction. To do that, you use an explicit BEGIN TRAN statement. The fetch requests an update (scroll) lock, and the lock is retained until the end of the transaction.

NOTE   Don't get confused between update and scroll locks. Scroll locks for cursor processing are a special type of update lock. Both scroll and update locks prevent other processes from acquiring exclusive locks, update locks, or scroll locks, but they don't prevent simple share (read) locks. The real difference between update locks and scroll locks is the length of time the lock is held. If there is no surrounding transaction, scroll locks are released when a new row is fetched or the cursor is closed. If there is a surrounding transaction, the scroll lock is held until the end of the transaction. (This is a slight oversimplification. We'll discuss the difference between scroll and update locks in more detail in Chapter 14.)

The following example shows optimistic concurrency control within a transaction. This means we do not want to acquire scroll locks. A simple share lock on the row is acquired while the row is being read, but it is released as soon as the row is read. If you use another connection to observe the locks, you'll see that the shared row locks are not held, although of course the exclusive locks, which are issued to carry out the actual update, are held until the transaction completes.

```
-- Be sure the default setting is in effect
SET TRANSACTION ISOLATION LEVEL READ COMMITTED
DECLARE my_curs CURSOR SCROLL FOR SELECT au_id, au_lname
    FROM authors
OPEN my_curs
BEGIN TRAN

FETCH FIRST FROM my_curs
IF (@@FETCH_STATUS <> 0) -- If not a valid fetch, get out
    PRINT 'Fetch is not valid'
-- Verify from another connection
-- that no lock held using sp_lock

UPDATE authors SET au_lname='Row1 Name' WHERE CURRENT OF my_curs

IF (@@ERROR <> 0)
    PRINT 'Update not valid'

FETCH LAST FROM my_curs

IF (@@FETCH_STATUS <> 0) -- If not a valid fetch, discontinue
    PRINT 'Fetch not valid'

-- Verify from another connection
-- and see the exclusive KEY lock from previous update

UPDATE authors SET au_lname='LastRow Name' WHERE CURRENT OF my_curs
IF (@@ERROR <> 0)
    PRINT 'Update not valid'
ROLLBACK TRANCLOSE my_curs
DEALLOCATE my_curs
```

The previous example uses a transaction, but it still uses optimistic concurrency control. If you want to be sure that a row doesn't change once you fetch it, you must hold the shared locks. You can do this by using the HOLDLOCK hint in the SELECT statement or by setting the isolation level to Repeatable Read (or Serializable), as in this example:

```
SET TRANSACTION ISOLATION LEVEL REPEATABLE READ
DECLARE my_curs CURSOR SCROLL FOR SELECT au_id, au_lname
    FROM authors
OPEN my_curs
BEGIN TRAN

FETCH FIRST FROM my_curs
IF (@@FETCH_STATUS <> 0) -- If not a valid fetch, discontinue
    PRINT 'Fetch not valid'
-- Check locks from another connection using sp_lock

UPDATE authors SET au_lname='Newer Row1 Name'
    WHERE CURRENT OF my_curs

IF (@@ERROR <> 0)
    PRINT 'Update not valid'

FETCH LAST FROM my_curs

IF (@@FETCH_STATUS <> 0) -- If not a valid fetch, discontinue
    PRINT 'Fetch not valid'

-- Verify from another connection
-- and see the exclusive KEY lock from previous update and
-- shared KEY from most recent FETCH


UPDATE authors SET au_lname='Newer LastRow Name'
    WHERE CURRENT OF my_curs
IF (@@ERROR <> 0)
    PRINT 'Update not valid'

ROLLBACK TRAN

CLOSE my_curs
DEALLOCATE my_curs
```

This example holds onto shared locks on all the rows that have been fetched. You can be sure that once a row is fetched, another user cannot change it while the transaction is in process. However, you cannot be sure that you can update the row. If you take this example and run it simultaneously in two SQL Query Analyzer windows, you might get the error shown on the following page in one of the two windows.

```
Msg 1205, Level 13, State 1
Your server command (process id 14) was deadlocked with another
process and has been chosen as deadlock victim. Re-run your command.
```

To increase the chance of deadlock (for illustrative purposes only—you'd never really want to increase your chances of deadlock), you can introduce a delay before each of the UPDATE statements:

```
WAITFOR DELAY '00:00:10'
```

This is a classic *conversion deadlock,* which occurs when each process holds a shared lock on a row and each needs an exclusive lock on the same row. Neither can get the exclusive lock because of the other process's shared lock. No matter how long the two processes wait, no resolution occurs because neither can get the lock it needs. SQL Server terminates one of the processes so that the other can conclude. (Chapter 14 describes such deadlocks in more detail. It also differentiates between ROW and KEY locks, which we're treating as the same thing in this discussion.) To avoid conversion deadlocks, you should use scroll locks instead of shared locks for any data you are reading if you intend to update it later. A scroll lock or an update lock does not prevent another process from reading the data, but it ensures that the holder of the update lock is next in line for an exclusive lock for that resource and thus eliminates the conversion deadlock problem by serializing access for the update lock resource.

The following code is a modification of the previous example that uses the SCROLL_LOCKS keyword in the cursor declaration. This forces SQL Server to acquire an update lock on the row being fetched, which is held until the next row is fetched. No other process can acquire another update lock on this same row. Since we're updating the fetched row, the update lock is converted into an exclusive lock, which is held until the end of the transaction. If we run 2 (or even 200) instances of this simultaneously, we do not get a deadlock. The scroll (update) lock acquired the first time the row is fetched makes the multiple instances run serially, since they must queue and wait for the update lock to be released:

```
-- We will use SCROLL_LOCKS, which are held until the
-- next row is fetched or until they convert into EXCLUSIVE locks.
-- So we do not require REPEATABLE READ. We can use the default
-- isolation level of READ COMMITTED.
SET TRANSACTION ISOLATION LEVEL READ COMMITTED

DECLARE my_curs CURSOR SCROLL SCROLL_LOCKS FOR SELECT au_id, au_lname
    FROM authors
OPEN my_curs
BEGIN TRAN
```

```
FETCH FIRST FROM my_curs
IF (@@FETCH_STATUS <> 0) -- If not a valid fetch, get out
    GOTO OnError
WAITFOR DELAY '00:00:10'

UPDATE authors SET au_lname='Newer Row1 Name'
    WHERE CURRENT OF my_curs

IF (@@ERROR <> 0)
    GOTO OnError

FETCH LAST FROM my_curs

IF (@@FETCH_STATUS <> 0) -- If not a valid fetch, get out
    GOTO OnError

-- Delay for 10 secs to increase chances of deadlocks
WAITFOR DELAY '00:00:10'

UPDATE authors SET au_lname='Newer LastRow Name'
    WHERE CURRENT OF my_curs
IF (@@ERROR <> 0)
    GOTO OnError

COMMIT TRAN
IF (@@ERROR=0)
    PRINT 'Committed Transaction'
GOTO Done

OnError:
PRINT 'Rolling Back Transaction'
ROLLBACK TRAN

Done:
CLOSE my_curs
DEALLOCATE my_curs
```

> **NOTE** If we didn't do an explicit BEGIN TRAN in the example above, we would still get an UPDATE lock on the most recently fetched row. This lock would then move to subsequent rows and be released from the earlier ones as we continue to fetch.

Optimistic Concurrency Control vs. Locking

Whether you should use optimistic concurrency control, use scroll locks, or hold shared locks depends on the degree to which you experience update conflicts or deadlocks. If the system is lightly updated or the updates tend to be quite dispersed and few conflicts occur, optimistic concurrency control will offer the best concurrency since locks are not held. But some updates will be rejected, and you have to decide how to deal with that. If updates are frequently rejected, you should probably move to the more pessimistic and traditional mode of locking. Holding shared locks prevents rows from being changed by someone else, but it can lead to deadlocks. If you are getting frequent deadlocks, you should probably use scroll locks.

Note that the FOR UPDATE OF modifier of the DECLARE statement does not affect locking behavior, and it does not mean that scroll (update) locks are used. The modifier's only purpose is to allow you to ensure that the cursor is updateable and that the user has the necessary permissions to make updates. Normal optimistic concurrency is used if SCROLL_LOCKS is not specified, which means that a shared lock is acquired on the row being read and is released as soon as the read is completed. If a cursor cannot be updated, you get an error message when a cursor is declared with FOR UPDATE OF. You could argue that FOR UPDATE OF should use update locks rather than shared locks on the fetched data, although there is certainly a case to be made for not doing it this way. Even though FOR UPDATE OF is specified, an update might never be made. If no update occurs, using shared locks is best because someone else can still declare the same cursor and there is no need to serialize the running of that batch. Concurrency therefore increases.

You should also realize that you do not have to issue the FOR UPDATE OF modifier to be able to do positioned updates via the cursor. You can update a cursor that does not have the FOR UPDATE OF modifier specified as long as the underlying declared cursor is updateable. A SELECT statement cannot be updated if it uses GROUP BY, HAVING, UNION, or CASE. But you do not get an error message stating that the SELECT statement cannot be updated until you actually try to do an update. By specifying FOR UPDATE OF in the DECLARE statement, you find out right away if the SELECT cannot be updated. You should consider always specifying FOR UPDATE OF for any cursor that you might later update.

If you will usually update fetched rows and there is contention for updates, you should use the SCROLL_LOCKS keyword. Yes, this serializes access to that resource, but the alternative is a high incidence of rejected updates with optimistic concurrency control or deadlocks with holding shared locks. Both of these require a lot of retries, which is wasteful. Using scroll locks in this type of scenario probably allows you to write the simplest application and gives you the best throughput for your system.

A final comment regarding concurrency options: if you use FOR UPDATE OF, you can update any column in the cursor. (You might be able to update any column if you don't specify the option, but you won't know that until you try the positioned update.) But if you use the FOR UPDATE OF *column_list* syntax and then try to update a column that is not in your specified list, you get error number 16932.

A lot of the discussion of cursor concurrency options ties in to modes and types of locking in SQL Server. You might consider rereading this section after you absorb all the details about locking in Chapter 14.

CURSOR VARIABLES

SQL Server 2000 lets you declare variables with a type of cursor. To assign a cursor to a cursor variable, you use the SET statement. Cursors variables cannot be assigned a value with an assignment SELECT, as scalar values can. Cursor variables can be either the source or the target in SET assignment statements, and they can be used as the type for OUTPUT parameters. They can be used in any of the cursor management statements: OPEN, FETCH, CLOSE, and DEALLOCATE. However, you cannot have a column in a table of type *cursor,* and input parameters to stored procedures cannot be cursors.

The following example declares a cursor and then sets a variable to reference the same result set:

```
DECLARE declared_cursor CURSOR FOR SELECT au_lname FROM authors
DECLARE @cursor_var CURSOR
SET @cursor_var = declared_cursor
```

The declared cursor and the cursor variable are almost synonymous. You can use either the declared name or the cursor variable name to open the cursor—they are two references to the same internal structure. You can open the cursor with this statement:

```
OPEN @cursor_var
```

Once you do this, the cursor is open. If you then try to open it with this declared name

```
OPEN declared_cursor
```

you get this error:

```
Msg 16905, Level 16, State 1
The cursor is already open.
```

If you issue one FETCH with the declared cursor, a subsequent FETCH from the cursor variable retrieves the next row. A CLOSE using either reference closes the cursor, and no more rows can be fetched. The only time the two references are treated differently is in the DEALLOCATE statement. Deallocating one of the references means only that you can no longer access the cursor using that reference. The internal data structures are not freed until the last reference is deallocated. If the cursor has not yet been closed, only the deallocation of the last reference closes it.

You can have more than one cursor variable referencing the same cursor, as the following example shows:

```
DECLARE declared_cursor CURSOR LOCAL
FOR SELECT title_id, price FROM titles
DECLARE @cursor_var_a CURSOR
DECLARE @cursor_var_b CURSOR
SET @cursor_var_a = declared_cursor
SET @cursor_var_b = @cursor_var_a
OPEN @cursor_var_a        -- Opens declared cursor
FETCH @cursor_var_b       -- Fetches row 1 from declared_cursor
FETCH declared_cursor     -- Fetches row 2
DEALLOCATE declared_cursor
-- Keeps cursor open since other references remain,
-- but can't use declared_cursor name to reference the cursor
```

One main use of cursor variables is for output parameters. There are four stored procedures for retrieving information about cursors, and each returns its information in a cursor. We'll look at these procedures in the next section.

Obtaining Cursor Information

Along with the wealth of cursor functionality in SQL Server 2000, you have access to a function and several procedures that provide you with information about your cursors. However, these procedures are not always easy to use, so I've provided some additional procedures that go beyond what is offered with the installed SQL Server product.

CURSOR_STATUS

The CURSOR_STATUS function determines the state of a particular cursor or cursor variable. Five possible values can be returned from this function, and the meaning of the values is slightly different depending on whether the argument is a cursor name or a cursor variable. The function takes two arguments; the first one indicates a global cursor, a local cursor, or a cursor variable (which is always local). Here's the syntax:

```
CURSOR_STATUS
(
{'local', 'cursor_name'}
| {'global', 'cursor_name'}
| {'variable', 'cursor_variable'}
)
```

Table 13-3 shows the five possible return values and their meanings.

Return Value	Cursor Name	Cursor Variable
1	The cursor is open, and for static and keyset cursors the result set has at least one row; for dynamic cursors, the result set can have zero, one, or more rows.	The cursor allocated to this variable is open, and for static and keyset cursors the result set has at least one row; for dynamic cursors, the result set can have zero, one, or more rows.
0	The result set of the cursor is empty. (Dynamic cursors never return this result.)	The cursor allocated to this variable is open, but the result set is empty. (Dynamic cursors never return this result.)
–1	The cursor is closed.	The cursor allocated to this variable is closed.
–2	Not applicable.	No cursor was assigned to this OUTPUT variable by the previously called procedure. *OR* A cursor was assigned by the previously called procedure, but it was in a closed state when the procedure completed. Therefore, the cursor is deallocated and not returned to the calling procedure. *OR* There is no cursor assigned to a declared cursor variable.
–3	A cursor with the specified name does not exist.	A cursor variable with the specified name does not exist. *OR* If one exists, it has not yet had a cursor allocated to it.

Table 13-3. *Meanings of return values from the CURSOR_STATUS function.*

We'll use the CURSOR_STATUS function in the example on the following page when we check the output parameter from the *sp_describe_cursor* stored procedure.

sp_describe_cursor

This procedure provides information on one cursor or cursor variable whose name must be passed to the procedure. Even though only one row of information is returned, you must supply the procedure with an output parameter of type *cursor*. After executing the procedure, you must use the cursor FETCH command to retrieve the information from the returned cursor. Here's the syntax for calling the stored procedure:

```
sp_describe_cursor [@cursor_return =] output_cursor_variable OUTPUT
{
[, [@cursor_source =] N'local',
    [@cursor_identity =] N'local_cursor_name'] |

[, [@cursor_source =] N'global',
    [@cursor_identity =] N'global_cursor_name'] |

[, [@cursor_source =] N'variable',
    [@cursor_identity =] N'input_cursor_variable']
}
```

Here's an example of using the procedure and then accessing the data returned in the cursor variable. *Authors_cursor* is the cursor for which we want information and *@Report* is a cursor variable to hold the results.

```
DECLARE authors_cursor CURSOR KEYSET FOR
SELECT au_lname
FROM authors
WHERE au_lname LIKE 'S%'

OPEN authors_cursor

-- Declare a cursor variable to hold the cursor output variable
-- from sp_describe_cursor
DECLARE @Report CURSOR

-- Execute sp_describe_cursor into the cursor variable
EXEC master.dbo.sp_describe_cursor
    @cursor_return = @Report OUTPUT,
    @cursor_source = 'global',
    @cursor_identity = 'authors_cursor'

-- Verify that the cursor variable contains information

IF cursor_status('variable', '@Report') != 1
    PRINT 'No information available from the cursor'

ELSE BEGIN
-- Fetch all the rows from the sp_describe_cursor output cursor
    WHILE (@@fetch_status = 0)
    BEGIN
        FETCH NEXT FROM @Report
    END
END
```

```
-- Close and deallocate the cursor from sp_describe_cursor
IF cursor_status('variable',  '@Report') >= -1
BEGIN
    CLOSE @Report
    DEALLOCATE @Report
END
GO

-- Close and deallocate the original cursor
CLOSE authors_cursor
DEALLOCATE authors_cursor
GO
```

Here's some of the information returned:

```
reference_name cursor_scope status model concurrency scrollable
-------------- ------------- ------ ----- ----------- ----------
authors_cursor 2             1      2     3           1


open_status cursor_rows fetch_status column_count row_count
----------- ----------- ------------ ------------ ---------
1           3           -9           1            0


last_operation
--------------
1
```

Table 13-4 explains some of the return values.

Result Column	Possible Return Values
CURSOR_SCOPE	1 = LOCAL 2 = GLOBAL
STATUS	The same values reported by the CURSOR_STATUS system function, described earlier.
MODEL	1 = Static 2 = Keyset 3 = Dynamic 4 = Fast forward
CONCURRENCY	1 = Read-only 2 = Scroll locks 3 = Optimistic
SCROLLABLE	0 = Forward-only 1 = Scrollable

Table 13-4. *Meaning of values returned by* sp_describe_cursor.   *(continued)*

Table 13-4 *continued*

Result Column	Possible Return Values
OPEN_STATUS	0 = Closed 1 = Open
CURSOR_ROWS	Number of qualifying rows in the result set.
FETCH_STATUS	The status of the last fetch on this cursor, as indicated by the @@FETCH_STATUS function. 0 = The fetch was successful. −1 = The fetch failed or is beyond the bounds of the cursor. −2 = The requested row is missing. −9 = There was no fetch on the cursor.
COLUMN_COUNT	The number of columns in the cursor result set.
ROW_COUNT	The number of rows affected by the last operation on the cursor, as indicated by the @@ROWCOUNT function.
LAST_OPERATION	The last operation performed on the cursor. 0 = No operations have been performed on the cursor. 1 = OPEN 2 = FETCH 3 = INSERT 4 = UPDATE 5 = DELETE 6 = CLOSE 7 = DEALLOCATE

sp_cursor_list

This procedure returns the same information as *sp_describe_cursor*, but it does so for all cursors. You can specify whether you want all global cursors, all local cursors, or both. Here's the syntax:

```
sp_cursor_list [@cursor_return =] cursor_variable_name OUTPUT,
[@cursor_scope =] cursor_scope
```

You can actually create your own stored procedure as a wrapper around *sp_cursor_list*. This allows you to avoid the declaration of the *@Report* cursor output parameter every time you want to look at cursor properties. You also do not have to code the repeated fetching of rows using this cursor variable. On the following page is an example of what such a procedure might look like. It uses a default of 3 for the value of *scope*, which means all cursors, but you can override that when you call this new *sp_cursor_info* procedure. You can pass a 1 to indicate local cursors only or a 2 to indicate global cursors only:

```
USE master
GO

CREATE PROC sp_cursor_info
(@scope int = 3)
AS
-- Declare a cursor variable to hold the cursor output variable
-- from sp_cursor_list

DECLARE @Report CURSOR
-- Execute sp_cursor_list into the cursor variable

EXEC master.dbo.sp_cursor_list @cursor_return = @Report OUTPUT,

@cursor_scope = @scope

-- Fetch all the rows from the sp_cursor_list output cursor
FETCH NEXT FROM @Report
WHILE (@@FETCH_STATUS = 0)
BEGIN
    FETCH NEXT FROM @Report
END

-- Close and deallocate the cursor from sp_cursor_list
CLOSE @Report
DEALLOCATE @Report
RETURN
GO
```

The procedure returns individual cursor rows, one for each cursor available in the session. You can expand this procedure even further to populate a temporary table with the values in the returned row. You can then use the CASE functionality to translate the integer code numbers returned into meaningful strings. The companion CD includes a script to build such a procedure, called *sp_cursor_details*, which calls *sp_cursor_list* and receives the results into a cursor variable. By creating the *sp_cursor_details* procedure in your *master* database, you can execute *sp_cursor_details* just like any other system-supplied stored procedure. I'll declare the same *authors_cursor* I declared earlier and then execute the *sp_cursor_details* procedure. The output is split into three sets of columns so it all fits on the page of this book, but the output in Query Analyzer would be all on one line.

```
DECLARE authors_cursor CURSOR KEYSET FOR
SELECT au_lname
FROM authors
WHERE au_lname LIKE 'S%'
GO
```

(continued)

```
OPEN authors_cursor
EXEC sp_cursor_details

OUTPUT:
Cursor Reference                          Declared Name                           Scope
------------------------------------      ------------------------------------    --------
authors_cursor                            authors_cursor                          global


Status Model             LOCKING         Scrolling     Open Qualifying Rows
------ -----------       -----------     -----------   ---- ----------------
open   keyset            optimistic      scrollable    yes  3


Fetch Status  Columns Rows for last operation Last operation Handle
------------- ------- ------------------------ -------------- ---------
no fetch done 1       0                        OPEN           180150000
```

sp_describe_cursor_tables

This procedure reports on the tables accessed by a given cursor. It returns its output in a cursor variable, with one row for each table in the specified cursor. It returns such information as the name of the table and any optimizer hints specified for the table. See the SQL Server online documentation for more details.

sp_describe_cursor_columns

This procedure reports the attributes of the columns in the result set of a given cursor. It returns its output in a cursor variable, with one row for each column in the SELECT list of the specified cursor. The information it returns includes the name of the column, the datatype, the ordinal position of the column, and the ID of the table from which the cursor is selected. See the SQL Server online documentation for more details.

WORKING WITH TEXT AND IMAGE DATA

SQL Server provides large object (LOB) support via the *ntext*, *text*, and *image* datatypes. I talked about their storage structure in Chapter 6. If you work with these datatypes, you might want to use the additional statements provided by SQL Server along with the standard SELECT, INSERT, UPDATE, and DELETE statements. Because a single LOB column can be as large as 2 GB, you frequently need to work with LOB data in chunks, and these additional statements (which we'll see in a moment) can help. I could have discussed this topic earlier, when I discussed Transact-SQL programming in Chapter 10. However, because you need some knowledge of isolation levels, transactions, and consistency issues to understand this topic, I've waited until after I covered most of those issues. In addition, one of the examples I'll show you involves cursors, so I really couldn't show that one before now.

For simplicity's sake, most of the discussion will deal with the *text* datatype. But everything here is also relevant to the *image* and *ntext* datatypes. These three datatypes are essentially the same internally. Recall that *ntext*, *text*, and *image* datatypes are special because they are normally not stored on the same data page as the rest of the row. Instead, the data row holds only a 16-byte pointer to an *ntext*, *text*, or *image* structure. Remember that you can choose to store LOB data in the row itself if the amount of data is small enough and the table option *text in row* has been enabled.

Although the space required by *text* data is managed much more efficiently in SQL Server 2000 than in earlier versions, functional drawbacks still exist. Although you can indeed use standard INSERT, UPDATE, DELETE, and SELECT statements with a *text* column, some significant restrictions apply. In a WHERE clause, you can search on the *text* column only with the LIKE operator or with the functions SUBSTRING and PATINDEX. Variables of type *text* cannot be declared or manipulated. You can declare a parameter in a stored procedure to be of type *text* (or *ntext* or *image*), but you can't do much besides pass a value to the procedure initially. For example, you cannot subsequently assign different values to the parameter or return it as an OUTPUT parameter. Because of these limitations, you'll want to use these special datatypes only when another datatype isn't a reasonable option. If a *varchar(8000)* column can work for you (or *nvarchar(4000)* for Unicode data), you can use it and avoid *text* or *ntext* altogether. But if you absolutely need a memo field, for example, and 8000 characters are not enough, you'll need to use *text* or denormalize the data and use multiple *varchar* columns.

If a *text* column makes the most sense for you despite its drawbacks, you need to understand how to work effectively with text. When you can, it is easiest to work with *text* datatypes using standard SELECT, INSERT, UPDATE, and DELETE statements. But if your text data gets large, you'll run into issues (such as how big a string your application can pass) that might make it necessary for you to deal with chunks of data at a time instead of the entire column.

The special statements for working with text data are WRITETEXT, READTEXT, and UPDATETEXT. Both READTEXT and UPDATETEXT let you work with chunks of a *text* column at a time. The WRITETEXT statement does not let you deal with chunks but rather with the entire column only.

You'll need to consider the overhead of transaction logging done with these operations. Unlike the normal INSERT, UPDATE, and DELETE operations that always cause the entire row to be logged, the amount of logging done by the WRITETEXT and UPDATETEXT operations depends on the recovery model you're using. These two operations are considered BULK operations, as I discussed in Chapter 5, which means that if you're in FULL or SIMPLE recovery mode, all the LOB data will be written to the log. If you're in BULK LOGGED mode, the LOB data isn't written directly to the log; instead, all pages modified by these BULK operations will be backed up when the transaction log is backed up. Also, if you use SQL Server replication to replicate *text* or *image* columns, any UPDATETEXT or WRITETEXT operations *must* be logged because the replication process looks for changes based on the transaction log.

The WRITETEXT, READTEXT, and UPDATETEXT statements all work with a *text pointer*. A text pointer is a unique *varbinary(16)* value for each *text, ntext,* or *image* column of each row. The following discussion of the three operations will talk about *text* data for simplicity, but in most cases it will apply to all three of the LOB datatypes.

WRITETEXT

WRITETEXT completely overwrites an existing *text* column. You provide the column name (qualified by the table name), the text pointer for the specific column of a specific row, and the actual data to be written. It might seem like a catch-22 when using WRITETEXT initially because you need to pass it a text pointer—but if the column is initially NULL, there *is* no text pointer. So how do you get one? You SELECT it using the TEXTPTR function. But if the *text* column has not been initialized, the TEXTPTR function returns NULL. To initialize a text pointer for a column of a row with *text* or *image* data, you can perform some variation of the following:

- Explicitly insert a non-null value in the *text* column when you use an INSERT statement. Recognize that WRITETEXT will completely overwrite the column anyway, so the value can always be something such as *A* or a space.

- Define a default on the column with a non-null value such as *A*. Then when you do the insert, you can specify DEFAULT or omit the column, which will result in the default value being inserted and the text pointer being initialized.

- Update the row after inserting it, explicitly setting it to anything, even NULL.

You then select the text pointer into a variable declared as *varbinary(16)* and pass that to WRITETEXT. You can't use SELECT statements or expressions in the WRITETEXT statement. This means that the statement is limited to being executed one row at a time, although it can be done from within a cursor. The SELECT statement that gets the text pointer should be known to return only one row, preferably by using an exact match on the primary key value in the WHERE clause because that will ensure that at most one row can meet the criteria. You can, of course, use @@ROWCOUNT to check this if you're not absolutely sure that the SELECT statement can return only one row. Before using the WRITETEXT statement, you should also ensure that you have a valid text pointer. If you find a row with the criteria you specified and the text pointer for that row was initialized, it will be valid. You can check it as a separate statement using the TEXTVALID function. Or you can check that you do not have a NULL value in your variable that was assigned the text pointer, as you'll see in the following example. Make sure that you don't have an old text pointer value from a previous use, which would make the IS NOT NULL check be TRUE. In this example, I do one variable assignment and the variable starts out NULL, so we can be sure that a non-null value means we have selected a valid text pointer:

```
-- WRITETEXT with an unprotected text pointer
DECLARE @mytextptr varbinary(16)
SELECT @mytextptr=TEXTPTR(pr_info)
    FROM pub_info WHERE pub_id='9999'
IF @mytextptr IS NOT NULL
    WRITETEXT pub_info.pr_info @mytextptr  'Hello Again'
```

In this example, the text pointer is not protected from changes made by others. Therefore, it is possible that the text pointer will no longer be valid by the time the WRITETEXT operation is performed. Suppose that you get a text pointer for the row with *pub_id='9999'*. But before you use it with WRITETEXT, another user deletes and reinserts the row for publisher 9999. In that case, the text pointer you're holding will no longer be valid. In the example above, the window for this occurrence is small, since we do the WRITETEXT immediately after getting the text pointer. *But there is still a window of vulnerability.* In your application, the window might be wider. If the text pointer is not valid when you do the WRITETEXT operation, you will get an error message like this:

```
Msg 7123, Level 16, State 1
Invalid text pointer value 000000000253f380.
```

You can easily see this for yourself if you add a delay (for example, *WAITFOR DELAY '00:00:15'*) after getting the text pointer and then delete the row from another connection. You'll get error 7123 when the WRITETEXT operation executes. If you think the chances of getting this error are slim, you can choose to simply deal with the error if it occurs.

You should instead consider using transaction protection to ensure that the text pointer will not change from the time you read it until you use it, and to serialize access for updates so that you do not encounter frequent deadlocks. Many applications use TEXTVALID to check right before operating—that's the right idea, but it's hardly foolproof. There's still a window between the TEXTVALID operation and the use of the text pointer during which the text pointer can be invalidated. The only way to close the window is to make both operations part of an atomic operation. This means using a transaction and having SQL Server protect the transaction with a lock. (For more about locking, see Chapter 14.)

By default, SQL Server operates with Read Committed isolation and releases a share (READ) lock after the page has been read. So simply putting the pointer in a transaction with the Read Committed isolation level, which is SQL Server's default, is not enough. You need to ensure that the lock is held until the text pointer is used.

You could change the isolation level to Repeatable Read, which is not a bad solution, but this changes the isolation behavior for all operations on that connection, so it might have a more widespread effect than you intend. (Although you could, of course, then change it right back.) Also, this approach doesn't guarantee that you will subsequently be able to get the exclusive lock required to do the WRITETEXT operation; it ensures only that when you get to the WRITETEXT operation, the text pointer will still be valid. You won't be sure that you're not in the lock queue behind another connection waiting to update the same row and column. In that case, your transaction and the competing one would both hold a share lock on the same row and would both need to acquire an exclusive lock. Since both transactions are holding a share lock, neither can get the exclusive lock and a deadlock results in one of the connections having its transaction automatically aborted. (In Chapter 14, you'll see that this is an example of a *conversion deadlock.*) If multiple processes are intending to modify the text and all transactions first request an update lock in a transaction when selecting the text pointer, conversion deadlocks will be avoided because only one process will get the update lock and the others will queue for it. But users' transactions that need only to read the row will not be affected because an update lock and a share lock are compatible.

Using the update lock on the text pointer is good for serializing access to the actual text data, even though the lock on the text data is distinct from the lock on the row with the text pointer. In this case, you essentially use the update lock on a text pointer as you would use an intent lock for the text data. This is conceptually similar to the intent locks that SQL Server uses on a table when a page-locking or row-locking operation for that table will take place. That operation recognizes that rows, pages, and tables have an implicit hierarchy. You can think of text pointers and text data as having a similar hierarchy and use the update lock on the text pointer to protect access to the associated text data.

Here is the improved version that protects the text pointer from getting invalidated and also reserves the transaction's spot in the queue so that it will get the exclusive lock that's necessary to change the column. This approach will avoid conversion deadlocks on the text pages:

```
-- WRITETEXT with a properly protected text pointer
BEGIN TRAN
DECLARE @mytextptr varbinary(16)
SELECT @mytextptr=TEXTPTR(pr_info)
    FROM pub_info (UPDLOCK) WHERE pub_id='9999'
IF @mytextptr IS NOT NULL
    WRITETEXT pub_info.pr_info @mytextptr 'Hello Again'
COMMIT TRAN
```

READTEXT

READTEXT is used in a similar way to WRITETEXT, except that READTEXT allows you to specify a starting position and the number of bytes to read. This is its basic syntax:

```
READTEXT [[database.]owner.]table_name.column_name
    text_ptr offset size [HOLDLOCK]
```

Unlike with WRITETEXT, with READTEXT you do not need to work with the entire contents of the data. You can specify the starting position (*offset*) and the number of bytes to read (*size*). READTEXT is often used with the PATINDEX function to find the offset (in number of characters) at which some string or pattern exists, and it's also used with DATALENGTH to determine the total size of the text column in bytes. If you're working with *ntext* data, you'll have to divide DATALENGTH by 2 to get the number of characters. But you cannot directly use these functions as the offset parameter. Instead, you must execute them beforehand and keep their values in a local variable, which you then pass. As I mentioned in the discussion of WRITETEXT, you'll want to protect your text pointer from becoming invalidated. In the next example, you'll read text without updating it. So you can use the HOLDLOCK lock hint on the SELECT statement for the text pointer (or set the isolation level to Repeatable Read).

Sometimes people think that transactions are used only for data modifications, but notice that in this case you use a transaction to ensure read repeatability (of the text pointer) even though you're not updating anything. You can optionally add HOLDLOCK to the READTEXT statement to ensure that the text doesn't change until the transaction has completed. But in the example below, we'll read the entire contents with just one read and we will not be rereading the contents, so there's no point in using HOLDLOCK. This example finds the pattern *Washington* in the *pr_info* column for *pub_id* 0877 and returns the contents of that column from that point on:

```
-- READTEXT with a protected text pointer
BEGIN TRAN
DECLARE @mytextptr varbinary(16), @sizeneeded int, @pat_offset int
SELECT @mytextptr=TEXTPTR(pr_info),
    @pat_offset=PATINDEX('%Washington%',pr_info) - 1,
    @sizeneeded=DATALENGTH(pr_info) -
        (PATINDEX('%Washington%',pr_info) - 1)
    FROM pub_info (HOLDLOCK) WHERE pub_id='0877'

IF @mytextptr IS NOT NULL AND @pat_offset >= 0 AND
    @sizeneeded IS NOT NULL
    READTEXT  pub_info.pr_info @mytextptr @pat_offset @sizeneeded

COMMIT TRAN
```

NOTE If you run the preceding query using SQL Query Analyzer, you might not see the entire text result. SQL Query Analyzer has a default limit of 256 characters that can be returned for a text column. You can use the Tools/Options command and go to the Results tab to change this limit.

The offset returned by PATINDEX and the offset used by READTEXT are unfortunately not consistent. READTEXT treats the first character as offset 0. (This makes sense because you can think of an offset as how many characters you have to move to get to the desired position—to get to the first character, you don't need to move at all.) But PATINDEX returns the value in terms of position, not really as an offset, and so the first character for it would be *1*. You could actually call this a minor bug. But people have adapted to it, so changing it would cause more problems than it would solve at this point. You should assume that this acts as intended and adjust for it. You need to fix this discrepancy by taking the result of PATINDEX and subtracting 1 from it. PATINDEX returns 0 if the pattern is not found. Since we subtract 1 from the value returned by PATINDEX, if the pattern was not found, the variable *@pat_offset* would be −1. We simply check that *@pat_offset* is not negative.

You also need to specify how many bytes you want to read. If you want to read from that point to the end of the column, for example, you can take the total length as returned from DATALENGTH and subtract the starting position, as shown in the preceding example. You cannot simply specify a buffer that you know is large enough to read the rest of the column into; that will result in error 7124:

```
The offset and length specified in the READTEXT command is greater
than the actual data length of %d.
```

If you could always perform a single READTEXT to handle your data, you'd probably not use it; instead, you could use SELECT. You need to use READTEXT when a *text* column is too long to reasonably bring back with just one statement. For example, the text size of the *pr_info* field for publisher 1622 is 18,518 bytes. You can't select this value in an application such as SQL Query Analyzer because it's longer than the maximum expected row length for a result set, so it would be truncated. But you can set up a simple loop to show the text in pieces. To understand this process, you need to be aware of the system function @@TEXTSIZE, which returns the maximum amount of text or image data that you can retrieve in a single statement. Of course, you need to make sure that the buffer in your application will also be large enough to accept the text. You can read chunks smaller than the @@TEXTSIZE limit, but not larger.

NOTE The value for @@TEXTSIZE is unrelated to the setting in SQL Query Analyzer for the maximum number of characters discussed in the previous note. @@TEXTSIZE is a server option, while the character limit controls the client tool's display.

You can change the value of @@TEXTSIZE for your connection by using SET TEXTSIZE *n*. The default value for @@TEXTSIZE is 64 KB. You should read chunks whose size is based on the amount of space available in your application buffer and based on the network packet size so that the text will fit in one packet, with an allowance for some additional space for metadata. For example, with the default network packet size of 4096 bytes (4 KB), a good read size would be about 4000 bytes, assuming that your application could deal with that size. You should also be sure that @@TEXTSIZE is at least equal to your read size. You can either check to determine its size or explicitly set it, as we do in the example below. Also notice the handy use of the CASE statement for a variable assignment to initialize the *@readsize* variable to the smaller of the total length of the column and the value of @@TEXTSIZE. In this example, I make the read size only 100 characters so that it displays easily in SQL Query Analyzer or in a similar query window. But this is too small for most applications and is used here for illustration only.

```
-- READTEXT in a loop to read chunks of text.
-- Instead of using HOLDLOCK, use SET TRANSACTION ISOLATION LEVEL
-- REPEATABLE READ (equivalent). Then set it back when done but
-- be sure to do so in a separate batch.
SET TRANSACTION ISOLATION LEVEL REPEATABLE READ
SET TEXTSIZE 100     --- Just for illustration; too small for
                     --- real world. 4000 would be a better value.
BEGIN TRAN

DECLARE @mytextptr varbinary(16), @totalsize int,
    @lastread int, @readsize int

SELECT
    @mytextptr=TEXTPTR(pr_info), @totalsize=DATALENGTH(pr_info),
    @lastread=0,
    -- Set the readsize to the smaller of the @@TEXTSIZE setting
    -- and the total length of the column
    @readsize=CASE WHEN (@@TEXTSIZE < DATALENGTH(pr_info)) THEN
        @@TEXTSIZE ELSE DATALENGTH(pr_info) END
     FROM pub_info WHERE pub_id='1622'

IF @mytextptr IS NOT NULL AND @readsize > 0
    WHILE (@lastread < @totalsize)
    BEGIN
        READTEXT pub_info.pr_info @mytextptr @lastread @readsize
        IF (@@error <> 0)
            BREAK     -- Break out of loop if an error on read
        -- Change offset to last char read
        SELECT @lastread=@lastread + @readsize
```

(continued)

```
                  -- If read size would go beyond end, adjust read size
                  IF ((@readsize + @lastread) > @totalsize)
                      SELECT @readsize=@totalsize - @lastread
            END

COMMIT TRAN
GO
--- Set it back, but in a separate batch
SET TRANSACTION ISOLATION LEVEL READ COMMITTED
```

Notice that in this example I need to ensure not only that the text pointer is still valid when we get to READTEXT but also that the column is not changed between iterations of READTEXT. If another connection simply updated the text in place, the text pointer would still be valid, although the read would be messed up since the contents and length were changed. I could use HOLDLOCK both on the READTEXT statement as well as for protecting the text pointer. But for illustration, I instead changed the isolation level to REPEATABLE READ.

> **NOTE**   If the *pub_info* table in your *pubs* database doesn't have any *text* data in the *pr_info* column, you can load it using a supplied script in the install directory of your SQL Server installation folder. The script called pubtext.bat requires two parameters: your *sa* password and the name of the SQL Server. There is also a script to load in image data for the logo column of *pub_info*, called pubimage.bat. Both of these scripts use the undocumented command-line utility called *textcopy*. (Although *textcopy* will allow image data to be copied into a SQL Server *image* column, there are no supplied facilities for displaying image data graphically. You'll need to use a client tool that provides this capability in order to "see" the graphics.)

Copying Text to Sequenced *varchar* Columns

As you've seen, the *text* datatype is sometimes awkward to work with. Many functions don't operate on text, stored procedures are limited in what they can do with text, and some tools don't deal with it well. If the amount of text isn't too big—and you get to be the judge of what is too big for you—you can covert a *text* column to a set of *varchar* columns. In SQL Server 2000, *varchar* columns can be up to 8000 bytes. Although the code that follows can produce columns of that size, that might still be too big to work with effectively. All of SQL Server's string functions will work on these columns, but if you want to print out each column, you might want to find something smaller that fits your needs better. The code below produces columns of length 200. You can take this code and substitute *varchar(8000)* or any other length up to 8000 for *varchar(200)*.

Like the previous example, the following procedure operates on the *pub_info* table from the *pubs* database. For a given *pub_id*, the procedure takes the text column of the row and does successive READTEXT operations in chunks of 200 until the entire text column has been read. After creating the procedure, we use a cursor to iterate for each row of *pub_info* and copy the text column into multiple rows of a temporary table. When we're done for a given *pub_id*, we take the temporary table's contents and add it to the permanent table. We truncate the temporary table and move on to the next *pub_id* value.

```
-- copy_text_to_varchar.sql
-- Proc get_text does READTEXT in a loop to read chunks of text
-- no larger than 200, or the column size or @@TEXTSIZE, and
-- produces as many rows as necessary to store the text column
-- as a series of sequenced varchar(200) rows
CREATE PROC get_text @pub_id char(4)
AS

DECLARE @mytextptr varbinary(16), @totalsize int, @lastread int,
    @readsize int
-- Use a TRAN and HOLDLOCK to ensure that textptr and text are
-- constant during the iterative reads
BEGIN TRAN
SELECT @mytextptr=TEXTPTR(pr_info), @totalsize=DATALENGTH(pr_info),
    @lastread=0,
    -- Set the readsize to the smaller of the @@TEXTSIZE settings,
    -- 200, and the total length of the column
    @readsize=CASE WHEN (200 < DATALENGTH(pr_info)) THEN 200
    ELSE DATALENGTH(pr_info) END
    FROM pub_info (HOLDLOCK) WHERE pub_id=@pub_id

-- If debugging, uncomment this to check values
-- SELECT @mytextptr, @totalsize, @lastread, @readsize

-- Do READTEXT in a loop to get next 200 characters until done
IF @mytextptr IS NOT NULL AND @readsize > 0
    WHILE (@lastread < @totalsize)
    BEGIN
        -- If readsize would go beyond end, adjust readsize
        IF ((@readsize + @lastread) > @totalsize)
            SELECT @readsize = @totalsize - @lastread

        -- If debugging, uncomment this to check values
        -- SELECT 'valid ptr?'=textvalid('pub_info.pr_info',
        --     @mytextptr), 'totalsize'=@totalsize,
        --     'lastread'=@lastread, 'readsize'=@readsize

        READTEXT pub_info.pr_info @mytextptr @lastread @readsize
        IF (@@ERROR <> 0)
            BREAK     -- Break out of loop if an error on read
        -- Change offset to last char read
        SELECT @lastread=@lastread + @readsize

    END
```

(continued)

```
COMMIT TRAN
GO

IF EXISTS (SELECT * FROM tempdb.dbo.sysobjects
    WHERE name='##mytmptext' AND type='U')
    DROP TABLE ##mytmptext
GO

-- Intermediate temp table that READTEXT will use.
-- This table is truncated after each pub_id value, so the Identity
-- property sequences the rows for each publisher separately.
CREATE TABLE ##mytmptext
(
    seq_no          int      IDENTITY,
    text_chunk      text
)
GO

IF EXISTS (SELECT * FROM sysobjects
    WHERE name='newprinfo' AND type='U')
    DROP TABLE newprinfo
GO

-- This is the new table that pub_info is copied to.
-- It keeps chunks of text and is sequenced for each pub_id.
CREATE TABLE newprinfo
(
    pub_id          char(4)     NOT NULL,
    seq_no          int         NOT NULL,
    text_chunk      varchar(200),
    CONSTRAINT PK PRIMARY KEY (pub_id, seq_no)
)
GO

-- Having created the procedure get_text, iterate for each pub_id
-- value, temporarily sequencing them in the temp table. Once done
-- for a given pub_id, copy them to the new permanent table. Then
-- truncate the temp table for use with reseeded Identity for next
-- pub_id row.
DECLARE @pub_id char(4)
DECLARE iterate_prinfo CURSOR FOR
    SELECT pub_id FROM pub_info ORDER BY pub_id

OPEN iterate_prinfo
    FETCH NEXT FROM iterate_prinfo INTO @pub_id
        BEGIN
        TRUNCATE TABLE ##mytmptext
```

```
        INSERT ##mytmptext
            EXEC get_text @pub_id

        INSERT newprinfo (pub_id, seq_no, text_chunk)
            SELECT @pub_id, SEQ_NO,
            CONVERT(varchar(200), TEXT_CHUNK)
            FROM ##mytmptext ORDER BY SEQ_NO

        FETCH NEXT FROM iterate_prinfo INTO @pub_id
        END

CLOSE iterate_prinfo
DEALLOCATE iterate_prinfo
GO


-- Simply verify contents of the new table
SELECT * FROM newprinfo ORDER BY pub_id,seq_no
GO
```

A subset of the output looks like the following:

```
pub_id   seq_no   text_chunk
------   ------   -------------------------------------------------
0736     1        This is sample text data for New Moon Books,
                  publisher 0736 in the pubs database. New Moon
                  Books is located in Boston, Massachusetts.
                  This is sample text data for New Moon Books,
                  publisher 0736 in
0736     2        the pubs database. New Moon Books is located in
                  Boston, Massachusetts.
                  This is sample text data for New Moon Books,
                  publisher 0736 in the pubs database. New Moon
                  Books is located in Boston, Massach
0736     3        usetts.
                  This is sample text data for New Moon Books,
                  publisher 0736 in the pubs database. New Moon
                  Books is located in Boston, Massachusetts.
                  This is sample text data for New Moon Books,
                  publish
```

UPDATETEXT

UPDATETEXT is a big improvement for text processing. If you had only WRITETEXT, you'd need to completely rewrite the entire column to make even a minor change. UPDATETEXT lets you work with text in pieces to insert, overwrite, or append data. Or you can copy data from another *text* column and append it or overwrite the column with it. Because of its additional capability and flexibility, the syntax for UPDATETEXT is a bit more complex, as you can see on the following page.

```
UPDATETEXT table_name.dest_column_name dest_text_ptr
    offset delete_length [inserted_data |
    table_name.src_column_name src_text_ptr ]
```

The destination column name and text pointer parameters point to the column that you will be updating; these parameters are required. As you would with WRITETEXT, you should use the UPDLOCK hint to protect the text pointer from becoming invalid and to serialize access to the text pages to prevent a conversion deadlock. The source column name parameters are used only when you copy data from another *text* column. Otherwise, you directly include in that spot the data you'll be adding or you omit the parameter if you're deleting data. The *offset* is the position at which you start your data modification. It should be NULL if you're appending to the current contents and 0 if you're starting from the beginning of the column. The *delete_length* parameter tells you how many characters (if any) to delete starting from the offset parameter. Use NULL for this parameter if you want to delete all contents from the offset up to the end of the column, and use 0 if you want to delete no bytes. As with READTEXT, the first character of the column is considered to have a 0 offset.

UPDATETEXT can do everything WRITETEXT can do, and much more. So you might choose to use only READTEXT and UPDATETEXT and forget about WRITETEXT. (WRITETEXT existed in versions of SQL Server before UPDATETEXT appeared; it is maintained for backward compatibility, but there isn't much need for it now.)

Following are some examples that illustrate the use of UPDATETEXT better than further explanation.

EXAMPLE 1

Use UPDATETEXT to completely replace the contents of a column:

```
-- Use UPDATETEXT to completely overwrite a text column.
-- Alternative to WRITETEXT.
DECLARE @mytextptr varbinary(16)
BEGIN TRAN

SELECT @mytextptr=TEXTPTR(pr_info) FROM pub_info (UPDLOCK) WHERE
    pub_id='9999'
IF @mytextptr IS NOT NULL
    UPDATETEXT pub_info.pr_info @mytextptr 0 NULL
        'New text for 9999'

COMMIT TRAN
```

EXAMPLE 2

Use UPDATETEXT to delete characters off the end; first notice that publisher 0877, Binnet & Hardley, has the following contents in the text column *pr_info*:

```
This is sample text data for Binnet & Hardley, publisher 0877 in
the pubs database. Binnet & Hardley is located in Washington,
D.C.
This is sample text data for Binnet & Hardley, publisher 0877 in
the pubs database. Binnet & Hardley is located in Washington,
D.C.
This is sample text data for Binnet & Hardley, publisher 0877 in
the pubs database. Binnet & Hardley is located in Washington,
D.C.
This is sample text data for Binnet & Hardley, publisher 0877 in
the pubs database. Binnet & Hardley is located in Washington,
D.C.
This is sample text data for Binnet & Hardley, publisher 0877 in
the pubs database. Binnet & Hardley is located in Washington,
D.C.
```

Because the text is repeated several times, we'll delete all characters that follow the first occurrence of *D.C.*:

```
DECLARE @mytextptr varbinary(16), @pat_offset int
BEGIN TRAN
SELECT @mytextptr=TEXTPTR(pr_info),
    @pat_offset=PATINDEX('%D.C.%', pr_info)-1+4
    -- For offset, subtract 1 for offset adjust but add 4 for
    -- length of "D.C."
    FROM pub_info (UPDLOCK) WHERE pub_id='0877'

IF @mytextptr IS NOT NULL AND @pat_offset >= 4
    UPDATETEXT pub_info.pr_info @mytextptr @pat_offset NULL

COMMIT TRAN
```

The column now has these contents (only):

```
This is sample text data for Binnet & Hardley, publisher 0877 in
the pubs database. Binnet & Hardley is located in Washington,
D.C.
```

EXAMPLE 3

With the small amount of text here, it wouldn't be bad to simply rewrite the column with new text. But if this were a large *text* column (you could literally store the contents of *War and Peace* in a single *text* column), it would be extremely inefficient to rewrite the entire column just to make a minor change. In this example, we'll add the text *Kimberly Tripp is president of the company.* to the current contents. We'll use UPDATETEXT to append text to the column:

```
DECLARE @mytextptr varbinary(16)
BEGIN TRAN
SELECT @mytextptr=TEXTPTR(pr_info) FROM pub_info (UPDLOCK)
    WHERE pub_id='0877'

IF @mytextptr IS NOT NULL
    UPDATETEXT pub_info.pr_info @mytextptr NULL NULL
        'Kimberly Tripp is president of the company.'

COMMIT TRAN
```

And the result:

```
This is sample text data for Binnet & Hardley, publisher 0877 in
the pubs database. Binnet & Hardley is located in Washington,
D.C.Kimberly Tripp is president of the company.
```

That worked exactly as specified, but you might wish we had skipped a line and then included a tab before adding the new sentence. We can easily add both a vertical and a horizontal tab, as you can see in the next example.

EXAMPLE 4

Use UPDATETEXT to insert some characters:

```
DECLARE @mytextptr varbinary(16), @pat_offset int,
    @mystring char(2)
BEGIN TRAN
SELECT
@mystring=char(13) + CHAR(9),    -- Vertical tab is code point 13.
                                 -- Tab is 9.
@pat_offset=PATINDEX('%Kim%', pr_info)-1,
@mytextptr=TEXTPTR(pr_info) FROM pub_info (UPDLOCK)
    WHERE pub_id='0877'

IF @mytextptr IS NOT NULL AND @pat_offset >= 0
    UPDATETEXT pub_info.pr_info @mytextptr @pat_offset 0
        @mystring

COMMIT TRAN
```

And the result:

```
This is sample text data for Binnet & Hardley, publisher 0877 in
the pubs database. Binnet & Hardley is located in Washington,
D.C.
     Kimberly Tripp is president of the company.
```

EXAMPLE 5

Oops! We just learned that the president has gotten married and changed her last name from *Tripp* to *Tripp-Simonnet*. We need to fix that. Use UPDATETEXT for search and replace:

```
-- UPDATETEXT for Search and Replace
DECLARE @mytextptr varbinary(16), @pat_offset int,
    @oldstring varchar(255), @newstring varchar(255),
    @sizeold int

BEGIN TRAN
SELECT @oldstring='Tripp', @newstring='Tripp-Simonnet'

SELECT @sizeold=DATALENGTH(@oldstring),
@pat_offset=PATINDEX('%' + @oldstring + '%', pr_info)-1,
@mytextptr=TEXTPTR(pr_info)
FROM pub_info (UPDLOCK) WHERE pub_id='0877'

IF @mytextptr IS NOT NULL AND @pat_offset >= 0
    UPDATETEXT pub_info.pr_info @mytextptr @pat_offset @sizeold
        @newstring

COMMIT TRAN
```

And the result:

```
This is sample text data for Binnet & Hardley, publisher 0877 in
the pubs database. Binnet & Hardley is located in Washington,
D.C.
     Kimberly Tripp-Simonnet is president of the company.
```

We used variables above and figured lengths and offsets using SQL Server's built-in functions. By doing this, we ensured that the procedure is pretty generic and that it can deal with changing the string to another string that is either longer or shorter than the original.

EXAMPLE 6

Suppose we want to append the contents of the text for publisher Scootney (*pub_id* 9952) to the text for Binnet (*pub_id* 0877). If we didn't have this option in UPDATETEXT, it would be necessary to bring all that text back to the client application, append it, and then send it back to the server. Over a slow network such as the Internet, this would not be practical if the *text* columns were large. But with UPDATETEXT, the whole operation is done on the server. In this example, notice that we protect the text pointer for the target with UPDLOCK, since we'll be updating that row. We can use HOLDLOCK for the source row since we're reading it only and we want to ensure that it hasn't changed.

We'll use UPDATETEXT to copy and append one text column to another:

```
-- UPDATETEXT to copy and append another text column
DECLARE @target_textptr varbinary(16),
    @source_textptr varbinary(16)
BEGIN TRAN

SELECT @target_textptr=TEXTPTR(pr_info) FROM pub_info (UPDLOCK)
WHERE pub_id='0877'
SELECT @source_textptr=TEXTPTR(pr_info) FROM pub_info (HOLDLOCK)
WHERE pub_id='9952'

IF @target_textptr IS NOT NULL AND @source_textptr IS NOT NULL
    UPDATETEXT pub_info.pr_info @target_textptr NULL NULL
        pub_info.pr_info @source_textptr

COMMIT TRAN
```

Text-in-Row Data

As discussed in Chapter 6, you can enable a table to store LOB data in the row itself. Most of the examples I've shown, as well as the details regarding the READTEXT, WRITETEXT, and UPDATEXT, apply equally to LOB data stored in a row or out of a row. However, the previous discussion of locking the text pointer applies only to LOB data that is stored outside of the data row. For tables that have *text in row* enabled, the locking issues with the text pointer are slightly different. When a text pointer is acquired for text data in a table with *text in row* enabled, the data row is locked with a share lock if the isolation level of the transaction is higher than READ UNCOMMIT-TED, and the database is not in read-only or single-user mode. The lock ensures that nobody else can modify or delete the row while you have a text pointer on a text value from that row. This lock is released when the text pointer becomes invalid. Since at the end of the transaction all text pointers are invalid, the locks are all released. You'll see a few more details about what kind of operations can invalidate a text pointer for in-row LOB data later in this section.

To illustrate the automatic locking of the row with in-row text data, let's see some basic examples. The share locks on rows with in-row text are held until the end of a transaction, and this means that we cannot get a text pointer for in-row text unless we are in a user defined transaction. This example shows an attempt to acquire a text pointer without an explicit transaction:

```
CREATE TABLE t1 (c1 int, c2 text)
EXEC sp_tableoption 't1', 'text in row', 'ON'
INSERT INTO t1 SELECT 1, 'hello there'
GO

DECLARE @ptrval varbinary(16)
SELECT @ptrval = TEXTPTR(c2) FROM t1 WHERE c1 = 1
READTEXT t1.c2 @ptrval 0 1

RESULTS:
Server: Msg 7101, Level 16, State 1, Line 3
You cannot use a text pointer for a table with option 'text in row'
set to ON.
Server: Msg 7133, Level 16, State 1, Line 4
NULL textptr (text, ntext, or image pointer) passed to
READTEXT function.
```

However, attempting to do the same text pointer assignment and READTEXT inside a user-defined transaction succeeds:

```
BEGIN TRAN
DECLARE @ptrval varbinary(16)
SELECT @ptrval = TEXTPTR(c2) FROM t1 WHERE c1 = 1
READTEXT t1.c2 @ptrval 0 1
COMMIT TRAN
```

To see that the shared locks are taken and held automatically, we can execute the same code shown earlier for the text data in the *pub_info* table, which was not stored in the row itself. If you actually ran that earlier example, the row with *pub_id 9999* is now gone, so I'll change the code to look for a row with *pub_id 1756*. I also must first enable the *text in row* option for the *pub_info* table and then use an explicit transaction.

```
-- WRITETEXT with text-in-row data
EXEC sp_tableoption pub_info, 'text in row', 'ON'
GO

BEGIN TRAN
DECLARE @mytextptr varbinary(16)
SELECT @mytextptr=TEXTPTR(pr_info)
    FROM pub_info WHERE pub_id='1756'
WAITFOR DELAY '00:00:20'
-- During the delay, you can attempt to delete
-- this row in another SQL Query Analyzer connection:
--        DELETE FROM pub_info WHERE pub_id='1756'
IF @mytextptr IS NOT NULL
    WRITETEXT pub_info.pr_info @mytextptr 'Hello Again'
COMMIT TRAN
```

If the isolation level of the transaction is READ UNCOMMITTED, any text pointer obtained from a table with *text in row* enabled is considered read-only and cannot be used to update LOB values. They can be used only to read the data. The example below creates a table with in-row text data and then sets the transaction isolation level to READ UNCOMMITTED. You can see that the READTEXT succeeds but the WRITETEXT does not.

```
CREATE TABLE t1 (c1 int, c2 text)
EXEC sp_tableoption 't1', 'text in row', 'ON'
INSERT INTO t1 SELECT 1, 'hello there'
GO

SET TRANSACTION ISOLATION LEVEL READ UNCOMMITTED
GO

BEGIN TRAN
DECLARE @ptr varbinary(16)
SELECT @ptr=textptr(c2) FROM t1 WHERE c1=1
READTEXT t1.c2 @ptr 0 5
COMMIT TRAN
GO

BEGIN TRAN
DECLARE @ptr varbinary(16)
SELECT @ptr=textptr(c2) FROM t1 WHERE c1=1
WRITETEXT t1.c2 @ptr 'xx'
COMMIT TRAN
GO
```

This is the error message returned by the WRITETEXT operation:

```
Server: Msg 7106, Level 16, State 1, Line 5
You cannot update a blob with a read-only text pointer
The statement has been terminated.
```

Note that the message uses the term *BLOB*, which should refer just to image fields; in my discussion, I've been using the term *LOB*, which refers to *text* and *ntext* as well as *image*.

Invalidating Text Pointers   As you saw earlier, if a table was not enabled for in-row text storage, no row lock is held for the text pointer. The only way you saw to lock the data row was to raise the isolation level to REPEATABLE READ. The drawback of using the isolation level to prolong the lock is that there is no way to choose to release the lock earlier. When working with LOB data in a table that has *text in row* enabled, you do have control over when the lock is released because it will be released whenever the text pointer becomes invalidated. I mentioned above that the end of a transaction will invalidate a text pointer, but that is not the only way.

Text pointers for in-row text data are also invalidated when certain DDL operations are performed on the table. Here are the DDL statements that invalidate your text pointers:

- CREATE CLUSTERED INDEX
- DROP CLUSTERED INDEX
- ALTER TABLE
- DROP TABLE
- TRUNCATE TABLE
- *sp_tableoption* with the *text in row* option
- *sp_indexoption*

Finally, you can invalidate a text pointer for in-row text data using a special stored procedure, *sp_invalidate_textptr*, which takes an argument of a text pointer.

You might need to force invalidation of text pointers because SQL Server sets an upper limit on the number of pointers for in-row text data. A limit is needed because SQL Server maintains internal memory for each valid text pointer, and we want to limit the amount of memory that can be used in this way. You can have up to 1024 valid text pointers per transaction per database. If your transaction spans two databases, you can have 1024 text pointers in each database. Within a transaction, obtaining a text pointer twice on the same LOB data gives you the same text pointer structure and will not count against your limit of 1024. Note that there is no limit on the number of pointers you can have for LOB data that is not stored in the row.

SUMMARY

In this chapter, we looked at two aspects of Transact-SQL programming that go beyond the set-based DML operations of SELECT, INSERT, UPDATE, and DELETE. First, I described server cursors in detail. Cursors are important tools that help you bridge the impedance mismatch between the set-oriented world of SQL Server and traditional record-oriented programming languages. When used properly, cursors are invaluable. When overused or used inappropriately, cursors can cause you to have a bad experience with SQL Server. SQL Server provides fully scrollable, updateable cursors.

SQL Server has four main cursor models: static, keyset, dynamic, and forward-only. Cursors can be accessed via syntax used directly in Transact-SQL or via function calls used in the programming interfaces to SQL Server (ODBC, OLE DB, and so on). These two types of cursors are called Transact-SQL cursors and API server cursors. This chapter focused on the Transact-SQL syntax, but the key points are relevant no matter what cursor interface you use with SQL Server.

Second, we looked at the processing of data that might be too large to store in the actual table rows. SQL Server provides the three datatypes—*text*, *ntext*, and *image*—to support LOB (large object) data, which can store up to 2 GB worth of data. You can use three special operators with LOB data: READTEXT, WRITETEXT, and UPDATETEXT. Because no datatypes can store this very large object, most manipulation of LOB data is done using text pointers. The three LOB operators take a text pointer as an argument and can allow you to access and manipulate only a subset of the data.

Part IV

Performance and Tuning

Chapter 14

Locking

Locking is a crucial function of any multiple-user database system, including Microsoft SQL Server. As you know, SQL Server manages multiple users simultaneously and ensures that all transactions observe the properties of the specified isolation level. At the highest isolation level, Serializable, SQL Server must make the multiple-user system yield results that are indistinguishable from those of a single-user system. It does this by automatically locking data to prevent changes made by one user from unexpectedly affecting work being done by another user on the same database at the same time.

THE LOCK MANAGER

SQL Server can lock data using several different modes. For example, read operations acquire shared locks and write operations acquire exclusive locks. Update locks are acquired during the initial portion of an update operation when the data is read. The SQL Server lock manager acquires and releases these locks. It also manages compatibility between lock modes, resolves deadlocks, and escalates locks if necessary. It controls locks on tables, on the pages of a table, on index keys, and on individual rows of data. Locks can also be held on system data—data that's private to the database system, such as page headers and indexes.

The lock manager provides two separate locking systems. The first system affects all fully shared data and provides row locks, page locks, and table locks for tables, data pages, text pages, and leaf-level index pages. The second system is used internally for index concurrency control, controlling access to internal data structures, and retrieving individual rows of data pages. This second system uses latches, which are less resource intensive than locks and provide performance optimization. You could use full-blown locks for all locking, but because of their complexity, they would slow down the system if they were used for all internal needs. If you examine locks using the *sp_lock* system stored procedure or a similar mechanism that gets information from the *syslockinfo* table, you cannot see latches—you see only information about locks for fully shared data.

Another way to look at the difference between locks and latches is that locks ensure the *logical* consistency of the data and latches ensure the *physical* consistency. Latching happens when you place a row physically on a page or move data in other ways, such as compressing the space on a page. SQL Server must guarantee that this data movement can happen without interference.

The Lock Manager and Isolation Levels

SQL Server supports all four transaction isolation levels specified by ANSI and ISO: Serializable, Repeatable Read, Read Committed, and Read Uncommitted. (See Chapter 3 and Chapter 12 for details.) To achieve the Serializable isolation level, you must prevent phantoms, because the transaction's behavior must be identical to what would have occurred had the transaction run on a single-user system. SQL Server provides serializability, which you can set using SET TRANSACTION ISOLATION LEVEL SERIALIZABLE. To support serializability, SQL Server locks index ranges using a special type of lock called a *key-range lock*. Such locks are held until the end of the transaction in order to prevent phantoms. If no index exists, the lock manager uses a table lock to guarantee serializability.

The lock manager provides fairly standard two-phase locking services. Although the names are similar, two-phase locking (2PL) and the two-phase commit (2PC) protocol are not directly related other than by the obvious fact that 2PC must use 2PL services. In 2PL, a transaction has a "growing" phase, during which it acquires locks, and a "shrinking" phase, during which it releases locks. To achieve serializability, all acquired locks are held until the end of the transaction and then are dropped all at once.

For a lower isolation level, such as Committed Read, locks can be released sooner—when the use of the object is completed. For example, if a range of data is being queried in the table, there will probably be shared locks outstanding. With Committed Read isolation, a shared lock is released as soon as the scan moves off one piece of data and onto the next. Exclusive locks, on the other hand, are always held until the end of the transaction so that the transaction can be rolled back if necessary.

With Serializable or Repeatable Read isolation, shared locks must be held until the end of the transaction to guarantee that the data that was read will not change or that new rows that meet the criteria of the query cannot be added while the transaction is in progress. Like shared locks, latches are not tied to the boundaries of a transaction because they are used to provide mutual exclusion (mutex) functionality rather than to directly lock data. For example, during a row insert in a table with a clustered index, the nearby index page is latched to prevent other inserts from colliding. The latches are needed to provide mutual exclusion only during long periods of time (that is, periods with more than a few instruction cycles).

Spinlocks

For shorter-term needs, SQL Server achieves mutual exclusion using a latch implemented with a spinlock. Spinlocks are used purely for mutual exclusion and never to lock user data. They are even more lightweight than latches, which are lighter than the full locks used for data and index leaf pages. The spinlock is the only functionality in SQL Server in which processor-specific assembly language is used. A spinlock is implemented in a few lines of assembly language specific to each processor type (such as *x*86/Pentium or Alpha). The requester of a spinlock repeats its request if the lock is not immediately available. (That is, the requester "spins" on the lock until it is free.)

Spinlocks are often used as mutexes within SQL Server for resources that are usually not busy. If a resource is busy, the duration of a spinlock is short enough that retrying is better than waiting and then being rescheduled by the operating system, which results in context switching between threads. The savings in context switches more than offsets the cost of spinning as long as you don't have to spin too long. Spinlocks are used for situations in which the wait for a resource is expected to be brief (or if no wait is expected).

Deadlocks

A deadlock occurs when two processes are waiting for a resource and neither process can advance because the other process prevents it from getting the resource. A true deadlock is a catch-22 in which, without intervention, neither process can ever progress. When a deadlock occurs, SQL Server intervenes automatically.

> **NOTE** A simple wait for a lock is not a deadlock. When the process that's holding the lock completes, the waiting process gets the lock. Lock waits are normal, expected, and necessary in multiple-user systems.

In SQL Server, two main types of deadlocks can occur: a cycle deadlock and a conversion deadlock. Figure 14-1 shows an example of a cycle deadlock. Process A starts a transaction, acquires an exclusive table lock on the *authors* table, and requests an exclusive table lock on the *publishers* table. Simultaneously, process B starts a transaction, acquires an exclusive lock on the *publishers* table, and requests an exclusive lock on the *authors* table. The two processes become deadlocked—caught in a "deadly embrace." Each process holds a resource needed by the other process.

Neither can progress, and, without intervention, both would be stuck in deadlock forever. You can actually generate the deadlock using SQL Query Analyzer, as follows:

1. Open a query window, and change your database context to the *pubs* database. Execute the following batch for process A:

   ```
   BEGIN TRAN
   UPDATE authors SET contract = 0
   GO
   ```

2. Open a second window, and execute this batch for process B:

   ```
   BEGIN TRAN
   UPDATE publishers SET city = 'Redmond', state = 'WA'
   GO
   ```

3. Go back to the first window, and execute this update statement:

   ```
   UPDATE publishers SET city = 'New Orleans', state = 'LA'
   GO
   ```

   At this point, the query should block. It is not deadlocked yet, however. It is waiting for a lock on the *publishers* table, and there is no reason to suspect that it won't eventually get that lock.

4. Go back to the second window, and execute this update statement:

   ```
   UPDATE authors SET contract = 1
   GO
   ```

   At this point, a deadlock occurs. The first connection will never get its requested lock on the *publishers* table because the second connection will not give it up until it gets a lock on the *authors* table. Since the first connection already has the lock on the *authors* table, we have a deadlock. One of the processes received the following error message. (Of course, the actual process ID reported will probably be different.)

   ```
   Server: Msg 1205, Level 13, State 1, Line 1
   Transaction (Process ID 55) was deadlocked on {lock} resources with
   another process and has been chosen as the deadlock victim. Rerun the
   transaction.
   ```

Figure 14-2 shows an example of a conversion deadlock. Process A and process B each hold a shared lock on the same page within a transaction. Each process wants to promote its shared lock to an exclusive lock but cannot do so because of the other process's lock. Again, intervention is required.

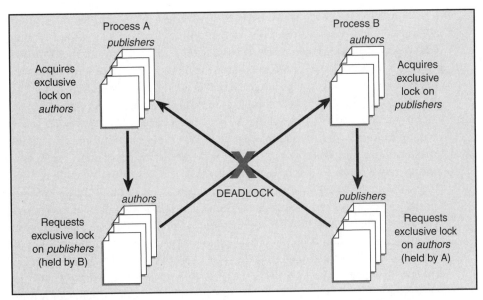

Figure 14-1. *A cycle deadlock resulting from each of two processes holding a resource needed by the other.*

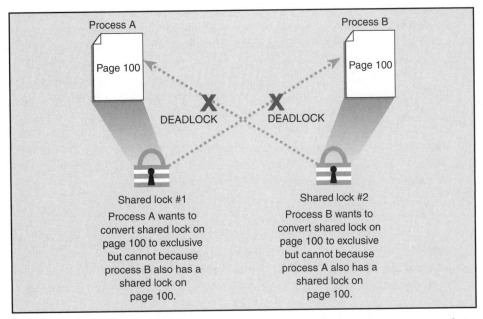

Figure 14-2. *A conversion deadlock resulting from two processes wanting to promote their locks on the same resource within a transaction.*

SQL Server automatically detects deadlocks and intervenes through the lock manager, which provides deadlock detection for regular locks. In SQL Server 2000, deadlocks can also involve resources other than locks. For example, if process A is holding a lock on Table1 and is waiting for memory to become available and process B has some memory it can't release until it acquires a lock on Table1, the processes will deadlock. Threads and communication buffers can also be involved in deadlocks. Latches are not involved in deadlock detection because SQL Server uses deadlock-proof algorithms when it acquires latches. When SQL Server detects a deadlock, it terminates one process's batch, rolling back the active transaction and releasing all that process's locks to resolve the deadlock.

In SQL Server 2000, a separate thread called LOCK_MONITOR checks the system for deadlocks every 5 seconds. The lock monitor also uses an internal counter called a *deadlock detection counter* to determine whether to check the system for deadlocks more often. The deadlock detection counter starts at a value of 3 and is reset to 3 if a deadlock occurs. If the LOCK_MONITOR thread finds no deadlocks when it checks at the end of its 5-second cycle, it decrements the deadlock detection counter. If the counter has a value greater than 0, the lock manager requests that the lock monitor also check all the locks for a deadlock cycle if a process requests a lock resource and is blocked. Thus, after 20 seconds of not finding any deadlocks, the deadlock detection counter is 0 and the lock manager stops requesting deadlock detection every time a process blocks on a lock. The deadlock detection counter stays at 0 most of the time and the checking for deadlocks happens only at the 5-second intervals of the lock monitor.

This LOCK_MONITOR thread checks for deadlocks by inspecting the list of waiting locks for any cycles, which indicate a circular relationship between processes holding locks and processes waiting for locks. SQL Server attempts to choose as the *victim* the process that would be the least expensive to roll back, considering the amount of work the process has already done. However, certain operations are marked as *golden,* or unkillable, and cannot be chosen as the deadlock victim. For example, a process involved in rolling back a transaction cannot be chosen as a deadlock victim because the changes being rolled back could be left in an indeterminate state, causing data corruption.

Using the SET DEADLOCK_PRIORITY LOW | NORMAL statement, you can make a process sacrifice itself as the victim if a deadlock is detected. If a process has a deadlock priority of LOW, it terminates when a deadlock is detected even if it is not the process that closed the loop. However, there is no counterpart SET option to set a deadlock priority to HIGH. As much as you might want your own processes to always come out the winner in a deadlock situation, this feature has not yet been implemented in SQL Server.

NOTE The lightweight latches and spinlocks used internally do not have deadlock detection services. Instead, deadlocks on latches and spinlocks are avoided rather than resolved. Avoidance is achieved via strict programming guidelines used by the SQL Server development team. These lightweight locks must be acquired in a hierarchy, and a process must not have to wait for a regular lock while holding a latch or spinlock. For example, one coding rule is that a process holding a spinlock must never directly wait for a lock or call another service that might have to wait for a lock, and a request can never be made for a spinlock that is higher in the acquisition hierarchy. By establishing similar guidelines for your development team for the order in which SQL Server objects are accessed, you can go a long way toward avoiding deadlocks in the first place.

In the example in Figure 14-1, the cycle deadlock could have been avoided if the processes had decided on a protocol beforehand—for example, if they had decided to always access the *authors* table first and the *publishers* table second. Then one of the processes would get the initial exclusive lock on the table being accessed first, and the other process would wait for the lock to be released. One process waiting for a lock is normal and natural. Remember, waiting is not a deadlock.

You should always try to have a standard protocol for the order in which processes access tables. If you know that the processes might need to update the row after reading it, they should initially request an update lock, not a shared lock. If both processes request an update lock rather than a shared lock, the process that is granted an update lock is assured that the lock can later be promoted to an exclusive lock. The other process requesting an update lock has to wait. The use of an update lock serializes the requests for an exclusive lock. Other processes needing only to read the data can still get their shared locks and read. Since the holder of the update lock is guaranteed an exclusive lock, the deadlock is avoided. We'll look in more detail at the compatibility of locks later in this chapter; additional information on deadlocks is presented in Chapter 16.

By the way, the time that your process holds locks should be minimal so other processes don't wait too long for locks to be released. Although you don't usually invoke locking directly, you can influence locking by keeping transactions as short as possible. For example, don't ask for user input in the middle of a transaction. Instead, get the input first and then quickly perform the transaction.

LOCK TYPES FOR USER DATA

Now we'll examine four aspects of locking user data. First, we'll look at the mode of locking (the type of lock). I already mentioned shared, exclusive, and update locks, and I'll go into more detail about these modes as well as others. Next, we'll look at the granularity of the lock, which specifies how much data is covered by a single lock. This can be a row, a page, an index key, a range of index keys, an extent, or an entire table. The third aspect of locking is the duration of the lock. As mentioned earlier, some locks are released as soon as the data has been accessed and some locks are held until the transaction commits or rolls back. For example, cursor scroll locks are held until a new FETCH operation is executed. The fourth aspect of locking concerns the ownership of the lock (the scope of the lock). Locks can be owned by a session, a transaction, or a cursor.

Lock Modes

SQL Server uses several locking modes, including shared locks, exclusive locks, update locks, and intent locks.

Shared Locks

Shared locks are acquired automatically by SQL Server when data is read. Shared locks can be held on a table, a page, an index key, or an individual row. Many processes can hold shared locks on the same data, but no process can acquire an exclusive lock on data that has a shared lock on it (unless the process requesting the exclusive lock is the same process as the one holding the shared lock). Normally, shared locks are released as soon as the data has been read, but you can change this by using query hints or a different transaction isolation level.

Exclusive Locks

SQL Server automatically acquires exclusive locks on data when it is modified by an insert, update, or delete operation. Only one process at a time can hold an exclusive lock on a particular data resource; in fact, as you'll see when we discuss lock compatibility, no locks of any kind can be acquired by a process if another process has the requested data resource exclusively locked. Exclusive locks are held until the end of the transaction. This means that the changed data is normally not available to any other process until the current transaction commits or rolls back. Other processes can decide to read exclusively locked data by using query hints.

Update Locks

Update locks are really not a separate kind of lock; they are a hybrid between shared and exclusive locks. They are acquired when SQL Server executes a data modification operation but first needs to search the table to find the resource that will be modified. Using query hints, a process can specifically request update locks, and in that case the update locks prevent the conversion deadlock situation presented in Figure 14-2.

Update locks provide compatibility with other current readers of data, allowing the process to later modify data with the assurance that the data hasn't been changed since it was last read. An update lock is not sufficient to allow you to change the data—all modifications require that the data resource being modified have an exclusive lock. An update lock acts as a serialization gate to queue future requests for the exclusive lock. (Many processes can hold shared locks for a resource, but only one process can hold an update lock.) As long as a process holds an update lock on a resource, no other process can acquire an update lock or an exclusive lock for that resource; instead, another process requesting an update or exclusive lock for the same resource must wait. The process holding the update lock can acquire an exclusive lock on that resource because the update lock prevents lock incompatibility with any other processes. You can think of update locks as "intent-to-update" locks, which is essentially the role they perform. Used alone, update locks are insufficient for updating data—an exclusive lock is still required for actual data modification. Serializing access for the exclusive lock lets you avoid conversion deadlocks.

Don't let the name fool you: update locks are not just for update operations. SQL Server uses update locks for any data modification operation that requires a search for the data prior to the actual modification. Such operations include qualified updates and deletes, as well as inserts into a table with a clustered index. In the latter case, SQL Server must first search the data (using the clustered index) to find the correct position at which to insert the new row. While SQL Server is only searching, it uses update locks to protect the data; only after it has found the correct location and begins inserting does it escalate the update lock to an exclusive lock.

Intent Locks

Intent locks are not really a separate mode of locking; they are a qualifier to the modes previously discussed. In other words, you can have intent shared locks, intent exclusive locks, and even intent update locks. Because SQL Server can acquire locks at different levels of granularity, a mechanism is needed to indicate that a component of a resource is already locked. For example, if one process tries to lock a table, SQL Server needs a way to determine whether a row (or a page) of that table is already locked. Intent locks serve this purpose. We'll discuss them in more detail when we look at lock granularity.

Special Lock Modes

SQL Server offers three additional lock modes: schema stability locks, schema modification locks, and bulk update locks. When queries are compiled, schema stability locks prevent other processes from acquiring schema modification locks, which are taken when a table's structure is being modified. A bulk update lock is acquired when the BULK INSERT command is executed or when the *bcp* utility is run to load data into a table. In addition, the copy operation must request this special lock by using the TABLOCK hint. Alternatively, the table can set the table option called *table lock on bulk load* to true, and then any bulk copy IN or BULK INSERT operation will automatically request a bulk update lock. If multiple connections have requested and received a bulk update lock, they can perform parallel loads into the same table.

Another lock mode that you might notice is the SIX lock. This mode is never requested directly by the lock manager but is the result of a conversion. If a transaction is holding a shared (S) lock on a resource and later an IX lock is needed, the lock mode will be indicated as SIX. For example, suppose you are operating at the Repeatable Read transaction isolation level and you issue the following batch:

```
SET TRANSACTION ISOLATION LEVEL REPEATABLE READ
BEGIN TRAN
SELECT * FROM bigtable
UPDATE bigtable
    SET col = 0
    WHERE keycolumn = 100
```

Assuming that the table is large, the SELECT statement will acquire a shared table lock. (If there are only a few rows in *bigtable*, SQL Server will acquire individual row or key locks.) The UPDATE statement will then acquire a single exclusive key lock to do the update of a single row, and the X lock at the key level will mean an IX lock at the page and table level. The table will then show SIX when viewed through *sp_lock*.

Table 14-1 shows most of the lock modes, as well as the abbreviations used in the output of *sp_lock*.

Abbreviation	*Lock Mode*	*Internal Code for Lock Mode*	*Description*
S	Shared	4	Allows other processes to read but not change the locked resource.
X	Exclusive	6	Prevents another process from modifying or reading data in the locked resource (unless the process is set to the Read Uncommitted isolation level).
U	Update	5	Prevents other processes from acquiring an update or exclusive lock; used when searching for the data to modify.

Table 14-1. *SQL Server lock modes.*

(continued)

Abbreviation	Lock Mode	Internal Code for Lock Mode	Description
IS	Intent shared	7	Indicates that a component of this resource is locked with a shared lock. This lock can be acquired only at the table or page level.
IU	Intent update	8	Indicates that a component of this resource is locked with an update lock. This lock can be acquired only at the table or page level.
IX	Intent exclusive	9	Indicates that a component of this resource is locked with an exclusive lock. This lock can be acquired only at the table or page level.
SIX	Shared with	11	Indicates that a resource intent exclusive lock holding a shared lock also has a component (a page or row) locked with an exclusive lock.
Sch-S	Schema stability	2	Indicates that a query using this table is being compiled.
Sch-M	Schema modification	3	Indicates that the structure of the table is being changed.
BU	Bulk update	13	Used when a bulk copy operation is copying data into a table and the TABLOCK hint is being applied (either manually or automatically).

Additional lock modes—called key-range locks—are taken only in Serializable isolation level for locking ranges of data. There are nine types of key-range locks, and each has a two-part name: The first part indicates the type of lock on the range of data between adjacent index keys, and the second part indicates the type of lock on the key itself. These nine types of key-range locks are described in Table 14-2.

Abbreviation	Internal Code for Lock Mode	Description
RangeS-S	14	Shared lock on the range between keys; shared lock on the key at the end of the range
RangeS-U	15	Shared lock on the range between keys; update lock on the key at the end of the range
RangeIn-Null	16	Exclusive lock to prevent inserts on the range between keys; no lock on the keys themselves
RangeX-X	22	Exclusive lock on the range between keys; exclusive lock on the key at the end of the range
RangeIn-S	17	Conversion lock created by S and RangeIn_Null lock
RangeIn-U	18	Conversion lock created by U and RangeIn_Null lock
RangeIn-X	19	Conversion of X and RangeIn_Null lock
RangeX-S	20	Conversion of RangeIn_Null and RangeS_S lock
RangeX-U	21	Conversion of RangeIn_Null and RangeS_U lock

Table 14-2. *Key-range locks.*

The RangeIn-Null lock is acquired when SQL Server attempts to insert into the range between keys. This type of lock is not often seen because it is typically very transient. It is held only until the correct location for insertion is found, and then the lock is escalated into an X lock. However, if you have one transaction scan a range of data using the Serializable isolation level and then another transaction tries to insert into that range, the second transaction will have a lock request in a WAIT state with the RangeIn-Null mode. You can observe this using the *sp_lock* command, as I'll describe in the section on viewing locks later in the chapter.

Lock Granularity

SQL Server can lock user data resources (not system resources, which are protected with latches) at the table, page, or row level. SQL Server also locks index keys and ranges of index keys. Figure 14-3 shows the possible lock levels in a table. Note that if the table has a clustered index, the data rows are at the leaf level of the clustered index and they are locked with key locks instead of row locks.

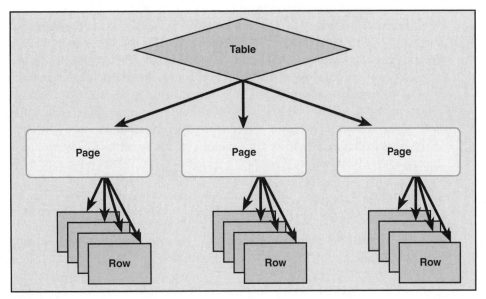

Figure 14-3. *Levels of granularity for SQL Server locks.*

The *syslockinfo* table keeps track of each lock by storing the type of resource locked (such as a row, key, or page), the mode of the lock, and an identifier for the specific resource. When a process requests a lock, SQL Server compares the lock requested to the resources already listed in the *syslockinfo* table and looks for an exact match on the resource type and identifier. (The lock modes don't have to be the same to yield an exact match.) However, if one process has a row exclusively locked in the *authors* table, for example, another process might try to get a lock on the entire *authors* table. Since these are two different resources, SQL Server does not find an exact match unless additional information is already stored in *syslockinfo*. This is what intent locks are for. The process that has the exclusive lock on a row of the *authors* table also has an intent exclusive lock on the page containing the row and another intent exclusive lock on the table containing the row. When the second process attempts to acquire the exclusive lock on the table, it finds a conflicting row already in the *syslockinfo* table on the same lock resource (the *authors* table). Not all requests for locks on resources that are already locked will result in a conflict. A conflict occurs when one process requests a lock on a resource that is already locked by another process in an incompatible lock mode. For example, two processes can each acquire shared locks on the same resource because shared locks are compatible with each other. I'll discuss lock compatibility in detail later in this chapter.

Key Locks

SQL Server 2000 supports two kinds of key locks, whose use depends on the isolation level of the current transaction. If the isolation level is Read Committed or Repeatable Read, SQL Server tries to lock the actual index keys accessed while processing the query. With a table that has a clustered index, the data rows are the leaf level of the index, and you will see key locks acquired. If the table is a heap, you might see key locks for the nonclustered indexes and row locks for the actual data.

If the isolation level is Serializable, the situation is special. We want to prevent phantoms, which means that if we have scanned a range of data within a transaction, we need to lock enough of the table to make sure that no one can insert a value into the range that was scanned. For example, we can issue the following query within an explicit transaction:

```
BEGIN TRAN
SELECT * FROM employees
WHERE salary BETWEEN 30000 AND 50000
```

Locks must be acquired to make sure that no new rows with *salary* values between 30000 and 50000 are inserted before the end of the transaction. Prior to version 7.0, SQL Server guaranteed this by locking whole pages or even the entire table. In many cases, however, this was too restrictive—more data was locked than the actual WHERE clause indicated, resulting in unnecessary contention. SQL Server 2000 uses key-range locks, which are associated with a particular key value in an index and indicate that all values between that key and the previous one in the index are locked.

Suppose we have an index on the *lastname* field in the *employees* table. We are in TRANSACTION ISOLATION LEVEL SERIALIZABLE and we issue this SELECT statement:

```
SELECT *
FROM employees
WHERE last_name BETWEEN 'Delaney' AND 'DuLaney'
```

If *Dallas*, *Donovan*, and *Duluth* are sequential leaf-level index keys in the table, the second two of these (*Donovan* and *Duluth*) acquire key-range locks (although only one row, for *Donovan*, is returned in the result set). The key-range locks prevent any inserts into the ranges ending with the two key-range locks. No values greater than *Dallas* and less than or equal to *Donovan* can be inserted, and no values greater than *Donovan* and less than or equal to *Duluth* can be inserted. Note that the key-range locks imply an open interval starting at the previous sequential key and a closed interval ending at the key on which the lock is placed. These two key-range locks prevent anyone from inserting either *Delany* or *Delanie*, which are in the range specified in the WHERE clause. However, the key-range locks would also prevent anyone from inserting *DeLancey* (which is greater than *Dallas* and less than *Donovan*) even though *DeLancey* is not in the query's specified range. Key-range locks are not perfect, but they do provide much greater concurrency than locking whole pages or tables, which was the only possibility in previous SQL Server versions.

Additional Lock Resources

Locking is also done on *extents*—units of disk space that are 64 KB in size (eight pages of 8 KB each). This kind of locking occurs automatically when a table or an index needs to grow and a new extent must be allocated. You can think of an extent lock as another type of special purpose latch, but it does show up in the output of the *sp_lock* procedure. Extents can have both shared extent and exclusive extent locks.

When you examine the output of *sp_lock*, notice that most processes hold a lock on at least one database. In fact, any process holding locks in any database other than *master* or *tempdb* will have a DB lock for that database. These are always shared locks and are used by SQL Server for determining when a database is in use. SQL Server detects DB locks when determining whether a database can be dropped, restored, or closed. Since *master* and *tempdb* cannot be dropped or closed, DB locks are unnecessary. In addition, *tempdb* is never restored, and to restore the *master* database the entire server must be started in single-user mode, so again, DB locks are unnecessary. Generally, you don't need to be concerned with extent or database locks, but you might see them if you are running *sp_lock* or perusing *syslockinfo*.

Application Locks

The method used by SQL Server to store information about locking and to check for incompatible locks is very straightforward and extensible. As you've seen, the SQL Server lock manager knows nothing about the object it is locking. It works only with strings representing the resources without knowing the actual structure of the item. If two processes are trying to obtain incompatible locks on the same resource, blocking will occur.

If the SQL Server developers were to decide to allow you to lock individual columns as well as rows, pages, and tables, they could simply decide on an internal code number for column locks, and then we could add that to the list of resources in Table 14-3.

Instead of adding new lock resources, SQL Server 2000 lets you extend the resources that can be locked. You can take advantage of the supplied mechanisms for detecting blocking and deadlocking situations, and you can choose to lock anything you like. These lock resources are called *application locks*. To define an application lock, you specify a name for the resource you are locking, a mode, an owner, and a timeout.

Two resources are considered to be the same resource and are subject to blocking if they have the same name and the same owner in the same database. Remember that by *lock owner* we mean the session, the transaction, or a cursor. For your own application locks, the only possible owners are transaction and session. Two requests for locks on the same resource can be granted if the modes of the locks requested are compatible. The locks are checked for compatibility using the same compatibility matrix used for SQL Server supplied locks.

For example, suppose you have a stored procedure that only one user at a time should execute. You can "lock" that procedure by using the *sp_getapplock* procedure to acquire a special lock, which means that someone is using this procedure. When the procedure is complete, you can use *sp_releaseapplock* to release the lock:

```
EXEC sp_getapplock 'ProcLock', 'Exclusive', 'session'
EXEC MySpecialProc <parameter list>
EXEC sp_releaseapplock 'ProcLock', 'session'
```

Until the lock is released using *sp_releaseapplock*, or until the session terminates, no other session can execute this procedure as long as it follows the protocol and uses *sp_getapplock* to request rights to the procedure before trying to execute it. SQL Server doesn't know what the resource *ProcLock* means. It just adds a row to the *syslockinfo* table that it will use to compare against other requested locks. Note that the procedure itself is not really locked. If another user or application doesn't know that this is a special procedure and tries to execute *MySpecialProc* without acquiring the application lock, SQL Server will not prevent the session from executing the procedure.

The resource name used in these procedures can be any identifier up to 255 characters long. The possible modes of the lock, which is used to check compatibility with other requests for this same resource, are Shared, Update, Exclusive, IntentExclusive, and IntentShared. There is no default; you must specify a mode. The possible values for lock owner, the third parameter, are transaction (the default) or session. A lock with an owner of transaction must be acquired with a user-defined transaction, and it will be automatically released at the end of the transaction without any need to call *sp_releaseapplock*. A lock with an owner of session will be released automatically only when the session disconnects.

Identifying Lock Resources

When the lock manager tries to determine whether a requested lock can be granted, it checks the *syslockinfo* table to determine whether a matching lock with a conflicting lock mode already exists. It compares locks by looking at the database ID (dbid), the object ID (objid), the type of resource locked, and the description of the specific resource referenced by the lock. The lock manager knows nothing about the meaning of the resource description. It simply compares the strings identifying the lock resources to look for a match. If it finds a match, it knows the resource is already locked; it then uses the lock compatibility matrix to determine whether the current lock is compatible with the one being requested. Table 14-3 shows all the lock resources, the abbreviations used in the output of *sp_lock*, and the information used to define the actual resource locked.

Resource	Abbre-viation	Internal Code for Resource	Resource Description	Example
Database	DB	2	None; the database is always indicated in the *dbid* column for every locked resource.	
Table	TAB	5	The table ID.	261575970 (Note that *sp_lock* shows the table ID in its own column rather than in the resource description column.)
Extent	EXT	8	File number:page number of the first page of the extent.	1:96
Page	PAG	6	File number:page number of the actual table or index page.	1:104
Index Key	KEY	7	A hashed value derived from all the key components and the locator. For a nonclustered index on a heap, where columns *c1* and *c2* are indexed, the hash would contain contributions from *c1*, *c2*, and the RID.	ac0001a10a00
Index Key Range	KEY	7	Same as Index Key.	ac0001a10a00
Row	RID	9	File number:page number:slot number of the actual row.	1:161:3
Application	APP	10	A hashed value derived from the name given to the lock	MyPr8adaea5f

Table 14-3. *Lockable resources in SQL Server.*

Note that key locks and key-range locks have identical resource descriptions. When we look at some examples of output from the *sp_lock* procedure, you'll see that you can distinguish between these types of locks by the value in the lock mode column.

Lock Duration

The length of time that a lock is held depends primarily on the mode of the lock and the transaction isolation level in effect. The default isolation level for SQL Server is Read Committed. At this level, shared locks are released as soon as SQL Server has read and processed the locked data. An exclusive lock is held until the end of the transaction, whether it is committed or rolled back. An update lock is also held until the end of the transaction unless it has been promoted to an exclusive lock, in which case the exclusive lock, as with all exclusive locks, remains for the duration of the transaction. If your transaction isolation level is Repeatable Read or Serializable, shared locks have the same duration as exclusive locks. That is, they are not released until the transaction is over.

In addition to changing your transaction isolation level, you can control the lock duration by using query hints. I'll discuss query hints for locking and for other purposes in Chapter 16.

Lock Ownership

Lock duration can also be affected by the lock ownership. There are three types of lock owners: transactions, cursors, and sessions. These are available through the *req_ownertype* column in the *syslockinfo* table. (This information is not visible through the *sp_lock* stored procedure.) A *req_ownertype* value of 1 indicates that the lock is owned by transaction, and its duration is as discussed as described in the previous section. Most of our locking discussion, in fact, deals with locks owned by a transaction.

A cursor lock has a *req_ownertype* value of 2. If a cursor is opened using a locking mode of SCROLL_LOCKS, a cursor lock is held on every row fetched until the next row is fetched or the cursor is closed. Even if the transaction commits before the next fetch, the cursor lock is not released.

Locks owned by a session have a *req_ownertype* value of 3. A session lock is one taken on behalf of a process that is outside the scope of a transaction. The most common example is a database lock, as discussed earlier. A process acquires a session lock on the database when it issues the USE database command, and that lock isn't released until another USE command is issued or until the process is disconnected.

Viewing Locks

To see the locks currently outstanding in the system as well as those that are being waited for, examine the *syslockinfo* system table or execute the system stored procedure *sp_lock*. The *syslockinfo* table is not really a system table. It is not maintained on disk because locks are not maintained on disk. Rather, it is materialized in table format based on the lock manager's current accounting of locks each time *syslockinfo* is queried. Another way to watch locking activity is with the excellent graphical representation of locking status provided by SQL Server Enterprise Manager. Even those who think that GUIs are for wimps can appreciate SQL Server Enterprise Manager's view of locking.

In some cases, the output of *sp_lock* can be voluminous. You can reduce the output by specifying one or two process ID values; *sp_lock* will then show you only locks held by those processes. The process ID for a particular connection is available using the system function @@spid. You can execute *sp_lock* and specify only your current connection:

```
EXEC sp_lock @@spid
```

However, even limiting the output to just the locks for the current connection can sometimes generate more output that you're interested in. To produce the lock output, SQL Server must translate internal ID numbers for the type of lock and mode of lock into the strings shown in Tables 14-1, 14-2, and 14-3. To do this translation, SQL Server uses the *spt_values* table in the *master* database as a giant lookup table. If you're using the Serializable isolation level, locks can be held on this table in the *master* database as well as on temporary tables in *tempdb*. Having to wade through these additional locks—which exist only because you're running *sp_lock* to examine your locks—can make it difficult to understand the locks on your user data. To help solve this problem, I have written a modified *sp_lock* procedure called *sp_lock2*, which does not print out any locks in the *master*, *model*, *tempdb*, or *msdb* databases. In addition, the procedure translates the database ID into the database name. You can find the script to create *sp_lock2* on the companion CD.

The following examples show what each of the lock types and modes discussed earlier look like when reported by the *sp_lock2* procedure. Note that the call to the *sp_lock2* procedure is preceded by the keyword EXECUTE, which is required when the call to a stored procedure is not the first item in a batch. Note also that the *sp_lock2* procedure is given an argument of @@spid so that we'll see only locks for the current process.

Example 1: SELECT with Default Isolation Level

SQL BATCH

```
USE PUBS
SET TRANSACTION ISOLATION LEVEL READ COMMITTED
BEGIN TRAN
SELECT * FROM authors
WHERE au_lname = 'Ringer'
EXEC sp_lock2 @@spid
COMMIT TRAN
```

OUTPUT OF sp_lock2

spid	Database	ObjId	IndId	Type	Resource	Mode	Status
52	pubs	0	0	DB		S	GRANT

The only lock we have is the DB lock. No locks on the *authors* table are held at this point because the batch was doing only select operations that acquired shared locks. By default, the shared locks are released as soon as the data has been read, so by the time *sp_lock2* is executed, the locks are no longer held.

Example 2: SELECT with Repeatable Read Isolation Level

SQL BATCH

```
USE PUBS
SET TRANSACTION ISOLATION LEVEL REPEATABLE READ
BEGIN TRAN
SELECT * FROM authors
WHERE au_lname = 'Ringer'
EXEC sp_lock2 @@spid
COMMIT TRAN
```

OUTPUT OF sp_lock2

spid	Database	ObjId	IndId	Type	Resource	Mode	Status
54	pubs	0	0	DB		S	GRANT
54	pubs	1977058079	2	KEY	(62039d7395e8)	S	GRANT
54	pubs	1977058079	1	PAG	1:88	IS	GRANT
54	pubs	1977058079	2	PAG	1:116	IS	GRANT
54	pubs	1977058079	1	KEY	(04015bb61919)	S	GRANT
54	pubs	1977058079	1	KEY	(1201b4159b48)	S	GRANT
54	pubs	1977058079	2	KEY	(6e021955d8e9)	S	GRANT
54	pubs	1977058079	0	TAB		IS	GRANT

Because the *authors* table has a clustered index, the rows of data are all index rows in the leaf level. The locks on the individual rows are marked as key locks instead of row locks. There are also key locks at the leaf level of the nonclustered index on the table. In the *authors* table, the nonclustered index is on the author's last name (*au_lname*) column, and that is the index being traversed to find the specified rows. You can tell the clustered and nonclustered indexes apart by the value in the *IndId* field: the data rows have an *IndId* value of 1, and the nonclustered index rows have an *IndId* value of 2. Because the transaction isolation level is Repeatable Read, the shared locks are held until the transaction is finished. Note that the two rows and two index rows have shared (S) locks, and the data and index pages, as well as the table itself, have intent shared (IS) locks.

Example 3: SELECT with Serializable Isolation Level

SQL BATCH

```
USE PUBS
SET TRANSACTION ISOLATION LEVEL SERIALIZABLE
BEGIN TRAN
SELECT * FROM authors
WHERE au_lname = 'Ringer'
EXEC sp_lock2 @@spid
COMMIT TRAN
```

OUTPUT OF *sp_lock2*

spid	Database	ObjId	IndId	Type	Resource	Mode	Status
56	pubs	0	0	DB		S	GRANT
56	pubs	1977058079	2	KEY	(62039d7395e8)	RangeS-S	GRANT
56	pubs	1977058079	1	PAG	1:88	IS	GRANT
56	pubs	1977058079	2	PAG	1:116	IS	GRANT
56	pubs	1977058079	1	KEY	(04015bb61919)	S	GRANT
56	pubs	1977058079	1	KEY	(1201b4159b48)	S	GRANT
56	pubs	1977058079	2	KEY	(6e021955d8e9)	RangeS-S	GRANT
56	pubs	1977058079	0	TAB		IS	GRANT
56	pubs	1977058079	2	KEY	(4903312f82bf)	RangeS-S	GRANT

The locks held with the Serializable isolation level are almost identical to those held with the Repeatable Read isolation level. The main difference is in the mode of the lock. The two-part mode RangeS-S indicates a key-range lock in addition to the lock on the key itself. The first part (RangeS) is the lock on the range of keys between (and including) the key holding the lock and the previous key in the index. The key-range locks prevent other transactions from inserting new rows into the table that meet the condition of this query; that is, no new rows with a last name of *Ringer* can be inserted. The key-range locks are held on ranges in the nonclustered index on *au_lname* and *au_fname* (*IndId* = 2) because that is the index used to find the qualifying rows. There are three key locks in the nonclustered index because three different ranges need to be locked. SQL Server must lock the range from the key preceding the first *Ringer* in the index up to the first *Ringer*, it must lock the range between the two instances of *Ringer*, and it must lock the range from the second *Ringer* to the next key in the index. (So actually nothing between *Ringer* and the previous key, *Panteley*, and nothing between *Ringer* and the next key, *Smith*, could be inserted. For example, we could not insert an author with the last name *Pike* or *Singh*.)

Example 4: Update Operations

SQL BATCH

```
USE PUBS
SET TRANSACTION ISOLATION LEVEL READ COMMITTED
BEGIN TRAN
UPDATE authors
SET contract = 0
WHERE au_lname = 'Ringer'
EXEC sp_lock2 @@spid
COMMIT TRAN
```

OUTPUT OF *sp_lock2*

spid	Database	ObjId	IndId	Type	Resource	Mode	Status
57	pubs	0	0	DB		S	GRANT
57	pubs	1977058079	1	PAG	1:88	IX	GRANT
57	pubs	1977058079	1	KEY	(04015bb61919)	X	GRANT
57	pubs	1977058079	1	KEY	(1201b4159b48)	X	GRANT
57	pubs	1977058079	0	TAB		IX	GRANT

The two rows in the leaf level of the clustered index are locked with X locks. The page and the table are then locked with IX locks. I mentioned earlier that SQL Server actually acquires update locks while it looks for the rows to update. However, these are escalated to X locks when the actual update is done, and by the time the *sp_lock2* procedure is run, the update locks are gone. Unless you actually force update locks with a query hint, you might never see them in the output of *sp_lock or sp_lock2*.

Example 5: Update with Serializable Isolation Level Using an Index

```
USE PUBS
SET TRANSACTION ISOLATION LEVEL SERIALIZABLE
BEGIN TRAN
UPDATE authors
SET contract = 0
WHERE au_lname = 'Ringer'
EXEC sp_lock2 @@spid
COMMIT TRAN
```

OUTPUT OF *sp_lock2*

spid	Database	ObjId	IndId	Type	Resource	Mode	Status
53	pubs	0	0	DB		S	GRANT
53	pubs	1977058079	2	KEY	(62039d7395e8)	RangeS-U	GRANT
53	pubs	1977058079	0	TAB		IX	GRANT
53	pubs	1977058079	2	KEY	(4903312f82bf)	RangeS-U	GRANT
53	pubs	1977058079	1	PAG	1:88	IX	GRANT
53	pubs	1977058079	2	KEY	(6e021955d8e9)	RangeS-U	GRANT
53	pubs	1977058079	2	PAG	1:116	IU	GRANT
53	pubs	1977058079	1	KEY	(04015bb61919)	X	GRANT
53	pubs	1977058079	1	KEY	(1201b4159b48)	X	GRANT

Again, notice that the key-range locks are on the nonclustered index used to find the relevant rows. The range interval itself needs only a share lock to prevent insertions, but the searched keys have U locks so that no other process can attempt to update them. The keys in the table itself (*IndId* = 1) obtain the exclusive lock when the actual modification is made.

Now let's look at an update operation with the same isolation level when no index can be used for the search.

Example 6: Update with Serializable Isolation Level Not Using an Index

```
USE PUBS
SET TRANSACTION ISOLATION LEVEL SERIALIZABLE
BEGIN TRAN
UPDATE authors
SET contract = 1
WHERE state = 'UT'
EXEC sp_lock2 @@spid
COMMIT TRAN
```

OUTPUT OF sp_lock2

```
spid Database ObjId         IndId  Type  Resource          Mode      Status
---- --------  -----------   ------ ----  ---------------   --------  ------
53   pubs      1977058079    1      KEY   (0b018636f9dc)    RangeS-U  GRANT
53   pubs      0             0      DB                      S         GRANT
53   pubs      1977058079    1      KEY   (100125852812)    RangeS-U  GRANT
53   pubs      1977058079    1      KEY   (1001898f02b5)    RangeS-U  GRANT
53   pubs      1977058079    1      KEY   (02010b688383)    RangeS-U  GRANT
53   pubs      1977058079    1      KEY   (0401c963b692)    RangeS-U  GRANT
53   pubs      1977058079    1      KEY   (06013d38d450)    RangeS-U  GRANT
53   pubs      1977058079    1      KEY   (0d01ac7ad21d)    RangeS-U  GRANT
53   pubs      1977058079    0      TAB                     IX        GRANT
53   pubs      1977058079    1      KEY   (0c01f170d106)    RangeS-U  GRANT
53   pubs      1977058079    1      KEY   (10018e6baefb)    RangeS-U  GRANT
53   pubs      1977058079    1      KEY   (0501dc9d152f)    RangeS-U  GRANT
53   pubs      1977058079    1      KEY   (0801c4f7a625)    RangeS-U  GRANT
53   pubs      1977058079    1      KEY   (0c019fc272ba)    RangeS-U  GRANT
53   pubs      1977058079    1      KEY   (0101aedb232b)    RangeS-U  GRANT
53   pubs      1977058079    1      KEY   (0601989a35e6)    RangeS-U  GRANT
53   pubs      1977058079    1      KEY   (0e01733a43ca)    RangeS-U  GRANT
53   pubs      1977058079    1      KEY   (0601d808a263)    RangeS-U  GRANT
53   pubs      1977058079    1      KEY   (070199a50c2d)    RangeS-U  GRANT
53   pubs      1977058079    1      PAG   1:88              IX        GRANT
53   pubs      1977058079    1      KEY   (100198c3f985)    RangeS-U  GRANT
53   pubs      1977058079    1      KEY   (ffffffffffff)    RangeS-U  GRANT
53   pubs      1977058079    1      KEY   (0701a9d28094)    RangeS-U  GRANT
53   pubs      1977058079    1      KEY   (02014f0bec4e)    RangeS-U  GRANT
53   pubs      1977058079    1      KEY   (0901ce1ba5f0)    RangeS-U  GRANT
53   pubs      1977058079    1      KEY   (04015bb61919)    RangeX-X  GRANT
53   pubs      1977058079    1      KEY   (1201b4159b48)    RangeX-X  GRANT
```

The locks here are similar to those in the previous example except that all the locks are on the table itself (*IndId* = 1). A clustered index scan (on the entire table) had to be done, so all keys initially received the RangeS-U lock, and when the two rows were eventually modified, the locks on those keys escalated to the RangeX-X lock.

Example 7: Creating a Table

SQL BATCH

```
USE PUBS
SET TRANSACTION ISOLATION LEVEL READ COMMITTED
BEGIN TRAN
SELECT *
INTO newTitles
FROM titles
WHERE price < 5
EXEC sp_lock2 @@spid
COMMIT TRAN
```

OUTPUT OF *sp_lock2*

spid	Database	ObjId	IndId	Type	Resource	Mode	Status
57	pubs	0	0	DB	[BULK-OP-LOG]	NULL	GRANT
57	pubs	0	0	DB		S	GRANT
57	pubs	0	0	DB	[BULK-OP-DB]	NULL	GRANT
57	pubs	1	0	TAB		IX	GRANT
57	pubs	3	0	TAB		IX	GRANT
57	pubs	2	0	TAB		IX	GRANT
57	pubs	3	2	KEY	(e40194df4eba)	X	GRANT
57	pubs	3	2	KEY	(7b0152f4ac0f)	X	GRANT
57	pubs	3	2	KEY	(ec01c5f30203)	X	GRANT
57	pubs	0	0	PAG	1:146	X	GRANT
57	pubs	0	0	PAG	1:145	X	GRANT
57	pubs	3	2	KEY	(410288dc0a1c)	X	GRANT
57	pubs	0	0	PAG	1:199	X	GRANT
57	pubs	0	0	PAG	1:198	X	GRANT
57	pubs	0	0	PAG	1:197	X	GRANT
57	pubs	0	0	PAG	1:196	X	GRANT
57	pubs	0	0	PAG	1:195	X	GRANT
57	pubs	0	0	PAG	1:194	X	GRANT
57	pubs	0	0	PAG	1:193	X	GRANT
57	pubs	0	0	PAG	1:192	X	GRANT
57	pubs	0	0	EXT	1:192	X	GRANT
57	pubs	3	1	KEY	(a1007beae6ee)	X	GRANT
57	pubs	3	1	KEY	(9a00f1a5ee93)	X	GRANT
57	pubs	3	1	KEY	(a000954553fc)	X	GRANT
57	pubs	3	1	KEY	(9d00c35530a4)	X	GRANT
57	pubs	3	1	KEY	(9c002dfa85b6)	X	GRANT
57	pubs	3	2	KEY	(4d02b937e929)	X	GRANT
57	pubs	3	2	KEY	(c6029c7b5ab8)	X	GRANT
57	pubs	1	1	KEY	(97009fa6c549)	X	GRANT
57	pubs	3	2	KEY	(d2016d108bf1)	X	GRANT
57	pubs	3	1	KEY	(98007a6de739)	X	GRANT
57	pubs	3	1	KEY	(990094c2522b)	X	GRANT
57	pubs	3	1	KEY	(9e00a6328c1c)	X	GRANT
57	pubs	3	1	KEY	(9b00489d390e)	X	GRANT
57	pubs	3	1	KEY	(9f00f022ef44)	X	GRANT
57	pubs	3	2	KEY	(d501db08ee70)	X	GRANT
57	pubs	3	2	KEY	(2f02d5933c81)	X	GRANT
57	pubs	0	0	IDX	IDX: 5:725577623	X	GRANT
57	pubs	725577623	0	TAB		Sch-M	GRANT
57	pubs	1	2	KEY	(2e02001f6a2c)	X	GRANT
57	pubs	2	1	KEY	(9700cdd96cc9)	X	GRANT
57	pubs	3	2	KEY	(6702012f70a8)	X	GRANT
57	pubs	1	3	KEY	(9700eaa6a30d)	X	GRANT

⋮

Very few of these locks are actually acquired on elements of the new table. In the *ObjId* column, notice that most of the objects have an ID of less than 100, which means that they are system tables. As the new *newTitles* table is built, SQL Server acquires locks on *sysobjects* and *syscolumns* to record information about this new table. Also notice the schema modification (Sch-M) lock on the new table as well as the extent (EXT) locks. While the table is being built, the extents are not marked as belonging to the table; you can see that the *ObjId* is 0. In the output in this example, the extent ID is shown as 1:192. This means that page 192 in file 1 is the first page of the extent. You can also see that the subsequent seven pages (193–199) in this extent are all exclusively locked while the table is being created.

Example 8: Row Locks

SQL BATCH

```
USE PUBS
SET TRANSACTION ISOLATION LEVEL READ COMMITTED
BEGIN TRAN
UPDATE newTitles
SET price = 3.99
WHERE type = 'business'
EXEC sp_lock2 @@spid
ROLLBACK TRAN
```

OUTPUT OF sp_lock2

spid	Database	ObjId	IndId	Type	Resource	Mode	Status
58	pubs	0	0	DB		S	GRANT
58	pubs	693577509	0	TAB		IX	GRANT
58	pubs	693577509	0	PAG	1:192	IX	GRANT
58	pubs	693577509	0	RID	1:192:0	X	GRANT

There are no indexes on the *newTitles* table, so the lock on the actual row meeting our criterion is an exclusive (X) lock on the row (RID). As expected, IX locks are taken on the page and the table.

LOCK COMPATIBILITY

Two locks are compatible if one lock can be granted while another lock on the same object held by a different process is outstanding. On the other hand, if a lock requested for an object is not compatible with a lock currently being held, the requesting connection must wait for the lock. For example, if a shared page lock exists on a page, another process requesting a shared page lock for the same page is granted the lock because the two lock types are compatible. But a process that requests an exclusive lock for the same page is not granted the lock because an exclusive lock is not compatible with the shared lock already held. Table 14-4 summarizes the compatibility of locks in SQL Server. *Yes* indicates that the lock held is compatible with the lock requested; *No* means that they're not compatible.

Requested Mode	Existing Granted Mode								
	IS	*S*	*U*	*IX*	*SIX*	*X*	*Sch-S*	*Sch-M*	*BU*
IS	Yes	Yes	Yes	Yes	Yes	No	Yes	No	No
S	Yes	Yes	Yes	No	No	No	Yes	No	No
U	Yes	Yes	No	No	No	No	Yes	No	No
IX	Yes	No	No	Yes	No	No	Yes	No	No
SIX	Yes	No	No	No	No	No	Yes	No	No
X	No	No	No	No	No	No	Yes	No	No
Sch-S	Yes	Yes	Yes	Yes	Yes	Yes	Yes	No	Yes
Sch-M	No	No	No	No	No	No	No	No	No
BU	No	No	No	No	No	No	Yes	No	Yes

Table 14-4. *SQL Server's lock compatibility matrix.*

Lock compatibility comes into play between locks on different resources, such as table locks and page locks. A table and a page obviously represent an implicit hierarchy since a table is made up of multiple pages. If an exclusive page lock is held on one page of a table, another process cannot get even a shared table lock for that table. This hierarchy is protected using intent locks. A process acquiring an exclusive page lock, update page lock, or intent exclusive page lock first acquires an intent exclusive lock on the table. This intent exclusive table lock prevents another process from acquiring the shared table lock on that table. (Remember that intent exclusive and shared locks are not compatible.)

Similarly, a process acquiring a shared row lock must first acquire an intent shared lock for the table, which prevents another process from acquiring an exclusive table lock. Or if the exclusive table lock already exists, the intent shared lock is not granted and the shared page lock has to wait until the exclusive table lock is released. Without intent locks, process A can lock a page in a table with an exclusive page lock and process B can place an exclusive table lock on the same table and hence think that it has a right to modify the entire table, including the page that process A has exclusively locked.

> **NOTE**   Obviously, lock compatibility is an issue only when the locks affect the same object. For example, two or more processes can each hold exclusive page locks simultaneously as long as the locks are on different pages or different tables.

Even if two locks are compatible, the requester of the second lock might still have to wait if an incompatible lock is waiting. For example, suppose that process A holds a shared page lock. Process B requests an exclusive page lock and must wait because the shared page lock and the exclusive page lock are not compatible. Process C requests a shared page lock that is compatible with the shared page already outstanding to process A. However, the shared page lock cannot be immediately granted. Process C must wait for its shared page lock because process B is ahead of it in the lock queue with a request (exclusive page) that is not compatible.

By examining the compatibility of locks not only with processes granted but also processes waiting, SQL Server prevents *lock starvation,* which can result when requests for shared locks keep overlapping so that the request for the exclusive lock can never be granted.

INTERNAL LOCKING ARCHITECTURE

Locks are not on-disk structures—you won't find a lock field directly on a data page or a table header—because it would be too slow to do disk I/O for locking operations. Locks are internal memory structures—they consume part of the memory used for SQL Server. Each locked data resource (a row, index key, page, or table) requires 64 bytes of memory to keep track of the database, the type of lock, and the information describing the locked resource. Each process holding a lock also must have a lock owner block of 32 bytes. A single transaction can have multiple lock owner blocks; a scrollable cursor sometimes uses several. Also, one lock can have many lock owner blocks, as in the case with a shared lock. Finally, each process waiting for a lock has a lock waiter block of another 32 bytes. Since lock owner blocks and lock waiter blocks have identical structures, I'll use the term *lock owner block* to refer to both of them.

The lock manager maintains a lock hash table. Lock resources, contained within a lock block, are hashed to determine a target hash slot in the hash table. (I'll discuss hashing in detail when I talk about the SQL Server hash join algorithm in Chapter 15.) All lock blocks that hash to the same slot are chained together from one entry in the hash table. Each lock block contains a 16-byte field that describes the locked resource. This 16-byte description is viewable in the *syslockinfo* table in the *rsc_bin* column. I'll dissect that column later in this section. The lock block also contains pointers to lists of lock owner blocks. A lock owner block represents a process that has been granted a lock, is waiting for the lock, or is in the process of converting to the lock. Figure 14-4 shows the general lock architecture.

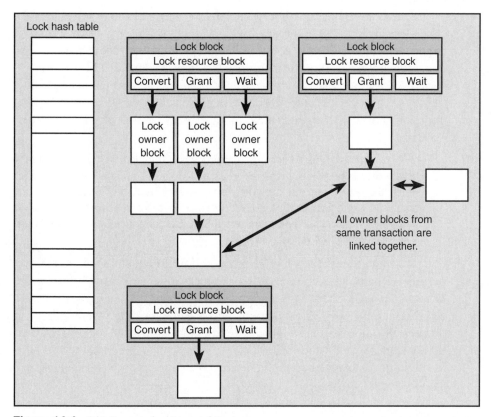

Figure 14-4. *SQL Server's locking architecture.*

The number of slots in the hash table is based on the system's physical memory, as shown in Table 14-5. All instances of SQL Server on the same machine will have a hash table with the same number of slots. Each entry in the lock hash table is 16 bytes in size and consists of a pointer to a list of lock blocks and a spinlock to guarantee nonconcurrent access to the same slot.

Physical Memory (MB)	Number of Slots	Memory Used
< 32	2^13 = 8K	128 KB
>= 32 and < 64	2^15 = 32K	512 KB
>= 64 and < 128	2^16= 64K	1 MB
>= 128 and < 512	2^17 = 128K	2 MB
>= 512 and < 1024	2^18 = 256K	4 MB
>= 1024	2^19 = 512K	8 MB

Table 14-5. *Number of slots in the internal lock hash table.*

The lock manager preallocates a number of lock blocks and lock owner blocks at server startup. If the number of locks is fixed by *sp_configure*, it allocates that configured number of lock blocks and the same number of lock owner blocks. If the number is not fixed (0 means auto-tune), it allocates 500 lock blocks on a SQL Server 2000, Desktop Edition server and 2500 lock blocks for the other editions. It allocates twice as many (2 * # lock blocks) of the lock owner blocks. At their maximum, the static allocations can't consume more than 25 percent of the committed buffer pool size.

> **NOTE**   In this context, I use the term *process* to refer to a SQL Server subtask. Every user connection is referred to as a process, as are the checkpoint manager, the lazywriter, the log writer, and the lock monitor. But these are only subtasks within SQL Server, not processes from the perspective of the operating system, which considers the entire SQL Server engine to be a single process with multiple threads.

When a request for a lock is made and no free lock blocks remain, the lock manager dynamically allocates new lock blocks instead of denying the lock request. The lock manager cooperates with the global memory manager to negotiate for server allocated memory. Each lock contains a flag indicating whether the block was dynamically allocated or preallocated. When necessary, the lock manager can free the dynamically allocated lock blocks. The lock manager is limited to 60 percent of the buffer manager's committed target size allocation to lock blocks and lock owner blocks.

Lock Blocks

The lock block is the key structure in SQL Server's locking architecture, as shown earlier in Figure 14-4. A lock block contains the following information:

- Lock resource name

- Pointers to connect the lock blocks to the lock hash table

- General summary information

- Pointer to a list of lock owner blocks for locks on this resource that have been granted (granted list)

- Pointer to a list of lock owner blocks for locks on this resource that are waiting to be converted to another lock mode (convert list)

- Pointer to a list of lock owner blocks for locks that have been requested on this resource but have not yet been granted (wait list)

The lock resource block is the most important element of the lock block. Its structure is shown in Figure 14-5. Each "row" in the figure represents 4 bytes, or 32 bits.

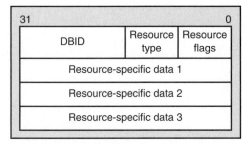

Figure 14-5. *The structure of a lock resource block.*

The meanings of the fields shown in Figure 14-5 are described in Table 14-6. The value in the "resource type" byte is one of the locking resources described earlier in Table 14-3 (page 789). The meaning of the values in the three data fields varies depending on the type of resource being described. SR indicates a subresource (which I'll describe shortly).

| | *Resource Contents* | | |
Resource Type	*Data 1*	*Data 2*	*Data 3*
Database (2)	SR	0	0
File (3)	File ID	0	0
Index (4)	Object ID	SR	Index ID
Table (5)	Object ID	SR	0
Page (6)	Page number		0
Key (7) (For a Key resource, Data2 is 2 bytes and Data3 is 6 bytes.)	Object ID	Index ID	Hashed key
Extent (8)	Extent ID		0
RID (9)	RID		0
Application (10) (For an Application resource, only the first 4 bytes of the name are used; the remaining bytes are hashed.)	Application resource name		

Table 14-6. *The meaning of fields in the lock resource block.*

Following are some of the possible SR (SubResouce) values:

- If the lock is on a DB resource, SR indicates one of the following:
  - ❏   Full database lock
  - ❏   Bulk operation lock
- If the lock is on a Table resource, SR indicates one of the following:
  - ❏   Full table lock (default)
  - ❏   Update statistics lock
  - ❏   Compile lock
- If the lock is on an Index resource, SR indicates one of the following:
  - ❏   Full index lock (default)
  - ❏   Index ID lock
  - ❏   Index name lock

Lock Owner Blocks

Each lock owned or waited for by a session is represented in a lock owner block. Lists of lock owner blocks form the grant, convert, and wait lists that hang off of the lock blocks. Each lock owner block for a granted lock is linked with all other lock owner blocks for the same transaction or session so that they can be freed as appropriate when the transaction or session ends.

Syslockinfo Table

The system procedures *sp_lock* and *sp_lock2* are based on information extracted from the *syslockinfo* table, which exists only in the *master* database. Lots more information, including the name of the lock owner, is kept in the *syslockinfo* table. Table 14-7 shows the columns in that table. Columns prefixed by *rsc_* are taken from a lock resource block. Columns prefixed by *req_* are taken from a lock owner block.

Column Name	Description
rsc_text	Textual description of a lock resource. Contains a portion of the resource name.
rsc_bin	Binary lock resource. Described in Figure 14-5 and Table 14-6.

Table 14-7. *Columns in the* syslockinfo *table.*   (continued)

Column Name	Description
rsc_valblk	Lock value block. Some resource types might include additional data in the lock resource that is not hashed by the lock manager to determine ownership of a particular lock resource. For example, page locks are not owned by a particular object ID. For lock escalation and other purposes, however, the object ID of a page lock might be placed in the lock value block.
rsc_dbid	Database ID.
rsc_indid	Index ID associated with the resource, if appropriate.
rsc_objid	Object ID associated with the resource, if appropriate.
rsc_type	Resource type from Table 14-3.
rsc_flag	Internal resource flags.
req_mode	Lock request mode. This column is the lock mode of the requester and represents either the granted mode or the convert or waiting mode. Can be any of the modes listed in Tables 14-1 or 14-2.
req_status	Status of the lock request. 1 = Granted 2 = Converting 3 = Waiting
req_refcnt	Lock reference count. Each time a transaction asks for a lock on a particular resource, a reference count is incremented. The lock cannot be released until the reference count equals 0.
req_cryrefcnt	Reserved for future use. Always set to 0.
req_lifetime	Lock lifetime bitmap. During certain query processing strategies, locks must be maintained on resources until the query processor has completed a particular phase of the query. The lock lifetime bitmap is used by the query processor and the transaction manager to denote groups of locks that can be released when a certain phase of a query is completed. Certain bits in the bitmap are used to denote locks that are held until the end of a transaction, even if their reference count equals 0.

(continued)

Table 14-7. *continued*

Column Name	Description
req_spid	Process ID of the session requesting the lock.
req_ecid	Execution context ID (ECID). Used to denote which thread in a parallel operation owns a particular lock.
req_ownertype	Type of object associated with the lock. Can be one of the following: 1 = Transaction 2 = Cursor 3 = Session 4 = ExSession Note that 3 and 4 represent a special version of session locks that track database and filegroup locks, respectively.
req_transactionID	Unique transaction ID used in *syslockinfo* and in SQL Profiler events.
req_transactionUOW	Identifies the Unit of Work (UOW) ID of the DTC transaction. For non–MS DTC transactions, UOW is set to 0.

In *syslockinfo*, you can analyze the *rsc_bin* field as the resource block. Here's an example:

```
SELECT rsc_bin FROM master..syslockinfo
```

Here's an example result row:

```
0x00070500AAA1534E01000800000000000000
```

From left to right, with the appropriate byte swapping within each field, this example means the following:

- Byte 0: Flag: 0x00

- Bytes 1: Resource Type: 0x07, a Key resource

- Bytes 2 through 3: DBID: 0x0005
  And since it is a Key resource:

- Bytes 4 through 7: ObjectID: 0x4E53A1AA (1314103722 decimal)

- Bytes 8 through 9: IndexID: 0x0001 (the clustered index)

- Bytes 10 through 16: Hash Key Name: 0x080000000000

BOUND CONNECTIONS

Remember that the issue of lock contention applies only between different SQL Server processes. A process holding locks on a resource does not lock itself from the resource—only other processes are denied access. But any other process (or connection to SQL Server) can actually execute as the same application and user. It is common for applications to have more than one connection to SQL Server. Every such connection is treated as an entirely different SQL Server process, and by default no sharing of the "lock space" occurs between connections, even if they belong to the same user and the same application.

However, two or more different connections can share a lock space and hence not lock each other out. This capability is known as a *bound connection*. With a bound connection, the first connection asks SQL Server to give out its bind token. The bind token is passed by the application (using a client-side global variable, shared memory, or another method) for use in subsequent connections. The bind token acts as a "magic cookie" so that other connections can share the lock space of the original connection. Locks held by bound connections do not lock each other. (The *sp_getbindtoken* and *sp_bindsession* system stored procedures get and use the bind token.)

Bound connections are especially useful if you're writing an extended stored procedure—a function written in your own DLL—and that extended stored procedure needs to call back into the database to do some work. Without a bound connection, the extended stored procedure collides with its own calling process's locks. When multiple processes share a lock space and a transaction space by using bound connections, a COMMIT or ROLLBACK affects all the participating connections. If you are going to use bound connections for the purpose of passing the bind token to an extended stored procedure to call back into the server, you must use a second parameter of the constant 1. If no parameter of 1 is passed, the token cannot be used in an extended stored procedure.

Here's an example of using bound connections between two different windows in SQL Query Analyzer. In SQL Server 2000, you must be inside of a transaction in order to get a bind token. Since we don't have a controlling application to declare and store the bind token in a client-side variable, we have to actually copy it from the first session and paste it into the second. So, in your first query window, you execute this batch:

```
DECLARE @token varchar(255)
BEGIN TRAN
EXEC sp_getbindtoken @token OUTPUT
SELECT @token
GO
```

This should return something like the following:

```
-----------dPe---5---.?j0U<_WP?1HMK-3/D8;@1
```

Normally, you wouldn't have to look at this messy string; your application would just store it and pass it on without your ever having to see it. But for a quick example using SQL Query Analyzer, it's necessary to actually see the value. You use your keyboard or mouse to select the token string that you received and use it in the following batch in a second SQL Query Analyzer window:

```
EXEC sp_bindsession 'dPe---5---.?j0U<_WP?1HMK-3/D8;@1'
GO
```

Now go back to the first query window and execute a command that locks some data. Remember that we have already begun a transaction in order to call *sp_getbindtoken*. You can use something like this:

```
USE pubs
UPDATE titles
SET price = $100
GO
```

This should exclusively lock every row in the *titles* table. Now go to the second query window and select from the locked table:

```
SELECT title_id, price FROM titles
GO
```

You should be able to see all the $100 prices in the *titles* table, just as if you were part of the same connection as the first query. Besides sharing lock space, the bound connection also shares transaction space. You can execute a ROLLBACK TRAN in the second window even though the first one began the transaction. If the first connection tries to then issue a ROLLBACK TRAN, it gets this message:

```
Server: Msg 3903, Level 16, State 1, Line 1
The ROLLBACK TRANSACTION request has no corresponding BEGIN TRANSACTION.
The transaction active in this session has been committed or aborted by
another session.
```

SQL Server keeps track of bound connections in an internal structure called the XCB (transaction control block), which is used to relate multiple connections in a bound session. You can actually see which connections are bound using SQL Query Analyzer and an undocumented DBCC command. First, you need the spid (Server Process ID) of any connections you're interested in. You can get this value using the function @@spid:

```
SELECT @@spid
```

The DBCC command is called DBCC PSS. Most of the information returned is meaningful and relevant only to Microsoft Product Support Services (PSS) engineers. It is really just a coincidence that Microsoft's support service is called PSS; in this case, PSS stands for Process Status Structure. As you saw earlier with DBCC PAGE, for most of the undocumented stored procedures you must first enable them using trace flag 3604. So suppose we've determined that the Process ID value of the first connection above, which is updating the prices in the *titles* table, is 51, and the connection we've bound to it is 54. The following command will print the PSS from both connections:

```
DBCC TRACEON(3604)
GO
DBCC PSS(1,51)
DBCC PSS(1,54)
```

Here's some partial output:

```
PSS:
----


PSS @0x193731D8
---------------
pspid = 51                    m_dwLoginFlags = 0x03e0   plsid = 422666344
pbackground = 0
pbSid
-----
01                                      .
sSecFlags = 0x12              pdeadlockpri = 0          poffsets = 0x0
pss_stats = 0x0              ptickcount = 16806736
pcputickcount = 3363174526155                          ploginstamp = 17
ptimestamp = 2000-08-13 12:31:47.793                   prowcount = 21
plangid = 0                  pdateformat = 1           pdatefirst = 7
Language = us_english        RemServer =               UserName = sa
poptions = 0x28480860        poptions2 = 0x3f438       pline = 1
pcurstepno = 0               prowcount = 18            pstatlist = 0
pcurcmd = 253                pseqstat = 0              ptextsize = 64512
pretstat = 0                 pslastbatchstarttime = 2000-08-13 13:13:03.423
pmemusage = 19               hLicense = 0              tpFlags = 0x1
isolation_level = 2          fips_flag = 0x0           sSaveSecFlags = 0x0
psavedb = 0                  pfetchstat = 0            pcrsrows = 0
pslastbatchtime = 2000-08-13 13:13:03.473              pubexecdb = 0
fInReplicatedProcExec = 0 pMsqlXact = 0x19373f88       presSemCount = [0]9951900
presSemCount = [0]9951900 pcputot = 180               pcputotstart = 170
pcpucmdstart = 170           pbufread = 32             pbufreadstart = 31
plogbufread = 533            plogbufreadstart = 428    pbufwrite = 5
pbufwritestart = 4           pLockTimeout = 4294967295 pUtilResultSet = 0x0
:
```

(continued)

```
PSS:
----

PSS @0x195B51D8
---------------
pspid = 54                 m_dwLoginFlags = 0x03e0   plsid = 422666344
pbackground = 0
pbSid
-----
01
sSecFlags = 0x12           pdeadlockpri = 0          poffsets = 0x0
pss_stats = 0x0            ptickcount = 18289118
pcputickcount = 3658807285722                        ploginstamp = 24
ptimestamp = 2000-08-13 12:56:30.107                 prowcount = 21
plangid = 0                pdateformat = 1           pdatefirst = 7
Language = us_english      RemServer =               UserName = sa
poptions = 0x28480860      poptions2 = 0x3f438       pline = 1
pcurstepno = 0             prowcount = 18            pstatlist = 0
pcurcmd = 253              pseqstat = 0              ptextsize = 64512
pretstat = 0               pslastbatchstarttime = 2000-08-13 13:13:56.380
pmemusage = 6              hLicense = 0              tpFlags = 0x1
isolation_level = 2        fips_flag = 0x0           sSaveSecFlags = 0x0
psavedb = 0               pfetchstat = 0            pcrsrows = 0
pslastbatchtime = 2000-08-13 13:13:56.420            pubexecdb = 0
fInReplicatedProcExec = 0 pMsqlXact = 0x195b5f88     presSemCount = [0]9951900
presSemCount = [0]9951900 pcputot = 40              pcputotstart = 30
pcpucmdstart = 30          pbufread = 3              pbufreadstart = 2
plogbufread = 56           plogbufreadstart = 33     pbufwrite = 0
pbufwritestart = 0         pLockTimeout = 4294967295 pUtilResultSet = 0x0
```

I won't even try to describe each of the values returned, mainly because I don't know them all. Some of them are pretty self-explanatory, such as *pslastbatchstarttime*, *Language*, and *UserName*. You might be able to guess the meaning of some of them. The value for the isolation level can be 0 through 4, with the numbers 1 through 4 mapping to the four transaction isolation levels. The value of 2 in my output means Read Committed. You will sometimes get a 0 for this value, which indicates the default isolation, which is Read Committed for SQL Server.

I have shown the Process ID value and a value called *plsid* in boldface. The *plsid* value is the transaction space identifier, although it doesn't look at all like the value returned in SQL Query Analyzer for the bind token. You can see that the *plsid* value is the same for these two connections. If you run DBCC PSS and look at other connections besides these two that have been bound together, you should notice that they all have different *plsid* values.

ROW-LEVEL VS. PAGE-LEVEL LOCKING

The debate over whether row-level locking is better than page-level locking or vice-versa has been one of those near-religious wars and warrants a few comments here. Although some people would have you believe that one is always better, it's not really that simple.

Prior to version 7, the smallest unit of data that SQL Server could lock was a page. Even though many people argued that this was unacceptable and it was impossible to maintain good concurrency while locking entire pages, many large and powerful applications were written and deployed using only page-level locking. If they were well designed and tuned, concurrency was not an issue, and some of these applications supported hundreds of active user connections with acceptable response times and throughput. However, with the change in page size from 2 KB to 8 KB for SQL Server 7, the issue has become more critical. Locking an entire page means locking four times as much data as in previous versions. Beginning with version 7, SQL Server implements full row-level locking, so any potential problems due to lower concurrency with the larger page size should not be an issue. However, locking isn't free. Considerable resources are required to manage locks. Recall that a lock is an in-memory structure of about 32 bytes, with another 32 bytes for each process holding the lock and each process waiting for the lock. If you need a lock for every row and you scan a million rows, you need more than 30 MB of RAM just to hold locks for that one process.

Beyond memory consumption issues, locking is a fairly processing-intensive operation. Managing locks requires substantial bookkeeping. Recall that, internally, SQL Server uses a lightweight mutex called a spinlock to guard resources, and it uses latches—also lighter than full-blown locks—to protect non–leaf-level index pages. These performance optimizations avoid the overhead of full locking. If a page of data contains 50 rows of data, all of which will be used, it is obviously more efficient to issue and manage one lock on the page than to manage 50. That's the obvious benefit of page locking—a reduction in the number of lock structures that must exist and be managed.

If two different processes each need to update a few separate rows of data and some of the rows needed by each process happen to exist on the same page, one process must wait until the page locks of the other process are released. If, in this case, you use row-level locking instead of page-level locking, the other process does not have to wait. The finer granularity of the locks means that no conflict occurs in the first place because each process is concerned with different rows. That's the obvious benefit of row-level locking. Which of these obvious benefits wins? Well, the decision isn't clear cut, and it depends on the application and the data. Each type of locking can be shown to be superior for different types of applications and usage.

The stored procedure *sp_indexoption* lets you manually control the unit of locking within an index. It also lets you disallow page locks or row locks within an index. Since these options are available only for indexes, there is no way to control the locking within the data pages of a heap. (But remember that if a table has a clustered index, the data pages are part of the index and are affected by the *sp_indexoption* setting.) The index options are set for each table or index individually. Two options, AllowRowLocks and AllowPageLocks, are both set to TRUE initially for every table and index. If both of these options are set to FALSE for a table, only full table locks are allowed.

As mentioned earlier, SQL Server determines at runtime whether to initially lock rows, pages, or the entire table. The locking of rows (or keys) is heavily favored. The type of locking chosen is based on the number of rows and pages to be scanned, the number of rows on a page, the isolation level in effect, the update activity going on, the number of users on the system needing memory for their own purposes, and so on.

Lock Escalation

SQL Server automatically escalates row, key, or page locks to coarser table locks as appropriate. This escalation protects system resources—it prevents the system from using too much memory for keeping track of locks—and increases efficiency. For example, after a query acquires many row locks, the lock level can be escalated to a table lock. If every row in a table must be visited, it probably makes more sense to acquire and hold a single table lock than to hold many row locks. A single table lock is acquired and the many row locks are released. This escalation to a table lock reduces locking overhead and keeps the system from running out of locks. Because a finite amount of memory is available for the lock structures, escalation is sometimes necessary to make sure the memory for locks stays within reasonable limits.

When the lock count for one transaction exceeds 1250 or when the lock count for one index or table scan exceeds 765, the lock manager looks to see how much memory is being used for all locks in the system. If more than 40 percent of the memory pool is being used for locks, SQL Server attempts to escalate multiple page, key, or RID locks into a table lock. SQL Server tries to find a table that is partially locked by the transaction and holds the largest number of locks for which no escalation has already been performed, and which is capable of escalation. Multiple RID, key, or page locks cannot be escalated to a table lock if some other processes hold incompatible locks on other RIDs, keys, or pages of the same table. SQL Server will keep looking for other tables partially locked by the same transaction until all possible escalations have taken place or the total memory used for locks drops under 40 percent. Note that SQL Server never escalates to page locks; the result of a lock escalation is always a table lock.

LOCKING HINTS AND TRACE FLAGS

Just as you can specify hints on queries to direct the query optimizer to choose a certain index or strategy in its query plan, you can specify hints for locking. For example, if you know that your query will scan so many rows that its page locks will escalate to table locks, you can direct the query to use table locks in the first place, which is more efficient. We'll look at locking hints and locking contention issues in detail in Chapter 16.

For now, armed with the knowledge of locking you've gained here, you can observe the locking activity of your system to understand how and when locks occur. Trace flag 1204 provides detailed information about deadlocks, and this information can help you understand why locks are occurring and how to change the order of access to objects to reduce them. Trace flag 1200 provides detailed locking information as every request for a lock is made. (But its output is voluminous.) You'll see details about these trace flags in Chapter 16.

SUMMARY

SQL Server lets you manage multiple users simultaneously and ensure that transactions observe the properties of the chosen isolation level. Locking guards data and the internal resources that make it possible for a multiple-user system to operate like a single-user system. In this chapter, we looked at the locking mechanisms in SQL Server, including full locking for data and leaf-level index pages and lightweight locking mechanisms for internally used resources.

We also looked at the types and modes of locks as well as lock compatibility and lock escalation. It is important to understand the issues of lock compatibility if you want to design and implement high-concurrency applications. We also looked at deadlocks and discussed ways to avoid them.

Chapter 15

The Query Processor

One of the most important components of the Microsoft SQL Server engine is the query processor. Actually, there is no specific component called the query processor; rather, several related components work closely together to process the queries that you or your applications submit to the SQL Server engine for processing. Some of these components are involved in parsing your queries and simplifying them in various ways. Others are involved in the actual execution of your query.

Probably the most important and sophisticated of all the components involved in processing your queries is the query optimizer. The optimizer's job is to produce an execution plan for your query or for each query in a batch or stored procedure. The plan lists the steps to be carried out in order to execute your query and includes such information as which index or indexes to use when accessing data from each table in the query. The plan also includes the strategy for processing each JOIN operation, each GROUP BY operation, and each sort.

In this chapter, we'll look at the phases of query processing, paying particular attention to the query optimizer. I'll show you the different ways that indexes can be used, and I'll describe strategies for processing the joining of tables or the grouping of data. You'll also learn about the statistical information that SQL Server has available to determine the optimum execution plan, as well as the various mechanisms that SQL Server can employ to reuse an execution plan that was developed for a previous query.

THE SQL MANAGER

The SQL manager, which we looked at in Chapter 3, is the driving force in much of SQL Server's query processing. You might say that it's the heart of SQL Server itself. The SQL manager deals with all of the requests to run stored procedures. It manages the procedure cache and the pseudo–system stored procedures, and it's involved in autoparameterization of ad hoc queries, which I'll discuss shortly.

Typically, the SQL manager is invoked with an RPC message when you ask SQL Server to do some work for you. However, when a SQL language statement comes in as an ad hoc SQL statement instead of as a procedure call, the SQL manager is also involved. It can be involved when a procedure or a batch has an EXEC statement in it because the EXEC is actually calling the SQL manager. If the SQL statement passes the autoparameterization template (which I'll discuss below), the SQL manager is called to parameterize the queries. It's also called when ad hoc queries need to be placed in the cache. The SQL manager really is the heart of SQL Server's query processing system.

COMPILATION AND OPTIMIZATION

It's important to be aware that compilation and execution are distinct phases of query processing and that the gap between when SQL Server compiles a query and when the query is executed can be as short as a few microseconds or as long as several days. Therefore, during compilation (which includes optimization), SQL Server has to determine what kind of available information will be useful during the compilation. Not everything that is true at compilation time will be true at execution time. For example, the optimizer might take into account how many concurrent users are trying to access the same data that your query is trying to access. However, the number of concurrent users can change dramatically from moment to moment. You really have to think of compilation and execution as two separate activities, even when you're submitting an ad hoc SQL statement through SQL Query Analyzer and executing it immediately.

When a query is ready to be processed by SQL Server, an execution plan for the query might already be available in SQL Server's cache. If not, the query must be compiled. You'll see more details about how execution plans can be saved and reused later in this chapter. The compilation process encompasses a few things. First, SQL Server goes through the phases of parsing and normalization. Parsing is the process of dissecting and transforming your SQL statements into compiler-ready data structures. Parsing also includes validation of the syntax to ensure that it is legal.

Parsing doesn't include things such as checking for valid table and column names, which are dealt with during normalization. The normalization process basically determines the characteristics of the objects that you reference inside your SQL statements and checks whether the semantics you're asking for make sense. For example, it is semantically illogical to try to execute a table.

The next step is the compilation of the Transact-SQL code. The difference between Transact-SQL and SQL itself can be confusing, and the developers at Microsoft use the two names as interchangeably as anyone else does. However, there's actually an important difference. When I talk about processing the SQL statements, this includes all of the DML statements: INSERT, UPDATE, DELETE, and SELECT. These are the only statements that can actually be optimized. SQL Server also has a language that wraps around these DML statements, called Transact-SQL, or TSQL. As you've seen in several previous chapters, Transact-SQL provides procedural constructs: IF statements, WHILE statements, local variable declarations, and so forth. These are treated very differently inside the query processor. The procedural logic of Transact-SQL is compiled by an engine that knows how to do procedural kinds of things.

The SQL statements themselves are compiled by the query optimizer. The optimizer has to translate the nonprocedural request of a set-based SQL statement into a procedure that can execute efficiently and return the desired results. Unless I indicate otherwise, when I talk about compilation I will mean both the compilation of the Transact-SQL and the optimization of the SQL statements.

After the plan is generated, it is placed in cache and then executed. I'll tell you more about the reuse of plans and what happens during execution later in the chapter.

Compilation

During the compilation process, SQL Server parses each statement and creates something called a *sequence tree*. This is one of the few data structures in SQL Server 2000 that has survived from SQL Server 6.5. The sequence tree is then normalized. The main function of the normalizer is to perform binding, which includes verifying that the tables and columns exist and loading the metadata for the tables and columns. Information about implicit conversions is also added to the sequence tree; for example, if the query is trying to add 10.0 to an integer value, SQL Server will insert an implicit convert into the tree. Normalization also replaces references to a view with the definition of that view. Finally, normalization includes a few syntax-based optimizations. If the statement is a DML statement, SQL Server extracts information from the sequence tree about that query and creates a special structure called a query graph, which is set up to let the optimizer work on it effectively. The query graph is then optimized and a plan is produced.

Figure 15-1 shows the flow of this compilation process.

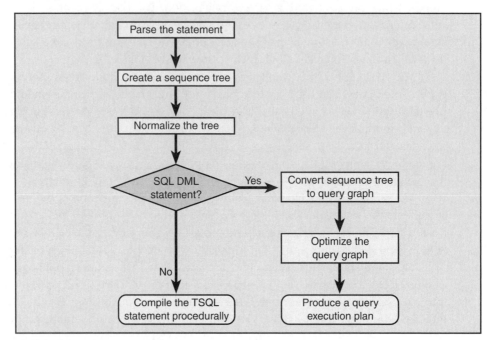

Figure 15-1. *The steps in compiling a statement.*

Optimization

SQL Server's query optimizer is a cost-based optimizer, which means that it tries to come up with the cheapest execution plan for each SQL statement. Each possible execution plan has an associated cost in terms of the amount of computing resources used. The query optimizer must analyze the possible plans and choose the one with the lowest estimated cost. Some complex SELECT statements have thousands of possible execution plans. In these cases, the query optimizer does not analyze all possible combinations. Instead, it tries to find an execution plan that has a cost reasonably close to the theoretical minimum. Later in this section, I'll tell you about some of the ways that the optimizer can reduce the amount of time it needs to spend on optimization.

The lowest estimated cost is not simply the lowest resource cost; the query optimizer chooses the plan that most quickly returns results to the user with a reasonable cost in resources. For example, processing a query in parallel (using multiple CPUs simultaneously for the same query) typically uses more resources than processing it serially using a single CPU, but the query completes much faster. The optimizer will choose a parallel execution plan to return results if the load on the server will not be adversely affected.

Optimization itself involves several steps. The first step is called *trivial plan optimization*. The idea behind trivial plan optimization is that cost-based optimization is expensive to run. The optimizer can try many possible variations in looking for the cheapest plan. If SQL Server knows that there is only one really viable plan for a query, it can avoid a lot of work. A common example is a query that consists of an INSERT with a VALUES clause. There is only one possible plan. Another example is a SELECT for which all the columns are among the keys of a unique composite index and that index is the only one that is relevant. No other index has that set of columns in it. In these two cases, SQL Server should just generate the plan and not try to find something better. The trivial plan optimizer finds the really obvious plans that are typically very inexpensive. This saves the optimizer from having to consider every possible plan, which can be costly and can outweigh any benefit provided by well-optimized queries.

If the trivial plan optimizer doesn't find a simple plan, SQL Server can perform some simplifications, which are usually syntactic transformations of the query itself, to look for commutative properties and operations that can be rearranged. SQL Server can perform operations that don't require looking at the cost or analyzing what indexes are available but that can result in a more efficient query. SQL Server then loads up the metadata, including the statistical information on the indexes, and then the optimizer goes through a series of phases of cost-based optimization.

The cost-based optimizer is designed as a set of transformation rules that try various permutations of indexes and join strategies. Because of the number of potential plans in SQL Server 2000, if the optimizer just ran through all the combinations and produced a plan, the optimization process would take a long time. So optimization is broken up into phases. Each phase is a set of rules. After each phase, SQL Server evaluates the cost of any resulting plan, and if the plan is cheap enough, it executes that plan. If the plan is not cheap enough, the optimizer runs the next phase, which is another set of rules. In the vast majority of cases, SQL Server finds a good plan in the preliminary phases.

If the optimizer goes through all the preliminary phases and still hasn't found a cheap plan, it examines the cost of the best plan it has so far. If the cost is above a particular threshold, the optimizer goes into a phase called full optimization. You can configure this threshold using the *cost threshold for parallelism* configuration option. The full optimization phase assumes that this plan should be run in parallel. However, the optimizer will not consider this option at all if the machine only has a single CPU available for SQL Server's use. If the machine is very busy, SQL Server might decide at execution time to run the plan on a single CPU, but the optimizer tries to produce a good parallel plan. If the cost is below the parallelism threshold, the full optimization phase just uses a brute force method to find a serial plan, checking every possible combination of indexes and processing strategies. Figure 15-2 shows the flow of processing through the optimizer.

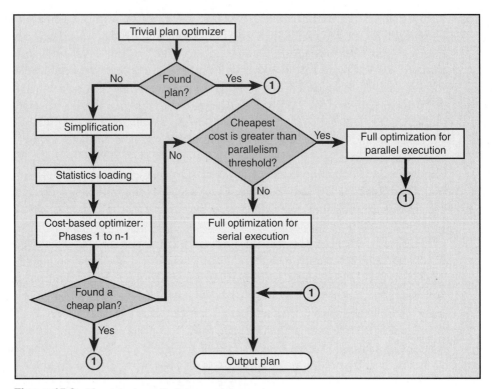

Figure 15-2. *The steps in optimizing a statement.*

How the Query Optimizer Works

Monitoring and tuning of queries are essential steps in optimizing performance. Knowing how the query optimizer works can be helpful as you think about how to write a good query or what indexes to define. However, you should guard against outsmarting yourself and trying to predict what the optimizer will do. You might miss some good options this way. Try to write your queries in the most intuitive way you can and then try to tune them only if their performance doesn't seem good enough.

Nevertheless, insight into how the optimizer works is certainly useful. It can help you understand why certain indexes are recommended over others and it can help you understand the query plan output in SQL Query Analyzer. For each table involved in the query, the query optimizer evaluates the search conditions in the WHERE clause and considers which indexes are available to narrow the scan of a table. That is, the optimizer evaluates to what extent an index can exclude rows from consideration. The more rows that can be excluded, the better, because that leaves fewer rows to process.

Joins can be processed using one of three methods: nested iteration, hashing, or merging. For any of these methods, the optimizer decides on the order in which the tables should be accessed. Because a nested iteration is a loop, order is important. The fewer the iterations through the loops, the less processing will be required. So it is useful to start with the table (or tables) that can exclude the most rows as the outer loops. The general strategy is to have the outer table limit the search the most, which results in the fewest total iterations (scans). With hash or merge joins, SQL Server builds an in-memory structure from one or both of the tables. To conserve memory resources, it tries to determine which is the smaller table or which will have the smallest number of qualifying rows after the WHERE conditions are applied. This table is typically chosen as the first table to be processed. We'll look at each of these join strategies again later in the chapter.

For each combination of join strategy, join order, and indexes, the query optimizer estimates a cost, taking into account the number of logical reads and the memory resources that are required and available. Then the optimizer compares the cost of each plan and chooses the plan with the lowest estimate. You can think of query optimization as happening in three main steps: query analysis, index selection, and join selection, although there is a lot of overlap between the index selection and join selection steps. The following sections discuss each step.

Query Analysis

During the query analysis phase, the query optimizer looks at each clause of the query and determines whether it can be useful in limiting how much data must be scanned— that is, whether the clause is useful as a search argument (SARG) or as part of the join criteria. A clause that can be used as a search argument is referred to as *sargable,* or *optimizable,* and can make use of an index for faster retrieval.

A SARG limits a search because it specifies an exact match, a range of values, or a conjunction of two or more items joined by AND. A SARG contains a constant expression (or a variable that is resolved to a constant) that acts on a column by using an operator. It has the form

```
column inclusive_operator <constant or variable>
```

   or

```
<constant or variable> inclusive_operator column
```

The column name can appear on one side of the operator, and the constant or variable can appear on the other side. If a column appears on both sides of the operator, the clause is not sargable. Sargable operators include =, >, <, =>, <=, BE-TWEEN, and sometimes LIKE. Whether LIKE is sargable depends on the type of wildcards (regular expressions) used. For example, *LIKE 'Jon%* is sargable but *LIKE*

'%Jon' is not because the wildcard (%) at the beginning prevents the use of an index. Here are some SARG examples:

```
name = 'jones'

salary > 40000

60000 < salary

department = 'sales'

name = 'jones' AND salary > 100000

name LIKE 'dail%'
```

A single SARG can include many conditions if they are AND'ed together. That is, one index might be able to operate on all the conditions that are AND'ed together. In the example above, there might be an index on (*name, salary*), so the entire clause *name = jones AND salary > 100000* can be considered one SARG and can be evaluated for qualifying rows using one index. If OR is used instead of AND in this example, a single index scan cannot be used to qualify both terms. The reason should be clear—if the lead field in the index key is *name*, the index is useful for finding just the *'jones'* rows. If the criterion in the WHERE clause includes AND *salary > 100000*, the second field of the index also qualifies those rows. That is, all the rows that have a *name* value of *'jones'* can be further restricted to find the rows with *'jones'* and an appropriate salary. The set of rows that meets both of the AND conditions is a subset of the rows that meet just the first condition on *name*. But if the second criterion is OR *salary > 100000*, the index is not useful in the same way because all the rows would need to be examined, not just the *'jones'* entries. The set of rows that meet either one of the conditions is a superset of the rows that meet just the first condition on *name*.

A phone book analogy can also be useful. If you want to find people who have the name *"jones"* AND live on 5th Avenue, using the phone book can help greatly reduce the size of your search. But if you want to find people who have the name *"Jones"* OR live on 5th Avenue, you have to scan every entry in the entire phone book. This assumes that you have only one phone book that is sorted alphabetically by name. If you have two phone books, one sorted by name and one sorted by street, that's another story, which I'll discuss a bit later.

An expression that is not sargable cannot limit the search. That is, SQL Server must evaluate every row to determine whether it meets the conditions in the WHERE clause. So an index is not useful to nonsargable expressions. Typical nonsargable expressions include negation operators such as NOT, !=, <>, !>, !<, NOT EXISTS, NOT IN, and NOT LIKE. Don't extrapolate too far and think that this means using a nonsargable clause always results in a table scan. An index is not useful to the nonsargable clause, but there might be indexes useful to other SARGs in the query. Queries often have multiple clauses, so a great index for one or more of the other clauses might be available. Here are some examples of nonsargable clauses:

```
ABS(price) < 4
```

```
name LIKE '%jon%'
```

```
name = 'jones' OR salary > 100000
```

> **NOTE** The last example above is not a single search argument, but each expression on either side of the OR is individually sargable. So a single index won't be used to evaluate both expressions, as it might if the operator is AND. A separate index can still be useful to each expression.

Expressions involving computations might be sargable because SQL Server 2000 can do scalar simplification in some cases. The following table shows examples of expressions that the query optimizer will simplify, along with the resultant simplified expression that is used to determine the usefulness of an index.

Original Expression	Simplified Expression
WHERE price * 12 = costs	WHERE price = costs/12
WHERE salary * 1 > 40000	WHERE salary > 40000

The simplified expression is not guaranteed to be exactly equivalent to the original, particularly if you have a mixture of datatypes and implicit conversions are occurring. However, the simplified expression is used only during optimization, to detect and measure the usefulness of a particular index. When determining whether a particular row actually qualifies for the result set, SQL Server always uses the original expression.

Let's look at a specific example. The *Northwind* database includes a table called *Order Details*, which has a nonclustered index on the column *ProductID*. When a query contains a SARG involving *ProductID*, the query optimizer has to determine whether using the nonclustered index will be the fastest way to access the qualifying rows. Remember that a nonclustered index contains every key value in its leaf level, with a bookmark pointing to the actual location of the row having that key. If too many rows satisfy the SARG's condition, the optimizer might decide it's too expensive to use the index and opt instead to scan the entire table. In addition to information about the key columns and the type of each index, the *sysindexes* system table contains a column called *statblob*, which holds statistical information about the distribution of all the different key values. We'll look at statistics in detail a bit later, but for now, be aware that examining the statistics is part of determining whether an index is useful.

The first query below has a SARG involving the *ProductID* column, and SQL Server is able to use the statistical information to estimate that five rows will meet the condition in the WHERE clause. The optimizer will choose to use the index on *ProductID*.

```
USE Northwind
SELECT * FROM [Order Details]
WHERE ProductID = 9
```

In the next query, because of the presence of the function ABS, there is no SARG and the index on *ProductID* is not even considered. The optimizer has no real choice other than to scan the entire table.

```
USE Northwind
SELECT * FROM [Order Details]
WHERE ABS(ProductID) = 9
```

In the third example, the optimizer can internally convert the condition in the WHERE clause into a SARG and correctly estimate the number of rows. However, the conversion is used only during optimization. During execution, the conversion cannot be done while traversing the index. The optimizer knows that SQL Server won't be able to do the repeated multiplication by 2 at every step in the index tree, so the final plan is to do a table scan. However, the optimizer used the index to come up with an estimate of the number of rows. In more complex queries, even if the index itself can't be used to locate the rows, knowing the number of qualifying rows can be useful in making other decisions about the best plan. The crucial point here is that when you used the function, the optimizer totally ignored the index. When you used an expression that was convertible to a SARG, the optimizer could examine the statistics, even if the index itself couldn't be used during execution.

```
USE Northwind
SELECT * FROM [Order Details]
WHERE ProductID * 2 = 18
```

How can you know what the plan is or what the optimizer is estimating for the number of rows? SQL Server 2000 provides several tools to help you analyze the optimizer's choices, and I'll go into much more detail on these tools in Chapter 16 when I tell you about tuning your queries. For now, let's just have a sneak preview of how to look at a graphical representation of the plan that the optimizer has chosen. If you type any of the three queries above into the SQL Query Analyzer query window, you can highlight the query and click the Display Estimated Execution Plan button just to the right of the database list. Alternatively, you can go to the Query menu and choose Display Estimated Execution Plan. Figure 15-3 shows the plan for the first query. If you place your cursor over the rightmost icon, you'll see the yellow box of details appear. The important thing to note is that the operation is Index Seek. Index Seek means that SQL Server will traverse the index from the root down to the leaf level, comparing the values in the SARG to the key values in the index rows to determine which page to look at next. Seeking through an index typically means a root-to-leaf traversal. Note also in Figure 15-3 that the estimated row count is five.

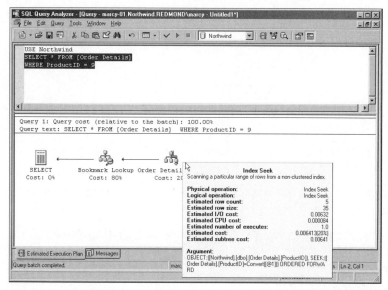

Figure 15-3. *A graphical query plan for an index seek operation.*

Figure 15-4 shows the plan for the second query, and you can see that the operation is Clustered Index Scan. A scan, the alternative to Index Seek, means that SQL Server will stay at the leaf level and traverse just that one level of the index from the first page to the last. I like to think of a seek as a vertical traversal of an index and a scan as a horizontal traversal. Remember that for a clustered index, the leaf level of the index is the table data itself, so scanning the clustered index really means scanning the table. In fact, the only time you'll see Table Scan as an operator in the plan is for heaps. Also notice in Figure 15-4 that the row count is nowhere close to reality. The index statistics were not used, and the optimizer just had to take a wild guess. I'll tell you a bit more about how and when the optimizer can "guess" later in this chapter.

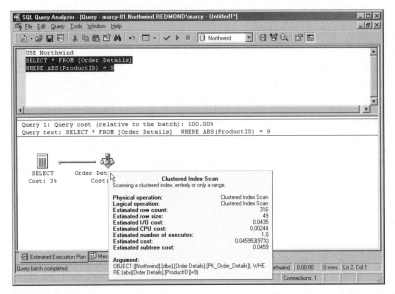

Figure 15-4. *A graphical query plan for a clustered index scan (table scan).*

Finally, Figure 15-5 shows the plan for the third query. Note that the row count is the same as in the first query, which means that the statistics can be used. But the operation to be performed is the index scan of the clustered index.

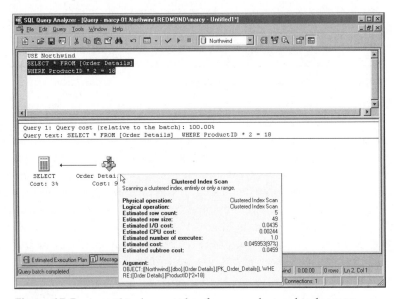

Figure 15-5. *A graphical query plan for a nonclustered index scan.*

As you saw in the second example, expressions that apply a function to a column are not sargable, and in SQL Server 2000, the optimizer does not attempt to internally convert them to something that is sargable. In some cases, however, you might be able to write an equivalent expression. For example, the *Orders* table has an index on the *CustomerID* column, which is a character string. The following two queries return the same three rows in their result set, but the first one does not use an index and the second one does:

```
SELECT * FROM Orders WHERE SUBSTRING(CustomerID, 1, 1) = 'N'

SELECT * FROM Orders WHERE CustomerID LIKE 'N%'
```

Future versions of SQL Server will address more issues of nonsargable clauses.

Index Selection

During the second phase of query optimization, index selection, the query optimizer determines whether an index exists for a sargable clause, assesses the index's usefulness by determining the selectivity of the clause (that is, how many rows will be returned), and estimates the cost of finding the qualifying rows. An index is potentially useful if its first column is used in the search argument and the search argument establishes a lower bound, upper bound, or both to limit the search. In addition, if an index contains every column referenced in a query, even if none of those columns is the first column of the index, the index is considered useful.

An index that contains all the referenced columns is called a *covering index* and is one of the fastest ways to access data. The data pages do not have to be accessed at all, which can mean a substantial savings in physical I/O. For example, suppose that the *Employees* table has an index on last name, first name, and date of hire. The following query is covered by this index:

```
SELECT LastName, HireDate
FROM Employees
WHERE FirstName = 'Sven'
```

You might have more covering indexes than you're aware of. In SQL Server 2000, a nonclustered index contains the clustered index key as part of the bookmark. So if the *Employees* table has a clustered index on the employee ID (*EmployeeID*) column, the nonclustered index described earlier, on *LastName*, *FirstName*, and *HireDate*, will also contain the *EmployeeID* for every data row, stored in the leaf level of the nonclustered index. Thus, the following is also a covered query:

```
SELECT EmployeeID, FirstName, LastName
FROM Employees
WHERE LastName LIKE 'B%'
```

Index Statistics

After the query optimizer finds a potentially useful index that matches the clause, it evaluates the index based on the selectivity of the clause. The optimizer checks the index's statistics—the histogram of values accessible through the index's row in the *sysindexes* table. The histogram is created when the index is created on existing data, and the values are refreshed each time UPDATE STATISTICS runs. If the index is created before data exists in the table, no statistics appear. The statistics will be misleading if they were generated when the dispersion of data values was significantly different from what appears in the current data in the table. However, SQL Server detects whether statistics are not up to date, and by default it automatically updates them during query optimization.

Statistics are a histogram consisting of an even sampling of values for the index key (or the first column of the key for a composite index) based on the current data. The histogram is stored in the *statblob* field of the *sysindexes* table, which is of type *image*. (As you know, *image* data is actually stored in structures separate from the data row itself. The data row merely contains a pointer to the *image* data. For simplicity's sake, I'll talk about the index statistics as being stored in the *image* field called *statblob*.) To fully estimate the usefulness of an index, the optimizer also needs to know the number of pages in the table or index; this information is stored in the *dpages* column of *sysindexes*.

The statistical information also includes details about the uniqueness (or *density*) of the data values encountered, which provides a measure of how selective the index is. Recall that the more selective an index is, the more useful it is, because higher selectivity means that more rows can be eliminated from consideration. A unique index, of course, is the most selective—by definition, each index entry can point to only one row. A unique index has a density value of $1/number\ of\ rows\ in\ the\ table$.

Density values range from 0 through 1. Highly selective indexes have density values of 0.10 or lower. For example, a unique index on a table with 8345 rows has a density of 0.00012 (1/8345). If a nonunique nonclustered index has a density of 0.2165 on the same table, each index key can be expected to point to about 1807 rows (0.2165 × 8345). This is probably not selective enough to be more efficient than just scanning the table, so this index is probably not useful. Because driving the query from a nonclustered index means that the pages must be retrieved in index order, an estimated 1807 data page accesses (or logical reads) are needed if there is no clustered index on the table and the leaf level of the index contains the actual RID of the desired data row. The only time a data page doesn't need to be reaccessed is when the occasional coincidence occurs in which two adjacent index entries happen to point to the same data page.

Assume in this example that about 40 rows fit on a page, so there are about 209 total pages. The chance of two adjacent index entries pointing to the same page is only about 0.5 percent (1/209). The number of logical reads for just the data pages, not even counting the index I/O, is likely to be close to 1807. If there is also a clustered index on the table, a couple of additional page accesses will be needed for each nonclustered key accessed. In contrast, the entire table can be scanned with just 209 logical reads—the number of pages in the table. In this case, the optimizer looks for better indexes or decides that a table scan is the best it can do.

The statistics histogram records steps (samples) for only the lead column of the index. This optimization takes into account that an index is useful only if its lead column is specified in a WHERE clause. However, density information is stored for multiple combinations of columns in a composite index. For example, if we have an index on (*lastname, firstname*), the *statblob* field will contain a density value for *lastname* and another density value for the combination of *lastname* and *firstname*. This will become clearer when we look at some actual statistics information.

SQL Server defines *density* as follows:

density = 1/cardinality of index keys

The cardinality means how many unique values exist in the data. Statistics for a single column index consist of one histogram and one *density* value. The multi-column statistics for one set of columns in a composite index consist of one histogram for the first column in the index and *density* values for each prefix combination of columns (including the first column alone). The fact that density information is kept for all columns helps the optimizer decide how useful the index is for joins.

Suppose, for example, that an index is composed of three key fields. The density on the first column might be 0.50, which is not too useful. But as you look at more key columns in the index, the number of rows pointed to is fewer than (or in the worst case, the same as) the first column, so the density value goes down. If you're looking at both the first and second columns, the density might be 0.25, which is somewhat better. And if you examine three columns, the density might be 0.03, which is highly selective. It doesn't make sense to refer to the density of only the second column. The lead column density is always needed.

The histogram contains up to 200 values of a given key column. In addition to the histogram, the *statblob* field contains the following information:

- The time of the last statistics collection
- The number of rows used to produce the histogram and density information
- The average key length
- Densities for other combinations of columns

The following example uses the *Orders* table in the *Northwind* database. Assume that we have built a nonclustered composite index (*cust_date_indx*) on *CustomerID* and *OrderDate*.

```
CREATE INDEX cust_date_indx ON Orders(CustomerID, OrderDate)
```

The existing clustered index is on *OrderID*, so *OrderID* is considered part of the key in every nonclustered index row. We can use DBCC SHOW_STATISTICS to display the statistics information for this index:

```
DBCC SHOW_STATISTICS('Orders', 'cust_date_indx')
```

Here are the results:

```
Statistics for INDEX 'cust_date_indx'.
```

Updated	Rows	Rows Sampled	Steps	Density	Average key length
Aug 31 2000	830	830	89	0.0	22.0

All density	Average Length	Columns
1.1235955E-2	10.0	CustomerID
1.2150669E-3	18.0	CustomerID, OrderDate
1.2048193E-3	22.0	CustomerID, OrderDate, OrderID

RANGE_HI_KEY	RANGE_ROWS	EQ_ROWS	DISTINCT_RANGE_ROWS	AVG_RANGE_ROWS
ALFKI	0.0	6.0	0	0.0
ANATR	0.0	4.0	0	0.0
ANTON	0.0	7.0	0	0.0
AROUT	0.0	13.0	0	0.0
BERGS	0.0	18.0	0	0.0
BLAUS	0.0	7.0	0	0.0
BLONP	0.0	11.0	0	0.0
BOLID	0.0	3.0	0	0.0
BONAP	0.0	17.0	0	0.0
BOTTM	0.0	14.0	0	0.0
BSBEV	0.0	10.0	0	0.0
CACTU	0.0	6.0	0	0.0
CENTC	0.0	1.0	0	0.0
CHOPS	0.0	8.0	0	0.0
COMMI	0.0	5.0	0	0.0
CONSH	0.0	3.0	0	0.0
DRACD	0.0	6.0	0	0.0
DUMON	0.0	4.0	0	0.0
EASTC	0.0	8.0	0	0.0
ERNSH	0.0	30.0	0	0.0

FAMIA	0.0	7.0	0	0.0
FOLIG	0.0	5.0	0	0.0
FOLKO	0.0	19.0	0	0.0
FRANK	0.0	15.0	0	0.0
FRANR	0.0	3.0	0	0.0
FRANS	0.0	6.0	0	0.0
FURIB	0.0	8.0	0	0.0
GALED	0.0	5.0	0	0.0
GODOS	0.0	10.0	0	0.0
GOURL	0.0	9.0	0	0.0
GREAL	0.0	11.0	0	0.0
GROSR	0.0	2.0	0	0.0
HANAR	0.0	14.0	0	0.0
HILAA	0.0	18.0	0	0.0
HUNGC	0.0	5.0	0	0.0
HUNGO	0.0	19.0	0	0.0
ISLAT	0.0	10.0	0	0.0
KOENE	0.0	14.0	0	0.0
LACOR	0.0	4.0	0	0.0
LAMAI	0.0	14.0	0	0.0
LAUGB	0.0	3.0	0	0.0
LAZYK	0.0	2.0	0	0.0
LEHMS	0.0	15.0	0	0.0
LETSS	0.0	4.0	0	0.0
LILAS	0.0	14.0	0	0.0
LINOD	0.0	12.0	0	0.0
LONEP	0.0	8.0	0	0.0
MAGAA	0.0	10.0	0	0.0
MAISD	0.0	7.0	0	0.0
MEREP	0.0	13.0	0	0.0
MORGK	0.0	5.0	0	0.0
NORTS	0.0	3.0	0	0.0
OCEAN	0.0	5.0	0	0.0
OLDWO	0.0	10.0	0	0.0
OTTIK	0.0	10.0	0	0.0
PERIC	0.0	6.0	0	0.0
PICCO	0.0	10.0	0	0.0
PRINI	0.0	5.0	0	0.0
QUEDE	0.0	9.0	0	0.0
QUEEN	0.0	13.0	0	0.0
QUICK	0.0	28.0	0	0.0
RANCH	0.0	5.0	0	0.0
RATTC	0.0	18.0	0	0.0
REGGC	0.0	12.0	0	0.0
RICAR	0.0	11.0	0	0.0
RICSU	0.0	10.0	0	0.0

(continued)

ROMEY	0.0	5.0	0	0.0
SANTG	0.0	6.0	0	0.0
SAVEA	0.0	31.0	0	0.0
SEVES	0.0	9.0	0	0.0
SIMOB	0.0	7.0	0	0.0
SPECD	0.0	4.0	0	0.0
SPLIR	0.0	9.0	0	0.0
SUPRD	0.0	12.0	0	0.0
THEBI	0.0	4.0	0	0.0
THECR	0.0	3.0	0	0.0
TOMSP	0.0	6.0	0	0.0
TORTU	0.0	10.0	0	0.0
TRADH	0.0	6.0	0	0.0
TRAIH	0.0	3.0	0	0.0
VAFFE	0.0	11.0	0	0.0
VICTE	0.0	10.0	0	0.0
VINET	0.0	5.0	0	0.0
WANDK	0.0	10.0	0	0.0
WARTH	0.0	15.0	0	0.0
WELLI	0.0	9.0	0	0.0
WHITC	0.0	14.0	0	0.0
WILMK	0.0	7.0	0	0.0
WOLZA	0.0	7.0	0	0.0

This output indicates that the statistics for this index were last updated on August 31, 2000. It also indicates that the table currently has 830 rows and that 89 different samples were used. The average key length in the first row is for all columns of the index.

The next section shows the density values for each left-based subset of key columns. There are 89 different values for *CustomerID*, so the density is 1/89 or 1.1235955E-2 or 0.011235955. There are 823 different values for the combination of *CustomerID* and *OrderDate*, so the density is 1/823 or 1.2150669E-3 or 0.0012150669. When the third key column of *OrderID* is included, the key is now unique, so the density is 1 divided by the number of rows in the name, or 1/830, which is 1.2048193E-3 or 0.0012048193.

In the *statblob* column, up to 200 sample values are stored; the range of key values between each sample value is called a *step*. The sample value is the endpoint of the range. Three values are stored along with each step: a value called EQ_ROWS, which is the number of rows that have a value equal to that sample value; a value called RANGE_ROWS, which specifies how many other values are inside the range (between two adjacent sample values); and the number of distinct values, or RANGE_DENSITY of the range. The DBCC SHOW_STATISTICS output shows us the first two of these three values, but not the range density. The RANGE_DENSITY is instead used to compute two additional values:

- DISTINCT_RANGE_ROWS—the number of distinct rows inside this range (not counting the RANGE_HI_KEY value itself). This is computed as 1/ RANGE_DENSITY.

- AVG_RANGE_ROWS—the average number of rows per distinct value, computed as RANGE_DENSITY * RANGE_ROWS.

In the output shown previously, all the distinct key values in the first column of the index were one of the sample values, so there were no additional values in between the range endpoints. That's why so many of the values are 0 in the output.

In addition to statistics on indexes, SQL Server can also keep track of statistics on columns with no indexes. Knowing the density, or the likelihood of a particular value occurring, can help the optimizer determine an optimum processing strategy, even if SQL Server can't use an index to actually locate the values. I'll discuss column statistics in more detail when we look at statistics management later in this section.

Query optimization is probability based, which means that its conclusions can be wrong. The optimizer can make decisions that are not optimal even if they make sense from a probability standpoint. (As an analogy, you can think of national election polls, which are based on relatively small samples. The famous headline "Dewey Defeats Truman!" proves that such statistical sampling can be wrong.)

> **NOTE** The above information on SHOW_STATISTICS values was adapted from a preliminary copy of a whitepaper by Lubor Kollar. I'm indebted to him for his assistance.

Index Cost

The second part of determining the selectivity of a SARG is calculating the estimated cost of the access methods that can be used. Even if a useful index is present, it might not be used if the optimizer determines that it is not the cheapest access method. One of the main components of the cost calculation, especially for queries involving only a single table, is the amount of logical I/O, which is the number of page accesses that are needed. Logical I/O is counted whether the pages are already in the memory cache or must be read from disk and brought into the cache. The term *logical I/O* is sometimes used to refer to I/O from cache, as if a read were either logical or physical, but this is a misnomer. As discussed in Chapter 3, pages are always retrieved from the cache via a request to the buffer manager, so all reads are logical. If the pages are not already in the cache, they must be brought in first by the buffer manager. In those cases, the read is also physical. Only the buffer manager, which serves up the pages, knows whether a page is already in cache or must be accessed from disk and brought into cache. The ratio of the I/O already in the cache to the logical I/O is referred to as the *cache-hit ratio,* an important metric to watch.

The optimizer evaluates indexes to estimate the number of likely "hits" based on the density and step values in the statistics. Based on these values, it estimates how many rows qualify for the given SARG and how many logical reads would retrieve those qualifying rows. It might find multiple indexes that can find qualifying rows, or it might determine that just scanning the table and checking all the rows is best. It tries to find the access method that will require the fewest logical reads.

Whether the access method uses a clustered index, one or more nonclustered indexes, a table scan, or another option determines the estimated number of logical reads. This number can be very different for each method. Using an index to find qualifying rows is frequently referred to as *an index driving the scan*. When a nonclustered index drives the scan, the query optimizer assumes that the page containing each identified qualifying row is probably not the same page accessed the last time. Because the pages must be retrieved according to the order of the index entries, retrieving the next row with a query driven by a nonclustered index will likely require that a different page than the one that contained the previous row be fetched because the two rows probably don't reside on the same page. They might reside on the same page by coincidence, but the optimizer correctly assumes that this will typically not be the case. (With 5000 pages, the chance of this occurring is 1/5000.) If the index is not clustered, data order is random with respect to the index key.

If the scan is driven from a clustered index, the next row is probably located on the same page as the previous row because the index leaf is, in fact, the data. The only time this is not the case when you use a clustered index is when the last row on a page has been retrieved; the next page must be accessed, and it will contain the next bunch of rows. But moving back and forth between the index and the data pages is not required.

There is, of course, a chance that a specific page might already be in cache when you use a nonclustered index. But a logical read will still occur even if the scan does not require physical I/O (a read from disk). Physical I/O is an order of magnitude more costly than I/O from cache. But don't assume that only the cost of physical I/O matters—reads from the cache are still far from free. To minimize logical I/O, the query optimizer tries to produce a plan that will result in the fewest number of page operations. In doing so, the optimizer will probably minimize physical I/O as well. For example, suppose we need to resolve a query with the following SARG:

```
WHERE Emp_Name BETWEEN 'Smith' AND 'Snow'
```

Here are the relevant index entries for a nonclustered index on *Emp_Name*:

```
Index_Key (Emp_Name)       Bookmarks: Found on Page(s)
--------------------       -------------------
Smith                      1:267, 1:384, 1:512
Smyth                      1:267
Snow                       1:384, 1:512
```

If this table is a heap, when we use this nonclustered index, six logical reads are required to retrieve the data pages in addition to the I/O necessary to read the index. If none of the pages is already cached, the data access results in three physical I/O reads, assuming that the pages remain in the cache long enough to be reused for the subsequent rows (which is a good bet).

Suppose that all the index entries are on one leaf page and the index has one intermediate level. In this case, three I/O reads (logical and probably physical) are necessary to read the index (one root level, one intermediate level, and one leaf level). So chances are that driving this query via the nonclustered index requires about nine logical I/O reads, six of which are probably physical if the cache started out empty. The data pages are retrieved in the following order:

Page 1:267 to get row with Smith
Page 1:384 for Smith
Page 1:512 for Smith
Page 1:267 (again) for Smyth
Page 1:384 (again) for Snow
Page 1:512 (again) for Snow

The number of logical reads would be more if the table also had a clustered index (for example, on the zip code field). Our leaf-level index entries might look like this:

```
Index_Key (Emp_Name)        Bookmarks: Clustered Key(s)
--------------------        ---------------------------
Smith                       06403, 20191, 98370
Smyth                       37027
Snow                        22241, 80863
```

For each of the six nonclustered keys, we have to traverse the clustered index. You typically see about three to four times as many logical reads for traversing a nonclustered index for a table that also has a clustered index. However, if the indexes for this table are re-created so that a clustered index exists on the *Emp_Name* column, all six of the qualifying rows are probably located on the same page. The number of logical reads is probably only three (the index root, the intermediate index page, and the leaf index page, which is the data page), plus the final read that will retrieve all the qualifying rows. This scenario should make it clear to you why a clustered index can be so important to a range query.

With no clustered index, the optimizer has to choose between a plan that does a table scan and a plan that uses one or more nonclustered indexes. The number of logical I/O operations required for a scan of the table is equal to the number of pages in the table. A table scan starts at the first page and uses the Index Allocation Map (IAM) to access all the pages in the table. As the pages are read, the rows are evaluated to see whether they qualify based on the search criteria. Clearly, if the table from the previous example had fewer than nine total data pages, fewer logical reads would be needed to scan the whole table than to drive the scan off the nonclustered index, which was estimated to take nine logical reads.

The estimated logical reads for scanning qualifying rows is summarized in Table 15-1. The access method with the least estimated cost is chosen based on this information.

Access Method	Estimated Cost (in Logical Reads)*
Table scan	The total number of data pages in the table.
Clustered index	The number of levels in the index plus the number of data pages to scan. (Data pages to be scanned = number of qualifying rows / rows per data page.)
Nonclustered index on a heap	The number of levels in the index plus the number of leaf pages plus the number of qualifying rows (a logical read for the data page of each qualifying row). The same data pages are often retrieved (from cache) many times, so the number of logical reads can be much higher than the number of pages in the table.
Nonclustered index on a table with a clustered index	The number of levels in the index plus the number of leaf pages plus the number of qualifying rows times the cost of searching for a clustered index key.
Covering nonclustered index	The number of levels in the index plus the number of leaf index pages (qualifying rows / rows per leaf page). The data page need not be accessed because all necessary information is in the index key.

* All computations are rounded up to the next integer

Table 15-1. *The cost of data access for tables with different index structures.*

Using Multiple Indexes

The query optimizer can decide to use two or more nonclustered indexes to satisfy a single query. When more than one index is considered useful because of two or more SARGs, the cost estimate changes a bit from the formulas given in Table 15-1. In addition to the I/O cost of finding the qualifying rows in each index, there is an additional cost of finding the intersection of the indexes so that SQL Server can determine which data rows satisfy all search conditions. Since each nonclustered index key contains a locator for the actual data, the results of the two index searches can be treated as worktables and joined together on the locator information.

Suppose we have the following query and we have indexes on both the *LastName* and *FirstName* columns. In this case, we have a clustered index on the ID number, which is a unique value.

```
SELECT FirstName, LastName, EmployeeID FROM Employees
WHERE LastName BETWEEN 'Smith' AND 'Snow'
AND FirstName BETWEEN 'Daniel' and 'David'
```

If the query optimizer decides to use both indexes, SQL Server will build two worktables with the results of each index search:

```
Index_Key (LastName)      Bookmark(Clustered Key)
--------------------      ----------------------
Smith                     66-712403
Smith                     87-120191
Smith                     76-137027
Smyth                     11-983770
Snow                      43-220191
Snow                      21-780863


Index_Key (FirstName)     Bookmark(Clustered Key)
--------------------      ----------------------
Daniel                    11-983770
Daniel                    77-321456
Danielle                  66-712403
David                     29-331218
```

These worktables are joined on the row locator information, which is unique for each row. Remember, even if you don't declare a clustered index as unique, SQL Server adds a special uniqueifier where needed so there is always a unique row locator in every nonclustered index. From the information above, we can see that only two rows have both their first name and last name values in the requested range. The result set is:

```
FirstName   LastName          EmployeeID
---------   ---------------   -----------
Daniel      Smythe            11-983770
Danielle    Smith             66-712403
```

In this example, the data in the two indexes is enough to satisfy the query. If we also want to see information such as address and phone number, the query optimizer uses the bookmark to find the actual data row by traversing the clustered index. It can also use multiple indexes if a single table has multiple SARGs that are

OR'ed together. In this case, SQL Server finds the UNION of the rows returned by each index to determine all the qualifying rows. You can see the main differences if you take the same query and data and write an OR query instead of an AND:

```
SELECT FirstName, LastName, EmployeeID FROM Employees
WHERE LastName BETWEEN 'Smith' AND 'Snow'
OR FirstName BETWEEN 'Daniel' AND 'David'
```

SQL Server can use the two indexes in the same way and build the same two worktables. However, it must UNION the two worktables together and remove duplicates. Once it removes the duplicates, it uses the bookmarks to find the rows in the table. All the result rows will have either a first name or a last name in the requested range, but not necessarily both. For example, we can return a row for Daniel Delaney or Bridgette Smith. If we don't remove duplicates, we end up with Daniel Smythe and Danielle Smith showing up twice because they meet both conditions of the SARGs.

Unusable Statistics

In two cases, the query optimizer can't use the statistics to estimate how many rows will satisfy a given SARG. First, if there are no statistics available, SQL Server obviously can't come up with any cost estimate. However, this situation is rare in SQL Server 2000 because by default every database has the two database options, *auto create statistics* and *auto update statistics*, set to TRUE. As you'll see later, you can turn this behavior off at the table level or the database level, but this is usually not recommended. The second situation in which there are no usable statistics is when the values in a SARG are variables. Consider this example:

```
DECLARE @name varchar(30)
SET @name = 'Zelda'
SELECT FirstName, LastName, EmployeeID FROM Employees
WHERE LastName > @name
```

When the preceding query is optimized, the SET statement has not been executed and the value of *@name* is unknown. No specific value can be used to compare the steps in the index's statistics information, so the query optimizer must guess.

> NOTE   Don't confuse variables with parameters even though their syntax is nearly identical. A variable's value is never known until the statement is actually executed; it is never known at compile time. Stored procedure parameters are known when the procedure is compiled because compilation and optimization don't even take place until the procedure is actually called with specific values for the parameters.

If the query optimizer can't use the statistics for either of the reasons mentioned, the server uses fixed percentages, shown here, depending on the operator. These fixed percentages can be grossly inaccurate for your specific data, however, so make sure that your statistics are up to date.

Operator	*Percentage of Rows*
=	10
>	30
<	30
BETWEEN	10

When the SARG involves an equality, the situation is usually handled in a special way. The 10 percent estimate shown above is actually used only in the unusual case in which there are no statistics at all. If there are statistics, they can be used. Even if we don't have a particular value to compare against the steps in the statistics histogram, the density information can be used. That information basically tells the query optimizer the expected number of duplicates, so when the SARG involves looking for one specific value, it assumes that the value occurs the average number of times.

An even more special case occurs when the query optimizer recognizes an equality in the WHERE clause and the index is unique. Because this combination yields an exact match and always returns at most one row, the query optimizer doesn't have to use statistics. For queries of one row that use an exact match such as a lookup by primary key, a unique nonclustered index is highly efficient. In fact, many environments probably shouldn't "waste" their clustered index on the primary key. If access via the complete primary key is common, it might be beneficial to specify NONCLUSTERED when you declare the primary key and save the clustered index for another type of access (such as a range query) that can benefit more from the clustered index.

Join Selection

Join selection is the third major step in query optimization. If the query is a multiple-table query or a self-join, the query optimizer evaluates join selection and selects the join strategy with the lowest cost. It determines the cost using a number of factors, including the expected number of reads and the amount of memory required. It can choose between three basic strategies for processing joins: nested loop joins, merge joins, and hash joins. In each method, the tables to be joined (or subsets of tables that have already been restricted with conditions in the WHERE clause) are called the *join inputs*.

Nested Loop Joins

Joins are frequently processed as nested iterations—a set of loops that take a row from the first table and use that row to scan the inner table, and so on, until the result that matches is used to scan the last table. The number of iterations through any of the loops equals the number of scans that must be done. This is not necessarily a table scan, since it is frequently done using an index. In fact, if no useful index is available to be used for an inner table, nested iteration probably isn't used and a hash join strategy is used instead. The result set is narrowed down as it progresses from table to table within each iteration in the loop. If you've done programming with an ISAM-type product, this should look familiar in terms of opening one "file" and then seeking into another in a loop. To process the following join

```
SELECT <some columns>
FROM departments dept JOIN employees empl
    ON dept.deptno=empl.deptno
```

you use pseudocode that looks something like this:

```
DO (until no more dept rows);
    GET NEXT dept row;
    {
        begin
            // Scan empl, hopefully using an index on empl.deptno
            GET NEXT empl row for given dept
        end
    }
```

Merge Joins

Merge joins were introduced in SQL Server 7. You can use a merge join when the two join inputs are both sorted on the join column. Consider the query we looked at in the previous section:

```
SELECT <some columns>
FROM departments dept JOIN employees empl
    ON dept.deptno=empl.deptno
```

If both the *departments* table and the *employees* table have clustered indexes on the *deptno* column, the query is a prime candidate for a merge join. You can think of merge joins as taking two sorted lists of values and merging them. Suppose you have two piles of contractor information. One pile contains the master contract that each contractor has signed, and the second contains descriptions of each project that the contractor has worked on. Both piles are sorted by contractor name. You need to merge the two piles of paperwork so that each contractor's master contract is placed with all the project descriptions for that contractor. You basically need to make just one pass through each stack.

Going back to the *employees* and *departments* query, our pseudocode would look something like this:

```
GET one dept row and one empl row
DO (until one input is empty);
    IF dept_no values are equal
        Return values from both rows
        GET next employee row
    ELSE IF empl.dept_no < dept.dept_no
        GET next employee row
    ELSE GET next department row
```

The query optimizer usually chooses the merge join strategy when both inputs are already sorted on the join column. In some cases, even if a sort must be done on one of the inputs, the query optimizer might decide that it is faster to sort one input and then do a merge join than to use any of the other available strategies. If the inputs are both already sorted, little I/O is required to process a merge join if the join is one to many. A many-to-many merge join uses a temporary table to store rows instead of discarding them. If there are duplicate values from each input, one of the inputs must rewind to the start of the duplicates as each duplicate from the other input is processed.

Hash Joins

Hash joins, also introduced in SQL Server 7, can be used when no useful index exists on the join column in either input. Hashing is commonly used in searching algorithms (as discussed in detail in Donald Knuth's classic *The Art of Computer Programming: Sorting and Searching*). We'll look at a simplified definition here. Hashing lets you determine whether a particular data item matches an already existing value by dividing the existing data into groups based on some property. You put all the data with the same value in what we can call a *hash bucket*. Then, to see if a new value has a match in existing data, you simply look in the bucket for the right value.

For example, suppose you need to keep all your wrenches organized in your workshop so that you can find the right size and type when you need it. You can organize them by their size property and put all half-inch wrenches (of any type) together, all 10-mm wrenches together, and so on. When you need to find a 15-mm box wrench, you simply go to the 15-mm drawer to find one (or see whether the last person who borrowed it has returned it). You don't have to look through all the wrenches, only the 15-mm ones, which greatly reduces your searching time. Alternatively, you can organize your wrenches by type and have all the box wrenches in one drawer, all the socket wrenches in another drawer, and so on.

Hashing data in a table is not quite so straightforward. You need a property by which to divide the data into sets of manageable size with a relatively equal membership. For integers, the hashing property might be something as simple as applying the modulo operator to each existing value. If you decide to hash on the operation modulo 13, every value is put in a hash bucket based on its remainder after dividing by 13. This means you need 13 buckets because the possible remainders are the integers 0 through 12. In real systems, the actual hash functions are substantially more complex; coming up with a good hash function is an art as well as a science.

When you use hashing to join two inputs, SQL Server uses one input, called the *build input,* to actually build the hash buckets. Then, one row at a time, it inspects the other input and tries to find a match in the existing buckets. The second input is called the *probe input.* Suppose we use modulo 3 as the hash function and join the two inputs shown in Figure 15-6. The rows not matching the SARGs are not shown, so the two inputs are reduced in size quite a bit. Here's the query:

```
SELECT Name, Manager
FROM employee empl JOIN department dept
ON dept.dept_no=empl.dept_no
WHERE <SARGs>
```

Department		Employee		
dept_no	Manager	ID	Name	dept_no
2	Laszlo	1	Pike	2
5	Wehland	2	Delaney	6
6	Graeffe	3	Harvey	7
8	Waymire	4	Moran	10
10	Aebi	5	Rogerson	14
13	Soukup	6	Karaszi	13
15	Berenson	7	Fields	11
		8	Robertson	4
		9	Pfeiff	1
		10	Hotz	7
		11	Dwyer	2
		12	Talmage	12

Figure 15-6. *Two inputs to a hash join operation.*

When processing hash joins, SQL Server tries to use the smaller input as the build input, so in this case we'll assume that the hash buckets have been built based on the *department* table values. The buckets are actually stored as linked lists, in which each entry contains only the columns from the build input that are needed. In this case, all we have to keep track of is the department number and manager name. The collection of these linked lists is called the *hash table.* Our hash table is shown in Figure 15-7. Our pseudocode looks something like this:

```
Allocate an Empty Hash Table
For Each Row in the Build Input
    Determine the hash bucket by applying the hash function
    Insert the relevant fields of the record into the bucket
For Each Record in the Probe Input
    Determine the hash bucket
    Scan the hash bucket for matches
    Output matches
Deallocate the Hash Table
```

Applying this algorithm to our two inputs, we get these results:

```
Name        Manager
--------    -------
Pike        Laszlo
Delaney     Graeffe
Moran       Aebi
Dwyer       Laszlo
Karaszi     Soukup
```

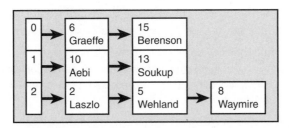

Figure 15-7. *A hash table built from the smaller (build) input.*

Hashing Variations

Although you can use hashing effectively when there are no useful indexes on your tables, the query optimizer might not always choose it as the join strategy because of its high cost in terms of memory required. Ideally, the entire hash table should fit into memory; if it doesn't, SQL Server must split both inputs into partitions, each containing a set of buckets, and write those partitions out to disk. As each partition (with a particular set of hash buckets) is needed, it is brought into memory. This increases the amount of work required in terms of I/O and general processing time. In the academic literature, you might see this type of hashing operation referred to as a *Grace hash*; the name comes from the project for which this technique was developed. SQL Server has another alternative, somewhere in between keeping everything in memory and writing everything out to disk. Partitions are only written out as needed, so you might have some partitions in memory and some out on disk.

To effectively use hashing, SQL Server must be able to make a good estimate of the size of the two inputs and choose the smaller one as the build input. Sometimes, during execution SQL Server will discover that the build input is actually the larger of the two. At that point, it can actually switch the roles of the build and probe input midstream, in a process called *role reversal*. Determining which input is smaller isn't too hard if there are no restrictive SARGs, as in this query:

```
SELECT Name, Manager
FROM employee empl JOIN department dept
ON dept.dept_no=empl.dept_no
```

SQL Server knows the sizes of the inputs because *sysindexes* keeps track of the size of each table. However, consider the case in which additional conditions are added to the query, as in this example:

```
WHERE empl.phone LIKE '425%'
```

It would help the query optimizer to know what percentage of the employees have phone numbers starting with 425. This is a case in which column statistics can be helpful. Statistics can tell the query optimizer the estimated number of rows that will meet a given condition, even if there is no actual index structure to be used.

> **NOTE** Hash and merge joins can be used only if the join is an equijoin—that is, if the join predicate compares columns from the two inputs for an equality match. If the join is not based on an equality, as in the example below, a nested loops join is the only possible strategy:
>
> ```
> WHERE table1.col1 BETWEEN table2.col2 AND table2.col3
> ```

The hashing and merging strategies can be much more memory intensive than the nested loops strategy, and because the query optimizer takes into account all available resources, you might notice that a system with little available memory might not use the hash and merge joins as often as systems with plenty of memory. Personal SQL Server installations are particularly vulnerable to memory pressure because you're more likely to have many competing applications running simultaneously. In most situations, there is limited memory for a desktop installation, so the query optimizer is much more pessimistic when it decides to use one of these two strategies.

Multiple-Table Joins

According to some folklore, SQL Server "does not optimize" joins of more than four tables. There was some truth to this in earlier versions of SQL Server, but in SQL Server 2000 optimization doesn't happen in the same way at all. There are so many different possible permutations of join strategies and index usage that the query optimizer goes through multiple optimization passes, each considering a larger set of the possible plans. On each pass, it keeps track of the best plan so far and uses a cost estimate to reduce the search in succeeding passes. If your query contains many tables, the query optimizer is likely to interrupt the last pass before completion because the last pass is quite exhaustive. The cheapest plan found will then be used.

Other Processing Strategies

Although our discussion of the query optimizer has dealt mainly with the choice of indexes and join strategies, the optimizer makes other decisions as well. It must decide how to process queries with GROUP BY, DISTINCT, and UNION, and it must decide how updates should be handled—either a row at a time or a table at a time. We looked at update strategies in Chapter 9. Here, I'll briefly discuss GROUP BY, DISTINCT, and UNION.

GROUP BY Operations

Prior to SQL Server 7, a GROUP BY operation was processed in only one way: SQL Server sorted the data (after applying any SARGs) and then formed the groups from the sorted data. SQL programmers noticed that queries involving grouping returned results in sorted order, although this was merely a by-product of the internal grouping mechanism. In SQL Server 2000, the query optimizer can choose to use hashing to organize the data into groups and compute aggregates. The pseudocode looks like this:

```
For Each Record in the Input
    Determine the hash bucket
    Scan the hash bucket for matches
    If a match exists
        Aggregate the new record into the old
        Drop the new record
    Otherwise
        Insert the record into the bucket
Scan and Output the Hash Table
```

If the query optimizer chooses to use hashing to process the GROUP BY, the data does not come back in any predictable order. The order actually depends on the order in which records appear in the hash buckets, but without knowing the specific hash function, you can't predict this order. If you use a lot of GROUP BY queries, you might be surprised that sometimes the results come back sorted and sometimes they don't. If you absolutely need your data in a particular order, you should use ORDER BY in your query.

> **NOTE** If a database has its compatibility level flag set to 60 or 65, the query processor automatically includes an ORDER BY in the query. This allows you to mimic the behavior of older SQL Server versions.

DISTINCT Operations

As with GROUP BY queries, the only way to remove duplicates before SQL Server 7 was to first sort the data. In SQL Server 2000, the query optimizer can choose to use hashing to return only the distinct result rows. The algorithm is much like the algorithm for hashing with GROUP BY, except that an aggregate does not need to be maintained:

```
For Each Record in the Input
    Determine the hash bucket
    Scan the hash bucket for matches
    If a match exists
        Drop the new record
    Otherwise
        Insert the record into the bucket
            and return the record as output
```

UNION Operations

The UNION operator in SQL Server has two variations for combining the result sets of two separate queries into a single result set. If you specify UNION ALL, SQL Server returns all rows from both inputs as the final result. If you don't specify ALL, SQL Server removes any duplicates before returning the results. For performance reasons, you should carefully evaluate your data, and if you know that the inputs are not overlapping, with no chance of duplicates, you should specify the ALL keyword to eliminate the overhead of removing duplicates. If SQL Server has to find the unique rows, it can do so in three ways: it can use hashing to remove the duplicates in a UNION, just as it does for DISTINCT; it can sort the inputs and then merge them; or it can concatenate the inputs and then sort them to remove the duplicates.

For GROUP BY, DISTINCT, and UNION operations, your best bet is to let the query optimizer decide whether to use hashing or sorting and merging. If you suspect that the query optimizer might not have made the best choice, you can use query hints to force SQL Server to use a particular processing strategy and compare the performance with and without the hints. In most cases, the query optimizer will have made the best choice after all. I'll tell you about query hints in Chapter 16.

Maintaining Statistics

As you've seen, the query optimizer uses statistics on both indexed and unindexed columns to determine the most appropriate processing strategy for any particular query. Whenever an index is created on a table containing data (as opposed to an empty table), the query optimizer collects statistics and stores them for that index in *sysindexes.statblob*. By default, the statistics are automatically updated whenever the query optimizer determines that they are out-of-date. In addition, the query optimizer generates statistics on columns used in SARGs when it needs them, and it updates them when needed.

As you've seen, the histogram for statistics on an index key or statistics on an unindexed column is a set of up to 200 values for that column. All of the values or a sampling of the values in a given column are sorted; the ordered sequence is divided into up to 199 intervals so that the maximum statistically significant information is captured. In general, these intervals are of nonequal size. SQL Server 2000 builds the histogram from the sorted set of column values in three passes. In the first pass, up to 200 values of RANGE_HI_KEY, EQ_ROWS, RANGE_ROWS, and DISTINCT_RANGE_ROWS are collected. Each additional key or column value is processed in the second pass; the value is either included in the last range (this is possible because the values are sorted) or a new range is created. If a new range is created, one pair of existing, adjacent ranges is collapsed into a single range so that the number of ranges (or steps) does not increase. The collapsed ranges are selected by considering the density information so that two neighboring ranges with the closest densities are collapsed in order to minimize information loss. In the third pass, more ranges might be collapsed if they have close densities. Therefore, even if the key column has more than 200 unique values, the histogram might have fewer than 200 steps.

You can specify the sampling interval when the indexes or statistics are initially created or at a later time using the statistics management tools. You can specify the FULLSCAN option, which means that all existing column values are sorted, or you can specify a percentage of the existing data values. By default, SQL Server uses a computed percentage that is a logarithmic function of the size of the table. If a table is less than 8 MB in size, a FULLSCAN is always done. When sampling, SQL Server randomly selects pages from the table by following the IAM chain. Once a particular page has been selected, all values from that page are used in the sample. Since disk I/O is the main cost of maintaining statistics, using all values from every page read minimizes that cost.

Statistics on nonindexed columns are built in exactly the same way as statistics on indexes. The system procedure *sp_helpstats* shows column statistics, in much the same way that *sp_helpindex* shows indexes on a table. If the statistics are created automatically, their names are very distinctive, as shown in this example:

```
EXEC sp_helpstats authors
```

RESULTS:

```
statistics_name                    statistics_keys
-------------------------------    ---------------------------------
_WA_Sys_au_fname_75D7831F          au_fname
_WA_Sys_state_75D7831F             state
city_stats                         city
```

We have three sets of statistics. The set of explicitly generated statistics is *city_stats*. The system-generated statistics are *_WA_Sys_au_fname_75D7831F* and *_WA_Sys_state_75D7831F*. To avoid long-term maintenance of unused statistics, SQL Server ages out the statistics that are automatically created on unindexed columns. After it updates the column statistics more than a certain number of times, the statistics are dropped rather than updated again. The *StatVersion* column of the *sysindexes* table shows how many times the statistics have been updated. Once *StatVersion* exceeds an internally generated threshold, the statistics are dropped. If they are needed in the future, they can be created again. There is no substantial cost difference between creating statistics and updating them. Statistics that are explicitly created (such as *city_stats* in the preceding example) are not automatically dropped.

Statistics are automatically updated when the query optimizer determines that they are out-of-date. This basically means that sufficient data modification operations have occurred since the last time they were updated to minimize their usefulness. The number of operations is tied to the size of the table and is usually something like $500 + 0.2 *$ (number of rows in the table). This means that the table must have at least 500 modification operations before statistics are updated during query optimization; for large tables, this threshold can be much larger. In this case, when I say "operation" I mean a single row modification. A single UPDATE statement that changes 1000 rows will be counted as 1000 modification operations. You can actually see the number of modification operations in the *sysindexes* table, in the *rowmodctr* column. The number of rows affected by every INSERT, UPDATE, or DELETE operation on a table is reflected in the *rowmodctr* column for the row representing the table itself. Remember that this will be the *sysindexes* row that has an *indid* value of either 0 (if the table is a heap) or 1 (if the table has a clustered index). Whenever statistics are updated, either manually or automatically, the *rowmodctr* value is reset to 0.

You can also manually force statistics to be updated in one of two ways. You can run the UPDATE STATISTICS command on a table or on one specific index or column statistics, or you can also execute the procedure *sp_updatestats*, which runs UPDATE STATISTICS against all user-defined tables in the current database.

You can create statistics on unindexed columns using the CREATE STATISTICS command or by executing *sp_createstats*, which creates single-column statistics for all eligible columns for all user tables in the current database. This includes all columns except computed columns and columns of the *ntext*, *text*, or *image* datatypes, and columns that already have statistics or are the first column of an index.

Every database is created with the database options *auto create statistics* and *auto update statistics* set to true, but you can turn either one off. You can also turn off automatic updating of statistics for a specific table in one of two ways:

- **sp_autostats** This procedure sets or unsets a flag for a table to indicate that statistics should or should not be updated automatically. You can also use this procedure with only the table name to find out whether the table is set to automatically have its index statistics updated.

- **UPDATE STATISTICS** In addition to updating the statistics, the option WITH NORECOMPUTE indicates that the statistics should not be automatically recomputed in the future. Running UPDATE STATISTICS again without the WITH NORECOMPUTE option enables automatic updates.

However, setting the database option *auto update statistics* to FALSE overrides any individual table settings. In other words, no automatic updating of statistics takes place. This is not a recommended practice unless thorough testing has shown you that you don't need the automatic updates or that the performance overhead is more than you can afford.

The Query Plan

The end product of the compilation phase of query processing is a query plan, which, with some exceptions, is put into the procedure cache. Cheap ad hoc SQL plans don't really go in the cache because it's not a good idea to flood the cache with plans that are unlikely to be reused. And ad hoc SQL is the least likely type of query to have its plan reused. If the statement is already so cheap to compile (less than 1/100 second), there is little to be gained by storing the plan in the cache.

Figure 15-8 shows the flow of compilation and execution. If a plan is not in cache initially, we must create one. This is shown on the left side of the flowchart. You can also see that after the plan has been put in cache, when it's time to execute it, SQL Server checks to see whether anything has changed and whether the plan must be recompiled. Even though it could be only microseconds separating compilation from execution, somebody could have executed a Data Definition Language (DDL) statement that added an index to a crucial table. This is admittedly unlikely, but it is possible, so SQL Server must account for it. There are a few things that will cause SQL Server to recompile a stored plan. Metadata changes such as adding or dropping indexes is the most likely reason. You need to make sure that the plan used reflects the current state of the indexes.

Another cause of recompilation is statistical changes. SQL Server keeps quite a bit of histogram information on the data that it processes. If the data distribution changes a lot, you'll likely need a different query plan to get the most efficient execution. If SQL Server has updated the statistics on an index used in the plan, a subsequent use of that plan invokes recompilation based on new distribution information.

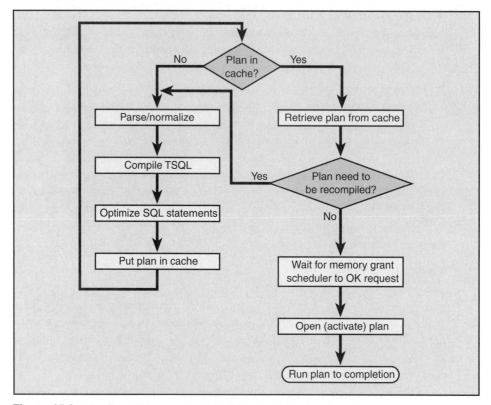

Figure 15-8. *The flow of query compilation and execution.*

Keep in mind that a change of actual parameter will *not* cause a plan to be recompiled, nor will environmental changes such as the amount of memory available or the amount of needed data that is already in cache. I'll give you more details about some special issues with stored procedure recompilation in the next section.

Execution is pretty straightforward, and if all you had were very simple queries such as "insert one row" or a singleton select from a table with a unique index, the processing would be very simple. But many queries require large amounts of memory to run efficiently, or at least could benefit from that memory. Starting with SQL Server 7, the SQL Server developers added the ability to use large amounts of memory for individual queries.

Another problem came up at this point. Once you start allowing queries to use very large amounts of memory, you have to decide how to arbitrate this memory use among many queries that might need that memory. SQL Server handles this as follows. When a query plan is optimized, the optimizer determines two pieces of information about memory use for that query: first, it picks a minimum amount of memory that the query needs in order to run effectively, and that value is stored with the query plan. It also determines a maximum amount of memory that the query could benefit from. For example, it doesn't help to give a sort operation 2 GB of memory if the entire table you're sorting fits into 100 MB. You really just want the 100 MB, and so that would be the value for the maximum amount of useful memory that's stored with the query plan.

When SQL Server goes to execute the plan, the plan gets passed to a routine called the *memory grant scheduler*. If the query it is looking at doesn't have a sort or a hash operation as part of the plan, SQL Server knows it doesn't use large amounts of memory. In this case, there is no waiting in the memory grant scheduler at all. The plan can be run immediately, so a typical transaction processing request bypasses this mechanism completely.

If there are very large queries, it's best to run a few of them at a time and let them get more of the memory they need. If at least half of the maximum memory requirement of the query is available, the query will run immediately with whatever memory it can get. Otherwise, the query will wait in the memory grant queue until half of the maximum memory requirement is available. At the same time, the SQL Server will never give out more than half of the remaining query memory to any one query. If you find that you're getting lots of memory timeout errors (error number 8645), this means your queries were waiting too long in the memory grant scheduler. By default, a query will wait only for an amount of time that is proportional to its estimated cost to run; at this time, that value is about 25 times the estimated number of seconds. With the default value, no query will wait less than 25 seconds because the query cost is rounded up to 1 if it is less than 1 second. If the time limit is exceeded, error 8645 is generated.

Once the scheduler allows memory to be allocated for a query's execution, SQL Server performs a step called "opening the plan," which starts the actual execution. From there, the plan runs to completion. If your query is using the default result set model, the plan will actually just run until it has produced all of its rows and they've all been sent back to the client. If you're using a cursor model, the processing is a bit different. Each client request is for just one block of rows, not all of them. After each block is sent back to the client, SQL Server must wait for the client to request the next block. While it's waiting, the entire plan is *quiesced*—that is, some of the locks are released, some resources are given up, and some positioning information is squirreled away. This information allows SQL Server to get back to where it was when the next block of rows is requested, and execution can continue.

I mentioned earlier that compilation and execution are two distinct phases of query processing, so one of the things the optimizer does is optimize based on a fairly stable state. SQL Server might recompile a statement depending on certain criteria being met, in which case the state isn't permanently stable but it must be something that you know doesn't change too often. If the optimizer were to use information that often changes dramatically, such as the number of concurrent processes or the number of locks held, you'd constantly be recompiling things. And compilation, especially in SQL Server 2000, tends to be pretty slow. For example, you might have a SQL statement that runs in 1/100 second, but it takes a ½ second to compile. It would be preferable to compile the statement once and let people execute it thousands or millions of times without repaying the compilation cost on every statement.

THE PROCEDURE CACHE

I've mentioned SQL Server's procedure cache several times. It's important to understand that the procedure cache in SQL Server 2000 is not actually a separate area of memory. Releases prior to SQL Server 7 had two effective configuration values to control the size of the procedure cache: one specifying a fixed size for SQL Server's total usable memory and one specifying a percentage of that memory (after fixed needs were satisfied) to be used exclusively for storing query plans. Also, in previous versions query plans for ad hoc SQL statements were never stored in the cache, only the plans for stored procedures. In SQL Server 2000, the total size of memory is by default dynamic and the space used for query plans is also very fluid.

One of the first things SQL Server determines when processing a query is whether the query is both ad hoc *and* cheap to compile; if so, SQL Server won't bother caching it at all. (In the next section, we'll look at what "ad hoc" actually means and compare it to the alternative types of queries: autoparameterized, prepared, and stored procedures.) It's not a good idea to flood the cache with things that probably won't be reused very often. It is cheaper to simply recompile if necessary. If the query is not ad hoc or is not cheap to compile, SQL Server will get some memory from the buffer cache. There is only one source of memory for 99 percent of the server's needs, and that is the buffer cache itself. In a few cases, SQL Server will go out and allocate large chunks of memory directly from the operating system, but those cases are extremely rare. For everything else, the management is centralized.

Plans are saved in cache along with a cost factor that reflects the cost of actually creating the plan by compiling the query. If the plan is ad hoc, SQL Server will set its cost to 0. The value 0 means that the plan is immediately available to be kicked out of the procedure cache. You're taking a chance that the plan might be reused, but the probability is low. If there's memory pressure on the system, plans for ad hoc statements should be the first to go. If the plan is not ad hoc, SQL Server sets the cost to the actual cost of compiling the query. These costs are basically in units of disk I/O. When a data page is read off the disk, it has a cost of 1 I/O. When this plan was built, information was read off the disk, including statistics and the text of the query itself. SQL did additional processing and that processing work is normalized to the cost of an I/O. Once the cost is computed, the plan is put into the cache. Figure 15-9 shows the flow of costing a plan and placing it in cache.

If another query comes along that can reuse that plan, SQL Server again determines what type of plan it is. If it's an ad hoc plan, SQL Server increments the cost by 1. So if ad hoc plans are really being reused, they'll stay in the cache for a little while longer as their cost factor increases. If the plan is reused frequently, the cost will keep getting bumped up by 1 until it reaches its actual creation cost—and that's as high as it will ever be set. But if it's reused a lot—if the same user or other users keep resubmitting the exact same SQL text—the plan will remain in cache.

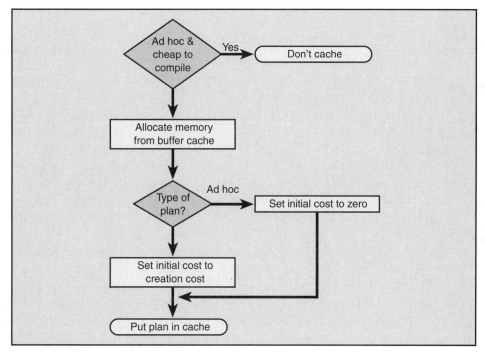

Figure 15-9. *Costing a query plan and placing it in cache.*

If the query is not ad hoc, which means that it's a stored procedure, a prepared query, or an autoparameterized query, the cost is set back up to the creation cost every time the plan is reused. As long as the plan is reused, it will stay in cache. Even if it's not used for a while, depending on how expensive it was to create initially, it can remain in cache for a fair amount of time. Figure 15-10 shows the flow of retrieving a plan from cache, and adjusting the cost.

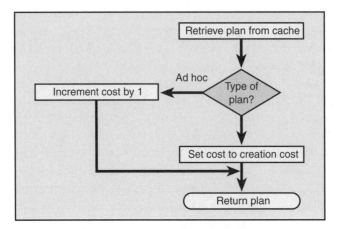

Figure 15-10. *Retrieving a plan from cache.*

The lazywriter is the mechanism that actually manages the cost of plans and is responsible for removing plans from cache when necessary. The lazywriter is actually part of the storage engine, but since it's so important to the query processing mechanism it needs to be mentioned here. The lazywriter uses the same mechanism for managing memory used by query plans that it does for managing data and index pages because plans are stored in the normal buffer cache. The lazywriter looks through all the buffer headers in the system. If there's very little memory pressure on the system, it looks very slowly; if memory pressure grows and the hit rates on the cached objects start going up, the lazywriter starts running more frequently. As the lazywriter runs, it looks at each buffer header and then at the current cost for the page that the buffer is holding. If the cost is 0, which means it hasn't been touched since the lazywriter's last pass through the cache, the lazywriter will release that page to get some free memory in the system to use for page I/O or for other plans. In addition, if the buffer contains a procedure plan, the lazywriter will call the SQL manager, which does some cleanup. Finally, the buffer is put on the free list for reuse.

If the cost associated with a buffer is greater than 0, the lazywriter decrements the cost and continues inspecting other buffers. The cost then actually indicates for how many cycles of the lazywriter something will stay in the cache without reuse before it's removed. This algorithm doesn't differentiate between query plans in cache and data or index pages in cache, with the exception of the step that calls the SQL manager if the object is a stored procedure. The lazywriter doesn't really know anything about an object being a query plan, and the algorithm balances the use of a cache for disk I/O versus the use of cache for a procedure plan. Figure 15-11 shows the flow of the lazywriter's processing of the cache.

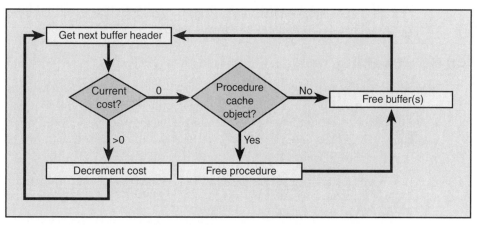

Figure 15-11. *The flow of the lazywriter's processing of plans in cache.*

You'll find that if you have something that is expensive to compile, even if it is not touched for a long time, it will stay in cache because its initial cost is so high. Anything that is reused frequently will sit in cache for a long time because its cost is also reset whenever it's used, and the lazywriter will never see it go to 0.

USING STORED PROCEDURES
AND CACHING MECHANISMS

Stored procedures are the most cost-effective mechanism for executing SQL commands from your applications, and I recommend that you use them whenever possible rather than passing ad hoc SQL statements from your applications. Chapters 3 and 11 discussed the efficiencies that stored procedures bring in terms of not requiring compilation of an execution plan for each execution. Plans can be reused and stay cached and available for subsequent use. Reusing a saved plan can provide a major performance advantage. The query optimizer might evaluate thousands of possible plans, so compilation and optimization time can end up being a more significant percentage of total execution time. It is critical that you understand when recompilation takes place and try to avoid it if at all possible.

SQL Server can save on recompilation using four mechanisms to make plan caching accessible in a wider set of scenarios than just using stored procedures:

- Ad hoc caching
- Autoparameterization
- The *sp_executesql* procedure
- The prepare and execute method

> **NOTE** The information here on caching query plans was adapted from a preliminary copy of a whitepaper by Peter Scharlock.

Ad Hoc Caching

SQL Server caches the plans from ad hoc queries, and if a subsequent batch matches exactly, the cached plan is used. This feature requires no extra work to use, but it is limited to exact textual matches. For example, if the following three queries are submitted in the *Northwind* database, the first and third queries will use the same plan but the second one will need to generate a new plan:

```
SELECT * FROM orders WHERE customerID = 'HANAR'
SELECT * FROM orders WHERE customerID = 'CHOPS'
SELECT * FROM orders WHERE customerID = 'HANAR'
```

Autoparameterization

For simple queries, SQL Server guesses which constants might really be parameters and attempts to treat them as parameters. If this is successful, subsequent queries that follow the same basic template can use the same plan. The following four templates can be used for autoparameterization. Note that *key-expression* is an expression involving only column names, constants, AND operators, and comparison operators (<, >, =, <=, >=, and <>).

```
INSERT table VALUES ({constant | NULL | DEFAULT}, ...)
DELETE table WHERE key-expression
UPDATE table SET colname = constant WHERE key-expression
SELECT {* | column-list} FROM table WHERE key-expression ORDER BY column-
    list
```

For example, these two queries will use the same plan:

```
SELECT firstname, lastname, title FROM employees WHERE employeeID = 6
SELECT firstname, lastname, title FROM employees WHERE employeeID = 2
```

Internally, SQL Server parameterizes these queries as follows:

```
SELECT firstname, lastname, title FROM employees WHERE employeeID = @p
```

SQL Server can allow other queries of the same template to use the same plan only if the template is *safe*. A template is safe if the plan selected will not change even if the actual parameters change. This ensures that autoparameterization won't degrade a query's performance.

The SQL Server query processor is much more conservative about deciding whether a template is safe than an application can be. SQL Server guesses which values are really parameters, whereas your application should actually know. Rather than rely on autoparameterization, you should use one of the following two mechanisms to mark parameters when they are known.

The *sp_executesql* Procedure

The stored procedure *sp_executesql* is halfway between ad hoc caching and stored procedures. Using *sp_executesql* requires that you identify the parameters but doesn't require all the persistent object management needed for stored procedures.

Here's the general syntax for the procedure:

```
sp_executesql @batch_text, @batch_parameter_definitions,
    param1,...paramN
```

Repeated calls with the same *batch_text* use the cached plan, with the new parameter values specified. The same cached plan is used in all the following cases:

```
EXEC sp_executesql N'SELECT firstname, lastname, title FROM employees
 WHERE employeeID = @p', N'@p tinyint', 6
EXEC sp_executesql N'SELECT firstname, lastname, title FROM employees
 WHERE employeeID = @p', N'@p tinyint', 2
EXEC sp_executesql N'SELECT firstname, lastname, title FROM employees
 WHERE employeeID = @p', N'@p tinyint', 6
```

ODBC and OLE DB expose this functionality via *SQLExecDirect* and *ICommand-WithParameters*. The ODBC and OLE DB documentation provide more details.

The Prepare and Execute Method

This last mechanism is like *sp_executesql* in that parameters to the batch are identified by the application, but there are some key differences. The prepare and execute method does not require the full text of the batch to be sent at each execution. Rather, the full text is sent once at prepare time; a handle that can be used to invoke the batch at execute time is returned. ODBC and OLE DB expose this functionality via *SQLPrepare/SQLExecute* and *ICommandPrepare*. You can also use this mechanism via ODBC and OLE DB when cursors are involved. When you use these functions, SQL Server is informed that this batch is meant to be used repeatedly.

Sharing Cached Plans

To allow users to share plans and thus maximize the effectiveness of the caching mechanisms, all users should execute in the same environment. Don't change SET options or database settings in the middle of an application or connection.

For all of the caching mechanisms, reusing a cached plan avoids recompilation and optimization. This saves compilation time, but it means that the same plan is used regardless of the particular parameter values passed in. If the optimal plan for a given parameter value is not the same as the cached plan, the optimal execution time will not be achieved. For this reason, SQL Server is very conservative about autoparameterization. When an application uses *sp_executesql*, prepare and execute, or stored procedures, the application developer is responsible for determining what should be parameterized. You should parameterize only constants whose range of values does not drastically affect the optimization choices.

The SQL Server Performance Monitor includes a counter called SQL Server:SQL Statistics that has several counters dealing with autoparameterization. You can monitor these counters to determine whether there are many unsafe or failed autoparameterization attempts. If these numbers are high, you can inspect your applications for situations in which the application can take responsibility for explicitly marking the parameters.

Examining the Plan Cache

The system table *syscacheobjects* keeps track of the compiled objects in cache at any time. Note that this table exists only in the *master* database and is really a pseudotable. It takes no space on disk and is materialized only when someone writes a query to access it. Table 15-2 lists some of the more useful columns in the *syscacheobjects* table.

Column Name	Description
bucketid	The bucket ID for this plan in an internal hash table; the bucket ID helps SQL Server locate the plan more quickly. Two rows with the same bucket ID refer to the same object (for example, the same procedure or trigger).
cacheobjtype	Type of object in the cache.
objtype	Type of object.
objid	One of the main keys used for looking up an object in the cache. This is the object ID stored in *sysobjects* for database objects (procedures, views, triggers, and so on). For cache objects such as ad hoc or prepared SQL, *objid* is an internally generated value.
dbid	Database ID in which the cache object was compiled.
uid	The creator of the plan (for ad hoc query plans and prepared plans).
refcounts	Number of other cache objects that reference this cache object.
usecounts	Number of times this cache object has been used since inception.

Table 15-2. *Useful columns in the* syscacheobjects *table.*   *(continued)*

Column Name	Description
pagesused	Number of memory pages consumed by the cache object.
setopts	SET option settings that affect a compiled plan. Changes to values in this column indicate that users have modified SET options.
langid	Language ID of the connection that created the cache object.
dateformat	Date format of the connection that created the cache object.
sql	Procedure name or first 128 characters of the batch submitted.

Cacheobjtype refers to the type of plan. It can have one of the following values:

- **Compiled Plan**   The actual plan generated during compilation and optimization. A compiled plan can be shared by sessions each running the same procedure or query.

- **Executable Plan**   The execution environment that runs the compiled plan. Each concurrent invocation of the same compiled plan will have its own executable plan. Caching this environment information saves setup costs, which can be significant for a frequently run query. All executable plans must have an associated compiled plan with the same *bucketid*, but not all compiled plans will have an associated executable plan saved.

- **Parse Tree**   The internal form of a query prior to compilation and optimization.

- **Cursor Parse Tree**   The parse tree for a cursor's query.

Objtype refers to the type of object whose plan is cached. It can have one of the following values:

- **Proc**   For both stored procedures and inline functions.

- **Prepared**   For queries submitted using *sp_executesql* and using the prepare and execute method and for queries that SQL Server has decided to autoparamaterize.

- **Ad hoc query**   For queries that don't fall into any other category (as discussed above).

- **ReplProc** For replication agents.

- **Trigger** A type whose plans are very similar to procedure or inline function plans.

- **View** A type for which you typically see only a parse tree, not a plan. You see this type not only when a view is accessed, but also when a non-inline function is encountered. The function does not have its own separate plan, but is expanded as part of whatever query it is part of.

- **Table** A type for which a user or system table will generate a parse tree object if it has computed columns.

- **Default, Check, Rule** Types that are expanded into parse trees and compiled as part of the query in which they are activated.

Two other columns, *refcount* and *usecount*, indicate how the plans are being used. The *refcount* value indicates how many times the plan has been referenced. An executable plan in cache will always have a *refcount* of 1. An executable plan might actually have a *refcount* greater than 1 if the plan is currently being executed, but that will not show up in the *syscacheobjects* table. The *refcount* for compiled plans is 1 + the number of execution plans, either in cache or in use. The *usecount* value refers to the number of times a cached object is used. Each time the plan is looked up and found, the *usecount* is incremented. If you see a value of 2 for *usecount* after the first execution of a procedure or query, that is because the plan is accessed once when it is created and stored in cache, and once again when it is retrieved from cache and executed.

Multiple Plans in Cache

SQL Server will try to limit the number of plans for a query or a procedure. Because plans are reentrant, this is easy to accomplish. You should be aware of some situations that will cause multiple plans for the same procedure to be saved in cache. The most likely situation is a difference in certain SET options, database options, or configuration options. For example, a stored procedure that concatenates strings might compile the concatenation differently depending on whether the option CONCAT_NULL_YIELDS_NULL is on or off or whether the corresponding database option is true or false. If a user executes the procedure with the option on, that person will use a different plan than if the option is off. The column *setopts* in the *syscacheobjects* table is a bitmap indicating which SET options were in effect when the plan was placed in cache. If you start a different session with different SET options enabled, SQL Server will always generate a new plan. The options included in the *setopts* field include:

```
ANSI_PADDING
FORCEPLAN
CONCAT_NULL_YIELDS_NULL
ANSI_WARNINGS
ANSI_NULLS
QUOTED_IDENTIFIER
ANSI_NULL_DFLT_ON
ANSI_NULL_DFLT_OFF
```

Two sessions that have set different languages or different *dateformat* values will also always generate separate plans. SQL Server must then also keep the *langid* value and *dateformat* value in *syscacheobjects* so that these values can be compared with future attempts to execute the same plan.

One other connection issue can affect whether a plan can be reused. If an owner name must be resolved implicitly, a plan cannot be reused. For example, suppose user *sue* issues the following SELECT statement:

```
SELECT * FROM mytable
```

SQL Server will first try to resolve the object by looking for an object called *mytable* owned by *sue*, and if no such object can be found, it will look for an object called *mytable* owned by the DBO. If user *dan* executes the exact same query, the object can be resolved in a completely different way (to a table owned by *dan*), so *sue* and *dan* could not share the plan generated for this query. However, the situation is different if *sue* issues this command:

```
SELECT * FROM dbo.mytable
```

Now there's no ambiguity. Anyone executing this exact query will always reference the same object. In the *syscacheobjects* table, the column *uid* indicates the user ID for the connection in which the plan was generated. Only another connection with the same user ID value can use the same plan. The one exception is if the user ID value is recorded as –2 in *syscacheobjects*, which indicates that the query submitted does not depend on implicit name resolution and can be shared among different users. This is the preferred method.

> **TIP** If your server has been running for a while, the *syscacheobjects* table can get quite large and awkward to work with. If you want to run your own tests to determine what gets put in cache, and when plans are reused, you will probably want to clear out the cache occasionally to keep its size manageable. This can be done with the command DBCC FREEPROCCACHE, which removes all cached plans from memory. In addition, DBCC FLUSHPROCINDB(<*dbid*>) can be used to clear all plans from one particular database. DO NOT use these commands on your production servers as it could impact the performance of your running applications.

When to Use Stored Procedures and Other Caching Mechanisms

Keep the following guidelines in mind when you are deciding whether to use stored procedures or one of the other mechanisms:

- **Stored procedures** Use when multiple applications are executing batches in which the parameters are known.

- **Ad hoc caching** Useful in limited scenarios. Don't design an application to use this.

- **Autoparameterization** Use for applications that cannot be easily modified. Don't design an application to use this.

- **The *sp_executesql* procedure** Use when a single user might use the same batch multiple times and when the parameters are known.

- **The prepare and execute method** Use when multiple users are executing batches in which the parameters are known, or when a single user will definitely use the same batch multiple times.

Recompiling Stored Procedures

In spite of the benefits of the mechanisms just discussed, you should still use stored procedures whenever possible. Besides giving you the benefits of precompilation, they minimize network traffic by reducing the text that needs to be sent from your application to SQL Server, and they provide a security mechanism to control who can access data and under what conditions. Stored procedures can be recompiled automatically or manually under various circumstances. Chapter 11 discussed some of these issues.

You can actually watch automatic recompilation occurring by using SQL Profiler: Choose to trace the event in the Stored Procedures category called SP:Recompile. If you also trace the event called SP:StmtStarting, you can see at what point in the procedure it is being recompiled. In particular, you might notice that stored procedures can be recompiled multiple times during their execution. For example, if you build a temporary table and later create an index on that table, and then add data to the table, your stored procedure will be recompiled numerous times. One way to avoid this is to include all data definition statements dealing with your temporary tables, as well as the insertion of rows into the temporary tables, right at the beginning of the procedure. So if the procedure must be recompiled, it won't happen more than once. Another way to prevent recompilations is to include the query hint KEEPPLAN in your statements that access the temporary tables. I'll discuss query hints in Chapter 16.

Although we've been assuming that recompilation is something you will usually want to avoid, this is not always the case. If you know that updated statistics can improve the query plan, or if you know that you have wildly different possible parameter values, recompilation can be a good thing.

As you saw, the system table *syscacheobjects* keeps track of the compiled objects in cache at any time. This table is accessible only by system administrators, but you can write your own stored procedures to provide information for your own tuning and testing purposes. You can use a procedure called *sp_procs_in_cache* (which is on the companion CD) to return a list of all procedure plans in cache and the number of times each plan occurs. The list is organized by database. If you execute the procedure without passing a parameter, you see procedures in your current database only. Alternatively, you can provide a specific database name or use the parameter *all* to indicate that you want to see procedure plans in cache from all databases. If you want to pull different information out of *syscacheobjects*, you can customize the procedure in any way you like. Remember to create the procedure in the *master* database so that it can be called from anywhere. Also remember to grant appropriate permissions if anyone other than a system administrator will be running it. The *sp_procs_in_cache* procedure shows both *compiled plans* and *executable plans*.

Other Benefits of Stored Procedures

Beyond the significant performance and security advantages, stored procedures can provide a valuable level of indirection between your applications and the database design. Suppose your application calls a procedure such as *get_customer_balance* and expects a result set to be returned. If the underlying database is then changed, the application can be totally unaffected and unaware of the change as long as the procedure also changes to return the result set as expected. For example, if you decide to denormalize your database design to provide faster query performance, you can change the stored procedure to respecify the query. If many applications call the procedure, you can simply change the stored procedure once and never touch the application. In fact, a running application doesn't even need to be restarted—it executes the new version of the stored procedure the next time it is called.

Another good reason to use stored procedures is to minimize round-trips on the network (that is, the conversational TDS traffic between the client application and SQL Server for every batch and result set). If you will take different actions based on data values, try to make those decisions directly in the procedure. Strictly speaking, you don't need to use a stored procedure to do this—a batch also provides this benefit. Issue as many commands as possible in a batch. You can try a simple test by inserting 100 rows first as a single batch and then as every insert in its own batch (that is, 100 batches). You'll see a performance improvement of an order of magnitude even on a LAN, and on a slow network the improvement will be stunning. While LAN speeds of 10 megabits per second (Mbps) are fast enough that the network is generally not a significant bottleneck, speeds can be tremendously different on a slow network. A modem operating at 28.8 kilobits per second (Kbps) is roughly 300 times slower than a LAN. Although WAN speeds vary greatly, they typically can be 100 to 200 times slower than a LAN. The fast LAN performance might hide inefficient network use. You can often see a prime example of this phenomenon when you use cursors. Fetching each row individually might be tolerable on a LAN, but it is intolerable when you use dial-up lines.

If a stored procedure has multiple statements, by default SQL Server sends a message to the client application at the completion of each statement to indicate the number of rows affected for each statement. In TDS-speak, this is known as a DONE_IN_PROC message. However, most applications do not need DONE_IN_PROC messages. So if you are confident that your applications do not need these messages, you can disable them, which can greatly improve performance on a slow network when there is otherwise little network traffic.

You can use the connection-specific option *SET NOCOUNT ON* to disable these messages for the application. While they are disabled, you cannot use the ODBC *SQLRowCount* function or its OLE DB equivalent. However, you can toggle NOCOUNT on and off as needed, and you can use *SELECT @@ROWCOUNT* even when NOCOUNT is on. You can also suppress the sending of DONE_IN_PROC messages by starting the server with trace flag 3640, which lets you suppress what might be needless overhead without touching your application. However, some ODBC applications depend on the DONE_IN_PROC message, so you should test your application before using trace flag 3640 in production—it can break applications that are written implicitly to expect that token.

You should keep an eye on the traffic between your client applications and the server. An application designed and tuned for slow networks works great on a fast network, but the reverse is not true. If you use a higher-level development tool that generates the SQL statements and issues commands on your behalf, it is especially important to keep an eye on what's moving across the network. You can use the SQL Profiler to watch all traffic into the server. Just to monitor network traffic, though, this might be overkill; a network sniffer such as Network Monitor (available with Microsoft Windows NT Server, Microsoft Windows 2000 Server, and Microsoft Systems Management Server) can work better if you want only to monitor network traffic. Network Monitor is easy to use, and even a networking neophyte can set it up quickly and with a few mouse clicks watch the traffic between machine pairs.

EXECUTION

The final step in query processing is execution. I'm not going to talk about execution in any detail other than this short paragraph. The execution engine takes the plan that the optimizer has produced and executes it. Along with the actual execution, the execution engine schedules the threads for the processes to run on and provides interthread communication.

SUMMARY

In this chapter, we looked at how SQL Server processes the queries that it receives from a client application. The most powerful and complex component of query processing is the query optimizer. We looked at the information that the optimizer uses to make its decisions about which indexes and which processing techniques should be used. Some of the most important information available to the optimizer is the statistics. Statistics can be automatically generated and maintained by SQL Server, and you can also manually update them.

We also looked at the caching of plans generated by the optimizer. SQL Server can cache and reuse plans not only from stored procedures, but also from ad hoc and autoparameterized queries. Because generation of query plans can be expensive, it is helpful to understand how and why query plans are reused and when they must be regenerated.

Chapter 16

Query Tuning

If you want to end up with a poorly performing application or a complete project failure, you should wait until the end of the project to deal with performance concerns. If, however, you want your application to be the best it can be, you must consider performance throughout the development cycle. In fact, you must consider performance before you even write your first line of code.

Every chapter of this book has included some information on performance. If you've turned directly to this chapter in hopes of finding the secret to improving your lackluster application, you'll be disappointed. I can offer only guidelines for you to keep in mind, along with some pointers that refer back to earlier information or to other helpful materials.

Microsoft SQL Server systems can be brilliantly fast with well-designed, well-implemented applications. SQL Server can support workloads of the type and size that no one dreamed possible back in 1988 when SQL Server first became available. But with a poorly planned or poorly implemented system, SQL Server can perform horribly. Statements like "SQL Server is slow" are not uncommon. Neither are such statements about other database products. Anytime you hear this from someone who has deployed a production application, your first thought should be that the person has dropped the ball somewhere along the line—or that SQL Server is unsuitable for the task at hand. (SQL Server can handle most systems, but some are still beyond its reach.)

If this is the first chapter you've turned to, please stop and go back at least to Chapter 3. All of the chapters from Chapter 3 to this one are relevant to performance issues. You might also revisit Chapter 13, which covers cursors, and Chapter 14, which covers locking. A thorough understanding of cursors and locking is a prerequisite for understanding the material in this chapter.

The big gains in query performance usually do not come from syntactic changes in the query but rather from a change in the database design or in indexing—or from taking a completely different approach to the query. For example, you might have to choose among the following approaches: writing a pretty complex query using a self-join or multilevel correlated subquery, using a cursor, or creating a solution that involves temporary tables. (You saw some of these techniques in Chapter 10.) Invariably, the only way you can determine which solution is best is to try all the queries. You might be surprised by the results.

Rather than trying to learn a bunch of tricks to do up front, you should be much more interested in doing the basics right. That is, you need to be sure that you've set up a good database structure—including perhaps some denormalization based on your CRUD analysis (described below)—and that you've created in advance what appear to be useful indexes. From there, you can test your queries and study the query plans generated for any queries that seem problematic.

THE DEVELOPMENT TEAM

A software project's success depends on the experience and skill of the staff developing it. Your second SQL Server development project will be better than your first, no matter how smart you are, so don't make your first project one that will have thousands of concurrent users, manage tens of gigabytes of data, and replicate data to 10 other servers. If you tackle such an extensive project your first time out, you'll probably fail (or at least finish late and over budget). And although it's useful to have experience working with other systems and environments, you can't expect successful SQL Server development on the first try.

The smartest companies start with a small, less-than-mission-critical system before moving many applications over to SQL Server. If management will not allow you the luxury of working on a "practice" system, you should at least try to augment your team with an experienced consultant or two. Look for someone who, at a minimum, is a Microsoft Certified Systems Engineer (MCSE) or Microsoft Certified Solution Developer (MCSD) who has taken both basic SQL Server exams—the Database Implementation and the Database Administration exams. In 1999, Microsoft introduced a Microsoft Certified DBA (MCDBA) certification, which indicates a similar level of qualification. This book, while it provides much useful information, can't replace other training. And skills such as database design, which transcend SQL Server specifically, are essential for a project's success.

APPLICATION AND DATABASE DESIGN

The biggest performance gains come from changes to the application and database design. You might change your configuration settings and add heftier hardware and be thrilled when performance doubles, but changes to the application can often result in even larger performance increases. There are as many approaches to software development as there are pages in this book. No single approach is the right approach—yours must be tailored to the size of the project, your team, and the skill level of the team members.

Take a look at the following list of suggestions for planning and implementing good performance in your system. I'll explain most of these items in detail in this chapter and in Chapter 17. (Chapter 4 discusses hardware.)

- Develop expertise on your development team.
- Understand that there is no substitute for solid application and database design.
- State performance requirements for peak, not average, use.
- Consider perceived response time for interactive systems.
- Prototype, benchmark, and test throughout the development cycle.
- Create useful indexes.
- Choose appropriate hardware.
- Use cursors judiciously.
- Use stored procedures almost all of the time.
- Minimize network round-trips.
- Understand concurrency and consistency tradeoffs.
- Analyze and resolve locking (blocking) problems.
- Analyze and resolve deadlock problems.
- Monitor and tune queries using SQL Profiler.
- Monitor Microsoft Windows 2000 system using System Monitor.
- Review and adjust operating system settings.
- Review and adjust SQL Server configuration settings.
- Make only one change at a time, and measure its effect.
- Do periodic database maintenance.

Normalize Your Database

I assume that if you're reading this book, you understand the concept of normalization and terms such as *third normal form*. (If you don't, see Candace Fleming and Barbara von Halle's *Handbook of Relational Database Design* [Addison-Wesley, 1988] and

Michael Hernandez's *Database Design for Mere Mortals* [Addison-Wesley, 1997]. A plethora of other books about database design and normalization are also available.)

A normalized database eliminates functional dependencies in the data so that updating the database is easy and efficient. But querying from that database might require a lot of joins between tables, so common sense comes into play. If the most important and time-critical function your system must perform is fast querying, it often makes sense to back off from a normalized design in favor of one that has some functional dependencies—that is, one that is not in third normal form or higher. Think of normalization as typically being good for updating but potentially bad for querying. Start with a normalized design, and then look at all the demands that will be placed on the system.

> **NOTE** There really isn't a binary concept of being "normalized" or "not normalized." There are only degrees of normalization. It's common to refer to a database that is at least in third normal form as *normalized* and to refer to a database at a lower level of normalization as *unnormalized* or *denormalized*. To keep the discussion simple, I'll use the terms in that way, as imprecise as that might be. Also note that the terms *unnormalized* and *denormalized* have slightly different meanings. An unnormalized database is one that has never been normalized. A denormalized database is one that was normalized at some point, but for specific performance-related reasons, the design was backed down from the normalized version. My apologies to those who make a living doing entity-relationship diagrams and are horrified by the loose use of these terms.

If you understand the data elements you need to record and you understand data modeling, producing a normalized design is not difficult. But it might take some time to learn about the way a business operates. If you already understand the underlying processes to be modeled and know how to do data modeling, the mechanics of producing a normalized database design are quite straightforward.

Once you produce a normalized design, which you can also think of as the *logical design,* you must decide if you can implement the design nearly "as is" or if you need to modify it to fit your performance characteristics. A lot of people have trouble with this. Rather than try to articulate specific performance characteristics, they generalize and strive for "as fast as possible" or "as many users as we can handle." Although goals can be difficult to articulate precisely, you should at least set relative goals. You should understand the tradeoffs between update and query performance, for example. If a salesperson must call up all of a customer's records while the customer is waiting on the phone, that action should be completed within a few seconds. Or if you want to run a bunch of batch processes and reports for your manufacturing operation each night and you have a window of four hours in which to do it, you have a pretty clear objective that must be met.

Evaluate Your Critical Transactions

One thing that you should do immediately is look at your critical transactions—that is, transactions whose performance will make or break the system. (In this context, I use the term *transaction* loosely, to mean any operation on the database.) Which tables and joins will be required for your critical transactions? Will data access be straightforward or complicated?

For example, if it is imperative that a given query have less than a 2-second response time but your normalized design would require a seven-way join, you should look at what denormalizing would cost. If tables are properly indexed, the query is well qualified, the search parameters are quite selective, and not a lot of data needs to be returned, the quick response might be possible. But you should note any seven-way joins and consider other alternatives. You should probably look for alternatives any time you get beyond a four-way join.

In our example, you might decide to carry a little redundant information in a couple of tables to make it just a three-way join. You'll incur some extra overhead to correctly update the redundant data in multiple places, but if update activity is infrequent or less important and the query performance is essential, altering your design is probably worth the cost. Or you might decide that rather than compute a customer's balance by retrieving a large amount of data, you can simply maintain summary values. You can use triggers to update the values incrementally when a customer's records change. For example, you can take the old value and add to or average it but not compute the whole thing from scratch each time. When you need the customer balance, it is available, already computed. You incur extra update overhead for the trigger to keep the value up-to-date, and you need a small amount of additional storage.

Proper indexes are extremely important for getting the query performance you need. But you must face query-vs.-update tradeoffs similar to those described earlier because indexes speed up retrieval but slow down updating. Chapter 9 explains the extra work required when your updates require index maintenance. You might want to lay out your critical transactions and look for the likely problems early on. If you can keep joins on critical transactions to four tables or less and make them simple equijoins on indexed columns, you'll be in good shape.

None of these considerations is new, nor are they specific to SQL Server. Back in the mainframe days, there was a technique known as "completing a CRUD chart." CRUD stands for Create-Retrieve-Update-Delete. In SQL, this would translate as ISUD—Insert-Select-Update-Delete. Conceptually, CRUD is pretty simple. You draw a matrix with critical transactions on the vertical axis and tables with their fields on the horizontal axis. The matrix gets very big very quickly, so creating it in Microsoft

Excel or in your favorite spreadsheet program can be helpful. For each transaction, you note which fields must be accessed and how they will be accessed, and you note the access as any combination of I, S, U, or D, as appropriate. You make the granularity at the field level so you can gain insight into what information you want in each table. This is the information you need if you decide to carry some fields redundantly in other tables to reduce the number of joins required. Of course, some transactions require many tables to be accessed, so be sure to note whether the tables are accessed sequentially or via a join. You should also indicate the frequency and time of day that a transaction runs, its expected performance, and how critical it is that the transaction meet the performance metric.

How far you carry this exercise is up to you. You should at least go far enough to see where the potential hot spots are for your critical transactions. Some people try to think of every transaction in the system, but that's nearly impossible. And what's more, it doesn't matter: only a few critical transactions need special care so they don't lead to problems. For example, if you have to do frequent select operations simultaneously on the tables that are updated most often, you might be concerned about locking conflicts. You need to consider what transaction isolation level to use and whether your query can live with Read Uncommitted and not conflict with the update activity. In addition, you shouldn't worry much about such things as noncritical reports that run only during off-hours.

If you're doing complex joins or expensive aggregate functions—SUM, AVG, and so on—for common or critical queries, you should explore techniques such as the following and you should understand the tradeoffs between query performance improvement and the cost to your update processes:

- Add logically redundant columns to reduce the number of tables to be joined.

- Use triggers to maintain aggregate summary data, such as customer balances, the highest value, and so forth. Such aggregates can usually be incrementally computed quickly. The update performance impact can be slight, but the query performance improvement can be dramatic.

- Define indexes on computed columns to maintain calculated data within a single table.

- Create indexed views to automatically maintain aggregated data or data from multiple tables that might need to be joined together. Just as with triggers, the update performance impact can be minimal, but the query performance improvement can be dramatic.

Keep Table Row Lengths and Keys Compact

When you create tables, you must understand the tradeoffs of using variable-length columns. (See Chapter 6.) As a general rule, data with substantial variance in the actual storage length is appropriate for variable-length columns. Also remember that the more compact the row length, the more rows will fit on a given page. Hence, a single I/O operation with compact rows is more efficient than an I/O operation with longer row lengths—it returns more rows and the data cache allows more rows to fit into a given amount of memory. In addition, if a variable-length column starts out with a small size and an UPDATE causes it to grow, the new size can end up causing the page to split, which can lead to extra overhead.

As with tables, when you create keys you should try to make the primary key field compact because it frequently occurs as a foreign key in other tables. If no naturally compact primary key exists, you might consider using an *identity* or *uniqueidentifier* column as a surrogate. And recall that if the primary key is a composite of multiple columns, the columns are indexed in the order that they are declared to the key. The order of the columns in the key can greatly affect how selective, and hence how useful, the index is.

Your clustered key should also be as compact as possible. If your clustered key is also your primary key (which is the default when you declare a PRIMARY KEY constraint), you might already have made it compact for the reason mentioned above. There are additional considerations for your clustered key because SQL Server automatically keeps the clustered key in all nonclustered indexes, along with the corresponding nonclustered key. For example, if your clustered index is on *zipcode* and you have a nonclustered index on *employee_id*, every row in the nonclustered index stores the corresponding *zipcode* value along with the *employee_id* value. I discussed the structure of indexes in Chapters 3 and 8, and I'll look at the topic again later in this chapter when I discuss how to choose the best indexes.

Occasionally, a table will have some columns that are infrequently used or modified and some that are very hot. In such cases, it can make sense to break the single table into two tables; you can join them back together later. This is kind of the reverse of denormalization as you commonly think of it. In this case, you do not carry redundant information to reduce the number of tables; instead, you increase the number of tables to more than are logically called for to put the hot columns into a separate, narrower table. With the more compact row length, you get more rows per page and potentially a higher cache-hit ratio. As with any deviation from the normalized model, however, you should do this only if you have good reason. After you complete a CRUD chart analysis, you might see that while your customer table is frequently accessed, 99 percent of the time this access occurs just to find out a customer's credit balance. You might decide to maintain this balance via a trigger rather than by recomputing it each time the query occurs. Information such as customer addresses, phone numbers, e-mail addresses, and so on are large fields that make the table have a wide row length. But not all that information is needed for critical transactions—only the customer balance is needed. In this case, splitting the table into two might result in the difference between fitting, say, 150 rows on a page instead of only 2 or 3 rows. A narrower table means a greater likelihood that the customer balance can be read from cache rather than by requiring physical I/O.

PLANNING FOR PEAK USAGE

People often ask questions such as, "Can SQL Server handle our system? We do a million transactions a day." To answer this question, you have to know exactly what transactions they have in mind. You also need to know the system's peak usage. If a million transactions a day are nicely spread out over 24 hours, that's less than 12 transactions per second. In general, a 12-TPS (transactions-per-second) system would be adequate. But if 90 percent of the million transactions come between 2 p.m. and 3 p.m., it's a very different situation. You'll have rates of about 275 TPS during that hour and probably peaks of more than 350 TPS. You can use benchmarks, such as Debit-Credit, in which SQL Server performs over 1500 TPS, but all transactions are different. It is meaningless to refer to transactions per second in SQL Server or any other system without also talking about the types of transactions. This is precisely the reason that standardized tests are available from the Transaction Processing Council for comparing database performance.

Regardless of the specific transactions, though, you must design and build your system to handle peak usage. In the case above, the important consideration is peak usage, which determines whether you should target your system to a volume of 350 TPS for unevenly distributed usage or to only 12 TPS with usage spread out evenly. Most systems experience peaks, and daily usage is not so nicely spread out.

PERCEIVED RESPONSE TIME FOR INTERACTIVE SYSTEMS

Systems are often built and measured without the appropriate performance goals in mind. When measuring query performance, for example, most designers tend to measure the time that it takes for the query to complete. By default, this is how SQL Server decides to cost query performance. But this might not be the way your users perceive system performance. To users, performance is often measured by the amount of time that passes between pressing the Enter key and getting some data. As a program designer, you can use this to your advantage. For example, you can make your application begin displaying results as soon as the first few rows are returned; if many rows will appear in the result set, you don't have to wait until they are all processed. You can use such approaches to dramatically improve the user's perception of the system's responsiveness. Even though the time required to get the last row might be about the same with both approaches, the time it takes to get the first row can be different—and the *perceived* difference can translate into the success or failure of the project.

By default, SQL Server optimizes a query based on the total estimated cost to process the query to completion. Recall from Chapter 3 that if a significant percentage of the rows in a table must be retrieved, it is better to scan the entire table than to use a nonclustered index to drive the retrieval. A clustered index, of course, would be ideal because the data would be physically ordered already. The discussion here pertains only to the performance tradeoff of scan-and-sort vs. using a nonclustered index.

Retrieving a page using the nonclustered index requires traversing the B-tree to get the address of a data page or the clustering key, retrieving that page (by using the RID to directly access it or traversing the clustered index to find the data page), and then traversing the nonclustered B-tree again to get the location information for the next data page and retrieve it...and so on. Many data pages are read many times each, so the total number of page accesses can be more than the total number of pages in the table. If your data and the corresponding nonclustered index are not highly selective, SQL Server usually decides not to use that nonclustered index. That is, if the index is not expected to eliminate more than about 90 percent of the pages from consideration, it is typically more efficient to simply scan the table than to do all the extra I/O of reading B-trees for both the nonclustered and clustered indexes as well as the data pages. And by following the index, each data page must frequently be accessed multiple times (once for every row pointed to by the index). Subsequent reads are likely to be from cache, not from physical I/O, but this is still much more costly than simply reading the page once for all the rows it contains (as happens in a scan).

Scanning the table is the strategy SQL Server chooses in many cases, even if a nonclustered index is available that could be used to drive the query, and even if it would eliminate a sort to return the rows based on an ORDER BY clause. A scan strategy can be much less costly in terms of total I/O and time. However, the choice of a full scan is based on SQL Server's estimate of how long it would take the query to complete in its entirety, not how long it would take for the first row to be returned. If an index exists with a key that matches the ORDER BY clause of the query and the index is used to drive the query execution, there is no need to sort the data to match the ORDER BY clause (because it's already ordered that way). The first row is returned faster by SQL Server chasing the index even though the last row returned might take much longer than if the table were simply scanned and the chosen rows sorted.

In more concrete terms, let's say that a query that returns many rows takes 1 minute to complete using the scan-and-sort strategy and 2 minutes using a nonclustered index. With the scan-and-sort strategy, the user doesn't see the first row until all the processing is almost done—for this example, about 1 minute. But with the index strategy, the user sees the first row within a subsecond—the time it takes to do, say, five I/O operations (read two levels of the nonclustered index, two levels of the clustered index, and then the data page). Scan-and-sort is faster in total time, but the nonclustered index is faster in returning the first row.

SQL Server provides a query hint called FAST that lets SQL Server know that having the first *n* rows returned quickly is more important than the total time, which would be the normal way query plans are costed. Later in this chapter, we'll look at some techniques for speeding up slow queries and discuss when it's appropriate to use the query hint. For now, you should understand the issues of *response time* (the time needed to get the first row) vs. *throughput* (the time needed to get all rows) when you think about your performance goals. Typically, highly interactive systems should be designed for best response time and batch-oriented systems should be designed for best throughput.

PROTOTYPING, BENCHMARKING, AND TESTING

As you make changes to your application design or hardware configuration, you should measure the effects of these changes. A simple benchmark test to measure differences is a tremendous asset. The benchmark system should correlate well with the expected performance of the real system, but it should be relatively easy to run. If you have a development "acceptance test suite" that you run before checking in any significant changes, you should add the benchmark to that test suite.

> **TIP**   You should measure performance with at least a proxy test; otherwise, you're setting yourself up for failure. Optimism without data to back it up is usually misguided.

Your benchmark doesn't have to be sophisticated initially. You can first create your database and populate it with a nontrivial amount of data—thousands of rows at a minimum. The data can be randomly generated, although the more representative you can make the data the better. Ideally, you should use data from the existing system, if there is one. For example, if a particular part represents 80 percent of your orders, you shouldn't make all your test data randomly dispersed. Any differences in the selectivity of indexes between your real data and the test data will probably cause significant differences in the execution plans you choose. You should also be sure that you have data in related tables if you use FOREIGN KEY constraints. As I explained earlier in this book, the enforcement of FOREIGN KEY constraints requires that those related tables (either referenced or referencing) be accessed if you're modifying data in a column that is participating in the constraint. So the execution plan is sometimes considerably more complicated than might be apparent due to the constraints, and a plethora of constraints can result in a system that has no simple operations.

As a rule of thumb, you should start with at least enough data so the difference between selecting a single row based on its primary key by using an index is dramatically faster than selecting such a row using a table scan. This assumes that the table in production will be large enough to reflect that difference. Remember that the system will perform much differently depending on whether I/O operations are physical or from the cache. So don't base your conclusions on a system that is getting high cache-hit ratios unless you have enough data to be confident that this behavior also will be true for your production system. In addition, keep in mind that running the same test multiple times might yield increasingly short response times. If you're testing on a dedicated machine, no other processes will be using SQL Server's memory and the data you read in from the disk the first time will already be in cache for subsequent tests.

> **TIP** If you want to run your tests repeatedly under the same conditions, use the command DBCC DROPCLEANBUFFERS after each test run to remove all data from memory and use DBCC FREEPROCCACHE to remove all query plans from memory.

Early in the development process, you should identify areas of lock contention between transactions and any specific queries or transactions that take a long time to run. SQL Profiler, discussed in Chapter 17, can be a wonderful tool for tracking down your long-running queries. And if table scans will be a drain on the production system, you should have enough data early on so that the drain is apparent when you scan. If you can run with several thousand rows of data without lock contention problems and with good response time on queries, you're in a good position to proceed with a successful development cycle. Of course, you must continue to monitor and make adjustments as you ramp up to the actual system and add more realistic amounts of data and simultaneous users. And, of course, your system test should take place on an ongoing basis before you deploy your application. It's not a one-time thing that you do the night before you go live with a new system.

Obviously, if your smallish prototype is exhibiting lock contention problems or the queries do not perform well within your desired goals, it's unlikely that your real system will perform as desired. Run the stored procedures that constitute your critical transactions. You can use a simple tool such as OSQL.EXE to dispatch them. First run each query or transaction alone; time it in isolation and check the execution plans using one of the SHOWPLAN options. Then run multiple sessions to simulate multiple users, either by manually firing off multiple OSQL commands or by using a third-party benchmarking or load stress tool. The SQL Server 2000 Resource Kit might include some tools for creating test simulations, but as of this writing, the content of the Resource Kit has not been finalized. A bit later, we'll look at how to analyze and improve a slow-running query.

> TIP   Before you roll out your production system, you should be able to conduct system tests with the same volumes of data and usage that the real system will have when it goes live. Crossing your fingers and hoping is not good enough. One handy tool for generating sample data, which is from the previous version of the Microsoft BackOffice Resource Kit, is included on this book's CD. The tool, called Filltabl.exe, allows you to add any number of rows to any table, as long as the table already exists and the user running the utility has insert permission on the table. If you run this executable from a command prompt, it will give you a usage message like this:
>
> usage: filltabl -Tdbtable -Ncount [-Uusername] [-Ppassword]
>   [-Sservername] [-Rrandomseed]
>
> note: there is no space between the option and the parameter
>   example: filltabl -Tpubs..authors -N20 -Usa -SMyServer
>
> Even though this utility was written for an older version of SQL Server, it will work with a named instance. Just use *ServerName\InstanceName* for the name of the server.

Also, based on your CRUD chart analysis (or on any analysis of critical transactions), you should identify tasks that will run at the same time as your critical transactions. Add these tasks to your testing routine to determine whether they will lead to contention when they run simultaneously with your critical transactions. For example, suppose *proc_take_orders* is your critical transaction. When it runs, some reports and customer status inquiries will also run. You should run some mixture of these types of processes when you analyze *proc_take_orders*. This will help you identify potential lock contention issues or other resource issues, such as high CPU usage or low cache.

You might also want to use benchmarking tools to launch and coordinate multiple client tasks simultaneously to time their work for throughput and response time. One such suite of benchmarking tools is available from Bluecurve, Inc. (now a subsidiary of Red Hat, Inc.) at www.redhat.com/services/bluecurve/bluecurve.html.

Development Methodologies

How much you spec, how you spec, when you start coding, and the role of prototyping are all matters on which there is no consensus; there is no one right answer. What's right for one team or project might be wrong for another. You must remember that the point of development is to ship products or deploy applications. Your ultimate purpose is not to produce specs and design documents.

The spec exists to clearly articulate and document how a module or system should work. It ensures that the developer thinks through the approach before writing code. It is also vitally important to others who come in later and are new to the system. While writing the design document, the developer might have to write some quick prototype code to help think through an issue. Or the developer should at least write some pseudocode and include it as part of the document.

Any development task that will take more than a couple of days to implement deserves a simple design document. Ideally, such a document should be at most 15 pages, and often about 3 succinct pages are ideal for even a complex component. The best design documents can be read in one sitting, and the reader should come away understanding clearly how the system will be built. Other developers should review the document before coding begins. This is best done in a positive, informal atmosphere in which others can contribute ideas. And, of course, in a healthy environment, developers are continually bouncing ideas off their peers.

The document should assume that the reader already knows *why* a module or component is needed. The document provides the *how*. Too many specs have 40 pages describing the market need for something or why a potential product would be really cool, and then they have 1 page that says, in essence, "We'll figure it out when we code it up."

No one can write a perfect spec up front. Prototyping the spec in an iterative fashion works far better. Areas that are clear don't need a prototype; use prototypes for areas fraught with risk, for your critical transactions, and for critical areas of the system in which multiple approaches are possible or reasonable. For the tricky stuff that you can't describe or predict a best performance, prototypes provide enormous benefits.

A useful prototype can be "quick and dirty." If you don't worry about all the failure cases and every conceivable state in which something can exist, useful prototype code can often be produced in 5 percent of the time that it takes to create production-caliber code (in which you must worry about those things). However, the production code might be 10 times better because you have recognized and corrected deficiencies early on. You'll either junk the prototype code or use it for the skeleton of the real system. Prototyping lets you learn and prove or disprove ideas, and then you can update the spec based on what you learn. And if you're selling your ideas to management or customers, your prototype can be useful to demonstrate proof of your concept.

As I mentioned before, every nontrivial development task deserves a brief design document. You need enough documentation to lay out the framework and system architecture and to detail how pieces fit together. But at the detailed levels, it's better to simply comment the source code liberally while you write and modify it. External design documentation rarely gets updated in a timely manner, so it quickly becomes useless. Explain operations when their purpose is not obvious. Don't assume that your readers will immediately grasp all the subtleties. And when you change something after the fact, add a comment about what you changed, when you changed it, and why. A module should be commented well enough so that testers or technical writers can gain a good understanding of what's going on just from reading the comments, even if they're not skilled programmers.

CREATING USEFUL INDEXES

Creating useful indexes is one of the most important tasks you can do to achieve good performance. Indexes can dramatically speed up data retrieval and selection, but they are a drag on data modification because along with changes to the data, the index entries must also be maintained and those changes must be logged. The key to creating useful indexes is understanding the uses of the data, the types and frequencies of queries performed, and how queries can use indexes to help SQL Server find your data quickly. A CRUD chart or similar analysis technique can be invaluable in this effort. You might want to quickly review the difference between clustered and nonclustered indexes because the difference is crucial in deciding what kind of index to create.

Clustered and nonclustered indexes are similar at the upper (node) levels—both are organized as B-trees. Index rows above the leaf level contain index key values and pointers to pages the next level down. Each row keeps track of the first key value on the page it points to. Figure 16-1 shows an abstract view of an index node for an index on a customer's last name. The entry *Johnson* indicates page 1:200 (file 1, page 200), which is at the next level of the index. Since *Johnson* and *Jones* are consecutive entries, all the entries on page 1:200 have values between *Johnson* (inclusive) and *Jones* (exclusive).

Key	Page Number
Jackson	1:147
Jensen	1:210
Johnson	1:200
Jones	1:186
Juniper	1:202

Figure 16-1. *An index node page.*

The leaf, or bottom, level of the index is where clustered and nonclustered indexes differ. For both kinds of indexes, the leaf level contains every key value in the table on which the index is built, and those keys are in sorted order. In a clustered index, the leaf level is the data level, so of course every key value is present. This means that the data in a table is sorted in order of the clustered index. In a nonclustered index, the leaf level is separate from the data. In addition to the key values, the index rows contain a bookmark indicating where to find the actual data. If the table has a clustered index, the bookmark is the clustered index key that corresponds to the nonclustered key in the row. (If the clustered key is composite, all parts of the key are included.)

Remember that clustered indexes are guaranteed to be unique in SQL Server 2000; if you don't declare them as unique, SQL Server adds a uniqueifier to every duplicate key to turn the index into a unique composite index. If our index on last name is a nonclustered index and the clustered index on the table is the zip code, a leaf-level index page might look something like Figure 16-2. The number in parentheses after the zip code is the uniqueifier and appears only when there are duplicate zip codes.

Key	Locator
Johnson	98004(1)
Johnson	06801(3)
Johnston	70118
Johnstone	33801(2)
Johnstone	95014(2)
Johnstone	60013
Jonas	80863(2)
Jonas	37027
Jonasson	22033(4)

Figure 16-2. *A leaf-level index page.*

Choose the Clustered Index Carefully

Clustered indexes are extremely useful for range queries (for example, *WHERE sales_quantity BETWEEN 500 and 1000*) and for queries in which the data must be ordered to match the clustering key. Only one clustered index can exist per table, since it defines the physical ordering of the data for that table. Since you can have only one clustered index per table, you should choose it carefully based on the most critical retrieval operations. Because of the clustered index's role in managing space within the table, nearly every table should have one. And if a table has only one index, it should probably be clustered.

If a table is declared with a primary key (which is advisable), by default the primary key columns form the clustered index. Again, this is because almost every table should have a clustered index, and if the table has only one index, it should probably be clustered. But if your table has several indexes, some other index might better serve as the clustered index. This is often true when you do single-row retrieval by primary key. A nonclustered, unique index works nearly as well in this case and still enforces the primary key's uniqueness. So save your clustered index for something that will benefit more from it by adding the keyword NONCLUSTERED when you declare the PRIMARY KEY constraint.

Make Nonclustered Indexes Highly Selective

A query using an index on a large table is often dramatically faster than a query doing a table scan. But this is not always true, and table scans are not all inherently evil. Nonclustered index retrieval means reading B-tree entries to determine the data page that is pointed to and then retrieving the page, going back to the B-tree, retrieving another data page, and so on until many data pages are read over and over. (Subsequent retrievals can be from cache.) With a table scan, the pages are read only once. If the index does not disqualify a large percentage of the rows, it is cheaper to simply scan the data pages, reading every page exactly once.

The query optimizer greatly favors clustered indexes over nonclustered indexes, because in scanning a clustered index the system is already scanning the data pages. Once it is at the leaf of the index, the system has gotten the data as well. So there is no need to read the B-tree, read the data page, and so on. This is why nonclustered indexes must be able to eliminate a large percentage of rows to be useful (that is, highly selective), whereas clustered indexes are useful even with less selectivity.

Indexing on columns used in the WHERE clause of frequent or critical queries is often a big win, but this usually depends on how selective the index is likely to be. For example, if a query has the clause *WHERE last_name = 'Stankowski'*, an index on *last_name* is likely to be very useful; it can probably eliminate 99.9 percent of the rows from consideration. On the other hand, a nonclustered index will probably not be useful on a clause of *WHERE sex = 'M'* because it eliminates only about half of the rows from consideration; the repeated steps needed to read the B-tree entries just to read the data require far more I/O operations than simply making one single scan through all the data. So nonclustered indexes are typically not useful on columns that do not have a wide dispersion of values.

Think of selectivity as the percentage of qualifying rows in the table (qualifying rows/total rows). If the ratio of qualifying rows to total rows is low, the index is highly selective and is most useful. If the index is used, it can eliminate most of the rows in the table from consideration and greatly reduce the work that must be performed. If the ratio of qualifying rows to total rows is high, the index has poor selectivity and will not be useful. A nonclustered index is most useful when the ratio is around 5 percent or less—that is, if the index can eliminate 95 percent of the rows from consideration. If the index has less than 5 percent selectivity, it probably will not be used; either a different index will be chosen or the table will be scanned. Recall that each index has a histogram of sampled data values for the index key, which the query optimizer uses to estimate whether the index is selective enough to be useful to the query.

Tailor Indexes to Critical Transactions

Indexes speed data retrieval at the cost of additional work for data modification. To determine a reasonable number of indexes, you must consider the frequency of updates vs. retrievals and the relative importance of the competing types of work. If your system is almost purely a decision-support system (DSS) with little update activity, it makes sense to have as many indexes as will be useful to the queries being issued. A DSS might reasonably have a dozen or more indexes on a single table. If you have a predominantly online transaction processing (OLTP) application, you need relatively few indexes on a table—probably just a couple carefully chosen ones.

Look for opportunities to achieve index coverage in queries, but don't get carried away. An index "covers" the query if it has all the data values needed as part of the index key. For example, if you have a query such as *SELECT emp_name, emp_sex FROM employee WHERE emp_name LIKE 'Sm%'* and you have a nonclustered index on *emp_name*, it might make sense to append the *emp_sex* column to the index key as well. Then the index will still be useful for the selection, but it will already have the value for *emp_sex*. The query optimizer won't need to read the data page for the row to get the *emp_sex* value; the query optimizer is smart enough to simply get the value from the B-tree key. The *emp_sex* column is probably a *char(1)*, so the column doesn't add greatly to the key length, and this is good.

Every nonclustered index is a covering index if all you are interested in is the key column of the index. For example, if you have a nonclustered index on first name, it covers all these queries:

- Select all the first names that begin with *K*.

- Find the first name that occurs most often.

- Determine whether the table contains the name *Melissa*.

In addition, if the table also has a clustered index, every nonclustered index includes the clustering key. So it can also cover any queries that need the clustered key value in addition to the nonclustered key. For example, if our nonclustered index is on the first name and the table has a clustered index on the last name, the following queries can all be satisfied by accessing only leaf pages of the B-tree:

- Select Tibor's last name.

- Determine whether any duplicate first and last name combinations exist.

- Find the most common first name for people with the last name *Wong*.

You can go too far and add all types of fields to the index. The net effect is that the index becomes a virtual copy of the table, just organized differently. Far fewer index entries fit on a page, I/O increases, cache efficiency is reduced, and much more disk space is required. The covered queries technique can improve performance in some cases, but you should use it with discretion.

A unique index (whether nonclustered or clustered) offers the greatest selectivity—that is, only one row can match—so it is most useful for queries that are intended to return exactly one row. Nonclustered indexes are great for single-row accesses via the PRIMARY KEY or UNIQUE constraint values in the WHERE clause.

Indexes are also important for data modifications, not just for queries. They can speed data retrieval for selecting rows, and they can speed data retrieval needed to find the rows that must be modified. In fact, if no useful index for such operations exists, the only alternative is for SQL Server to scan the table to look for qualifying rows. Update or delete operations on only one row are common; you should do these operations using the primary key (or other UNIQUE constraint index) values to be assured that there is a useful index to that row and no others.

A need to update indexed columns can affect the update strategy chosen. For example, to update a column that is part of the key of the clustered index on a table, you must process the update as a delete followed by an insert rather than as an update-in-place. When you decide which columns to index, especially which columns to make part of the clustered index, consider the effects the index will have on the update method used. (Review the discussion of updates in Chapter 9.)

SQL Server 2000 provides a new function that can give us a workaround if you need to index a large character field. The CHECKSUM function computes a checksum on a row or a column, and its value is always a 4-byte integer. You can create a computed column to be the checksum of your large character field and then build an index on that computed column. The values returned by CHECKSUM are not guaranteed to be absolutely unique, but there will be few duplicates. Since there is the possibility of two character string values having the same value for the checksum, your queries will need to include the full string that you're looking for.

Here's an example. Suppose we're expecting the *titles* table in the *pubs* database to grow to over a million titles by the end of the year. We want to be able to do quick lookups on book names, but since the *title* field is 80 characters wide, we know that an index on *title* is not ideal. (In fact, the *titles* table does have an index on *title*, but since it's not really such a good idea, we'll drop it.) So we'll create a computed column using CHECKSUM and index that:

```
DROP INDEX titles.titleind
GO
ALTER TABLE titles
ADD hash_title AS CHECKSUM(title)
GO
CREATE INDEX hash_index ON titles(hash_title)
GO
```

First let's try just searching for a particular title:

```
SELECT * FROM titles
WHERE title = 'Cooking with Computers: Surreptitious Balance Sheets'
```

If you look at the query plan for this SELECT, you'll see that a clustered index scan is done, which means the whole table must be searched. Instead, let's also query on the checksum value in the *hash_title* column:

```
SELECT * FROM titles
WHERE title = 'Cooking with Computers: Surreptitious Balance Sheets'
AND hash_title =
    CHECKSUM('Cooking with Computers: Surreptitious Balance Sheets')
```

The query plan will now show that SQL Server can do an index seek on the computed column *hash_title.* We'll look at query plans in detail later in this chapter.

Pay Attention to Column Order

At the risk of stating the obvious, an index can be useful to a query only if the criteria of the query match the columns that are leftmost in the index key. For example, if an index has a composite key of *last_name,first_name,* that index is useful for a query such as *WHERE last_name = 'Smith' or WHERE last_name = 'Smith'* AND *first_name = 'John'*. But it is not useful for a query such as *WHERE first_name = 'John'.* Think of using the index like a phone book. You use a phone book as an index on last name to find the corresponding phone number. But the standard phone book is useless if you know only a person's first name because the first name might be located on any page.

You should put the most selective columns leftmost in the key of nonclustered indexes. For example, an index on *emp_name,emp_sex* is useful for a clause such as *WHERE emp_name = 'Smith'* AND *emp_sex = 'M'*. But if the index is defined as *emp_sex,emp_name,* it isn't useful for most retrievals. The leftmost key, *emp_sex,* cannot rule out enough rows to make the index useful. Be especially aware of this when it comes to indexes that are built to enforce a PRIMARY KEY or UNIQUE constraint defined on multiple columns. The index is built in the order that the columns are defined for the constraint. So you should adjust the order of the columns in the constraint to make the index most useful to queries; doing so will not affect its role in enforcing uniqueness.

Index Columns Used in Joins

Index columns are frequently used to join tables. When you create a PRIMARY KEY or UNIQUE constraint, an index is automatically created for you. But no index is automatically created for the referencing columns in a FOREIGN KEY constraint. Such columns are frequently used to join tables, so they are almost always among the most likely ones on which to create an index. If your primary key and foreign key columns are not naturally compact, consider creating a surrogate key using an identity column (or a similar technique). As with row length for tables, if you can keep your index keys compact, you can fit many more keys on a given page, which results in less physical I/O and better cache efficiency. And if you can join tables based on integer values such as an identity, you avoid having to do relatively expensive character-by-character comparisons. Ideally, columns used to join tables are integer columns—fast and compact.

I talked about density in the statistics discussion in Chapter 15. When determining the density of a search argument (SARG), the query optimizer can look up a specific value in the statistics histogram to get an estimate of the number of occurrences. However, when it looks at whether an index is useful for a join operation, there is no specific value that it can look up. The query optimizer needs to know how many rows in one table are likely to match the join columns value from the other table. In other words, if two tables are related in a one-to-many relationship, how many is "many"? We use the term *join density* to mean the average number of rows in one table that match a row in the table it is being joined to. You can also think of join density as the average number of duplicates for an index key. A column with a unique index has the lowest possible join density (there can be no duplicates) and is therefore extremely selective for the join. If a column being joined has a large number of duplicates, it has a high density and is not very selective for joins.

As you learned in Chapter 15, joins are frequently processed as nested loops. For example, if while joining the *orders* table with *order_items* the system starts with the *orders* table (the outer table), and then for each qualifying order row the inner table is searched for corresponding rows. Think of the join being processed as, "Given a specific row in the outer table, go find all corresponding rows in the inner table." If you think of joins in this way, you'll realize that it's important to have a useful index on the inner table, which is the one being searched for a specific value. For the most common type of join, an equijoin that looks for equal values in columns of two tables, the query optimizer automatically decides which is the inner table and which is the outer table of a join. The table order that you specify for the join doesn't matter in the equijoins case. However, the order for outer joins must match the semantics of the query, so the resulting order is dependent on the order specified.

Create or Drop Indexes as Needed

If you create indexes but find that they aren't used, you should drop them. Unused indexes slow data modification without helping retrieval. You can determine whether indexes are used by watching the plans produced via the SHOWPLAN options. However, this isn't easy if you're analyzing a large system with many tables and indexes. There might be thousands of queries that can be run and no way to run and analyze the SHOWPLAN output for all of them. An alternative is to use the Index Tuning

Wizard to generate a report of current usage patterns. The wizard is designed to determine which new indexes to build, but you can use it simply as a reporting tool to find out what is happening in your current system. We'll look at the wizard in the next section.

Some batch-oriented processes that are query intensive can benefit from certain indexes. Such processes as complex reports or end-of-quarter financial closings often run infrequently. If this is the case, remember that creating and dropping indexes is simple. Consider a strategy of creating certain indexes in advance of your batch processes and then dropping them when those batch processes are done. In this way, the batch processes benefit from the indexes but do not add overhead to your OLTP usage.

The Index Tuning Wizard

You've seen that the query optimizer can come up with a reasonably effective query plan even in the absence of well-planned indexes on your tables. However, this does not mean that a well-tuned database doesn't need good indexes. The query plans that don't rely on indexes frequently consume additional system memory, and other applications might suffer. In addition, having appropriate indexes in place can help solve many blocking problems.

Designing the best possible indexes for the tables in your database is a complex task; it not only requires a thorough knowledge of how SQL Server uses indexes and how the query optimizer makes its decisions, but it requires that you be intimately familiar with how your data will actually be used. The SQL Server 2000 Index Tuning Wizard is a powerful tool for helping you design the best possible indexes.

You can access the Index Tuning Wizard from the Wizards list in SQL Server Enterprise Manager or from the Tools menu in SQL Profiler. You can also access the wizard from the Query menu in SQL Query Analyzer. The wizard tunes a single database at a time, and it bases its recommendations on a workload file that you provide. The workload file can be a file of captured trace events that contains at least the RPC and SQL Batch starting or completed events, as well as the text of the RPCs and batches. It can also be a file of SQL statements. If you use SQL Query Analyzer to invoke the wizard, you also have the option of tuning just the current queries in your SQL Query Analyzer window. If you use SQL Profiler to create the workload file, you can capture all SQL statements submitted by all users over a period of time. The wizard can then look at the data access patterns for all users, for all tables, and can make recommendations with everyone in mind.

You can check the Microsoft web site periodically to see if any new whitepapers have been posted. The best place to look is http://msdn.microsoft.com/library/default.asp?URL=/library/techart/itwforsql.htm. The CD includes a set of lab exercises in a file called Analysis Labs.doc that allow new users to get a feel for the graphical tools in SQL Server 2000. This document includes a lab exercise for exploring the

Index Tuning Wizard. To go along with these lab exercises, the companion CD also contains a sample database called PierrotImports, which is available as two files, PierrotImports.mdf and PierrotImports_log.ldf. You can add the PierrotImports database to your system using the procedure *sp_attach_db*. An example of using this command is in the file Attach_Pierrot.sql. Finally, the CD includes a sample workload file (PierrotQueries.sql) composed of SQL statements that access the PierrotImports database.

When the wizard gets a workload file, it tunes the first 32,767 parsable queries and produces nine reports. You can choose to make the analysis more exhaustive or less exhaustive. You can choose to have the wizard keep all existing indexes, or you can have it come up with a totally new set of index recommendations, which might mean dropping some or all of your existing indexes. Finally, you can choose whether or not the Index Tuning Wizard will recommend building indexed views.

After the wizard generates its reports, which you can save to disk, you can implement the suggestions immediately, schedule the implementation for a later time, or save the script files for the creation (and optional dropping) of indexes. Once the scripts are saved, you can run them later or just inspect them to get ideas of possible indexes to create.

You can also use the wizard purely for analyzing your existing design. One of the reports, Index Usage Report (Current Configuration), shows what percentage of the queries in the submitted workload make use of each of your existing indexes. You can use this information to determine whether an index is being used at all and get rid of any unused indexes along with their space and maintenance overhead.

The current version of the wizard cannot completely tune cross-database queries. It inspects the local tables involved in the queries for index recommendations, but it ignores the tables in other databases. Also, if you're using Unicode data, the wizard does not recognize Unicode constants (such as *N'mystring'*) in your queries and cannot optimize for them. Future versions of the wizard will address these issues and probably add new features as well.

> **NOTE**   If you're going to use SQL Profiler to capture a workload file, you should consider tracing events at several periods throughout the day. This can give you a more balanced picture of the kinds of queries that are actually being executed in your database. If you define your trace using SQL Profiler procedures, you can set up a SQL Server Agent job to start and stop the trace at predefined times, appending to the same workload file each time.

You can also run the Index Tuning Wizard from a command prompt. This capability allows you to define the tuning activities you're interested in but schedule the activity for a later time when the system might not be so busy. Any command prompt activity can be a job step for the SQL Server Agent to run at a predetermined schedule, or you can use the operating system's scheduler to run the command. For details, look up the *itwiz* utility in *SQL Server Books Online*.

MONITORING QUERY PERFORMANCE

Before you think about taking some action to make a query faster, such as adding an index or denormalizing, you should understand how a query is currently being processed. You should also get some baseline performance measurements so you can compare behavior both before and after making your changes. SQL Server provides these tools (SET options) for monitoring queries:

- STATISTICS IO
- STATISTICS TIME
- SHOWPLAN

You enable any of these SET options before you run a query, and they will produce additional output. Typically, you run your query with these options set in a tool such as SQL Query Analyzer. When you're satisfied with your query, you can cut and paste it into your application or into the script file that creates your stored procedures. If you use the SET commands to turn these options on, they apply only to the current connection. SQL Query Analyzer provides check boxes for turning any or all of these options on or off for all connections.

STATISTICS IO

Don't let the term *statistics* fool you. STATISTICS IO doesn't have anything to do with the statistics used for storing histograms and density information in *sysindexes*. This option provides statistics on how much work SQL Server did to process your query. When this option is set to ON, you get a separate line of output for each query in a batch that accesses any data objects. (You don't get any output for statements that don't access data, such as PRINT, SELECT the value of a variable, or call a system function.) The output from SET STATISTICS IO ON includes the values Logical Reads, Physical Reads, Read Ahead Reads, and Scan Count.

Logical Reads

This value indicates the total number of page accesses needed to process the query. Every page is read from the data cache, whether or not it was necessary to bring that page from disk into the cache for any given read. This value is always at least as large and usually larger than the value for Physical Reads. The same page can be read many times (such as when a query is driven from an index), so the count of Logical Reads for a table can be greater than the number of pages in a table.

Physical Reads

This value indicates the number of pages that were read from disk; it is always less than or equal to the value of Logical Reads. The value of the Buffer Cache Hit Ratio, as displayed by System Monitor, is computed from the Logical Reads and Physical Reads values as follows:

Cache-Hit Ratio = (Logical Reads – Physical Reads) / Logical Reads

Remember that the value for Physical Reads can vary greatly and decreases substantially with the second and subsequent execution because the cache is loaded by the first execution. The value is also affected by other SQL Server activity and can appear low if the page was preloaded by read ahead activity. For this reason, you probably won't find it useful to do a lot of analysis of physical I/O on a per-query basis. When you're looking at individual queries, the Logical Reads value is usually more interesting because the information is consistent. Physical I/O and achieving a good cache-hit ratio is crucial, but they are more interesting at the all-server level. Pay close attention to Logical Reads for each important query, and pay close attention to physical I/O and the cache-hit ratio for the server as a whole.

STATISTICS IO acts on a per-table, per-query basis. You might want to see the *physical_io* column in *sysprocesses* corresponding to the specific connection. This column shows the cumulative count of synchronous I/O that has occurred during the *spid*'s existence, regardless of the table. It even includes any Read Ahead Reads that were made by that connection.

Read Ahead Reads

The Read Ahead Reads value indicates the number of pages that were read into cache using the read ahead mechanism while the query was processed. These pages are not necessarily used by the query. If a page is ultimately needed, a logical read is counted but a physical read is not. A high value means that the value for Physical Reads is probably lower and the cache-hit ratio is probably higher than if a read ahead was not done. In a situation like this, you shouldn't infer from a high cache-hit ratio that your system can't benefit from additional memory. The high ratio might come from the read ahead mechanism bringing much of the needed data into cache. That's a good thing, but it might be better if the data simply remains in cache from previous use. You might achieve the same or a higher cache-hit ratio without requiring the Read Ahead Reads.

You can think of read ahead as simply an optimistic form of physical I/O. In full or partial table scans, the table's IAMs are consulted to determine which extents belong to the object. The extents are read with a single 64-KB scatter read, and because of the way that the IAMs are organized, they are read in disk order. If the table is spread across multiple files in a file group, the read ahead attempts to keep at least eight of the files busy instead of sequentially processing the files. Read Ahead Reads are asynchronously requested by the thread that is running the query; because they are asynchronous, the scan doesn't block while waiting for them to complete. It blocks only when it actually tries to scan a page that it thinks has been brought into cache and the read hasn't finished yet. In this way, the read ahead neither gets too ambitious (reading too far ahead of the scan) nor too far behind.

Scan Count

The Scan Count value indicates the number of times that the corresponding table was accessed. Outer tables of a nested loop join have a Scan Count of 1. For inner tables, the Scan Count might be the number of times "through the loop" that the table was accessed. The number of Logical Reads is determined by the sum of the Scan Count times the number of pages accessed on each scan. However, even for nested loop joins, the Scan Count for the inner table might show up as 1. SQL Server might copy the needed rows from the inner table into a worktable in cache and use this worktable to access the actual data rows. When this step is used in the plan, there is often no indication of it in the STATISTICS IO output. You must use the output from STATISTIC TIME, as well as information about the actual processing plan used, to determine the actual work involved in executing a query. Hash joins and merge joins usually show the Scan Count as 1 for both tables involved in the join, but these types of joins can involve substantially more memory. You can inspect the *memusage* value in *sysprocesses* while the query is being executed, but unlike the *physical_io* value, this is not a cumulative counter and is valid only for the currently running query. Once a query finishes, there is no way to see how much memory it used.

Troubleshooting Example Using STATISTICS IO

The following situation is based on a real problem I encountered when doing a simple SELECT * from a table with only a few thousand rows. The amount of time this simple SELECT took seemed to be out of proportion to the size of the table. We can create a similar situation here by making a copy of the *orders* table in the *Northwind* database and adding a new column to it with a default value of 2000-byte character field.

```
SELECT *
INTO neworders
FROM orders
GO
ALTER TABLE neworders
ADD full_details CHAR(2000) NOT NULL DEFAULT 'full details'
```

We can gather some information about this table with the following command:

```
EXEC sp_spaceused neworders, true
```

The results will tell us that there are 830 rows in the table, 3240 KB for data, which equates to 405 data pages. That doesn't seem completely unreasonable, so we can try selecting all the rows after enabling STATISTICS IO:

```
SET STATISTICS IO ON
GO
SELECT * FROM neworders
```

The results now show that SQL Server had to perform 1945 logical reads for only 405 data pages. There is no possibility that a nonclustered index is being used inappropriately because I just created this table, and there are no indexes at all on it. So where are all the reads coming from?

Recall that if a row is increased in size so that it no longer fits on the original page, it will be moved to a new page and SQL Server will create a forwarding pointer to the new location from the old location. In Chapter 9, I told you about two ways to find out how many forwarding pointers were in a table: we could use the undocumented trace flag 2509, or we could run DBCC SHOWCONTIG with the TABLERESULTS options. Here, I'll use the trace flag:

```
DBCC TRACEON (2509)
GO
DBCC CHECKTABLE (neworders)

RESULTS:
DBCC execution completed. If DBCC printed error messages, contact your
system administrator.
DBCC results for 'neworders'.
There are 830 rows in 405 pages for object 'neworders'.
Forwarded Record count = 770
```

If you play around with the numbers a bit, you might realize that 2*770 + 405 equals 1945, the number of reads we ended up performing with the table scan. What I realized was happening was that when scanning a table, SQL Server will read every page (there are 405 of them) and each time a forwarding pointer is encountered, SQL Server will jump ahead to that page to read the row and then jump back to the page where the pointer was and read the original page again. So for each forwarding pointer, there are two additional logical reads. SQL Server is doing a lot of work here for a simple table scan.

The "fix" to this problem is to regularly check the number of forwarding pointers, especially if a table has variable-length fields and is frequently updated. If you notice a high number of forwarding pointers, you can rebuild the table by creating a clustered index. If for some reason I don't want to keep the clustered index, I can drop it. But the act of creating the clustered index will reorganize the table.

```
SET STATISTICS IO OFF
GO
CREATE CLUSTERED INDEX orderID_cl ON neworders(orderID)
GO
DROP INDEX neworders.orderID_cl
GO
EXEC sp_spaceused neworders, true
SET STATISTICS IO ON
GO
SELECT ROWS = count(*) FROM neworders
```

```
RESULTS:

name            rows     reserved    data      index_size    unused
--------------- -------- ----------- --------- ------------- ------
neworders       830      2248 KB     2216 KB   8 KB          24 KB

ROWS
-----------
830

(1 row(s) affected)
```

Table 'neworders'. Scan count 1, logical reads 277, physical reads 13, read-ahead reads 278.

This output shows us that not only did the building of the clustered index reduce the number of pages in the table, from 405 to 277, but the cost to read the table is now the same as the number of pages in the table.

STATISTICS TIME

The output of SET STATISTICS TIME ON is pretty self-explanatory. It shows the elapsed time and CPU time required to process the query. In this context, it means the time not spent waiting for resources such as locks or reads to complete. The times are separated into two components: the time required to parse and compile the query and the time required to execute the query. For some of your testing, you might find it just as useful to look at the system time with *getdate* before and after a query if all you need to measure is elapsed time. However, if you want to compare elapsed time vs. actual CPU time or if you're interested in how long compilation and optimization took, you must use STATISTICS TIME.

In many cases, you'll notice that the output includes two sets of data for parse and compile time. This happens when the plan is being added to *syscacheobjects* for possible reuse. The first line is the actual parse and compile before placing the plan in cache, and the second line appears when SQL Server is retrieving the plan from cache. Subsequent executions will still show the same two lines, but if the plan is actually being reused, the parse and compile time for both lines will be 0.

Showplan

In SQL Server 2000, there is not just a single option for examining the execution plan for a query. You can choose to see the plan in a text format, with or without additional performance estimates, or you can see a graphical representation of the processing plan. In Chapter 15, I gave you a sneak preview of the graphical showplan. Now I'll go into more detail.

The output of any of the showplan options shows some basic information about how the query will be processed. The output will tell you, for each table in the query, whether indexes are being used or whether a table scan is necessary. It will also tell you the order that all the different operations of the plan are to be carried out. Reading showplan output is as much an art as it is a science, but for the most part it just takes a lot of practice to get really comfortable with its interpretation. I hope that the examples in this section will be enough to give you a good start.

SHOWPLAN_TEXT and SHOWPLAN_ALL

The two SET options SHOWPLAN_TEXT and SHOWPLAN_ALL let you see the estimated query plan without actually executing the query. Both options also automatically enable the SET NOEXEC option, so you don't see any results from your query—you see only the way that SQL Server has determined is the best method for processing the query. Turning NOEXEC ON can be a good thing while tuning a query. For example, if you have a query that takes 20 minutes to execute, you might try to create an index that will allow it to run faster. However, immediately after creating a new index, you might just want to know whether the query optimizer will even choose to use that index. If you were actually executing the query every time you looked at its plan, it would take you 20 minutes for every tuning attempt. Setting NOEXEC ON along with the showplan option will allow you to see the plan without actually executing all the statements.

> **WARNING**   Since turning on SHOWPLAN_TEXT or SHOWPLAN_ALL implies that NOEXEC is also on, you must set the SHOWPLAN option to OFF before you do anything else. For example, you must set SHOWPLAN_TEXT to OFF before setting SHOWPLAN_ALL to ON.

SHOWPLAN_TEXT shows you all the steps involved in processing the query, including the type of join used, the order of table accesses, and which index or indexes are used for each table. Any internal sorts are also shown. Here's an example of a simple two-table join from the *Northwind* database:

```
SET SHOWPLAN_TEXT ON
GO
SELECT ProductName, Products.ProductId
FROM [Order Details] JOIN Products
ON [Order Details].ProductID = Products.ProductId
WHERE Products.UnitPrice > 10
GO

OUTPUT:
StmtText
--------------------------------------------------------------------
|--Nested Loops(Inner Join, OUTER REFERENCES:([Products].[ProductID]))
  |--Clustered Index Scan
    (OBJECT:([Northwind].[dbo].[Products].[PK_Products]),
     WHERE:([Products].[UnitPrice]>10.00))
  |--Index Seek
```

```
(OBJECT:([Northwind].[dbo].[Order Details].[ProductID]),
SEEK:([Order Details].[ProductID]=[Products].[ProductID])
ORDERED FORWARD)
```

The output tells us that the query plan is performing an inner join on the two tables. Inner Join is the logical operator, as requested in the query submitted. The way that this join is actually carried out is the physical operator; in this case, the query optimizer chose to use nested loops. The outer table in the join is the *Products* table, and a Clustered Index Scan is the physical operator. In this case, there is no separate logical operator—the logical operator and the physical operator are the same. Remember that since a clustered index contains all the table data, scanning the clustered index is equivalent to scanning the whole table. The inner table is the *Order Details* table, which has a nonclustered index on the *ProductID* column. The physical operator used is Index Seek. The Object reference after the Index Seek operator shows us the full name of the index used: *:([Northwind].[dbo].[Order Details].[ProductID]*. In this case, it is a bit confusing because the name of the index is the same as the name of the join column. For this reason, I recommend not giving indexes the same names as the columns they will access.

SHOWPLAN_ALL provides this information plus estimates of the number of rows that are expected to meet the queries' search criteria, the estimated size of the result rows, the estimated CPU time, and the total cost estimate that was used internally when comparing this plan to other possible plans. I won't show you the output from SHOWPLAN_ALL because it's too wide to fit nicely on a page of this book. But the information returned is the same as the information you'll be shown with the graphical showplan, and I'll show you a few more examples of graphical plans in this chapter.

When using showplan to tune a query, you typically add one or more indexes that you think might help speed up a query and then you use one of these showplan options to see whether any of your new indexes were actually used. If showplan indicates that a new index is being used, you should then actually execute the query to make sure that the performance is improved. If an index is not going to be used or is not useful in terms of performance improvement and you're not adding it to maintain a PRIMARY KEY or UNIQUE constraint, you might as well not add it. If an index is not useful for queries, the index is just overhead in terms of space and maintenance time. After you add indexes, be sure to monitor their effect on your updates because indexes can add overhead to data modification (inserts, deletes, and updates).

If a change to indexing alone is not the answer, you should look at other possible solutions, such as using an index hint or changing the general approach to the query. In Chapter 10, you saw that several different approaches can be useful to some queries—ranging from the use of somewhat tricky SQL to the use of temporary tables and cursors. If these approaches also fail to provide acceptable performance, you should consider changes to the database design using the denormalization techniques discussed earlier.

Graphical Showplan

You can request a graphical representation of a query's estimated execution plan in SQL Query Analyzer either by using the Display Estimated Execution Plan toolbar button immediately to the right of the database drop-down list or by choosing Display Estimated Execution Plan from the Query menu. Like the SET options SHOWPLAN_TEXT and SHOWPLAN_ALL, by default your query is not executed when you choose to display the graphical showplan output. The graphical representation contains all the information available through SHOWPLAN_ALL, but not all of it is visible at once. You can, however, move your cursor over any of the icons in the graphical plan to see the additional performance estimates.

Figure 16-3 shows the graphical query plan for the same query I used in the previous section, and I've put my cursor over the icon for the nested loop join so you can see the information box. When reading the graphical showplan, you need to read from right to left. When you look at the plan for a JOIN, the table listed on the top is the first one processed. For a LOOP join, the top table is the outer table, and for a HASH join, the top table is the build table. The figure shows that the *Products* table is accessed first as the outer table in a Nested Loop join, and the other table would be the inner table. You can't see the other table in the figure because the information box is covering it up. The final step in the plan, shown on the far left, is to actually SELECT the qualifying rows and return them to the client.

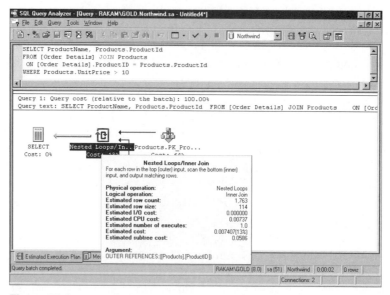

Figure 16-3. *A graphical showplan showing a nested loop join operation.*

Table 16-1, taken from *SQL Server Books Online*, describes the meaning of each of the output values that you can see in the details box for the Nested Loops icon. Some of these values (for example, StmtId, NodeId, and Parent) do not show up in the graphical representation—only in the SHOWPLAN_ALL output.

Column	What It Contains
StmtText	The text of the Transact-SQL statement.
StmtId	The number of the statement in the current batch.
NodeId	The ID of the node in the current query.
Parent	The node ID of the parent step.
PhysicalOp	The physical implementation algorithm for the node.
LogicalOp	The relational algebraic operator that this node represents.
Argument	Supplemental information about the operation being performed. The contents of this column depend on the physical operator.
DefinedValues	A comma-separated list of values introduced by this operator. These values can be computed expressions that were present in the current query (for example, in the SELECT list or WHERE clause) or internal values introduced by the query processor in order to process this query. These defined values can then be referenced elsewhere within this query.
EstimateRows	The estimated number of rows output by this operator.
EstimateIO	The estimated I/O cost for this operator.
EstimateCPU	The estimated CPU cost for this operator.
AvgRowSize	The estimated average row size (in bytes) of the row being passed through this operator.
TotalSubtreeCost	The estimated (cumulative) cost of this operation and all child operations.
OutputList	A comma-separated list of columns being projected by the current operation.
Warnings	A comma-separated list of warning messages relating to the current operation.
Type	The node type. For the parent node of each query, this is the Transact-SQL statement type (for example, SELECT, INSERT, EXECUTE, and so on). For subnodes representing execution plans, the type is PLAN_ROW.
Parallel	0 = Operator is not running in parallel. 1 = Operator is running in parallel.
EstimateExecutions	The estimated number of times this operator will be executed while running the current query.

Table 16-1. *Values available in the showplan output.*

Let's look at a slightly more complex query plan for this query based on a four-table join and a GROUP BY with aggregation.

```
USE Northwind
SELECT e.LastName, p.ProductName, sum(d.Quantity * d.UnitPrice)
FROM [Order Details] d JOIN Orders o
    ON o.OrderID = d.OrderID
JOIN Products p
    ON d.ProductID = p.ProductID
JOIN  Employees e
    ON e.EmployeeID = o.EmployeeID
GROUP BY e.LastName, p.ProductName
```

You can see most of the graphical showplan in Figure 16-4. Because there are four tables, the plan shows three join operators. You need to read the plan from right to left, and you can see that the *Employees* and *Orders* tables are joined with a Nested Loops join, and then the result of that first join is joined with the *Order Details* table, again using Nested Loops. Finally, the result of the second join is joined with the *Products* table using hashing. Note that the order in which the joins are processed in the plan is not at all the same order used when writing the query. The query optimizer attempts to find the best plan regardless of how the query was actually submitted. The final step is to do the grouping and aggregation, and the graphical plan shows us that this was done using hashing.

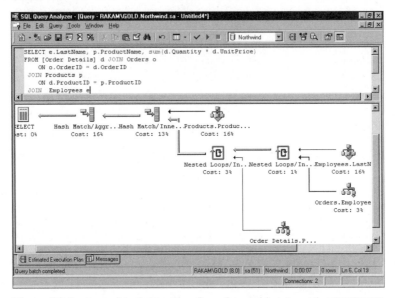

Figure 16-4. *A graphical showplan for a four-table join with GROUP BY aggregation.*

WARNING In order to generate the graphical showplan, SQL Server must make sure that both SHOWPLAN_TEXT and SHOWPLAN_ALL are in the OFF state so that the NOEXEC option is also OFF. If you've been tuning queries using the SHOWPLAN_TEXT option and you then decide to look at a graphical showplan, the NOEXEC option will be left in the OFF state after you view the graphical plan. If you then try to go back to looking at SHOWPLAN_TEXT, you'll find that it has been turned off, and any queries you run will actually be executed.

Troubleshooting with Showplan

One of the first things to look for in your showplan output is whether there are any warning messages. Warning messages might include the string *"NO STATS:()"* with a list of columns. This warning message means that the query optimizer attempted to make a decision based on the statistics for this column but that no statistics were available. Consequently, the query optimizer had to make a guess, which might have resulted in the selection of an inefficient query plan. Warnings can also include the string *MISSING JOIN PREDICATE*, which means that a join is taking place without a join predicate to connect the tables. Accidentally dropping a join predicate might result in a query that takes much longer to run than expected and returns a huge result set. If you see this warning, you should verify that the absence of a join predicate is what you wanted, as in the case of a CROSS JOIN.

Another area where SHOWPLAN can be useful is for determining why an index wasn't chosen. You can look at the estimated row counts for the various search arguments. Remember that a nonclustered index will mainly be useful if only a very small percentage of rows in the table will qualify; if the showplan output shows hundreds of rows meeting the condition, that can be a good indication of why a nonclustered index was not chosen. However, if the row estimate is very different from what you know it to actually be, you can look in two places for the reason. First make sure statistics are updated or that you haven't turned off the option to automatically update statistics on indexes. Second, make sure your WHERE clause actually contains a SARG and that you haven't invalidated the use of the index by applying a function or other operation to the indexed column. You saw an example of this problem in Chapter 15, and the plan was shown in Figure 15-4.

Another thing to remember from Chapter 15 is that there is no guarantee that the query optimizer will find the fastest plan. It will search until it finds a good plan; there might actually be a faster plan, but the query optimizer might take twice as long to find it. The query optimizer decides to stop searching when it finds a "good enough" plan because the added cost of continued searching might offset whatever slight savings in execution time you'd get with a faster plan.

Here's an example. We'll build a table with big rows, each of which has a *char(7000)*, so it needs one page per row. We'll then populate this table with 1000 rows of data and build three indexes:

```
CREATE TABLE emps(
empid int not null identity(1,1),
fname varchar(10) not null,
lname varchar(10) not null,
hiredate datetime not null,
salary money not null,
resume char(7000) not null)
GO

-- populate with 1000 rows, each of which will fill a page
SET NOCOUNT ON
DECLARE @i AS int
SET @i = 1
WHILE @i <= 1000
BEGIN
INSERT INTO emps VALUES('fname' + cast(@i AS varchar(5)),
'lname' + cast(@i AS varchar(5)),
getdate() - @i,
1000.00 + @i % 50,
'resume' + cast(@i AS varchar(5)))
    SET @i = @i + 1
END
GO

CREATE CLUSTERED INDEX idx_ci_empid ON [dbo].[emps] ([empid])
CREATE NONCLUSTERED INDEX idx_nci_lname ON [dbo].[emps] ([lname])
CREATE NONCLUSTERED INDEX idx_nci_fname ON [dbo].[emps] ([fname])
GO
```

The query we'll execute will only access the *fname* and *lname* columns. As you've seen, SQL Server uses the index intersection technique to use two nonclustered indexes to determine the qualifying rows and join the results from the two indexes together. However, the optimizer decided not to use that plan in this case:

```
SELECT fname, lname
FROM emps
```

The plan shows a clustered index scan, which means that the entire table is examined. The number of logical reads is about equal to the number of pages in the table (1002). However, if we apply a SARG that actually includes the whole table, we'll find that the query optimizer will use the index intersection technique. Here's the query:

```
SELECT fname, lname
FROM emps
WHERE fname BETWEEN 'fname' and 'fname9999'
```

Figure 16-5 shows the query plan using an index seek on the nonclustered index on *fname* and an index scan on the nonclustered index on *lname*, and then using a hash join to combine the result sets of the two index operations. If we turn on STATISTICS IO, the logical reads are reported to be only 8 pages. It might seem as if the difference between 8 logical reads and 1000 logical reads is a lot, but in the grand scheme of things, it really isn't all that much. Reading 1000 pages is still a very fast operation, and the query optimizer decided not to search further. It will only consider the index intersection case if it already is doing index seek operations, and with no SARGs in the query, index seek is not an option.

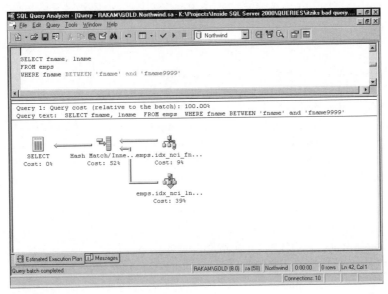

Figure 16-5. *A graphical showplan for an index intersection when index seek operations are used.*

However, if the table has more than 1000 rows, the situation changes. If we drop the *emps* table and re-create it with 10,000 rows instead of 1000, the cost of doing the simple clustered index scan becomes 10,000 logical reads. In this case, that is deemed too expensive, so the query optimizer will keep searching for a better plan. With 10,000 rows in the *emps* table, the index intersection technique is evaluated and found to be faster. In fact, it will take only about 60 logical reads, which *is* a big improvement over 10,000.

Logical and Physical Operators

The logical and physical operators describe how a query or update was executed. The physical operators describe the physical implementation algorithm used to process a statement—for example, scanning a clustered index or performing a merge join. Each step in the execution of a query involves a physical operator. The logical operators describe the relational algebraic operation used to process a statement—for example, performing an aggregation or an inner join. Not all steps used to process a query or update involve logical operations.

Logical operators map pretty closely to what is contained in the query itself. As you've seen, you might have an inner join for the logical operator. The physical operator is then how the query optimizer decided to process that join—for example as a nested loop join, a hash join, or a merge join. Aggregation is a logical operator because the query actually specifies a GROUP BY with an aggregate and the corresponding physical operator, as chosen by the query optimizer, could be stream aggregate (if the grouping is done by sorting) or hash match (if the grouping is done by hashing).

You might see some types of joins that you don't recognize. I've already talked about inner joins; left, right, and full outer joins; and cross joins. You might also see the following logical operators: *Left Semi Join, Right Semi Join, Left Anti Semi Join*, and *Right Anti Semi Join*. These sound mysterious, but they're really not. Normally, in a join, you're interested in columns from both tables. But if you use a subquery with an EXISTS or IN predicate, you're saying that you're not interested in retrieving data from the inner table and you're using it only for lookup purposes. So instead of needing data from both tables, you need data from only one of the tables, and this is a *Semi Join*. If you're looking for data from the outer table that doesn't exist in the inner table, it becomes an *Anti Semi Join*.

Here's an example in the *pubs* database that retrieves all the names of publishers that don't have corresponding *pub_id* values in the *titles* table—in other words, publishers who haven't published any books:

```
USE pubs
GO
SELECT pub_name
FROM publishers
WHERE pub_id  NOT IN (SELECT pub_id FROM titles)
```

Here's the SHOWPLAN_TEXT output that the query generates. You can see the *Left Anti Semi Join* operator.

```
StmtText
-----------------------------------------------------------------------

  |--Nested Loops(Left Anti Semi Join, WHERE:([titles].[pub_id]=NULL OR
            [publishers].[pub_id]=[titles].[pub_id]))
       |--Clustered Index
             Scan(OBJECT:([pubs].[dbo].[publishers].[UPKCL_pubind]))
       |--Clustered Index
             Scan(OBJECT:([pubs].[dbo].[titles].[UPKCL_titleidind]))
```

Displaying the Actual Plan

All of the showplan options discussed so far show the estimated query plan. As long as the query is not actually being executed, you can only see an estimate. As you saw in Chapter 15, conditions such as memory resources might change before you actually run the query, so the estimated plan might not be the actual plan. If you need to see the actual plan at the time the query is executed, you have three options:

■   Choose Show Execution Plan from the Query menu in SQL Query Analyzer. Unlike the Display Estimated Execution Plan option, this one acts like a toggle. Once you select it, it stays selected until you deselect it. You'll see two tabs of results for every query you run until you deselect Show Execution Plan. The first tab shows the actual query output, and the second shows the graphical showplan.

■   Set STATISTICS PROFILE to ON. This option gives you the query results followed by the STATISTICS_ALL output in the same results pane.

■   Set up a trace in SQL Profiler to capture the Execution Plan events. This displays from the same information as SHOWPLAN_TEXT in the trace output for every query that is executed. We'll look at tracing in more detail in Chapter 17.

Other SQL Query Analyzer Tools

In SQL Server 2000, SQL Query Analyzer provides other troubleshooting information besides SHOWPLAN and statistical output. Two additional options on the Query menu act as toggles to provide more information for every query that you run: Show Server Trace and Show Client Statistics. Each of these options, when enabled, adds another tab to the results window. The Server Trace output gives information similar to what you might see when you use SQL Profiler, which I'll discuss in Chapter 17. The Client Statistics output can give you a set of very useful data that indicates how much work the client had to do to submit this query and retrieve the results from SQL Server. It includes information that can also be returned by other means, such as the time spent and the number of rows affected, and it can also give additional information such as the number of bytes sent and received across the network.

Let's look at one of the *Northwind* queries I ran earlier and see what the client statistics look like when I execute it. Here's the query again:

```
SELECT e.LastName, p.ProductName, sum(d.Quantity * d.UnitPrice)
FROM [Order Details] d JOIN Orders o
    ON o.OrderID = d.OrderID
JOIN Products p
```

(continued)

```
    ON d.ProductID = p.ProductID
JOIN  Employees e
    ON e.EmployeeID = o.EmployeeID
GROUP BY e.LastName, p.ProductName
```

Here's the information that Client Statistics returned:

Counter	Value	Average
Application Profile Statistics:		
Timer resolution (milliseconds)	0	0
Number of INSERT, UPDATE, DELETE statements	0	0
Rows effected by INSERT, UPDATE, DELETE statements	0	0
Number of SELECT statements	1	1
Rows effected by SELECT statements	588	588
Number of user transactions	1	1
Average fetch time	0	0
Cumulative fetch time	0	0
Number of fetches	0	0
Number of open statement handles	0	0
Max number of opened statement handles	0	0
Cumulative number of statement handles	0	0
Network Statistics:		
Number of server roundtrips	1	1
Number of TDS packets sent	1	1
Number of TDS packets received	9	9
Number of bytes sent	552	552
Number of bytes received	35,921	35,921
Time Statistics:		
Cumulative client processing time	223	223
Cumulative wait time on server replies	3	3

The number in the *Value* column pertains only to the most recently run batch. The number in the *Average* column is a cumulative average since you started collecting client statistics for this session. If you turn off the option to collect client statistics and then turn it on again, the numbers in the *Average* column will be reset.

There are a few other interesting features in SQL Query Analyzer that you should know about. I don't want to go into a lot of detail because this isn't a book about pointing and clicking your way through the tools and most of these tools aren't directly related to tuning your queries. But the more fluent you are in your use of this tool, the more you can use it to maximum benefit when you perform troubleshooting and tuning operations. This is not a complete list of all the capabilities of SQL Query Analyzer. I suggest you read SQL Server Books Online thoroughly and spend some time just exploring this tool even if you already think you know how to use it. I'll bet you'll discover something new. For a start, take a look at these options:

Object Browser　　The Object Browser is a tree-based tool window for navigating through the database objects of a selected SQL Server. Besides navigation, the Object Browser offers object scripting and procedure execution. To limit the overhead of using the Object Browser, only one server can be active at a time. The drop-down list box at the top of the Object Browser presents a distinct list of server names to which you can connect, and this means that you must have a connection already open to a server before you can use the Object Browser. The Object Browser has no explicit connect logic: it piggybacks on the existing query window connection's information.

Changing Fonts　　You can right-click in almost any window and choose the option to change your font. Alternatively, you can choose Options from the Tools menu and go to the Fonts tab, where you can set the font of any type of window.

Quick Edit　　From the Edit menu, you can choose to set or clear bookmarks, go to a specific line in the query window, change text to uppercase or lowercase, indent or unindent a block of code, or comment out a whole block of code.

Shortcut Keys　　You can configure the Ctrl+1 through Ctrl+0 and Alt+F1 and Ctrl+F1 keys as query shortcuts. Choose Customize from the Tools menu to bring up a dialog box in which you can define a command or stored procedure (either system or user defined) to be run when that key combination is entered. The command itself won't be displayed in the query window, but the result of running the defined command will appear in the results pane of the active query window. By default, the Alt+F1 combination executes *sp_help*, but you can change this.

Any text highlighted in the query window will be appended to the command that is executed as a single string. If the command is a stored procedure, the highlighted text will then be interpreted as a single parameter to that stored procedure. If this text is not compatible with the parameter the procedure is expecting, an error will result. To prevent too many errors, SQL Server will check if the procedure accepts parameters; if not, no parameters will be sent, regardless of what is highlighted in the query window.

Although the Customize dialog box indicates that it accepts only stored procedures as text, this is not completely true. You can type in a complete SQL statement, such as *SELECT getdate()*. However, if you define something other than a stored procedure as the executed text for the shortcut, any highlighted text in the query window is ignored. For example, you might want to have the text associated with a key combination to be SELECT * FROM so that you can type a table name into the query window, highlight it, and use the keyboard shortcut to get all the rows from that table. (That is, you want to execute *SELECT * FROM <highlighted table name>*). Since the text associated with the keystroke is not a stored procedure, your highlighted text will be ignored and you'll end up with a syntax error.

Finally, keep in mind that the command to be executed will run in the current database context. System stored procedures will never cause any problems, but executing a local stored procedure or selecting from a table might cause an error if you're not in the right database when you use the shortcut. Alternatively, you can fully qualify the name of the referenced object in the shortcut definition.

> **TIP** There are dozens of predefined shortcuts for SQL Server 2000 SQL Query Analyzer. For a complete list, see the file called SQL QA Shortcut Matrix.xls on the companion CD.

Customizing the Toolbar   You can add additional icons to the SQL Query Analyzer toolbar by double-clicking (or right-clicking) on any open area of the toolbar to bring up the Customize Toolbar dialog box. In the Customize Toolbar dialog box, you can add almost any of the commands available through the menus as buttons on the toolbar. You can also use this dialog box to change the position of existing buttons.

Object Search   Object Search, available from the Tools menu, is an alternative way to locate objects besides using the tree-based metaphor available through the Object Browser. You can specify the name of an object to search for, the database name (or all databases), and the types of objects you're interested in. If the server is case sensitive, you can make the search either case sensitive or case insensitive; if the server is case insensitive, the search can be case insensitive only and the Case-Sensitive check box will be disabled. By default, the Object Search imposes a hit limit on the search of 100 objects returned, but you can change this limit.

There can be multiple instances of the Object Search, each connected to the same or to different servers. The Object Search is a child window like the query window. Each Object Search window has one dedicated connection. When you open the Object Search window, it connects to the same server that the active query window is connected to.

The searching is performed using a stored procedure called *sp_MSobjsearch*. This procedure is undocumented, but it exists in the *master* database, so you can use *sp_helptext* to see its definition. It is fairly well commented, at least as far as listing what parameters it expects and the default values for those parameters.

The results of the stored procedure are displayed in the grid of the Object Search window. From there, the same functionality is available as in the Object Browser. You can drag a row into the query editor while holding down the secondary mouse button to initiate a script option.

Transact-SQL Debugger   You can use the Transact-SQL Debugger to control and monitor the execution of stored procedures and support traditional debugger functionality such as setting breakpoints, defining watch expressions, and single-stepping through procedures. The debugger lets you step through nested procedure calls, and you can debug a trigger by creating a simple procedure that performs the firing action on the trigger's table. The trigger is then treated as a nested procedure. Note that the default behavior of the debugger is to roll back any changes that have taken place, so even though you're executing data modification operations, the changes to your tables will not be permanent. You can, however, change this default behavior and choose to *not* roll back any changes. To debug a user-defined function you can write a procedure that includes a SELECT statement containing the function call. (You can't debug system supplied functions because they're not written using Transact-SQL.)

If you're interested in working with the debugger, I suggest that you thoroughly read the article in *SQL Server Books Online* titled "Troubleshooting the Transact-SQL Debugger" and spend a bit of time getting very familiar with the tool. To invoke the debugger, choose a particular database in the Object Browser and open the Stored Procedures folder for that database. Right-click on a procedure name, and select Debug on the context menu. If the procedure expects parameters, you'll be prompted for them.

Here are a few issues that deserve special attention:

■   Try to include the RETURN keyword in all your procedures and triggers that you might end up needing to debug. In some cases, the debugger might not be able to correctly step back to the calling procedure if a RETURN is not encountered.

■   Because the debugger starts a connection to the server in a special mode that allows single stepping, you cannot use the debugger to debug concurrency or blocking issues.

■   To use all the features of the debugger, the SQL Server must be running under a real account and not using Local System. The Local System special account cannot access network resources, and even if you're running the debugger on the same machine on which the server is running, the debugger uses DCOM to communicate between the client and the server. DCOM requires a real operating system account. The initial release of SQL Server 2000 has an additional problem with this requirement. When the debugger is first invoked, the code checks only the account that the default instance is running under. If that is Local System, you'll get a warning and will be able to choose whether or not to continue. There are two problems with this. First of all, if you're connecting to a named instance and that instance is using a valid account, you'll still get this warning if the default instance is using Local System. Second, if the default instance is using a real account but the instance you're connecting to is not, you won't get the warning but the debugger will not be fully functional.

Using Query Hints

As you know, SQL Server performs locking and query optimization automatically. But because the query optimizer is probability based, it sometimes makes wrong predictions. For example, to eliminate a deadlock, you might want to force an update lock. Or you might want to tell the query optimizer that you value the speed of returning the first row more highly than total throughput. You can specify these and other behaviors by using query hints. The word *hint* is a bit of a misnomer in this context because it is handled as a directive rather than as a suggestion. SQL Server provides the following four general types of hints:

■ Join hints, which specify the join technique that will be used

■ Index hints, which specify one or more specific indexes that should be used to drive a search or a sort

■ Query processing hints, which specify that a particular processing strategy should be used

■ Lock hints, which specify a particular locking mode that should be used

If you've made it this far in this book, you probably understand the various issues related to hints—locking, how indexes are selected, overall throughput vs. the first row returned, and how join order is determined. Understanding these issues is the key to effectively using hints and intelligently instructing SQL Server to deviate from "normal" behavior when necessary. Hints are simply syntactic hooks that override default behavior; you should now have insight into those behaviors so you can make good decisions about when such overrides are warranted.

Query hints should be used for special cases—not as standard operating procedure. When you specify a hint, you constrain SQL Server. For example, if you indicate in a hint that a specific index should be used and later you add another index that would be even more useful, the hint prevents the query optimizer from considering the new index. In future versions of SQL Server, you can expect new query optimization strategies, more access methods, and new locking behaviors. If you bind your queries to one specific behavior, you forgo your chances of benefiting from such improvements. SQL Server offers the nonprocedural development approach—that is, you don't have to tell SQL Server *how* to do something. Rather, you tell it *what* to do. Hints run contrary to this approach. Nonetheless, the query optimizer isn't perfect and never can be. In some cases, hints can make the difference between a project's success and failure, if they're used judiciously.

When you use a hint, you must have a clear vision of how it might help. It's a good idea to add a comment to the query to justify the hint. Then you should test your hypothesis by watching the output of STATISTICS IO, STATISTICS TIME, and one of the showplan options both with and without your hint.

> **TIP** Since your data is constantly changing, a hint that works well today might not indicate the appropriate processing strategy next week. In addition, the query optimizer is constantly evolving, and the next upgrade or service pack you apply might invalidate the need for that hint. You should periodically retest all queries that rely on hinting to verify that the hint is still useful.

Join Hints

You can use join hints only when you use the ANSI-style syntax for joins—that is, when you actually use the word JOIN in the query. In addition, the hint comes between the type of join and the word JOIN, so you can't leave off the word INNER for an inner join. Here's an example of forcing SQL Server to use a HASH JOIN:

```
SELECT title_id, pub_name, title
FROM titles INNER HASH JOIN publishers
    ON titles.pub_id = publishers.pub_id
```

Alternatively, you can specify a LOOP JOIN or a MERGE JOIN. You can use another join hint, REMOTE, when you have defined a linked server and are doing a cross-server join. REMOTE specifies that the join operation is performed on the site of the right table—that is, the table after the word JOIN. This is useful when the left table is a local table and the right table is a remote table. You should use REMOTE only when the left table has fewer rows than the right table.

Index Hints

You can specify that one or more specific indexes be used by naming them directly in the FROM clause. You can also specify the indexes by their *indid* value, but this makes sense only when you specify *not* to use an index or to use the clustered index, whatever it is. Otherwise, the *indid* value is prone to change as indexes are dropped and re-created. You can use the value 0 to specify that no index should be used—that is, to force a table scan. And you can use the value 1 to specify that the clustered index should be used regardless of the columns on which it exists. The index hint syntax looks like this:

```
SELECT select_list
FROM table [(INDEX ({index_name | index_id}
            [, index_name | index_id ...]))]
```

This example forces the query to do a table scan:

```
SELECT au_lname, au_fname
FROM authors (INDEX(0))
WHERE au_lname LIKE 'C%'
```

This example forces the query to use the index named *aunmind*:

```
SELECT au_lname, au_fname
FROM authors (INDEX(aunmind))
WHERE au_lname LIKE 'C%'
```

The following example forces the query to use both indexes 2 and 3. Note, however, that identifying an index by *indid* is dangerous. If an index is dropped and re-created in a different place, it might take on a different *indid*. If you don't have an index with a specified ID, you get an error message. The clustered index is the only index that will always have the same *indid* value, which is 1. Also, you cannot specify index 0 (no index) along with any other indexes.

```
SELECT au_lname, au_fname
FROM authors (INDEX (2,3))
WHERE au_lname LIKE 'C%'
```

We could use index hints in the example shown earlier, in which the query optimizer was not choosing to use an index intersection. We could force the use of two indexes using this query:

```
SELECT fname, lname
FROM emps (INDEX (idx_nci_fname, idx_nci_lname))
```

A second kind of index hint is FASTFIRSTROW, which tells SQL Server to use a nonclustered index leaf level to avoid sorting the data. This hint has been preserved only for backward compatibility; it has been superseded by the processing hint FAST *n*, which is one of the query processing hints, as discussed in the next section.

Query Processing Hints

Query processing hints follow the word OPTION at the very end of your SQL statement and apply to the entire query. If your query involves a UNION, only the last SELECT in the UNION can include the OPTION clause. You can include more than one OPTION clause, but you can specify only one hint of each type. For example, you can have one GROUP hint and also use the ROBUST PLAN hint. Here's an example of forcing SQL Server to process a GROUP BY using hashing:

```
SELECT type, count(*)
FROM titles
GROUP BY type
OPTION (HASH GROUP)
```

This example uses multiple query processing hints:

```
SELECT pub_name, count(*)
FROM titles JOIN publishers
    ON titles.pub_id = publishers.pub_id
GROUP BY pub_name
OPTION (ORDER GROUP, ROBUST PLAN, MERGE JOIN)
```

There are eight different types of processing hints, most of which are fully documented in SQL Server Books Online. The key aspects of these hints are described here:

Grouping Hints   You can specify that SQL Server use a HASH GROUP or an ORDER GROUP to process GROUP BY operations.

Union Hints   You can specify that SQL Server form the UNION of multiple result sets by using HASH UNION, MERGE UNION, or CONCAT UNION. HASH UNION and MERGE UNION are ignored if the query specifies UNION ALL because UNION ALL does not need to remove duplicates. UNION ALL is always carried out by simple concatenation.

Join Hints   As discussed in the earlier section on join hints, you can specify join hints in the OPTION clause as well as in the JOIN clause, and any join hint in the OPTION clause applies to all the joins in the query. OPTION join hints override those in the JOIN clause. You can specify LOOP JOIN, HASH JOIN, or MERGE JOIN.

FAST number_rows   This hint tells SQL Server to optimize so that the first rows come back as quickly as possible, possibly reducing overall throughput. You can use this option to influence the query optimizer to drive a scan using a nonclustered index that matches the ORDER BY clause of a query rather than using a different access method and then doing a sort to match the ORDER BY clause. After the first *number_rows* are returned, the query continues execution and produces its full result set.

FORCE ORDER   This hint tells SQL Server to process the tables in exactly the order listed in your FROM clause. However, if any of your joins is an OUTER JOIN, this hint might be ignored.

MAXDOP number   This hint overrides the *max degree of parallelism* configuration option for only the query specifying this option. I'll discuss parallelism when we look at server configuration in Chapter 17.

ROBUST PLAN   This hint forces the query optimizer to attempt a plan that works for the maximum potential row size, even if it means degrading performance. This is particularly applicable if you have wide *varchar* columns. When the query is processed, some types of plans might create intermediate tables. Operators might need to store and process rows that are wider than any of the input rows, which might exceed SQL Server's internal row size limit. If this happens, SQL Server produces an error during query execution. If you use ROBUST PLAN, the query optimizer will not consider any plans that might encounter this problem.

KEEP PLAN   This hint ensures that a query is not recompiled as frequently when there are multiple updates to a table. This can be particularly useful when a stored procedure does a lot of work with temporary tables, which might cause frequent recompilations.

Stored Procedure Optimization

So far, I've been talking about tuning and optimizing individual queries. But what if you want to optimize an entire stored procedure? In one sense, there's nothing special about optimizing a stored procedure because each statement inside the procedure is optimized individually. If every statement has good indexes to use and each one performs optimally, the procedure should also perform optimally. However, since the execution plan for a stored procedure is a single unit, there are some additional issues to be aware of. The main issue is how often the entire procedure is recompiled. In Chapter 11, we looked at how and when you might want to force a procedure to be recompiled, either on an occasional basis or every time it is executed. I also mentioned some situations in which SQL Server will automatically recompile a stored procedure.

For a complex procedure or function, recompilation can take a substantial amount of time. As I've mentioned, in some cases you must recompile the entire procedure to get the optimum plan, but you don't want the procedure to be recompiled more often than necessary. Tuning a stored procedure, as opposed to tuning individual queries, involves making sure that the procedure is not recompiled more often than it needs to be. In fact, a badly tuned stored procedure can end up being recompiled numerous times for every single execution.

In this section, I'll mention three specific situations that can cause a run-time recompilation of a stored procedure or function:

- Data in a table referenced by the routine has changed.

- The procedure contains a mixture of DDL and DML operations.

- Certain operations on temporary tables are performed.

These situations are actually discussed in detail in Microsoft Knowledge Base article Q243586, which is included on the companion CD. In this section, I'll just mention the most important issues.

Data Changing in a Referenced Table

You saw in Chapter 15 that SQL Server 2000 will automatically update index statistics if more than a certain number of row modification operations have been performed on a table. And, if any table referenced by a procedure has had its statistics updated, the procedure will automatically be updated the next time it is executed. This is particularly common when your procedure creates a temporary table. When the table is first created, it has no rows in it, so any added rows can invoke an update of statistics and thus a recompile. In fact, query plans involving temporary tables are more likely to be recompiled than query plans involving permanent tables because only six modification operations have to occur in order to force an update of statistics.

If you find that your stored procedures are being recompiled more often than you think is necessary, you can use the KEEP PLAN query hint. Note that the KEEP PLAN hint applies only to recompiling a procedure due to row modifications for a temporary table.

You can use SQL Profiler to determine if and when your procedures are being recompiled. (Knowledge Base article Q243586 supplies a lot of detail on using SQL Profiler.)

Mixing DDL and DML

If any DDL operations are performed, either on a temporary table or a permanent table, the procedure is always recompiled as soon as another DML operation is encountered. This situation is called *interleaving* of DDL and DML. DDL operations can include creating a table, modifying a table, adding or changing a table constraint, or adding an index to a table. If you have a procedure that creates a table, selects from it, creates an index, and then selects from the table again, the procedure will be recompiled twice while it is running. And this doesn't take into account the fact that it might have been compiled before it ever started execution the first time, perhaps due to not having a plan available in cache.

To avoid this situation, you should have all the DDL right at the beginning of the procedure so that there is no interleaving. The procedure will then have to be recompiled only once, while it is executing.

Other Operations on Temporary Tables

Certain other operations on temporary tables will cause recompiles even though these same operations on a permanent table might not cause a procedure to be recompiled. You can minimize these recompiles by making sure that your procedures meet the following conditions:

■   All references to a temporary table refer to a table created locally, not to temporary tables created in the calling procedure or batch.

■ The procedure does not declare any cursors that reference a temporary table.

■ The procedure does not create temporary tables inside a conditionally executed statement such as IF/ELSE or WHILE.

CONCURRENCY AND CONSISTENCY TRADEOFFS

If you're designing a multiuser application that will both query and modify the same data, you need a good understanding of concurrency and consistency. Concurrency is the ability to have many simultaneous users operating at once. The more users who can work well simultaneously, the higher your concurrency. Consistency is the level at which the data in multiuser scenarios exhibits the same behavior that it would if only one user were operating at a time. Consistency is expressed in terms of isolation levels. At the highest isolation level, Serializable, the multiuser system behaves just as it would if users submitted their requests serially. At the Serializable level, you have a greater need to protect resources, which you do by locking, which in turn reduces concurrency. (Locking is discussed in Chapter 14. You should also understand transactional concepts, which are covered in Chapter 12.)

In many typical environments, an ongoing struggle occurs between the OLTP demands on the database and the DSS demands. OLTP is characterized by relatively high volumes of transactions that modify data. The transactions tend to be relatively short and usually don't query large amounts of data. DSS is read intensive, often with complex queries that can take a long time to complete and thus hold locks for a long time. The exclusive locks needed for data modification with OLTP applications block the shared locks used for DSS. And DSS tends to use many shared locks and often holds them for long periods and thus stalls the OLTP applications, which must wait to acquire the exclusive locks required for updating. DSS also tends to benefit from many indexes and often from a denormalized database design that reduces the number of tables to be joined. Large numbers of indexes are a drag on OLTP because of the additional work to keep them updated. And denormalization means redundancy—a tax on the update procedures.

You need to understand the isolation level required by your application. Certainly, you do not want to request Serializable (or, equivalently, use the HOLDLOCK or SERIALIZABLE hint) if you need only Read Committed. And it might become clear that some queries in your application require only Read Uncommitted (dirty read) because they look for trends and don't need guaranteed precision. If that's the case, you might have some flexibility in terms of queries not requiring shared locks, which keeps them from being blocked by processes modifying the database and from blocking those modifying processes. But even if you can live with a dirty-read level, you should use it only if necessary. This isolation level means that you might read data that logically never existed; this can create some weird conditions in the application. For example, a row that's just been read will seem to vanish because it gets rolled back. If your application can live with a dirty-read isolation level, it might be comforting to have that as a fallback. However, you should probably first try to make your application work with the standard isolation level of Read Committed and fall back to dirty read only if necessary.

RESOLVING BLOCKING PROBLEMS

Many applications suffer from poor performance because processes are backed up waiting to acquire locks or because of deadlocks. A smooth, fast application should minimize the time spent waiting for locks, and it should avoid deadlocks. The most important step you can take is to first understand how locking works.

A process *blocks* when it stalls while waiting to acquire a lock that is incompatible with a lock held by some other process. This condition is often, but erroneously, referred to as a "deadlock." As long as the process being stalled is not, in turn, stalling the offending process—which results in a circular chain that will never work itself out without intervention—you have a blocking problem, not a deadlock. If the blocking process is simply holding on to locks or is itself blocked by some other process, this is not a deadlock either. The process requesting the lock must wait for the other process to release the incompatible lock; when it does, all will be fine. Of course, if the process holds that lock excessively, performance still grinds to a halt and you must deal with the blocking problem. Your process will suffer from bad performance and might also hold locks that stall other processes; every system on the network will appear to hang.

The following guidelines will help you avoid or resolve blocking problems:

- Keep transactions as short as possible. Ideally, a BEGIN TRAN...COMMIT TRAN block should include only the actual DML statements that must be included in the explicit transaction. As much as possible, do conditional logic, variable assignment, and other "setup" work before the BEGIN TRAN. The shorter the duration of the transaction, the shorter the time that locks will be held. Keep the entire transaction within one batch if possible.

- Never add a pause within a transaction for user input. This rule is basically a part of the previous one, but it is especially important. Humans are slow and unreliable compared to computers. Do not add a pause in the middle of the transaction to ask a user for input or to confirm some action. The person might decide to get up to take a coffee break, stalling the transaction and making it hold locks that cause blocking problems for other processes. If some locks must be held until the user provides more information, you should set timers in your application so that even if the user decides to go to lunch, the transaction will be aborted and the locks will be released. Similarly, give your applications a way to cancel out of a query if such an action is necessary. Alternatively, you can use the LOCK_TIMEOUT session option to control when SQL Server automatically cancels out of a locking situation. We'll look at this option later in this chapter.

■ When you process a result set, process all rows as quickly as possible. Recall from Chapter 3 that an application that stops processing results can prevent the server from sending more results and stall the scanning process, which requires locks to be held much longer.

■ For browsing applications, consider using cursors with optimistic concurrency control. An address book application is a good example of a browsing application: users scroll around to look at data and occasionally update it. But the update activity is relatively infrequent compared to the time spent perusing the data. Using scrollable cursors with the OPTIMISTIC locking mode is a good solution for such applications. Instead of locking, the cursor's optimistic concurrency logic determines whether the row has changed from the copy that your cursor read. If the row has not changed during the lengthy period in which the user is perusing the data, the update is made without holding locks. If the row has changed, the UPDATE statement produces an error and the application can decide how to respond. Although I strenuously cautioned you against the misuse of cursors in Chapter 13, they are ideally suited to browsing applications.

You can also implement your own optimistic locking mechanism without using cursors. Save the values of the data you selected, and add a WHERE clause to your update that checks whether the values in the current data are the same as those you retrieved. Or, rather than use the values of the data, use a SQL Server *rowversion* column—an ever-increasing number that's updated whenever the row is touched, unrelated to the system time. If the values or rowversion are not identical, your update will not find any qualifying row and will not affect anything. You can also detect changes with @@ROWCOUNT and decide to simply abort, or more typically, you can indicate to the user that the values have changed and then ask whether the update should still be performed. But between the time the data was initially retrieved and the time the update request was issued, shared locks are not held, so the likelihood of blocking and deadlocks is significantly reduced.

Indexes and Blocking

I've already recommended that you choose your indexes wisely, strictly for performance reasons. However, concurrency concerns are also a reason to make sure you have good indexes on your tables. (Of course, better concurrency can also lead to better performance.) You saw in Chapter 14 that SQL Server acquires row (or key) locks whenever possible. However, this does not always mean that no other rows are affected if you're updating only one row in a table. Remember that to find the row to update, SQL Server must first do a search and acquire UPDATE locks on the resources it inspects. If SQL Server doesn't have a useful index to help find the desired row, it uses a table scan. This means every row in the table acquires an update lock, and the row actually being updated acquires an exclusive lock, which is not released until the end of the transaction. Here's a small example that illustrates the crucial relationship between indexes and concurrency:

```
USE pubs
GO
DROP TABLE t1
GO
/* First create and populate a small table */
CREATE TABLE t1 (a int)
GO
INSERT INTO t1 VALUES (1)
INSERT INTO t1 VALUES (3)
INSERT INTO t1 VALUES (5)
GO

BEGIN tran
UPDATE t1
SET a = 7 WHERE a = 1

EXEC sp_lock @@spid
/* The output here should show you one X lock, on a RID; that is the
   row that has been updated */

/* In another query window, run this batch before rollback is
   issued: */

USE pubs
UPDATE t1
SET a = 10
WHERE a = 3

/* Execute the rollback in the first window */
ROLLBACK TRAN
```

You should have noticed that the second connection was unable to proceed. To find the row where a = 3, it tries to scan the table, first acquiring update locks. However, it cannot obtain an update lock on the first row, which now has a value of 7 for *a*, because that row is exclusively locked. Since SQL Server has no way to know whether that is a row it is looking for without being able to look at it, this second connection blocks. When the rollback occurs in the first connection, the locks are released and the second connection can finish.

Let's see what happens if we put an index on the table. We'll run the same script again, except this time we'll build a nonclustered index on column *a*:

```
USE pubs
GO
DROP TABLE t1
GO
/* First create and populate a small table */
CREATE TABLE t1 ( a int)
GO
CREATE INDEX idx1 ON t1(a)
GO
INSERT INTO t1 VALUES (1)
INSERT INTO t1 VALUES (3)
INSERT INTO t1 VALUES (5)
GO

BEGIN tran
UPDATE t1
SET a = 7 WHERE a = 1

EXEC sp_lock @@spid
/* In this case, the output should show you three X locks (one again on
a RID) and two KEY locks. When the key column a is changed, the leaf
level of the nonclustered index is adjusted. Since the leaf level of
the index keeps all the keys in sorted order, the old key with the
value 1 is moved from the beginning of the leaf level to the end
because now its value is 7. However, until the transaction is over, a
ghost entry is left in the original position and the key lock is
maintained. So there are two key locks: one for the old value and one
for the new. */

/* In another query window, run this batch before rollback is issued: */

USE pubs
UPDATE t1
SET a = 10
WHERE a = 3

/* Execute the rollback in the first window */
ROLLBACK TRAN
```

This time, the second query succeeded, even though the first query held X locks on the keys in the leaf level of the index. The second connection was able to generate the lock resource string for the keys it needed to lock and then request locks only on those particular keys. Since the keys that the second connection requested were not the same as the keys that the first connection locked, there was no conflict over locking resources and the second connection could proceed.

RESOLVING DEADLOCK PROBLEMS

Deadlocks befuddle many programmers and are the bane of many applications. A deadlock occurs when, without some intervening action, processes cannot get the locks they need no matter how long they wait. Simply waiting for locks is *not* a deadlock condition. SQL Server automatically detects the deadlock condition and terminates one of the processes to resolve the situation. The process gets the infamous error message 1205 indicating that it was selected as the "victim" and that its batch and the current transaction have been canceled. The other process can then get the locks it needs and proceed. The two general forms of deadlocks are *cycle deadlocks* and *conversion deadlocks*. (See Chapter 14 for more on these two kinds of deadlocks.)

Cycle Deadlock Example

If you repeatedly run the following two transactions simultaneously from different OSQL.EXE sessions, you're nearly assured of encountering a "deadly embrace" (cycle deadlock) almost immediately from one of the two processes. It should be clear why: One of the processes gets an exclusive lock on a row in the *authors* table and needs an exclusive lock on a row in the *employee* table. The other process gets an exclusive lock on the row in *employee*, but it needs an exclusive lock for the same row in *authors* that the first process has locked.

```
-- Connection 1
USE pubs
WHILE (1=1)
BEGIN
    BEGIN TRAN
    UPDATE employee SET lname='Smith' WHERE emp_id='PMA42628M'
    UPDATE authors SET au_lname='Jones' WHERE au_id='172-32-1176'
    COMMIT TRAN
END

-- Connection 2
USE pubs
WHILE (1=1)
```

(continued)

```
BEGIN
    BEGIN TRAN
    UPDATE authors SET au_lname='Jones' WHERE au_id='172-32-1176'
    UPDATE employee SET lname='Smith' WHERE emp_id='PMA42628M'
    COMMIT TRAN
END
```

The result is the dreaded error 1205 (shown here) from one of the connections. The other connection continues along as if no problem has occurred.

```
Server: Msg 1205, Level 13, State 50, Line 1
Transaction (Process ID 52) was deadlocked on {lock} resources with
another process and has been chosen as the deadlock victim. Rerun the
transaction.
```

If you simply rewrite one of the batches so that both batches first update *authors* and then update *employee*, the two connections will run forever without falling into a cycle deadlock. Or you can first update *employee* and then update *authors* from both connections. Which table you update first doesn't matter, but the updates must be consistent, and you must follow a known protocol. If your application design specifies a standard protocol for accessing the tables consistently, one of the connections gets the exclusive page lock on the first table and the other process must wait for the lock to be released. Simply waiting momentarily for a lock is normal and usually fast, and it happens frequently without your realizing it. It is *not* a deadlock.

Conversion Deadlock Example

Now run the following transaction simultaneously from two different OSQL.EXE or SQL Query Analyzer sessions. You're running the same script, so it's obvious that the two processes follow a consistent order for accessing tables. But this example quickly produces a deadlock. A delay has been added so that you encounter the race condition more quickly, but the condition is lurking there even without the WAITFOR DELAY—the delay just widens the window.

```
USE pubs
SET TRANSACTION ISOLATION LEVEL REPEATABLE READ
BEGIN TRAN
SELECT * FROM authors WHERE au_id='172-32-1176'
-- Add 5 sec sleep to widen the window for the deadlock
WAITFOR DELAY '00:00:05'
UPDATE authors SET au_lname='Updated by '
    + CONVERT(varchar, @@spid) WHERE au_id='172-32-1176'
COMMIT TRAN
```

You can correct this example in a couple of ways. Does the isolation level need to be Repeatable Read? If Read Committed is sufficient, you can simply change the isolation level to get rid of the deadlock and to provide better concurrency. If you use Read Committed isolation, the shared locks can be released after the SELECT, and then one of the two processes can acquire the exclusive lock it needs. The other process waits for the exclusive lock and acquires it as soon as the first process finishes its update. All operations progress smoothly, and the queuing and waiting happen invisibly and so quickly that it is not noticeable to the processes.

But suppose that you need Repeatable Read (or Serializable) isolation. In this case, you should serialize access by using an update lock, which you request using the UPDLOCK hint. Recall from Chapter 14 that an update lock is compatible with a shared lock for the same resource. But two update locks for the same resource are not compatible, and update and exclusive locks are also not compatible. Acquiring an update lock does not prevent others from reading the same data, but it does ensure that you're first in line to upgrade your lock to an exclusive lock if you subsequently decide to modify the locked data. (The important issue here is that the exclusive lock can be acquired, so this technique works equally well even if that second statement is a DELETE and not an UPDATE, as in this example.)

By serializing access to the exclusive lock, you prevent the deadlock situation. The serialization also reduces concurrency, but that's the price you must pay to achieve the high level of transaction isolation. A modified example follows; multiple simultaneous instances, of this example will not deadlock. Try running about 20 simultaneous instances and see for yourself. None of the instances deadlocks and all complete, but they run serially. With the built-in 5-second sleep, it takes about 100 seconds for all 20 connections to complete because one connection completes about every 5 seconds. This illustrates the lower concurrency that results from the need for higher levels of consistency (in this case, Repeatable Read).

```
USE pubs
SET TRANSACTION ISOLATION LEVEL REPEATABLE READ
BEGIN TRAN
SELECT * FROM authors (UPDLOCK) WHERE au_id='172-32-1176'
-- Add 5 sec sleep to widen the window for the deadlock
WAITFOR DELAY '00:00:05'
UPDATE authors SET au_lname='Updated by '
    + CONVERT(varchar, @@spid) WHERE au_id='172-32-1176'
COMMIT TRAN
```

As a general strategy, you should add the UPDLOCK hint (or some other serialization) if you discover during testing that conversion deadlocks are occurring. Or add UPDLOCK from the outset if you detect from your CRUD analysis that deadlocks are likely, and then try backing it off during multiuser testing to see if it is absolutely necessary. Either approach is viable. If you know that in most cases the read-for-update (discussed later) will follow with an actual update, you might opt for the UPDLOCK hint from the outset and see if you can back it off later. But if the transaction is short and you will later update the data in most cases, there isn't much point in backing off the update lock. The shared lock will need to upgrade to an exclusive lock, so getting the update lock in the first place makes good sense.

Preventing Deadlocks

Deadlocks can usually be avoided, although you might have to do some detailed analysis to solve the problems that cause them. Sometimes the cure is worse than the ailment, and you're better off handling deadlocks rather than totally preventing them, as we'll discuss in the next section. Preventing deadlocks (especially conversion deadlocks) requires a thorough understanding of lock compatibility. These are the main techniques you can use to prevent deadlocks:

- To prevent cycle deadlocks, make all processes access resources in a consistent order.

- Reduce the transaction isolation level if it's suitable for the application.

- To prevent conversion deadlocks, explicitly serialize access to a resource.

Deadlock prevention is a good reason to use stored procedures. By encapsulating the data access logic in stored procedures, it's easier to impose consistent protocols for the order in which resources (for example, tables) are accessed, which can help you avoid cycle deadlocks. But in so doing, you do not reduce the likelihood of conversion deadlocks. As noted above, conversion deadlocks are best dealt with by serializing access to a resource or by lowering the transaction isolation level if appropriate. The most common scenario for conversion deadlocks is the read-for-update situation. If a resource will be read within a transaction requiring Repeatable Read or Serializable isolation and will be updated later, you should request an update lock on the read using the UPDLOCK hint. The update lock will let other users read the data but will prevent them from updating the data or doing a read-for-update. The net effect is that once the update lock is acquired, the process will be next in line for the exclusive lock needed to actually modify it.

Handling Deadlocks

The cost of serializing access is that other users wanting to read-for-update (or actually update or delete) must wait. If you are not experiencing deadlocks, serializing access might needlessly reduce concurrency. You might have a case in which a transaction often does a read-for-update but only infrequently does the update. In this case, deadlocks might be infrequent. The best course of action might be to *not* prevent deadlocks and simply deal with them when they occur.

Preventing deadlocks can significantly reduce concurrency because the read-for-update would be blocked. Instead, you can simply write your applications to handle deadlocking. Check for deadlock message 1205, and retry the transaction. With retry logic, you can live with moderate deadlock activity without adding a lot of serialization to the application. It's still a good idea to keep count of how often you experience deadlocks; if the incidence is high, the wasted effort and constant retrying are likely to be worse than the cost of preventing the deadlock in the first place. How you write the deadlock handler will depend on the language or tool you use to build your application. But an application that is prone to deadlocks should have a deadlock handler that retries. Such a handler must be written in the host language. There is no way to do a retry directly within a stored procedure or a batch because deadlock error 1205 terminates the batch.

Volunteering to Be the Deadlock Victim

Recall from Chapter 14 that the LOCK_MONITOR process in SQL Server attempts to choose as the deadlock victim the process that would be the least expensive to roll back, considering the amount of work the process has already done. But a process can also offer to "sacrifice itself" as the victim for deadlock resolution. You can make this happen by using the *SET DEADLOCK_PRIORITY LOW | NORMAL* statement. If a process has a deadlock priority of LOW and the other participating process is NOR-MAL (the default), the LOW process is chosen as the victim even if it was not the process that closed the loop.

Adding *SET DEADLOCK_PRIORITY LOW* to one of the connections (and not the other) indicates that it will be selected as the victim, even if it will be more expensive to roll back. You might find this useful if, for example, you are building summary tables for reporting purposes and also performing OLTP activities on the same database, and you occasionally have deadlocks and know that one process is more important than the other. You set the less important process to LOW. It might also be useful if one application was written with a good deadlock handler and the other was not. Until the application without the handler can be fixed, the "good" application can make the simple change of volunteering itself and then handle a deadlock with retry logic when the deadlock occurs later.

Watching Locking Activity

Locking problems often result from locks that you don't even realize are being taken. You might be updating only table A, but blocking issues arise on table B because of relationships that you don't realize exist. If, for example, a foreign key relationship exists between table A and table B and the update on A is causing some query activity to B, some shared locks must exist. Or a trigger or a nested call to another procedure might cause some locking that isn't obvious to you.

In cases like these, you must be able to watch locks to look for locking operations that you weren't aware of. The graphical lock display of SQL Server Enterprise Manager is the most convenient way to watch locking in many cases. However, SQL Server Enterprise Manager provides only a snapshot of the current state of locking; you can miss a lot of locking activity that occurs in the time it takes you to refresh the display.

Identifying the Culprit

As with most debugging situations, the hardest part of solving a problem with locking is understanding the problem. If you get complaints that "the system is hung," it's a good bet that you have a blocking problem. Most blocking problems happen because a single process holds locks for an extended period of time. A classic case (as I discussed earlier) is an interactive application that holds locks until the user at the other end takes an action, such as clicking a button to commit the transaction or scrolling to the end of the output, which causes all the results to be processed. If the user goes to lunch and doesn't take that action, everyone else might as well grab lunch too because they're not going to get much work done. Locks pile up, and the system seems to hang. The locks in the system are reported in the pseudo–system table, *syslockinfo*, in the *master* database. I'll talk about a related pseudo–system table, *sysprocesses*, later in the chapter.

> **NOTE** The pseudo–system tables are not maintained as on-disk structures. Locking and process data are by definition relevant only at runtime. So *syslockinfo* and *sysprocesses* are presented as system tables, and although they can be queried just like other system tables, they do not have on-disk storage as normal tables do.

A big challenge in trying to identify the cause of blocking is that when you experience such problems, you probably have hundreds or thousands of locks piled up. At these times, it's hard to see the trees through the forest. Usually, you just want to see which process is holding up everyone else. Once you identify it, of course, you need to immediately get it out of the way, either by forcing it to complete or, if necessary, by issuing the KILL command on the connection. The longer-term solution is to rework the application so that it will not hold locks indefinitely.

SQL Server Enterprise Manager provides a graphical way to watch locking activity, as shown in Figure 16-6; this is the best method most of the time. From the Management folder, choose Current Activity. You can look at locks either by process or by object. If you select the Locks / Process ID option, the graphic shows which processes are blocked and which processes are blocking. When you double-click on the process in the right pane, you see the last command the process issued. This is what Figure 16-6 shows. You can then send a message to the offending user to complete the transaction (although this is a short-term solution at best). Or you can kill the process from SQL Server Enterprise Manager, which isn't ideal but is sometimes the best short-term course of action. You can select a particular process from the left pane, under the Locks / Process ID option, and the right pane will show all the locks held by that process.

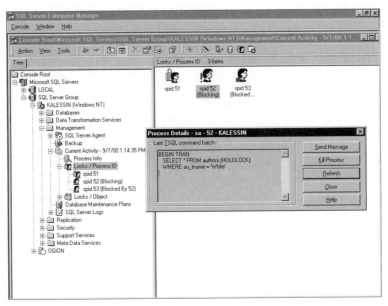

Figure 16-6. *Viewing the last batch issued by a blocking process in SQL Server Enterprise Manager.*

Alternatively, you can select the Locks / Object option under Current Activity. The left pane displays a graphic of each locked object. If you then select one of these objects, the right pane shows which processes have that object locked. Again, when you double-click on the process in the right pane, you see the last command the process issued.

But sometimes even SQL Server Enterprise Manager can get blocked by locking activity in *tempdb*, so it's useful to know how to monitor-lock the old-fashioned way, by using system stored procedures or by querying directly from the *syslockinfo* table. You start by running *sp_who2* and *sp_lock*. Most people are familiar with *sp_who* but not *sp_who2*, which works in almost the same way but formats the output in a more readable way and contains more of the columns from the *sysprocesses* table. However, *sysprocesses* contains additional information that neither *sp_who* nor *sp_who2* reports, so you might even want to write your own *sp_who3*! We'll look at the *sysprocesses* table in more detail later in this chapter.

The *BlkBy* column of the *sp_who2* output shows the ID (*spid*) of a blocking process. The procedure *sp_lock* provides a formatted and sorted listing of *syslockinfo* that decodes the lock types into mnemonic forms, such as *IS (Intent-Shared)* instead of *type 7*. In Chapter 14, we looked at output from *sp_lock* to watch the various types and modes of locking. If your users say that the system is hung, try to log on and execute *sp_who2* and *sp_lock*. If you can log on and execute these procedures, you immediately know that the system is not hung. If you see a nonzero *spid* in the *BlkBy* column of the *sp_who2* output or if the Status value is WAIT in the *sp_lock* output, blocking is occurring. It's normal for some blocking to occur—it simply indicates that one process is waiting for a resource held by another. If such contention didn't exist, you wouldn't even need to lock. But if you reissue the query for lock activity a moment later, you expect to find that same blockage cleared up. In a smoothly running system, the duration that locks are held is short, so long pileups of locks don't occur.

When a major lock pileup occurs, you can get a lengthy chain of processes blocking other processes. It can get pretty cumbersome to try to track this manually. You can create a procedure such as the following to look for the process at the head of a blocking chain:

```
USE master
GO
CREATE PROCEDURE sp_leadblocker
AS
IF EXISTS
    (SELECT * FROM master.dbo.sysprocesses
    WHERE spid IN (SELECT blocked FROM master.dbo.sysprocesses))
    SELECT spid, status, loginame=SUBSTRING(loginame,1,12),
        hostname=substring(hostname, 1, 12),
            blk=CONVERT(char(3), blocked),
        dbname=SUBSTRING(DB_NAME(dbid), 1, 10), cmd, waittype
        FROM master.dbo.sysprocesses
        WHERE spid IN (SELECT blocked FROM master.dbo.sysprocesses)
            AND blocked=0
ELSE
SELECT 'No blocking processes found!'
```

Once you identify the connection (*spid*) causing the problem, check to see the specific locks that it is holding. You can query from *syslockinfo* for this, but simply running *sp_lock spid* will probably give you exactly what you need. There might be multiple separate lock chains, in which case the batch will return more than one *spid*. You can follow the same procedure for each one.

The *syslockinfo* Table

If a lot of blocking is going on, you might want to take a look at all locks held that are blocking other users. You can use the procedure *sp_blockinglocks* (which is not a part of the installed SQL Server product but is included on the companion CD) to print out a list of all locks held that are blocking other processes. The procedure examines the *syslockinfo* table for resources that have more than one lock listed and are held by different processes with different status values. For example, if process

52 has an X lock on the *sales* table with a status of GRANT and process 53 is trying to read from that table, the output of *sp_blockinglocks* looks like this:

```
spid   db     ObjId         IndId  Type Resource           Mode     Status
------ -----  -----------   ------ ---- ---------------    --------  ------
52     pubs   149575571     0      TAB                     X         GRANT
53     pubs   149575571     0      TAB                     IS        WAIT
```

It can also be useful to see the last command issued by a blocking process; you can do this by double-clicking on a process ID in the Current Activity panes of SQL Server Enterprise Manager. You can also use *DBCC INPUTBUFFER (spid)* for this—which is the same thing SQL Server Enterprise Manager does when you double-click on a process. DBCC INPUTBUFFER reads the memory from within the server that was used for the last command. So DBCC INPUTBUFFER can access whatever command is still in the buffer for a given connection, even if it has already been executed.

Usually, by this point you have enough of a handle on the problem to turn your attention to the application, which is where the resolution will ultimately lie. But if you need or want to go a bit further, you can find out the depth at which the connection is nested within a transaction. Blocking problems often happen because the connection doesn't realize the nested depth and hasn't applied the correct pairing of COMMIT commands. (Chapter 12 discusses the scoping and nesting levels of transactions.) A connection can determine its own nesting depth by querying @@TRANCOUNT. Starting with SQL Server 7, you can also determine the nesting level of any current connection, not just your own. This involves inspecting the *sysprocesses* table directly because the information is not included in either *sp_who* or *sp_who2*.

The *sysprocesses* Table

As I've mentioned, some columns in the *sysprocesses* table don't show up in the output of either *sp_who* or *sp_who2*. Table 16-2 describes these columns.

Column Name	*Data Type*	*Description*
waittype	*binary(2)*	The *waittypes* of 1 through 15 correspond to the mode of lock being waited on. (See the list on page 931.) Hex values 0x40 through 0x4f correspond to miscellaneous waits. 0x81 is a wait to write to the log. 0x400 through 0x40f are latch waits. 0x800 is a wait on a network write.
waittime	*int*	Indicates the current wait time in milliseconds. The value is 0 when the process is not waiting.

Table 16-2. *Columns in the* sysprocesses *table that aren't available via* sp_who *or* sp_who2. *(continued)*

Table 16-2. *continued*

Column Name	Data Type	Description
lastwaittype	*nchar(32)*	A string indicating the name of the last or current wait type.
waitresource	*nchar(32)*	A textual representation of a lock resource.
memusage	*int*	Indicates the number of pages in the memory cache that are currently allocated to this process. A negative number means that the process is freeing memory allocated by another process.
login_time	*datetime*	Indicates the time when a client process logged on to the server. For system processes, it indicates the time when SQL Server startup occurred.
ecid	*smallint*	An execution context ID that uniquely identifies the subthreads operating on behalf of a single process.
kpid	*smallint*	The operating system thread ID.
open_tran	*smallint*	Indicates the current transaction nesting depth for the process.
uid	*smallint*	The user ID for the user who executed the command.
sid	*binary(85)*	A globally unique identifier (GUID) for the login.
nt_domain	*nchar(128)*	The operating system domain for the client.
nt_username	*nchar(128)*	The operating system username for the process.
net_address	*nchar(12)*	An assigned unique identifier for the network interface card on each user's workstation.
net_library	*nchar(12)*	The name of the client's network library DLL.

The procedure *sp_who2* translates the *dbid* into a database name and translates the numeric value for its status into a string. The most common status values you'll see are BACKGROUND, ROLLBACK, DORMANT (used when a connection is being retained while waiting for remote procedure call [RPC] processing), SLEEPING, and RUNNABLE.

The values that the *sysprocesses* table holds in the *waittype* column are the same ones you'll see in the *req_mode* column of *syslockinfo*. They can be translated as follows:

```
Lock Mode    value
-----------  -------
NULL         1
Sch-S        2
Sch-M        3
S            4
U            5
X            6
IS           7
IU           8
IX           9
SIU          10
SIX          11
UIX          12
BU           13
RangeS-S     14
RangeS-U     15
RangeIn-Nul  16
RangeIn-S    17
RangeIn-U    18
RangeIn-X    19
RangeX-S     20
RangeX-U     21
RangeX-X     22
```

> **NOTE**   These values are not the same as the values shown in SQL Server Books Online under the description for the *syslockinfo* table. The values in SQL Server Books Online are incorrect.

The Trace Flag for Analyzing Deadlock Activity

Trace flags are useful for analyzing deadlock situations. When a process is part of a deadlock, the victim process realizes that the deadlock occurred when it gets error message 1205. Any other process participating in the deadlock is unaware of the situation. To resolve the deadlock, you probably want to see both processes; trace flag 1204 provides this information.

The following is a fragment of the output from SQLSERVR.EXE, which was started from the command line using –T1204. This example uses the conversion deadlock script that we used previously—issuing the same batch from two connections—to illustrate the output of trace flag 1204. To capture deadlock information, you must start SQL Server from a command prompt; the output of the trace flag will be displayed in the command window. If you're running a named instance of SQL Server 2000, you must be in the binn directory for that instance (such as \mssql$MyInstanceName\binn), and you must also supply the instance name with the *-s* parameter.

```
sqlservr -c -T1204 -s MyInstance
Deadlock encountered .... Printing deadlock information
Wait-for graph
Node:1
KEY: 5:1977058079:1 (02014f0bec4e) CleanCnt:2 Mode: S Flags: 0x0
 Grant List::
   Owner:0x192713e0 Mode: S   Flg:0x0 Ref:1 Life:02000000 SPID:52 ECID:0
   SPID: 52 ECID: 0 Statement Type: UPDATE Line #: 7
   Input Buf: Language Event: USE pubs
SET TRANSACTION ISOLATION LEVEL REPEATABLE READ
BEGIN TRAN
SELECT * FROM authors WHERE au_id='172-32-1176'
-- Add 5 sec sleep to widen the window for the deadlock
WAITFOR DELAY '00:00:05'
UPDATE authors SET au_lname='Updated by '
    + CO
 Requested By:
   ResType:LockOwner Stype:'OR' Mode: X SPID:51 ECID:0 Ec:(0x192794e8)
   Value:0x19271400 Cost:(0/0)

Node:2
KEY: 5:1977058079:1 (02014f0bec4e) CleanCnt:2 Mode: S Flags: 0x0
 Grant List::
   Owner:0x192712e0 Mode: S   Flg:0x0 Ref:1 Life:02000000 SPID:51 ECID:0
   SPID: 51 ECID: 0 Statement Type: UPDATE Line #: 7
   Input Buf: Language Event: USE pubs
SET TRANSACTION ISOLATION LEVEL REPEATABLE READ
BEGIN TRAN
SELECT * FROM authors WHERE au_id='172-32-1176'
-- Add 5 sec sleep to widen the window for the deadlock
WAITFOR DELAY '00:00:05'
UPDATE authors SET au_lname='Updated by '
    + CO
 Requested By:
   ResType:LockOwner Stype:'OR' Mode: X SPID:52 ECID:0 Ec:(0x192c34e8)
   Value:0x1926d400 Cost:(0/0)
Victim Resource Owner:
 ResType:LockOwner Stype:'OR' Mode: X SPID:52 ECID:0 Ec:(0x192c34e8)
 Value:0x1926d400 Cost:(0/0)
```

This output shows the *spid* for both processes affected, shows a fragment of their input buffer (but not the entire command), and notes that neither process can upgrade its locks because of the circular relationship. Process 52 requests an update lock on a key that process 51 already has an update lock on. At the same time, process 51 requests an exclusive lock on a key that process 52 already has a shared lock on.

Thus, the two processes are in a circular relationship. The output can help you solve the problem—you know the processes involved and the locks that could not be acquired, and you have an idea of the commands being executed.

> **NOTE** The number assigned to trace flag 1204 is intended to be easy to remember. Recall that error 1205 is the well-known error message that an application receives when it is chosen as the deadlock victim.

Lock Hints

You can specify a lock type or duration with syntax similar to that for specifying index hints. Chapter 14 explains lock compatibility and other issues that are essential to using lock hints properly. Lock hints work only in the context of a transaction, so if you use these hints, you must use BEGIN TRAN/COMMIT (or ROLLBACK) TRAN blocks (or you must run with implicit transactions set to ON). The lock hint syntax is as follows:

```
SELECT select_list
FROM table_name [(lock_type)]
```

> **TIP** Remember to put the lock hint in parentheses; if you don't, it will be treated as an alias name for the table instead of as a lock hint.

You can specify one of the following keywords for *lock_type*:

HOLDLOCK

This is equivalent to the SERIALIZABLE hint described on the following page. This option is similar to specifying SET TRANSACTION ISOLATION LEVEL SERIALIZABLE, except that the SET option affects all tables, not only the one specified in this hint.

UPDLOCK

This takes update page locks instead of shared page locks while reading the table and holds them until the end of the transaction. Taking update locks can be an important technique for eliminating conversion deadlocks.

TABLOCK

This takes a shared lock on the table even if page locks would be taken otherwise. This option is useful when you know you'll escalate to a table lock or if you need to get a complete snapshot of a table. You can use this option with HOLDLOCK if you want the table lock held until the end of the transaction block (REPEATABLE READ).

PAGLOCK

This keyword takes shared page locks when a single shared table lock might otherwise be taken. (To request an exclusive page lock, you must use the XLOCK hint along with the PAGLOCK hint.)

TABLOCKX

This takes an exclusive lock on the table that is held until the end of the transaction block. (All exclusive locks are held until the end of a transaction, regardless of the isolation level in effect. This hint has the same effect as specifying both the TABLOCK and the XLOCK hints together.)

ROWLOCK

This specifies that a shared row lock be taken when a single shared page or table lock is normally taken.

READUNCOMMITTED | READCOMMITTED | REPEATABLEREAD | SERIALIZABLE

These hints specify that SQL Server should use the same locking mechanisms as when the transaction isolation level is set to the level of the same name. However, the hint controls locking for a single table in a single statement, as opposed to locking of all tables in all statements in a transaction.

NOLOCK

This allows uncommitted, or dirty, reads. Shared locks are not issued by the scan, and the exclusive locks of others are not honored. This hint is equivalent to READUNCOMMITTED.

READPAST

This specifies that locked rows are skipped (read past). READPAST applies only to transactions operating at READ COMMITTED isolation and reads past row-level locks only.

XLOCK

This takes an exclusive lock that will be held until the end of the transaction on all data processed by the statement. This lock can be specified with either PAGLOCK or TABLOCK, in which case the exclusive lock applies to the appropriate level of granularity.

Setting a Lock Timeout

Although it is not specifically a query hint, SET LOCK_TIMEOUT also lets you control SQL Server locking behavior. By default, SQL Server does not time out when waiting for a lock; it assumes optimistically that the lock will be released eventually. Most client programming interfaces allow you to set a general timeout limit for the connection so that a query is automatically canceled by the client if no response comes back after a specified amount of time. However, the message that comes back when the time period is exceeded does not indicate the cause of the cancellation; it could be because of a lock not being released, it could be because of a slow network, or it could just be a long running query.

Like other SET options, SET LOCK_TIMEOUT is valid only for your current connection. Its value is expressed in milliseconds and can be accessed by using the system function @@LOCK_TIMEOUT. This example sets the LOCK_TIMEOUT value to 5 seconds and then retrieves that value for display:

```
SET LOCK_TIMEOUT 5000
SELECT @@LOCK_TIMEOUT
```

If your connection exceeds the lock timeout value, you receive the following error message:

```
Server: Msg 1222, Level 16, State 50, Line 0
Lock request time out period exceeded.
```

Setting the LOCK_TIMEOUT value to 0 means that SQL Server does not wait at all for locks. It basically cancels the entire statement and goes on to the next one in the batch. This is not the same as the READPAST hint, which skips individual rows.

The following example illustrates the difference between READPAST, READUNCOMMITTED, and setting LOCK_TIMEOUT to 0. All of these techniques let you "get around" locking problems, but the behavior is slightly different in each case.

1. In a new query window, execute the following batch to lock one row in the *titles* table:

   ```
   USE pubs
   BEGIN TRANSACTION
   UPDATE titles
   SET price = price * 10
   WHERE title_id = 'BU1032'
   ```

2. Open a second connection, and execute the following statements:

   ```
   USE pubs
   SET LOCK_TIMEOUT 0
   SELECT * FROM titles
   SELECT * FROM authors
   ```

   Notice that after error 1222 is received, the second select statement is executed, returning all the rows from the *authors* table.

3. Open a third connection, and execute the following statements:

   ```
   USE pubs
   SELECT * FROM titles (READPAST)
   SELECT * FROM authors
   ```

   SQL Server skips (reads past) only one row, and the remaining 17 rows of *titles* are returned, followed by all the *authors* rows.

4. Open a fourth connection, and execute the following statements:

```
USE pubs
SELECT * FROM titles (READUNCOMMITTED)
SELECT * FROM authors
```

In this case, SQL Server does not skip anything. It reads all 18 rows from *titles*, but the row for title BU1032 shows the dirty data that you changed in step 1. This data has not yet been committed and is subject to being rolled back.

NOTE The NOLOCK, READUNCOMMITTED, and READPAST table hints are not allowed for tables that are targets of delete, insert, or update operations.

Combining Hints

You can combine index and lock hints and use different hints for different tables, and you can combine HOLDLOCK with the level of shared locks. Here's an example:

```
BEGIN TRAN
SELECT title, au_lname
FROM titles (TABLOCK) JOIN titleauthor
    ON titles.title_id=titleauthor.title_id
JOIN authors (PAGLOCK, HOLDLOCK, INDEX(1))
ON authors.au_id=titleauthor.au_id
```

SEGREGATING OLTP AND DSS APPLICATIONS

Sometimes it makes sense to split up your OLTP and DSS applications. This can be an excellent strategy if your DSS applications don't need immediate access to information. This is a reason for the recent popularity of data warehousing, data marts, and other data management systems, although these concepts have been around for years.

You can use a separate database (on the same server or on different servers) for DSS and OLTP, and the DSS database can be much more heavily indexed than the OLTP database. The DSS database will not have exclusive locks holding up queries, and the OLTP database's transactions will not get held up by the shared locks of the DSS. SQL Server's built-in replication capabilities make it relatively easy to publish data from the OLTP server and subscribe to it from your reporting server. SQL Server's replication capabilities can propagate data in near real time, with latency between the servers of just a few seconds. However, for maintaining a DSS server, it is best to propagate the changes during off-peak hours. Otherwise, the locks acquired during propagation at the subscribing site will affect the DSS users, just as any other update activity would. In addition, if for most of the day the DSS server is only executing SELECT queries, you can enable the database option *read only*. This means that SQL Server will not acquire or check locks for any queries because they will all be shared and therefore compatible. Completely bypassing lock maintenance can lead to noticeable performance improvements for the SELECT queries.

ENVIRONMENTAL CONCERNS

To finish this discussion of query tuning, we'll briefly look at some of the environmental concerns that you need to be aware of in your programming—for example, we'll discuss case sensitivity, which can greatly affect your applications. We'll also look at nullability issues and ANSI compatibility.

Case Sensitivity

Various options and settings affect the semantics of Transact-SQL statements. You must be sure that your Transact-SQL code can work regardless of the setting, or you must control the environment so that you know what the setting is.

Case sensitivity is by far the most common environmental problem, and it is simple to avoid. You should seriously consider doing most of your development in a case-sensitive environment, even if you will deploy your application mostly in a case-insensitive environment. The reason is simple: nearly all operations that work in a case-sensitive environment will also work in a case-insensitive environment, but the converse is not true.

For example, if we write the statement *select * from authors* in the *pubs* database of a case-sensitive environment, it will work equally well in a case-insensitive environment. On the other hand, the statement *SELECT * FROM AUTHORS* will work fine in a case-insensitive environment but will fail in a case-sensitive environment. The table in *pubs* is actually named *authors*, which is lowercase. The only statement that would work in a case-sensitive environment but fail in a case-insensitive environment is the declaration of an object name, a column name, or a variable name. For example, with the statement *declare @myvar int*, another statement declaring *@MYVAR int* would work fine in a case-sensitive environment because the two names are distinct, but it would fail in a case-insensitive environment because the names would be considered duplicates.

The easiest way to determine whether your environment is case sensitive is to perform a SELECT statement with a WHERE clause that compares a lowercase letter with its uppercase counterpart—you don't need to access a table to do this. The simple SELECT statement on the following page returns 1 if the environment is case sensitive and 0 if the environment is not case sensitive.

```
SELECT CASE
    WHEN ('A'='a') THEN 0
    ELSE 1
END
```

I use the term "environment" here because in SQL Server 2000 you can control the case sensitivity at different levels. Recall from Chapter 4 that your SQL Server instance will have a default collation, which determines both the character set and the sort order used. Each database can specify the collation it will use in the CREATE DATABASE command, or you can change the collation using the ALTER DATABSE command. If you don't specify a collation for a database, it will use the server's default. Case sensitivity is just one of the issues surrounding the character set used by SQL Server. The character set choice affects both the rows selected and their ordering in the result set for a query such as this:

```
SELECT au_lname, au_fname FROM authors
    WHERE au_lname='José'
ORDER BY au_lname, au_fname
```

If you never use characters that are not in the standard ASCII character set, case sensitivity is really your primary issue. But if your data has special characters such as the *é* in the example above, be sure that you understand all the issues surrounding different collations. For more information, see Chapter 4.

Nullability and ANSI Compliance Settings

To be recognized as ANSI compliant, various options had to be enabled in SQL Server because of subtle differences in semantics between the traditional SQL Server behavior and what is mandated by ANSI. I already covered the majority of these issues in earlier chapters. To preserve backward compatibility, the prior behavior couldn't simply be changed. So options were added (or in a few cases, previous options were toggled on) to change the semantics to comply with the ANSI SQL requirements. These options are summarized in Table 16-3, along with the statement used to change the behavior.

All of the options listed in the table can be set individually, but you might want to avoid doing that because there are 128 (2^7) permutations to consider. You might want to set just a few of the options individually, such as SET ANSI_WARNINGS. But by and large, you should either leave them all at their default settings or change them as a group to the ANSI SQL-92 behavior. You can enable these options as a group by setting SET ANSI_DEFAULTS ON. A good reason to use all the ANSI-compliant options is that several of the new features of SQL Server 2000, such as Indexed Views, require that almost all of these options be set for compliance.

ANSI SQL Requirement	SQL Server Statement
Disable SQL Server's = NULL extension	SET ANSI_NULLS ON
Automatically display a warning if a truncation would occur because the target column is too small to accept a value. By default, SQL Server truncates without any warning.	SET ANSI_WARNINGS ON
Always right-pad *char* columns, and don't trim trailing blanks that were entered in *varchar* columns, as SQL Server would do by default.	SET ANSI_PADDING ON
Make all statements implicitly part of a transaction, requiring a subsequent COMMIT or ROLLBACK.	SET IMPLICIT_TRANSACTIONS ON
Close any open cursors upon COMMIT of a transaction. By default, SQL Server keeps the cursor open so that it can be re-used without incurring the overhead of reopening it.	SET CURSOR_CLOSE_ON_COMMIT ON
Allow identifier names to include SQL Server keywords if the identifier is included in double quotation marks, which by default is not allowed. This causes single and double quotation marks to be treated differently.	SET QUOTED_IDENTIFIER ON
By default, create as NULL a column in a CREATE TABLE statement that is not specified as NULL or NOT NULL. The statement toggles this so that the column can be created with NULL. (I recommend that you always specify NULL or NOT NULL so that this setting option is irrelevant.)	SET ANSI_NULL_DFLT_ON ON

Table 16-3. *ANSI SQL requirements satisfied by SQL Server options.*

The ability to set these options on a per-connection basis makes life interesting for you as a SQL Server application programmer. Your challenge is to recognize and deal with the fact that these settings will change the behavior of your code. Basically, that means you need to adopt some form of the following four strategies:

- **The Optimistic approach**   Hope that none of your users or the person doing database administration will change such a setting. Augment your optimism by educating users not to change these settings.

- **The Flexible approach**   Try to write all your procedures to accommodate all permutations of the settings of all the various options. (This approach is usually not practical.)

- **The Hard-Line approach**   Explicitly set your preferences at startup and periodically recheck them to determine that they have not been subsequently altered. Simply refuse to run if the settings are not exactly what you expect.

- **The Clean Room approach**   Have a "sealed" system that prevents anyone from having direct access to change such a setting.

The approach you take is your choice, but recognize that if you don't think about the issue at all, you have basically settled for the Optimistic approach. This approach is certainly adequate for many applications for which it's pretty clear that the user community would have neither the desire nor the ability to make environmental changes. But if you're deploying an application and the machine running SQL Server will be accessed by applications that you don't control, it's probably an overly simplistic approach. Philosophically, the Flexible approach is nice, but it probably isn't realistic unless the application is quite simple.

You can change the SQL Server default values for the server as a whole by using *sp_configure 'user options'*. A specific user connection can then further refine the environment by issuing one of the specific SET statements just discussed. The system function @@OPTIONS can then be examined by any connection to see the current settings for that connection. The @@OPTIONS function and the value to be set using *sp_configure 'user options'* are a bit mask with the values depicted in Table 16-4.

By default, none of these options is enabled for SQL Server itself. So in a brand-new installation, the run value for *sp_configure 'user options'* will be 0. A system administrator can set this so that all connections have the same initial default settings. If you query the value of @@OPTIONS from an application that has not modified the environment, the value will also be 0. However, be aware that many applications, or even the SQL Server ODBC or OLE DB drivers that the applications use, might have changed the environment. Note that this includes SQL Query Analyzer, which uses ODBC. To change the default behavior, simply set the corresponding bit by doing a bitwise OR with the previous value. For example, suppose your run value is 512, which indicates that NOCOUNT is the only option turned on. You want to leave

NOCOUNT enabled, but you also want to enable option value 32, which controls how NULLs are handled when using equality comparisons. You'd simply pass the decimal value 544 (or 0x220) to *sp_configure 'user options'*, which is the result of doing a bitwise OR between the two options (for example, SELECT 32|512).

Decimal Value	Hexadecimal Value	Option	Description
2	0x0002	IMPLICIT_ TRANSACTIONS	Controls whether a transaction is started implicitly when a statement is executed.
4	0x0004	CURSOR_CLOSE_ ON_COMMIT	Controls behavior of cursors once a commit has been performed.
8	0x0008	ANSI_WARNINGS	Controls truncation and NULL in aggregate warnings.
16	0x0010	ANSI_PADDING	Controls padding of variables.
32	0x0020	ANSI_NULLS	Controls NULL handling by using equality operators.
64	0x0040	ARITHABORT	Terminates a query when an overflow or divide-by-zero error occurs during query execution.
128	0x0080	ARITHIGNORE	Returns NULL when an overflow or divide-by-zero error occurs during a query.
256	0x0100	QUOTED_ IDENTIFIER	Differentiates between single and double quotation marks when evaluating an expression, allowing object names to include characters that would otherwise not conform to naming rules or would collide with a reserved word or a keyword.

Table 16-4. *Bitmask values for SQL Server options.* *(continued)*

Table 16-4. *continued*

Decimal Value	Hexadecimal Value	Option	Description
512	0x0200	NOCOUNT	Turns off the message returned at the end of each statement that states how many rows were affected by the statement.
1024	0x0400	ANSI_NULL_ DFLT_ON	Alters the session's behavior to use ANSI compatibility for nullability. New columns defined without explicit nullability will be defined to allow NULLs.
2048	0x0800	ANSI_NULL_ DFLT_OFF	Alters the session's behavior to not use ANSI compatibility for nullability. New columns defined without explicit nullability will be defined to prohibit NULLs.

You can use DBCC USEROPTIONS to examine current options that have been set. The output is similar to the following code:

```
Set Option    Value
----------    ----------
textsize      64512
language      us_english
dateformat    mdy
datefirst     7
arithabort    SET
nocount       SET
```

This DBCC command shows only options that have been set—it doesn't show all the current settings for *sp_configure 'user options'*. But you can also decode your current connection settings pretty easily from @@OPTIONS using something like this:

```
SELECT 'IMPLICIT TRANSACTIONS' AS 'OPTION', CASE WHEN
    (@@OPTIONS & 0x0002 > 0) THEN 'ON' ELSE 'OFF' END
UNION
```

```
SELECT 'CURSOR_CLOSE_ON_COMMIT', CASE WHEN
    (@@OPTIONS & 0x0004 > 0) THEN 'ON' ELSE 'OFF' END
UNION
SELECT 'ANSI_WARNINGS',CASE WHEN (@@OPTIONS & 0x0008 > 0) THEN
    'ON' ELSE 'OFF' END
UNION
SELECT 'ANSI_PADDINGS', CASE WHEN (@@OPTIONS & 0x0010 > 0) THEN
    'ON' ELSE 'OFF' END
UNION
SELECT 'ANSI_NULLS', CASE WHEN (@@OPTIONS & 0x0020 > 0) THEN 'ON'
    ELSE 'OFF' END
UNION
SELECT 'ARITHABORT', CASE WHEN (@@OPTIONS & 0x0040 > 0) THEN 'ON'
    ELSE 'OFF' END
UNION
SELECT 'ARITHIGNORE', CASE WHEN (@@OPTIONS & 0x0080 > 0)
    THEN 'ON' ELSE 'OFF' END
UNION
SELECT 'QUOTED_IDENTIFIER', CASE WHEN (@@OPTIONS & 0x0100 > 0)
    THEN 'ON' ELSE 'OFF' END
UNION
SELECT 'NOCOUNT', CASE WHEN (@@OPTIONS & 0x0200 > 0) THEN 'ON'
    ELSE 'OFF' END
UNION
SELECT 'ANSI_NULL_DFLT_ON', CASE WHEN (@@OPTIONS & 0x0400 > 0)
    THEN 'ON' ELSE 'OFF' END
UNION
SELECT 'ANSI_NULL_DFLT_OFF', CASE WHEN (@@OPTIONS & 0x0800 > 0)
    THEN 'ON' ELSE 'OFF' END
ORDER BY 'OPTION'
```

Here's the result:

```
OPTION                      SETTING
--------------------------  -------
ANSI_NULL_DFLT_OFF          OFF
ANSI_NULL_DFLT_ON           ON
ANSI_NULLS                  ON
ANSI_PADDINGS               ON
ANSI_WARNINGS               ON
ARITHABORT                  ON
ARITHIGNORE                 OFF
CURSOR_CLOSE_ON_COMMIT      OFF
IMPLICIT TRANSACTIONS       OFF
NOCOUNT                     OFF
QUOTED_IDENTIFIER           ON
```

Unfortunately, running the previous SELECT statement will not give you a complete picture. As you saw in Chapter 5, many of the options, especially those involving NULL handling, can also be changed at the database level by using *sp_dboption*. To really get the full picture, you must examine @@OPTIONS for your current session in addition to *sp_dboption* for your current database.

Locale-Specific SET Options

Beware of the locale-specific SET options. SET DATEFORMAT and SET DATEFIRST change the recognized default date format. If DATEFORMAT is changed to *dmy* instead of the (U.S.) default *mdy*, a date such as *12/10/98* will be interpreted as October 12, 1998. A good strategy for dates is to always use the ISO format *yyyymmdd*, which is recognized no matter what the setting of DATEFORMAT is.

DATEFIRST affects what is considered the first day of the week. By default (in the United States), it has the value 7 (Sunday). Date functions that work with the day-of-week as a value between 1 and 7 will be affected by this setting. These day-of-week values can be confusing because their numbering depends on the DATEFIRST value, but the values for DATEFIRST don't change. For example, as far as DATEFIRST is concerned, Sunday's value is always 7. But if you've designated Sunday (7) as DATEFIRST, if you execute the statement *SELECT DATEPART(dw,GETDATE())* and your date falls on a Sunday, the statement will return 1. You just defined Sunday to be the first day of the week, so 1 is correct.

SUMMARY

This chapter walked you through performance-related topics that you should consider when designing and implementing a high-performance application. As a starting point, skilled team members are vital. More than anything else, a skilled and experienced staff is the best predictor and indicator of a project's potential success. You must establish performance criteria and prototype, test, and monitor performance throughout development.

We also looked at techniques that you can use in database design and in making indexing decisions. We discussed how to deal with lock contention issues and how to resolve deadlocks.

As you make and monitor changes, remember to change just one variable at a time. When you change multiple variables at the same time, it becomes impossible to evaluate the effectiveness of any one of them. This goes for all changes, whether they're related to design, indexing, the use of a query optimizer hint, or a configuration setting. This is a fundamental aspect of all performance optimization. In the next chapter, we'll look at configuration and performance monitoring.

Configuration and Performance Monitoring

In the previous chapter, we looked at the most important aspects of performance—those affected by design, prototyping, indexing, and query writing. You can also improve system performance by tuning your system configuration, but this is unlikely to yield as much gain as a design change. It's even more critical that your system not be misconfigured. You might see only a 5 percent improvement in performance by moving from a reasonable configuration to an ideal configuration, but a badly misconfigured system can kill your application's performance.

This chapter discusses configuration options for Microsoft Windows NT and Windows 2000 and Microsoft SQL Server 2000. It includes guidelines for setting important values and suggests improvements (which will often be minor at best). You'll also learn how to use the two most essential monitoring tools: SQL Profiler and System Monitor.

OPERATING SYSTEM CONFIGURATION SETTINGS

As mentioned previously, a badly configured system can destroy performance. For example, a system with an incorrectly configured memory setting can break an application. SQL Server dynamically adjusts the most important configuration options for you; you should accept these defaults unless you have a good reason to change them. In certain cases, tweaking the settings rather than letting SQL Server dynamically adjust them might lead to a tiny performance improvement, but your time is probably better spent on application and database design, indexing, query tuning, and other such activities.

Task Management

As you saw in Chapter 3, the operating system schedules all threads in the system for execution. Each thread of every process has a priority, and Windows NT and Windows 2000 execute the next available thread with the highest priority. By default, the OS gives active applications a higher priority. But this priority setting is not appropriate for a server application that's running in the background, such as SQL Server. To remedy this situation, SQL Server's installation program eliminates the Windows NT and Windows 2000 favoring of foreground applications by modifying the priority setting. It's not a bad idea to periodically double-check this setting in case someone sets it back. From Control Panel in Windows NT or Windows 2000, double-click on the System icon to open the System Properties dialog box. In Windows 2000, you can select the Advanced tab and then click the Performance Options button. Under Optimize Performance For, be sure that the button for Background Services is selected, and not the one for Applications. In Windows NT, you can select the Performance tab, and in the Application Performance section, slide the Select The Performance Boost For The Foreground Application control to the None setting.

Resource Allocation

A computer running Windows NT Server or Windows 2000 Server for file and print services will want to use the most memory for file caching. But if it is also running SQL Server, it makes sense for more memory to be available for SQL Server's use. In Windows 2000, you can change the properties for file and print services by right-clicking on My Network Places and choosing Properties. Then right-click on Local Area Connection and again choose Properties. Select File And Printer Sharing For Microsoft Networks and click the Properties button. In Windows NT, you can configure the server's resource allocation (and associated nonpaged memory pool usage) in the Server dialog box of the Network applet. Double-click on the Network icon in Control Panel and click on the Services tab. The Server dialog box appears, as shown in Figure 17-1. This dialog box is almost identical to the one you get in Windows 2000.

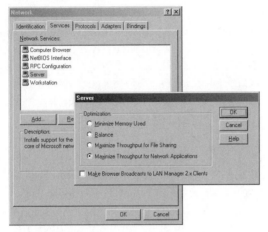

Figure 17-1. *Configuring the server file and print service settings.*

The Maximize Throughput For Network Applications setting is best for running SQL Server. You need high network throughput with minimal memory devoted to file caching so more memory is available to SQL Server. When this option is set, network applications such as SQL Server have priority over the file cache for access to memory. Although you might expect that the Minimize Memory Used option would help, it minimizes the memory available for some internal network settings that are needed to support a lot of SQL Server users.

PAGEFILE.SYS Location

If possible, you should place the operating system paging file on a different drive than the files used by SQL Server. This is vital if your system will be paging. However, an even better approach is to add memory or change the SQL Server memory configuration to effectively eliminate paging. So little page file activity will occur that the file's location will be irrelevant.

File System Selection

As I discussed in Chapter 4, whether you use the FAT or NTFS file system doesn't have much effect on system performance. You should use NTFS in most cases for reasons of security and robustness, not performance.

Nonessential Services

You should disable any services you don't need. In Windows 2000, you can right-click on My Computer and choose Manage, and in Windows NT, you can use the Services icon in Control Panel. Unnecessary services add overhead to the system and use resources that could otherwise go to SQL Server. If possible, don't use the server that's running SQL Server as a domain controller (DC), the group's file or print server, the Web server, the DHCP server, and so on. You should also consider disabling the Alerter, ClipBook, Computer Browser, Messenger, Network DDE, and Task Scheduler services that are enabled by default but are not needed by SQL Server.

Network Protocols

You should run only the network protocols you actually need for connectivity. Installing multiple network protocols (such as TCP/IP, NWLink, NetBEUI, DLC, and Appletalk) on your system is so easy that some systems run protocols that aren't even used. But this adds overhead. If you legitimately need to use multiple protocols, you should make sure that the highest binding is set for the most often used protocol.

SQL SERVER CONFIGURATION SETTINGS

Configuration changes can degrade system performance just as easily as they can improve it. This is particularly true in SQL Server 2000, for which most performance-oriented configuration settings are fully automatic. SQL Server 2000 has only 10 configuration options that are not considered "advanced," and none of these directly affects performance. To see all the configuration options, you must change the value of the Show Advanced Options setting:

```
EXEC sp_configure 'show advanced options', 1
GO

RECONFIGURE
GO
```

You should change configuration options only when you have a clear reason for doing so, and you should closely monitor the effects of each change to determine whether the change improved or degraded performance. Always make and monitor changes one at a time.

Serverwide Options

The serverwide options discussed here are set via the *sp_configure* system stored procedure. Many of them can also be set from SQL Server Enterprise Manager, but there is no single dialog box from which all configuration settings can be seen or changed. Most of the options that can be changed from SQL Server Enterprise Manager user interface are controlled from one of the Properties tabs that you reach by right-clicking on your server. If you use the *sp_configure* stored procedure, no changes take effect until the RECONFIGURE command (or RECONFIGURE WITH OVERRIDE, in some cases) is issued. Some changes (dynamic changes) take effect immediately upon reconfiguration, but others do not take effect until the server is restarted. If an option's *run_value* and *config_value* as displayed by *sp_configure* are different, you must restart the server in order for the *config_value* to take effect.

We won't look at every configuration option here—only those that relate directly to performance. In most cases, we'll discuss options that you should *not* change. Some of these are resource settings that relate to performance only in that they consume memory (for example, *open objects*). But if they are configured too high, they can rob a system of memory and degrade performance. I'll group the *sp_configure* settings by functionality. Keep in mind that SQL Server sets almost all of these options automatically, and your applications will work well without you ever looking at these options.

Memory Options

Before SQL Server 7, you had to manually configure memory options; this is no longer the case. In Chapter 3, you saw how SQL Server uses memory, including how it allocates memory for different uses and when it reads data from or writes data to disk. But we did not discuss how much memory SQL Server actually uses for these purposes or how to monitor the amount of the system's memory resources it uses.

min server memory and *max server memory*

By default, SQL Server automatically adjusts the total amount of the memory resources it will use. However, you can use the *min server memory* and *max server memory* configuration options to take manual control. The default setting for *min server memory* is 0 (MB), and the default setting for *max server memory* is 2147483647. If you use the *sp_configure* stored procedure to change both of these options to the same value, you basically take full control and tell SQL Server to use a fixed memory size. This mimics the memory configuration behavior prior to SQL Server 7. You can also use SQL Server Enterprise Manager to set a minimum and maximum value for memory, using the Memory tab of the SQL Server Properties dialog box (shown in Figure 17-2). To bring up the dialog box, right-click on the name of your server and then choose Properties.

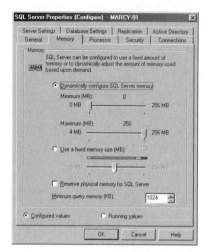

Figure 17-2. *The Memory tab of the SQL Server Properties dialog box.*

You can set the minimum and maximum memory using slider bars. Note that the maximum allowed is slightly less than the amount of physical memory in the machine. The absolute maximum of 2147483647 MB previously mentioned is actually the largest value that can be stored in the integer field of the *sysconfigures* table. It is not related to the actual resources of your system. You can select a separate option button to indicate that you want to use a fixed size. Setting the minimum and maximum sliders to the same value has the same effect.

set working set size   The Memory tab of the SQL Server Properties dialog box also includes a check box labeled Reserve Physical Memory For SQL Server. Selecting this is equivalent to setting the configuration option *set working set size* to 1, which reserves physical memory space for SQL Server that is equal to the server memory setting. Do this only if you don't want SQL Server to dynamically adjust its memory usage. Setting *set working set size* means that the operating system does not swap out SQL Server pages even if they can be used more readily by another process when SQL Server is idle. If the operating system's virtual memory manager must page, it must do so from other processes. These other processes can include other instances of SQL Server. This setting defaults to 0, which allows the Windows NT or Windows 2000 virtual memory manager to determine the working set size of SQL Server.

As I've mentioned, you should generally let SQL Server take full control of the memory values, especially if you have multiple instances running, but if your server might be inactive for long periods, you can manually set *min server memory* so that when someone finally submits a query, memory will be available and the query can be processed quickly. If you have other critical applications on your server that might have inactive periods, you can manually set *max server memory* so that SQL Server will not use too much system memory and so that when the other application becomes active again, memory will be available for it to use.

When SQL Server uses memory dynamically, the lazywriter queries the system periodically to determine the amount of free physical memory available. The lazywriter expands or shrinks the buffer cache to keep the operating system's free physical memory at 5 MB plus or minus 200 KB to prevent paging. If less than 5 MB is free, the lazywriter releases memory to the operating system that usually goes on the free list. If more than 5 MB of physical memory is free, the lazywriter recommits memory to the buffer cache. The lazywriter recommits memory to the buffer cache only when it repopulates the free list; a server at rest does not grow its buffer cache.

SQL Server also releases memory to the operating system if it detects that too much paging is taking place. You can tell when SQL Server increases or decreases its total memory use by using SQL Profiler to monitor the Server Memory Change event (in the Server category). An event is generated whenever SQL Server's memory increases or decreases by 1 MB or 5 percent of the maximum server memory, whichever is greater. You can look at the value of the data element called Event Sub Class to see whether the change was an increase or a decrease. An Event Sub Class value of 1 means a memory increase; a value of 2 means a memory decrease. We'll look at SQL Profiler in more detail later in this chapter.

awe enabled   A third memory option, called *awe enabled*, is available only for SQL Server 2000 Enterprise (or Developer) Edition running under Windows 2000 Advanced Server or DataCenter Server. This option enables the use of the Windows 2000 Address Windowing Extensions (AWE) API to support very large memory sizes. SQL Server 2000 can use as much memory as Windows 2000 Advanced Server or Windows 2000 DataCenter Server allows. Instances of SQL Server 2000 do not dynamically manage the size of the address space when you enable AWE memory. Therefore, when you enable AWE memory and start an instance of SQL Server 2000, one of the following occurs:

- If less than 3 GB of free memory is available on the computer, memory is dynamically allocated and, regardless of the parameter setting for *awe enabled*, SQL Server will run in non-AWE mode.

- If *sp_configure max server memory* has been set and at least 3 GB of free memory is available on the computer, the instance acquires the amount of memory specified in *max server memory*. If the amount of memory available on the computer is less than *max server memory* (but more than 3 GB) or if *max server memory* has not been set, the instance acquires almost all of the available memory and can leave up to only 128 MB of memory free.

If you're running multiple instances of SQL Server 2000 on the same computer and each instance uses AWE memory, you must pay close attention to certain configuration issues. The following list is taken from *SQL Server Books Online*, which documents that you must ensure the following:

- Each instance has a *max server memory* setting.

- The sum of the *max server memory* values for all the instances is less than the amount of physical memory in the computer.

If the sum of the settings exceeds the physical memory on the computer, some of the instances either will not start or will have less memory than is specified in *max server memory*. For example, suppose a computer has 16 GB of physical RAM and has three instances of SQL Server 2000 running on it. Furthermore, *max server memory* is set to 8 GB for each instance. If you stop and restart all three instances:

- The first instance will start with the full amount of 8 GB of memory.

- The second instance will start, but with slightly less than 8 GB of memory (up to 128 MB less).

- The third instance will start in dynamic memory mode and will have 128 MB or less memory available to it.

user connections   SQL Server 2000 dynamically adjusts the number of simultaneous connections to the server if the *user connections* configuration setting is left at its default of 0. Even if you set this value to a different number, SQL Server does not actually allocate the full amount of memory needed for each user connection until a user actually connects. When SQL Server starts up, it allocates an array of pointers with as many entries as the configured value for user connections. Each entry uses less than 1000 bytes of memory. Each user who connects to SQL Server is allocated 24 KB for three memory objects of one page (8 KB) each. These memory objects keep track of things such as the Process Status Structure (PSS) for each connection and the context area needed by the User Mode Scheduler (UMS) to keep track of the user's context as it moves the wait queue to a CPU and back again.

You should always let SQL Server dynamically adjust the value of the *user connections* option. If you configure the value too low, future connections will be denied access to SQL Server. Even if you're trying to limit the number of actual simultaneous users, this can backfire because connections are not the same as users. One user can open multiple connections through the same application. If you're using a query tool such as SQL Query Analyzer, each time you click the New Query button you start a new connection to the server that counts against the total.

locks The *locks* configuration option sets the number of available locks (of all types). The default is 0, which means that SQL Server adjusts this value dynamically. It starts by allocating 2 percent of the memory allotted to SQL Server to an initial pool of lock structures. When the pool of locks is exhausted, it allocates additional locks. The dynamic lock pool does not allocate more than 40 percent of the memory allocated to SQL Server. If too much memory is being used for locks, SQL Server escalates row locks into table locks wherever possible. You should leave this value at its default. If you manually supply a value for the maximum number of locks, once that number of locks is reached, any query that requests additional lock resources will receive an error message and the batch will terminate.

Scheduling Options

SQL Server 2000 has a special algorithm for scheduling user processes, which uses UMS threads (as described in Chapter 3). There is one UMS thread per processor, and the UMS makes sure that only one process can run on a scheduler at any given time. The UMS manages assignment of user connections to UMS threads to keep the number of users per CPU as balanced as possible. Four configuration options affect the behavior of the scheduler: *lightweight pooling*, *affinity mask*, *priority boost*, and *max worker threads*.

lightweight pooling By default, SQL Server operates in thread mode, which means that the UMS schedules the operating system threads. However, SQL Server also lets user connections run in fiber mode; fibers are less expensive to manage than threads. The *lightweight pooling* option has a value of 0 or 1; 1 means that SQL Server should run in fiber mode. Using fibers can yield a minor performance advantage, perhaps as much as a 5 percent increase in throughput when all of the available CPUs are operating at 100 percent. However, the tradeoff is that certain operations, such as running queries on linked servers or executing extended stored procedures, must run in thread mode. The cost of switching from fiber to thread mode for those connections can be noticeable, and in some cases will offset any benefit of operating in fiber mode.

If you're running in an environment with multiple CPUs, all of which are operating at 100 percent capacity, and if System Monitor shows a lot of context switching, setting *lightweight pooling* to 1 might yield some performance benefit. With a system using more than four processors, the performance improvements should be even greater.

affinity mask You can use the *affinity mask* setting to bind all the threads (or fibers) handled by one UMS thread to a certain processor. You should avoid doing this because this setting prevents the operating system from using whatever processor is currently most available; each UMS must then schedule its threads on the same processor.

You can also use this setting to limit the number of processors that SQL Server can use. For example, on an eight-processor system, setting *affinity mask* to 63 decimal or 00111111 binary means that SQL Server can use only processors 0 through 5. Two processors are reserved for other, non–SQL Server activity.

The *affinity mask* option was added in version 6.5 at the request of some major customers who ran SMP hardware with more than four processors. These sites were accustomed to similar options on UNIX or mainframe systems. Most sites do not need this option.

priority boost   If the *priority boost* setting is enabled, SQL Server runs at a higher scheduling priority. The default is 0, which means that SQL Server runs at normal priority whether you're running it on a single-processor machine or on an SMP machine. Enabling the priority boost option allows the SQL Server process to run at high priority. There are probably very few sites or applications for which setting this option will make much difference, so I recommend leaving it alone. But if your machine is totally dedicated to running SQL Server, you might want to enable this option (set it to 1) to see for yourself. It can potentially offer a performance advantage on a heavily loaded, dedicated system. Contrary to some folklore, this setting does not make SQL Server run at the highest operating system priority.

max worker threads   SQL Server uses the operating system's thread services by keeping a pool of worker threads (or fibers) that take requests off the queue. It attempts to evenly divide the worker threads among the UMS schedulers so the number of threads available to each UMS is the setting of *max worker threads* divided by the number of CPUs. With 100 or fewer users, there are usually as many worker threads as active users (not just connected users who are idle). With more users, it often makes sense to have fewer worker threads than active users. Although some user requests have to wait for a worker thread to become available, total throughput increases because less context switching occurs.

The *max worker threads* setting is somewhat autoconfigured. The default is 255, which does not mean that 255 worker threads are in the pool. It means that if a connection is waiting to be serviced and no thread is available, a new thread is created if the thread total is currently below 255. If this setting is configured to 255 and the highest number of simultaneously executing commands is, say, 125, the actual number of worker threads will not exceed 125. It might be even less than that because SQL Server destroys and trims away worker threads that are no longer being used. You should probably leave this setting alone if your system is handling 100 or fewer simultaneous connections. In that case, the worker thread pool will not be greater than 100.

Even systems that handle 4000 or more connected users run fine with the default setting of 255. When thousands of users are simultaneously connected, the actual worker thread pool is usually well below 255 because from the back-end database perspective most connections are idle, even though the user might be doing plenty of work on the front end.

Disk I/O Options

No options are available for controlling SQL Server's disk read behavior. All the tuning options to control read-ahead in previous versions of SQL Server are now handled completely internally. One option is available to control disk write behavior. This option controls how frequently the checkpoint process writes to disk.

recovery interval The *recovery interval* option can be automatically configured. SQL Server setup sets it to 0, which means autoconfiguration. In SQL Server 2000, this means a recovery time of less than one minute, but that might change in later releases or service packs. This option lets the database administrator control the checkpoint frequency by specifying the maximum number of minutes that recovery should take.

Prior to SQL Server 7, the recovery interval was set in terms of minutes; the default was 5. In practice, this meant a checkpoint every 30,000 log records, which was almost always much less than every 5 minutes because the implementation was not scaled for today's faster systems. In SQL Server 2000, recovery is more likely to match the *recovery interval* option, assuming that the system was busy before it came down. For databases with more than 20 MB of log records, the recovery interval directly corresponds to the checkpoint frequency. Thus, a recovery interval of 5 means that checkpoints occur only every 5 minutes and all dirty pages are written to disk.

Query Processing Options

SQL Server has several options for controlling the resources available for processing queries. As with all the other tuning options, your best bet is to leave these options at their default values unless thorough testing indicates that a change might help.

min memory per query When a query requires additional memory resources, the number of pages it gets is determined partly by the *min memory per query* option. This option is relevant for sort operations that you specifically request using an ORDER BY clause, and it also applies to internal memory needed by merge join operations and by hash join and hash grouping operations This configuration option allows you to specify a minimum amount of memory (specified in kilobytes) that any of these operations should be granted before they are executed. Sort, merge, and hash operations receive memory in a very dynamic fashion, so you rarely need to adjust this value. In fact, on larger machines, your sort and hash queries typically get much more than the *min memory per query* setting, so you shouldn't restrict yourself unnecessarily. If you need to do a lot of hashing or sorting, however, and you have few users or a lot of available memory, you might improve performance by adjusting this value. On smaller machines, setting this value too high can cause virtual memory to page, which hurts server performance.

query wait   The *query wait* option controls how long a query that needs additional memory waits, if that memory is not available. A setting of −1 means that the query waits 25 times the estimated execution time of the query, but it will always wait at least 25 seconds with this setting. A value of 0 or more specifies the number of seconds that a query will wait. If the wait time is exceeded, SQL Server generates error 8645:

```
Server: Msg 8645, Level 17, State 1, Line 1
A time out occurred while waiting for memory resources to execute the
query. Re-run the query.
```

Even though memory is allocated dynamically, SQL Server can still run out if the memory resources on the machine are exhausted. If your queries time out with error 8645, you can try increasing the paging file size or even add more physical memory. You can also try tuning the query by creating more useful indexes so that hash or merge operations aren't needed. Keep in mind that this option affects only queries that have to wait for memory needed by hash and merge operations. Queries that have to wait for other reasons will be unaffected.

index create memory   The *min memory per query* option applies only to sorting and hashing used during query execution; it does not apply to the sorting that takes place during index creation. Another option, *index create memory*, lets you allocate a specific amount of memory for index creation. Its value is also specified in kilobytes.

query governor cost limit   You can use the *query governor cost limit* option to set a maximum length of time that a query will run. SQL Server will not execute queries that the optimizer estimates will take longer than this. The option is specified in seconds, but it might not map exactly to seconds on your machine. You should think of the value as an abstract cost of the query rather than an actual number of seconds. The cost figure was correlated to seconds on one test machine in the SQL Server development group, and no information is available on the exact specs of that machine.

You can come up with your own correlation using SQL Profiler. If you capture the *Performance: Execution Plan* events, the data element called Binary Data reflects the optimizer's estimated cost for each SQL statement. This value is compared to the *query governor cost limit* value. If you then also capture the Duration data for each SQL statement, you can compare the estimated cost with the actual duration. For example, if, on average, queries that show a cost (in the SQL Profiler trace) of 8 seconds take 10 seconds to run, you should specify a *query governor cost limit* of about 80 percent of what you really want to allow. If you want to block all queries that are estimated to take longer than 1 minute to run, you should set the option to 48 (80 percent of 60 seconds). We'll look at SQL Profiler in more detail later in this chapter.

max degree of parallelism and cost threshold for parallelism   SQL Server 2000 lets you run certain kinds of complex queries simultaneously on two or more processors. The queries must lend themselves to being executed in sections. Here's an example:

```
SELECT AVG(charge_amt), category
FROM charge
GROUP BY category
```

If the *charge* table has 100,000 rows and there are 10 different values for *category*, SQL Server can split the rows into groups and have only a subset of the groups processed on each processor. For example, with a 4-CPU machine, categories 1 through 3 can be averaged on the first processor, categories 4 through 6 on the second processor, categories 7 and 8 on the third, and categories 9 and 10 on the fourth. Each processor can come up with averages for only its groups, and the separate averages are brought together for the final result.

During optimization, the optimizer always finds the cheapest possible serial plan before considering parallelism. If this serial plan costs less than the configured value for the *cost threshold for parallelism* option, no parallel plan is generated. The *cost threshold for parallelism* option refers to the cost of the query in seconds, but just like the *query governor cost limit* option, the value is not in actual clock seconds. The default value for the *cost threshold for parallelism* option is 5. Otherwise, if the cheapest serial plan costs more than this configured threshold, a parallel plan is produced based on some assumptions about how many processors and how much memory will actually be available at run time. This parallel plan cost is compared with the serial plan cost and the cheaper one is chosen. The other plan is discarded.

When the parallel plan is created, the optimizer inserts exchange operators into the query execution plan to prepare the query for parallel execution. An exchange operator is an operator in a query execution plan that provides process management, data redistribution, and flow control. The two main types of exchange operators that you'll observe if parallel plans are generated are the *distribute* operator, which separates the processing into multiple streams, and the *gather* operator, which retrieves the separate results and combines them into a single result. Occasionally, you'll also see a *redistribute* operator if the original streams need to be moved onto different processors at some point during the processing.

A parallel query execution plan can use more than one thread; a serial execution plan, which is used by a nonparallel query, uses only a single thread. The actual number of threads used by a parallel query is determined at query plan execution initialization and is called the degree of parallelism (DOP). This is the algorithm for determining what DOP to run at, based on the state of the system:

1. The maximum DOP of a query is the minimum of the configured *max degree of parallelism* value, the OPTION query hint MAXDOP, if any was specified, and the number of schedulers in the system:

```
MaxDOP = min ('max degree of parallelism',
              'OPTION MAXDOP', #schedulers)
```

2. The maximum DOP is further limited by dividing half the number of free threads available at the time the query starts by the number of concurrent "branches" the query might run. Each branch represents one stage of the query. For example, a branch might be a parallel scan or a parallel hash join. Note, however, that because SQL Server does not reserve these threads in any way, it might still run short of threads at runtime and get an 8642 error. If this happens, you should consider increasing the *max worker threads* configuration parameter:

```
MaxDOP = min (MaxDOP, 0.5 * #free threads
                    / #concurrent branches in this statement)
```

3. Next, SQL Server determines whether the query is a "large" query. If so, the query will run at the MaxDOP determined in the previous steps. In SQL Server 2000, a query is considered "large" if the serial cost of the query is greater than 600 (10 minutes). This limit was added to avoid situations in which a long-running query starts running at a low DOP because the system is busy and continues to run at that low DOP even if the system becomes less busy and more resources become available. (See the next step for more details.)

```
If (optimizer's parallel cost * optimizer's estimated DOP > 600)
                    Then DOP = MaxDOP
```

4. If the query is not a large query, SQL Server looks at how busy the system is to decide its DOP. First, it looks at how many active threads are in the system. A thread is determined to be active if it is being used by some connection, so this does not include internal system tasks. If there are more than four active threads per scheduler, SQL Server is very conservative with DOP and runs with DOP 0, which is in effect a serial plan:

```
If (#active threads > 4 * #schedulers) Then DOP = 0
```

5.   Otherwise, if there are no more than four active threads per scheduler, SQL
     Server looks at how many schedulers are currently idle (have no worker
     threads that are running or capable of running at that instant). This value
     is then used as the DOP:

```
DOP = #idle schedulers
```

Once a query starts executing on multiple threads for parallel execution, it uses
the same number of threads until completion. Each time a parallel query execution
plan is retrieved from the cache, SQL Server reexamines the optimal number of threads
specified. One execution of a query can result in the use of a single thread, and
another execution of the same query (at a different time) can result in using two or
more threads.

As you can see in the calculations above, the *max degree of parallelism* option
indicates the maximum number of processors that are used to run queries in parallel. The default value of 0 means that SQL Server should use the number of available CPUs. A value of 1 means that SQL Server should suppress parallelism completely.
Any other value restricts the degree of parallelism below the number of CPUs. If your
computer has only one processor, the *max degree of parallelism* value is ignored.

Be careful when you use the *max degree of parallelism* or *cost threshold for
parallelism* options—they have serverwide impact. You can also use trace flag 8687
to turn off parallelism for individual connections.

You can use SQL Profiler to trace the degree of parallelism for each query captured. If you choose to monitor events in the Performance category, you'll see four
different events for Degree Of Parallelism. This is so you can use the SQL Server 2000
Profiler to trace a SQL Server 7 server. In that case, a different one of the options is
used for each different DML statement (Delete, Insert, Select, or Update). In SQL
Server 2000, tracing any of these four events will write a row to the trace output
for every query indicating its degree of parallelism. The Event Sub Class data is a number
indicating which DML statement was run: 1 = SELECT, 2 = INSERT, 3 = UPDATE, and
4 = DELETE. The value in the Binary Data column indicates the degree of parallelism
actually used for that query—that is, the number of CPUs used to perform the
operation.

Database Options

Several database options can affect performance. The *read only* and *single user*
options affect performance because they eliminate locking in some cases. If your
database is used only for decision support (for example, a data mart), it might make
sense to set your database to *read only*, as follows:

```
ALTER DATABASE dbname SET READ_ONLY
```

In this way, no locking is performed in the database; this greatly reduces overhead. This option prevents changes from being made to the database. You can easily toggle it off to perform tasks such as bulk loading of data. For an operation in which the data is changed via large batch jobs that can run during off-hours and the normal workload is query only, *read only* is a good choice.

Even if your database is not read only, you might want to perform off-hour maintenance tasks and bulk loading operations with the *single user* option enabled, as shown here:

```
ALTER DATABASE dbname SET SINGLE_USER
```

This option also eliminates the need for locking because only one connection can use the database at a time. Of course, you need locking to make a multiuser system behave like a single-user system. But in this case, it *is* a single-user system, so locking is not required. If you need to do a big bulk load and index creation at night while no one else is using the system, you can eliminate the need to take locks during the bulk load.

Two other options are particularly useful if you're running SQL Server Desktop Edition on a small machine and your resources are extremely limited: *autoclose* and *autoshrink*. The *autoclose* option causes the database to shut down cleanly and free resources after the last user exits. By default, it is set to TRUE for all databases when SQL Server runs on Windows 98. The database reopens automatically when a user tries to use the database. The *autoshrink* option (discussed in Chapter 5) can be useful if your disk space resources are extremely limited, but there is a performance tradeoff. Shrinking a database is a CPU-intensive operation and takes a long time. All indexes on heaps affected by the shrink must be adjusted because the row locators change.

Finally, two database options control the automatic gathering of statistics: *auto create statistics* and *auto update statistics*. These were both discussed in Chapter 15.

Buffer Manager Options

In Chapter 3, we saw how the buffer manager (also known as the cache manager) uses a queue of "favored pages," which you can think of as a least recently used (LRU) algorithm, but no queue list of buffers is maintained in the order of most recent access. You can use the *pintable* option to directly influence the favoring behavior.

Pinning a Table in the Cache

You can permanently remove a table from the queue of pages examined by the lazywriter so that once they are read into the data cache, they are never forced from cache. (This favors them permanently, although it is really more than that: they are entirely exempted.) You can enable this option using the *sp_tableoption* stored procedure with the *pintable* option.

The *pintable* option is not appropriate for most sites. But if you get very random cache hits and you have some relatively small tables that are hot compared to other larger tables, this option might be beneficial. If those small, hot tables keep getting forced out by the random access to larger tables and you have plenty of memory, you can pin those small tables. By pinning, you override the buffer manager. But you take away the pages in cache used for each small table, so you give the buffer manager less memory to work with. Pinning a table does not initially read it in; pinning just makes the table "sticky" so that once a page of the table is in the cache, it doesn't get forced out. If you want the table preloaded and sticky, you can enable the option and then do *SELECT * FROM table* to read all the pages into cache. Be careful when you use this option; the table shouldn't be so big that you eat up more memory than your system can afford to use.

Monitoring Buffer Manager Performance

Two DBCC commands exist to monitor the performance of the buffer manager: SQLPERF(WAITSTATS) and SQLPERF(LRUSTATS). DBCC SQLPERF(WAITSTATS) not only provides an overview of the buffer manager, it helps identify where a transaction is delayed. It shows the total milliseconds of wait time and how much of the time is due to waiting for reads, waiting for different types of locks, waiting to add a log record to the log buffer, and waiting for log buffers to be physically written. The command DBCC SQLPERF(LRUSTATS) gives details on the lazywriter and the state of the cache, such as the cache-hit ratio, the size of the cache, the average number of pages scanned to find an available buffer, and the number of free pages. Although this information is available through System Monitor, the DBCC SQLPERF command lets you capture the output to a table and save the data for analysis.

For example, to capture the DBCC SQLPERF(WAITSTATS) output, you can create a table with four columns and use the dynamic EXECUTE command to populate the table. The following script shows one way to define and populate such a table. It actually adds a fifth column to the table, which indicates the current date and time that the rows were inserted into the table.

```
CREATE TABLE waitstats
(
wait_type       varchar(20),
requests        numeric(10, 0),
wait_time       numeric(12, 2),
signal_wait     numeric(12, 0),
recorded_time   datetime DEFAULT GETDATE()
)
GO

INSERT INTO waitstats (wait_type, requests, wait_time, signal_wait)
    EXEC ('DBCC SQLPERF(WAITSTATS)')
```

Startup Parameters on SQLSERVR.EXE

You can alter startup parameters used by the SQL Server process to tune performance by disabling the performance statistics collection or specifying trace flags.

Disabling the Performance Collection

Normally, SQL Server keeps performance statistics such as CPU usage and amount of I/O on a per-user basis. The values are materialized in the *sysprocesses* table when queried. If you never query or monitor these values, the work to keep track of them is unnecessary. You can eliminate the calls that produce these performance statistics by passing the *-x* startup flag to SQLSERVR.EXE. Or you can add *-x* as an additional parameter from the Setup program via the Set Server Options dialog box.

Specifying Trace Flags

We've discussed the use of trace flags several times, and you've seen how to enable them using DBCC TRACEON. You can also specify a trace flag at server startup; some trace flags make the most sense if they are specified serverwide rather than on a per-user basis. For example, trace flag 1204, which records information to the error log when a deadlock occurs, doesn't make sense for a specific connection because you probably have no idea ahead of time which connections will encounter deadlocks. To enable a trace flag serverwide, you add the flag as a parameter when you start SQL Server from the command line (for example, *sqlservr.exe -c -t1204*).

SYSTEM MAINTENANCE

SQL Server requires much less regular system maintenance than most comparable products. For example, because pages are automatically split, it maintains data clustering characteristics; most products that support data clustering make you do data reorganization to keep the data clustered. However, you should perform a couple of regular maintenance tasks for performance reasons. You can easily schedule these tasks (such as updating statistics and rebuilding your clustered index) using the SQL Server Agent service or the Database Maintenance Plan Wizard.

In the earlier discussion of tuning queries, I explained the importance of index distribution statistics. If you have not enabled automatic updating of statistics, you should update statistics frequently so that any significant changes in the volumes or distribution of data are reflected. Although it's not essential to dump and reload tables to keep clustering properties intact, doing so can be useful in rebuilding tables to reestablish fill factors and avoid page splits. The simple way to do this is to rebuild the clustered index on the table using the DROP_EXISTING option. When you use this option, the existing nonclustered indexes do not have to be re-created because the clustering key will stay the same. You can also use the DBCC DBREINDEX command to rebuild all the indexes on a table. Rebuilding the clustered index helps keep a table from becoming fragmented and makes read ahead more effective. You can use DBCC SHOWCONTIG to determine how much fragmentation a table has. To remove fragmentation without incurring the overhead of completely rebuilding indexes, you can use DBCC INDEXDEFRAG. Of course, you should also regularly do other tasks, such as performing backups and periodically checking the structural integrity of the database (for example, by using DBCC CHECKDB), but these are not performance-related tasks.

MONITORING SYSTEM BEHAVIOR

Throughout this book, we've looked at statements that are useful for monitoring some aspect of SQL Server's performance. These include procedures such as *sp_who2*, *sp_lock*, SET SHOWPLAN_TEXT ON, DBCC SQLPERF, and various trace flags for analyzing deadlock issues. SQL Server Enterprise Manager provides a graphical display that is a combination of *sp_who2* and *sp_lock*, and you should make use of it. In addition, two other tools let you monitor the behavior of your SQL Server system: SQL Profiler and System Monitor (Performance Monitor in Windows NT).

SQL Profiler

SQL Profiler has been completely rewritten for SQL Server 2000 because of the need to absolutely guarantee that no trace records will be lost under stress. SQL Server 2000 must support C2 auditing, and losing any trace information is unacceptable if auditing is enabled. In addition, if records are missing, it is much more difficult for Product Support to use SQL Profiler for reproducing problems.

History of SQL Profiler

The original tracing tool, which appeared in version 6.5, was called SQL Trace and was basically an "ODS Sniffer." SQL Trace was itself based on an earlier freeware product called SQLEye. SQLEye was essentially a filter that listened on the network using the ODS API for all the batches that were sent to a specified SQL Server. When SQLEye received an incoming batch, it could apply one of several filters to it and record in a file all batches that satisfied the filters' conditions. In version 6.5, the same developer who wrote SQLEye put a GUI wrapper around its configuration and specification commands and created the SQL Trace tool.

Because SQL Trace worked only at the ODS layer, it could capture only the commands that were actually being sent to SQL Server. Once SQL Server received the command, SQL Trace had no further knowledge of what SQL Server did with it. For example, if a client connection sent a batch to SQL Server that consisted of only a stored procedure call, that is all SQL Trace could capture and record. It could not record all the statements that were executed within the stored procedure, and it had no knowledge of other procedures that were called by the original stored procedure.

SQL Profiler in SQL Server 7 and SQL Server 2000 belongs to a new generation of profiling tools. Not only can it keep track of every statement executed and every statement within every stored procedure, but it can keep track of every time a table is accessed, every time a lock is acquired, and every time an error occurs.

Tracing in SQL Server 2000

SQL Server 2000 divides the tracing functionality into two separate but connected components. On the server side is the SQL Trace facility, which manages queues of events generated by event producers. A consumer thread reads events off of the queues and filters them before sending them to the process that requested them. Events are the main unit of activity as far as tracing is concerned, and an event can be anything that happens inside SQL Server, or between SQL Server and a client. For example, opening a table to access its data is an event, executing a stored procedure is an event, and sending a T-SQL batch from a client to the SQL Server is an event. There is a set of system store procedures that you can use to define which events should be traced, what data for each event you're interested in, and where you want to save the information collected from the events. You can specify filters to apply to the events in order to reduce the amount of information collected and stored. We'll see some examples of the use of these procedures later in this section.

Figure 17-3 shows the general architecture of the SQL Trace server component. (Event *producers* are server components such as the lock manager, buffer manager, and ODS, which generate the events recorded in the queue.)

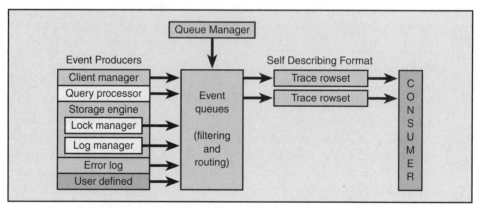

Figure 17-3. *The SQL Trace architecture.*

As an alternative to using the system procedures to define the events to trace, you can use the client-side component called SQL Profiler. Using this tool, you can select the events and data columns from a list and then specify how you want to filter the events. The tool then displays every event that meets your criteria as it occurs.

You incur a lot more overhead when you use SQL Profiler to capture and save events. The server-side consumer thread returns OLE-DB row sets to the client-side consumer, and then SQL Profiler must display the data from the row sets appropriately. To reduce the amount of data sent from the server to the client, each row contains only a minimum amount of information—basically an event code, a data column code, and a value for that data column. For example, if through SQL Profiler we have asked to keep track of the text of every single stored procedure when it completes and we want to know what time it completes, how much time it took to execute the procedure, the name of the procedure, and the login ID of the user who executed it, the server trace will send multiple rows to the client every time a stored procedure completes. Each row will contain the event code (43 for Stored Procedure Completed events) and one of the requested data column codes. There will be one row for the text (the name) of the procedure call, one row for the end time, one row for the user's login name, and so forth. There will be other rows for data columns we didn't explicitly request because a set of default data columns is returned with every trace. SQL Profiler must read these rows and pivot them to produce one row for each event for display purposes.

When you configure the client-side trace using SQL Profiler, you can choose to save the captured data to a file or a table, in addition to displaying it in the SQL Profiler UI. Once you save trace data, you can again use SQL Profiler to read the saved data for display or analysis purposes. Figure 17-4 shows the client-side architecture. The controller can either get the data from the consumer, which received currently active trace information from the server, or it can read data from a saved location, such as a table or a file. On the left, you can see all the different data sources that can be read. SQL Server 2000's Profiler can read trace data saved with the SQL Server 7 Profiler, and it can read script files saved using the trace facility in SQL Server 6.5.

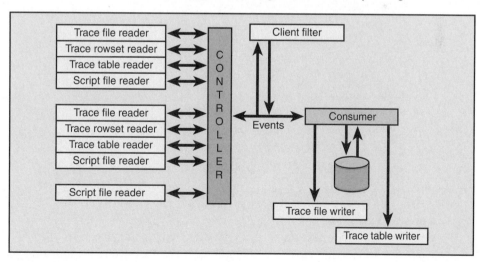

Figure 17-4. *The SQL Profiler architecture.*

SQL Server 2000 provides more than 100 predefined events, and you can configure 10 additional events of your own. SQL Profiler is more than just the user interface that is available through the SQL Profiler icon. You use the interface for defining traces from a client machine, watching the events recorded by those client-side traces, and replaying traces. SQL Profiler can also define server-side traces that run invisibly, using extended stored procedures. One of the advantages of server-side traces is that they can be configured to start automatically. We'll see more on server-side traces later.

Defining a Trace

We'll look at how to define a trace by using the SQL Profiler interface, but the details regarding the types of events, data elements available, and filters are equally applicable to server-side traces defined using the system stored procedures. To start a new trace, choose New and then Trace from the File menu in SQL Profiler. You'll be asked to log in to a particular SQL Server server, and then you'll see a dialog box similar to the one shown in Figure 17-5, with four tabs for defining the trace properties. Alternatively, you can choose File, Open, Trace Template, and then select from 8 predefined trace definitions. You'll get the same tabbed dialog box, but much of the information will be predefined. From the File menu, you can also open a saved trace file or a trace table that you saved previously.

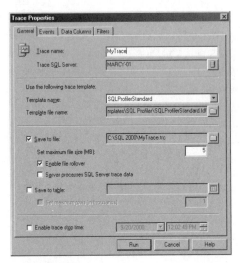

Figure 17-5. *The Trace Properties dialog box.*

General Tab

When you define a new trace, you give the trace a name and select the SQL Server server you want to monitor. The default is the server that you just logged on to, but you can select another SQL Server server. You can choose to base your new trace on one of the existing templates by specifying either the name of a template or the file location where the template is stored. Optionally, you can save the information to a file while it is being captured. The file can be processed from either the client or the server. If it is processed from the client (SQL Profiler), each row is processed individually. Writing to a server-side file is done using the same mechanism as log writes use, and the file is opened for pure sequential writing. You can set a maximum file size in megabytes, and you can configure the trace for automatic file rollover. This means that when the file reaches the maximum size you specified, SQL Server will automatically start a new file with a numeric suffix added to the name. This allows the trace files to stay smaller and be managed more easily. Finally, you can set the trace to stop at a specified time; it will start as soon as you click the Run button.

If you use the SQL Profiler interface to create a server-side file, two traces are actually created—one on the server to write to the file and one on the client for display purposes. This does not mean that the events are raised twice; they're raised only once, and the queue filter will manage the fact that there are two subscribers for the same information.

Events Tab

On the Events tab, you can select from over 100 available events, which are grouped into 13 categories. You can select an entire category or select events from within a category. The online documentation gives a complete description of each event. The Events tab is shown in Figure 17-6.

Figure 17-6. *The Events tab of the Trace Properties dialog box.*

Data Columns Tab

You can specify which data items you want to record for each event. For example, you might want to keep track of only the SQL Server user, the application being used, and the text of the SQL statement being executed. Or you might want to record performance information such as the duration of the event, the table or index accessed, the severity of an error, and the start and end time of the event. Three data elements—BinaryData, IntegerData, and EventSubClass—have different meanings depending on what event is being captured. For example, if you're capturing the Execution Plan event, BinaryData reflects the estimated cost of the query and IntegerData reflects the estimate of the number of rows to be returned. If you're capturing the Server Memory event, EventSubClass data can be 1, which means that the server memory was increased, or it can be 2, which means it was decreased. The IntegerData column reflects the new memory size in megabytes. Not all events have meaningful values for every possible data element. Again, details are available in the online documentation, but they might be a little hard to find. Figure 17-7 shows you where in SQL Server Books Online you can find the details. The figure shows the section on Monitoring Server Performance And Activity, which is in the Administering SQL Server volume. Under Monitoring With SQL Profiler Event Categories is a section for each different category. The figure shows the Performance Event Category, and the right pane shows the top part of the article on Performance Data Columns. The table displays the meaning of the data columns for each possible event. For the Degree Of Parallelism1 Event Class, the EventSubClass column indicates the type of operation being performed, the IntegerData column indicates the pages used in memory for the query plan, and the BinaryData column indicates the actual DOP.

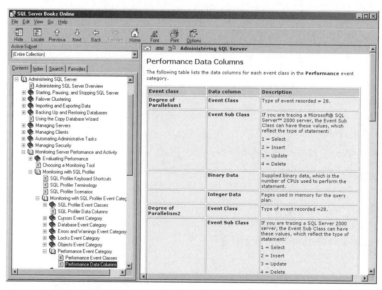

Figure 17-7. *Finding the details of each of the data columns in Books Online.*

It might seem strange that there are four different events for degree of parallelism, but this is necessary for backward compatibility, so that SQL Profiler can be used to trace activity on a SQL Server 7 server. If you are tracing events on a SQL Server 2000 server, all four events will provide the same functionality (for example, any of the four can be used to get the same DOP information). If you are tracing a SQL Server 7 server, each DOP event will trace only one kind of DML statement: Degree Of Parallelism1 traces INSERT statements, Degree Of Parallelism2 traces UDPATE statements, Degree Of Parallelism3 traces DELETE statements, and Degree Of Parallelism4 traces SELECT statements. The Data Columns tab is shown in Figure 17-8.

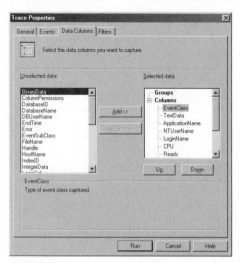

Figure 17-8. *The Data Columns tab of the Trace Properties dialog box.*

NOTE The companion CD includes a spreadsheet called SQL Trace Event Summary.xls that lists each possible event, its event ID, and the data columns available for that event.

Filters Tab

Using the Filters tab, you can filter out events that aren't of interest. Two types of filters are available—string filters and numeric filters. Each data element can be filtered in only one of these ways. For data values that are strings, such as ApplicationName or DatabaseName, you can apply a pattern matching string using either LIKE or NOT LIKE, and wildcard characters are allowed. For example, if I want to trace events only from databases that have *history* in their name, I can supply a filter LIKE '%history%'. Of course, I also have to capture the DatabaseName column in order to have this filter available. For numeric values such as DatabaseID or Duration (in milliseconds), you can apply filters that check for the data being equal to, not equal to, less than or equal to, or greater than or equal to. For example, if I want to trace only events that took longer than 1000 milliseconds to execute, I can set the Duration filter to *'greater than or equal' 1000*. For data that represents datetime values, only the greater than and less than filters are available.

By default, all traces exclude events originating from SQL Profiler because typically you don't want to trace the events that are involved in the actual tracing. Figure 17-9 shows the Filters tab of the Trace Properties dialog box.

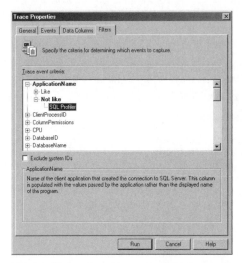

Figure 17-9. *The Filters tab of the Trace Properties dialog box.*

The online documentation provides full details of all the filters and describes which data elements allow which filters. Note that you can supply multiple values for a condition. For example, if you want to trace events that occur only in databases with ID 5 or 6, you can enter both 5 and 6 under the Equals condition.

The Filters tab includes a check box labeled Exclude System IDs. Selecting this box allows you to capture fewer trace events by excluding most of the events that reference system objects. Selecting this option sets the ObjectID filter to greater than or equal to 100, thus eliminating most of the system objects from the trace, and possibly reducing the number of events captured by up to 25 percent.

As a security mechanism, SQL Profiler automatically omits from the trace any of the security-related stored procedures affecting passwords, and this behavior is always in effect and nonconfigurable. This includes procedures such as *sp_addapprole*, *sp_password*, *sp_addlogin,* and *sp_addlinkedsrvlogin*, as well as many of the procedures for configuring replication.

You can save and restart traces that you define using SQL Profiler. You can also copy the definition to another machine and start it from the SQL Profiler user interface there.

Information gathered by SQL Profiler or SQL Trace can be extremely useful for tracking all kinds of performance problems. By saving the captured events to a table, you can analyze usage patterns and query behavior using Transact-SQL stored procedures. By saving your captured events to a file, you can copy that file to another machine or e-mail it to a central location (or even to your support provider).

Defining a Server-Side Trace

If you want to start a particular trace programmatically (or automatically), you must define a server-side trace using the *sp_trace_** internal stored procedures. You can include the calls to these procedures in any SQL Server stored procedure or batch. To define a server-side trace, client programs such as SQL Query Analyzer have to know only four procedures.

1. *sp_trace_create* sets up the trace and configures a file to keep the captured events. It returns a trace ID number that is then used in the other three procedures to further define and manipulate the trace.

2. *sp_trace_setevent* is then called once for each data column of every event that you want to capture.

3. *sp_trace_setfilter* can be called once for each filter you want to define on any of the events' data columns.

4. *sp_trace_setstatus* is called to start, stop, or remove the trace.

A fifth procedure, *sp_trace_generateevent*, can optionally be called to generate user-defined events.

The trickiest part of setting up a server-side trace is that you must use ID numbers when specifying the events and data columns. Fortunately, the page in *Microsoft SQL Server Books Online* that documents the *sp_trace_setevent* procedure provides the ID number for each event and each data column. The following example creates a trace that writes events to a file called C:\TraceSELECT.trc. It will capture the start time, text, and database ID of each SQL:BatchCompleted event, but the filter restricts the trace to only capturing events that have the substring 'SELECT' in the text data column.

```
DECLARE @RC int, @TraceID int, @ON bit
SET @ON = 1
EXEC @RC = sp_trace_create @TraceID OUTPUT, 0, N'C:\TraceSELECT.trc'
SELECT 'RC'= @RC, 'TraceID'= @TraceID

-- SQL:BatchCompleted Event, Start Time column
EXEC @RC = sp_trace_setevent @TraceID, 12, 14, @ON
-- SQL:BatchCompleted Event, Database ID Column
EXEC @RC = sp_trace_setevent @TraceID, 12, 3, @ON
-- SQL:BatchCompleted Event, Text Column
EXEC @RC = sp_trace_setevent @TraceID, 12, 1, @ON
-- Audit Login event, Start Column
EXEC @RC = sp_trace_setevent @TraceID, 14, 14, @ON

-- Set filter for Column 1 (text), data = 'select'
EXEC @RC = sp_trace_setfilter @TraceID, 1, 0, 0, N'select'

-- Start Trace (status 1 = start)
EXEC @RC = sp_trace_setstatus @TraceID, 1
```

One crucial aspect of these stored procedures is that their parameters must be passed with the correct datatype. The filename parameter for *sp_trace_create* is of type *nvarchar*, so a Unicode constant with the *N* prefix must be supplied for the filename. The last parameter of the *sp_trace_setevent* procedure, which sets the tracing of that data for that event to either ON or OFF, must be of type *bit*. Because I can't do a CAST or CONVERT in the procedure call to force a constant of 1 to be a bit, I defined a bit variable to hold the value, and I pass that variable to every call. To modify this trace at a later time, I would need to pass a bit value of 0 to disable the capturing of a particular data column.

Let's look at the procedure that creates the trace in a bit more detail. Here's the syntax:

```
sp_trace_create [ @traceid = ] trace_id OUTPUT
    , [ @options = ] option_value
    , [ @tracefile = ] 'trace_file'
    [ , [ @maxfilesize = ] max_file_size ]
    [ , [ @stoptime = ] 'stop_time' ]
```

The *@traceid* parameter returns an integer ID that is used to modify a trace, stop or restart it, or look at its properties. The preceding script printed out the value of the trace ID just for informational purposes. The *@options* parameter allows us to specify one or more options for this trace. Here are the possible values:

0	No options set.
1	Trace should produce a rowset.
2	Start a new trace file when the current file reaches its maximum size. If no maximum size has been specified, the default is 5 MB. This is equivalent to using the Enable File Rollover option in the General tab of the Trace Properties dialog box.
4	SQL Server should shut down if the file cannot be written to. This is needed for servers that are being audited.
8	Produce a Blackbox.trc file, which is a record of the last 5 MB of trace information gathered by the server; cannot be used with any other options.

A value of 1 means that the trace will produce a rowset that will be sent to the SQL Profiler UI, and cannot be used if we are capturing to a server-side file.

You might find it useful to have certain traces running constantly, but be careful about the amount of information you capture. Trace files can grow quite large if they are left running the entire time SQL Server is running. To configure a trace to start automatically every time SQL Server starts, you can put the trace definition into a stored procedure, and then use *sp_procoption* to set that procedure's startup property to ON.

SQL Server 2000 provides several functions to inspect the status of your traces. The most useful is probably *fn_trace_getinfo,* which reports all the parameters specified in the *sp_trace_create* procedure, as well as the status of the trace (1 = currently running). Here's an example of its use:

```
SELECT * FROM :: fn_trace_getinfo(default)
```

We could supply a particular trace ID instead of the word "default," but if we don't know the trace ID, using this form shows all the traces. Here's my output:

```
traceid     property    value
----------- ----------- --------------------
1           1           0
1           2           C:\TraceSELECT.trc
1           3           5
1           4           NULL
1           5           1
```

The row with property 1 contains the value of the *@options* parameter, as shown in the preceding chart. If you see a trace with a value of 1 for property 1, it is most likely a trace that was started from the SQL Profiler UI. The row with property 2 contains the trace filename, if any. Note that SQL Server will automatically append the trc suffix to your filename, even if you already supplied that suffix. The row with property 3 contains the maximum file size, which defaults to 5 MB, and the row with property 4 contains the stop time, which has no value for my trace. Finally, the row with property 5 is the trace status; a 0 means the trace is stopped, a 1 means the trace is running.

The *fn_trace_geteventinfo* function will show you what events and data columns you are capturing for a particular trace. The data is returned with the event and data column IDs, so you'll have to do a little work to translate. The function *fn_trace_getfilterinfo* will return information about the filters on a particular trace.

You might have noticed that there is nothing in the supplied procedures to allow capturing trace data to a table for traces that you define on the server. This is by design, because writing to a table cannot be done as quickly as writing to a file, and it is imperative that the trace capturing operations not lose any events, no matter how busy your server is. If you want to view your trace data in a table, so that you can analyze it using SQL queries, you can copy the data from a trace file to a table using the function *fn_trace_gettable*.

Server-side traces are wonderfully useful in all kinds of situations and much more efficient that client-side tracing with SQL Profiler. If you are avoiding them because you think it's too hard to write all the procedure calls and look up all the necessary event and data column ID information, take heart. You can use the SQL Profiler UI to define all the events, all the data columns, and all the filters that you want, and then use the item in the File menu called Script Trace, which will produce all the calls to the stored procedures that correspond to the trace elements you select. The only change you'll need to make is to provide a filename to hold the captured data, and then you can run the newly created script through SQL Query Analyzer to start your trace running as a server-side trace.

Gathering Diagnostic Information

A lot of the information that your traces gather can help your support provider trouble-shoot system problems. However, this information is usually not enough by itself. Support providers ask a standard set of questions when you call. A special utility in SQL Server 2000 helps you gather this information with a single command: *sqldiag*. It can work with a SQL Server trace if you have enabled automatic query recording using the blackbox functionality. I'll talk about this blackbox later in this section. When you execute *sqldiag* from a command prompt while SQL Server is running, it gathers the following information:

- Text of all error logs (unless the -X, option has been supplied)
- Registry information
- DLL version information
- Output from:
  - ❏ *sp_configure*
  - ❏ *sp_who*
  - ❏ *sp_lock*
  - ❏ *sp_helpdb*
  - ❏ *xp_msver*
  - ❏ *sp_helpextendedproc*
  - ❏ *sysprocesses*
- Input buffer SPIDs/deadlock information
- Microsoft Diagnostics Report for the server, including:
  - ❏ Contents of *<servername>*.txt file
  - ❏ Operating System Version Report
  - ❏ System Report
  - ❏ Processor List
  - ❏ Video Display Report
  - ❏ Hard Drive Report
  - ❏ Memory Report
  - ❏ Services Report
  - ❏ Drivers Report
  - ❏ IRQ and Port Report

❏   DMA and Memory Report

❏   Environment Report

❏   Network Report

The information is stored in a file with the default name of sqldiag.txt; you can specify a different filename in the command line for *sqldiag*. The default directory is the \LOG directory of your SQL Server installation. Obviously, if SQL Server is not running, some of the information in the preceding list won't be available, but any blackbox information will be captured.

To enable blackbox recording, create and start a trace with an option value of 8; when executing the *sp_trace_create* procedure, don't specify a filename or any other parameters. A trace file called blackbox.trc will automatically be captured in the default \Data directory of your SQL Server installation. If you look at your trace properties with *fn_trace_getinfo* you can see the exact name of the file. The following example shows the creation of the blackbox trace, and the trace info returned by the *fn_trace_getinfo* function:

```
DECLARE @rc int, @TraceID int
EXEC @rc = sp_trace_create @TraceID output, 8
SELECT TraceID = @traceID, error = @rc

EXEC sp_trace_setstatus @traceID, 1
SELECT * from ::fn_trace_getinfo(@TraceID)

RESULTS:
TraceID     error
----------- -----------
1           0

(1 row(s) affected)

traceid     property    value
----------- ----------- ----------------------------------------
1           1           8
1           2           C:\Program Files\Microsoft SQL Server
                            \MSSQL\data\blackbox
1           3           5
1           4           NULL
1           5           1

(5 row(s) affected)
```

If blackbox recording has been enabled, running *sqldiag* will copy the blackbox.trc file to sqldiag.trc in the same directory as the sqldiag.txt file. If you specify a name other than *sqldiag* for the text file, the blackbox file will also be copied to the \LOG directory with a different name. For example, if you specify a *sqldiag* output filename as MyReport.txt, the blackbox trace file will be renamed to MyReport.trc. I mentioned earlier that even if SQL Server is not running when *sqldiag* is executed, the blackbox file will still be available. This can be very useful if SQL Server failed because of an error; the blackbox trace file will contain a record of what queries were executed immediately before the failure. You might consider creating a stored procedure to enable blackbox tracing, and marking that procedure for autostart. In this case, you'll know that you'll always have a record of the queries that were executed, any time an unexpected failure occurs. On the companion CD, I have included a script to create such a procedure and mark the procedure for autostart.

When you first enable blackbox tracing, you should see the blackbox.trc file in the \Data directory, but you might notice that the size of file looks like it is staying at 0. In fact, you might not actually see a positive size reported for the blackbox.trc file until one of the following occurs:

■   **The size of the trace exceeds 5 MB.**   The blackbox trace is automatically configured for a maximum file size of 5 MB and also configured to rollover and start a new file called blackbox_1.trc when the initial 5 MB is exceeded. If this second trace exceeds 5 MB in size, the trace reverts to the initial *blackbox.trc* file. Until the first rollover occurs, the operating system file might show a size of 0, even though trace information is being collected.

■   **You execute *sqldiag*.**   When you run *sqldiag* and the trace has more than 128 KB of data, the blackbox trace information will be written to the blackbox.trc file on disk in the \Data directory and copied to the \LOG directory as sqldiag.trc. Note that while the trace is running, information is written to the blackbox.trc file in 128 KB chunks, so that the trace file might not contain the most recent events. If you need the blackbox.trc file or the sqldiag.trc file to have all the events up to a specific time, you must use one of the following two options:

   ❑   **The blackbox trace is stopped and removed.**   When the blackbox trace is closed, SQL Server writes the contents to the blackbox.trc file. If you subsequently run *sqldiag*, the complete blackbox.trc file is copied to the \Data directory as sqldiag.trc. If you know the trace ID number, you can use the *sp_trace_setstatus* procedure to both stop and remove the trace, as shown in these examples:

```
EXEC sp_trace_setstatus <TraceID>, 0 -- Stop the trace

EXEC sp_trace_setstatus <TraceID>, 2 -- Remove the trace
```

❑ **You stop SQL Server.** Shutting down SQL Server effectively stops and closes the trace. This means that if SQL Server stops because of an error condition and you have previously enabled blackbox tracing, you will have a record of the events just before SQL Server stopped.

To enable blackbox tracing to start automatically when SQL Server starts, you must create the trace in a stored procedure. Other traces can also be defined inside stored procedures, even if you don't mark them for autostart. You might consider creating a number of procedures that capture events relevant to different performance conditions. For example, one trace might capture events related to stored procedure recompilation, another trace might capture information relating to automatic growth of a database, and another might capture deadlock information. You could then set up an alert to watch related Performance Counters using SQL Server Agent, and when a certain situation is encountered or a threshold is crossed, you could start a trace to gather more data. You'll probably want to limit the size of the trace file and not allow it to roll over and start a new file.

Tracing and Auditing

C2 auditing is necessary if you are running a C2 certified system. A C2 certified system meets a strict government standard that defines the database security level. To have a C2 certified SQL Server, you must configure SQL Server in the evaluated C2 configuration. You must enable *c2 audit mode* as a server-wide configuration option, and this will automatically start tracing a large number of events specifically designed for auditing purposes. If you look at the list of possible events, you'll see several dozen of them are in the Security Audit category. For more information about C2 certification, see the C2 Administrator's and User's Security Guide, which you can find at http://www.microsoft.com/downloads/release.asp?ReleaseID=24481.

PERFORMANCE CONSIDERATIONS

SQL Server tracing uses a "pay as you go" model. No overhead is incurred for events that are not captured. Most events need very few resources. SQL Profiler becomes expensive only if you trace all of the more than 100 event classes and capture all data from those events. Early testing shows an absolute maximum of 5 to 10 percent overhead if you capture everything. Most of the performance hit is due to a longer code path; the actual resources needed to capture the event data are not particularly CPU intensive. In addition, to minimize the performance hit, you should define all your traces as server-side traces, and avoid the overhead of producing row sets to send to the SQL Profiler client.

System Monitor

You can use SQL Profiler to monitor the behavior of your server on a query-by-query or event-by-event basis. But if you want to monitor your server's performance as an entire system, the best tool is System Monitor. This tool is extensible, which allows SQL Server to export its performance statistics so that you can monitor your entire system. That's crucial because such important statistics as CPU use must be monitored for the entire system, not just for SQL Server. In fact, many of the most important counters to watch while performance tuning SQL Server don't even belong to any of the SQL Server objects.

System Monitor comes with your Windows 2000 operating system. In Windows NT, the equivalent tool was called Performance Monitor. The discussion here will be relevant no matter which version you are using. Traditionally, in mainframe and minicomputer systems, you had to buy a separate system monitor—at considerable expense—or use a hodgepodge of utilities, some to monitor the operating system and others to monitor the database. Then, if you worked on some other system, it didn't have the same set of tools you were accustomed to using.

In the Programs/Administrative Tools folder, click on the Performance icon to start System Monitor

System Monitor provides a huge set of counters. Probably no one understands all of them, so don't be intimidated. Peruse all the objects and counters and note which ones have separate instances. Don't confuse System Monitor's use of the word "instance" with a SQL Server 2000 instance. System Monitor uses instance to refer to a particular occurrence of a counter. For example, the SQLServer:Databases object has counters for things like number of active transactions, log file size, and transactions per second. But since there are lots of different databases in a SQL Server instance (such as master, Northwind, and pubs), you also need to choose a particular database from the instance list. Other counters, such as SQLServer:Memory Manager, apply to the entire SQL Server installation, and there are no separate instances to deal with. If you want to monitor separate SQL Server instances, there are separate counters to use. For example, the SQLServer:Memory Manager object, which I just mentioned, pertains only to the default instance of SQL Server on the machine. If I also have a named instance called ENT2, there will be an entire set of objects and counters for that instance, including an object called MSSQL$ENT2:Memory Manager. For more information about performance counters, click the Explain button in the Select Counters dialog box, or see the SQL Server and operating system documentation.

SEE ALSO For general information about using System Monitor, look at the Windows 2000 Server Operations Guide in the Windows 2000 Server Resource Kit, particularly Chapters 5 through 10. If you're running Performance Monitor on Windows NT 4, you can look at the Windows NT Workstation Resource Kit Version 4.0 (Chapters 9 through 16). (Prior to Windows NT 4, the Performance Monitor section of the resource kit was contained in a separate volume called *Optimizing Windows NT* by Russ Blake, and this has lots of information that is still very useful.)

Performance Monitor Counters

In this section, we'll look at several important counters. I'll briefly explain how they can be useful and what actions you should consider based on the information they provide. Often, of course, the appropriate action is generic: for example, if CPU usage is high, you should try to reduce it. The methods you can use to make such adjustments are varied and vast—from redesigning your application to reworking some queries, adding indexes, or getting faster or additional processors.

Object: Processor
Counter: % Processor Time

This counter monitors systemwide CPU usage. If you use multiple processors, you can set up an instance for each processor. Each processor's CPU usage count should be similar. If not, you should examine other processes on the system that have only one thread and are executing on a given CPU. Ideally, your system shouldn't consistently run with CPU usage of 80 percent or more, although short spikes of up to 100 percent are normal, even for systems with plenty of spare CPU capacity. If your system runs consistently above 80 percent or will grow to that level soon, or if it frequently spikes above 90 percent and stays there for 10 seconds or longer, you should try to reduce CPU usage.

First, consider making your application more efficient. High CPU usage counts can result from just one or two problematic queries. The queries might get high cache-hit ratios but still require a large amount of logical I/O. Try to rework those queries or add indexes. If the CPU usage count continues to be high, you might consider getting a faster processor or adding processors to your system. If your system is running consistently with 100 percent CPU usage, look at specific processes to see which are consuming the CPUs. It's likely that the offending process is doing some polling or is stuck in a tight loop; if so, the application needs some work, such as adding a sleep.

You should also watch for excessively low CPU usage, which indicates that your system is stalled somewhere. If locking contention is occurring, your system might be running at close to 0 percent CPU usage when no productive work is happening! Very low CPU usage can be a bigger problem than very high CPU usage. If you have poor overall throughput and low CPU usage, your application has a bottleneck somewhere and you must find and clear it.

Note that Task Manager (Ctrl+Shift+Escape) in Windows NT 4 and Windows 2000 also provides a way to monitor CPU usage. Task Manager is even easier to use than System Monitor.

Object: PhysicalDisk
Counter: Disk Transfers/sec

This counter shows physical I/O rates for all activity on the machine. You can set up an instance for each physical disk in the system or watch it for the total of all disks. SQL Server does most I/O in 8-KB chunks, although read-ahead I/O is essentially done with an I/O size of 64 KB. Watch this counter to be sure that you're not maxing out the I/O capacity of your system or of a particular disk. The I/O capacity of disk drives and controllers varies considerably depending on the hardware. But today's typical SCSI hard drive can do 80 to 90 random 8-KB reads per second, assuming that the controller can drive it that hard. If you see I/O rates approaching these rates *per drive,* you should verify that your specific hardware can sustain more. If not, add more disks and controllers, add memory, or rework the database to try to get a higher cache-hit ratio and require less physical I/O (via better design, better indexes, possible denormalization, and so on).

To see any of the counters from the PhysicalDisk object, you must reboot your computer with the Diskperf service started. You do this from a command prompt, with the command DISKPERF. Using the -Y option sets the system to start all the disk performance counters when the system is restarted. After you're done monitoring, disable Diskperf.

Object: PhysicalDisk
Counter: Current Disk Queue Length

This counter indicates the number of reads that are currently outstanding for a disk. Occasional spikes are OK, especially when an operation that generates a lot of asynchronous I/O, such as a checkpoint, is activated. But for the most part, the disks should not have a lot of queued I/O. Those operations, of course, must ultimately complete, so if more than one operation is queued consistently, the disk is probably overworked. You should either decrease physical I/O or add more I/O capacity.

Object: Memory
Counter: Pages/sec and Page Faults/sec

These counters watch the amount of paging on the system. As the system settles into a steady state, you want these values to be 0—that is, no paging going on in the system. In fact, if you allow SQL Server to automatically adjust its memory usage, it will reduce its memory resources when paging occurs. You should find that any paging that does occur is not due to SQL Server. If your system does experience regular paging, perhaps due to other applications running on the machine, you should consider adding more physical memory.

Object: Process
Counter: % Processor Time

Typically, you run this counter for the SQL Server process instance, but you might want to run it for other processes. It confirms that SQL Server (or some other process) is using a reasonable amount of CPU time. (It doesn't make much sense to spend a lot of time reducing SQL Server's CPU usage if some other process on the machine is using the larger percentage of the CPU to drive the total CPU usage near capacity.)

Object: Process
Counter: Virtual Bytes

You use this counter to see the total virtual memory being used by SQL Server, especially when a large number of threads and memory are being consumed. If this number gets too high, you might see Out Of Virtual Memory errors.

Object: Process
Counter: Private Bytes

This counter shows the current number of bytes allocated to a process that cannot be shared with other processes. It is probably the best System Monitor counter for viewing the approximate amount of memory committed by any threads within the *sqlservr.exe* process space. Additional SQL Server 2000 instances will be labeled sqlservr#1, sqlservr#2, and so on.

Object: Process
Counter: Working Set

This counter shows the amount of memory recently used by a process. For a SQL Server process instance, this counter can actually be a valuable indicator of how much memory has been allocated within the SQL Server process space, especially for a dedicated server (because working-set trimming will likely not happen much). The value recorded by the working set should be very close to the value reported in Task Manager, on the Processes tab, as the Mem Usage value for the instance of *sqlservr.exe*. Working Set is the current memory that SQL Server (and any components loaded in it) is currently accessing. It might not reflect the total amount of memory that SQL Server (and any component loaded in its process space) has allocated. Here, we use the term "allocated" to mean memory that has been committed to SQL Server. As long as no trimming has occurred, Working Set is the best counter for seeing how much memory has been allocated within the SQL Server process space.

Process:Private Bytes (described above) does not show all the memory committed, but the value can be more stable than Working Set if trimming occurs. You should consider monitoring both Private Bytes and Working Set. If you see Working Set dip below Private Bytes, you should look at Private Bytes. If Working Set dips below Private Bytes, the operating system must be trimming SQL Server's Working Set. This means other processes are competing for memory that SQL Server might need to get back, and you should evaluate what other processes are competing with SQL Server for memory resources.

Object: SQLServer:Buffer Manager
Counter: Buffer Cache Hit Ratio

There is no right value for the buffer cache-hit ratio because it is application specific. If your system has settled into a steady state, ideally you want to achieve rates of 90 percent or higher, but this is not always possible if the I/O is random. Keep adding more physical memory as long as this value continues to rise or until you run out of money.

Object: SQLServer:Memory Manager
Counter: Total Server Memory (KB)

This counter can be useful, but it doesn't reflect all memory allocated within a SQL Server process space. It reflects only memory allocated in the SQL Server buffer pool. Note that the buffer pool is not just for data pages; it is also for other memory allocations within the server, including plans for stored procedures and for ad hoc queries. Certain components can be loaded into the SQL Server process space and allocate memory that is not under SQL Server's direct control. These include extended stored procedures, OLE Automation objects, and OLE DB provider DLLs. The memory space needed for these types of objects is included in SQL Server's Working Set but not in the Total Server Memory counter.

Object: SQLServer:Cache Manager

This object contains counters for monitoring how the cache is being used for various types of objects, including ad hoc query plans, procedure plans, trigger plans, and prepared SQL plans. A separate Cache Hit Ratio counter is available for each type of plan, as is a counter showing the number of such objects and the number of pages used by the objects.

Object: SQLServer:Buffer Manager
Counter: Page Reads/sec

Watch this counter in combination with the counters from the PhysicalDisk object. If you see rates approaching the capacity of your hardware's I/O rates (use 80 to 90 I/Os per disk per second as a guide), you should reduce I/O rates by making your application more efficient (via better design, better indexes, denormalization, and so on). Or you can increase the hardware's I/O capacity. This statistic measures only read operations, not writes, and it does so only for SQL Server, so you don't see the whole picture.

Object: SQLServer:Buffer Manager
Counter: Page Writes/sec

This value keeps track of all physical writes done by SQL Server, for any reason. It includes checkpoint writes, lazywriter writes, and large block writes done during index creation or bulk copy operations. Separate counters are available for checkpoint writes and lazywriter writes; you're probably better off using these more specific counters.

Object: SQLServer:Databases
Counter: Log Flushes/sec

This value should be well below the capacity of the disk on which the transaction log resides. It is best to place the transaction log on a separate physical disk drive (or on a mirrored drive) so that the disk drive is always in place for the next write, since transaction log writes are sequential. There is a separate counter for each database, so make sure you're monitoring the right database instance.

Object: SQLServer:Databases
Counter: Transactions/sec

This counter measures actual transactions—either user-defined transactions surrounded by BEGIN TRAN and COMMIT TRAN or individual data modification statements if no BEGIN TRAN has been issued. For example, if you have a batch that contains two individual INSERT statements, this counter records two transactions. The counter has a separate instance for each database and there is no way to keep track of total transactions for all of SQL Server. Use it only as a general indication of your system's throughput. There is obviously no "correct" value—just the higher the better.

User-Defined Counter

SQL Server 2000 offers a performance monitor counter for keeping track of any data or information that is useful to you. The counter, called Query, is under the SQL Server:User Settable object, and there are 10 instances to choose from. Ten stored procedures are available for specifying a value that System Monitor will chart for a particular instance. For example, if you want to use User Counter 1 to keep track of how many rows are in the *invoices* table, you can create triggers on the *invoices* table so that every time a row is inserted or deleted, the stored procedure *sp_user_counter1* is executed. You can include the following code in the triggers:

```
DECLARE @numrows int
SELECT @numrows = COUNT(*) FROM invoices
EXEC sp_user_counter1 @numrows
```

Once it is assigned a value, an instance of the user counter maintains that value until a new value is assigned. Note that the value passed to the stored procedure must be a constant, a variable, or a parameterless system function starting with @@, and it must have an integer datatype.

Other Performance Monitor Counters

The counters mentioned in this chapter are just the tip of the iceberg. SQL Server has dozens of others, for monitoring almost every aspect of SQL Server behavior discussed in this book. The best way to learn about them is to experiment with System Monitor. Look through the list of available objects and counters, select a few for viewing, and see what results you get. You'll probably find a few that you'll want to use all the time, and others that you'll be interested in only occasionally. But do revisit the complete list because there are too many to remember. A month from now, you'll discover a counter that you completely overlooked the first time. You should also revisit the available objects and counters after every service pack upgrade because new ones might be added as the SQL Server development team gets feedback.

Tables 17-1 through 17-5 show some of the counters you might want to experiment with; the descriptions are adapted from the online documentation.

Counter	Description
Extents Allocated/sec	Number of extents allocated per second to database objects used for storing index or data records.
Forwarded Records/sec	Number of records per second fetched through forwarded record pointers.
Full Scans/sec	Number of unrestricted full scans per second. These can be either base-table or full-index scans.
Index Searches/sec	Number of index searches per second. These are used to start range scans and single-index record fetches and to reposition an index.
Page Splits/sec	Number of page splits per second that occur as the result of overflowing index pages.
Pages Allocated/sec	Number of pages allocated per second to database objects used for storing index or data records.
Probe Scans/sec	Number of probe scans per second. These are used to find rows in an index or base table directly.
Range Scans/sec	Number of qualified range scans through indexes per second.

Table 17-1. *Counters for the SQLServer:Access Methods object.*   (continued)

Counter	Description
Skipped Ghosted Records/sec	Number of ghosted records per second skipped during scans.
Table Lock Escalations/sec	Number of times locks on a table were escalated.
Worktables Created/sec	Number of worktables created per second.

Counter*	Description
Active Transactions	Number of active transactions for the database.
Bulk Copy Rows/sec	Number of rows bulk copied per second.
Bulk Copy Throughput/sec	Amount (in kilobytes) of data bulk copied per second.
Data File(s) Size (KB)	Cumulative size (in kilobytes) of all the data files in the database, including any automatic growth. This counter is useful for determining the correct size of *tempdb*, for example.
Log Cache Hit Ratio	Percentage of log cache reads satisfied from the log cache.
Log File(s) Size (KB)	Cumulative size (in kilobytes) of all the transaction log files in the database.
Log Growths	Total number of times the transaction log for the database has been expanded.
Log Shrinks	Total number of times the transaction log for the database has been shrunk.
Log Truncations	Total number of times the transaction log for the database has been truncated.
Percent Log Used	Percentage of space in the log that is in use.
Shrink Data Movement Bytes/sec	Amount of data being moved per second by autoshrink operations or by DBCC SHRINKDATABASE or DBCC SHRINKFILE statements.
Transactions/sec	Number of transactions started for the database per second.

* Separate instances of these counters exist for each database.

Table 17-2. *Counters for the SQLServer:Databases object.*

Counter	Description
Average Wait Time (ms)	Average amount of wait time (in milliseconds) for each lock request that resulted in a wait.
Lock Requests/sec	Number of new locks and lock conversions per second requested from the lock manager.
Lock Timeouts/sec	Number of lock requests per second that timed out, including internal requests for NOWAIT locks.
Lock Wait Time (ms)	Total wait time (in milliseconds) for locks in the last second.
Lock Waits/sec	Number of lock requests per second that could not be satisfied immediately and required the caller to wait.
Number of Deadlocks/sec	Number of lock requests per second that resulted in a deadlock.

Table 17-3. *Counters for the SQLServer:Locks object.*

Counter	Description
Connection Memory (KB)	Total amount of dynamic memory the server is using for maintaining connections.
Lock Memory (KB)	Total amount of dynamic memory the server is using for locks.
Maximum Workspace Memory (KB)	Maximum amount of memory available for executing processes such as hash, sort, bulk copy, and index creation operations.
Memory Grants Outstanding	Total number of processes per second that have successfully acquired a workspace memory grant.
Memory Grants Pending	Total number of processes per second waiting for a workspace memory grant.
Optimizer Memory (KB)	Total amount of dynamic memory the server is using for query optimization.
SQL Cache Memory (KB)	Total amount of dynamic memory the server is using for the dynamic SQL cache.
Target Server Memory (KB)	Total amount of dynamic memory the server is willing to consume.
Total Server Memory (KB)	Total amount (in kilobytes) of dynamic memory that the server is currently using.

Table 17-4. *Counters for the SQLServer:Memory Manager object.*   *(continued)*

Counter	Description
Auto-Param Attempts/sec	Number of autoparameterization attempts per second. Total should be the sum of the failed, safe, and unsafe autoparameterizations. Auto-parameterization occurs when SQL Server attempts to reuse a cached plan for a previously executed query that is similar to, but not exactly the same as, the current query.
Batch Requests/sec	Number of Transact-SQL command batches received per second.
Failed Auto-Params/sec	Number of failed autoparameterization attempts per second. This value should be small.
Safe Auto-Params/sec	Number of safe autoparameterization attempts per second.
SQL Compilations/sec	Number of SQL compilations per second. Indicates the number of times the compile code path is entered. Includes compiles due to recompiles. Once SQL Server user activity is stable, this value should reach a steady state.
Unsafe Auto-Params/sec	Number of unsafe autoparameterization attempts per second. The table has characteristics that prevent the cached plan from being shared. These are designated as *unsafe*. The fewer of these that occur the better.

Table 17-5. *Counters for the SQLServer:SQL Statistics object.*

Other Performance Monitoring Considerations

Any time you monitor performance, you also slightly alter performance simply because of the overhead cost of monitoring. It can be helpful to run System Monitor on a separate machine from SQL Server to reduce that overhead. The SQL Server–specific counters are obtained by querying SQL Server, so they use connections to SQL Server. (System Monitor always uses Windows Authentication to connect to the SQL Server.) It is best to monitor only the counters you are interested in.

SUMMARY

Configuration alone can rarely turn your slow, plodding application into a screamer. In fact, you're more likely to misconfigure your system by taking manual control of the options that SQL Server sets automatically. Knowing what each configuration option does can keep you from misconfiguring your system.

In this chapter, we looked at the configuration options and discussed some guidelines for their use. I also discussed how to monitor the effects on your system's performance using SQL Profiler, server traces, and System Monitor. SQL Server tracing lets you determine which queries, procedures, or users have the biggest performance impact. System Monitor gives you a scientific method of holding constant all but one variable within the system as a whole so that you can measure the effect as you vary it.

Bibliography and Suggested Reading

Despite this book's considerable length, it doesn't touch on every important area relating to Microsoft SQL Server, and it assumes that readers have some knowledge of relational database management systems (RDBMSs). This section includes other recommended resources for learning about the SQL language, the fundamentals of using Microsoft SQL Server, and related technologies. However, the most important recommendation I can make is to read, cover to cover, the SQL Server documentation.

One of the CDs included with this book contains an evaluation copy of the complete SQL Server 2000 product. To access the product documentation, you can run the setup program and choose to install only the Books Online from the Client Utilities. The other CD contains some valuable whitepapers. You should start there. This second CD also contains some tools for use with SQL Server as well as an on-line Transact-SQL language reference compiled by a member of the SQL Server development team. Although the reference is a Microsoft Word file, it contains many cross-linked references and is intended for online use.

You can augment your reading with the following books and other resources. I've listed them in order from introductory materials to the more detailed or specialized materials.

SQL (Osborne's Complete Reference Series) by James R. Groff and Paul N. Weinberg (Osborne McGraw-Hill, 1999). An excellent primer for users who are new to SQL.

An Introduction to Database Systems, 7ᵗʰ Edition, by C. J. Date (Addison-Wesley, 1999). A new revision of a classic book, written by a giant in the field, that covers general relational database concepts. A must-read for everyone in the database industry.

Microsoft SQL Server 7.0 Database Implementation Training Kit and ***Microsoft SQL Server 7.0 System Administration Training Kit*** (Microsoft Press, 1999). Self-paced training with plenty of information about administration and security. These kits are fairly introductory and are suitable for those newer to SQL Server. The 1999 edition is based on SQL Server 7. The SQL Server 2000 version should be available soon. Check the Microsoft Press Web site (http://mspress.microsoft.com) periodically for details.

Database Design for Mere Mortals by Michael J. Hernandez (Addison-Wesley, 1997). A very readable approach to the daunting task of designing a relational database to solve real-world problems. The book is written in a database-independent format, so the details can be applied to SQL Server as well as to other RDBMSs you might use.

Handbook of Relational Database Design by Candace C. Fleming and Barbara Vonhalle (Addison-Wesley, 1988). A fine book that discusses general logical database design and data modeling approaches and techniques.

SAMS Teach Yourself Microsoft SQL Server 2000 in 21 Days by Richard Waymire and Rick Sawtell (SAMS Publishing, 2000). A good first book on SQL Server 2000 in tutorial format that gets readers up to speed quickly. One of the coauthors is a program manager on the SQL Server development team. This title includes self-test questions for each of the 21 "days."

Database: Principles, Programming, Performance by Patrick O'Neil (Morgan Kaufmann Publishers, 1994). This thorough textbook provides excellent introductory materials, so I've placed it high on the list. It also carefully details a broad spectrum of database topics, including buffer management and transaction semantics.

Understanding the New SQL: A Complete Guide by Jim Melton and Alan R. Simon (Morgan Kaufmann Publishers, 2000). Melton is an active participant in the SQL standards work and was the editor of the ANSI SQL-92 standard. Although you can get the ANSI SQL specification directly from ANSI, this book translates the standard into English.

SQL-99 Complete, Really by Peter Gulutzan and Trudy Pelzer (R&D Books, 1999). An excellent reference that I consult frequently for issues regarding ANSI SQL-99 semantics and conformance.

A Guide to the SQL Standard by C. J. Date with Hugh Darwen (Addison-Wesley, 1997). Similar in purpose and focus to the Melton and Simon book, this book offers more compact coverage, provides additional insight into why things work the way they do, and includes more discussion of semantics. It is an especially good reference on the use of NULL.

Optimizing Transact-SQL: Advanced Programming Techniques by David Rozenshtein, Anatoly Abramovich, and Eugene Birger (Coriolis Group, 1997). A book that offers lots of clever queries and solutions written with Transact-SQL. (Note, however, that the solutions here were authored before SQL Server had the CASE construct, and CASE can sometimes provide easier, more straightforward solutions.)

Joe Celko's SQL for Smarties: Advanced SQL Programming by Joe Celko (Morgan Kaufmann Publishers, 1999). An excellent book for insight into subtle but powerful ways to write nonintuitive queries. In places, this one is truly the SQL book for the Mensa crowd—it's loaded with mind-bending puzzles about writing SQL queries to perform nonobvious tasks. It contains many examples—probably more than any other book on this list—and you're likely to find solutions to problems similar in scope to ones you might face.

Hitchhiker's Guide to Visual Basic and SQL Server by William Vaughn (Microsoft Press, 1998). A good book that discusses the various programming interfaces available through Microsoft Visual Basic, especially when you're accessing SQL Server.

Inside ODBC by Kyle Geiger (Microsoft Press, 1995). The finest book available on ODBC, period. Written by the "Father of ODBC." A must for C programmers who work with ODBC and SQL Server. It includes a fine discussion of cursors as well. Although this book is out of print, you might know someone who has a copy, or you can check at used bookstores.

SQL Server: Common Problems, Tested Solutions by Neil Pike (APress, 2000). An expanded FAQ list, originally compiled by SQL Server MVP Pike, with contributions by most of the other SQL Server MVPs. Lots of details on frequently confusing issues that arise in working with all versions of SQL Server, from 6 to 2000. The solutions are either undocumented or poorly explained in the product documentation. Some answers are very short, others are pretty extensive, depending on the question. The book provides many possible answers and ways of doing things.

Microsoft Developer Network (MSDN) Library. Various articles and resources (available on line at http://msdn.microsoft.com/library/default.asp) from Microsoft. Like Microsoft Knowledge Base, the MSDN library contains information about all the Microsoft development products. A must for serious developers.

Professional SQL Server 7.0 Programming by Rob Vieira (WROX Press, 1999). A book that has it all, from basic database design and stored procedures, to advanced queries and linked servers, to advanced topics such as performance tuning and security. It also has a solid description of OLAP Services and Data Transformation Services. A SQL Server 2000 version of this book is in the works.

The Guru's Guide to Transact-SQL by Ken Henderson (Addison Wesley, 1999). A book that offers the most complete set of code examples I have seen—over 600 of them! These examples not only illustrate important concepts and best practices, but they can be incorporated into real-world applications. Henderson has a very good discussion of SOUNDEX and a proposal for an alternative implementation. The book covers basic material as well as advanced topics such as OLE automation and full-text searching. It was because of this book that I finally started to understand and get excited about the power of full-text searching and the CONTAINSTABLE function.

Advanced Transact-SQL for SQL Server 2000 by Itzik Ben-Gan and Tom Moreau (APress, 2000). A book by two writers who really know Transact-SQL—in fact, they probably dream in T-SQL. Anything written by Ben-Gan is guaranteed to be a gold mine. Ben-Gan and Moreau provide lots of details on new SQL Server 2000 features such as user-defined functions (UDFs), indexed views, cascading actions, federated views, and hierarchical structures.

Microsoft SQL Server 7.0 Performance Tuning Technical Reference by Steve Adrien Deluca (Editor), Marcilina S. Garcia, Jamie Reding, and Edward Whalen (Microsoft Press, 2000). Provides information that database administrators need in order to configure a SQL Server 7 RDBMS for optimum performance and scalability. Unlike many tuning books on the market, it teaches not just about SQL Server but also about the underlying operating system and hardware. A SQL Server 2000 version is in the works.

Performance Tuning and Optimization of Microsoft SQL Server 7.0 (Microsoft Authorized Training Course #2013). Recommended for people who are interested in becoming the SQL Server performance expert on their team. This course is available from authorized training centers. A separate SQL Server 2000 version of this course won't be offered because much of the relevant information has been included in this course and in the other SQL Server 2000 curricula. Check the Microsoft training and certification Web site (http://www.microsoft.com/train_cert) periodically for details.

Transaction Processing: Concepts and Techniques by Jim Gray and Andreas Reuter (Morgan Kaufmann Publishers, 1992). Without a doubt, the best book with in-depth explanations of such issues as locking, logging and recovery, and transactional semantics. This book is unusual (and terrific!) in that it is packed with detailed information but is still readable and understandable—unlike many of the overly academic papers that seem more suitable for graduate school classes than for people trying to build actual solutions.

Principles of Database Query Processing for Advanced Applications by Clement T. Yu and Weiyi Meng (Morgan Kaufmann Publishers, 1998). For those who want to know what happens under the hood. This is a textbook-style guide to an important area of database theory—how queries work in a variety of databases and the strategies and algorithms used to optimize them. The book covers topics relevant to relational databases, object-oriented databases, and distributed databases.

In Search of Clusters: The Ongoing Battle in Lowly Parallel Computing by Gregory F. Pfister (Prentice Hall, 1998). A good source of information on scalability limits of symmetric multiprocessing (SMP) systems, such as Amdahl's law, the Von Neumann bottleneck, and other considerations for SMP systems.

I'd also like to recommend the following resources:

Transaction Processing Council (TPC) Web site and full disclosure reports (FDRs). Invaluable resources available at http://www.tpc.org. The Web site allows you to stay abreast of current performance levels of competing hardware and software solutions. It also has plenty of information regarding benchmarks. You also might want to order one of the FDRs for a benchmark that uses SQL Server to determine the exact hardware and software configuration used. If you plan to run a very large system, such an FDR can be a good template to use.

Microsoft Knowledge Base. Various articles (available at *http://www.microsoft.com*) that contain helpful information, tips, and answers to common questions. The site is frequently updated and of high quality. A must for serious developers who use any Microsoft development product, not just SQL Server.

Index

Note: Page numbers in italics refer to figures, tables, or code listings.

H

hardware components
  disk arrays, 125–26, 137–38 (*see also* redundant array of inexpensive disks (RAID))
  disk controllers, 125–26, 137–38
  disk drives, 125–26, 137–38
  disk subsystem, 139–40
  fallback server compatibility, 140–41
  introduced, 121–22, *122*
  memory, 124–25
  other considerations, 141
  processor (CPU), 122–23
  uninterruptible power supply (UPS), 138–39
hardware guidelines, 119–21
hardware requirements, *122*
hash buckets, 92, 93, 841
hashes, Grace, 843
hashing, 92
hashing variations, 843–44
hash joins, 841–43, *842, 843,* 909
hash tables, 842–43, *843*
HAVING clause, 371
HCL (Windows Hardware Compatibility List), 119–20
heaps, 83
  deleting rows from, 482, *483,* 484, *484,* 485
history of SQL Server. *See* Microsoft SQL Server evolution

HOLDLOCK hint, 755, 758, 931, 934
horizontal partitions, 51
HOST_ID function, *556*
HOST_NAME function, *556*
hot-standby drives, 137
hot swappable drives, 137
Hungarian-style notation for column names, 226

I

IAM (Index Allocation Map) pages, 195–96
IBM OS/2
  Extended Edition, 3–4
  joint development agreement with Microsoft
  end, 13
  OS/2 2.0 release on hold, 14
  SQL Server 1.11, 11–12
  SQL Server 4.2, 13–15
  SQL Server for Windows NT, 15–21
  start, 3–4
IDENT_CURRENT function, 244
identifiers, delimited, 224–25
IDENT_INCR function, 241, *556*
IDENTITYCOL keyword, 235, 242–43
identity columns, 570–73
@@IDENTITY function, 243, 244
IDENTITY function, 458–59
IDENTITY_INSERT option, 452
IDENTITY property, 38–39, 241–44, 271, 272, 298, 452

Kalen Delaney has worked with SQL Server extensively since joining the technical support group at Sybase in 1987, shortly after the company's first public product release. Kalen soon began teaching Sybase's Performance and Tuning course. She received the company's Instructor of the Year Award in 1990. Kalen left Sybase in 1992 to become an independent Microsoft SQL Server trainer and consultant. Kalen has been the primary Subject Matter Expert (SME) for two Microsoft SQL Server courses and has helped Microsoft develop training materials for bringing their product support specialists up to speed on the new capabilities and internal behavior of new versions of SQL Server. She teaches these special classes to SQL Server support engineers throughout the United States and around the world.

Kalen has worked for more than 22 years with computer and database systems since earning her M.S. degree in computer science at the University of California, Berkeley. She has published numerous articles in *SQL Server Professional* and *Windows 2000 Magazine* and currently is a contributing editor and regular columnist for *SQL Server Magazine*. She lives with her husband and four children in the Pacific Northwest, just a ferryboat ride from Microsoft's Redmond campus.

The manuscript for this book was prepared using Microsoft Word 97. Pages were composed by Microsoft Press using Adobe PageMaker 6.52 for Windows, with text in Garamond and display type in Helvetica Black. Composed pages were delivered to the printer as electronic prepress files.

Cover Graphic Designer
Girvin | Strategic Branding and Design

Cover Illustrator
Glenn Mitsui

Interior Graphic Artist
Michael Kloepfer

Principal Compositor
Daniel Latimer

Principal Proofreader/Copy Editor
Crystal Thomas

Indexer
Hugh Maddocks

Get a **Free**
e-mail newsletter, updates,
special offers, links to related books,
and more when you

register online!

Register your Microsoft Press® title on our Web site and you'll get
a FREE subscription to our e-mail newsletter, *Microsoft Press
Book Connections.* You'll find out about newly released and upcoming
books and learning tools, online events, software downloads, special
offers and coupons for Microsoft Press customers, and information
about major Microsoft® product releases. You can also read useful
additional information about all the titles we publish, such as detailed book descriptions, tables of contents and indexes, sample
chapters, links to related books and book series, author biographies,
and reviews by other customers.

Registration is easy. Just visit this Web page and fill in your information:
http://www.microsoft.com/mspress/register

Microsoft®

Proof of Purchase

Use this page as proof of purchase if participating in a promotion or rebate offer on
this title. Proof of purchase must be used in conjunction with other proof(s) of
payment such as your dated sales receipt—see offer details.

Inside Microsoft® SQL™ Server 2000
0-7356-0998-5

CUSTOMER NAME

Microsoft Press, PO Box 97017, Redmond, WA 98073-9830

MICROSOFT LICENSE AGREEMENT

Book Companion CD

IMPORTANT—READ CAREFULLY: This Microsoft End-User License Agreement ("EULA") is a legal agreement between you (either an individual or an entity) and Microsoft Corporation for the Microsoft product identified above, which includes computer software and may include associated media, printed materials, and "online" or electronic documentation ("SOFTWARE PRODUCT"). Any component included within the SOFTWARE PRODUCT that is accompanied by a separate End-User License Agreement shall be governed by such agreement and not the terms set forth below. By installing, copying, or otherwise using the SOFTWARE PRODUCT, you agree to be bound by the terms of this EULA. If you do not agree to the terms of this EULA, you are not authorized to install, copy, or otherwise use the SOFTWARE PRODUCT; you may, however, return the SOFTWARE PRODUCT, along with all printed materials and other items that form a part of the Microsoft product that includes the SOFTWARE PRODUCT, to the place you obtained them for a full refund.

SOFTWARE PRODUCT LICENSE

The SOFTWARE PRODUCT is protected by United States copyright laws and international copyright treaties, as well as other intellectual property laws and treaties. The SOFTWARE PRODUCT is licensed, not sold.

1. **GRANT OF LICENSE.** This EULA grants you the following rights:

   a. **Software Product.** You may install and use one copy of the SOFTWARE PRODUCT on a single computer. The primary user of the computer on which the SOFTWARE PRODUCT is installed may make a second copy for his or her exclusive use on a portable computer.

   b. **Storage/Network Use.** You may also store or install a copy of the SOFTWARE PRODUCT on a storage device, such as a network server, used only to install or run the SOFTWARE PRODUCT on your other computers over an internal network; however, you must acquire and dedicate a license for each separate computer on which the SOFTWARE PRODUCT is installed or run from the storage device. A license for the SOFTWARE PRODUCT may not be shared or used concurrently on different computers.

   c. **License Pak.** If you have acquired this EULA in a Microsoft License Pak, you may make the number of additional copies of the computer software portion of the SOFTWARE PRODUCT authorized on the printed copy of this EULA, and you may use each copy in the manner specified above. You are also entitled to make a corresponding number of secondary copies for portable computer use as specified above.

   d. **Sample Code.** Solely with respect to portions, if any, of the SOFTWARE PRODUCT that are identified within the SOFTWARE PRODUCT as sample code (the "SAMPLE CODE"):

      i. **Use and Modification.** Microsoft grants you the right to use and modify the source code version of the SAMPLE CODE, *provided* you comply with subsection (d)(iii) below. You may not distribute the SAMPLE CODE, or any modified version of the SAMPLE CODE, in source code form.

      ii. **Redistributable Files.** Provided you comply with subsection (d)(iii) below, Microsoft grants you a nonexclusive, royalty-free right to reproduce and distribute the object code version of the SAMPLE CODE and of any modified SAMPLE CODE, other than SAMPLE CODE, or any modified version thereof, designated as not redistributable in the Readme file that forms a part of the SOFTWARE PRODUCT (the "Non-Redistributable Sample Code"). All SAMPLE CODE other than the Non-Redistributable Sample Code is collectively referred to as the "REDISTRIBUTABLES."

      iii. **Redistribution Requirements.** If you redistribute the REDISTRIBUTABLES, you agree to: (i) distribute the REDISTRIBUTABLES in object code form only in conjunction with and as a part of your software application product; (ii) not use Microsoft's name, logo, or trademarks to market your software application product; (iii) include a valid copyright notice on your software application product; (iv) indemnify, hold harmless, and defend Microsoft from and against any claims or lawsuits, including attorney's fees, that arise or result from the use or distribution of your software application product; and (v) not permit further distribution of the REDISTRIBUTABLES by your end user. Contact Microsoft for the applicable royalties due and other licensing terms for all other uses and/or distribution of the REDISTRIBUTABLES.

2. **DESCRIPTION OF OTHER RIGHTS AND LIMITATIONS.**

   - **Limitations on Reverse Engineering, Decompilation, and Disassembly.** You may not reverse engineer, decompile, or disassemble the SOFTWARE PRODUCT, except and only to the extent that such activity is expressly permitted by applicable law notwithstanding this limitation.

   - **Separation of Components.** The SOFTWARE PRODUCT is licensed as a single product. Its component parts may not be separated for use on more than one computer.

   - **Rental.** You may not rent, lease, or lend the SOFTWARE PRODUCT.

   - **Support Services.** Microsoft may, but is not obligated to, provide you with support services related to the SOFTWARE PRODUCT ("Support Services"). Use of Support Services is governed by the Microsoft policies and programs described in the user manual, in "online" documentation, and/or in other Microsoft-provided materials. Any supplemental software code provided to you as part of the Support Services shall be considered part of the SOFTWARE PRODUCT and subject to the terms and conditions of this EULA. With respect to technical information you provide to Microsoft as part of the Support Services, Microsoft may use such information for its business purposes, including for product support and development. Microsoft will not utilize such technical information in a form that personally identifies you.

- **Software Transfer.** You may permanently transfer all of your rights under this EULA, provided you retain no copies, you transfer all of the SOFTWARE PRODUCT (including all component parts, the media and printed materials, any upgrades, this EULA, and, if applicable, the Certificate of Authenticity), **and** the recipient agrees to the terms of this EULA.

- **Termination.** Without prejudice to any other rights, Microsoft may terminate this EULA if you fail to comply with the terms and conditions of this EULA. In such event, you must destroy all copies of the SOFTWARE PRODUCT and all of its component parts.

3. **COPYRIGHT.** All title and copyrights in and to the SOFTWARE PRODUCT (including but not limited to any images, photographs, animations, video, audio, music, text, SAMPLE CODE, REDISTRIBUTABLES, and "applets" incorporated into the SOFTWARE PRODUCT) and any copies of the SOFTWARE PRODUCT are owned by Microsoft or its suppliers. The SOFTWARE PRODUCT is protected by copyright laws and international treaty provisions. Therefore, you must treat the SOFTWARE PRODUCT like any other copyrighted material **except** that you may install the SOFTWARE PRODUCT on a single computer provided you keep the original solely for backup or archival purposes. You may not copy the printed materials accompanying the SOFTWARE PRODUCT.

4. **U.S. GOVERNMENT RESTRICTED RIGHTS.** The SOFTWARE PRODUCT and documentation are provided with RESTRICTED RIGHTS. Use, duplication, or disclosure by the Government is subject to restrictions as set forth in subparagraph (c)(1)(ii) of the Rights in Technical Data and Computer Software clause at DFARS 252.227-7013 or subparagraphs (c)(1) and (2) of the Commercial Computer Software—Restricted Rights at 48 CFR 52.227-19, as applicable. Manufacturer is Microsoft Corporation/One Microsoft Way/Redmond, WA 98052-6399.

5. **EXPORT RESTRICTIONS.** You agree that you will not export or re-export the SOFTWARE PRODUCT, any part thereof, or any process or service that is the direct product of the SOFTWARE PRODUCT (the foregoing collectively referred to as the "Restricted Components"), to any country, person, entity, or end user subject to U.S. export restrictions. You specifically agree not to export or re-export any of the Restricted Components (i) to any country to which the U.S. has embargoed or restricted the export of goods or services, which currently include, but are not necessarily limited to, Cuba, Iran, Iraq, Libya, North Korea, Sudan, and Syria, or to any national of any such country, wherever located, who intends to transmit or transport the Restricted Components back to such country; (ii) to any end user who you know or have reason to know will utilize the Restricted Components in the design, development, or production of nuclear, chemical, or biological weapons; or (iii) to any end user who has been prohibited from participating in U.S. export transactions by any federal agency of the U.S. government. You warrant and represent that neither the BXA nor any other U.S. federal agency has suspended, revoked, or denied your export privileges.

DISCLAIMER OF WARRANTY

NO WARRANTIES OR CONDITIONS. MICROSOFT EXPRESSLY DISCLAIMS ANY WARRANTY OR CONDITION FOR THE SOFTWARE PRODUCT. THE SOFTWARE PRODUCT AND ANY RELATED DOCUMENTATION ARE PROVIDED "AS IS" WITHOUT WARRANTY OR CONDITION OF ANY KIND, EITHER EXPRESS OR IMPLIED, INCLUDING, WITHOUT LIMITATION, THE IMPLIED WARRANTIES OF MERCHANTABILITY, FITNESS FOR A PARTICULAR PURPOSE, OR NONINFRINGEMENT. THE ENTIRE RISK ARISING OUT OF USE OR PERFORMANCE OF THE SOFTWARE PRODUCT REMAINS WITH YOU.

LIMITATION OF LIABILITY. TO THE MAXIMUM EXTENT PERMITTED BY APPLICABLE LAW, IN NO EVENT SHALL MICROSOFT OR ITS SUPPLIERS BE LIABLE FOR ANY SPECIAL, INCIDENTAL, INDIRECT, OR CONSEQUENTIAL DAMAGES WHATSOEVER (INCLUDING, WITHOUT LIMITATION, DAMAGES FOR LOSS OF BUSINESS PROFITS, BUSINESS INTERRUPTION, LOSS OF BUSINESS INFORMATION, OR ANY OTHER PECUNIARY LOSS) ARISING OUT OF THE USE OF OR INABILITY TO USE THE SOFTWARE PRODUCT OR THE PROVISION OF OR FAILURE TO PROVIDE SUPPORT SERVICES, EVEN IF MICROSOFT HAS BEEN ADVISED OF THE POSSIBILITY OF SUCH DAMAGES. IN ANY CASE, MICROSOFT'S ENTIRE LIABILITY UNDER ANY PROVISION OF THIS EULA SHALL BE LIMITED TO THE GREATER OF THE AMOUNT ACTUALLY PAID BY YOU FOR THE SOFTWARE PRODUCT OR US$5.00; PROVIDED, HOWEVER, IF YOU HAVE ENTERED INTO A MICROSOFT SUPPORT SERVICES AGREEMENT, MICROSOFT'S ENTIRE LIABILITY REGARDING SUPPORT SERVICES SHALL BE GOVERNED BY THE TERMS OF THAT AGREEMENT. BECAUSE SOME STATES AND JURISDICTIONS DO NOT ALLOW THE EXCLUSION OR LIMITATION OF LIABILITY, THE ABOVE LIMITATION MAY NOT APPLY TO YOU.

MISCELLANEOUS

This EULA is governed by the laws of the State of Washington USA, except and only to the extent that applicable law mandates governing law of a different jurisdiction.

Should you have any questions concerning this EULA, or if you desire to contact Microsoft for any reason, please contact the Microsoft subsidiary serving your country, or write: Microsoft Sales Information Center/One Microsoft Way/Redmond, WA 98052-6399.